Ted Smith

EACC
2424 CALifORNIA Rd
ELKHART, IN 46514

Cisco IOS

Configuration Fundamentals

Cisco Systems, Inc.

Macmillan Technical Publishing
201 West 103rd Street
Indianapolis, IN 46290 USA

Cisco IOS Configuration Fundamentals

Cisco Systems, Inc.

Copyright© 1998 Cisco Systems, Inc.

Cisco Press logo is a trademark of Cisco Systems, Inc.

Published by:
Macmillan Technical Publishing
201 West 103rd Street
Indianapolis, IN 46290 USA

Printed in the United States of America 2 3 4 5 6 7 8 9 0

Library of Congress Cataloging-in-Publication: 97-81047

ISBN: 1-57870-044-2

Feedback Information

At Cisco Press, our goal is to create in-depth technical books of the highest quality and value. Each book is crafted with care and precision, undergoing rigorous development that involves the unique expertise of members from the professional technical community.

Readers' feedback is a natural continuation of this process. If you have any comments regarding how we could improve the quality of this book, or otherwise alter it to better suit your needs, you can contact us at `ciscopress@mcp.com`. Please make sure to include the book title and ISBN in your message.

We greatly appreciate your assistance.

Associate Publisher	Jim LeValley
Executive Editor	Julie Fairweather
Cisco Systems Program Manager	H. Kim Lew
Managing Editor	Caroline Roop
Acquisitions Editors	Tracy Hughes
	Lynette Quinn
Development Editor	Liz Green
Project Editor	Sherri Fugit
Team Coordinator	Amy Lewis
Book Designer	Louisa Klucznik
Cover Designer	Jean Bisesi
Production Team	Kim Cofer
	Nicole Ritch
Indexer	Tim Wright

Trademark
Acknowledgments

Acknowledgments

The Cisco IOS Reference Library is the result of collaborative efforts of many Cisco technical writers and editors over the years. This bookset represents the continuing development and integration of user documentation for the ever-increasing set of Cisco IOS networking features and functionality.

The current team of Cisco IOS technical writers and editors includes Katherine Anderson, Jennifer Bridges, Joelle Chapman, Christy Choate, Meredith Fisher, Tina Fox, Marie Godfrey, Dianna Johansen, Sheryl Kelly, Yvonne Kucher, Doug MacBeth, Lavanya Mandavilli, Mary Mangone, Spank McCoy, Greg McMillan, Madhu Mitra, Oralee Murillo, Vicki Payne, Jane Phillips, George Powers, Teresa Oliver Schick, Wink Schuetz, Karen Shell, Grace Tai, and Bethann Watson.

The writing team wants to acknowledge the many engineering, customer support, and marketing subject-matter experts for their participation in reviewing draft documents and, in many cases, providing source material from which this bookset is developed.

Contents at a Glance

Table of Contents

About the Cisco IOS Reference Library

The Cisco IOS Reference Library books are Cisco documentation that describe the tasks and commands necessary to configure and maintain your Cisco IOS network.

The Cisco IOS software bookset is intended primarily for users who configure and maintain access servers and routers, but are not necessarily familiar with the tasks, the relationship between tasks, or the commands necessary to perform particular tasks.

CISCO IOS REFERENCE LIBRARY ORGANIZATION

The Cisco IOS Reference library consists of eight books. Each book contains technology-specific configuration chapters with corresponding command reference chapters. Each configuration chapter describes Cisco's implementation of protocols and technologies, related configuration tasks, and contains comprehensive configuration examples. Each command reference chapter complements the organization of its corresponding configuration chapter and provides complete command syntax information.

OTHER BOOKS AVAILABLE IN THE CISCO IOS REFERENCE LIBRARY

- *Cisco IOS Dial Solutions*, 1-57870-055-8; March 1998

  This book provides readers with real-world solutions and how to implement them on a network. Customers interested in implementing dial solutions across their network environment include remote sites dialing in to a central office, Internet Service Providers (ISPs), ISP customers at home offices, and enterprise WAN system administrators implementing dial-on-demand routing (DDR).

- *Cisco IOS Wide Area Networking Solutions*, 1-57870-054-x; March 1998

  This book offers thorough, comprehensive coverage of internetworking technologies, particularly ATM, Frame Relay, SMDS, LAPB, and X.25, teaching the reader how to configure the technologies in a LAN/WAN environment.

- *Cisco IOS Switching Services*, 1-57870-053-1; March 1998

  This book is a comprehensive guide detailing available Cisco IOS switching alternatives. Cisco's switching services range from fast switching and Netflow switching to LAN Emulation.

- *Cisco IOS Network Protocols*, Vol. I IP. 1-57870-049-3; April 1998

  This book is a comprehensive guide detailing available IP and IP routing alternatives. It describes how to implement IP addressing and IP services and how to configure support for a wide range of IP routing protocols, including BGP for ISP networks and basic and advanced IP Multicast functionality.

- *Cisco IOS Networking Protocols, Vol. II IPX, AppleTalk, and More*, 1-57870-050-7; April 1998

  This book is a comprehensive guide detailing available network protocol alternatives. It describes how to implement various protocols in your network. This book includes documentation of the latest functionality for the IPX and AppleTalk desktop protocols as well as the following network protocols: Apollo Domain, Banyan VINES, DECNet, ISO CLNS, and XNS.

- *Cisco IOS Bridging and IBM Network Solutions*, 1-57870-051-5; April 1998

  This book describes Cisco's support for networks in IBM and bridging environments. Support includes: transparent and source-route transparent bridging, source-route bridging (SRB), remote source-route bridging (RSRB), data link switching plus (DLS+), serial tunnel and block serial tunnel, SDLC and LLC2 parameter, IBM network media translation, downstream physical unit and SNA service point, SNA Frame Relay access support, Advanced Peer-to-Peer Networking, and native client interface architecture (NCIA).

- *Cisco IOS Network Security*, 1-57870-057-4; May 1998

  This book documents security configuration from a remote site and for a central enterprise or service provider network. It describes AAA, Radius, TACACS+, and Kerberos network security features. It also explains how to encrypt data across enterprise networks. The book includes many illustrations that show configurations and functionality, along with a discussion of network security policy choices and some decision-making guidelines.

BOOK CONVENTIONS

Software and hardware documentation uses the following conventions:

- The caret character (^) represents the Control key.

  For example, the key combinations ^D and Ctrl-D are equivalent: Both mean hold down the Control key while you press the D key. Keys are indicated in capitals, but are not case-sensitive.

- A string is defined as a nonquoted set of characters.

  For example, when setting an SNMP community string to *public*, do not use quotation marks around the string; otherwise, the string will include the quotation marks.

Command descriptions use these conventions:

- Vertical bars (|) separate alternative, mutually exclusive, elements.
- Square brackets ([ ]) indicate optional elements.
- Braces ({ }) indicate a required choice.
- Braces within square brackets ([{ }]) indicate a required choice within an optional element.
- **Boldface** indicates commands and keywords that are entered literally as shown.
- *Italic* indicates arguments for which you supply values; in contexts that do not allow italic, arguments are enclosed in angle brackets (< >).

Examples use these conventions:

- Examples that contain system prompts denote interactive sessions, indicating that the user enters commands at the prompt. The system prompt indicates the current command mode. For example, the prompt `Router(config)#` indicates global configuration mode.
- Terminal sessions and information the system displays are in `screen` font.
- Information you enter is in `boldface screen` font.
- Nonprinting characters, such as passwords, are in angle brackets (< >).
- Default responses to system prompts are in square brackets ([ ]).
- Exclamation points (!) at the beginning of a line indicate a comment line. They are also displayed by the Cisco IOS software for certain processes.

CAUTION

Means *reader be careful*. In this situation, you might do something that could result in equipment damage or loss of data.

NOTES

Means *reader take note*. Notes contain helpful suggestions or references to materials not contained in this manual.

TIMESAVER

Means *the described action saves time*. You can save time by performing the action described in the paragraph.

Within the Cisco IOS Reference Library, the term *router* is used to refer to both access servers and routers. When a feature is supported on the access server only, the term *access server* is used. When a feature is supported on one or more specific router platforms (such as the Cisco 4500), but not on other platforms (such as the Cisco 2500), the text specifies the supported platforms.

Within examples, routers and access servers are alternately shown. These products are used only for example purposes—an example that shows one product does not indicate that the other product is not supported.

Configuration Fundamentals Overview

This chapter provides an overview of Cisco IOS software configuration, describes the chapters in this document, and suggests sections to read based on various situations. This chapter contains the following sections:

- Overview of Router Configuration Tasks
- Cisco IOS User Interfaces
- File Management
- Interface Configuration
- System Management
- Guide to This Book
- Other Documentation

OVERVIEW OF ROUTER CONFIGURATION TASKS

To configure your router or access server, perform the following steps:

Step 1   Before confiuring your router or access server, you must determine the following:

- Which network protocols you are supporting (for example, AppleTalk, IP, Novell IPX, and so on)

- The addressing plan for each network protocol

- Which routing protocol you will use for each network protocol

- Which WAN protocols you will run on each interface (for example: Frame Relay, HDLC, SMDS, X.25, and so on)

Refer to the *Cisco Product Catalog* and the release notes for a list of Cisco-supported protocols, interfaces, and platforms.

Step 2   Set up the hardware as described in the documentation shipped with your product.

Step 3   Initially configure the software as described in the documentation shipped with your product.

Step 4   Configure any user interface, file management, or interface management tasks as described in this book.

NOTES

The Cisco IOS documentation set is intended for network administrators who already have completed the setup and configuration tasks described in the documentation shipped with individual products. The Cisco IOS documentation set describes advanced configuration tasks, not hardware setup and initial software configuration. Refer to the documentation shipped with your product for this information.

Step 5 Configure protocol-specific features on your router or access server as described in the appropriate chapters of the other Cisco IOS software books.

Step 6 If desired, perform system management tasks to monitor and fine-tune the performance of your router in the network.

CISCO IOS USER INTERFACES

The user interface chapters describe the different methods of entering commands into the router and altering the user environment.

The Cisco IOS software provides a command line interface that allows you to configure and manage the router or access server. If you are unfamiliar with the Cisco IOS command line interface, you should read Chapter 1, "Using the Command Line Interface." This chapter discusses the different command modes, context-sensitive help, and editing features. This chapter also describes the Web browser interface, which can be used to configure and monitor the router as well.

Cisco provides some configuration alternatives to the command line interface. If you wish to use AutoInstall to configure a new router or setup to change the configuration, read Chapter 3, "Using Configuration Tools." This chapter also mentions other configuration tools that are available, but it does not provide detailed documentation.

To use the command line interface, your terminal must be connected to the router through the console port or one of the TTY lines. By default, the terminal is configured to a basic configuration, which should work for most terminal sessions. However, you might want to alter the terminal settings. See Chapter 5, "Configuring Operating Characteristics for Terminals," for information.

You also can make connections to other hosts from the router. Chapter 7, "Managing Connections and System Banners," describes how to manage these connections. Alternatively, users can connect to your router. You can display messages to the terminals of these users. These tasks are also described in Chapter 7.

FILE MANAGEMENT

The file management chapters describe the different types of files you can manipulate on the router, such as configuration files, images, and microcode.

Chapter 9, "Modifying, Downloading, and Maintaining Configuration Files," discusses how to modify configuration files, download configuration files for servers, store configuration files on servers, and configure the router to load a configuration file at system startup. In order to customize your router's operation to your needs, you will need to alter the configuration file. This chapter describes how to do this task, while the other chapters in the Cisco IOS documentation set describe the specific commands that are added to the configuration.

Chapter 11, "Loading and Maintaining System Images and Microcode," discusses how to download images from servers, store images on servers, specify which image is loaded at system startup, and specify which microcode images to use. If you are not storing or upgrading your system image and you do not wish to change image booting procedures, you do not need to read this chapter.

Chapter 13, "Maintaining Router Memory," deals with the different types of memory your router might have and how to use this memory to manage files. This chapter also contains information on how to upgrade images on some platforms. Read this chapter if you are upgrading your system image or deleting files in Flash memory.

Chapter 15, "Rebooting a Router," focuses on tasks related to the rebooting procedure. Read this chapter if you wish to change which image or configuration file is loaded at system startup. This chapter also discusses ROM Monitor mode, which allows you to boot the router manually.

Chapter 17, "Configuring Additional File Transfer Functions," describes how to configure your router to be a server or use rsh and rcp. As a TFTP server, your router can provide other routers with images and configuration files over the network. The remote shell and remote copy functions allow users to execute commands remotely or copy files to or from another host.

INTERFACE CONFIGURATION

The interface configuration chapters consist of the following:

- Chapter 19, "Overview of Interface Configuration," provides an overview of configuring interfaces on Cisco routers. This chapter describes configuration tasks that can be performed on any type of interface.

- Chapter 20, "Configuring LAN Interfaces," describes configuration processes for configuring interfaces related to local-area networks, including

  - Ethernet and Fast Ethernet interfaces

  - Fiber Distributed Data Interfaces (FDDI)

  - Hub interfaces

  - Packet OC-3 interfaces

  - Token Ring interfaces

- Chapter 21, "Configuring Serial Interfaces," describes how to configure serial interfaces on Cisco IOS devices. Interfaces described in this chapter include

  - High-Speed serial interfaces (HSSI)

  - Low-speed serial interfaces

  - Serial interfaces for CSU/DSU service modules

  - Synchronous serial interfaces

- Chapter 22, "Configuring Logical Interfaces," provides configuration guidelines for loopback, null, and tunnel interfaces.

Commands used to illustrate configuration tasks in these chapters are documented in Chapter 23, "Interface Commands."

SYSTEM MANAGEMENT

The system management chapters discuss tasks that allow you to maintain your router after it is configured with the network, routing, and WAN protocols. These chapters discuss ways you can fine-tune the router and maintain it over time.

SNMP, RMON, Cisco Discovery Protocol, and Response Time Reporter are described in Chapter 24, "Monitoring the Router and Network." You can use these protocols to gather information about the router and network usage.

If you want to improve the basic performance of the router, read Chapter 26, "Managing System Performance." This chapter discusses queuing and congestion strategies, traffic shaping, switching and scheduling priorities, and other general system performance tasks.

Chapter 28, "Troubleshooting the Router," provides an introduction to troubleshooting techniques, error message logging, and debugging commands. If you are troubleshooting a particular protocol, read this chapter to learn how to log system error messages and use debugging commands. Then, refer to the chapter in the documentation set that documents your protocol.

Chapter 30, "Performing Basic System Management," discusses basic optional tasks. For example, you can change the name of the router, create command aliases, enable minor services, and set time and calendar services.

GUIDE TO THIS BOOK

The previous sections listed common tasks found in each chapter. However, some common tasks require information in more than one chapter. This section suggests sections in different chapters of *Cisco IOS Configuration Fundamentals* that are useful to read based on your situation.

Learning the Cisco IOS Command Line Interface

If you are not familiar with the Cisco IOS command line interface, read the following sections to gain a basic understanding of the user interface and basic configuration tasks:

In Chapter 1, "Using the Command Line Interface," see:

- Accessing Each Command Mode
- Using the No and Default Forms of Commands
- Getting Context-Sensitive Help
- Checking Command Syntax
- Using the Command History Features
- Using the Editing Features

In Chapter 9, "Modifying, Downloading, and Maintaining Configuration Files," see:

- Displaying Configuration File Information
- Understanding Configuration Files
- Entering Configuration Mode and Selecting a Configuration Source
- Configuring the Cisco IOS Software from the Terminal
- Reexecuting the Configuration Commands in Startup Configuration
- Clearing the Configuration Information

In Chapter 30, "Performing Basic System Management," see:

- Setting the Router Name

In addition, Chapter 19, "Overview of Interface Configuration," provides an overview of configuring interfaces on Cisco routers.

Storing or Obtaining Configuration Files or Images from a Server

You might want to save a configuration or image on a server or upgrade your image to a different release. If you will be storing or obtaining configuration files or images from a server, read the following sections:

In Chapter 9, "Modifying, Downloading, and Maintaining Configuration Files," see:

- Copying Configuration Files from the Router to a Network Server

- Copying Configuration Files from a Network Server to the Router

- Copying Images from Flash Memory to a Network Server

- Copying Images from a Network Server to Flash Memory

In Chapter 13, "Maintaining Router Memory," see:

- Partitioning Flash Memory

- Using Flash Load Helper to Upgrade Software on Run-from-Flash Systems

Changing the Image or Configuration File Loaded by the Router

If you wish to change the image or configuration file used when the system reloads, read the following sections:

In Chapter 9, "Modifying, Downloading, and Maintaining Configuration Files," see:

- Specifying the Startup Configuration File

In Chapter 11, "Loading and Maintaining System Images and Microcode," see:

- Specifying the Startup System Image in the Configuration File

In Chapter 15, "Rebooting a Router," see:

- Displaying Booting Information

- Rebooting Procedures

- Modifying the Configuration Register Boot Field

- Setting Environment Variables

OTHER DOCUMENTATION

Other documentation for Cisco routers and access servers is available.

- Refer to the documentation shipped with your platform for hardware and platform-specific information.

- For the latest information about the software, including new features added since the documentation was printed and additional caveats about using the software, refer to the release note that accompanies the software.

- Refer to the *Cisco IOS Software Command Summary* for summarized command information.

- Refer to the *System Error Messages* publication for information about system software, internal hardware, and communication line error messages.

PART I

Cisco IOS User Interfaces

## CHAPTER 1

Using the Command Line Interface

Cisco IOS commands can be entered at a terminal connected to the access server or router using the command line interface (CLI). Commands also can be entered using the Cisco Web browser interface. This chapter describes how to use the Cisco IOS command line interface and Web page interface. It describes command modes, help features, command editing and history features, and menus.

For a complete description of the user interface commands in this chapter, see Chapter 2, "Basic Command Line Interface Commands."

USER INTERFACE TASK LIST

You can perform the tasks in the following sections to familiarize yourself with the Cisco IOS user interface. If you are not familiar with the Cisco IOS command line interface, read the first six sections to gain a basic understanding of the user interface.

- Accessing Each Command Mode
- Using the No and Default Forms of Commands
- Getting Context-Sensitive Help
- Checking Command Syntax
- Using the Command History Feature
- Using the Editing Features
- Creating Menus
- Using the Cisco Web Browser Interface to Issue Commands
- Customizing the User Interface on a Web Browser
- Displaying 8-bit and Multibyte Character Sets

ACCESSING EACH COMMAND MODE

The Cisco IOS user interface is divided into many different modes. The commands available to you at any given time depend on which mode you currently are using. Entering a question mark (?) at the system prompt allows you to obtain a list of commands available for each command mode.

When you start a session on the router, you begin in user mode, often called EXEC mode. Only a limited subset of the commands are available in EXEC mode. In order to have access to all commands, you must enter privileged EXEC mode. Normally, you must enter a password to enter privileged EXEC mode. From privileged mode, you can enter any EXEC command or enter global configuration mode. Most of the EXEC commands are one-time commands, such as **show** commands, which show the current status of something, and **clear** commands, which clear counters or interfaces. The EXEC commands are not saved across reboots of the router.

The configuration modes allow you to make changes to the running configuration. If you later save the configuration, these commands are stored across router reboots. In order to get to the various configuration modes, you must start at global configuration mode. From global configuration mode, you can enter interface configuration mode, subinterface configuration mode, and a variety of protocol-specific modes.

ROM monitor mode is a separate mode used when the router cannot boot properly. If your router or access server does not find a valid system image when it is booting, or if its configuration file is corrupted at startup, the system might enter read-only memory (ROM) monitor mode.

The following sections describe how to access each of the Cisco IOS command modes:

- User EXEC Mode
- Privileged EXEC Mode
- Global Configuration Mode
- Interface Configuration Mode
- Subinterface Configuration Mode
- ROM Monitor Mode

User EXEC Mode

After you log in to the router or access server, you are automatically in user EXEC command mode. The EXEC commands available at the user level are a subset of those available at the privileged level. In general, the user EXEC commands allow you to connect to remote devices, change terminal settings on a temporary basis, perform basic tests, and list system information.

To list the user EXEC commands, complete the following task:

Task	Command
List the user EXEC commands.	?

The user-level prompt consists of the host name followed by the angle bracket (>):

```
Router>
```

The default host name is Router unless it has been changed during initial configuration using the **setup** command. Refer to the product user guide for information on the **setup** facility. You also can change the host name using the **hostname** global configuration command described in Chapter 30, "Basic System Management Commands."

To list the commands available in user EXEC mode, enter a question mark (?) as shown in the following example:

```
Router> ?
Exec commands:
  <1-99>           Session number to resume
  connect          Open a terminal connection
  disconnect       Disconnect an existing telnet session
  enable           Turn on privileged commands
  exit             Exit from the EXEC
  help             Description of the interactive help system
  lat              Open a lat connection
  lock             Lock the terminal
  login            Log in as a particular user
  logout           Exit from the EXEC
  menu             Start a menu-based user interface
  mbranch          Trace multicast route for branch of tree
  mrbranch         Trace reverse multicast route to branch of tree
  mtrace           Trace multicast route to group
  name-connection  Name an existing telnet connection
  pad              Open a X.29 PAD connection
  ping             Send echo messages
  resume           Resume an active telnet connection
  show             Show running system information
  systat           Display information about terminal lines
  telnet           Open a telnet connection
  terminal         Set terminal line parameters
  tn3270           Open a tn3270 connection
  trace            Trace route to destination
  where            List active telnet connections
  x3               Set X.3 parameters on PAD
  xremote          Enter XRemote mode
```

The list of commands might vary slightly from this example, depending on the software feature set and configuration of your Cisco routing product.

Privileged EXEC Mode

Because many of the privileged commands set operating parameters, privileged access should be password-protected to prevent unauthorized use. The privileged command set includes those commands contained in user EXEC mode, as well as the **configure** command, through which you can access the remaining command modes. Privileged EXEC mode also includes high-level testing commands, such as **debug**.

The privileged EXEC mode prompt consists of the devices's host name followed by the pound sign (#). (If the router or access server was named with the **hostname** command, that name would appear as the prompt instead of "Router").

```
Router#
```

To access and list the privileged EXEC commands, complete the following tasks:

Task	Command
Step 1 Enter the privileged EXEC mode.	enable [*password*]
Step 2 List privileged EXEC commands.	?

To return from privileged EXEC mode to user EXEC mode, perform the following task:

Task	Command
Move from privileged EXEC mode to user EXEC mode.	**disable**

If the system administrator has set a password, you are prompted to enter it before being allowed access to privileged EXEC mode. The password is not displayed on the screen and is case-sensitive. If an enable password has not been set, enable mode can be accessed only from the router console. The system administrator uses the **enable password** global configuration command to set the password that restricts access to privileged mode.

The following example shows how to access privileged EXEC mode:

```
Router> enable
Password:
Router#
```

From the privileged level, you can access global configuration mode. For instructions, see the next section, "Global Configuration Mode."

Global Configuration Mode

Global configuration commands apply to features that affect the system as a whole, rather than just one protocol or interface. Use the **configure terminal** privileged EXEC command to enter global configuration mode.

Commands to enable a particular routing or bridging function are also global configuration commands.

To access and list the global configuration commands, complete the following tasks:

Task	Command
Step 1 At the terminal, from the privileged EXEC mode, enter global configuration mode.	**configure terminal**
Step 2 List the global configuration commands.	?

The following example shows how to access global configuration mode:

```
Router# configure terminal
Enter configuration commands, one per line. End with CNTL/Z.
Router(config)#
```

To exit global configuration mode and return to privileged EXEC mode, use one of the following commands:

Task	Command
Exit global configuration mode.	**exit** **end** **Ctrl-Z**

From global configuration mode, you can access a number of other command modes. These command modes are described in the sections that follow. For a complete list of these modes, see the section "Other Configuration Modes."

Interface Configuration Mode

Many features are enabled on a per-interface basis. Interface configuration commands modify the operation of an interface such as an Ethernet, FDDI, or serial port. Interface configuration commands always follow an **interface** global configuration command, which defines the interface type.

For details on interface configuration commands that affect general interface parameters, such as bandwidth, clock rate, and so on, see Chapter 23, "Interface Commands."

To access and list the interface configuration commands, complete the following tasks:

Task	Command
Step 1 From global configuration mode, enter interface configuration mode.	**interface** *type number*
Step 2 List the interface configuration commands.	?

In the following example, serial interface 0 is about to be configured. The new prompt
Router(config-if)# indicates interface configuration mode.

```
Router(config)# interface serial 0 <CR>
Router(config-if)#
```

To exit interface configuration mode and return to global configuration mode, enter the **exit** command. To exit configuration mode and return to privileged EXEC mode, use the **end** command or
press **Ctrl-Z**.

Subinterface Configuration Mode

You can configure multiple virtual interfaces (called subinterfaces) on a single physical interface.
Subinterfaces appear to be distinct physical interfaces to the various protocols. For example,
Frame Relay networks provide multiple point-to-point links called permanent virtual circuits
(PVCs). PVCs can be grouped under separate subinterfaces that, in turn, are configured on a single
physical interface. From a bridging spanning-tree viewpoint, each subinterface is a separate bridge
port, and a frame arriving on one subinterface can be sent out on another subinterface.

Subinterfaces also allow multiple encapsulations for a protocol on a single interface. For example,
a router or access server can receive an ARPA-framed IPX packet and forward the packet back out
the same physical interface as a SNAP-framed IPX packet.

To access and list the subinterface configuration commands, complete the following tasks:

Task	Command
Step 1 From interface configuration mode, configure a virtual interface.	See the example that follows. For information on interface commands that allow subinterface implementation, see the protocol-specific chapter later in this book.
Step 2 List the subinterface configuration commands.	?

In the following example, a subinterface is configured for serial line 2, which is configured for
Frame Relay encapsulation. The subinterface is called 2.1 to indicate that it is subinterface 1 of
serial interface 2. The new prompt Router(config-subif)# indicates that you are in subinterface
configuration mode. The subinterface can be configured to support one or more Frame Relay PVCs.

```
Router(config)# interface serial 2
Router(config-if)# encapsulation frame-relay
Router(config-if)# interface serial 2.1
Router(config-subif)#
```

To exit subinterface configuration mode and return to global configuration mode, enter the **exit**
command. To exit configuration mode and return to privileged EXEC mode, press **Ctrl-Z**.

ROM Monitor Mode

If your router or access server does not find a valid system image, or if you interrupt the boot sequence, the system might enter read-only memory (ROM) monitor mode. From ROM monitor mode, you can boot the device or perform diagnostic tests.

You also can enter ROM monitor mode by entering the **reload** EXEC command and then pressing the Break key during the first 60 seconds of startup. If you have changed the configuration, use the **copy running-config startup-config** command and then issue the **reload** command to save your configuration changes.

To access and list the ROM monitor configuration commands, complete the following tasks:

Task	Command
Step 1 Enter ROM monitor mode from privileged EXEC mode.	**reload** Press the Break key during the first 60 seconds while the system is booting.
Step 2 List the ROM monitor commands.	**?**

The ROM monitor prompt is the angle bracket (>):

```
> ?
$ state       Toggle cache state (? for help)
B [filename]  [TFTP Server IP address ¦ TFTP Server Name]
              Load and execute system image from ROM or from TFTP server
C [address]   Continue execution [optional address]
D /S M L V    Deposit value V of size S into location L with modifier M
E /S M L      Examine location L with size S with modifier M
G [address]   Begin execution
H             Help for commands
I             Initialize
K             Stack trace
L [filename]  [TFTP Server IP address ¦ TFTP Server Name]
              Load system image from ROM or from TFTP server, but do not
              begin execution
O             Show configuration register option settings
P             Set the break point
S             Single step next instruction
T function    Test device (? for help)
Deposit and Examine sizes may be B (byte), L (long) or S (short).
Modifiers may be R (register) or S (byte swap).
Register names are: D0-D7, A0-A6, SS, US, SR, and PC
```

To return to user EXEC mode, type **continue**. To initialize the router or access server, enter the **i** command. The **i** command causes the bootstrap program to reinitialize the hardware, clear the contents of memory, and boot the system. (It is best to issue the **i** command before you run any tests or boot software). To boot the system image file, use the **b** command (see Chapter 15, "Rebooting a Router"). For details on ROM monitor mode commands, refer to the appropriate hardware installation guide.

Summary of Main Command Modes

Table 1–1 summarizes the main command modes of the Cisco IOS software.

Table 1–1 *Summary of Main Command Modes*

Command Mode	Access Method	Prompt	Exit Method
User EXEC	Log in.	`Router>`	Use the **logout** command.
Privileged EXEC	From user EXEC mode, use the **enable** EXEC command.	`Router#`	To exit back to user EXEC mode, use the **disable** command. To enter global configuration mode, use the **configure terminal** privileged EXEC command.
Global configuration	From privileged EXEC mode, use the **configure terminal** privileged EXEC command.	`Router(config)#`	To exit to privileged EXEC mode, use the **exit** or **end** command or press **Ctrl-Z**. To enter interface configuration mode, enter an **interface** configuration command.
Interface configuration	From global configuration mode, enter by specifying an interface with an **interface** command.	`Router(config-if)#`	To exit to global configuration mode, use the **exit** command. To exit to privileged EXEC mode, use the **exit** command or press **Ctrl-Z**. To enter subinterface configuration mode, specify a subinterface with the **interface** command.

Table 1–1 *Summary of Main Command Modes, Continued*

Command Mode	Access Method	Prompt	Exit Method
Subinterface configuration	From interface configuration mode, specify a subinterface with an **interface** command.	`Router(config-subif)#`	To exit to global configuration mode, use the **exit** command. To enter privileged EXEC mode, use the **end** command or press **Ctrl-Z**.
ROM monitor	From privileged EXEC mode, use the **reload** EXEC command. Press the Break key during the first 60 seconds while the system is booting.	`>`	To exit to user EXEC mode, type **continue**.

Other Configuration Modes

The following sections describe the other configuration modes:

- Access-List Configuration Mode
- APPN Command Modes
- Controller Configuration Mode
- Crypto Map Configuration Mode
- Hex Input Mode
- Hub Configuration Mode
- IBM Channel Attach Command Modes
- IPX-Router Configuration Mode
- Key Chain Configuration Mode
- LANE Database Configuration Mode
- Line Configuration Mode
- Map-Class Configuration Mode
- Map-List Configuration Mode
- Response Time Reporter Configuration Mode
- Route-Map Configuration Mode
- Router Configuration Mode
- TN3270 Server Command Modes

Most of these modes can be entered from global configuration mode. In these modes, the **exit** command returns you to the global configuration mode. Other modes must be entered from another configuration mode. Entering the **exit** command in one of these modes returns you to the configuration mode you used to enter the mode.

In any configuration mode, to enter privileged EXEC mode and leave configuration mode entirely, use the **end** command or press **Ctrl-Z**.

Table 1–2 in the "Summary of Configuration Command Modes" section lists how to enter each mode.

Access-List Configuration Mode

All IP and IPX access lists can be identified by a number. Alternatively, some IP and IPX access lists can be identified by a name. Use access-list configuration mode when you are creating a named IP or IPX access list.

APPN Command Modes

Advanced Peer-to-Peer Networking (APPN) is the second generation of SNA. APPN provides support for client/server applications and offers more dynamics than traditional hierarchical SNA, such as dynamic directory and routing services.

APPN allows you to define attributes of the APPN network that can become quite complex. To easily manage the details of APPN, special configuration command modes and conventions have been developed.

Because APPN offers a large number of configuration options, specific configuration dialogs are used for each major APPN configuration item. When you define the major item, you automatically will enter the detailed configuration mode for that item. There are two options to exit the detailed configuration mode. Use the **complete** command to exit the detailed configuration mode and update the APPN subsystem with the changes. Use the **exit** command to leave the definition in "no complete" state without updating the APPN subsystem.

The following are the APPN modes:

- APPN Control Point Mode
- APPN Port Mode
- APPN Link Station Mode
- APPN Connection Network Mode
- APPN Class of Service Mode
- APPN Mode Configuration Mode
- APPN Partner LU Location Mode
- APPN Subsystem Mode

Controller Configuration Mode

You can configure channelized T1 in the controller configuration mode.

Crypto Map Configuration Mode

Use crypto map configuration mode to create or alter the definition of a crypto map. Crypto maps are part of an authentication/encryption router configuration.

Hex Input Mode

Use hex input mode to enter a public key for an encrypting peer router. The public key data is entered in hexadecimal form, and it will take more than one command line to enter. To continue entering the public key data on a new line, press **Return**. When the public key is completely entered, press Return to get a new line, then type **quit** to return to the global configuration mode.

Hub Configuration Mode

Hub configuration commands configure hub functionality for an Ethernet interface on the Cisco 2500. They always follow a **hub** global configuration command. See Chapter 20, "Configuring LAN Interfaces," and Chapter 23, "Interface Commands."

IBM Channel Attach Command Modes

The Channel Interface Processor (CIP) supports the IBM channel attach feature. This configuration is an ideal connectivity hub for large corporate networks that provide routing services between mainframes and LANs.

Interface Channel Configuration Mode

Before you configure your channel attach interface, you must select an interface. The following mode is valid only for port 2 on a CIP board. Ports 0 and 1 represent real, physical ports. Port 2 is an internal, virtual port.

Internal LAN Configuration Mode

Use the IBM channel internal LAN configuration mode to configure an internal LAN on a CIP interface and configure Cisco Systems Network Architecture (CSNA) parameters.

Internal Adapter Configuration Mode

Internal adapter commands allow you to configure the link characteristics for the internal LAN adapter and name the internal LAN adapter.

To configure an internal adapter interface, you must first use the bridge-group internal LAN configuration command or the source-bridge internal LAN configuration command to configure bridging type.

IPX-Router Configuration Mode

Internet Packet Exchange (IPX) is a Novell network-layer protocol. The IPX-router configuration mode is used to configure IPX routing.

Key Chain Configuration Mode

From key chain configuration mode, you can manage authentication keys.

Key management controls the authentication keys that routing protocols use. To enter key chain configuration mode, identify or define a key chain using the **keychain** command. From key chain configuration mode, you can identify or define key numbers.

Key Chain Key Configuration Mode

Once you define a key chain, use the key chain key configuration mode to configure the keys on the key chain.

LANE Database Configuration Mode

LAN emulation (LANE) clients consult the LANE configuration server for information such as the location of the LANE server. The configuration server looks up the configuration information in its name database.

A LANE database contains entries that bind an emulated LAN name to the ATM address of the LANE server, bind LANE client MAC addresses to an emulated LAN name, and bind LANE client ATM address templates to an emulated LAN name.

In LANE database configuration mode, you can use the **client-atm-address name**, **default name**, **mac-address name**, and **name server-atm-address** commands to create entries in the specified database.

Line Configuration Mode

Line configuration commands modify the operation of an auxiliary, console, physical, or virtual terminal line. Line configuration commands always follow a **line** command, which defines a line number. These commands generally are used to connect to remote routers or access servers, change terminal parameter settings either on a line-by-line basis or for a range of line, and set up the auxiliary port modem configuration to support dial-on-demand routing (DDR).

Map-Class Configuration Mode

Cisco IOS software allows you to specify parameters that control the traffic that the source router will send over a switched virtual circuit (SVC).

Map-List Configuration Mode

Cisco IOS ATM and Frame Relay software supports static mapping schemes that identify the protocol addresses of remote hosts or routers.

Map-list configuration commands configure a map list. They always follow a **map-list** global configuration command.

Response Time Reporter Configuration Mode

Use the response time reporter configuration mode to configure a probe to measure response times and availability. See Chapter 24, "Monitoring the Router and Network."

Route-Map Configuration Mode

Use the route-map configuration mode to configure routing table and source and destination information.

Router Configuration Mode

Router configuration commands configure an IP routing protocol and always follow a **router** command.

TN3270 Server Command Modes

The TN3270 server provides a set of command modes. The TN3270 server can be configured only on Port 2, the internal LAN port, of a Channel Interface Processor (CIP) card.

The following are the TN3270 server command modes:

- TN3270 server configuration mode
- DLUR configuration mode
- DLUR SAP configuration mode
- PU configuration mode

Summary of Configuration Command Modes

Table 1–2 lists the command modes, how to access and exit each mode, the prompt while in each mode, and an example of how to get to the mode. The exit method is only listed if the **exit** command does not return you to global configuration mode or if you must use a different command to exit the mode. The prompts listed assume that the default device name is "Router."

Table 1–2   *Summary of Command Modes*

Command Mode	Access and Exit Method	Prompt	Example

Access-list configuration	From global configuration mode, use the **ip access-list** or **ipx access-list** command. **ip access-list** {**standard** | **extended**} *name*
	
	or
	
	ipx access-list {**standard** | **extended** | **sap** | **summary**} *name*
		`Router(config-std-nacl)#`
		or
		`Router(config-ext-nacl)#`
			`Router(config)#` **ip access-list extended flag**
			`Router (config-ext-nacl)#`

APPN configuration	From global configuration mode, use the **appn mode** command.	`Router(appn)#`	`Router(config)#` **appn mode** `Router(appn)#`
Controller configuration	From global configuration mode, use the **controller t1** *slot/port* command to configure a channelized T1 interface.	`Router(config-controller)#`	`Router(config)#` **controller t1 0/0** `Router(config-controller)#`
Crypto map configuration	From global configuration mode, use the **crypto map** *map-name* [*seq-num*] command.	`Router(config-crypto-map)#`	`Router(config)#` **crypto map Research 10** `Router(config-crypto-map)#`

Table 1–2 *Summary of Command Modes, Continued*

Command Mode	Access and Exit Method	Prompt	Example

Hex input	From global configuration mode, use the **crypto public-key** command. **crypto public-key** *key-name serial-number*
	
	To exit hex input mode, use the **quit** command.
		`Router(config-pubkey)#`	`Router(config)#` **`crypto public-key`** **`BananaCryptoEngine`** **`01709644`**
			
			`Enter a public key as a hexadecimal number`
			`....`
			
			`Router(config-pubkey)#` **`C31260F4`** **`BD8A5ACE 2C1B1E6C`** **`8B0ABD27 01493A50`**
			
			`Router(config-pubkey)#` **`A6A66946`**
			
			`Router(config-pubkey)#` **`quit`**
			
			`Router(config)#`

Hub configuration	From global configuration mode, enter by specifying a hub with the **hub** *number port* [*port*] command.	`Router(config-hub)#`	`Router(config)#` **`hub`** **`ethernet 0 1 3`** `Router(config-hub)#`
Interface channel configuration	From global configuration mode, use the **interface channel** *slot/port* command.	`Router(config)#`	`Router(config)#` **`interface channel 0/1`** `Router(config)#`
Internal LAN configuration	From interface configuration mode, use the **lan [ethernet | tokenring | fddi]** *lan-id* command. To exit to interface configuration mode, use the **exit** command.	`Router(config-if)#`	`Router(config)#` **`lan`** **`ethernet 10`** `Router(cfg-lan-Ether 10)#`

Table 1–2   *Summary of Command Modes, Continued*

Command Mode	Access and Exit Method	Prompt	Example

Internal adapter configuration	From internal LAN configuration mode, enter the **adapter** *adapter-number mac-address* command.
	
	To exit to Internal LAN configuration mode, use the **exit** command.
		`Router(config-lan)#`	`Router(config)# lan ethernet 10`
			
			`Router(cfg-lan-Ether 10)# adapter 1 4.5.6`
			
			`Router(cfg-adap-Ether 10-1)#`

IPX-router configuration	From global configuration mode, enter by issuing the **ipx routing** command, then a command that begins with **ipx router** (such as **ipx router eigrp**). **ipx router {eigrp** *autonomous-system-number* | **nlsp** [*tag*] | **rip}**	`Router(config-ipx-router)#`	`Router(config)# ipx router rip`
			
			`Router(config-ipx-router)#`

Key chain configuration	From global configuration mode, use the **keychain** command. **keychain** *name-of-chain*	`Router(config-keychain)#`	`Router(config)# keychain blue`
			
			`Router(config-keychain)#`

Key chain key configuration	From key chain configuration mode, use the **key** *number* command.
	
	To exit to key chain configuration mode, use the **exit** command.
		`Router(config-keychain-key)#`	`Router(config)# keychain blue`
			
			`Router(config-keychain)# key 10`
			
			`Router(config-keychain-key)#`

LANE database configuration	From global configuration mode, use the **lane database** command. **lane database** [*database-name*]	`Router(lane-config-datab)#`	`Router(config)# lane database red`
			
			`Router(lane-config-datab)#`

Table 1–2 *Summary of Command Modes, Continued*

Command Mode	Access and Exit Method	Prompt	Example
Line configuration	From global configuration mode, enter by specifying a line with a **line** {**aux** | **con** | **tty** | **vty**} *line-number* [*ending-line-number*] command.	`Router(config-line)#`	`Router(config)#` **`line vty 0 4`** `Router(config-line)#`

Map-class configuration	From global configuration mode, configure a map class with the **map-class** *encapsulation class-name* command.	`Router(config-map-class)#`	`Router(config)#`
			`map-class atm aaa`
			`Router(config-map-class)#`

Map-list configuration	From global configuration mode, define a map list with the **map-list** *name* command.	`Router(config-map-list)#`	`Router(config)#`
			`map-list atm`
			`Router(config-map-list)#`

Response time reporter configuration	From global configuration mode, use the **rtr** command. **rtr** *probe*	`Router(config-rtr)#`	`Router(config)#` **`rtr 1`** `Router(config-rtr)#`

Route-map configuration	From global configuration mode, enter by specifying the **route-map** [*map-tag*] command.	`Router(config-route-map)#`	`Router(config)#`
			`route-map arizona`
			`Router(config-route-map)#`

Router configuration	From global configuration mode, enter by issuing the **router** [*keyword*] command (such as **router igrp**).	`Router(config-router)#`	`Router(config)#`
			`router rip`
			`Router(config-router)#`

Table 1–2 *Summary of Command Modes, Continued*

Command Mode	Access and Exit Method	Prompt	Example
TN3270 server configuration	From interface configuration mode, use the **tn3270-server** command. To exit to interface configuration mode, use the **exit** command.	`Router(tn3270-server)#`	`Router(config)#` **`tn3270-server`** `Router(tn3270-server)#`
DLUR configuration	From TN3270 configuration mode, use the **dlur** command. To exit to TN3270 configuration mode, use the **exit** command.	`Router(tn3270-dlur)#`	`Router(config)#` **`tn3270-server`** `Router(tn3270-server)#` **`dlur`** `Router(tn3270-dlur)#`
DLUR SAP configuration	From DLUR configuration mode, use the **lsap** command. To exit to DLUR configuration mode, use the **exit** command.	`Router(tn3270-dlur-sap)#`	`Router(config)#` **`tn3270-server`** `Router(tn3270-server)#` **`dlur`** `Router(tn3270-dlur)#` **`lsap`** `Router(tn3270-dlur-sap)#`
PU configuration	From TN3270 server configuration mode or from DLUR configuration mode, use the **PU** command. To exit PU configuration mode, use the **exit** command.	`Router(tn3270-pu)#` `Router(tn3270-dlur-pu)#`	`Router(config)#` **`tn3270-server`** `Router(tn3270-server)#` **`pu PU1`** **`05d00001`** `10.0.0.1` **`token-adapter 1 8`** **`rmac 4000.0000.0001`** **`rsap 4`** `Router(tn3270-pu)#`

USING THE NO AND DEFAULT FORMS OF COMMANDS

Almost every configuration command also has a **no** form. In general, use the **no** form to disable a feature or function. Use the command without the keyword **no** to re-enable a disabled feature or to enable a feature that is disabled by default. For example, IP routing is enabled by default. To disable IP routing, specify the **no ip routing** command and specify **ip routing** to re-enable it.

Configuration commands also can have a **default** form. The **default** form of a command returns the command setting to its default. Most commands are disabled by default, so the **default** form is the same as the **no** form. However, some commands are enabled by default and have variables set to certain default values. In these cases, the **default** command enables the command and sets variables to their default values.

GETTING CONTEXT-SENSITIVE HELP

Entering a question mark (?) at the system prompt displays a list of commands available for each command mode. You also can get a list of any command's associated keywords and arguments with the context-sensitive help feature.

To get help specific to a command mode, a command, a keyword, or arguments, perform one of the following tasks:

Task	Command
Obtain a brief description of the help system in any command mode.	**help**
Obtain a list of commands that begin with a particular character string.	*abbreviated-command-entry*?
Complete a partial command name.	*abbreviated-command-entry*<**Tab**>
List all commands available for a particular command mode.	?
List a command's associated keywords.	*command* ?
List a keyword's associated arguments.	*command keyword* ?

When using context-sensitive help, the space (or lack of a space) before the question mark (?) is significant. To obtain a list of commands that begin with a particular character sequence, type in those characters followed immediately by the question mark (?). Do not include a space. This form of help is called *word help*, because it completes a word for you.

To list keywords or arguments, enter a question mark (?) in place of a keyword or argument. Include a space before the ?. This form of help is called *command syntax help*, because it reminds you which keywords or arguments are applicable based on the command, keywords, and arguments you already have entered.

You can abbreviate commands and keywords to the number of characters that allow a unique abbreviation. For example, you can abbreviate the **show** command to **sh.**

Enter the **help** command (which is available in any command mode) for a brief description of the help system:

```
Router# help
Help may be requested at any point in a command by entering
a question mark '?'. If nothing matches, the help list will
be empty and you must back up until entering a '?' shows the
available options.
Two styles of help are provided:
1. Full help is available when you are ready to enter a
   command argument (e.g. 'show ?') and describes each possible
   argument.
2. Partial help is provided when an abbreviated argument is entered
   and you want to know what arguments match the input
   (e.g. 'show pr?'.)
```

As described in the **help** command output, you can enter a partial command name and a question mark (?) to obtain a list of commands beginning with a particular character set. (See the section "Completing a Partial Command Name" later in this chapter for more details.)

Example of Context Sensitive Help

The following example illustrates how the context-sensitive help feature enables you to create an access list from configuration mode.

Enter the letters **co** at the system prompt followed by a question mark (?). Do not leave a space between the last letter and the question mark (?). The system provides the commands that begin with **co.**

```
Router# co?
configure  connect  copy
```

Enter the **configure** command followed by a space and a question mark (?) to list the command's keywords and a brief explanation:

```
Router# configure ?
  memory    Configure from NV memory
  network   Configure from a TFTP network host
  terminal  Configure from the terminal
  <cr>
```

Enter the **terminal** keyword to enter configuration mode from the terminal:

```
Router# configure terminal
Enter configuration commands, one per line. End with CNTL/Z.
Router(config)#
```

Enter the **access-list** command followed by a space and a question mark (?) to list the command's keywords:

```
Router(config)# access-list ?
  <1-99>      IP standard access list
  <100-199>   IP extended access list
  <1000-1099> IPX SAP access list
  <1100-1199> Extended 48-bit MAC address access list
  <200-299>   Protocol type-code access list
  <300-399>   DECnet access list
  <400-499>   XNS standard access list
  <500-599>   XNS extended access list
  <600-699>   Appletalk access list
  <700-799>   48-bit MAC address access list
  <800-899>   IPX standard access list
  <900-999>   IPX extended access list
```

The two numbers within the angle brackets represent an inclusive range. Enter the access-list number **99** and then enter another question mark (?) to see the arguments that apply to the keyword and brief explanations:

```
Router(config)# access-list 99 ?
  deny    Specify packets to reject
  permit  Specify packets to forward
```

Enter the **deny** argument followed by a question mark (?) to list additional options:

```
Router(config)# access-list 99 deny ?
  A.B.C.D  Address to match
```

Generally, uppercase letters represent variables, though this is not always the case. Enter the IP address followed by a question mark (?) to list additional options:

```
Router(config)# access-list 99 deny 131.108.134.0 ?
  A.B.C.D  Mask of bits to ignore
  <cr>
```

The <cr> symbol appears in the list to indicate that one of your options is to press Return to execute the command.

The other option is to add a wildcard mask. Enter the wildcard mask followed by a question mark (?) to list further options.

```
Router(config)# access-list 99 deny 131.108.134.0 0.0.0.255 ?
  <cr>

Router(config)# access-list 99 deny 131.108.134.0 0.0.0.255
```

The <cr> symbol by itself indicates there are no more keywords or arguments. Press Return to execute the command. The system adds an entry to access list 99 that denies access to all hosts on subnet 131.108.134.0.

Displaying Help for All User-Level Commands

To configure a line to display help for the full set of user-level commands during all sessions, perform the following task in line configuration mode:

Task	Command
Configure a line or lines to receive help for the full set of user-level commands when a user presses ?.	**full-help**

To configure the current session to display help for the full set of user-level commands, perform the following task in user **exec** mode:

Task	Command
Configure this session to provide help for the full set of user-level commands.	**terminal full-help**

The **full-help** and **terminal full-help** commands enable (or disable) a display of all help messages available from the terminal. They are used with the **show** command.

The following example is output for **show ?** with **terminal full-help** disabled and then enabled:

```
Router> show ?
  bootflash  Boot Flash information
  calendar   Display the hardware calendar
  clock      Display the system clock
  context    Show context information
  dialer     Dialer parameters and statistics
  history    Display the session command history
  hosts      IP domain-name, lookup style, nameservers, and host table
  isdn       ISDN information
  kerberos   Show Kerberos Values
  modemcap   Show Modem Capabilities database
  ppp        PPP parameters and statistics
  rmon       rmon statistics
  sessions   Information about Telnet connections
  snmp       snmp statistics
  terminal   Display terminal configuration parameters
  users      Display information about terminal lines
  version    System hardware and software status

Router> terminal full-help
Router> show ?
  access-expression  List access expression
  access-lists       List access lists
  aliases            Display alias commands
  apollo             Apollo network information
  appletalk          AppleTalk information
```

```
arp             ARP table
async           Information on terminal lines used as router interfaces
bootflash       Boot Flash information
bridge          Bridge Forwarding/Filtering Database [verbose]
bsc             BSC interface information
bstun.          BSTUN interface information
buffers         Buffer pool statistics
calendar        Display the hardware calendar
cdp             CDP information
clns            CLNS network information
clock           Display the system clock
cls             DLC user information
cmns            Connection-Mode networking services (CMNS) information
...
x25             X.25 information
xns             XNS information
xremote         XRemote statistics
```

CHECKING COMMAND SYNTAX

The user interface provides error isolation in the form of an error indicator, a caret symbol (^). The ^ symbol appears at the point in the command string where you have entered an incorrect command, keyword, or argument.

In the following example, suppose you want to set the clock. Use context-sensitive help to check the syntax for setting the clock.

```
Router# clock ?
  set  Set the time and date
Router# clock
```

The help output shows that the set keyword is required. Check the syntax for entering the time:

```
Router# clock set ?
hh:mm:ss   Current time
Router# clock set
```

Enter the current time:

```
Router# clock set 13:32:00
% Incomplete command.
```

The system indicates that you need to provide additional arguments to complete the command. Press **Ctrl-P** (see the next section, "Using the Command History Feature" to repeat automatically the previous command entry. Then add a space and question mark (?) to reveal the additional arguments:

```
Router# clock set 13:32:00 ?
  <1-31>     Day of the month
  January    Month of the year
  February
  March
  April
  May
  June
```

```
July
August
September
October
November
December
```

Now you can complete the command entry:

```
Router# clock set 13:32:00 23 February 97
                                         ^
% Invalid input detected at '^' marker.
```

The caret symbol (^) and help response indicate an error at 97. To list the correct syntax, enter the command up to the point where the error occurred and then enter a question mark (?):

```
Router# clock set 13:32:00 23 February ?
  <1993-2035> Year
Router# clock set 13:32:00 23 February
```

Enter the year using the correct syntax and press Return to execute the command.

```
Router# clock set 13:32:00 23 February 1997
```

USING THE COMMAND HISTORY FEATURE

With the current Cisco IOS release, the user interface provides a history, or record, of commands that you have entered. This feature is particularly useful for recalling long or complex commands or entries, including access lists. With the command history feature, you can complete the tasks in the following sections:

- Setting the Command History Buffer Size
- Recalling Commands
- Disabling the Command History Feature

Setting the Command History Buffer Size

By default, the system records 10 command lines in its history buffer. To set the number of command lines that the system will record during the current terminal session, complete the following task in EXEC mode:

Task	Command
Enable the command history feature for the current terminal session.	**terminal history** [size *number-of-lines*]

The **terminal no history size** command resets the number of lines saved in the history buffer to the default of 10 lines.

To configure the number of command lines the system will record for all sessions on a particular line, complete the following task in line configuration mode:

Task	Command
Enable the command history feature.	**history** [**size** *number-of-lines*][1]

[1] The **no history** command turns off command history for the line.

Recalling Commands

To recall commands from the history buffer, perform one of the following tasks:

Task	Key Sequence/Command
Recall commands in the history buffer, beginning with the most recent command. Repeat the key sequence to recall successively older commands.	Press **Ctrl-P** or the up arrow key.[1]
Return to more recent commands in the history buffer after recalling commands with Ctrl-P or the up arrow key. Repeat the key sequence to recall successively more recent commands.	Press **Ctrl-N** or the down arrow key.[1]
While in EXEC mode, list the last several commands you have just entered.	**show history**

[1] The arrow keys function only on ANSI-compatible terminals such as VT100s.

Disabling the Command History Feature

The command history feature is automatically enabled. To disable it during the current terminal session, complete the following task in EXEC mode:

Task	Command
Disable the command history feature for the current session.	**terminal no history**

To configure a specific line so that the command history feature is disabled, complete the following task in line configuration mode:

Task	Command
Configure the line so that the command history feature is disabled.	**no history**

USING THE EDITING FEATURES

The current software release includes an enhanced editing mode that provides a set of editing key functions similar to those of the Emacs editor.

You can enter commands in uppercase, lowercase, or a mix of both. Only passwords are case sensitive. You can abbreviate commands and keywords to the number of characters that allow a unique abbreviation. For example, you can abbreviate the **show** command to **sh**. After entering the command line at the system prompt, press the Return key to execute the command.

The following subsections are included in this section:

- Enabling Enhanced Editing Mode
- Moving Around on the Command Line
- Completing a Partial Command Name
- Pasting in Buffer Entries
- Editing Command Lines that Wrap
- Deleting Entries
- Scrolling Down a Line or a Screen
- Redisplaying the Current Command Line
- Transposing Mistyped Characters
- Controlling Capitalization
- Designating a Keystroke as a Command Entry
- Disabling Enhanced Editing Mode

Enabling Enhanced Editing Mode

Although enhanced editing mode is automatically enabled with the current Cisco IOS release, you can disable it and revert to the editing mode of previous Cisco IOS releases. (See the section "Disabling Enhanced Editing Mode" later in this chapter.)

To re-enable the enhanced editing mode for the current terminal session, complete the following task in EXEC mode:

Task	Command
Enable the enhanced editing features for the current terminal session.	**terminal editing**

To reconfigure a specific line to have enhanced editing mode, complete the following task in line configuration mode:

Task	Command
Enable the enhanced editing features.	**editing**

Moving Around on the Command Line

Perform the following tasks to move the cursor around on the command line to make corrections or changes:

Task	Keystrokes
Step 1 Move the cursor back one character.	Press **Ctrl-B** or press the left arrow key.[1]
Step 2 Move the cursor forward one character.	Press **Ctrl-F** or press the right arrow key.[1]
Step 3 Move the cursor to the beginning of the command line.	Press **Ctrl-A**.
Step 4 Move the cursor to the end of the command line.	Press **Ctrl-E**.
Step 5 Move the cursor back one word.	Press **Esc B**.
Step 6 Move the cursor forward one word.	Press **Esc F**.

[1] The arrow keys function only on ANSI-compatible terminals such as VT100s.

Completing a Partial Command Name

If you cannot remember a complete command name, press the Tab key to allow the system to complete a partial entry. To do so, perform the following task:

Task	Keystrokes
Complete a command name.	Enter the first few letters and press the Tab key.

If your keyboard does not have a Tab key, press **Ctrl-I** instead.

In the following example, when you enter the letters **conf** and press the Tab key, the system provides the complete command:

```
Router# conf<Tab>
Router# configure
```

If you enter a set of characters that could indicate more than one command, the system beeps to indicate an error. Enter a question mark (**?**) to obtain a list of commands that begin with that set of characters. Do not leave a space between the last letter you enter and the question mark (**?**).

For example, there are three commands in privileged mode that start with co. To see what they are, type **co?** at the privileged EXEC prompt:

```
Router# co?
configure  connect  copy
Router# co
```

Pasting in Buffer Entries

The system provides a buffer that contains the last 10 items you deleted. To recall these items and paste them in the command line, perform the following tasks:

Task	Keystrokes
Step 1 Recall the most recent entry in the buffer.	Press **Ctrl-Y**.
Step 2 Recall the next buffer entry.	Press **Esc Y**.

The buffer contains only the last 10 items you have deleted or cut. If you press **Esc Y** more than 10 times, you will cycle back to the first buffer entry.

Editing Command Lines that Wrap

The new editing command set provides a wraparound feature for commands that extend beyond a single line on the screen. When the cursor reaches the right margin, the command line shifts

10 spaces to the left. You cannot see the first ten characters of the line, but you can scroll back and check the syntax at the beginning of the command. To scroll back, perform the following task:

Task	Keystrokes
Return to the beginning of a command line to verify that you have entered a lengthy command correctly.	Press **Ctrl-B** or the left arrow key repeatedly until you scroll back to the beginning of the command entry, or press **Ctrl-A** to return directly to the beginning of the line.[1]

[1] The arrow keys function only on ANSI-compatible terminals such as VT100s.

In the following example, the **access-list** command entry extends beyond one line. When the cursor first reaches the end of the line, the line is shifted 10 spaces to the left and redisplayed. The dollar sign ($) indicates that the line has been scrolled to the left. Each time the cursor reaches the end of the line, the line is again shifted 10 spaces to the left.

```
Router(config)# access-list 101 permit tcp 131.108.2.5 255.255.255.0 131.108.1
Router(config)# $ 101 permit tcp 131.108.2.5 255.255.255.0 131.108.1.20 255.25
Router(config)# $t tcp 131.108.2.5 255.255.255.0 131.108.1.20 255.255.255.0 eq
Router(config)# $108.2.5 255.255.255.0 131.108.1.20 255.255.255.0 eq 45
```

When you have completed the entry, press **Ctrl-A** to check the complete syntax before pressing the Return key to execute the command. The dollar sign ($) appears at the end of the line to indicate that the line has been scrolled to the right:

```
Router(config)# access-list 101 permit tcp 131.108.2.5 255.255.255.0 131.108.1$
```

The Cisco IOS software assumes you have a terminal screen that is 80 columns wide. If you have a width other than that, use the **terminal width** command to set the width of your terminal.

Use line wrapping in conjunction with the command history feature to recall and modify previous complex command entries. See the section "Recalling Commands" earlier in this chapter for information about recalling previous command entries.

Deleting Entries

Perform any of the following tasks to delete command entries if you make a mistake or change your mind:

Task	Keystrokes
Erase the character to the left of the cursor.	Press the Delete or Backspace key.
Delete the character at the cursor.	Press **Ctrl-D**.
Delete all characters from the cursor to the end of the command line.	Press **Ctrl-K**.

Task	Keystrokes
Delete all characters from the cursor to the beginning of the command line.	Press **Ctrl-U** or **Ctrl-X**.
Delete the word to the left of the cursor.	Press **Ctrl-W**.
Delete from the cursor to the end of the word.	Press **Esc D**.

Scrolling Down a Line or a Screen

When you use the help facility to list the commands available in a particular mode, the list is often longer than the terminal screen can display. In such cases, a - - -More- - - prompt is displayed at the bottom of the screen. To view the next line or screen, complete the following tasks:

Task	Keystrokes
Step 1 Scroll down one line.	Press the Return key.
Step 2 Scroll down one screen.	Press the Space bar.

NOTES

The - - -More- - - prompt is used for any output that has more lines than can be displayed on the terminal screen, including **show** command output. You can use the keystrokes listed above whenever you see the - - -More- - - prompt.

Redisplaying the Current Command Line

If you are entering a command and the system suddenly sends a message to your screen, you can easily recall your current command line entry. To do so, perform the following task:

Task	Keystrokes
Redisplay the current command line.	Press **Ctrl-L** or **Ctrl-R**.

Transposing Mistyped Characters

If you have mistyped a command entry, you can transpose the mistyped characters by performing the following task:

Task	Keystrokes
Transpose the character to the left of the cursor with the character located at the cursor.	Press **Ctrl-T.**

Controlling Capitalization

You can capitalize or lowercase words or capitalize a set of letters with simple keystroke sequences. To do so, perform the following tasks:

Task		Keystrokes
Step 1	Capitalize at the cursor.	Press **Esc C.**
Step 2	Change the word at the cursor to lowercase.	Press **Esc L.**
Step 3	Capitalize letters from the cursor to the end of the word.	Press **Esc U.**

Designating a Keystroke as a Command Entry

Sometimes you might want to use a particular keystroke as an executable command, perhaps as a shortcut. Complete the following task to insert a system code for this purpose:

Task	Keystrokes
Insert a code to indicate to the system that the keystroke immediately following should be treated as a command entry, *not* an editing key.	Press **Ctrl-V** or **Esc Q.**

Disabling Enhanced Editing Mode

To globally disable enhanced editing mode and revert to the editing mode of previous software releases, perform the following task in line configuration mode:

Task	Command
Disable the enhanced editing features for a particular line.	**no editing**

To disable enhanced editing mode and revert to the editing mode of software releases before Cisco IOS release 9.21 for the current terminal session, perform the following task in EXEC mode:

Task	Command
Disable the enhanced editing features for the local line.	**terminal no editing**

For example, you might disable enhanced editing if you have prebuilt scripts that conflict when enhanced editing is enabled. You can re-enable enhanced editing mode with the **editing** command or **terminal editing** command.

The editing keys and functions of software releases before 9.21 are listed in Table 1–3.

Table 1–3   *Editing Keys and Functions for Software Release 9.1 and Earlier*

Key	Function
Delete or Backspace	Erases the character to the left of the cursor.
Ctrl-W	Erases a word.
Ctrl-U	Erases a line.
Ctrl-R	Redisplays a line.
Ctrl-Z	Ends configuration mode and returns to the EXEC prompt.
Return	Executes single-line commands.

CREATING MENUS

A menu is a displayed list of actions from which you can select without having to know anything about the underlying command-level details. A menu system effectively controls which functions a user can access. Figure 1–1 illustrates the parts that make up a typical menu.

CREATING A MENU TASK LIST

To create menus, perform the tasks in the following sections:

- Specifying the Menu Title
- Understanding Menu Guidelines
- Specifying the Menu Item Text

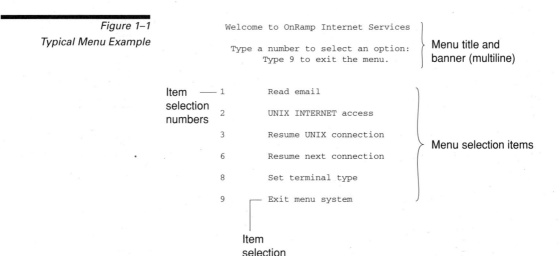

Figure 1–1
Typical Menu Example

• Specifying the Underlying Command for the Menu Item
• Creating a Submenu
• Creating Hidden Menu Entries
• Specifying Menu Display Configuration Options
• Invoking the Menu
• Deleting the Menu from the Configuration

Understanding Menu Guidelines

Anyone who can enter configuration mode can create these menus. Keep the following guidelines in mind when you create menus:

• Each menu item represents a single user command.
• The menu system default is a standard "dumb" terminal that only displays text in a 24-line-by-80-column format.
• A menu can have a maximum of 18 menu items. Menus containing more than nine menu items are automatically configured as single-spaced menus; menus containing nine or fewer menu items are automatically configured as double-spaced menus, but can be configured as single-spaced menus using the **single-space** option of the **menu** command. (For more information about menu display configuration options, see the section "Specifying Menu Display Configuration Options" later in this chapter.)

- When you construct a menu, always specify how a user exits a menu and where the user goes. If you do not provide an exit from a menu—such as with the **menu-exit** command (described in the section "Specifying the Underlying Command for the Menu Item" later in this chapter), there is no way to exit the menu.

- The **exec-timeout** command can be used to close and clean up an idle menu; the **session-timeout** command can be used to clean up a menu with an open connection.

Specifying the Menu Title

You can specify an identifying title for the menu. To specify the menu title, perform the following task in global configuration mode:

Task	Command
Specify the title for the menu.	**menu** *name* **title** *delimiter title delimiter*

The following example specifies the title that is displayed when the OnRamp menu is selected. The following four main elements create the title:

- The **menu title** command
- Delimiter characters that open and close the title text
- Escape characters to clear the screen (optional)
- Title text

The following example shows the command used to create the title for the menu shown in Figure 1.1, at the beginning of this section:

```
Router(config)# menu OnRamp title /^[[H^[[J
Enter TEXT message.  End with the character '/'.
        Welcome to OnRamp Internet Services


        Type a number to select an option;
            Type 9 to exit the menu.
/
Router(config)#
```

You can position the title of the menu horizontally by preceding the title text with blank characters. You also can add lines of space above and below the title by pressing **Return**.

In this example, the title text consists of the following:

- One-line title
- Space
- Two-line menu instruction banner

Title text must be enclosed within text delimiter characters—the slash character (/) in this example. Title text delimiters are characters that ordinarily do not appear within the text of a title, such as slash (/), double quote ("), or tilde (~). You can use any character that is not likely to be used within the text of the title as delimiter characters. Ctrl-C is reserved for special use and should not be used in the text of the title.

This title text example also includes an escape character sequence to clear the screen before displaying the menu. In this case, the string ^[[H^[[J is an escape string used by many VT100-compatible terminals to clear the screen. To enter it, you must enter **Ctrl-V** before each escape character (^[).

You also can use the **clear-screen** option of the **menu** command to clear the screen before displaying menus and submenus, instead of embedding a terminal-specific string in the menu title. This option uses a terminal-independent mechanism based on termcap entries defined in the router and the terminal type configured for the user's terminal. The **clear-screen** option allows the same menu to be used on multiple types of terminals instead of having terminal-specific strings embedded within menu titles. If the termcap entry does not contain a clear string, the menu system inserts 24 new lines, causing all existing text to scroll off the top of the terminal screen.

To add the **clear-screen** option to a menu, perform the following task in global configuration mode:

Task	Command
Specify screen clearing before displaying menus and submenus.	**menu** *name* **clear-screen**

The following example specifies the **clear-screen** option for the OnRamp menu:

```
Router(config)# menu OnRamp clear-screen
```

The terminal screen will be cleared before each menu or submenu is displayed.

Specifying the Menu Item Text

Each displayed menu entry consists of the selection number and the text describing the action to be performed. You can specify descriptive text for a maximum of 18 menu items. Because each menu entry represents a single user interface command, you must specify the menu item text one entry at a time. To specify the menu item text, perform the following task in global configuration mode:

Task	Command
Specify the text for the menu item.	**menu** *name* **text** *number text*

The following example specifies the text that is displayed for the three entries in the OnRamp menu:

```
Router(config)# menu OnRamp text 1 Read email
Router(config)# menu OnRamp text 2 UNIX Internet Access
Router(config)# menu OnRamp text 9 Exit menu system
```

You can provide access to context-sensitive help by creating a "help server" host and using a menu entry to make a connection to that host.

Menu selection numbers do not need to be contiguous. You can provide consistency across menus by assigning a particular number to a special function—such as Help or Exit—regardless of the number of menu entries in a given menu. For example, menu entry 1 could be reserved for help across all menus, and the last menu entry (for example, 9) could be reserved for the exit.

When more than nine menu items are defined in a menu, the **line-mode** and **single-space** options to the **menu** command are activated automatically, but also can be configured explicitly for menus of nine items or fewer. For more information on these commands, refer to the section "Specifying Menu Display Configuration Options" later in this chapter.

Specifying the Underlying Command for the Menu Item

Each displayed menu entry issues a user interface command when the user enters its number. Each menu entry can have only a single command associated with it. To specify the menu item command, perform the following task in global configuration mode:

Task	Command
Specify the command to be performed when the menu item is selected.	**menu** *name* **command** *number command*

The following example specifies the commands that are associated with the three entries in the OnRamp menu:

```
Router(config)# menu OnRamp command 1 rlogin mailsys
Router(config)# menu OnRamp command 2 rlogin unix.cisco.com
Router(config)# menu OnRamp command 9 menu-exit
```

The **menu-exit** command is available only from within menus. This command provides a way to return to a higher-level menu or to exit the menu system.

When a menu item allows connections (their normal use), the menu item also should contain entries that can be used to resume connections; otherwise, when a user escapes from a connection and returns to the menu, there is no way to resume the session and it will sit idle until the user logs off.

You can build the **resume connection** EXEC command into a menu entry so that the user can resume a connection, or you can configure the line using the **escape-char none** command to prevent users from escaping their sessions.

To specify connection resumption as part of the menu item command, perform the following task in global configuration mode:

Task	Command
Specify the command to be performed when the menu item is selected.	menu *name* **command** *number* **resume** [*connection*] **/connect** [*connect string*]

Embedding the **resume** command within the **menu** command permits a user to resume the named connection or make another connection using the specified name, if there is no active connection by that name. As an option, you also can supply the connect string needed to connect initially. When you do not supply this connect string, the command uses the specified connection name.

You can use the **resume** command in a menu in the following functions:

- Embedded in a menu entry
- As a separate, specific menu entry
- As a "rotary" menu entry

In the following example, the **resume** command is embedded in the **menu** command so that selecting the menu item either starts the specified connection session (if one is not already open) or resumes the session (if one is already open):

```
Router(config)# menu Duluth text 1 Read email
Router(config)# menu Duluth command 1 resume mailsys /connect rlogin mailsys
```

In the following example, the **resume** command is used in a separate menu entry (entry 3) to resume a specific connection:

```
Router(config)# menu Duluth text 3 Resume UNIX Internet Access
Router(config)# menu Duluth command 3 resume unix.cisco.com
```

You use the **resume/next** command to resume the next open connection in the user's list of connections. This command allows you to create a single menu entry that steps through all of the user's connections. To specify **resume/next** connection resumption as part of the menu item command, perform the following task in global configuration mode:

Task	Command
Specify **resume/next** connection resumption.	menu *name* **command** *number* **resume /next**

The following example shows a menu entry (entry 6) created to step through all of the user's connections:

```
Router(config)# menu Duluth text 6 Resume next connection
Router(config)# menu Duluth command 6 resume /next
```

Creating a Submenu

To create submenus that are opened by selecting a higher-level menu entry, use the **menu** command to invoke a menu in a line menu entry. To specify a submenu item command, perform the following tasks in global configuration mode:

Task		Command
Step 1	Specify the menu item that invokes the submenu.	**menu** *name* **text** *number text*
Step 2	Specify the command to be performed when the menu item is selected.	**menu** *name* **command** *number* **menu** *name2*
Step 3	Specify the title for the submenu.	**menu** *name2* **title** *delimiter title2 delimiter*
Step 4	Specify the submenu item.	**menu** *name2* **text** *number text*
Step 5	Specify the commands to be performed when the submenu item is selected.	**menu** *name2* **command** *number command*

The following example specifies that the menu item (entry 8) activates the submenu in the OnRamp menu:

```
Router(config)# menu OnRamp text 8 Set terminal type
```

The following example specifies the command that is performed when the menu item (entry 8) is selected in the OnRamp menu:

```
Router(config)# menu OnRamp command 8 menu Terminals
```

The following example specifies the title for the Terminals submenu:

```
Router(config)# menu Terminals title /
            Supported Terminal Types


        Type a number to select an option;
        Type 9 to return to the previous menu.
```

The following example specifies the submenu items for the Terminals submenu:

```
Router(config)# menu Terminals text 1 DEC VT420 or similar
Router(config)# menu Terminals text 2 Heath H-19
Router(config)# menu Terminals text 3 IBM 3051 or equivalent
Router(config)# menu Terminals text 4 Macintosh with gterm emulator
Router(config)# menu Terminals text 9 Return to previous menu
```

The following example specifies the commands associated with the items in the Terminals submenu:

```
Router(config)# menu Terminals command 1 term terminal-type vt420
Router(config)# menu Terminals command 2 term terminal-type h19
Router(config)# menu Terminals command 3 term terminal-type ibm3051
Router(config)# menu Terminals command 4 term terminal-type gterm
Router(config)# menu Terminals command 9 menu-exit
```

When you select entry 8 on the main menu, the Terminals submenu appears:

```
Supported Terminal Types

   Type a number to select an option;
Type 9 to return to the previous menu.

1      DEC VT420 or similar

2      Heath H-19

3      IBM 3051 or equivalent

4      Macintosh with gterm emulator

9      Return to previous menu
```

NOTES

If you nest too many levels of menus, the system prints an error message on the terminal and returns to the previous menu level.

Creating Hidden Menu Entries

A hidden menu entry is a menu item that contains a selection number but no associated text describing the action to be performed. Include this type of menu entry to aid system administrators who help users. The normal procedure is to specify a menu command but omit specifying any text for the item. To specify a hidden menu item, perform the following task in global configuration mode:

Task	Command
Specify the command to be performed when the hidden menu entry is selected.	**menu** *name* **command** *number command*

The following example shows the command associated with the submenu entry in the OnRamp menu:

```
Router(config)# menu OnRamp command 7 show whoami
```

The **show whoami** command can be included in menus to aid system administrators who help users. If text is included as an argument in the command, that text is displayed as part of the additional data about the line, and helps identify exactly which menu or submenu the user is accessing. Because the **show whoami** command is hidden inside the menu entry, this information might not be otherwise available. For example, the hidden menu entry created by the line in the configuration file `menu OnRamp command 7 show whoami Terminals submenu of OnRamp Internet Access` menu might display information similar to the following:

```
Comm Server "cs101", Line 0 at 0 bps. Location "Second floor, West"
Additional data: Terminals submenu of OnRamp Internet Access menu
```

To prevent the information from being lost if the menu display clears the screen, this command always displays a ---More--- prompt before returning.

Specifying Menu Display Configuration Options

In addition to the **clear-screen** option in the **menu** command, described in the section "Specifying the Menu Title," the following are the three other **menu** command options that define menu functions:

- line-mode
- single-space
- status-line

Using Line Mode in Menus

In a menu of nine or fewer items, you ordinarily select a menu item by entering the item number. In line mode, you select a menu entry by entering the item number and pressing Return. The line mode allows you to backspace over the selected number and enter another before pressing Return to perform the command. This function allows you to change the selection number before you invoke the command.

To invoke the **line-mode** option, perform the following task in global configuration mode:

Task	Command
Specify line-mode operation.	**menu** *name* **line-mode**

The line-mode option is invoked automatically when more than nine menu items are defined, but it also can be configured explicitly for menus of nine items or fewer.

Displaying Single-Spaced Menus

If there are nine or fewer menu items, the Cisco IOS software ordinarily displays the menu items double-spaced. In a menu of more than nine items, the **single-space** option is activated automatically to fit the menu into a normal 24-line terminal screen. However, the single-space option also can be configured explicitly for menus of nine or fewer items.

To invoke the **single-space** option, perform the following task in global configuration mode:

Task	Command
Specify single-space operation.	**menu** *name* **single-space**

Displaying an Informational Status Line

The **status-line** option displays a line of status information about the current user at the top of the terminal screen before the menu title is displayed. This status line includes the router's host name, the user's line number, and the current terminal type and keymap type (if any).

To display the **status-line** option, perform the following task in global configuration mode:

Task	Command
Display a status line when using a menu.	**menu** *name* **status-line**

Invoking the Menu

To invoke the menu, perform the following task at the EXEC prompt:

Task	Command
Invoke the menu by specifying the name of the menu.	**menu** *name*

You can define menus containing privileged EXEC commands, but users must have privileged access when they start up the menu.

To ensure that a menu is automatically invoked on a line, make sure the menu does not have any exit paths that leave users in an interface they cannot operate, then configure that line with the command **autocommand menu** *menu_name*.

Menus also can be invoked on a per-user basis by defining an **autocommand** for that local user-name.

Invoke a Menu Example

The following example invokes the *OnRamp* menu:

```
Router> menu OnRamp

    Welcome to OnRamp Internet Services

    Type a number to select an option;
        Type 9 to exit the menu.
```

```
1    Read email

2    UNIX Internet access

3    Resume UNIX connection


6    Resume next connection

9    Exit menu system
```

Deleting the Menu from the Configuration

To delete the menu from the configuration, perform the following task in global configuration mode:

Task	Command
Delete the menu by specifying the menu name.	**no menu** *name*

The following example deletes the OnRamp menu from the configuration:
```
Router(config)# no menu OnRamp
```

USING THE CISCO WEB BROWSER INTERFACE TO ISSUE COMMANDS

You can issue most of the Cisco IOS commands using a Web browser. This Cisco IOS feature is accessed by using the Cisco Web browser interface, which is accessed from the router's home page. (All Cisco routers and access servers loaded with the latest version of Cisco IOS software have a home page, which is password-protected.)

From the router's home page, you click on a hypertext link titled "Monitor the Router." This link takes you to a Web page that has a "Command" field. You can type commands in this field as if you were entering commands at a terminal connected to the router. The page also displays a list of commands. You can execute these commands by clicking on them, as if you were clicking hypertext links.

Cisco Web Browser Interface Task List

To use the Cisco Web browser interface to issue commands, perform the tasks in the following sections:

- Configuring the Cisco Web Browser Interface
- Using the Correct Hardware and Software
- Accessing Your Router's Home Page

- Issuing Commands Using the Cisco Web Browser Interface
  - ○ Entering Commands Using Hypertext Links
  - ○ Entering Commands Using the Command Field
  - ○ Entering Commands Using the URL Window

Configuring the Cisco Web Browser Interface

You can enable the Cisco Web browser interface on any router running Cisco IOS Release 11.0(6) or later software. Once enabled, you will be able to issue Cisco IOS commands to your router using a Web browser.

The Web browser interface is automatically enabled when you use ClickStart to configure a Cisco 1003, Cisco 1004, or Cisco 1005 router.

If you have any other Cisco router, you must enable the Web browser interface by altering the routers' configuration. To do this, perform the tasks in the following list. The first task is required; the remaining are optional.

- Enabling the Cisco Web Browser Interface
- Changing the Cisco Web Browser Interface Port Number
- Controlling Access to the Cisco Web Browser Interface
- Specifying the Method for User Authentication

Enabling the Cisco Web Browser Interface

To enable a Cisco router to be configured from a browser using the Cisco Web browser interface, perform the following task in global configuration mode:

Task	Command
Enable a router to be reconfigured using the Cisco Web browser interface.	**ip http server**

Now that the Cisco Web browser interface is enabled, you can perform any of the optional tasks or proceed to configure a router using the Cisco Web browser interface.

Changing the Cisco Web Browser Interface Port Number

By default, the Cisco Web browser interface uses port 80 on the router. To assign the Cisco Web browser interface to a different port, perform the following task in global configuration mode:

Task	Command
Assign a port number to be used by the Cisco Web browser interface.	**ip http port** *number*

Controlling Access to the Cisco Web Browser Interface

To control which hosts can access the http server used by the Cisco Web browser interface, perform the following task in global configuration mode:

Task	Command
Control access to the http server used by the Cisco Web browser interface.	**ip http access-class** {*access-list-number* | *name*}

Specifying the Method for User Authentication

To specify how HTTP server users are authenticated, perform the following task in global configuration mode:

Task	Command
Specify how HTTP server users are authenticated.	**ip http authentication** {aaa | enable | local | tacacs}

Using the Correct Hardware and Software

To use the Cisco Web browser interface, your computer must have a World Wide Web browser. The Cisco Web browser interface works with most browsers, including Netscape Navigator. Your Web browser must be able read and submit forms. The original versions of Mosaic might have problems using the Cisco Web browser interface, because they either cannot submit forms or have difficulty doing so.

The computer must be connected to the same network that the router or access server is on.

Accessing Your Router's Home Page

Cisco IOS Release 11.0(6) or later software allows users with a default privilege level of 15 to access a predefined home page for a router or access server. If you have been assigned a privilege level other than 15, Cisco IOS Release 11.3 or later software allows you to issue Cisco IOS commands from a Web page where the commands defined for your specific user privilege level will be displayed.

To access the home page for your router or access server with a default privilege level of 15, perform the following steps:

Step 1   Enter the following command in the URL field of your Web browser and press return: **http://**_router-name_**/**. (For example, to access a Cisco router named _cacophony_ with a default privilege level of 15, type http://cacophony/). The browser then prompts you for the password.

Step 2   Enter the password.

NOTES

The name and password for your router and access server are designated in their configuration. Contact your network administrator if you do not have this information.

The browser should display the home page for your router or access server.

The router's home page looks something like the Cisco 7200 home page shown in Figure 1–2.

Figure 1–2

Example of a Home Page for a Cisco 7200

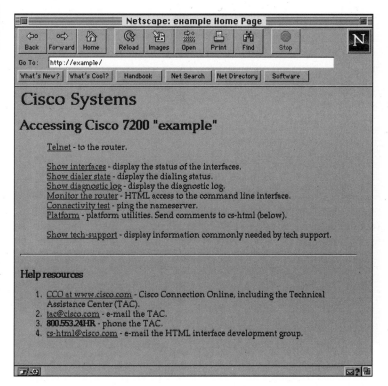

To access a router Web page for a preassigned privilege level other than the default of 15, perform the following steps:

Step 1   Enter the following command in the URL field of your Web browser and press return: **http://***router-name***/level/***level***/***mode***/***command*. (For example, to request a user privilege level of 12 on a Cisco router named *cacophony*, type http://cacophony/level/12/exec).The browser then prompts you for the username and/or password.

Step 2   Depending on your authentication method, enter your username and/or password and press return. The Web browser should display a Web page specific to your user privilege level, mode, and the command you have requested.

Table 1–4   lists the URL arguments you must use when requesting a Web page.

Table 1–4   *Description of the URL Arguments*

Argument	Description
router-name	Name of the router being configured.
level	The privilege level you are requesting.
mode	The mode the command will be executed in, such as EXEC, configure, and interface.
command	(Optional) The command you want to execute. If you specify a command, your browser will display a Web page showing the results of the requested command. If you do not specify a command in the URL, your browser will display a Web page listing all of the commands available for your privilege level.

Issuing Commands Using the Cisco Web Browser Interface

To issue commands using the Cisco Web browser interface, click the link "Monitor the router" in the first list of hypertext links on the home page. This displays the Web page shown in Figure 1–3.

Entering Commands Using Hypertext Links

To enter a command using hypertext links, scroll through the commands listed at the bottom of the screen and click the one you want to execute. If the link is a complete command, it is executed. If the command has more parameters, another list of command hypertext links is displayed. Scroll through this second list and click the one you want to execute.

If the command is a request for information, like a **show** command, the information is displayed in the Web browser window.

If the command requires a variable, a form in which you can enter the variable is displayed.

Figure 1–3

The "Command" Field Web Page for a Router Named "example"

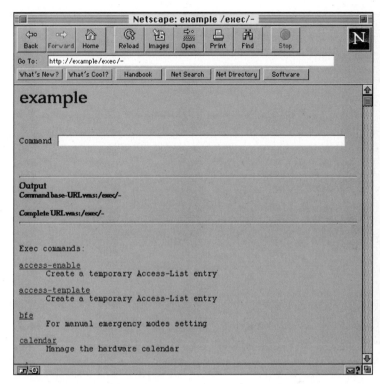

Entering Commands Using the Command Field

Entering the command in the command field is just like entering it at a terminal console. Enter the command using the syntax documented in the Cisco IOS command reference. If you are uncertain of the options available for a particular command, type a question mark (**?**).

For example, entering **show ?** in the command field displays the parameters for the **show** command. The Cisco Web browser interface displays the parameters as hypertext links. To select a parameter, you can either click one of the links, or you can enter the parameter in the command field.

Entering Commands Using the URL Window

You can issue a command using the URL window for the Web browser.

For example, to execute a **show configuration** command on a router named *example*, you would enter the following in the URL window:

```
http://example/exec/show/configuration
```

The Web browser then displays the configuration for the "example" router. To save effort, modify the URL in the URL window in the browser control bar instead of retyping the entire URL.

The difference between entering a command in the command field and entering a command in the URL window is that in the URL window, command modes, keywords, and options should be separated by slashes, not spaces.

CUSTOMIZING THE USER INTERFACE ON A WEB BROWSER

You can customize HTML pages to display Cisco IOS command output and Cisco IOS platform-specific variables (for example, a router host name or router address typically used in router setup pages) for a Web browser. You can display this information using HTML-formatted Server Side Includes (SSIs) that you insert into your custom HTML pages. SSIs are a Cisco IOS software feature described in the following sections.

Definition of SSIs

SSIs are HTML-formatted commands or variables that you insert into HTML pages when you customize Cisco IOS platform configuration pages for a Web browser. These SSI commands and SSI variables display Cisco IOS command output and Cisco IOS platform-specific variables.

The Cisco IOS software supports two HTML SSI commands defined for customizing HTML pages: the SSI EXEC command and the SSI ECHO command. The HTML format of the SSI EXEC command is **<!--#exec cmd=**"*xxx*"**-->**, and the HTML format of the SSI ECHO command is **<!--#echo var=**"*yyy*"**-->**. (See the section "Customizing HTML Pages Using SSIs" later in this chapter for a description of how to use these commands.)

In addition to the two SSI commands, the Cisco IOS software supports several SSI variables defined for customizing HTML pages. SSI variables are used with the SSI ECHO command. There is one SSI variable defined for all Cisco IOS platforms (SERVER_NAME) and other SSI variables specifically defined for ISDN, Frame Relay, and asynchronous serial platforms. The format and a description of all the available SSI variables are provided in Table 1–5. (See the section "Customizing HTML Pages Using SSIs" later in this chapter for a description of how to use these SSI variables with the SSI ECHO command.)

The SSI EXEC command is supported on all platforms. The SSI ECHO command, used with SSI variables, is supported on all platforms listed in Table 1–5.

Table 1–5   *Description of SSI Variables*

HTML Format of SSI Variable	Description of Variable Displayed on Browser Page	Cisco IOS Platform(s) This SSI Is Supported On
SERVER_NAME	Host name of the HTTP server.	All Cisco IOS platforms
EZSETUP_PASSWORD	Enable password (currently left blank).	Cisco 1000 series
EZSETUP_PASSWORD_ VERIFY	Repeat of the enable password to verify accuracy (currently left blank).	Cisco 1000 series

Table 1–5 *Description of SSI Variables, Continued*

HTML Format of SSI Variable	Description of Variable Displayed on Browser Page	Cisco IOS Platform(s) This SSI Is Supported On
EZSETUP_ETHERNET0_ADDRESS	IP address of the Ethernet 0 interface.	Cisco 1000 series
EZSETUP_ETHERNET0_MASK	IP mask of the Ethernet 0 interface.	Cisco 1000 series
EZSETUP_DNS_ADDRESS	DNS address used by the router.	Cisco 1000 series
EZSETUP_STANDARD_DEBUG_Y	Standard debug variable. Returns CHECKED if set to TRUE; otherwise, it is blank.	Cisco 1000 series
EZSETUP_STANDARD_DEBUG_N	Standard debug variable. Returns CHECKED if set to FALSE; otherwise, it is blank.	Cisco 1000 series
EZSETUP_ISDN_SWITCHTYPE	ISDN Switch type.	Cisco 1003 and Cisco 1004
EZSETUP_ISDN_REMOTE_NAME	Name of remote ISDN system.	Cisco 1003 and Cisco 1004
EZSETUP_ISDN_REMOTE_NUMBER	Phone number of remote ISDN system.	Cisco 1003 and Cisco 1004
EZSETUP_ISDN_CHAP_PASSWORD	CHAP password of remote ISDN system.	Cisco 1003 and Cisco 1004
EZSETUP_ISDN_SPID1	ISDN SPID 1.	Cisco 1003 and Cisco 1004
EZSETUP_ISDN_SPID2	ISDN SPID 2.	Cisco 1003 and Cisco 1004
EZSETUP_ISDN_SPEED_56	Speed of ISDN interface. Returns CHECKED if set to 56k; otherwise, it is blank.	Cisco 1003 and Cisco 1004
EZSETUP_ISDN_SPEED_64	Speed of ISDN interface. Returns CHECKED if set to 64k; otherwise, it is blank.	Cisco 1003 and Cisco 1004
EZSETUP_FR_ADDRESS	Frame-Relay IP address.	Cisco 1005
EZSETUP_FR_MASK	Frame-Relay IP mask.	Cisco 1005

Table 1–5 *Description of SSI Variables, Continued*

HTML Format of SSI Variable	Description of Variable Displayed on Browser Page	Cisco IOS Platform(s) This SSI Is Supported On
EZSETUP_FR_DLCI	Frame-Relay DLCI.	Cisco 1005
EZSETUP_ASYNC_ REMOTE_NAME	Name of remote system.	Cisco 1005
EZSETUP_ASYNC_ REMOTE_NUMBER	Phone number of remote system.	Cisco 1005
EZSETUP_ASYNC_ CHAP_PASSWORD	CHAP password for remote system.	Cisco 1005
EZSETUP_ASYNC_ LINE_PASSWORD	Async line password.	Cisco 1005
EZSETUP_ASYNC_ MODEM_SPEED	Speed of async modem (either 14.4k or 28.8k).	Cisco 1005
EZSETUP_ASYNC_ MODEM_SPEED_144K	Returns CHECKED if async modem speed is 14.4k; otherwise it is blank.	Cisco 1005
EZSETUP_ASYNC_ MODEM_SPEED_288K	Returns CHECKED if async modem speed is 28.8k; otherwise it is blank.	Cisco 1005

How SSIs Work

Once you have designed a set of HTML pages that include SSIs, you can copy these pages to a Cisco IOS platform's Flash memory. (See the section "Copying HTML Pages to Flash Memory" for instructions on storing HTML pages in Flash memory later in this section.) When you retrieve these pages from Flash memory and display them using a Web browser, any SSI command that was designed into these pages will either display Cisco IOS command output or display a current variable or identifier defined in Table 1–5. For example, the SSI ECHO command with the variable SERVER_NAME will display the current host name of the HTTP server you are using, and the SSI ECHO command with the variable EZSETUP_ISDN_SWITCHTYPE will display the current ISDN switch type you are using.

Benefits of Customizing Web Pages with SSIs

Using SSIs, you can customize one set of international HTML pages (for example, in Japanese) and copy these pages to Flash memory on multiple Cisco IOS platforms. When you retrieve these pages from the Flash memory of a Cisco IOS platform, current variables and identifiers associated with the platform you are currently using are displayed. SSIs save you from having to duplicate these international pages (considered relatively large images that contain 8-bit or multibyte characters) and store them in the source code for each platform you are using. (Refer to Table 1–5 to determine which Cisco IOS platforms support which SSIs variables.)

User Interface Customization Task List

To customize your HTML pages and view them for the user interface, perform the tasks in the following sections:

- Customizing HTML Pages Using SSIs
- Copying HTML Pages to Flash Memory
- Enabling the Cisco Web Browser Interface
- Viewing Your HTML File Containing SSIs

Customizing HTML Pages Using SSIs

When you are customizing an HTML page for a Web browser, type **<!--#exec cmd="***xxx***"-->** in your HTML file where you want Cisco IOS command output to appear on the browser page. Replace *xxx* with a Cisco IOS command that can be executed in the router's EXEC mode. (See the "SSI EXEC Command Example" section later in this chapter.)

When you are customizing an HTML page for a Web browser, type **<!--#echo var="***yyy***"-->** in your HTML file where you want a value or identifier associated with a particular Cisco IOS platform (for example, an ISDN or Frame Relay platform) to appear on the browser page. Replace *yyy* with an SSI variable described in Table 1–5. (See the "SSI ECHO Command Example" section later in this chapter.)

Copying HTML Pages to Flash Memory

Once you have customized HTML pages using SSIs, copy your HTML pages to a Cisco IOS platform's Flash memory. To do this, save your pages using a filename appended with ".shtml" (for example, *filename*.shtml) and copy your file to Flash memory using a **copy** command (for example, the **copy tftp flash** command). (Refer to the Cisco IOS command references for a **copy** command compatible with your Cisco IOS platform.)

Enabling the Cisco Web Browser Interface

To view the HTML pages you have just customized, you must first enable the Cisco Web browser interface. To enable the Cisco Web browser interface, perform the following task in global configuration mode:

Task	Command
Enable the Cisco Web browser interface.	**ip http server**

Refer to the section "Configuring the Cisco Web Browser Interface" earlier in this chapter for more information on configuring the Cisco Web browser interface.

Viewing Your HTML File Containing SSIs

Once the Cisco Web browser interface is enabled, you can retrieve your HTML page from Flash memory and view it on the Cisco Web browser by typing the URL **http://*router*/flash/*filename*** in the URL window. Replace *router* with the host name or IP address of the current Cisco IOS platform you are using, and replace *filename* with the name of the file you created with ".shtml" appended. For example, http://myrouter/flash/ssi_file.shtml.

SSI Configuration Examples

This section provides the following configuration examples:

- SSI EXEC Command Example
- SSI ECHO Command Example

SSI EXEC Command Example

The following is an example of the HTML SSI EXEC command used to display the Cisco IOS **show users** EXEC command output:

Contents of the HTML file in Flash memory:

```
<HTML>
<HEAD>
<TITLE> SSI EXEC Command Example</TITLE>
</HEAD>
<BODY>
This is an example of the SSI EXEC command
<HR>
<PRE>
<!--#exec cmd="show users"-->
</PRE>
<HR>
</BODY>
</HTML>
```

Contents that the Web browser receives when the HTML file is retrieved from Flash memory:

```
<HTML>
<HEAD>
<TITLE> SSI EXEC Command Example</TITLE>
</HEAD>
<BODY>
This is an example of the SSI EXEC command
<HR>
<PRE>

Line    User   Host(s) Idle  Location
0 con 0         idle     12
```

```
2 vty 0      idle      0  router.cisco.com
</PRE>
<HR>
</BODY>
</HTML>
```

SSI ECHO Command Example

The following is an example of the HTML SSI ECHO command used with the SSI variable *SERVER_NAME* (see Table 1–5) to display the Cisco IOS platform host name *rain*:

Contents of the HTML file in Flash memory:

```
<HTML>
<HEAD>
<TITLE>SSI Echo Command Example</TITLE>
</HEAD>
<BODY>
This is an example of the SSI echo command
<HR>
<!--#echo var="SERVER_NAME"-->
<HR>
</BODY>
</HTML>
```

Contents that the Web browser receives when the HTML file is retrieved from Flash memory:

```
<HTML>
<HEAD>
<TITLE>SSI Echo Command Example</TITLE>
</HEAD>
<BODY>
This is an example of the SSI echo command
<HR>
rain
<HR>
</BODY>
</HTML>
```

DISPLAYING 8-BIT AND MULTIBYTE CHARACTER SETS

Your Cisco IOS platform automatically will display 8-bit and multibyte character sets and print the ESC character as a single character instead of as the caret and bracket symbols (^[) when the Cisco Web browser interface is enabled with the **ip http server** command. (See the section "Configuring the Cisco Web Browser Interface" for more information on configuring the Cisco Web browser interface.)

If you are Telneting to a Cisco IOS platform, perform the following task in line configuration mode to display 8-bit and multibyte international character sets and print the ESC character as a single character instead of "^[":

Task	Command
Configure a router to display 8-bit and multibyte international character sets and print the ESC character as a single character instead of "^[" when Telneting to a Cisco IOS platform.	**international**

If you are Telneting to a Cisco IOS platform, perform the following task in EXEC mode to display 8-bit and multibyte international characters sets and print the ESC character as a single character instead of "^[" for the current Telnet session:

Task	Command
Configure a router to display 8-bit and multibyte international character sets and print the ESC character as a single character instead of "^[" when Telneting to a Cisco IOS platform for the current session.	**terminal international**

## CHAPTER 2

Basic Command Line Interface Commands

This chapter describes the commands used to enter and exit the various Cisco IOS configuration command modes. It provides a description of the **help** command and help features, lists the command editing keys and functions, and details the command history feature.

You can abbreviate the syntax of Cisco IOS configuration commands. The software recognizes a command when you enter enough characters of the command to uniquely identify it.

For user interface task information and examples, see Chapter 1, "Using the Command Line Interface."

DISABLE

To exit privileged EXEC mode and return to user EXEC mode, enter the **disable** EXEC command.

> **disable** [*level*]

Syntax	Description
level	(Optional) Specifies the user-privilege level.

NOTES

The **disable** command is associated with privilege level 0. If you configure AAA authorization for a privilege level greater than 0, this command will not be included in the command set for that privilege level.

Command Mode

EXEC

Usage Guidelines

This command first appeared in Cisco IOS Release 10.0.

Use this command with the **level** option to reduce the user-privilege level. If a level is not specified, it defaults to the user EXEC mode, which is level 1.

Example

In the following example, entering the **disable** command causes the system to exit privileged EXEC mode and return to user EXEC mode as indicated by the angle bracket (>):

```
Router# disable
Router>
```

Related Commands

enable

EDITING

To enable enhanced editing mode for a particular line, use the **editing** line configuration command. To disable the enhanced editing mode, use the **no** form of this command.

editing
no editing

Syntax   Description

This command has no arguments or keywords.

Default

Enabled

Command Mode

Line configuration

Usage Guidelines

This command first appeared in Cisco IOS Release 10.0.

Table 2–1 provides a description of the keys used to enter and edit commands. Ctrl indicates the Control key. It must be pressed simultaneously with its associated letter key. Esc indicates the Escape key. It must be pressed first, followed by its associated letter key. Keys are case sensitive.

Table 2–1 *Editing Keys and Functions for Cisco IOS Release 9.21 and Later*

Keys	Function
Tab	Completes a partial command-name entry. When you enter a unique set of characters and press the Tab key, the system completes the command name. If you enter a set of characters that could indicate more than one command, the system beeps to indicate an error. Enter a question mark (?) immediately following the partial command (no space). The system provides a list of commands that begin with that string.
Delete or Backspace	Erases the character to the left of the cursor.
Return	At the command line, pressing the Return key performs the function of processing a command. At the "`---More---`" prompt on a terminal screen, pressing the Return key scrolls down a line.
Space Bar	Allows you to see more output on the terminal screen. Press the space bar when you see the line "`---More---`" on the screen to display the next screen.
Left Arrow[1]	Moves the cursor one character to the left. When you enter a command that extends beyond a single line, you can press the Left Arrow key repeatedly to scroll back toward the system prompt and verify the beginning of the command entry.
Right Arrow[1]	Moves the cursor one character to the right.
Up Arrow[1] or Ctrl-P	Recalls commands in the history buffer, beginning with the most recent command. Repeat the key sequence to recall successively older commands.
Down Arrow[1] or Ctrl-N	Return to more recent commands in the history buffer after recalling commands with the Up Arrow or Ctrl-P. Repeat the key sequence to recall successively more recent commands.
Ctrl-A	Moves the cursor to the beginning of the line.
Ctrl-B	Moves the cursor back one character.
Ctrl-D	Deletes the character at the cursor.
Ctrl-E	Moves the cursor to the end of the command line.
Ctrl-F	Moves the cursor forward one character.
Ctrl-K	Deletes all characters from the cursor to the end of the command line.
Ctrl-L and Ctrl-R	Redisplays the system prompt and command line.

Table 2–1   *Editing Keys and Functions for Cisco IOS Release 9.21 and Later, Continued*

Keys	Function
Ctrl-T	Transposes the character to the left of the cursor with the character located at the cursor.
Ctrl-U and Ctrl-X	Deletes all characters from the cursor back to the beginning of the command line.
Ctrl-V and Esc Q	Inserts a code to indicate to the system that the keystroke immediately following should be treated as a command entry, *not* as an editing key.
Ctrl-W	Deletes the word to the left of the cursor.
Ctrl-Y	Recalls the most recent entry in the delete buffer. The delete buffer contains the last ten items you have deleted or cut. Ctrl-Y can be used in conjunction with Esc Y.
Ctrl-Z	Ends configuration mode and returns you to the EXEC prompt.
Esc B	Moves the cursor back one word.
Esc C	Capitalizes the word from the cursor to the end of the word.
Esc D	Deletes from the cursor to the end of the word.
Esc F	Moves the cursor forward one word.
Esc L	Changes the word to lowercase at the cursor to the end of the word.
Esc U	Capitalizes from the cursor to the end of the word.
Esc Y	Recalls the next buffer entry. The buffer contains the last ten items you have deleted. Press Ctrl-Y first to recall the most recent entry. Then press Esc Y up to nine times to recall the remaining entries in the buffer. If you bypass an entry, continue to press Esc Y to cycle back to it.

[1] The arrow keys function only with ANSI-compatible terminals.

Table 2–2 lists the editing keys and functions of the earlier software release.

Table 2–2   *Editing Keys and Functions for Cisco IOS Release 9.1 and Earlier*

Key	Function
Delete or Backspace	Erases the character to the left of the cursor.
Ctrl-W	Erases a word.
Ctrl-U	Erases a line.

Table 2–2 *Editing Keys and Functions for Cisco IOS Release 9.1 and Earlier, Continued*

Key	Function
Ctrl-R	Redisplays a line.
Ctrl-Z	Ends configuration mode and returns to the EXEC prompt.
Return	Executes single-line commands.

Example

In the following example, enhanced editing mode is disabled on line 3:

```
line 3
no editing
```

Related Commands

terminal editing

ENABLE

To enter privileged EXEC mode, use the **enable** EXEC command.

enable [*level*]

Syntax	*Description*
level	(Optional) Privileged level on which to log in.

> **NOTES**
>
> The **enable** command is associated with privilege level 0. If you configure AAA authorization for a privilege level greater than 0, this command will not be included in the command set for that privilege level.

Command Mode

EXEC

Usage Guidelines

This command first appeared in Cisco IOS Release 10.0.

Because many of the privileged commands set operating parameters, privileged access should be password-protected to prevent unauthorized use. If the system administrator has set a password with the **enable password** global configuration command, you are prompted to enter it before being allowed access to privileged EXEC mode. The password is case sensitive.

If an enable password has not been set, enable mode can be accessed only from the router console. If a level is not specified, it defaults to the privileged EXEC mode, which is level 15.

Example

In the following example, the user enters the **enable** command and is prompted to enter a password. The password is not displayed on the screen. After the user enters the correct password, the system enters privileged command mode as indicated by the pound sign (#).

```
Router> enable
Password:
Router#
```

Related Commands

disable
enable password

END

To exit configuration mode, or any of the configuration submodes, use the **end** global configuration command.

> **end**

Syntax   Description

This command has no arguments or keywords.

Command Mode

Global configuration

Usage Guidelines

This command first appeared in Cisco IOS Release 10.0.

You also can press **Ctrl-Z** to exit configuration mode.

Example

In the following example, the name is changed to *george* using the **hostname** global configuration command. Entering the **end** command causes the system to exit configuration mode and return to EXEC mode.

```
Router(config)# hostname george
george(config)# end
george#
```

Related Commands

hostname

EXIT

To exit any configuration mode or close an active terminal session and terminate the EXEC, use the **exit** command at the system prompt.

> **exit**

Syntax   Description

This command has no arguments or keywords.

Command Mode

Available in all command modes.

Usage Guidelines

This command first appeared in Cisco IOS Release 10.0.

Use the **exit** command at the EXEC levels to exit the EXEC mode. Use the **exit** command at the configuration level to return to privileged EXEC mode. Use the **exit** command in interface, line, router, IPX-router, and route-map command modes to return to global configuration mode. Use the **exit** command in subinterface configuration mode to return to interface configuration mode. You also can press **Ctrl-Z,** or use the **end** command from any configuration mode to return to privileged EXEC mode.

NOTES

The **exit** command is associated with privilege level 0. If you configure AAA authorization for a privilege level greater than 0, this command will not be included in the command set for that privilege level.

Examples

In the following example, the user exits subinterface configuration mode to return to interface configuration mode:

```
Router(config-subif)# exit
Router(config-if)#
```

The following example shows how to exit an active session.

```
Router> exit
```

Related Commands

disconnect
end
logout

FULL-HELP

To get help for the full set of user-level commands, use the **full-help** line configuration command.

> **full-help**

Syntax   Description

This command has no arguments or keywords.

Default

Disabled

Command Mode

Line configuration

Usage Guidelines

This command first appeared in Cisco IOS Release 10.0.

The **full-help** command enables (or disables) an unprivileged user to see all of the help messages available. It is used with the **show ?** command.

Example

The following example is output for the **show ?** command with **full-help** disabled and then enabled:

```
Router> show ?
  bootflash  Boot Flash information
  calendar   Display the hardware calendar
  clock      Display the system clock
  context    Show context information
  dialer     Dialer parameters and statistics
  history    Display the session command history
  hosts      IP domain-name, lookup style, nameservers, and host table
  isdn       ISDN information
  kerberos   Show Kerberos Values
  modemcap   Show Modem Capabilities database
  ppp        PPP parameters and statistics
  rmon       rmon statistics
  sessions   Information about Telnet connections
  snmp       snmp statistics
  terminal   Display terminal configuration parameters
  users      Display information about terminal lines
  version    System hardware and software status

Router> enable
Password:
Router# configure terminal
Enter configuration commands, one per line.  End with CNTL/Z.
```

```
Router(config)# line console 0
Router(config-line)# full-help
Router(config-line)# end
Router#
%SYS-5-CONFIG_I: Configured from console by console
Router# disable
Router> show ?
  access-expression  List access expression
  access-lists       List access lists
  aliases            Display alias commands
  apollo             Apollo network information
  appletalk          AppleTalk information
  arp                ARP table
  async              Information on terminal lines used as router interfaces
  bootflash          Boot Flash information
  bridge             Bridge Forwarding/Filtering Database [verbose]
  bsc                BSC interface information
  bstun              BSTUN interface information
  buffers            Buffer pool statistics
  calendar           Display the hardware calendar
  ...
  translate          Protocol translation information
  ttycap             Terminal capability tables
  users              Display information about terminal lines
  version            System hardware and software status
  vines              VINES information
  vlans              Virtual LANs Information
  whoami             Info on current tty line
  x25                X.25 information
  xns                XNS information
  xremote            XRemote statistics
```

Related Commands

help

HELP

To display a brief description of the help system, enter the **help** command.

help

Syntax   Description

This command has no arguments or keywords.

Command Mode

Available in all command modes.

Usage Guidelines

This command first appeared in Cisco IOS Release 10.0.

The **help** command provides a brief description of the context-sensitive help system.

- To list all commands available for a particular command mode, enter a question mark (?) at the system prompt.

- To obtain a list of commands that begin with a particular character string, enter the abbreviated command entry immediately followed by a question mark (?). This form of help is called word help, because it lists only the keywords or arguments that begin with the abbreviation you entered.

- To list a command's associated keywords or arguments, enter a question mark (?) in place of a keyword or argument on the command line. This form of help is called command syntax help, because it lists the keywords or arguments that apply based on the command, keywords and arguments you have entered already.

NOTES

The **help** command is associated with privilege level 0. If you configure AAA authorization for a privilege level greater than 0, this command will not be included in the command set for that privilege level.

Examples

Enter the **help** command for a brief description of the help system:

```
Router# help
Help may be requested at any point in a command by entering
a question mark '?'. If nothing matches, the help list will
be empty and you must backup until entering a '?' shows the
available options.
Two styles of help are provided:
1. Full help is available when you are ready to enter a
   command argument (e.g. 'show ?') and describes each possible
   argument.
2. Partial help is provided when an abbreviated argument is entered
   and you want to know what arguments match the input
   (e.g. 'show pr?'.)
```

The following example shows how to use word help to display all the privileged EXEC commands that begin with the letters "co":

```
Router# co?
configure  connect  copy
```

The following example shows how to use command syntax help to display the next argument of a partially complete **access-list** command. One option is to add a wildcard mask. The <cr> symbol indicates that the other option is to press Return to execute the command.

```
Router(config)# access-list 99 deny 131.108.134.234 ?
  A.B.C.D  Mask of bits to ignore
<cr>
```

Related Commands

full-help

HISTORY

To enable the command history function or to change the command history buffer size for a particular line, use the **history** line configuration command. To disable the command history feature, use the **no** form of this command.

> **history** [**size** *number-of-lines*]
> **no history** [**size** *number-of-lines*]

Syntax	Description
size *number-of-lines*	(Optional) Specifies the number of command lines that the system will record in its history buffer. The range is 0 to 256. The default is 10.

Default

10 lines

Command Mode

Line configuration

Usage Guidelines

This command first appeared in Cisco IOS Release 10.0.

The **history** command without the **size** keyword and the *number-of-lines* argument enables the history function with the last buffer size specified or with the default of 10 lines, if there was not a prior setting.

The **no history** command without the **size** keyword and the *number-of lines* argument disables the history feature but remembers the buffer size if it was something other than the default. The **no history size** command resets the buffer size to 10.

NOTES

The **history size** command only sets the size of the buffer; it does not reenable the history feature. If the **no history** command is used, the **history** command must be used to reenable this feature.

The command history feature provides a record of EXEC commands that you have entered. This feature is particularly useful for recalling long or complex commands or entries, including access lists.

Table 2–3 lists the keys and functions you can use to recall commands from the command history buffer.

Table 2–3   *History Keys*

Key	Functions
Ctrl-P or Up Arrow[1]	Recalls commands in the history buffer in a backward sequence, beginning with the most recent command. Repeat the key sequence to recall successively older commands.
Ctrl-N or Down Arrow[1]	Returns to more recent commands in the history buffer after recalling commands with Ctrl-P or the Up Arrow. Repeat the key sequence to recall successively more recent commands.

[1] The arrow keys function only with ANSI-compatible terminals such as VT100s.

Example

In the following example, line 4 is configured with a history buffer size of 35 lines:

```
line 4
history size 35
```

Related Commands

show history
terminal history size

INTERNATIONAL

If you are Telneting to a Cisco IOS platform and you want to display 8-bit and multibyte international characters (for example, Japanese) and print the ESC character as a single character instead of as the caret and bracket symbols (^[), use the **international** line configuration command. Use the **no** form of this command to display characters in 7-bit format.

    international
    no international

Syntax   Description

This command has no arguments or keywords.

Default

Disabled

Command Mode

Line configuration

Usage Guidelines

This command first appeared in Cisco IOS Release 11.3.

If you are configuring a Cisco IOS platform using the Cisco Web browser interface, this feature is enabled automatically when you enable the Cisco Web browser using the **ip http server** command.

Example

The following example enables a Cisco IOS platform to display 8-bit and multibyte characters and print the ESC character as a single character instead of as the caret and bracket symbols (^[) when you are Telneting to the platform:

```
international
```

Related Commands

terminal international

IP HTTP ACCESS-CLASS

To assign an access list to the HTTP server used by the Cisco IOS ClickStart software or the Cisco Web browser interface, use the **ip http access-class** global configuration command. To remove the assigned access list, use the **no** form of this command.

> **ip http access-class** {*access-list-number* | *name*}
> **no ip http access-class** {*access-list-number* | *name*}

Syntax	Description
access-list-number	Standard IP access-list number in the range 0 to 99, as configured by the **access-list** (**standard**) command.
name	Name of a standard IP access list, as configured by the **ip access-list** command.

Default

There is no access list applied to the HTTP server.

Command Mode

Global configuration

Usage Guidelines

This command first appeared in Cisco IOS Release 11.2.

If this command is configured, the specified access list is assigned to the HTTP server. Before the HTTP server accepts a connection, it checks the access list. If the check fails, the HTTP server does not accept the request for a connection.

Example

The following command assigns the access list named *marketing* to the HTTP server:

```
ip http access-class marketing
ip access-list standard marketing
 permit 192.5.34.0  0.0.0.255
 permit 128.88.0.0  0.0.255.255
 permit 36.0.0.0  0.255.255.255
 ! (Note: all other access implicitly denied)
```

Related Commands

ip access-list
ip http server

IP HTTP AUTHENTICATION

Use the **ip http authentication** global configuration command to specify a particular authentication method for HTTP server users. Use the **no** form of this command to disable a configured authentication method.

> **ip http authentication** {aaa | enable | local | tacacs}
> **no ip http authentication** {aaa | enable | local | tacacs}

Syntax	Description
aaa	Indicates that the AAA facility is used for authentication.
enable	Indicates that the enable password method, which is the default method of HTTP server user authentication, is used for authentication.
local	Indicates that the local user database as defined on the Cisco router or access server is used for authentication.
tacacs	Indicates that the TACACS or XTACACS server is used for authentication.

Default

The default method of authentication for the HTTP server interface is the enable password method.

Command Mode

Global configuration

Usage Guidelines

This command first appeared in Cisco IOS Release 11.2 F.

The **ip http authentication** command enables you to specify a particular authentication method for HTTP server users. The HTTP server uses the enable password method to authenticate a user at privilege level 15. The **ip http authentication** command now lets you specify enable, local, TACACS, or AAA HTTP server user authentication.

Example

The following example specifies TACACS as the method of HTTP server user authentication:

```
ip http authentication tacacs
```

Related Commands

ip http server

IP HTTP PORT

To specify the port to be used by the Cisco IOS ClickStart software or the Cisco Web browser interface, use the **ip http port** global configuration command. To use the default port, use the **no** form of this command.

ip http port *number*
no ip http port

Syntax	Description
number	Port number for use by ClickStart or the Cisco Web browser interface. The default is 80.

Default

80

Command Mode

Global configuration

Usage Guidelines

This command first appeared in Cisco IOS Release 11.2.

Use this command if ClickStart or the Cisco Web browser interface cannot use port 80.

Example

The following command configures the router so that you can use ClickStart or the Cisco Web browser interface via port 60:

```
ip http server
ip http port 60
```

Related Commands

ip http server

IP HTTP SERVER

To enable a Cisco 1003, Cisco 1004, or Cisco 1005 router to be configured from a browser using the Cisco IOS ClickStart software and to enable any router to be monitored or have its configuration modified from a browser using the Cisco Web browser interface, use the **ip http server** global configuration command. To disable this feature, use the **no** form of this command.

ip http server
no ip http server

Syntax   Description

This command has no arguments or keywords.

Default

This feature is enabled on Cisco 1003, Cisco 1004, and Cisco 1005 routers that have not yet been configured. For Cisco 1003, Cisco 1004, and Cisco 1005 routers that already have been configured, and for all other routers, this feature is disabled.

Command Mode

Global configuration

Usage Guidelines

This command first appeared in Cisco IOS Release 11.2.

Example

The following command configures the router so that you can use the Cisco Web browser interface to issue commands to it:

```
ip http server
```

Related Commands

ip http access-class
ip http port

MENU (EXEC)

Use the **menu** EXEC command to invoke a user menu.

> **menu** *name*

Syntax	Description
name	The configuration name of the menu.

Command Mode

User EXEC mode or privileged EXEC mode

Usage Guidelines

This command first appeared in Cisco IOS Release 10.0.

A menu can be invoked at either the user or privileged EXEC level, but if an item in the menu contains a privileged EXEC command, the user must be logged in at the privileged level for the command to succeed.

Example

The following example shows how to invoke the menu named *Access1*:

```
menu Access1
```

Related Commands

menu (global)

MENU (GLOBAL)

Use the **menu** global configuration command with the appropriate keyword to specify menu-display options. Use the **no** form of the global configuration command to delete a specified, or named, menu from the configuration.

> **menu** *name* [**clear-screen** | **line-mode** | **single-space** | **status-line**]
> **no menu** *name*

Syntax	Description
name	The configuration name of the menu.
clear-screen	(Optional) Clears the terminal screen before displaying a menu.

Syntax	Description
line-mode	(Optional) In a menu of nine or fewer items, you ordinarily select a menu item by entering the item number. In line mode, you select a menu entry by entering the item number and pressing Return. Line mode allows you to backspace over the selected number and enter another number before pressing Return to execute the command. This option is activated automatically when more than nine menu items are defined but also can be configured explicitly for menus of nine or fewer items.
single-space	(Optional) Displays menu items single-spaced rather than double-spaced. This option is activated automatically when more than nine menu items are defined but also can be configured explicitly for menus of nine or fewer items.
status-line	(Optional) Displays a line of status information about the current user.

Default

Disabled

Command Mode

Global configuration

Usage Guidelines

This command first appeared in Cisco IOS Release 10.0.

The **clear-screen** option uses a terminal-independent mechanism based on termcap entries defined in the router and the terminal type configured for the user's terminal. The **clear-screen** option allows the same menu to be used on multiple types of terminals instead of having terminal-specific strings embedded within menu titles. If the termcap entry does not contain a clear string, the menu system enters 24 new lines, causing all existing text to scroll off the top of the terminal screen.

The **status-line** option displays the status information at the top of the screen before the menu title is displayed. This status line includes the router's host name, the user's line number, and the current terminal type and keymap type (if any).

A menu can be activated at the user EXEC level or at the privileged EXEC level, depending upon whether the given menu contains menu entries using privileged commands.

When a particular line should always display a menu, that line can be configured with an **autocommand** configuration command. The menu should not contain any exit paths that leave users in an unfamiliar interface environment.

Menus can be run on a per-user basis by defining a similar autocommand for that local username.

Examples

The following example invokes the menu named *Access1*:

```
menu Access1
```

The following example displays the status information using the **status-line** option for the menu named *Access1*:

```
menu Access1 status-line
```

Related Commands

menu command
menu text
menu title
resume

MENU COMMAND

Use the **menu command** global configuration command to specify underlying commands for user interface menus.

  menu *name* **command** *number*

Syntax	Description
name	The configuration name of the menu. You can specify a maximum of 20 characters.
number	The selection number associated with the menu entry. This number is displayed to the left of the menu entry. You can specify a maximum of 18 menu entries. When the tenth item is added to the menu, the line-mode and single-space options are activated automatically.

Default

Disabled

Command Mode

Global configuration

Usage Guidelines

This command first appeared in Cisco IOS Release 10.0.

The **menu command** and **menu text** commands define a menu entry. These commands must use the same menu name and menu selection number.

The **menu command** has a special option, **menu-exit**, that is available only within menus. It is used to exit a submenu and return to the previous menu level or exit the menu altogether and return to the EXEC command prompt.

You can create submenus that are opened by selecting a higher-level menu entry. Use the **menu** command to invoke a menu as the command in a line specifying a higher-level menu entry.

NOTES

If you nest too many levels of menus, the system prints an error message on the terminal and returns to the previous menu level.

When a menu allows connections (their normal use), the command for an entry activating the connection should contain a **resume** command, or the line should be configured to prevent users from escaping their sessions with the **escape-char none** command. Otherwise, when they escape from a connection and return to the menu, there will be no way to resume the session and it will sit idle until the user logs off.

Specifying the **resume** command as the action that is performed for a selected menu entry permits a user to resume a named connection or connect using the specified name if there is no active connection by that name. As an option, you also can supply the connect string needed to connect initially. When you do not supply this connect string, the command uses the specified connection name.

You also can use the **resume/next** command, which resumes the next connection in the user's list of connections. This function allows you to create a single menu entry that steps through all of the user's connections.

Example

The following example specifies the commands to be executed when a user enters the selection number associated with the menu entry for the menu named *Access1*:

```
menu Access1 command 1 tn3270 vms.cisco.com
menu Access1 command 2 rlogin unix.cisco.com
menu Access1 command 3 menu-exit
```

Related Commands

menu (global)
menu text
menu title
resume

MENU TEXT

Use the **menu text** global configuration command to specify the text of a menu item in a user interface menu.

> **menu** *name* **text** *number*

Syntax	Description
name	The configuration name of the menu. You can specify a maximum of 20 characters.
number	The selection number associated with the menu item. This number is displayed to the left of the menu item. You can specify a maximum of 18 menu items. When the tenth item is added to the menu, the **line-mode** and **single-space** options are activated automatically.

Default

No text appears for the menu item.

Command Mode

Global configuration

Usage Guidelines

This command first appeared in Cisco IOS Release 10.0.

The **menu text** command and the **menu command** define a menu item. These commands must use the same menu name and menu selection number.

You can specify a maximum of 18 items in a menu.

Example

The following example specifies the descriptive text for the three entries in the menu *Access1*:

```
menu Access1 text 1 IBM Information Systems
menu Access1 text 2 UNIX Internet Access
menu Access1 text 3 Exit menu system
```

Related Commands

menu (global)
menu command
menu title
resume

MENU TITLE

Use the **menu title** global configuration command to create a title, or banner, for a user menu.

> **menu** *name* **title** *delimiter title delimiter*

Syntax	Description
name	The configuration name of the menu. You can specify a maximum of 20 characters.
delimiter	Characters that mark the beginning and end of a title. Text delimiters are characters that do not ordinarily appear within the text of a title, such as slash (/), double quote ("), and tilde (~). Ctrl-C is reserved for special use and should not be used in the text of the title.
title	The lines of text to appear at the top of the menu.

Default

The menu does not have a title.

Command Mode

Global configuration

Usage Guidelines

This command first appeared in Cisco IOS Release 10.0.

The **menu title** command must use the same menu name used with the **menu text** and **menu command** commands used to create a menu.

You can position the title of the menu horizontally by preceding the title text with blank characters. You also can add lines of space above and below the title by pressing Return.

Follow the **title** keyword with one or more blank characters and a delimiting character of your choice. Then enter one or more lines of text, ending the title with the same delimiting character. You cannot use the delimiting character within the text of the message.

When you are configuring from a terminal and are attempting to include special control characters, such as a screen-clearing string, you must use Ctrl-V before the special control characters so that they are accepted as part of the title string. The string ^[[H^[[J is an escape string used by many VT100-compatible terminals to clear the screen. To use a special string, you must enter **Ctrl-V** before each escape character.

You also can use the **clear-screen** option of the **menu** command to clear the screen before displaying menus and submenus, instead of embedding a terminal-specific string in the menu title. The **clear-screen** option allows the same menu to be used on different types of terminals.

Example

The following example specifies the title that will be displayed when the menu *Access1* is invoked. Press the Return key after the second slash (/) to display the prompt.

```
Router(config)# menu Access1 title /^[[H^[[J
Enter TEXT message.  End with the character '/'.
               Welcome to Access1 Internet Services

             Type a number to select an option;
                  Type 9 to exit the menu.
/
Router(config)#
```

Related Commands

menu (global)
menu command
menu text
resume

SHOW HISTORY

To list the commands you have entered in the current EXEC session, use the **show history** EXEC command.

show history

Syntax   Description

This command has no arguments or keywords.

Command Mode

EXEC

Usage Guidelines

This command first appeared in Cisco IOS Release 10.0.

The command history feature provides a record of EXEC commands you have entered. The number of commands that the history buffer will record is determined by the **history size** line configuration command or the **terminal history size** EXEC command.

Table 2–4 lists the keys and functions you can use to recall commands from the command history buffer.

Table 2–4   *History Keys*

Key	Function
Ctrl-P or Up Arrow	Recalls commands in the history buffer in a backward sequence, beginning with the most recent command. Repeat the key sequence to recall successively older commands.
Ctrl-N or Down Arrow	Returns to more recent commands in the history buffer after recalling commands with Ctrl-P or the Up Arrow. Repeat the key sequence to recall successively more recent commands.

Sample Display

The following is sample output from the **show history** command, which lists the commands the user has entered in EXEC mode for this session:

```
Router# show history
  help
  where
  show hosts
  show history
Router#
```

Related Commands

history size
terminal history size

TERMINAL EDITING

To enable the enhanced editing mode on the local line, use the **terminal editing** EXEC command. To disable the enhanced editing mode on the current line, use the **no** form of this command.

    terminal editing
    terminal no editing

Syntax   Description

This command has no arguments or keywords.

Default

Enabled

Command Mode

EXEC

Usage Guidelines

This command first appeared in Cisco IOS Release 10.0.

Table 2–5 provides a description of the keys used to enter and edit commands. Ctrl indicates the Control key. It must be pressed simultaneously with its associated letter key. Esc indicates the Escape key. It must be pressed first, followed by its associated letter key. Keys are *not* case sensitive.

Table 2–5 *Command Editing Keys and Functions*

Keys	Function
Tab	Completes a partial command-name entry. When you enter a unique set of characters and press the Tab key, the system completes the command name. If you enter a set of characters that could indicate more than one command, the system beeps to indicate an error. Enter a question mark (?) immediately following the partial command (no space). The system provides a list of commands that begin with that string.
Delete or Backspace	Erases the character to the left of the cursor.
Return	At the command line, pressing the Return key performs the function of processing, or carrying out, a command. At the "---More---" prompt on a terminal screen, pressing the Return key scrolls down a line.
Space Bar	Scrolls down a page on the terminal screen. Press the space bar when you see the line "---More---" on the screen to display the next screen.
Left arrow[1]	Moves the cursor one character to the left. When you enter a command that extends beyond a single line, you can continue to press the left arrow key at any time to scroll back toward the system prompt and verify the beginning of the command entry.
Right arrow[1]	Moves the cursor one character to the right.
Up arrow[1] or Ctrl-P	Recalls commands in the history buffer, beginning with the most recent command. Repeat the key sequence to recall successively older commands.
Down arrow[1] or Ctrl-N	Return to more recent commands in the history buffer after recalling commands with the Up arrow or Ctrl-P. Repeat the key sequence to recall successively more recent commands.
Ctrl-A	Moves the cursor to the beginning of the line.
Ctrl-B	Moves the cursor back one character.
Ctrl-D	Deletes the character at the cursor.
Ctrl-E	Moves the cursor to the end of the command line.

Table 2–5 *Command Editing Keys and Functions, Continued*

Keys	Function
Ctrl-F	Moves the cursor forward one character.
Ctrl-K	Deletes all characters from the cursor to the end of the command line.
Ctrl-L and Ctrl-R	Redisplays the system prompt and command line.
Ctrl-T	Transposes the character to the left of the cursor with the character located at the cursor.
Ctrl-U and Ctrl-X	Deletes all characters from the cursor back to the beginning of the command line.
Ctrl-V and Esc Q	Inserts a code to indicate to the system that the key stroke immediately following should be treated as a command entry, *not* as an editing key.
Ctrl-W	Deletes the word to the left of the cursor.
Ctrl-Y	Recalls the most recent entry in the delete buffer. The delete buffer contains the last ten items you have deleted or cut. Ctrl-Y can be used in conjunction with Esc Y.
Ctrl-Z	Ends configuration mode and returns you to the EXEC prompt.
Esc B	Moves the cursor back one word.
Esc C	Capitalizes the word at the cursor.
Esc D	Deletes from the cursor to the end of the word.
Esc F	Moves the cursor forward one word.
Esc L	Changes the word at the cursor to lowercase.
Esc U	Capitalizes from the cursor to the end of the word.
Esc Y	Recalls the next buffer entry. The buffer contains the last ten items you have deleted. Press Ctrl-Y first to recall the most recent entry. Then press Esc Y up to nine times to recall the remaining entries in the buffer. If you bypass an entry, continue to press Esc Y to cycle back to it.

[1] The arrow keys function only with ANSI-compatible terminals.

The editing keys and functions for Software Release 9.1 and earlier are listed Table 2–6.

Table 2–6 *Editing Keys and Functions for Software Release 9.1 and Earlier*

Key	Function
Delete or Backspace	Erases the character to the left of the cursor.
Ctrl-W	Erases a word.
Ctrl-U	Erases a line.
Ctrl-R	Redisplays a line.
Ctrl-Z	Ends configuration mode and returns to the EXEC prompt.
Return	Executes single-line commands.

Example

In the following example, enhanced mode editing is reenabled for the current terminal session:

```
terminal editing
```

Related Commands

editing

TERMINAL FULL-HELP

To get help for the full set of user-level commands, use the **terminal full-help** EXEC command.

terminal full-help

Syntax   Description

This command has no arguments or keywords.

Default

Disabled

Command Mode

EXEC

Usage Guidelines

This command first appeared in Cisco IOS Release 10.0.

The **terminal full-help** command enables (or disables) a user to see all of the help messages available from the terminal. It is used with the **show ?** command.

Example

The following example is output for the **show ?** command with **terminal full-help** disabled and then enabled:

```
Router> show ?
  bootflash  Boot Flash information
  calendar   Display the hardware calendar
  clock      Display the system clock
  context    Show context information
  dialer     Dialer parameters and statistics
  history    Display the session command history
  hosts      IP domain-name, lookup style, nameservers, and host table
  isdn       ISDN information
  kerberos   Show Kerberos Values
  modemcap   Show Modem Capabilities database
  ppp        PPP parameters and statistics
  rmon       rmon statistics
  sessions   Information about Telnet connections
  snmp       snmp statistics
  terminal   Display terminal configuration parameters
  users      Display information about terminal lines
  version    System hardware and software status

Router> terminal full-help
Router> show ?
  access-expression  List access expression
  access-lists       List access lists
  aliases            Display alias commands
  apollo             Apollo network information
  appletalk          AppleTalk information
  arp                ARP table
  async              Information on terminal lines used as router interfaces
  bootflash          Boot Flash information
  bridge             Bridge Forwarding/Filtering Database [verbose]
  bsc                BSC interface information
  bstun              BSTUN interface information
  buffers            Buffer pool statistics
  calendar           Display the hardware calendar
  cdp                CDP information
  clns               CLNS network information
  clock              Display the system clock
  cls                DLC user information
  cmns               Connection-Mode networking services (CMNS) information
  compress           Show compression statistics.
  ...
  x25                X.25 information
  xns                XNS information
  xremote            XRemote statistics
```

Related Commands
full-help
help

TERMINAL HISTORY

To enable the command history feature for the current terminal session or change the size of the command history buffer for the current terminal session, use the **terminal history** EXEC command. To disable the command history feature or reset the command history buffer to its default size, use the **no** form of this command.

> **terminal history** [size *number-of-lines*]
> **terminal no history** [size]

Syntax	Description
size	(Optional) Sets command history buffer size.
number-of-lines	(Optional) Specifies the number of command lines that the system will record in its history buffer. The range is 0 to 256. The default is 10.

Default
10 lines

Command Mode
EXEC

Usage Guidelines
This command first appeared in Cisco IOS Release 10.0.

The **terminal history** command without the **size** keyword and argument enables the command history feature with the last buffer size specified or the default size. The **terminal no history** command without the **size** keyword disables the command history feature. The **terminal no history size** command resets the buffer size to the default of 10 command lines.

The **terminal history** command provides a record of EXEC commands you have entered. This feature is particularly useful to recall long or complex commands or entries, including access lists.

Table 2–7 lists the keys and functions you can use to recall commands from the history buffer.

Table 2-7   *History Keys*

Key	Function
Ctrl-P or up arrow[1]	Recalls commands in the history buffer in a backward sequence, beginning with the most recent command. Repeat the key sequence to recall successively older commands.
Ctrl-N or down arrow[1]	Returns to more recent commands in the history buffer after recalling commands with Ctrl-P or the up arrow. Repeat the key sequence to recall successively more recent commands.

[1] The arrow keys function only with ANSI-compatible terminals such as VT100s.

Example

In the following example, the number of command lines recorded is set to 15 for the local line:

```
terminal history size 15
```

Related Commands

history
show history

TERMINAL INTERNATIONAL

If you are Telneting to a Cisco IOS platform and you want to display 8-bit and multibyte international characters (for example, Japanese) and print the ESC character as a single character instead of as the caret and bracket symbols (^[) for a current Telnet session, use the **terminal international** EXEC command. Use the **no** form of this command to display characters in 7-bit format for a current Telnet session.

> **terminal international**
> **no terminal international**

Syntax   Description

This command has no arguments or keywords.

Default

Disabled

Command Mode

EXEC

Usage Guidelines

This command first appeared in Cisco IOS Release 11.3.

If you are configuring a Cisco IOS platform using the Cisco Web browser interface, this feature is enabled automatically when you enable the Cisco Web browser using the **ip http server** command.

Example

The following example enables a Cisco IOS platform to display 8-bit and multibyte characters and print the ESC character as a single character instead of as the caret and bracket symbols (^[) when you are Telneting to the platform for the current Telnet session:

```
terminal international
```

Related Commands

international

## CHAPTER 3

Using Configuration Tools

Cisco IOS includes a number of configuration tools that simplify the process of setting up the initial configuration of a router or access server. This chapter describes the following configuration tools:

- Using AutoInstall
- Using Setup for Configuration Changes
- Using Other Configuration Tools

For a complete description of the configuration tools commands in this chapter, see Chapter 4, "Configuration Tools Commands."

USING AUTOINSTALL

This section provides information about AutoInstall, a procedure that allows you to configure a new router automatically and dynamically. The AutoInstall procedure involves connecting a new router to a network where an existing router is preconfigured, turning on the new router, and enabling it with a configuration file that is automatically downloaded from a Trivial File Transfer Protocol (TFTP) server.

The following sections provide the requirements for AutoInstall and an overview of how the procedure works. To start the procedure, see the "Performing the AutoInstall Procedure" section later in this chapter.

AutoInstall Requirements

For the AutoInstall procedure to work, your system must meet the following requirements:

- Routers must be physically attached to the network using one or more of the following interface types: Ethernet, Token Ring, Fiber Distributed Data Interface (FDDI), serial with High-Level Data-Link Control (HDLC) encapsulation, or serial with Frame Relay encapsulation. HDLC is the default serial encapsulation. If the AutoInstall process fails over HDLC, the Cisco IOS software automatically configures Frame Relay encapsulation.

- The existing preconfigured router must be running Software Release 9.1 or later. For AutoInstall over Frame Relay, this router must be running Cisco IOS Release 10.3 or later.

- The new router must be running Software Release 9.1 or later. For AutoInstall over Frame Relay, the new router must be running Cisco IOS Release 10.3 or later.

NOTES

Of Token Ring interfaces, only those that set ring speed with physical jumpers support AutoInstall. AutoInstall does not work with Token Ring interfaces for which the ring speed must be set with software configuration commands. If the ring speed is not set, the interface is set to shutdown mode.

- You must complete procedure 1 and either procedure 2 or 3:

  - Procedure 1: A configuration file for the new router must reside on a TFTP server. This file can contain the full configuration or the minimum needed for the administrator to Telnet into the new router for configuration. In addition, make sure to complete one of the following procedures.

  - Procedure 2: A file named *network-confg* also must reside on the server. The file must have an Internet Protocol (IP) host name entry for the new router. The server must be reachable from the existing router.

  - Procedure 3: An IP address-to-host name mapping for the new router must be added to a Domain Name System (DNS) database file.

- If the existing router is to help automatically install the new router via an HDLC-encapsulated serial interface using Serial Line Address Resolution Protocol (SLARP), that interface must be configured with an IP address whose host portion has the value 1 or 2. (AutoInstall over Frame Relay does not have this address constraint.) Subnet masks of any size are supported.

- If the existing router is to help automatically install the new router using a Frame Relay-encapsulated serial interface, that interface must be configured with the following:

  - An IP helper address pointing to the TFTP server. In the following example, 171.69.2.75 is the address of the TFTP server:

    ```
    ip helper 171.69.2.75
    ```

  - A Frame Relay map pointing back to the new router. In the following example, 172.21.177.100 is the IP address of the *new* router's serial interface, and 100 is the PVC identifier:

    ```
    frame-relay map ip 172.21.177.100 100 dlci
    ```

- If the existing router is to help automatically install the new router via an Ethernet, Token Ring, or FDDI interface using BOOTP or Reverse Address Resolution Protocol (RARP), a

BOOTP or RARP server also must be set up to map the new router's Media Access Control (MAC) address to its IP address.

- IP helper addresses might need to be configured to forward the TFTP and DNS broadcast requests from the new router to the host that is providing those services.

Using a DOS-Based TFTP Server

AutoInstall over Frame Relay and other WAN encapsulations support downloading configuration files from UNIX-based and DOS-based TFTP servers. Other booting mechanisms such as RARP and SLARP also support UNIX-based and DOS-based TFTP servers.

The DOS format of the UNIX network-confg file that must reside on the server must be eight characters or fewer, with a three-letter extension. Therefore, when an attempt to load network-confg fails, AutoInstall automatically attempts to download the file *cisconet.cfg* from the TFTP server.

If cisconet.cfg exists and is downloaded successfully, the server is assumed to be a DOS machine. The AutoInstall program then attempts to resolve the host name for the router through host commands in cisconet.cfg.

If cisconet.cfg does not exist or cannot be downloaded, or if the program is unable to resolve a host name, DNS attempts to resolve the host name. If DNS cannot resolve the host name, the router attempts to download ciscortr.cfg. If the host name is longer than eight characters, it is truncated to eight characters. For example, a router with a host name "australia" will be treated as "australi" and AutoInstall will attempt to download australi.cfg.

The format of cisconet.cfg and ciscortr.cfg is to be the same as those described for network-confg and hostname-confg.

If neither network-confg nor cisconet.cfg exists and DNS is unable to resolve the host name, AutoInstall attempts to load router-confg, and then ciscortr.cfg if router-confg does not exist or cannot be downloaded. The cycle is repeated three times.

How AutoInstall Works

Once the requirements for using AutoInstall are met, the dynamic configuration of the new router occurs in the following order:

1. The new router acquires its IP address. Depending on the interface connection between the two routers and/or access servers, the new router's IP address is dynamically resolved by either SLARP requests or BOOTP or RARP requests.

2. The new router resolves its name through network-confg, cisconet.cfg, or DNS.

3. The new router automatically requests and downloads its configuration file from a TFTP server.

4. If a host name is not resolved, the new router attempts to load router-confg or ciscortr.cfg.

Acquiring the New Router's IP Address

The new router (*newrouter*) resolves its interface's IP addresses by one of the following means:

- If *newrouter* is connected by an HDLC-encapsulated serial line to the existing router (*existing*), *newrouter* sends a SLARP request to *existing*.

- If *newrouter* is connected by an Ethernet, Token Ring, or FDDI interface, it broadcasts BOOTP and RARP requests.

- If *newrouter* is connected by a Frame Relay-encapsulated serial interface, it first attempts the HDLC automatic installation process and then attempts the BOOTP or RARP process over Ethernet, Token Ring, or FDDI. If both attempts fail, the new router attempts to install automatically over Frame Relay. In this case, a BOOTP request is sent over the lowest numbered serial or HSSI interface.

The existing router (*existing*) responds in one of the following ways, depending on the request type:

- In response to a SLARP request, *existing* sends a SLARP reply packet to *newrouter*. The reply packet contains the IP address and netmask of *existing*. If the host portion of the IP address in the SLARP response is 1, *newrouter* configures its interface using the value 2 as the host portion of its IP address and vice versa. (See Figure 3–1.)

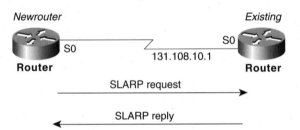

Figure 3–1

Using SLARP to Acquire the New Router's IP Address

The IP address of *existing* is 131.108.10.1. The network mask of *existing's* interface is 255.255.255.0. Therefore, *newrouter* learns that its IP address is 131.108.10.2

- In response to BOOTP or RARP requests, an IP address is sent from the BOOTP or RARP server to *newrouter*.

  A BOOTP or RARP server must have been set up already to map *newrouter*'s MAC address to its IP address. If the BOOTP server does not reside on the directly attached network segment, routers between *newrouter* and the BOOTP server can be configured with the **ip helper-address** command to allow the request and response to be forwarded between segments, as shown in Figure 3–2.

  AutoInstall over Frame Relay is a special case in that the existing router acts as a BOOTP server and responds to the incoming BOOTP request. Only a helper address and a Frame Relay map need to be set up. No MAC-to-IP address map is needed on the existing router.

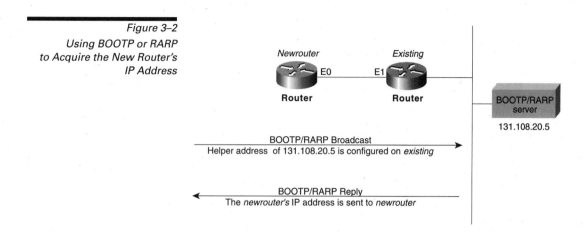

Figure 3–2
Using BOOTP or RARP
to Acquire the New Router's
IP Address

As of Software Release 9.21, routers can be configured to act as RARP servers.

Because the router attempts to resolve its host name as soon as one interface resolves its IP address, only one IP address needs to be set up with SLARP, BOOTP, or RARP.

Resolving the IP Address to the Host Name

The new router resolves its IP address-to-host name mapping by sending a TFTP broadcast requesting the file network-confg, as shown in Figure 3–3.

The network-confg file is a configuration file generally shared by several routers. In this case, it is used to map the IP address of the new router (just obtained dynamically) to the name of the new router. The file network-confg must reside on a reachable TFTP server and must be globally readable.

The following is an example of a minimal network-confg file that maps the IP address of the new router (131.108.10.2) to the name *newrouter*. The address of the new router was learned via SLARP and is based on *existing*'s IP address of 131.108.10.1.

```
ip host newrouter 131.108.10.2
```

If you are not using AutoInstall over Frame Relay, the host portion of the address must be 1 or 2. AutoInstall over Frame Relay does not have this addressing constraint.

If *newrouter* does not receive a network-confg or a cisconet.cfg file, or if the IP address-to-host-name mapping does not match the newly acquired IP address, *newrouter* sends a DNS broadcast. If DNS is configured and has an entry that maps *newrouter*'s SLARP, BOOTP, or RARP-acquired IP address to its name, *newrouter* successfully resolves its name.

If DNS does not have an entry that maps the new router's SLARP, BOOTP, or RARP-acquired address to its name, the new router cannot resolve its host name. The new router attempts to download a default configuration file as described in the next section, and failing that, enters **setup** mode—or enters user EXEC mode with AutoInstall over Frame Relay.

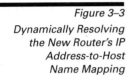

Figure 3–3
Dynamically Resolving
the New Router's IP
Address-to-Host
Name Mapping

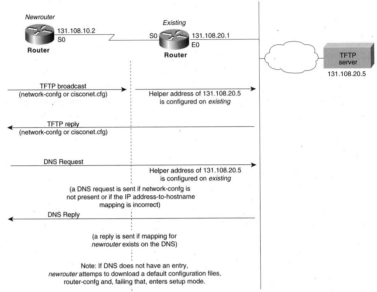

Downloading the New Router's Host Configuration File

After the router successfully resolves its host name, *newrouter* sends a TFTP broadcast requesting the file newrouter-confg or newrouter.cfg. The name *newrouter-confg* must be in all lowercase letters, even if the true host name is not. If *newrouter* cannot resolve its host name, it sends a TFTP broadcast requesting the default host configuration file router-confg. The file is downloaded to *newrouter*, where the configuration commands take effect immediately.

When using AutoInstall over Frame Relay, you are put into **setup** mode while the AutoInstall process is running. If the configuration file is successfully installed, the **setup** process is terminated. If you expect the AutoInstall process to be successful, either do *not* respond to the **setup** prompts or respond to the prompts as follows:

```
Would you like to enter the initial configuration dialog? [yes]: no
Would you like to terminate autoinstall? [yes]: no
```

If you do not expect the AutoInstall process to be successful, create a configuration file by responding to the **setup** prompts. The AutoInstall process is terminated transparently.

You will see the following display as the AutoInstall operation is in progress:

```
Please Wait. AutoInstall being attempted!!!!!!!!!!!!!!!!!!!!!
```

If the host configuration file contains only the minimal information, you must connect using Telnet into *existing*, from there connect via Telnet to *newrouter*, and then run the **setup** command to configure *newrouter.* See the "Using Setup for Configuration Changes" section later in this chapter for details on the **setup** command.

If the host configuration file is complete, *newrouter* should be fully operational. You can enter the **enable** command (with the system administrator password) at the system prompt on *newrouter,* and then issue the **copy running-config startup-config** command to save the information in the recently obtained configuration file into nonvolatile random-access memory (NVRAM) or to the location specified by the CONFIG_FILE environment variable. If it must reload, *newrouter* simply loads its configuration file from NVRAM.

If the TFTP request fails, or if *newrouter* still has not obtained the IP addresses of all its interfaces, and those addresses are not contained in the host configuration file, then *newrouter* enters **setup** mode automatically. **Setup** mode prompts you for manual configuration of the Cisco IOS software at the console. The new router continues to issue broadcasts to attempt to learn its host name and obtain any unresolved interface addresses. The broadcast frequency will dwindle to every 10 minutes after several attempts. See the "Using Setup for Configuration Changes" section later in this chapter for details on the **setup** command.

Performing the AutoInstall Procedure

To dynamically configure a new router using AutoInstall, complete the following tasks. Steps 1, 2, and 3 are completed by the central administrator. Step 4 is completed by the person at the remote site.

Step 1   Modify the existing router's configuration to support the AutoInstall procedure.

Step 2   Set up the TFTP server to support the AutoInstall procedure.

Step 3   Set up the BOOTP or RARP server if needed. A BOOTP or RARP server is required for AutoInstall using an Ethernet, Token Ring, FDDI, or Frame Relay-encapsulated serial interface. With a Frame Relay-encapsulated serial interface, the existing router acts as the BOOTP server. A BOOTP or RARP server is not required for AutoInstall using an HDLC-encapsulated serial interface.

Step 4   Connect the new router to the network.

Modifying the Existing Router's Configuration

You can use any of the following types of interfaces:

- An HDLC-encapsulated serial line (the default configuration for a serial line)
- An Ethernet, Token Ring, FDDI interface
- A Frame Relay-encapsulated serial line

Using an HDLC-Encapsulated Serial Interface Connection

To set up AutoInstall via a serial line with HDLC encapsulation (the default), you must configure the existing router. Perform the following steps, beginning in global configuration mode:

Task	Command
Step 1 Configure the serial interface that connects to the new router with HDLC encapsulation (the default), and enter interface configuration mode.	**interface serial** *interface-number*
Step 2 Enter an IP address for the interface. The host portion of the address must have a value of 1 or 2. (AutoInstall over Frame Relay does not have this address constraint.)	**ip address** *address mask*
Step 3 Configure a helper address for the serial interface to forward broadcasts associated with the TFTP, BOOTP, and DNS requests.	**ip helper-address** *address*
Step 4 Optionally, configure a DCE clock rate for the serial line, unless an external clock is being used. This step is needed only for DCE appliques.	**clock rate** *bps*
Step 5 Exit configuration mode.	**^Z**
Step 6 Save the configuration file to your startup configuration. On most platforms, this step saves the configuration to NVRAM. On the Cisco 7000 family, this step saves the configuration to the location specified by the CONFIG_FILE environment variable.	**copy running-config startup-config**

In the following example, the existing router's configuration file contains the commands needed to configure the router for AutoInstall on a serial line using HDLC encapsulation:

```
Router# configure terminal
interface serial 0
 ip address 172.31.10.1 255.255.255.0
 ip helper-address 172.31.20.5
 Ctrl-Z
Router(config)# copy running-config startup-config
```

Using an Ethernet, Token Ring, or FDDI Interface Connection

To set up AutoInstall using an Ethernet, Token Ring, or FDDI interface, you must modify the configuration of the existing router. Perform the following steps, beginning in global configuration mode:

Task		Command
Step 1	Configure a LAN interface, and enter interface configuration mode.	**interface {ethernet | tokenring | fddi}** *interface-number*
Step 2	Enter an IP address for the interface.	**ip address** *address mask*
Step 3	Optionally, configure a helper address to forward broadcasts associated with the TFTP, BOOTP, and DNS requests.	**ip helper-address** *address*
Step 4	Exit configuration mode.	**^Z**
Step 5	Save the configuration file to your startup configuration. On most platforms, this step saves the configuration to NVRAM. On the Cisco 7000 family, this step saves the configuration to the location specified by the CONFIG_FILE environment variable.	**copy running-config startup-config**

Typically, the local-area network (LAN) interface and IP address are already configured on the existing router. You might need to configure an IP helper address if the TFTP server is not on the same network as the new router.

In the following example, the existing router's configuration file contains the commands needed to configure the router for AutoInstall on an Ethernet interface:

```
Router# configure terminal
interface Ethernet 0
 ip address 172.31.10.1 255.255.255.0
 ip helper-address 172.31.20.5
 Ctrl-Z
Router(config)# copy running-config startup-config
```

Using a Frame Relay-Encapsulated Serial Interface Connection

To set up AutoInstall via a serial line with Frame Relay encapsulation, you must configure the existing router. Perform the following tasks, beginning in global configuration mode:

Task	Command
Step 1 Configure the serial interface that connects to the new router, and enter interface configuration mode.	**interface serial 0**
Step 2 Configure Frame Relay encapsulation on the interface that connects to the new router.	**encapsulation frame-relay**
Step 3 Create a Frame Relay map pointing back to the new router. or For point-to-point subinterfaces, assign a data-link connection identifier (DLCI) to the interface that connects to the new router, and provide the IP address of the serial port on the new router.	**frame-relay map ip** *ip-address dlci* or **frame-relay interface-dlci** *dlci option* [**protocol ip** *ip-address*]
Step 4 Enter an IP address for the interface. This step sets the IP address of the existing router.	**ip address** *address mask*
Step 5 Configure a helper address for the TFTP server.	**ip helper-address** *address*
Step 6 Optionally, configure a DCE clock rate for the serial line, unless an external clock is being used. This step is needed only for DCE appliques.	**clock rate** *bps*
Step 7 Exit configuration mode.	**^Z**
Step 8 Save the configuration file to your startup configuration. On most platforms, this step saves the configuration to NVRAM. On the Cisco 7000 family, this step saves the configuration to the location specified by the CONFIG_FILE environment variable.	**copy running-config startup-config**

You must use a DTE interface on the new router, because the network always provides the clock signal.

In the following example, the existing router's configuration file contains the commands needed to configure the router for Frame Relay AutoInstall on a serial line:

```
Router# configure terminal
interface serial 0
 ip address 172.31.20.20 255.255.255.0
 encapsulation frame-relay
 frame-relay map ip 172.31.10.1 255.255.255.0 48
 ip helper-address 172.31.20.5
```

Setting Up the TFTP Server

For AutoInstall to work correctly, the new router must be able to resolve its host name and then download a *name*-confg or a *name*.cfg file from a TFTP server. The new router can resolve its host name by using a network-confg or a cisconet.cfg file downloaded from a TFTP server or by using the DNS.

To set up a TFTP server to support AutoInstall, complete the following tasks. Step 2 includes two ways to resolve the new router's host name. Use the first method if you want to use a network-config file to resolve the new router's host name. Use the second method if you want to use DNS to resolve the new router's host name.

Task	Command
Step 1 Enable TFTP on a server.	Consult your host vendor's TFTP server documentation and RFCs 906 and 783.
Step 2 If you want to use a network-confg or cisconet.cfg file to resolve the new router's name, create the network-confg or cisconet.cfg file containing an IP address-to-host name mapping for the new router. Enter the **ip host** command into the TFTP config file, not into the router. The IP address must match the IP address that is to be dynamically obtained by the new router.	**ip host** *hostname address*
or	
If you want to use DNS to resolve the new router's name, create an address-to-name mapping entry for the new router in the DNS database. The IP address must match the IP address that is to be obtained dynamically by the new router.	Contact the DNS administrator or refer to RFCs 1101 and 1183.

Task	Command
Step 3 Create the *name*-confg or *name*.cfg file, which should reside in the tftpboot directory on the TFTP server. The *name* part of *name*-confg or *name*.cfg filename must match the host name you assigned for the new router in the previous step. Enter configuration commands for the new router into this file.	See the appropriate chapter in this book for specific commands.

The *name*-confg or the *name*.cfg file can contain either the new router's full configuration or a minimal configuration.

The minimal configuration file is a virtual terminal password and an enable password. It allows an administrator to Telnet into the new router to configure it. If you are using BOOTP or RARP to resolve the address of the new router, the minimal configuration file also must include the IP address to be obtained dynamically using BOOTP or RARP.

You can use the **copy running-config tftp** command to help you generate the configuration file that you will download during the AutoInstall process.

— **NOTES**

The existing router might need to forward TFTP requests and response packets if the TFTP server is not on the same network segment as the new router. When you modified the existing router's configuration, you specified an IP helper address for this purpose.

You can save a minimal configuration under a generic newrouter-confg file. Use the **ip host** command in the network-confg or cisconet.cfg file to specify *newrouter* as the host name with the address you will be resolving dynamically. The new router should then resolve its IP address, host name, and minimal configuration automatically. Use Telnet to connect to the new router from the existing router and use the **setup** facility to configure the rest of the interfaces. For example, the line in the network-confg or cisconet.cfg file could be similar to the following:

```
ip host newrouter 131.108.170.1
```

The following host configuration file contains the minimal set of commands needed for AutoInstall using SLARP or BOOTP:

```
enable-password letmein
!
line vty 0
password letmein
!
end
```

The preceding example shows a minimal configuration for connecting from a router one hop away. From this configuration, use the **setup** facility to configure the rest of the interfaces. If the router is more than one hop away, you also must include routing information in the minimal configuration.

The following minimal network configuration file maps the new router's IP address, 131.108.10.2, to the host name *newrouter*. The new router's address was learned via SLARP and is based on the existing router's IP address of 131.108.10.1.

```
ip host newrouter 131.108.10.2
```

Setting Up the BOOTP or RARP Server

If the new router is connected to the existing router using an Ethernet, Token Ring, or FDDI interface, you must configure a BOOTP or RARP server to map the new router's MAC address to its IP address. If the new router is connected to the existing router using a serial line with HDLC encapsulation or if you are configuring AutoInstall over Frame Relay, the tasks in this section are not required.

To configure a BOOTP or RARP server, complete one of the following tasks:

Task	Command
If BOOTP is to be used to resolve the new router's IP address, configure your BOOTP server.	Refer to your host vendor's manual pages and to RFCs 951 and 1395
If RARP is to be used to resolve the new router's IP address, configure your RARP server.	Refer to your host vendor's manual pages and to RFC 903

NOTES

If the RARP server is not on the same subnet as the new router, use the **ip rarp-server** command to configure the existing router to act as a RARP server.

The following host configuration file contains the minimum set of commands needed for AutoInstall using RARP. It includes the IP address that will be obtained dynamically via BOOTP or RARP during the AutoInstall process. When RARP is used, this extra information is needed to specify the proper netmask for the interface.

```
interface ethernet 0
 ip address 131.108.10.2 255.255.255.0
enable-password letmein
!
line vty 0
 password letmein
!
end
```

Connecting the New Router to the Network

Connect the new router to the network using either an HDLC-encapsulated or Frame Relay-encapsulated serial interface or an Ethernet, Token Ring, or FDDI interface. After the router successfully resolves its host name, *newrouter* sends a TFTP broadcast requesting the file *name*-confg or *name*.cfg. The router name must be in all lowercase, even if the true host name is not. The file is downloaded to the new router, where the configuration commands take effect immediately. If the configuration file is complete, the new router should be fully operational. To save the complete configuration to NVRAM, complete the following tasks in privileged EXEC mode:

Task	Command
Step 1 Enter privileged mode at the system prompt on the new router.	**enable** *password*
Step 2 Save the information from the *name*-config file into your startup configuration. On most platforms, this step saves the configuration to NVRAM. On the Cisco 7000 family, this step saves the configuration to the location specified by the CONFIG_FILE environment variable.	**copy running-config startup-config**

CAUTION

Verify that the existing and new routers and/or access servers are connected before entering the **copy running-config startup-config** EXEC command to save configuration changes. Use the **ping** EXEC command to verify connectivity. If an incorrect configuration file is downloaded, the new router will load NVRAM configuration information before it can enter AutoInstall mode.

If the configuration file is a minimal configuration file, the new router comes up, but with only one interface operational. Complete the following steps to connect to the new router and configure it:

Task	Command
Step 1 Establish a Telnet connection to the existing router.	**telnet** *existing*
Step 2 From the existing router, establish a Telnet connection to the new router.	**telnet** *newrouter*
Step 3 Enter privileged EXEC mode.	**enable** *password*
Step 4 Enter **setup** mode to configure the new router.	**setup**

USING SETUP FOR CONFIGURATION CHANGES

The **setup** command facility is an interactive facility that allows you to perform first-time configuration and other basic configuration procedures on all routers. The facility prompts you to enter basic information needed to start a router functioning quickly and uneventfully.

Although the **setup** command facility is a quick way to "set up" a router, you also can use it after first-time startup to perform basic configuration changes. This section focuses on the following:

- How to use the **setup** command facility after first-time startup
- How to use the streamlined **setup** facility

Refer to your hardware platform's user guide for more information on how to use **setup** for first-time startup.

Whenever you use the **setup** command facility, be sure that you know the following:

- Interfaces the router has
- Protocols the router is routing
- Whether the router is to perform bridging
- Network addresses for the protocols being configured
- Password strategy for your environment

Setup Command Facility Task List

You can perform the tasks in the following sections to make configuration changes using the **setup** command facility. Both tasks are optional.

- Using Setup after First-Time Startup
- Using the Streamlined Setup Facility

Using Setup after First-Time Startup

The command parser allows you to make very detailed changes to your configurations. However, some major configuration changes do not require the granularity provided by the command parser. In these cases, you can use the **setup** command facility to make major enhancements to your configurations. For example, you might want to use **setup** to add a protocol suite, to make major addressing scheme changes, or to configure a newly installed interface. Although you can use the command parser to make these major changes, the **setup** command facility provides you with a high-level view of the configuration and guides you through the configuration change process.

Additionally, if you are not familiar with Cisco products and the command parser, the **setup** command facility is a particularly valuable tool, because it asks you the questions required to make configuration changes.

NOTES

If you use **setup** to modify a configuration because you have added or modified the hardware, be sure to verify the physical connections using the **show version** command. Also, verify the logical port assignments using the **show running-config** command to ensure that you configure the proper port. Refer to your platform's hardware publications for details on physical and logical port assignments.

To enter the **setup** command facility, perform the following task in privileged EXEC mode:

Task	Command
Enter the **setup** command facility.	**setup**

When you enter the **setup** command facility after first-time startup, an interactive dialog called the System Configuration Dialog appears on the system console screen. The System Configuration Dialog guides you through the configuration process. It prompts you first for global parameters and then for interface parameters. The values shown in brackets next to each prompt are the default values last set using either the **setup** command facility or the **configure** command.

NOTES

The prompts and the order in which they appear on the screen vary depending on the platform and the interfaces installed in the device.

You must run through the entire System Configuration Dialog until you come to the item that you intend to change. To accept default settings for items that you do not want to change, press the Return key.

To return to the privileged EXEC prompt without making changes and without running through the entire System Configuration Dialog, press **Ctrl-C**.

The facility also provides help text for each prompt. To access help text, press the question mark (?) key at a prompt.

When you complete your changes, the **setup** command facility shows you the configuration command script that was created during the **setup** session. It also asks you if you want to use this configuration. If you answer Yes, the configuration is saved to NVRAM. If you answer No, the configuration is not saved and the process begins again. There is no default for this prompt; you must answer either Yes or No.

If any problems exist with the configuration file pointed to in NVRAM, or if the ignore NVRAM bit is set in the configuration register, the router enters the streamlined **setup** command facility. See the "Using the Streamlined Setup Facility" section for more information.

The following example shows how to use the **setup** command facility to configure interface serial 0 and to add ARAP and IP/IPX PPP support on the asynchronous interfaces:

```
Router# setup

        --- System Configuration Dialog ---

At any point you may enter a question mark '?' for help.
Use ctrl-c to abort configuration dialog at any prompt.
Default settings are in square brackets '[]'.

Continue with configuration dialog? [yes]:

First, would you like to see the current interface summary? [yes]:

Interface          IP-Address      OK? Method  Status                 Protocol
Ethernet0          172.16.72.2     YES manual  up                     up
Serial0            unassigned      YES not set administratively down  down
Serial1            172.16.72.2     YES not set up                     up

Configuring global parameters:

  Enter host name [Router]:

The enable secret is a one-way cryptographic secret used
instead of the enable password when it exists.

  Enter enable secret [<Use current secret>]:

The enable password is used when there is no enable secret
and when using older software and some boot images.

  Enter enable password [ww]:
  Enter virtual terminal password [ww]:
  Configure SNMP Network Management? [yes]:
    Community string [public]:
  Configure DECnet? [no]:
  Configure AppleTalk? [yes]:
    Multizone networks? [no]: yes
  Configure IPX? [yes]:
  Configure IP? [yes]:
    Configure IGRP routing? [yes]:
      Your IGRP autonomous system number [15]:
  Configure Async lines? [yes]:
    Async line speed [9600]: 57600
    Configure for HW flow control? [yes]:
```

```
       Configure for modems? [yes/no]: yes
          Configure for default chat script? [yes]: no
       Configure for Dial-in IP SLIP/PPP access? [no]: yes
          Configure for Dynamic IP addresses? [yes]: no
          Configure Default IP addresses? [no]: yes
          Configure for TCP Header Compression? [yes]: no
          Configure for routing updates on async links? [no]:
       Configure for Async IPX? [yes]:
       Configure for Appletalk Remote Access? [yes]:
          AppleTalk Network for ARAP clients [1]: 20
          Zone name for ARAP clients [ARA Dialins]:

Configuring interface parameters:

Configuring interface Ethernet0:
   Is this interface in use? [yes]:
   Configure IP on this interface? [yes]:
     IP address for this interface [172.16.72.2]:
     Number of bits in subnet field [8]:
     Class B network is 172.16.0.0, 8 subnet bits; mask is /24
   Configure AppleTalk on this interface? [yes]:
     Extended AppleTalk network? [yes]:
     AppleTalk starting cable range [1]:
     AppleTalk ending cable range [1]:
     AppleTalk zone name [Sales]:
     AppleTalk additional zone name:
   Configure IPX on this interface? [yes]:
     IPX network number [1]:

Configuring interface Serial0:
   Is this interface in use? [no]: yes
   Configure IP on this interface? [no]: yes
   Configure IP unnumbered on this interface? [no]: yes
     Assign to which interface [Ethernet0]:
   Configure AppleTalk on this interface? [no]: yes
     Extended AppleTalk network? [yes]:
     AppleTalk starting cable range [2]: 3
     AppleTalk ending cable range [3]: 3
     AppleTalk zone name [myzone]: ZZ Serial
     AppleTalk additional zone name:
   Configure IPX on this interface? [no]: yes
     IPX network number [2]: 3

Configuring interface Serial1:
   Is this interface in use? [yes]:
   Configure IP on this interface? [yes]:
   Configure IP unnumbered on this interface? [yes]:
     Assign to which interface [Ethernet0]:
   Configure AppleTalk on this interface? [yes]:
     Extended AppleTalk network? [yes]:
     AppleTalk starting cable range [2]:
     AppleTalk ending cable range [2]:
     AppleTalk zone name [ZZ Serial]:
     AppleTalk additional zone name:
   Configure IPX on this interface? [yes]:
     IPX network number [2]:
```

```
Configuring interface Async1:
    IPX network number [4]:
    Default client IP address for this interface [none]: 172.16.72.4
Configuring interface Async2:
    IPX network number [5]:
    Default client IP address for this interface [172.16.72.5]:
Configuring interface Async3:
    IPX network number [6]:
    Default client IP address for this interface [172.16.72.6]:
Configuring interface Async4:
    IPX network number [7]:
    Default client IP address for this interface [172.16.72.7]:
Configuring interface Async5:
    IPX network number [8]:
    Default client IP address for this interface [172.16.72.8]:
Configuring interface Async6:
    IPX network number [9]:
    Default client IP address for this interface [172.16.72.9]:
Configuring interface Async7:
    IPX network number [A]:
    Default client IP address for this interface [172.16.72.10]:
Configuring interface Async8:
    IPX network number [B]:
    Default client IP address for this interface [172.16.72.11]:
Configuring interface Async9:
    IPX network number [C]:
    Default client IP address for this interface [172.16.72.12]:
Configuring interface Async10:
    IPX network number [D]:
    Default client IP address for this interface [172.16.72.13]:
Configuring interface Async11:
    IPX network number [E]:
    Default client IP address for this interface [172.16.72.14]:
Configuring interface Async12:
    IPX network number [F]:
    Default client IP address for this interface [172.16.72.15]:
Configuring interface Async13:
    IPX network number [10]:
    Default client IP address for this interface [172.16.72.16]:
Configuring interface Async14:
    IPX network number [11]:
    Default client IP address for this interface [172.16.72.17]:
Configuring interface Async15:
    IPX network number [12]:
    Default client IP address for this interface [172.16.72.18]:
Configuring interface Async16:
    IPX network number [13]:
    Default client IP address for this interface [172.16.72.19]:

The following configuration command script was created:

hostname Router
enable secret 5 $1$krIg$emfYm/1OwHVspDuS8Gy0K1
enable password ww
```

```
line vty 0 4
password ww
snmp-server community public
!
no decnet routing
appletalk routing
ipx routing
ip routing
!
line 1 16
speed 57600
flowcontrol hardware
modem inout
!
arap network 20 ARA Dialins
line 1 16
arap enable
autoselect
!
! Turn off IPX to prevent network conflicts.
interface Ethernet0
no ipx network
interface Serial0
no ipx network
interface Serial1
no ipx network
!
interface Ethernet0
ip address 172.16.72.2 255.255.255.0
appletalk cable-range 1-1 1.204
appletalk zone Sales
ipx network 1
no mop enabled
!
interface Serial0
no shutdown
no ip address
ip unnumbered Ethernet0
appletalk cable-range 3-3
appletalk zone ZZ Serial
ipx network 3
no mop enabled
!
interface Serial1
no ip address
ip unnumbered Ethernet0
appletalk cable-range 2-2 2.2
appletalk zone ZZ Serial
ipx network 2
no mop enabled
!
Interface Async1
ipx network 4
ip unnumbered Ethernet0
```

```
peer default ip address 172.16.72.4
async mode interactive
!
Interface Async2
ipx network 5
ip unnumbered Ethernet0
peer default ip address 172.16.72.5
async mode interactive
!
Interface Async3
ipx network 6
ip unnumbered Ethernet0
peer default ip address 172.16.72.6
async mode interactive
!
Interface Async4
ipx network 7
ip unnumbered Ethernet0
peer default ip address 172.16.72.7
async mode interactive
async dynamic address
!
Interface Async5
ipx network 8
ip unnumbered Ethernet0
peer default ip address 172.16.72.8
async mode interactive
!
Interface Async6
ipx network 9
ip unnumbered Ethernet0
peer default ip address 172.16.72.9
async mode interactive
!
Interface Async7
ipx network A
ip unnumbered Ethernet0
peer default ip address 172.16.72.10
async mode interactive
!
Interface Async8
ipx network B
ip unnumbered Ethernet0
peer default ip address 172.16.72.11
async mode interactive
!
Interface Async9
ipx network C
ip unnumbered Ethernet0
peer default ip address 172.16.72.12
async mode interactive
!
Interface Async10
ipx network D
```

```
ip unnumbered Ethernet0
peer default ip address 172.16.72.13
async mode interactive
!
Interface Async11
ipx network E
ip unnumbered Ethernet0
peer default ip address 172.16.72.14
async mode interactive
!
Interface Async12
ipx network F
ip unnumbered Ethernet0
peer default ip address 172.16.72.15
async mode interactive
!
Interface Async13
ipx network 10
ip unnumbered Ethernet0
peer default ip address 172.16.72.16
async mode interactive
!
Interface Async14
ipx network 11
ip unnumbered Ethernet0
peer default ip address 172.16.72.17
async mode interactive
!
Interface Async15
ipx network 12
ip unnumbered Ethernet0
peer default ip address 172.16.72.18
async mode interactive
!
Interface Async16
ipx network 13
ip unnumbered Ethernet0
peer default ip address 172.16.72.19
async mode interactive
!
router igrp 15
network 172.16.0.0
!
end

Use this configuration? [yes/no]: yes

Building configuration...

Use the enabled mode 'configure' command to modify this configuration.

Router#
```

Using the Streamlined Setup Facility

The streamlined **setup** command facility is available only if your router is running from ROM monitor and has RXBOOT ROMs installed. The following routers can have this type of ROM installed:

- Cisco 2500 running the IGS-RXBOOT image
- Cisco 3000 running the IGS-RXBOOT image
- Cisco 4000 running the XX-RXBOOT image
- Other routers running the RXBOOT image

The streamlined **setup** command facility permits your router to load a system image from a network server when there are problems with the startup configuration. The Cisco IOS software automatically puts you in the streamlined **setup** command facility when your router is accidentally or intentionally rebooted (or you are attempting to load a system image from a network server) after any of the following circumstances:

- You issued an **erase startup-config** command, thereby deleting the startup configuration file.
- You have bit 6 (ignore NVRAM configuration) set in the configuration register.
- Your startup configuration has been corrupted.
- You configured the router to boot from a network server (the last four bits of the configuration register are not equal to 0 or 1) and there is no Flash or no valid image in Flash.
- You configured the router to boot the RXBOOT image.

The streamlined **setup** command facility differs from the standard **setup** command facility, because the streamlined facility does not ask you to configure global router parameters. You are prompted only to configure interface parameters, which permit your router to boot.

The following example shows a router entering the streamlined **setup** command facility:

```
          --- System Configuration Dialog ---

Default settings are in square brackets '[]'.

Configuring interface IP parameters for netbooting:
```

NOTES

The message "Configuring interface IP parameters for netbooting" only appears if you are booting over a network server and your configuration has insufficient IP information.

The streamlined **setup** command facility continues by prompting you for interface parameters for each installed interface. The facility asks whether an interface is in use. If so, the facility then prompts you to provide an IP address and subnet mask bits for the interface. Enter the subnet mask bits as a decimal value, such as 5.

The following example shows the portion of the streamlined **setup** command facility that prompts for interface parameters. In the example, the facility is prompting for Ethernet0 interface parameters and Serial0 interface parameters:

```
Configuring interface Ethernet0:
  Is this interface in use? [yes]:
  Configure IP on this interface? [yes]:
    IP address for this interface: 192.195.78.50
    Number of bits in subnet field [0]: 5
    Class C network is 192.195.78.0, 5 subnet bits; mask is 255.255.255.248

Configuring interface Serial0:
  Is this interface in use? [yes]:
  Configure IP on this interface? [yes]:
    IP address for this interface: 192.195.78.34
    Number of bits in subnet field [5]:
    Class C network is 192.195.78.0, 5 subnet bits; mask is 255.255.255.248
```

The configuration information you provide on this screen is *temporary* and exists only so that you can proceed with booting your system. When you reload the system, your original configuration is left intact. If your startup configuration is corrupted, enter the **setup** command facility, and configure the basic parameters. Then issue the **copy running-config startup-config** command to write this configuration to NVRAM.

USING OTHER CONFIGURATION TOOLS

You also can configure the Cisco IOS using one of the following tools:

- ClickStart
- ConfigMaker

For more information on using these configuration tools, refer to the documentation shipped with your product or configuration tool.

ClickStart

ClickStart enables you to configure and monitor a router using a World Wide Web browser. ClickStart can be used to configure a router to connect a small office or home PC to the Internet or to another network. In this environment, your PC is connected to the router via an Ethernet connection. You configure the router to dial your Internet service provider, and your Internet service provider supplies an ISDN, Frame Relay, or Asynchronous Serial connection to the Internet. You do not need to have an extensive background in networks and routers to configure your router using ClickStart.

You can use ClickStart to configure a Cisco 1003 or Cisco 1004 ISDN router running Cisco IOS Release 11.0(6) or later software, or Cisco IOS Release 11.1(2) or later software. You also can use ClickStart to configure a Cisco 1005 Frame Relay or Asynchronous Serial router running Cisco IOS Release 11.1(5) or later software. ClickStart is also available for the Cisco 1600 series and Cisco 700 series.

ConfigMaker

Use Cisco ConfigMaker on a Windows 95 or Windows NT system to quickly and easily configure Cisco 1000 series, Cisco 1600 series, Cisco 2500 series, and Cisco 3600 series routers and access servers from a single PC. Use this application to create a network of devices, make connections between devices, automatically assign addresses, and deliver configurations to routers by using the COM port on the computer. Cisco ConfigMaker is designed for resellers and network administrators of small to medium-sized businesses who are proficient in LAN fundamentals and basic network design.

ConfigMaker makes configuring a High-Level Data-Link Control (HDLC), Frame Relay or ISDN wide-area network connection between routers or the Internet as easy as drawing a network diagram. The tool guides users step-by-step through network design and addressing tasks and automatically delivers configuration files to individual routers on the network. ConfigMaker provides a graphical view of the entire network and lets the user build network diagrams using standard copy/paste, drag/drop, and online editing functions. ConfigMaker enables the user to monitor router and network configuration status at a glance with simple color codes.

CHAPTER 4

Configuration Tools Commands

AutoInstall and Setup are facilities that assist in setting up the initial configuration of a Cisco product. The AutoInstall facility has no unique commands. Its functionality is built on other Cisco IOS commands.

The **setup** command facility is an interactive facility that enables you to perform first-time configuration and other basic configuration procedures on all routers. The facility prompts you to enter basic information needed to start a router functioning quickly and uneventfully.

While the **setup** command facility is a quick way to "set up" a router, you also can use it after first-time startup to perform basic configuration changes. The command in this chapter focuses on using **setup** after first-time startup.

Refer to your hardware platform's user guide for details on how to use **setup** for first-time startup.

SETUP

To enter the **setup** command facility, use the **setup** privileged EXEC command.

> **setup**

Syntax   Description

This command has no arguments or keywords.

Command Mode

Privileged EXEC

Usage Guidelines

This command first appeared in Cisco IOS Release 11.1.

You can use the **setup** command facility to make major enhancements to your configurations. For example, you might want to use **setup** to add a protocol suite, to make major addressing scheme changes, or to configure a newly installed interface. While you can use the command parser to make these major changes, the **setup** command facility provides you with a high-level view of the configuration and guides you through the configuration change process.

Also, if you are not familiar with Cisco products and the command parser, the **setup** command facility is a particularly valuable tool, because it asks you the questions required to make configuration changes.

NOTES

If you use **setup** to modify a configuration because you have added or modified the hardware, be sure to verify the physical connections using the **show version** command. Also, verify the logical port assignments using the **show running-config** command to ensure that you configure the correct port. See your platform's hardware publications for details on physical and logical port assignments.

Whenever you use the **setup** command facility, be sure that you have the following information:

- Interfaces the router has
- Protocols the router is routing
- Whether the router is to perform bridging
- Network addresses for the protocols being configured
- Password strategy for your environment

When you enter the **setup** command facility after first-time startup, an interactive dialog called the System Configuration Dialog appears on the system console screen. The System Configuration Dialog guides you through the configuration process. It prompts you first for global parameters and then for interface parameters. The values shown in brackets next to each prompt are the default values last set using either the **setup** command facility or the **configure** command.

NOTES

The prompts and the order in which they appear on the screen vary depending on the platform and the interfaces installed in the device.

You must run through the entire System Configuration Dialog until you come to the item that you intend to change. To accept default settings for items that you do not want to change, press the Return key.

To return to the privileged EXEC prompt without making changes and without running through the entire System Configuration Dialog, press **Ctrl-C**.

The facility also provides help text for each prompt. To access help text, press the question mark (?) key at a prompt.

When you complete your changes, the **setup** command facility shows you the configuration command script that was created during the **setup** session. It also asks you if you want to use this configuration. If you answer Yes, the configuration is saved to NVRAM. If you answer No, the configuration is not saved and the process begins again. There is no default for this prompt; you must answer either Yes or No.

The Cisco IOS software automatically puts you in the streamlined **setup** command facility when your router is accidentally or intentionally rebooted (or you are attempting to load a system image from a network server) after any of the following circumstances:

- You issued an **erase startup-config** command, thereby deleting the startup configuration file.

- You have bit 6 (ignore NVRAM configuration) set in the configuration register.

- Your startup configuration has been corrupted.

- You configured the router to boot from a network server (the last four bits of the configuration register are not equal to 0 or 1) and there is no Flash or no valid image in Flash.

- You configured the router to boot the RXBOOT image.

The streamlined **setup** command facility permits your router to load a system image from a network server when there are problems with the startup configuration.

The streamlined **setup** command facility differs from the standard **setup** command facility because the streamlined facility does not ask you to configure global router parameters. You are prompted only to configure interface parameters, which permit your router to boot.

The streamlined **setup** command facility is available only if your router is running from ROM monitor and has RXBOOT ROMs installed. The following routers can have this type of ROM installed:

- Cisco 2500 running the IGS-RXBOOT image

- Cisco 3000 running the IGS-RXBOOT image

- Cisco 4000 running the XX-RXBOOT image

- Other routers running the RXBOOT image

Examples

The following example shows how to use the **setup** command facility to configure interface serial 0 and to add ARAP and IP/IPX PPP support on the asynchronous interfaces.

```
Router# setup

        --- System Configuration Dialog ---

At any point you may enter a question mark '?' for help.
Use ctrl-c to abort configuration dialog at any prompt.
Default settings are in square brackets '[]'.

Continue with configuration dialog? [yes]:

First, would you like to see the current interface summary? [yes]:

Interface        IP-Address      OK? Method  Status                 Protocol
Ethernet0        172.16.72.2     YES manual  up                     up
Serial0          unassigned      YES not set administratively down  down
Serial1          172.16.72.2     YES not set up                     up

Configuring global parameters:

  Enter host name [Router]:

The enable secret is a one-way cryptographic secret used
instead of the enable password when it exists.

  Enter enable secret [<Use current secret>]:

The enable password is used when there is no enable secret
and when using older software and some boot images.

  Enter enable password [ww]:
  Enter virtual terminal password [ww]:
  Configure SNMP Network Management? [yes]:
    Community string [public]:
  Configure DECnet? [no]:
  Configure AppleTalk? [yes]:
    Multizone networks? [no]: yes
  Configure IPX? [yes]:
  Configure IP? [yes]:
    Configure IGRP routing? [yes]:
      Your IGRP autonomous system number [15]:
  Configure Async lines? [yes]:
    Async line speed [9600]: 57600
    Configure for HW flow control? [yes]:
    Configure for modems? [yes/no]: yes
      Configure for default chat script? [yes]: no
    Configure for Dial-in IP SLIP/PPP access? [no]: yes
      Configure for Dynamic IP addresses? [yes]: no
      Configure Default IP addresses? [no]: yes
      Configure for TCP Header Compression? [yes]: no
      Configure for routing updates on async links? [no]:
```

```
   Configure for Async IPX? [yes]:
   Configure for Appletalk Remote Access? [yes]:
     AppleTalk Network for ARAP clients [1]: 20
     Zone name for ARAP clients [ARA Dialins]:

Configuring interface parameters:

Configuring interface Ethernet0:
  Is this interface in use? [yes]:
  Configure IP on this interface? [yes]:
    IP address for this interface [172.16.72.2]:
    Number of bits in subnet field [8]:
    Class B network is 172.16.0.0, 8 subnet bits; mask is /24
  Configure AppleTalk on this interface? [yes]:
    Extended AppleTalk network? [yes]:
    AppleTalk starting cable range [1]:
    AppleTalk ending cable range [1]:
    AppleTalk zone name [Sales]:
    AppleTalk additional zone name:
  Configure IPX on this interface? [yes]:
    IPX network number [1]:

Configuring interface Serial0:
  Is this interface in use? [no]: yes
  Configure IP on this interface? [no]: yes
  Configure IP unnumbered on this interface? [no]: yes
    Assign to which interface [Ethernet0]:
  Configure AppleTalk on this interface? [no]: yes
    Extended AppleTalk network? [yes]:
    AppleTalk starting cable range [2]: 3
    AppleTalk ending cable range [3]: 3
    AppleTalk zone name [myzone]: ZZ Serial
    AppleTalk additional zone name:
  Configure IPX on this interface? [no]: yes
    IPX network number [2]: 3

Configuring interface Serial1:
  Is this interface in use? [yes]:
  Configure IP on this interface? [yes]:
  Configure IP unnumbered on this interface? [yes]:
    Assign to which interface [Ethernet0]:
  Configure AppleTalk on this interface? [yes]:
    Extended AppleTalk network? [yes]:
    AppleTalk starting cable range [2]:
    AppleTalk ending cable range [2]:
    AppleTalk zone name [ZZ Serial]:
    AppleTalk additional zone name:
  Configure IPX on this interface? [yes]:
    IPX network number [2]:
Configuring interface Async1:
    IPX network number [4]:
    Default client IP address for this interface [none]: 172.16.72.4
```

```
Configuring interface Async2:
   IPX network number [5]:
   Default client IP address for this interface [172.16.72.5]:
Configuring interface Async3:
   IPX network number [6]:
   Default client IP address for this interface [172.16.72.6]:
Configuring interface Async4:
   IPX network number [7]:
   Default client IP address for this interface [172.16.72.7]:
Configuring interface Async5:
   IPX network number [8]:
   Default client IP address for this interface [172.16.72.8]:
Configuring interface Async6:
   IPX network number [9]:
   Default client IP address for this interface [172.16.72.9]:
Configuring interface Async7:
   IPX network number [A]:
   Default client IP address for this interface [172.16.72.10]:
Configuring interface Async8:
   IPX network number [B]:
   Default client IP address for this interface [172.16.72.11]:
Configuring interface Async9:
   IPX network number [C]:
   Default client IP address for this interface [172.16.72.12]:
Configuring interface Async10:
   IPX network number [D]:
   Default client IP address for this interface [172.16.72.13]:
Configuring interface Async11:
   IPX network number [E]:
   Default client IP address for this interface [172.16.72.14]:
Configuring interface Async12:
   IPX network number [F]:
   Default client IP address for this interface [172.16.72.15]:
Configuring interface Async13:
   IPX network number [10]:
   Default client IP address for this interface [172.16.72.16]:
Configuring interface Async14:
   IPX network number [11]:
   Default client IP address for this interface [172.16.72.17]:
Configuring interface Async15:
   IPX network number [12]:
   Default client IP address for this interface [172.16.72.18]:
Configuring interface Async16:
   IPX network number [13]:
   Default client IP address for this interface [172.16.72.19]:
```

The following configuration command script was created:

```
hostname Router
enable secret 5 $1$krIg$emfYm/1OwHVspDuS8Gy0K1
enable password ww
line vty 0 4
password ww
snmp-server community public
!
no decnet routing
appletalk routing
ipx routing
ip routing
!
line 1 16
speed 57600
flowcontrol hardware
modem inout
!
arap network 20 ARA Dialins
line 1 16
arap enable
autoselect
!
! Turn off IPX to prevent network conflicts.
interface Ethernet0
no ipx network
interface Serial0
no ipx network
interface Serial1
no ipx network
!
interface Ethernet0
ip address 172.16.72.2 255.255.255.0
appletalk cable-range 1-1 1.204
appletalk zone Sales
ipx network 1
no mop enabled
!
interface Serial0
no shutdown
no ip address
ip unnumbered Ethernet0
appletalk cable-range 3-3
appletalk zone ZZ Serial
ipx network 3
no mop enabled
!
interface Serial1
no ip address
ip unnumbered Ethernet0
```

```
appletalk cable-range 2-2 2.2
appletalk zone ZZ Serial
ipx network 2
no mop enabled
!
Interface Async1
ipx network 4
ip unnumbered Ethernet0
peer default ip address 172.16.72.4
async mode interactive
!
Interface Async2
ipx network 5
ip unnumbered Ethernet0
peer default ip address 172.16.72.5
async mode interactive
!
Interface Async3
ipx network 6
ip unnumbered Ethernet0
peer default ip address 172.16.72.6
async mode interactive
!
Interface Async4
ipx network 7
ip unnumbered Ethernet0
peer default ip address 172.16.72.7
async mode interactive
async dynamic address
!
Interface Async5
ipx network 8
ip unnumbered Ethernet0
peer default ip address 172.16.72.8
async mode interactive
!
Interface Async6
ipx network 9
ip unnumbered Ethernet0
peer default ip address 172.16.72.9
async mode interactive
!
Interface Async7
ipx network A
ip unnumbered Ethernet0
peer default ip address 172.16.72.10
async mode interactive
!
Interface Async8
ipx network B
ip unnumbered Ethernet0
```

```
peer default ip address 172.16.72.11
async mode interactive
!
Interface Async9
ipx network C
ip unnumbered Ethernet0
peer default ip address 172.16.72.12
async mode interactive
!
Interface Async10
ipx network D
ip unnumbered Ethernet0
peer default ip address 172.16.72.13
async mode interactive
!
Interface Async11
ipx network E
ip unnumbered Ethernet0
peer default ip address 172.16.72.14
async mode interactive
!
Interface Async12
ipx network F
ip unnumbered Ethernet0
peer default ip address 172.16.72.15
async mode interactive
!
Interface Async13
ipx network 10
ip unnumbered Ethernet0
peer default ip address 172.16.72.16
async mode interactive
!
Interface Async14
ipx network 11
ip unnumbered Ethernet0
peer default ip address 172.16.72.17
async mode interactive
!
Interface Async15
ipx network 12
ip unnumbered Ethernet0
peer default ip address 172.16.72.18
async mode interactive
!
Interface Async16
ipx network 13
ip unnumbered Ethernet0
peer default ip address 172.16.72.19
async mode interactive
```

```
!
router igrp 15
network 172.16.0.0
!
end

Use this configuration? [yes/no]: yes

Building configuration...

Use the enabled mode 'configure' command to modify this configuration.

Router#
```

The following example shows a router entering the streamlined **setup** command facility:

```
--- System Configuration Dialog ---

Default settings are in square brackets '[]'.

Configuring interface IP parameters for netbooting:
```

NOTES

The message "Configuring interface IP parameters for netbooting" only appears if you are booting over a network server and your configuration has insufficient IP information.

The streamlined **setup** command facility continues by prompting you for interface parameters for each installed interface. The facility asks whether an interface is in use. If so, the facility then prompts you to provide an IP address and subnet mask bits for the interface. Enter the subnet mask bits as a decimal value, such as 5. Continuing with the streamlined **setup** command facility example, the following output shows the portion of the facility that prompts for interface parameters. In the example, the facility is prompting for Ethernet 0 interface parameters and Serial 0 interface parameters:

```
Configuring interface Ethernet0:
  Is this interface in use? [yes]:
  Configure IP on this interface? [yes]:
    IP address for this interface: 192.195.78.50
    Number of bits in subnet field [0]: 5
    Class C network is 192.195.78.0, 5 subnet bits; mask is 255.255.255.248

Configuring interface Serial0:
  Is this interface in use? [yes]:
  Configure IP on this interface? [yes]:
    IP address for this interface: 192.195.78.34
    Number of bits in subnet field [5]:
    Class C network is 192.195.78.0, 5 subnet bits; mask is 255.255.255.248
```

The configuration information you provide on this screen is *temporary* and exists only so that you can proceed with booting your system. When you reload the system, your original configuration is left intact. If your startup configuration is corrupted, enter the **setup** command facility, and configure the basic parameters. Then issue the **copy running-config startup-config** command to write this configuration to NVRAM.

Related Commands

copy running-config startup-config
erase startup-config
show running-config
show version

## CHAPTER 5

Configuring Operating Characteristics for Terminals

This chapter describes how to configure operating characteristics for terminals. For a complete description of the terminal operation commands in this chapter, see Chapter 6, "Terminal Operating Characteristics Commands."

To configure operating characteristics for terminals, perform any of the tasks in the following sections:

- Displaying Information about Current Terminal Session
- Setting Local Terminal Parameters
- Saving Local Settings Between Sessions
- Ending a Session
- Changing Terminal Session Parameters
- Recording the Device Location
- Changing the Retry Interval for a Terminal Port Queue
- LPD Protocol Support

DISPLAYING INFORMATION ABOUT CURRENT TERMINAL SESSION

The **show whoami** command displays information about the current user's terminal line, including host name, line number, line speed, and location. To display line information, perform the following task at the EXEC prompt:

Task	Command
Display line information.	**show whoami** *text*

If text is included as an argument in the command, that text is displayed as part of the additional data about the line.

The following example shows sample output of the **show whoami** command:

```
Router> show whoami

Comm Server "Router", Line 0 at 0bps.  Location "Second floor, West"

--More--
Router>
```

To prevent the information from being lost, this command always displays a ---More--- prompt before returning. Press the space bar to return to the prompt.

SETTING LOCAL TERMINAL PARAMETERS

The **terminal** EXEC commands enable or disable features for the current session only. You can use these commands to temporarily change terminal line settings without changing the stored configuration file.

To see a list of the commands for setting terminal parameters for the current session, perform the following task in user EXEC mode:

Task	Command
List the commands for setting terminal parameters.	**terminal ?**

The following example shows the type of output **terminal ?** could generate:

```
Router> terminal ?
  autohangup            Automatically hangup when last connection closes
  data-character-bits   Size of characters being handled
  databits              Set number of data bits per character
  dispatch-character    Define the dispatch character
  dispatch-timeout      Set the dispatch timer
  download              Put line into 'download' mode
  editing               Enable command line editing
  escape-character      Change the current line's escape character
  exec-character-bits   Size of characters to the command exec
  flowcontrol           Set the flow control
  full-help             Provide help to unprivileged user
  help                  Description of the interactive help system
  history               Enable and control the command history function
  hold-character        Define the hold character
  ip                    IP options
  keymap-type           Specify a keymap entry to use
  lat                   DEC Local Area Transport (LAT) protocol-specific
                        configuration
  length                Set number of lines on a screen
  no                    Negate a command or set its defaults
```

```
notify                  Inform users of output from concurrent sessions
padding                 Set padding for a specified output character
parity                  Set terminal parity
rxspeed                 Set the receive speed
special-character-bits  Size of the escape (and other special) characters
speed                   Set the transmit and receive speeds
start-character         Define the start character
stop-character          Define the stop character
stopbits                Set async line stop bits
telnet                  Telnet protocol-specific configuration
telnet-transparent      Send a CR as a CR followed by a NULL instead of a CR
                        followed by a LF
terminal-type           Set the terminal type
transport               Define transport protocols for line
txspeed                 Set the transmit speeds
width                   Set width of the display terminal
```

Throughout this chapter, many terminal settings can be configured for all terminal sessions or for just the current terminal session. The commands will be in two forms. The basic form will be in line configuration mode and can be saved permanently so that all terminal sessions are affected. The **terminal** form of the command is entered in EXEC mode and only affects the current session.

SAVING LOCAL SETTINGS BETWEEN SESSIONS

You can configure the Cisco IOS software to save local parameters set with **terminal** EXEC commands between sessions. Saving local settings ensures that the parameters the user sets will remain in effect between terminal sessions. This function is useful for servers in private offices. To save local settings between sessions, perform the following task in line configuration mode:

Task	Command
Save local settings between sessions.	**private**

By default, user-set terminal parameters are cleared when the session ends with either the **exit** EXEC command, or when the interval set with the **exec-timeout** line configuration command has passed.

ENDING A SESSION

To end a session, perform the following steps:

Task	Command
Enter the quit EXEC command.	**quit**

See Chapter 7, "Managing Connections and System Banners," for more information on exiting sessions and closing connections.

CHANGING TERMINAL SESSION PARAMETERS

This section explains how to change terminal and line settings both for a particular line and locally. The local settings are set with the EXEC **terminal** commands. They temporarily override the settings made by the system administrator and remain in effect only until you exit the system. In line configuration mode, you can set terminal operation characteristics that will be in operation for that line until the next time you change the line parameters.

The following sections describe the more common changes to the terminal and line settings:

- Defining Escape Character and Other Key Sequences
- Specifying Telnet Operation Characteristics
- Configuring Data Transparency for File Transfers
- Specifying an International Character Display

The following sections describe the less common changes to the terminal and line settings:

- Setting Character Padding
- Specifying the Terminal and Keyboard Type
- Changing the Terminal Screen Length and Width
- Changing Pending Output Notification
- Creating Character and Packet Dispatch Sequences
- Displaying Debug Messages on the Console and Terminals
- Changing Flow Control for the Current Session
- Setting a Terminal-Locking Mechanism
- Configuring Automatic Baud Rate Detection
- Setting a Line as Insecure
- Configuring Communication Parameters for Terminal Ports

Defining Escape Character and Other Key Sequences

You can define or modify the default key sequences to execute functions for system escape, terminal activation, disconnect, and terminal pause.

Globally Defining Escape Character and Other Key Sequences

To define or change the default key sequence, perform one or more of the following tasks in line configuration mode:

Task	Command
Change the system escape sequence. The escape sequence indicates that the codes that follow have special meaning. The default escape sequence is Ctrl-^.[1]	**escape-character** *ascii-number*
Define a session activation sequence or character. Entering this sequence at a vacant terminal begins a terminal session. The default activation sequence is the Return key.	**activation-character** *ascii-number*
Define the session disconnect sequence or character. Entering this sequence at a terminal ends the session with the router. There is no default disconnect sequence.	**disconnect-character** *ascii-number*
Define the hold sequence or character that causes output to the terminal screen to pause. To continue the output, enter any character after the hold character. To use the hold character in normal communications, precede it with the escape character. There is no default sequence.	**hold-character** *ascii-number*

[1] Pressing **Ctrl** displays a caret (^) character. The escape sequence is **Ctrl-Shift-6**.

You can reinstate the default value for the escape character or activation character by using the **no** form of the command. For example, issuing the **no escape-character** line configuration command returns the escape character to Ctrl-^.

NOTES

If you are using the **autoselect** function, the activation character should not be changed from the default value of Return. If you change this default, the **autoselect** feature might not function immediately.

Defining Escape and Pause Characters for the Current Session

For the current terminal session, you can modify key sequences to execute functions for system escape and terminal pause. To modify these sequences, perform one or more of the following tasks in EXEC mode:

Task	Command
Change the system escape sequence for the current session. The escape sequence indicates that the codes that follow have special meaning. The default sequence is Ctrl-^.	**terminal escape-character** *ASCII-number*
Define the hold sequence or character that causes output to the terminal screen to pause for this session. There is no default sequence. To continue the output, type any character after the hold character. To use the hold character in normal communications, precede it with the escape character. You cannot suspend output on the console terminal.	**terminal hold-character** *ASCII-number*

The **terminal escape-character** command is useful, for example, if you have the default escape character defined for a different purpose in your keyboard file. Entering the escape character followed by the X key returns you to EXEC mode when you are connected to another computer.

Specifying Telnet Operation Characteristics

The following sections discuss Telnet operation characteristics tasks:

- Generating a Hardware Break Signal for a Reverse Telnet Connection
- Setting the Line to Refuse Full-Duplex, Remote Echo Connections
- Allowing Transmission Speed Negotiation
- Synchronizing the Break Signal
- Changing the End-of-Line Character

Generating a Hardware Break Signal for a Reverse Telnet Connection

To cause the router to generate a hardware Break signal on the EIA/TIA-232 line that is associated with a reverse Telnet connection for the current line and session, perform the following task in EXEC mode:

Task	Command
Generate a hardware Break signal on the EIA/TIA-232 line that is associated with a reverse Telnet connection for the current line and session.	**terminal telnet break-on-ip**

The hardware Break signal occurs when a Telnet Interrupt-Process command is received on that connection. This command can be used to control the translation of Telnet IP commands into X.25 Break indications.

This command is also a useful workaround in the following situations:

- Several user Telnet programs send an Interrupt-Process command but cannot send a Telnet Break signal.

- Some Telnet programs implement a Break signal that sends an Interrupt-Process command.

Some EIA/TIA-232 hardware devices use a hardware Break signal for various purposes. A hardware Break signal is generated when a Telnet Break command is received.

NOTES

This command applies only to access server products. It is not supported on stand-alone routers.

Setting the Line to Refuse Full-Duplex, Remote Echo Connections

You can set the line to allow the Cisco IOS software to refuse full-duplex, remote echo connection requests from the other end. This refusal suppresses negotiation of the Telnet Remote Echo and Suppress Go Ahead options. To set the current line to refuse to negotiate full-duplex, remote echo options on incoming connections for the current session, perform the following task in EXEC mode:

Task	Command
Set the current line to refuse to negotiate full-duplex for the current session.	**terminal telnet refuse-negotiations**

NOTES

This command applies only to access server products. It is not supported on stand-alone routers.

Allowing Transmission Speed Negotiation

To allow the Cisco IOS software to negotiate transmission speed for the current line and session, perform the following task in EXEC mode:

Task	Command
Allow the Cisco IOS software to negotiate transmission speed for the current line and session.	**terminal telnet speed** *default-speed maximum-speed*

You can match line speeds on remote systems in reverse Telnet, on host machines that connect to the network through an access server, or on a group of console lines hooked up to an access server when disparate line speeds are in use at the local and remote ends of the connection. Line speed negotiation adheres to the Remote Flow Control option, defined in RFC 1080.

NOTES

This command applies only to access server products. It is not supported on stand-alone routers.

Synchronizing the Break Signal

You can set lines on the access server to cause a reverse Telnet line to send a Telnet Synchronize signal when it receives a Telnet Break signal. The TCP Synchronize signal clears the data path, but interprets incoming commands. To cause the Cisco IOS software to send a Telnet Synchronize signal when it receives a Telnet Break signal on the current line and session, perform the following task in EXEC mode:

Task	Command
Cause the Cisco IOS software to send a Telnet Synchronize signal when it receives a Telnet Break signal on the current line and session.	**terminal telnet sync-on-break**

NOTES

This command applies only to access server products. It is not supported on stand-alone routers.

Changing the End-of-Line Character

The end of each line typed at the terminal is ended with a Return (CR). To cause the current terminal line to send a CR as a CR followed by a NULL instead of a CR followed by a line feed (LF), perform the following task in EXEC mode:

Task	Command
Cause the current terminal line to send a CR as a CR followed by a NULL instead of a CR followed by a line feed (LF).	**terminal telnet transparent**

This command ensures interoperability with different interpretations of end-of-line handling in the Telnet protocol specification.

NOTES

This command applies only to access servers. It is not supported on stand-alone routers.

Configuring Data Transparency for File Transfers

Data transparency enables the Cisco IOS software to pass data on a terminal connection without the data being interpreted as a control character.

During terminal operations, some characters are reserved for special functions. For example, **Ctrl-Shift-6-X** (^^x) suspends a session. When transferring files over a terminal connection (using the Xmodem or Kermit protocols, for example), you must suspend the recognition of these special characters to allow a successful file transfer. This process is called *data transparency.*

You can set a line to act as a transparent pipe so that programs such as Kermit, Xmodem, or CrossTalk can download a file across a terminal line. To temporarily configure a line to act as a pipe for file transfers, perform the following task in EXEC mode

Task	Command
Set up the terminal line to act as a transparent pipe for file transfers.	**terminal download**

The **terminal download** command is equivalent to entering all the following commands.

- **terminal telnet transparent**
- **terminal no escape-character**

- terminal no hold-character
- terminal no padding 0
- terminal no padding 128
- terminal parity none
- terminal databits 8

Specifying an International Character Display

The classic U.S. ASCII character set is limited to 7 bits (128 characters), which adequately represents most displays in the U.S. Most defaults on the modem router work best on a 7-bit path. However, international character sets and special symbol display can require an 8-bit wide path and other handling.

You can use a 7-bit character set (such as ASCII), or you can enable a full 8-bit international character set (such as ISO 8859). This allows special graphical and international characters for use in banners and prompts, and adds special characters such as software flow control. Character settings can be configured globally, per line, or locally at the user level. Use the following criteria for determining which configuration mode to use when you set this international character display:

- If a large number of connected terminals support nondefault ASCII bit settings, use the global configuration commands.
- If only a few of the connected terminals support nondefault ASCII bit settings, use line configuration commands or the EXEC local terminal setting commands.

NOTES

Setting the EXEC character width to an 8-bit character set can cause failures. If a user on a terminal that is sending parity enters the **help** command, an "unrecognized command" message appears because the system is reading all eight bits, although the eighth bit is not needed for **help**.

NOTES

If you are using the **autoselect** function, the activation character should be set to the default Return, and the EXEC character bit should be set to 7. If you change these defaults, the application does not recognize the activation request.

Specifying the International Character Display for All Lines

To specify a character set for all lines, perform one or both of the following tasks in global configuration mode:

Task	Command
Specify the character set used in EXEC and configuration command characters.	**default-value exec-character-bits** {7	8}
Specify the character set used in special characters such as software flow control, hold, escape, and disconnect characters.	**default-value special-character-bits** {7	8}

Specifying the International Character Display on a Hardware, Software, or Per-line Basis

To specify a character set based on hardware, software, or on a per-line basis, perform any of the following tasks in line configuration mode:

Task	Command
Set the number of data bits per character that are generated and interpreted by hardware.	**databits** {5	6	7	8}
Set the number of data bits per character that are generated and interpreted by software.	**data-character-bits** {7	8}
Specify the character set used in EXEC and configuration command characters on a per-line basis.	**exec-character-bits** {7	8}
Specify the character set used in special characters such as software flow control, hold, escape, and disconnect characters on a per-line basis.	**special-character-bits** {7	8}

Specifying an International Character Display for the Current Session

To specify a character set based on hardware, software, or on a per-line basis for the current terminal session, perform the following appropriate tasks in EXEC mode:

Task	Command
Set the number of data bits per character that are generated and interpreted by hardware for the current session.	**terminal databits** {5 | 6 | 7 | 8}
Set the number of data bits per character that are generated and interpreted by software for the current session.	**terminal data-character-bits** {7 | 8}
Specify the character set used in EXEC and configuration command characters on a per-line basis for the current session.	**terminal exec-character-bits** {7 | 8}
Specify the character set used in special characters (such as software flow control, hold, escape, and disconnect characters) on a per-line basis for the current session.	**terminal special-character-bits** {7 | 8}

Setting Character Padding

Character padding adds a number of null bytes to the end of the string and can be used to make a string an expected length for conformity. You can change the character padding on a specific output character.

Globally Setting Character Padding

To set character padding, perform the following task in line configuration mode:

Task	Command
Set padding on a specific output character for the specified line.	**padding** *ascii-number count*

Changing Character Padding for the Current Session

To change character padding on a specific output character for the current session, perform the following task in EXEC mode:

Task	Command
Set padding on a specific output character for the specified line for this session.	**terminal padding** *ASCII-number count*

Specifying the Terminal and Keyboard Type

You can specify the type of terminal connected to a line. This feature has two benefits: It provides a record of the type of terminal attached to a line, and it can be used in Telnet terminal negotiations to inform the remote host of the terminal type for display management.

Globally Specifying the Terminal Type

To specify the terminal type, perform the following task in line configuration mode:

Task	Command
Specify the terminal type.	**terminal-type** {*terminal-name*	*terminal-type*}

This feature is used by TN3270 terminals to identify the keymap and ttycap passed by the Telnet protocol to the end host.

Changing the Terminal and Keyboard Type for the Current Session

To specify the type of terminal connected to the current line for the current session, perform the following task in EXEC mode:

Task	Command
Specify the terminal type for this session.	**terminal terminal-type** *terminal-type*

Indicate the terminal type if it is different from the default of VT100. This default is used by TN3270 for display management and by Telnet and rlogin to inform the remote host of the terminal type.

To specify the current keyboard type for a session, perform the following task in EXEC mode:

Task	Command
Specify the keyboard type for this session.	**terminal keymap-type** *keymap-name*

You must specify the keyboard type when you use a keyboard other than the default of VT100. The system administrator can define other keyboard types and give you their names.

Changing the Terminal Screen Length and Width

By default, the Cisco IOS software provides a screen display of 24 lines by 80 characters. You can change these values if they do not meet the requirements of your terminal. The screen values you set are passed during rsh and rlogin sessions.

The screen values set can be learned by some host systems that use this type of information in terminal negotiation. To disable pausing between screens of output, set the screen length to a zero.

The screen length specified can be learned by remote hosts. For example, the rlogin protocol uses the screen length to set up terminal parameters on a remote UNIX host. The width specified also can be learned by remote hosts.

Globally Changing the Terminal Screen Length and Width

To set the terminal screen length and width, perform the following tasks in line configuration mode:

Task	Command
Step 1 Set the screen length.	**length** *screen-length*
Step 2 Set the screen width.	**width** *characters*

Changing the Terminal Screen Length and Width for the Current Session

To set the number of lines or character columns on the current terminal screen for the current session, perform one of the following tasks in EXEC mode:

Task	Command
Set the screen length for the current session.	**terminal length** *screen-length*
Set the screen width for the current session.	**terminal width** *characters*

Changing Pending Output Notification

You can set up a line to inform a user who has multiple, concurrent Telnet connections when output is pending on a connection other than the active one. For example, you might want to know when another connection receives mail or a message.

Globally Setting Pending Output Notification

To set pending output notification, perform the following task in line configuration mode:

Task	Command
Set up a line to notify a user of pending output.	notify

Setting Pending Output Notification for the Current Session

To set pending output notification for the current session, perform the following task in EXEC mode:

Task	Command
Set up a line to notify a user of pending output for the current session.	terminal notify

Creating Character and Packet Dispatch Sequences

The Cisco IOS software supports dispatch sequences and TCP state machines that transmit data packets only when they receive a defined character or sequence of characters. You can set up dispatch characters that allow packets to be buffered, then transmitted upon receipt of a character. You can set up a state machine that allows packets to be buffered, then transmitted upon receipt of a sequence of characters. This feature enables packet transmission when the user presses a function key, which is typically defined as a sequence of characters, such as "Esc I C."

TCP state machines can control TCP processes with a set of predefined character sequences. The current state of the device determines what happens next, given an expected character sequence. The state-machine commands configure the server to search for and recognize a particular sequence of characters, then cycle through a set of states. The user defines these states—up to eight states can be defined. (Think of each state as a task that the server performs based on the assigned configuration commands and the type of character sequences received).

The Cisco IOS software supports user-specified state machines for determining whether data from an asynchronous port should be sent to the network. This functionality extends the concept of the dispatch character and allows the equivalent of multicharacter dispatch strings.

Up to eight states can be set up for the state machine. Data packets are buffered until the appropriate character or sequence triggers the transmission. Delay and timer metrics allow for more efficient use of system resources. Characters defined in the TCP state machine take precedence over those defined for a dispatch character.

Setting Character and Packet Dispatch Sequences for a Line

Perform the following tasks in line configuration mode, as needed, for your particular system needs:

Task	Command
Step 1 Specify the transition criteria for the states in a TCP state machine.	**state-machine** *name state firstchar lastchar* [*nextstate* | **transmit**]
Step 2 Specify the state machine for TCP packet dispatch.	**dispatch-machine** *name*
Step 3 Define a character that triggers packet transmission.	**dispatch-character** *ASCII-number* [*ASCII-number2 . . . ASCII-number*]
Step 4 Set the dispatch timer.	**dispatch-timeout** *milliseconds*

Changing the Packet Dispatch Character for the Current Session

To change the packet dispatch character for the current session, perform the following task in EXEC mode:

Task	Command
Define a character that triggers packet transmission for the current session.	**terminal dispatch-character** *ASCII-number1* [*ASCII-number2 . . . ASCII-number*]

Displaying Debug Messages on the Console and Terminals

To display **debug** command output and system error messages in EXEC mode on the current terminal, perform the following task in privileged EXEC mode:

Task	Command
Display debug command output and system error messages in EXEC mode on the current terminal.	**terminal monitor**

Remember that all terminal parameter-setting commands are set locally and do not remain in effect after a session is ended. You must perform this task at the privileged-level EXEC prompt at each session to see the debugging messages.

Changing Flow Control for the Current Session

To configure flow control between the router and attached device for this session, perform one of the following tasks in EXEC mode:

Task	Command
Set the terminal flow control for this session.	**terminal flowcontrol {none	software [in	out]	hardware}**
Set the flow control start character in the current session.	**terminal start-character** *ASCII-number*[1]
Set the flow control stop character in the current session.	**terminal stop-character** *ASCII-number*[1]

[1] This command is seldom used. Typically, you only need to use the **terminal flowcontrol** command.

Setting a Terminal-Locking Mechanism

You can enable a terminal-locking mechanism that allows a terminal to be temporarily locked by performing the following task in line configuration mode:

Task	Command
Enable a temporary terminal locking mechanism.	**lockable**

After you configure the line as lockable, you still must issue the **lock** EXEC command to lock the keyboard.

Configuring Automatic Baud Rate Detection

You can configure a terminal to detect the baud rate being used over an asynchronous serial line automatically. To set up automatic baud detection, perform the following task in line configuration mode:

Task	Command
Set the terminal to detect automatically the baud rate.	**autobaud**

NOTES

Do not use the **autobaud** command with the **autoselect** command.

To start communications using automatic baud detection, enter multiple Returns at the terminal. A 600-, 1,800-, or 19,200- baud line requires three Returns to detect the baud rate. A line at any other baud rate requires only two Returns. If you enter extra Returns after the baud rate is detected, the EXEC facility simply displays another system prompt.

Setting a Line as Insecure

You can set up a terminal line to appear as an insecure dial-up line. The information is used by the LAT software, which reports such dial-up connections to remote systems.

To set a line as insecure, perform the following task in line configuration mode:

Task	Command
Set the line as a dial-up line.	insecure

In the previous releases of Cisco IOS software, any line that used modem control was reported as a dial-up connection through the LAT protocol; this feature allows more direct control of your line.

Configuring Communication Parameters for Terminal Ports

You can change these parameters as necessary to meet the requirements of the terminal or host to which you are attached. To do so, perform one or more of the following tasks in EXEC mode:

Task	Command
Set the line speed for the current session. Choose from line speed, transmit speed, or receive speed.	terminal speed *bps* terminal txspeed *bps* terminal rxspeed *bps*
Set the data bits for the current session.	terminal databits {5 | 6 | 7 | 8}
Set the stop bits for the current session.	terminal stopbits {1 | 1.5 | 2}
Set the parity bit for the current session.	terminal parity {none | even | odd | space | mark}

RECORDING THE DEVICE LOCATION

You can record the location of a serial device. The text provided for the location appears in the output of the EXEC monitoring commands. To record the device location, perform the following task in line configuration mode:

Task	Command
Record the location of a serial device.	**location** *text*

CHANGING THE RETRY INTERVAL FOR A TERMINAL PORT QUEUE

If you attempt to connect to a remote device (such as a printer) that is busy, the connection attempt is placed in a terminal port queue. If the retry interval is set too high, and several routers or other devices are connected to the remote device, your connection attempt can have long delays. To change the retry interval for a terminal port queue, perform the following task in global configuration mode:

Task	Command
Change the retry interval for a terminal port queue.	**terminal-queue entry-retry-interval** *interval*

LPD PROTOCOL SUPPORT

The Cisco IOS software supports a subset of the Berkeley UNIX Line Printer Daemon (LPD) protocol used to send print jobs between UNIX systems. This subset of the LPD protocol permits the following:

- Improved status information
- Cancellation of print jobs
- Confirmation of successful printing and automatic retry for common print failures
- Use of standard UNIX software

The Cisco implementation of LPD permits you to configure a printer to allow several types of data to be sent as print jobs (for example, PostScript or raw text).

To configure a printer for the LPD protocol, perform the following task in global configuration mode:

Task	Command
Configure printer and specify a TTY line (or lines) for the device.	**printer** *printername* {**line** *number* | **rotary** *number*} [**newline-convert**]

If you use the **printer** command, you also must modify the */etc/printcap* file on the UNIX system to include the definition of the remote printer on the router. Use the optional **newline-convert** keyword on UNIX systems that do not handle single character line terminators to convert a new line to a character Return, line-feed sequence.

The following example includes the configuration of the printer Saturn on the host Memphis:

```
comm1pt¦Printer on cisco AccessServer:\
    :rm=memphis:rp+saturn:\
    :sd+/usr/spool/lpd/comm1pt:\
    :lf=?var/log/lpd/comm1pt:
```

The content of the actual file might differ, depending on the configuration of your UNIX system.

To print, users use the standard **UNIX lpr** command.

Support for the LPD protocol allows you to display a list of currently defined printers and current usage statistics for each printer. To do so, perform the following task in EXEC mode:

Task	Command
List currently defined printers and their usage statistics.	**show printer**

To provide access to LPD features, your system administrator must configure a printer and assign a TTY line (or lines) to the printer. The administrator must also modify */etc/printcap* on your UNIX system to include the definition of the remote printer in the Cisco IOS software.

## CHAPTER 6

Terminal Operating Characteristics Commands

This chapter describes the commands used to control terminal operating characteristics.

For terminal operating characteristic task information and examples, see Chapter 5, "Configuring Operating Characteristics for Terminals."

ACTIVATION-CHARACTER

To define the character you enter at a vacant terminal to begin a terminal session, use the **activation-character** line configuration command. Use the **no** form of this command to make any character activate a terminal.

> **activation-character** *ascii-number*
> **no activation-character**

Syntax	Description
ascii-number	Decimal representation of the activation character.

Default
Return (decimal 13)

Command Mode
Line configuration

Usage Guidelines
This command first appeared in Cisco IOS Release 10.0.

See Appendix A, "ASCII Character Set," for a list of ASCII characters.

NOTES

If you are using the **autoselect** function, set the activation character to the default, Return, and exec-character-bits to 7. If you change these defaults, the application will not recognize the activation request.

Example

The following example sets the activation character for the console to Delete, which is Decimal 127:

```
line console
  activation-character 127
```

AUTOBAUD

To set the line for automatic baud detection, use the **autobaud** line configuration command. Use the **no** form of this command to restore the default.

    autobaud
    no autobaud

Syntax   Description

This command has no arguments or keywords.

Default

No autobaud detection

Command Mode

Line configuration

Usage Guidelines

This command first appeared in Cisco IOS Release 10.0.

The autobaud detection supports a range from 300 to 19,200 baud. A line set for autobaud cannot be used for outgoing connections, nor can you set autobaud capability on a line using 19,200 baud when the parity bit is set (because of hardware limitations).

Example

The following example sets the auxiliary port for autobaud detection:

```
line 5
  autobaud
```

DATABITS

To set the number of data bits per character that are interpreted and generated by the router hardware, use the **databits** line configuration command. Use the **no** form of the command to restore the default value.

>   **databits** {5 | 6 | 7 | 8}
>   **no databits**

Syntax	Description
5	Five data bits per character.
6	Six data bits per character.
7	Seven data bits per character.
8	Eight data bits per character.

Default

8 data bits per character

Command Mode

Line configuration

Usage Guidelines

This command first appeared in Cisco IOS Release 10.0.

The **databits** line configuration command can be used to mask the high bit on input from devices that generate 7 data bits with parity. If parity is being generated, specify 7 data bits per character. If no parity generation is in effect, specify 8 data bits per character. The other keywords are supplied for compatibility with older devices and generally are not used.

Example

The following example changes the data bits to 7 on line 4:

```
line 4
 databits 7
```

Related Commands

data-character-bits
terminal databits
terminal data-character-bits

DATA-CHARACTER-BITS

To set the number of data bits per character that are interpreted and generated by the Cisco IOS software, use the **data-character-bits** line configuration command. Use the **no** form of the command to restore the default value.

> **data-character-bits** {7 | 8}
> **no data-character-bits**

Syntax	Description
7	Seven data bits per character.
8	Eight data bits per character.

Default

8 data bits per character

Command Mode

Line configuration

Usage Guidelines

This command first appeared in Cisco IOS Release 10.0.

The **data-character-bits** line configuration command is used primarily to strip parity from X.25 connections on routers with the protocol translation software option. The **data-character-bits** line configuration command does not work on hard-wired lines.

Example

The following example sets the number of data bits per character for virtual terminal line 1 to 7:

```
line vty 1
 data-character-bits 7
```

Related Commands

terminal data-character-bits

DEFAULT-VALUE EXEC-CHARACTER-BITS

To define the EXEC character width for either 7 bits or 8 bits, use the **default-value exec-character-bits** global configuration command. Use the **no** form of the command to restore the default value.

> **default-value exec-character-bits** {7 | 8}
> **no default-value exec-character-bits**

Syntax	Description
7	Selects the 7-bit ASCII character set.
8	Selects the full 8-bit ASCII character set.

Default

7-bit ASCII character set

Command Mode

Global configuration

Usage Guidelines

This command first appeared in Cisco IOS Release 10.0.

Configuring the EXEC character width to 8 bits allows you to add graphical and international characters in banners, prompts, and so forth. However, setting the EXEC character width to 8 bits can also cause failures. If a user on a terminal that is sending parity enters the command **help**, an "unrecognized command" message appears because the system is reading all 8 bits, although the eighth bit is not needed for the **help** command.

Example

The following example selects the full 8-bit ASCII character set for EXEC banners and prompts:

```
default-value exec-character-bits 8
```

Related Commands

default-value special-character-bits
exec-character-bits
length
terminal exec-character-bits
terminal special-character-bits

DEFAULT-VALUE SPECIAL-CHARACTER-BITS

To configure the flow control default value from a 7-bit width to an 8-bit width, use the **default-value special-character-bits** global configuration command. Use the **no** form of the command to restore the default value.

> **default-value special-character-bits {7 | 8}**
> **no default-value special-character-bits**

Syntax	Description
7	Selects the 7-bit character set.
8	Selects the full 8-bit character set.

Default
7-bit character set

Command Mode
Global configuration

Usage Guidelines
This command first appeared in Cisco IOS Release 10.0.

Configuring the special character width to 8 bits allows you to add graphical and international characters in banners, prompts, and so forth.

Example
The following example selects the full 8-bit special character set:

```
default-value special-character-bits 8
```

Related Commands
default-value exec-character-bits
exec-character-bits
length
terminal exec-character-bits
terminal special-character-bits

DISCONNECT-CHARACTER

To define a character to disconnect a session, use the **disconnect-character** line configuration command. Use the **no** form of this command to remove the disconnect character.

> **disconnect-character** *ascii-number*
> **no disconnect-character**

Syntax	Description
ascii-number	Decimal representation of the session disconnect character.

Default
No disconnect character is defined.

Command Mode

Line configuration

Usage Guidelines

This command first appeared in Cisco IOS Release 10.0.

The Break character is represented by zero; NULL cannot be represented.

To use the session-disconnect character in normal communications, precede it with the escape character. See Appendix A, "ASCII Character Set," for a list of ASCII characters.

Example

The following example sets the disconnect character for virtual terminal line 4 to Escape, which is decimal character 27:

```
line vty 4
 disconnect-character 27
```

DISPATCH-CHARACTER

To define a character that causes a packet to be sent, use the **dispatch-character** line configuration command. Use the **no** form of this command to remove the definition of the specified dispatch character.

> **dispatch-character** *ascii-number1 [ascii-number2 . . . ascii-number]*
> **no dispatch-character** *ascii-number1* [ascii-number2 . . . ascii-number]

Syntax	Description
ascii-number	Decimal representation of the character, such as Return (decimal 13) for line-at-a-time transmissions.

Default

No dispatch character is defined.

Command Mode

Line configuration

Usage Guidelines

This command first appeared in Cisco IOS Release 10.0.

The **dispatch-character** command defines a dispatch character that causes a packet to be sent even if the dispatch timer has not expired. It causes the Cisco IOS software to attempt to buffer characters into larger-sized packets for transmission to the remote host.

Enable the **dispatch-character** command from the session that initiates the connection, not from the incoming side of a streaming Telnet session.

This command can take multiple arguments, so you can define any number of characters as dispatch characters.

Example

The following example specifies the Return character (decimal 13) as the dispatch character:

```
line vty 4
  dispatch-character 13
```

Related Commands

dispatch-machine
dispatch-timeout
state-machine
terminal dispatch-character

DISPATCH-MACHINE

To specify an identifier for a TCP packet dispatch state machine on a particular line, use the **dispatch-machine** line configuration command. Use the **no** form of the command to disable a state machine on a particular line

> **dispatch-machine** *name*
> **no dispatch-machine**

Syntax	Description
name	Name of the state machine that determines when to send packets on the asynchronous line.

Default

No dispatch state machine identifier is defined.

Command Mode

Line configuration

Usage Guidelines

This command first appeared in Cisco IOS Release 10.0.

When the **dispatch-timeout** command is specified, a packet being built will be sent when the timer expires, and the state will be reset to zero.

Any dispatch characters specified using the **dispatch-character** command are ignored when a state machine is also specified.

If a packet becomes full, it will be sent regardless of the current state, but the state is not reset. The packet size depends on the traffic level on the asynchronous line and the dispatch-timeout value. There is always room for 60 data bytes. If the dispatch-timeout value is greater than or equal to 100 ms, a packet size of 536 (data bytes) is allocated.

Example

The following example specifies the name *linefeed* for the state machine:

```
state-machine linefeed 0 0 9 0
state-machine linefeed 0 11 255 0
state-machine linefeed 0 10 10 transmit

line 1
 dispatch-machine linefeed
```

Related Commands

dispatch-character
dispatch-timeout
state-machine

DISPATCH-TIMEOUT

To set the character dispatch timer, use the **dispatch-timeout** line configuration command. Use the **no** form of this command to remove the timeout definition.

> **dispatch-timeout** *milliseconds*
> **no dispatch-timeout**

Syntax

milliseconds

Description

Integer that specifies the number of milliseconds that the Cisco IOS software waits after putting the first character into a packet buffer before sending the packet. During this interval, more characters might be added to the packet, which increases the processing efficiency of the remote host.

Default

No dispatch timeout is defined.

Command Mode

Line configuration

Usage Guidelines

This command first appeared in Cisco IOS Release 10.0.

The **dispatch-timeout** line configuration command causes the software to buffer characters into packets for transmission to the remote host. The Cisco IOS software sends a packet a specified amount of time after the first character is put into the buffer. You can use the **dispatch-timeout** and **dispatch-character** line configuration commands together. In this case, the software dispatches a packet each time the dispatch character is entered, or after the specified dispatch timeout interval, depending on which condition is met first.

NOTES

The software's response might appear intermittent if the timeout interval is greater than 100 ms and remote echoing is used. For lines with a reverse-Telnet connection, use a dispatch-timeout value less than 10 ms.

Example

The following example sets the dispatch timer to 80 ms:

```
line vty 0 4
  dispatch-timeout 80
```

Related Commands

dispatch-character
dispatch-machine
state-machine

ESCAPE-CHARACTER

To define a system escape character, use the **escape-character** line configuration command. Use the **no** form of this command to set the escape character to Break.

escape-character *ascii-number* | **none**
no escape-character

Syntax	Description
ascii-number	Either the decimal representation of the character or a control sequence (Ctrl-E, for example).
none	Disables escape entirely.

Default

Ctrl-^

Command Mode

Line configuration

Usage Guidelines

This command first appeared in Cisco IOS Release 10.0.

The Break key cannot be used as an escape character on the console terminal because the Cisco IOS software interprets Break as an instruction to halt the system. To send the escape character to the other side, press **Ctrl-^** twice.

See Appendix A, "ASCII Character Set," for a list of ASCII characters.

Example

The following example sets the escape character to Ctrl-P, which is decimal character 16:

```
line console
  escape-character 16
```

Related Commands

terminal escape-character

EXEC-CHARACTER-BITS

To configure the character widths of EXEC and configuration command characters, use the **exec-character-bits** line configuration command. Use the **no** form of the command to restore the default value.

> **exec-character-bits {7 | 8}**
> **no exec-character-bits**

Syntax	Description
7	Selects the 7-bit character set.
8	Selects the full 8-bit character set for use of international and graphical characters in banner messages, prompts, and so forth.

Default

7-bit ASCII character set

Command Mode

Line configuration

Usage Guidelines

This command first appeared in Cisco IOS Release 10.0.

Setting the EXEC character width to 8 allows you to use special graphical and international characters in banners, prompts, and so forth. However, setting the EXEC character width to 8 bits can cause failures. If a user on a terminal that is sending parity enters the **help** command, an "unrecognized command" message appears because the system is reading all 8 bits, and the eighth bit is not needed for the **help** command.

NOTES

If you are using the **autoselect** function, set the activation-character to the default, Return, and **exec-character-bits** to 7. If you change these defaults, the application will not recognize the activation request.

Example

The following example enables full 8-bit international character sets, except for the console, which is an ASCII terminal. It illustrates use of the **default-value exec-character-bits** global configuration command and the **exec-character-bits** line configuration command.

```
default-value exec-character-bits 8
line 0
 exec-character-bits 7
```

Related Commands

default-value exec-character-bits
default-value special-character-bits
length
terminal exec-character-bits
terminal special-character-bits

HOLD-CHARACTER

To define the local hold character used to pause output to the terminal screen, use the **hold-character** line configuration command. Use the **no** form of this command to restore the default.

    hold-character *ascii-number*
    no hold-character

Syntax	Description
ascii-number	Either the decimal representation of the hold character or a control sequence (for example, Ctrl-P).

Default

No hold character is defined.

Command Mode

Line configuration

Usage Guidelines

This command first appeared in Cisco IOS Release 10.0.

The Break character is represented by zero; NULL cannot be represented. To continue the output, enter any character after the hold character. To use the hold character in normal communications, precede it with the escape character. See Appendix A, "ASCII Character Set," for a list of ASCII characters.

Example

The following example sets the hold character to Ctrl-S, which is decimal 19:

```
line 8
  hold-character 19
```

Related Commands

terminal hold-character

INSECURE

To set the line as an insecure location, use the **insecure** line configuration command. Use the **no** form of this command to disable this feature.

insecure
no insecure

Syntax   Description

This command has no arguments or keywords.

Default

Disabled

Command Mode

Line configuration

Usage Guidelines

This command first appeared in Cisco IOS Release 10.0.

Example

The following example sets up line 10 as a dial-up line that is used by the LAT software to report the line as available to remote hosts:

```
line 10
  insecure
```

LENGTH

To set the terminal screen length, use the **length** line configuration command. Use the **no** form of the command to restore the default value.

   length *screen-length*
   no length

Syntax   *Description*

screen-length   Number of lines on the screen. A value of zero disables pausing between
                               screens of output.

Default

24 lines

Command Mode

Line configuration

Usage Guidelines

This command first appeared in Cisco IOS Release 10.0.

The Cisco IOS software uses the value of this command to determine when to pause during multiple-screen output. Not all commands recognize the configured screen length. For example, the **show terminal** command assumes a screen length of 24 lines or more.

Example

The following example illustrates how to disable the screen pause function on the terminal connected to line 6:

```
line 6
  terminal-type VT220
  length 0
```

Related Commands

terminal length

LOCATION

To record the location of a serial device, use the **location** line configuration command. Use the **no** form of this command to remove the description.

> **location** *text*
> **no location**

Syntax	Description
text	Location description.

Default

None

Command Mode

Line configuration

Usage Guidelines

This command first appeared in Cisco IOS Release 10.0.

The **location** command enters information about the device location and status. Use the **show users all** EXEC command to display the location information.

Example

The following example identifies the location of the console:

```
line console
  location Building 3, Basement
```

LOCKABLE

To enable the **lock** EXEC command, use the **lockable** global configuration command. Use the **no** form of this command to reinstate the default—the terminal cannot be locked.

> **lockable**
> **no lockable**

Syntax	Description
This command has no arguments or keywords.	

Default

Not lockable

Command Mode

Global configuration

Usage Guidelines

This command first appeared in Cisco IOS Release 10.0.

This command activates a temporary password, which is set up with the **lock** EXEC command, so that a terminal is temporarily inaccessible.

Example

The following example sets the terminal to the lockable state:

```
lockable
```

Related Commands

lock

LOGOUT-WARNING

To warn users of an impending forced timeout, use the **logout-warning** line configuration command. Use the **no** form of this command to restore the default.

    logout-warning [*number*]

Syntax	*Description*
number	(Optional) Number of seconds that are counted down before session termination. If no number is specified, the default of 20 seconds is used.

Default

No warning is sent to the user.

Command Mode

Line configuration

Usage Guidelines

This command first appeared in Cisco IOS Release 10.3.

This command notifies the user of an impending forced timeout, set by using the **absolute-timeout** command, or another method such as ARAP.

Example

The following example sets a countdown value of 30 seconds:

```
line 5
 logout-warning 30
```

Related Commands

absolute-timeout
session-timeout

NOTIFY

To enable terminal notification about pending output from other Telnet connections, use the **notify** line configuration command. Use the **no** form of this command to end notification.

> notify
> **no notify**

Syntax   Description

This command has no arguments or keywords.

Default

Disabled

Command Mode

Line configuration

Usage Guidelines

This command first appeared in Cisco IOS Release 10.0.

This command sets a line to inform a user who has multiple, concurrent Telnet connections when output is pending on a connection other than the current one.

Example

The following example sets up notification of pending output from connections on virtual terminal lines 0 to 4:

```
line vty 0 4
  notify
```

Related Commands

terminal notify

PADDING

To set the padding on a specific output character, use the **padding** line configuration command. Use the **no** form of this command to remove padding for the specified output character.

> **padding** *ascii-number count*
> **no padding** *ascii-number*

Syntax	Description
ascii-number	Decimal representation of the character.
count	Number of NULL bytes sent after that character, up to 255 padding characters in length.

Default

None

Command Mode

Line configuration

Usage Guidelines

This command first appeared in Cisco IOS Release 10.0.

Use this command when the attached device is an old terminal that requires padding after certain characters (such as ones that scrolled or moved the carriage). See Appendix A, "ASCII Character Set," for a list of ASCII characters.

Example

The following example pads a Return (decimal 13) with 25 NULL bytes:

```
line console
  padding 13 25
```

Related Commands

terminal padding

PARITY

To define generation of a parity bit, use the **parity** line configuration command. Use the **no** form of the command to specify no parity.

> **parity {none | even | odd | space | mark}**
> **no parity**

Syntax	Description
none	No parity.
even	Even parity.
odd	Odd parity.
space	Space parity.
mark	Mark parity.

Default

No parity

Command Mode

Line configuration

Usage Guidelines

This command first appeared in Cisco IOS Release 10.0.

Communication protocols provided by devices such as terminals and modems often require a specific parity-bit setting.

Example

The following example changes the default of no parity to even parity:

```
line 34
  parity even
```

Related Commands

terminal parity

PRINTER (LPD)

To configure a printer and assign a server TTY line (or lines) to it, use the **printer** global configuration command. Use the **no** form of the command to disable printing on a TTY line.

> **printer** *printer-name* {**line** *number* | **rotary** *number*} [**newline-convert** | **formfeed**]
> **no printer**

Syntax	*Description*
printer-name	Printer name.
line *number*	Assigns a TTY line to the printer.
rotary *number*	Assigns a rotary group of TTY lines to the printer.
newline-convert	(Optional) Converts newline (linefeed) characters to a two-character sequence "carriage-return, linefeed."
formfeed	(Optional) Causes the Cisco IOS software to send a form-feed character (ASCII 0x0C) to the printer TTY line immediately following each print job received from the network.

Default

No printers are defined by default.

Command Mode

Global configuration

Usage Guidelines

This command first appeared in Cisco IOS Release 10.3.

This command enables you to configure a printer for operations and assign either a single TTY line or a group of TTY lines to it. To make multiple printers available through the same printer name, specify the number of a rotary group.

In addition to configuring the printer with the **printer** command, you also must modify the file */etc/printcap* on your UNIX system to include the definition of the remote printer in the Cisco IOS software.

Use the optional **newline-convert** keyword in UNIX environments that cannot handle single-character line terminators. This converts newline characters to a carriage-return, linefeed sequence. Use the **formfeed** keyword when using the line printer daemon (lpd) protocol to print and when your system is unable to separate individual output jobs with a form feed (page eject). You can enter the **newline-convert** and **formfeed** keywords together and in any order.

Example

The following example configures a printer named printer1 and assigns its output to the single TTY line 4:

```
printer printer1 line 4
```

Related Commands

clear line
show printer

PRIVATE

To save user EXEC command changes between terminal sessions, use the **private** line configuration command. Use the **no** form of this command to restore the default condition.

> **private**
> **no private**

Syntax   Description

This command has no arguments or keywords.

Default

User-set configuration options are cleared with the EXEC command **exit** or when the interval set with the **exec-timeout** line configuration command has passed.

Command Mode

Line configuration

Usage Guidelines

This command first appeared in Cisco IOS Release 10.0.

This command ensures that the terminal parameters set by the user remain in effect between terminal sessions. This behavior is desirable for terminals in private offices.

Example

The following example sets up virtual terminal line 1 to keep all user-supplied settings at system restarts:

```
line 15
  private
```

Related Commands

exec-timeout
exit

SHOW WHOAMI

To display information about the current user's terminal line, including hostname, line number, line speed, and location, use the **show whoami** EXEC command.

show whoami [*text*]

Syntax	Description
text	(Optional) Additional data to print to the screen.

Command Mode

EXEC

Usage Guidelines

This command first appeared in Cisco IOS Release 10.0.

If text is included as an argument in the command, that text is displayed as part of the additional data about the line.

To prevent the information from being lost if the menu display clears the screen, this command always displays a ---More--- prompt before returning. Press the space bar to return to the prompt.

Sample Display

The following example shows sample output of the **show whoami** command:

```
Router> show whoami


Comm Server "Router", Line 0 at 0bps.  Location "Second floor, West"

--More--
Router>
```

SPECIAL-CHARACTER-BITS

To configure the number of data bits per character for special characters such as software flow control characters and escape characters, use the **special-character-bits** line configuration command. Use the **no** form of the command to restore the default value.

special-character-bits {7 | 8}
no special-character-bits

Syntax	Description
7	Selects the 7-bit ASCII character set.
8	Selects the full 8-bit character set for special characters.

Default

7-bit ASCII character set

Command Mode

Line configuration

Usage Guidelines

This command first appeared in Cisco IOS Release 10.0.

Setting the special character bits to 8 allows you to use twice as many special characters as with the 7-bit ASCII character set. The special characters affected by this setting are the escape, hold, stop, start, disconnect, and activation characters.

Example

The following example allows the full 8-bit international character set for special characters on line 5:

```
line 5
 special-character-bits 8
```

Related Commands

default-value exec-character-bits
default-value special-character-bits
exec-character-bits
terminal exec-character-bits
terminal special-character-bits

STATE-MACHINE

To specify the transition criteria for the state of a particular state machine, use the **state-machine** global configuration command. Use the **no** form of the command to delete a particular state machine.

> **state-machine** *name state firstchar... lastchar* [*nextstate* | **transmit**]
> **no state-machine** *name*

Syntax	*Description*
name	Specifies the name for the state machine (used in the **dispatch-machine** line command). The user can specify any number of state machines, but each line can have only one state machine associated with it.
state	Defines which state is being modified. There are a maximum of eight states per state machine. Lines are initialized to state 0 and return to state 0 after a packet is transmitted.
firstchar... lastchar	Specify a range of characters. If the state machine is in the indicated state, and the next character input is within this range, the process goes to the specified next state. Full 8-bit character comparisons are done, so the maximum value is 255. Take care that the line is configured to strip parity bits (or not generate them), or duplicate the low characters in the upper half of the space.
nextstate	(Optional) Defines the state to enter if the character is in the specified range.
transmit	(Optional) Causes the packet to be transmitted and the state machine to be reset to state 0. Recurring characters that have not been explicitly defined to have a particular action return the state machine to state 0.

Default

No transition criteria are specified.

Command Mode

Global configuration

Usage Guidelines

This command first appeared in Cisco IOS Release 10.0.

This command is paired with the **dispatch-machine** line configuration command, which defines the line on which the state machine is effective.

Example

The following example uses a dispatch machine named *function* to ensure that the function key characters on an ANSI terminal are lumped together in one packet. Because the default in the example is to remain in state 0 without transmitting anything, normal key signals are transmitted immediately.

```
line 1 20
 dispatch-machine function
!
state-machine function 0 0 255 transmit
```

Related Commands

dispatch-character
dispatch-machine
dispatch-timeout

STOPBITS

To set the number of the stop bits transmitted per byte, use the **stopbits** line configuration command. Use the **no** form of the command to restore the default value.

stopbits {1 | 1.5 | 2}
no stopbits

Syntax	Description
1	One stop bit.
1.5	One and one-half stop bits.
2	Two stop bits.

Default

2 stop bits

Command Mode

Line configuration

Usage Guidelines

This command first appeared in Cisco IOS Release 10.0.

Communication protocols provided by devices such as terminals and modems often require a specific stop-bit setting.

Example

The following example changes the default from 2 stop bits to 1 as a performance enhancement:

```
line 4
 stopbits 1
```

Related Commands

terminal stopbits

TERMINAL DATABITS

To change the number of data bits per character for the current terminal line for this session, use the **terminal databits** EXEC command.

    terminal databits {5 | 6 | 7 | 8}

Syntax	Description
5	Five data bits per character.
6	Six data bits per character.
7	Seven data bits per character.
8	Eight data bits per character.

Default

8 data bits per character

Command Mode

EXEC

Usage Guidelines

This command first appeared in a release prior to Cisco IOS Release 10.0.

Communication protocols provided by devices such as terminals and modems often require a specific data bit setting. The **terminal databits** command can be used to mask the high bit on input from devices that generate seven data bits with parity. If parity is being generated, specify seven data bits per character. If no parity generation is in effect, specify eight data bits per character. The other keywords (5 and 6) are supplied for compatibility with older devices and are generally not used.

Example

The following example shows how to change the databits per character to seven:

```
Router> terminal databits 7
```

Related Commands

databits

TERMINAL DATA-CHARACTER-BITS

To set the number of data bits per character that are interpreted and generated by the Cisco IOS software for the current line and session, use the **terminal data-character-bits** EXEC command.

terminal data-character-bits {7 | 8}

Syntax	Description
7	Seven data character bits.
8	Eight data character bits.

Default

8 data bits per character

Command Mode

EXEC

Usage Guidelines

This command first appeared in a release prior to Cisco IOS Release 10.0.

This command is used primarily to strip parity from X.25 connections on routers with the protocol translation software option. The **terminal data-character-bits** command does not work on hard-wired lines.

Example

The following example sets the data bits per character on the current line to 7:

```
Router> terminal data-character-bits 7
```

Related Commands

data-character-bits

TERMINAL DISPATCH-CHARACTER

To define a character that causes a packet to be sent for the current session, use the **terminal dispatch-character** EXEC command.

terminal dispatch-character *ASCII-number1* [*ASCII-number2 . . . ASCII-number*]

Syntax	Description
ASCII-number	The ASCII decimal representation of the character, such as Return (ASCII character 13) for line-at-a-time transmissions. The command can take multiple arguments, so you can define any number of characters as the dispatch character.

Command Mode

EXEC

Usage Guidelines

This command first appeared in a release prior to Cisco IOS Release 10.0.

At times, you might want to queue up a string of characters until they fill a complete packet and then transmit the packet to a remote host. This can make more efficient use of a line, because the access server or router normally dispatches each character as it is entered.

Example

The following example defines the characters Ctrl-D (ASCII decimal character 4) and Ctrl-Y (ASCII decimal character 25) as the dispatch characters:

```
Router> terminal dispatch-character 4 25
```

Related Commands

dispatch-character

TERMINAL DISPATCH-TIMEOUT

To set the character dispatch timer for the current terminal line for the current session, use the **terminal dispatch-timeout** EXEC command.

terminal dispatch-timeout *milliseconds*

Syntax	Description
milliseconds	An integer that specifies the number of milliseconds that the router waits after it puts the first character into a packet buffer before sending the packet. During this interval, more characters can be added to the packet, which increases processing efficiency of the remote host.

Command Mode

EXEC

Usage Guidelines

This command first appeared in a release prior to Cisco IOS Release 10.0.

Use this command to increase the processing efficiency of the remote host.

NOTES

The router's response might appear intermittent if the timeout interval is greater than 100 milliseconds and remote echoing is used.

Example

The following example sets the dispatch timer to 80 milliseconds:

```
Router> terminal dispatch-timeout 80
```

Related Commands

dispatch-timeout

TERMINAL DOWNLOAD

To temporarily set the capability of a line to act as a transparent pipe for file transfers for the current session, use the **terminal download** EXEC command.

>   **terminal download**

Syntax   Description

This command has no arguments or keywords.

Default

Disabled

Command Mode

EXEC

Usage Guidelines

This command first appeared in a release prior to Cisco IOS Release 10.0.

You can use this feature to run a program such as KERMIT, XMODEM, or CrossTalk that downloads a file across an access server or router line. This command sets up the terminal line to transmit data and is equivalent to entering all the following commands:

- **terminal telnet transparent**
- **terminal no escape-character** (see **terminal escape-character**)
- **terminal no hold-character** (see **terminal hold-character**)
- **terminal no padding 0** (see **terminal padding**)
- **terminal no padding 128** (see **terminal padding**)
- **terminal parity none**
- **terminal databits 8**

Example

The following configures a line to act as a transparent pipe:

```
Router> terminal download
```

TERMINAL ESCAPE-CHARACTER

To set the escape character for the current terminal line for the current session, use the **terminal escape-character** EXEC command.

> **terminal escape-character** *ASCII-number*

Syntax	Description
ASCII-number	Either the ASCII decimal representation of the escape character or a control sequence (Ctrl-P, for example). Entering the escape character followed by X returns you to the EXEC when you are connected to another computer. See Appendix A, "ASCII Character Set," for a list of ASCII characters.

Default

Ctrl-^ (which is **Ctrl-Shift-6**)

Command Mode

EXEC

Usage Guidelines

This command first appeared in a release prior to Cisco IOS Release 10.0.

This command is useful, for example, if you have the default escape character defined for a different purpose in your keyboard file. Entering the escape character followed by the X key returns you to EXEC mode when you are connected to another computer.

NOTES

The Break key cannot be used as an escape character on the console terminal, because the operating software interprets BREAK as an instruction to halt the system.

Example

The following example sets the escape character to Ctrl-P (ASCII decimal 16):

```
Router> terminal escape-character 16
```

Related Commands

escape-character

TERMINAL EXEC-CHARACTER-BITS

To locally change the ASCII character set used in EXEC and configuration command characters for the current session, use the **terminal exec-character-bits** EXEC command.

   terminal exec-character-bits {7 | 8}

Syntax	Description
7	Selects the 7-bit ASCII character set.
8	Selects the full 8-bit character set.

Default

7-bit ASCII character set (unless set otherwise in global configuration mode)

Command Mode

EXEC

Usage Guidelines

This command first appeared in a release prior to Cisco IOS Release 10.0.

This EXEC command overrides the **default-value exec-character-bits** global configuration command. Configuring the EXEC character width to 8 bits enables you to add special graphical and international characters in banners, prompts, and so forth.

When the user exits the session, the character width is reset to the default value established by the default value EXEC-character-bits global configuration command. However, setting the EXEC character width to 8 bits also can cause failures. If a user on a terminal that is sending parity enters the **help** command, an "unrecognized command" message appears, because the system is reading all 8 bits, and the eighth bit is not needed for the **help** command.

Example

The following example temporarily configures a router to use a full 8-bit user interface for system banners and prompts, allowing the use of additional graphical and international characters.

```
terminal exec-character-bits 8
```

Related Commands

exec-character-bits

TERMINAL FLOWCONTROL

To set flow control for the current terminal line for the current session, use the **terminal flowcontrol** EXEC command.

    terminal flowcontrol {none | software [in | out] | hardware}

Syntax	Description
none	Prevents flow control.
software	Sets software flow control.
**in	out**	(Optional) Specifies the direction: **in** causes the router to listen to flow control from the attached device, and **out** causes the router to send flow control information to the attached device. If you do not specify a direction, both directions are assumed.
hardware	Sets hardware flow control. For information about setting up the RS-232 line, see the manual that was shipped with your product.

Default

None

Command Mode

EXEC

Usage Guidelines

This command first appeared in a release prior to Cisco IOS Release 10.0.

Flow control enables you to regulate the rate at which data can be transmitted from one point so that it is equal to the rate at which it can be received at another point. Flow control protects against loss of data because the terminal is not capable of receiving data at the rate it is being sent. You can set up data flow control for the current terminal line in one of two ways: software flow control, which you do with control key sequences, and hardware flow control, which you do at the device level.

For software flow control, the default stop and start characters are Ctrl-S and Ctrl-Q (XOFF and XON). You can change them with the **terminal stop-character** and **terminal start-character** commands.

Example

The following example sets incoming software flow control:

```
Router> terminal flowcontrol software in
```

Related Commands

flowcontrol

TERMINAL HOLD-CHARACTER

To set or change the hold character for the current session, use the **terminal hold-character** EXEC command. Use the **terminal no hold-character** command to delete the hold character.

> **terminal hold-character** *ASCII-number*
> **terminal no hold-character**

Syntax   Description

ASCII-number   Either the ASCII decimal representation of the hold character or a control sequence (for example, Ctrl-P). By default, no local hold character is set. The Break character is represented by zero; NULL cannot be represented.

Default

None

Command Mode

EXEC

Usage Guidelines

This command first appeared in Cisco IOS Release 10.0.

You can define a local hold character that temporarily suspends the flow of output on the terminal. When information is scrolling too quickly, you can enter the hold character to pause the screen output, then enter any other character to resume the flow of output.

You cannot suspend output on the console terminal. To send the hold character to the host, precede it with the escape character.

Example

The following example removes the previously set hold character:

```
Router> terminal no hold-character
```

Related Commands

hold-character

TERMINAL KEYMAP-TYPE

To specify the current keyboard type for the current session, use the **terminal keymap-type** EXEC command.

> **terminal keymap-type** *keymap-name*

Syntax	Description
keymap-name	Name defining the current keyboard type.

Default

VT100

Command Mode

EXEC

Usage Guidelines

This command first appeared in Cisco IOS Release 11.2.

You must use this command when you are using a keyboard other than the default of VT100. The system administrator can define other keyboard types and give you their names.

Example

The following example specifies a VT220 keyboard as the current keyboard type:

```
Router> terminal keymap-type vt220
```

TERMINAL LENGTH

To set the number of lines on the current terminal screen for the current session, use the **terminal length** EXEC command.

> **terminal length** *screen-length*

Syntax	*Description*
screen-length	Your desired number of lines on the screen. The router uses this value to determine when to pause during multiple-screen output. A value of zero prevents the router from pausing between screens of output. When the output exceeds the screen length, it scrolls past.

Default
24 lines

Command Mode
EXEC

Usage Guidelines
This command first appeared in a release prior to Cisco IOS Release 10.0.

Some types of terminal sessions do not require you to specify the screen length, because the screen length specified can be learned by some remote hosts. For example, the rlogin protocol uses the screen length to set up terminal parameters on a remote UNIX host.

Example
The following example prevents the router from pausing between multiple screens of output:

```
Router> terminal length 0
```

Related Commands
length

TERMINAL MONITOR

To display **debug** command output and system error messages for the current terminal and session, use the **terminal monitor** EXEC command.

> **terminal monitor**

Syntax   *Description*

This command has no arguments or keywords.

Default
Disabled

Command Mode

EXEC

Usage Guidelines

This command first appeared in a release prior to Cisco IOS Release 10.0.

Remember that all terminal parameter-setting commands are set locally and do not remain in effect after a session is ended. You must perform this task at the privileged-level EXEC prompt at each session to see the debugging messages.

For more information about privileged-level EXEC mode, See Chapter 1, "Using the Command Line Interface."

Example

The following example displays **debug** command output and error messages during the current terminal session:

```
Router> terminal monitor
```

TERMINAL NOTIFY

To configure a line to inform a user who has multiple concurrent Telnet connections when output is pending on a connection other than the current one, use the **terminal notify** EXEC command.

terminal notify

Syntax   Description

This command has no arguments or keywords.

Default

None

Command Mode

EXEC

Usage Guidelines

This command first appeared in a release prior to Cisco IOS Release 10.0.

You might want to know, for example, when another connection receives mail or a message.

Example

The following example configures a line to inform a user with multiple connections when output is pending on a non-current connection:

```
Router> terminal notify
```

Related Commands

notify

TERMINAL PADDING

To change the character padding on a specific output character for the current session, use the **terminal padding** EXEC command.

> **terminal padding** *ASCII-number count*

Syntax	Description
ASCII-number	The ASCII decimal representation of the character.
count	The number of NULL bytes sent after that character, up to 255 padding characters in length.

Default

No padding

Command Mode

EXEC

Usage Guidelines

This command first appeared in a release prior to Cisco IOS Release 10.0.

Character padding adds a number of null bytes to the end of the string and can be used to make a string an expected length for conformity.

Example

The following example pads Ctrl-D (ASCII decimal character 4) with 164 NULL bytes:

```
Router> terminal padding 4 164
```

Related Commands

padding

TERMINAL PARITY

To define the generation of the parity bit for the current terminal line for the current session, use the **terminal parity** EXEC command.

> **terminal parity** {**none** | **even** | **odd** | **space** | **mark**}

Syntax	Description
none	No parity. This is the default.
even	Even parity.
odd	Odd parity.
space	Space.
mark	Mark.

Default

None

Command Mode

EXEC

Usage Guidelines

This command first appeared in a release prior to Cisco IOS Release 10.0.

Communication protocols provided by devices such as terminals and modems often require a specific parity bit setting.

Example

The following example shows how to set the parity bit to odd:

```
Router> terminal parity odd
```

Related Commands

parity

TERMINAL-QUEUE ENTRY-RETRY-INTERVAL

To change the retry interval for a terminal port queue, use the **terminal-queue** global configuration command. Use the **no** form of this command to restore the default terminal port queue interval.

terminal-queue entry-retry-interval *interval*
no terminal-queue

Syntax	Description
interval	Number of seconds between terminal port retries.

Default

60 seconds

Command Mode

Global configuration

Usage Guidelines

This command first appeared in Cisco IOS Release 11.1.

If a remote device (such as a printer) is busy, the connection attempt is placed in a terminal port queue. If you want to decrease the waiting period between subsequent connection attempts, decrease the default of 60 to an interval of 10 seconds. Decrease the time between subsequent connection attempts when, for example, a printer queue stalls for long periods.

Example

The following example changes the terminal port queue retry interval from the default of 60 seconds to 10 seconds:

```
terminal-queue entry-retry-interval 10
```

TERMINAL RXSPEED

To set the terminal receive speed (how fast information is sent to the terminal) for the current line and session, use the **terminal rxspeed** EXEC command.

    terminal rxspeed *bps*

Syntax	Description
bps	Baud rate in bits per second (bps).

Default

9,600 bps

Command Mode

EXEC

Usage Guidelines

This command first appeared in a release prior to Cisco IOS Release 10.0.

Example

The following example sets the current auxiliary line receive speed to 115,200 bps:

```
Router> terminal rxspeed 115200
```

Related Commands

rxspeed

TERMINAL SPECIAL-CHARACTER-BITS

To change the ASCII character widths to accept special characters for the current terminal line and session, use the **terminal special-character-bits** EXEC command.

  terminal special-character-bits {7 | 8}

Syntax	Description
7	Selects the 7-bit ASCII character set.
8	Selects the full 8-bit ASCII character set. Configuring the width to 8 bits enables you to use twice as many special characters as with the 7-bit setting. This selection enables you to add special graphical and international characters in banners, prompts, and so forth.

Default

7-bit ASCII character set

Command Mode

EXEC

Usage Guidelines

This command first appeared in a release prior to Cisco IOS Release 10.0.

This command is useful, for example, if you want the router to provide temporary support for international character sets. It overrides the **default-value special-character-bits** global configuration command and is used to compare character sets typed by the user with the special character available during a data connection, which includes software flow control and escape characters.

When you exit the session, the character width is reset to the default value established by the global configuration command. However, setting the EXEC character width to eight bits can cause failures. If a user on a terminal that is sending parity enters the **help** command, an "unrecognized command" message appears, because the Cisco IOS software is reading all eight bits, and the eighth bit is not needed for the **help** command.

Example

The following example temporarily configures a router to use a full 8-bit user interface for system banners and prompts. When you exit the system, character width is reset to the width established by the **default-value exec-character-bits** global configuration command.

```
Router> terminal special-character-bits 8
```

Related Commands

special-character-bits

TERMINAL SPEED

To set the transmit and receive speeds of the current terminal line for the current session, use the **terminal speed** EXEC command.

> **terminal speed** *bps*

Syntax	Description
bps	The baud rate in bits per second (bps).

Default

9,600 bps

Command Mode

EXEC

Usage Guidelines

This command first appeared in a release prior to Cisco IOS Release 10.0.

Set the speed to match the transmission rate of whatever device you have connected to the port. Some baud rates available on devices connected to the port might not be supported on the router. The router indicates whether the speed you selected is not supported.

Example

The following example restores the transmit and receive speed on the current line to 9,600 bps.

```
router> terminal speed 9600
```

Related Commands

speed

TERMINAL START-CHARACTER

To change the flow control start character for the current session, use the **terminal start-character** EXEC command.

> **terminal start-character** *ASCII-number*

Syntax	Description
ASCII-number	The ASCII decimal representation of the start character.

Default

Ctrl-Q (ASCII decimal character 17)

Command Mode

EXEC

Usage Guidelines

This command first appeared in a release prior to Cisco IOS Release 10.0.

The flow control start character signals the start of data transmission when software flow control is in effect.

Example

The following example changes the start character to Ctrl-O (ASCII decimal character 15):

```
Router> terminal start-character 15
```

Related Commands

start-character

TERMINAL STOPBITS

To change the number of stop bits transmitted per byte by the current terminal line during an active session, use the **terminal stopbits** EXEC command.

   terminal stopbits {1 | 1.5 | 2}

Syntax	Description
1	One stop bit.
1.5	One and a half stop bits.
2	Two stop bits.

Default

Two stop bits

Command Mode

EXEC

Usage Guidelines

This command first appeared in a release prior to Cisco IOS Release 10.0.

Communication protocols provided by devices such as terminals and modems often require a specific stop-bit setting.

Example

The following example illustrates how to change the stop bits to one:

```
router> terminal stopbits 1
```

Related Commands

stopbits

TERMINAL STOP-CHARACTER

To change the flow control stop character for the current session, use the **terminal stop-character** EXEC command.

 terminal stop-character *ASCII-number*

Syntax	*Description*
ASCII-number	The ASCII decimal representation of the stop character.

Default

Ctrl-S (ASCII character 19)

Command Mode

EXEC

Usage Guidelines

This command first appeared in a release prior to Cisco IOS Release 10.0.

The flow control stop character signals the end of data transmission when software flow control is in effect.

Example

The following example changes the stop character to Ctrl-E (ASCII character 5).

```
Router> terminal stop-character 5
```

Related Commands

stop-character

TERMINAL TELNET BREAK-ON-IP

To cause the access server to generate a hardware Break signal on the RS-232 line, which is associated with a reverse Telnet connection, for the current line and sessions, use the **terminal telnet break-on-ip** EXEC command.

 terminal telnet break-on-ip

Syntax   Description

This command has no arguments or keywords.

Default

Disabled

Command Mode

EXEC

Usage Guidelines

This command first appeared in a release prior to Cisco IOS Release 10.0.

The hardware Break signal occurs when a Telnet Interrupt-Process (IP) command is received on that connection. The **terminal telnet break-on-ip** command can be used to control the translation of Telnet IP commands into X.25 Break indications.

This command is also a useful workaround in the following situations:

- Several user Telnet programs send an IP command, but cannot send a Telnet Break signal.

- Some Telnet programs implement a Break signal that sends an IP command.

Some RS-232 hardware devices use a hardware Break signal for various purposes. A hardware Break signal is generated when a Telnet Break command is received.

_____ **NOTES** _____

This command applies only to access servers. It is not supported on stand-alone routers.

_____

Example

The following example shows how to generate a Break signal on the asynchronous TTY line 4:

```
line tty 4
terminal telnet break-on-ip
```

TERMINAL TELNET REFUSE-NEGOTIATIONS

To set the current line to refuse to negotiate full-duplex, remote echo options on incoming connections for current sessions, use the **terminal telnet refuse-negotiations** EXEC command.

> **terminal telnet refuse-negotiations**

Syntax   Description

This command has no arguments or keywords.

Default

Disabled

Command Mode

EXEC

Usage Guidelines

This command first appeared in a release prior to Cisco IOS Release 10.0.

You can set the line to allow the access server to refuse full-duplex, remote echo connection requests from the other end. This task suppresses negotiation of the Telnet Remote Echo and Suppress Go Ahead options.

NOTES

This command applies only to access servers. It is not supported on stand-alone routers.

Example

The following example shows how to set an asynchronous interface to refuse full-duplex, remote echo requests:

```
line async 1
terminal telnet refuse-negotiations
```

TERMINAL TELNET SPEED

To allow the access server to negotiate transmission speed for the current line and session, use the **terminal telnet speed** EXEC command.

terminal telnet speed *default-speed maximum-speed*

Syntax	Description
default-speed	Line speed (in bps) that the access server will use if the device on the other end of the connection has not specified a speed.
maximum-speed	Maximum line speed (in bps) that the device on the other end of the connection can use.

Default

9,600 bps (unless otherwise set using the **speed**, **txspeed** or **rxspeed** line configuration commands)

Command Mode

EXEC

Usage Guidelines

This command first appeared in a release prior to Cisco IOS Release 10.0.

You can match line speeds on remote systems in reverse Telnet, on host machines hooked up to an access server to access the network, or on a group of console lines hooked up to the access server, when disparate line speeds are in use at the local and remote ends of the connection. Line speed negotiation adheres to the Remote Flow Control option, defined in RFC 1080.

NOTES

This command applies only to access servers. It is not supported on stand-alone routers.

Example

The following example enables the access server to negotiate a bit rate on the line using the Telnet option. If no speed is negotiated, the line will run at 2,400 bps. If the remote host requests a speed greater than 9,600 bps, then 9,600 bps will be used.

```
line async 7
terminal telnet speed 2400 9600
```

TERMINAL TELNET SYNC-ON-BREAK

To cause the access server to send a Telnet Synchronize signal when it receives a Telnet Break signal on the current line and session, use the **terminal telnet sync-on-break** EXEC command.

terminal telnet sync-on-break

Syntax   Description

This command has no arguments or keywords.

Default

Disabled

Command Mode

EXEC

Usage Guidelines

This command first appeared in a release prior to Cisco IOS Release 10.0.

You can set the line to cause a reverse Telnet line to send a Telnet Synchronize signal when it receives a Telnet Break signal. The TCP Synchronize signal clears the data path, but still interprets incoming commands.

NOTES ──

This command applies only to access servers. It is not supported on stand-alone routers.

Example

The following example shows how to set an asynchronous line to cause the access server to send a Telnet synchronize signal:

```
line async 15
terminal telnet sync-on-break
```

TERMINAL TELNET TRANSPARENT

To cause the current terminal line to send a Return character (CR) as a CR followed by a NULL instead of a CR followed by a Line Feed (LF) for the current session, use the **terminal telnet transparent** EXEC command.

   terminal telnet transparent

Syntax   Description

This command has no arguments or keywords.

Default

CR followed by an LF

Command Mode

EXEC

Usage Guidelines

This command first appeared in a release prior to Cisco IOS Release 10.0.

The end of each line typed at the terminal is ended with a Return (CR). This command permits interoperability with different interpretations of end-of-line demarcation in the Telnet protocol specification.

NOTES ──

This command applies only to access server products. It is not supported on stand-alone routers.

Example

The following example configures a line to send a CR as a CR followed by a NULL:

```
Router> terminal telnet transparent
```

TERMINAL TERMINAL-TYPE

To specify the type of terminal connected to the current line for the current session, use the **terminal terminal-type** EXEC command.

terminal terminal-type *terminal-type*

Syntax	*Description*
terminal-type	Defines the terminal name and type and permits terminal negotiation by hosts that provide that type of service.

Default

VT100

Command Mode

EXEC

Usage Guidelines

This command first appeared in a release prior to Cisco IOS Release 10.0.

Indicate the terminal type if it is different from the default of VT100. The terminal type name is used by TN3270 for display management and by Telnet and rlogin to inform the remote host of the terminal type.

Example

The following example defines the terminal on line 7 as a VT220:

```
Router> terminal terminal-type VT220
```

Related Commands

terminal-type
terminal keymap-type

TERMINAL TXSPEED

To set the terminal transmit speed (how fast the terminal can send information) on the current line and session, use the **terminal txspeed** EXEC command.

terminal txspeed *bps*

Syntax	*Description*
bps	Baud rate in bits per second (bps).

Default
9,600 bps

Command Mode
EXEC

Usage Guidelines
This command first appeared in Cisco IOS Release 10.0.

Example
The following example sets the current auxiliary line transmit speed to 2,400 bps:
```
Router> terminal txspeed 2400
```

Related Commands
txspeed
terminal keymap-type
terminal terminal-type

TERMINAL-TYPE

To specify the type of terminal connected to a line, use the **terminal-type** line configuration command. Use the **no** form of this command to remove any information about the type of terminal and reset the line to the default terminal emulation.

> **terminal-type** {*terminal-name* | *terminal-type*}
> **no terminal-type**

Syntax	*Description*
terminal-name	Terminal name.
terminal-type	Terminal type.

Default
VT100

Command Mode
Line configuration

Usage Guidelines
This command first appeared in Cisco IOS Release 10.0.

This command records the type of terminal connected to the line. The argument *terminal-name* provides a record of the terminal type and allows terminal negotiation of display management by hosts that provide that type of service.

For TN3270 applications, this command must follow the corresponding ttycap entry in the configuration file.

Example

The following example defines the terminal on line 7 as a VT220:

```
line 7
  terminal-type VT220
```

TERMINAL WIDTH

To set the number of character columns on the terminal screen for the current line for a session, use the **terminal width** EXEC command.

> **terminal width** *characters*

Syntax	Description
characters	Number of character columns displayed on the terminal.

Default

80 characters

Command Mode

EXEC

Usage Guidelines

This command first appeared in a release prior to Cisco IOS Release 10.0.

By default, the route provides a screen display width of 80 characters. You can reset this value if it does not meet the needs of your terminal. The width specified can be learned by remote hosts.

Example

The following example sets the terminal character columns to 132:

```
terminal width 132
```

Related Commands

width

WIDTH

To set the terminal screen width, use the **width** line configuration command. This command sets the number of character columns displayed on the attached terminal. Use the **no** form of this command to return to the default screen width.

> **width** *characters*
> **no width**

Syntax

characters

Description

Integer that specifies the number of character columns displayed on the terminal.

Default

80 character columns

Command Mode

Line configuration

Usage Guidelines

This command first appeared in Cisco IOS Release 10.0.

The rlogin protocol uses the *characters* argument to set up terminal parameters on a remote host.

Some hosts can learn the values for both length and width specified with the **line** and **width** commands.

Example

The following example changes the character columns to 132 for the terminal on line 7:

```
line 7
 location console terminal
 width 132
```

Related Commands

terminal width

## CHAPTER 7

Managing Connections and System Banners

This chapter describes how to manage connections to other hosts and set banner messages for router users. For a complete description of the connections and system banner commands in this chapter, see Chapter 8, "Connections and System Banners Commands."

The following sections describe the connections and system banners tasks:

- Managing Connections
- Setting Up Terminal Banner Messages

MANAGING CONNECTIONS

This section describes session-management activities. The following sections describe connection-management activities that apply to all supported connection protocols:

- Escaping to the EXEC Prompt
- Switching to Another Connection
- Assigning a Logical Name to a Connection
- Changing a Login Name
- Locking Access to a Terminal
- Specifying a TACACS Host
- Sending Messages to Other Terminals
- Clearing TCP/IP Connections
- Exiting a Session Started from a Router
- Logging Out of a Router
- Disconnecting a Line

Escaping to the EXEC Prompt

After you have started a connection, you can escape out of the current session and return to the EXEC prompt by using the escape sequence command (**Ctrl-Shift-6** then **x** [**Ctrl^x**] by default). You can type the command character as you hold down the **Ctrl** key or with the **Ctrl** key released; you can type either uppercase or lowercase letters.

NOTES

In screen output examples that show two caret (^^) symbols together, the first caret represents the Control key (**Ctrl**) and the second caret represents the keystroke sequence **Shift-6**. The double-caret combination (^^) means hold down the **Ctrl** key while you press the **Shift** and the **6** key.

By default, the escape sequence is **Ctrl^x**. If you press the escape key (**Escape-Char**), you change the **Shift-Ctrl-6** sequence to whatever you want. For example, if you press **Escape-Char Break**, the **Break** key becomes the new escape character to suspend a session and to access the EXEC prompt.

Switching to Another Connection

You can have several concurrent sessions open and switch back and forth between them.

The number of sessions that can be open is defined by the **session-limit** command.

To switch between sessions by escaping one session and resuming a previously opened session, perform the following tasks:

Task		Command
Step 1	Escape the current connection and return to the EXEC prompt.	**Ctrl-Shift-6** then **x** (**Ctrl^x**) by default
Step 2	List the open sessions. All open sessions associated with the current terminal line are displayed.	**where**
Step 3	Make the connection.	**resume** [*connection*] [*keyword*]

The **Ctrl^x**, **where**, and **resume** commands are available with all supported connection protocols.

You also could make a new connection while you are at the EXEC prompt.

Assigning a Logical Name to a Connection

To assign a logical name to a connection, perform the following task in EXEC mode:

Task	Command
Assign a logical name to a connection.	name-connection

The logical name can be useful for keeping track of multiple connections.

You are prompted for the connection number and name to assign. The **where** command displays a list of the assigned logical connection names.

Changing a Login Name

You can change a login username if you must match outgoing access list requirements or other login prompt requirements. To change a login username, perform the following task in user EXEC mode:

Task	Command
Change a login username.	login

When you enter this command, the system prompts you for a username and password. Enter the new username and the original password. If the username does not match, but the password does, the Cisco IOS software updates the session with the new username used by **login** command attempt.

If no username and password prompts appear, the network administrator did not specify that a username and password be required at login time. If both the username and password are entered correctly, the session becomes associated with the specified username.

When you access a system with TACACS security, you can enter your login name or specify a TACACS server by using the following argument when the "Username:" prompt appears:

    user @tacacs-server

The router must be one of the routers defined in a router configuration. For more information, refer to the "Specifying a TACACS Host Example" section later in this chapter.

If you do not specify a host, the router tries each of the TACACS servers in the list until it receives a response.

If you specify a host that does not respond, no other TACACS server will be queried. The router either denies access or function, according to the action specified by the **tacacs-server last-resort** command, if it is configured.

If you specified a TACACS server host with the *user @tacacs-server* argument, the TACACS server specified is used for all subsequent authentication or notification queries, with the possible exception of SLIP address queries.

For an example of changing a login name, see the "Changing a Login Name Example" section at the end of this chapter.

Locking Access to a Terminal

You can prevent access to your terminal session while keeping your connection open by setting up a temporary password. To lock access to the terminal, perform the following tasks in EXEC mode:

Task	Command
Step 1 Issue the **lock** command. The system prompts you for a password.	**lock**
Step 2 Enter a password, which can be any arbitrary string. The screen clears and displays the message "Locked."	*password*
Step 3 To regain access to your sessions, re-enter the password.	*password*

The Cisco IOS software honors session timeouts on a locked line. You must clear the line to remove this feature. The system administrator must set up the line to allow use of the temporary locking feature.

Specifying a TACACS Host

You can specify a TACACS host when you dial in or use the **login** command. Only the specified host is accessed for user authentication information.

To specify the name of a TACACS host at login, perform the following task in EXEC mode:

Task	Command
Specify the name of a TACACS host at login.	*user@hostname*

For an example of specifying a TACACS host, see the "Specifying a TACACS Host Example" section at the end of this chapter.

Sending Messages to Other Terminals

You can send messages to one or all terminal lines. A common reason for doing this is to inform users of an impending shutdown. To send a message to other terminals, perform the following task in EXEC mode:

Task	Command
Send a message to other terminals.	**send** {*line-number* | ***}

The system prompts for the message, which can be up to 500 characters long. Enter **Ctrl-Z** to end the message. Enter **Ctrl-C** to abort the command.

Clearing TCP/IP Connections

To clear a TCP connection, perform the following task in privileged EXEC mode:

Task	Command
Clear a TCP connection.	**clear tcp** {**line** *line-number*	**local** *host-name port* **remote** *host-name port*	**tcb** *address*}

The **clear tcp** command is particularly useful for clearing hung TCP connections.

The **clear tcp line** *line-number* command terminates the TCP connection on the specified TTY line. Additionally, all TCP sessions initiated from that TTY line are terminated.

The **clear tcp local** *host-name port* **remote** *host-name port* command terminates the specific TCP connection identified by the host name/port pair of the local and remote router.

Exiting a Session Started from a Router

The protocol used to initiate a session determines how you exit that session.

To exit XRemote, you must quit all active X connections, usually with a command supported by your X client system. Usually, when you quit the last connection (all client processes are stopped), XRemote closes, and you return to the EXEC prompt. Check your X client system documentation for specific information about exiting an XRemote session.

To exit a SLIP and PPP, you must hang up the dial-in connection, usually with a command that your dial-in software supports.

To exit a LAT, Telnet, rlogin, TN3270, and X.3 PAD session begun from the router to a remote device, enter the escape sequence (**Ctrl-Shift-6** then **x** [**Ctrl^x**] by default) and enter the **disconnect** command at the EXEC prompt. You also can log off the remote system.

Except for XRemote, you also can escape to the EXEC prompt and enter either of the following commands to terminate an active terminal session:

- **exit**
- **logout**

To exit a Telnet session *to* a router, see the "Logging Out of a Router" section that follows.

Logging Out of a Router

The method you use to disconnect from a router depends on where you are located in relation to the router, and the port on the router to which you log in. Keep the following in mind:

- If your terminal or computer running a terminal-emulation application is connected physically to the console port of the router, you can disconnect from the console port by physically disconnecting the cable from the console port of the router.

- If your terminal or computer running a terminal-emulation application is remotely connected to the console port of the router, you disconnect by issuing the command or key sequence used by your terminal-emulation package. For example, if you are on a Macintosh computer running the application "TCP/Connect" from InterCon Corporation, you would press **Ctrl-]** at the user or privileged EXEC prompt to disconnect.

- If you are on a remote terminal and connect to a VTY line through a synchronous interface on the router, you can issue any of the following commands to disconnect:

  ○ **close**

  ○ **exit**

  ○ **logout**

  ○ **quit**

Disconnecting a Line

To disconnect a line, perform the following task in EXEC mode:

Task	Command
Disconnect a line.	**disconnect** [*connection*]

Avoid disconnecting a line to end a session. Instead, log off the host to allow the router to clear the connection. Then end the session. Only if you cannot log out of an active session should you disconnect the line.

SETTING UP TERMINAL BANNER MESSAGES

The types of messages that can be displayed to terminal users who connect to the router are described in the following sections:

- Configuring a Message-of-the-Day (MOTD) Banner
- Configuring a Line-Activation Message
- Configuring an Incoming Message Banner
- Configuring an Idle Terminal Message
- Displaying a "Line in Use" Message
- Displaying a "Host Failed" Message

You also can turn off message displays, as described in the "Enabling or Disabling the Display of Messages" section.

For an example of displaying terminal banner messages, see the "Banner Message Example" section at the end of this chapter.

Configuring a Message-of-the-Day (MOTD) Banner

You can configure a message-of-the-day (MOTD) to be displayed on all connected terminals. This message is displayed at login and is useful for sending messages that affect all network users (such as impending system shutdowns). To do so, perform the following task in global configuration mode:

Task	Command
Configure a MOTD banner.	**banner motd** *d message d*

Configuring a Line-Activation Message

You can configure a line-activation message to be displayed when an EXEC process (such as a line-activation or incoming connection to a VTY line) is created. To do so, perform the following task in global configuration mode:

Task	Command
Configure a message to be displayed on terminals with an interactive EXEC session.	**banner exec** *d message d*

Configuring an Incoming Message Banner

You can configure a message to be displayed on terminals connected to reverse Telnet lines. This message is useful for providing instructions to users of these types of connections.

To configure messages that are sent on incoming connections, perform the following task in global configuration mode:

Task	Command
Configure messages to display on terminals connected to reverse Telnet lines.	**banner incoming** *d message d*

Configuring an Idle Terminal Message

You can configure messages to be displayed on a console or terminal not in use. Also called a *vacant message*, this message is different from the banner message displayed when an EXEC process is activated. To configure an idle terminal message, perform the following task in line configuration mode:

Task	Command
Display an idle terminal message.	**vacant-message** [*d message d*]

Displaying a "Line in Use" Message

You can display a "line-in-use" message when an incoming connection is attempted and all rotary group or other lines are in use. Perform the following task in line configuration mode:

Task	Command
Display a "line-in-use" message.	**refuse-message** *d message d*

If you do not define such a message, the user receives a system-generated error message when all lines are in use. You also can use this message to provide the user with further instructions.

Displaying a "Host Failed" Message

You can display a "host failed" message when a Telnet connection with a specific host fails. Perform the following task in line configuration mode:

Task	Command
Display a "host failed" message.	**busy-message** *hostname d message d*

Enabling or Disabling the Display of Messages

You can control display of the message-of-the-day and line-activation banners. By default, these banners are displayed on all lines. To suppress or reinstate the display of such messages, perform one of the following tasks in line configuration mode:

Task		Command
Step 1	Suppress banner display.	**no exec-banner**
Step 2	Reinstate the display of the EXEC or MOTD banners.	**exec-banner**

Managing Connections and System Banners Examples

This section contains the following examples:

- Changing a Login Name Example
- Specifying a TACACS Host Example
- Clearing TCP/IP Connection Examples
- Banner Message Example

Changing a Login Name Example

The following example shows how login usernames and passwords can be changed. In this example, a user currently logged on under the username *user1* attempts to change that login name to *user2*. After entering the **login** command, the user enters the new username, but enters an incorrect password. Because the password does not match the original password, the system rejects the attempt to change the username.

```
Router> login
Username: user2
Password:
% Access denied
Still logged in as "user1"
```

Next, the user attempts the login change again, with the username *user2*, but enters the correct (original) password. This time, the password matches the current login information, the login username is changed to *user2*, and the user is allowed access to the EXEC at the user-level.

```
router> login
Username: user2
Password:
router>
```

Specifying a TACACS Host Example

In the following example, *user1* specifies the TACACS host *host1* to authenticate the password:

```
router> login
Username: user1@host1
Translating "HOST1"...domain server (131.108.1.111) [OK]
```

Clearing TCP/IP Connection Examples

The following example clears a TCP connection using its TTY line number. The **show tcp** command displays the line number (tty2) that is used in the **clear tcp** command.

```
Router# show tcp

    tty2, virtual tty from host router20.cisco.com
    Connection state is ESTAB, I/O status: 1, unread input bytes: 0
    Local host: 171.69.233.7, Local port: 23
    Foreign host: 171.69.61.75, Foreign port: 1058

    Enqueued packets for retransmit: 0, input: 0, saved: 0

    Event Timers (current time is 0x36144):
    Timer          Starts    Wakeups          Next
    Retrans          4          0             0x0
    TimeWait         0          0             0x0
    AckHold          7          4             0x0
    SendWnd          0          0             0x0
    KeepAlive        0          0             0x0
    GiveUp           0          0             0x0
    PmtuAger         0          0             0x0
```

```
      iss: 4151109680   snduna: 4151109752   sndnxt: 4151109752     sndwnd:    24576
      irs: 1249472001   rcvnxt: 1249472032   rcvwnd:         4258 delrcvwnd:       30

      SRTT: 710 ms, RTTO: 4442 ms, RTV: 1511 ms, KRTT: 0 ms
      minRTT: 0 ms, maxRTT: 300 ms, ACK hold: 300 ms

Router# clear tcp line 2
   [confirm]
    [OK]
```

The following example clears a TCP connection by specifying its local router host name and port
and its remote router host name and port. The **show tcp brief** command displays the local (Local
Address) and remote (Foreign Address) host names and ports to use in the **clear tcp** command.

```
Router# show tcp brief
   TCB          Local Address          Foreign Address        (state)
   60A34E9C   router1.cisco.com.23      router20.cisco.1055   ESTAB

Router# clear tcp local router1 23 remote router20 1055
   [confirm]
    [OK]
```

The following example clears a TCP connection using its TCB address. The **show tcp brief** command displays the TCB address to use in the **clear tcp** command.

```
Router# show tcp brief
   TCB          Local Address          Foreign Address        (state)
   60B75E48   router1.cisco.com.23      router20.cisco.1054   ESTAB

Router# clear tcp tcb 60B75E48
   [confirm]
    [OK]
```

Banner Message Example

The following example shows how to use the **banner** global configuration command and the **no
exec-banner** line configuration command to notify your users that the server is going to be reloaded
with new software:

```
! Both messages are inappropriate for the VTYs.
line vty 0 4
 no exec-banner
!
banner exec /
 This is Cisco Systems training group router.

 Unauthorized access prohibited.
 /
!
banner incoming /
 You are connected to a Hayes-compatible modem.

 Enter the appropriate AT commands.
 Remember to reset anything to change before disconnecting.
 /
```

```
!
banner motd /
 The router will go down at 6pm for a software upgrade
 /
```

## CHAPTER 8

Connections and System Banners Commands

This chapter describes the connections and system banner commands.

For connection and system banner task information and examples, see Chapter 7, "Managing Connections and System Banners."

BANNER EXEC

To display a message on terminals with an interactive EXEC, use the **banner exec** global configuration command. This command specifies a message to be displayed when an EXEC process is created (a line is activated, or an incoming connection is made to a VTY). The **no** form of this command disables the EXEC banner.

> **banner exec** *d message d*
> **no banner exec**

Syntax	Description
d	Delimiting character of your choice—a pound sign (#) for example. You cannot use the delimiting character in the banner message.
message	Message text.

Default

None

Command Mode

Global configuration

Usage Guidelines

This command first appeared in Cisco IOS Release 10.0.

Follow this command with one or more blank spaces and a delimiting character of your choice. Then enter one or more lines of text, terminating the message with the second occurrence of the delimiting character.

Example

The following example sets an EXEC message. The dollar sign ($) is used as a delimiting character.

```
banner exec $
Session activated. Enter commands at the prompt.
$
```

Related Commands

banner incoming
banner motd
exec-banner

BANNER INCOMING

To specify a message used when you have an incoming connection to a line from a host on the network, use the **banner incoming** global configuration command. The **no** form of this command disables the incoming connection banner.

> **banner incoming** *d message d*
> **no banner incoming**

Syntax	Description
d	Delimiting character of your choice—a pound sign (#) for example. You cannot use the delimiting character in the banner message.
message	Message text.

Default

None

Command Mode

Global configuration

Usage Guidelines

This command first appeared in Cisco IOS Release 10.0.

Follow this command with one or more blank spaces and a delimiting character of your choice. Then enter one or more lines of text, terminating the message with the second occurrence of the delimiting character.

An *incoming connection* is one initiated from the network side of the router. The EXEC banner can be suppressed on certain lines using the **no exec-banner** line configuration command. This line should *not* display the EXEC or MOTD banners when an EXEC is created.

Example

The following example sets an incoming connection message. The pound sign (#) is used as a delimiting character.

```
banner incoming #
Welcome to Reuses.
#
```

Related Commands

banner exec
banner motd
exec-banner

BANNER MOTD

To specify a message-of-the-day (MOTD) banner, use the **banner motd** global configuration command. The **no** form of this command disables the MOTD banner.

banner motd *d message d*
no banner motd

Syntax	Description
d	Delimiting character of your choice—a pound sign (#) for example. You cannot use the delimiting character in the banner message.
message	Message text.

Default

None

Command Mode

Global configuration

Usage Guidelines

This command first appeared in Cisco IOS Release 10.0.

Follow this command with one or more blank spaces and a delimiting character of your choice. Then enter one or more lines of text, terminating the message with the second occurrence of the delimiting character.

This MOTD banner is displayed to all terminals connected and is useful for sending messages that affect all users (such as impending system shutdowns).

The **banner** command without any keywords specified defaults to the **banner motd** command. When a new **banner motd** command is added to the configuration, it overwrites the existing **banner** command if no keyword is specified. Similarly, if a **banner** command is added to the configuration, any existing **banner motd** command is overwritten.

Example

The following example sets a MOTD banner. The pound sign (#) is used as a delimiting character:

```
banner motd #
Building power will be off from 7:00 AM until 9:00 AM this coming Tuesday.
#
```

Related Commands

banner exec
banner incoming
exec-banner

BUSY-MESSAGE

To create a "host failed" message that displays when a connection fails, use the **busy-message** global configuration command. Use the **no** form of this command to disable the "host failed" message from displaying on the specified host.

> **busy-message** *hostname d message d*
> **no busy-message** *hostname*

Syntax	Description
hostname	Name of the host that cannot be reached.
d	Delimiting character of your choice—a pound sign (#) for example. You cannot use the delimiting character in the message.
message	Message text.

Default

None

Command Mode

Global configuration

Usage Guidelines

This command first appeared in Cisco IOS Release 10.0.

This command applies only to Telnet connections.

Follow the **busy-message** command with one or more blank spaces and a delimiting character of your choice. Then enter one or more lines of text, terminating the message with the second occurrence of the delimiting character.

Defining a "host failed" message for a host prevents all Cisco IOS software-initiated user messages, including the initial message that indicates the connection is "Trying..." The **busy-message** command can be used in the **autocommand** command to suppress these messages.

Example

The following example displays a message on the terminal whenever an attempt to connect to the host named *dross* fails. The pound sign (#) is used as a delimiting character.

```
busy-message dross #
Cannot connect to host. Contact the computer center.
#
```

CLEAR TCP

To clear a TCP connection, use the **clear tcp** privileged EXEC command.

    clear tcp {**line** *line-number* | **local** *host-name port* **remote** *host-name port* | **tcb** *address*}

Syntax	Description
line *line-number*	TTY line number of the TCP connection to clear.
local *host-name port* **remote** *host-name port*	Local router's host name and port and remote router's host name and port of the TCP connection to clear.
tcb *address*	Transmission Control Block (TCB) address of the TCP connection to clear. The TCB address is an internal identifier for the end point.

Command Mode

Privileged EXEC

Usage Guidelines

This command first appeared in Cisco IOS Release 11.1.

The **clear tcp** command is particularly useful for clearing hung TCP connections.

The **clear tcp line** *line-number* command terminates the TCP connection on the specified TTY line. Also, all TCP sessions initiated from that TTY line are terminated.

The **clear tcp local** *host-name port* **remote** *host-name port* command terminates the specific TCP connection identified by the host name/port pair of the local and remote router.

The **clear tcp tcb** *address* command terminates the specific TCP connection identified by the TCB address.

Examples

The following example clears a TCP connection using its TTY line number. The **show tcp** command displays the line number (tty2) that is used in the **clear tcp** command.

```
Router# show tcp

    tty2, virtual tty from host router20.cisco.com
    Connection state is ESTAB, I/O status: 1, unread input bytes: 0
    Local host: 171.69.233.7, Local port: 23
    Foreign host: 171.69.61.75, Foreign port: 1058

    Enqueued packets for retransmit: 0, input: 0, saved: 0

    Event Timers (current time is 0x36144):
    Timer        Starts    Wakeups          Next
    Retrans          4         0          0x0
    TimeWait         0         0          0x0
    AckHold          7         4          0x0
    SendWnd          0         0          0x0
    KeepAlive        0         0          0x0
    GiveUp           0         0          0x0
    PmtuAger         0         0          0x0

    iss: 4151109680  snduna: 4151109752  sndnxt: 4151109752     sndwnd:  24576
    irs: 1249472001  rcvnxt: 1249472032  rcvwnd:         4258  delrcvwnd:   30

    SRTT: 710 ms, RTTO: 4442 ms, RTV: 1511 ms, KRTT: 0 ms
    minRTT: 0 ms, maxRTT: 300 ms, ACK hold: 300 ms

Router# clear tcp line 2
    [confirm]
    [OK]
```

The following example clears a TCP connection by specifying its local router host name and port and its remote router host name and port. The **show tcp brief** command displays the local (Local Address) and remote (Foreign Address) host names and ports to use in the **clear tcp** command.

```
Router# show tcp brief
    TCB      Local Address           Foreign Address        (state)
    60A34E9C  router1.cisco.com.23    router20.cisco.1055   ESTAB

Router# clear tcp local router1 23 remote router20 1055
    [confirm]
    [OK]
```

The following example clears a TCP connection using its TCB address. The **show tcp brief** command displays the TCB address to use in the **clear tcp** command.

```
Router# show tcp brief
    TCB        Local Address          Foreign Address       (state)
    60B75E48   router1.cisco.com.23      router20.cisco.1054   ESTAB

Router# clear tcp tcb 60B75E48
    [confirm]
      [OK]
```

Related Commands

show tcp
show tcp brief

EXEC

To allow an EXEC process on a line, use the **exec** line configuration command. Use the **no** form of this command to turn off the EXEC process for the specified line.

exec
no exec

Syntax   Description

This command has no arguments or keywords.

Default

The EXEC processes start is activated automatically on all lines.

Command Mode

Line configuration

Usage Guidelines

This command first appeared in Cisco IOS Release 10.0.

When you want to allow an outgoing connection *only* for a line, use the **no exec** command. When a user tries to Telnet to a line with the **no exec** command configured, the user will get no response when pressing the Return key at the login screen.

Example

The following example illustrates how to turn off the EXEC on line 7. You might want to do this on the auxiliary port if the attached device (for example, the control port of a rack of modems) sends unsolicited data. If this happens, an EXEC process starts, which makes the line unavailable.

```
line 7
 no exec
```

EXEC-BANNER

To control whether banners are displayed or suppressed, use the **exec-banner** line configuration command. Use the **no** form of this command to suppress the banner messages.

> **exec-banner**
> **no exec-banner**

Syntax   Description

This command has no arguments or keywords.

Default

The messages defined with **banner motd** and **banner exec** commands are displayed on all lines.

Command Mode

Line configuration

Usage Guidelines

This command first appeared in Cisco IOS Release 10.0.

This command determines whether the router will display the EXEC banner or the message-of-the-day (MOTD) banner when an EXEC is created.

Example

The following example suppresses the banner on virtual terminal lines 0 to 4:

```
line 0 4
 no exec-banner
```

Related Commands

banner exec
banner motd

EXEC-TIMEOUT

To set the interval that the EXEC command interpreter waits until user input is detected, use the **exec-timeout** line configuration command. Use the **no** form of this command to remove the timeout definition.

> **exec-timeout** *minutes* [*seconds*]
> **no exec-timeout**

Syntax	Description
minutes	Integer that specifies the number of minutes.
seconds	(Optional) Additional time intervals in seconds.

Default

10 minutes

Command Mode

Line configuration

Usage Guidelines

This command first appeared in Cisco IOS Release 10.0.

If no input is detected during the interval, the EXEC facility resumes the current connection. If no connections exist, the EXEC facility returns the terminal to the idle state and disconnects the incoming session.

To specify no timeout, enter the **exec-timeout 0 0** command.

Examples

The following example sets a time interval of 2 minutes, 30 seconds:

```
line console
  exec-timeout 2 30
```

The following example sets a time interval of 10 seconds:

```
line console
  exec-timeout 0 10
```

NAME-CONNECTION

To assign a logical name to a connection, use the **name-connection** user EXEC command.

> **name-connection**

Syntax   Description

This command has no arguments or keywords.

Default

None

Command Mode

User EXEC

Usage Guidelines

This command first appeared in a release prior to Cisco IOS Release 10.0.

This command can be useful for keeping track of multiple connections.

You are prompted for the connection number and name to assign. The **where** command displays a list of the assigned logical connection names.

Example

The following example assigns the logical name *blue* to the connection:

```
Router> where
Conn Host                Address              Byte  Idle Conn Name
*  1 doc-2509             172.30.162.131          0     0 doc-2509

Router> name-connection
Connection number: 1
Enter logical name: blue
Connection 1 to doc-2509 will be named "BLUE" [confirm]
```

Related Commands

where

REFUSE-MESSAGE

To define a line-in-use message, use the **refuse-message** line configuration command. Use the **no** form of this command to disable the message.

refuse-message *d message d*
no refuse-message

Syntax	Description
d	Delimiting character of your choice—a pound sign (#) for example. You cannot use the delimiting character in the message.
message	Message text.

Default

No line-in-use message is defined.

Command Mode

Line configuration

Usage Guidelines

This command first appeared in Cisco IOS Release 10.0.

Follow this command with one or more blank spaces and a delimiting character of your choice. Then enter one or more lines of text, terminating the message with the second occurrence of the delimiting character. You cannot use the delimiting character within the text of the message.

When you define a message using this command, the Cisco IOS software does the following:

1. Accepts the connection.
2. Prints the custom message.
3. Clears the connection.

Example

In the following example, line 5 is configured with a line-in-use message, and the user is instructed to try again later:

```
line 5
refuse-message  /The dial-out modem is currently in use.

Please try again later./
```

SEND

To send messages to one or all terminal lines, use the **send** EXEC command.

send {*line-number* | * | **aux** *number* | **console** *number* | **tty** *number* | **vty** *number*}

Syntax	Description
line-number	Line number to which the message will be sent.
*	Sends a message to all TTY lines.
aux *number*	Sends a message to the AUX port.
console *number*	Sends a message to the console port.
tty *number*	Sends a message to an asynchronous line.
vty *number*	Sends a message to a VTY line.

Default

None

Command Mode

EXEC

Usage Guidelines

This command first appeared in Cisco IOS Release 11.2.

The system prompts for the message, which can be up to 500 characters long. Enter **Ctrl-Z** to end the message. Enter **Ctrl-C** to abort this command.

Example

The following example sends a message to all lines:

```
2509# send *
Enter message, end with CTRL/Z; abort with CTRL/C:
The system 2509 will be shut down in 10 minutes for repairs.^Z
Send message? [confirm]
2509#


***
***
*** Message from tty0 to all terminals:
***
The system 2509 will be shut down in 10 minutes for repairs.


2509#
```

SERVICE LINENUMBER

To configure the Cisco IOS software to display line number information after the EXEC or incoming banner, use the **service linenumber** global configuration command. Use the **no** form of this command to disable this function.

> service linenumber
> no service linenumber

Syntax   Description

This command has no arguments or keywords.

Default

Disabled

Command Mode

Global configuration

Usage Guidelines

This command first appeared in Cisco IOS Release 10.0.

With the **service linenumber** command, you can have the Cisco IOS software display the host name, line number, and location each time an EXEC process is started, or an incoming connection is made. The line number banner appears immediately after the EXEC banner or incoming banner. This feature is useful for tracking problems with modems, because the host and line for the modem connection are listed. Modem type information also can be included.

Example

In the following example, a user Telnets to Router2 before and after the **service linenumber** command is enabled. The second time, information about the line is displayed after the banner.

```
Router1> telnet Router2
Trying Router2 (172.30.162.131)... Open

Welcome to Router2.

User Access Verification

Password:
Router2> enable
Password:
Router2# configure terminal
Enter configuration commands, one per line.  End with CNTL/Z.
Router2(config)# service linenumber
Router2(config)# end
Router2# logout

[Connection to Router2 closed by foreign host]
Router1> telnet Router2
Trying Router2 (172.30.162.131)... Open

Welcome to Router2.

Router2 line 10


User Access Verification

Password:
Router2>
```

Related Commands

show users

SHOW HOSTS

To display the default domain name, the style of name lookup service, a list of name server hosts, and the cached list of host names and addresses on the network to which you can connect, use the **show hosts** user EXEC command.

   show hosts

Syntax   Description

This command has no arguments or keywords.

Command Mode

User EXEC

Usage Guidelines

This command first appeared in a release prior to Cisco IOS Release 10.0.

Sample Display

The following is a sample display from the **show hosts** output:

```
Router# show hosts

Default domain is CISCO.COM
Name/address lookup uses domain service
Name servers are 255.255.255.255
Host                 Flags       Age   Type     Address(es)
SLAG.CISCO.COM       (temp, OK)  1     IP       131.108.4.10
CHAR.CISCO.COM       (temp, OK)  8     IP       192.31.7.50
CHAOS.CISCO.COM      (temp, OK)  8     IP       131.108.1.115
DIRT.CISCO.COM       (temp, EX)  8     IP       131.108.1.111
DUSTBIN.CISCO.COM    (temp, EX)  0     IP       131.108.1.27
DREGS.CISCO.COM      (temp, EX)  24    IP       131.108.1.30
```

Table 8–1 describes significant fields shown in the display.

Table 8–1 *Show Hosts Field Descriptions*

Field	Description
Host	Name of server host.
Flags	A temporary entry is entered by a name server; the server removes the entry after 72 hours of inactivity.
	A permanent entry is entered by a configuration command and is not timed out. Entries marked "OK" are believed to be valid. Entries marked "??" are considered suspect and subject to revalidation. Entries marked "EX" are expired.
Age	Indicates the number of hours since the Cisco IOS software last referred to the cache entry.
Type	Identifies the type of address (for example, IP, CLNS, or X.121). If you used the **ip hp-host** global configuration command, the **show hosts** command displays these host names as type HP-IP.
Address(es)	Shows the address of the host. One host can have up to eight addresses.

SYSTAT

The **show users** command replaces the **systat** command. Refer to the description of the **show users** command for more information.

VACANT-MESSAGE

To display an idle terminal message, use the **vacant-message** line configuration command. Use the **no** form of this command to remove the default vacant message or any other vacant message that might have been set.

> **vacant-message** [*d message d*]
> **no vacant-message**

Syntax	Description
d	(Optional) A delimiting character of your choice—a pound sign (#), for example. You cannot use the delimiting character in the banner message.
message	(Optional) Vacant terminal message.
d	(Optional) A delimiting character of your choice.

Default

The format of the default vacant message is as follows:

```
<blank lines>
hostname tty# is now available
<blank lines>
Press RETURN to get started.
```

This message is generated by the system.

Command Mode

Line configuration

Usage Guidelines

This command first appeared in Cisco IOS Release 10.0.

This command enables the banner to be displayed on the screen of an idle terminal. The **vacant-message** command without any arguments restores the default message.

Follow this command with one or more blank spaces and a delimiting character of your choice. Then enter one or more lines of text, terminating the message with the second occurrence of the delimiting character.

NOTES

For a rotary group, you need to define the message for only the first line in the group.

Example

The following example turns on the system banner and displays this message:

```
line 0
vacant-message #
                Welcome to Cisco Systems, Inc.
                Press Return to get started.
```

PART II

File Management

## CHAPTER 9

Modifying, Downloading, and Maintaining Configuration Files

This chapter describes how to load and maintain configuration files. Configuration files contain commands entered to customize the function of the Cisco IOS software.

To benefit most from the instructions and organization of this chapter, your router must contain a minimal configuration that allows you to interact with the system software. You can create a basic configuration file using the **setup** command facility. See the user guide for your hardware platform for more information on using **setup** at first-time startup. See the "Using Setup for Configuration Changes" section in Chapter 3, "Using Configuration Tools," for information on using **setup** after first-time startup.

For a complete description of the configuration file commands in this chapter, see Chapter 10, "Configuration File Commands."

NOTES

One or more of the commands that previously appeared in this chapter have been replaced by new commands. Table 9–1 maps the old commands to their replacements. The old commands continue to perform their normal functions in the current release, but support for these commands will cease in a future release.

Table 9–1 *Mapping Old Commands to New Commands*

Old Command	New Command
configure network	copy rcp running-config (for an rcp server)
	copy tftp running-config (for a TFTP server)
configure overwrite-network	copy rcp startup-config (for an rcp server)
	copy tftp startup-config (for a TFTP server)

Table 9–1   *Mapping Old Commands to New Commands, Continued*

Old Command	New Command
show configuration	show startup-config
write erase	erase startup-config
write memory	copy running-config startup-config
write network	copy running-config rcp (for an rcp server)
	copy running-config tftp (for a TFTP server)
write terminal	show running-config

CONFIGURATION FILE TASK LIST

To load and maintain configuration files needed for startup, complete any of the tasks in the following sections:

- Displaying Configuration File Information
- Understanding Configuration Files
- Entering Configuration Mode and Selecting a Configuration Source
- Configuring the Cisco IOS Software from the Terminal
- Copying Configuration Files from the Router to a Network Server
- Copying Configuration Files from a Network Server to the Router
- Maintaining Configuration Files Larger than NVRAM
- Copying Configuration Files between Different Locations
- Reexecuting the Configuration Commands in Startup Configuration
- Clearing the Configuration Information
- Specifying the Startup Configuration File

NOTES

These tasks assume you have a minimal configuration that you want to modify.

DISPLAYING CONFIGURATION FILE INFORMATION

Perform the following tasks in EXEC mode to display information about configuration files:

Task		Command
Step 1	List the contents of the BOOT environment variable, the name of the configuration file pointed to by the CONFIG_FILE environment variable, and the contents of the BOOTLDR environment variable.	**show boot** (Cisco 3600 series, Cisco 7000 family only)
Step 2	List the configuration information stored in a specified file.	**show file** *device:filename* (Cisco 7000 family only)
Step 3	List the configuration information in running memory.	**show running-config**
Step 4	List the startup configuration information.	**show startup-config**
Step 5	On all platforms except the Cisco 7000 family[1], the startup configuration is usually NVRAM. On the Cisco 7000 family, the CONFIG_FILE environment variable points to the startup configuration. The CONFIG_FILE variable defaults to NVRAM.	

[1] The Cisco 7000 family consists of Cisco 7000 series routers with RSP7000, Cisco 7200 series routers, and Cisco 7500 series routers.

UNDERSTANDING CONFIGURATION FILES

Configuration files contain the commands the router uses to customize the function of the Cisco IOS software. The **setup** command facility helps you create a basic configuration file. However, you can manually change the configuration by typing commands in a configuration mode.

Types of Configuration Files

Startup configuration files are used during system startup to configure the software. Running configuration files contain the current configuration of the software. The two configuration files can be different. For example, you might want to change the configuration for a short time period rather than permanently. In this case, you would change the running configuration using the **configure terminal** command, but not save the configuration using the **copy running-config startup-config** command.

To change the running configuration, use the **configure terminal** command, as described in the "Configuring the Cisco IOS Software from the Terminal" section earlier in this chapter. To change the startup-config, you can either save the running configuration file to the startup configuration using the **copy running-config startup-config** command (which is also described in the "Configuring the Cisco IOS Software from the Terminal" section) or copy commands from a file directory to the startup configuration without affecting the running configuration (see the "Copying Configuration Files from a Network Server to the Router" section).

Location of Configuration Files

The configuration files are stored in the following places:

- The running configuration is stored in RAM.
- On all platforms except the Cisco 7000 family, the startup configuration is stored in non-volatile random-access memory (NVRAM).
- On the Cisco 7000 family, the startup configuration is stored in the location specified by the CONFIG_FILE environment variable. The CONFIG_FILE variable defaults to NVRAM and can be a file in the following devices:
  - **nvram:** (NVRAM)
  - **bootflash:** (Internal Flash memory)
  - **slot0:** (First PCMCIA slot)
  - **slot1:** (Second PCMCIA slot)

ENTERING CONFIGURATION MODE AND SELECTING A CONFIGURATION SOURCE

To enter configuration mode, enter the **configure** command at the privileged EXEC prompt. The Cisco IOS software responds with the following prompt asking you to specify the terminal, memory, or a file stored on a network server (network) as the source of configuration commands:

```
Configuring from terminal, memory, or network [terminal]?
```

Configuring from the terminal allows you to enter configuration commands at the command line. See the "Configuring the Cisco IOS Software from the Terminal" section for details. Configuring from memory reexecutes the commands in the startup configuration file. See the "Reexecuting the Configuration Commands in Startup Configuration" section for more details. Configuring from the network allows you to load and execute configuration commands over the network. See the "Copying Configuration Files from a Network Server to the Router" section for more details.

CONFIGURING THE CISCO IOS SOFTWARE FROM THE TERMINAL

The Cisco IOS software accepts one configuration command per line. You can enter as many configuration commands as you want.

You can add comments to a configuration file describing the commands you have entered. Precede a comment with an exclamation point (!). Because comments are *not* stored in NVRAM or in the active copy of the configuration file, comments do not appear when you list the active configuration with the **show running-config** EXEC command. Also, when the startup configuration is NVRAM, comments do not show up when you list the startup configuration with the **show startup-config** EXEC command. Comments are stripped out of the configuration file when it is loaded onto the router. However, you can list the comments in configuration files stored on a TFTP, rcp, or MOP server.

When you configure the software from the terminal, the software executes the commands you enter at the system prompts. To configure the software from the terminal, complete the following tasks:

Task	Command
Step 1 Enter configuration mode and select the terminal option.	**configure terminal**
Step 2 Enter the necessary configuration commands.	See the appropriate chapter for specific configuration commands.
Step 3 Quit configuration mode.	**end** or press Ctrl-Z (^Z)
Step 4 Save the configuration file to your startup configuration. On most platforms, this step saves the configuration to NVRAM. On the Cisco 7000 family, this step saves the configuration to the location specified by the CONFIG_FILE environment variable. The CONFIG_FILE variable defaults to NVRAM.	**copy running-config startup-config**

In the following example, the software is configured from the terminal. The comment The follow-ing command provides the router host name identifies the purpose of the next command line. The **hostname** command changes the router name from *router1* to *router2*. By pressing **Ctrl-Z** (^Z) or entering the command **end**, the user quits configuration mode. Finally, the **copy running-config startup-config** command saves the current configuration to the startup configuration.

```
Router1# configure terminal
Router1(config)# !The following command provides the router host name.
Router1(config)# hostname router2
Router2(config)# end
Router2# copy running-config startup-config
```

When the startup configuration is NVRAM, it stores the current configuration information in text format as configuration commands, *recording only nondefault settings*. The memory is check-summed to guard against corrupted data.

> **CAUTION**
>
> Some specific commands might not get saved to NVRAM. You will have to enter these commands again if you reboot the machine. These commands are noted in the documentation. We recommend that you keep a listing of these settings, so you can quickly reconfigure your router after rebooting.

COPYING CONFIGURATION FILES FROM THE ROUTER TO A NETWORK SERVER

You can copy configuration files from the router to a TFTP server or rcp server. You might do this task to back up a current configuration file to a server before changing its contents, thereby allowing you to later restore the original configuration file from the server. The following sections describe these tasks:

- Copying a Configuration File from the Router to a TFTP Server
- Copying a Configuration File from the Router to an rcp Server

The protocol you use depends on which type of server you are using. The rcp transport mechanism provides faster performance and more reliable delivery of data than TFTP. These improvements are possible because rcp is built on and uses the Transmission Control Protocol/Internet Protocol (TCP/IP) stack, which is connection-oriented.

Copying a Configuration File from the Router to a TFTP Server

In some implementations of TFTP, you must create a dummy file on the TFTP server and give it read, write, and execute permissions before copying a file over it. Refer to your TFTP documentation for more information.

To store configuration information on a TFTP network server, complete the following tasks in the EXEC mode:

Task	Command
Step 1 Specify that the running or startup configuration file be stored on a network server.	**copy running-config tftp** or **copy startup-config tftp**
Step 2 Enter the IP address of the network server.	*ip-address*
Step 3 Enter the name of the configuration file to store on the server.	*filename*
Step 4 Confirm the entry.	y

The command prompts you for the destination host's address and a filename, as the following example illustrates.

The following example copies a configuration file from a router to a TFTP server:

```
Tokyo# copy running-config tftp
Remote host [172.16.2.155]?
Name of configuration file to write [tokyo-confg]?
Write file tokyo-confg on host 172.16.2.155? [confirm] y
#
Writing tokyo-confg!!! [OK]
```

Copying a Configuration File from the Router to an rcp Server

You can copy a configuration file from the router to an rcp server.

If you copy the configuration file to a personal computer used as a file server, the computer must support rsh.

Understanding the rcp Username

The rcp protocol requires a client to send a remote username on each rcp request to a server. When you copy a configuration file from the router to a server using rcp, the Cisco IOS software sends the first valid username in the following list:

1. The username set by the **ip rcmd remote-username** command, if the command is configured.

2. The remote username associated with the current TTY (terminal) process. For example, if the user is connected to the router through Telnet and was authenticated through the **username** command, the router software sends the Telnet username as the remote username.

3. The router host name.

For the rcp copy request to execute successfully, an account must be defined on the network server for the remote username. If the server has a directory structure, the configuration file or image is written to or copied from the directory associated with the remote username on the server. Use the **ip rcmd remote-username** command to specify which directory on the server to use. For example, if the system image resides in the home directory of a user on the server, you can specify that user's name as the remote username.

If you are writing to the server, the rcp server must be properly configured to accept the rcp write request from the user on the router. For UNIX systems, you must add an entry to the *.rhosts* file for the remote user on the rcp server. For example, suppose the router contains the following configuration lines:

```
hostname Rtr1
ip rcmd remote-username User0
```

If the router's IP address translates to Router1.company.com, then the *.rhosts* file for User0 on the rcp server should contain the following line:

```
Router1.company.com Rtr1
```

Refer to the documentation for your rcp server for more details.

Copying a Configuration File from the Router to the rcp Server Tasks

To copy a startup configuration file or a running configuration file from the router to an rcp server, complete the following tasks:

Task		Command
Step 1	Enter configuration mode from the terminal. This step is required only if you override the default remote username (see Step 2).	configure terminal
Step 2	Specify the remote username. This step is optional, but recommended.	ip rcmd remote-username *username*
Step 3	Exit configuration mode.	end
Step 4	Specify that the router's running configuration or startup configuration file be stored on an rcp server.	copy running-config rcp or copy startup-config rcp
Step 5	Enter the IP address of the network server.	*ip-address*
Step 6	Enter the name of the configuration file to store on the server.	*filename*
Step 7	Confirm the entry.	y

Storing a Running Configuration File on a Server Example

The following example copies the running configuration file named *rtr2-confg* to the *netadmin1* directory on the remote host with an IP address of 172.16.101.101:

```
Router# configure terminal
Router(config)# ip rcmd remote-username netadmin1
Router(config)# end
Router# copy running-config rcp
Remote host[]? 172.16.101.101
Name of configuration file to write [Rtr2-confg]?
Write file rtr2-confg on host 172.16.101.101?[confirm]
Building configuration...[OK]
Connected to 172.16.101.101
Router#
```

Storing a Startup Configuration File on a Server Example

The following example shows how to store a startup configuration file on a server by using rcp to copy the file:

```
Rtr2# configure terminal
Rtr2(config)# ip rcmd remote-username netadmin2
```

```
Rtr2(config)# end
Rtr2# copy startup-config rcp
Remote host[]? 172.16.101.101
Name of configuration file to write [rtr2-confg]?
Write file rtr2-confg on host 172.16.101.101?[confirm]
![OK]
```

COPYING CONFIGURATION FILES FROM A NETWORK SERVER TO THE ROUTER

You can copy configuration files from a TFTP server or an rcp server to the running configuration or startup configuration of the router. You might want to do this for one of the following reasons:

- To restore a backed-up configuration file.

- To use the configuration file for another router. For example, you may add another router to your network and want it to have a similar configuration to the original router. By copying the file to the new router, you can change the relevant parts rather than re-creating the whole file.

- To load the same configuration commands on to all the routers in your network so that all the routers have similar configurations.

The **copy tftp running-config** and **copy rcp running-config** commands, load the configuration files into the router as if you were typing the commands in at the command line. They do not erase the existing running configuration before adding the commands. If a command in the copied configuration file replaces a command in the existing configuration file, the existing command will be erased. For example, if the copied configuration file contains a different IP address in a particular command than the existing configuration, the IP address in the copied configuration will be used. However, some commands in the existing configuration may not be replaced or negated. In this case, the resulting configuration file will be a mixture of the existing configuration file and the copied configuration file, with the copied configuration file having precedence.

In order to restore a configuration file to an exact copy of a file stored on a server, you need to copy the configuration file directly to the startup configuration (using the **copy tftp startup-config** or **copy rcp startup-config** command) and reload the router.

The following sections describe these tasks:

- Copying a Configuration File from a TFTP Server to the Router
- Copying a Configuration File from an rcp Server to the Router

You can copy configuration files from a TFTP or rcp server. The protocol you use depends on which type of server you are using. The rcp transport mechanism provides faster performance and more reliable delivery of data than TFTP. These improvements are possible because the rcp transport mechanism is built on and uses the Transmission Control Protocol/Internet Protocol (TCP/IP) stack, which is connection-oriented.

Copying a Configuration File from a TFTP Server to the Router

To copy a configuration file from a TFTP server to the router, complete the following tasks from EXEC mode:

Task	Command
Step 1 Copy a file from a TFTP server to the router.	**copy tftp running-config** or **copy tftp startup-config**
Step 2 When prompted, enter the IP address or domain name of the server.	*ip-address* or *name*
Step 3 If prompted, enter the filename of the configuration file.	*filename*
Step 4 Confirm the entry.	**y**

In the following example, the software is configured from the file *tokyo-config* at IP address 172.16.2.155:

```
Router1# copy tftp running-config
Host or network configuration file [host]?
IP address of remote host [255.255.255.255]? 172.16.2.155
Name of configuration file [tokyo-confg]?
Configure using tokyo-confg from 172.16.2.155? [confirm] y
Booting tokyo-confg from 172.16.2.155:!!! [OK - 874/16000 bytes]
```

Copying a Configuration File from an rcp Server to the Router

You can copy configuration files from an rcp server to the router.

If you copy the configuration file to a personal computer used as a file server, the computer must support rsh.

Understanding the rcp Username

The rcp protocol requires a client to send a remote username on each rcp request to a server. When you copy a configuration file from the router to a server using rcp, the Cisco IOS software sends the first valid username in the following list:

1. The username set by the **ip rcmd remote-username** command, if the command is configured.

2. The remote username associated with the current TTY (terminal) process. For example, if the user is connected to the router through Telnet and was authenticated through the **username** command, the router software sends the Telnet username as the remote username.

3. The router host name.

For the rcp copy request to execute successfully, an account must be defined on the network server for the remote username. If the server has a directory structure, the configuration file or image is written to or copied from the directory associated with the remote username on the server. Use the **ip rcmd remote-username** command to specify which directory on the server to use. For example, if the system image resides in the home directory of a user on the server, you can specify that user's name as the remote username.

Copying a Configuration File from an rcp Server to the Router Tasks

To copy a configuration file from an rcp server to the running configuration or startup configuration, perform the following tasks:

Task		Command
Step 1	Enter configuration mode from the terminal. This step is required only if you override the default remote username (see Step 2).	**configure terminal**
Step 2	Specify the remote username. This step is optional, but recommended.	**ip rcmd remote-username** *username*
Step 3	Exit configuration mode.	**end**
Step 4	Using rcp, copy the configuration file from a network server to running memory or the startup configuration.	**copy rcp running-config** or **copy rcp startup-config**
Step 5	When prompted, enter the IP address of the server.	*ip-address*
Step 6	When prompted, enter the name of the configuration file.	*filename*
Step 7	Confirm the entry.	**y**

Copying rcp Running-Config Example

The following example copies a host configuration file named *host1-confg* from the *netadmin1* directory on the remote server with an IP address of 172.16.101.101, and loads and runs those commands on the router:

```
Router# configure terminal
Router(config)# ip rcmd remote-username netadmin1
Router(config)# end
Router# copy rcp running-config
Host or network configuration file [host]?
Address of remote host [255.255.255.255]? 172.16.101.101
```

```
Name of configuration file [Router-confg]? host1-confg
Configure using host1-confg from 172.16.101.101? [confirm]
Connected to 172.16.101.101
Loading 1112 byte file host1-confg:![OK]
Router#
%SYS-5-CONFIG: Configured from host1-config by rcp from 172.16.101.101
```

Copying rcp Startup-Config Example

The following example specifies a remote username of *netadmin1*. Then it copies the configuration file *host2-confg* from the *netadmin1* directory on the remote server with an IP address of 172.16.101.101 to the startup configuration.

```
Rtr2# configure terminal
Rtr2(config)# ip rcmd remote-username netadmin1
Rtr2(config)# end
Rtr2# copy rcp startup-config
Address of remote host [255.255.255.255]? 172.16.101.101
Name of configuration file[rtr2-confg]? host2-confg
Configure using host2-confg from 172.16.101.101?[confirm]
Connected to 172.16.101.101
Loading 1112 byte file host2-confg:![OK]
[OK]
Rtr2#
%SYS-5-CONFIG_NV:Non-volatile store configured from host2-config by rcp from
172.16.101.101
```

MAINTAINING CONFIGURATION FILES LARGER THAN NVRAM

To maintain a configuration file that exceeds size of NVRAM, perform one of the tasks in the following sections:

- Compressing the Configuration File
- Storing the Configuration in Flash Memory (Cisco 7000 family)
- Loading the Configuration Commands from the Network

Compressing the Configuration File

The **service compress-config** global configuration command specifies that the configuration file is to be stored compressed in NVRAM. Once the configuration file has been compressed, the router functions normally. When the system is booted, it recognizes that the configuration file is compressed, expands it, and proceeds normally. The **show startup-config** EXEC command expands the configuration before displaying it.

To compress configuration files, perform the following tasks, beginning in global configuration mode:

Task	Command
Step 1 Verify that your system's ROMs support file compression. If not, you can install new ROMs that support file compression.	Refer to the appropriate hardware installation and maintenance publication.
Step 2 Specify that the configuration file is to be compressed.	**service compress-config**
Step 3 Exit global configuration mode.	**end**
Step 4 Enter the new configuration.	Use TFTP or rcp to copy the new configuration. If you try to load a configuration that is more than three times larger than the NVRAM size, the following error message is displayed: "[buffer overflow - *file-size/buffer-size* bytes]." or **configure terminal**
Step 5 When you have finished changing the running configuration, save the new configuration.	**copy running-config startup-config**

The size of the configuration must not exceed three times the NVRAM size. For a 128 KB size NVRAM, the largest expanded configuration file size is 384 KB.

The **service compress-config** command works only if you have Cisco IOS Software Release 10 boot ROMs or later. Installing new ROMs is a one-time operation and is necessary only if you do not have Cisco IOS Release 10 in ROM already. If the boot ROMs do not recognize a compressed configuration, the following message is displayed:

```
Boot ROMs do not support NVRAM compression Config NOT written to NVRAM
```

The example below compresses a 129 KB configuration file to 11 KB.

```
Router# configure terminal
Router(config)# service compress-config
Router(config)# end
Router# copy tftp running-config
Host or network configuration file [host]?
IP address of remote host [255.255.255.255]? 172.16.2.155
```

```
Name of configuration file [tokyo-confg]?
Configure using tokyo-confg from 172.16.2.155? [confirm] y
Booting tokyo-confg from 172.16.2.155:!!! [OK - 874/16000 bytes]
Router# copy running-config startup-config
Building configuration...
Compressing configuration from 129648 bytes to 11077 bytes
[OK]
```

Storing the Configuration in Flash Memory (Cisco 7000 family)

On the Cisco 7000 family routers, you can store the startup configuration in Flash memory by setting the environment variable CONFIG_FILE to a file in internal Flash memory or Flash memory in a PCMCIA slot.

To store the startup configuration in Flash memory, perform the following tasks, beginning in privileged EXEC mode:

Task		Command
Step 1	Copy the current startup configuration to the new location to create the configuration file.	copy startup-config *device:filename*
Step 2	Enter global configuration mode.	configure terminal
Step 3	The buffer that holds the configuration file is usually the size of NVRAM. Larger configurations need larger buffers. Change the size of the buffer that holds the configuration commands.	boot buffersize *bytes*
Step 4	Specify that the startup configuration file is to be stored in Flash memory by setting the CONFIG_FILE variable.	boot config *device:filename*
Step 5	Exit global configuration mode.	end
Step 6	Enter the new configuration.	Use TFTP or rcp to copy the new configuration. If you try to load a configuration that is more than three times larger than the NVRAM size, the following error message is displayed: "[buffer overflow - *file-size/buffer-size* bytes]." or configure terminal

Task	Command
Step 7 When you have finished changing the running configuration, save the new configuration.	**copy running-config startup-config**

See the "Specifying the CONFIG_FILE Environment Variable (Cisco 7000 family)" section for more information.

The following example stores the configuration file in slot 0:

```
Router# copy startup-config slot0:router-config
Router# configure terminal
Router(config)# boot buffersize 129000
Router(config)# boot config slot0:router-config
Router(config)# end
Router# copy running-config startup-config
```

Care must be taken when editing or changing a large configuration. Flash memory space is used every time a **copy running-config startup-config** is issued. Because file management for Flash memory, such as optimizing free space, is not done automatically, you must pay close attention to available Flash memory. Cisco recommends that you use a large-capacity Flash card of at least 20 MB.

Loading the Configuration Commands from the Network

You also can store large configurations on TFTP or rcp servers and download them at system startup. To use a network server to store large configurations, perform the following tasks, beginning in privileged EXEC mode:

Task	Command
Step 1 Save the running configuration to a TFTP or rcp server.	**copy running-config {tftp	rcp}**
Step 2 Enter global configuration mode.	**configure terminal**
Step 3 The buffer that holds the configuration file is usually the size of NVRAM. Larger configurations need larger buffers. Change the size of the buffer that holds the configuration commands.	**boot buffersize** *bytes*
Step 4 Specify that the startup configuration file is to be loaded from the network server at startup.	**boot network [tftp	rcp]** *filename* [*ip-address*]
Step 5 Exit global configuration mode.	**end**
Step 6 Save the configuration.	**copy running-config startup-config**

See "Copying Configuration Files from the Router to a Network Server" and "Configuring the Router to Download Configuration Files" for more information on these tasks.

COPYING CONFIGURATION FILES BETWEEN DIFFERENT LOCATIONS

On many platforms, such as the Cisco 1600 series, Cisco 3600 series, and Cisco 7000 family routers, you can copy files from one Flash memory device, such as internal Flash memory or a Flash memory card in a PCMCIA slot, to other locations. You also can copy configuration files from a TFTP or rcp server to Flash memory.

Copying Configuration Files from Flash Memory to the Startup or Running Configuration

To copy a configuration file from Flash memory directly to your startup configuration in NVRAM or your running configuration, enter one of the following commands in EXEC mode:

Task	Command
Load a configuration file directly into NVRAM.	**copy** *device*:[*partition-number*:][*filename*] **startup-config** (Cisco 1600 series and Cisco 3600 series)
	copy [*device*:]*filename* **startup-config** (Cisco 7000 family)
Copy a configuration file to your running configuration.	**copy** *device*:[*partition-number*:][*filename*] **running-config** (Cisco 1600 series and Cisco 3600 series)
	copy [*device*:]*filename* **running-config** (Cisco 7000 family)

The following example copies the file *ios-upgrade-1* from partition 4 of the Flash memory PC Card in slot 0 to the router's startup configuration on a Cisco 3600 series.

For a Cisco 1600 series router, the process will be the same, except the device used in the **copy** command must be **flash:**

```
Router# copy slot0:4:ios-upgrade-1 startup-config

Copy 'ios-upgrade-1' from flash device
  as 'startup-config' ? [yes/no] yes
[OK]
```

Copying Configuration Files between Flash Memory Devices

On Cisco 3600 series and Cisco 7000 family routers, you can copy files from one Flash memory device, such as internal Flash memory or a Flash memory card in a PCMCIA slot, to another Flash memory device. Copying files to different Flash memory devices lets you create backup copies of working configurations and duplicate configurations for other routers.

To copy a configuration file between Flash memory devices, follow these steps in EXEC mode:

Task	Command
Step 1 Display the layout and contents of Flash memory to verify the file name.	**show** *device*: [**all** | **chips** | **detailed** | **err** | **partition** *number* | **summary**]
Step 2 Copy a configuration file between Flash memory devices.	**copy** *device*:[*partition-number*:][*filename*] *device*:[*partition-number*:][*filename*]
Step 3 Verify the checksum of the file you copied.	**verify** *device*: [*partition-number*:][*filename*]

NOTES

The source device and the destination device cannot be the same. For example, the command **copy slot1: slot1:** is invalid.

Copying a Configuration File between Local Flash Memory Devices Example

The following example copies the file *running-config* from partition 1 of internal Flash memory to partition 1 of slot 1 on a Cisco 3600 series router. In this example, the source partition is not specified, so the router prompts for the partition number.

```
Router# copy flash: slot1:

System flash

Partition   Size    Used    Free    Bank-Size  State       Copy Mode
    1       4096K   3070K   1025K   4096K      Read/Write  Direct
    2       16384K  1671K   14712K  8192K      Read/Write  Direct

[Type ?<no> for partition directory; ? for full directory; q to abort]
Which partition? [default = 1]

System flash directory, partition 1:
File  Length   Name/status
  1   3142748  dirt/network/mars-test/c3600-j-mz.latest
  2   850      running-config
[3143728 bytes used, 1050576 available, 4194304 total]

PCMCIA Slot1 flash directory:
File  Length   Name/status
  1   1711088  dirt/gate/c3600-i-mz
  2   850      running-config
[1712068 bytes used, 2482236 available, 4194304 total]

Source file name? running-config
```

```
Destination file name [running-config]?
Verifying checksum for 'running-config' (file # 2)...  OK

Erase flash device before writing? [confirm]
Flash contains files. Are you sure you want to erase? [confirm]

Copy 'running-config' from flash: device
  as 'running-config' into slot1: device WITH erase? [yes/no] yes
Erasing device... eeeeeeeeeeeeeeeeeeeeeeeeeeeeeeeeeeeeeeeeeeeeeeeeeeeeeeeeeeeeeeeeeee
...erased
!
 [OK - 850/4194304 bytes]

Flash device copy took 00:00:30 [hh:mm:ss]
Verifying checksum...  OK (0x16)
```

Copying a Configuration File from a Server to Flash Memory

To copy a configuration file from an rcp server to a Flash memory device, perform the following tasks in privileged EXEC mode:

Task		Command
Step 1	Enter configuration mode from the terminal. This step is required only if you override the default remote username (see Step 2).	**configure terminal**
Step 2	Specify the remote username. This step is optional, but recommended.	**ip rcmd remote-username** *username*
Step 3	Exit configuration mode.	**end**
Step 4	Using rcp, copy the configuration file from a network server to the Flash memory device.	**copy rcp** *device*:[*partition-number*:][*filename*]
Step 5	When prompted, enter the IP address of the server.	*ip-address*
Step 6	When prompted, enter the name of the configuration file.	*filename*
Step 7	Confirm the entry.	**y**

To copy a configuration file from a TFTP server to the router, complete the following task from EXEC mode:

Task	Command
Step 1 Copy the file from a TFTP server to the Flash memory device.	**copy tftp** *device*:[*partition-number*:][*filename*]
Step 2 When prompted, enter the IP address or domain name of the server.	*ip-address* or *name*
Step 3 If prompted, enter the filename of the configuration file.	*filename*
Step 4 Confirm the entry.	**y**

Copying TFTP Example for Cisco 7000 Family

On the Cisco 7000 family, the following example copies the *router-config* file from a TFTP server to the Flash memory card inserted in slot 0 of the Network Processing Engine (NPE) or Route Switch Processor (RSP) card. The copied file has the name *new-config*.

```
Router# copy tftp:router-config slot0:new-config
```

RE-EXECUTING THE CONFIGURATION COMMANDS IN STARTUP CONFIGURATION

To re-execute the commands located in the startup configuration, complete the following task in privileged EXEC mode:

Task	Command
Reexecute the configuration commands located in the startup configuration.	**configure memory**

CLEARING THE CONFIGURATION INFORMATION

You can clear the configuration information from the startup configuration. If you reboot the router with no startup configuration, the router will enter the setup facility so that you can configure the router from scratch.

Erasing the Startup Configuration

To clear the contents of your startup configuration, perform the following task in EXEC mode:

Task	Command
Clear the contents of your startup configuration.	**erase startup-config**

For all platforms except the Cisco 7000 family, this command erases NVRAM. The startup configuration file cannot be restored once it has been deleted.

On the Cisco 7000 family, when you use the **erase startup-config** command, the router erases or deletes the configuration pointed to by CONFIG_FILE environment variable. If this variable points to NVRAM, the router erases NVRAM. If the CONFIG_FILE environment variable specifies a Flash memory device and configuration filename, the router deletes the configuration file. That is, the router marks the file as "deleted," rather than erasing it. This feature allows you to recover a "deleted" file.

Erasing a Stored Configuration File

To erase or delete a saved configuration file from a specific Flash device, complete one of the following tasks in EXEC mode:

Task	Command
For the Cisco 7000 family, delete a specified configuration file on a specified Flash device.	**delete** [*device:*]*filename* (Cisco 7000 family)
For the Cisco 1600 series and Cisco 3600 series routers, erase a specified configuration file, all files on a device, or all files in a partition.	**erase** *device:*[*partition-number*] (Cisco 1600 series and Cisco 3600 series only)

When you delete a specific file in Flash memory, the system marks the file as deleted, allowing you to recover later a "deleted" file using the **undelete** command. Erased files cannot be recovered.

For the Cisco 7000 family, if you omit the device name, the Cisco IOS software uses the default device specified by the **cd** command.

If you attempt to erase or delete the configuration file specified by the CONFIG_FILE environment variable, the system prompts you to confirm the deletion.

The **erase** [*device:*]*filename* command differs from the **erase flash** command. The **erase** [*device:*]*filename* command erases a specified file located in internal Flash memory or on the Flash memory card inserted in a PCMCIA slot. The **erase flash** command erases internal Flash memory.

The following example erases the *myconfig* file from a Flash memory card inserted in slot 0:

```
Router# erase slot0:myconfig
```

The following example deletes the *myconfig* file from a Flash memory card inserted in slot 0:

```
Router# delete slot0:myconfig
```

SPECIFYING THE STARTUP CONFIGURATION FILE

Normally, the router uses the startup configuration file in NVRAM or the device specified by the CONFIG_FILE environment variable (Cisco 7000 family) at startup. See the "Specifying the CONFIG_FILE Environment Variable (Cisco 7000 family)" section for details on setting the CONFIG_FILE variable.

You also can configure the router to request and receive two configuration files automatically from the network server at startup. See the "Configuring the Router to Download Configuration Files" section for details.

Specifying the CONFIG_FILE Environment Variable (Cisco 7000 family)

On the Cisco 7000 family, you can configure the Cisco IOS software to load the startup configuration file specified by the CONFIG_FILE environment variable. The CONFIG_FILE variable defaults to NVRAM. To change the CONFIG_FILE variable, complete the following task, beginning in EXEC mode:

Task	Command
Step 1 Copy the configuration file to the device from which the router will load the file upon restart.	**copy [flash | mop | rcp | tftp | running-config | startup-config]** *device:filename*
Step 2 Enter configuration mode from the terminal.	**configure terminal**
Step 3 Set the CONFIG_FILE environment variable. This step modifies the runtime CONFIG_FILE environment variable.	**boot config** *device:filename*
Step 4 Exit configuration mode.	**end**

Task	Command
Step 5 Save this runtime CONFIG_FILE environment variable to your startup configuration.	**copy running-config startup-config**
Step 6 Optionally, verify the contents of the CONFIG_FILE environment variable.	**show boot**

Possible devices are **nvram, bootflash, slot0,** and **slot1.**

When saving the runtime CONFIG_FILE environment variable to the startup configuration, the router saves a complete version of the configuration file to the location specified by the CONFIG_FILE environment variable and a distilled version to NVRAM. A distilled version is one that does not contain access list information. If NVRAM contains a complete configuration file, the router prompts you to confirm your overwrite of the complete version with the distilled version. If NVRAM contains a distilled configuration, the router does not prompt you for confirmation and proceeds with overwriting the existing distilled configuration file in NVRAM.

NOTES ───

If you specify a file in a Flash device as the CONFIG_FILE variable, every time you save your configuration file with the **copy running-config startup-config** command, the old configuration file is marked as deleted, and the new configuration file is saved to that device. Eventually, Flash memory will be full, because the old configuration files still take up memory. Use the **squeeze** command to delete the old configuration files permanently and reclaim the space.

The following example copies the running configuration file to the first PCMCIA slot of the RSP card in a Cisco 7500 series. This configuration is then used as the startup configuration when the system is restarted.

```
Router# copy running-config slot0:config2
Router# configure terminal
Router(config)# boot config slot0:config2
Router(config)# end
Router# copy running-config startup-config
[ok]
Router# show boot
BOOT variable = slot0:rsp-boot-m
CONFIG_FILE variable = nvram:
Current CONFIG_FILE variable = slot0:config2

Configuration register is 0x010F
```

Configuring the Router to Download Configuration Files

You can configure the router to load one or two configuration files at system startup. The configuration files are loaded into memory and read in as if you were typing the commands at the command line. Thus, the configuration for the router will be a mixture of the original startup configuration and the one or two downloaded configuration files.

Network Versus Host Configuration Files

For historical reasons, the first file the router downloads is called the network configuration file. The second file the router downloads is called the host configuration file. Two configuration files can be used when all of the routers on a network use many of the same commands. The network configuration file contains the standard commands used to configure all of the routers. The host configuration files contain the commands specific to one particular host. If you are loading two configuration files, the host configuration file should be the configuration file that you want to have precedence over the other file. Both the network and host configuration files must reside on a network server reachable via TFTP, rcp, or MOP, and must be readable.

Understanding the rcp Username

The rcp protocol requires a client to send a remote username on each rcp request to a server. When you copy a configuration file from a server to the router using rcp, the Cisco IOS software sends the first valid username in the following list:

1. The username set by the **ip rcmd remote-username** command, if the command is configured.

2. The remote username associated with the current TTY (terminal) process. For example, if the user is connected to the router through Telnet and was authenticated through the **username** command, the router software sends the Telnet username as the remote username.

3. The router host name.

For the rcp copy request to execute successfully, an account must be defined on the network server for the remote username. If the server has a directory structure, the configuration file or image is written to or copied from the directory associated with the remote username on the server. Use the **ip rcmd remote-username** command to specify which directory on the server to use. For example, if the system image resides in the home directory of a user on the server, you can specify that user's name as the remote username.

If you copy the configuration file to a personal computer used as a file server, the computer must support rsh.

Configuring the Router to Download Configuration Files Task List

You can specify an ordered list of network configuration and host configuration filenames. The Cisco IOS software scans this list until it successfully loads the appropriate network or host configuration file.

To configure the router to download configuration files at system startup, perform at least one of the tasks described in the following sections:

- Configuring the Router to Download the Network Configuration File
- Configuring the Router to Download the Host Configuration File

If the network server fails to load a configuration file during startup, it tries again every ten minutes (the default setting) until a host provides the requested files. With each failed attempt, the network server displays a message on the console terminal. If the network server is unable to load the specified file, it displays the following message:

```
Booting host-confg... [timed out]
```

If there are any problems with the startup configuration file, or if the configuration register is set to ignore NVRAM, the router enters the **setup** command facility. See the "Using Setup for Configuration Changes" section in Chapter 3, "Using Configuration Tools," for details on the **setup** command.

Configuring the Router to Download the Network Configuration File

To configure the Cisco IOS software to download a network configuration file from a server at startup, complete the following task:

Task	Command
Step 1 Enter configuration mode from the terminal.	**configure terminal**
Step 2 Enter the network configuration filename to download a file using TFTP, rcp, or MOP.	**boot network mop** *filename* [*mac-address*] [*interface*] **boot network [tftp	rcp]** *filename* [*ip-address*]
Step 3 Enable the router to load the network file automatically upon restart.	**service config**
Step 4 Exit configuration mode.	**end**
Step 5 Save the configuration file to your startup configuration.	**copy running-config startup-config**

For Step 2, if you do not specify a network configuration filename, the Cisco IOS software uses the default filename *network-confg*. If you omit both the **tftp** and the **rcp** keywords, the software assumes that you are using TFTP to transfer the file and that the server whose IP address you specify supports TFTP. If you omit the address, the router uses the broadcast address.

You can specify more than one network configuration file. The software tries them in order entered until it loads one successfully. This procedure can be useful for keeping files with different configuration information loaded on a network server.

Configuring the Router to Download the Host Configuration File

To configure the Cisco IOS software to download a host configuration file from a server at startup, complete the following task.

Task	Command
Step 1 Enter configuration mode from the terminal.	**configure terminal**
Step 2 Enter the host configuration filename to be downloaded using MOP, rcp, or TFTP.	**boot host mop** *filename* [*mac-address*] [*interface*] **boot host** [**tftp** | **rcp**] *filename* [*ip-address*]
Step 3 Enable the device to load the host file automatically upon restart.	**service config**
Step 4 Exit configuration mode.	**end**
Step 5 Save the configuration file to your startup configuration.	**copy running-config startup-config**

If you do not specify a host configuration filename, the router uses its own name to form a host configuration filename by converting the name to all lowercase letters, removing all domain information, and appending *-confg*. If no host name information is available, the software uses the default host configuration filename *router-confg*. If you omit both the **tftp** and the **rcp** keywords, the software assumes that you are using TFTP to transfer the file and that the server whose IP address you specify supports TFTP. If you omit the address, the router uses the broadcast address.

You can specify more than one host configuration file. The Cisco IOS software tries them in order entered until it loads one successfully. This procedure can be useful for keeping files with different configuration information loaded on a network server.

Configuring the Router to Download Configuration Files at System Startup Example

In the following example, a router is configured to download the host configuration file *hostfile1* and the network configuration file *networkfile1*: The router uses TFTP and the broadcast address to obtain the file.

```
Router# configure terminal
Router(config)# boot host hostfile1
Router(config)# boot network networkfile1
Router(config)# service config
Router(config)# end
Router# copy running-config startup-config
```

CHAPTER 10

Configuration File Commands

This chapter provides detailed descriptions of the commands used to load and copy configuration files. Configuration files contain commands entered to customize the function of the Cisco IOS software.

NOTES

Commands in this chapter that have been replaced by new commands continue to perform their normal functions in the current release but are no longer documented. Support for these commands will cease in a future release. Table 10–1 maps the old commands with their replacements.

Table 10–1 *Mapping Old Commands to New Commands*

Old Command	New Command
configure network	copy rcp running-config (for an rcp server)
	copy tftp running-config (for a TFTP server)
configure overwrite-network	copy rcp startup-config (for an rcp server)
	copy tftp startup-config (for a TFTP server)
show configuration	show startup-config
write erase	erase startup-config
write memory	copy running-config startup-config
write network	copy running-config rcp (for an rcp server)
	copy running-config tftp (for a TFTP server)
write terminal	show running-config

For configuration information and examples, see Chapter 9, "Modifying, Downloading, and Maintaining Configuration Files."

BOOT BUFFERSIZE

To modify the buffer size used to load configuration files, use the **boot buffersize** global configuration command. Use the **no** form of this command to return to the default setting.

> **boot buffersize** *bytes*
> **no boot buffersize**

Syntax	Description
bytes	Specifies the size of the buffer to be used. There is no minimum or maximum size that can be specified.

Default

Buffer size of the NVRAM

Command Mode

Global configuration

Usage Guidelines

This command first appeared in Cisco IOS Release 10.0.

Normally, the Cisco IOS software uses a buffer the size of the system NVRAM to hold configuration commands read from the network. You can increase this size if you have a very complex configuration.

Example

The following example sets the buffer size to 64000 bytes:

```
boot buffersize 64000
```

BOOT CONFIG

On the Cisco 7000 family, to specify the device and filename of the configuration file from which the router configures itself during initialization (startup), use the **boot config** global configuration command. Use the **no** form of the command to remove this specification.

> **boot config** *device:filename*
> **no boot config**

Syntax	Description
device:	Device containing the configuration file. The colon (:) is required. Valid devices are as follows:
	• **bootflash**—Internal Flash memory.
	• **nvram**—Nonvolatile random-access memory (NVRAM). If you specify NVRAM, omit the filename.
	• **slot0**—First PCMCIA slot.
	• **slot1**—Second PCMCIA slot.
filename	Name of the configuration file. The configuration file must be an ASCII file. The maximum filename length is 63 characters.

Default

NVRAM (**nvram:**)

Command Mode

Global configuration

Usage Guidelines

This command first appeared in Cisco IOS Release 11.0.

Use this command only with the Cisco 7000 family. You set the CONFIG_FILE environment variable in the current running memory when you use the **boot config** command. This variable specifies the configuration file used for initialization (startup).

— **NOTES** —————————————————————————

When you use this global configuration command, you affect only the running configuration. You must save the environment variable setting to your startup configuration to place the information under ROM monitor control and to have the environment variable function as expected. Use the **copy running-config startup-config** command to save the environment variable from your running configuration to your startup configuration.

If you specify **nvram:** as the device, and it contains only a distilled version of the configuration, the Cisco IOS software displays an error message and does not update the CONFIG_FILE environment variable. (A distilled configuration is one that does not contain access lists.) If you specify a configuration file in the *filename* argument that does not exist or is not valid, the software displays an error message and does not update the CONFIG_FILE environment variable.

The router uses the NVRAM configuration during initialization when the CONFIG_FILE environment variable does not exist or when it is null (such as at first-time startup). If the software detects

Part II

Command Reference

a problem with NVRAM or the configuration it contains, the device enters **setup** mode. See Chapter 3, "Using Configuration Tools," for more information on the **setup** command facility.

When you use the **no** form of this command, the router returns to using the NVRAM configuration as the startup configuration.

Examples

In the following example, the first line specifies that a Cisco 7000 series router should use the configuration file *router-config* located in internal Flash memory to configure itself during initialization. The second line copies the specification to the startup configuration, ensuring that this specification will take effect upon the next reload:

```
Router (config)# boot config flash:router-config
Router (config)# end
Router# copy running-config startup-config
```

The following example instructs a Cisco 7500 series router to use the configuration file *router-config* located on the Flash memory card inserted in the second PCMCIA slot of the RSP card during initialization. The second line copies the specification to the startup configuration, ensuring that this specification will take effect upon the next reload:

```
Router (config)# boot config slot1:router-config
Router (config)# end
Router# copy running-config startup-config
```

Related Commands

copy running-config startup-config
show boot
show flash

BOOT HOST

To change the default name of the host configuration filename from which you want to load configuration commands, use the **boot host** global configuration command. Use the **no** form of this command to restore the host configuration filename to the default.

boot host mop *filename* [*mac-address*] [*interface*]
no boot host mop *filename* [*mac-address*] [*interface*]

boot host [**tftp** | **rcp**] *filename* [*ip-address*]
no boot host [**tftp** | **rcp**] *filename* [*ip-address*]

Syntax	Description
mop	Configures the router from a configuration file stored on a DEC MOP server.
filename	Name of the file from which you want to load configuration commands.

Syntax	Description
mac-address	(Optional) MAC address of the MOP server on which the file resides. If the MAC address argument is not included, a broadcast message is sent to all MOP boot servers. The first MOP server to indicate that it has the file is the server from which the router gets the boot image.
interface	(Optional) Interface on which the router should send MOP requests to reach the MOP server. The interface options are **async, dialer, ethernet, serial,** and **tunnel.** If the interface argument is not specified, a request is sent on all interfaces that have MOP enabled. The interface from which the first response is received is the interface used to load the software.
tftp	(Optional) Configures the router from a configuration file stored on a TFTP server.
rcp	(Optional) Configures the router from a configuration file stored on an rcp server.
ip-address	(Optional) IP address of the TFTP server on which the file resides. If omitted, this value defaults to the IP broadcast address of *255.255.255.255.*

Part II

Command Reference

Default

The router uses its host name to form a host configuration filename. To form this name, the router converts its name to all lowercase letters, removes all domain information, and appends *-confg.*

Command Mode

Global configuration

Usage Guidelines

This command first appeared in Cisco IOS Release 10.0.

Use the **service config** command to enable the loading of the specified configuration file at reboot time. Without this command, the router ignores the **boot host** command and uses the configuration information in NVRAM. If the configuration information in NVRAM is invalid or missing, the **service config** command is enabled automatically.

The network server will attempt to load two configuration files from remote hosts. The first is the network configuration file containing commands that apply to all network servers on a network. The second is the host configuration file containing commands that apply to one network server in particular.

Example

The following example sets the host filename to *wilma-confg* at address 192.168.7.19:

```
boot host /usr/local/tftpdir/wilma-confg 192.168.7.19
```

Related Commands

boot network
service config

BOOT NETWORK

To change the default name of the network configuration file from which you want to load configuration commands, use the **boot network** global configuration command. Use the **no** form of this command to restore the network configuration filename to the default.

> **boot network mop** *filename* [*mac-address*] [*interface*]
> **no boot network mop** *filename* [*mac-address*] [*interface*]
>
> **boot network** [**tftp** | **rcp**] *filename* [*ip-address*]
> **no boot network** [**tftp** | **rcp**] *filename* [*ip-address*]

Syntax	Description
mop	Configures the router to download the configuration file from a network server using the Digital Maintenance Operation Protocol (MOP).
filename	Name of the file from which you want to load configuration commands. The default filename is *network-config*.
mac-address	(Optional) If **mop** is specified, the MAC address of the network server on which the file resides. If the MAC address argument is not included, a broadcast message is sent to all MOP boot servers. The first server to indicate that it has the file is the server from which the router gets the boot image.
interface	(Optional) If **mop** is specified, the interface on which the router should send MOP requests to reach the server. The interface options are **async, dialer, ethernet, serial,** and **tunnel.** If the interface argument is not specified, a request will be sent on all interfaces that have MOP enabled, and the interface from which the first response is received will be used to load the software.
tftp	(Optional) Configures the router to download the configuration file from a network server using TFTP. If omitted and **rcp** is not specified, defaults to **tftp.**

Syntax	Description
rcp	(Optional) Configures the router to download the configuration file from a network server using rcp. If omitted, defaults to **tftp**.
ip-address	(Optional) If **rcp** or **tftp** is specified, the IP address of the network server on which the compressed image file resides. If the IP address is omitted, this value defaults to the IP broadcast address of 255.255.255.255.

Default

The default filename is *network-config*. The default transfer protocol type is TFTP, if neither **tftp** nor **rcp** is specified.

Command Mode

Global configuration

Usage Guidelines

This command first appeared in Cisco IOS Release 10.0.

When booting from a network server, routers ignore routing information, static IP routes, and bridging information. As a result, intermediate routers are responsible for handling rcp or TFTP requests. Before booting from a network server, verify that a server is available by using the **ping** command.

Use the **service config** command to enable the loading of the specified configuration file at reboot time. Without this command, the router ignores the **boot network** command and uses the configuration information in NVRAM. If the configuration information in NVRAM is invalid or missing, the **service config** command is enabled automatically.

The network server will attempt to load two configuration files from remote hosts. The first is the network configuration file containing commands that apply to all network servers on a network. Use the **boot network** command to identify the network configuration file.

The rcp software requires that a client send the remote username on each rcp request to the network server. When the **boot network rcp** command is executed, the Cisco IOS software sends the host name as the both the remote and local usernames. The rcp implementation searches for the configuration files to be used relative to the account directory of the remote username on the network server, if the server has a directory structure, for example, as do UNIX systems.

NOTES

For rcp, if you do not explicitly specify a remote username by issuing the **ip rcmd remote-username** command and the host name is used, an account for the host name must be defined on the destination server. If the network administrator of the destination server did not establish an account for the host name, this command will not execute successfully.

If you copy the system image to a personal computer used as a file server, the remote host computer must support the remote shell (rsh) protocol.

Examples

The following example changes the network configuration filename to *bridge_9.1* and uses the default broadcast address:

```
boot network bridge_9.1
service config
```

The following example changes the network configuration filename to *bridge_9.1*, specifies that rcp is to be used as the transport mechanism, and gives 172.16.1.111 as the IP address of the server on which the network configuration file resides:

```
boot network rcp bridge_9.1 172.16.1.111
service config
```

Related Commands

boot host
service config

CONFIGURE

To enter global configuration mode, use the **configure** privileged EXEC command. You must be in global configuration mode to enter global configuration commands.

    configure {terminal | memory | network}

Syntax	Description
terminal	Executes configuration commands from the terminal.
memory	For all platforms except the Cisco 7000 family, executes the commands stored in NVRAM.
	For the Cisco 7000 family, executes the configuration specified by the CONFIG_FILE environment variable.
network	The **copy rcp running-config** or **copy tftp running-config** command replaces the **configure network** command. If you use rcp, see the **copy rcp** command for more information on **copy rcp running-config**. If you use TFTP, see the **copy tftp** command for more information on **copy tftp running-config**.

Default

For all platforms except the Cisco 7000 family, there is no default.

For the Cisco 7000 family, the router uses the NVRAM configuration (if valid) when the CONFIG_FILE environment variable does not exist or is null (such as at first-time startup).

Command Mode

Privileged EXEC

Usage Guidelines

This command first appeared in Cisco IOS Release 10.0.

If you do not specify **terminal** or **memory,** the Cisco IOS software prompts you for the source of configuration commands. If you specify **terminal**, the software executes the commands you enter at the system prompts.

On all platforms except the Cisco 7000 family, if you specify **memory,** the software executes the commands located in NVRAM. On the Cisco 7000 family, if you specify **memory,** the router executes the commands pointed to by the CONFIG_FILE environment variable. The CONFIG_FILE environment variable specifies the device and filename of the configuration file that the router uses to configure itself during initialization. Possible devices are as follows:

- **bootflash:**—This device is the internal Flash memory.
- **nvram:**—This device is the router's NVRAM.
- **slot0:**—This device is the first PCMCIA slot. This device is the initial default device.
- **slot1:**—This device is the second PCMCIA slot.

When the CONFIG_FILE environment variable specifies NVRAM, the router executes the NVRAM configuration only if it is an entire configuration, not a distilled version. A *distilled configuration* is one that does not contain access lists.

To view the contents of the CONFIG_FILE environment variable, use the **show boot** command. To modify the CONFIG_FILE environment variable, use the **boot config** command and then save your changes by issuing the **copy running-config startup-config** command.

After you enter the **configure** command, the system prompt changes from `<router-name>#` to `<router-name>(config)#`, indicating that you are in global configuration mode. To leave global configuration mode and return to the privileged EXEC prompt, press **Ctrl-Z.**

> **NOTES**

The commands **configure net network** and **configure net host** no longer clear line parameters.

Examples

In the following example, a router is configured from the terminal:

```
Router# configure

Configuring from terminal, memory, or network [terminal]?
Enter configuration commands, one per line. End with CTRL/Z.
Router(config)#
```

In the following example, a Cisco 7000 family router executes the commands pointed to by the CONFIG_FILE environment variable:

```
configure memory
```

Related Commands

boot config
copy running-config startup-config
show boot
show running-config
show startup-config

CONFIGURE OVERWRITE-NETWORK

The **copy rcp startup-config** or **copy tftp startup-config** command replaces the **configure overwrite-network** command. See the **copy** command in Chapter 14, "Router Memory Commands," for more information on **copy rcp startup-config** and **copy tftp startup-config**.

ERASE STARTUP-CONFIG

To erase a saved configuration, use the **erase startup-config** EXEC command. The **erase startup-config** command replaces the **write erase** command.

        erase startup-config

Syntax   Description

This command has no arguments or keywords.

Command Mode

EXEC

Usage Guidelines

This command first appeared in Cisco IOS Release 11.0.

On all platforms except the Cisco 7000 family, this command erases the startup configuration in NVRAM.

When you use the **erase startup-config** command on the Cisco 7000 family, the router erases or deletes the configuration pointed to by CONFIG_FILE environment variable. The CONFIG_FILE environment variable specifies the configuration file used for initialization. If the CONFIG_FILE environment variable points to NVRAM, the router erases NVRAM. If the CONFIG_FILE environment variable specifies a Flash memory device and configuration filename, the Cisco IOS software deletes the configuration file. That is, the software marks the file as "deleted."

Examples

The following example erases the configuration located in NVRAM or specified by the CONFIG_FILE environment variable:

```
erase startup-config
```

Related Commands

boot config
delete
show boot
show startup-config
undelete

SERVICE COMPRESS-CONFIG

To compress configuration files, use the **service compress-config** global configuration command. To disable compression, use the **no** form of this command.

service compress-config
no service compress-config

Syntax   Description

This command has no arguments or keywords.

Default

Disabled

Command Mode

Global configuration

Usage Guidelines

This command first appeared in Cisco IOS Release 10.0.

If the file compression completes successfully, the following message is displayed:

```
Compressing configuration from configuration-size to compressed-size
[OK]
```

If the boot ROMs do not recognize a compressed configuration, the following message is displayed:

```
Boot ROMs do not support NVRAM compression Config NOT written to NVRAM
```

If the file compression fails, the following message is displayed:

```
Error trying to compress nvram
```

One way to determine whether a configuration file will compress enough to fit into NVRAM is to use a text editor to enter the configuration, then use the UNIX **compress** command to check the compressed size. To get a closer approximation of the compression ratio, use the UNIX command **compress -b12**.

Once the configuration file has been compressed, the router functions normally. A **show startup-config** command would uncompress the configuration before displaying it. At boot time, the system would recognize that the configuration file was compressed, uncompress it, and proceed normally.

To disable compression of the configuration file, enter configuration mode and specify the **no service compress-config** command. Then enter the **copy running-config startup-config** command. The router displays an OK message if it is able to write the uncompressed configuration to NVRAM. Otherwise, the router displays an error message indicating that the configuration is too large to store. If the configuration file is larger than the physical NVRAM, the following message is displayed:

```
##Configuration too large to fit uncompressed in NVRAM Truncate configuration? [confirm]
```

To truncate and save the configuration, type **Y**. To not truncate and not save the configuration, type **N**.

Example

In the following example, the configuration file is compressed:

```
service compress-config
```

Related Commands

show startup-config

SERVICE CONFIG

To enable autoloading of configuration files from a network server, use the **service config** global configuration command. Use the **no** form of this command to restore the default.

service config
no service config

Syntax   Description

This command has no arguments or keywords.

Default

Disabled, except on systems without NVRAM or with invalid or incomplete information in NVRAM. In these cases, autoloading of configuration files from a network server is enabled automatically.

Command Mode

Global configuration

Usage Guidelines

This command first appeared in Cisco IOS Release 10.0.

Usually, the **service config** command is used in conjunction with the **boot host** or **boot network** command. You must enter the **service config** command to enable the router to configure the system automatically from the file specified by the **boot host** or **boot network** command.

The **service config** command also can be used without the **boot host** or **boot network** command. If you do not specify host or network configuration filenames, the router uses the default configuration files. The default network configuration file is *network-confg*. The default host configuration file is *host-confg*, where host is the host name of the router. If the Cisco IOS software cannot resolve its host name, the default host configuration file is *router-confg*.

Example

In the following example, a router is configured to autoload the default host configuration file:

```
service config
```

Related Commands

boot host
boot network

SHOW CONFIGURATION

The **show startup-config** command replaces this command. Refer to the description of the **show startup-config** command for more information.

SHOW FILE

To display the configuration stored in a specified file on the Cisco 7000 family, use the **show file** EXEC command.

show file [*device*:] *filename*

Syntax	Description
device:	(Optional) Device containing the configuration file. The colon (:) is required. Valid devices are as follows:

- **bootflash**—Internal Flash memory.
- **slot0**—First PCMCIA slot. This device is the initial default device.
- **slot1**—Second PCMCIA slot.
- **nvram**—Router's NVRAM. If you specify NVRAM, omit the filename. The colon (:) is required.
- **slavebootflash**—Internal Flash memory on the slave RSP card of a Cisco 7507 or Cisco 7513 configured for HSA.
- **slaveslot0**—First PCMCIA slot of the slave RSP card on a Cisco 7507 or Cisco 7513 configured for HSA.
- **slaveslot1**—Second PCMCIA slot of the slave RSP card on a Cisco 7507 or Cisco 7513 configured for HSA.
- **slavenvram**—NVRAM of the slave RSP card on a Cisco 7507 or Cisco 7513 configured for HSA. If you specify the slave NVRAM, omit the filename.

If you omit the *device*: argument, the system uses the default device specified by the **cd** command.

filename	Name of the file. The file can be of any type. The maximum filename length is 63 characters.

Command Mode
EXEC

Usage Guidelines
This command first appeared in Cisco IOS Release 11.0.

Use this command for the Cisco 7000 family. When showing the configuration, the Cisco IOS software informs you whether the displayed configuration is a complete configuration or a distilled version. A distilled configuration is one that does not contain access lists.

Sample Display
The following is sample output from the **show file** command:

```
Router# show file slot0:router-config

Using 534 out of 129016 bytes
!
version 10.3
```

```
!
hostname Cyclops
!
enable-password xxxx
service pad
!
boot system dross-system 172.16.13.111
boot system dross-system 172.16.1.111
!
exception dump 172.16.13.111
!
no ip ipname-lookup
!
decnet routing 13.1
decnet node-type area
decnet max-address 1023
!
interface Ethernet 0
ip address 172.16.1.1 255.255.255.0
ip helper-address 172.31.1.0
ip accounting
ip gdp
decnet cost 3
!
ip domain-name CISCO.COM
ip name-server 255.255.255.255
!
end
```

Related Commands

boot buffersize
cd
configure
dir

SHOW RUNNING-CONFIG

To display the configuration information currently running on the terminal, use the **show running-config** EXEC command. This command replaces the **write terminal** command.

     show running-config

Syntax   Description

This command has no arguments or keywords.

Command Mode

EXEC

Usage Guidelines

This command first appeared in Cisco IOS Release 11.0.

Use this command in conjunction with the **show startup-config** command to compare the information in running memory to the information stored in NVRAM or in a location specified by the CONFIG_FILE environment variable. On the Cisco 7000 family, this variable specifies the configuration file used for initialization (startup). Use the **boot config** command in conjunction with the **copy running-config startup-config** command to set the CONFIG_FILE environment variable.

Sample Display

The following partial sample output displays the running configuration:

```
Router2# show running-config

Building configuration...

Current configuration:
!
version 11.2
no service udp-small-servers
no service tcp-small-servers
!
hostname Router2
!
...
!
end
```

Related Commands

boot config
configure
copy running-config startup-config
show startup-config

SHOW STARTUP-CONFIG

To display the contents of NVRAM (if present and valid) or to show the configuration file pointed to by the CONFIG_FILE environment variable, use the **show startup-config** EXEC command. This command replaces the **show configuration** command.

> show startup-config

Syntax   Description

This command has no arguments or keywords.

Command Mode

EXEC

Usage Guidelines

This command first appeared in Cisco IOS Release 11.0.

NVRAM stores the configuration information on the network server in text form as configuration commands. For all platforms except the Cisco 7000 family, the **show startup-config** command shows the version number of the software used when you last executed the **copy running-config startup-config** command.

For the Cisco 7000 family, the **show startup-config** command shows the configuration file specified by the CONFIG_FILE environment variable. The Cisco IOS software informs you whether the displayed configuration is a complete configuration or a distilled version. A distilled configuration is one that does not contain access lists. If the CONFIG_FILE environment variable does not exist or is not valid, the software displays the NVRAM configuration (if it is a valid, complete configuration).

Sample Displays

The following sample output from the **show startup-config** command displays the contents of NVRAM:

```
Router# show startup-config

Using 5057 out of 32768 bytes
!
version 10.3
!
enable-password xxxx
service pad
!
boot system dross-system 172.16.13.111
boot system dross-system 172.16.1.111
!
exception dump 172.16.13.111
!
no ip ipname-lookup
!
decnet routing 13.1
decnet node-type area
decnet max-address 1023
!
interface Ethernet 0
ip address 172.16.1.1 255.255.255.0
ip helper-address 172.30.1.0
ip accounting
ip gdp
decnet cost 3
```

```
!
ip domain-name CISCO.COM
ip name-server 255.255.255.255
!
end
```

The following is partial sample output from the **show startup-config** command when the configuration file has been compressed:

```
Router# show startup-config

Using 21542 out of 65536 bytes, uncompressed size = 142085 bytes
!
version 9.22
service compress-config
!
hostname rose
!
boot system flash gs7-k.sthormod_clean
boot system rom
```

Related Commands

configure
copy running-config startup-config
description
service compress-config
show boot
show running-config

WRITE ERASE

The **erase startup-config** command replaces this command. Refer to the description of the **erase startup-config** command for more information.

WRITE MEMORY

The **copy running-config startup-config** command replaces this command. Refer to the description of the **copy** command in Chapter 14, "Router Memory Commands," for more information on **copy running-config startup-config**.

WRITE NETWORK

The **copy running-config rcp** or **copy running-config tftp** command replaces this command. See the description of the **copy** command in Chapter 14, "Router Memory Commands," for more information on **copy running-config rcp** or **copy running-config tftp**.

WRITE TERMINAL

The **show running-config** command replaces this command. Refer to the description of **show running-config** for more information.

## CHAPTER 11

Loading and Maintaining System Images and Microcode

This chapter describes how to load and maintain system images and microcode. System images contain the system software. Microcode images contain microcode to be downloaded to various hardware devices.

To benefit most from the instructions and organization of this chapter, your router must contain a minimal configuration that allows you to interact with the system software. You can create a basic configuration file using the **setup** command facility. See the user guide for your hardware platform for more information on using **setup** at first-time startup. See the "Using Setup for Configuration Changes" section in Chapter 3, "Using Configuration Tools," for information on using **setup** after first-time startup.

For a complete description of the system image and microcode commands mentioned in this chapter, see Chapter 12, "System Image and Microcode Commands."

NOTES

One or more of the commands that previously appeared in this chapter have been replaced by new commands. Table 11–1 maps the old commands to their replacements. The old commands continue to perform their normal functions in the current release, but support for these commands will cease in a future release.

Table 11-1 *Mapping Old Commands to New Commands*

Old Command	New Command
copy erase flash	erase flash
copy verify or copy verify flash	verify flash (on all systems except Cisco 1600 series, Cisco 3600 series, Cisco 7000 family) verify (on Cisco 1600 series, Cisco 3600 series, Cisco 7000 family)
copy verify bootflash	verify bootflash

SYSTEM IMAGES AND MICROCODE TASK LIST

You can perform the tasks involving images described in the following sections:

- Displaying System Image Information
- Understanding Images
- Copying Images from Flash Memory to a Network Server
- Copying Images from a Network Server to Flash Memory
- Copying Images between Local Flash Memory Devices
- Specifying the Startup System Image in the Configuration File
- Recovering a System Image Using Xmodem or Ymodem (Cisco 1600 series and Cisco 3600 series only)
- Loading and Displaying Microcode Images

NOTES

These tasks assume you have a minimal configuration that you want to modify.

DISPLAYING SYSTEM IMAGE INFORMATION

Perform the following tasks in EXEC mode to display information about system software:

Task	Command
Step 1 List the contents of the BOOT environment variable, the name of the configuration file pointed to by the CONFIG_FILE environment variable, and the contents of the BOOTLDR environment variable.	**show boot** (Cisco 3600 series, Cisco 7000 family only)

Task	Command
Step 2 List information about Flash memory, including system image filenames and amounts of memory used and remaining.	**show flash**
Step 3 List the names of the Flash devices currently supported on the router.	**show flash devices** (Cisco 7000 family only)
Step 4 List information about Flash memory, including system image filenames, amounts of memory used and remaining, and Flash partitions.	**show** *device*: [**all** | **chips** | **detailed** | **err** | **partition** *number* | **summary**] (Cisco 1600 series and Cisco 3600 series)
	show flash [**all** | **chips** | **filesys**] [*device*:] (Cisco 7000 family only)
	show flash [**all** | **chips** | **detailed** | **err** | **partition** *number* [**all** | **chips** | **detailed** | **err**] | **summary**] (all other platforms)
Step 5 Display microcode information.	**show microcode**
Step 6 List the system software release version, configuration register setting, and other information.	**show version**

UNDERSTANDING IMAGES

System images contain the Cisco IOS software. Your router already has an image on it when you receive it. However, you might want to load a different image onto the router at some point. For example, you might wish to upgrade your software to the latest release or use the same version of the software for all the routers in a network.

Types of Images

The following are two main types of images your router may use:

- System image—The complete Cisco IOS software. This image is loaded when your router boots and is used most of the time.

  On all platforms except the Cisco 1600 series, Cisco 3600 series, and Cisco 7000 family, the image is located in Flash memory. See Table 11–2 for places where the images can be located on the Cisco 1600 series, Cisco 3600 series, and Cisco 7000 family routers.

Table 11–2   *Possible System and Boot Image Locations*

Router	Flash (flash:)	Bootflash (bootflash:)	first PCMCIA slot (slot0:)	Second PCMCIA slot (slot1:)
Cisco 7000 family		yes	yes	yes
Cisco 3600 series	yes		yes	yes
Cisco 1600 series	yes			

Refer to your hardware documentation for information about where these images are located by default.

- Boot image—A subset of the Cisco IOS software. This image is used to perform network booting or to load Cisco IOS images onto the router. This image is also used if the router cannot find a valid system image. Depending on your platform, this image might be called xboot image, rxboot image, bootstrap image, or boot loader/helper image.

On some platforms, the boot image is contained in ROM. In others, the boot image can be stored in Flash memory. On these platforms, you can specify which image should be used as the boot image using the **boot bootldr** command.

Refer to your hardware documentation for information about the boot image used on your router.

Image Naming Conventions

You can identify the platform, features, and image location by the name of the image. The naming convention for images that are stored on a UNIX system is as follows:

platform-features-type

The *platform* variable indicates which platforms can use this image. Examples of *platform* variables are rsp (Cisco 7000 series with RSP7000 and Cisco 7500 series), c1600 (Cisco 1600 series), or c1005 (Cisco 1005).

The *feature* variable identifies the feature sets supported by the image.

The *type* field can contain the following characters:

- f—The image runs from Flash memory.
- m—The image runs from RAM.
- r—The image runs from ROM.
- l—The image is relocatable.
- z—The image is zip compressed.
- x—The image is mzip compressed.

COPYING IMAGES FROM FLASH MEMORY TO A NETWORK SERVER

You can copy system images from Flash memory to a TFTP server or to an rcp server. You can use this server copy of the system image as a backup copy, or you can use it to verify that the copy in Flash is the same as the original file on disk. The following sections describe these tasks:

- Copying an Image from Flash or Bootflash Memory to a TFTP Server
- Copying an Image from Flash Memory to an rcp Server

The protocol you use depends on which type of server you are using. The rcp transport mechanism provides faster performance and more reliable delivery of data than TFTP. These improvements are possible because the rcp transport mechanism is built on and uses the Transmission Control Protocol/Internet Protocol (TCP/IP) stack, which is connection-oriented.

Copying an Image from Flash or Bootflash Memory to a TFTP Server

You can copy a system image to a TFTP network server. In some implementations of TFTP, you must first create a "dummy" file on the TFTP server and give it read, write, and execute permissions before copying a file over it. Refer to your TFTP documentation for more information.

To copy a system image to a TFTP network server, perform the following tasks in EXEC mode:

Task		Command
Step 1	(Optional) If you do not already know it, learn the exact spelling of the system image filename in Flash memory.	**show flash all**
		show flash [*device*:] (Cisco 7000 family only)
	On the Cisco 1600 series, Cisco 3600 series, and Cisco 7000 family, you can learn the spelling of the system image filename on a specified Flash memory device.	**show** *device*: **all** (Cisco 1600 series and Cisco 3600 series)
		show bootflash (Cisco 4500 series only)
	On a Cisco 4500 series, you can learn the spelling of the boot image filename in boot Flash memory.	

Task	Command
Step 2 Copy the system image from Flash memory to a TFTP server. On the Cisco 1600 series, Cisco 3600 series, and Cisco 7000 family, you can copy the system image from a specified Flash memory device to a TFTP server. On the Cisco 4500 series, you can copy the boot image from boot Flash memory to a TFTP server.	**copy flash tftp** **copy** *device*:[*partition-number*:][*filename*] **tftp** (Cisco 1600 series and Cisco 3600 series only) **copy** *file-id* **tftp** (Cisco 7000 family only) or **copy bootflash tftp** (Cisco 4500 series only)
Step 3 When prompted, enter the IP address or domain name of the TFTP server.	*ip-address* or *name*
Step 4 When prompted, enter the filename of the system image in Flash memory.	*filename*

To stop the copy process, press **Ctrl-^**.

In the output, an exclamation point (!) indicates that the copy process is taking place. Each exclamation point (!) indicates that ten packets have been transferred successfully.

Copying Flash TFTP Example Using Show Flash All

The following example uses the **show flash all** command to learn the name of the system image file and the **copy flash tftp** command to copy the system image to a TFTP server. The name of the system image file (xk09140z) is listed near the end of the **show flash all** output.

```
Router# show flash all
2048K bytes of flash memory on embedded flash (in XX).
  ROM   socket   code   bytes        name
    0     U42     89BD   0x40000    INTEL 28F020
    1     U44     89BD   0x40000    INTEL 28F020
    2     U46     89BD   0x40000    INTEL 28F020
    3     U48     89BD   0x40000    INTEL 28F020
    4     U41     89BD   0x40000    INTEL 28F020
    5     U43     89BD   0x40000    INTEL 28F020
    6     U45     89BD   0x40000    INTEL 28F020
    7     U47     89BD   0x40000    INTEL 28F020
  security jumper(12V) is installed,
  flash memory is programmable.
file   offset     length      name
 0     0x40       1204637     xk09140z
  [903848/2097152 bytes free]
```

```
Router# copy flash tftp
IP address of remote host [255.255.255.255]? 172.16.13.110
filename to write on tftp host? xk09140z
writing xk09140z !!!!...
successful tftp write.
Router#
```

Copying Flash TFTP Example for Cisco 7000 Family

The following example uses the **show flash** [*device*:] command on a Cisco 7000 family to display the name of the system image file to copy. In the example, the Flash memory device containing the system image is the second PCMCIA slot. The file to copy is *test*. The example uses the **copy** *file-id* **tftp** command to copy *test* to a TFTP server.

```
Router#show flash slot1:

-#- ED --type-- --crc--- -seek-- nlen -length- -----date/time------ name
 1  .. 1         46A11866 2036C    4    746      May 16 1995 16:24:37 test

Router#copy slot1:test tftp
IP address of remote host [255.255.255.255]? 172.16.13.110
filename to write on tftp host? [test]y
writing test!!!!...
successful tftp write.
```

Copying by Specifying a Source Partition Number (Cisco 1600 series and Cisco 3600 series) Example

In this example, the file *your-ios* is copied from partition 2 of the Flash memory PC card in slot 0 of a Cisco 3600 series router to the TFTP server at 172.23.1.129. The source partition number is specified in the command line. The file will be saved with the name *server-ios* in the /sysadmin/images directory.

For the Cisco 1600 series router, the process will be the same except the device used in the **copy** command must be **flash:** and the directory listed will show System Flash rather than slot 0.

```
Router# copy slot0:2 tftp

PCMCIA Slot0 flash directory, partition 2:
File  Length    Name/status
  1   3141700   your-ios
[3141764 bytes used, 1052540 available, 4194304 total]
Address or name of remote host [172.23.1.129]?
Source file name? your-ios
Destination file name [your-ios]? /sysadmin/images/server-ios
Verifying checksum for 'your-ios' (file # 1)...  OK
Copy 'your-ios' from Flash to server
  as '/sysadmin/images/server-ios'? [yes/no] yes
!!!!!!!!!!!!!!!!!!!!!!!!!!!!!!!!!!!!!!!!!!!!!!!!!!!!!!!!!!!!!!!!!!!!!!!!!!!!!!!!!!!!
!!!!!!!!!!!!!!!!!!!!!!!!!!!!!!!!!!!!!!!!!!!!!!!!!!!!!!!!!!!!!!!!!!!!!!!!!!!!!!!!!!!!
!!!!!!!!!!!!!!!!!!!!!!!!!!!!!!!!!!!!!!!!!!!!!!!!!!!!!!!!!!!!!!!!!!!!!!!!!!!!!!!!!!!!
!!!!!!!!!!!!!!!!!!!!!!!!!!!!!!!!!!!!!!!!!!!!!!!!!!!!!!!!!!!!!!!!!!!!!!!!!!!!!!!!!!!!
```

```
!!!!!!!!!!!!!!!!!!!!!!!!!!!!!!!!!!!!!!!!!!!!!!!!!!!!!!!!!!!!!!!!!!!!!!!!!!!!!!!!!!!!!!!!!!!!
!!!!!!!!!!!!!!!!!!!!!!!!!!!!!!!!!!!!!!!!!!!!!!!!!!!!!!!!!!!!!!!!!!!!!!!!!!!!!!!!!!!!!!!!!!!!
!!!!!!!!!!!!!!!!!!!!!!!!!!!!!!!!!!!!!!!!!!!!!!!!!!!!!!!!!!!!!!!!!!!!!!!!!!!!!!!!!!!!!!!!!!!!
Upload to server done
Flash device copy took 00:00:41 [hh:mm:ss]
```

Copying by Specifying a Source Partition and Filename (Cisco 1600 series and Cisco 3600 series)

In this example, the file *your-ios* is copied from partition 4 of the Flash memory PC card in slot 0 of a Cisco 3600 series router to the TFTP server at 172.23.1.129. Because all required information is specified in the command line, the software does not display Flash memory contents. The file will be saved with the name *c3640-j-mz* in the dirt/images directory relative to the directory of the remote username.

For the Cisco 1600 series router, the process will be the same, except the device used in the **copy** command must be **flash:**

```
Router# copy slot0:4:your-ios tftp

Address or name of remote host [172.23.1.129]?
Destination file name [your-ios]? dirt/images/c3640-j-mz
Verifying checksum for 'your-ios' (file # 2)...  OK
Copy 'your-ios' from Flash to server
  as 'dirt/images/c3640-j-mz'? [yes/no] yes
!!!!!!!!!!!!!!!!!!!!!!!!!!!!!!!!!!!!!!!!!!!!!!!!!!!!!!!!!!!!!!!!!!!!!!!!!!!!!!!!!!!!!!!!!!!!
!!!!!!!!!!!!!!!!!!!!!!!!!!!!!!!!!!!!!!!!!!!!!!!!!!!!!!!!!!!!!!!!!!!!!!!!!!!!!!!!!!!!!!!!!!!!
!!!!!!!!!!!!!!!!!!!!!!!!!!!!!!!!!!!!!!!!!!!!!!!!!!!!!!!!!!!!!!!!!!!!!!!!!!!!!!!!!!!!!!!!!!!!
!!!!!!!!!!!!!!!!!!!!!!!!!!!!!!!!!!!!!!!!!!!!!!!!!!!!!!!!!!!!!!!!!!!!!!!!!!!!!
Upload to server done
Flash device copy took 00:00:20 [hh:mm:ss]
```

Copying by Not Specifying a Source Partition (Cisco 1600 series and Cisco 3600 series)

In this example, the file *your-ios* is copied from partition 1 of the Flash memory PC card in slot 0 of a Cisco 3600 series router to the TFTP server at 172.23.1.129. Because the partition number and filename are not specified, the software displays the contents of the Flash memory PC card. The file will be saved with the name *your-ios* in the dirt/sysadmin directory relative to the directory of the remote username.

For the Cisco 1600 series router, the process will be the same except the device used in the **copy** command must be **flash:** and the directories listed will show System Flash rather than slot 0.

```
Router# copy slot0: tftp

PCMCIA Slot0 flash

Partition   Size    Used     Free     Bank-Size   State        Copy Mode
    1       4096K   1671K    2424K    4096K       Read/Write   Direct
    2       4096K   3068K    1027K    4096K       Read/Write   Direct
    3       4096K   1671K    2424K    4096K       Read/Write   Direct
    4       4096K   3825K     270K    4096K       Read/Write   Direct
```

```
[Type ?<no> for partition directory; ? for full directory; q to abort]
Which partition? [default = 1]

PCMCIA Slot0 flash directory, partition 1:
File  Length    Name/status
   1   1711088  your-ios
[1711152 bytes used, 2483152 available, 4194304 total]

Address or name of remote host [172.23.1.129]?
Source file name? your-ios
Destination file name [your-ios]? dirt/sysadmin/your-ios
Verifying checksum for 'your-ios' (file # 1)...  OK
Copy 'your-ios' from Flash to server
  as 'dirt/sysadmin/ios-2'? [yes/no] yes
!!!!!!!!!!!!!!!!!!!!!!!!!!!!!!!!!!!!!!!!!!!!!!!!!!!!!!!!!!!!!!!!!!!!!!!!!!!!!!!!!!!!!!!!!!!
!!!!!!!!!!!!!!!!!!!!!!!!!!!!!!!!!!!!!!!!!!!!!!!!!!!!!!!!!!!!!!!!!!!!!!!!!!!!!!!!!!!!!!!!!!!
!!!!!!!!!!!!!!!!!!!!!!!!!!!!!!!!!!!!!!!!!!!!!!!!!!!!!!!!!!!!!!!!!!!!!!!!!!!!!!!!!!!!!!!!!!!
!!!!!!!!!!!!!!!!!!!!!!!!!!!!!!!!!!!!!!!!!!!!!!!!!!!!!!!!!!!!!!!!!!!!!!!!!!!!!
Upload to server done
Flash device copy took 00:00:23 [hh:mm:ss]
```

Copying an Image from Flash Memory to an rcp Server

You can copy a system image from Flash memory to an rcp network server.

If you copy the configuration file to a personal computer used as a file server, the computer must support rsh.

To stop the copy process, press **Ctrl-^**.

Understanding the rcp Username

The rcp protocol requires a client to send a remote username on each rcp request to a server. When you copy an image from the router to a server using rcp, the Cisco IOS software sends the first valid username in the following list:

1. The username set by the **ip rcmd remote-username** command, if the command is configured.

2. The remote username associated with the current TTY (terminal) process. For example, if the user is connected to the router through Telnet and was authenticated through the **username** command, the router software sends the Telnet username as the remote username.

3. The router host name.

For the rcp copy request to execute successfully, an account must be defined on the network server for the remote username. If the server has a directory structure, the configuration file or image is written or copied relative to the directory associated with the remote username on the server. The path for all files and images to be copied begins at the remote user's home directory. Use the **ip rcmd remote-username** command to specify which directory on the server to use. For example, if the system image resides in the home directory of a user on the server, you can specify that user's name as the remote username.

If you are writing to the server, the rcp server must be properly configured to accept the rcp write request from the user on the router. For UNIX systems, you must add an entry to the *.rhosts* file for the remote user on the rcp server. For example, suppose the router contains the following configuration lines:

```
hostname Rtr1
ip rcmd remote-username User0
```

If the router's IP address translates to Router1.company.com, then the *.rhosts* file for User0 on the rcp server should contain the following line:

```
Router1.company.com Rtr1
```

Refer to the documentation for your rcp server for more details.

Copying from Flash Memory to an rcp Server Tasks

To copy the system image from Flash memory to a network server, perform the following tasks:

Task	Command
Step 1 (Optional) If you do not already know it, learn the exact spelling of the system image filename in Flash memory.	**show flash all**
	show flash [*device*:] (Cisco 7000 family only)
On the Cisco 1600 series, Cisco 3600 series, and Cisco 7000 family, you can learn the spelling of the system image filename on a specified Flash memory device.	**show** *device*: **all** (Cisco 1600 series and Cisco 3600 series)
	show bootflash (Cisco 4500 series only)
On a Cisco 4500 series, you can learn the spelling of the boot image filename in boot Flash memory	
Step 2 Enter configuration mode from the terminal. This step is required only if you are going to override the default remote username (see Step 3).	**configure terminal**
Step 3 Specify the remote username. This step is optional, but recommended.	**ip rcmd remote-username** *username*
Step 4 Exit configuration mode.	**end**

Task	Command
Step 5 Copy the system image from Flash memory to a network server using rcp. On the Cisco 1600 series, Cisco 3600 series, and Cisco 7000 family, you can copy the system image from a specified Flash memory device to an rcp server. On the Cisco 4500 series, you can copy the boot image from boot Flash memory to an rcp server.	**copy flash rcp** **copy** *device*:[*partition-number*:][*filename*] **rcp** (Cisco 1600 series and Cisco 3600 series only) **copy** *file-id* **rcp** (Cisco 7000 family only) or **copy bootflash rcp** (Cisco 4500 series only)
Step 6 When prompted, enter the IP address or domain name of the rcp server.	*ip-address* or *name*
Step 7 When prompted, enter the filename of the system image in Flash memory.	*filename*

To stop the copy process, press **Ctrl-^**.

Copying Flash rcp Example

The following example copies the system image *c5200-ds-l* to a network server using rcp:

```
Router# configure terminal
Router(config)# ip rcmd remote-username netadmin1
Router(config)# end
Router# copy flash rcp
System flash directory:
File name/status
  1 c5200-ds-l
[2076072 bytes used, 21080 bytes available]

Name of file to copy? c5200-ds-l
Address or name of remote host [UNKNOWN]? 172.16.1.111
File name to write to? c5200-ds-l
Verifying checksum for 'c5200-ds-l' (file # 1)...[OK]
Writing c5200-ds-l -
```

Copying File-id rcp Example for Cisco 7000 Family

The following example copies a system image file called *test* from the second PCMCIA slot on a Cisco 7000 family router to a network server using rcp:

```
Router# configure terminal
Router(config)# ip rcmd remote-username netadmin1
Router(config)# end
```

```
Router# copy slot1:test rcp
System flash directory:
File name/status
  1 test
[2076072 bytes used, 21080 bytes available]

Name of file to copy? [test] y
Address or name of remote host [UNKNOWN]? 172.16.1.111
File name to write to? test
Verifying checksum for 'test' (file # 1)...[OK]
Writing test!!!!...
```

The exclamation point (!) indicates that the copy process is taking place. Each exclamation point (!) indicates that ten packets have been transferred successfully.

Copying by not Specifying a Source Partition and Filename (Cisco 1600 series and Cisco 3600)

In this example, the file *your-ios* is copied from partition 1 of the Flash memory PC card in slot 1 of a Cisco 3600 series router to the rcp server at 172.23.1.129. Because the partition number and filename are not specified, the software displays the contents of the Flash memory PC card. The file will be saved with the name *your-ios* in the /sysadmin/images directory.

For the Cisco 1600 series router, the process will be the same except the device used in the **copy** command must be **flash:** and the directory listed will be the "System flash directory."

```
Router# copy slot1: rcp

PCMCIA Slot1 flash directory:
File  Length   Name/status
  1   1711088  your-ios
[1711152 bytes used, 2483152 available, 4194304 total]

Address or name of remote host [172.23.1.129]?
Source file name? your-ios
Destination file name [your-ios]? /sysadmin/images/your-ios
Verifying checksum for 'your-ios' (file # 1)...  OK
Copy 'your-ios' from Flash to server
  as '/sysadmin/images/your-ios'? [yes/no] yes
Writing /sysadmin/images/your-ios
!!!!!!!!!!!!!!!!!!!!!!!!!!!!!!!!!!!!!!!!!!!!!!!!!!!!!!!!!!!!!!!!!!!!!!!!!!!!!!!!!!!
!!!!!!!!!!!!!!!!!!!!!!!!!!!!!!!!!!!!!!!!!!!!!!!!!!!!!!!!!!!!!!!!!!!!!!!!!!!!!!!!!!!
!!!!!!!!!!!!!!!!!!!!!!!!!!!!!!!!!!!!!!!!!!!!!!!!!!!!!!!!!!!!!!!!!!!!!!!!!!!!!!!!!!!
!!!!!!!!!!!!!!!!!!!!!!!!!!!!!!!!!!!!!!!!!!!!!!!!!!!!!!!!!!!!!!!
Upload to server done
Flash device copy took 00:00:08 [hh:mm:ss]
```

Copying by Specifying a Source Partition and Filename (Cisco 1600 series and Cisco 3600 series)

In this example, the file *your-ios* is copied from partition 1 of the Flash memory PC card in slot 1 of a Cisco 3600 series router to the rcp server at 172.23.1.129. Because all required information is specified in the command line, the software does not display Flash memory contents. The file will be saved with the name *your-ios* in the /sysadmin/images directory.

For the Cisco 1600 series router, the process will be the same except the device used in the **copy** command must be **flash:**

```
Router# copy slot1:1:your-ios rcp

Address or name of remote host [172.23.1.129]?
Destination file name [your-ios]? /sysadmin/images/your-ios
Verifying checksum for 'your-ios' (file # 1)...  OK
Copy 'your-ios' from Flash to server
  as '/sysadmin/images/your-ios'? [yes/no] yes
Writing /sysadmin/images/your-ios
!!!!!!!!!!!!!!!!!!!!!!!!!!!!!!!!!!!!!!!!!!!!!!!!!!!!!!!!!!!!!!!!!!!!!!!!!!!!!!!!!!!!!
!!!!!!!!!!!!!!!!!!!!!!!!!!!!!!!!!!!!!!!!!!!!!!!!!!!!!!!!!!!!!!!!!!!!!!!!!!!!!!!!!!!!!
!!!!!!!!!!!!!!!!!!!!!!!!!!!!!!!!!!!!!!!!!!!!!!!!!!!!!!!!!!!!!!!!!!!!!!!!!!!!!!!!!!!!!
!!!!!!!!!!!!!!!!!!!!!!!!!!!!!!!!!!!!!!!!!!!!!!!!!!!!!!!!!!!!!!!!!!!!!!!!!
Upload to server done
Flash device copy took 00:00:08 [hh:mm:ss]
```

COPYING IMAGES FROM A NETWORK SERVER TO FLASH MEMORY

You can copy system images or boot image from a TFTP, rcp, or MOP server to Flash memory or boot Flash memory to upgrade or change the IOS software or boot image on your router.

The protocol you use depends on which type of server you are using. The rcp transport mechanism provides faster performance and more reliable delivery of data than TFTP. These improvements are possible because the rcp transport mechanism is built on and uses the Transmission Control Protocol/Internet Protocol (TCP/IP) stack, which is connection-oriented.

The following sections describe the copying tasks. The first two tasks and the last task are required. If you have a Run-from-Flash system, the third section is required. Perform one of the remaining tasks, depending on which file transfer protocol you use.

- Understanding Flash Memory Space Considerations
- Outputting for Image Downloading Process
- Copying to Flash Memory Tasks for Run-from-Flash Systems
- Copying an Image from a TFTP Server to Flash Memory or Boot Flash Memory
- Copying an Image from an rcp Server to Flash Memory or Boot Flash Memory
- Copying an Image from a MOP Server to Flash Memory or Boot Flash Memory
- Verifying the Image in Flash Memory

See Chapter 13, "Maintaining Router Memory," for an explanation of the Flash memory card that can be used on the Cisco 3600 series and Cisco 7000 family.

NOTES

When you are upgrading or changing to a different Cisco IOS release, refer to the appropriate release notes for information on system requirements and limitations.

Filenames in Flash memory can be up to 63 characters long; they are not case sensitive and are always converted to lowercase.

NOTES

The destination filename must be an alphanumeric expression. For example, the filename 1 is invalid.

Understanding Flash Memory Space Considerations

Be sure there is enough space available before copying a file to Flash memory. Use the **show flash** command, and compare the size of the file you want to copy to the amount of Flash memory available. If the space available is less than the amount needed, the **copy** command is partially executed, but the entire file is not copied into Flash memory. The failure message "buffer overflow - *xxxx/xxxx*" appears, where *xxxx/xxxx* is the number of bytes read from the source file and the number of bytes available on the destination device.

CAUTION

Do not reboot the router if there is no valid image in Flash memory.

NOTES

For the Cisco 3600 series, if you do not have access to a network server and need to download a system image, you can copy an image from a local or remote computer (such as a PC, UNIX workstation, or Macintosh) using the Xmodem or Ymodem protocols. See the section "Recovering a System Image Using Xmodem or Ymodem (Cisco 1600 series and Cisco 3600 series only)" later in this chapter.

The **copy** command automatically displays the Flash memory directory, including the amount of free space. On Cisco 2500, Cisco 3000, and Cisco 4000 systems, if the file being downloaded to Flash memory is an uncompressed system image, the **copy** command automatically determines the size of the file being downloaded and validates it with the space available in Flash memory.

The router gives you the option of erasing the existing contents of Flash memory before writing to it. *If there is no free Flash memory available, or if no files have ever been written to Flash memory, the erase routine is required before new files can be copied.* If there is enough free Flash memory, the router gives you the option of erasing the existing Flash memory before writing to it. The system will inform you of these conditions and prompt you for a response.

NOTES

If you enter **n** after the "Erase flash before writing?" prompt, the copy process continues. If you enter **y** and confirm the erasure, the erase routine begins. Be sure to have ample Flash memory space before entering **n** at the erasure prompt.

If you attempt to copy a file into Flash memory that is already there, a prompt informs you that a file with the same name already exists. This file is "deleted" when you copy the new file into Flash. The first copy of the file still resides within Flash memory, but it is rendered unusable in favor of the newest version, and is listed with the "deleted" tag when you use the **show flash** command. If you terminate the copy process, the newer file is marked "deleted," because the entire file was not copied and is not valid. In this case, the original file in Flash memory is valid and available to the system.

You can copy normal or compressed images to Flash memory. You can produce a compressed system image on any UNIX platform using the **compress** command. Refer to your UNIX platform's documentation for the exact usage of the **compress** command.

On some platforms, the Flash security jumper must be installed in order to write to Flash memory. In addition, some platforms have a write-protect switch which must be set to *unprotected* in order to write to Flash memory.

Outputting for Image Downloading Process

The output and dialogue might vary depending on the platform.

Outputting for Partitioned Flash Memory

One of the following prompts displayed after the command indicates how the file can be downloaded:

- None—The file cannot be copied.
- RXBOOT-Manual—You must manually reload to the rxboot image in ROM to copy the image.
- RXBOOT-FLH—The copy is done automatically via the Flash load helper software in boot ROMs.
- Direct—The copy can be done directly.

If the file can be downloaded into more than one partition, you are prompted for the partition number. To obtain help, enter any of the following at the partition number prompt:

- ?—Display the directory listings of all partitions.
- ?1—Display the directory of the first partition.
- ?2—Display the directory of the second partition.
- q—Quit the copy command.

General Output Conventions

During a copy operation, a pound sign (#) generally means that a Flash memory device is being cleared and initialized. (Different platforms use different ways of indicating that Flash is being cleared.) An exclamation point (!) means that ten packets have been transferred successfully. A series of "V" characters means that a checksum verification of the file is occurring after the file is written to Flash memory. An "O" means an out-of-order packet. A period (.) means a timeout. The last line in the output indicates whether the copy was successful.

To interrupt a copy operation, press **Ctrl-^** or **Ctrl-Shift-6**. The operation terminates, but any partial file copied remains until Flash memory is erased.

Copying to Flash Memory Tasks for Run-from-Flash Systems

You cannot run the system from Flash memory and copy to it at the same time. Therefore, for systems that run from Flash, do *one* of the following before copying to Flash:

- Partition Flash memory or use Flash load helper to allow the system to run from Flash memory while you copy to it.
- Reload the system to use a system image from boot ROMs. See the "Modifying the Configuration Register Boot Field" section for more information.

See "Comparing Types of Memory" in Chapter 13, "Maintaining Router Memory," for more information on Run-from-Flash systems.

Refer to the appropriate hardware installation and maintenance publication for information about the jumper settings required for your configuration.

Copying an Image from a TFTP Server to Flash Memory or Boot Flash Memory

To copy a system image from a Trivial File Transfer Protocol (TFTP) server to Flash memory or to copy a boot image to boot Flash memory (Cisco 4500 Series only), complete the following tasks:

Task	Command
Step 1 Make a backup copy of the current software image or bootstrap image.	See the instructions in the section "Copying Images from Flash Memory to a Network Server."
Step 2 Copy a system image to Flash memory or Copy a boot image to boot Flash memory (Cisco 4500 Series only)	**copy tftp flash** **copy tftp** *file-id* (Cisco 7000 family only) **copy tftp bootflash** (Cisco 4500 Series only) **copy tftp** *device*:[*partition-number*:][*filename*] (Cisco 1600 series and Cisco 3600 series)

Task		Command
Step 3	When prompted, enter the IP address or domain name of the server.	*ip-address* or *name*
Step 4	If prompted, enter the filename of the server system image.	*filename*
Step 5	If prompted, enter the Flash memory device that is to receive the copy of the system image.	*device*

For the Cisco 7000 family, the *file-id* argument of the **copy tftp** *file-id* command specifies a device and filename as the destination of the copy operation. You can omit the device, entering only **copy tftp** *filename*. When you omit the device, the system uses the default device specified by the **cd** command.

Copying TFTP Flash Example

The following example shows how to use the **copy tftp flash** command to copy a system image named *igs-p-l* when Flash memory is too full to copy the file. The filename *igs-p-l* can be in either lowercase or uppercase; the system sees *IGS-P-L* as *igs-p-l*. If more than one file of the same name is copied to Flash, regardless of case, the last file copied becomes the valid file.

```
Router# copy tftp flash
IP address or name of remote host [255.255.255.255]? dirt
Translating "DIRT"...domain server (255.255.255.255) [OK]

Name of file to copy? igs-p-l
Copy igs-p-l from 172.16.13.111 into flash memory? [confirm]
Flash is filled to capacity.
Erasure is needed before flash may be written.
Erase flash before writing? [confirm]
Erasing flash EPROMs bank 0

Zeroing bank...zzzzzzzzzzzzzzzz
Verify zeroed...vvvvvvvvvvvvvvvv
Erasing bank...eeeeeeeeeeeeeeee

Erasing flash EPROMs bank 1

Zeroing bank...zzzzzzzzzzzzzzzz
Verify zeroed...vvvvvvvvvvvvvvvv
Erasing bank...eeeeeeeeeeeeeeee

Erasing flash EPROMs bank 2

Zeroing bank...zzzzzzzzzzzzzzzz
Verify zeroed...vvvvvvvvvvvvvvvv
Erasing bank...eeeeeeeeeeeeeeee
```

```
Erasing flash EPROMs bank 3

Zeroing bank...zzzzzzzzzzzzzzzz
Verify zeroed...vvvvvvvvvvvvvvvv
Erasing bank...eeeeeeeeeeeeeeee

Loading from 172.16.1.111:!!!!...
 [OK - 1906676/4194240 bytes]
Verifying via checksum...
vvvvvvvvvvvvvvvvvvvvvvvvvvvvvvvvvvvvvvvvvvvvvvvvvvvvvvvvvvvvvvvvvvvvvvvvvvvvvvvvvvv
vvvvvvvvvvvvvvvvvvvvvvvvvvvvvvvvvvvvvvvvvvvvvvvvvvvvvvvvvvvvvvvvvvvvvvvvvvvvvvvvvvv
vvvvvvvvvvvvvvvvvvvvvvvvvvvvvvvvvvvvvvvvvvvvvvvvvvvvvvvvvvvvvvvvvvvvvvvvvvvvvvvvvvv
vvvvvvvvvvvvvvvvvvvvvvvvvvvvvvvvvvvvvvvvvvvvvvvvvvvvvvvvvvvvvvvvvvvvvvvvvvvvvvvvvvv
vvvvvvvvvvvvvvvvvvvvvvvvvvvvv
Flash verification successful. Length = 1906676, checksum = 0x12AD
```

Copying TFTP Flash Example When File by the Same Name Already Exists

The following example shows how to copy a system image named *igs-p-l* into the current Flash configuration in which a file named *igs-p-l* already exists:

```
Router# copy tftp flash
IP address or name of remote host [172.16.13.111]?
Name of file to copy? igs-p-l
File igs-p-l already exists; it will be invalidated!
Copy igs-p-l from 172.16.13.111 into flash memory? [confirm]
2287500 bytes available for writing without erasure.
Erase flash before writing? [confirm]n
Loading from 172.16.1.111:!!!!...
[OK - 1906676/2287500 bytes]
Verifying via checksum...
vvvvvvvvvvvvvvvvvvvvvvvvvvvvvvvvvvvvvvvvvvvvvvvvvvvvvvvvvvvvvvvvvvvvvvvvvvvvvvvvvvv
vvvvvvvvvvvvvvvvvvvvvvvvvvvvvvvvvvvvvvvvvvvvvvvvvvvvvvvvvvvvvvvvvvvvvvvvvvvvvvvvvvv
vvvvvvvvvvvvvvvvvvvvvvvvvvvvvvvvvvvvvvvvvvvvvvvvvvvvvvvvvvvvvvvvvvvvvvvvvvvvvvvvvvv
vvvvvvvvvvvvvvvvvvvvvvvvvvvvvvvvvvvvvvvvvvvvvvvvvvvvvvvvvvvvvvvvvvvvvvvvvvvvvvvvvvv
vvvvvvvvvvvvvvvvvvvvvvvvvvvvv
Flash verification successful. Length = 1902192, checksum = 0x12AD
```

Copying TFTP Flash Example with Security Jumper not Installed

In the following example, the Flash security jumper is not installed, so you cannot write files to Flash memory.

```
Router# copy tftp flash
Flash: embedded flash security jumper(12V)
       must be strapped to modify flash memory
```

Copying by Specifying Destination Partition and Filename for Cisco 1600 Series and Cisco 3600 Series

In the following example, the file *c3600-i-mz* on the TFTP server at 172.23.1.129 is copied to the first partition of internal Flash memory of a Cisco 3600 series router.

For the Cisco 1600 series router, the process will be the same except the device used in the **copy** command must be **flash:** and the directory listed will be the "System flash directory."

```
Router# copy tftp flash:1:c3600-i-mz

System flash directory, partition 1:
File  Length   Name/status
   1   1711088  current-ios
[1711152 bytes used, 2483152 available, 4194304 total]

Address or name of remote host [172.23.1.129]?
Source file name [c3600-i-mz]?
Accessing file 'c3600-i-mz' on 172.23.1.129...
Loading c3600-i-mz from 172.23.1.129 (via Ethernet1/0): ! [OK]
Erase flash device before writing? [confirm]
Flash contains files. Are you sure you want to erase? [confirm]
Copy 'c3600-i-mz' from server
  as 'c3600-i-mz' into Flash WITH erase? [yes/no] yes
Erasing device... eeeeeeeeeeeeeeee ...erased
Loading c3600-i-mz from 172.23.1.129 (via Ethernet1/0):
!!!!!!!!!!!!!!!!!!!!!!!!!!!!!!!!!!!!!!!!!!!!!!!!!!!!!!!!!!!!!!!!!!!!!!!!!!!!!!!!!!!!
!!!!!!!!!!!!!!!!!!!!!!!!!!!!!!!!!!!!!!!!!!!!!!!!!!!!!!!!!!!!!!!!!!!!!!!!!!!!!!!!!!!!
!!!!!!!!!!!!!!!!!!!!!!!!!!!!!!!!!!!!!!!!!!!!!!!!!!!!!!!!!!!!!!!!!!!!!!!!!!!!!!!!!!!!
!!!!!!!!!!!!!!!!!!!!!!!!!!!!!!!!!!!!!!!!!!!!!!!!!!!!!!!!!!!!!!!!!!!!!!!!!
[OK - 1711088/4194304 bytes]

Verifying checksum...  OK (0xF89A)
Flash device copy took 00:00:17 [hh:mm:ss]
```

Copying by Not Specifying Destination Partition and Filename for Cisco 1600 Series and Cisco 3600 Series

In the following example, the file *images/3600/c3600-i-mz* on the TFTP server at 172.23.1.129 is copied to the first partition of internal Flash memory of a Cisco 3600 series router. The software prompts for the destination partition since it was not provided in the command line.

For the Cisco 1600 series router, the process will be the same except the device used in the **copy** command must be **flash:** and the directory listed will be the "System flash directory."

```
Router# copy tftp flash:

System flash

Partition   Size    Used    Free    Bank-Size  State       Copy Mode
   1        4096K   1671K   2424K   4096K      Read/Write  Direct
   2        16384K  1671K   14712K  8192K      Read/Write  Direct

[Type ?<no> for partition directory; ? for full directory; q to abort]
Which partition? [default = 1]

System flash directory, partition 1:
File  Length   Name/status
   1   1711088 c3600-i-mz
[1711152 bytes used, 2483152 available, 4194304 total]
```

```
Address or name of remote host [172.23.1.129]?
Source file name? images/3600/c3600-i-mz
Destination file name [images/3600/c3600-i-mz]?
Accessing file 'images/3600/c3600-i-mz' on 172.23.1.129...
Loading images/3600/c3600-i-mz from 172.23.1.129 (via Ethernet1/0): ! [OK]
Erase flash device before writing? [confirm]
Flash contains files. Are you sure you want to erase? [confirm]
Copy 'images/3600/c3600-i-mz' from server
   as 'images/3600/c3600-i-mz' into Flash WITH erase? [yes/no] yes
Erasing device... eeeeeeeeeeeeeeee ...erased
Loading images/3600/c3600-i-mz from 172.23.1.129 (via Ethernet1/0):
   !!!!!!!!!!!!!!!!!!!!!!!!!!!!!!!!!!!!!!!!!!!!!!!!!!!!!!!!!!!!!!!!!!!!!!!!!!!!!!!!
   !!!!!!!!!!!!!!!!!!!!!!!!!!!!!!!!!!!!!!!!!!!!!!!!!!!!!!!!!!!!!!!!!!!!!!!!!!!!!!!!
   !!!!!!!!!!!!!!!!!!!!!!!!!!!!!!!!!!!!!!!!!!!!!!!!!!!!!!!!!!!!!!!!!!!!!!!!!!!!!!!!
   !!!!!!!!!!!!!!!!!!!!!!!!!!!!!!!!!!!!!!!!!!!!!!!!!!!!!!!!!!!!!!!!!
[OK - 1711088/4194304 bytes]

Verifying checksum...  OK (0xF89A)
Flash device copy took 00:00:17 [hh:mm:ss]
```

Copying an Image from an rcp Server to Flash Memory or Boot Flash Memory

You can copy a system image from an rcp network server to Flash memory. You also can copy a boot image from an rcp network server to boot Flash memory.

If you copy the configuration file to a personal computer used as a file server, the computer must support rsh.

Understanding the rcp Username

The rcp protocol requires a client to send a remote username on each rcp request to a server. When you copy a configuration file from the router to a server using rcp, the Cisco IOS software sends the first valid username in the following list:

1. The username set by the **ip rcmd remote-username** command, if the command is configured.

2. The remote username associated with the current TTY (terminal) process. For example, if the user is connected to the router through Telnet and was authenticated through the **username** command, the router software sends the Telnet username as the remote username.

3. The router host name.

For the rcp copy request to execute successfully, an account must be defined on the network server for the remote username. If the server has a directory structure, the configuration file or image is written to or copied from the directory associated with the remote username on the server. Use the **ip rcmd remote-username** command to specify which directory on the server to use. For example, if the system image resides in the home directory of a user on the server, you can specify that user's name as the remote username.

Copying from an rcp Server to Flash Memory Tasks

To copy a system image from an rcp server to Flash memory or to copy a boot image to boot Flash memory, complete the following tasks:

Task	Command
Step 1 Make a backup copy of the current system or bootstrap software image.	See the instructions in the section "Copying Images from Flash Memory to a Network Server."
Step 2 Enter configuration mode from the terminal. This step is required only if you override the default remote username (see Step 3).	**configure terminal**
Step 3 Specify the remote username. This step is optional, but recommended.	**ip rcmd remote-username** *username*
Step 4 Exit configuration mode.	**end**
Step 5 Copy the system image from an rcp server to Flash memory, or Copy the boot image from an rcp server to boot Flash memory.	**copy rcp flash** **copy rcp bootflash** **copy rcp** *file-id* (Cisco 7000 family only) **copy rcp** *device*:[*partition-number*:][*filename*] (Cisco 1600 series and Cisco 3600 series)
Step 6 When prompted, enter the IP address or domain name of the network server.	*ip-address* or *name*
Step 7 When prompted, enter the filename of the server system image to be copied.	*filename*

Copying rcp Flash Example

The following example shows how to copy a system image named *mysysim1* from the *netadmin1* directory on the remote server named *SERVER1.CISCO.COM* with an IP address of 172.16.101.101 to Flash memory. To ensure that enough Flash memory is available to accommodate the system image to be copied, the Cisco IOS software allows you to erase the contents of Flash memory first.

```
Router1# configure terminal
Router1(config)# ip rcmd remote-username netadmin1
Router1(config)# end
Router# copy rcp flash

System flash directory:
File name/status
    1 mysysim1
[2076072 bytes used, 21080 bytes available]

Address or name of remote host[UNKNOWN]? 172.16.101.101
Name of file to copy? mysysim1
Copy mysysim1 from SERVER1.CISCO.COM?[confirm]

Checking for file 'mysysim1' on SERVER1.CISCO.COM...[OK]

Erase Flash device before writing?[confirm]
Are you sure?[confirm]
Erasing device...ezeeze...erased.

Connected to 172.16.101.101

Loading 2076007 byte file mysysim1:!!!!...
[OK]

Verifying checksum... (0x87FD)...[OK]
Router#
```

Copying rcp Example Using RSP Card

The following example uses the **copy rcp** *file-id* command to copy the *router-image* file from a network server using rcp to the Flash memory card inserted in slot 0 of the RSP card:

```
Router1# configure terminal
Router1(config)# ip rcmd remote-username netadmin1
Router1(config)# end
Router1# copy rcp slot0:router-image
```

Copying rcp Boot Flash Example

The following copies a bootstrap image from the rcp server to boot Flash memory:

```
Router1# configure terminal
Router1(config)# ip rcmd remote-username netadmin1
Router1(config)# end
Router1# copy rcp bootflash

System flash directory:
File name/status
    1 btxx
[2076072 bytes used, 21080 bytes available]

Address or name of remote host[UNKNOWN]? 172.16.1.111
Name of file to copy? btxx
Copy btxx from UTOPIA.CISCO.COM?[confirm]
```

```
Checking for file 'btxx' on UTOPIA.CISCO.COM...[OK]

Erase flash device before writing?[confirm]
Are you sure?[confirm]
Erasing device...ezeeze...erased.

Connected to 172.16.1.111

Loading 2076007 byte file btxx:!!!!...
[OK]

Verifying checksum... (0x87FD)...[OK]
```

Copying by Specifying a Destination Partition
(Cisco 1600 series and Cisco 3600 series)

In the following example, the file */tftpboot/gate/c3600-i-mz* on the rcp server at 172.23.1.129 is copied to partition 3 in slot 0 of a Cisco 3600 series router.

For the Cisco 1600 series router, the process will be the same except the device used in the **copy** command must be **flash:** and the directory listed will be the "System flash directory."

```
Router# copy rcp slot0:3
PCMCIA Slot0 flash directory, partition 3:
File  Length    Name/status
  1   426       running-config
[492 bytes used, 4193812 available, 4194304 total]

Address or name of remote host [172.23.1.129]?
Source file name? /tftpboot/gate/c3600-i-mz

Destination file name [/tftpboot/gate/c3600-i-mz]?
Accessing file '/tftpboot/gate/c3600-i-mz' on 172.23.1.129...
Connected to 172.23.1.129
Loading 1711088 byte file c3600-i-mz: ! [OK]

Erase flash device before writing? [confirm]
Flash contains files. Are you sure you want to erase? [confirm]
Copy '/tftpboot/gate/c3600-i-mz' from server
  as '/tftpboot/gate/c3600-i-mz' into Flash WITH erase? [yes/no] yes
Erasing device... eeeeeeeeeeeeeeeeeeeeeeeeeeeeeeeee ...erased
Connected to 172.23.1.129
Loading 1711088 byte file c3600-i-mz:
!!!!!!!!!!!!!!!!!!!!!!!!!!!!!!!!!!!!!!!!!!!!!!!!!!!!!!!!!!!!!!!!!!!!!!!!!!!!!!!!!!
!!!!!!!!!!!!!!!!!!!!!!!!!!!!!!!!!!!!!
!!!!!!!!!!!!!!!!!!!!!!!!!!!!!!!!!!!!!!!!!!!!!!!!!!!!!!!!!!!!!!!!!!!!!!!!!!!!!!!!!!
!!!!!!!!!!!!!!!!!!!!!!!!!!!!!!!!!!!!!!!!!!!!!!!!!!!!!!!!!!!!!!!!!!!!!!!!!!!!!!!!!!
!!!!!!!!!!!!!!!!!!!!!!!!!!!!!!!!!!!!!!!!! [OK]

Verifying checksum...  OK (0xF89A)
Flash device copy took 00:00:16 [hh:mm:ss]
```

Copying by not Specifying a Destination Partition
(Cisco 1600 series and Cisco 3600 series)

In the following example, the file */tftpboot/gate/c3600-i-mz* on the rcp server at 172.23.1.129 is copied to the first partition of slot 0 of a Cisco 3600 series router. The software prompts for the destination partition, because it was not provided in the command line.

For the Cisco 1600 series router, the process will be the same except the device used in the **copy** command must be **flash:** and the directories listed will be for the System Flash directory.

```
Router# copy rcp slot0:
PCMCIA Slot0 flash

Partition   Size    Used    Free    Bank-Size  State        Copy Mode
   1        4096K   3068K   1027K   4096K      Read/Write   Direct
   2        4096K   1671K   2424K   4096K      Read/Write   Direct
   3        4096K     0K    4095K   4096K      Read/Write   Direct
   4        4096K   3825K    270K   4096K      Read/Write   Direct

[Type ?<no> for partition directory; ? for full directory; q to abort]
Which partition? [default = 1]
PCMCIA Slot0 flash directory, partition 1:
File  Length    Name/status
   1  3142288   c3600-j-mz
[3142352 bytes used, 1051952 available, 4194304 total]

Address or name of remote host [172.23.1.129]?
Source file name? /tftpboot/gate/c3600-i-mz
Destination file name [/tftpboot/gate/c3600-i-mz]?
Accessing file '/tftpboot/gate/c3600-i-mz' on 172.23.1.129...
Connected to 172.23.1.129
Loading 1711088 byte file c3600-i-mz: ! [OK]

Erase flash device before writing? [confirm]
Flash contains files. Are you sure you want to erase? [confirm]

Copy '/tftpboot/gate/c3600-i-mz' from server
  as '/tftpboot/gate/c3600-i-mz' into Flash WITH erase? [yes/no] yes
Erasing device... eeeeeeeeeeeeeeeeeeeeeeeeeeeeeeeee ...erased
Connected to 172.23.1.129
Loading 1711088 byte file c3600-i-mz:
!!!!!!!!!!!!!!!!!!!!!!!!!!!!!!!!!!!!!!!!!!!!!!!!!!!!!!!!!!!!!!!!!!!!!!!!!!!!!!!!!!!
!!!!!!!!!!!!!!!!!!!!!!!!!!!!!!!!!!!!!!!!!!!!!!!!!!!!!!!!!!!!!!!!!!!!!!!!!!!!!!!!!!!
!!!!!!!!!!!!!!!!!!!!!!!!!!!!!!!!!!!!!!!!!!!!!!!!!!!!!!!!!!!!!!!!!!!!!!!!!!!!!!!!!!!
!!!

Verifying checksum... OK (0xF89A)
Flash device copy took 00:00:18 [hh:mm:ss]
```

Copying an Image from a MOP Server to Flash Memory or Boot Flash Memory

On all platforms except the Cisco 7200 series and Cisco 7500 series, you can copy a system image from a Maintenance Operation Protocol (MOP) server to Flash memory or a boot image to boot Flash memory. To do so, perform the following task in EXEC mode:

Task	Command
Copy a boot image using MOP to Flash	**copy mop flash**
or	**copy mop bootflash**
Copy a boot image to boot Flash.	**copy mop** *device*:[*partition-number*:][*filename*] (Cisco 3600 series)

Copying MOP Flash Example

The following example shows a sample output from the **copy mop flash** command. In this example, the system image *routerimage*, which already exists in Flash memory, is copied to Flash memory. Although there is enough memory to copy the file without erasing any existing files, Flash memory is erased.

```
Router# copy mop flash

System flash directory:
File  Length    Name/status
  1   984         routerimage[deleted]
  2   984         routerimage
[2096 bytes used, 8386512 available, 8388608 total]
Source file name? routerimage
Destination file name [routerimage]?

Erase flash device before writing? [confirm]
Flash contains files. Are you sure you want to erase? [confirm]

Copy 'routerimage' from server
  as 'routerimage' into Flash WITH erase? [yes/no]yes
Erasing device... eeeeeeeeeeeeeeeeeeeeeeeeeeeeeee...erased
Loading routerimage from 1234.5678.9abc via Ethernet0: !
[OK - 984/8388608 bytes]

Verifying checksum... OK (0x14B3)
Flash copy took 0:00:01 [hh:mm:ss]
```

Copying MOP Example for the Cisco 1600 Series and Cisco 3600 Series

In the following example, the system image *routerimage*, which already exists in internal Flash memory, is copied from a MOP server to the first partition of internal Flash memory. Although there is enough memory to copy the file without erasing any existing files, Flash memory is erased.

```
Router# copy mop flash:

System flash
Partition   Size     Used      Free      Bank-Size  State        Copy Mode
   1        4096K    1671K     2424K     4096K      Read/Write   Direct
   2       16384K    1671K    14712K     8192K      Read/Write   Direct

[Type ?<no> for partition directory; ? for full directory; q to abort]
Which partition? [default = 1]

System flash directory, partition 1:
File  Length    Name/status
  1    984         routerimage[deleted]
  2    984         routerimage
[2096 bytes used, 8386512 available, 8388608 total]

Source file name? routerimage
Destination file name [routerimage]?
Erase flash device before writing? [confirm]
Flash contains files. Are you sure you want to erase? [confirm]
Copy 'routerimage' from server
  as 'routerimage' into Flash WITH erase? [yes/no]yes
Erasing device... eeeeeeeeeeeeeeeeeeeeeeeeeeeeeeee ...erased
Loading routerimage from 1234.5678.9abc via Ethernet1/0: !
[OK - 984/8388608 bytes]

Verifying checksum... OK (0x14B3)
Flash copy took 0:00:01 [hh:mm:ss]
```

Verifying the Image in Flash Memory

Before booting from Flash memory, verify that the checksum of the image in Flash memory matches the checksum listed in the README file that was distributed with the system software image by using the **verify** command. The checksum of the image in Flash memory is displayed at the bottom of the screen when you issue the **copy tftp, copy rcp, copy rcp,** or **copy mop** command to copy an image. The README file was copied to the network server automatically when you installed the system software image on the server.

CAUTION

If the checksum value does not match the value in the README file, do not reboot the router. Instead, issue the **copy** command and compare the checksums again. If the checksum is repeatedly wrong, copy the original system software image back into Flash memory *before* you reboot the router from Flash memory. If you have a corrupted image in Flash memory and you try to boot from Flash, the router will start the system image contained in ROM (assuming that booting from a network server is not configured). If ROM does not contain a fully functional system image, the router will not function and must be reconfigured through a direct console port connection.

The Flash memory content listing does not include the checksum of individual files. To recompute and verify the image checksum after an image is copied into Flash memory or a Flash memory device, complete the following task in EXEC mode:

Task	Command
Recompute and verify the image checksum after the image is copied into Flash memory. See Table 11–2, "Possible System and Boot Image Locations," for valid Flash devices for the Cisco 1600, Cisco 3600, and Cisco 7000 family.	**verify flash**
	verify bootflash (Cisco 4500 Series only)
	verify *device*:[*partition-number*:][*filename*] (Cisco 1600 series and Cisco 3600 series only)
	verify [*device*:]*filename* (Cisco 7000 family)

When you enter the **verify flash** command, the screen prompts you for the filename to verify. By default, it prompts for the last (most recent) file in Flash. Press **Return** to recompute the default file checksum or enter the filename of a different file at the prompt. Note that the checksum for microcode images is always 0x0000.

The following example illustrates how to use the **verify flash** command:

```
Router# verify flash

Name of file to verify [gsxx]?
Verifying via checksum...
vvvvvvvvvvvvvvvvvvvvvvvvvvvvvvvv

Flash verification successful. Length = 1923712, checksum = 0xA0C1
```

The following example verifies the *gsxx* file on the Flash memory card inserted in slot 0 of a Cisco 7000 family:

```
Router# verify slot0:gsxx
cccccccccccccccccccccccccccccccccccccccccccccccccccccccccccccccccccccccccccc
File slot0:gsxx verified OK
```

Verifying Checksum Example for Cisco 1600 series and Cisco 3600 series

The following example verifies the checksum of the file *c3600-i-mz.test* in the fourth partition of the Flash memory card in slot 0. For the Cisco 1600 series router, the process will be the same, except the device used in the **verify** command must be **flash:** and the directories listed will be for System Flash.

```
Router# verify slot0:
PCMCIA Slot0 flash

Partition   Size    Used    Free    Bank-Size   State        Copy Mode
   1        4096K   3069K   1026K   4096K       Read/Write   Direct
   2        4096K   3069K   1026K   4096K       Read/Write   Direct
```

```
3         4096K     0K     4096K     4096K     Read/Write     Direct
4         4096K   3826K     269K     4096K     Read/Write     Direct

[Type ?<no> for partition directory; ? for full directory; q to abort]
Which partition? [default = 1] 4

PCMCIA Slot0 flash directory, partition 4:
File  Length    Name/status
  1   2205860   dirt/images/c3600-d-mz
  2   1711128   c3600-i-mz.test
  3   850       alz
[3918032 bytes used, 276272 available, 4194304 total]

Name of file to verify? c3600-i-mz.test
Verifying checksum for 'c3600-i-mz.test' (file # 2)...  OK
```

COPYING IMAGES BETWEEN LOCAL FLASH MEMORY DEVICES

On Cisco 3600 series and Cisco 7000 family routers, you can copy images from one Flash memory device, such as internal Flash memory or a Flash memory card in a PCMCIA slot, to another Flash memory device, as shown in Figure 11–1. One reason to copy the image to a different flash device is to make a backup copy of it.

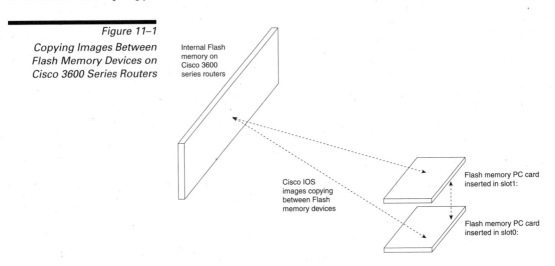

Figure 11–1

Copying Images Between Flash Memory Devices on Cisco 3600 Series Routers

Internal Flash memory on Cisco 3600 series routers

Cisco IOS images copying between Flash memory devices

Flash memory PC card inserted in slot1:

Flash memory PC card inserted in slot0:

To copy an image between Flash memory devices, follow these steps in EXEC mode:

Task	Command
Step 1 Display the layout and contents of Flash memory.	**show** *device*: [**all** | **chips** | **detailed** | **err** | **partition** *number* | **summary**]

Task	Command
Step 2 Copy an image between Flash memory devices.	**copy** *device***:**[*partition-number*:][*filename*] *device***:**[*partition-number*:][*filename*]
Step 3 Verify the checksum of the image you copied.	**verify** *device***:** [*partition-number*:][*filename*]

NOTES

The source device and the destination device cannot be the same. For example, the command **copy slot1: slot1:** is invalid.

Copying a File between Local Flash Memory Devices Examples for Cisco 3600—Source Partition Specified

The following example copies the file admin/images/new-ios from partition 1 of internal Flash memory to partition 1 of slot 0.

```
Router# copy flash:1 slot0:

System flash directory, partition 1:
File  Length    Name/status
  1   3142748 admin/images/new-ios
[3142812 bytes used, 1051492 available, 4194304 total]

PCMCIA Slot0 flash
Partition  Size   Used    Free    Bank-Size  State       Copy Mode
  1        4096K  1671K   2424K   4096K      Read/Write  Direct
  2        4096K  3069K   1026K   4096K      Read/Write  Direct
  3        4096K  1671K   2424K   4096K      Read/Write  Direct
  4        4096K  3826K    269K   4096K      Read/Write  Direct

[Type ?<no> for partition directory; ? for full directory; q to abort]
Which partition? [default = 1]

PCMCIA Slot0 flash directory, partition 1:
File  Length    Name/status
  1   1711088 /tftpboot/gate/c3600-i-mz
[1711152 bytes used, 2483152 available, 4194304 total]

Source file name? admin/images/new-ios
Destination file name [admin/images/new-ios]?
Verifying checksum for 'admin/images/new-ios' (file # 1)...  OK

Erase flash device before writing? [confirm]
Flash contains files. Are you sure you want to erase? [confirm]
Copy 'admin/images/new-ios' from flash: device
  as 'admin/images/new-ios' into slot0: device WITH erase? [yes/no] yes
```

```
Erasing device... eeeeeeeeeeeeeeeeeeeeeeeeeeeeeeee ...erased
!!!!!!!!!!!!!!!!!!!!!!!!!!!!!!!!!!!!!!!!!!!!!!!!!!!!!!!!!!!!!!!!!!!!!!!!!!!!!!!!!!!!
!!!!!!!!!!!!!!!!!!!!!!!!!!!!!!!!!!!!!!!!!!!!!!!!!!!!!!!!!!!!!!!!!!!!!!!!!!!!!!!!!!!!
!!!!!!!!!!!!!!!!!!!!!!!!!!!!!!!!!!!!!!!!!!!!!!!!!!!!!!!!!!!!!!!!!!!!!!!!!!!!!!!!!!!!
!!!!!!!!!!!!!!!!!!!!!!!!!!!!!!!!!!!!!!!!!!!!!!!!!!!!!!!!!!!!!!!!!!!!!!!!!!!!!!!!!!!!
!!!!!!!!!!!!!!!!!!!!!!!!!!!!!!!!!!!!!!!!!!!!!!!!!!!!!!!!!!!!!!!!!!!!!!!!!!!!!!!!!!!!
!!!!!!!!!!!!!!!!!!!!!!!!!!!!!!!!!!!!!!!!!!!!!!!!!!!!!!!!!!!!!!!!!!!!!!!!!!!!!!!!!!!!
!!!!!!!!!!!!!!!!!!!!!!!!!!!!!!!!!!!!!!!!!!!!!!!!!!!!!!!!!!!!!!!!!!!!!!!!!!!!!!!!!!!!
!!!!!!!!!!!!!!!!!!!!!!!!!!!!!!!!!!!!!!!!!!!!!!!!!!!!!!!!!!!!!!!!!!!!!!!!!!!!!!!!!!!!
!!!!!!!!!!!!!!!!!!!!!!!!!!!!!!!!!!!!!!!!!!!!!!!!!!!!!!!!!!!!!!!!
[OK - 3142748/4194304 bytes]

Flash device copy took 00:00:50 [hh:mm:ss]
Verifying checksum... OK (0xB732)
```

SPECIFYING THE STARTUP SYSTEM IMAGE IN THE CONFIGURATION FILE

You can enter multiple boot commands in the startup configuration file or in the BOOT environment variable to provide backup methods for loading a system image onto the router. The following are three ways to load a system image:

- From Flash memory—Flash memory allows you to copy new system images without changing ROM. Information stored in Flash memory is not vulnerable to network failures that might occur when loading system images from servers.

- From a network server—In case Flash memory becomes corrupted, you can specify that a system image to be loaded from a network server using TFTP, rcp, or MOP as a backup boot method. For some platforms, you can specify a boot image to be loaded from a network server using TFTP or rcp.

- From ROM—In case of both Flash memory corruption and network failure, specifying a system image to be loaded from ROM provides a final backup boot method. System images stored in ROM might not always be as current as those stored in Flash memory or on network servers.

NOTES

The Cisco 7000 family cannot boot from ROM.

You can enter the different types of boot commands in any order in the startup configuration file or in the BOOT environment variable. If you enter multiple boot commands, the Cisco IOS software tries them in the order they are entered.

NOTES

Booting from ROM is faster than booting from Flash memory. However, booting from Flash memory is faster and more reliable than booting from a network server.

Loading the System Image from Flash Memory

Use the following sections to configure your router to boot from Flash memory. Flash memory can reduce the effects of network failure by reducing dependency on files that can only be accessed over the network.

Flash Memory Configuration Process

To configure the router to load a system image in Flash memory, perform the following steps:

Step 1	(Optional) Copy a system image or boot image to Flash memory using TFTP, rcp, and MOP. See the "Copying Images from a Network Server to Flash Memory" section for more information on performing this step.
Step 2	Configure the system to automatically boot from the desired file and location in Flash memory or boot Flash memory. See the "Configuring the Router to Boot Automatically from an Image in Flash Memory" section.
Step 3	(Optional) Depending on the current configuration register setting, you might need to change the configuration register value.
Step 4	(Optional) For some platforms, to change the location of the boot image, set the BOOTLDR environment variable.
Step 5	Save your configurations.
Step 6	Power-cycle and reboot your system to ensure that all is working as expected.

Configuring the Router to Boot Automatically from an Image in Flash Memory

To configure a router to boot automatically from an image in Flash memory, perform the following tasks:

Task	Command
Step 1 Enter configuration mode from the terminal.	**configure terminal**
Step 2 Enter the filename of an image stored in Flash memory.	**boot system flash** [*filename*]
	boot system flash [*partition-number*:][*filename*]
	boot system flash [*device*:][*filename*] (Cisco 7000 family)
	boot system flash [*device*:][*partition-number*:] *filename* (Cisco 1600 series and Cisco 3600 series)
Step 3 Set the configuration register to enable loading of the system image specified in the configuration file.	**config-register** *value*

Task	Command
Step 4 Exit configuration mode.	**end**
Step 5 Save the configuration file to your startup configuration.	**copy running-config startup-config**
Step 6 Optionally, verify the contents of the startup configuration.	**show startup-config**
Step 7 Power cycle and reboot the system to ensure that all works as expected.	**reload**

For routers that are partitioned, if you do not specify a partition, the router boots from the first partition. If you do not specify a filename, the router boots from the first valid image found in the partition.

If you enter more than one image filename, the router tries them in the order entered.

To remove a filename from the configuration file, enter the **no boot system flash** command and specify the file location.

NOTES

The **no boot system** configuration command disables all **boot system** configuration commands regardless of argument. Specifying the **flash** keyword or the *filename* argument with the **no boot system** command disables only the commands specified by these arguments.

The following example shows how to configure the router to boot automatically from an image in Flash memory:

```
Router# configure terminal
Router(config)# boot system flash gsnew-image
Router(config)# config-register 0x010F
Router(config)# end
Router# copy running-config startup-config
[ok]
Router# reload
[confirm]

%SYS-5-RELOAD: Reload requested
System Bootstrap, Version 4.6(0.16), BETA SOFTWARE
Copyright (c) 1986-1995 by cisco Systems
RP1 processor with 16384 Kbytes of memory
F3: 1871404+45476+167028 at 0x1000
```

```
Booting gsnew-image from flash memory RRRRRRRRRRRRRRRRRRRRRRRRRRRRR
RRRRRRRRRRRRRRRRRRRRRRRRRRRRRRRRRRRRRRRRRRRRRRRRRRRRRRRRRRRRRRRRRRRRR
RRRRRRRRRRRRRRRRRRRRRRRRRRRRRRRRRRRRRRRRRRRRRRRRRRRRRRRRRRRRRRRRRRRRR
RRRRRRRRRRRRRRRRRRRRRRRRRRRRRRRRRRRRRRRRRRRRRRRRRRRRRRRRRRRRRRRRRRRRR
RRRRRRRRRRRRRRRRRRRRRRRRRRRRRRRRRRRRRRRRRRRRRRRRRRRRRRRRRRRRRRRRRRRRR
RRRRRRRRRRRRRRRRRRRRRRRRRRRRRRRRRRRRRRRRRRRRRRR [OK - 1916912/13767448 bytes]
F3: 1871404+45476+167028 at 0x1000

                 Restricted Rights Legend

Use, duplication, or disclosure by the Government is
subject to restrictions as set forth in subparagraph
(c) of the Commercial Computer Software - Restricted
Rights clause at FAR sec. 52.227-19 and subparagraph
(c) (1) (ii) of the Rights in Technical Data and Computer
Software clause at DFARS sec. 252.227-7013.

cisco Systems, Inc.
            170 West Tasman Drive
            San Jose, California 95134

GS Software (GS7), Version 10.2,
Copyright (c) 1986-1995 by cisco Systems, Inc.
Compiled Thu 05-Nov-94 14:16 by mlw
```

Loading the System Image from a Network Server

You can configure the Cisco IOS software to load a system image file from a network server using TFTP, rcp, or MOP.

If you do not boot from a network server using MOP and you do not specify either TFTP or rcp, by default the system image that you specify is booted from a network server via TFTP.

NOTES

If you are using a Sun workstation as a network server and TFTP to transfer the file, set up the workstation to enable verification and generation of User Datagram Protocol (UDP) checksums. See the Sun documentation for details.

For increased performance and reliability, use rcp to boot a system image from a network server. The rcp implementation uses the Transmission Control Protocol (TCP), which ensures reliable delivery of data.

You cannot explicitly specify a remote username when you issue the **boot** command. Instead, the host name of the router is used. If the remote server has a directory structure, as do UNIX systems, and you boot the router from a network server using rcp, the Cisco IOS software searches for the system image on the server relative to the directory of the remote username.

You also can boot from a compressed image on a network server. One reason to use a compressed image is to ensure that there is enough memory available for storage. On routers that do not contain a run-from-ROM image in EPROM, when the router boots software from a network server, the image being booted and the running image both must fit into memory. If the running image is large, there might not be room in memory for the image being booted from the network server.

If there is not enough room in memory to boot a regular image from a network server, you can produce a compressed software image on any UNIX platform using the **compress** command. Refer to your UNIX platform's documentation for the exact usage of the **compress** command.

To specify the loading of a system image from a network server, complete the following tasks:

Task	Command
Step 1 Enter configuration mode from the terminal.	**configure terminal**
Step 2 Specify the system image file to be booted from a network server using rcp, TFTP, or MOP.	**boot system [rcp	tftp]** *filename* [*ip-address*] **boot system mop** *filename* [*mac-address*] [*interface*]
Step 3 Set the configuration register to enable loading of the image specified in the configuration file.	**config-register** *value*
Step 4 Exit configuration mode.	**end**
Step 5 Save the configuration file to your startup configuration.	**copy running-config startup-config**

In the following example, a router uses rcp to boot from the *testme5.tester* system image file on a network server at IP address 172.16.0.1:

```
Router# configure terminal
Router(config)# boot system rcp testme5.tester 172.16.0.1
Router(config)# config-register 0x010F
Router(config)# end
Router# copy running-config startup-config
```

Loading the System Image from ROM

To specify the use of the ROM system image as a backup to other boot instructions in the configuration file, complete the following tasks:

Task	Command
Step 1 Enter configuration mode from the terminal.	**configure terminal**
Step 2 Specify use of the ROM system image as a backup image.	**boot system rom**
Step 3 Set the configuration register to enable loading of the system image specified in the configuration file.	**config-register** *value*
Step 4 Exit configuration mode.	**end**
Step 5 Save the configuration file to your startup configuration.	**copy running-config startup-config**

In the following example, a router is configured to boot from ROM:

```
Router# configure terminal
Router(config)# boot system rom
Router(config)# config-register 0x010F
Router(config)# end
Router# copy running-config startup-config
```

NOTES

The Cisco 7000 family cannot load from ROM.

Using a Fault-Tolerant Booting Strategy

Occasionally network failures make booting from a network server impossible. To lessen the effects of network failure, consider the following booting strategy. After Flash is installed and configured, you might want to configure the router to boot in the following order:

1. Boot an image from Flash.
2. Boot an image from a system file on a network server.
3. Boot from ROM image.

This boot order provides the most fault-tolerant booting strategy. Perform the following tasks to allow the router to boot first from Flash, then from a system file from a network server, and finally from ROM:

Task		Command
Step 1	Enter configuration mode from the terminal.	**configure terminal**
Step 2	Configure the router to boot from Flash memory.	**boot system flash** [*filename*]
		boot system flash [*partition-number*:][*filename*]
		boot system flash [*device*:][*filename*] (Cisco 7000 family)
		boot system flash [*device*:][*partition-number*:] *filename* (Cisco 1600 series and Cisco 3600 series)
Step 3	Configure the router to boot from a network server.	**boot system** [**rcp**	**tftp**] *filename* [*ip-address*]
Step 4	Configure the router to boot from ROM.	**boot system rom**
Step 5	Set the configuration register to enable loading of the system image specified in the configuration file.	**config-register** *value*
Step 6	Exit configuration mode.	**end**
Step 7	Save the configuration file to your startup configuration.	**copy running-config startup-config**

In the example, a router is configured to first boot an internal Flash image called *gsxx*. Should that image fail, the router will boot the configuration file *gsxx* from a network server. If that method should fail, then the system will boot from ROM.

```
Router# configure terminal
Router(config)# boot system flash gsxx
Router(config)# boot system gsxx 172.16.101.101
Router(config)# boot system rom
Router(config)# config-register 0x010F
Router(config)# end
Router# copy running-config startup-config
[ok]
```

Using this strategy, a router has three alternative sources from which to boot. These alternative sources help lessen the negative effects of a failure on network or file server.

RECOVERING A SYSTEM IMAGE USING XMODEM OR YMODEM (CISCO 1600 SERIES AND CISCO 3600 SERIES ONLY)

If you do not have access to a network server and need to download a system image (to update it, or if all the system images in Flash memory somehow are damaged or erased) you can copy an image from a local or remote computer (such as a PC, UNIX workstation, or Macintosh) using the Xmodem or Ymodem protocols. This functionality primarily serves as a disaster recovery technique and is illustrated in Figure 11–2.

Xmodem and Ymodem are common protocols used for transferring files and are included in applications such as Windows 3.1 (TERMINAL.EXE), Windows 95 (HyperTerminal), Windows NT 3.5x (TERMINAL.EXE), Windows NT 4.0 (HyperTerminal), and Linux UNIX freeware (minicom).

Cisco 3600 series routers do not support XBOOT functionality, a disaster recovery technique for Cisco IOS software, and do not have a separate boot helper (rxboot) image.

Xmodem and Ymodem downloads are slow, so you should use them only when you do not have access to a network server. You can speed up the transfer by setting the transfer port speed to 115,200 bps.

On the Cisco 3600 series, you can perform the file transfer using Cisco IOS software or, if all local system images are damaged or erased, the ROM monitor. When you use Cisco IOS software for an Xmodem or Ymodem file transfer, the transfer can occur on either the AUX port or the console port. The AUX port, which supports hardware flow control, is recommended. File transfers from the ROM monitor must use the console port.

On the Cisco 1600 series, you can only perform the file transfer from the ROM monitor over the console port.

Figure 11–2

Copying a System Image to a Cisco 3600 Series Router with Xmodem or Ymodem

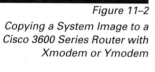

Cisco 3600 series router downloading a Cisco IOS software image from a remote or local PC

Local PC running terminal emulation software and Xmodem

Remote PC running terminal emulation software and Xmodem

To copy a Cisco IOS image from a computer or workstation to a router using the Xmodem or Ymodem protocol, enter one of the following commands:

Task	Command
For the Cisco 3600 only, copy a system image from a computer to Flash memory using Cisco IOS software in EXEC mode.	**copy xmodem** *device*:[*partition*:][*filename*] or **copy ymodem** *device*:[*partition*:][*filename*]
Copy a system image from a computer to Flash memory using the ROM monitor.	**xmodem** [**-y**] [**-c**] [**-e**] [**-f**] [**-r**] [**-x**] [**-s** *data-rate*] [*filename*] (Cisco 1600 series only) **xmodem** [**-c** | **-y** | **-r** | **-x**] [*filename*] (Cisco 3600 series only) The **-c** option provides CRC-16 checksumming; **-y** uses the Ymodem protocol; **-e** erases the first partition in Flash memory; **-f** erases all of Flash memory; **-r** downloads the image to DRAM (the default is Flash memory); and **-x** prevents the image from executing after download; and **-s** sets the console port data rate.

The computer from which you transfer the Cisco IOS image must be running terminal emulation software and the Xmodem or Ymodem protocol.

For the Cisco 1600 series, if you include the **-r** option (download to DRAM), your router must have enough DRAM to hold the file being transferred. To run from Flash memory, an image must be positioned as the first file in Flash memory. If you are copying a new image to boot from Flash memory, erase all existing files first.

Xmodem Transfer Example Using the Cisco IOS Software (Cisco 3600 series only)

This example shows a file transfer using Cisco IOS software and the Xmodem protocol. The Ymodem protocol follows a similar procedure, using the **copy ymodem** command.

To transfer a Cisco IOS image from a computer running terminal emulation software and the Xmodem protocol, follow these steps:

Step 1   Place a Cisco IOS software image on the remote computer's hard drive. You can download an image from Cisco Connection Online.

Step 2   To transfer from a remote computer, connect a modem to the AUX port of your Cisco 3600 series router and to the standard telephone network. The AUX port is set by default to a speed of 9,600 bps, 2 stop bits, and no parity. The maximum speed is 115,200 bps. Configure the router for both incoming and outgoing calls by entering the **modem inout** command.

Connect a modem to the remote computer and to the telephone network. The remote computer dials through the telephone network and connects to the router.

To transfer from a local computer, connect the router's AUX port to a serial port on the computer, using a null-modem cable. The AUX speed configured on the router must match the transfer speed configured on the local computer.

Step 3 At the EXEC prompt in the terminal emulator window of the computer, enter the **copy xmodem flash:** command:

```
Router# copy xmodem flash:
                **** WARNING ****
x/ymodem is a slow transfer protocol limited to the current speed
settings of the auxiliary/console ports. The use of the auxiliary
port for this download is strongly recommended.
During the course of the download no exec input/output will be
available.
            ---- ******* ----
```

Press **Enter** to continue.

Step 4 Specify whether to use cyclic redundancy check (CRC) block checksumming, which verifies that your data has been correctly transferred from the computer to the router. If your computer does not support CRC block checksumming, answer **no** at the prompt:

```
Proceed? [confirm]
Use crc block checksumming? [confirm] no
```

Step 5 Determine how many times the software should try to receive a bad block of data before it declares the copy operation a failure. The default is 10 retries. A higher number might be needed for noisy telephone lines. You can configure an unlimited number of retries.

```
Max Retry Count [10]: 7
```

Step 6 Decide whether you want to check that the file is a valid Cisco 3600 series image:

```
Perform image validation checks? [confirm]
Xmodem download using simple checksumming with image validation
Continue? [confirm]
```

After the transfer has begun, and if the image is valid, the software checks to see whether enough Flash memory space exists on the router to accommodate the transfer:

```
System flash directory:
File  Length   Name/status
  1   1738244  images/c3600-i-mz
[1738308 bytes used, 2455996 available, 4194304 total]
```

Step 7 Enter the destination filename:

```
Destination file name ? new-ios-image
```

Step 8   If you don't want the contents of internal Flash memory erased before the file transfer, enter **no**:

```
Erase flash device before writing? [confirm] no

Copy '' from server
  as 'new-ios-image' into Flash WITHOUT erase? [yes/no] yes
Ready to receive file...........
```

Step 9   Start an Xmodem or Ymodem send operation with the terminal emulation software on the computer that is sending the system image to the router. See your emulation software application's manual for instructions on how to execute a file transfer. Depending on the application you use, the emulation software might display the progress of the file transfer.

Xmodem Transfer Example Using the ROM Monitor

This example shows a file transfer using the ROM monitor and the Xmodem protocol. To transmit with the Ymodem protocol, use the **xmodem -y** command.

For the Cisco 3600, the router must have enough DRAM to hold the file being transferred, even if you are copying to Flash memory. The image is copied to the first file in internal Flash memory. Any existing files in Flash memory are erased. Copying files to Flash partitions or to the second-file position is not supported.

CAUTION

A modem connection from the telephone network to your console port introduces security issues that you should consider before enabling the connection. For example, remote users can dial into your modem and access the router's configuration settings.

Step 1   Place a Cisco IOS software image on the remote computer's hard drive. You can download an image from Cisco Connection Online or from the Feature Pack (Cisco 1600 series only).

Step 2   To transfer from a remote computer, connect a modem to the console port of your router and to the standard telephone network. The modem and console port must communicate at the same speed, which can be from 9600 to 115200 bps (Cisco 3600 series) or from 1200 to 115200 bps (Cisco 1600 series), depending on the speed supported by your modem. Use the **confreg** ROM monitor command to configure the console port transmission speed for the router. For the Cisco 1600 series, you also can set the transmission speed with the **-s** option.

Connect a modem to the remote computer and to the telephone network. The remote computer dials through the telephone network and connects to the router.

To transfer from a local computer, connect the router's console port to a serial port on the computer, using a null-modem cable. The console port speed configured on the router must match the transfer speed configured on the local computer.

NOTES

If you are transferring from a local computer, you might need to configure the terminal emulation program to ignore RTS/DTR signals.

Step 3   You should see a ROM monitor prompt in the terminal emulation window:

```
rommon >
```

Enter the **xmodem** ROM monitor command, along with any desired copy options and, optionally, the filename of the Cisco IOS image. The image loads into Flash memory by default; to download to DRAM instead, use the -r option. The image is normally executed on completion of the file transfer; to prevent execution, use the -x option. The -c option specifies CRC-16 checksumming, which is more sophisticated and thorough than standard checksumming, if it is supported by the computer:

```
rommon > xmodem -c new-ios-image
Do not start the sending program yet...
          File size          Checksum    File name
    1738244 bytes (0x1a8604)    0xdd25 george-admin/c3600-i-mz

WARNING: All existing data in flash will be lost!
Invoke this application only for disaster recovery.
Do you wish to continue? y/n  [n]:  yes
Ready to receive file new-ios-image ...
```

Step 4   Start an Xmodem send operation, which is initiated from the terminal emulation software on the remote computer that is sending the system image to the router. See your emulation software application's manual for instructions on how to execute a Xmodem file transfer.

Step 5   The Cisco IOS image is transferred and executed. If you are transferring from a remote computer, the computer maintains control of your console port even after the new Cisco IOS image is running. To release control to a local terminal, reconfigure the speed of the router's console port to match the speed of the local terminal by entering the **speed** *bps* configuration command from the remote computer at the router prompt:

```
Router# configure terminal
Router(config)# line 0
Router(config-line)# speed 9600
```

The remote connection is broken, and you can disconnect the modem from the console port and reconnect the terminal line.

LOADING AND DISPLAYING MICROCODE IMAGES

On the Cisco 7000 series with RSP7000 and Cisco 7500 series, you also can load and display microcode images, as described in the following sections:

- Understanding Microcode Images
- Specifying the Location of the Microcode Images
- Reloading the Microcode Image
- Displaying Microcode Image Information

Understanding Microcode Images

Microcode images contain microcode that runs on various hardware devices. By default, the system loads the microcode bundled with the system software. However, you can configure the router to use microcode stored in Flash.

Cisco 7000 series with a RSP7000 and Cisco 7500 series each have a writable control store (WCS) that stores microcode. You can load updated microcode onto the WCS from boot Flash or a Flash memory card inserted in one of the PCMCIA slots of the RSP card.

You can update microcode without having physical access to the router.

Specifying the Location of the Microcode Images

By default, the system loads the microcode bundled with the system software. However, you can configure the router to load different microcode.

To specify the location of the microcode to use, complete the following tasks:

Task		Command
Step 1	(Optional) Copy microcode files into Flash. You only need to if you are loading the microcode from Flash. See the section "Copying Images from a Network Server to Flash Memory" for more information about how to copy TFTP images to Flash memory.	**copy tftp flash** or **copy tftp** *file-id*
Step 2	Enter configuration mode.	**configure terminal**
Step 3	Configure the router to load microcode into the WCS from Flash memory or the system image. By default, the microcode bundled with the system image is loaded.	**microcode** *interface* [**flash** *filename* [*slot*] | **system** [*slot*]]
Step 4	Exit configuration mode.	**end**

Task	Command
Step 5 Retain new configuration information when the system is rebooted.	**copy running-config startup-config**

If an error occurs when you are attempting to download microcode, the system loads the default system microcode image, which is bundled with the system software.

NOTES

Microcode images cannot be compressed.

Reloading the Microcode Image

The configuration commands specifying the microcode are implemented following one of three events:

- The system is booted.
- A card is inserted or removed.
- The configuration command **microcode reload** is issued.

After you have entered a microcode configuration command and one of these events has taken place, all cards are reset, loaded with microcode from the appropriate sources, tested, and enabled for operation.

To signal to the system that all microcode configuration commands have been entered and the processor cards should be reloaded, complete the following task in global configuration mode:

Task	Command
Notify the system that all microcode configuration commands have been entered and the processor cards should be reloaded.	**microcode reload**

If Flash memory is busy because a card is being removed or inserted, or a **microcode reload** command is executed while Flash is locked, the files will not be available and the onboard ROM microcode will be loaded. Issue another **microcode reload** command when Flash memory is available, and the proper microcode will be loaded. The **show flash** command will show if another user or process has locked Flash memory.

NOTES

The **microcode reload** command should not be used while Flash is in use. For example, do not use this command when a **copy tftp flash** or **show flash** command is active.

The **microcode reload** command is automatically added to your running configuration when you issue a microcode command that changes the system's default behavior of loading all processors from ROM.

Displaying Microcode Image Information

To display microcode information, perform the following task in EXEC mode:

Task	Command
Display microcode information.	**show microcode**

## CHAPTER 12

System Image and Microcode Commands

This chapter provides detailed descriptions of the commands used to load and copy system images and microcode images. System images contain the system software. Microcode images contain microcode to be downloaded to various hardware devices.

NOTES

Commands in this chapter that have been replaced by new commands continue to perform their normal functions in the current release but are no longer documented. Support for these commands will cease in a future release. Table 12–1 maps the old commands with their replacements.

Table 12–1 *Mapping Old Commands to New Commands*

Old Command	New Command
copy erase flash	erase flash
copy verify or copy verify flash	verify flash or verify
copy verify bootflash	verify bootflash

For configuration information and examples, see Chapter 11, "Loading and Maintaining System Images and Microcode."

COPY VERIFY

The **verify** or **verify flash** command replaces this command. Refer to the descriptions of the **verify** and **verify flash** commands for more information.

COPY VERIFY BOOTFLASH

The **verify bootflash** command replaces this command. Refer to the description of the **verify boot-flash** command for more information.

COPY XMODEM

To copy a Cisco IOS image from a local or remote computer (such as a PC, Macintosh, or UNIX workstation) to Flash memory on a Cisco 3600 series router using the Xmodem protocol, use the **copy xmodem** EXEC command.

> **copy xmodem** *device*:[*partition-number*:][*filename*]

Syntax	Description
device	One of the following devices, which must be followed by a colon (:):
	• **flash** – Internal Flash memory
	• **slot0** – Flash memory card in PCMCIA slot 0
	• **slot1** – Flash memory card in PCMCIA slot 1
partition-number	(Optional) Partition number of the destination Flash memory device. You must enter a colon (:) after the partition number if a filename follows it.
filename	• (Optional) Name of the destination file.

Command Mode
EXEC

Usage Guidelines
This command first appeared in Cisco IOS Release 11.2 P.

The **copy tftp flash:** and **copy rcp flash:** commands are much faster than the **copy xmodem flash:** command. Use the **copy xmodem flash:** command only if you do not have access to a TFTP or rcp server.

This copy operation is performed through the console or AUX port. The AUX port, which supports hardware flow control, is recommended.

No output is displayed on the port over which the transfer is occurring. You can use the **logging buffered** command to log all router messages sent to the console port during the file transfer.

Example

The following command initiates a file transfer from a local or remote computer to the router's internal Flash memory using the Xmodem protocol:

```
copy xmodem flash:
```

Related Commands

copy ymodem
xmodem

COPY YMODEM

To copy a Cisco IOS image from a local or remote computer (such as a PC, Macintosh, or UNIX workstation) to Flash memory on a Cisco 3600 series router using the Ymodem protocol, use the **copy ymodem** EXEC command.

copy ymodem *device*:[*partition-number*:][*filename*]

Syntax	Description
• *device*	• One of the following devices, which must be followed by a colon (:):
	• **flash** — Internal Flash memory
	• **slot0** — Flash memory card in PCMCIA slot 0
	• **slot1** — Flash memory card in PCMCIA slot 1
partition-number	(Optional) Partition number of the destination Flash memory device. You must enter a colon (:) after the partition number if a filename follows it.
filename	(Optional) Name of the destination file.

Command Mode

EXEC

Usage Guidelines

This command first appeared in Cisco IOS Release 11.2 P.

The **copy tftp flash:** and **copy rcp flash:** commands are much faster than the **copy ymodem flash:** command. Use the **copy ymodem flash:** command only if you do not have access to a TFTP or rcp server.

This copy operation is performed through the console or AUX port. The AUX port, which supports hardware flow control, is recommended.

No output is displayed on the port over which the transfer is occurring. You can use the **logging buffered** command to log all router messages sent to the console port during the file transfer.

Part II

Command Reference

Example

The following command initiates a file transfer from a local or remote computer to the router's internal Flash memory using the Ymodem protocol:

```
copy ymodem flash:
```

Related Commands

copy xmodem

MICROCODE

To specify the location of the microcode that you want to download from Flash memory into the writable control store (WCS) on a Cisco 7000 series with RSP7000 or Cisco 7500 series, use the **microcode** global configuration command. Use the **no** form of this command to load the microcode bundled with the system image.

> **microcode** *interface* [**flash** *file-id* [*slot*] | **system** [*slot*]]
> **no microcode** *interface* [**flash** *file-id* [*slot*] | **system** [*slot*]]

Syntax	Description
interface	One of the following interface processor names: **aip, cip, eip, feip, fip, fsip, hip, mip, sip, sp, ssp, trip, vip,** or **vip2.**
flash	(Optional) If the **flash** keyword is specified, a *file-id* argument is required, unless you are using the **no microcode** *interface* **flash** command.
filename	(Optional) Filename of the microcode in Flash memory that you want to download. This argument is only used with the **flash** keyword. If you use the **flash** keyword, the name of the microcode file in Flash is required unless the command is **no microcode** *interface* **flash.** (This command results in the same default condition as the command **microcode** *interface* **rom,** which indicates that the card should be loaded from its onboard ROM microcode.)
file-id	Specifies a *device:filename* of the microcode file to download. The colon (:) is required. Valid devices are as follows: • **bootflash**—Internal Flash memory. • **slot0**—First PCMCIA slot. • **slot1**—Second PCMCIA slot. Slave devices such as slaveslot0 are invalid. The slave's file system is not available during microcode reloads. The *filename* is the name of the microcode file.

Syntax	Description
slot	Number of the slot. Range is 0 to 15.
system	(Optional) If **system** is specified, the router loads the microcode from the microcode bundled into the system image you are running for that interface type.

Default

The default is to load from the microcode bundled in the system image.

Command Mode

Global configuration

Usage Guidelines

This command first appeared in Cisco IOS Release 11.0.

When using HSA for simple hardware backup, ensure that the master and slave RSP card contain the same microcode image in the same location when the router is to load the interface processor microcode from a flash *file-id*. Thus, if the slave RSP becomes the master, it will be able to find the microcode image and download it to the interface processor.

Example

In the following example, all FIP cards will be loaded with the microcode found in Flash memory file *fip.v141-7* when the system is booted, when a card is inserted or removed, or when the **microcode reload** global configuration command is issued. The configuration is then written to the startup configuration file.

```
Router(config)# microcode fip flash slot0:fip.v141-7
Router(config)# end
Router# copy running-config startup-config
```

Related Commands

microcode reload

MICROCODE RELOAD

To signal to the Cisco 7000 series with RSP7000 or Cisco 7500 series that all microcode configuration commands have been entered and the processor cards should be reloaded, use the **microcode reload** global configuration command.

microcode reload

Syntax   Description

This command has no arguments or keywords.

Command Mode

Global configuration

Usage Guidelines

This command first appeared in Cisco IOS Release 10.3.

You must be in configuration mode to enter this command. Immediately after you enter the **micro-code reload** command and press **Return**, the system reloads all microcode. Global configuration mode remains enabled; after the reload is complete, enter the **exit** command to return to the EXEC system prompt.

Example

In the following example, all controllers are reset, the specified microcode is loaded, and the CxBus complex is reinitialized according to the microcode configuration commands that have been written to memory:

```
Router# configure terminal
Router(config)# microcode reload
Router(config)# end
```

Related Commands

microcode

SHOW FLH-LOG

To view the system console output generated during the Flash load helper operation, use the **show flh-log** privileged EXEC command.

show flh-log

Syntax   Description

This command has no arguments or keywords.

Command Mode

Privileged EXEC

Usage Guidelines

This command first appeared in Cisco IOS Release 10.3.

If you are a remote Telnet user performing the Flash upgrade without a console connection, this command enables you to retrieve console output when your Telnet connection has terminated due to the switch to the ROM image. The output indicates what happened during the download, and is particularly useful if the download fails.

Sample Display

The following is sample output from the **show flh-log** command:

```
Router# show flh-log

%FLH: abc/igs-kf.914 from 172.16.1.111 to flash...

System flash directory:
File  Length    Name/status
  1   2251320   abc/igs-kf.914

[2251384 bytes used, 1942920 available, 4194304 total]
Accessing file 'abc/igs-kf.914' on 172.16.1.111...
Loading from 172.16.13.111:

Erasing device...... erased
Loading from 172.16.13.111:
- [OK -
2251320/4194304 bytes]

Verifying checksum... OK (0x97FA)
Flash copy took 79292 msecs
%FLH: Re-booting system after download
Loading abc/igs-kf.914 at 0x3000040, size = 2251320 bytes [OK]

F3: 2183364+67924+259584 at 0x3000060


               Restricted Rights Legend

Use, duplication, or disclosure by the Government is
subject to restrictions as set forth in subparagraph
(c) of the Commercial Computer Software - Restricted
Rights clause at FAR sec. 52.227-19 and subparagraph
(c) (1) (ii) of the Rights in Technical Data and Computer
Software clause at DFARS sec. 252.227-7013.

            cisco Systems, Inc.
            170 West Tasman Drive
            San Jose, California 95134


Cisco Internetwork Operating System Software
Cisco IOS (tm) GS Software (GS7), Version 11.0
Copyright (c) 1986-1995 by cisco Systems, Inc.
Compiled Tue 06-Dec-94 14:01 by smith
Image text-base: 0x00001000, data-base: 0x005A9C94

cisco 2500 (68030) processor (revision 0x00) with 4092K/2048K bytes of
memory.
Processor board serial number 00000000
```

```
DDN X.25 software, Version 2.0, NET2 and BFE compliant.
ISDN software, Version 1.0.
Bridging software.
Enterprise software set supported. (0x0)
1 Ethernet/IEEE 802.3 interface.
2 Serial network interfaces.
 --More--

1 ISDN Basic Rate interface.
32K bytes of non-volatile configuration memory.

4096K bytes of processor board System flash (Read ONLY)
```

SHOW MICROCODE

To show the microcode bundled into a Cisco 7000 series with RSP7000 or Cisco 7500 series system, use the **show microcode** EXEC command.

show microcode

Syntax   Description

This command has no arguments or keywords.

Command Mode

EXEC

Usage Guidelines

This command first appeared in Cisco IOS Release 10.0.

Sample Display

The following is sample output from the **show microcode** command:

```
Router# show microcode

Microcode bundled in system

Card    Microcode   Target Hardware   Description
Type    Version     Version
----    ---------   ---------------   ----------
SP      2.3         11.x              SP version 2.3
EIP     1.1         1.x               EIP version 1.1
TRIP    1.2         1.x               TRIP version 1.2
FIP     1.4         2.x               FIP version 1.4
HIP     1.1         1.x               HIP version 1.1
SIP     1.1         1.x               SIP version 1.1
FSIP    1.1         1.x               FSIP version 1.1
```

VERIFY

On the Cisco 1600 series, Cisco 3600 series, and Cisco 7000 family, to verify the checksum of a file on a Flash memory device, use the **verify** EXEC command. This command replaces the **copy verify** and **copy verify flash** commands.

> **verify** [*device*:] *filename* (Cisco 7000 family)
>
> **verify** *device*:[*partition-number*:][*filename*] (Cisco 1600 series and Cisco 3600 series)

Syntax	Description
device:	(Optional for Cisco 7000 family) Device containing the file whose checksum is being verified. The colon (:) is required. Valid devices are as follows:
	• **flash**—Internal Flash memory in the Cisco 1600 series and Cisco 3600 series. This is the only valid device for the Cisco 1600 series.
	• **bootflash**—Internal Flash memory in the Cisco 7000 family.
	• **slot0**—First PCMCIA slot on the Cisco 3600 series and Cisco 7000 family.
	• **slot1**—Flash memory in the second PCMCIA slot on the Cisco 3600 series and Cisco 7000 family.
	• **slavebootflash**—Internal Flash memory on the slave RSP card of a Cisco 7507 or Cisco 7513 configured for HSA.
	• **slaveslot0**—First PCMCIA slot of the slave RSP card on a Cisco 7507 or Cisco 7513 configured for HSA.
	• **slaveslot1**—Second PCMCIA slot of the slave RSP card on a Cisco 7507 or Cisco 7513 configured for HSA.
	When you omit this argument, the system verifies the checksum of the specified file on the current working device.
filename	Name of a file on the specified Flash device. The file can be of any type. The maximum filename length is 63 characters. The filename is optional for the Cisco 1600 series and Cisco 3600 series.
partition-number	(Optional) Partition number to verify. You must enter a colon (:) after the partition number if a filename follows it.

Default

The current working device is the default device.

Command Mode

EXEC

Usage Guidelines

This command first appeared in Cisco IOS Release 11.0.

Use the **verify** command to verify the checksum of a file before using it. When you omit the *device*: argument, the system verifies the checksum of the specified file on the current working device.

Examples

The following example verifies the *gsxx* file on the Flash memory card inserted in slot 0:

```
verify slot0:gsxx
```

The following example verifies the checksum of the file *alz*, located in the fourth partition of the Flash memory card in slot 0 of a Cisco 3600 series router:

```
Router# verify slot0:4

PCMCIA Slot0 flash directory, partition 4:
File   Length   Name/status
  1    2205860  dirt/images/c3600-d-mz
  2    1711128  dirt/images/c3600-i-mz.test
  3    850      alz
[3918032 bytes used, 276272 available, 4194304 total]

Name of file to verify? alz
Verifying checksum for 'alz' (file # 3)...  OK
```

The following example verifies the checksum of the file *alz*, located in the fourth partition of the Flash memory card on a Cisco 1600 series:

```
Router# verify flash:4

System flash directory, partition 4:
File   Length   Name/status
  1    2205860  dirt/images/c1600-d-mz
  2    1711128  dirt/images/c1600-i-mz.test
  3    850      alz
[3918032 bytes used, 276272 available, 4194304 total]

Name of file to verify? alz
Verifying checksum for 'alz' (file # 3)...  OK
```

Related Commands

cd
copy flash
copy verify
ip rcmd remote-username
pwd
show flash

VERIFY BOOTFLASH

To verify the checksum of a boot image in boot Flash memory, use the **verify bootflash** EXEC command. This command replaces the **copy verify bootflash** command.

verify bootflash

Syntax   Description

This command has no arguments or keywords.

Command Mode

EXEC

Usage Guidelines

This command first appeared in Cisco IOS Release 11.0.

You can use this command only on routers that have two banks of Flash: one bank for the boot image and the second bank for the system image.

Each boot software image that is distributed on disk uses a single checksum for the entire image. This checksum is displayed only when the image is copied into Flash memory; it is not displayed when the image file is copied from one disk to another.

The README file, which is included with the image on the disk, lists the name, file size, and checksum of the image. Review the contents of the README file before loading or duplicating the new image so that you can verify the checksum when you copy it into Flash memory or onto a server.

To display the contents of boot Flash memory, use the **show bootflash** command. The Flash contents listing does not include the checksum of individual files. To recompute and verify the image checksum after the image has been copied into Flash memory, use the **verify bootflash** command. When you enter the command, the system prompts you for the filename to verify. By default, it prompts for the last file (most recent) in Flash. Press **Return** to recompute the default file checksum, or enter the name of a different file at the prompt.

Example

The following example verifies the boot file *c4500-xboot*:

```
Router# verify bootflash

Boot flash directory:
File  name/status
   1   c4500-xboot
[1387336 bytes used, 2806968 bytes available]

Name of file to verify? c4500-xboot
Verifying checksum for 'c4500-xboot' (file # 1)... [OK]
```

Related Commands

copy bootflash tftp
copy mop bootflash
copy tftp bootflash
erase bootflash
show flh-log

VERIFY FLASH

To verify the checksum of Flash memory, use the **verify flash** EXEC command. This command replaces the **copy verify** and **copy verify flash** commands.

     verify flash

Syntax   Description

This command has no arguments or keywords.

Command Mode

EXEC

Usage Guidelines

This command first appeared in Cisco IOS Release 10.3.

The **verify flash** command is not supported on the Cisco 1600 series, Cisco 3600 series, Cisco 7000 series with RSP7000 and the Cisco 7500 series.

Each system software or microcode image that is distributed on disk uses a single checksum for the entire image. This checksum is displayed only when the image is copied into Flash memory; it is *not* displayed when the image file is copied from one disk to another.

The README file (which is included with the image on the disk) lists the name, file size, and checksum of the image. Review the contents of the README file before loading or duplicating the new image so that you can verify the checksum when you copy it into the Flash memory or onto a TFTP server.

To display the contents of Flash memory, use the **show flash** command. The Flash content listing does not include the checksum of individual files. To recompute and verify the image checksum after the image file is copied into Flash memory, use the **verify flash** command. When you enter the command, the screen prompts you for the filename to verify. By default, it prompts for the last file in Flash (most recent). Press **Return** to recompute the default file checksum, or enter the filename of a different file at the prompt.

Examples

The following example verifies the file *gsxx* in Flash memory:

```
Router# verify flash

Name of file to verify [gsxx]?
Verifying via checksum...
vvvvvvvvvvvvvvvvvvvvvvvvvvvvvvvv

Flash verification successful. Length = 1923712, checksum = 0xA0C1
```

The following example verifies an image when more than one Flash memory partition exists:

```
Router# verify flash

System flash partition information:
Partition   Size    Used    Free    Bank-Size   State       Copy-Mode
    1       4096K   2048K   2048K   2048K       Read Only   RXBOOT-FLH
    2       4096K   2048K   2048K   2048K       Read/Write  Direct

[Type ?<no> for partition directory; ? for full directory; q to abort]
```

The system prompts only if there are two or more read/write partitions. If the partition entered is not valid, the process terminates. You can enter a partition number, a question mark (**?**) for a directory display of all partitions, or a question mark and a number (**?***number*) for directory display of a particular partition. The default is the first partition.

```
File  Length   Name/status
  1   3459720  master/igs-j.111.1.0
[3459784 bytes used, 734520 available, 4194304 total]

Name of file to verify? master/igs-j.111.1.0
Verifying checksum for 'master/igs-j.111.1.0' (file # 1)... OK
```

Related Commands

show flash
verify

XMODEM

To copy a Cisco IOS image to a Cisco 1600 series or Cisco 3600 series router using the ROM monitor and the Xmodem or Ymodem protocol, use the **xmodem** ROM monitor command.

xmodem [-c] [-y] [-e] [-f] [-r] [-x] [-s *data-rate*] [*filename*]

Syntax	Description
-c	(Optional) CRC-16 checksumming, which is more sophisticated and thorough than standard checksumming.
-y	(Optional) Uses Ymodem protocol for higher throughput.

Syntax	Description
-e	(Optional) Erases the first partition in Flash memory before starting the download. This option is only valid for the Cisco 1600.
-f	(Optional) Erases all of Flash memory before starting the download. This option is only valid for the Cisco 1600.
-r	(Optional) Downloads the file to DRAM. The default is Flash memory.
-x	(Optional) Do not execute Cisco IOS image on completion of the download.
-s *data-rate*	(Optional) Sets the console port's data rate during file transfer. Values are 1,200, 2,400, 4,800, 9,600, 19,200, 38,400, and 115,200 bps. The default rate is specified in the configuration register. This option is only valid for the Cisco 1600 series.
filename	(Optional) Filename to copy. This argument is ignored when -r is specified, because only one file can be copied to DRAM. On the Cisco 1600 series, files are loaded to the ROM for execution.

Default

Xmodem protocol with 8-bit CRC, file downloaded into Flash memory and executed on completion.

Command Mode

ROM monitor

Usage Guidelines

This command first appeared in Cisco IOS Release 11.2 P.

The Cisco 3600 series does not support XBOOT functionality. If your Cisco IOS image is erased or damaged, you cannot load a new image over the network.

Use the **xmodem** ROM monitor command to download a new system image to your router from a local personal computer (such as a PC, Mac, or UNIX workstation), or a remote computer over a modem connection, to the router's console port. The computer must have a terminal emulation application that supports these protocols.

For the Cisco 3600 series, your router must have enough DRAM to hold the file being transferred, even if you are copying to Flash memory. The image is copied to the first file in internal Flash memory. Any existing files in Flash memory are erased. There is no support for partitions or copying as a second file.

For the Cisco 1600 series, if you include the -r option, your router must have enough DRAM to hold the file being transferred. To run from Flash, an image must be positioned as the first file in Flash memory. If you are copying a new image to boot from Flash, erase all existing files first.

CAUTION

A modem connection from the telephone network to your console port introduces security issues that you should consider before enabling the connection. For example, remote users can dial into your modem and access the router's configuration settings.

NOTES

If the file to be downloaded is not a valid router image, the copy operation is automatically terminated.

Example

The following example uses the **xmodem -c** *filename* ROM monitor command to copy the file *new-ios-image* from a remote or local computer:

```
rommon > xmodem -c new-ios-image
Do not start the sending program yet...
        File size          Checksum   File name
    1738244 bytes (0x1a8604)    0xdd25 george-admin/c3600-i-mz

WARNING: All existing data in bootflash will be lost!
Invoke this application only for disaster recovery.
Do you wish to continue? y/n  [n]:  yes
Ready to receive file new-ios-image ...
```

Related Commands

copy xmodem
copy ymodem

13

Maintaining Router Memory

This chapter describes how to maintain and use the different types of memory on your router.

To benefit most from the instructions and organization of this chapter, your router must contain a minimal configuration that allows you to interact with the system software. You can create a basic configuration file using the **setup** command facility. See the user guide for your hardware platform for more information on using **setup** at first-time startup. See the "Using Setup for Configuration Changes" section in Chapter 3, "Using Configuration Tools," for information on using **setup** after first-time startup.

For a complete description of the memory commands mentioned in this chapter, see Chapter 14, "Router Memory Commands."

NOTES

One or more of the commands that previously appeared in this chapter have been replaced by new commands. Table 13–1 maps the old commands to their replacements. The old commands continue to perform their normal functions in the current release, but support for these commands will cease in a future release.

Table 13–1 *Mapping Old Commands to New Commands*

Old Command	New Command
copy erase flash	erase flash
copy verify or copy verify flash	verify flash (on all systems except Cisco 1600 series, Cisco 3600 series, Cisco 7000 family)
	verify (on Cisco 1600 series, Cisco 3600 series, Cisco 7000 family)
copy verify bootflash	verify bootflash

Maintaining Router Memory Task List

You can perform the tasks related to Flash memory in the following sections:

- Displaying Memory Information
- Comparing Types of Memory
- Reallocating DRAM Memory (Cisco 3600 series only)
- Partitioning Flash Memory
- Using Flash Load Helper to Upgrade Software on Run-from-Flash Systems
- Using Flash Upgrade Features (Cisco 3000 and Cisco 4000 series)
- Formatting Flash Memory (Cisco 7000 family)
- Device Management
- Erasing Boot Flash Memory on a Cisco 4500
- Deleting, Erasing, and Recovering Files on a Device

Format Flash Memory is a required first task if you are using a new PCMCIA Flash memory card on the Cisco 7000 family.

NOTES

These tasks assume you have a minimal configuration that you want to modify.

Displaying Memory Information

Perform the following tasks in EXEC mode to display information about system memory:

Task	Command
Step 1 List information about Flash memory, including system image filenames and amounts of memory used and remaining.	**show flash**
Step 2 List the names of the Flash devices currently supported on the router.	**show flash devices** (Cisco 7000 family only)
Step 3 List information about Flash memory, including system image filenames, amounts of memory used and remaining, and Flash partitions.	**show** *device***: [all	chips	detailed	err	partition** *number* **	summary]** (Cisco 1600 series and Cisco 3600 series)
	**show flash [all	chips	filesys]** [*device***:]** (Cisco 7000 family only)
	**show flash [all	chips	detailed	err	partition** *number* **[all	chips	detailed	err]	summary]** (all other platforms)

COMPARING TYPES OF MEMORY

Your router has many different locations where it can store images, configuration files, and microcode. Refer to your hardware documentation for details on the following:

- Which types of memory your router contains
- Where files can be located
- Where images and boot images are located by default

DRAM

Dynamic random-access memory contains two types of memory:

- Primary, main, or processor memory, which is reserved for the CPU to execute Cisco IOS software and to hold the running configuration and routing tables.
- Shared, packet, or I/O memory, which buffers data transmitted or received by the router's network interfaces.

On the Cisco 3600 series routers, you can use the **memory-size iomem** command to configure the proportion of DRAM devoted to main memory and to shared memory.

EPROM

Erasable Programmable Read Only Memory (EPROM). This memory is often referred to simply as ROM. It sometimes contains the following:

- ROM Monitor, which provides a user interface when the router cannot find a valid image.
- The boot loader/helper software (also called the boot image), which helps the router boot when it cannot find a valid Cisco IOS image in Flash memory.

NVRAM

Non-volatile Random Access Memory (NVRAM) stores the following information:

- Startup configuration file for every platform except the Cisco 7000 family.
- For the Cisco 7000 family, the location of the startup configuration depends on the CONFIG_FILE Environment Variable.
- The software configuration register, which is used to determine which image to use when booting the router.

Flash

Flash memory stores the Cisco IOS software image. On some platforms, it can store configuration files or boot images. This section contains the following sections:

- Types of Flash Memory
- Flash Memory Device Naming Conventions

Types of Flash Memory

Depending on the hardware platform, Flash memory might be available as EPROMs, single in-line memory modules (SIMMs), or Flash memory cards. Check the appropriate hardware installation and maintenance guide for information about types of Flash memory available on a specific platform.

Depending on the platform, Flash memory is available in the following forms:

- Internal Flash memory
    - Internal Flash memory often contains the system image.
    - Some platforms have two or more banks of Flash memory on one single in-line memory module (SIMM). If the SIMM has two banks, it is sometimes referred to as *dual-bank Flash memory*. The banks can be partitioned into separate logical devices. See the "Partitioning Flash Memory" section for information about how to partition Flash memory.
- Bootflash
    - Bootflash often contains the boot image.
    - Bootflash sometimes contains the ROM Monitor.
- Flash memory PC cards or PCMCIA cards

    A Flash memory card that is inserted into a Personal Computer Memory Card International Association (PCMCIA) slot. This card is used to store system images, boot images, and configuration files.

    The following platforms contains PCMCIA slots:

    - The Cisco 1600 series routers include one PCMCIA slot.
    - The Cisco 3600 series routers include two PCMCIA slots.
    - The Cisco 7200 series Network Processing Engine (NPE) contains two PCMCIA slots.
    - The Cisco 7000 RSP700 card and the Cisco 7500 series Route Switch Processor (RSP) card contain two PCMCIA slots.

    Because the Cisco 3600 series and Cisco 7000 family can boot images and load configuration files from several locations, these systems use special ROM monitor environment variables to specify the location and filename of images and configuration files that the router is to use for various functions.

    Some ciscoFlash MIB variables support the Flash file system on the Cisco 7000 family.

    Note that the internal Flash and the Flash memory card cannot be used as a contiguous bank of Flash memory.

Flash Memory Device Naming Conventions

Many commands use the *device*: argument to specify a Flash memory device. A colon (:) always follows the device type. The available devices are as follows:

- For Cisco 1600 series routers, the device can be only the Flash memory card inserted into the PCMCIA slot (**flash:**).

- For Cisco 3600 series routers, the device can be internal Flash memory (**flash:**) or a Flash memory PC card inserted in one of the PCMCIA slots (**slot0:** or **slot1:**).

- For Cisco 7000 family routers, the device can be internal Flash memory (**bootflash:**) or a Flash memory PC card inserted in one of the PCMCIA slots (**slot0:** or **slot1:**).

For the Cisco 1600 series and Cisco 3600 series, some commands also include a partition number or a filename in the form *device*:[*partition-number*:][*filename*]. If a filename follows the partition number, you must also enter a colon after the partition number.

For example, **flash:** means internal Flash memory; **flash:1** means the first partition in internal Flash memory; and **flash:1:c3620-i-mz.112-5P** means a particular file in the first partition in internal Flash memory.

What You Can Do from Flash Memory

You can perform the following tasks using flash memory:

- Copy a system image from a server to Flash memory using TFTP or rcp.

- Copy a system image from Flash memory to a network server using TFTP or rcp.

- Copy an image from a Flash device to another Flash device (Cisco 3600 series and Cisco 7000 family).

- For the Cisco 4500 series and Cisco 7000 family, copy a boot image to Flash memory using TFTP or rcp.

- For the Cisco 4500 series and Cisco 7000 family, copy the Flash memory boot image to a network server using TFTP or rcp.

- Boot a router from a software image stored in Flash memory either automatically or manually.

NOTES

The system image stored in Flash memory can be changed only from privileged EXEC level on the console terminal.

Write Protection

Flash memory provides write protection against accidental erasing or reprogramming.

- Some platforms have a write-protect jumper that can be removed to prevent reprogramming of Flash memory. You must install the jumper when programming is required.

- Some platforms have write-protect switched on Flash memory cards that you can use to protect data. You must set the switch to *unprotected* to write data to the Flash memory card.

Refer to your hardware documentation for information on security jumpers and write-protect switches.

Run-from-Flash Systems

Many Cisco routers load the system image from Flash storage into RAM in order to run the Cisco IOS. However, some platforms, such as the Cisco 1600 Series and Cisco 2500 Series, execute the Cisco IOS directly in Flash memory. These platforms are "run-from-Flash memory" systems.

If you want to partition Flash memory, you must use a relocatable image. Relocatable images can be run from any location in Flash and can download images to any location. If you are upgrading from a nonrelocatable image to a relocatable image, you must erase Flash memory during the download so that the image is downloaded as the first file in Flash memory. All images for run-from-Flash platforms from Cisco IOS Release 11.0 and on are relocatable. See the "Image Naming Conventions" section in Chapter 11, "Loading and Maintaining System Images and Microcode" to determine whether your images are run-from-Flash images or are relocatable.

REALLOCATING DRAM MEMORY (CISCO 3600 SERIES ONLY)

DRAM memory in Cisco 3600 series routers is organized as one contiguous address space divided between processor memory and I/O memory. Depending on the type and number of network interfaces you have configured in the router, you might need to reallocate the DRAM memory partitioned to processor memory and I/O memory.

Cisco manufacturing configures most Cisco 3600 series routers to have 25 percent of the address space allocated to I/O memory and 75 percent allocated to processor memory. But for customer orders that require two or more ISDN PRI interfaces, DRAM memory is configured to provide 40 percent of the address space for I/O memory and 60 percent for processor memory. (See Figure 13–1.) Cisco Systems performs these DRAM memory adjustments before it ships each router.

NOTES

Routers running two or more ISDN PRI interfaces or 12 or more ISDN BRI interfaces require a DRAM memory configuration of 40 percent I/O memory and 60 percent processor memory.

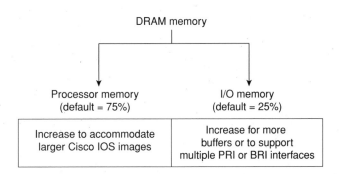

Figure 13–1

Components and Uses of DRAM Memory for Cisco 3600 Series Routers

However, there are cases where you might have to reallocate manually the DRAM memory split between processor memory and I/O memory after you have received a router from Cisco Systems.

For example, suppose you receive a Cisco 3640 router with the following running configuration:

- 2 Ethernet and 2 WAN interface card
- 8-port ISDN BRI with an NT1 network module
- IP feature set
- 16 MB of DRAM memory (by default, processor memory = 75%, I/O memory = 25%)
- 4 MB of Flash memory

Later, however, you add a 4-port ISDN BRI network module to the router. You now have 12 ISDN BRI interfaces running on the router. At this point, you must use the **memory-size iomem** command to configure 40 percent of the address space for I/O memory and 60 percent for processor memory.

To view your current mix of processor and I/O memory and reassign memory distribution accordingly, enter the following commands beginning in privileged EXEC mode:

Task	Command
Step 1 View the total amount of memory loaded on the router.	**show version**
Step 2 Determine the amount of free memory.	**show memory**[1]
Step 3 Enter global configuration mode.	**configure terminal**
Step 4 Allocate processor memory and I/O memory.	**memory-size iomem** *I/O-memory-percentage*[2]

Task	Command
Step 5 Exit global configuration mode.	exit
Step 6 Save the configuration to NVRAM.	copy running-config startup-config
Step 7 Reload the router to run the new image.	reload

[1] The Free(b) column in the **show memory** command's output shows how much I/O memory is available.
[2] The default is 40 percent for I/O memory and 60 percent for processor memory.

Valid I/O memory percentage values are 25, 30, 40 (the default), and 50. I/O memory size is the specified percentage of total memory size, rounded down to the nearest multiple of 1 MB. The remaining memory is processor memory.

The **memory-size iomem** command does not take effect until you save it to NVRAM using the **copy running-config startup-config** EXEC command and reload the router. However, when you enter the command, the software checks whether the new memory distribution leaves enough processor memory for the currently running Cisco IOS image. If not, the following message appears:

CAUTION

Attempting a memory partition that does not provide enough Processor memory for the current image. If you write memory now, this version of software may not be able to run.

When you enter the **reload** command to run a new image, the software calculates the new processor and I/O memory split. If there is not enough processor memory, it automatically reduces I/O memory to an alternative setting to load the image. If there is still not enough processor memory for the image to run, then you do not have enough DRAM.

Reallocating Processor Memory and I/O Memory Example

The following example allocates 40 percent of DRAM to I/O memory and the remaining 60 percent to processor memory. The example views the current allocation of memory, changes the allocation, saves the allocation, and reloads the router so the changes can take effect. In the **show memory** command output, the Free(b) column shows how much I/O memory is available

```
Router# show memory
                Head    Total(b)    Used(b)    Free(b)   Lowest(b)  Largest(b)
Processor   60913730    3066064     970420    2095644    2090736    2090892
      I/O     C00000    4194304    1382712    2811592    2811592    2805492
--More--

Router# configure terminal
Enter configuration commands, one per line.  End with CNTL/Z.
Router(config)# memory-size iomem 40
Router(config)# exit
Router#
```

```
Router# copy running-config startup-config
Building configuration...
[OK]

Router# reload

rommon > boot
program load complete, entry point: 0x80008000, size: 0x32ea24
Self decompressing the image :
##############################################################################
##############################################################################
################################################################ [OK]
```

PARTITIONING FLASH MEMORY

On the Cisco 1003, Cisco 1600 series, Cisco 2500 series, Cisco 3000, Cisco 3600 series, Cisco 4000, Cisco 4500, AS5100 series, and the AccessPro card, you can partition banks of Flash memory into separate, logical devices so that the router can hold and maintain two or more different software images. This partitioning allows you to write software into Flash memory while running software in another bank of Flash memory.

Systems that Support Partitioning

To partition Flash memory, you must have at least two banks of Flash memory; a bank is a set of four chips. This requirement includes systems that support a single SIMM that has two banks of Flash memory. The minimum partition size is the size of a bank.

CiscoFlash MIB variables support partitioned Flash.

Benefits of Partitioning Flash Memory

Partitioning Flash memory provides the following benefits:

- For any system, partitioning—rather than having one logical Flash memory device—provides a cleaner way of managing different files in Flash memory, especially if the Flash memory size is large.

- For systems that execute code out of Flash memory, partitioning allows you to download a new image into the file system in one Flash memory bank while an image is being executed from the file system in the other bank. The download is simple and causes no network disruption or downtime. After the download is complete, you can switch over to the new image at a convenient time.

- One system can hold two different images, one image acting as a backup for the other. Therefore, if a downloaded image fails to boot for some reason, the earlier running, good image is still available. Each bank is treated as a separate device.

Flash Load Helper versus Dual Flash Bank

Flash load helper is a software option that enables you to upgrade system software on run-from-Flash systems that have a single bank of Flash memory. It is a lower-cost software upgrade solution than dual-bank Flash, which requires two banks of Flash memory on one SIMM. Flash load helper is only available on the Cisco 2500 series and Cisco 3000.

You might use Flash load helper rather than partitioning Flash into two banks for one of the following reasons:

- If you want to download a new file into the same bank from which the current system image is executing.
- If you want to download a file that is larger than the size of a bank, and hence want to switch to a single-bank mode.
- If you have only one single-bank Flash SIMM installed. In this case, Flash load helper is the best option for upgrading your software.

See the "Using Flash Load Helper to Upgrade Software on Run-from-Flash Systems" section for information about using Flash load helper.

Partitioning Flash Memory

To partition Flash memory, perform the following task in global configuration mode:

Task	Command
Partition Flash memory.	**partition flash** *partitions* [*size1 size2*]
	partition *device*: [*number-of-partitions*][*partition-size*] (Cisco 1600 series and Cisco 3600 series)

This task will succeed only if the system has at least two banks of Flash and the partitioning does not cause an existing file in Flash memory to be split across the partitions.

For all platforms except the Cisco 1600 series and Cisco 3600 series, Flash memory can be partitioned only into two partitions.

For the Cisco 1600 series and Cisco 3600 series, the number of partitions that you can create in a Flash memory device equals the number of banks in the device. Enter the **show** *device*: **all** command to view the number of banks on the Flash memory device. The number of partition size entries you set must be equal to the number of specified partitions. For example, the **partition slot0: 2 8 8** command configures two partitions to be 8 MB in size each. The first 8 corresponds to the first partition; the second 8 corresponds to the second partition.

USING FLASH LOAD HELPER TO UPGRADE SOFTWARE ON RUN-FROM-FLASH SYSTEMS

Flash load helper is a software option that enables you to upgrade system software on run-from-Flash systems that have a single bank of Flash memory. It is a lower-cost software upgrade solution than dual-bank Flash, which requires two banks of Flash memory on one SIMM.

The Flash load helper software upgrade process is simple and does not require additional hardware; however, it does require some brief network downtime. A system image running from Flash can use Flash load helper only if the boot ROMs support Flash load helper. Otherwise, you must perform the Flash upgrade manually.

Flash load helper is an automated procedure that reloads the ROM-based image, downloads the software to Flash memory, and reboots to the system image in Flash memory. Flash load helper performs checks and validations to maximize the success of a Flash upgrade and minimize the chance of leaving Flash memory either in an erased state or with a file that cannot boot.

In run-from-Flash systems, the software image is stored in and executed from the Flash EPROM rather than from RAM. This method reduces memory cost. A run-from-Flash system requires enough Flash EPROM to hold the image and enough main system RAM to hold the routing tables and data structures. The system does not need the same amount of main system RAM as a run-from-RAM system, because the full image does not reside in RAM. Run-from-Flash systems include the Cisco 2500 series and some Cisco 3000 series.

Flash Load Helper Features

Flash load helper includes the following features:

- Confirms access to the specified source file on the specified server before erasing Flash memory and reloading to the ROM image for the actual upgrade.
- Warns you if the image being downloaded is not appropriate for the system.
- Prevents reloads to the ROM image for a Flash upgrade if the system is not set up for automatic booting and the user is not on the console terminal. In the event of a catastrophic failure during the upgrade, Flash load helper can bring up the boot ROM image as a last resort rather than force the system to wait at the ROM monitor prompt for input from the console terminal.
- Retries Flash downloads automatically up to six times. The retry sequence is as follows:
  - First try
  - Immediate retry
  - Retry after 30 seconds
  - Reload ROM image and retry
  - Immediate retry
  - Retry after 30 seconds

- Allows you to save any configuration changes made before you exit out of the system image.
- Notifies users logged in to the system of the impending switch to the boot ROM image so that they do not lose their connections unexpectedly.
- Logs console output during the Flash load helper operation into a buffer that is preserved through system reloads. You can retrieve the buffer contents from a running image. The output is useful when console access is unavailable or a failure occurs in the download operation.

Flash load helper also can be used on systems with multiple banks of Flash memory that support Flash memory partitioning. Flash load helper enables you to download a new file into the same partition from which the system is executing an image.

For information about how to partition multiple banks of Flash memory so your system can hold two different images, see the "Partitioning Flash Memory" section.

Flash Load Helper Configuration Task List

Perform the tasks in the following sections to use and monitor Flash load helper:

- Downloading a File Using Flash Load Helper
- Monitoring Flash Load Helper

Downloading a File Using Flash Load Helper

To download a new file to Flash memory using Flash load helper, check to make sure that your boot ROMs support Flash load helper and then perform the following task in privileged EXEC mode:

Task	Command
Download a new file to Flash memory.	**copy tftp flash**
	or
	copy mop flash

The following error message displays if you are in a Telnet session and the system is set for manual booting (the boot bits in the configuration register are zero):

```
ERR: Config register boot bits set for manual booting
```

In case of any catastrophic failure in the Flash memory upgrade, this error message helps to minimize the chance of the system going down to ROM monitor mode and being taken out of the remote Telnet user's control.

The system tries to bring up at least the boot ROM image if it cannot boot an image from Flash memory. Before reinitiating the **copy tftp flash** command, you must set the configuration register boot field to a nonzero value, using the **config-register** global configuration command.

The **copy tftp flash** command initiates a series of prompts to which you must provide responses. The dialog is similar to the following:

```
Router# copy tftp flash

*************************** NOTICE ******************************
Flash load helper v1.0
This process will accept the TFTP copy options and then terminate
the current system image to use the ROM based image for the copy.
Router functionality will not be available during that time. If
you are logged in via telnet, this connection will terminate. Users
with console access can see the results of the copy operation.
****************************************************************
```

If terminals other than the one on which this command is being executed are active, the following message appears:

```
There are active users logged into the system.

Proceed? [confirm] y
System flash directory:
File Length  Name/status
1    2251320 abc/igs-kf.914
[2251384 bytes used, 1942920 available, 4194304 total]
```

Enter the IP address or the name of the remote host from which you are copying:

```
Address or name of remote host [255.255.255.255]? 172.16.1.111
```

Enter the name of the file you want to copy:

```
Source file name? abc/igs-kf.914
```

Enter the name of the destination file:

```
Destination file name [default = source name]? <Return>
Accessing file 'abc/igs-kf.914' on 172.16.1.111....
Loading from 172.16.13.111:
Erase flash device before writing? [confirm] <Return>
```

If you choose to erase Flash memory, the dialog continues as follows. The **copy tftp flash** operation verifies the request from the running image by trying to copy a single block from the remote TFTP server. Then the Flash load helper is executed, causing the system to reload to the ROM-based system image.

```
Erase flash device before writing? [confirm] y
Flash contains files. Are you sure? [confirm] y
```

If the file does not seem to be a valid image for the system, a warning is displayed and a separate confirmation is sought from you.

```
Copy 'abc/igs-kf.914' from TFTP server
as 'abc/igs-kf.914' into Flash WITH erase? y

%SYS-5-RELOAD: Reload requested
%FLH: rxboot/igs-kf.914r from 172.16.1.111 to flash...
```

If you choose not to erase Flash memory and there is no file duplication, the dialog continues as follows:

```
Erase flash device before writing? [confirm] n
Copy 'abc/igs-kf.914' from TFTP server
as 'abc/igs-kf.914' into Flash WITHOUT erase? y
```

If you choose not to erase Flash memory, and there was file duplication, the dialog continues as follows:

```
Erase flash device before writing? [confirm] n
File 'abc/igs-kf.914' already exists; it will be invalidated!
Invalidate existing copy of 'abc/igs-kf' in flash memory? [confirm] y
Copy 'abc/igs-kf.914' from TFTP server
as 'abc/igs-kf.914' into Flash WITHOUT erase? y
```

If the configuration has been modified but not yet saved, you are prompted to save the configuration:

```
System configuration has been modified. Save? [confirm]
```

If you confirm to save the configuration, you might also receive this message:

```
Warning: Attempting to overwrite an NVRAM configuration previously
written by a different version of the system image. Overwrite the
previous NVRAM configuration? [confirm]
```

Users with open Telnet connections are notified of the system reload, as follows:

```
**System going down for Flash upgrade**
```

If the TFTP process fails, the copy operation is retried up to three times. If the failure happens in the middle of a copy operation so that only part of the file has been written to Flash memory, the retry does not erase Flash memory unless you specified an erase operation. The partly written file is marked as deleted, and a new file is opened with the same name. If Flash memory runs out of free space in this process, the copy operation is terminated.

After Flash load helper finishes copying (whether the copy operation is successful or not), it automatically attempts an automatic or a manual boot, depending on the value of bit zero of the configuration register boot field according to the following:

- If bit zero equals 0, the system attempts a default boot from Flash memory to load up the first bootable file in Flash memory. This default boot is equivalent to a manual **boot flash** command at the ROM monitor prompt.

- If bit zero equals 1, the system attempts to boot based on the boot configuration commands. If no boot configuration commands exist, the system attempts a default boot from Flash memory; that is, it attempts to load the first bootable file in Flash memory.

Monitoring Flash Load Helper

To view the system console output generated during the Flash load helper operation, use the image that has been booted up after the Flash memory upgrade. Perform the following task in privileged EXEC mode:

Task	Command
View the console output generated during the Flash load helper operation.	**show flh-log**

If you are a remote Telnet user performing the Flash upgrade without a console connection, this task allows you to retrieve console output when your Telnet connection has terminated due to the switch to the ROM image. The output indicates what happened during the download, and is particularly useful if the download fails.

USING FLASH UPGRADE FEATURES (CISCO 3000 AND CISCO 4000 SERIES)

On the Cisco 3000 series and Cisco 4000 series systems that do not run from Flash memory, the upgrade feature of checks and validations are performed to maximize the success of a Flash upgrade and minimize the chances of leaving Flash memory in either an erased state or with a nonbootable file. The software performs the following checks:

- Confirms that the file will fit into Flash memory (based on the erase option and presence of files in Flash memory). This check is done only for uncompressed system images.

- Attempts to recognize the type of file being downloaded and displays warnings where necessary.

FORMATTING FLASH MEMORY (CISCO 7000 FAMILY)

On the Cisco 7000 family, you must format a new Flash memory card before using it in a PCMCIA slot. You also can format internal Flash memory (bootflash).

Flash memory cards have sectors that can fail. You can reserve certain Flash memory sectors as "spares" for use when other sectors fail. Use the **format** command to specify between 0 and 16 sectors as spares. If you reserve a small number of spare sectors for emergencies, you do not waste space because you can use most of the Flash memory card. If you specify zero spare sectors and some sectors fail, you must reformat the Flash memory card and thereby erase all existing data.

The format operation requires at least Cisco IOS Release 11.0 system software.

Formatting Flash Memory Process

CAUTION

The following formatting procedure erases all information in Flash memory. To prevent the loss of important data, proceed carefully.

Use the following procedure to format Flash memory. If you are formatting bootflash, you can skip the first step. If you are formatting a Flash memory card, complete both steps.

Step 1   Insert the new Flash memory card into a PCMCIA slot. Refer to instructions on maintaining the router and replacing PCMCIA cards in your router's hardware documentation for instructions on performing this step.

Step 2   Format Flash memory.

To format Flash memory, complete the following task in EXEC mode:

Task	Command
Format Flash memory.	**format** [**spare** *spare-number*] *device1*: [[*device2*:][*monlib-filename*]]

The following example shows the **format** command that formats a Flash memory card inserted in slot 0.

```
Router# format slot0:
Running config file on this device, proceed? [confirm]y
All sectors will be erased, proceed? [confirm]y
Enter volume id (up to 31 characters): <Return>
Formatting sector 1 (erasing)
Format device slot0 completed
```

When the router returns you to the EXEC prompt, the new Flash memory card is successfully formatted and ready to use.

Recovering from Locked Blocks

To recover from locked blocks, reformat the Flash memory card. A locked block of Flash memory occurs when power is lost or a Flash memory card is unplugged during a write or erase operation. When a block of Flash memory is locked, it cannot be written to or erased, and the operation will consistently fail at a particular block location. The only way to recover from locked blocks is by reformatting the Flash memory card with the **format** command.

CAUTION

Formatting a Flash memory card to recover from locked blocks causes existing data to be lost.

DEVICE MANAGEMENT

If your router has multiple Flash memory devices, you can perform tasks such as changing the default directory, displaying the current device, and listing the files in the device.

Setting the System Default Flash Device

You can specify the Flash device that the system uses as the default device. Setting the default Flash device allows you to omit an optional *device*: argument from related commands. For all EXEC commands that have an optional *device*: argument, the system uses the device specified by the **cd** command when you omit the optional *device*: argument. For example, the **dir** command contains an optional *device*: argument and displays a list of files on a Flash memory device.

To specify a default Flash device, complete the following task from EXEC mode:

Task	Command
Set a default Flash memory device.	**cd** *device*:

The following example sets the default device to the Flash memory card inserted in slot 0:
```
cd slot0:
```

Displaying the Current Default Flash Device

To display the current default Flash device specified by the **cd** command, complete the following task from EXEC mode:

Task	Command
Display the current Flash memory device.	**pwd**

The following example shows that the present working device specified by the **cd** command is slot 0:

```
Router> pwd
slot0
Router>
```

The following example uses the **cd** command to change the present working device to bootflash and then uses the **pwd** command to display that present working device:

```
Router> cd bootflash:
Router> pwd
bootflash
Router>
```

Showing a List of Files on a Flash Device

You can view a list of the contents of a Flash memory device before manipulating its contents. For example, before copying a new configuration file to a Flash device, you might want to verify that the device does not already contain a configuration file with the same name. Similarly, before copying a Flash configuration file to another location, you might want to verify its filename for use in another command. You can check the contents a Flash device with the **dir** EXEC command.

To show a list of files on a specified Flash device, complete the following task from EXEC mode:

Task	Command
Display a list of files on a Flash memory device.	**dir** [/**all**	/**deleted**] [/**long**] [*device*:][*filename*]

The following example instructs the router to list undeleted files for the default device specified by the **cd** command. Notice that the router displays the information in short format because no keywords are used:

```
Router# dir
-#- -length- -----date/time------ name
1    620       May 4 1993 21:38:04 config1
2    620       May 4 1993 21:38:14 config2

7993896 bytes available (1496 bytes used)
```

The following example displays the long version of the same device:

```
Router# dir /long
.-#- ED --type-- --crc--- -seek-- nlen -length- -----date/time------ name
1    ... 1         37CEC52E 202EC   7    620       May 4  1993 21:38:04 config1
2    ... 1         37CEC52E 205D8   7    620       May 4  1993 21:38:14 config2

7993896 bytes available (1496 bytes used)
```

ERASING BOOT FLASH MEMORY ON A CISCO 4500

To erase the contents of boot Flash memory, perform the following task at the EXEC prompt:

Task	Command
Erase boot Flash memory.	**erase bootflash**

DELETING, ERASING, AND RECOVERING FILES ON A DEVICE

Depending on your particular platform, you can erase files, delete files, and recover files in Flash memory.

Erasing Files on a Flash Device

When you no longer need a file on a Flash memory device, you can erase it. Erased files cannot be recovered.

To erase a file on a specified Flash device, complete the following task from EXEC mode:

Task	Command
Erase a file in Flash memory.	**erase** [*device:*]*filename*

Erasing a File Example

The following example erases all files in the second partition in Flash memory:

```
Router# erase flash:2

System flash directory, partition 2:
File  Length   Name/status
  1   1711088  dirt/gate/c1600-i-mz
[1711152 bytes used, 15066064 available, 16777216 total]

Erase flash device, partition 2? [confirm]
Are you sure? [yes/no]: yes
Erasing device... eeeeeeeeeeeeeeeeeeeeeeeeeeeeeeeeeeeeeeeeeeeeeeeeeeeeeeeee ...erased
```

Deleting Files on a Flash Device

When you no longer need a file on a Flash memory device, you can delete it. When you delete a file, the router simply marks the file as deleted, but does not erase the file. This feature allows you to recover a "deleted" file, as discussed in the following section. You might want to recover a "deleted" image or configuration file if the new image or configuration file becomes corrupted.

To delete a file from a specified Flash device, complete the following task from EXEC mode:

Task	Command
Delete a file from a Flash memory device.	**delete** [*device:*]*filename*

If you omit the device, the router uses the default device specified by the **cd** command.

If you attempt to delete the configuration file specified by the CONFIG_FILE or BOOTLDR environment variable, the system prompts you to confirm the deletion. Also, if you attempt to delete the last valid system image specified in the BOOT environment variable, the system prompts you to confirm the deletion.

The following example deletes the *myconfig* file from a Flash memory card inserted in slot 0:

```
delete slot0:myconfig
```

Recovering Deleted Files on a Flash Device

You can undelete a deleted file. For example, you might want to revert to a previous configuration file because the current one is corrupt.

To undelete a deleted file on a Flash memory device, complete the following task from EXEC mode:

Task	Command
Undelete a deleted file on a Flash memory device.	**undelete** *index* [*device*:]

You must undelete a file by its index, because you can have multiple deleted files with the same name. For example, the "deleted" list could contain multiple configuration files with the name *router-config*. You undelete by index to indicate which of the many *router-config* files from the list to undelete. Use the **dir** command to learn the index number of the file you want to undelete.

You cannot undelete a file if a valid (undeleted) one with the same name exists. Instead, you first delete the existing file and then undelete the file you want. For example, if you had an undeleted version of the *router-config* file and you wanted to use a previous, deleted version instead, you cannot simply undelete the previous version by index. You must first delete the existing *router-config* file and then undelete the previous *router-config* file by index. You can undelete a file as long as the file has not been permanently erased via the **squeeze** command. You can delete and undelete a file up to 15 times.

The following example recovers the deleted file whose index number is 1 to the Flash memory card inserted in slot 0:

```
undelete slot0: 1
```

Permanently Deleting Files on a Flash Device

When a Flash memory device is full, you might need to rearrange the files so that the space used by the "deleted" files can be reclaimed. To determine whether a Flash memory device is full, use the **show flash** command.

To permanently delete files on a Flash memory device, complete the following task from privileged EXEC mode:

Task	Command
Permanently delete all deleted file on a Flash memory card.	**squeeze** *device*:

When you issue the **squeeze** command, the router copies all valid files to the beginning of Flash memory and erases all files marked "deleted." At this point, you cannot recover "deleted" files, and you now can write to the reclaimed Flash memory space.

NOTES

The squeeze operation can take as long as several minutes, because it can involve erasing and rewriting almost an entire Flash memory space.

## CHAPTER 14

Router Memory Commands

This chapter provides detailed descriptions of the commands used to maintain router memory.

NOTES

Commands in this chapter that have been replaced by new commands continue to perform their normal functions in the current release, but are no longer documented. Support for these commands will cease in a future release. Table 14–1 maps the old commands with their replacements.

Table 14–1 *Mapping Old Commands to New Commands*

Old Command	New Command
copy erase flash	erase flash
copy verify or copy verify flash	verify flash (on all systems except the Cisco 700 family)
	verify (on the Cisco 700 family)
copy verify bootflash	verify bootflash

For configuration information and examples, see Chapter 13, "Maintaining Router Memory."

CD

To set the default Flash device for the system, use the **cd** EXEC command.

    cd [*device:*]

Syntax	Description
device:	(Optional) Default device. The colon (:) is required. Valid devices are as follows:

- **bootflash**—Internal Flash memory in the Cisco 7000 family.
- **slot0**—First PCMCIA slot on the Cisco 7000 family. For the Cisco 7000 family, this device is the initial default device and the default device when you omit the *device*: argument.
- **slot1**—Second PCMCIA slot on the Cisco 7000 family.

Default

For the Cisco 7000 family, **slot0** is the initial default device and the default device when you omit the *device*: argument.

Command Mode

EXEC

Usage Guidelines

This command first appeared in Cisco IOS Release 11.0.

Use this command only with the Cisco 7000 family. For all EXEC commands that have an optional *device*: argument, the system uses the device specified by the **cd** command when you omit the optional *device*: argument. For example, the **dir** command contains an optional *device*: argument and displays a list of files on a Flash memory device. When you omit this *device*: argument, the system shows a list of the files on the Flash device specified by the **cd** command.

Example

The following example sets the default device to the Flash memory card inserted in the slot 0:

```
cd slot0:
```

Related Commands

copy
delete
dir
pwd
show flash
undelete

COPY

To copy any file from a source to a destination, use the **copy** EXEC command.

The **copy running-config startup-config** command replaces the **write memory** command. The **copy running-config rcp** or **copy running-config tftp** command replaces the **write network** command. The **copy rcp running-config** or **copy tftp running-config** command replaces the **configure network** command. The **copy rcp startup-config** or **copy tftp startup-config** command replaces the **configure overwrite-network** command.

copy *source destination*

Syntax	Description
source	The source location for the file to be copied. See Table 14–2 for a list of possible sources.
destination	Destination of the copied file. See Table 14–2 for a list of possible destinations.

Part II

Command Reference

Table 14–2   *Copy Command Sources and Destinations*

Keyword	Source or Destination
running-config	The current running configuration.
startup-config	The configuration used for initialization. The startup configuration is contained in NVRAM for all platforms except the Cisco 7000 family. The CONFIG_FILE environment variable specifies the startup configuration on a Cisco 7000 family. The Cisco 4500 series cannot use the copy running startup command.
tftp	A TFTP server.
rcp	An rcp server.
mop	A MOP server. This option is not valid for the Cisco 7500 series. This keyword cannot be used as a destination of a **copy** command.
flash	Internal Flash memory for all platforms except the Cisco 1600, Cisco 3600, and the Cisco 7000 family. On the Cisco 7000 family, this keyword can be used only as the source; in this case, the software prompts you for the device and filename. This keyword is never valid on Cisco 1600 series and Cisco 3600.
bootflash	Boot Flash memory. This keyword is only valid on platforms which have boot Flash memory.

Table 14–2   *Copy Command Sources and Destinations, Continued*

Keyword	Source or Destination
device:[*partition-number:*][*filename*]	A file in a partition in Flash memory device. This option is only valid on the Cisco 1600 and Cisco 3600 series. *device*—The colon (:) is required in the device name. See Table 14–3 for valid devices. *partition-number*—You must enter a colon (:) after the partition number if a filename follows it. *filename*—Name of the source or destination file. Wildcards are not permitted. The maximum filename length is 63 characters. If you omit the destination filename, the software uses the source filename.
[device:]filename	A file in a Flash memory device. This option is only valid on the Cisco 7000 family. *device*—The device is optional. If you omit the source or destination device, the Cisco IOS software uses the default device, as specified by the **cd** command. If a device is listed, the colon (:) is required. See Table 14–3 for valid devices. *filename*—Name of the source or destination file. Wildcards are not permitted. The maximum filename length is 63 characters. The source filename is required. If you omit the destination filename, the software uses the source filename.

Table 14–3   *Devices*

Keyword	Device
flash	Internal Flash memory on the Cisco 3600 series. On Cisco 1600 series routers, the keyword specifies the local Flash memory device, a Flash memory PC card inserted in a PCMCIA slot. This is the only valid device for the Cisco 1600 series.
bootflash	Internal Flash memory in the Cisco 7000 family.
slot0	First PCMCIA slot on the Cisco 3600 series and Cisco 7000 family.
slot1	Second PCMCIA slot on the Cisco 3600 series and Cisco 7000 family.

Table 14-3 *Devices, Continued*

Keyword	Device
nvram	Router's NVRAM. If you specify NVRAM, omit the filename. The colon (:) is required. Some platforms, such as the Cisco 1600 series and Cisco 3600 series, cannot use this keyword.
slavebootflash	Internal Flash memory on the slave RSP card of a Cisco 7507 or Cisco 7513 configured for HSA.
slaveslot0	First PCMCIA slot of the slave RSP card on a Cisco 7507 or Cisco 7513 configured for HSA.
slaveslot1	Second PCMCIA slot of the slave RSP card on a Cisco 7507 or Cisco 7513 configured for HSA.
slavenvram	NVRAM of the slave RSP card on a Cisco 7507 or Cisco 7513 configured for HSA. If you specify NVRAM, omit the filename.

Command Mode

EXEC

Usage Guidelines

This command first appeared in Cisco IOS Release 11.0.

If you do not specify a filename, the router prompts you for it.

This section contains usage guidelines for the following situations:

- Invalid Combinations of Source and Destination
- Copying Character Descriptions
- Partitions
- Using rcp
- Using TFTP
- Using MOP
- Storing Images on Servers
- Copying from a Server to Flash
- Verifying Images
- Copying a Configuration File from a Server to the Running Configuration
- Copying a Configuration File from a Server to the Startup Configuration
- Storing the Running or Startup Configuration on a Server
- Saving the Running Configuration to the Startup Configuration

Part II

Command Reference

- CONFIG_FILE, BOOT, and BOOTLDR Environment Variables
- High System Availability

Invalid Combinations of Source and Destination

Some invalid combinations exist. Specifically, you cannot copy:

- A running configuration to a running configuration.
- A startup configuration to a startup configuration.
- From a server to a server.
- From a device to the same device (for example, the **copy flash: flash:** command is invalid).

Copying Character Descriptions

Table 14–4 describes the characters that you might see during processing of the **copy** command.

Table 14–4 *Copy Character Descriptions*

Character	Description
!	An exclamation point indicates that the copy process is taking place. Each exclamation point indicates that ten packets (512 bytes each) have been successfully transferred.
.	A period indicates the copy process timed out. Many periods in a row typically mean that the copy process might fail.
O	An uppercase O indicates a packet was received out of order and the copy process might fail.
e	A lowercase e indicates a device is being erased.
E	An uppercase E indicates an error and the copy process might fail.
V	A series of uppercase Vs indicates the progress during the verification of the image checksum.

Partitions

You cannot copy an image or configuration file to a Flash partition from which you are currently running. For example, if partition 1 is running the current system image, copy the configuration file or image to partition 2. Otherwise, the copy operation will fail.

On the Cisco 3600 series, you can identify the available device partitions by entering the **show flash:, show slot0:,** or **show slot1:** command.

Using rcp

The rcp protocol requires a client to send a remote username on each rcp request to a server. When you copy a configuration file or image between the router and a server using rcp, the Cisco IOS software sends the first valid username in the following list:

1. The username set by the **ip rcmd remote-username** command, if the command is configured.

2. The remote username associated with the current TTY (terminal) process. For example, if the user is connected to the router through Telnet and was authenticated through the **username** command, the router software sends the Telnet username as the remote username.

3. The router host name.

For the rcp copy request to execute successfully, an account must be defined on the network server for the remote username. If the network administrator of the destination server did not establish an account for the remote username, this command will not execute successfully. If the server has a directory structure, the configuration file or image is written to or copied from the directory associated with the remote username on the server. Use the **ip rcmd remote-username** command to specify which directory on the server to use. For example, if the system image resides in the home directory of a user on the server, you can specify that user's name as the remote username.

If you are writing to the server, the rcp server must be properly configured to accept the rcp write request from the user on the router. For UNIX systems, you must add an entry to the *.rhosts* file for the remote user on the rcp server. Suppose the router contains the following configuration lines:

```
hostname Rtr1
ip rcmd remote-username User0
```

If the router's IP address translates to Router1.company.com, then the *.rhosts* file for User0 on the rcp server should contain the following line:

```
Router1.company.com Rtr1
```

Refer to the documentation for your rcp server for more details.

If you are using a personal computer as a file server, the computer must support rsh.

Using TFTP

The system prompts for the address of the TFTP server and TFTP filename if you do not provide them at the command line. When copying to internal Flash memory, the system provides an option to erase existing internal Flash memory before writing onto it. The entire copying process takes several minutes and differs from network to network.

Using MOP

You do not need to specify the address of a MOP server. The Cisco IOS software automatically solicits a MOP boot server for the specified file by sending a multicast file-request message.

Use the **copy mop flash** or **copy mop bootflash** command to copy a system or bootstrap image from a MOP server to Flash memory. MOP must be enabled on the relevant interfaces before you can use these commands.

The router prompts for the name of the image file. It provides an option to erase the existing boot image in Flash before writing the new image into Flash. If no free space is available, or if files have never been written to Flash memory, you must erase Flash memory before copying the MOP image.

Storing Images on Servers

Use the **copy flash rcp, copy flash tftp, copy bootflash rcp, copy bootflash tftp** or **copy** *file-id* command to copy a system image or boot image from Flash memory to a network server. You can use the copy of the image as a backup copy. You also can use it to verify that the copy in Flash memory is the same as the original file.

Copying from a Server to Flash

Use the **copy rcp flash, copy tftp flash, copy mop flash, copy rcp bootflash, copy tftp bootflash, copy mop bootflash, copy rcp file-id,** or **copy tftp file-id** command to copy an image from a server to Flash memory.

If you are using rcp or TFTP, the Cisco IOS software prompts for the address of the server and source filename. If you are using MOP, the router prompts for the source filename.

The system provides an option to erase existing Flash memory before writing onto it. The entire copying process takes several minutes and differs from network to network.

CAUTION

Verify the image in Flash memory before booting the image.

Verifying Images

Before booting from Flash memory, verify that the checksum of the image in Flash memory matches the checksum listed in the README file that was distributed with the image. The checksum of the image in Flash memory is displayed when the **copy** command completes. The README file was copied to the server automatically when you installed the image.

CAUTION

If the checksum values do not match, do not reboot the router. Instead, reissue the **copy** command and compare the checksums again. If the checksum is repeatedly wrong, copy the original software image back into Flash memory *before* you reboot the router from Flash memory. If you have a corrupted image in Flash memory and try to boot from Flash memory, the router will start the system image contained in ROM (assuming booting from a network server is not configured). If ROM does not contain a fully functional system image, the router might not function and will have to be reconfigured through a direct console port connection.

Copying a Configuration File from a Server to the Running Configuration

Use the **copy rcp running-config** or **copy tftp running-config** command to load a configuration file from a network server to the router's running configuration. The configuration will be added to the running configuration as if the commands were typed in the command line interface. Thus, the resulting configuration will be a combination of the previous running configuration and the loaded configuration file, with the loaded configuration file having precedence.

You can copy either a host configuration file or a network configuration file. Accept the default value of *host* to copy and load a host configuration file containing commands that apply to one network server in particular. Enter *network* to copy and load a network configuration file containing commands that apply to all network servers on a network.

NOTES

The **copy rcp startup-config** and **copy tftp startup-config** commands replaces the **configure network** command.

Copying a Configuration File from a Server to the Startup Configuration

Use the **copy rcp startup-configuration** or **copy tftp startup-configuration** command to copy a configuration file from a network server to the router's startup configuration. These commands replace the startup configuration file with the copied configuration file.

NOTES

When using rcp, the **copy rcp startup-config** command replaces the **configure overwrite-network** command.

Storing the Running or Startup Configuration on a Server

Use the **copy running-config {rcp | tftp}** command to copy the current configuration file to a network server using rcp or TFTP. Use the **copy startup-config {rcp | tftp}** command to copy the startup configuration file to a network server using rcp or TFTP. The configuration file copy can serve as a backup copy. You are prompted for a destination host and filename.

Saving the Running Configuration to the Startup Configuration

On all platforms except the Cisco 7000 family, the **copy running-config startup-config** command copies the currently running configuration to NVRAM. Use this command in conjunction with the **reload** command to restart the router with the configuration information stored in NVRAM.

CAUTION

Some specific commands might not get saved to NVRAM. You will have to enter these commands again if you reboot the machine. These commands are noted in the documentation. Cisco recommends that you keep a listing of these settings, so you quickly can reconfigure your router after rebooting.

If you issue the **copy running-config startup-config** command from a bootstrap system image, you receive a warning instructing you to indicate whether you want your previous NVRAM configuration to be overwritten and configuration commands lost. This warning does not appear if NVRAM contains an invalid configuration or if the previous configuration in NVRAM was generated by a bootstrap system image.

On the Cisco 7000 family, the **copy running-config startup-config** command copies the currently running configuration to the location specified by the CONFIG_FILE environment variable. This variable specifies the device and configuration file used for initialization. When the CONFIG_FILE environment variable points to NVRAM, or when this variable does not exist (such as at first-time startup), the software writes the current configuration to NVRAM. If the current configuration is too large for NVRAM, the software displays a message and stops executing the command. Use this command in conjunction with the **reload** command to restart the router with the configuration information stored in the CONFIG_FILE environment variable.

When the CONFIG_FILE environment variable specifies a valid device other than **nvram:** (that is, **flash, bootflash, slot0,** or **slot1**), the software writes the current configuration to the specified device and filename and stores a distilled version of the configuration in NVRAM. A distilled version of the configuration is one that does not contain access-list information. If NVRAM already contains a copy of a complete configuration, the router prompts you to confirm the copy.

CONFIG_FILE, BOOT, and BOOTLDR Environment Variables

For the Cisco 7000 family:

- The CONFIG_FILE environment variable specifies the configuration file used during router initialization.

- The BOOTLDR environment variable specifies the Flash device and filename containing the rxboot image that ROM uses for booting.

- The BOOT environment variable specifies a list of bootable images on various devices.

For the Cisco 3600:

- There is no CONFIG_FILE environment variable. The startup configuration is always the configuration in NVRAM.

- Cisco 3600 routers do not use a dedicated boot helper image (rxboot), which many other routers use to help with the boot process. Instead, the BOOTLDR ROM monitor environment variable identifies the Flash memory device and filename that are used as the boot helper; the default is the first system image in Flash memory.

- The BOOT environment variable specifies a list of bootable images on various devices.

To view the contents of environment variables, use the **show boot** command. To modify the CONFIG_FILE environment variable, use the **boot config** command. To modify the BOOTLDR environment variable, use the **boot bootldr** command. To modify the BOOT environment variable, use the **boot system** command. To save your modifications, use the **copy running-config startup-config** command.

When the destination is specified by the CONFIG_FILE or BOOTLDR environment variable, the router prompts you for confirmation before proceeding with the copy. When the destination is the only valid image in the BOOT environment variable, the router also prompts you for confirmation before proceeding with the copy.

High System Availability

High System Availability (HSA) refers to how quickly your router returns to an operational status after a failure occurs. On the Cisco 7507 and Cisco 7513, you can install two RSP cards in a single router to improve system availability.

On a Cisco 7507 or Cisco 7513 configured for HSA, the **copy rcp startup-configuration** command used with automatic synchronization disabled causes the system to ask you if you also want to copy the file to the slave's startup configuration. The default answer is **yes**. If automatic synchronization is enabled, the system automatically copies the file to the slave's startup configuration each time you use this command.

Examples

The following examples illustrate uses of the **copy** command. Depending on your platform, the output might be different from the output shown in the example.

- Copying from a Server to Flash Memory Examples
- Saving a Copy of an Image on a Server Examples
- Copying from a Server to the Startup Configuration Example
- Copying from a Server to the Running Configuration Example
- Copying the Running Configuration to a Server Example
- Copying the Startup Configuration to a Server Example
- Saving the Current Running Configuration Example
- Moving Configuration Files to Other Locations Examples

Copying from a Server to Flash Memory Examples

The following example uses a **copy rcp**, **copy tftp**, or **copy mop** command to copy an image from a server to Flash memory.

- Copying an Image from a Server to Flash Memory

  This example copies a system image named *file1* from the *netadmin1* directory on the remote rcp server with an IP address of 172.16.101.101 to Flash memory. To ensure that enough Flash memory is available to accommodate the system image to be copied, the Cisco IOS software allows you to erase the contents of Flash memory first.

For a TFTP server, use the **copy tftp flash** command. You do not need to specify a remote username with the **ip rcmd remote-username** command.

For a MOP server, use the **copy mop flash** command. You do not need to specify a remote username with the **ip rcmd remote-username** command. In addition, you do not specify an address for the remote host.

```
Router# configure terminal

Router(config)# ip rcmd remote-username netadmin1
Router(config)# end
Router# copy rcp flash

System flash directory, partition 2:
File  Length   Name/status
  1   984      file1 [deleted]
  2   984      file1
[2096 bytes used, 8386512 available, 8388608 total]
Address or name of remote host [255.255.255.255]? 172.16.101.101
Source file name? file1
Destination file name [file1]?
Accessing file 'file1' on 172.16.101.101...
Loading file1 from 172.16.101.101 (via Ethernet0): ! [OK]

Erase flash device before writing? [confirm]
Flash contains files. Are you sure you want to erase? [confirm]

Copy 'file1' from server
  as 'file1' into Flash WITH erase? [yes/no] yes
Erasing device... eeeeeeeeeeeeeeeeeeeeeeeeeeeeeeee...erased
Loading file1 from 172.16.101.101 (via Ethernet0): !
[OK - 984/8388608 bytes]

Verifying checksum... OK (0x14B3)
Flash copy took 0:00:01 [hh:mm:ss]
```

The exclamation point (!) indicates that the copy process is taking place. Each exclamation point (!) indicates that ten packets have been transferred successfully. A series of "V" characters indicates that a checksum verification of the image is occurring after the image is written to Flash memory.

- Copying a Boot Image from a Server to Bootflash Memory Example

The following example shows how to use the **copy mop bootflash** command to copy the bootstrap image *c4500-xboot.101*.

To use TFTP for the copy operation, use the **copy tftp bootflash** command; you will be prompted for the IP address of the TFTP server.

To use rcp, first specify a remote username with the **ip rcmd remote-username** global configuration command. Then, in privileged EXEC mode, enter the **copy rcp bootflash** command.

```
Router# copy mop bootflash
Boot flash directory:
File  Length    Name/status
  1   2622607   c4500-xboot
[2622672 bytes used, 1571632 available, 4194304 total]

Source file name? c4500-xboot.101
Destination file name [c4500-xboot.101]?

Erase flash device before writing? [confirm]
Flash contains files. Are you sure you want to erase? [confirm]

Copy 'c4500-xboot.101' from server into
    bootflash as 'c4500-xboot.101' WITH erase? [yes/no] yes
Erasing device... eeeeeeeeeeeeeeee...erased
Loading c4500-xboot.101 from 1234.5678.9abc via Ethernet0: !
!!!!!!!!!!!!!!!!!!!!!!!!!!!!!!!!!!!!!!!!!!!!!!!!!!!!!!!!!!!!!!!!!!!!!!!!!!!
!!!!!!!!!!!!!!!!!!!!!!!!!!!!!!!!!!
[OK - 2622607/4194304 bytes]

Verifying checksum... OK (0xE408)
Flash copy took 0:00:10 [hh:mm:ss]
```

The exclamation point (!) indicates that the copy process is taking place. Each exclamation point (!) indicates that ten packets have been transferred successfully.

- Copying from a Server to a Flash Memory Using Flash Load Helper Example

  The following example copies a system image into a partition of Flash memory. The system will prompt for a partition number only if there are two or more read/write partitions or one read-only and one read/write partition and dual Flash bank support in boot ROMs. If the partition entered is not valid, the process terminates. You can enter a partition number, a question mark (?) for a directory display of all partitions, or a question mark and a number (?*number*) for directory display of a particular partition. The default is the first read/write partition. In this case, the partition is read-only and has dual Flash bank support in boot ROM, so the system uses Flash load helper.

  For an rcp server, first specify a remote username with the **rcmd remote-username** command. Then use the **copy rcp flash** command. The dialogue will be similar.

  For a MOP server, use the **copy mop flash** command. You do not specify an address for the remote host.

```
Router# copy tftp flash

System flash partition information:
Partition  Size   Used   Free   Bank-Size  State       Copy-Mode
    1      4096K  2048K  2048K  2048K      Read Only   RXBOOT-FLH
    2      4096K  2048K  2048K  2048K      Read/Write  Direct
```

```
[Type ?<no> for partition directory; ? for full directory; q to abort]
Which partition? [default = 2]

                          **** NOTICE ****
Flash load helper v1.0
This process will accept the copy options and then terminate
the current system image to use the ROM based image for the copy.
Routing functionality will not be available during that time.
If you are logged in via telnet, this connection will terminate.
Users with console access can see the results of the copy operation.
                     ---- ******** ----
Proceed? [confirm]
System flash directory, partition 1:
File  Length   Name/status
  1   3459720  master/igs-bfpx.100-4.3
[3459784 bytes used, 734520 available, 4194304 total]
Address or name of remote host [255.255.255.255]? 172.16.1.1
Source file name? master/igs-bfpx-100.4.3
Destination file name [default = source name]?

Loading master/igs-bfpx.100-4.3 from 172.16.1.111: !
Erase flash device before writing? [confirm]
Flash contains files. Are you sure? [confirm]
Copy 'master/igs-bfpx.100-4.3' from TFTP server
as 'master/igs-bfpx.100-4.3' into Flash WITH erase? [yes/no] yes
```

- Copying an Image from a Server to a Flash Memory Card Partition Example

  The following example copies the file c3600-i-mz from the rcp server at IP address
  172.23.1.129 to the Flash memory card in slot 0 of a Cisco 3600 series router, which has
  only one partition. As the operation progresses, the Cisco IOS software asks you to erase
  the files on the Flash memory PC card to accommodate the incoming file. This entire
  operation takes 18 seconds to perform, as indicated at the end of the example.

  If you use TFTP rather than rcp, type **copy tftp slot0:** instead. Most of the dialogue remains
  the same, although some of the output may vary slightly.

```
Router# copy rcp slot0:
PCMCIA Slot0 flash

Partition   Size   Used    Free    Bank-Size   State        Copy Mode
   1        4096K   3068K   1027K   4096K       Read/Write   Direct
   2        4096K   1671K   2424K   4096K       Read/Write   Direct
   3        4096K     0K    4095K   4096K       Read/Write   Direct
   4        4096K   3825K    270K   4096K       Read/Write   Direct

[Type ?<no> for partition directory; ? for full directory; q to abort]
Which partition? [default = 1]

PCMCIA Slot0 flash directory, partition 1:
File  Length   Name/status
  1   3142288  c3600-j-mz.test
```

```
[3142352 bytes used, 1051952 available, 4194304 total]
Address or name of remote host [172.23.1.129]?
Source file name? /tftpboot/images/c3600-i-mz
Destination file name [/tftpboot/images/c3600-i-mz]?
Accessing file '/tftpboot/images/c3600-i-mz' on 172.23.1.129...
Connected to 172.23.1.129
Loading 1711088 byte file c3600-i-mz: ! [OK]

Erase flash device before writing? [confirm]
Flash contains files. Are you sure you want to erase? [confirm]

Copy '/tftpboot/images/c3600-i-mz' from server
  as '/tftpboot/images/c3600-i-mz' into Flash WITH erase? [yes/no] yes
Erasing device... eeeeeeeeeeeeeeeeeeeeeeeeeeeeeeeeeee ...erased
Connected to 172.23.1.129
Loading 1711088 byte file c3600-i-mz:
!!!!!!!!!!!!!!!!!!!!!!!!!!!!!!!!!!!!!!!!!!!!!!!!!!!!!!!!!!!!!!!!!!!!!!!!!!!!!!!!!!!!!
!!!!!!!!!!!!!!!!!!!!!!!!!!!!!!!!!!!!!!!!!!!!!!!!!!!!!!!!!!!!!!!!!!!!!!!!!!!!!!!!!!!!!
!!!!!!!!!!!!!!!!!!!!!!!!!!!!!!!!!!!!!!!!!!!!!!!!!!!!!!!!!!!!!!!!!!!!!!!!!!!!!!!!!!!!!
!!!

Verifying checksum...  OK (0xF89A)
Flash device copy took 00:00:18 [hh:mm:ss]
```

Saving a Copy of an Image on a Server Examples

The following examples use **copy flash** or **copy file-id** commands to copy images to a server for storage.

- Copying an Image from Flash Memory to an rcp Server Example

  The following example illustrates how to copy a system image from Flash Memory to an rcp server. To copy to a TFTP server, use the **copy flash tftp** command instead.

```
Router# copy flash rcp
IP address of remote host [255.255.255.255]? 172.16.13.110
Name of file to copy? gsxx
writing gsxx - copy complete
```

- Copying an Image from a Partition of Flash Memory to a Server Example

  The following example illustrates how to use the **copy flash rcp** command when copying from a particular partition of Flash memory. The process is similar using **copy flash tftp**.

  The system will prompt if there are two or more partitions. If the partition entered is not valid, the process terminates. You have the option to enter a partition number, a question mark (?) for a directory display of all partitions, or a question mark and a number (?*number*) for a directory display of a particular partition. The default is the first partition.

```
Router# configure terminal
Router# ip rcmd remote-username netadmin1
Ctrl-Z
Router# copy flash rcp
System flash partition information:
```

```
Partition   Size    Used    Free    Bank-Size   State       Copy-Mode
   1        4096K   2048K   2048K   2048K       Read Only   RXBOOT-FLH
   2        4096K   2048K   2048K   2048K       Read/Write  Direct
[Type ?<number> for partition directory; ? for full directory; q to abort]
Which partition? [1] 2

System flash directory, partition 2:
File  Length    Name/status
  1   3459720   master/igs-bfpx.100-4.3
[3459784 bytes used, 734520 available, 4194304 total]
Address or name of remote host [ABC.CISCO.COM]?
Source file name? master/igs-bfpx.100-4.3
Destination file name [master/igs-bfpx.100-4.3]?
Verifying checksum for 'master/igs-bfpx.100-4.3' (file # 1)... OK
Copy 'master/igs-bfpx.100-4.3' from Flash to server
as 'master/igs-bfpx.100-4.3'? [yes/no] yes
!!!!...
Upload to server done
Flash copy took 0:00:00 [hh:mm:ss]
```

The exclamation point (!) indicates that the copy process is taking place. Each exclamation point (!) indicates that ten packets have been transferred successfully.

- Copying an Image from a Flash Memory Device to a Server

    The following example copies the file *c3600-i-mz* from partition 1 of the Flash memory card in slot 0 to a TFTP server that has IP address 172.23.1.129. Because the Flash memory card has multiple partitions, and a partition number and filename are not specified in the command line, you must provide this information during the copy operation.

```
Router# copy slot0: tftp
PCMCIA Slot0 flash

Partition   Size    Used    Free    Bank-Size   State       Copy Mode
   1        4096K   1671K   2424K   4096K       Read/Write  Direct
   2        4096K   3068K   1027K   4096K       Read/Write  Direct
   3        4096K   1671K   2424K   4096K       Read/Write  Direct
   4        4096K   3825K    270K   4096K       Read/Write  Direct

[Type ?<no> for partition directory; ? for full directory; q to abort]
Which partition? [default = 1] 1

PCMCIA Slot0 flash directory, partition 1:
File  Length    Name/status
  1   1711088   /tftpboot/cisco_rules/c3600-i-mz
[1711152 bytes used, 2483152 available, 4194304 total]
Address or name of remote host [172.23.1.129]?
Source file name? /tftpboot/cisco_rules/c3600-i-mz
Destination file name [/tftpboot/cisco_rules/c3600-i-mz]? dirt/cisco_rules/c3700-i-mz
Verifying checksum for '/tftpboot/cisco_rules/c3600-i-mz' (file # 1)...  OK
Copy '/tftpboot/cisco_rules/c3600-i-mz' from Flash to server
  as 'dirt/cisco_rules/c3700-i-mz'? [yes/no] yes
```

```
!!!!!!!!!!!!!!!!!!!!!!!!!!!!!!!!!!!!!!!!!!!!!!!!!!!!!!!!!!!!!!!!!!!!!!!!!!!!!!!!!!!!!!!!!!!!
!!!!!!!!!!!!!!!!!!!!!!!!!!!!!!!!!!!!!!!!!!!!!!!!!!!!!!!!!!!!!!!!!!!!!!!!!!!!!!!!!!!!!!!!!!!!
!!!!!!!!!!!!!!!!!!!!!!!!!!!!!!!!!!!!!!!!!!!!!!!!!!!!!!!!!!!!!!!!!!!!!!!!!!!!!!!!!!!!!!!!!!!!
!!!!!!!!!!!!!!!!!!!!!!!!!!!!!!!!!!!!!!!!!!!!!!!!!!!!!!!!!!!!!!!!!!!!!!!!!!!!
Upload to server done
Flash device copy took 00:00:23 [hh:mm:ss]
```

- Copying an Image from Boot Flash Memory to a Server

    The following example shows how to use the **copy bootflash rcp** command on a Cisco 4500 router. To use TFTP, use the **copy bootflash tftp** command; you do not need to enter the **ip rcmd remote-username** command.

```
Router(config)# ip rcmd remote-username netadmin1
Router(config)# end
Router# copy bootflash rcp

System flash directory, partition 2:
File  Length   Name/status
  1   984      file1
[1048 bytes used, 8387560 available, 8388608 total]
Address or name of remote host [223.255.254.254]?
Source file name? file1
Destination file name [file1]? file1
Verifying checksum for 'file1' (file # 1)... OK
Copy 'file1' from Flash to server
  as 'file1'? [yes/no]y
!!!!...
Upload to server done
Flash copy took 0:00:00 [hh:mm:ss]
```

    The exclamation point (!) indicates that the copy process is taking place. Each exclamation point (!) indicates that ten packets have been transferred successfully.

Copying from a Server to the Running Configuration Example

The following example shows how to use the **copy rcp running-config** command. This example specifies a remote username of *netadmin1*. Then it copies and runs a host configuration filename *host1-confg* from the *netadmin1* directory on the remote server with an IP address of 172.16.101.101.

```
Router# configure terminal
Router(config)# ip rcmd remote-username netadmin1
Router(config)# Ctrl-Z
Router# copy rcp running-config

Host or network configuration file [host]?
Address of remote host [255.255.255.255]? 172.16.101.101
Name of configuration file [Router-confg]? host1-confg
Configure using host1-confg from 172.16.101.101? [confirm]
Connected to 172.16.101.101
Loading 1112 byte file host1-confg:![OK]
Router#
%SYS-5-CONFIG: Configured from host1-config by rcp from 172.16.101.101
```

Copying from a Server to the Startup Configuration Example

The following example shows how to use **copy rcp startup-config** command. This example specifies a remote username of *netadmin1*. Then it copies and stores a configuration file *host2-confg* from the *netadmin1* directory on the remote server with an IP address of 172.16.101.101.

```
Router# configure terminal
Router(config)# ip rcmd remote-username netadmin1
Router(config)# end
Router# copy rcp startup-config

Address of remote host [255.255.255.255]? 172.16.101.101
Name of configuration file[rtr2-confg]? host2-confg
Configure using rtr2-confg from 172.16.101.101?[confirm]
Connected to 172.16.101.101
Loading 1112 byte file rtr2-confg:![OK]
[OK]
Router#
%SYS-5-CONFIG_NV:Non-volatile store configured from rtr2-config by
rcp from 172.16.101.101
```

Copying the Running Configuration to a Server Example

The following example shows how to use the **copy running-config rcp** command. This example specifies a remote username of *netadmin1*. Then it copies the running configuration file, named *Rtr2-confg* to the *netadmin1* directory on the remote host with an IP address of 172.16.101.101.

```
Router# configure terminal
Router(config)# ip rcmd remote-username netadmin1
Router(config)# Ctrl-Z
Router# copy running-config rcp
Remote host[]? 172.16.101.101

Name of configuration file to write [Rtr2-confg]?
Write file rtr2-confg on host 172.16.101.101?[confirm]
Building configuration...[OK]
Connected to 172.16.101.101
```

Copying the Startup Configuration to a Server Example

The following example shows how to use the **copy startup-config rcp** command.

```
Router# configure terminal
Router(config)# ip rcmd remote-username netadmin2
Router(config)# end
Router# copy startup-config rcp
Remote host[]? 172.16.101.101

Name of configuration file to write [rtr2-confg]? <cr>
Write file rtr2-confg on host 172.16.101.101?[confirm] <cr>
![OK]
```

Saving the Current Running Configuration Example

The following example copies the running configuration to the startup configuration. On a Cisco 7000 family router, this command copies the running configuration to the startup configuration specified by the CONFIG_FILE variable:

```
copy running-config startup-config
```

The following example shows the **copy running-config startup-config** command and the warning the system provides if you are trying to save configuration information from bootstrap into the system:

```
Router(boot)# copy running-config startup-config

Warning: Attempting to overwrite an NVRAM configuration written
by a full system image. This bootstrap software does not support
the full configuration command set. If you perform this command now,
some configuration commands may be lost.
Overwrite the previous NVRAM configuration?[confirm]
```

Enter **no** to escape writing the configuration information to memory.

Moving Configuration Files to Other Locations Examples

On some routers, you can store copies of configuration files on a Flash memory device.

- Copying the Startup Configuration to a Flash Memory Device Example

  The following example uses the **copy startup-config** command to copy the startup configuration file (specified by the CONFIG_FILE environment variable) to a Flash memory card inserted in slot 0. To copy the running configuration file instead, use the **copy running-config** command instead.

```
copy startup-config slot0:router-confg
```

- Copying the Running Configuration to a Flash Memory Device Example

  The following example copies the running configuration from the router to the Flash memory PC card in slot 1:

```
Router# copy running-config slot1:

PCMCIA Slot1 flash directory:
File  Length   Name/status
  1   1711088  dirt/images/c3600-i-mz
[1711152 bytes used, 2483152 available, 4194304 total]
Destination file name [running-config]?
Building configuration...

Erase flash device before writing? [confirm] no

Copy 'running-config'
  as 'running-config' into flash device WITHOUT erase? [yes/no] yes
!
 [OK - 850/2483152 bytes]
```

```
Verifying checksum... OK (0x16)
Flash device copy took 00:00:00 [hh:mm:ss]
```

- Copying to the Running Configuration from a Flash Memory Device Example

    The next example copies the file *ios-upgrade-1* from the Flash memory card in slot 0 on a Cisco 3600 series to the running configuration.

```
Router# copy slot0:4:ios-upgrade-1 running-config

Copy 'ios-upgrade-1' from flash device
  as 'running-config' ? [yes/no] yes
```

- Copying to the Startup Configuration from a Flash Memory Device Example

    The following example copies the *router-image* file from the Flash memory card inserted in the slot 0 on a Cisco 7000 family to the startup configuration:

```
copy slot0:router-image startup-config
```

- Copying a Configuration File from One Flash Device to Another Example

    This example copies the file *running-config* from the first partition in internal Flash memory to the Flash memory PC card in slot 1 on a Cisco 3600 series. The file's checksum is verified, and its copying time of 30 seconds is displayed:

```
Router# copy flash: slot1:
System flash

Partition   Size    Used     Free    Bank-Size  State        Copy Mode
 1          4096K   3070K    1025K   4096K      Read/Write   Direct
 2          16384K  1671K    14712K  8192K      Read/Write   Direct

[Type ?<no> for partition directory; ? for full directory; q to abort]
Which partition? [default = 1]

System flash directory, partition 1:
File  Length   Name/status
 1    3142748  dirt/images/mars-test/c3600-j-mz.latest
 2    850      running-config
[3143728 bytes used, 1050576 available, 4194304 total]

PCMCIA Slot1 flash directory:
File  Length   Name/status
 1    1711088  dirt/images/c3600-i-mz
 2    850      running-config
[1712068 bytes used, 2482236 available, 4194304 total]
Source file name? running-config
Destination file name [running-config]?
Verifying checksum for 'running-config' (file # 2)... OK
Erase flash device before writing? [confirm]
Flash contains files. Are you sure you want to erase? [confirm]

Copy 'running-config' from flash: device
```

```
     as 'running-config' into slot1: device WITH erase? [yes/no] yes
Erasing device... eeeeeeeeeeeeeeeeeeeeeeeeeeeeeeeeeeeeeeeeeeeeeeeeeeeeee ...erased
!
 [OK - 850/4194304 bytes]

Flash device copy took 00:00:30 [hh:mm:ss]
Verifying checksum...  OK (0x16)
```

Copying an Image from the Master RSP Card to the Slave RSP Card Example

The following example copies the *router-image* file from the Flash memory card inserted in slot 1 of the master RSP card to slot 0 of the slave RSP card in the same router:

```
copy slot1:router-image slaveslot0:
```

Related Commands

boot config
boot system flash
cd
copy xmodem flash
copy ymodem flash
delete
dir
erase bootflash
ip rcmd remote-username
reload
show boot
show bootflash
slave auto-sync config
verify
verify bootflash
write erase

COPY VERIFY

The **verify** or **verify flash** command replaces this command. Refer to the descriptions of the **verify** and **verify flash** commands in Chapter 12, "System Image and Microcode Commands," for more information.

COPY VERIFY BOOTFLASH

The **verify bootflash** command replaces this command. Refer to the description of the **verify bootflash** command in Chapter 12 for more information.

DELETE

To delete any file on a Flash memory device of the Cisco 7000 family, use the **delete** EXEC command.

> **delete** [*device*:]*filename*

Syntax	Description
device:	(Optional) Device containing the file to be deleted. The colon (:) is required. Valid devices are as follows:
	• **bootflash**—Internal Flash memory in the Cisco 7000 family.
	• **slot0**—First PCMCIA slot on the Cisco 7000 family. For the Cisco 7000 family, this device is the initial default device.
	• **slot1**—Second PCMCIA slot on the Cisco 7000 family.
	• **slavebootflash**—Internal Flash memory on the slave RSP card of a Cisco 7507 or Cisco 7513 configured for HSA.
	• **slaveslot0**—First PCMCIA slot of the slave RSP card on a Cisco 7507 or Cisco 7513 configured for HSA.
	• **slaveslot1**—Second PCMCIA slot of the slave RSP card on a Cisco 7507 or Cisco 7513 configured for HSA.
filename	Name of the file to be deleted. The maximum filename length is 63 characters.

Default

For the Cisco 7000 family, the initial default device is **slot0:**. Otherwise, the default device is that specified by the **cd** command.

Command Mode

EXEC

Usage Guidelines

This command first appeared in Cisco IOS Release 11.0.

Use this command only with the Cisco 7000 family.

If you omit the device, the Cisco IOS software uses the default device specified by the **cd** command.

If you attempt to delete the configuration file specified by the CONFIG_FILE or BOOTLDR environment variable, the system prompts you to confirm the deletion. Also, if you attempt to delete the last valid system image specified in the BOOT environment variable, the system prompts you to confirm the deletion. When you delete a file, the software simply marks the file as deleted, but does not erase the file. This feature allows you to later recover a "deleted" file using the **undelete** command. You can delete and undelete a file up to 15 times. To permanently delete all "deleted" files on a Flash memory device, use the **squeeze** command.

Example

The following example deletes the *router-backupconfig* file from the Flash card inserted in slot 0:

```
delete slot0:router-backupconfig
```

Related Commands

cd
dir
show boot
squeeze
undelete

DIR

To display a list of files on a Flash memory device of the Cisco 7000 family, use the **dir** EXEC command.

> **dir** [/**all** | /**deleted** | /**long**] [*device*:][*filename*]

Syntax	Description
/**all**	(Optional) Lists deleted files, undeleted files, and files with errors.
/**deleted**	(Optional) Lists only the deleted files.
/**long**	(Optional) Lists only valid files. Valid files are those that are undeleted and without errors.
device:	(Optional) Device containing the file(s) to list. The colon (:) is required. Valid devices are as follows:
	• **bootflash**—Internal Flash memory in the Cisco 7000 family.
	• **slot0**—First PCMCIA slot on the Cisco 7000 family. For the Cisco 7000 family, this device is the initial default device.
	• **slot1**—Second PCMCIA slot on the Cisco 7000 family.
	• **slavebootflash**—Internal Flash memory on the slave RSP card of a Cisco 7507 or Cisco 7513 configured for HSA.
	• **slaveslot0**—First PCMCIA slot of the slave RSP card on a Cisco 7507 or Cisco 7513 configured for HSA.
	• **slaveslot1**—Second PCMCIA slot of the slave RSP card on a Cisco 7507 or Cisco 7513 configured for HSA.
filename	(Optional) Name of the file(s) to display on a specified device. The files can be of any type. You can use wildcards in the filename. A wildcard character (*) matches all patterns. Strings after a wildcard are ignored.

Part II

Command Reference

Default

For the Cisco 7000 family, the initial default device is **slot0:**. Otherwise, the default device is that specified by the **cd** command. When you omit all keywords and arguments, the Cisco IOS software displays only undeleted files for the default device specified by the **cd** command in short format.

Command Mode

EXEC

Usage Guidelines

This command first appeared in Cisco IOS Release 11.0.

Use this command only with the Cisco 7000 family. If you omit the device, the software uses the default device specified by the **cd** command.

When you use one of the keywords (**/all, /deleted, /long**), the system displays file information in long format. The long format includes the following categories:

- File's index number (#).
- Whether the file contains an error (*E*) or is deleted (*D*).
- File's *type* (1 = configuration file, 2 = image file). The software displays these values only when the file's type is certain. When the file's type is unknown, the system displays a zero or FFFFFFFF in this field.
- File's cyclic redundant check (*crc*).
- Offset into the file system of the next file (*seek*).
- Length of the file's name (*nlen*).
- Length of the file itself (*length*).
- Date and time the file was created (*date/time*).
- File's name (*name*).

When you omit all keywords (**/all, /deleted, /long**), the system displays file information in short format. Short format includes the following categories:

- File's index number (#)
- Length of the file itself (*length*)
- Date and time the file was created (*date/time*)
- File's name (*name*)

Examples

The following example instructs a router to list undeleted files for the default device specified by the **cd** command. Notice that the router displays the information in short format because no keywords are used.

```
Router# dir
-#- -length- -----date/time------ name
1   620       May 4  1993 21:38:04 config1
2   620       May 4  1993 21:38:14 config2

7993896 bytes available (1496 bytes used)
```

The following example displays the long version of the same device:

```
Router# dir /long
-#- ED --type-- --crc--- -seek-- nlen -length- -----date/time------ name
1   .. 1        37CEC52E 202EC   7    620       May 4  1993 21:38:04 config1
2   .. 1        37CEC52E 205D8   7    620       May 4  1993 21:38:14 config2

7993896 bytes available (1496 bytes used)
```

Related Commands

cd
delete
undelete

ERASE

To erase a file, use one of the **erase** EXEC commands.

> **erase** *device*:[*partition-number*] (Cisco 1600 series and Cisco 3600 only)

Syntax	Description
device:	Device containing the file to delete. The colon (:) is required. Valid devices are as follows:
	• **flash**—Internal Flash memory in the Cisco 1600 series and Cisco 3600 series. This device is the initial default device. This is the only valid device for the Cisco 1600 series.
	• **slot0**— Flash memory card in PCMCIA slot 0 on the Cisco 3600 series.
	• **slot1**—Flash memory card in PCMCIA slot 1 on the Cisco 3600 series.
partition-number	(Optional) Partition number to erase.
filename	Name of the file to delete. The files can be of any type. This command does not support wildcards in the filename.

Command Mode

EXEC

Usage Guidelines

This command first appeared in Cisco IOS Release 11.0.

For the Cisco 1600 and Cisco 3600 series, you cannot erase a single filename. You can erase only an entire Flash memory device or a specified partition.

If you attempt to erase the configuration file specified by the CONFIG_FILE or BOOTLDR environment variable, the system prompts you to confirm the deletion. Also, if you attempt to erase the last valid system image specified in the BOOT environment variable, the system prompts you to confirm the deletion.

Examples

The following example deletes the *myconfig* file from a Flash memory card inserted in the slot 0:

```
erase slot0:myconfig
```

The following example erases all of partition 2 in internal Flash memory on a Cisco 3600 series:

```
Router# erase flash:2

System flash directory, partition 2:
File  Length   Name/status
   1   1711088  dirt/images/c3600-i-mz
[1711152 bytes used, 15066064 available, 16777216 total]

Erase flash device, partition 2? [confirm]
Are you sure? [yes/no]: yes
Erasing device... eeeeeeeeeeeeeeeeeeeeeeeeeeeeeeeeeeeeeeeeeeeeeeeeeeeeeeee ...erased
```

The following example erases all of partition 2 in Flash memory on a Cisco 1600 series:

```
Router# erase flash:2

System flash directory, partition 2:
File  Length   Name/status
   1   1711088  dirt/images/c1600-i-mz
[1711152 bytes used, 15066064 available, 16777216 total]

Erase flash device, partition 2? [confirm]
Are you sure? [yes/no]: yes
Erasing device... eeeeeeeeeeeeeeeeeeeeeeeeeeeeeeeeeeeeeeeeeeeeeeeeeeeeeeee ...erased
```

Related Commands

boot config
delete
show boot
undelete

ERASE BOOTFLASH

To erase the boot image in boot Flash memory, use the **erase bootflash** EXEC command.

erase bootflash

Syntax   Description

This command has no arguments or keywords.

Command Mode

EXEC

Usage Guidelines

This command first appeared in Cisco IOS Release 10.3.

You can use this command only on routers that have two banks of Flash memory: one bank for the boot image and the second bank for the system image.

Example

The following example erases the boot image in Flash memory:

```
erase bootflash
```

Related Commands

copy bootflash tftp
copy mop bootflash
copy tftp bootflash
show bootflash
verify bootflash

ERASE FLASH

To erase internal Flash memory, use the **erase flash** EXEC command. This command replaces the **copy erase flash** command.

erase flash

Syntax   Description

This command has no arguments or keywords.

Command Mode

EXEC

Usage Guidelines

This command first appeared in Cisco IOS Release 10.3.

The Cisco 7000 family routers do not support this command.

Example

The following example illustrates how to use this command. Note that this example reflects the dual Flash bank feature available only on low-end systems (the AccessPro PC card, Cisco 2500 series, Cisco 3000 series, and Cisco 4000 series).

```
Router# erase flash

System flash partition information:
Partition   Size    Used    Free    Bank-Size   State       Copy-Mode
    1        4096K   2048K   2048K   2048K       Read Only   RXBOOT-FLH
    2        4096K   2048K   2048K   2048K       Read/Write  Direct

[Type ?<no> for partition directory; ? for full directory; q to abort]
Which partition? [default = 2]
```

The system will prompt only if there are two or more read/write partitions. If the partition entered is not valid or is the read-only partition, the process terminates. You can enter a partition number, a question mark (?) for a directory display of all partitions, or a question mark and a number (?*number*) for directory display of a particular partition. The default is the first read/write partition.

```
System flash directory, partition 2:
File  Length   Name/status
  1   3459720  master/igs-bfpx.100-4.3
[3459784 bytes used, 734520 available, 4194304 total]

Erase flash device, partition 2? [confirm] <Return>
```

FORMAT

To format Flash memory on the Cisco 7000 family, use the **format** EXEC command.

format [spare *spare-number*] *device1*: [[*device2*:][*monlib-filename*]]

CAUTION

The following formatting procedure erases all information in the Flash memory. To prevent the loss of important data, proceed carefully.

Syntax	Description
spare	(Optional) Reserves spare sectors as specified by the *spare-number* argument when formatting a device.
spare-number	(Optional) Number of the spare sectors to reserve on formatted device. Valid values are 0 to 16. The default value is zero.
device1:	Device to format. The colon (:) is required. Valid devices are as follows:
	• **bootflash**—Internal Flash memory in the Cisco 7000 family.
	• **slot0**—First PCMCIA slot on the Cisco 7000 family.
	• **slot1**—Second PCMCIA slot on the Cisco 7000 family.
	• **slavebootflash**—Internal Flash memory on the slave RSP card of a Cisco 7507 or Cisco 7513 configured for HSA.
	• **slaveslot0**—First PCMCIA slot of the slave RSP card on a Cisco 7507 or Cisco 7513 configured for HSA.
	• **slaveslot1**—Second PCMCIA slot of the slave RSP card on a Cisco 7507 or Cisco 7513 configured for HSA.
device2:	(Optional) Device containing the monlib file to use for formatting *device1*. The colon (:) is required. Valid devices are as follows:
	• **bootflash**—Internal Flash memory in the Cisco 7000 family.
	• **slot0**—First PCMCIA slot on the Cisco 7000 family. For the Cisco 7000 family, this device is the initial default device.
	• **slot1**—Second PCMCIA slot on the Cisco 7000 family.
monlib-filename	(Optional) Name of the ROM monitor library file (monlib file) to use for formatting *device1*. The default monlib file is the one bundled with the system software.
	When used with HSA and you do not specify the *monlib-filename*, the system takes the ROM monitor library file from the slave image bundle. If you specify the *monlib-filename*, the system assumes that the files reside on the slave devices.

Default

The default monlib file is the one bundled with the system software.

Command Mode

EXEC

Usage Guidelines

This command first appeared in Cisco IOS Release 11.0.

Use this command with the Cisco 7000 family to format internal Flash memory (boot Flash) or your Flash memory cards.

In some cases, you might need to insert a new PCMCIA Flash memory card and load images or backup configuration files onto it. Before you can use a new Flash memory card, you must format it.

Flash memory cards have sectors that can fail. On the Cisco 7000 family, you can reserve certain Flash memory sectors as "spares" for use when other sectors fail. Use the **format** command to specify between 0 and 16 sectors as spares. If you reserve a small number of spare sectors for emergencies, you do not waste space, because you can use most of the Flash memory card. If you specify zero spare sectors and some sectors fail, you must reformat the Flash memory card and thereby erase all existing data.

The monlib file is the ROM monitor library, which is contained in the Cisco IOS system software. The ROM monitor uses the monlib file to access files in the Flash file system.

In the command syntax, *device1* is the device to format and *device2* contains the monlib file to use. When you omit the [[*device2*:][*monlib-filename*]] argument, the system formats *device1* using the monlib that is bundled with the system software. When you omit *device2* from the [[*device2*:][*monlib-filename*]] argument, the system formats *device1* using the named monlib file from the device specified by the **cd** command. When you omit *monlib-filename* from the [[*device2*:][*monlib-filename*]] argument, the system formats *device1* using *device2*'s monlib file. When you specify the whole [[*device2*:][*monlib-filename*]] argument, the system formats *device1* using the specified monlib file from the specified device. Note that you can specify *device1*'s own monlib file in this argument. When the system cannot find a monlib file, the system terminates the formatting process.

CAUTION

You can read from or write to Flash memory cards formatted for Cisco 7000 series Route Processor (RP) cards in your Cisco 7200 series and Cisco 7500 series, but you cannot boot the Cisco 7200 series and Cisco 7500 series from a Flash memory card that is formatted for the Cisco 7000 series. Similarly, you can read from or write to Flash memory cards formatted for the Cisco 7200 series and Cisco 7500 series in your Cisco 7000 series, but you cannot boot the Cisco 7000 series from a Flash memory card that is formatted for the Cisco 7200 series and Cisco 7500 series.

Example

The following example shows the **format** command that formats a Flash memory card inserted in slot 0:

```
Router# format slot0:
Running config file on this device, proceed? [confirm]y
All sectors will be erased, proceed? [confirm]y
Enter volume id (up to 31 characters): <Return>
Formatting sector 1 (erasing)
Format device slot0 completed
```

When the Cisco IOS software returns you to the EXEC prompt, the new Flash memory card is successfully formatted and ready for use.

Related Commands

copy
delete
dir
show file
show flash
squeeze
undelete

MEMORY-SIZE IOMEM

To reallocate the percentage of DRAM memory to use for I/O memory and processor memory on Cisco 3600 series routers, use the **memory-size iomem** global configuration command. The **no** form of this command reverts to the default allocation of 25 percent I/O memory and 75 percent processor memory.

> **memory-size iomem** *I/O-memory-percentage*
> **no memory-size iomem** *I/O-memory-percentage*

Syntax	Description
I/O-memory-percentage	The percentage of DRAM allocated to I/O memory. The values permitted are **25, 30, 40,** and **50** percent.

Default

The default allocation is 25 percent I/O memory and 75 percent processor memory.

Command Mode

Global configuration

Usage Guidelines

This command first appeared in Cisco IOS Release 11.2 P.

When you specify the percentage of I/O memory in the command line, processor memory automatically acquires the remaining percentage of DRAM memory.

Example

The following configuration allocates 40 percent of the DRAM memory to I/O memory and the remaining 60 percent to processor memory.

```
Router# configure terminal
Enter configuration commands, one per line.  End with CNTL/Z.
Router(config)# memory-size iomem 40
Router(config)# exit
Router# copy running-config startup-config
Building configuration...
[OK]

Router# reload

rommon 1 > boot
program load complete, entry point: 0x80008000, size: 0x32ea24
Self decompressing the image :
###############################################################################
###############################################################################
################################################################### [OK]
```

PARTITION

To separate Flash memory into partitions on the Cisco 1600 series and Cisco 3600 series, use the **partition** global configuration command. Use the **no** form of this command to undo partitioning and to restore Flash memory to one partition.

> **partition** *device*: [*number-of-partitions*][*partition-size*]
> **no partition** *device*:

Syntax	Description
device	One of the following devices, which must be followed by a colon (:). The Cisco 1600 series can use only the flash keyword.
	• **flash**—Internal Flash memory
	• **slot0**—Flash memory card in PCMCIA slot 0
	• **slot1**—Flash memory card in PCMCIA slot 1
number-of-partitions	(Optional) Number of partitions in Flash memory.
partition-size	(Optional) Size of each partition. The number of partition size entries must be equal to the number of specified partitions.

Default

Flash memory consists of one partition.

If the partition size is not specified, partitions of equal size are created.

Command Mode

Global configuration

Part
II

Usage Guidelines

To undo partitioning, use the **partition** *device*:**1** or **no partition** *device*: command. If there are files in a partition other than the first, you must use the command **erase** *device*:*partition-number* to erase the partition before reverting to a single partition.

When creating two partitions, you must not truncate a file or cause a file to spill over into the second partition.

Examples

The following example divides the Flash memory card in slot 0 into two partitions, each 8 MB in size on the Cisco 3600:

```
Router# configure terminal
Enter configuration commands, one per line.  End with CNTL/Z.
Router(config)# partition slot0: 2 8 8
```

The following example creates four partitions of equal size in the card in slot 0 on the Cisco 3600.

```
Router# configure terminal
Enter configuration commands, one per line.  End with CNTL/Z.
Router(config)# partition slot0: 4
```

The following example divides the Flash memory card into two partitions, each 4 MB in size on a Cisco 1600 series:

```
Router# configure terminal
Enter configuration commands, one per line.  End with CNTL/Z.
Router(config)# partition flash: 2 4 4
```

The following example creates four partitions of equal size in the card on a Cisco 1600 series:

```
Router# configure terminal
Enter configuration commands, one per line.  End with CNTL/Z.
Router(config)# partition flash: 4
```

PARTITION FLASH

To separate Flash memory into two partitions, use the **partition flash** global configuration command. Use the **no** form of this command to undo partitioning and restore Flash memory to one partition.

> **partition flash** *partitions* [*size1 size2*]
> **no partition flash**

Syntax	Description
partitions	Number of partitions in Flash memory. Can be 1 or 2.
size1	(Optional) Size of the first partition in megabytes.
size2	(Optional) Size of the second partition in megabytes.

Default

Flash memory consists of one partition.

If this command is entered, but partition size is not specified, two partitions of equal size will be created.

Command Mode

Global configuration

Usage Guidelines

This command first appeared in Cisco IOS Release 10.3.

Although the software supports up to eight partitions, current hardware allows only two. To undo partitioning, use either the **partition flash 1** or **no partition flash** command. If one or more files exist in the second partition, you must manually erase the second partition with the **erase flash** command before reverting to a single partition.

When creating two partitions, you must not truncate a file or cause the spillover of a file into the second partition.

Example

The following example creates two partitions of 4 MB each in Flash memory:

```
partition flash 2 4 4
```

PWD

To show the current setting of the **cd** command on the Cisco 7000 family, use the **pwd** EXEC command.

    pwd

Syntax   Description

This command has no arguments or keywords.

Default

This command has no default.

Command Mode

EXEC

Usage Guidelines

This command first appeared in Cisco IOS Release 11.0.

Use this command with the Cisco 7000 family.

Use the **pwd** command to show what device is specified as the system's default device by the **cd** command. For all EXEC commands that have an optional *device*: argument, the system uses the device specified by the **cd** command when you omit the optional *device*: argument.

For example, the **dir** command contains an optional *device*: argument and displays a list of files on a Flash memory device. When you omit this *device*: argument, the system shows a list of the files on the Flash device specified by the **cd** command.

Examples

The following example shows that the present working device specified by the **cd** command is slot 0:

```
Router> pwd
slot0
```

The following example uses the **cd** command to change the present working device to slot 1 and then uses the **pwd** command to display that present working device:

```
Router> cd slot1:
Router> pwd
slot1
```

Similarly, the following example uses the **cd** command on the Cisco 7500 series to change the present working device to boot Flash and then uses the **pwd** command to display that present working device:

```
Router> cd bootflash:
Router> pwd
bootflash
```

Related Commands

cd

SHOW BOOTFLASH

To display information about boot Flash memory, use the **show bootflash** EXEC command.

show bootflash

Syntax   Description

This command has no arguments or keywords.

Command Mode

EXEC

Usage Guidelines

This command first appeared in Cisco IOS Release 10.3.

You can use this command only on routers that have two banks of Flash: one bank for the boot image and the second bank for the system image.

The **show bootflash** command displays the type of boot Flash memory present, any files that might currently exist in boot Flash memory, and the amount of boot Flash memory used and remaining.

Sample Display

The following is sample output from the **show bootflash** command:

```
Router# show bootflash
Boot flash directory:
File  name/status
   1  c4500-xboot
[1387336 bytes used, 2806968 bytes available]
```

Table 14–5 describes the fields shown in the output.

Table 14–5 *Show Bootflash Field Descriptions*

Field	Description
Boot File	Number of the boot file.
flash directory: name/status	Name and status of the boot file. The status is displayed if appropriate and can be one of the following: • [deleted]—File has been deleted. • [invalid checksum]—File has an incorrect checksum.

SHOW FLASH

To display the layout and contents of Flash memory, use one of the following **show flash** EXEC commands:

show flash [all | chips | detailed | err | partition *number* [all | chips | detailed | err] | summary]

show *device*: [all | chips | detailed | err | partition *number* | summary] (Cisco 1600 series and Cisco 3600 series)

show flash [all | chips | filesys] [*device*:] (Cisco 7000 family only)

Syntax	Description
all	(Optional) On all platforms except the Cisco 7000 family, **all** shows complete information about Flash memory, including information about the individual ROM devices in Flash memory and the names and sizes of all system image files stored in Flash memory, including those that are invalid. On the Cisco 7000 family, **all** shows the following information: • The information displayed by the **dir** command when you use the **/all** and **/long** keywords together. • The information displayed by the **filesys** keyword. • The information displayed by the **chips** keyword.
chips	(Optional) Shows information per partition and per chip, including which bank the chip is in plus its code, size, and name.
detailed	(Optional) Shows detailed file directory information per partition, including file length, address, name, Flash memory checksum, computer checksum, bytes used, bytes available, total bytes, and bytes of system Flash memory.
err	(Optional) Shows write or erase failures in the form of number of retries.
partition *number*	(Optional) Shows output for the specified partition number. If you specify the **partition** keyword, you must specify a partition number. You can use this keyword only when Flash memory has multiple partitions.
summary	(Optional) Shows summary information per partition, including the partition size, bank size, state, and method by which files can be copied into a particular partition. You can use this keyword only when Flash memory has multiple partitions.
filesys	(Optional) Shows the Device Info Block, the Status Info, and the Usage Info.

Part
II

Command Reference

Syntax	*Description*
device:	(Optional for the Cisco 7000 family) Specifies the device about which to show Flash information.

For the Cisco 7000 family, the device is optional; but when it is used, the colon (:) is required. When it is omitted, the default device is that specified by the **cd** command.

Valid devices are as follows:

- **bootflash**—Internal Flash memory in the Cisco 7000 family.

- **flash**—Internal Flash memory in the Cisco 3600 series. A Flash memory PC card on the Cisco 1600 series. This is the only valid device for the Cisco 1600 series.

- **slot0**—First PCMCIA slot on the Cisco 3600 series and Cisco 7000 family.

- **slot1**—Second PCMCIA slot on the Cisco 3600 series and Cisco 7000 family.

- **slavebootflash**—Internal Flash memory on the slave RSP card of a Cisco 7507 or Cisco 7513 configured for HSA.

- **slaveslot0**—First PCMCIA slot of the slave RSP card on a Cisco 7507 or Cisco 7513 configured for HSA.

- **slaveslot1**—Second PCMCIA slot of the slave RSP card on a Cisco 7507 or Cisco 7513 configured for HSA.

Command Mode

EXEC

Usage Guidelines

The **show flash all** command first appeared in Cisco IOS Release 10.0. The remaining commands, such as **chips** and **detailed**, first appeared in Cisco IOS Release 10.3.

The **show flash** command displays the type of Flash memory present, any files that currently exist in Flash memory, and the amounts of Flash memory used and remaining.

For the Cisco 7000 family, when you specify a PCMCIA slot as the device, the router displays the layout and contents of the Flash memory card inserted in the specified slot of the RP or RSP card. When you omit the *device*: argument, the router displays the default device specified by the **cd** command. Use the **pwd** command to show the current default device.

Sample Displays

The output of the **show flash** command depends on the platform. This section contains the following examples:

- Show Flash Example
- Show Flash Example with Partitioned Memory
- Show Flash All Example
- Show Flash All Example with Security Jumper Not Installed
- Show Flash All Example with Partitioned Memory
- Show Flash Chips Example with Partitioned Memory
- Show Flash Detailed Example with Partitioned Memory
- Show Flash Err Example with Partitioned Memory
- Show Flash Summary Example with Partitioned Memory
- Show Flash Examples for Cisco 7000 Family
- Show Flash Examples for Cisco 1600 Series and Cisco 3600 Series

Show Flash Example

The following is sample output from the **show flash** command. The output might vary for your platform.

```
Router# show flash

4096K bytes of flash memory sized on embedded flash.

File    name/status
0       ahp4/gs7-k
1       micro/eip1-0
2       micro/sp1-3
3       micro/trip1-1
4       micro/hip1-0
5       micro/fip1-1
6       flyspecked
7       spucode
8       tripucode
9       fipucode
10      eipucode
11      hipucode
12      sipucode
13      sp_q160-1
14      ahp4/sp160-3 [deleted]
15      ahp4/sp160-3
[682680/4194304 bytes free/total]
```

Table 14–6 describes the **show flash** fields in this display.

Table 14–6 *Show Flash Field Descriptions*

Field	Description
File	Number of file in Flash memory.
name/status	Files that currently exist in Flash memory.
bytes free	Amount of Flash memory remaining.
[deleted]	Flag indicating that another file exists with the same name or that the process has been abnormally terminated.

As the display shows, the Flash memory can store and display multiple, independent software images for booting itself or for TFTP server software for other products. This feature is useful for storing default system software. These images can be stored in compressed format (but cannot be compressed by the router).

To eliminate any files from Flash memory (invalidated or otherwise) and free up all available memory space, the entire Flash memory must be erased; individual files cannot be erased from Flash memory.

Show Flash Example with Partitioned Memory

The following is a sample output from the **show flash** command on a router that has Flash memory partitioned:

```
Router# show flash

System flash directory, partition 1:
  File  Length    Name/status
    1   3459720   master/igs-bfpx.100-4.3
  [3459784 bytes used, 734520 available, 4194304 total]
4096K bytes of processor board System flash (Read Only)

System flash directory, partition 2:
  File  Length    Name/status
    1   3459720   igs-kf
  [3459784 bytes used, 734520 available, 4194304 total]
  4096K bytes of processor board System flash (Read/Write)
```

Show Flash All Example

The following is a sample output from the **show flash all** command. The format of your display might differ.

```
Router# show flash all

4096K bytes of flash memory sized on embedded flash.
  Chip    socket    code     bytes      name
    0       U63      89BD    0x040000   INTEL 28F020
    1       U62      89BD    0x040000   INTEL 28F020
```

```
 2      U61     89BD    0x040000    INTEL 28F020
 3      U60     89BD    0x040000    INTEL 28F020
 4      U48     89BD    0x040000    INTEL 28F020
 5      U47     89BD    0x040000    INTEL 28F020
 6      U46     89BD    0x040000    INTEL 28F020
 7      U45     89BD    0x040000    INTEL 28F020
 8      U30     89BD    0x040000    INTEL 28F020
 9      U29     89BD    0x040000    INTEL 28F020
10      U28     89BD    0x040000    INTEL 28F020
11      U27     89BD    0x040000    INTEL 28F020
12      U17     89BD    0x040000    INTEL 28F020
13      U16     89BD    0x040000    INTEL 28F020
14      U15     89BD    0x040000    INTEL 28F020
15      U14     89BD    0x040000    INTEL 28F020

Flash file directory:
File  name/status
addr           length       fcksum      ccksum
0   gs7-k
0x12000080     2601100      0x4015      0x4015
1   micro/eip1-0
0x1227B14C     53364        0x0         0x0
2   micro/sp1-3
0x12288200     55418        0x0         0x0
3   micro/trip1-1
0x12295ABC     105806       0x0         0x0
4   micro/hip1-0
0x122AF84C     35528        0x0         0x0
5   micro/fip1-1
0x122B8354     97070        0x0         0x0
6   fsipucode
0x122CFEC4     6590         0x0         0x0
7   spucode
0x122D18C4     55418        0x0         0x0
8   tripucode
0x122DF180     105806       0x0         0x0
9   fipucode
0x122F8F10     97070        0x0         0x0
10  eipucode
0x12310A80     53330        0x60A1      0x60A1
11  hipucode
0x1231DB14     35528        0x0         0x0
12  sipucode
0x1232661C     54040        0x0         0x0
13  sp_q160-1
0x1233974      42912        0x0         0x0
14  ahp4/sp160-3 [deleted]
0x1233E154     55730        0x0         0x0
15  ahp4/sp160-3
0x1234BB48     55808        0x0         0x0
[682680/4194304 bytes free/total]
```

Table 14–7 describes the **show flash all** display fields.

Table 14–7   *Show Flash All Field Descriptions*

Field	Description
bytes of flash memory sized on embedded flash	Total amount of Flash memory present.
Chip	Identifies the ROM unit.
socket	Location of the ROM unit.
code	Vendor code identifying the vendor of the ROM unit.
bytes	Size of the ROM unit (in hex bytes).
name (in row beginning with Chip)	Vendor name and chip part number of the ROM unit.
security jumper, flash memory	Security jumper is/is not installed. Flash memory is programmable or read-only. If the security jumper is not installed, you will see the **show flash** display with a message indicating that the jumper is not installed.
File	Number of the system image file. If no filename is specified in the **boot system flash** command, the router boots the system image file with the lowest file number.
name/status	Filename and status of a system image file. The status [invalidated] appears when a file has been rewritten (recopied) into Flash memory. The first (now invalidated) copy of the file is still present within Flash memory, but it is rendered unusable in favor of the newest version. The [invalidated] status also can indicate an incomplete file that results from the user abnormally terminating the copy process, a network timeout, or a Flash memory overflow.
addr	Address of the file in Flash memory.
length	Size of the system image file (in bytes).
fcksum	Checksum recorded in Flash memory.
ccksum	Computer checksum.
[deleted]	Flag indicating that another file exists with the same name or that process has been abnormally terminated.
bytes free/total	Amount of Flash memory used/total amount of Flash memory.

Show Flash All Example with Security Jumper Not Installed

In the following example, the security jumper is not installed. You cannot write to Flash memory until the security jumper is installed:

```
Router# show flash all

4096K bytes of flash memory on embedded flash (in RP1).
 security jumper(12V) is not installed,
flash memory is read-only.

file    offset      length       name
0       0xDCD0      1903892      gs7-k [deleted]
1       0x1DEA24    1903912      gs7-k
 [329908/4194304 bytes free]
```

Show Flash All Example with Partitioned Memory

The following is sample output for the **show flash all** command on router that has Flash memory partitioned:

```
Router# show flash all

System flash partition information:
Partition   Size    Used     Free     Bank-Size    State        Copy-Mode
    1       4096K    3459K    637K     4096K        Read Only    RXBOOT-FLH
    2       4096K    3224K    872K     4096K        Read/Write   Direct

System flash directory, partition 1:
File    Length      Name/status
        addr    fcksum      ccksum
  1     3459720     master/igs-bfpx.100-4.3
        0x40    0x3DE1      0x3DE1
[3459784 bytes used, 734520 available, 4194304 total]
4096K bytes of processor board System flash (Read ONLY)

    Chip    Bank    Code     Size     Name
     1       1      89A2     1024KB   INTEL 28F008SA
     2       1      89A2     1024KB   INTEL 28F008SA
     3       1      89A2     1024KB   INTEL 28F008SA
     4       1      89A2     1024KB   INTEL 28F008SA
Executing current image from System flash [partition 1]

 System flash directory, partition2:
File    Length      Name/status
        addr    fcksum      ccksum
  1     3224008     igs-kf.100
        0x40    0xEE91      0xEE91
[3224072 bytes used, 970232 available, 4194304 total]
4096K bytes of processor board System flash (Read/Write)

    Chip    Bank    Code     Size     Name
     1       2      89A2     1024KB   INTEL 28F008SA
```

Part
II

Command Reference

```
2       2        89A2      1024KB    INTEL 28F008SA
3       2        89A2      1024KB    INTEL 28F008SA
4       2        89A2      1024KB    INTEL 28F008SA
```

Table 14–8 describes the additional fields in the display.

Table 14–8   *Show Flash All Fields for Partitioned Flash Memory*

Field	Description
Partition	Partition number in Flash memory.
Size	Size of partition in bytes.
Used	Number of bytes used in partition.
Free	Number of bytes free in partition.
Bank-Size	Size of bank in bytes.
State	State of the partition. It can be one of the following values: • Read-Only indicates the partition that is being executed from. • Read/Write is a partition that can be copied to.
Copy-Mode	Method by which the partition can be copied to: • RXBOOT-FLH indicates copy via Flash load helper. • Direct indicates user can copy directly into Flash memory. • None indicates that it is not possible to copy into that partition.
System flash directory, partition 1	Flash directory and its contents.
File	Number of the system image file. If no filename is specified in the **boot system flash** command, the router boots the system image file with the lowest file number.
Length	Size of the system image file (in bytes).
Name/status	Filename and status of a system image file. The status [invalidated] appears when a file has been rewritten (recopied) into Flash memory. The first (now invalidated) copy of the file is still present within Flash memory, but it is rendered unusable in favor of the newest version. The [invalidated] status also can indicate an incomplete file that results from the user abnormally terminating the copy process, a network timeout, or a Flash memory overflow.
addr	Address of the file in Flash memory.
fcksum	Checksum recorded in Flash memory.

Table 14–8 *Show Flash All Fields for Partitioned Flash Memory, Continued*

Field	Description
ccksum	Computer checksum.
Chip	Chip number.
Bank	Bank number.
Code	Code number.
Size	Size of chip.
Name	Name of chip manufacturer and chip type.

Show Flash Chips Example with Partitioned Memory

The following is sample output for the **show flash chips** command on a router that has Flash memory partitioned:

```
Router# show flash chips

System flash partition 1:
4096K bytes of processor board System flash (Read ONLY)

   Chip   Bank   Code     Size      Name
    1      1     89A2     1024KB     INTEL 28F008SA
    2      1     89A2     1024KB     INTEL 28F008SA
    3      1     89A2     1024KB     INTEL 28F008SA
    4      1     89A2     1024KB     INTEL 28F008SA
Executing current image from System flash [partition 1]

System flash partition 2:
4096K bytes of processor board System flash (Read/Write)

   Chip   Bank   Code     Size      Name
    1      2     89A2     1024KB     INTEL 28F008SA
    2      2     89A2     1024KB     INTEL 28F008SA
    3      2     89A2     1024KB     INTEL 28F008SA
    4      2     89A2     1024KB     INTEL 28F008SA
```

Show Flash Detailed Example with Partitioned Memory

The following is sample output for the **show flash detailed** command on a router that has Flash memory partitioned:

```
Router# show flash detailed

System flash directory, partition 1:
File  Length    Name/status
        addr       fcksum   ccksum
  1   3224008   igs-kf.100
```

```
        0x40      0xEE91  0xEE91
[3224072 bytes used, 970232 available, 4194304 total]
4096K bytes of processor board System flash (Read/Write)

System flash directory, partition 2:
File  Length   Name/status
         addr      fcksum  ccksum
  1   3224008  igs-kf.100
        0x40      0xEE91  0xEE91
[3224072 bytes used, 970232 available, 4194304 total]
4096K bytes of processor board System flash (Read/Write)
```

Show Flash Err Example with Partitioned Memory

The following is sample output for the **show flash err** command on a router that has Flash memory partitioned:

```
Router# show flash err

System flash directory, partition 1:
File  Length   Name/status
  1   37376    master/igs-bfpx.100-4.3  [invalid checksum]
[37440 bytes used, 4156864 available, 4194304 total]
4096K bytes of processor board System flash (Read/Write)

    Chip    Bank    Code    Size     Name               erase  write
     1       1      89A2    1024KB   INTEL 28F008SA       0      0
     2       1      89A2    1024KB   INTEL 28F008SA       0      0
     3       1      89A2    1024KB   INTEL 28F008SA       0      0
     4       1      89A2    1024KB   INTEL 28F008SA       0      0
Executing current image from System flash [partition 1]

System flash directory, partition 2:
File  Length   Name/status
  1   37376    master/igs-bfpx.100-4.3  [invalid checksum]
[37440 bytes used, 4156864 available, 4194304 total]
4096K bytes of processor board System flash (Read/Write)

    Chip    Bank    Code    Size     Name               erase  write
     1       2      89A2    1024KB   INTEL 28F008SA       0      0
     2       2      89A2    1024KB   INTEL 28F008SA       0      0
     3       2      89A2    1024KB   INTEL 28F008SA       0      0
     4       2      89A2    1024KB   INTEL 28F008SA       0      0
```

Show Flash Summary Example with Partitioned Memory

The following is sample output for the **show flash summary** command on a router that has Flash memory partitioned. The partition in the Read Only state is the partition from which the Cisco IOS image is being executed.

```
Router# show flash summary

System flash partition information:
Partition   Size    Used    Free    Bank-Size   State       Copy-Mode
    1       4096K   2048K   2048K   2048K       Read Only   RXBOOT-FLH
    2       4096K   2048K   2048K   2048K       Read/Write  Direct
```

The following are possible values for Copy-Mode:

- RXBOOT-MANUAL—User can copy manually by reloading to the boot ROM image.

- RXBOOT-FLH—User can copy via Flash load helper.

- Direct—User can copy directly into Flash memory.

- None—Copy not allowed into that partition.

Show Flash Examples for Cisco 7000 Family

The following sample output shows the **show flash** command on a Cisco 7000 family:

```
Router# cd slot1:
Router# show flash
-#- ED --type-- --crc--- -seek-- nlen -length- -----date/time------ name
 1   .. 1       46A11866 2036C   4    746      May 16 1995 16:24:37 test
```

If you do not use the **cd** command to change the present working device to slot 1, you can display the same sample output with the following command:

```
Router# show flash slot1:
-#- ED --type-- --crc--- -seek-- nlen -length- -----date/time------ name
 1   .. 1       46A11866 2036C   4    746      May 16 1995 16:24:37 test
```

The following is sample output for the **show flash filesys** command on a Cisco 7000 family:

```
Router# show flash filesys slot1:

-------- F I L E   S Y S T E M   S T A T U S --------
  Device Number = 1
DEVICE INFO BLOCK: test
  Magic Number          = 6887635   File System Vers = 10000    (1.0)
  Length                = 800000    Sector Size      = 20000
  Programming Algorithm = 4         Erased State     = FFFFFFFF
  File System Offset     = 20000    Length = 7A0000
  MONLIB Offset         = 100       Length = A140
  Bad Sector Map Offset = 1FFF8     Length = 8
  Squeeze Log Offset    = 7C0000    Length = 20000
  Squeeze Buffer Offset = 7E0000    Length = 20000
  Num Spare Sectors     = 0
    Spares:
STATUS INFO:
  Writable
  NO File Open for Write
  Complete Stats
  No Unrecovered Errors
  Squeeze in progress
```

```
USAGE INFO:
  Bytes Used       = 36C    Bytes Available = 79FC94
  Bad Sectors      = 0      Spared Sectors = 0
  OK Files         = 1      Bytes = 2EC
  Deleted Files    = 0      Bytes = 0
  Files w/Errors   = 0      Bytes = 0
```

The following is sample output for the **show flash chips bootflash:** command on a Cisco 7000 family:

```
Router# show flash chips bootflash:
******** RSP Internal Flash Bank -- Intel Chips ********
Flash SIMM Reg: 401
  Flash SIMM PRESENT
  2 Banks
  Bank Size = 4M
  HW Rev = 1

Flash Status Registers: Bank 0
  Intelligent ID Code: 89898989 A2A2A2A2
  Status Reg: 80808080

Flash Status Registers: Bank 1
  Intelligent ID Code: 89898989 A2A2A2A2
  Status Reg: 80808080
```

In the following example, the present working device is bootflash on a Cisco 7000 family. The sample output displays the **show flash all** output.

```
Router# cd bootflash:
Router# show flash all
-#- ED --type-- --crc--- -seek-- nlen -length- -----date/time------ name
1   .. FFFFFFFF 49B403EE 3D0510  21   3736719  May 30 1995 17:47:54 dirt/yanke/m

3865328 bytes available (3736848 bytes used)

------- F I L E   S Y S T E M   S T A T U S --------
  Device Number = 2
DEVICE INFO BLOCK: test
  Magic Number        = 6887635   File System Vers = 10000    (1.0)
  Length              = 800000    Sector Size      = 40000
  Programming Algorithm = 5       Erased State     = FFFFFFFF
  File System Offset  = 40000     Length = 740000
  MONLIB Offset       = 100       Length = A270
  Bad Sector Map Offset = 3FFFC   Length = 4
  Squeeze Log Offset  = 780000    Length = 40000
  Squeeze Buffer Offset = 7C0000  Length = 40000
  Num Spare Sectors   = 0
    Spares:
STATUS INFO:
  Writable
  NO File Open for Write
  Complete Stats
  No Unrecovered Errors
  Squeeze in progress
```

```
USAGE INFO:
  Bytes Used      = 390510 Bytes Available = 3AFAF0
  Bad Sectors     = 0      Spared Sectors = 0
  OK Files        = 1      Bytes = 390490
  Deleted Files   = 0      Bytes = 0
  Files w/Errors  = 0      Bytes = 0


******** RSP Internal Flash Bank -- Intel Chips ********
Flash SIMM Reg: 401
  Flash SIMM PRESENT
  2 Banks
  Bank Size = 4M
  HW Rev = 1


Flash Status Registers: Bank 0
  Intelligent ID Code: 89898989 A2A2A2A2
  Status Reg: 80808080


Flash Status Registers: Bank 1
  Intelligent ID Code: 89898989 A2A2A2A2
  Status Reg: 80808080


Router# show flash chips bootflash:

******** RSP Internal Flash Bank -- Intel Chips ********
Flash SIMM Reg: 401
  Flash SIMM PRESENT
  2 Banks
  Bank Size = 4M
  HW Rev = 1


Flash Status Registers: Bank 0
  Intelligent ID Code: 89898989 A2A2A2A2
  Status Reg: 80808080


Flash Status Registers: Bank 1
  Intelligent ID Code: 89898989 A2A2A2A2
  Status Reg: 80808080
```

Show Flash Examples for Cisco 1600 Series and Cisco 3600 Series

The following example shows detailed information about the second partition in internal Flash memory on a Cisco 3600 series router:

```
Router# show flash: partition 2

System flash directory, partition 2:
File  Length    Name/status
  1   1711088   dirt/images/c3600-i-mz
[1711152 bytes used, 15066064 available, 16777216 total]
16384K bytes of processor board System flash (Read/Write)
```

The following example shows copy and file space information about each partition in the card in slot 1 on a Cisco 3600 series router:

```
Router# show slot1: summary
```

The following example shows the state of the Flash memory PC card on a Cisco 1600 series router:

```
Router# show flash: all
```

The following example illustrates the **show flash: chips** command on a Cisco 1600 series router:

```
Router# show flash: chips
```

The following example illustrates the **show flash: detailed** command:

```
Router# show flash: detailed
```

The following example illustrates the **show flash: err** command:

```
Router# show flash: err
```

SHOW FLASH DEVICES

To display the names of the Flash devices supported on the Cisco 7000 family, use the **show flash devices** EXEC command.

```
show flash devices
```

Syntax   *Description*

This command has no arguments or keywords.

Command Mode

EXEC

Usage Guidelines

This command first appeared in Cisco IOS Release 11.1.

Use this command for the Cisco 7200 series or a Cisco 7507 or Cisco 7513 that is configured for High System Availability (HSA). HSA refers to how quickly your router returns to an operational status after a failure occurs. On the Cisco 7507 and Cisco 7513, you can install two RSP cards in a single router to improve system availability.

When you issue this command, the router returns a list of valid Flash devices supported on the NPE card (for a Cisco 7200 series) and both RSP cards (for a Cisco 7507 or Cisco 7513). Use this command to learn the names of the Flash devices that the NPE card or slave RSP supports.

Sample Display

In the following example, the Flash devices for a Cisco 7507 or Cisco 7513 are displayed:

```
slot-10# show flash devices
nvram, tftp, rcp, slot0, slot1, bootflash, slaveslot0,
slaveslot1, slavebootflash, slavenvram
slot-10#
```

SQUEEZE

To delete Flash files permanently on the Cisco 7000 family, use the **squeeze** EXEC command.

   squeeze *device*:

Syntax	Description
device:	Flash device from which to permanently delete files. The colon (:) is required. Valid devices are as follows:

- **bootflash**—Internal Flash memory on the Cisco 7000 family.
- **slot0**—First PCMCIA slot on the Cisco 7000 family.
- **slot1**—Second PCMCIA slot on the Cisco 7000 family.
- **slavebootflash**—Internal Flash memory on the slave RSP card of a Cisco 7507 or Cisco 7513 configured for HSA.
- **slaveslot0**—First PCMCIA slot of the slave RSP card on a Cisco 7507 or Cisco 7513 configured for HSA.
- **slaveslot1**—Second PCMCIA slot of the slave RSP card on a Cisco 7507 or Cisco 7513 configured for HSA.

Command Mode

EXEC

Usage Guidelines

This command first appeared in Cisco IOS Release 11.1.

Use this command with the Cisco 7000 family.

When Flash memory is full, you might need to rearrange the files so that the space used by the "deleted" files can be reclaimed. When you issue the **squeeze** command, the router copies all valid files to the beginning of Flash memory and erases all files marked "deleted." At this point, you cannot recover "deleted" files and you can write to the reclaimed Flash memory space.

In addition to removing deleted files, the **squeeze** command removes any files that the system has marked as error. An error file is created when a file write fails (for example, because the device is full) and is automatically deleted. To remove error files, you must use the **squeeze** command.

NOTES

The squeeze operation might take as long as several minutes, because it can involve erasing and rewriting almost an entire Flash memory space.

Part
II

Command Reference

Example

The following example instructs the router to erase permanently the files marked "deleted" from the Flash memory card inserted in slot 1:

```
squeeze slot1:
```

Related Commands

delete
dir
undelete

UNDELETE

To recover a deleted file on a specified device of the Cisco 7000 family, use the **undelete** EXEC command.

undelete *index* [*device*:]

Syntax	Description
index	Number that indexes the file in the **dir** command output.
device:	(Optional) Device to contain the recovered configuration file. The colon (:) is required. Valid devices are as follows:

- **bootflash**—Internal Flash memory in the Cisco 7000 family.
- **slot0**—First PCMCIA slot on the Cisco 7000 family.
- **slot1**—Second PCMCIA slot on the Cisco 7000 family.
- **slavebootflash**—Internal Flash memory on the slave RSP card of a Cisco 7507 or Cisco 7513 configured for HSA.
- **slaveslot0**—First PCMCIA slot of the slave RSP card on a Cisco 7507 or Cisco 7513 configured for HSA.
- **slaveslot1**—Second PCMCIA slot of the slave RSP card on a Cisco 7507 or Cisco 7513 configured for HSA.

Default

The default device is the one specified by the **cd** command.

Command Mode

EXEC

Usage Guidelines

This command first appeared in Cisco IOS Release 11.0.

Use this command with the Cisco 7000 family.

When you delete a file, the Cisco IOS software simply marks the file as deleted, but does not erase the file. This command allows you to recover a "deleted" file on a specified Flash memory device. You must undelete a file by its index, because you could have multiple deleted files with the same name. For example, the "deleted" list could contain multiple configuration files with the name *router-config*. You undelete by index to indicate which of the many *router-config* files from the list to undelete. Use the **dir** command to learn the index number of the file you want to undelete.

You cannot undelete a file if a valid (undeleted) one with the same name exists. Instead, you first delete the existing file and then undelete the file you want. For example, if you had an undeleted version of the *router-config* file and you wanted to use a previous, deleted version instead, you could not simply undelete the previous version by index. You would first delete the existing *router-config* file and then undelete the previous *router-config* file by index. You can delete and undelete a file up to 15 times.

If you try to recover the configuration file pointed to by the CONFIG_FILE environment variable, the system prompts you to confirm recovery of the file. This prompt reminds you that the CONFIG_FILE environment variable points to an undeleted file. To permanently delete all "deleted" files on a Flash memory device, use the **squeeze** command. If you try to recover a file that has the same name as an existing valid file, the system displays an error message.

Example

The following example recovers the deleted file whose index number is 1 to the Flash memory card inserted in slot 0:

```
undelete 1 slot0:
```

Related Commands

delete
dir
squeeze

## CHAPTER 15

Rebooting a Router

This chapter describes the basic procedure a router follows when it reboots, how to alter the procedure, and how to use the ROM Monitor.

For a complete description of the booting commands mentioned in this chapter, see Chapter 16, "Booting Commands."

REBOOTING A ROUTER TASK LIST

You can perform the tasks related to rebooting discussed in the following sections:

- Displaying Booting Information
- Rebooting Procedures
- Modifying the Configuration Register Boot Field
- Setting Environment Variables
- Scheduling a Reload of the System Image
- Configuring High System Availability Operation (Cisco 7500 series)
- Stopping Booting and Entering ROM Monitor Mode
- Manually Loading a System Image from ROM Monitor

DISPLAYING BOOTING INFORMATION

Perform the following tasks in EXEC mode to display information about system software, system image files, and configuration files:

Task	Command
Step 1 List the contents of the BOOT environment variable, the name of the configuration file pointed to by the CONFIG_FILE environment variable, and the contents of the BOOTLDR environment variable.	**show boot** (Cisco 3600 series, Cisco 7000 family only)
Step 2 List the startup configuration information. On all platforms except the Cisco 7000 family, the startup configuration is usually in NVRAM. On the Cisco 7000 family, the CONFIG_FILE environment variable points to the startup configuration, defaulting to NVRAM.	**show startup-config**
Step 3 List the system software release version, configuration register setting, and other information.	**show version**

You also can use the **o** command (the **confreg** command for some platforms) in ROM monitor mode to list the configuration register settings on some models.

REBOOTING PROCEDURES

The following sections describe what happens when the router reboots:

- What Configuration File Does the Router Use Upon Startup?
- What Image Does the Router Use Upon Startup?

What Configuration File Does the Router Use Upon Startup?

On all platforms, except the Cisco 7000 family:

- If the configuration register is set to ignore NVRAM, the router enters setup mode.
- If the configuration register is not set to ignore NVRAM, then:
  - The startup software checks for configuration information in NVRAM.
  - If NVRAM holds valid configuration commands, the Cisco IOS software executes the commands automatically at startup.
  - If the software detects a problem with NVRAM or the configuration it contains (a CRC checksum error), it enters **setup** mode and prompts for configuration.

On the Cisco 7000 family:

- If the configuration register is set to ignore NVRAM, the router enters setup mode.
- If the configuration register is not set to ignore NVRAM, then:
  - The startup software uses the configuration pointed to by the CONFIG_FILE environment variable.
  - When the CONFIG_FILE environment variable does not exist or is null (such as at first-time startup), the router uses NVRAM as the default startup device.
  - When the router uses NVRAM to start up and the system detects a problem with NVRAM or the configuration it contains, the router enters **setup** mode.

Problems can include a bad checksum for the information in NVRAM or an empty NVRAM with no configuration information. See the "Using Setup for Configuration Changes" section in Chapter 3, "Using Configuration Tools," for details on the **setup** command facility. For more information on environment variables, see the "Setting Environment Variables" section.

What Image Does the Router Use Upon Startup?

When a router is powered on or rebooted, the following events happen:

- The ROM monitor initializes.
- The ROM monitor checks the configuration register boot field (the lowest four bits in the register).
  - If the boot field is 0x0, the system does not boot an IOS image and waits for user intervention at the ROM monitor prompt.
  - If the boot field is 0x1, the ROM monitor boots the boot helper image. (On some platforms, the boot helper image is specified by the BOOTLDR environment variable.)
  - If the boot field is 0x2 through 0xF, the ROM monitor boots the first valid image specified in the configuration file or specified by the BOOT environment variable.

When the boot field is 0x2 through 0xF, the router goes through each command in order until it boots a valid image. If bit 13 in the configuration register is set, each command will be tried once. If bit 13 is not set, the **boot system** commands specifying a network server will be tried up to five more times. The timeouts between each consecutive attempt are two seconds, four seconds, 16 seconds, 256 seconds, and 300 seconds. If it cannot find a valid image, the following events happen:

- If all boot commands in the system configuration file specify booting from a network server and all commands fail, the system attempts to boot the first valid file in Flash memory.
- If the "boot-default-ROM-software" option in the configuration register is set, the router will start the boot image (the image contained in boot ROM or specified by the BOOTLDR environment variable).
- If the "boot-default-ROM-software" option in the configuration register is not set, the system waits for user intervention at the ROM monitor prompt. You must boot the router manually.

- If a fully functional system image is not found, the router will not function and must be reconfigured through a direct console port connection.

NOTES

Refer to your platform documentation for information on the default location of the boot image.

When looking for a bootable file in Flash memory:

- The system searches for the filename in Flash memory. If a filename is not specified, the software searches through the entire Flash directory for a bootable file instead of picking only the first file.
- The system attempts to recognize the file in Flash memory. If the file is recognized, the software decides whether it is bootable by performing the following checks:
  - For run-from-Flash images, the software determines whether it is loaded at the correct execution address.
  - For run-from-RAM images, the software determines whether the system has enough RAM to execute the image.

Figure 15–1 illustrates the basic booting decision process.

MODIFYING THE CONFIGURATION REGISTER BOOT FIELD

The configuration register boot field determines whether the router loads an operating system image, and if so, where it obtains this system image. This section contains the following topics:

- How the Router Uses the Boot Field
- Hardware Versus Software Configuration Register Boot Fields
- Modifying the Software Configuration Register Boot Field
- Modifying the Software Configuration Register Boot Field Example

Refer to the documentation for your platform for more information on the configuration register.

How the Router Uses the Boot Field

The lowest four bits of the 16-bit configuration register (bits 3, 2, 1, and 0) form the boot field. The following boot field values determine whether the router loads an operating system and where it obtains the system image:

- When the entire boot field equals 0-0-0-0 (0x0), the router does not load a system image. Instead, it enters ROM monitor or "maintenance" mode, from which you can enter ROM monitor commands to load a system image manually. See the "Manually Loading a System Image from ROM Monitor" section for details on ROM monitor mode.

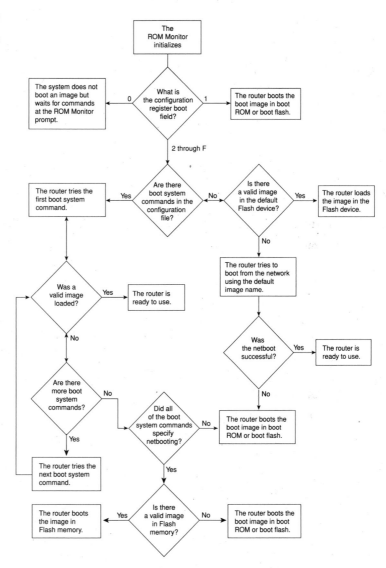

Figure 15–1
Booting Process

- When the entire boot field equals 0-0-0-1 (0x1), the router loads the boot helper or rxboot image.
- When the entire boot field equals a value between 0-0-1-0 (0x2) and 1-1-1-1 (0xF), the router loads the system image specified by **boot system** commands in the startup configuration file. When the startup configuration file does not contain **boot system** commands, the router tries to load a default system image stored on a network server.

When loading a default system image from a network server, the router uses the configuration register settings to determine the default system image filename for booting from a network server. The router forms the default boot filename by starting with the word *cisco* and then appending the octal equivalent of the boot field number in the configuration register, followed by a hyphen (-) and the processor type name (cisco*nn-cpu*). See the appropriate hardware installation guide for details on the configuration register and the default filename.

Hardware Versus Software Configuration Register Boot Fields

You modify the boot field from either the hardware configuration register or the software configuration register, depending on the platform.

Most platforms have a software configuration register. Refer to your hardware documentation for information on the configuration register for your platform.

The hardware configuration register can be changed only on the processor card with dual in-line package (DIP) switches located at the back of the router. For information on modifying the hardware configuration register, refer to the appropriate hardware installation guide.

Modifying the Software Configuration Register Boot Field

To modify the software configuration register boot field, complete the following tasks:

Task	Command
Step 1 Obtain the current configuration register setting. The configuration register is listed as a hexadecimal value.	**show version**
Step 2 Enter configuration mode, selecting the terminal option.	**configure terminal**
Step 3 Modify the existing configuration register setting to reflect the way in which you want to load a system image. The configuration register value is in hexadecimal form with a leading "0x."	**config-register** *value*
Step 4 Exit configuration mode.	**end**
Step 5 Verify that the configuration register setting is correct. Repeat steps 2 through 5 again if the setting is not correct.	**show version**
Step 6 Reboot the router to make your changes take effect.	**reload**

In ROM monitor mode, use the **o** command or the **confreg** command on some platforms to list the value of the configuration register boot field.

Modify the current configuration register setting to reflect the way in which you want to load a system image. To do so, change the least significant hexadecimal digit to one of the following:

- 0 to load the system image manually using the **boot** command in ROM monitor mode.

- 1 to load the system image from boot ROMs. On the Cisco 7200 series and Cisco 7500 series, this setting configures the system to load the system image automatically from boot Flash.

- 2–F to load the system image from **boot system** commands in the startup configuration file or from a default system image stored on a network server.

For example, if the current configuration register setting is 0x101 and you want to load a system image from **boot system** commands in the startup configuration file, you would change the configuration register setting to 0x102.

Modifying the Software Configuration Register Boot Field Example

In the following example, the **show version** command indicates that the current configuration register is set so that the router does not automatically load an operating system image. Instead, it enters ROM monitor mode and waits for user-entered ROM monitor commands. The new setting instructs the router to a load a system image from commands in the startup configuration file or from a default system image stored on a network server.

```
Router1# show version

Cisco Internetwork Operating System Software
IOS (tm) 4500 Software (C4500-J-M), Version 11.1(10.4), MAINTENANCE INTERIM SOFTWARE
Copyright (c) 1986-1997 by cisco Systems, Inc.
Compiled Mon 07-Apr-97 19:51 by dschwart
Image text-base: 0x600088A0, data-base: 0x60718000

ROM: System Bootstrap, Version 5.1(1) [daveu 1], RELEASE SOFTWARE (fc1)
FLASH: 4500-XBOOT Bootstrap Software, Version 10.1(1), RELEASE SOFTWARE (fc1)

Router1 uptime is 6 weeks, 5 days, 2 hours, 22 minutes
System restarted by error - a SegV exception, PC 0x6070F7AC
System image file is "c4500-j-mz.111-current", booted via flash

cisco 4500 (R4K) processor (revision 0x00) with 32768K/4096K bytes of memory.
Processor board ID 01242622
R4600 processor, Implementation 32, Revision 1.0
G.703/E1 software, Version 1.0.
Bridging software.
SuperLAT software copyright 1990 by Meridian Technology Corp).
X.25 software, Version 2.0, NET2, BFE and GOSIP compliant.
TN3270 Emulation software (copyright 1994 by TGV Inc).
Basic Rate ISDN software, Version 1.0.
2 Ethernet/IEEE 802.3 interfaces.
2 Token Ring/IEEE 802.5 interfaces.
4 ISDN Basic Rate interfaces.
128K bytes of non-volatile configuration memory.
8192K bytes of processor board System flash (Read/Write)
4096K bytes of processor board Boot flash (Read/Write)
```

```
Configuration register is 0x2100

Router1# configure terminal
Router1(config)# config-register 0x210F
Router1(config)# end
Router1# reload
```

SETTING ENVIRONMENT VARIABLES

Because many platforms can boot images from several locations, these systems use special ROM monitor environment variables to specify the location and filename of images that the router is to use. In addition, Cisco 7000 family can load configuration files from several locations and use an environment variable to specify startup configurations.

These special environment variables are as follows:

- BOOT
- BOOTLDR
- CONFIG_FILE

BOOT Environment Variable

The BOOT environment variable specifies a list of bootable system images on various devices. See "Specifying the Startup System Image in the Configuration File" section in Chapter 11, "Loading and Maintaining System Images and Microcode." After you save the BOOT environment variable to your startup configuration, the router checks the variable upon startup to determine the device and filename of the image to boot.

The router tries to boot the first image in the BOOT environment variable list. If the router is unsuccessful at booting that image, it tries to boot the next image specified in the list. The router tries each image in the list until it successfully boots. If the router cannot boot any image in the BOOT environment variable list, the router attempts to boot the boot image.

If an entry in the BOOT environment variable list does not specify a device, the router assumes the device is **tftp**. If an entry in the BOOT environment variable list specifies an invalid device, the router skips that entry.

BOOTLDR Environment Variable

The BOOTLDR environment specifies the Flash device and filename containing the boot image that the ROM monitor uses if it cannot find a valid system image. In addition, a boot image is required to boot the router with an image from a network server.

You can change the BOOTLDR environment variable on platforms that use a software boot image rather than boot ROMs. On these platforms, the boot image can be changed without having to replace the boot ROM.

This environment variable allows you to have several boot images. After you save the BOOTLDR environment variable to your startup configuration, the router checks the variable upon startup to determine which boot image to use if the system cannot be loaded.

NOTES

Refer to your platform documentation for information on the default location of the boot image.

CONFIG_FILE Environment Variable

The CONFIG_FILE environment variable specifies the device and filename of the configuration file to use for initialization (startup). For the Cisco 7000 family, valid devices are **nvram:, bootflash:, slot0:**, and **slot1:**. See "Location of Configuration Files" section in Chapter 9, "Modifying, Downloading, and Maintaining Configuration Files," for more information on devices. After you save the CONFIG_FILE environment variable to your startup configuration, the router checks the variable upon startup to determine the location and filename of the configuration file to use for initialization.

The router uses the NVRAM configuration during initialization when the CONFIG_FILE environment variable does not exist or when it is null (such as at first-time startup). If the router detects a problem with NVRAM or a checksum error, the router enters **setup** mode. See "Using Setup for Configuration Changes" in Chapter 3, "Using Configuration Tools," for more information on the **setup** command facility.

Controlling Environment Variables

Although the ROM monitor controls environment variables, you can create, modify, or view them with certain commands. To create or modify the BOOT, BOOTLDR, and CONFIG_FILE environment variables, use the **boot system, boot bootldr,** and **boot config** global configuration commands, respectively.

See the "Specifying the Startup System Image in the Configuration File" section in Chapter 11, "Loading and Maintaining System Images and Microcode," for details on setting the BOOT environment variable. See "Specifying the Startup Configuration File" section in Chapter 9, "Modifying, Downloading, and Maintaining Configuration Files," for details on setting the CONFIG_FILE variable.

NOTES

When you use these three global configuration commands, you affect only the running configuration. You must save the environment variable settings to your startup configuration to place the information under ROM monitor control and for the environment variables to function as expected. Use the **copy running-config startup-config** command to save the environment variables from your running configuration to your startup configuration.

You can view the contents of the BOOT, BOOTLDR, and the CONFIG_FILE environment variables by issuing the **show boot** command. This command displays the settings for these variables as they exist in the startup configuration as well as in the running configuration, if a running configuration setting differs from a startup configuration setting.

Use the **show startup-config** command to display the contents of the configuration file pointed to by the CONFIG_FILE environment variable.

Setting the BOOTLDR Environment Variable

To set the BOOTLDR environment variable, perform the following tasks, beginning in privileged EXEC mode:

Task		Command
Step 1	Verify that internal Flash or boot Flash contains the boot helper image.	**dir** [/all	/deleted] [/long] [*device*:][*filename*]
Step 2	Enter the configuration mode from the terminal.	**configure terminal**
Step 3	Set the BOOTLDR environment variable to specify the Flash device and filename of the boot helper image. This step modifies the runtime BOOTLDR environment variable.	**boot bootldr** *device:filename*
Step 4	Exit configuration mode.	**end**
Step 5	Save this runtime BOOTLDR environment variable to your startup configuration.	**copy running-config startup-config**
Step 6	Optionally, verify the contents of the BOOTLDR environment variable.	**show boot**

The following example sets the BOOTLDR environment to change the location of the boot helper image from internal Flash to slot 0.

```
Router# dir bootflash:
-#- -length- -----date/time------ name
1   620       May 04 1995 26:22:04 rsp-boot-m
2   620       May 24 1995 21:38:14 config2

7993896 bytes available (1496 bytes used)
Router# configure terminal
Router (config)# boot bootldr slot0:rsp-boot-m
^Z
Router# copy running-config startup-config
[ok]
Router# show boot
```

```
BOOT variable = slot0:rsp-boot-m
CONFIG_FILE variable = nvram:
Current CONFIG_FILE variable = slot0:router-config

Configuration register is 0x0

Router#
```

SCHEDULING A RELOAD OF THE SYSTEM IMAGE

You might want to schedule a reload of the system image to occur on the router at a later time (for example, late at night or during the weekend when the router is used less), or you might want to synchronize a reload network-wide (for example, to perform a software upgrade on all routers in the network).

NOTES

A scheduled reload must take place within approximately 24 days.

Configuring a Scheduled Reload

To configure the router to reload the Cisco IOS software at a later time, perform one of the following tasks in privileged EXEC command mode:

Task	Command
Schedule a reload of the software to take effect in the specified minutes or hours and minutes.	**reload in** [*hh*:]*mm* [*text*]
Schedule a reload of the software to take place at the specified time (using a 24-hour clock).	**reload at** *hh*:*mm* [*month day* | *day month*] [*text*]

If you specify the month and day, the reload is scheduled to take place at the specified time and date. If you do not specify the month and day, the reload takes place at the specified time on the current day (if the specified time is later than the current time), or on the next day (if the specified time is earlier than the current time). Specifying 00:00 schedules the reload for midnight.

NOTES

The **at** keyword can be used only if the system clock has been set on the router (either through NTP, the hardware calendar, or manually). The time is relative to the configured time zone on the router. To schedule reloads across several routers to occur simultaneously, the time on each router must be synchronized with NTP.

The following example illustrates how to use the **reload** command to reload the software on the router on the current day at 7:30 p.m.:

```
Router# reload at 19:30
Reload scheduled for 19:30:00 UTC Wed Jun 5 1996 (in 2 hours and 25 minutes)
Proceed with reload? [confirm]
```

The following example illustrates how to use the **reload** command to reload the software on the router at a future time:

```
Router# reload at 02:00 jun 20
Reload scheduled for 02:00:00 UTC Thu Jun 20 1996 (in 344 hours and 53 minutes)
Proceed with reload? [confirm]
```

Displaying Information about a Scheduled Reload

To display information about a previously scheduled reload or to determine whether a reload has been scheduled on the router, perform the following task in EXEC command mode:

Task	Command
Display reload information, including the time the reload is scheduled to occur, and the reason for the reload if it was specified when the reload was scheduled.	show reload

Canceling a Scheduled Reload

To cancel a previously scheduled reload, perform the following task in privileged EXEC command mode:

Task	Command
Cancel a previously scheduled reload of the software.	reload cancel

The following example illustrates how to use the **reload cancel** command to stop a scheduled reload:

```
Router# reload cancel
Router#
***
*** --- SHUTDOWN ABORTED ---
***
```

CONFIGURING HIGH SYSTEM AVAILABILITY OPERATION (CISCO 7500 SERIES)

High System Availability (HSA) refers to how quickly your router returns to an operational status after a failure occurs. On the Cisco 7507 and Cisco 7513, you can install two RSP cards in a single router to improve system availability.

Two RSP cards in a router provide the most basic level of increased system availability through a "cold restart" feature. A "cold restart" means that when one RSP card fails, the other RSP card reboots the router. In this way, your router is never in a failed state for very long, thereby increasing system availability.

When one RSP card takes over operation from another, system operation is interrupted. This change is similar to issuing the **reload** command. The following events occur when one RSP card fails and the other takes over:

- The router stops passing traffic.

- Route information is lost.

- All connections are lost.

- The backup or "slave" RSP card becomes the active or "master" RSP card that reboots and runs the router. Thus, the slave has its own image and configuration file so that it can act as a single processor.

NOTES

HSA does not affect performance in terms of packets per second or overall bandwidth. Also, HSA does not provide fault-tolerance or redundancy.

Understanding Master and Slave Operation

A router configured for HSA operation has one RSP card that is the master and one that is the slave. The master RSP card functions as if it were a single processor, controlling all functions of the router. The slave RSP card does nothing but actively monitor the master for failure.

A system crash can cause the master RSP to fail or go into a nonfunctional state. When the slave RSP detects a nonfunctional master, the slave resets itself and takes part in *master-slave arbitration*. Master-slave arbitration is a ROM monitor process that determines which RSP card is the master and which is the slave upon startup (or reboot).

If a system crash causes the master RSP to fail, the slave RSP becomes the new master RSP and uses its own system image and configuration file to reboot the router. The failed RSP card now becomes the slave. The failure state of the slave (formerly the master) can be accessed from the console via the **show stacks** command.

With HSA operation, the following items are important to note:

- An RSP card that acts as the slave runs a different software version than it does when it acts as the master. The slave mode software is a subset of the master mode software.

- The two RSP cards do not have to run the same master software image and configuration file. When the slave reboots the system and becomes the new master, it uses its own system image and configuration file to reboot the router.

- When enabled, automatic synchronization mode automatically ensures that the master and slave RSP cards have the same configuration file.

- Both hardware and software failures can cause the master RSP to enter a nonfunctional state, but the system does not indicate the type of failure.

- The console is always connected to the master. A Y cable is shipped with your Cisco 7507 or Cisco 7513. The "top" of the Y cable plugs into the console port on each RSP card, while the "bottom" of the Y cable plugs into a terminal or terminal server. The master RSP card has ownership of the Y cable in that the slave Universal Asynchronous Receiver Transmitter (UART) drivers are disabled. Thus, no matter which RSP card has mastership of the system, your view of the internetwork environment is always from the master's perspective. Refer to your product's hardware installation and maintenance publication for information on properly installing the Y cable.

Understanding Implementation Methods

There are two common ways to use HSA. You can use HSA for:

- Simple hardware backup

  Use this method to protect against an RSP card failure. With this method, you configure both RSP cards with the same software image and configuration information. Also, you configure the router to synchronize configuration information automatically on both cards when changes occur.

- Software error protection

  Use this method to protect against critical Cisco IOS software errors in a particular release. With this method, you configure the RSP cards with different software images, but with the same configuration information. If you are using new or experimental Cisco IOS software, consider using the software error protection method.

You also can use HSA for advanced implementations. For example, you can configure the RSP cards with the following:

- Similar software versions, but different configuration files
- Different software images *and* different configuration files
- Widely varied configuration files (for example, various features or interfaces can be turned off and on per card).

NOTES

While other uses are possible, the configuration information in this guide describes tasks for only the two common methods—simple hardware backup and software error protection.

Understanding System Requirements

To configure HSA operation, you must have a Cisco 7507 or Cisco 7513 containing two RSP processor cards and Cisco IOS Release 11.1 or later.

Configuring HSA Operation Task List

When configuring HSA operation, complete the tasks in the following sections. The first two and last two tasks are required for both implementations. The third task relates to simple hardware backup. The fourth task relates to software error protection only.

- Specifying the Default Slave RSP (both implementations)
- Ensuring that Both RSP Cards Contain the Same Configuration File (both implementations)
- Ensuring that Both RSP Cards Contain the Same System Image (simple hardware backup only)
- Ensuring that Both RSP Cards Contain the Same Microcode Image (simple hardware backup only)
- Specifying Different Startup Images for the Master and Slave RSP (software error protection only)
- Setting Environment Variables on the Master and Slave RSP (both implementations)
- Monitoring and Maintaining HSA Operation (both implementations)

Specifying the Default Slave RSP

Because your view of the environment is always from the master RSP perspective, you define a default slave RSP. The router uses the default slave information when booting as follows:

- If a system boot is due to powering up the router or using the **reload** command, then the specified default slave will be the slave RSP.
- If a system boot is due to a system crash or hardware failure, then the system ignores the default slave designation and makes the crashed or faulty RSP the slave RSP.

To define the default slave RSP, perform the following task, beginning in privileged EXEC mode:

Task	Command
Step 1 Enter the configuration mode from the terminal.	**configure terminal**
Step 2 Define the default slave RSP.	**slave default-slot** *processor-slot-number*
Step 3 Exit configuration mode.	**^Z**
Step 4 Save this information to your startup configuration.	**copy running-config startup-config**

Upon the next system reboot, the above changes take effect (if both RSP cards are operational). Thus, the specified default slave becomes the slave RSP card. The other RSP card takes over mastership of the system and controls all functions of the router.

If you do not specifically define the default slave RSP, the RSP card located in the higher number processor slot is the default slave. On the Cisco 7507, processor slot 3 contains the default slave RSP. On the Cisco 7513, processor slot 7 contains the default slave RSP.

The following example sets the default slave RSP to processor slot 2 on a Cisco 7507:

```
Router# configure terminal
Router (config)# slave default-slot 2
^Z
Router# copy running-config startup-config
```

Ensuring that Both RSP Cards Contain the Same Configuration File

With both the simple hardware backup and software error protection implementation methods, you always want your master and slave configuration files to match. To ensure that they match, turn on automatic synchronization. In automatic synchronization mode, the master copies its startup configuration to the slave's startup configuration when you issue a **copy** command that specifies the master's startup configuration (**startup-config**) as the target.

Automatic synchronization mode is on by default; however, to turn it on manually, perform the following tasks, beginning in privileged EXEC mode:

Task		Command
Step 1	Enter the configuration mode from the terminal.	configure terminal
Step 2	Turn on automatic synchronization mode.	slave auto-sync config
Step 3	Exit configuration mode.	^Z
Step 4	Save this information to your startup configuration and copy the configuration to the slave's startup configuration.	copy running-config startup-config

The following example turns on automatic configuration file synchronization:

```
Router# configure terminal
Router (config)# slave auto-sync config
^Z
Router# copy running-config startup-config
```

Ensuring that Both RSP Cards Contain the Same System Image

For simple hardware backup, ensure that both RSP cards have the same system image.

To ensure that both RSP cards have the same system image, perform the following tasks in EXEC mode:

Task	Command
Step 1 Display the contents of the BOOT environment variable to learn the current booting parameters for the master and slave RSP.	**show boot**
Step 2 Verify the location and version of the master RSP software image.	**dir** [/**all**	/**deleted**] [/**long**] {**bootflash**	**slot0**	**slot1**} [*filename*]
Step 3 Determine whether the slave RSP contains the same software image in the same location.	**dir** [/**all**	/**deleted**] [/**long**] {**slavebootflash**	**slaveslot0**	**slaveslot1**} [*filename*]
Step 4 If the slave RSP does not contain the same system image in the same location, copy the master's system image to the appropriate slave location.	**copy** *file-id* {**slavebootflash**	**slaveslot0**	**slaveslot1**} Note that you might also have to use the **delete** and/or **squeeze** command in conjunction with the **copy** command to accomplish this step.

The following example ensures that both RSP cards have the same system image. Note that because no environment variables are set, the default environment variables are in effect for both the master and slave RSP. Therefore, the router will boot the image in slot 0.

```
Router# show boot

BOOT variable =
CONFIG_FILE variable =
Current CONFIG_FILE variable =
BOOTLDR variable does not exist

Configuration register is 0x0

current slave is in slot 7
BOOT variable =
CONFIG_FILE variable =
BOOTLDR variable does not exist

Configuration register is 0x0
```

```
Router# dir slot0:
-#- -length- -----date/time------ name
1    3482498  May 4 1993 21:38:04 rsp-k-mz11.2

7993896 bytes available (1496 bytes used)

Router# dir slaveslot0:
-#- -length- -----date/time------ name
1    3482498  May 4 1993 21:38:04 rsp-k-mz11.1

7993896 bytes available (1496 bytes used)

Router# delete slaveslot0:rsp-k-mz11.1
Router# copy slot0:rsp-k-mz11.2 slaveslot0:rsp-k-mz11.2
```

Ensuring that Both RSP Cards Contain the Same Microcode Image

To ensure that interface processors will load the same microcode, regardless of which RSP is used, perform the following tasks beginning in privileged EXEC mode:

Task	Command
Step 1 Determine the microcode images used on the interface processors. If all interface processors are running from the bundled system microcode, no further action is required.	**show controller cbus**
Step 2 If any interface processors are running from the Flash file system, verify the location and version of the master RSP's supplementary microcode.	**dir [/all | /deleted] [/long] {bootflash | slot0 | slot1}** [*filename*]
Step 3 Determine whether the slave RSP contains the same microcode image in the same location.	**dir [/all | /deleted] [/long] {slavebootflash | slaveslot0 | slaveslot1}** [*filename*]
Step 4 If the slave RSP does not contain the same microcode image in the same location, copy the master's microcode image to the appropriate slave location.	**copy** *file-id* **{slavebootflash | slaveslot0 | slaveslot1}** Note that you might also have to use the **delete** and/or **squeeze** command in conjunction with the **copy** command to accomplish this step.

The following example ensures that both RSP cards have the same microcode image. Notice that slots 0, 1, 4, 9, and 10 load microcode from the bundled software, as noted by the statement *software loaded from system*. Slot 11, the (Fast Serial Interface Processor) FSIP processor, does not use the microcode bundled with the system. Instead, it loads the microcode from *slot0:pond/bath/rsp_fsip20-1*. Thus, you must ensure that the slave RSP has a copy of the same FSIP microcode in the same location.

```
Router# show controller cbus

MEMD at 40000000, 2097152 bytes (unused 416, recarves 3, lost 0)
  RawQ 48000100, ReturnQ 48000108, EventQ 48000110
  BufhdrQ 48000128 (2948 items), LovltrQ 48000140 (5 items, 1632 bytes)
  IpcbufQ 48000148 (16 items, 4096 bytes)
  3571 buffer headers (48002000 - 4800FF20)
  pool0: 28 buffers, 256 bytes, queue 48000130
  pool1: 237 buffers, 1536 bytes, queue 48000138
  pool2: 333 buffers, 4544 bytes, queue 48000150
  pool3: 4 buffers, 4576 bytes, queue 48000158
  slot0: EIP, hw 1.5, sw 20.00, ccb 5800FF30, cmdq 48000080, vps 4096
    software loaded from system
    Ethernet0/0, addr 0000.0ca3.cc00 (bia 0000.0ca3.cc00)
      gfreeq 48000138, lfreeq 48000160 (1536 bytes), throttled 0
      rxlo 4, rxhi 42, rxcurr 0, maxrxcurr 2
      txq 48000168, txacc 48000082 (value 27), txlimit 27
          ........
  slot1: FIP, hw 2.9, sw 20.02, ccb 5800FF40, cmdq 48000088, vps 4096
    software loaded from system
    Fddi1/0, addr 0000.0ca3.cc20 (bia 0000.0ca3.cc20)
      gfreeq 48000150, lfreeq 480001C0 (4544 bytes), throttled 0
      rxlo 4, rxhi 165, rxcurr 0, maxrxcurr 0
      txq 480001C8, txacc 480000B2 (value 0), txlimit 95
  slot4: AIP, hw 1.3, sw 20.02, ccb 5800FF70, cmdq 480000A0, vps 8192
    software loaded from system
    ATM4/0, applique is SONET (155Mbps)
      gfreeq 48000150, lfreeq 480001D0 (4544 bytes), throttled 0
      rxlo 4, rxhi 165, rxcurr 0, maxrxcurr 0
      txq 480001D8, txacc 480000BA (value 0), txlimit 95
  slot9: MIP, hw 1.0, sw 20.02, ccb 5800FFC0, cmdq 480000C8, vps 8192
    software loaded from system
    T1 9/0, applique is Channelized T1
      gfreeq 48000138, lfreeq 480001E0 (1536 bytes), throttled 0
      rxlo 4, rxhi 42, rxcurr 0, maxrxcurr 0
      txq 480001E8, txacc 480000C2 (value 27), txlimit 27
          .......
  slot10: TRIP, hw 1.1, sw 20.00, ccb 5800FFD0, cmdq 480000D0, vps 4096
    software loaded from system
    TokenRing10/0, addr 0000.0ca3.cd40 (bia 0000.0ca3.cd40)
      gfreeq 48000150, lfreeq 48000200 (4544 bytes), throttled 0
      rxlo 4, rxhi 165, rxcurr 1, maxrxcurr 1
      txq 48000208, txacc 480000D2 (value 95), txlimit 95
          .........
```

```
slot11: FSIP, hw 1.1, sw 20.01, ccb 5800FFE0, cmdq 480000D8, vps 8192
    software loaded from flash slot0:pond/bath/rsp_fsip20-1
    Serial11/0, applique is Universal (cable unattached)
        gfreeq 48000138, lfreeq 48000240 (1536 bytes), throttled 0
        rxlo 4, rxhi 42, rxcurr 0, maxrxcurr 0
        txq 48000248, txacc 480000F2 (value 5), txlimit 27
            . . . . . . . . . . .

Router# dir slot0:pond/bath/rsp_fsip20-1
-#- -length- -----date/time------ name
3   10242    Jan 01 1995 03:46:31 pond/bath/rsp_fsip20-1

Router# dir slaveslot0:pond/bath/rsp_fsip20-1
No such file

4079832 bytes available (3915560 bytes used)

Router# copy slot0:pond/bath/rsp_fsip20-1 slaveslot0:
4079704 bytes available on device slaveslot0, proceed? [confirm]

Router# dir slaveslot0:pond/bath/rsp_fsip20-1
-#- -length- -----date/time------ name
3   10242    Mar 01 1993 02:35:04 pond/bath/rsp_fsip20-1

4069460 bytes available (3925932 bytes used)
```

Specifying Different Startup Images for the Master and Slave RSP

For software error protection, the RSP cards should have different system images.

When the factory sends you a new Cisco 7507 or Cisco 7513 with two RSPs, you receive the same system image on both RSP cards. For the software error protection method, you need two different software images on the RSP cards. Thus, you copy a desired image to the master RSP card and modify the **boot system** commands to reflect booting two different system images. Each RSP card uses its own image to boot the router when it becomes the master.

To specify different startup images for the master and slave RSP, perform the following tasks beginning in EXEC mode:

Task		Command
Step 1	Verify the location and version of the master RSP software image.	**dir** [/**all**	/**deleted**] [/**long**] {**bootflash**	**slot0**	**slot1**} [*filename*]
Step 2	Determine whether the slave RSP contains the same software image in the same location.	**dir** [/**all**	/**deleted**] [/**long**] {**slavebootflash**	**slaveslot0**	**slaveslot1**} [*filename*]

Task	Command
Step 3 Copy a different system image to the master RSP.	copy *file-id* {**bootflash** | **slot0** | **slot1**} copy **flash** {**bootflash** | **slot0** | **slot1**} copy **rcp** {**bootflash** | **slot0** | **slot1**} copy **tftp** {**bootflash** | **slot0** | **slot1**}
Step 4 Enter configuration mode from the terminal.	**configure terminal**
Step 5 From global configuration mode, configure the master RSP to boot the new image from the appropriate location.	**boot system flash bootflash:**[*filename*] **boot system flash slot0:**[*filename*] **boot system flash slot1:**[*filename*]
Step 6 Also, add a **boot system** command that specifies the slave's boot image and location. This is the boot image that the slave uses when it becomes the master RSP and boots the system. Note that because the slave will boot this image when the slave is actually the new master RSP, the command syntax does not use a "**slave**" prefix.	**boot system flash bootflash:**[*filename*] **boot system flash slot0:**[*filename*] **boot system flash slot1:**[*filename*]
Step 7 (Optional) Configure the master RSP to boot from a network server.	**boot system** [**rcp** | **tftp**] *filename* [*ip-address*]
Step 8 Set the configuration register to enable the system to load the system image from a network server or from Flash.	**config-register** *value*[1]
Step 9 Exit configuration mode.	**end**
Step 10 Save the configuration file to the master's startup configuration. Because automatic synchronization is turned on, this step saves the **boot system** commands to the master and slave startup configuration.	**copy running-config startup-config**
Step 11 Reset the router with the new configuration information.	**reload**

[1] See the section "Modifying the Configuration Register Boot Field" for more information on systems that can use this command to modify the software configuration register.

HSA: Upgrading to a New Software Version Example

In this example, assume the following:

- The master RSP is in processor slot 6 and the slave RSP is in processor slot 7 of a Cisco 7513.
- The system has the same image *rsp-k-mz11.1* in PCMCIA slot 0 of both the master and slave RSP cards.
- You want to upgrade to Cisco IOS Release 11.2, but you want to guard against software failures. So, you configure HSA operation for software error protection.

Figure 15–2 illustrates the software error protection configuration for this example. The configuration commands for this configuration follow the figure.

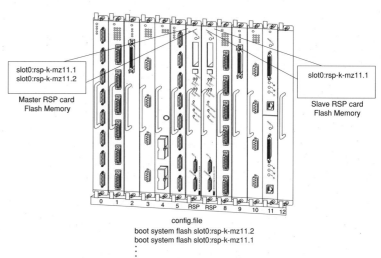

Figure 15–2

Software Error Protection: Upgrading to a New Software Version

slot0:rsp-k-mz11.1
slot0:rsp-k-mz11.2

Master RSP card
Flash Memory

slot0:rsp-k-mz11.1

Slave RSP card
Flash Memory

config.file
boot system flash slot0:rsp-k-mz11.2
boot system flash slot0:rsp-k-mz11.1

Because you always view the environment from the master RSP perspective, in the following command you view the master's slot 0 to verify the location and version of the master's software image:

```
Router# dir slot0:
-#- -length- -----date/time------ name
1    3482496   May 4 1993 21:38:04 rsp-k-mz11.1

7993896 bytes available (1496 bytes used)
```

Now view the slave's software image location and version:

```
Router# dir slaveslot0:
-#- -length- -----date/time------ name
1    3482496   May 4 1993 21:38:04 rsp-k-mz11.1

7993896 bytes available (1496 bytes used)
```

Because you want to run the Release 11.2 system image on one RSP card and the Release 11.1 system image on the other RSP card, copy the Release 11.2 system image to the master's slot 0:

```
Router# copy tftp slot0:rsp-k-mz11.2
```

Enter global configuration mode and configure the system to boot first from a Release 11.2 system image and then from a Release 11.1 system image.

```
Router# configure terminal
Router (config)# boot system flash slot0:rsp-k-mz11.2
Router (config)# boot system flash slot0:rsp-k-mz11.1
```

With this configuration, when the slot 6 RSP card is master, it looks first in its PCMCIA slot 0 for the system image file *rsp-k-mz11.2* to boot. Finding this file, the router boots from that system image. When the slot 7 RSP card is master, it also looks first in its slot 0 for the system image file *rsp-k-mz11.2* to boot. Because that image does not exist in that location, the slot 7 RSP card looks for the system image file *rsp-k-mz11.1* in slot 0 to boot. Finding this file in its PCMCIA slot 0, the router boots from that system image. In this way, each RSP card can reboot the system using its own system image when it becomes the master RSP card.

Configure the system further with a fault-tolerant booting strategy:

```
Router (config)# boot system tftp rsp-k-mz11.1 192.168.1.25
```

Set the configuration register to enable loading of the system image from a network server or from Flash and save the changes to the master and slave startup configuration file:

```
Router (config)# config-register 0x010F
Router (config)# end
Router# copy running-config startup-config
```

Reload the system so that the master RSP uses the new Release 11.2 system image:

```
Router# reload
```

HSA: Backing Up with an Older Software Version Example

In this example scenario, assume the following:

- The master RSP is in processor slot 6 and the slave RSP is in processor slot 7 of a Cisco 7513.
- The system has the same image *rsp-k-mz11.2* in PCMCIA slot 0 of both the master and slave RSP cards.
- You want to use Cisco IOS Release 11.1 as backup to guard against software failures. So, you configure HSA operation for software error protection.

In this scenario, you begin with the configuration shown in Figure 15–3.

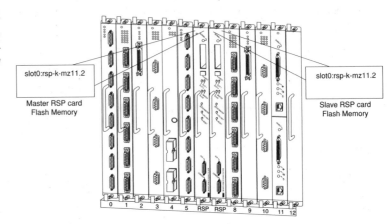

Figure 15–3

Software Error Protection: Backing Up with an Older Software Version, Part I

First, copy the *rsp-k-mz11.1* image to the master and slave RSP cards, as shown in Figure 15–4.

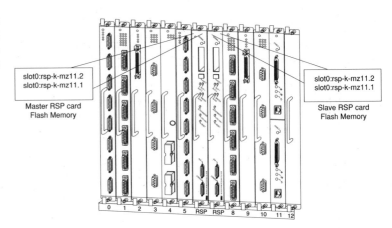

Figure 15–4

Software Error Protection: Backing Up with an Older Software Version, Part II

Next, you delete the *rsp-k-mz11.2* image from the slave RSP card. The final configuration is shown in Figure 15–5.

The following commands configure software error protection for this example scenario.

View the master and slave slot 0 to verify the location and version of their software images:

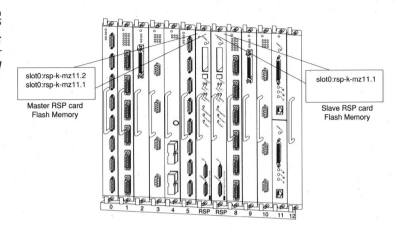

Figure 15–5
Software Error Protection: Backing Up with an Older Software Version, Part III

slot0:rsp-k-mz11.2
slot0:rsp-k-mz11.1

Master RSP card
Flash Memory

slot0:rsp-k-mz11.1

Slave RSP card
Flash Memory

```
Router# dir slot0:
-#- -length- -----date/time------ name
1    3482498   May 4 1993 21:38:04 rsp-k-mz11.2

7993896 bytes available (1496 bytes used)

Router# dir slaveslot0:
-#- -length- -----date/time------ name
1    3482498   May 4 1993 21:38:04 rsp-k-mz11.2

7993896 bytes available (1496 bytes used)
```

Copy the Release 11.1 system image to the master and slave slot 0:

```
Router# copy tftp slot0:rsp-k-mz11.1
Router# copy tftp slaveslot0:rsp-k-mz11.1
```

Delete the *rsp-k-mz11.2* image from the slave RSP card:

```
Router# delete slaveslot0:rsp-k-mz11.2
```

Configure the system to boot first from a Release 11.2 system image and then from a Release 11.1 system image.

```
Router# configure terminal
Router (config)# boot system flash slot0:rsp-k-mz11.2
Router (config)# boot system flash slot0:rsp-k-mz11.1
```

Configure the system further with a fault-tolerant booting strategy:

```
Router (config)# boot system tftp rsp-k-mz11.1 192.168.1.25
```

Set the configuration register to enable loading of the system image from a network server or from Flash and save the changes to the master and slave startup configuration files:

```
Router (config)# config-register 0x010F
Router (config)# end
Router# copy running-config startup-config
```

NOTES

You do not need to reload the router in this example, because the router is currently running the Release 11.2 image.

Setting Environment Variables on the Master and Slave RSP

You can set environment variables on both RSP cards in a Cisco 7507 and Cisco 7513. For more information on environment variables, see the "Setting Environment Variables" section.

NOTES

When configuring HSA operation, Cisco recommends that you use the default environment variables. If you change the variables, Cisco recommends setting the same device for equivalent environment variables on each RSP card. For example, if you set one RSP card's CONFIG_FILE environment variable device to NVRAM, set the other RSP card's CONFIG_FILE environment variable device to NVRAM also.

You set environment variables on the master RSP just as you would if it were the only RSP card in the system. Refer to the following sections for more information on these steps:

- Controlling Environment Variables
- Specifying the Startup System Image in the Configuration File (in Chapter 11, "Loading and Maintaining System Images and Microcode").
- Setting the BOOTLDR Environment Variable
- Specifying the CONFIG_FILE Environment Variable (Cisco 7000 family) (in Chapter 9, "Modifying, Downloading, and Maintaining Configuration Files").

You can set the same environment variables on the slave RSP card, manually or automatically. The following sections describe these two methods:

- Automatically Setting Environment Variables on the Slave RSP
- Manually Setting Environment Variables on the Slave RSP

Automatically Setting Environment Variables on the Slave RSP

With automatic synchronization turned on, the system automatically saves the same environment variables to the slave's startup configuration when you set the master's environment variables and save them.

NOTES

Automatic synchronization mode is on by default. To turn off automatic synchronization, use the **no slave auto-sync config** global configuration command.

To set environment variables on the slave RSP when automatic synchronization is on, perform the following steps beginning in global configuration mode:

Task	Command
Step 1 Set the master's environment variables as described in the "Controlling Environment Variables," and "Setting the BOOTLDR Environment Variable."	**boot system** **boot bootldr** **boot config**
Step 2 Save the settings to the startup configuration. This also puts the information under that RSP card's ROM monitor control.	**copy running-config startup-config**
Step 3 Verify the environment variable settings.	**show boot**

Manually Setting Environment Variables on the Slave RSP

If you disable automatic synchronization of configuration files, you must manually synchronize the slave's configuration file to the master's configuration file to store environment variables on the slave RSP.

Once you set the master's environment variables, you can manually set the same environment variables on the slave RSP card using the **slave sync config** command.

To set environment variables on the slave RSP manually, perform the following steps beginning in global configuration mode:

Task	Command
Step 1 Set the master's environment variables as described in the "Controlling Environment Variables," and "Setting the BOOTLDR Environment Variable."	**boot system** **boot bootldr** **boot config**
Step 2 Exit global configuration mode.	**end**
Step 3 Save the settings to the startup configuration. This also puts the information under that RSP card's ROM monitor control.	**copy running-config startup-config**
Step 4 Save the same environment variables to the slave RSP by manually synchronizing their configuration files.	**slave sync config**
Step 5 Verify the environment variable settings.	**show boot**

Monitoring and Maintaining HSA Operation

To monitor and maintain HSA operation, complete the tasks in the following sections:

- Overriding the Slave Image Bundled with the Master Image
- Manually Synchronizing Configuration Files
- Troubleshooting a Failed RSP Card
- Displaying Information about Master and Slave RSP Cards

Overriding the Slave Image Bundled with the Master Image

You can override the slave image that is bundled with the master image. To do so, perform the following task in global configuration mode:

Task	Command
Specify which image the slave runs.	**slave image** {**system** | *device:filename*}

Manually Synchronizing Configuration Files

You can manually synchronize configuration files and ROM monitor environment variables on the master and slave RSP cards. To do so, perform the following task in privileged EXEC mode:

Task	Command
Manually synchronize master and slave configuration files.	slave sync config

---

CAUTION

When you install a second RSP card for the first time, you *must* immediately configure it using the **slave sync config** command. This ensures that the new slave is configured consistently with the master. Failure to do so can result in an unconfigured slave RSP card taking over mastership of the router when the master fails, rendering the network inoperable.

The **slave sync config** command is also a useful tool for more advanced implementation methods not discussed in this chapter.

Troubleshooting a Failed RSP Card

When a new master RSP card takes over mastership of the router, it automatically reboots the failed RSP card as the slave RSP card. You can access the state of the failed RSP card in the form of a stack trace from the master console using the **show stacks** command.

You also can reload a failed, inactive RSP card manually from the master console. This task returns the card to the active slave state. If the master RSP fails, the slave will be able to become the master. To manually reload the inactive RSP card, perform the following task from global configuration mode:

Task	Command
Reload the inactive slave RSP card.	slave reload

Displaying Information about Master and Slave RSP Cards

You also can display information about both the master and slave RSP cards. To do so, perform any of the following tasks from EXEC mode:

Task	Command
Display the environment variable settings and configuration register settings for both the master and slave RSP cards.	show boot

Task	Command
Show a list of Flash devices currently supported on the router.	**show flash devices**
Display the software version running on the master and slave RSP cards.	**show version**
Display the stack trace and version information of the master and slave RSP cards.	**show stacks**

STOPPING BOOTING AND ENTERING ROM MONITOR MODE

During the first 60 seconds of startup, you can force the router to stop booting. The router will enter ROM monitor mode, where you can change the configuration register value or boot the router manually.

To stop booting and enter ROM monitor mode, complete the following tasks:

Task		Command
Step 1	Restart the router.	reload
Step 2	Press the **Break** key during the first 60 seconds while the system is starting up. If you are connected via a Telnet session, issue a **send break** command.	Break[1]

[1] This key will not work on the Cisco 7000 unless it has at least Cisco IOS Release 10 boot ROMs.

MANUALLY LOADING A SYSTEM IMAGE FROM ROM MONITOR

If your router does not find a valid system image, or if its configuration file is corrupted at startup, and the configuration register is set to enter ROM monitor mode, the system enters ROM monitor mode. From this mode, you can load a system image manually from the following locations:

- Internal Flash memory or a Flash memory PC card
- A network server file
- ROM
- A local or remote computer, using the Xmodem or Ymodem protocol (Cisco 1600 series and Cisco 3600 series only)

You may boot from a location only if the router can store an image there. Therefore, not all platforms can load manually from these locations.

You also can enter ROM monitor mode by restarting the router and then pressing the **Break** key or issuing a **send break** command from a Telnet session during the first 60 seconds of startup.

Manually Booting from Flash Memory

To manually boot from Flash memory, complete the following task in ROM monitor mode:

Task	Command
Manually boot the router from Flash. Refer to your hardware documentation for the correct form of this command to use.	**boot flash** [*filename*]
	boot flash *partition-number*:[*filename*]
	boot flash flash:[*partition-number*:] [*filename*]
	boot [*device*:][*partition-number*:][*filename*] (Cisco 1600 series and Cisco 3600 series)
	boot *device*:[*filename*] (Cisco 7000 family)

If the filename is not specified, the first bootable file found in the device and partition is used.

In the following example, a router is manually booted from Flash memory. Because the optional *filename* argument is absent, the first valid file in Flash memory is loaded.

```
> boot flash
F3: 1858656+45204+166896 at 0x1000

Booting gs7-k from flash memory RRRRRRRRRRRRRRRRRRRRRRRRRRRRRRRRRRRRRRRR
RRRRRRRRRRRRRRRRRRRRRRRRRRRRRRRRRRRRRRRRRRRRRRRRRRRRRRRRRRRRRRRRRRRRRRRRRRRRRRRRRR
RRRRRRRRRRRRRRRRRRRRRRRRRRRRRRRRRRRRRRRRRRRRRRRRRRRRRRRRRRRRRRRRRRRRRRRRRRRRRRRRRR
RRRRRRRRRRRRRRRRRRRRRRRRRRRRRRRRRRRRRRRRRRRRRRRRRRRRRRRRRRRRRRRRRRRRRRRRRRRRRRRRRR
RRRRRRRRRRRRRRRRRRRRRRRRRRRRRRRRRRRRRRRRRRRRRRRRRRRRRRRRRRRRRRRRRRRRRRRRRRR [OK -
1903912/13765276 bytes]
F3: 1858676+45204+166896 at 0x1000

                 Restricted Rights Legend

Use, duplication, or disclosure by the Government is
subject to restrictions as set forth in subparagraph
(c) of the Commercial Computer Software - Restricted
```

In the following example, the **boot flash** command is used with the filename *gs7-k*—the name of the file that is loaded:

```
> boot flash gs7-k
F3: 1858656+45204+166896 at 0x1000

Booting gs7-k from flash memory RRRRRRRRRRRRRRRRRRRRRRRRRRRRRRRRRRRRRRRR
RRRRRRRRRRRRRRRRRRRRRRRRRRRRRRRRRRRRRRRRRRRRRRRRRRRRRRRRRRRRRRRRRRRRRRRRRRRRRRRRRR
RRRRRRRRRRRRRRRRRRRRRRRRRRRRRRRRRRRRRRRRRRRRRRRRRRRRRRRRRRRRRRRRRRRRRRRRRRRRRRRRRR
RRRRRRRRRRRRRRRRRRRRRRRRRRRRRRRRRRRRRRRRRRRRRRRRRRRRRRRRRRRRRRRRRRRRRRRRRRRRRRRRRR
RRRRRRRRRRRRRRRRRRRRRRRRRRRRRRRRRRRRRRRRRRRRRRRRRRRRRRRRRRRRRRRRRRRRRRRRRRRRRRRRRR
RRRRRRRRRRRRRR [OK - 1903912/13765276 bytes]
F3: 1858676+45204+166896 at 0x1000
```

```
                        Restricted Rights Legend

      Use, duplication, or disclosure by the Government is
      subject to restrictions as set forth in subparagraph
      (c) of the Commercial Computer Software - Restricted
      System Bootstrap, Version 4.6(1012) [mlw 99], INTERIM SOFTWARE
      Copyright (c) 1986-1992 by cisco Systems
      RP1 processor with 16384 Kbytes of memory
```

The following command instructs the ROM monitor to boot the first file in the first partition of internal Flash memory:

> **boot flash:**

This command instructs the ROM monitor to boot the first file in the second partition of the Flash memory card in slot 0:

> **boot slot0:2:**

In this example, the ROM monitor boots the file named *imagename* from the third partition of the Flash memory card in slot 0:

> **boot slot0:3:imagename**

The following command fails to specify a valid device type (**flash:**, **slot0:**, or **slot1:**), so the ROM monitor invokes the boot helper to boot a system image.

> **boot flash**

Manually Booting from a Network File

To boot from a network file manually, complete the following task in EXEC mode:

Task	Command
Manually boot the router from a network file.	**boot** *filename* [*ip-address*]

In the following example, a router is manually booted from the network file *network1*:

> **boot network1**

Manually Booting from ROM

To boot the router manually from ROM, complete the following step in EXEC mode:

Task	Command
Manually boot the router from ROM.	**boot**

On the Cisco 7200 series and Cisco 7500 series, the **boot** command loads the first bootable image located in boot Flash.

In the following example, a router is manually booted from ROM:

```
>boot
```

Manually Booting Using MOP

You can boot system software interactively using MOP. Typically, you do this to verify that system software has been properly installed on the MOP boot server before configuring the router to boot the system software image automatically.

To boot the router manually using MOP, perform the following task in EXEC mode:

Task	Command
Manually boot the router using MOP.	**boot mop** *filename* [*mac-address*] [*interface*]

The Cisco 7200 series and Cisco 7500 series do not support the **boot mop** command.

In the following example, a router is manually booted from a MOP server:

```
>boot mop network1
```

Using the System Image Instead of Reloading

To return to EXEC mode from the ROM monitor to use the system image instead of reloading, perform the following task in ROM monitor mode:

Task	Command
Return to EXEC mode to use the system image.	**continue**

## CHAPTER 16

Booting Commands

This chapter provides detailed descriptions of the commands used to modify the rebooting procedures of the router.

For configuration information and examples, see Chapter 15, "Rebooting a Router."

BOOT

To boot the router manually from the prompt, use the **boot** ROM monitor command.

This manual reload is only used for troubleshooting purposes, and the options directly depend upon hardware possibilities.

The ROM monitor prompt is either ">" or for newer platforms "rommon *x*>". Enter only lowercase commands.

These commands work only if there is a valid image to boot. Also, from the ROM monitor prompt, issuing a prior reset command is necessary for the boot to be always successful.

    boot
    boot *filename* [*ip-address*]
    boot flash [*filename*]
    boot flash [*partition-number*:] [*filename*]
    boot *device*:[*filename*] (Cisco 7000 family)
    boot [*device*:][*partition-number*:][*filename*] (Cisco 1600 and Cisco 3600 series)

Syntax	Description
filename	When used in conjunction with the *ip-address* argument, the *filename* argument is the name of the system image file to boot from a network server. The filename is case sensitive.
	When used in conjunction with the **flash** keyword, the *filename* argument is the name of the system image file to boot from Flash memory. On all platforms except the Cisco 1600 series, Cisco 3600 series, and Cisco 7000 family, the system obtains the image file from internal Flash memory. On the Cisco 1600 series, Cisco 3600 series and Cisco 7000 family, the *device*: argument specifies the Flash memory device from which to obtain the system image. See the *device*: argument later in this table for valid device values. The filename is case sensitive. Without *filename*, the first valid file in Flash memory is loaded.
ip-address	(Optional) IP address of the TFTP server on which the system image resides. If omitted, this value defaults to the IP broadcast address of 255.255.255.255.
flash	(Optional) Boots the router from Flash memory.
device:	Only newer ROM monitors support the device:filename format. Specifying the device is optional for all platforms except the Cisco 7000 family. Possible devices are: • **flash:**—Internal Flash memory on the Cisco 1600 series and Cisco 3600 series. This is the only valid device for the Cisco 1600 series. • **bootflash:**—Internal Flash memory on the Cisco 7000 family. • **slot0:**—Flash memory card in first PCMCIA slot on the Cisco 7000 family and Cisco 3600 series. • **slot1:**—Flash memory card in second PCMCIA slot on the Cisco 7000 family and Cisco 3600 series.
partition-number:	(Optional) Boots the router from Flash memory with the optional filename of the image you want loaded from the specified Flash partition. If you do not specify a filename, the first valid file in the specified partition of Flash memory is loaded. This option is relevant to platforms such as the 2500, where the Flash may be partitioned.

Default

For most platforms, if you enter the **boot** command and press Return, the router boots from ROM by default. However, for some platforms, such as the Cisco 3600 series, if you enter the **boot** command and press **Enter,** the router boots the first image in Flash memory. Refer to the documentation for your platform for information about the default image.

If you enter the **boot flash** command without a *filename*, the first valid file in Flash memory is loaded.

For other defaults, see the Syntax Description section.

Command Mode

ROM monitor

Usage Guidelines

This command first appeared in Cisco IOS Release 10.3.

Use this command only when your router cannot find the boot configuration information needed in nonvolatile random-access memory (NVRAM). To get to the ROM monitor prompt (>), use one of the following methods:

- Enter the **reload** EXEC command, then press the **Break** key during the first 60 seconds of startup.

- Set configuration register bits 0 to 3 to zero (manual booting) and enter the **reload** command.

Refer to the your hardware documentation for information on correct jumper settings for your platform.

Examples

In the following example, a router is manually booted from ROM (except the Cisco 3600 series):

```
> boot
F3:
(ROM Monitor copyrights)
```

In the following example, a router boots the file *routertest* from a network server with the IP address 172.16.15.112:

```
> boot routertest 172.16.15.112
F3:
(ROM Monitor copyrights)
```

The following example shows the **boot flash** command without the *filename* argument. The first valid file in Flash memory is loaded.

```
> boot flash
F3: 1858656+45204+166896 at 0x1000
Booting gs7-k from flash memory RRRRRRRRRRRRRRRRRRRRRRRRRRRRRRRRRRRRRRRR
RRRRRRRRRRRRRRRRRRRRRRRRRRRRRRRRRRRRRRRRRRRRRRRRRRRRRRRRRRRRRRRRRRRRRRRRRRR
```

```
RRRRRRRRRRRRRRRRRRRRRRRRRRRRRRRRRRRRRRRRRRRRRRRRRRRRRRRRRRRRRRRRRRRRRRRRRR
RRRRRRRRRRRRRRRRRRRRRRRRRRRRRRRRRRRRRRRRRRRRRRRRRRRRRRRRRRRRRRRRRRRRRRRRRR
RRRRRRRRRRRRRRRRRRRRRRRRRRRRRRRRRRRRRRRRRRRRRRRRRRRRRRRRRRRRRRRRRRRRRRRRRR
RRRRRRRRRRRRRRRRRRRRRRRRRRRRRRRRRRRR [OK - 1903912/13765276 bytes]
F3: 1858676+45204+166896 at 0x1000
(ROM Monitor copyrights)
```

In the following example, the **boot flash** command is used with the filename *gs7-k*. That is the file that will be loaded.

```
> boot flash gs7-k
F3: 1858656+45204+166896 at 0x1000

Booting gs7-k from flash memory RRRRRRRRRRRRRRRRRRRRRRRRRRRRRRRRRRRRRRRRRR
RRRRRRRRRRRRRRRRRRRRRRRRRRRRRRRRRRRRRRRRRRRRRRRRRRRRRRRRRRRRRRRRRRRRRRRRRR
RRRRRRRRRRRRRRRRRRRRRRRRRRRRRRRRRRRRRRRRRRRRRRRRRRRRRRRRRRRRRRRRRRRRRRRRRR
RRRRRRRRRRRRRRRRRRRRRRRRRRRRRRRRRRRRRRRRRRRRRRRRRRRRRRRRRRRRRRRRRRRRRRRRRR
RRRRRRRRRRRRRRRRRRRRRRRRRRRRRRRRRRRRRRRRRRRRRRRRRRRRRRRRRRRRRRRRRRRRRRRRRR
RRRRRRRRRRRRRR [OK - 1903912/13765276 bytes]
F3: 1858676+45204+166896 at 0x1000

(ROM Monitor copyrights)
```

In the following example, the **boot flash flash:** command boots the relocatable image file *igs-bpx-l* from partition 2 in Flash memory:

```
> boot flash flash:2:igs-bpx-l
F3: 3562264+98228+303632 at 0x30000B4

(ROM Monitor copyrights)
```

Use the following example if the boot image has been inadvertently erased. (The IOS is directly launched from the ROM monitor without the intermediate boot stage. This startup requires less system memory.)

```
> boot flash:c4500-j-mz.103-7
```

In the following example, the Cisco 7000 family accepts the **flash** keyword for compatibility but ignores it, and boots from slot 0:

```
> boot flash slot0:gs7-k-mz.103-9
F3: 8468+3980384+165008 at 0x1000
```

In the following example, the new rommon requires new syntax.

```
rommon 8 > b flash flash:c4500-j-mz.103-12
boot of "flash flash:c4500-j-mz.103-12" using boot helper "bootflash:c4500-xboot.101-1"
failed
```

In the following example, the command did not function because it must be entered in lowercase.

```
rommon 10 > BOOT
command "BOOT" not found
```

The following example shows the ROM monitor booting the first file in the first partition of internal Flash memory of a Cisco 3600 series:

```
> boot flash:
```

This example boots the first image file in the first partition of the Flash memory card in slot 0 of a Cisco 3600 series:

```
> boot slot0:
```

The following example shows the ROM monitor booting the first file in the first Flash memory partition on a Cisco 1600 series:

```
> boot flash:
```

Related Commands

continue

BOOT BOOTLDR

To specify a Flash device and filename containing the boot image that ROM uses for booting, use the **boot bootldr** global configuration command. Use the **no** form of the command to remove this boot image specification.

boot bootldr *device*: *filename*
no boot bootldr

Syntax

Syntax	Description
device:	Device containing the boot image that ROM uses. The colon (:) is required. Valid values are as follows: • **bootflash**—Internal Flash memory. • **slot0**—First PCMCIA slot. • **slot1**—Second PCMCIA slot.
filename	Name of the boot image file. The maximum filename length is 63 characters.

Default

There is no default Flash device or filename.

Command Mode

Global configuration

Usage Guidelines

This command first appeared in Cisco IOS Release 11.0.

The **boot bootldr** command sets the BOOTLDR environment variable in the current running configuration. You must specify both the device and the filename.

NOTES

When you use this global configuration command, you affect only the running configuration. You must save the environment variable setting to your startup configuration to place the information under ROM monitor control and to have the environment variable function as expected. Use the **copy running-config startup-config** command to save the environment variable from your running configuration to your startup configuration.

The **no** form of the command sets the BOOTLDR environment variable to a null string. On the Cisco 7000 family, a null string causes the first image file in boot Flash to be used as the boot image that ROM uses for booting.

Examples

In the following example, the internal Flash memory contains the boot image:

```
boot bootldr bootflash:boot-image
```

The following example specifies that the Flash memory card inserted in slot 0 contains the boot image:

```
boot bootldr slot0:boot-image
```

Related Commands

copy running-config startup-config
show boot
show flash

BOOT BOOTSTRAP

To configure the filename that is used to boot a secondary bootstrap image, use the **boot bootstrap** global configuration command. Use the **no** form of this command to disable booting from a secondary bootstrap image.

> **boot bootstrap flash** [*filename*]
> **no boot bootstrap flash** [*filename*]
>
> **boot bootstrap mop** *filename* [*mac-address*] [*interface*]
> **no boot bootstrap mop** *filename* [*mac-address*] [*interface*]
>
> **boot bootstrap** [tftp] *filename* [*ip-address*]
> **no boot bootstrap** [tftp] *filename* [*ip-address*]

Syntax	Description
flash	Boots the router from Flash memory.
filename	(Optional with **flash**) Name of the system image to boot from a network server or from Flash memory. If you omit the filename when booting from Flash memory, the router uses the first system image stored in Flash memory.
mop	Boots the router from a system image stored on a DEC MOP server.
mac-address	(Optional) MAC address of the MOP server on which the file resides. If the MAC address argument is not included, a broadcast message is sent to all MOP boot servers. The first MOP server to indicate that it has the file is the server from which the router gets the boot image.
interface	(Optional) Interface out which the router should send MOP requests to reach the MOP server. The interface options are **async, dialer, Ethernet, loopback, null, serial,** and **tunnel.** If the interface argument is not specified, a request is sent on all interfaces that have MOP enabled. The interface from which the first response is received is the interface used to load the software.
tftp	(Optional) Boots the router from a system image stored on a TFTP server.
ip-address	(Optional) IP address of the TFTP server on which the system image resides. If omitted, this value defaults to the IP broadcast address of 255.255.255.255.

Default

No secondary bootstrap

Command Mode

Global configuration

Usage Guidelines

This command first appeared in Cisco IOS Release 10.0.

The **boot bootstrap** command causes the router to load a secondary bootstrap image over the network. The secondary bootstrap image then loads the specified system image file. See the appropriate hardware installation guide for details on the configuration register and secondary bootstrap filename.

Use this command when you have attempted to load a system image but have run out of memory even after compressing the system image. Secondary bootstrap allows you to load a larger system image through a smaller secondary image.

Example

In the following example, the system image file *sysimage-2* will be loaded by using a secondary bootstrap image:

```
boot bootstrap sysimage-2
```

BOOT SYSTEM

To specify the system image that the router loads at startup, use one of the following **boot system** global configuration commands. Use a **no** form of this command to remove the startup system image specification.

boot system flash [*device*:][*partition-number*:][*filename*] (Cisco 1600 series and Cisco 3600 series)
no boot system flash [*device*:][*partition-number*:][*filename*]

boot system flash [*device*:][*filename*] (Cisco 7000 family)
no boot system flash [*device*:][*filename*]

boot system flash (remaining platforms)
no boot system flash

boot system mop *filename* [*mac-address*] [*interface*]
no boot system mop *filename* [*mac-address*] [*interface*]

boot system rom
no boot system rom

boot system [**rcp** | **tftp**] *filename* [*ip-address*]
no boot system [**rcp** | **tftp**] *filename* [*ip-address*]

no boot system

Syntax	Description
flash	On all platforms except the Cisco 1600 series, Cisco 3600 series, and Cisco 7000 family, this keyword boots the router from internal Flash memory. If you omit all arguments that follow this keyword, the system searches internal Flash for the first bootable image.

Syntax	Description
	On the Cisco 1600 series, Cisco 3600 series, and Cisco 7000 family, this keyword boots the router from a Flash device, as specified by the device: argument. On the Cisco 1600 series and Cisco 3600 series, if you omit all optional arguments, the router searches internal Flash memory for the first bootable image. On the Cisco 7000 family, when you omit all arguments that follow this keyword, the system searches the PCMCIA slot 0 for the first bootable image.
device:	(Optional) Device containing the system image to load at startup. The colon (:) is required. Valid devices are as follows:
	• **flash:**—Internal Flash memory on the Cisco 1600 series and Cisco 3600 series. For the Cisco 1600 series and Cisco 3600 series, this device is the default if you do not specify a device. This is the only valid device for the Cisco 1600 series,
	• **bootflash**—Internal Flash memory in the Cisco 7000 family.
	• **slot0**—First PCMCIA slot on the Cisco 3600 series and Cisco 7000 family. For the Cisco 7000 family, this device is the default if you do not specify a device.
	• **slot1**—Flash memory card in the second PCMCIA slot on the Cisco 3600 series and Cisco 7000 family.
partition-number:	(Optional) Number of the Flash memory partition that contains the system image to boot, specified by the optional *filename* argument. If you do not specify a filename, the router loads the first valid file in the specified partition of Flash memory. This argument is only valid on routers that can be partitioned.
filename	(Optional when used with **boot system flash**) Name of the system image to load at startup. It is case sensitive. If you do not specify a filename, the router loads the first valid file in the specified Flash device, the specified partition of Flash memory, or the default Flash device if you also omit the *device*: argument.
mop	Boots the router from a system image stored on a Digital MOP server. Do not use this keyword with the Cisco 3600 series or Cisco 7000 family.

Part II

Command Reference

Syntax	Description
mac-address	(Optional) Media Access Control (MAC) address of the MOP server containing the specified system image file. If you do not include the MAC address argument, the router sends a broadcast message to all MOP boot servers. The first MOP server to indicate that it has the specified file is the server from which the router gets the boot image.
interface	(Optional) Interface the router uses to send out MOP requests to the MOP server. The interface options are **async, dialer, ethernet, serial,** and **tunnel.** If you do not specify the interface argument, the router sends a request out on all interfaces that have MOP enabled. The interface that receives the first response is the interface the router uses to load the software.
rom	Boots the router from ROM. Do not use this keyword with the Cisco 3600 series or Cisco 7000 family.
rcp	(Optional) Boots the router from a system image stored on a network server using rcp. If you omit this keyword, the transport mechanism defaults to **tftp.**
tftp	(Optional) Boots the router from a system image stored on a TFTP server. This is the default when you do not specify any keyword (**flash, mop, rom, tftp,** or **rcp.**)
ip-address	(Optional) IP address of the TFTP server containing the system image file. If omitted, this value defaults to the IP broadcast address of 255.255.255.255.

Default

If you configure the router to boot from a network server but do not specify a system image file with the **boot system** command, the router uses the configuration register settings to determine the default system image filename. The router forms the default boot filename by starting with the word *cisco* and then appending the octal equivalent of the boot field number in the configuration register, followed by a hyphen (-) and the processor type name (cisco*nn-cpu*). See the appropriate hardware installation guide for details on the configuration register and default filename. See also the **config-register** or **confreg** command and the "Syntax" section preceding this section.

If you omit a keyword (**flash, mop, rom, rcp,** or **tftp**) from the **boot system** command, the system defaults to booting from a system image stored on a TFTP server.

Command Mode

Global configuration

Usage Guidelines

This command first appeared in Cisco IOS Release 10.0.

For this command to work, the **config-register** command must be set properly.

Enter several **boot system** commands to provide a fail-safe method for booting your router. The router stores and executes the **boot system** commands in the order in which you enter them in the configuration file. If you enter multiple boot commands of the same type—for example, if you enter two commands that instruct the router to boot from different network servers—then the router tries them in the order in which they appear in the configuration file. If a **boot system** command entry in the list specifies an invalid device, the router skips that entry. Use the **boot system rom** command to specify use of the ROM system image as a backup to other **boot** commands in the configuration.

For some platforms, the boot image must be loaded before the system image is loaded. However, on many platforms, the boot image is only loaded if the router is booting from a network server or the Flash device is not specified. If the device is specified, the router will boot faster, because it does not have to load the boot image first.

This section contains the following usage guideline sections:

- Changing the List of Boot System Commands
- Booting Compressed Images
- Understanding the rcp Protocol
- Stopping Booting and Entering ROM Monitor Mode
- Cisco 1600 series, Cisco 3600 series, and Cisco 7000 Family Notes

Changing the List of Boot System Commands

To remove a single entry from the bootable image list, use the **no** form of the command with an argument. For example, to remove the entry that specifies a bootable image on a Flash memory card inserted in the second slot, use the **no boot system flash slot1:**[*filename*] command. All other entries in the list remain.

To eliminate all entries in the bootable image list, use the **no boot system** command. At this point, you can redefine the list of bootable images using the previous **boot system** commands. Remember to save your changes to your startup configuration by issuing the **copy running-config startup-config** command.

Each time you write a new software image to Flash memory, you must delete the existing filename in the configuration file with the **no boot system flash** *filename* command. Then add a new line in the configuration file with the **boot system flash** *filename* command.

NOTES

If you want to rearrange the order of the entries in the configuration file, you must first issue the **no boot system** command and then redefine the list.

Part II

Command Reference

Booting Compressed Images

You can boot the router from a compressed image on a network server. When a network server boots software, both the image being booted and the running image must fit into memory. Use compressed images to ensure that enough memory is available to boot the router. You can compress a software image on any UNIX platform using the **compress** command. Refer to your UNIX platform's documentation for the exact usage of the **compress** command. (You also can uncompress data with the UNIX **uncompress** command.)

Understanding the rcp Protocol

The rcp protocol requires that a client send the remote username in an rcp request to a server. When the router executes the **boot system rcp** command, the Cisco IOS software sends the host name as both the remote and local usernames by default. For the rcp protocol to execute properly, an account must be defined on the network server for the remote username configured on the router.

If the server has a directory structure, the rcp software searches for the system image to boot from the remote server relative to the directory of the remote username.

By default, the router software sends the host name as the remote username. You can override the default remote username by using the **ip rcmd remote-username** command. For example, if the system image resides in the home directory of a user on the server, you can specify that user's name as the remote username.

Stopping Booting and Entering ROM Monitor Mode

During the first 60 seconds of startup, you can force the router to stop booting by pressing the **Break** key. The router will enter ROM monitor mode, where you can change the configuration register value or boot the router manually.

Cisco 1600 series, Cisco 3600 series, and Cisco 7000 Family Notes

For the Cisco 3600 series and Cisco 7000 family, the **boot system** command modifies the BOOT environment variable in the running configuration. The BOOT environment variable specifies a list of bootable images on various devices.

NOTES

When you use the **boot system** global configuration command on the Cisco 1600 series, Cisco 3600 series, and Cisco 7000 family, you affect only the running configuration. You must save the BOOT environment variable settings to your startup configuration to place the information under ROM monitor control and to have the environment variable function as expected. Use the **copy running-config startup-config** command to save the environment variable from your running configuration to your startup configuration.

To view the contents of the BOOT environment variable, use the **show boot** command.

Examples

The following example illustrates a list specifying two possible internetwork locations for a system image, with the ROM software being used as a backup:

```
boot system cs3-rx.90-1 192.168.7.24
boot system cs3-rx.83-2 192.168.7.19
boot system rom
```

The following example boots the system boot relocatable image file *igs-bpx-l* from partition 2 of the Flash device:

```
boot system flash flash:2:igs-bpx-l
```

The following example instructs the router to boot from an image located on the Flash memory card inserted in slot 0 of the Cisco 7000 RSP7000 card, Cisco 7200 NPE card, or Cisco 7500 series RSP card:

```
boot system flash slot0:new-config
```

This example specifies the file *new-ios-image* as the system image for a Cisco 3600 series router to load at startup. This file is located in the fourth partition of the Flash memory card in slot 0:

```
Router# configure terminal
Enter configuration commands, one per line.  End with CNTL/Z.
Router(config)# boot system flash slot0:4:dirt/images/new-ios-image
```

This example boots from the image file *c1600-y-l* in partition 2 of Flash memory of a Cisco 1600 series:

```
Router# configure terminal
Enter configuration commands, one per line.  End with CNTL/Z.
Router(config)# boot system flash flash:2:c1600-y-l
```

Related Commands

config-register
copy
copy flash rcp
copy flash tftp
copy verify flash
copy running-config startup-config
copy tftp flash
ip rcmd remote-username
show boot

CONFIG-REGISTER

To change the configuration register settings, use the **config-register** global configuration command.

> **config-register** *value*

Syntax	*Description*
value	Hexadecimal or decimal value that represents the 16-bit configuration register value that you want to use the next time the router is restarted. The value range is from 0x0 to 0xFFFF (0 to 65535 in decimal).

Default

Refer to your platform documentation for the default configuration register value.

Command Mode

Global configuration

Usage Guidelines

This command first appeared in Cisco IOS Release 10.0.

This command applies only to platforms that use a software configuration register.

The lowest four bits of the configuration register (bits 3, 2, 1, and 0) form the boot field. The boot field determines whether the router boots manually, from ROM, or from Flash or the network. To change the boot field value and leave all other bits set to their default values, follow these guidelines:

- If you set the configuration register boot field to 0x0, you must boot the operating system manually with the **boot** command.
- If you set the configuration register boot field to 0x1, the router boots using the default ROM software.
- If you set the configuration register boot field to any value from 0x2 to 0xF, the router uses the boot field value to form a default boot filename for booting from a network server.

For more information about the configuration register bit settings and default filenames, see the appropriate router hardware installation guide.

Example

In the following example, the configuration register is set to boot the system image from Flash memory:

```
config-register 0x210F
```

Related Commands

boot system
confreg
o
show version

CONFREG

To change the configuration register settings while in ROM monitor mode, use the **confreg** ROM monitor command.

    confreg [*value*]

Syntax	Description
value	(Optional) Hexadecimal value that represents the 16-bit configuration register value that you want to use the next time the router is restarted. The value range is from 0x0 to 0xFFFF.

Default

Refer to your platform documentation for the default configuration register value.

Command Mode

ROM monitor

Usage Guidelines

This command first appeared in Cisco IOS Release 10.0.

Not all versions in the ROM monitor support this command. Refer to your platform documentation for more information on ROM monitor mode.

If you use this command without specifying the configuration register value, the router prompts for each bit of the configuration register.

The lowest four bits of the configuration register (bits 3, 2, 1, and 0) form the boot field. The boot field determines whether the router boots manually, from ROM, from Flash or the network. To change the boot field value and leave all other bits set to their default values, follow these guidelines:

- If you set the configuration register boot field to 0x0, you must boot the operating system manually with the **boot** command.

- If you set the configuration register boot field to 0x1, the router boots using the default ROM software.

- If you set the configuration register boot field to any value from 0x2 to 0xF, the router uses the boot field value to form a default boot filename for booting from a network server.

For more information about the configuration register bit settings and default filenames, see the appropriate router hardware installation guide.

Example

In the following example, the configuration register is set to boot the system image from Flash memory:

```
confreg 0x210F
```

In the following example, no configuration value is entered, so the system prompts for each bit in the register:

```
rommon 7 > confreg

        Configuration Summary
enabled are:
console baud: 9600
boot: the ROM Monitor

do you wish to change the configuration? y/n  [n]:  y
enable  "diagnostic mode"? y/n  [n]:  y
enable  "use net in IP bcast address"? y/n  [n]:

enable  "load rom after netboot fails"? y/n  [n]:
enable  "use all zero broadcast"? y/n  [n]:
enable  "break/abort has effect"? y/n  [n]:
enable  "ignore system config info"? y/n  [n]:
change console baud rate? y/n  [n]:  y
enter rate: 0 = 9600, 1 = 4800, 2 = 1200, 3 = 2400  [0]:  0
change the boot characteristics? y/n  [n]:  y
enter to boot:
 0 = ROM Monitor
 1 = the boot helper image
 2-15 = boot system
    [0]:  0

        Configuration Summary
enabled are:
diagnostic mode
console baud: 9600
boot: the ROM Monitor

do you wish to change the configuration? y/n  [n]:

You must reset or power cycle for new config to take effect.
rommon 8>
```

CONTINUE

To return to the EXEC mode from ROM monitor mode, use the **continue** ROM monitor command.

    continue

Syntax   *Description*

This command has no arguments or keywords.

Command Mode

ROM monitor

Usage Guidelines

This command first appeared in Cisco IOS Release 11.0.

Use this command when you are in ROM monitor mode, and you want to return to EXEC mode to use the system image instead of reloading. On older platforms, the angle bracket (>) indicates that you are in ROM monitor mode. On newer platforms, "rommon *number*>" is the default ROM monitor prompt. Typically, you are in ROM monitor mode when you manually load a system image or perform diagnostic tests. Otherwise, you will most likely never be in this mode.

CAUTION

While in ROM monitor mode, the Cisco IOS system software is suspended until you issue either a reset or the **continue** command.

Example

In the following example, the **continue** command takes you from ROM monitor to EXEC mode:

```
> continue
Router#
```

Related Commands

boot

o

To list the value of the boot field (bits 0-3) in the configuration register, use the ROM monitor **o** command. To reset the value of the boot field so that the router boots from ROM, use the ROM monitor **o/r** command.

> o
> o/r

Syntax   Description

This command has no arguments or keywords.

Default

Refer to the appropriate hardware installation guide for default values.

Command Mode

ROM monitor

Usage Guidelines

This command first appeared in Cisco IOS Release 10.0.

Not all platforms support the **o** command.

To get to the ROM monitor prompt, use the **reload** EXEC command if the configuration register has a boot value of 0. (For systems with a software configuration register, a value can be included on the **o/r** command line.) Use the **i** command in conjunction with the **o/r** command to initialize the router. (The **i** command is documented in the hardware installation and maintenance publication for your product.) The **o/r** command resets the configuration register to 0x141, which disables the **Break** key, ignores the NVRAM configuration, and boots the default system image from ROM.

Examples

The following is a sample display from the **o** command:

```
> o
Bit#   Configuration register option settings:
15     Diagnostic mode disabled
14     IP broadcasts do not have network numbers
13     Do not boot default ROM software if network boot fails
12-11  Console speed is 9600 baud
10     IP broadcasts with ones
09     Do not use secondary bootstrap
08     Break enabled
07     OEM disabled
06     Ignore configuration disabled
03-00  Boot to ROM monitor
>
```

The following is an example of the **o/r** and **i** commands used to reset and boot the default system image from ROM:

```
> o/r
> i
```

Related Commands

config-register

RELOAD

To reload the operating system, use the **reload** EXEC command.

> **reload** [*text*] | [**in** [*hh:*]*mm* [*text*]] | [**at** *hh:mm* [*month day* | *day month*] [*text*]] | [**cancel**]

Syntax	Description
text	(Optional) Reason for the reload, 1 to 255 characters long.
in [*hh*:]*mm*	(Optional) Schedule a reload of the software to take effect in the specified minutes or hours and minutes. The reload must take place within approximately 24 days.
at *hh:mm*	(Optional) Schedule a reload of the software to take place at the specified time (using a 24-hour clock). If you specify the month and day, the reload is scheduled to take place at the specified time and date. If you do not specify the month and day, the reload takes place at the specified time on the current day (if the specified time is later than the current time), or on the next day (if the specified time is earlier than the current time). Specifying 00:00 schedules the reload for midnight. The reload must take place within approximately 24 days.
month	(Optional) Name of the month, any number of characters in a unique string.
day	(Optional) Number of the day in the range 1 to 31.
cancel	(Optional) Cancel a scheduled reload.

Command Mode
EXEC

Usage Guidelines
This command first appeared in Cisco IOS Release 10.0.

The **reload** command halts the system. If the system is set to restart on error, it reboots itself. Use the **reload** command after configuration information is entered into a file and saved to the startup configuration.

You cannot reload from a virtual terminal if the system is not set up for automatic booting. This prevents the system from dropping to the ROM monitor and thereby taking the system out of the remote user's control.

If you modify your configuration file, the system prompts you to save the configuration. During a save operation, the system asks you whether you want to proceed with the save if the CONFIG_FILE environment variable points to a startup configuration file that no longer exists. If you say "yes" in this situation, the system goes to **setup** mode upon reload.

When you schedule a reload to occur at a later time, it must take place within approximately 24 days.

The **at** keyword can be used only if the system clock has been set on the router (either through NTP, the hardware calendar, or manually). The time is relative to the configured time zone on the router.

To schedule reloads across several routers to occur simultaneously, the time on each router must be synchronized with NTP.

To display information about a scheduled reload, use the **show reload** command.

Examples

The following example illustrates how to use the **reload** command to reload the software on the router immediately:

```
Router# reload
```

The following example illustrates how to use the **reload** command to reload the software on the router in 10 minutes:

```
Router# reload in 10
Router# Reload scheduled for 11:57:08 PDT Fri Apr 21 1996 (in 10 minutes)
Proceed with reload? [confirm]
Router#
```

The following example illustrates how to use the **reload** command to reload the software on the router at 1 p.m. today:

```
Router# reload at 13:00
Router# Reload scheduled for 13:00:00 PDT Fri Apr 21 1996 (in 1 hour and 2 minutes)
Proceed with reload? [confirm]
Router#
```

The following example illustrates how to use the **reload** command to reload the software on the router on April 20 at 2 a.m.:

```
Router# reload at 02:00 apr 20
Router# Reload scheduled for 02:00:00 PDT Sat Apr 20 1996 (in 38 hours and 9 minutes)
Proceed with reload? [confirm]
Router#
```

The following example illustrates how to use the **reload** command to cancel a pending reload:

```
Router# reload cancel
%Reload cancelled.
```

Related Commands

copy running-config startup-config
show reload

SHOW BOOT

To display the contents of the BOOT environment variable, the name of the configuration file pointed to by the CONFIG_FILE environment variable, the contents of the BOOTLDR environment variable, and the configuration register setting, use the **show boot** EXEC command.

show boot

Syntax   Description

This command has no arguments or keywords.

Command Mode

EXEC

Usage Guidelines

This command first appeared in Cisco IOS Release 11.0.

Use this command with the Cisco 7000 family. The **show boot** command allows you to view the current settings for the following environment variables:

- BOOT
- CONFIG_FILE
- BOOTLDR

The BOOT environment variable specifies a list of bootable images on various devices. The CONFIG_FILE environment variable specifies the configuration file used during system initialization. The BOOTLDR environment variable specifies the Flash device and filename containing the rxboot image that ROM uses for booting. You set these environment variables with the **boot system, boot config,** and **boot bootldr** commands, respectively.

When you use this command on a Cisco 7507 or Cisco 7513 configured for High System Availability (HSA), this command also shows you the environment variable settings for both the master and slave RSP card.

HSA refers to how quickly your router returns to an operational status after a failure occurs. On the Cisco 7507 and Cisco 7513, you can install two RSP cards in a single router to improve system availability.

Sample Displays

The following is sample output from the **show boot** command:

```
Cyclone# show boot
BOOT variable =
CONFIG_FILE variable = nvram:
Current CONFIG_FILE variable = slot0:router-config
BOOTLDR variable not exist

Configuration register is 0x0

Cyclone#
```

In the sample output, the BOOT environment variable contains a null string. That is, a list of bootable images is not specified.

The CONFIG_FILE environment variable points to the configuration file in NVRAM as the startup (initialization) configuration. The run-time value for the CONFIG_FILE environment variable points to the *router-config* file on the Flash memory card inserted in the first slot of the RSP card. That is, during the run-time configuration, you have modified the CONFIG_FILE environment variable using the **boot config** command, but you have not saved the run-time configuration to the startup configuration. To save your run-time configuration to the startup configuration, use the **copy running-config startup-config** command. If you do not save the run-time configuration to the startup configuration, then the system reverts back to the saved CONFIG_FILE environment variable setting for initialization information upon reload. In this sample, the system reverts back to NVRAM for the startup configuration file.

The BOOTLDR environment variable does not yet exist. That is, you have not created the BOOTLDR environment variable using the **boot bootldr** command.

The following example is output from the **show boot** command for a Cisco 7513 configured for HSA:

```
Router# show boot
BOOT variable =
CONFIG_FILE variable =
Current CONFIG_FILE variable =
BOOTLDR variable does not exist

Configuration register is 0x0

current slave is in slot 7
BOOT variable =
CONFIG_FILE variable =
BOOTLDR variable does not exist

Configuration register is 0x0

Router#
```

Related Commands

boot bootstrap
boot config
boot system
show version

SHOW RELOAD

To display the reload status on the router, use the **show reload** EXEC command.

   show reload

Syntax   Description

This command has no arguments or keywords.

Command Mode

EXEC

Usage Guidelines

This command first appeared in Cisco IOS Release 11.2.

You can use the **show reload** command to display a pending software reload. To cancel the reload, use the **reload cancel** privileged EXEC command.

Sample Display

The following sample output from the **show reload** command shows that a reload is schedule for 12 a.m. (midnight) on Saturday, April 20:

```
Router# show reload

Reload scheduled for 00:00:00 PDT Sat April 20 1996 (in 12 hours and 12 minutes)
Router#
```

Related Commands

reload

SHOW VERSION

To display the configuration of the system hardware, the software version, the names and sources of configuration files, and the boot images, use the **show version** EXEC command.

   show version

Syntax   Description

This command has no arguments or keywords.

Command Mode

EXEC

Usage Guidelines

This command first appeared in Cisco IOS Release 10.0.

You also can use this command with a Cisco 7507 or Cisco 7513 configured with High System Availability (HSA). HSA refers to how quickly your router returns to an operational status after a failure occurs. On the Cisco 7507 and Cisco 7513, you can install two RSP cards in a single router to improve system availability.

When used with HSA, this command also displays the currently running slave RSP card and the Cisco IOS release that it is running.

Sample Displays

The following is sample output from the **show version** command:

```
Router> show version

GS Software (GS7), Version 10.0
Copyright (c) 1986-1993 by cisco Systems, Inc.
Compiled Mon 11-Jan-93 14:44

System Bootstrap, Version 4.6(1)

Current date and time is Fri 2-26-1993 2:18:52
Boot date and time is Fri 1-29-1993 11:42:38
Router uptime is 3 weeks, 6 days, 14 hours, 36 minutes
System restarted by power-on
Running default software
Network configuration file is "Router", booted via tftp from 172.16.2.333

RP1 (68040) processor with 16384K bytes of memory.
X.25 software.
Bridging software.
1 CIP controller (3 IBM Channels).
1 CIP2 controller (3 IBM Channels).
1 Switch Processor.
1 TRIP controller (4 Token Ring).
4 Token Ring/IEEE 802.5 interface.
1 AIP controller (1(ATM)
1 ATM network interface
4096K bytes of flash memory on embedded flash (in RP1).
Configuration register is 0x0
```

Table 16–1 describes significant fields shown in these displays.

Table 16–1   *Show Version Field Descriptions*

Field	Description
GS Software (GS7), Version 10.0	Always specify the complete version number when reporting a possible software problem. In the example output, the version number is 10.0.
System Bootstrap, Version	Bootstrap version string.
Current date and time Boot date and time Router uptime is	Current date and time, the date and time the system was last booted, and *uptime*, or the amount of time the system has been up and running.

Table 16–1 *Show Version Field Descriptions, Continued*

Field	Description
System restarted by power-on	Also displayed is a log of how the system was last booted, both as a result of normal system startup and of system error. For example, information can be displayed to indicate a bus error that is generally the result of an attempt to access a nonexistent address, as follows: System restarted by bus error at PC 0xC4CA, address 0x210C0C0
Running default software	If the software was booted over the network, the Internet address of the boot host is shown. If the software was loaded from onboard ROM, this line reads "running default software." In addition, the names and sources of the host and network configuration files are shown.
RP1....	The remaining output in each display shows the hardware configuration and any nonstandard software options. The configuration register contents are displayed in hexadecimal notation.

Part II

Command Reference

The output of the **show version** EXEC command also can provide certain messages, such as bus error messages. If such error messages appear, report the complete text of this message to your technical support specialist.

The following is sample output from the **show version** command on a Cisco 7500 series router with an RSP2 and three VIP2s with a variety of interfaces.

```
Router# show version

Cisco Internetwork Operating System Software
IOS (tm) GS Software (RSP-JV-M), Experimental Version 11.1(12816)
[getchell 108]
Copyright (c) 1986-1996 by cisco Systems, Inc.
Compiled Mon 03-Jun-96 11:39 by getchell
Image text-base: 0x600108A0, data-base: 0x60910000

ROM: System Bootstrap, Version 5.3(16645) [szhang 571], INTERIM SOFTWARE

Router uptime is 4 minutes
System restarted by reload
System image file is "slot0:dirt/vip2/master/rsp-jv-mz.960603", booted via tftp from
172.18.2.3

cisco RSP2 (R4600) processor with 24576K bytes of memory.
R4600 processor, Implementation 32, Revision 2.0
Last reset from power-on
G.703/E1 software, Version 1.0.
```

```
SuperLAT software copyright 1990 by Meridian Technology Corp).
Bridging software.
X.25 software, Version 2.0, NET2, BFE and GOSIP compliant.
TN3270 Emulation software (copyright 1994 by TGV Inc).
Primary Rate ISDN software, Version 1.0.
Chassis Interface.
1 CIP controller (3 IBM Channels).
1 CIP2 controller (3 IBM Channels).
1 EIP controller (6 Ethernet).
1 HIP controller (1 HSSI).
1 FSIP controller (8 Serial).
1 AIP controller (1 ATM).
1 TRIP controller (4 Token Ring).
1 FIP controller (1 FDDI).
1 MIP controller (2 T1).
3 VIP2 controllers (1 FastEthernet)(13 Ethernet)(4 Serial)(4 Token Ring)(1
Fddi).
1 FEIP controller (1 FastEthernet).
19 Ethernet/IEEE 802.3 interfaces.
2 FastEthernet/IEEE 802.3 interfaces.
8 Token Ring/IEEE 802.5 interfaces.
12 Serial network interfaces.
1 HSSI network interface.
2 FDDI network interfaces.
1 ATM network interface.
2 Channelized T1/PRI ports.
125K bytes of non-volatile configuration memory.

8192K bytes of Flash PCMCIA card at slot 0 (Sector size 128K).
8192K bytes of Flash PCMCIA card at slot 1 (Sector size 128K).
8192K bytes of Flash internal SIMM (Sector size 256K).
No slave installed in slot 7.
Configuration register is 0x0
```

Table 16–2 describes the fields in this display for Cisco 7500 series routers with an RSP2 route switch processor.

Table 16–2 *Show Version Field Descriptions on Cisco 7500 Series Routers*

Field	Description
IOS (tm) GS Software, Version 11.1	Always specify the complete version number when reporting a possible software problem. In the example output, the version number is 11.1.
ROM: System Bootstrap, Version 5.3(16645) [szhang 571], INTERIM SOFTWARE	Bootstrap version string.

Table 16–2 *Show Version Field Descriptions on Cisco 7500 Series Routers, Continued*

Field	Description
Router uptime is... System restarted by... System image file is...	The amount of time the system has been up and running, how the system was restarted, and the name of the system image file.
System last reset by	Also displayed is a log of how the system was last booted, both as a result of normal system startup and of system error. For example, information can be displayed to indicate a bus error that is generally the result of an attempt to access a nonexistent address, as follows: System restarted by bus error at PC 0xC4CA, address 0x210C0C0
cisco RSP2 (R4600) processor...	The remaining output in each display shows the software currently running, hardware configuration, and any nonstandard software options. The configuration register contents are displayed in hexadecimal notation.

The following is sample output of the **show version** command from a Cisco 7513. In this example, the current slave is processor slot 7.

```
Router# show version

Cisco Internetwork Operating System Software
IOS (tm) GS Software (RSP-P-M), Experimental Version 11.1(5479) [dbath 119]
Copyright (c) 1986-1995 by cisco Systems, Inc.
Compiled Wed 08-Nov-95 17:51 by dbath
Image text-base: 0x600088A0, data-base: 0x603B6000

ROM: System Bootstrap, Version 5.3(18168) [mansonw 63], INTERIM SOFTWARE

Router uptime is 4 days, 31 minutes
System restarted by reload
System image file is "slot0:dirt/dbath/rsp-p-mz-ark-1", booted via tftp from 172.31.7.19


cisco RSP2 (R4600) processor with 16384K bytes of memory.
R4600 processor, Implementation 32, Revision 2.0
Last reset from power-on
G.703/E1 software, Version 1.0.
Primary Rate ISDN software, Version 1.0.
Chassis Interface.
1 CIP controller (3 IBM Channels).
1 CIP2 controller (3 IBM Channels).
1 EIP controller (6 Ethernet).
```

```
1 FSIP controller (8 Serial).
1 AIP controller (1 ATM).
1 TRIP controller (4 Token Ring).
1 FIP controller (1 FDDI).
1 MIP controller (2 T1).
6 Ethernet/IEEE 802.3 interfaces.
4 Token Ring/IEEE 802.5 interfaces.
8 Serial network interfaces.
1 FDDI network interface.
1 ATM network interface.
2 Channelized T1/PRI ports.
125K bytes of non-volatile configuration memory.

8192K bytes of Flash PCMCIA card at slot 0 (Sector size 128K).
8192K bytes of Flash internal SIMM (Sector size 256K).

Slave in slot 7 is running Cisco Internetwork Operating System Software
IOS (tm) GS Software (RSP-DW-M), Experimental Version 11.1(5479) [dbath 118]
Copyright (c) 1986-1995 by cisco Systems, Inc.
Compiled Wed 08-Nov-95 16:57 by dbath

Configuration register is 0x0
```

Related Commands

reload

SLAVE AUTO-SYNC CONFIG

To turn on automatic synchronization of configuration files for a Cisco 7507 or Cisco 7513 that is configured for High System Availability (HSA), use the **slave auto-sync config** global configuration command. To turn off automatic synchronization, use the **no** form of the command.

> **slave auto-sync config**
> **no slave auto-sync config**

Syntax   Description

This command has no arguments or keywords.

Default

Enabled

Command Mode

Global configuration

Usage Guidelines

This command first appeared in Cisco IOS Release 11.1.

Use this command for a Cisco 7507 or Cisco 7513 that is configured for High System Availability (HSA). HSA refers to how quickly your router returns to an operational status after a failure occurs. On the Cisco 7507 and Cisco 7513, you can install two RSP cards in a single router to improve system availability.

In automatic synchronization mode, when you issue a **copy** EXEC command that specifies the master's startup configuration (**startup-config**) as the target, the master also copies the same file to the slave's startup configuration (**slave-startup-config**). Use this command when implementing HSA for simple hardware backup or for software error protection to ensure that the master and slave RSP contain the same configuration files.

Example

The following example turns on automatic configuration file synchronization. When the **copy running-config startup-config** command is issued, the running configuration is saved to the startup configurations of both the master RSP and the slave RSP.

```
Router(config)# slave auto-sync config
Router(config)# end
Router# copy running-config startup-config
```

Related Commands

slave sync config

SLAVE DEFAULT-SLOT

To specify the default slave RSP card on a Cisco 7507 or Cisco 7513, use the **slave default-slot** global configuration command.

> **slave default-slot** *processor-slot-number*

Syntax	Description
processor-slot-number	Number of processor slot that contains the default slave RSP. On the Cisco 7507, valid values are 2 or 3. On the Cisco 7513, valid values are 6 or 7. The default is the higher-number processor slot.

Default

The default slave is the RSP card located in the higher-number processor slot. On the Cisco 7507, processor slot 3 contains the default slave RSP. On the Cisco 7513, processor slot 7 contains the default slave RSP.

Command Mode

Global configuration

Usage Guidelines

This command first appeared in Cisco IOS Release 11.1.

Use this command for a Cisco 7507 or Cisco 7513 that is configured for High System Availability (HSA). HSA refers to how quickly your router returns to an operational status after a failure occurs. On the Cisco 7507 and Cisco 7513, you can install two RSP cards in a single router to improve system availability.

The router uses the default slave information when booting if:

- A system boot is due to powering up the router or using the **reload** command, then the specified default slave will be the slave RSP.

- A system boot is due to a system crash or hardware failure, then the system ignores the default slave designation and makes the crashed or faulty RSP card the slave RSP.

Example

The following example sets the default slave RSP to processor slot 2 on a Cisco 7507:

```
slave default-slot 2
```

Related Commands

reload

SLAVE IMAGE

To specify the image that the slave RSP runs on a Cisco 7507 or Cisco 7513, use the **slave image** global configuration command.

> **slave image** {**system** | **flash** *file-id*}

Syntax	Description
system	(Optional) Loads the slave image that is bundled with the master system image. This is the default.
flash	(Optional) Loads the slave image from the Flash device specified by the *file-id* argument.

Syntax	Description
file-id	Specifies a *device:filename* of the slave image file to download. The colon (:) is required. Valid devices are as follows:

- **bootflash**—Internal Flash memory in the Cisco 7500 series.
- **slot0**—PCMCIA slot on the Cisco 7000 series RP card or the first PCMCIA slot on the Cisco 7500 series RSP card.
- **slot1**—Second PCMCIA slot on the Cisco 7500 series RSP card.

The *filename* argument is the name of a file on the specified Flash device. The file can be of any type. The maximum filename length is 63 characters. The first file on the specified device is the default file.

Default

The default is to load the image from the system bundle.

Command Mode

Global configuration

Usage Guidelines

This command first appeared in Cisco IOS Release 11.1.

Use this command for a Cisco 7507 or Cisco 7513 that is configured for High System Availability (HSA). HSA refers to how quickly your router returns to an operational status after a failure occurs. On the Cisco 7507 and Cisco 7513, you can install two RSP cards in a single router to improve system availability.

Use the **slave image** command to override the slave image that is bundled with the master image.

When using HSA for simple hardware backup, ensure that the slave image is in the same location on the master and the slave RSP card. Thus, if the slave RSP card becomes the master, it will be able to find the slave image and download it to the new slave.

Example

The following example specifies that the slave RSP run the *rsp-dw-mz.ucode.111-3.2* image from slot 0.

```
slave image flash slot0:rsp-dw-mz.ucode.111-3.2
```

Related Commands

slave reload

SLAVE RELOAD

To force a reload of the image that the slave RSP card is running on a Cisco 7507 or Cisco 7513, use the **slave reload** global configuration command.

> **slave reload**

Syntax   Description

This command has no arguments or keywords.

Command Mode

Global configuration

Usage Guidelines

This command first appeared in Cisco IOS Release 11.1.

Use this command for a Cisco 7507 or Cisco 7513 that is configured for High System Availability (HSA). HSA refers to how quickly your router returns to an operational status after a failure occurs. On the Cisco 7507 and Cisco 7513, you can install two RSP cards in a single router to improve system availability.

After using the **slave image** global configuration command to specify the image that the slave RSP runs on a Cisco 7507 or Cisco 7513, use the **slave reload** command to reload the slave with the new image. The **slave reload** command also can be used to force the slave to reboot its existing image.

Example

The following example reloads an inactive slave RSP card. If the slave successfully reloads, it will return to an active slave state. If the master RSP fails, the slave RSP will become the master.

```
slave reload
```

Related Commands

slave image

SLAVE SYNC CONFIG

To synchronize configuration files manually on the master and slave RSP cards of a Cisco 7507 or Cisco 7513, use the **slave sync config** privileged EXEC command.

> **slave sync config**

Syntax   Description

This command has no arguments or keywords.

Default

Automatic synchronization is turned on.

Command Mode

Privileged EXEC

Usage Guidelines

This command first appeared in Cisco IOS Release 11.1.

Use this command for a Cisco 7507 or Cisco 7513 that is configured for High System Availability (HSA). HSA refers to how quickly your router returns to an operational status after a failure occurs. On the Cisco 7507 and Cisco 7513, you can install two RSP cards in a single router to improve system availability.

This command allows you to synchronize the configuration files of the master and slave RSP cards on a case-by-case basis when you do not have automatic synchronization turned on. This command copies the master's configuration file to the slave RSP card.

NOTES

You *must* use this command when you insert a new slave RSP card into a Cisco 7507 or Cisco 7513 for the first time to ensure the new slave is configured consistently with the master.

Example

The following example synchronizes the configuration files on the master and slave RSP cards:

```
slave sync config
```

Related Commands

slave auto-sync config

CHAPTER 17

Configuring Additional File Transfer Functions

This chapter describes how to configure a router as a server, change MOP parameters, configure the router to forward extended BOOTP requests over asynchronous interfaces, and configure rcp and rsh.

For a complete description of the file transfer function commands mentioned in this chapter, see Chapter 18, "Additional File Transfer Function Commands."

ADDITIONAL FUNCTIONS TASK LIST

To configure additional file transfer functions, perform any of the tasks in the following sections:

- Configuring a Router as a Server
- Changing MOP Request Parameters
- Specifying Asynchronous Interface Extended BOOTP Requests
- Configuring a Router to Use rsh and rcp

CONFIGURING A ROUTER AS A SERVER

It is too costly and inefficient to have a machine that only acts as server on every network segment. However, when you do not have a server on every segment, your network operations can incur enormous time delays across network segments. You can configure a router to serve as a RARP or TFTP server to reduce costs and time delays in your network while allowing you to use your router for its regular functions.

Typically, a router that is configured as a server provides other routers with operating system images from its Flash memory. You also can configure the router to respond to other types of service requests, such as Reverse Address Resolution Protocol (RARP) requests.

To configure the router as a server, perform any of the tasks in the following sections. The tasks are not mutually exclusive.

- Configuring a Router as a TFTP Server
- Configuring a Router as a RARP Server

In addition, you can configure the Cisco IOS software to forward extended BOOTP requests over asynchronous interfaces.

Configuring a Router as a TFTP Server

As a TFTP server host, the router responds to TFTP Read Request messages by sending a copy of the system image contained in ROM or one of the system images contained in Flash memory to the requesting host. The TFTP Read Request message must use one of the filenames that are specified in the configuration.

NOTES

For the Cisco 7000 family, the filename used must represent a software image that is present in Flash memory. If no image resides in Flash memory, the client router will boot the server's ROM image as a default.

Flash memory can be used as a TFTP file server for other routers on the network. This feature allows you to boot a remote router with an image that resides in the Flash server memory.

With Cisco IOS Release 11.0, the Cisco 7000 family allows you to specify one of the different Flash memory devices (**bootflash:, slot0:, slot1:, slavebootflash:, slaveslot0:, or slaveslot1:**) as the TFTP server.

In the description that follows, one Cisco 7000 router is referred to as the *Flash server*, and all other routers are referred to as *client routers*. Example configurations for the Flash server and client routers include commands as necessary.

Configuring a Router as a TFTP Server Task List

To configure a router as a TFTP server, perform the tasks in the following sections:

- Performing Prerequisite Tasks
- Configuring the Server
- Configuring the Client Router

Performing Prerequisite Tasks

The server and client router must be able to reach each other before the TFTP function can be implemented. Verify this connection by pinging between the server and client router (in either direction) with the **ping** command.

An example use of the **ping** command is as follows:

```
Router# ping 172.16.101.101
```

In this example, the Internet Protocol (IP) address of 172.16.101.101 belongs to the client router. Connectivity is indicated by a series of exclamation points (!), while a series of periods (.) plus *[timed out]* or *[failed]* indicates no connection. If the connection fails, reconfigure the interface, check the physical connection between the Flash server and client router, and ping again.

After you verify the connection, ensure that a TFTP-bootable image is present on the server. This is the system software image the client router will boot. Note the name of this software image so you can verify it after the first client boot.

CAUTION

For full functionality, the software image sent to the client must be the same type as the ROM software installed on the client router. For example, if the server has X.25 software, and the client does not have X.25 software in ROM, the client will not have X.25 capabilities after booting from the server's image in Flash memory.

Configuring the Server

To specify TFTP server operation, complete the following tasks:

Task	Command
Step 1 Enter configuration mode from the terminal.	**configure terminal**
Step 2 Specify the system image to send in response to Read Requests. You can enter multiple lines to specify multiple images.	**tftp-server flash** [*partition-number:*]*filename1* [**alias** *filename2*] [*access-list-number*]
	tftp-server flash *device:filename* (Cisco 7000 family only)
	tftp-server flash [*device:*][*partition-number:*]*filename* (Cisco 1600 series and Cisco 3600 series only)
	tftp-server rom alias *filename1* [*access-list-number*]
Step 3 Exit configuration mode.	**end**
Step 4 Save the configuration file to your startup configuration.	**copy running-config startup-config**

The TFTP session can sometimes fail. TFTP generates the following special characters to help you determine why a TFTP session fails:

- An "E" character indicates that the TFTP server received an erroneous packet.
- An "O" character indicates that the TFTP server received an out-of-sequence packet.
- A period (.) indicates a timeout.

The transfer session might still succeed even if TFTP generates these characters, but the output is useful for diagnosing the transfer failure.

In the following example, the system can use TFTP to send copies of the Flash memory file *version-10.3* in response to a TFTP Read Request for that file. The requesting host is checked against access list 22.

```
tftp-server flash version-10.3 22
```

In the following example, the system can use TFTP to send a copy of the ROM image *gs3-k.101* in response to a TFTP Read Request for the *gs3-k.101* file:

```
tftp-server rom alias gs3-k.101
```

In the following example, the system can use a router to send a copy of the file *gs7-k.9.17* in Flash memory in response to a TFTP Read Request. The client router must reside on a network specified by access list 1. Thus, in the example, any clients on network 172.16.101.0 are permitted access to the file.

```
Server# configure terminal
Enter configuration commands, one per line. End with CTRL/Z
Server(config)# tftp-server flash gs7-k.9.17 1
Server(config)# access-list 1 permit 172.16.101.0 0.0.0.255
Server(config)# end
Server# copy running-config startup-config
[ok]
Server#
```

Configuring the Client Router

Configure the client router to load a system image from the server first. As a backup, configure the client router to then load its own ROM image if the load from a server fails. To configure the client router, perform the following tasks, beginning in privileged EXEC mode:

Task	Command
Step 1 Enter configuration mode from the terminal.	**configure terminal**
Step 2 Remove all previous **boot system** statements from the configuration file.	**no boot system**
Step 3 Specify that the client router load a system image from the server.	**boot system** [**tftp**] *filename* [*ip-address*]

Task	Command
Step 4 As a backup, specify that the client router loads its own ROM image.	**boot system rom**
Step 5 Set the configuration register to enable the client router to load a system image from a network server.	**config-register** *value*
Step 6 Exit configuration mode.	**end**
Step 7 Save the configuration file to your startup configuration.	**copy running-config startup-config**
Step 8 Reload the router to make your changes take effect.	**reload**
Step 9 After the router reboots, verify that the client router booted the correct image from the TFTP server.	**show version**

CAUTION

Using the **no boot system** command, as in the following example, will invalidate *all* other boot system commands currently in the client router system configuration. Before proceeding, determine whether the system configuration stored in the client router should first be saved (uploaded) to a TFTP file server so you have a backup copy.

The following example shows how to configure a router to use a TFTP server:

```
Client# configure terminal
Enter configuration commands, one per line. End with CTRL/Z
Client(config)# no boot system
Client(config)# boot system gs7-k.9.17 172.31.111.111
Client(config)# boot system rom
Client(config)# config-register 0x010F
Client(config)# end
Client# copy running-config startup-config
[ok]
Client# reload
```

In this example, the **no boot system** command invalidates all other **boot system** commands currently in the configuration memory, and any **boot system** commands entered after this command will be executed first. The second command, **boot system** *filename address*, tells the client router to look for the file *gs7-k.9.17* on the TFTP server with an IP address of 172.31.111.111. Failing this, the client router will boot from its system ROM in response to the **boot system rom** command, which is included as a backup in case of a network problem. The **copy running-config startup-config** command copies the configuration to the startup configuration, and the **reload** command boots the system.

CAUTION

The system software (*gs7-k.9.17* in the example) to be booted from the server (172.31.111.111 in the example) *must* reside in Flash memory on the server. If it is not in Flash memory, the client router will boot the server's system ROM.

The following example shows sample output of the **show version** command after the router has rebooted:

```
Client> show version
GS Software (GS7), Version 9.1.17
Copyright (c) 1986-1992 by cisco Systems, Inc.
Compiled Wed 21-Oct-92 22:49

System Bootstrap, Version 4.6(0.15)

Current date and time is Thu 10-22-1992 13:15:03
Boot date and time is Thu 10-22-1992 13:06:55
env-chassis uptime is 9 minutes
System restarted by power-on
System image file is "gs7-k.9.17", booted via tftp from 172.31.111.111

RP1 (68040) processor with 16384K bytes of memory.
X.25 software.
Bridging software.
1 Switch Processor.
1 EIP controller (6 Ethernet).
6 Ethernet/IEEE 802.3 interface.
128K bytes of non-volatile configuration memory.
4096K bytes of flash memory on embedded flash (in RP1).
Configuration register is 0x010F
```

The important information in this example is contained in the first line "GS Software..." and in the line that begins "System image file...." The "GS Software..." line shows the version of the operating system in the client router's RAM. The "System image file...." line shows the filename of the system image loaded from the TFTP server.

Configuring a Router as a RARP Server

You can configure the router as a RARP server. This feature enables the Cisco IOS software to answer RARP requests, making diskless booting of various systems possible (for example, Sun workstations or PCs on networks where the client and server are on separate subnets).

To configure the router as a RARP server, perform the following task in interface configuration mode:

Task	Command
Configure the router as a RARP server.	**ip rarp-server** *ip-address*

Figure 17–1 illustrates a network configuration in which a router is configured to act as a RARP server.

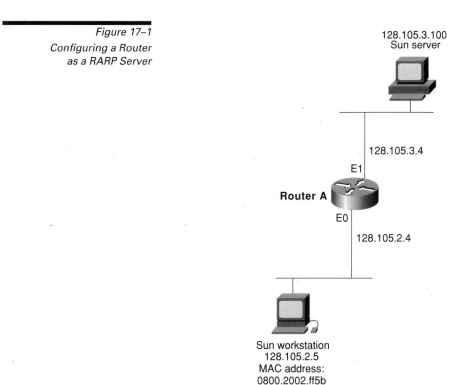

Figure 17–1

Configuring a Router as a RARP Server

128.105.3.100
Sun server

128.105.3.4

E1

Router A

E0

128.105.2.4

Sun workstation
128.105.2.5
MAC address:
0800.2002.ff5b

Router A's configuration

```
! Allow the router to forward broadcast portmapper requests
ip forward-protocol udp 111
! Provide the router with the IP address of the diskless sun
arp 172.30.2.5 0800.2002.ff5b arpa
interface ethernet 0
! Configure the router to act as a RARP server, using the Sun Server's IP
! address in the RARP response packet.
ip rarp-server 172.30.3.100
! Portmapper broadcasts from this interface are sent to the Sun Server.
ip helper-address 172.30.3.100
```

The Sun client and server's IP addresses must use the same major network number because of a limitation with the current SunOS *rpc.bootparamd* daemon.

Figure 17–2 illustrates a similar configuration with an access server.

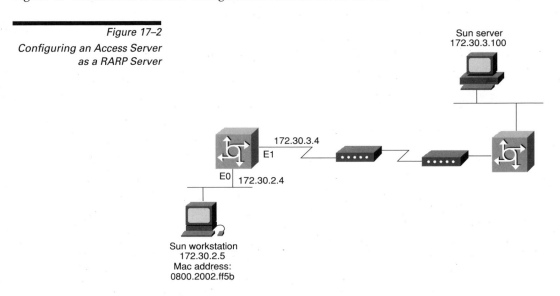

Figure 17–2

Configuring an Access Server as a RARP Server

In the following example, the access server is configured to act as a RARP server. Figure 17–2 illustrates the network configuration.

```
! Allow the access server to forward broadcast portmapper requests
ip forward-protocol udp 111
! Provide the access server with the IP address of the diskless sun
arp 172.30.2.5 0800.2002.ff5b arpa
interface ethernet 0
! Configure the access server to act as a RARP server, using the Sun Server's
! IP address in the RARP response packet.
ip rarp-server 172.30.3.100
! Portmapper broadcasts from this interface are sent to the Sun Server.
ip helper-address 172.30.3.100
```

The Sun client and server's IP addresses must use the same major network number because of a limitation with the current SunOS *rpc.bootparamd* daemon.

CHANGING MOP REQUEST PARAMETERS

By default, when the software transmits a request that requires a response from a MOP boot server and the server does not respond, the message will be retransmitted after four seconds. The message will be retransmitted a maximum of eight times. The MOP device code is set to the Cisco device code by default.

If the MOP boot server and router are separated by a slow serial link, it might take longer than four seconds for the router to receive a response to its message. Therefore, you might want to configure the software to wait longer than four seconds before retransmitting the message if you are using such a link. You might also want to change the maximum number of retries for the MOP request or the MOP device code.

To change the Cisco IOS software parameters for transmitting boot requests to a MOP server, complete the following tasks, starting in privileged EXEC mode:

Task	Command
Step 1 Enter configuration mode from the terminal.	**configure terminal**
Step 2 Change MOP server parameters.	**mop device-code** {cisco I ds200}
	mop retransmit-timer *seconds*
	mop retries *count*
Step 3 Exit configuration mode.	**end**
Step 4 Save the configuration file to your startup configuration.	**copy running-config startup-config**

In the following example, if the MOP boot server does not respond within ten seconds after the router sends a message, the software retransmits the message:

```
Router# configure terminal
Router (config)# mop retransmit-timer 10
Router (config)# end
Router# copy running-config startup-config
```

SPECIFYING ASYNCHRONOUS INTERFACE EXTENDED BOOTP REQUESTS

The Boot Protocol (BOOTP) server for asynchronous interfaces supports the extended BOOTP requests specified in RFC 1084. The following command is useful in conjunction with using the auxiliary port as an asynchronous interface.

To configure extended BOOTP requests for asynchronous interfaces, perform the following task in global configuration mode:

Task	Command
Configure extended BOOTP requests for asynchronous interfaces.	**async-bootp** *tag* [:*hostname*] *data*

You can display the extended BOOTP requests by performing the following task in EXEC mode:

Task	Command
Show parameters for BOOTP requests.	**show async-bootp**

CONFIGURING A ROUTER TO USE RSH AND RCP

Remote shell (rsh) gives users the capability to execute commands remotely. Remote copy (rcp) allows users to copy files to and from a file system residing on a remote host or server on the network. Cisco's implementation of rsh and rcp interoperates with standard implementations.

This section is divided into the following sections:

- Configuring a Router to Use rsh
- Configuring a Router to Use rcp
- Configuring rsh and rcp Security (optional)

Configuring a Router to Use rsh

You can use rsh to execute commands on remote systems to which you have access. When you issue the **rsh** command, a shell is started on the remote system. The shell allows you to execute commands on the remote system without having to log in to the target host.

You do not need to connect to the system, router, or access server and then disconnect after you execute a command if you use rsh. For example, you can use rsh to look remotely at the status of other devices *without* connecting to the target device, executing the command, and then disconnecting. This capability is useful for looking at statistics on many different routers.

Maintaining rsh Security

To gain access to a remote system running rsh, such as a UNIX host, an entry must exist in the system's *.rhosts* file or its equivalent identifying you as a user who is authorized to execute commands remotely on the system. On UNIX systems, the *.rhosts* file identifies users who can execute commands on the system remotely.

You can enable rsh support on a router to allow users on remote systems to execute commands. However, Cisco's implementation of rsh does not support an *.rhosts* file. Instead, you must configure a local authentication database to control access to the router by users attempting to execute commands remotely using rsh. A local authentication database is similar to a UNIX *.rhosts* file. Each entry that you configure in the authentication database identifies the local user, the remote host, and the remote user.

Configuring the Router to Allow Remote Users to Execute Commands Using rsh

To configure the router as an rsh server, complete the following tasks in global configuration mode:

Task		Command
Step 1	Create an entry in the local authentication database for each remote user who is allowed to execute **rsh** commands.	**ip rcmd remote-host** *local-username* {*ip-address* | *host*} *remote-username* [**enable** [*level*]]

Task	Command
Step 2 Enable the software to support incoming **rsh** commands.	**ip rcmd rsh-enable**

To disable the software from supporting incoming **rsh** commands, use the **no ip rcmd rsh-enable** command.

NOTES

When support of incoming **rsh** commands is disabled, you still can issue an **rsh** command to be executed on other routers that support the remote shell protocol and on UNIX hosts on the network.

The following example shows how to add two entries for remote users to the authentication database, and enable a router to support **rsh** commands from remote users:

```
ip rcmd remote-host Router1 172.16.101.101 rmtnetad1
ip rcmd remote-host Router1 172.16.101.101 netadmin4 enable
ip rcmd rsh-enable
```

The users, named *rmtnetad1* and *netadmin4*, are both on the remote host at IP address 172.16.101.101. Although both users are on the same remote host, you must include a unique entry for each user. Both users are allowed to connect to the router and remotely execute **rsh** commands on it after the router is enabled for rsh. The user named *netadmin4* is allowed to execute privileged EXEC mode commands on the router. Both authentication database entries give the router's host name *Router1* as the local username. The last command enables the router to support **rsh** commands issued by remote users.

Remotely Executing Commands Using rsh

You can use rsh to execute commands remotely on network servers that support the remote shell protocol. To use this command, the *.rhosts* files (or equivalent files) on the network server must include an entry that permits you to execute commands remotely on that host.

If the remote server has a directory structure, as do UNIX systems, the **rsh** command that you issue is executed remotely from the directory of the account for the remote user that you specify through the **/user** *username* keyword and argument pair.

If you do not specify the **/user** keyword and argument, the Cisco IOS software sends a default remote username. As the default value of the remote username, the software sends the remote username associated with the current TTY process, if that name is valid. If the TTY remote username is invalid, the software uses the router host name as the both the remote and local usernames.

To execute a command remotely on a network server using rsh, perform the following tasks in privileged EXEC mode:

Task	Command
Step 1 Enter privileged EXEC mode.	**enable** [*password*]
Step 2 Enter the **rsh** command to be executed remotely.	**rsh** {*ip-address* | *host*} [**/user** *username*] *remote-command*

The following example executes the "ls -a" command in the home directory of the user sharon on mysys.cisco.com using rsh:

```
Router# enable
Router# rsh mysys.cisco.com /user sharon ls -a
.
..
.alias
.cshrc
.emacs
.exrc
.history
.login
.mailrc
.newsrc
.oldnewsrc
.rhosts
.twmrc
.xsession
jazz
Router#
```

Configuring a Router to Use rcp

The rcp copy commands rely on the rsh server (or daemon) on the remote system. To copy files using rcp, you do not need to create a server for file distribution, as you do with TFTP. You need only to have access to a server that supports the remote shell (rsh). (Most UNIX systems support rsh.) Because you are copying a file from one place to another, you must have read permission on the source file and write permission on the destination file. If the destination file does not exist, rcp creates it for you.

Although Cisco's rcp implementation emulates the functions of the UNIX rcp implementation—copying files among systems on the network—Cisco's command syntax differs from the UNIX rcp command syntax. Cisco software rcp support offers a set of copy commands that uses rcp as the transport mechanism. These rcp copy commands are similar in style to our TFTP copy commands, but they offer an alternative that provides faster performance and reliable delivery of data. These improvements are possible because the rcp transport mechanism is built on and uses the Transmission Control Protocol/Internet Protocol (TCP/IP) stack, which is connection oriented. You can use rcp commands to copy system images and configuration files from the router to a network server and vice versa.

You also can enable rcp support to allow users on remote systems to copy files to and from the router.

Configuring the Router to Accept rcp Requests from Remote Users

To configure the Cisco IOS software to support incoming rcp requests, complete the following tasks in global configuration mode:

Task	Command
Step 1 Create an entry in the local authentication database for each remote user who is allowed to execute rcp commands.	**ip rcmd remote-host** *local-username* {*ip-address* | *host*} *remote-username* [**enable** [*level*]]
Step 2 Enable the software to support incoming rcp requests.	**ip rcmd rcp-enable**

To disable the software from supporting incoming rcp requests, use the **no ip rcmd rcp-enable** command.

— **NOTES**

When support for incoming rcp requests is disabled, you still can use the **rcp** commands to copy images from remote servers. The support for incoming rcp requests is distinct from its capability to handle outgoing rcp requests.

The following example shows how to add two entries for remote users to the authentication database and then enable the software to support remote copy requests from remote users. The users, named *netadmin1* on the remote host at IP address 172.16.15.55 and *netadmin3* on the remote host at IP address 172.16.101.101, are both allowed to connect to the router and remotely execute **rcp** commands on it after the router is enabled to support rcp. Both authentication database entries give the host name *Router1* as the local username. The last command enables the router to support rcp requests from remote users.

```
ip rcmd remote-host Router1 172.16.15.55 netadmin1
ip rcmd remote-host Router1 172.16.101.101 netadmin3
ip rcmd rcp-enable
```

Configuring the Remote to Send rcp Requests

The rcp protocol requires a client to send a remote username on each rcp request to a server. When you copy a configuration file from a server to the router using rcp, the Cisco IOS software sends the first valid username in the following list:

1. The username set by the **ip rcmd remote-username** command, if the command is configured.

2. The remote username associated with the current TTY (terminal) process. For example, if the user is connected to the router through Telnet and was authenticated through the **username** command, the router software sends the Telnet username as the remote username.

NOTES

For Cisco, TTYs are commonly used in access servers. The concept of TTY originated with UNIX. For UNIX systems, each physical device is represented in the file system. Terminals are called *TTY devices*, which stands for *teletype*, the original UNIX terminal.

---

3. The router host name.

For **boot** commands using rcp, the software sends the router host name; you cannot configure the remote username explicitly.

For the rcp copy request to execute successfully, an account must be defined on the network server for the remote username.

If you are writing to the server, the rcp server must be configured properly to accept the rcp write request from the user on the router. For UNIX systems, you must add an entry to the *.rhosts* file for the remote user on the rcp server. For example, if the router contains the following configuration lines:

```
hostname Rtr1
ip rcmd remote-username User0
```

and the router's IP address translates to Router1.company.com, then the *.rhosts* file for User0 on the rcp server should contain the following line:

```
Router1.company.com Rtr1
```

Refer to the documentation for your rcp server for more details.

If the server has a directory structure, the configuration file or image is written or copied relative to the directory associated with the remote username on the server. Use the **ip rcmd remote-username** command to specify which directory on the server to use. For example, if the system image resides in the home directory of a user on the server, you can specify that user's name as the remote username.

If you copy the configuration file to a personal computer used as a file server, the computer must support rsh.

To override the default remote username sent on rcp requests, complete the following tasks starting in privileged EXEC mode:

Task	Command
Step 1 Enter configuration mode from the terminal.	**configure terminal**
Step 2 Specify the remote username.	**ip rcmd remote-username** *username*

To remove the remote username and return to the default value, use the **no ip rcmd remote-username** command.

Configuring rsh and rcp Security

You configure a local authentication database to control access to the router by remote users. To allow remote users to execute **rcp** or **rsh** commands, configure entries for those users in the router's authentication database.

Each entry configured in the authentication database identifies the following:

- Local Username
- Remote Username
- Remote Host Name

To execute commands remotely on the router, the remote user must correctly specify all three values. For rsh users, you also can grant a user permission to execute privileged EXEC commands remotely.

To ensure security, the Cisco IOS software is *not* enabled to support rcp requests from remote users by default. When the software is not enabled to support rcp, the authorization database has no effect.

Local Username

You can specify the router host name as the local username.

To make the local username available to remote users, you must communicate the username to the network administrator or the remote user.

Remote Username

Each entry in the authentication database also requires a remote username. The network administrator must know what remote usernames remote users will specify.

Remote Host Name

The Cisco IOS software uses Domain Name System (DNS) to check the host name sent by the client with the client's IP address. Because DNS can return several valid IP addresses for a host name, the software checks the address of the requesting client against all IP addresses for the named host. If the address sent by the requester does not match any address listed with DNS for the host name, then the software rejects the remote command execution request.

If no DNS servers are configured, the software cannot authenticate the host in this manner. In this case, the software sends a broadcast request to attempt to gain access to DNS services on another server.

If DNS services are not available or you do not want to use DNS for authentication, you must use the **no ip domain-lookup** command to disable the router's attempt to gain access to a DNS server by sending a broadcast request.

To bypass the DNS security check for rsh and rcp, perform the following task in global configuration mode:

Task	Command
Bypass the DNS security check.	**no ip rcmd domain-lookup**

The Cisco IOS software accepts the request to execute a command remotely only if all three values sent with the request match exactly the values configured for an entry in the local authentication file.

## CHAPTER 18

Additional File Transfer Function Commands

This chapter provides detailed descriptions of commands used to configure the router for additional file transfer functions.

NOTES

Commands in this chapter that have been replaced by new commands continue to perform their normal functions in the current release, but are no longer documented. Support for these commands will cease in a future release. Table 18–1 maps the old commands with their replacements.

Table 18–1 *Mapping Old Commands to New Commands*

Old Command	New Command
tftp-server system	tftp-server

For configuration information and examples, see Chapter 17, "Configuring Additional File Transfer Functions."

ASYNC-BOOTP

To configure extended BOOTP requests for asynchronous interfaces as defined in RFC 1084, use the **async-bootp** global configuration command. Use the **no** form of this command to restore the default.

> **async-bootp** *tag* [*:hostname*] *data*
> **no async-bootp**

Syntax	Description
tag	Item being requested; expressed as filename, integer, or IP dotted-decimal address. See Table 18–2 for possible keywords.
:hostname	(Optional) This entry applies only to the host specified. The argument *:hostname* accepts both an IP address and a logical host name.
data	List of IP addresses entered in dotted-decimal notation or as logical host names, a number, or a quoted string.

Table 18–2   *Async-BOOTP Tag Keywords*

Keyword	Description
bootfile	Specifies use of a server boot file from which to download the boot program. Use the optional *:hostname* and *data* arguments to specify the filename.
subnet-mask *mask*	Dotted-decimal address specifying the network and local subnetwork mask (as defined by RFC 950).
time-offset *offset*	Signed 32-bit integer specifying the time offset of the local subnetwork in seconds from Universal Coordinated Time (UTC).
gateway *address*	Dotted-decimal address specifying the IP addresses of gateways for this subnetwork. A preferred gateway should be listed first.
time-server *address*	Dotted-decimal address specifying the IP address of time servers (as defined by RFC 868).
IEN116-server *address*	Dotted-decimal address specifying the IP address of name servers (as defined by IEN 116).
DNS-server *address*	Dotted-decimal address specifying the IP address of domain name servers (as defined by RFC 1034).
log-server *address*	Dotted-decimal address specifying the IP address of an MIT-LCS UDP log server.
quote-server *address*	Dotted-decimal address specifying the IP address of Quote of the Day servers (as defined in RFC 865).
lpr-server *address*	Dotted-decimal address specifying the IP address of Berkeley UNIX Version 4 BSD servers.
impress-server *address*	Dotted-decimal address specifying the IP address of Impress network image servers.

Table 18–2 *Async-BOOTP Tag Keywords, Continued*

Keyword	Description
rlp-server *address*	Dotted-decimal address specifying the IP address of Resource Location Protocol (RLP) servers (as defined in RFC 887).
hostname *name*	The name of the client, which might or might not be domain qualified, depending upon the site.
bootfile-size *value*	A two-octet value specifying the number of 512-octet (byte) blocks in the default boot file.

Default

If no extended BOOTP commands are entered, the Cisco IOS software generates a gateway and subnet mask appropriate for the local network.

Command Mode

Global configuration

Usage Guidelines

This command first appeared in Cisco IOS Release 10.0.

Use the EXEC command **show async-bootp** to list the configured parameters. Use the **no async-bootp** command to clear the list.

Examples

The following example illustrates how to specify different boot files: one for a PC, and one for a Macintosh. With this configuration, a BOOTP request from the host on 172.30.1.1 results in a reply listing the boot filename as *pcboot*. A BOOTP request from the host named *mac* results in a reply listing the boot filename as *macboot*.

```
async-bootp bootfile :172.30.1.1 "pcboot"
async-bootp bootfile :mac "macboot"
```

The following example specifies a subnet mask of 255.255.0.0:

```
async-bootp subnet-mask 255.255.0.0
```

The following example specifies a negative time offset of the local subnetwork of -3600 seconds:

```
async-bootp time-offset -3600
```

The following example specifies the IP address of a time server:

```
async-bootp time-server 128.128.1.1
```

Related Commands

show async-bootp

IP RARP-SERVER

Use the **ip rarp-server** interface configuration command to enable the router to act as a Reverse Address Resolution Protocol (RARP) server. Use the **no** form of this command to restore the interface to the default of no RARP server support.

> **ip rarp-server** *ip-address*
> **no ip rarp-server** *ip-address*

Syntax	*Description*
ip-address	IP address that is to be provided in the source protocol address field of the RARP response packet. Normally, this is set to whatever address you configure as the primary address for the interface.

Default

Disabled

Command Mode

Interface configuration

Usage Guidelines

This command first appeared in Cisco IOS Release 10.0.

This feature makes diskless booting of clients possible between network subnets where the client and server are on separate subnets.

RARP server support is configurable on a per interface basis, so that the router does not interfere with RARP traffic on subnets that do not need RARP assistance.

The Cisco IOS software answers incoming RARP requests only if both of the following two conditions are met:

- The **ip rarp-server** command has been configured for the interface on which the request was received.
- There is a static entry found in the IP ARP table that maps the MAC address contained in the RARP request to an IP address.

Use the **show ip arp** EXEC command to display the contents of the IP ARP cache.

Sun Microsystems, Inc. makes use of RARP and UDP-based network services to facilitate network-based booting of SunOS on their workstations. By bridging RARP packets and using both the **ip helper-address** interface configuration command and the **ip forward-protocol** global configuration command, the Cisco IOS software should be able to perform the necessary packet switching to enable booting of Sun workstations across subnets. Unfortunately, some Sun workstations assume that the sender of the RARP response, in this case the router, is the host that the client can contact to TFTP load the bootstrap image. This causes the workstations to fail to boot.

By using the **ip rarp-server** feature, the Cisco IOS software can be configured to answer these RARP requests, and the client machine should be able to reach its server by having its TFTP requests forwarded through the router that acts as the RARP server.

In the case of RARP responses to Sun workstations attempting to diskless boot, the IP address specified in the **ip rarp-server** interface configuration command should be the IP address of the TFTP server. In addition to configuring RARP service, the Cisco IOS software must also be configured to forward UDP-based Sun portmapper requests to completely support diskless booting of Sun workstations. This can be accomplished using configuration commands of the form:

ip forward-protocol udp 111
interface *interface name*
ip helper-address *target-address*

RFC 903 documents the Reverse Address Resolution Protocol.

Examples

The following partial example configures a router to act as a RARP server. The router is configured to use the primary address of the specified interface in its RARP responses.

```
arp 172.30.2.5 0800.2002.ff5b arpa
interface ethernet 0
ip address 172.30.3.100 255.255.255.0
ip rarp-server 172.30.3.100
```

In the following example, a router is configured to act as a RARP server, with TFTP and portmapper requests forwarded to the Sun server:

```
! Allow the router to forward broadcast portmapper requests
ip forward-protocol udp 111
! Provide the router with the IP address of the diskless sun
arp 172.30.2.5 0800.2002.ff5b arpa
interface ethernet 0
! Configure the router to act as a RARP server, using the Sun Server's IP
! address in the RARP response packet.
ip rarp-server 172.30.3.100
! Portmapper broadcasts from this interface are sent to the Sun Server.
ip helper-address 172.30.3.100
```

Related Commands

ip forward-protocol
ip helper-address

IP RCMD DOMAIN-LOOKUP

Use the **ip rcmd domain-lookup** global configuration command to enable Domain Name System (DNS) security for rcp and rsh. To bypass DNS security for rcp and rsh, use the **no** form of this command.

> ip rcmd domain-lookup
> no ip rcmd domain-lookup

Syntax   Description

This command has no arguments or keywords.

Default

Enabled

Command Mode

Global configuration

Usage Guidelines

This command first appeared in Cisco IOS Release 10.3.

If you do not want to use DNS for rcmd queries, but DNS has been enabled with the **ip domain-lookup** command, use the **no ip rcmd domain-lookup** command.

This command will turn off DNS lookups for rsh and rcp only. The **no ip domain-lookup** command takes precedence over the **ip rcmd domain-lookup** command. If **ip domain-lookup** is disabled with the **no ip domain-lookup** command, DNS will be bypassed for rcp and rsh, even if **ip rcmd domain-lookup** is enabled.

NOTES

Cisco IOS Release 10.3 added the **ip** keyword to **rcmd** commands. If you are upgrading from Release 10.2 to Release 10.3 or later, this keyword is automatically added to any **rcmd** commands you have in your Release 10.2 configuration files.

Example

In the following example, DNS security is enabled for rcp and rsh:

```
ip rcmd domain-lookup
```

Related Commands

ip domain-lookup

IP RCMD RCP-ENABLE

To configure the Cisco IOS software to allow remote users to copy files to and from the router, use the **ip rcmd rcp-enable** global configuration command. Use the **no** form of this command to disable a router that is enabled for rcp.

> **ip rcmd rcp-enable**
> **no ip rcmd rcp-enable**

Syntax   Description

This command has no arguments or keywords.

Default

To ensure security, the router is not enabled for rcp by default.

Command Mode

Global configuration

Usage Guidelines

This command first appeared in Cisco IOS Release 10.3.

To allow a remote user to execute **rcp** commands on the router, you must also create an entry for the remote user in the local authentication database.

The **no ip rcmd rcp-enable** command does not prohibit a local user from using rcp to copy system images and configuration files to and from the router.

To protect against unauthorized users copying the system image or configuration files, the router is not enabled for rcp by default.

─── **NOTES** ──────────────────────────────────────

Cisco IOS Release 10.3 added the **ip** keyword to **rcmd** commands. If you are upgrading from Release 10.2 to Release 10.3 or later, this keyword is automatically added to any **rcmd** commands you have in your Release 10.2 configuration files.

───

Example

The following example shows how to enable the router for rcp:

```
rcp-enable
```

Related Commands

ip rcmd remote-host

IP RCMD REMOTE-HOST

To create an entry for the remote user in a local authentication database so that remote users can execute commands on the router using rsh or rcp, use the **ip rcmd remote-host** global configuration command. Use the **no** form of this command to remove an entry for a remote user from the local authentication database.

> **ip rcmd remote-host** *local-username* {*ip-address* | *host*} *remote-username* [enable [*level*]]
> **no ip rcmd remote-host** *local-username* {*ip-address* | *host*} *remote-username* [enable [*level*]]

Syntax	Description
local-username	Name of the user on the local router. You can specify the router host name as the username. This name needs to be communicated to the network administrator or the user on the remote system. To be allowed to execute commands remotely on the router, the remote user must specify this value correctly.
ip-address	IP address of the remote host from which the local router will accept remotely executed commands. Either the IP address or the host name is required.
host	Name of the remote host from which the local router will accept remotely executed commands. Either the host name or the IP address is required.
remote-username	Name of the user on the remote host from which the router will accept remotely executed commands.
enable *level*	(Optional) Enables the remote user to execute privileged EXEC commands using rsh or to copy files to the router using rcp. The range is 1 to 15. The default is 15.

Default

There are no entries in the local authentication database.

Command Mode

Global configuration

Usage Guidelines

This command first appeared in Cisco IOS Release 10.3.

A TCP connection to a router is established using an IP address. Using the host name is valid only when you are initiating an **rcp** or **rsh** command from a local router. The host name is converted to an IP address using DNS or host-name aliasing.

To allow a remote user to execute **rcp** or **rsh** commands on a local router, you must create an entry for the remote user in the local authentication database. You must also enable the router to act as an rsh or rcp server.

To enable the router to act as an rsh server, issue the **ip rcmd rsh-enable** command. To enable the router to act as an rcp server, issue the **ip rcmd rcp-enable** command. The router cannot act as a server for either of these protocols unless you explicitly enable the capacity.

A local authentication database, which is similar to a UNIX *.rhosts* file, is used to enforce security on the router through access control. Each entry that you configure in the authentication database identifies the local user, the remote host, and the remote user. To permit a remote user of rsh to execute commands in privileged EXEC mode or to permit a remote user of rcp to copy files to the router, specify the **enable** keyword and level.

An entry that you configure in the authentication database differs from an entry in a UNIX *.rhost* file in the following aspect. Because the *.rhosts* file on a UNIX system resides in the home directory of a local user account, an entry in a UNIX *.rhosts* file does not need to include the local username; the local username is determined from the user account. To provide equivalent support on a router, specify the local username along with the remote host and remote username in each authentication database entry that you configure.

For a remote user to be able to execute commands on the router in its capacity as a server, the local username, host address or name, and remote username sent with the remote client request must match values configured in an entry in the local authentication file.

A remote client host should be registered with DNS. The Cisco IOS software uses DNS to authenticate the remote host's name and address. Because DNS can return several valid IP addresses for a host name, the Cisco IOS software checks the address of the requesting client against all of the IP addresses for the named host returned by DNS. If the address sent by the requester is considered invalid, that is, it does not match any address listed with DNS for the host name, then the software will reject the remote command execution request.

Note that if no DNS servers are configured for the router, then that device cannot authenticate the host in this manner. In this case, the Cisco IOS software sends a broadcast request to attempt to gain access to DNS services on another server. If DNS services are not available, you must use the **no ip domain-lookup** command to disable the attempt to gain access to a DNS server by sending a broadcast request.

If DNS services are not available and, therefore, you bypass the DNS security check, the software will accept the request to execute a command remotely *only if* all three values sent with the request match exactly the values configured for an entry in the local authentication file.

NOTES

Cisco IOS Release 10.3 added the **ip** keyword to **rcmd** commands. If you are upgrading from Release 10.2 to Release 10.3 or later, this keyword is automatically added to any **rcmd** commands you have in your Release 10.2 configuration files.

Example

The following example allows the remote user *netadmin3* on a remote host with the IP address 172.16.101.101 to execute commands on *router1* using the rsh or rcp protocol. User *netadmin3* is allowed to execute commands in privileged EXEC mode.

```
ip rcmd remote-host router1 172.16.101.101 netadmin3 enable
```

Related Commands

ip rcmd rcp-enable
ip rcmd rsh-enable
no ip domain-lookup

IP RCMD REMOTE-USERNAME

To configure the remote username to be used when requesting a remote copy using rcp, use the **ip rcmd remote-username** global configuration command. To remove from the configuration the remote username, use the **no** form of this command.

    ip rcmd remote-username *username*
    no ip rcmd remote-username *username*

CAUTION

The remote username must be associated with an account on the destination server.

Syntax	*Description*
username	Name of the remote user on the server. This name is used for rcp copy requests. All files and images to be copied are searched for or written relative to the directory of the remote user's account, if the server has a directory structure, for example, as do UNIX systems.

Default

If you do not issue this command, the Cisco IOS software sends the remote username associated with the current TTY process, if that name is valid, for **rcp** copy commands. For example, if the user is connected to the router through Telnet and the user was authenticated through the **username** command, then the software sends that username as the remote username.

If the username for the current TTY process is not valid, the Cisco IOS software sends the host name as the remote username. For **rcp** boot commands, the Cisco IOS software sends the access server host name by default.

NOTES

For Cisco, TTY lines are commonly used for access services. The concept of TTYs originated with UNIX. For UNIX systems, each physical device is represented in the file system. Terminals are called TTY devices (which stands for teletype, the original UNIX terminal).

Command Mode

Global configuration

Usage Guidelines

This command first appeared in Cisco IOS Release 10.3.

The rcp protocol requires that a client send the remote username on an rcp request to the server. Use this command to specify the remote username to be sent to the server for an rcp copy request. If the server has a directory structure, as do UNIX systems, all files and images to be copied are searched for or written relative to the directory of the remote user's account.

NOTES

Cisco IOS Release 10.3 added the **ip** keyword to **rcmd** commands. If you are upgrading from Release 10.2 to Release 10.3 or later, this keyword is automatically added to any **rcmd** commands you have in your Release 10.2 configuration files.

Example

The following example configures the remote username to *netadmin1*:

```
ip rcmd remote-username netadmin1
```

Related Commands

boot network rcp
boot system rcp
copy
copy flash rcp
copy verify bootflash
copy verify flash
copy verify running-config
copy verify startup-config
copy running-config rcp
copy startup-config rcp

IP RCMD RSH-ENABLE

To configure the router to allow remote users to execute commands on it using rsh, use the **ip rcmd rsh-enable** global configuration command. Use the **no** form of this command to disable a router that is enabled for rsh.

    ip rcmd rsh-enable
    no ip rcmd rsh-enable

Syntax   Description

This command has no arguments or keywords.

**Part
II**

Command Reference

Default

To ensure security, the router is not enabled for rsh by default.

Command Mode

Global configuration

Usage Guidelines

This command first appeared in Cisco IOS Release 10.3.

Use this command to enable the router to receive rsh requests from remote users. In addition to issuing this command, you must create an entry for the remote user in the local authentication database to allow a remote user to execute **rsh** commands on the router.

The **no ip rcmd rsh-enable** command does not prohibit a local user of the router from executing a command on other routers and UNIX hosts on the network using rsh. It disables a router that is enabled for rsh.

NOTES

Cisco IOS Release 10.3 added the **ip** keyword to **rcmd** commands. If you are upgrading from Release 10.2 to Release 10.3 or later, this keyword is automatically added to any **rcmd** commands you have in your Release 10.2 configuration files.

Example

The following example shows how to enable a router as an rsh server:

```
ip rcmd rsh-enable
```

Related Commands

ip rcmd remote-host

MOP DEVICE-CODE

To identify the type of device sending MOP sysid messages and request program messages, use the **mop device-code** global configuration command. Use the **no** form of this command to set the identity to the default value.

    mop device-code {cisco | ds200}
    no mop device-code {cisco | ds200}

Syntax	Description
cisco	Denotes a Cisco device code.
ds200	Denotes a DECserver 200 device code.

Default

Cisco device code

Command Mode

Global configuration

Usage Guidelines

This command first appeared in Cisco IOS Release 10.0.

The sysid messages and request program messages use the identity information indicated by this command.

Example

The following example identifies a DECserver 200 device as sending MOP sysid and request program messages:

```
mop device-code ds200
```

Related Commands

mop sysid

MOP RETRANSMIT-TIMER

To configure the length of time that the Cisco IOS software waits before retransmitting boot requests to a MOP server, use the **mop retransmit-timer** global configuration command. Use the **no** form of this command to reinstate the default value.

> **mop retransmit-timer** *seconds*
> **no mop retransmit-timer**

Syntax	Description
seconds	Sets the length of time, in seconds, that the software waits before retransmitting a message. The value is a number from 1 to 20.

Default

four seconds

Command Mode

Global configuration

Usage Guidelines

This command first appeared in Cisco IOS Release 10.0.

By default, when the software transmits a request that requires a response from a MOP boot server and the server does not respond, the message is retransmitted after four seconds. If the MOP boot server and router are separated by a slow serial link, it might take longer than four seconds for the software to receive a response to its message. Therefore, you might want to configure the software to wait longer than four seconds before retransmitting the message if you are using such a link.

Example

In the following example, if the MOP boot server does not respond within 10 seconds after the router sends a message, the server will retransmit the message:

```
mop retransmit-timer 10
```

Related Commands

mop device-code
mop retries
mop enabled

MOP RETRIES

To configure the number of times the Cisco IOS software will retransmit boot requests to a MOP server, use the **mop retries** global configuration command. Use the **no** form of this command to reinstate the default value.

> **mop retries** *count*
> **no mop retries**

Syntax	Description
count	Indicates the number of times the software will retransmit a MOP boot request. The value is a number from 3 to 24.

Default

8 times

Command Mode

Global configuration

Usage Guidelines

This command first appeared in Cisco IOS Release 10.0.

Example

In the following example, the software will attempt to retransmit a message to an unresponsive host 11 times before declaring a failure:

```
mop retries 11
```

Related Commands

mop device-code
mop retransmit-timer
mop enabled

RSH

To execute a command remotely on a remote rsh host, use the **rsh** privileged EXEC command.

rsh {*ip-address* | *host*} [**/user** *username*] *remote-command*

Syntax	Description
ip-address	IP address of the remote host on which to execute the **rsh** command. Either the IP address or the host name is required.
host	Name of the remote host on which to execute the command. Either the host name or the IP address is required.
/user *username*	(Optional) Remote username.
remote-command	Command to be executed remotely. This is a required parameter.

Default

If you do not specify the **/user** keyword and argument, the Cisco IOS software sends a default remote username. As the default value of the remote username, the software sends the username associated with the current TTY process if that name is valid. For example, if the user is connected to the router through Telnet and the user was authenticated through the **username** command, then the software sends that username as the remote username. If the TTY username is invalid, the software uses the host name as the both the remote and local usernames.

NOTES

For Cisco, TTY lines are commonly used for access services. The concept of TTY originated with UNIX. For UNIX systems, each physical device is represented in the file system. Terminals are called *TTY devices*, which stands for *teletype*, the original UNIX terminal.

Command Mode

Privileged EXEC

Usage Guidelines

This command first appeared in Cisco IOS Release 10.0.

Use the **rsh** command to execute commands remotely. The host on which you remotely execute the command must support the rsh protocol, and the *.rhosts* files on the rsh host must include an entry that permits you to execute commands remotely on that host.

For security reasons, the software does not default to a remote login if no command is specified, as does UNIX. Instead, the router provides Telnet and connect services that you can use rather than rsh.

Example

The following command specifies that user *sharon* attempts to execute the UNIX **ls** command remotely with the *-a* argument on the remote host *mysys.cisco.com*. The command output resulting from the remote execution follows the command example:

```
Router1# rsh mysys.cisco.com /user sharon ls -a
.
..
.alias
.cshrc
.emacs
.exrc
.history
.login
.mailrc
.newsrc
.oldnewsrc
.rhosts
.twmrc
.xsession
jazz
```

SHOW ASYNC-BOOTP

To display the extended BOOTP request parameters that have been configured for asynchronous interfaces, use the **show async-bootp** privileged EXEC command.

> **show async-bootp**

Syntax   Description

This command has no arguments or keywords.

Command Mode

Privileged EXEC

Usage Guidelines

This command first appeared in Cisco IOS Release 10.0.

Sample Display

The following is a sample output of the **show async-bootp** command:

```
Router# show async-bootp

The following extended data will be sent in BOOTP responses:

bootfile (for address 192.168.1.1) "pcboot"
bootfile (for address 172.16.1.111) "dirtboot"
subnet-mask 255.255.0.0
time-offset -3600
time-server 192.168.1.1
```

Table 18–3 describes significant fields shown in the display.

Table 18–3   *Show Async-BOOTP Field Descriptions*

Field	Description
bootfile... "pcboot"	Boot file for address 192.168.1.1 is named pcboot.
subnet-mask 255.255.0.0	Subnet mask.
time-offset -3600	Local time is one hour (3600 seconds) earlier than UTC time.
time-server 192.168.1.1	Address of the time server for the network.

Related Commands

async-bootp

TFTP-SERVER

To configure a router or a Flash memory device on the router as a TFTP server, use one of the following **tftp-server** global configuration commands. This command replaces the **tftp-server system** command. To remove a previously defined filename, use the **no tftp-server** command with the appropriate filename.

tftp-server flash [*partition-number*:]*filename1* [alias *filename2*] [*access-list-number*] (all others)

tftp-server rom alias *filename1* [*access-list-number*] (all others)

no tftp-server {flash [*partition-number*:]*filename1* | rom alias *filename2*} (all others)

tftp-server flash [*device*:][*partition-number*:]*filename* (Cisco 1600 series and Cisco 3600 series)

no tftp-server flash [*device*:][*partition-number*:]*filename* (Cisco 1600 series and Cisco 3600 series)

tftp-server flash *device:filename* (Cisco 7000 family)
no tftp-server flash *device:filename*

Syntax	Description
flash	Specifies TFTP service of a file in Flash memory.
rom	Specifies TFTP service of a file in ROM.
filename1	Name of a file in Flash or in ROM that the TFTP server uses in answering TFTP Read Requests.
alias	Specifies an alternate name for the file that the TFTP server uses in answering TFTP Read Requests.
filename2	Alternate name of the file that the TFTP server uses in answering TFTP Read Requests. A client of the TFTP server can use this alternate name in its Read Requests.
access-list-number	(Optional) Basic IP access-list number. Valid values are 0 to 99.
partition-number:	(Optional) Specifies TFTP service of a file in the specified partition of Flash memory. If the partition number is not specified, the file in the first partition is used.
	For the Cisco 1600 series and Cisco 3600 series, you must enter a colon (:) after the partition number if a filename follows it.
device:	Specifies TFTP service of a file on a Flash memory device in the Cisco 1600 series, Cisco 3600 series and Cisco 7000 family. The colon (:) is required. Valid devices are as follows:
	• **flash**—Internal Flash memory on the Cisco 1600 series and Cisco 3600 series. This is the only valid device for the Cisco 1600.
	• **bootflash**—Internal Flash memory in the Cisco 7000 family.
	• **slot0**—First PCMCIA slot on the Cisco 3600 series and Cisco 7000 family.
	• **slot1**—Second PCMCIA slot on the Cisco 3600 series and Cisco 7000 family.
	• **slavebootflash**—Internal Flash memory on the slave RSP card of a Cisco 7507 or Cisco 7513 configured for HSA.
	• **slaveslot0**—First PCMCIA slot of the slave RSP card on a Cisco 7507 or Cisco 7513 configured for HSA.
	• **slaveslot1**—Second PCMCIA slot of the slave RSP card on a Cisco 7507 or Cisco 7513 configured for HSA.

Syntax	Description
filename	Name of the file on a Flash memory device that the TFTP server uses in answering a TFTP Read Request. Use this argument only with the Cisco 1600 series, Cisco 3600 series, Cisco 7000 series or Cisco 7500 series.

Default

Disabled

Command Mode

Global configuration

Usage Guidelines

This command first appeared in Cisco IOS Release 11.0.

You can specify multiple filenames by repeating the **tftp-server** command. The system sends a copy of the system image contained in ROM or one of the system images contained in Flash memory to any client that issues a TFTP Read Request with this filename.

If the specified *filename1* or *filename2* exists in Flash memory, a copy of the Flash image is sent. On systems that contain a complete image in ROM, the system sends the ROM image if the specified *filename1* or *filename2* is not found in Flash memory.

Images that run from ROM cannot be loaded over the network. Therefore, it does not make sense to use TFTP to offer the ROMs on these images.

On the Cisco 7000 family, the system sends a copy of the file contained on one of the Flash memory devices to any client that issues a TFTP Read Request with its filename.

Examples

In the following example, the system uses TFTP to send a copy of the *version-10.3* file located in Flash memory in response to a TFTP Read Request for that file. The requesting host is checked against access list 22.

```
tftp-server flash version-10.3 22
```

In the following example, the system uses TFTP to send a copy of the ROM image *gs3-k.101* in response to a TFTP Read Request for the *gs3-k.101* file:

```
tftp-server rom alias gs3-k.101
```

In the following example, the system uses TFTP to send a copy of the *version-11.0* file in response to a TFTP Read Request for that file. The file is located on the Flash memory card inserted in slot 0.

```
tftp-server flash slot0:version-11.0
```

The following example enables a Cisco 3600 series router to operate as a TFTP server. The source file c3640-i-mz is in the second partition of internal Flash memory:

```
Router# configure terminal
Enter configuration commands, one per line.  End with CNTL/Z.
router(config)# tftp-server flash flash:2:dirt/gate/c3640-i-mz
```

In the next example, the source file is in the second partition of the Flash memory PC card in slot 0 on a Cisco 3600 series:

```
Router# configure terminal
Enter configuration commands, one per line.  End with CNTL/Z.
router(config)# tftp-server flash slot0:2:dirt/gate/c3640-j-mz
```

The following example enables a Cisco 1600 series router to operate as a TFTP server. The source file c1600-i-mz is in the second partition of Flash memory:

```
router# configure terminal
Enter configuration commands, one per line.  End with CNTL/Z.
router(config)# tftp-server flash flash:2:dirt/gate/c1600-i-mz
```

Related Commands

access-list

PART III

Interface Configuration

## CHAPTER 19

Overview of Interface Configuration

Use the information in this chapter to understand the types of interfaces supported on Cisco routers and access servers and to locate configuration information for various types of interfaces.

For a complete description of the interface commands used in this and other chapters that describe interface configuration, see Chapter 23, "Interface Commands."

This chapter contains general information that applies to all interface types; it includes these sections:

- Interface Types Supported on Cisco Routers
- Understanding Interface Configuration
- Understanding Subinterfaces
- Configuring Features Available on any Interface
- Understanding Online Insertion and Removal (OIR)
- Understanding Fast Switching Support
- Monitoring and Maintaining the Interface

For examples of configuration tasks discussed in this chapter, see "Interface Configuration Examples" at the end of this chapter.

NOTES

In Cisco IOS Release 11.3, all commands supported on the Cisco 7500 series are also supported on the Cisco 7000 series.

INTERFACE TYPES SUPPORTED ON CISCO ROUTERS

Two types of interfaces are supported: physical and virtual interfaces. The types of physical interfaces on a device depend on its interface processors or port adapters. The virtual interfaces that Cisco routers and access servers support include subinterfaces and IP tunnels.

Cisco routers and access servers support the following types of interfaces:

- Asynchronous serial
- Asynchronous Transfer Mode (ATM)
- Channelized E1
- Channelized T1
- Dialer
- Ethernet
- Fast Ethernet
- Fiber Distributed Data Interface (FDDI)
- Fractional T1/T1
- High-Speed Serial Interface (HSSI)
- ISDN Basic Rate Interface (BRI)
- ISDN Multiple Basic Rate Interface (MBRI)
- ISDN Primary Rate Interface (PRI)
- LAN Extender
- Loopback
- Low-Speed Serial
- Null
- Packet OC-3
- Synchronous serial
- Token Ring
- Tunnel

Also, the Cisco IOS software supports subinterfaces.

For hardware technical descriptions and information about installing interfaces, refer to the hardware installation and maintenance publication for your product. For command descriptions and usage information, see Chapter 23, "Interface Commands."

UNDERSTANDING INTERFACE CONFIGURATION

These general instructions apply to all interface configuration processes. Begin interface configuration in global configuration mode. To configure an interface, follow these steps:

Step 1   Enter the **configure** EXEC command at the privileged EXEC prompt to enter global configuration mode.

Step 2   Once in the global configuration mode, start configuring the interface by entering the **interface** command. Identify the interface type followed by the number of the connector or interface card. These numbers are assigned at the factory at the time of installation or when cards are added to a system and can be displayed with the **show interfaces** EXEC command. A report is provided for each interface that the device supports, as seen in the following partial sample display:

```
Router# show interfaces
Serial 0 is administratively down, line protocol is down
Hardware is MCI Serial
MTU 1500 bytes, BW 1544 Kbit, DLY 20000 usec, rely 255/255, load 1/255
Encapsulation HDLC, loopback not set, keepalive set (10 sec)
```

Use the **show hardware** EXEC command to see a list of the system software and hardware.

To begin configuring serial interface 0, you add the following line to the configuration file:

```
interface serial 0
```

NOTES

It is not necessary to add a space between the interface type and interface number. For example, in the preceding line, you can specify either *serial 0* or *serial0*. The command works either way.

Step 3   Follow each **interface** command with the interface configuration commands your particular interface requires. The commands you enter define the protocols and applications that will run on the interface. The commands are collected and applied to the **interface** command until you enter another **interface** command, a command that is not an interface configuration command, or until you type the Ctrl-Z sequence to get out of configuration mode and return to privileged EXEC mode.

Step 4   Once an interface is configured, you can check its status by entering the EXEC **show** commands described after the task tables that follow.

NOTES

Configuring channelized T1 and E1 interfaces requires additional steps. When you configure channelized T1 or channelized E1, you must first define the channels and the time slots that comprise the channels by using the **controller t1** and the **channel-group** controller configuration commands. Then configure the virtual serial interfaces using the **interface serial** global configuration commands.

UNDERSTANDING SUBINTERFACES

Configuring multiple virtual interfaces, or subinterfaces, on a single physical interface allows greater flexibility and connectivity on the network. A subinterface is a mechanism that allows a single physical interface to support multiple logical interfaces or networks. That is, several logical interfaces or networks can be associated with a single hardware interface. Subinterfaces are implemented in various WAN and LAN protocols, including ATM, Frame Relay, SMDS, X.25, and Novell IPX. For more information about using subinterfaces, refer to the appropriate protocol chapter.

NOTES

The Cisco IOS software can support a maximum of 300 interfaces and subinterfaces.

CONFIGURING FEATURES AVAILABLE ON ANY INTERFACE

The following sections describe optional tasks that you can perform on any type of interface:

- Adding a Description for an Interface
- Configuring MOP
- Controlling Interface Hold-Queue Limits
- Setting Bandwidth
- Setting Interface Delay
- Adjusting Timers
- Limiting Transmit Queue Size
- Adjusting Maximum Packet Size or MTU Size

Adding a Description for an Interface

You can add a description about an interface to help you remember what is attached to it. This description is meant solely as a comment to help identify what the interface is being used for. The description will appear in the output of the following commands: **show configuration, show running-config,** and **show interfaces.** When you add a description for a T1 controller interface, it will appear in the output of the **show controllers t1** and **show running-config** commands.

To add a description for any interface but a T1 or E1 controller interface, perform the following task in interface configuration mode. To add a description for a T1 or E1 controller in a Cisco 4500 series, Cisco 7200 series, or Cisco 7500 series routers, perform the following task in controller configuration mode:

Task	Command
Add a description for an interface.	**description** *string*

For examples of adding interface descriptions, see the section "Interface Description Examples" at the end of this chapter.

Configuring MOP

You can enable MOP on an interface by performing the following task in interface configuration mode:

Task	Command
Enable MOP.	**mop enabled**

You can enable an interface to send out periodic MOP system identification messages on an interface by performing the following task in interface configuration mode:

Task	Command
Enable MOP message support.	**mop sysid**

Controlling Interface Hold-Queue Limits

Each interface has a hold-queue limit. This limit is the number of data packets that the interface can store in its hold queue before rejecting new packets. When the interface empties one or more packets from the hold queue, it can accept new packets again. You can specify the hold-queue limit of an interface in interface configuration mode as follows:

Task	Command
Specify the maximum number of packets allowed in the hold queue.	**hold-queue** *length* {**in** | **out**}

Setting Bandwidth

Higher-level protocols use bandwidth information to make operating decisions. For example, IGRP uses the minimum path bandwidth to determine a routing metric. TCP adjusts initial retransmission parameters based on the apparent bandwidth of the outgoing interface. Perform the following task in interface configuration mode to set a bandwidth value for an interface:

Task	Command
Set a bandwidth value.	**bandwidth** *kilobits*

The bandwidth setting is a routing parameter only; it does not affect the physical interface.

Setting Interface Delay

Higher-level protocols might use delay information to make operating decisions. For example, IGRP can use delay information to differentiate between a satellite link and a land link. To set a delay value for an interface, perform the following task in interface configuration mode:

Task	Command
Set a delay value for an interface.	delay *tens-of-microseconds*

Setting the delay value sets an informational parameter only; you cannot adjust the actual delay of an interface with this configuration command.

Adjusting Timers

To adjust the frequency of update messages, perform the following task in interface configuration mode:

Task	Command
Adjust the frequency with which the Cisco IOS software sends messages to itself (Ethernet and Token Ring) or to the other end (HDLC-serial and PPP-serial links) to ensure that a network interface is alive for a specified interface.	keepalive [*seconds*]

You also can configure the *keepalive* interval, the frequency at which the Cisco IOS software sends messages to itself (Ethernet and Token Ring) or to the other end (HDLC-serial, PPP-serial) to ensure that a network interface is alive. The interval in some previous software versions was 10 seconds; it is now adjustable in one-second increments down to one second. An interface is declared down after three update intervals have passed without receiving a keepalive packet.

When adjusting the keepalive timer for a very low bandwidth serial interface, large packets can delay the smaller keepalive packets long enough to cause the line protocol to go down. You might need to experiment to determine the best value.

Limiting Transmit Queue Size

You can control the size of the transmit queue available to a specified interface on the MCI and SCI cards. To limit the size, perform the following task in interface configuration mode:

Task	Command
Limit the size of the transmit queue.	tx-queue-limit *number*

Adjusting Maximum Packet Size or MTU Size

Each interface has a default maximum packet size or maximum transmission unit (MTU) size. This number generally defaults to 1,500 bytes. On serial interfaces, the MTU size varies, but cannot be set smaller than 64 bytes. To adjust the maximum packet size, perform the following task in interface configuration mode:

Task	Command
Adjust the maximum packet size or MTU size.	**mtu** *bytes*

UNDERSTANDING ONLINE INSERTION AND REMOVAL (OIR)

The online insertion and removal (OIR) feature—supported on the Cisco 7200 series and the Cisco 7500 series routers only—allows you to remove and replace interface processors while the system is online. You can shut down the interface processor before removal and restart it after insertion without causing other software or interfaces to shut down.

NOTES

Do not remove or install more that one interface processor at one time. After a removal or installation, observe the LEDs before continuing.

You do not need to notify the software that you are going to remove or install an interface processor. When the route processor is notified by the system that an interface processor has been removed or installed, it stops routing and scans the system for a configuration change. All interface processors are initialized, and each interface type is verified against the system configuration; then the system runs diagnostics on the new interface. There is no disruption to normal operation during interface processor insertion or removal.

Only an interface of a type that has been configured previously will be brought on line; others require configuration. If a newly installed interface processor does not match the system configuration, the interface is left in an administratively down state until the system operator configures the system with the new interfaces.

Hardware (MAC-level) addresses for all interfaces on the Cisco 7500 routers are stored on an electronically erasable programmable read-only memory (EEPROM) component in the Route Processor (RP) instead of on the individual interface boards. On the Cisco 7500, an address allocator in the EEPROM contains a sequential block of 40 addresses (5 interface slots times a maximum of 8 possible ports per slot; each address is assigned to a specific slot and port address in the chassis, regardless of how the interfaces are configured. On the Cisco 7200 series, hardware addresses are stored in a midplane EEPROM that supports 1,024 addresses per box.

Storage of hardware addresses in EEPROM allows interfaces to be replaced online without requiring the system to update switching tables and data structures. Regardless of the types of interfaces installed, the hardware addresses do not change unless you replace the system RP. If you do replace the RP, the hardware addresses of *all* ports change to those specified in the address allocator on the new RP.

UNDERSTANDING FAST SWITCHING SUPPORT

Switching is the process by which packets are forwarded. The Cisco IOS software supports multiple methods of switching. Cisco routers fast switch Layer 2 Forwarding (L2F) traffic. In stack group environments in which some L2F traffic is offloaded to a powerful router, fast switching provides improved scalability.

MONITORING AND MAINTAINING THE INTERFACE

You can perform the tasks in the following sections to monitor and maintain the interfaces:

- Monitoring Interface and Controller Status
- Monitoring the T1 or E1 Controller
- Monitoring and Maintaining CSU/DSU Service Modules
- Monitoring the LAN Extender Interface
- Monitoring and Maintaining a Hub
- Monitoring IP Tunnels
- Clearing and Resetting the Interface
- Shutting Down and Restarting the Interface
- Configuring Loopback Detection
- Running Interface Loopback Diagnostics
- Enabling Loopback Testing of Fractional T1/T1

Monitoring Interface and Controller Status

The software contains commands that you can enter at the EXEC prompt to display information about the interface, including the version of the software and the hardware, the controller status, and statistics about the interfaces. The following table lists some of the interface monitoring tasks.

(You can display the full list of **show** commands by entering the **show ?** command at the EXEC prompt.)

Perform the following commands in EXEC mode:

Task		Command
Step 1	Display the status of the asynchronous interface.	**show async status** **show interfaces async**
Step 2	Display compression statistics on a serial interface.	**show compress**
Step 3	Display current internal status information for the interface controller cards.	**show controllers** [{bri | cbus | fddi | lance | mci | serial | token}]
Step 4	Display information about the Switch Processor (SP) controller on the Cisco 7500 series.	**show controllers cbus**
Step 5	Display current internal status information for the interface controller cards.	**show controllers** [{e1 | ethernet | fastethernet | fddi | serial | t1 | token}]
Step 6	Display current internal status information for the interface controller cards on the Cisco 7200 and Cisco 7500 series routers.	**show controllers** {ethernet | fastethernet | fddi | serial | token}
Step 7	Display diagnostic information about the controller, interface processor, and port adapters associated with a specified slot of a Cisco 7200 series, or Cisco 7500 series router.	**show diagbus** [*slot*]
Step 8	If accounting is configured, display the number of packets of each protocol type that has been sent through the interface.	**show interfaces** [*type number*] [*first*] [*last*] [**accounting**]
	For Cisco 7500 series with a Packet over SONET Interface Processor.	**show interfaces** [*type slot/port*] [**accounting**]
	For the Cisco 7500 series with VIP or VIP2 cards.	**show interfaces** [*type slot/port-adapter/port*] [**accounting**]

Task	Command
Step 9 Display information about the Cisco 7500 with a Packet over SONET Interface Processor.	**show interfaces posi** [*slot/port*]
Step 10 Display the number of packets of each protocol type that has been sent through the asynchronous serial line.	**show interfaces async** [*number*] [**accounting**]
Step 11 Display the currently running configuration in RAM.	**show running-config**
Step 12 Display the current contents of the routing information field (RIF) cache.	**show rif**
Step 13 Display the global (system-wide) and interface-specific status of any configured Level 3 protocol.	**show protocols**
Step 14 Display the hardware configuration, software version, the names and sources of configuration files, and the boot images.	**show version**

Monitoring the T1 or E1 Controller

This section applies to channelized T1 or E1 interfaces. Because the T1 or E1 link itself is viewed as the controller, perform the following tasks in EXEC mode to display information about activity on the T1 or E1 line.

Task	Command
Step 1 Display information about the T1 link.	**show controller t1**
Step 2 Display information about the E1 link.	**show controller e1**

Alarms, line conditions, and other errors are displayed. The data is updated every 10 seconds. Every 15 minutes, the cumulative data is stored and retained for 24 hours. This means at any one time, up to 96, 15-minute accumulations are counted in the data display.

Monitoring and Maintaining CSU/DSU Service Modules

This section describes how to monitor and maintain service modules. Tasks involved to monitor and maintain service modules are described in these sections:

- Performing a Self-Test
- Displaying a Performance Report
- Performing Loopback Tests
- Resetting the CSU/DSU

Performing a Self Test

To perform a self test on the integrated CSU/DSU, perform the following task in privileged EXEC mode:

Task	Command
Perform a self test. Specify the interface type and number.	**test service-module** *interface*

This command cannot be used if a DTE, line, or remote loopback is in progress. A series of tests, including a ROM checksum test, RAM test, EEPROM checksum test, Flash checksum test, and a DTE loopback with an internal pattern test, are performed on the CSU/DSU. This self test is also performed at power on.

Data transmission is interrupted for five seconds when you issue this command. To view the output of the most recent self test, enable the **show service-module** command.

Displaying a Performance Report

To display the performance report for an integrated CSU/DSU, perform one of the following tasks in privileged EXEC mode:

Task	Command
Display a performance report. Choose either serial interface 1 or 0.	**show service-module** *interface*
Display the CSU/DSU performance statistics for the past 24 hours. This command applies only to the FT1/T1 module.	**show service-module** *interface* **performance-statistics** [*interval-range*]

The *interval-range* value specifies the number of 15-minute intervals displayed in the report. You can choose a range from 1 to 96, where each value represents the CSU/DSU activity performed in that 15-minute interval. For example, a range of 2-3 displays the performance statistics for the intervals two and three.

Performing Loopback Tests

You can loop packets back to the network from the integrated CSU/DSU and loop packets through a local CSU/DSU to a remote CSU/DSU.

Performing Loopback Line Test

To loop data received from the line at the integrated CSU/DSU and loop packets back to the line, perform the following tasks in interface configuration mode:

Task	Command
Step 1 Perform loopback at a point close to the network to CSU/DSU interface.	**loopback line**
Step 2 Perform loopback at a point close to the interface between the CSU/DSU and the router.	**loopback line payload**

Packets are looped from an incoming network transmission back into the network at a CSU or DSU loopback point.

When the **loopback line** command is configured on the 2-wire 56-kbps CSU/DSU module or the 4-wire 56/64-kbps CSU/DSU modules installed on a Cisco 2524 or Cisco 2525 router, the network data loops back at the CSU and the router data loops back at the DSU. If the CSU/DSU is configured for switched mode, you must have an established connection to perform a payload-line loopback. When the **loopback line payload** command is configured, the CSU/DSU module loops the data through the DSU portion of the module. Data is not looped back to the serial interface.

If you enable the **loopback line** command on the fractional T1/T1 module, the CSU/DSU performs a full-bandwidth loopback through the CSU portion of the module and data transmission through the serial interface is interrupted for the duration of the loopback. No reframing or corrections of bipolar violation errors or cyclic redundancy check (CRC) errors are performed. When you configure the **line loopback payload** command on the FT1/T1 module, the CSU/DSU performs a loopback through the DSU portion of the module. The **line loopback payload** command reframes the data link, regenerates the signal, and corrects bipolar violations and Extended Super Frame CRC errors.

When performing a T1-line loopback with Extended Super Framing, communication over the facilities data link is interrupted but performance statistics are still updated. To show interfaces currently in loopback operation, use the **show service-module** EXEC command.

Performing Loopback DTE

To loop packets back to DTE from within the local CSU/DSU, perform the following task:

Task	Command
Loop packets to DTE.	**loopback dte**

Packets are looped from within the CSU/DSU back to the serial interface of the router. Send a test ping to see if the packets successfully looped back. To cancel the loopback test, use the **no loopback dte** command.

When using the 4-wire 56/64-kbps CSU/DSU module, an out-of-service signal is transmitted to the remote CSU/DSU.

Performing a Remote Loopback Test Using the FT1/T1 CSU/DSU Module

This command applies only when the remote CSU/DSU device is configured for this function. It is used for testing the data communication channels along with or without remote CSU/DSU circuitry. The loopback is usually performed at the line port, rather than the DTE port, of the remote CSU/DSU.

On the integrated FT1/T1 CSU/DSU module installed on a Cisco 2524 and Cisco 2525 router, the **loopback remote full** command sends the loopup code to the remote CSU/DSU. The remote CSU/DSU should perform a full-bandwidth loopback through the CSU portion of the module. The **loopback remote payload** command sends the loopup code on the configured timeslots, while maintaining the D4-Extended Super Framing. The remote CSU/DSU performs the equivalent of a loopback line payload request. The remote CSU/DSU loops back only those timeslots that are configured on the remote end. This loopback reframes the data link, regenerates the signal, and corrects bipolar violations and Extended Super Frame CRC errors. The **loopback remote smart-jack** command sends a loopup code to the remote smart jack. You cannot put the local smart jack into loopback.

To loop packets on the integrated FT1/T1 CSU/DSU module, perform the following task:

Task	Command
Loop packets at a remote CSU/DSU using the fractional T1/T1 CSU/DSU module.	**loopback remote {full	payload	smart-jack} [0in1	1in1	1in2	1in5	1in8	3in24	qrw	user-pattern** 24bit-binary value]

Failure to loop up or initiate a remote loopback request could be caused by enabling the **no service-module t1 remote-loopback** command or having an alternate remote-loopback code configured on the remote end. When the loopback is terminated, the result of the pattern test is displayed.

NOTES

If the FT1/T1 CSU/DSU module is configured to provide internal clocking, the module ceases to generate clocking when it is placed into loopback.

Two- and Four-Wire 56/64-kbps CSU/DSU Modules

This command applies only when the remote CSU/DSU device is configured for this function. It is used for testing the data communication channels along with or without remote CSU/DSU circuitry. The loopback is usually performed at the line port, rather than the DTE port, of the remote CSU/DSU.

On the 2- and 4-wire 56/64-kbps CSU/DSU modules, an active connection is required before a loopup can be initiated while in switched mode. When transmitting V.54 loopbacks, the remote device is commanded into loopback using V.54 messages. Failure to loop up or initiate a remote loopback request could be caused by enabling the **no service-module 56k remote-loopback** command.

To loop packets at the remote CSU/DSU, perform the following task:

Task	Command
Loop packets at a remote CSU/DSU using the 2- and 4-wire 56/64-kbps CSU/DSU modules.	**loopback remote [2047 | 511 | stress-pattern** *pattern number*]

To show interfaces currently in loopback operation, use the **show interfaces loopback** EXEC command.

Resetting the CSU/DSU

To reset the CSU/DSU, perform the following task in privileged EXEC mode:

Task	Command
Reset the CSU/DSU. Specify the interface type and number.	**clear service-module** *interface*

Use this command only in severe circumstances (for example, when the router is not responding to a CSU/DSU configuration command).

This command terminates all DTE and line loopbacks that are locally or remotely configured. It also interrupts data transmission through the router for up to 15 seconds. The software performs an automatic software reset in case of two consecutive configuration failures.

The CSU/DSU module is not reset with the **clear interface** command.

CAUTION

If you experience technical difficulties with your router and intend to contact customer support, refrain from using this command. The command erases the router's past CSU/DSU performance statistics. To clear only the CSU/DSU performance statistics, issue the **clear counters** command.

Monitoring the LAN Extender Interface

To monitor the LAN Extender interface, the Ethernet interface that resides on the LAN Extender, the serial interface that resides on the LAN Extender, or the serial interface connected to the LAN Extender, perform one or more of the following tasks at the EXEC prompt:

Task	Command
Display hardware and software information about the LAN Extender.	**show controllers lex** [*number*]
Display information on the Cisco 7500 series.	**show controllers lex** [*slot/port*]
Display statistics about the LAN Extender interface.	**show interfaces lex** *number* [**ethernet** | **serial**]
Display statistics about the serial interface on the host router that is physically connected to the LAN Extender.	**show interfaces serial** *number* [**accounting**]
Display statistics on the Cisco 7500 series.	**show interfaces serial** *slot/port* [**accounting**]

Monitoring and Maintaining a Hub

You can perform the tasks in the following sections to monitor and maintain the hub:

- Shutting Down the Hub Port
- Resetting the Hub or Clearing the Hub Counters
- Monitoring the Hub

Shutting Down the Hub Port

To shut down or disable a hub port, perform the following tasks, beginning in global configuration mode:

Task	Command
Step 1 Specify the hub number and the hub port (or range of hub ports) and place you in hub configuration mode.	**hub ethernet** *number port* [*end-port*]
Step 2 Shut down the hub port.	**shutdown**

See the examples of shutting down a hub port at the end of Chapter 20, "Configuring LAN Interfaces" in the section "Hub Configuration Examples."

Resetting the Hub or Clearing the Hub Counters

To reset the hub or clear the hub counters, perform one of the following tasks in EXEC mode:

Task	Command
Reset and reinitialize the hub hardware.	**clear hub ethernet** *number*
Clear the hub counters displayed by the **show hub** command.	**clear hub counters** [**ethernet** *number* [*port* [*end-port*]]]

Monitoring the Hub

To display hub information, perform the following task in EXEC mode:

Task	Command
Display hub statistics.	**show hub** [**ethernet** *number* [*port* [*end-port*]]]

Monitoring Tunnels

Complete any of the following tasks in EXEC mode to monitor the IP tunnels you have configured:

Task	Command
List tunnel interface information.	**show interfaces tunnel** *unit* [**accounting**]
List the routes that go through the tunnel.	**show** *protocol* **route**

Task	Command
List the route to the tunnel destination.	show ip route

Clearing and Resetting the Interface

To clear the interface counters shown with the **show interfaces** command, enter the following command at the EXEC prompt:

Task	Command
Step 1 Clear the interface counters.	**clear counters** [*type number*] [**ethernet** | **serial**]
Step 2 Clear interface counters for the FastEthernet NIM on the Cisco 4000 series or Cisco 4500 series.	**clear counters fastethernet** *number*
Step 3 Clear interface counters for the Cisco 7200 series.	**clear counters** [*type slot/port*]
Step 4 Clear interface counters for the Cisco 7500 series with VIP or VIP2 Interface Processors.	**clear counters** [*type slot/port-adaptor*]

The command clears all the current interface counters from the interface unless the optional arguments are specified to clear only a specific interface type from a specific slot and port number.

― **NOTES** ―――――――――――――――――――――――――――――

This command will not clear counters retrieved using SNMP, but only those seen with the EXEC **show interfaces** command.

Complete the following tasks in EXEC mode to clear and reset interfaces. Under normal circumstances, you do not need to clear the hardware logic on interfaces.

Task	Command
Step 1 Reset the hardware logic on an interface.	**clear interface** *type number*
Step 2 Reset the hardware logic on an asynchronous serial line.	**clear line** [*number*]
Step 3 Clear the entire Token Ring RIF cache.	**clear rif-cache**

Shutting Down and Restarting the Interface

You can disable an interface. Doing so disables all functions on the specified interface and marks the interface as unavailable on all monitoring command displays. This information is communicated to other network servers through all dynamic routing protocols. The interface will not be mentioned in any routing updates. On serial interfaces, shutting down an interface causes the DTR signal to be dropped. On Token Ring interfaces, shutting down an interface causes the interface to de-insert from the ring. On FDDIs, shutting down an interface causes the optical bypass switch, if present, to go into bypass mode.

To shut down an interface and then restart it, perform the following tasks in interface configuration mode:

Command	Task
Step 1 Shut down an interface.	**shutdown**
Step 2 Re-enable an interface.	**no shutdown**

To check whether an interface is disabled, use the EXEC command **show interfaces**. An interface that has been shut down is shown as administratively down in the **show interfaces** command display. See examples in the section "Interface Shutdown Examples" at the end of this chapter.

One reason to shut down an interface is if you want to change the electrical interface type or mode of a Cisco 7500 series port on line. You replace the serial adapter cable and use software commands to restart the interface, and, if necessary, reconfigure the port for the new interface. At system startup or restart, the FSIP polls the interfaces and determines the electrical interface type of each port (according to the type of port adapter cable attached). However, it does not necessarily repoll an interface when you change the adapter cable on line. To ensure that the system recognizes the new interface type, shut down using the **shutdown** command, and re-enable the interface after changing the cable. Refer to your hardware documentation for more details.

Configuring Loopback Detection

When an interface has a backup interface configured, it is often desirable that the backup interface be enabled when the primary interface is either down or in loopback. By default, the backup is only enabled if the primary interface is down. By using the **down-when-looped** command, the backup interface also will be enabled if the primary interface is in loopback. To achieve this condition, perform the following task in interface configuration mode:

Task	Command
Configure an interface to tell the system it is down when loopback is detected.	**down-when-looped**

If testing an interface with the **loopback** command, you should not have loopback detection configured, or packets will not be transmitted out the interface that is being tested.

Running Interface Loopback Diagnostics

You can use a loopback test on lines to detect and distinguish equipment malfunctions between line and modem or Channel Service Unit/Digital Service Unit (CSU/DSU) problems on the network server. If correct data transmission is not possible when an interface is in loopback mode, the interface is the source of the problem. The DSU might have similar loopback functions you can use to isolate the problem if the interface loopback test passes. If the device does not support local loopback, this function will have no effect.

You can specify hardware loopback tests on the Ethernet and synchronous serial interfaces, and all Token Ring interfaces that are attached to CSU/DSUs and that support the local loopback signal. The CSU/DSU acts as a Data Communications Equipment (DCE) device; the router or access server acts as a Data Terminal Equipment (DTE) device. The local loopback test generates a CSU loop—a signal that goes through the CSU/DSU to the line, then back through the CSU/DSU to the router or access server. The **ping** command also can be useful during loopback operation.

The loopback tests are available on the following interfaces:

- High-Speed Serial Interface (HSSI), including the High-Speed Communications Interface (HSCI) card ribbon cable
- Cisco Multiport Communications Interface (MCI) and Cisco Serial Communication Interface (SCI) synchronous serial interfaces
- MCI and Cisco Multiport Ethernet Controller (MEC) Ethernet interfaces; an Ethernet loopback server also is provided on the Ethernet interfaces.
- Ethernet loopback server
- Channelized E1 interfaces (local loopback only)
- Channelized T1 interfaces (local and remote loopback)
- Fractional T1/T1 Interfaces
- Token Ring interfaces
- Channelized E1 controller and interface (local loopback only)
- Channelized T1 controller and interface (local and remote loopback)
- Troubleshooting channelized E1 and channelized T1

The following sections describe each test.

NOTES

Loopback does not work on an X.21 DTE because the X.21 interface definition does not include a loopback definition.

Enabling Loopback Testing on the HSSI

The HSSI allows you to perform the tasks described in these sections:

- Enabling Loopback Test to the DTE
- Enabling Loopback Test through the CSU/DSU
- Enabling Loopback Test over Remote DS-3 Link

These tests apply only when the device supports them and are used to check the data communications channels. The tests are usually performed at the line port rather than the DTE port of the remote CSU/DSU.

The internal loopback concepts are illustrated in Figure 19–1.

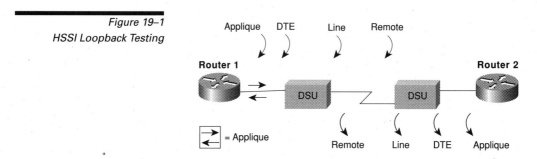

Figure 19–1
HSSI Loopback Testing

Enabling Loopback Test to the DTE

You can loop packets to DTE within the CSU/DSU at the DTE interface when the device supports this function. Doing so is useful for testing the DTE-to-DCE cable. To loop the packets to DTE, perform the following task in interface configuration mode:

Task	Command
Loop packets to DTE internally.	**loopback dte**

Enabling Loopback Test through the CSU/DSU

You can loop packets completely through the CSU/DSU to configure a CSU loop when the device supports this feature. Doing so is useful for testing the DCE device (CSU/DSU) itself. To configure a CSU loop, perform the following task in interface configuration mode:

Task	Command
Loop packets completely through the CSU/DSU.	**loopback line**

Enabling Loopback Test over Remote DS-3 Link

You can loop packets through the CSU/DSU, over the Digital signal level 3 (DS-3) link, and to the remote CSU/DSU and back. To do so, perform the following task in interface configuration mode:

Task	Command
Loop packets through the CSU/DSU to a remote CSU/DSU over the DS-3 link.	loopback remote

This command applies only when the device supports the remote function. It is used for testing the data communication channels. The loopback usually is performed at the line port, rather than the DTE port, of the remote CSU/DSU.

Configuring the Ethernet Loopback Server

The router software provides an Ethernet loopback server that supports Digital Equipment Corporation (Digital), Intel, and Xerox systems specified by the "blue book," a joint specification written by Digital, Intel, and Xerox that defines the Ethernet protocol. The loopback server responds to forward data loopback messages sent either to the server's MAC address or to the broadcast address. Currently, the Ethernet loopback server does not respond to the loopback assistance multicast address.

Use the Ethernet loopback server to test communications between your internetworking products and Digital systems that do not support the IP **ping** command, such as DECnet-only VMS systems.

To originate a loop test on your VMS system with a Cisco server, use the Digital Network Control Program (NCP) command **loop circuit**. For more information about the **loop circuit** command, consult the DECnet VAX documentation. Cisco network servers support all options that can be specified by the VMS hosts.

Enabling Loopback on Token Ring Cards

You can place all of the Token Ring interface cards into loopback mode by performing the following task in interface configuration mode:

Task	Command
Enable loopback to verify that the Token Ring interface receives back every packet it sends.	loopback

Enabling Loopback Testing of Fractional T1/T1

For information, see "Performing Loopback Tests" in the "Monitoring and Maintaining CSU/DSU Service Modules" section earlier in this chapter.

INTERFACE CONFIGURATION EXAMPLES

Examples are included in this section to illustrate configuration tasks described in this chapter. These configuration examples are provided:

- Enabling Interface Configuration Examples
- Interface Description Examples
- Interface Shutdown Examples
- Backup Interface Examples

Enabling Interface Configuration Examples

The following example illustrates how to begin interface configuration on a serial interface. It assigns Point-to-Point (PPP) encapsulation to serial interface 0.

```
interface serial 0
encapsulation ppp
```

The same example on a Cisco 7500 requires the following commands:

```
interface serial 1/0
encapsulation ppp
```

Configuring Specific IP Addresses for an Interface Example

This example shows how to configure the access server so that it will use the default address pool on all interfaces except interface 7, on which it will use an address pool called lass:

```
ip address-pool local
ip local-pool lass 172.30.0.1
 async interface
 interface 7
 peer default ip address lass
```

Interface Description Examples

The following example illustrates how to add a description about an interface that will appear in configuration files and monitoring command displays:

```
interface ethernet 0
description First Ethernet in network 1
ip address 101.13.15.78 255.255.255.0
```

The following example for a Cisco 7500 describes an administration network attached to the Ethernet processor in slot 2, port 4:

```
interface ethernet 2/4
description 2nd floor administration net
```

Interface Shutdown Examples

The following example turns off the Ethernet interface in slot 2 at port 4:

```
interface ethernet 2/4
shutdown
```

The following example turns the interface back on:

```
interface ethernet 2/4
no shutdown
```

The following example illustrates how to shut down a Token Ring interface:

```
interface tokenring 0
shutdown
```

The following example shuts down a T1 circuit number 23 running on a Cisco 7500:

```
interface serial 4/0:23
shutdown
```

The following example shuts down the entire T1 line physically connected to a Cisco 7500:

```
controller t1 4/0
shutdown
```

Backup Inte\rface Examples

The following sections present examples of backup interfaces configured to be activated in three different circumstances:

- The primary line goes down.
- The load on the primary line reaches a certain threshold.
- The load on the primary line exceeds a specified threshold.

## CHAPTER 20

Configuring LAN Interfaces

Use the information in this chapter to configure LAN interfaces supported on Cisco routers and access servers.

This chapter describes the processes for configuring LAN interfaces. It contains these sections:

- Configuring an Ethernet or Fast Ethernet Interface
- Configuring a Fiber Distributed Data Interface (FDDI)
- Configuring a Hub Interface
- Configuring a LAN Extender Interface
- Configuring a Token Ring Interface

For examples of configuration tasks, see "LAN Interface Configuration Examples" at the end of this chapter.

For hardware technical descriptions and information about installing interfaces, refer to the hardware installation and maintenance publication for your product. For a complete description of the LAN interface commands used in this chapter, see Chapter 23, "Interface Commands."

NOTES

In Cisco IOS Release 11.3, all commands supported on the Cisco 7500 series are also supported on the Cisco 7000 series.

CONFIGURING AN ETHERNET OR FAST ETHERNET INTERFACE

Cisco supports both 10 Mbps Ethernet and 100 Mbps Fast Ethernet.

Support for the 10 Mbps and 100 Mbps Ethernet interface is supplied on various Ethernet network interface cards or systems.

The Fast Ethernet NP-1FE Module, for example, provides the following benefits:

- VLAN routing—Virtual LAN (VLAN) support enables network managers to group users logically rather than by physical location. The high performance of the underlying Cisco 4700, combined with the feature-rich NP-1FE, makes it an ideal combination for a low-density, higher-performance application such as inter-VLAN routing.

- High-speed interconnections—The Fast Ethernet interface enables network managers to implement Fast-Ethernet routing solutions for optimal cost and performance across a wide range of applications, including campus or enterprise backbones and data centers. It is also a low-cost way to provide Fast-Ethernet access to traditional low-speed WAN services.

- Local area network aggregation—The Cisco 4500 or the Cisco 4700 can support as many as 12 Ethernets, four Token Rings, or one FDDI segment. ISDN interfaces are also supported.

  With the Catalyst 3000 or Catalyst 5000 system, the Fast Ethernet processor can be used to aggregate up to 12, 10-Mbps LANs and give them high-speed access to Layer 3 routing services, such as providing firewalls and maintaining access lists.

Refer to the *Cisco Product Catalog* for specific platform and hardware compatibility information.

Use the **show interfaces, show controllers mci,** and **show controllers cbus** EXEC commands to display the Ethernet port numbers. These commands provide a report for each interface supported by the router or access server.

Use the **show interface fastethernet** command to display interface statistics, and use the **show controller fastethernet** to display the information about the Fast Ethernet controller chip. The output shows statistics, including information about initialization block information, transmit ring, receive ring, and errors.

Ethernet and Fast Ethernet Interface Configuration Task List

Perform the tasks in the following sections to configure features on an Ethernet or Fast Ethernet interface. The first task is required; the remaining tasks are optional.

- Specifying an Ethernet or Fast Ethernet Interface
- Specifying an Ethernet Encapsulation Method
- Specifying the Media and Connector Type (Cisco 4000)
- Extending the 10BaseT Capability (Cisco 4000 and Cisco 4500 only) (Does not apply to the Fast Ethernet Interface)
- Configuring the 100VG-AnyLAN Port Adapter

Specifying an Ethernet or Fast Ethernet Interface

To specify an Ethernet interface and enter interface configuration mode, perform one of the following tasks in global configuration mode:

Task	Command
Begin interface configuration.	**interface ethernet** *number*
Begin interface configuration for the Cisco 7200 and 7500 series.	**interface ethernet** *slot/port*
Begin interface configuration for Cisco 7500 series.	**interface ethernet** *slot/port-adapter/port*
Begin interface configuration for the Cisco 4000 series with a Fast Ethernet NIM installed.	**interface fastethernet** *number*
Specify a Fast Ethernet interface and enter interface configuration mode on the Cisco 7200 series or the Cisco 7500 series.	**interface fastethernet** *slot/port*
Specify a Fast Ethernet interface and enter interface configuration mode on the Cisco 7500.	**interface fastethernet** *slot/port-adapter/port*

Use the **show interfaces fastethernet** command to display the Fast Ethernet slots and ports. The Fast Ethernet NIM and the FEIP default to half-duplex mode.

Specifying an Ethernet Encapsulation Method

Currently, there are three common Ethernet encapsulation methods:

- The standard ARPA Ethernet Version 2.0 encapsulation, which uses a 16-bit protocol type code (the default encapsulation method)
- SAP IEEE 802.3 encapsulation, in which the type code becomes the frame length for the IEEE 802.2 LLC encapsulation (destination and source Service Access Points, and a control byte)
- The SNAP method, as specified in RFC 1042, which allows Ethernet protocols to run on IEEE 802.2 media

The encapsulation method you use depends upon the routing protocol you are using, the type of Ethernet media connected to the router or access server, and the routing or bridging application you configure.

Establish Ethernet encapsulation of IP packets by performing one of the following tasks in interface configuration mode:

Task	Command
Select ARPA Ethernet encapsulation.	encapsulation arpa
Select SAP Ethernet encapsulation.	encapsulation sap
Select SNAP Ethernet encapsulation.	encapsulation snap

For an example of selecting Ethernet encapsulation for IP, see the section "Enabling Ethernet Encapsulation Example" at the end of this chapter. Also, see the chapters describing specific protocols or applications.

Specifying the Media and Connector Type (Cisco 4000)

You can specify that the Ethernet network interface module (NIM) on the Cisco 4000 uses either the default of an AUI and a 15-pin connector, or 10BaseT and an RJ45 connector. To do so, perform one of the following tasks in interface configuration mode:

Task	Command
Select a 15-pin Ethernet connector.	media-type aui
Select an RJ45 Ethernet connector.	media-type 10baset

Extending the 10BaseT Capability (Cisco 4000 and Cisco 4500 only)

On a Cisco 4000 or Cisco 4500, you can extend the twisted-pair 10BaseT capability beyond the standard 100 meters by reducing the *squelch* (signal cutoff time). This feature applies only to the LANCE controller 10BaseT interfaces. LANCE is the AMD controller chip for the Cisco 4000 and Cisco 4500 Ethernet interface.

To reduce squelch, perform the first task that follows in interface configuration mode. You can later restore the squelch by performing the second task.

Task	Command
Reduce the squelch.	squelch reduced
Return squelch to normal.	squelch normal

Configuring the 100VG-AnyLAN Port Adapter

The 100VG-AnyLAN port adapter (PA-100VG) is available on Cisco 7200 series routers and on Cisco 7500 series routers.

The PA-100VG provides a single interface compatible with and specified by IEEE 802.12 to support 100 Mbps over Category 3 or Category 5 unshielded twisted-pair (UTP) cable with RJ-45 terminators. The PA-100VG supports 802.3 Ethernet packets and can be monitored with the IEEE 802.12 Interface MIB.

To configure the PA-100VG port adapter, perform the following tasks beginning in global configuration mode:

Task	Command
Step 1 Specify a 100VG-AnyLAN interface and enter interface configuration.	**interface vg-anylan** *slot/port-adapter/port* (Cisco 7500)
	interface vg-anylan *slot/port* (Cisco 7200)
Step 2 Specify the IP address and subnet mask to the interface.	**ip address** *ip-address mask*
Step 3 Configure the frame type. Currently, only Ethernet frames are supported. The frame type defaults to Ethernet.	**frame-type ethernet**

NOTES

The port number for the 100VG-AnyLAN port adapter is always 0.

Configuring the PA-100VG interface is similar to configuring an Ethernet or Fast Ethernet interface. To display information about the 100VG-AnyLAN port adapter, use the **show interfaces vg-anylan** EXEC command.

CONFIGURING A FIBER DISTRIBUTED DATA INTERFACE (FDDI)

The Fiber Distributed Data Interface (FDDI) is an ANSI-defined standard for timed 100-Mbps token passing over fiber-optic cable. FDDI is not supported on access servers.

An FDDI network consists of two counter token-passing fiber-optic rings. On most networks, the primary ring is used for data communication, and the secondary ring is used as a hot standby. The FDDI standard sets a total fiber length of 200 kilometers. (The maximum circumference of the FDDI network is only half the specified kilometers because of the *wrapping* or looping back of the signal that occurs during fault isolation.)

The FDDI standard allows a maximum of 500 stations with a maximum distance between active stations of two kilometers when interconnecting them with multimode fiber or ten kilometers when interconnected via single mode fiber, both of which are supported by our FDDI interface controllers. The FDDI frame can contain a minimum of 17 bytes and a maximum of 4500 bytes. Cisco's implementation of FDDI supports Station Management (SMT) Version 7.3 of the X3T9.5 FDDI specification, offering a single MAC dual-attach interface that supports the fault-recovery methods of the dual attachment stations (DASs). The mid-range platforms also support single attachment stations (SASs).

Refer to the *Cisco Product Catalog* for specific information on platform and interface compatibility. For installation and configuration information, refer to the installation and configuration publication for the appropriate interface card or port adapter.

Source-Route Bridging over FDDI on Cisco 4000-M, Cisco 4500-M, and Cisco 4700-M Routers

Source-route bridging (SRB) is supported on the FDDI interface to the Cisco 4000-M, Cisco 4500-M, and Cisco 4700-M routers.

Particle-Based Switching of Source-Route Bridge Packets on Cisco 7200 Series Routers

Source-route bridging (SRB) is supported over Fiber Distributed Data Interface (FDDI).

Particle-based switching is supported for SRB packets (over FDDI and Token Ring) by default.

Particle-based switching adds scatter-gather capability to SRB to improve performance. Particles represent a communications data packet as a collection of noncontiguous buffers. The traditional Cisco IOS packet has a packet type control structure and a single contiguous data buffer. A particle packet has the same packet type control structure but also maintains a queue of particle type structures, each of which manages its own block.

The scatter-gather architecture used by particle-based switching provides the following advantages:

- Allows drivers to use memory more efficiently (especially when using media that has a large maximum transmission unit [MTU]). For example, Token Ring buffers could be 512 bytes rather than 16 KB.

- Allows concurrent use of the same region of memory. For example, on IP multicast, a single packet is received and sent out on multiple interfaces simultaneously.

- Allows insertion or deletion of memory at any location in a packet (not just at the beginning or end).

Using Connection Management (CMT) Information

Connection management (CMT) is an FDDI process that handles the transition of the ring through its various states (off, on, active, connect, and so on) as defined by the X3T9.5 specification. The FIP provides CMT functions in microcode.

A partial sample output of the **show interfaces fddi** command follows, along with an explanation of how to interpret the CMT information in the output.

```
Phy-A state is active, neighbor is B, cmt signal bits 08/20C, status ALS
Phy-B state is active, neighbor is A, cmt signal bits 20C/08, status ILS
CFM is thru A, token rotation 5000 usec, ring operational 0:01:42
Upstream neighbor 0800.2008.C52E, downstream neighbor 0800.2008.C52E
```

The **show interfaces fddi** example shows that Physical A (Phy-A) completed CMT with its neighbor. The state is active and the display indicates a Physical B-type neighbor.

The sample output indicates CMT signal bits 08/20C for Phy-A. The transmit signal bits are 08. Looking at the PCM state machine, 08 indicates that the port type is A, the port compatibility is set, and the LCT duration requested is short. The receive signal bits are 20C, which indicates the neighbor type is B, port compatibility is set, there is a MAC on the port output, and so on.

The neighbor is determined from the received signal bits, as follows:

Bit Positions	9 8 7 6 5 4 3 2 1 0
Value Received	1 0 0 0 0 0 1 1 0 0

Interpreting the bits in the diagram above, the received value equals 0x20C. Bit positions 1 and 2 (0 1) indicate a Physical B-type connection.

The transition states displayed indicate that the CMT process is running and actively trying to establish a connection to the remote physical connection. The CMT process requires state transition with different signals being transmitted and received before moving on to the state Ahead as indicated in the PCM state machine. The ten bits of CMT information are transmitted and received in the Signal State. The NEXT state is used to separate the signaling performed in the Signal State. Therefore, in the preceding sample output, the NEXT state was entered 11 times.

NOTES

The display line showing transition states is not generated if the FDDI interface has been shut down, or if the **cmt disconnect** command has been issued, or if the **fddi if-cmt** command has been issued. (The **fddi if-cmt** command applies to the Cisco 7500 only.)

The CFM state is through A in the sample output, which means this interface's Phy-A has successfully completed CMT with the Phy-B of the neighbor and Phy-B of this interface has successfully completed CMT with the Phy-A of the neighbor.

The display (or nondisplay) of the upstream and downstream neighbor does not affect the ability to route data. Because the upstream neighbor is also its downstream neighbor in the sample, there are only two stations in the ring: the network server and the router at address 0800.2008.C52E.

FDDI Configuration Task List

Perform the tasks in the following sections to configure an FDDI interface. The first task is required; the remaining tasks are optional.

- Specifying an FDDI
- Enabling FDDI Bridging Encapsulation
- Enabling Full-Duplex Mode on the FDDI
- Setting the Token Rotation Time
- Setting the Transmission Valid Timer
- Controlling the Transmission Timer
- Modifying the C-Min Timer
- Modifying the TB-Min Timer
- Modifying the FDDI Timeout Timer
- Controlling SMT Frame Processing
- Enabling Duplicate Address Checking
- Setting the Bit Control
- Controlling the CMT Microcode
- Starting and Stopping FDDI
- Controlling the FDDI SMT Message Queue Size
- Preallocating Buffers for Bursty FDDI Traffic

Specifying an FDDI

To specify an FDDI interface and enter interface configuration mode, perform one of the following tasks in global configuration mode:

Task	Command
Begin interface configuration.	**interface fddi** *number*
Begin interface configuration for the Cisco 7200 or Cisco 7500 series.	**interface fddi** *slot/port*

Enabling FDDI Bridging Encapsulation

Cisco FDDI by default uses the SNAP encapsulation format defined in RFC 1042. It is not necessary to define an encapsulation method for this interface when using the FIP.

FIP fully supports transparent and translational bridging for the following configurations:

- FDDI-to-FDDI
- FDDI-to-Ethernet
- FDDI-to-Token Ring

Enabling FDDI bridging encapsulation places the FIP into encapsulation mode when doing bridging. In transparent mode, the FIP interoperates with earlier versions of encapsulating interfaces when performing bridging functions on the same ring. When using the FIP, you can specify the encapsulation method by performing the following task in interface configuration mode:

Task	Command
Specify the encapsulation method for the FIP.	**fddi encapsulate**

When you are doing translational bridging, you have to route routable protocols and use translational bridging for the rest (such as LAT).

NOTES

Bridging between dissimilar media presents several problems that can prevent communication. These problems include bit-order translation (using MAC addresses as data), maximum transfer unit (MTU) differences, frame status differences, and multicast address usage. Some or all of these problems might be present in a multimedia-bridged LAN and might prevent communication. These problems are most prevalent in networks that bridge between Token Rings and Ethernet networks or between Token Rings and FDDI because of the different ways Token Ring is implemented by the end nodes.

Cisco currently is aware of problems with the following protocols when bridged between Token Ring and other media: AppleTalk, DECnet, IP, Novell IPX, Phase IV, VINES, and XNS. Further, the following protocols might have problems when bridged between FDDI and other media: Novell IPX and XNS. Cisco recommends that these protocols be routed whenever possible.

Enabling Full-Duplex Mode on the FDDI

To enable full-duplex mode on the PA-F/FD-SM and PA-F/FD-MM port adapters, perform the following task in interface configuration mode:

Task	Command
Enable full-duplex on the FDDI interface of the PA-F/FD-SM and PA-F/FD-MM port adapter.	**full-duplex** or **no half-duplex**

Setting the Token Rotation Time

You can set the FDDI token rotation time to control ring scheduling during normal operation and to detect and recover from serious ring error situations. To do so, perform the following task in interface configuration mode:

Task	Command
Set the FDDI token rotation time.	**fddi token-rotation-time** *microseconds*

The FDDI standard restricts the allowed time to be greater than 4,000 microseconds and less than 165,000 microseconds. As defined in the X3T9.5 specification, the value remaining in the token rotation timer (TRT) is loaded into the token holding timer (THT). Combining the values of these two timers provides the means to determine the amount of bandwidth available for subsequent transmissions.

Setting the Transmission Valid Timer

You can set the transmission timer to recover from a transient ring error by performing the following task in interface configuration mode:

Task	Command
Set the FDDI valid transmission timer.	**fddi valid-transmission-time** *microseconds*

Controlling the Transmission Timer

You can set the FDDI control transmission timer to control the FDDI TL-Min time, which is the minimum time to transmit a Physical Sublayer or PHY line state before advancing to the next Physical Connection Management or PCM state as defined by the X3T9.5 specification. To do so, perform the following task in interface configuration mode:

Task	Command
Set the FDDI control transmission timer.	**fddi tl-min-time** *microseconds*

Modifying the C-Min Timer

You can modify the C-Min timer on the PCM from its default value of 1,600 microseconds by performing the following task in interface configuration mode:

Task	Command
Set the C-Min timer on the PCM.	fddi c-min *microseconds*

Modifying the TB-Min Timer

You can change the TB-Min timer in the PCM from its default value of 100 milliseconds. To do so, perform the following task in interface configuration mode:

Task	Command
Set TB-Min timer in the PCM.	fddi tb-min *milliseconds*

Modifying the FDDI Timeout Timer

You can change the FDDI timeout timer in the PCM from its default value of 100 milliseconds. To do so, perform the following task in interface configuration mode:

Task	Command
Set the timeout timer in the PCM.	fddi t-out *milliseconds*

Controlling SMT Frame Processing

You can disable and re-enable SMT frame processing for diagnostic purposes. To do so, perform one of the following tasks in interface configuration mode:

Task	Command
Disable SMT frame processing.	no fddi smt-frames
Enable SMT frame processing.	fddi smt-frames

Enabling Duplicate Address Checking

You can enable the duplicate address detection capability on the FDDI. If the FDDI finds a duplicate address, it displays an error message and shuts down the interface. To enable duplicate address checking, perform the following task in interface configuration mode:

Task	Command
Enable duplicate address checking capability.	**fddi duplicate-address-check**

Setting the Bit Control

You can set the FDDI bit control to control the information transmitted during the Connection Management (CMT) signaling phase. To do so, perform the following task in interface configuration mode:

Task	Command
Set the FDDI bit control.	**fddi cmt-signal-bits** *signal-bits* [phy-a | phy-b]

Controlling the CMT Microcode

You can control whether the CMT onboard functions are on or off. The FIP provides CMT functions in microcode. These functions are separate from those provided on the processor card and are accessed through EXEC commands.

The default is for the FIP CMT functions to be on. A typical reason to disable is when you work with new FDDI equipment and have problems bringing up the ring. If you disable the CMT microcode, the following actions occur:

- The FIP CMT microcode is disabled.
- The main system code performs the CMT function while debugging output is generated.

To disable the CMT microcode, perform the following task in interface configuration mode:

Task	Command
Disable the FCIT CMT functions.	**no fddi if-cmt**

Starting and Stopping FDDI

In normal operation, the FDDI interface is operational once the interface is connected and configured. You can start and stop the processes that perform the CMT function and allow the ring on one fiber to be stopped. To do so, perform either of the following tasks in EXEC mode:

Task	Command
Start CMT processes on FDDI ring.	cmt connect [*interface-name* [phy-a	phy-b]]
Stop CMT processes on FDDI ring.	cmt disconnect [*interface-name* [phy-a	phy-b]]

Do not do either of the preceding tasks during normal operation of FDDI; they are performed during interoperability tests.

Controlling the FDDI SMT Message Queue Size

You can set the maximum number of unprocessed FDDI Station Management (SMT) frames that will be held for processing. Setting this number is useful if the router you are configuring gets bursts of messages arriving faster than the router can process them. To set the number of frames, perform the following task in global configuration mode:

Task	Command
Set SMT message queue size.	smt-queue-threshold *number*

Preallocating Buffers for Bursty FDDI Traffic

The FCI card preallocates three buffers to handle bursty FDDI traffic (for example, NFS bursty traffic). You can change the number of preallocated buffers by performing the following task in interface configuration mode:

Task	Command
Preallocate buffers to handle bursty FDDI traffic.	fddi burst-count

CONFIGURING A HUB INTERFACE

The Cisco 2500 series includes routers that have hub functionality for an Ethernet interface. The hub is a multiport repeater. The advantage of an Ethernet interface over a hub is that the hub provides a star-wiring physical network configuration while the Ethernet interface provides 10BaseT physical network configuration. The router models with hub ports and their configurations are as follows:

- Cisco 2505—1 Ethernet (8 ports) and 2 serial
- Cisco 2507—1 Ethernet (16 ports) and 2 serial
- Cisco 2516—1 Ethernet (14 ports), 2 serial, and 1 ISDN BRI

Cisco provides SNMP management of the Ethernet hub as specified in RFC 1516.

To configure hub functionality on an Ethernet interface, perform the tasks in the following sections. The first task is required; the remaining are optional.

- Enabling a Hub Port
- Disabling or Enabling Automatic Receiver Polarity Reversal
- Disabling or Enabling the Link Test Function
- Enabling Source Address Control
- Enabling SNMP Illegal Address Trap

See the "Hub Configuration Examples" section at the end of this chapter.

Enabling a Hub Port

To enable a hub port, perform the following tasks in global configuration mode:

Task	Command
Step 1 Specify the hub number and the hub port (or range of hub ports) and enter hub configuration mode.	**hub ethernet** *number port* [*end-port*]
Step 2 Enable the hub ports.	**no shutdown**

Disabling or Enabling Automatic Receiver Polarity Reversal

On Ethernet hub ports only, the hub ports can invert, or correct, the polarity of the received data if the port detects that the received data packet waveform polarity is reversed due to a wiring error. This receive-circuitry polarity correction allows the hub to repeat subsequent packets with correct polarity. When enabled, this function is executed once after reset of a link fail state.

Automatic receiver polarity reversal is enabled by default. To disable this feature on a per-port basis, perform the following task in hub configuration mode:

Task	Command
Disable automatic receiver polarity reversal.	**no auto-polarity**

To re-enable automatic receiver polarity reversal on a per-port basis, perform the following task in hub configuration mode:

Task	Command
Re-enable automatic receiver polarity reversal.	**auto-polarity**

Disabling or Enabling the Link Test Function

The link test function applies to Ethernet hub ports only. The Ethernet ports implement the link test function as specified in the 802.3 10BaseT standard. The hub ports will transmit link test pulses to any attached twisted pair device if the port has been inactive for more than 8 to 17 milliseconds.

If a hub port does not receive any data packets or link test pulses for more than 65 to 132 milliseconds and the link test function is enabled for that port, that port will enter link fail state and be disabled from transmit and receive functions. The hub port will be re-enabled when it receives four consecutive link test pulses or a data packet.

The link test function is enabled by default. To allow the hub to interoperate with 10BaseT twisted-pair networks that do not implement the link test function, the hub's link test receive function can be disabled on a per-port basis. To do so, perform the following task in hub configuration mode:

Task	Command
Disable the link test function.	**no link-test**

To re-enable the link test function on a hub port connected to an Ethernet interface, perform the following task in hub configuration mode:

Task	Command
Enable the link test function.	**link-test**

Enabling Source Address Control

On an Ethernet hub port only, you can configure a security measure such that the port accepts packets only from a specific MAC address. For example, suppose your workstation is connected to port 3 on a hub, and source address control is enabled on port 3. Your workstation has access to the network, because the hub accepts any packet from port 3 with your workstation's MAC address. Any packets arriving with a different MAC address cause the port to be disabled. The port is re-enabled after 1 minute and the MAC address of incoming packets is checked again.

To enable source address control on a per-port basis, perform the following task in hub configuration mode:

Task	Command
Enable source address control.	source-address [*mac-address*]

If you omit the optional MAC address, the hub remembers the first MAC address it receives on the selected port, and allows only packets from the learned MAC address.

See the examples of establishing source address control at the end of this chapter in "Hub Configuration Examples."

Enabling SNMP Illegal Address Trap

To enable the router to issue an SNMP trap when an illegal MAC address is detected on an Ethernet hub port, perform the following tasks in hub configuration mode:

Task	Command
Step 1 Specify the hub number and the hub port (or range of hub ports), and enter hub configuration mode.	**hub ethernet** *number port* [*end-port*]
Step 2 Enable the router to issue an SNMP trap when an illegal MAC address is detected on the hub port.	**snmp trap illegal-address**

You might need to set up a host receiver for this trap type (snmp-server host) for a Network Management System (NMS) to receive this trap type. The default is no trap. For an example of configuring an SNMP trap for an Ethernet hub port, see the section "Hub Configuration Examples" at the end of this chapter.

CONFIGURING A LAN EXTENDER INTERFACE

The Cisco 1001 and Cisco 1002 LAN Extenders are two-port chassis that connect a remote Ethernet LAN to a core router at a central site (see Figure 20–1). The LAN Extender is intended for small networks at remote sites. Overview information for LAN Extender interfaces is provided in these sections:

- Connecting a LAN Extender to a Core Router
- Installing a LAN Extender at a Remote Site
- Discovering the MAC Address

- Upgrading Software for the LAN Extender
- Configuring the LAN Extender

Connecting a LAN Extender to a Core Router

The remote site can have one Ethernet network. The core router can be a Cisco 2500 series, Cisco 4000 series, Cisco 4500 series, Cisco 4700 series, Cisco 7500 series, or AGS+ router running Cisco IOS Release 10.2(2) or later, which all support the LAN Extender host software. The connection between the LAN Extender and the core router is made via a short leased serial line, typically a 56-kbps or 64-kbps line. However, the connection also can be via T1 or E1 lines.

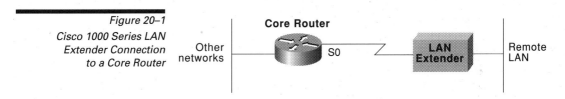

Figure 20–1
Cisco 1000 Series LAN Extender Connection to a Core Router

Expanded View of the Connection to a Core Router

Figure 20–2 is an expanded view of Figure 20–1 that shows all the components of the LAN Extender connection to a core router. On the left is the core router, which is connected to the LAN Extender, as well as to other networks. In the core router, you configure a LAN Extender interface, which is a logical interface that connects the core router to the LAN Extender chassis. In the core router, you also configure a serial interface, which is the physical interface that connects the core router to the LAN Extender. You then bind, or associate, the LAN Extender interface to the physical serial interface.

Figure 20–2 shows the actual physical connection between the core router and the LAN Extender. The serial interface on the core router is connected by a leased serial line to a serial port on the LAN Extender. This creates a virtual Ethernet connection, which is analogous to having inserted an Ethernet interface processor into the core router.

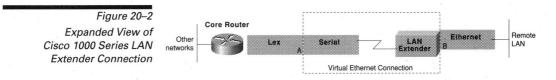

Figure 20–2
Expanded View of Cisco 1000 Series LAN Extender Connection

Management of the LAN Extender Interface

Although there is a physical connection between the core router and the LAN Extender, what you actually manage is a remote Ethernet LAN. Figure 20–3 shows the connection you are managing, which is a LAN Extender interface connected to an Ethernet network. The virtual Ethernet connection (the serial interface and LAN Extender) has been removed from the figure, and points A and B, which in Figure 20–2 were separated by the virtual Ethernet connection, are now adjacent. All LAN Extender interface configuration tasks described in this chapter apply to the interface configuration shown in Figure 20–3.

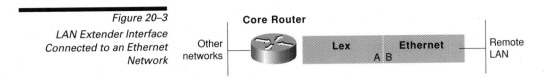

Figure 20–3
LAN Extender Interface
Connected to an Ethernet
Network

Installing a LAN Extender at a Remote Site

To install a LAN Extender at a remote site, see the *Cisco 1000 Series Hardware Installation* publication.

Discovering the MAC Address

After the LAN Extender has been installed at the remote site, you need to obtain its MAC address. Each LAN Extender is preconfigured with a permanent (burned-in) MAC address. The address is assigned at the factory; you cannot change it. The MAC address is printed on the LAN Extender's packing box. (If necessary, you also can display the MAC address with the **debug ppp negotiation** command.) The first three octets of the MAC address (the vendor code) are always the hexadecimal digits 00.00.0C.

Upgrading Software for the LAN Extender

You can upgrade software for the LAN Extender on the host router with a TFTP server that is local to the host router.

The LAN Extender and core router communicate using the Point-to-Point Protocol (PPP). Before you can configure the LAN Extender from the core router, you must first enable PPP encapsulation on the serial interface to which the LAN Extender is connected.

Configuring the LAN Extender

You configure the LAN Extender from the core router—either a Cisco 4000 series or Cisco 7000 series router—as if it were simply a network interface board. The LAN Extender cannot be managed or configured from the remote Ethernet LAN or via a Telnet session.

To configure the LAN Extender, you configure a logical LAN Extender interface on the core router and assign the MAC address from your LAN Extender to that interface. Subsequently, during the PPP negotiation on the serial line, the LAN Extender sends its preconfigured MAC address to the core router. The core router then searches for an available (preconfigured) LAN Extender interface, seeking one to which you have already assigned that MAC address. If the core router finds a match, it binds, or associates, that LAN Extender interface to the serial line on which that MAC address was negotiated. At this point, the LAN Extender interface is created and is operational. If the MAC address does not match one that is configured, the connection request is rejected. Figure 20–4 illustrates this binding process.

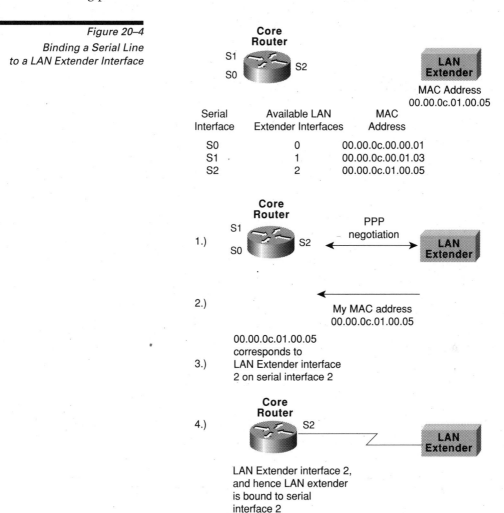

Figure 20–4
Binding a Serial Line
to a LAN Extender Interface

Serial Interface	Available LAN Extender Interfaces	MAC Address
S0	0	00.00.0c.00.00.01
S1	1	00.00.0c.00.01.03
S2	2	00.00.0c.01.00.05

LAN Extender Interface Configuration Task List

To configure a LAN Extender interface, perform the tasks described in the following sections. The first task is required; the remainder are optional.

- Configuring and Creating a LAN Extender Interface
- Defining Packet Filters

- Controlling Priority Queuing
- Controlling the Sending of Commands to the LAN Extender
- Shutting Down and Restarting the LAN Extender's Ethernet Interface
- Restarting the LAN Extender
- Downloading a Software Image to the LAN Extender
- Troubleshooting the LAN Extender

To monitor the LAN Extender interface, see the section "Monitoring and Maintaining the Interface" in Chapter 19, "Overview of Interface Configuration." For configuration examples, see the "Enabling a LAN Extender Interface Example" and the "LAN Extender Interface Access List Examples" sections at the end of this chapter.

Configuring and Creating a LAN Extender Interface

To configure and create a LAN Extender interface, you configure the LAN Extender interface itself and the serial interface to which the LAN Extender is physically connected. The order in which you configure these two interfaces does not matter. However, you must first configure both interfaces in order for the LAN Extender interface to bind (associate) to the serial interface.

To create and configure a LAN Extender interface, perform the following tasks:

Task	Command
Step 1 Configure a LAN Extender interface in global configuration mode and enter interface configuration mode. or Configure a LAN Extender on a Cisco 7000.	**interface lex** *number* **interface lex** *slot/port*
Step 2 Assign the burned-in MAC address from your LAN Extender to the LAN Extender interface.	**lex burned-in-address** *ieee-address*
Step 3 Assign a protocol address to the LAN Extender interface.	**ip address** *ip-address mask*
Step 4 Return to global configuration mode.	**exit**
Step 5 Configure a serial interface in global configuration mode and enter interface configuration mode.	**interface serial** *number*
Step 6 Enable PPP encapsulation on the serial interface in interface configuration mode.	**encapsulation ppp**

Task	Command
Step 7 Exit interface configuration mode.	**Ctrl-Z**
Step 8 Save the configuration to memory.	**copy running-config startup-config**

Note that there is no correlation between the number of the serial interface and the number of the LAN Extender interface. These interfaces can have the same or different numbers.

NOTES

Do not configure the MTU to a value other than the default value when you are configuring a LAN Extender interface.

Defining Packet Filters

You can configure specific administrative filters that filter frames based on their source MAC address. The LAN Extender forwards packets between a remote LAN and a core router. It examines frames and transmits them through the internetwork according to the destination address, and it does not forward a frame back to its originating network segment.

You define filters on the LAN Extender interface in order to control which packets from the remote Ethernet LAN are permitted to pass to the core router. (See Figure 20–5.) These filters are applied only on traffic passing from the remote LAN to the core router. Filtering on the LAN Extender interface is actually performed in the LAN Extender, not on the core router. This means that the filtering is done using the LAN Extender CPU, thus off-loading the function from the core router. This process also saves bandwidth on the WAN, because only the desired packets are forwarded from the LAN Extender to the core router. Whenever possible, you should perform packet filtering on the LAN Extender.

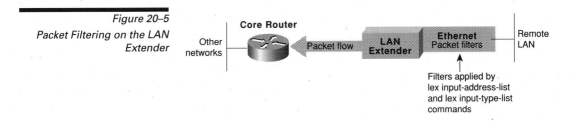

Figure 20–5
Packet Filtering on the LAN
Extender

You also can define filters on the core router to control which packets from the LAN Extender interface are permitted to pass to other interfaces on the core router. (See Figure 20–6.) You do this using the standard filters available on the router. This means that all packets are sent across the WAN before being filtered and that the filtering is done using the core router's CPU.

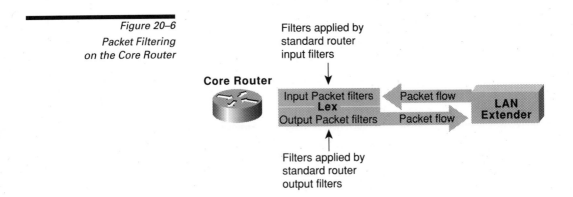

Figure 20–6
Packet Filtering
on the Core Router

The major reason to create access lists on a LAN Extender interface is to prevent traffic that is local to the remote Ethernet LAN from traversing the WAN and reaching the core router. You can filter packets by MAC address, including vendor code, and by Ethernet type code. To define filters on the LAN Extender interface, perform the tasks described in one or both of the following sections:

- Filtering by MAC Address and Vendor Code
- Filtering by Protocol Type

NOTES

When setting up administrative filtering, remember that there is virtually no performance penalty when filtering by vendor code, but there can be a performance penalty when filtering by protocol type.

When defining access lists, keep the following points in mind:

- You can assign only one vendor code access list and only one protocol-type access list to an interface.
- The conditions in the access list are applied to all outgoing packets from the LAN Extender.
- The entries in an access list are scanned in the order you enter them. The first entry that matches the outgoing packet is used.
- An implicit "deny everything" entry is automatically defined at the end of an access list unless you include an explicit "permit everything" entry at the end of the list. This means that unless you have an entry at the end of an access list that explicitly permits all packets that do not match any of the other conditions in the access list, these packets will not be forwarded out the interface.
- All new entries to an existing list are placed at the end of the list. You cannot add an entry to the middle of a list.
- If you do not define any access lists on an interface, it is as if you had defined an access list with only a "permit all" entry. All traffic passes across the interface.

Filtering by MAC Address and Vendor Code

You can create access lists to filter MAC addresses administratively. These access lists can filter groups of MAC addresses, including those with particular vendor codes. There is no noticeable performance loss in using these access lists, and the lists can be of indefinite length. You can filter groups of MAC addresses with particular vendor codes by performing the tasks that follow:

Step 1   Create a vendor code access list.

Step 2   Apply an access list to an interface.

To create a vendor code access list, perform the following task in global configuration mode:

Task	Command
Create an access list to filter frames by canonical (Ethernet-ordered) MAC address.	access-list *access-list-number* {permit | deny} *address mask*

NOTES

Token Ring and FDDI networks swap their MAC address bit ordering, but Ethernet networks do not. Therefore, an access list that works for one medium might not work for others.

Once you have defined an access list to filter by a particular vendor code, you can assign this list to a particular LAN Extender interface so that the interface will then filter based on the MAC source addresses of packets received on that LAN Extender interface. To apply the access list to an interface, perform the following task in interface configuration mode:

Task	Command
Assign an access list to an interface for filtering by MAC source addresses.	lex input-address-list *access-list-number*

For an example of creating an access list and applying it to a LAN Extender interface, see the section "LAN Extender Interface Access List Examples" in the section "LAN Interface Configuration Examples" at the end of this chapter.

Filtering by Protocol Type

You can filter by creating a type-code access list and applying it to a LAN Extender interface.

The LAN Extender interface can filter only on bytes 13 and 14 of the Ethernet frame. In Ethernet packets, these two bytes are the type field. In 802.3 packets, these two bytes are the length field.

To filter by protocol type, perform the following tasks:

Step 1   Create a protocol-type access list.

Step 2   Apply the access list to an interface.

NOTES

Type-code access lists can have an impact on system performance; therefore, keep the lists as short as possible and use wildcard bit masks whenever possible.

To create a protocol-type access list, perform the following task in global configuration mode:

Task	Command
Create an access list to filter frames by protocol type.	**access-list** *access-list-number* {**permit** | **deny**} *type-code wild-mask*

To apply an access list to an interface, perform the following task in interface configuration mode:

Task	Command
Add a filter for Ethernet- and SNAP-encapsulated packets on input.	**lex input-type-list** *access-list-number*

For an example of creating an access list and applying it to a LAN Extender interface, see the section "LAN Extender Interface Access List Examples" in the section "LAN Interface Configuration Examples" at the end of this chapter.

Controlling Priority Queuing

Priority output queuing is an optimization mechanism that allows you to set priorities on the type of traffic passing through the network. Packets are classified according to various criteria, including protocol and subprotocol type. Packets are then queued on one of four output queues. For more information about priority queuing, see Chapter 26, "Managing System Performance."

To control priority queuing on a LAN Extender interface, perform the following tasks:

- Set the priority by protocol type.
- Assign a priority group to an interface.

To establish queuing priorities based on the protocol type, perform the following task in global configuration mode:

Task	Command
Establish queuing priorities based on the protocol type.	**priority-list** *list* **protocol** *protocol* {**high** | **medium** | **normal** | **low**} or **priority-list** *list* **protocol bridge** {**high** | **medium** | **normal** | **low**} **list** *list-number*

You then assign a priority list to an interface. You can assign only one list per interface. To assign a priority list to a LAN Extender interface, perform the following task in interface configuration mode:

Task	Command
Assign a priority list to a LAN Extender interface, thus activating priority output queuing on the LAN Extender.	**lex priority-group** *group*

Controlling the Sending of Commands to the LAN Extender

Each time the core router sends a command to the LAN Extender, the LAN Extender responds with an acknowledgment. The core router waits for the acknowledgment for a predetermined amount of time. If it does not receive an acknowledgment in this time period, the core router resends the command.

By default, the core router waits two seconds for an acknowledgment from the LAN Extender. You might want to change this interval if your connection to the LAN Extender requires a different amount time. To determine whether commands to the LAN Extender are timing out, use the **debug lex rcmd** privileged EXEC command. To change this interval, perform the following task in interface configuration mode:

Task	Command
Set the amount of time that the core router waits to receive an acknowledgment from the LAN Extender.	**lex timeout** *milliseconds*

By default, the core router sends each command ten times before giving up. The core router displays an error message when it gives up sending commands to the LAN Extender. To change this default, perform the following task in interface configuration mode:

Task	Command
Set the number of times the core router sends a command to the LAN Extender before giving up.	**lex retry-count** *number*

Shutting Down and Restarting the LAN Extender's Ethernet Interface

From the core router, you can shut down the LAN Extender's Ethernet interface. This stops traffic on the remote Ethernet LAN from reaching the core router, but leaves the LAN Extender interface that you created intact.

Note that logically, it makes no sense to shut down the serial interface on the LAN Extender. There are no commands that might allow you to do this.

To shut down the LAN Extender's Ethernet interface, perform the following task in interface configuration mode:

Task	Command
Shut down the LAN Extender's Ethernet interface.	**shutdown**

To restart the LAN Extender's Ethernet interface, perform the following task in interface configuration mode:

Task	Command
Restart the LAN Extender's Ethernet interface.	**no shutdown**

Restarting the LAN Extender

To reboot the LAN Extender and reload the software, perform the following tasks in privileged EXEC mode:

Task		Command
Step 1	Halt operation of the LAN Extender and have it perform a cold restart.	**clear controller lex** *number* [**prom**]
Step 2	Halt operation of the LAN Extender on a Cisco 7000.	**clear controller lex** *slot*/*port* [**prom**]

Downloading a Software Image to the LAN Extender

When the LAN Extender is powered on, it runs the software image that is shipped with the unit. You can download a new software image from Flash memory on the core router or from a TFTP server or from Flash memory on the core router to the LAN Extender.

To download a software image to the LAN Extender, perform one of the following tasks in privileged EXEC mode:

Task	Command
Download a software image from Flash memory on the core router.	**copy flash lex** *number*
Download a software image from a TFTP server.	**copy tftp lex** *number*
Download a software image from Flash memory.	**copy flash lex** *number*

Troubleshooting the LAN Extender

The primary method of troubleshooting the LAN Extender is by using the light-emitting diodes (LEDs) that are present on the chassis. This section helps you assist the remote user at the LAN Extender site who can observe the LEDs.

The key to problem solving is to try to isolate the problem to a specific subsystem. By comparing what the system is doing to what it should be doing, the task of isolating a problem is greatly simplified.

The Cisco 1000 series LAN Extender uses multiple LEDs to indicate its current operating condition. By observing the LEDs, any fault conditions that the unit is encountering can be observed. The system LEDs are located on the front panel of your LAN Extender (see Figure 20–7).

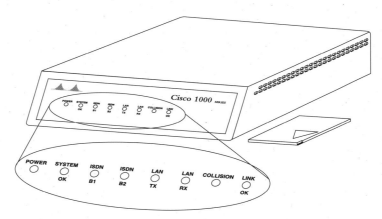

Figure 20–7
LAN Extender LEDs

When there is a problem with the LAN Extender, a user at the remote site should contact you and report the condition of the LEDs located on the front panel of the LAN Extender. You then can use this information to diagnose or verify the operation of the system.

Table 20–1   *LED Trouble Indicators*

LED	Condition	Meaning
POWER	On Steady	The POWER LED indicates that 12 Volts DC is being supplied to the LAN Extender.
	Off	If the POWER LED is off, power is not reaching the unit. Verify that the power supply is plugged into the wall receptacle, and that the cable from the power supply to the unit is connected.
SYSTEM OK	On Steady	The SYSTEM OK LED is lit when the unit passes the power on diagnostics. This indicates proper operation.
	Blinking	The system will blink while running its startup diagnostics and then will go to a steady "on" position. Blinking after the startup diagnostics indicates that a system error has been encountered. Contact your system administrator, who will have you disconnect and then reconnect the power to recycle your LAN Extender. If the blinking continues, check your WAN connection and the RX and TX LEDs.
	Off	An error condition has occurred. Contact your system administrator, who will ask you to disconnect the power cord and then reconnect it to re-establish power to your LAN Extender.
SERIAL TX and SERIAL RX	Flicker	The serial line is transmitting and receiving packets normally.

Table 20–1 *LED Trouble Indicators, Continued*

LED	Condition	Meaning
	Blinking	A line fault has been detected. The LEDs will go on for several seconds and then they will blink a certain number of times to indicate a particular error. The LEDs will blink at a rate of one to two blinks per second. The following are the errors that can be encountered: 1 blink = The serial line is down. 2 blinks = No clock signal was received. 3 blinks = An excessive number of cyclic redundancy check (CRC) errors has been received. 4 blinks = The line is noisy. 5 blinks = A loopback condition has occurred. 6 blinks = The PPP link has failed. Contact your system administrator.
LAN TX and LAN RX	Flicker	The Ethernet LAN connection is transmitting and receiving data normally.
COLLISION		Data collisions are being detected.
LINK OK	Steady	This indicates the serial link is up and functioning.

CONFIGURING A TOKEN RING INTERFACE

Cisco supports various Token Ring interfaces. Refer to the *Cisco Product Catalog* for information about platform and hardware compatibility.

The Token Ring interface supports both routing (Layer 3 switching) and source-route bridging (Layer 2 switching). Routing and bridging function on a per-protocol basis. For example, IP traffic could be routed while SNA traffic is bridged. Routing features enhance source-route bridges.

The Token Ring MIB variables support the specification in RFC 1231, "IEEE 802.5 Token Ring MIB," by K. McCloghrie, R. Fox, and E. Decker, May 1991. The mandatory Interface Table and Statistics Table are implemented, but the optional Timer Table of the Token Ring MIB is not. The Token Ring MIB has been implemented for the TRIP.

Use the **show interfaces, show controllers token,** and **show controllers cbus** EXEC commands to display the Token Ring numbers. These commands provide a report for each ring that Cisco IOS software supports.

NOTES

If the system receives an indication of a cabling problem from a Token Ring interface, it puts that interface into a reset state and does not attempt to restart it. It functions this way because periodic attempts to restart the Token Ring interface drastically affect the stability of routing tables. Once you have again plugged the cable into the MAU, restart the interface by entering the **clear interface tokenring** command, where the *number* argument is the interface number.

By default, the Token Ring interface uses the SNAP encapsulation format defined in RFC 1042. It is not necessary to define an encapsulation method for this interface.

Particle-Based Switching of Source-Route Bridge Packets on Cisco 7200 Series Routers

Particle-based switching is supported for SRB packets (over FDDI and Token Ring) by default.

Particle-based switching adds scatter-gather capability to SRB to improve performance. Particles represent a communications data packet as a collection of noncontiguous buffers. The traditional Cisco IOS packet has a packet type control structure and a single contiguous data buffer. A particle packet has the same packet type control structure, but it also maintains a queue of particle type structures, each of which manages its own block.

The scatter-gather architecture used by particle-based switching provides the following advantages:

- Allows drivers to use memory more efficiently (especially when using media that has a large maximum transmission unit [MTU]). For example, Token Ring buffers could be 512 bytes rather than 16 KB.

- Allows concurrent use of the same region of memory. For example, on IP multicast, a single packet is received and sent out on multiple interfaces simultaneously.

- Allows insertion or deletion of memory at any location in a packet (not just at the beginning or end).

Token Ring Interface Configuration Task List

Perform the tasks in the following sections to configure a Token Ring interface. The first task is required; the remaining tasks are optional.

- Specifying a Token Ring Interface
- Enabling Early Token Release
- Configuring PCbus Token Ring Interface Management

Specifying a Token Ring Interface

To specify a Token Ring interface and enter interface configuration mode, perform one of the following tasks in global configuration mode:

Task	Command
Begin interface configuration.	**interface tokenring** *number*
Begin interface configuration for the Cisco 7200 or Cisco 7500 series.	**interface tokenring** *slot/port*
Begin interface configuration for the Cisco 7500 series.	**interface tokenring** *slot/port-adapter/port*

Enabling Early Token Release

Cisco Token Ring interfaces support early token release, a method whereby the interface releases the token back onto the ring immediately after transmitting rather than waiting for the frame to return. This feature can help to increase the total bandwidth of the Token Ring. To configure the interface for early token release, perform the following task in interface configuration mode:

Task	Command
Enable early token release.	**early-token-release**

Configuring PCbus Token Ring Interface Management

The Token Ring interface on the AccessPro PC card can be managed by a remote LAN manager over the PCbus interface. Currently, the LanOptics Hub Networking Management software running on an IBM-compatible PC is supported.

To enable LanOptics Hub Networking Management of a PCbus Token Ring interface, perform the following task in interface configuration mode:

Task	Command
Enable PCbus LAN management.	**local-lnm**

LAN INTERFACE CONFIGURATION EXAMPLES

This section provides examples to illustrate configuration tasks described in this chapter. These examples are included:

- Enabling Interface Configuration Examples
- Enabling Ethernet Encapsulation Example

- PA-VG100 Port Adapter Configuration Example
- Hub Configuration Examples
- Enabling a LAN Extender Interface Example
- LAN Extender Interface Access List Examples
- Packet OC-3 Interface Configuration Examples

Enabling Interface Configuration Examples

The following example illustrates how to begin interface configuration on a serial interface. It assigns Point-to-Point (PPP) encapsulation to serial interface 0.

```
interface serial 0
 encapsulation ppp
```

The same example on a Cisco 7500 requires the following commands:

```
interface serial 1/0
 encapsulation ppp
```

Configuring Specific IP Addresses for an Interface Example

This example shows how to configure the access server so that it will use the default address pool on all interfaces except interface 7, on which it will use an address pool called lass:

```
ip address-pool local
ip local-pool lass 172.30.0.1
 async interface
 interface 7
 peer default ip address lass
```

Enabling Ethernet Encapsulation Example

These commands enable standard Ethernet Version 2.0 encapsulation on the Ethernet interface processor in slot 4 on port 2 of a Cisco 7500:

```
interface ethernet 4/2
 encapsulation arpa
```

PA-VG100 Port Adapter Configuration Example

Following is an example of a basic configuration for the PA-VG100 port adapter interface in slot 1 on a Cisco 7500 series router. In this example, IP routing is enabled on the router, so an IP address and subnet mask are assigned to the interface.

```
configure terminal
interface vg-anylan 1/0/0
 ip address 1.1.1.10 255.255.255.0
 no shutdown
 exit
exit
```

Hub Configuration Examples

The following sections provide examples of hub configuration:

- Hub Port Startup Examples
- Source Addressing for an Ethernet Hub Port Configuration Examples
- Hub Port Shutdown Examples
- Enabling SNMP Illegal Address Trap for Hub Port Example

Hub Port Startup Examples

The following example configures port 1 on hub 0 of Ethernet interface 0:

```
hub ethernet 0 1
no shutdown
```

The following example configures ports 1 through 8 on hub 0 of Ethernet interface 0:

```
hub ethernet 0 1 8
no shutdown
```

Source Addressing for an Ethernet Hub Port Configuration Examples

The following example configures the hub to allow only packets from MAC address 1111.2222.3333 on port 2 of hub 0:

```
hub ethernet 0 2
source-address 1111.2222.3333
```

The following example configures the hub to remember the first MAC address received on port 2 and to allow only packets from that learned MAC address:

```
hub ethernet 0 2
source-address
```

Hub Port Shutdown Examples

The following example shuts down ports 3 through 5 on hub 0:

```
hub ethernet 0 3 5
shutdown
```

The following example shuts down port 3 on hub 0:

```
hub ethernet 0 3
shutdown
```

Enabling SNMP Illegal Address Trap for Hub Port Example

The following example specifies the gateway IP address, enables an SNMP trap to be issued to the host 172.69.40.51 when a MAC address violation is detected on hub ports 2, 3, or 4, and specifies that interface Ethernet 0 is the source for all traps on the router. The community string is defined as the string *public* and the read/write parameter is set.

```
ip route 0.0.0.0 0.0.0.0 172.22.10.1
snmp-server community public rw
snmp-server trap-source ethernet 0
snmp-server host 172.69.40.51 public
hub ethernet 0 2 4
snmp trap illegal-address
```

Enabling a LAN Extender Interface Example

The following simple example configures and creates a LAN Extender interface. In this example, the MAC address of the LAN Extender is 0000.0c00.0001.

```
interface serial 4
 encapsulation ppp
interface lex 0
 lex burned-in-address 0000.0c00.0001
 ip address 131.108.172.21 255.255.255.0
```

LAN Extender Interface Access List Examples

This section provides these examples of LAN Extender interface configuration:

- Filtering by MAC Address Example
- Filtering by Ethernet Type Code Example

Filtering by MAC Address Example

The following is an example that controls which traffic from Macintosh computers on the remote Ethernet LAN reaches the core router:

```
access-list 710 permit 0800.0298.0000 0000.0000.FFFF
access-list 710 deny 0800.0276.2917 0000.0000.0000
access-list 710 permit 0800.0000.0000 0000.FFFF.FFFF
interface lex 0
 lex input-address-list 710
```

The first line of this access list permits traffic from any Macintosh whose MAC address starts with 0800.0298. The remaining two octets in the MAC address can be any value because the mask for these octets is FFFF ("don't care" bits).

The second line specifically rejects all traffic originating from a Macintosh with the MAC address of 0800.0276.2917. Note that none of the mask bits are "don't care" bits.

The third line specifically permits all traffic from other Macintoshes whose MAC addresses start with 0800. Note that in the mask, the "don't care" bits are the rest of the address.

At the end of the list is an implicit "deny everything" entry, meaning that any address that does not match an address or address group on the list is rejected.

Filtering by Ethernet Type Code Example

Using the same configuration as in the previous section, you could allow only the Macintosh traffic by Ethernet type code with the following access list:

```
access-list 220 permit 0x809B 0x0000
interface lex 0
 lex input-type-list 220
```

This access list permits only those messages whose protocol number matches the masked protocol number in the first line. The implicit last entry in the list is a "deny everything" entry.

Packet OC-3 Interface Configuration Examples

The examples in this section include a simple configuration and a configuration for two routers back to back.

Packet OC-3 Configuration with Default Values Accepted

In the following example, the default framing, MTU, and clock source are accepted, and the interface is configured for the IP protocol:

```
interface posi 3/0
 ip address 172.18.2.3 255.0.0.0
```

Two Routers Connected Back to Back

To connect two routers, attach the cable between the Packet OC-3 port on each. By default, the POSIP uses loop timing mode. For back-to-back operation, only one of the POSIPs may be configured to supply its internal clock to the line.

In the following example, two routers are connected back to back through their Packet OC-3 interfaces:

First router

```
interface posi 3/0
 ip address 170.1.2.3 255.0.0.0
 no keepalive
 pos internal-clock
```

Second router

```
interface posi 3/0
 ip address 170.1.2.4 255.0.0.0
 no keepalive
```

The following example shuts down the entire T1 line physically connected to a Cisco 7500:

```
controller t1 4/0
shutdown
```

CHAPTER 21

Configuring
Serial Interfaces

Use the information in this chapter to configure serial interfaces.

For information on configuring an Asynchronous Transfer Mode (ATM) interface, see the section "Invoking ATM over a Serial Line" in the section "Configuring a Synchronous Serial Interface" later in this chapter.

For hardware technical descriptions and information about installing interfaces, refer to the hardware installation and maintenance publication for your product. For a complete description of serial interface commands used in this chapter, see Chapter 23, "Interface Commands."

The following sections are included in this chapter:

- Configuring a High-Speed Serial Interface (HSSI)
- Configuring a Synchronous Serial Interface
- Configuring a Packet OC-3 Interface
- Configuring Serial Interfaces for CSU/DSU Service Modules
- Configuring Low-Speed Serial Interfaces

For examples of configuration tasks, see "Serial Interface Configuration Examples" at the end of this chapter.

NOTES

In Cisco IOS Release 11.3, all commands supported on the Cisco 7500 series are also supported on the Cisco 7000 series.

CONFIGURING A HIGH-SPEED SERIAL INTERFACE (HSSI)

The HSSI Interface Processor (HIP) provides a single HSSI network interface. The network interface resides on a modular interface processor that provides a direct connection between the high-speed CiscoBus and an external network.

HSSI Configuration Task List

Perform the tasks in the following sections to configure an HSSI interface. The first task is required; the remaining tasks are optional.

- Specifying an HSSI
- Specifying HSSI Encapsulation
- Invoking ATM on an HSSI Line
- Converting HSSI to Clock Master

Specifying an HSSI

To specify an HSSI and enter interface configuration mode, perform one of the following tasks in global configuration mode:

Task	Command
Begin interface configuration.	**interface hssi** *number*
Begin interface configuration for the Cisco 7500 series.	**interface hssi** *slot/port*

Specifying HSSI Encapsulation

The HSSI supports the serial encapsulation methods, except for X.25-based encapsulations. The default method is HDLC. You can define the encapsulation method by performing the following task in interface configuration mode:

Task	Command
Configure HSSI encapsulation.	**encapsulation {atm-dxi	hdlc	frame-relay	ppp	sdlc-primary	sdlc-secondary	smds	stun}**

Invoking ATM on an HSSI Line

If you have an ATM DSU, you can invoke ATM over an HSSI line. You do so by mapping an ATM virtual path identifier (VPI) and virtual channel identifier (VCI) to a DXI frame address. ATM-DXI encapsulation defines a data exchange interface that allows a DTE (such as a router) and a DCE (such as an ATM DSU) to cooperate to provide a User-Network Interface (UNI) for ATM networks.

To invoke ATM over a serial line, perform the following tasks in interface configuration mode:

Task	Command
Step 1 Specify the encapsulation method.	**encapsulation atm-dxi**
Step 2 Map a given VPI and VCI to a DXI frame address.	**dxi map** *protocol address vpi vci* [**broadcast**]

You also can configure the **dxi map** command on a serial interface.

Converting HSSI to Clock Master

You can convert the HSSI interface into a 45-MHz clock master by performing the following task in interface configuration mode:

Task	Command
Convert the HSSI interface into a 45-MHz clock master.	**hssi internal-clock**

CONFIGURING A SYNCHRONOUS SERIAL INTERFACE

Synchronous serial interfaces are supported on various serial network interface cards or systems. These interfaces support full-duplex operation at T1 (1.544 Mbps) and E1 (2.048 Mbps) speeds. Refer to the *Cisco Product Catalog* for specific information regarding platform and hardware compatibility.

Synchronous Serial Configuration Task List

Perform the tasks in the following sections to configure a synchronous serial interface. The first task is required; the remaining tasks are optional.

- Specifying a Synchronous Serial Interface
- Specifying Synchronous Serial Encapsulation
- Configuring a Channelized T3 Interface Processor
- Configuring Half-Duplex for Synchronous Serial Port Adapters on Cisco 7200 Series Routers
- Configuring Compression Service Adapters on Cisco 7500 Series Routers
- Configuring Compression of HDLC Data
- Configuring Real-Time Transport Protocol Header Compression

- Invoking ATM over a Serial Line
- Configuring the CRC
- Using the NRZI Line-Coding Format
- Inverting the Data
- Enabling the Internal Clock
- Setting Transmit Delay
- Configuring DTR Signal Pulsing
- Ignoring DCD and Monitor DSR as Line Up/Down Indicator
- Specifying the Serial Network Interface Module Timing
- Specifying G.703 Interface Options

See the "Serial Interface Configuration Examples" section at the end of this chapter for examples of configuration tasks.

Specifying a Synchronous Serial Interface

To specify a synchronous serial interface and to enter interface configuration mode, perform one of the following tasks in global configuration mode:

Task	Command
Begin interface configuration.	**interface serial** *number*
Begin interface configuration for the Cisco 7205 or Cisco 7200 series.	**interface serial** *slot/port*
Begin interface configuration for the Cisco 7500 series.	**interface serial** *slot/port-adapter/port*
Begin interface configuration for a channelized T1 or E1 interface.	**interface serial** *slot/port:channel-group* (Cisco 7000 series) **interface serial** *number:channel-group* (Cisco 4000 series)

Specifying Synchronous Serial Encapsulation

By default, synchronous serial lines use the High-Level Data Link Control (HDLC) serial encapsulation method, which provides the synchronous framing and error detection functions of HDLC without windowing or retransmission. The synchronous serial interfaces support the following serial encapsulation methods:

- Asynchronous Transfer Mode-Data Exchange Interface (ATM-DXI)
- High-Level Data Link Control (HDLC)

- Frame Relay
- Point-to-Point Protocol (PPP)
- Synchronous Data Link Control (SDLC)
- Switched Multimegabit Data Services (SMDS)
- Cisco Serial Tunnel (STUN)
- X.25-based encapsulations

You can define the encapsulation method by performing the following task in interface configuration mode:

Task	Command
Configure synchronous serial encapsulation.	encapsulation {atm-dxi | hdlc | frame-relay | ppp | sdlc-primary | sdlc-secondary | smds | stun | x25}

Encapsulation methods are set according to the type of protocol or application you configure in the Cisco IOS software. ATM-DXI is described in this chapter in the section "Invoking ATM over a Serial Line." The remaining encapsulation methods are defined in chapters describing the protocols or applications. Serial encapsulation methods are also discussed in Chapter 23 under the **encapsulation** command.

By default, synchronous interfaces operate in full-duplex mode. To configure an SDLC interface for half-duplex mode, perform the following task in interface configuration mode:

Task	Command
Configure an SDLC interface for half-duplex mode.	half-duplex

BSC is a half-duplex protocol. Each block of transmission is acknowledged explicitly. To avoid the problem associated with simultaneous transmission, there is an implicit role of primary and secondary stations. The primary resends the last block if there is no response from the secondary within the period of block-receive timeout.

To configure the serial interface for full-duplex mode, perform the following task in interface configuration mode:

Task	Command
Specify that the interface can run BSC using switched RTS signals.	full-duplex

Configuring a Channelized T3 Interface Processor

The CT3IP is a fixed-configuration interface processor based on the second-generation Versatile Interface Processor (VIP2). It is supported on the Cisco 7500 series routers. The CT3IP has four T1 connections via DB-15 connectors and one DS3 connection via BNC connectors. Each DS3 interface can provide up to 28 T1 channels (a single T3 group). Each channel is presented to the system as a serial interface that can be configured individually. The CT3IP can transmit and receive data bidirectionally at the T1 rate of 1.536 Mbps. The four T1 connections use 100-ohm twisted-pair serial cables to external channel service units (CSUs) or to a MultiChannel Interface Processor (MIP) on the same router or on another router. For wide-area networking, the CT3IP can function as a concentrator for a remote site.

The CT3IP provides 28 T1 channels for serial transmission of data. Each T1 channel can be configured to use a portion of the T1 bandwidth or the entire T1 bandwidth for data transmission. Bandwidth for each T1 channel can be configured for n x 56 kbps or n x 64 kbps (where n is 1 to 24). The unused portion of the T1 bandwidth, when not running at full T1 speeds, is filled with idle channel data. The CT3IP does not support the aggregation of multiple T1 channels (called *inverse muxing* or *bonding*) for higher bandwidth data rates.

The first three T1 channels of the CT3IP can be broken out to the three DSUP-15 connectors on the CPT3IP so the T1 can be demultiplexed further by the MIP on the same router or on another router, or by other multiplexing equipment. When connecting to the MIP, you configure a channelized T1 as described in the "Configuring External T1 Channels" section. This is referred to as an external T1 channel.

The CT3IP supports RFC 1406 and RFC 1407 (CISCO-RFC-1407-CAPABILITY.my). For information on Cisco MIBs, refer to the current Cisco IOS release note for the location of the Management Information Base (MIB) online reference.

For RFC 1406, Cisco supports all tables except the "Frac" table. For RFC 1407, Cisco supports all tables except the "FarEnd" tables.

The CT3IP supports the following WAN protocols:

- Frame Relay
- HDLC
- PPP
- SMDS Data Exchange Interface (DXI)

The CT3IP meets ANSI T1.102-1987 and BELCORE TR-TSY-000499 specifications for T3 and meets ANSI 62411 and BELCORE TR499 specifications for T1. The CT3IP provides internal CSU functionality and includes reporting performance data statistics, transmit and receive statistics, and error statistics. The CT3IP supports RFC 1406 (T1 MIB) and RFC 1407 (T3 MIB).

External T1 channels do not provide CSU functionality and must connect to an external CSU.

The CT3IP supports RFC 1406 (T1 MIB) and RFC 1407 (T3 MIB).

Channelized T3 Configuration Task List

Perform the tasks in the following sections to configure the CT3IP (all tasks are optional except for the second task):

- Configuring the T3 Controller
- Configuring Each T1 Channel
- Configuring External T1 Channels
- Troubleshooting the T3 and T1 Channels
- Looping Back T1 Channels
- Looping Back T3 Lines
- Monitoring and Maintaining the CT3IP
- Configuring Maintenance Data Link (MDL) Messages
- Enabling Performance Report Monitoring
- Enabling BERT Test Pattern
- Enabling Remote FDL Loopbacks

After you configure the T1 channels on the CT3IP, you can continue configuring it as you would a normal serial interface. All serial interface commands might not be applicable to the T1 channel. For more information, see the "Configuring a Synchronous Serial Interface" section earlier in this chapter.

For CT3IP configuration examples, see the "Channelized T3 Interface Processor Configuration Examples" section later in this chapter.

Configuring the T3 Controller

If you do not modify the configuration of the CT3IP, the configuration defaults shown in Table 21–1 are used.

Table 21–1 *CT3IP Controller Defaults*

Attribute	Default Value
Framing	auto-detect
Cable length	224 feet
Clock source	internal

If you must change any of the default configuration attributes, complete the first task in global configuration mode followed by any of the optional tasks in controller configuration mode:

Task	Command
Select the CT3IP and enter controller configuration mode.	**controller t3** *slot/port-adapter/port*
Change the framing format.	**framing {c-bit | m23 | auto-detect}**
Change the cable length (values are 0 to 450 feet).	**cablelength** *feet*
Change the clock source used by the T3 controller.	**clock source {internal | line}**

NOTES

The port adapter and port numbers for the CT3IP are 0.

NOTES

Although you can specify a cable length from 0 to 450 feet, the hardware only recognizes two ranges: 0 to 224 and 225 to 450. For example, entering 150 feet uses the 0 to 224 range. If you later change the cable length to 200 feet, there is no change because 200 is within the 0 to 224 range. However, if you change the cable length to 250, the 225 to 450 range is used. The actual number you enter is stored in the configuration file.

Configuring Each T1 Channel

You must configure the timeslots used by each T1 channel on the CT3IP. Optionally, you can specify the speed, framing format, and clock source used by each T1 channel. If you do not specify the speed, framing format, and clock source used by each T1 channel, the configuration defaults shown in Table 21–2 are used.

Table 21–2 *CT3IP T1 Channel Defaults*

Attribute	Default Value
Speed	64 kbps
Framing	esf
Clock source	internal
Line code	b8zs
T1 yellow alarm	detection and generation

To specify the timeslots used by each T1 channel, complete the following tasks beginning in global configuration mode:

Task	Command
Step 1 Select the CT3IP and enter controller configuration mode.	**controller t3** *slot/port-adapter/port*
Step 2 Configure the timeslots (values are 1 to 24) for the T1 channel (values are 1 to 28) and optionally specify the speed for each T1 channel.	**t1** *channel* **timeslot** *range* [**speed** {56	64}]

NOTES

The 56-kbps speed is valid only for T1 channels 21 through 28.

NOTES

T1 channels on the CT3IP are numbered 1 to 28 rather than the more traditional zero-based scheme (0 to 27) used with other Cisco products. This is to ensure consistency with telco numbering schemes for T1 channels within channelized T3 equipment.

If you need to change any of the default configuration attributes, complete the first task in global configuration mode followed by any of the optional tasks in controller configuration mode:

Task	Command
Select the CT3IP and enter controller configuration mode.	**controller t3** *slot/port-adapter/port*
Change the framing format used by the T1 channel (values are 1 to 28).	**t1** *channel* **framing** {esf	sf}
Change the clock source used by the T1 channel (values are 1 to 28).	**t1** *channel* **clock source** {internal	line}
Change the line coding used by the T1 channel (values are 1 to 28).	**t1** *channel* **linecode** {ami	b8zs}
Disable detection or generation of a yellow alarm on the T1 channel (values are 1 to 28).	**no t1** *channel* **yellow** {detection	generation}

NOTES

If you select **ami** line coding, you also must invert the data on the T1 channel by using the **invert data** interface command. To do so, first use the **interface serial** *slot/port-adapter/port:t1-channel* global configuration command to select the T1 channel and enter interface configuration mode.

NOTES

If you select **sf** framing, you should consider disabling yellow alarm detection, because the yellow alarm can be incorrectly detected with **sf** framing.

After you configure the T1 channels on the CT3IP, you can continue configuring it as you would a normal serial interface. All serial interface commands might not be applicable to the T1 channel. For more information, see the "Configuring a Synchronous Serial Interface" section in this chapter.

To enter interface configuration mode and configure the serial interface that corresponds to a T1 channel, perform the following task in global configuration mode:

Task	Command
Define the serial interface for a T1 channel (values are 1 to 28) and enter interface configuration mode.	**interface serial** *slot/port-adapter/port:t1-channel*

NOTES

The port adapter and port numbers for the CT3IP are 0.

In addition to the commands in the "Configuring a Synchronous Serial Interface" section, the **invert data** interface command can be used to configure the T1 channels on the CT3IP. If the T1 channel on the CT3IP is using AMI line coding, you must invert the data. For information on the **invert data** interface command, see "Inverting the Data" later in this chapter. For more information, see the **t1 linecode** controller command.

Configuring External T1 Channels

The first three T1 channels (1, 2, and 3) of the CT3IP can be broken out to the DSUP-15 connectors on the CPT3IP so the T1 channel can be demultiplexed further by the MIP on the same router, another router, or other multiplexing equipment.

— NOTES ——————————————————————————

If a T1 channel that was configured previously as a serial interface is broken out to the external T1 port, that interface and its associated configuration remain intact while the channel is broken out to the external T1 port. The serial interface is not usable during the time the T1 channel is broken out to the external T1 port; however, the configuration remains to facilitate the return of the T1 channel to a serial interface with the **no t1 external** command.

To configure a T1 channel as an external port, complete the following tasks beginning in EXEC mode:

Task	Command
Step 1 Determine whether the external device connected to the external T1 port is configured and cabled correctly by locating the line Ext1... in the display output. If the line status is OK, a valid signal is being received and the signal is not an all-ones signal.	**show controller t3** *slot/port-adapter/port*
Step 2 Enter configuration mode.	**configure terminal**
Step 3 Select the CT3IP and enter controller configuration mode.	**controller t3** *slot/port-adapter/port*
Step 4 Configure the T1 channel (values are 1, 2, and 3) as an external port and optionally specify the cable length and line code. The default cable length is 133 feet, and the default line code is b8zs.	**t1 external** *channel* [**cablelength** *feet*] [**linecode** {**ami** | **b8zs**}]

— NOTES ——————————————————————————

Only T1 channels 1 through 3 can be configured as external T1.

— NOTES ——————————————————————————

Although you can specify a cable length from 0 to 655 feet, the hardware only recognizes the following ranges: 0 to 133, 134 to 266, 267 to 399, 400 to 533, and 534 to 655. For example, entering 150 feet uses the 134 to 266 range. If you later change the cable length to 200 feet, there is no change because 200 is within the 134 to 266 range. However, if you change the cable length to 399, the 267 to 399 range is used. The actual number you enter is stored in the configuration file.

After you configure the external T1 channel, you can continue configuring it as a channelized T1 from the MIP. All channelized T1 commands might not be applicable to the T1 interface. To define the T1 controller and enter controller configuration mode, perform the following task in global configuration mode:

Task	Command
Select the MIP and enter controller configuration mode.	**controller t1** *slot*/*port*

After you configure the channelized T1 on the MIP, you can continue configuring it as you would a normal serial interface. All serial interface commands might not be applicable to the T1 interface. To enter interface configuration mode and configure the serial interface that corresponds to a T1 channel group, perform the following task beginning in global configuration mode:

Task	Command
Define the serial interface for a T1 channel on the MIP (values are 1 to 28) and enter interface configuration mode.	**interface serial** *slot*/*port*:*t1-channel*

For more information, see "Configuring a Channelized T3 Interface Processor" and "Configuring a Synchronous Serial Interface" earlier in this chapter.

For an example of configuring an external T1 channel, see "Channelized T3 Interface Processor Configuration Examples" later in this chapter.

Troubleshooting the T3 and T1 Channels

You can use the following methods to troubleshoot the CT3IP using Cisco IOS software:

- Testing the T1 by using the **t1 test** controller configuration command and the test port.
- Looping back the T1 by using **loopback** interface configuration commands.
- Looping back the T3 by using **loopback** controller configuration commands.

Enabling Test Port

You can use the T1 test port available on the CT3IP to break out any of the 28 T1 channels for testing (for example, 24-hour BERT testing as is commonly done by telephone companies before a line is brought into service).

The T1 test port is also available as an external port. For more information on configuring an external port, see the previous section, "Configuring External T1 Channels."

NOTES

If a T1 channel that was configured previously as a serial interface is broken out to the T1 port test, that interface and its associated configuration remain intact while the channel is broken out to the T1 port test. The serial interface is not usable during the time the T1 channel is broken out to the T1 test port; however, the configuration remains to facilitate the return of the T1 channel to a serial interface with the **no t1 test** command.

To enable a T1 channel as a test port, complete the following tasks beginning in global configuration mode:

Task		Command
Step 1	Determine whether the external device connected to the external T1 port is configured and cabled correctly by locating the line Ext1... in the display output. If the line status is OK, a valid signal is being received and the signal is not an all-ones signal.	**show controller t3** *slot/port-adapter/port*
Step 2	Select the CT3IP and enter controller configuration mode.	**controller t3** *slot/port-adapter/port*
Step 3	Enable the T1 channel (values are 1 to 28) as a test port and optionally specify the cable length and line code. The default cable length is 133 feet, and the default line code is b8zs.	**t1 test** *channel* [**cablelength** *feet*] [**linecode** {**ami** | **b8zs**}]

To disable a T1 channel as a test port, complete the following tasks beginning in global configuration mode:

Task		Command
Step 1	Select the CT3IP and enter controller configuration mode.	**controller t3** *slot/port-adapter/port*
Step 2	Disable the T1 channel (values are 1 to 28) as a test port.	**no t1 test** *channel*

NOTES

Although you can specify a cable length from 0 to 655 feet, the hardware only recognizes the following ranges: 0 to 133, 134 to 266, 267 to 399, 400 to 533, and 534 to 655. For example, entering 150 feet uses the 134 to 266 range. If you later change the cable length to 200 feet, there is no change because 200 is within the 134 to 266 range. However, if you change the cable length to 399, the 267 to 399 range is used. The actual number you enter is stored in the configuration file.

Looping Back T1 Channels

You can perform the following types of loopbacks on a T1 channel:

- Local—Loops the router output data back toward the router at the T1 framer and sends an AIS signal out toward the network (see Figure 21–1).

- Network line—Loops the data back toward the network before the T1 framer and automatically sets a local loopback (see Figure 21–2).

- Network payload—Loops just the payload data back toward the network at the T1 framer and automatically sets a local loopback (see Figure 21–3).

- Remote line inband—Sends a repeating 5-bit inband pattern (00001) to the remote end requesting that it enter into a network line loopback (see Figure 21–4).

To enable loopbacks on a T1 channel, complete the first task beginning in global configuration mode followed by any one of the following tasks:

Task	Command
Select the T1 channel (values are 1 to 28) on the CT3IP and enter interface configuration mode.	**interface serial** *slot/port-adapter/port:t1-channel*
Enable the local loopback on the T1 channel.	**loopback local**
Enable the network line loopback on the T1 channel.	**loopback network line**
Enable the network payload loopback on the T1 channel.	**loopback network payload**
Enable the remote line inband loopback on the T1 channel.	**loopback remote line inband**

NOTES

The port adapter and port numbers for the CT3IP are 0.

Figure 21–1 shows an example of a local loopback in which the loopback occurs in the T1 framer.

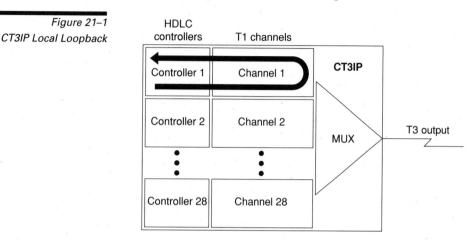

Figure 21–1
CT3IP Local Loopback

Figure 21–2 shows an example of a network line loopback in which just the data is looped back toward the network (before the T1 framer).

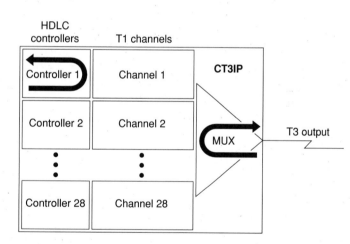

Figure 21–2
CT3IP Network Line Loopback

Figure 21–3 shows an example of a network payload loopback in which just the payload data is looped back toward the network at the T1 framer.

Figure 21–4 shows an example of a remote inband loopback in which the network line enters a line loopback.

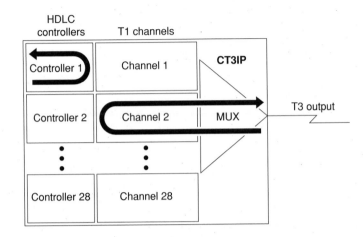

Figure 21–3
CT3IP Network Payload Loopback

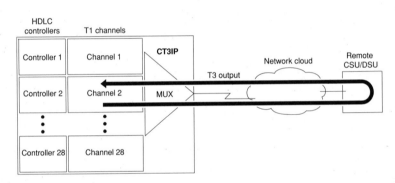

Figure 21–4
CT3IP Remote Loopback

Looping Back T3 Lines

You can put the entire T3 line into loopback mode (that is, all T1 channels are looped) by using the following types of loopbacks:

- Local—Loops the router output data back toward the router at the T1 framer and sends an AIS signal out toward the network.

- Network—Loops the data back toward the network (before the T1 framer).

- Remote —Sends a FEAC (far-end alarm control) request to the remote end requesting that it enter into a network line loopback. FEAC requests (and therefore remote loopbacks) are only possible when the T3 is configured for C-bit framing. The type of framing used is determined by the equipment to which you are connecting. (For more information, see the **framing** controller command.)

To enable loopbacks on the T3 (and all T1 channels), complete the first task beginning in global configuration mode followed by any one of the following tasks:

Task	Command
Select the CT3IP and enter controller configuration mode.	**controller t3** *slot/port-adapter/port*
Enable the local loopback.	**loopback local**
Enable the network loopback.	**loopback network**
Enable the remote loopback.	**loopback remote**

NOTES

The port adapter and port numbers for the CT3IP are 0.

Monitoring and Maintaining the CT3IP

After configuring the new interface, you can monitor the status and maintain the CT3IP in the Cisco 7000 series routers with an RSP7000. You can monitor the status and maintain the CT3IP in the Cisco 7500 series routers by using the **show** commands. To display the status of any interface, complete one of the following tasks in EXEC mode:

Task	Command
Display the internal status of each interface processor and list each interface.	**show controller cbus**
Display the status of the T3 and T1 channels (values are 1 to 28), including the T3 alarms and T1 alarms for all 28 T1 channels or only the T1 channel specified.	**show controller t3** [*slot/port-adapter/port*[:*t1-channel*]] [**brief	tabular**]
Display statistics about the serial interface for the specified T1 channel (values are 1 to 28) on the router.	**show interfaces serial** *slot/port-adapter/port:t1-channel* [**accounting	crb**]

Configuring Maintenance Data Link (MDL) Messages

The CT3IP can be configured to send a Maintenance Data Link (MDL) message as defined in the ANSI T1.107a-1990 specification. To specify the transmission of the MDL messages, complete the following tasks beginning in global configuration mode:

Task	Command
Step 1 Select the CT3IP and enter controller configuration mode.	**controller t3** *slot/port-adapter/port*
Step 2 Configure the Maintenance Data Link (MDL) message.	**mdl** {transmit {path | idle-signal | test-signal} | string {eic | lic | fic | unit | pfi | port | generator} *string*}

NOTES

Specify one **mdl** command for each message. For example, use **mdl string eic Router A** to transmit "Router A" as the equipment identification code and use **mdl string lic Test Network** to transmit "Test Network" as the location identification code.

Use the **show controllers t3** command to display MDL information (received strings). MDL information is displayed only when framing is set to C-bit.

Enabling Performance Report Monitoring

The CT3IP supports performance reports via the Facility Data Link (FDL) per ANSI T1.403. By default, performance reports are disabled. To enable FDL performance reports, complete the following tasks beginning in global configuration mode:

Task	Command
Step 1 Select the CT3IP and enter controller configuration mode.	**controller t3** *slot/port-adapter/port*
Step 2 Enable one-second transmission of the performance report for a specific T1 channel (values are 1 to 28).	**t1** *channel* **fdl ansi**

NOTES

Performance reporting is available only on T1 channels configured for ESF framing.

To display the remote performance report information, complete the following task in EXEC command mode:

Task	Command
Display the remote performance report information for the T1 channel (values are 1 to 28).	**show controller t3** [*slot/port-adapter/port*[*:t1-channel*]] **remote performance** [**brief** | **tabular**]

Enabling BERT Test Pattern

To enable and disable generation of a bit error rate testing (BERT) test pattern for a specified interval for a specific T1 channel, complete the following tasks beginning in global configuration mode:

	Task	Command
Step 1	Select the CT3IP and enter controller configuration mode.	**controller t3** *slot/port-adapter/port*
Step 2	Enable a BERT test pattern on a T1 channel (values are 1 to 28).	**t1** *channel* **bert pattern** {0s | 1s | 2^15 | 2^20 | 2^23} **interval** *minutes*
Step 3	Disable a BERT test pattern on a T1 channel (values are 1 to 28).	**no t1** *channel* **bert pattern** {0s | 1s | 2^15 | 2^20 | 2^23} **interval** *minutes*

The BERT test patterns from the CT3IP are framed test patterns (that is, the test patterns are inserted into the payload of the framed T1 signal).

To view the BERT results, use the **show controller t3** or **show controller t3 brief** EXEC command. The BERT results include the following information:

- Type of test pattern selected
- Status of the test
- Interval selected
- Time remaining on the BERT test
- Total bit errors
- Total bits received

When the T1 channel has a BERT test running, the line state is DOWN. Also, when the BERT test is running and the Status field is Not Sync, the information in the total bit errors field is not valid. When the BERT test is done, the Status field is not relevant.

The **t1 bert pattern** command is not written to NVRAM, because it is only used for testing the T1 channel for a short predefined interval and to avoid accidentally saving the command, which could cause the interface not to come up the next time the router reboots.

Enabling Remote FDL Loopbacks

You can perform the following types of remote Facility Data Link (FDL) loopbacks on a T1 channel:

- Remote payload FDL ANSI—Sends a repeating, 16-bit ESF data link code word (00010100 11111111) to the remote end requesting that it enter into a network payload loopback.
- Remote line FDL ANSI—Sends a repeating, 16-bit ESF data link code word (00001110 11111111) to the remote end requesting that it enter into a network line loopback.

To enable loopbacks on a T1 channel, complete the first task beginning in global configuration mode followed by Step 2 or Step 3 depending on the type of loopback you want to perform:

Task	Command
Step 1 Select the T1 channel (values are 1 to 28) on the CT3IP and enter interface configuration mode.	**interface serial** *slot*/*port-adapter*/*port*:*t1-channel*
Step 2 Enable the remote payload FDL ANSI bit loopback on the T1 channel.	**loopback remote payload [fdl] [ansi]**
Step 3 Enable the remote line FDL ANSI bit loopback on the T1 channel.	**loopback remote line [fdl] [ansi]**

─── **NOTES** ───────────────────────────────────

The port adapter and port numbers for the CT3IP are 0.

Configuring Half-Duplex for Synchronous Serial Port Adapters on Cisco 7200 Series Routers

The synchronous serial port adapters (PA-8T-V35, PA-8T-X21, PA-8T-232, and PA-4T+) on Cisco 7200 series routers support half-duplex carrier modes and timers.

In half-duplex mode, data is sent one direction at a time. Direction is controlled by handshaking the RST and CTS control lines. This is described in the following section.

For more information about the PA-8T-V35, PA-8T-X21, PA-8T-232, and PA-4T+ synchronous serial port adapters, refer to the following publications:

- *PA-8T-V35 Synchronous Serial Port Adapter Installation and Configuration*
- *PA-8T-X21 Synchronous Serial Port Adapter Installation and Configuration*
- *PA-8T-232 Synchronous Serial Port Adapter Installation and Configuration*
- *PA-4T+ Synchronous Serial Port Adapter Installation and Configuration*

Configuring Half-Duplex Carrier Modes and Timers

This section describes how to configure the synchronous serial port adapters (PA-8T-V35, PA-8T-X21, PA-8T-232, and PA-4T+) on Cisco 7200 series routers. To configure the half-duplex feature on synchronous serial port adapters, perform the tasks described in the following sections in this chapter:

- Understanding Half-Duplex DTE and DCE State Machines
- Changing Between Controlled-Carrier and Constant-Carrier Modes
- Tuning Half-Duplex Timers

Configuring Compression Service Adapters on Cisco 7500 Series Routers

The SA-Comp/1 and SA-Comp/4 data compression service adapters (CSAs) are available on Cisco 7200 series routers and on second-generation Versatile Interface Processors (VIP2s) in Cisco 7500 series routers. (CSAs require VIP2 model VIP2-40.)

These service adapters provide high-performance, hardware-based data compression capabilities via simultaneous Stacker compression data compression algorithms with independent full-duplex compression and decompression capabilities on point-to-point (PPP) encapsulated packets.

The SA-Comp/1 supports up to 64 WAN interfaces and the SA-Comp/4 supports up to 256 WAN interfaces.

On the Cisco 7200 series routers, you can specify optionally which CSA the interface uses to perform hardware compression.

You can configure point-to-point compression on serial interfaces that use PPP encapsulation. Compression reduces the size of a PPP frame via lossless data compression. PPP encapsulations support both predictor and Stacker compression algorithms.

If the majority of your traffic is already compressed files, do not use compression.

When you configure Stacker compression on Cisco 7200 series routers, and on Cisco 7500 series routers, there are three methods of compression: hardware compression, distributed compression, and software compression. Specifying the **compress stac** command with no options causes the router to use the fastest available compression method, as described here:

- If the router contains a compression service adapter (CSA), compression is performed in the CSA hardware (hardware compression).

- If the CSA is not available, compression is performed in the software installed on the VIP2 (distributed compression).

- If the VIP2 is not available, compression is performed in the router's main processor (software compression).

Using hardware compression in the CSA frees the router's main processor for other tasks. You also can configure the router to use the VIP2 to perform compression by using the **distributed** option, or to use the router's main processor by using the **software** option. If the VIP2 is not available, compression is performed in the router's main processor.

When compression is performed in software installed in the router's main processor, it might affect system performance significantly. You should disable compression in the router's main processor if the router CPU load exceeds 40 percent. To display the CPU load, use the **show process cpu** EXEC command.

Configuring Compression of HDLC Data

You can configure point-to-point software compression on serial interfaces that use HDLC encapsulation. Compression reduces the size of an HDLC frame via lossless data compression. The compression algorithm used is a Stacker (LZS) algorithm.

Compression is performed in software and might affect system performance significantly. Cisco recommends that you disable compression if CPU load exceeds 65 percent. To display the CPU load, use the **show process cpu** EXEC command.

If the majority of your traffic is already compressed files, you should not use compression.

To configure compression over HDLC, perform the following tasks in interface configuration mode:

Task	Command
Step 1 Enable encapsulation of a single protocol on the serial line.	**encapsulation hdlc**
Step 2 Enable compression.	**compress stac**

Configuring Real-Time Transport Protocol Header Compression

Real-time Transport Protocol (RTP) is a protocol used for carrying packetized audio and video traffic over an IP network. RTP is described in RFC 1889. RTP is not intended for data traffic, which uses TCP or UDP. RTP provides end-to-end network transport functions intended for applications with real-time requirements, such as audio, video, or simulation data over multicast or unicast network services.

Invoking ATM over a Serial Line

If you have an ATM DSU, you can invoke ATM over a serial line. You do so by mapping an ATM virtual path identifier (VPI) and virtual channel identifier (VCI) to a DXI frame address. ATM-DXI encapsulation defines a data exchange interface that allows a DTE (such as a router) and a DCE (such as an ATM DSU) to cooperate for providing a User-Network Interface (UNI) for ATM networks.

To invoke ATM over a serial line, perform the following tasks in interface configuration mode:

Task	Command
Step 1 Specify the encapsulation method.	**encapsulation atm-dxi**
Step 2 Map a given VPI and VCI to a DXI frame address.	**dxi map** *protocol address vpi vci* [**broadcast**]

You also can configure the **dxi map** command on an HSSI interface.

Configuring the CRC

The cyclic redundancy check (CRC) on a serial interface defaults to a length of 16 bits. To change the length of the CRC to 32 bits on an FSIP or HIP of the Cisco 7500 series only, complete the following task in interface configuration mode:

Task	Command
Set the length of the CRC.	**crc** *size*

Using the NRZI Line-Coding Format

All Fast Serial Interface Processor (FSIP) interface types on the Cisco 7500 and the PA-8T and PA-4T+ synchronous serial port adapters on the Cisco 7000 series routers with RSP7000, Cisco 7200 series routers, and Cisco 7500 series routers support nonreturn-to-zero (NRZ) and nonreturn-to-zero inverted (NRZI) format. This is a line-coding format that is required for serial connections in some environments. NRZ encoding is most common. NRZI encoding is used primarily with EIA/TIA-232 connections in IBM environments.

The default configuration for all serial interfaces is NRZ format. The default is **no nrzi-encoding**.

To enable NRZI format, complete the following task in interface configuration mode:

Task	Command
Enable NRZI encoding format.	**nrzi-encoding**
	or
	nrzi-encoding [mark] (Cisco 7200 series routers and Cisco 7500 series routers)

Enabling the Internal Clock

When a DTE does not return a transmit clock, use the following interface configuration command on the Cisco 7000 series to enable the internally generated clock on a serial interface:

Task	Command
Enable the internally generated clock on a serial interface.	**transmit-clock-internal**

Inverting the Transmit Clock Signal

Systems that use long cables or cables that are not transmitting the TxC signal (transmit echoed clock line, also known as TXCE or SCTE clock) can experience high error rates when operating at the higher transmission speeds. For example, if the interface on the PA-8T and PA-4T+ synchronous serial port adapters is reporting a high number of error packets, a phase shift might be the problem. Inverting the clock signal can correct this shift. To invert the clock signal, complete the following task in interface configuration mode:

Task	Command
Invert the clock signal on an interface.	**invert txclock**

Inverting the Data

If the interface on the PA-8T and PA-4T+ synchronous serial port adapters is used to drive a dedicated T1 line that does not have B8ZS encoding, you must invert the data stream on the connecting CSU/DSU or on the interface. Be careful not to invert data on both the CSU/DSU and the interface, because two data inversions will cancel each other out.

If the T1 channel on the CT3IP is using alternate mark inversion (AMI) line coding, you must invert the data. For more information, see the **t1 linecode** controller command. For more information on the CT3IP, refer to the "Configuring a Channelized T3 Interface Processor" section earlier in this chapter.

To invert the data stream, complete the following task in interface configuration mode:

Task	Command
Invert the data on an interface.	**invert data**

Setting Transmit Delay

It is possible to send back-to-back data packets over serial interfaces faster than some hosts can receive them. You can specify a minimum dead time after transmitting a packet to alleviate this condition. This setting is available for serial interfaces on the MCI and SCI interface cards and for the HSSI or MIP. Perform one of the following tasks, as appropriate for your system, in interface configuration mode:

Task	Command
Set the transmit delay on the MCI and SCI synchronous serial interfaces.	**transmitter-delay** *microseconds*
Set the transmit delay on the HSSI or MIP.	**transmitter-delay** *hdlc-flags*

Configuring DTR Signal Pulsing

You can configure pulsing DTR signals on all serial interfaces. When the serial line protocol goes down (for example, because of loss of synchronization) the interface hardware is reset and the DTR signal is held inactive for at least the specified interval. This function is useful for handling encrypting or other similar devices that use the toggling of the DTR signal to resynchronize. To configure DTR signal pulsing, perform the following task in interface configuration mode:

Task	Command
Configure DTR signal pulsing.	**pulse-time** *seconds*

Ignoring DCD and Monitoring DSR as Line Up/Down Indicator

This task applies to Quad Serial NIM interfaces on the Cisco 4000 series and Hitachi-based serial interfaces on the Cisco 2500 series and Cisco 3000 series.

By default, when the serial interface is operating in DTE mode, it monitors the Data Carrier Detect (DCD) signal as the line up/down indicator. By default, the attached DCE device sends the DCD signal. When the DTE interface detects the DCD signal, it changes the state of the interface to up.

In some configurations, such as an SDLC multidrop environment, the DCE device sends the Data Set Ready (DSR) signal instead of the DCD signal, which prevents the interface from coming up.

To tell the interface to monitor the DSR signal instead of the DCD signal as the line up/down indicator, perform the following task in interface configuration mode:

Task	Command
Configure the serial interface to monitor the DSR signal as the line up/down indicator.	**ignore-dcd**

> **CAUTION**
>
> Unless you know for certain that you really need this feature, be very careful using this command. It will hide the real status of the interface. The interface could actually be down and you will not know by looking at show displays.

Specifying the Serial Network Interface Module Timing

On Cisco 4000 series routers, you can specify the serial Network Interface Module timing signal configuration. When the board is operating as a DCE and the DTE provides terminal timing (SCTE or TT), you can configure the DCE to use SCTE from the DTE. When running the line at high speeds and long distances, this strategy prevents phase shifting of the data with respect to the clock.

To configure the DCE to use SCTE from the DTE, perform the following task in interface configuration mode:

Task	Command
Configure the DCE to use SCTE from the DTE.	**dce-terminal-timing enable**

When the board is operating as a DTE, you can invert the TXC clock signal it gets from the DCE that the DTE uses to transmit data. Invert the clock signal if the DCE cannot receive SCTE from the DTE, the data is running at high speeds, and the transmission line is long. Again, this prevents phase shifting of the data with respect to the clock.

To configure the interface so that the router inverts the TXC clock signal, perform the following task in interface configuration mode:

Task	Command
Specify timing configuration to invert TXC clock signal.	**dte-invert-txc**

Specifying G.703 Interface Options

This section describes the optional tasks for configuring a G.703 serial interface (a serial interface that meets the G.703 electrical and mechanical specifications and operates at E1 data rates). G.703 interfaces are available on port adapters for the Fast Serial Interface Processor (FSIP) on a Cisco 4000 series or Cisco 7500 series router. Configuration tasks are described in these sections:

- Enabling Framed Mode
- Enabling CRC4 Generation
- Using Time Slot 16 for Data
- Specifying a Clock Source

Enabling Framed Mode

G.703 interfaces have two modes of operation: framed and unframed. By default, G.703 serial interfaces are configured for unframed mode. To enable framed mode, perform the following task in interface configuration mode:

Task	Command
Enable framed mode.	timeslot *start-slot - stop-slot*

To restore the default, use the **no** form of this command or set the starting time slot to 0.

Enabling CRC4 Generation

By default, the G.703 CRC4, which is useful for checking data integrity while operating in framed mode, is not generated. To enable generation of the G.703 CRC4, perform the following task in interface configuration mode:

Task	Command
Enable CRC4 generation.	crc4

Using Time Slot 16 for Data

By default, time slot 16 is used for signaling. It also can be used for data. To specify the use of time slot 16 for data, perform the following task in interface configuration mode:

Task	Command
Specify that time slot 16 is used for data.	ts16

Specifying a Clock Source

A G.703 interface can clock its transmitted data from either its internal clock or from a clock recovered from the line's receive data stream. By default, the interface uses the line's receive data stream. To control which clock is used, perform the following task in interface configuration mode:

Task	Command
Specify the clock used for transmitted data.	**clock source** {**line**	**internal**}

CONFIGURING A PACKET OC-3 INTERFACE

The Cisco Packet OC-3 Interface Processor (POSIP) is available on Cisco 7500 series routers.

The POSIP is a fixed-configuration interface processor that uses second-generation Versatile Interface Processor (VIP2) technology. The POSIP provides a single 155.520-Mbps, OC-3 physical layer interface for packet-based traffic. This OC-3 interface is fully compatible with SONET and Synchronous Digital Hierarchy (SDH) network facilities and is compliant with RFC 1619, "PPP over SONET/SDH," and RFC 1662, "PPP in HDLC-like Framing." The Packet-over-SONET specification is primarily concerned with the use of the PPP encapsulation over SONET/SDH links.

Table 21–3 describes the default values set in the initial configuration of a Packet OC-3 interface.

Table 21–3   *Packet OC-3 Interface Default Configuration*

Attribute	Default Value
Maximum transmission unit (MTU)	4470 bytes
Framing	SONET STS-3c framing
Loopback internal	No internal loopback
Loopback line	No line loopback
Transmit clocking	Recovered receive clock
Enabling	Shut down

Because the Packet OC-3 interface is partially configured, you might not need to change its configuration before enabling it. However, when the router is powered up, a new Packet OC-3 interface is shut down. To enable the Packet OC-3 interface, you must enter the **no shutdown** command in the global configuration mode.

Packet OC-3 Interface Configuration Task List

The values of all Packet OC-3 configuration parameters can be changed to match your network environment. Perform the optional tasks in the following sections if you need to customize the POSIP configuration:

- Selecting a Packet OC-3 Interface
- Setting the MTU Size
- Configuring Framing
- Configuring an Interface for Internal Loopback
- Configuring an Interface for Line Loopback
- Setting the Source of the Transmit Clock
- Enabling the Packet OC-3 Interface
- Assigning a Network Protocol Address
- Saving the Configuration

For Packet OC-3 interface configuration examples, see the "CSU/DSU Service Module Examples" section later in this chapter.

Selecting a Packet OC-3 Interface

The Packet OC-3 interface is referred to as *pos* in the configuration commands. An interface is created for each POSIP found in the system at reset time.

If you need to change any of the default configuration attributes or otherwise reconfigure the Packet OC-3 interface, first complete the following task in global configuration mode:

Task	Command
Select the Packet OC-3 interface and enter interface configuration mode.	**interface pos** *slot*/*port*

Setting the MTU Size

To set the maximum transmission unit (MTU) size for the interface, complete the following task in interface configuration mode:

Task	Command
Set the MTU size.	**mtu** *bytes*

The value of the *bytes* argument is in the range 64 to 4,470 bytes; the default is 4,470 bytes. (Here, 4,470 bytes exactly matches FDDI and HSSI interfaces for autonomous switching). The **no** form of the command restores the default.

Configuring Framing

To configure framing on the Packet OC-3 interface, complete one of the following tasks in interface configuration mode:

Task	Command
Select SDH STM-1 framing.	**pos framing-sdh**
Revert to the default SONET STS-3c framing.	**no pos framing-sdh**

Configuring an Interface for Internal Loopback

With the **loopback internal** command, packets from the router are looped back in the framer. Outgoing data gets looped back to the receiver without actually being transmitted. With the **loopback line** command, the receive (RX) fiber is logically connected to the transmit fiber (TX) so that packets from the remote router are looped back to it. Incoming data gets looped around and retransmitted without actually being received.

To enable or disable internal loopback on the interface, complete one of the following tasks in interface configuration mode:

Task	Command
Enable internal loopback.	**loop internal**
Disable internal loopback.	**no loop internal**

Local loopback is useful for checking that the POSIP is working. Packets from the router are looped back in the framer.

Configuring an Interface for Line Loopback

Line loopback is used primarily for debugging purposes.

To enable or disable an interface for line loopback, complete one of the following tasks in interface configuration mode:

Task	Command
Enable line loopback.	**loop line**

Task	Command
Disable line loopback.	**no loop line**

The receive fiber (RX) is logically connected to the transmit fiber (TX) so that packets from the remote router are looped back to it.

Setting the Source of the Transmit Clock

By default, the Packet OC-3 interface uses the recovered receive clock to provide transmit clocking. To change the transmit clock source, complete one of the following tasks in interface configuration mode:

Task	Command
Set the internal clock as the transmit clock source.	**pos internal-clock**
Set the recovered receive clock to provide transmit clocking.	**no pos internal-clock**

Enabling the Packet OC-3 Interface

To enable the Packet OC-3 interface when it is first installed or after it has been disabled, complete the following task in interface configuration mode:

Task	Command
Enable the interface.	**no shutdown**

Assigning a Network Protocol Address

You now can enter one or more network protocol addresses and otherwise configure the interface for LAN or WAN uses. For example, if IP routing is enabled on the system, perform the following task in interface configuration mode:

Task	Command
Assign an IP address and subnet mask to the interface.	**ip address** *ip-address mask*

Saving the Configuration

To save the new configuration to memory, complete the following task in privileged EXEC mode.

Task	Command
Write the new configuration to memory.	**copy running-config startup-config**

CONFIGURING SERIAL INTERFACES FOR CSU/DSU SERVICE MODULES

This section describes how to configure the router to support channel service unit (CSU) and data service unit (DSU) service modules:

- Fractional T1/T1 CSU/DSU
- Two-Wire and four-Wire 56/64-kbps CSU/DSU

Fractional T1/T1 CSU/DSU Service Module Configuration Task List

To configure fractional T1 and T1 (FT1/T1) service modules, perform the tasks described in these sections:

- Specifying the Clock Source
- Enabling Data Inversion before Transmission
- Specifying the Frame Type of a FT/T1 Line
- Specifying the CSU Line Build Out
- Specifying FT1/T1 Line-Code Type
- Enabling Remote Alarms
- Enabling Loopcodes that Initiate Remote Loopbacks
- Specifying Timeslots

Specifying the Clock Source

To specify the clock source for the FT1/T1 CSU/DSU module, perform the following task in interface configuration mode:

Task	Command
Specify the clock source for the CSU/DSU internal clock or the line clock.	**service-module t1 clock source {internal | line}**

Enabling Data Inversion before Transmission

Data inversion is used to guarantee the ones density requirement on an alternate mark inversion (AMI) line when using bit-oriented protocols such as High-Level Data Link Control (HDLC), Point-to-Point Protocol (PPP), X.25, and Frame Relay.

To guarantee the ones density requirement on an AMI line using the FT1/T1 CSU/DSU module, perform the following task in interface configuration mode:

Task	Command
Invert bit codes by changing all 1 bits to 0 bits and all 0 bits to 1 bits.	**service-module t1 data-coding inverted**

If the timeslot speed is set to 56 kbps, this command is rejected because line density is guaranteed when transmitting at 56 kbps. Use this command with the 64 kbps line speed. If you transmit inverted bit codes, both CSU/DSUs must have this command configured for successful communication.

To enable normal data transmission on a FT1/T1 network, perform the following task in interface configuration mode:

Task	Command
Enable normal data transmission on a T1 network.	**service-module tx1 data-coding normal** or **no service-module t1 data-coding inverted**

Specifying the Frame Type of a FT/T1 Line

To specify the frame type for a line using the FT1/T1 CSU/DSU module, perform the following task in interface configuration mode:

Task	Command
Specify a FT1/T1 frame type. Choose either D4 Super Frame (sf) or Extended Super Frame (esf).	**service-module t1 framing {sf	esf}**

In most cases, the service provider determines which framing type, either **esf** or **sf**, is required for your circuit.

Specifying the CSU Line Build Out

To decrease the outgoing signal strength to an optimum value for the telecommunication carrier network, perform the following task on the FT1/T1 CSU/DSU module in interface configuration mode:

Task	Command
Decrease the outgoing signal strength in decibels.	service-module t1 lbo {-15 db	-7.5 db}

To transmit packets without decreasing outgoing signal strength, perform the following task in interface configuration mode:

Task	Command
Transmit packets without decreasing outgoing signal strength.	service-module t1 lbo none

The ideal signal strength should be between -15 dB and -22 dB, which is calculated by adding the phone company loss + cable length loss + line build out.

You may use this command in back-to-back configurations, but it is not needed on most actual T1 lines.

Specifying FT1/T1 Line-Code Type

To configure the line code for the FT1/T1 CSU/DSU module, perform the following task in interface configuration mode:

Task	Command
Specify a line-code type. Choose alternate mark inversion (AMI) or binary 8 zero substitution (B8ZS).	service-module t1 linecode {ami	b8zs}

Configuring B8ZS is a method of ensuring the ones density requirement on a T1 line by substituting intentional bipolar violations in bit positions four and seven for a sequence of eight, zero bits. When the CSU/DSU is configured for AMI, you must guarantee the ones density requirement in your router configuration using the **service-module t1 data-coding inverted** command or the **service-module t1 timeslots speed 56** command.

In most cases, your T1 service provider determines which line-code type, either **ami** or **b8zs**, is required for your T1 circuit.

Enabling Remote Alarms

To generate remote alarms (yellow alarms) at the local CSU/DSU or detect remote alarms sent from the remote CSU/DSU, perform the following task in interface configuration mode:

Task	Command
Enable remote alarms.	service-module t1 remote-alarm-enable

Remote alarms are transmitted by the CSU/DSU when it detects an alarm condition, such as a red alarm (loss of signal) or blue alarm (unframed 1's). The receiving CSU/DSU then knows there is an error condition on the line.

With D4 super frame configured, a remote alarm condition is transmitted by setting the bit 2 of each time slot to zero. For received user data that has the bit 2 of each time slot set to zero, the CSU/DSU interprets the data as a remote alarm and interrupts data transmission, which explains why remote alarms are disabled by default. With Extended Super Frame configured, the remote alarm condition is signalled out of band in the facility data link.

You can see if the FT1/T1 CSU/DSU is receiving a remote alarm (yellow alarm) by issuing the **show service-module** command.

To disable remote alarms, perform the following task in interface configuration mode:

Task	Command
Disable remote alarms.	no service-module t1 remote-alarm-enable

Enabling Loopcodes that Initiate Remote Loopbacks

To specify if the fractional T1/T1 CSU/DSU module goes into loopback when it receives a loopback code on the line, perform the following task in interface configuration mode:

Task		Command
Step 1	Configure the remote loopback code used to transmit or accept CSU loopback requests.	service-module t1 remote-loopback full
Step 2	Configure the loopback code used by the local CSU/DSU to generate or detect **payload-loopback** commands.	service-module t1 remote-loopback payload [alternate	v54]

NOTES

By entering the **service-module t1 remote-loopback** command without specifying any keywords, you enable the standard-loopup codes, which use a 1-in-5 pattern for loopup and a 1-in-3 pattern for loopdown.

You can configure the **full** and **payload** loopback points simultaneously. However, only one loopback payload code can be configured at a time. For example, if you configure the **service-module t1 remote-loopback payload alternate** command, a payload v.54 request, which is the industry standard and default, cannot be transmitted or accepted. Full and payload loopbacks with standard-loopup codes are enabled by default.

The **no** form of this command disables loopback requests. For example, the **no service-module t1 remote-loopback full** command ignores all full-bandwidth loopback transmissions and requests. Configuring the **no** form of the command might not prevent telco line providers from looping your router in esf mode, because fractional T1/T1 telcos use facilities data-link messages to initiate loopbacks.

If you enable the **service-module t1 remote-loopback** command, the **loopback remote** commands on the FT1/T1 CSU/DSU module will not be successful.

Specifying Timeslots

To define timeslots for FT1/T1 module, perform the following task in interface configuration mode:

Task	Command
Specify timeslots.	service-module t1 timeslots {*range*	all} [speed {56	64}]

This command specifies which timeslots are used in fractional T1 operation and determines the amount of bandwidth available to the router in each timeslot.

The *range* specifies the DS0 timeslots that constitute the FT1/T1 channel. The range is from 1 to 24, where the first timeslot is numbered 1 and the last timeslot is numbered 24. Specify this field by using a series of subranges separated by commas. The timeslot range must match the timeslots assigned to the channel group. In most cases, the service provider defines the timeslots that comprise a channel group. Use the **no** form of this command to select all FT1/T1 timeslots transmitting at 64 kbps, which is the default.

To use the entire T1 line, enable the **service-module T1 timeslots all** command.

Two-Wire and Four-Wire 56/64-kbps CSU/DSU Service Module Configuration Task List

To configure two- and four-wire 56/64 kbps service modules, perform the tasks described in these sections:

- Setting the Clock Source
- Setting the Network Line Speed
- Enabling Scrambled Data Coding
- Changing Between Digital Data Service and Switched Dial-Up Modes
- Enabling Acceptance of a Remote Loopback Request
- Selecting a Service Provider

Setting the Clock Source

In most applications, the CSU/DSU should be configured with the **service-module 56k clock source line** command. For back-to-back configurations, use the **internal** keyword to configure one CSU/DSU and use the **line** keyword to configure the other CSU/DSU.

To configure the clock source for a 4-wire 56/64-kbps CSU/DSU module, perform the following task for a serial interface in interface configuration mode:

Task	Command
Configure the clock source.	service-module 56k clock source {line | internal}

Use the **no** form of this command to revert to the default clock source, which is the line clock.

Setting the Network Line Speed

To configure the network line speed for a 4-wire 56/64-kbps CSU/DSU module, perform the following task for a serial interface in interface configuration mode:

Task	Command
Set the network line speed.	service-module 56k clock rate *speed*

You can use the following line speed settings: 2.4, 4.8, 9.6, 19.2, 38.4, 56, 64 kpbs, and an **auto** setting.

The 64-kbps line speed cannot be used with back-to-back digital data service (DDS) lines. The subrate line speeds are determined by the service provider.

Only the 56-kbps line speed is available in switched mode. Switched mode is the default on the two-wire CSU/DSU and is enabled by the **service-module 56k network-type** interface configuration command on the four-wire CSU/DSU.

The **auto** linespeed setting enables the CSU/DSU to decipher current line speed from the sealing current running on the network. Because back-to-back DDS lines do not have sealing current, use the **auto** setting only when transmitting over telco DDS lines and using the line clock as the clock source.

Use the **no** form of this command to enable a network line speed of 56 kbps, which is the default.

Enabling Scrambled Data Coding

To prevent application data from replicating loopback codes when operating at 64-kbps on a 4-wire CSU/DSU, perform the following task for a serial interface in interface configuration mode:

Task	Command
Scramble bit codes before transmission.	service-module 56k data-coding scrambled

Enable the scrambled configuration only in 64-kbps digital data service (DDS) mode. If the network type is set to switched, the configuration is refused.

If you transmit scrambled bit codes, both CSU/DSUs must have this command configured for successful communication.

To enable normal data transmission for the 4-wire 56/64-kbps module, perform the following task for a serial interface in interface configuration mode:

Task	Command
Specify normal data transmission.	service-module 56k data-coding normal
	or
	no service-module 56k data-coding

Changing Between Digital Data Service and Switched Dial-Up Modes

To transmit packets in Digital Data Service (DDS) mode or switched dial-up mode using the 4-wire 56/64-kbps CSU/DSU module, perform the following task for a serial interface in interface configuration mode:

Task	Command
Transmit packets in switched dial-up mode or DDS mode.	service-module 56k network-type dds
	or
	service-module 56k network-type switched

Use the **no** form of these commands to transmit from a dedicated leased line in DDS mode. DDS is enabled by default for the four-wire CSU/DSU. Switched is enabled by default for the two-wire CSU/DSU.

In switched mode, you need additional dialer configuration commands to configure dial-out numbers. Before you enable the **service-module 56k network-type switched** command, both CSU/DSU's must use a clock source coming from the line and the clock rate configured to **auto** or **56k** kbps. If the clock rate is not set correctly, this command will not be accepted.

The two-wire and four-wire 56/64-kbps CSU/DSU modules use V.25 *bis* dial commands to interface with the router. Therefore, the interface must be configured using the **dialer in-band** command. DTR dial is not supported.

NOTES

Any loopbacks in progress are terminated when switching between modes.

Enabling Acceptance of a Remote Loopback Request

To enable the acceptance of a remote loopback request on a two- or four-wire 56/64-kbps CSU/DSU module, perform the following task for a serial interface in interface configuration mode:

Task	Command
Enable a remote loopback request.	service-module 56k remote-loopback

The **no service-module 56k remote-loopback** command prevents the local CSU/DSU from being placed into loopback by remote devices on the line. Unlike the T1 module, the two- or four-wire 56/64-kbps CSU/DSU module can still initiate remote loopbacks with the **no** form of this command configured.

Selecting a Service Provider

To select a service provider to use with a two- or four-wire 56/64 kbps dial-up line, perform the following task for a serial interface in interface configuration mode:

Task	Command
Select a service provider for a two- or four-wire switched 56/64 kbps dialup line.	service-module 56k switched-carrier {att | other | sprint}

The **att** keyword specifies AT&T or another digital network service provider as the line carrier, which is the default for the four-wire 56/64-kbps CSU/DSU module. The **sprint** keyword specifies

Sprint or another service provider whose network carries mixed voice and data as the line carrier, which is the default for the two-wire switched 56-kbps CSU/DSU module.

In a Sprint network, echo-canceler tones are sent during call setup to prevent echo cancelers from damaging digital data. The transmission of these cancelers might increase call setup times by eight seconds on the four-wire module. Having echo cancellation enabled does not affect data traffic.

This configuration command is ignored if the network type is DDS.

Use the **no** form of this command to enable the default service provider. AT&T is enabled by default on the four-wire 56/64 module. Sprint is enabled by default on the two-wire switched 56 module.

CONFIGURING LOW-SPEED SERIAL INTERFACES

This section describes how to configure low-speed serial interfaces. In addition to the background information described in the "Understanding Half-Duplex DTE and DCE State Machines" section, these configuration guidelines are provided for configuring low-speed serial interfaces:

- Changing between Controlled-Carrier and Constant-Carrier Modes
- Tuning Half-Duplex Timers
- Changing between Synchronous and Asynchronous Modes

See the "Serial Interface Configuration Examples" section at the end of this chapter for configuration examples.

Understanding Half-Duplex DTE and DCE State Machines

The following section describes the communication between half-duplex DTE transmit and receive state machines and half-duplex DCE transmit and receive state machines.

Half-Duplex DTE State Machines

As shown in Figure 21–5, the half-duplex DTE transmit state machine for low-speed interfaces remains in the ready state when it is quiescent. When a frame is available for transmission, the state machine enters the transmit delay state and waits for a time period, which is defined by the **half-duplex timer transmit-delay** command. The default is 0 milliseconds. Transmission delays are used for debugging half-duplex links and assisting lower-speed receivers that cannot process back-to-back frames.

After idling for a defined number of milliseconds, the state machine asserts a request to send (RTS) signal and changes to the wait-clear-to-send (CTS) state for the data communications equipment (DCE) to assert CTS. A timeout timer with a value set by the **half-duplex timer rts-timeout** command starts. This default is three milliseconds. If the timeout timer expires before CTS is asserted, the state machine returns to the ready state and deasserts RTS. If CTS is asserted prior to the timer's expiration, the state machine enters the transmit state and sends the frames.

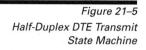

Figure 21–5
Half-Duplex DTE Transmit
State Machine

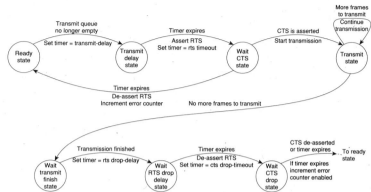

Once there are no more frames to transmit, the state machine transitions to the wait transmit finish state. The machine waits for the transmit first in first out (FIFO) in the serial controller to empty, starts a delay timer with a value defined by the **half-duplex timer rts-drop-delay** interface command, and transitions to the wait RTS drop delay state.

When the timer in the wait RTS drop delay state expires, the state machine deasserts RTS and transitions to the wait CTS drop state. A timeout timer with a value set by the **half-duplex timer cts-drop-timeout** interface command starts, and the state machine waits for the CTS to de-assert. The default is 250 milliseconds. Once the CTS signal is de-asserted or the timeout timer expires, the state machine transitions back to the ready state. If the timer expires before CTS is de-asserted, an error counter is incremented. The error counter can be displayed by issuing the **show controllers** command for the serial interface in question.

As shown in Figure 21–6, a half-duplex DTE receive state machine for low-speed interfaces idles and receives frames in the ready state. A giant frame is any frame whose size exceeds the maximum transmission unit (MTU). If the beginning of a giant frame is received, the state machine transitions to the in-giant state and discards frame fragments until it receives the end of the giant frame. At this point, the state machine transitions back to the ready state and waits for the next frame to arrive.

Figure 21–6
Half-Duplex DTE
Receive State Machine

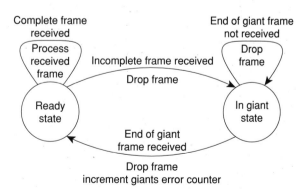

An error counter is incremented upon receipt of the giant frames. To view the error counter, enter the **show interface** command for the serial interface in question.

Half-Duplex DCE State Machines

As shown in Figure 21–7, for a low-speed serial interface in DCE mode, the half-duplex DCE transmit state machine idles in the ready state when it is quiescent. When a frame is available for transmission on the serial interface, such as when the output queues are no longer empty, the state machine starts a timer (based on the value of the **transmit-delay** command, in milliseconds) and transitions to the transmit delay state. Similar to the DTE transmit state machine, the transmit delay state gives you the option of setting a delay between the transmission of frames; for example, this feature lets you compensate for a slow receiver that loses data when multiple frames are received in quick succession. The default **transmit-delay** value is 0 milliseconds. Use the **half-duplex timer transmit-delay** interface configuration command to specify a delay value not equal to 0.

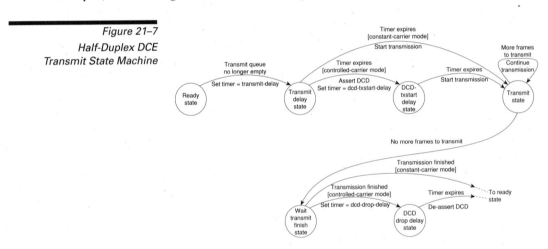

Figure 21–7
Half-Duplex DCE
Transmit State Machine

After the transmit delay state, the next state depends on whether the interface is in constant-carrier mode (the default) or controlled-carrier mode.

If the interface is in constant-carrier mode, it passes through the following states:

1. The state machine passes to the transmit state when the **transmit-delay** timer expires. The state machine stays in the transmit state until there are no more frames to transmit.

2. When there are no more frames to transmit, the state machine passes to the wait transmit finish state, where it waits for the transmit FIFO to empty.

3. Once the FIFO empties, the DCE passes back to the ready state and waits for the next frame to appear in the output queue.

If the interface is in controlled-carrier mode, the interface performs a handshake using the data carrier detect (DCD) signal. In this mode, DCD is de-asserted when the interface is idle and has nothing to transmit. The transmit state machine transitions through the states as follows:

1. After the **transmit-delay** timer expires, the DCE asserts DCD and transitions to the DCD-txstart delay state to ensure a time delay between the assertion of DCD and the start of transmission. A timer with the value **dcd-txstart-delay** is started. (This timer has a default value of 100 milliseconds; use the **half-duplex timer dcd-txstart-delay** interface configuration command to specify a delay value.)

2. When this delay timer expires, the state machine transitions to the transmit state and transmits frames until there are no more frames to transmit.

3. After the DCE transmits the last frame, it transitions to the wait transmit finish state, where it waits for transmit FIFO to empty and the last frame to transmit to the wire. Then DCE starts a delay timer with the value **dcd-drop-delay**. (This timer has the default value of 100 milliseconds; use the **half-duplex timer dcd-drop-delay** interface configuration command to specify a delay value.)

4. The DCE transitions to the wait DCD drop delay state. This state causes a time delay between the transmission of the last frame and the de-assertion of DCD in the controlled-carrier mode for DCE transmits.

5. When the timer expires, the DCE de-asserts DCD and transitions back to the ready state and stays there until there is a frame to transmit on that interface.

As shown in Figure 21–8, the half-duplex DCE receive state machine idles in the ready state when it is quiescent. It transitions out of this state when the DTE asserts RTS. In response, the DCE starts a timer with the value **cts-delay**. This timer delays the assertion of CTS because some DTE interfaces expect this delay. (The default value of this timer is 0 milliseconds; use the **half-duplex timer cts-delay** interface configuration command to specify a delay value.)

Figure 21–8

Half-Duplex DCE Receive State Machine

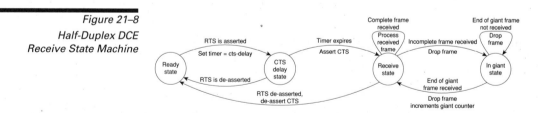

When the timer expires, the DCE state machine asserts CTS and transitions to the receive state. It stays in the receive state until there is a frame to receive. If the beginning of a giant frame is received, it transitions to the in-giant state and keeps discarding all the fragments of the giant frame and transitions back to the receive state.

Transitions back to the ready state occur when RTS is de-asserted by the DTE. The response of the DCE to the de-assertion of RTS is to de-assert CTS and go back to the ready state.

Changing Between Controlled-Carrier and Constant-Carrier Modes

The **half-duplex controlled-carrier** command enables you to change between controlled-carrier and constant-carrier modes for low-speed serial DCE interfaces in half-duplex mode. Configure a serial interface for half-duplex mode by using the **half-duplex** command. Full-duplex mode is the default for serial interfaces. This interface configuration is available on Cisco 2520 through Cisco 2523 routers.

Controlled-carrier operation means that the DCE interface will have DCD de-asserted in the quiescent state. When the interface has something to transmit, it will assert DCD, wait a user-configured amount of time, then start the transmission. When it has finished transmitting, it will again wait a user-configured amount of time, then de-assert DCD.

Placing a Low-Speed Serial Interface in Controlled-Carrier Mode

To place a low-speed serial interface in controlled-carrier mode, perform the following task in interface configuration mode:

Task	Command
Place a low-speed serial interface in controlled-carrier mode.	**half-duplex controlled-carrier**

Placing a Low-Speed Serial Interface in Constant-Carrier Mode

To return a low-speed serial interface to constant-carrier mode from controlled-carrier mode, perform the following task in interface configuration mode:

Task	Command
Place a low-speed serial interface in constant-carrier mode.	**no half-duplex controlled-carrier**

Tuning Half-Duplex Timers

To tune half-duplex timers, perform the following task in interface configuration mode:

Task	Command
Tune half-duplex timers.	**half-duplex timer** {**cts-delay** *value*	**cts-drop-timeout** *value*	**dcd-drop-delay** *value*	**dcd-txstart-delay** *value*	**rts-drop-delay** *value*	**rts-timeout** *value*	**transmit-delay** *value*}

The timer tuning commands permit you to adjust the timing of the half-duplex state machines to suit the particular needs of their half-duplex installation.

Note that the **half-duplex timer** command and its options deprecates the following two timer tuning commands that are available only on high-speed serial interfaces:

- sdlc cts-delay
- sdlc rts-timeout

Changing Between Synchronous and Asynchronous Modes

To specify the mode of a low-speed serial interface as either synchronous or asynchronous, perform the following task in interface configuration mode:

Task	Command
Specify the mode of a low-speed interface as either synchronous or asynchronous.	**physical-layer {sync	async}**

This command applies only to low-speed serial interfaces available on Cisco 2520 through Cisco 2523 routers.

In synchronous mode, low-speed serial interfaces support all interface configuration commands available for high-speed serial interfaces, except the following two commands:

- sdlc cts-delay
- sdlc rts-timeout

When placed in asynchronous mode, low-speed serial interfaces support all commands available for standard asynchronous interfaces. The default is synchronous mode.

Note that when you enter this command, it does not appear in the output of **show running config** and **show startup config** commands, because these are physical-layer commands.

Returning a Low-Speed Serial Interface to Synchronous Mode

To return to the default mode (synchronous) of a low-speed serial interface on a Cisco 2520 through Cisco 2523 router, perform the following task in interface configuration mode:

Task	Command
Return the interface to its default mode, which is synchronous.	**no physical-layer**

SERIAL INTERFACE CONFIGURATION EXAMPLES

This section includes the following example groups:

- Channelized T3 Interface Processor Configuration Examples
- Low-Speed Serial Interface Examples
- CSU/DSU Service Module Examples

Channelized T3 Interface Processor Configuration Examples

The examples in this section show how to configure the Channelized T3 Interface Processor (CT3IP). The first example shows how to configure two of the T1 channels of the channelized T3 controller. The second example shows how to configure one of the T1 channels of the channelized T3 controller as an external port for further channelization on the Multichannel Interface Processor (MIP).

For more information, see "Configuring the T3 Controller" and "Configuring External T1 Channels" earlier in this chapter. Examples included in this section are the following:

- CT3IP Configuration with Default Values Accepted Example
- CT3IP External Ports Configuration Example
- CT3IP Maintenance Data Link (MDL) Example
- CT3IP Performance Monitoring Example
- CT3IP BERT Test Pattern Example
- CT3IP Remote FDL Loopback Example

CT3IP Configuration with Default Values Accepted Example

In the following example, timeslots 1 through 24 (the entire T1 bandwidth) are assigned to T1 channel 16 and timeslots 1 through 5 and 20 through 23 (fractional T1 bandwidth) are assigned to T1 channel 10 for the CT3IP in slot 9. The default framing, cable length, and clock source are accepted for the T3, and the default speed, framing, clock source, and line code are accepted for each T1 channel. Each T1 channel is assigned an IP address. Other interface configuration commands can be assigned to the T1 channel at this time.

```
controller t3 9/0/0
 t1 16 timeslot 1-24
 t1 10 timeslot 1-5,20-23
interface serial 9/0/0:16
 ip address 10.20.20.1 255.255.255.0
interface serial 9/0/0:10
 ip address 10.20.20.3 255.255.255.0
```

CT3IP External Ports Configuration Example

In the following example, T1 channel 1 on the CT3IP in slot 9 is broken out as an external port so that it can be further channelized on the MIP in slot 3. The cable length is 300 feet, and the default line coding format on the T1 channel is used. Because the default line coding format on the T1 channel is B8ZS and the default line coding on the MIP is AMI, the line coding on the MIP is changed to B8ZS.

```
controller t3 9/0/0
 t1 external 1 cablelength 300
controller t1 3/0
 linecode b8zs
 channel-group 1 timeslots 1
interface serial 3/0:1
 ip address 10.20.20.5 255.255.255.0
```

CT3IP Maintenance Data Link (MDL) Example

The following examples show several of the Maintenance Data Link (MDL) messages for the CT3IP in slot 9:

```
controller t3 9/0/0
 mdl string eic Router C
 mdl string lic Network A
 mdl string fic Bldg 102
 mdl string unit 123ABC
```

CT3IP Performance Monitoring Example

In the following example, the performance reports are generated for T1 channel 6 on the CT3IP in slot 9:

```
controller t3 9/0/0
 t1 6 fdl ansi
```

CT3IP BERT Test Pattern Example

The following example shows how to enable a BERT test pattern that consists of a repeating pattern of ones (...111...) and runs for 30 minutes for T1 channel 8 on CT3IP in slot 9:

```
controller t3 9/0/0
 t1 8 bert pattern 1s interval 30
```

CT3IP Remote FDL Loopback Example

The following example shows how to enable a remote payload FDL ANSI bit loopback for T1 channel 6 on CT3IP in slot 3:

```
interface serial 3/0/0:6
 loopback remote payload fdl ansi
```

Low-Speed Serial Interface Examples

These configuration examples are provided for low-speed serial interfaces:

- Setting Synchronous or Asynchronous Mode Examples
- Changing between Controlled-Carrier and Constant-Carrier Modes Examples

- Tuning Half-Duplex Timers Example
- Cisco 40000 Series Router with 2T16S Serial Network Processor Example

Setting Synchronous or Asynchronous Mode Examples

The following example shows how to change a low-speed serial interface from synchronous to asynchronous mode:

```
interface serial 2
 physical-layer async
```

The following examples show how to change a low-speed serial interface from asynchronous mode back to its default synchronous mode:

```
interface serial 2
 physical-layer sync
```

   or

```
interface serial 2
 no physical-layer
```

The following example shows some typical asynchronous interface configuration commands:

```
interface serial 2
 physical-layer async
 ip address 1.0.0.2 255.0.0.0
 async default ip address 1.0.0.1
 async mode dedicated
 async default routing
```

The following example shows some typical synchronous serial interface configuration commands available when the interface is in synchronous mode:

```
interface serial 2
 physical-layer sync
 ip address 1.0.0.2 255.0.0.0
 no keepalive
 ignore-dcd
 nrzi-encoding
 no shutdown
```

Changing Between Controlled-Carrier and Constant-Carrier Modes Examples

The following example shows how to change to controlled-carrier mode from the default of constant-carrier operation:

```
interface serial 2
 half-duplex controlled-carrier
```

The following example shows how to change to constant-carrier mode from controlled-carrier mode:

```
interface serial 2
 no half-duplex controlled-carrier
```

Tuning Half-Duplex Timers Example

The following examples show how to set the cts-delay timer to 1,234 milliseconds and the transmit-delay timer to 50 milliseconds.

```
interface serial 2
 half-duplex timer cts-delay 1234
 half-duplex timer transmit-delay 50
```

Cisco 40000 Series Router with 2T16S Serial Network Processor Example

The 2T16S network processor module provides high-density serial interfaces for the Cisco 4000 series routers. This module has two high-speed interfaces that support full-duplex T1 and E1 rates (up to 2 MB per second) and 16 low-speed interfaces. The 16 lower-speed ports can be individually configured as either synchronous ports at speeds up to 128 kbps or as asynchronous ports at speeds up to 115 kbps.

For the slow-speed interfaces, both synchronous and asynchronous serial protocols are supported. For the high-speed interfaces, only the synchronous protocols are supported. Synchronous protocols include IBM's BSC, SDLC, and HDLC. Asynchronous protocols include PPP, SLIP, and ARAP for dial-up connections using external modems.

This example shows a Cisco 4500 router equipped with two 2T16S serial network processor modules and two conventional Ethernet ports.

This router is configured for WAN aggregation using X.25, Frame Relay, PPP, and HDLC encapsulation. Serial interfaces 0, 1, 18, and 19 are the synchronous high-speed interfaces. Serial interfaces 2 through 17 and 20 through 35 are the synchronous/asynchronous low-speed interfaces.

```
version 11.2
!
hostname c4X00
!
username brad password 7 13171F1D0A080139
username jim password 7 104D000A0618
!
```

Ethernet interfaces and their subinterfaces are configured for LAN access.

```
interface Ethernet0
 ip address 10.1.1.1 255.255.255.0
 media-type 10BaseT
!
interface Ethernet1
 ip address 10.1.2.1 255.255.255.0
 media-type 10BaseT
!
```

Interfaces Serial 0 and Serial 1 are the high-speed serial interfaces on the first 2T16S module. In this example, subinterfaces are also configured for remote offices connected to interface Serial 0.

```
interface Serial0
 description Frame relay configuration sample
 no ip address
 encapsulation frame-relay
!
interface Serial0.1 point-to-point
 description PVC to first office
 ip address 10.1.3.1 255.255.255.0
 frame-relay interface-dlci 16
!
interface Serial0.2 point-to-point
 description PVC to second office
 ip address 10.1.4.1 255.255.255.0
 frame-relay interface-dlci 17
!
interface Serial1
 description X25 configuration sample
 ip address 10.1.5.1 255.255.255.0
 no ip mroute-cache
 encapsulation x25
 x25 address 6120184321
 x25 htc 25
 x25 map ip 10.1.5.2 6121230073
```

Serial interfaces 2 to 17 are the low-speed interfaces on the 2T16S network processor module. In this example, remote routers are connected to various configurations.

```
interface Serial2
 description DDR connection router dial out to remote sites only
 ip address 10.1.6.1 255.255.255.0
 dialer in-band
 dialer wait-for-carrier-time 60
 dialer string 0118527351234
 pulse-time 1
 dialer-group 1
!
interface Serial3
 description DDR interface to answer calls from remote office
 ip address 10.1.7.1 255.255.255.0
 dialer in-band
!
interface Serial4
 description configuration for PPP interface
 ip address 10.1.8.1 255.255.255.0
 encapsulation ppp
!
interface Serial5
 description Frame relay configuration sample
 no ip address
 encapsulation frame-relay
```

```
!
interface Serial5.1 point-to-point
 description PVC to first office
 ip address 10.1.9.1 255.255.255.0
 frame-relay interface-dlci 16
!
interface Serial5.2 point-to-point
 description PVC to second office
 ip address 10.1.10.1 255.255.255.0
 frame-relay interface-dlci 17
!
interface Serial6
 description configuration for PPP interface
 ip address 10.1.11.1 255.255.255.0
 encapsulation ppp
!
interface Serial7
 no ip address
 shutdown
!
interface Serial8
 ip address 10.1.12.1 255.255.255.0
 encapsulation ppp
 async default routing
 async mode dedicated
!
interface Serial9
 physical-layer async
 ip address 10.1.13.1 255.255.255.0
 encapsulation ppp
 async default routing
 async mode dedicated
!
interface Serial10
 physical-layer async
 no ip address
!
interface Serial11
 no ip address
 shutdown
!
interface Serial12
 physical-layer async
 no ip address
 shutdown
!
interface Serial13
 no ip address
 shutdown
!
interface Serial14
 no ip address
 shutdown
```

```
!
interface Serial15
 no ip address
 shutdown
!
interface Serial16
 no ip address
 shutdown
!
interface Serial17
 no ip address
 shutdown
```

Interface serial 18 is the first high-speed serial interface of the second 2T16S module. Remote sites on different subnets are dialing in to this interface with point-to-point and multipoint connections.

```
interface Serial18
 description Frame relay sample
 no ip address
 encapsulation frame-relay
!
interface Serial18.1 point-to-point
 description Frame relay subinterface
 ip address 10.1.14.1 255.255.255.0
 frame-relay interface-dlci 16
!
interface Serial18.2 point-to-point
 description Frame relay subinterface
 ip address 10.1.15.1 255.255.255.0
 frame-relay interface-dlci 17
!
interface Serial18.3 point-to-point
 description Frame relay subinterface
 ip address 10.1.16.1 255.255.255.0
 frame-relay interface-dlci 18
!
interface Serial18.5 multipoint
 ip address 10.1.17.1 255.255.255.0
 frame-relay map ip 10.1.17.2 100 IETF
```

This second high-speed serial interface is configured to connect an X.25 link. Serial interfaces 20 through 35 are the low-speed interfaces. However, some of the interfaces are not displayed in this example.

```
interface Serial19
 description X25 sample config
 ip address 10.1.18.1 255.255.255.0
 no ip mroute-cache
 encapsulation x25
 x25 address 6120000044
 x25 htc 25
 x25 map ip 10.1.18.2 6120170073
!
interface Serial20
 ip address 10.1.19.1 255.255.255.0
!
```

```
interface Serial21
 physical-layer async
 ip unnumbered e0
 encap ppp
 async mode dedicated
 async dynamic routing
 ipx network 45
 ipx watchdog-spoof
 dialer in-band
 dialer-group 1
 ppp authentication chap
!
interface Serial22
 no ip address
 shutdown
!
interface Serial23
 no ip address
 shutdown
!
interface Serial24
 no ip address
 shutdown
!
!Serial interfaces 23 through 35 would appear here.
!...

 router eigrp 10
 network 10.0.0.0
!
 dialer-list 1 protocol ip permit
!
 line con 0
 exec-timeout 15 0
 password david
 login
```

The following basic line configuration configures some of the modules' low-speed serial interfaces.

```
line 8 10
 modem InOut
 transport input all
 rxspeed 64000
 txspeed 64000
 flowcontrol hardware
line 12
 transport input all
 rxspeed 64000
 txspeed 64000
 flowcontrol hardware
 modem chat-script generic
```

```
line 21
 transport input all
 rxspeed 64000
 txspeed 64000
 flowcontrol hardware
!
 end
```

CSU/DSU Service Module Examples

Two main categories of service module examples are provided:

- FT1/T1 Examples
- 2- and 4-Wire 56/64 kpbs Service Module Examples

FT1/T1 Examples

FT1/T1 examples are provided for these configurations:

- Specifying a T1 Frame Type Example
- Specifying the CSU Line Build Out Example
- Specifying T1 Line-Code Type Example
- Enabling Loopcodes Example
- Specifying Timeslots Example
- Displaying a Performance Report Example
- Enabling Loopback Line Examples
- Looping Back DTE Example
- Setting the Clock Source Example

Specifying a T1 Frame Type Example

The following example enables super frame as the FT1/T1 frame type:

```
service-module t1 framing sf
```

Specifying the CSU Line Build Out Example

The following example shows a line build out setting of -7.5 dB:

```
service-module t1 lbo -7.5db
```

Specifying T1 Line-Code Type Example

The following example specifies AMI as the line-code type:

```
service-module t1 linecode ami
```

Enabling Loopcodes Example

The following interactive example displays two routers connected back-to-back through an FT1/T1 line:

```
router# no service-module t1 remote-loopback full
router# service-module t1 remote-loopback payload alternate

router# loopback remote full
%SERVICE_MODULE-5-LOOPUPFAILED: Unit 0 - Loopup of remote unit failed

router# service-module t1 remote-loopback payload v54
router# loopback remote payload
%SERVICE_MODULE-5-LOOPUPFAILED: Unit 0 - Loopup of remote unit failed

router# service-module t1 remote-loopback payload alternate
router# loopback remote payload
%SERVICE_MODULE-5-LOOPUPREMOTE: Unit 0 - Remote unit placed in loopback
```

Specifying Timeslots Example

The following example displays a series of timeslot ranges and a speed of 64 kbps:

```
Router# service-module t1 timeslots 1-10,15-20,22 speed 64
```

Displaying a Performance Report Example

The following example is sample output from the **show service-module** command:

```
Router1# show service-module s 0
Module type is T1/fractional
    Hardware revision is B, Software revision is 1.1i,
    Image checksum is 0x21791D6, Protocol revision is 1.1
Receiver has AIS alarm,
Unit is currently in test mode:
    line loopback is in progress
Framing is ESF, Line Code is B8ZS, Current clock source is line,
Fraction has 24 timeslots (64 Kbits/sec each), Net bandwidth is 1536 Kbits/sec.
Last user loopback performed:
    remote loopback
    Failed to loopup remote
Last module self-test (done at startup): Passed
Last clearing of alarm counters 0:05:50
    loss of signal     :   1, last occurred 0:01:50
    loss of frame      :   0,
    AIS alarm          :   1, current duration 0:00:49
    Remote alarm       :   0,
    Module access errors  :   0,
Total Data (last 0 15 minute intervals):
    1466 Line Code Violations, 0 Path Code Violations
    0 Slip Secs, 0 Fr Loss Secs, 0 Line Err Secs, 0 Degraded Mins
    0 Errored Secs, 0 Bursty Err Secs, 0 Severely Err Secs, 0 Unavail Secs
```

```
Data in current interval (351 seconds elapsed):
    1466 Line Code Violations, 0 Path Code Violations
    25 Slip Secs, 49 Fr Loss Secs, 40 Line Err Secs, 1 Degraded Mins
    0 Errored Secs, 0 Bursty Err Secs, 0 Severely Err Secs, 49 Unavail Secs
```

Enabling Loopback Line Examples

The following example shows how to configure a payload loopback:

```
Router1# loopback line payload
Loopback in progress
Router1# no loopback line
```

The following example shows the output when you loop a packet in switched mode without an active connection:

```
Router1# service-module 56k network-type switched
Router1# loopback line payload
Need active connection for this type of loopback
% Service module configuration command failed: WRONG FORMAT.
```

Looping Back DTE Example

The following example loops a packet from a module to the serial interface:

```
Router1# loopback dte
Loopback in progress
Router1# ping 12.0.0.1
Type escape sequence to abort.
Sending 5, 100-byte ICMP Echos to 12.0.0.1, timeout is 2 seconds:
!!!!!
Success rate is 100 percent (5/5), round-trip min/avg/max = 8/12/28 ms
```

Setting the Clock Source Example

The following example shows a router using internal clocking while transmitting frames at 38.4 kbps:

```
Router1# service-module 56k clock source internal
Router1# service-module 56k clock rate 38.4
```

2- and 4-Wire 56/64 kpbs Service Module Examples

Two- and four-wire 56/64 kpbs service module examples are provided for these configurations:

- Setting the Network Line Speed Examples
- Enabling Scrambled Data Coding Example
- Enabling Switched Dial-Up Mode Example
- Displaying a Performance Report Example
- Remote Loopback Request Example
- Selecting a Service Provider Example

Setting the Network Line Speed Examples

The following interactive example displays two routers connected in back-to-back DDS mode. However, the configuration fails because the **auto** rate is used.

```
Router1# service-module 56k clock source internal
Router1# service-module 56k clock rate 38.4

Router2# service-module 56k clock rate auto
% WARNING - auto rate will not work in back-to-back DDS.

a1# ping 10.1.1.2
Type escape sequence to abort.
Sending 5, 100-byte ICMP Echos to 10.1.1.2, timeout is 2 seconds:
.....
Success rate is 0 percent (0/5)

Router2# service-module 56k clock rate 38.4

Router1# ping 10.1.1.2
Type escape sequence to abort.
Sending 5, 100-byte ICMP Echos to 10.1.1.2, timeout is 2 seconds:
!!!!!
Success rate is 100 percent (5/5), round-trip min/avg/max = 52/54/56 ms
```

When transferring from DDS mode to switched mode, you must set the correct clock rate, as shown in the following example:

```
Router2# service-module 56k network-type dds
Router2# service-module 56k clock rate 38.4
Router2# service-module 56k network-type switched
% Have to use 56k or auto clock rate for switched mode
% Service module configuration command failed: WRONG FORMAT.

Router2# service-module 56k clock rate auto
% WARNING - auto rate will not work in back-to-back DDS.
Router2# service-module 56k network-type switched
```

Enabling Scrambled Data Coding Example

The following example scrambles bit codes in 64 kbps DDS mode:

```
Router# service-module 56k clock rate 56
Router# service-module 56k data-coding scrambled
Can configure scrambler only in 64k speed DDS mode
% Service module configuration command failed: WRONG FORMAT.
Router# service-module 56k clock rate 64
Router# service-module 56k data-coding scrambled
```

Enabling Switched Dial-Up Mode Example

The following example displays transmission in switched dial-up mode:

```
Router# service-module 56k clock rate 19.2
Router# service-module 56k network-type switched
```

```
% Have to use 56k or auto clock rate for switched mode
% Service module configuration command failed: WRONG FORMAT.
Router# service-module 56k clock rate auto
Router# service-module 56k network-type switched
Router# dialer in-band
Router# dialer string 2576666
Router# dialer-group 1
```

Displaying a Performance Report Example

The following example is sample output from the **show service-module serial** command:

```
Router1# show service-module serial 1

Module type is 4-wire Switched 56
    Hardware revision is B, Software revision is X.07,
    Image checksum is 0x45354643, Protocol revision is 1.0
Connection state: active,
Receiver has loss of signal, loss of sealing current,
Unit is currently in test mode:
    line loopback is in progress
Current line rate is 56 Kbits/sec
Last user loopback performed:
    dte loopback
    duration 00:00:58
Last module self-test (done at startup): Passed
Last clearing of alarm counters 0:13:54
    oos/oof              :   3, last occurred 0:00:24
    loss of signal       :   3, current duration 0:00:24
    loss of sealing curren:   2, current duration 0:04:39
    loss of frame        :   0,
    rate adaption attempts:   0,
```

Remote Loopback Request Example

The following example enables you to transmit and receive remote loopbacks using the **service-module 56k remote-loopback** command:

```
service-module 56k remote-loopback
```

Selecting a Service Provider Example

The following example selects AT&T as the service provider:

```
service-module 56k network-type switched
service-module 56k switched-carrier att
```

## CHAPTER 22

Configuring Logical Interfaces

Use the information in this chapter to understand and configure the types of logical, or virtual, interfaces supported on Cisco routers and access servers. This chapter includes the following configuration instructions and examples:

- Configuring a Loopback Interface
- Configuring a Null Interface
- Configuring a Tunnel Interface

For examples of configuration tasks, see "Logical Interface Configuration Examples" later in this chapter.

For hardware technical descriptions and information about installing interfaces, refer to the hardware installation and maintenance publication for your product. For complete descriptions of the logical interface commands, see Chapter 23, "Interface Commands."

NOTES

In Cisco IOS Release 11.3, all commands supported on the Cisco 7500 series are also supported on the Cisco 7000 series.

CONFIGURING A LOOPBACK INTERFACE

You can specify a software-only interface called a *loopback interface* to emulate an interface. It is supported on all platforms. A *loopback interface* is a virtual interface that is always up and enables BGP and Remote Source-Route Bridging (RSRB) sessions to stay up even if the outbound interface is down.

You can use the loopback interface as the termination address for BGP sessions, for RSRB connections, or to establish a Telnet session from the device's console to its auxiliary port when all other interfaces are down. You also can use a loopback interface to configure IPX-PPP on asynchronous interfaces. To do so, you must associate an asynchronous interface with a loopback interface configured to run IPX. In applications where other routers or access servers attempt to reach this loopback interface, you should configure a routing protocol to distribute the subnet assigned to the loopback address.

Packets routed to the loopback interface are rerouted back to the router or access server and processed locally. IP packets routed out the loopback interface but not destined to the loopback interface are dropped. This means that the loopback interface serves as the Null 0 interface also.

NOTES

Loopback does not work on an X.21 DTE, because the X.21 interface definition does not include a loopback definition.

To specify a loopback interface and enter interface configuration mode, perform one of the following tasks in global configuration mode:

Task	Command
Step 1 Begin interface configuration.	**interface loopback** *number*
Step 2 Begin interface configuration for the Cisco 7200 series or the Cisco 7500 series.	**interface loopback** *slot/port*
Step 3 Begin interface configuration for the Cisco 7500 series.	**interface loopback** *slot/port-adapter/port*

See "Running Interface Loopback Diagnostics" in Chapter 19, "Overview of Interface Configuration."

CONFIGURING A NULL INTERFACE

The Cisco IOS software supports a "null" interface. This pseudo interface functions similarly to the null devices available on most operating systems. This interface is always up and can never forward or receive traffic; encapsulation always fails. The only interface configuration command that you can specify for the null interface is **no ip unreachables**.

The null interface provides an alternative method of filtering traffic. You can avoid the overhead involved with using access lists by directing undesired network traffic to the null interface.

To specify the null interface, perform the following task in global configuration mode:

Task	Command
Begin interface configuration.	**interface null 0**

Specify null 0 (or null0) as the interface type and number. The null interface can be used in any command that has an interface type as an argument. The following example configures a null interface for IP route 127.0.0.0:

```
ip route 127.0.0.0 255.0.0.0 null 0
```

CONFIGURING A TUNNEL INTERFACE

Tunneling provides a way to encapsulate arbitrary packets inside of a transport protocol. This feature is implemented as a virtual interface to provide a simple interface for configuration. The tunnel interface is not tied to specific "passenger" or "transport" protocols, but rather, it is an architecture that is designed to provide the services necessary to implement any standard point-to-point encapsulation scheme. Because tunnels are point-to-point links, you must configure a separate tunnel for each link.

Tunneling has the following three primary components:

- Passenger protocol, which is the protocol you are encapsulating (AppleTalk, Banyan VINES, CLNP, DECnet, IP, or IPX)
- Carrier protocol, which is one of the following encapsulation protocols:
  - Generic route encapsulation (GRE), Cisco's multiprotocol carrier protocol
  - Cayman, a proprietary protocol for AppleTalk over IP
  - EON, a standard for carrying CLNP-over-IP networks
  - NOS, IP over IP compatible with the popular KA9Q program
  - Distance Vector Multicast Routing Protocol (DVMRP) (IP in IP tunnels, defined by RFC 20036)
- Transport protocol, which is the protocol used to carry the encapsulated protocol (IP only)

Figure 22–1 illustrates IP tunneling terminology and concepts.

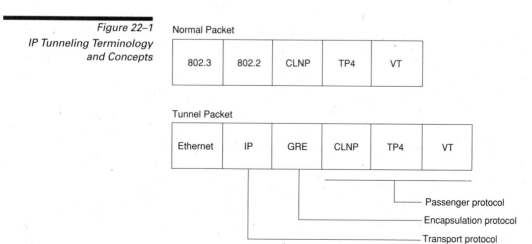

Figure 22–1
IP Tunneling Terminology and Concepts

To understand the process of tunneling, consider connecting two AppleTalk networks with a non-AppleTalk backbone, such as IP. The relatively high bandwidth consumed by the broadcasting of Routing Table Maintenance Protocol (RTMP) data packets can hamper the backbone's network performance severely. This problem can be solved by tunneling AppleTalk through a foreign protocol, such as IP. Tunneling encapsulates an AppleTalk packet inside the foreign protocol packet, which is then sent across the backbone to a destination router. The destination router then de-encapsulates the AppleTalk packet, and if necessary, routes the packet to a normal AppleTalk network. Because the encapsulated AppleTalk packet is sent in a directed manner to a remote IP address, bandwidth usage is greatly reduced. Furthermore, the encapsulated packet benefits from any features normally enjoyed by IP packets, including default routes and load balancing.

Advantages of Tunneling

The following are several situations where encapsulating traffic in another protocol is useful:

- To provide multiprotocol local networks over a single-protocol backbone
- To provide workarounds for networks containing protocols that have limited hop counts; for example, AppleTalk (see Figure 22–2)
- To connect discontinuous subnetworks
- To allow virtual private networks across wide-area networks (WANs)

Figure 22–2
Providing Workarounds
for Networks with Limited
Hop Counts

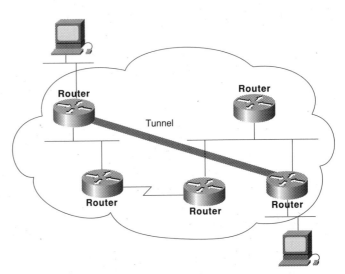

If the path between two computers has more than 15 hops, they cannot talk to each other, but it is possible to hide some of the hops inside the network with a tunnel.

Special Considerations

The following are considerations and precautions to observe when you configure tunneling:

- Encapsulation and decapsulation at the tunnel end points are slow operations; in general, only processor switching is supported. However, fast switching of GRE tunnels was introduced in version 11.1 for the Cisco 2500 series and the Cisco 4000 series of routers.

- Consider security and topology issues. Be careful not to violate access control lists. You can configure a tunnel with a source and destination that are not restricted by firewall routers.

- Tunneling might create problems with transport protocols with limited timers (for example, DECnet) due to increased latency.

- Be aware of the environments across which you create tunnels. You might be tunneling across fast FDDI rings or through slow 9600-bps phone lines; some passenger protocols behave poorly in mixed media networks.

- Multiple point-to-point tunnels can saturate the physical link with routing information.

- Routing protocols that make their decisions based solely on hop count often will prefer a tunnel over a multipoint real link. A tunnel might appear to be a one-hop, point-to-point link and have the lowest-cost path, but might actually cost more. For example, in the topology shown in Figure 22–3, packets from Host 1 will travel across networks w, q, and z to get to Host 2 instead of taking the path w, x, y, z, because the first path "appears" shorter.

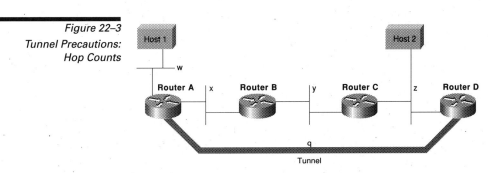

Figure 22–3
Tunnel Precautions:
Hop Counts

- An even worse problem occurs if routing information from the tunneled network mixes with the transport network's information. In this case, the best path to the "tunnel destination" is via the tunnel itself. This is called a *recursive route*, and it will cause the tunnel interface to shut down temporarily. To avoid recursive routing problems, keep passenger and transport network routing information disjointed:

  ○ Use a different AS number or tag.

  ○ Use a different routing protocol.

  ○ Use static routes to override the first hop (but watch for routing loops).

- If you see line protocol down, as in the following example, it might be because of a recursive route:

```
%TUN-RECURDOWN Interface Tunnel 0
temporarily disabled due to recursive routing
```

IP Tunneling Configuration Task List

If you want to configure IP tunneling, you must perform the tasks in the following sections:

- Specifying the Tunnel Interface
- Configuring the Tunnel Source
- Configuring the Tunnel Destination

The tasks in the following tunnel configuration sections are optional:

- Configuring the Tunnel Mode
- Configuring End-to-End Checksumming
- Configuring a Tunnel Identification Key
- Configuring a Tunnel Interface to Drop Out-of-Order Datagrams
- Configuring Asynchronous Host Mobility

For commands that monitor IP tunnels, see the section "Monitoring and Maintaining the Interface" in Chapter 19, "Overview of Interface Configuration." For examples of configuring tunnels, see the section "IP Tunneling Examples" at the end of this chapter.

Specifying the Tunnel Interface

To specify a tunnel interface and enter interface configuration mode, perform one of the following tasks in global configuration mode:

Task	Command
Begin interface configuration.	**interface tunnel** *number*
Begin interface configuration for the Cisco 7500 series.	**interface tunnel** *slot/port*

Configuring the Tunnel Source

You must specify the tunnel interface's source address by performing the following task in interface configuration mode:

Task	Command
Configure the tunnel source.	**tunnel source** {*ip-address*	*type number*}

You cannot have two tunnels using the same encapsulation mode with exactly the same source and destination address. The workaround is to create a loopback interface and source packets off of the loopback interface.

Configuring the Tunnel Destination

You must specify the tunnel interface's destination by performing the following task in interface configuration mode:

Task	Command
Configure the tunnel destination.	**tunnel destination** {*hostname*	*ip-address*}

Configuring the Tunnel Mode

The encapsulation mode for the tunnel interface defaults to generic route encapsulation (GRE), so this task is considered optional. However, if you want a mode other than GRE, you must configure it by performing the following task in interface configuration mode:

Task	Command
Configure the tunnel mode.	**tunnel mode** {**aurp**	**cayman**	**dvmrp**	**eon**	**gre ip**	**nos**}

If you are tunneling AppleTalk, you must use either the AppleTalk Update Routing Protocol (AURP), Cayman, or GRE tunneling mode. Cayman tunneling is designed by Cayman Systems and enables routers and access servers to interoperate with Cayman GatorBoxes. You can have Cisco devices at either end of the tunnel, or you can have a GatorBox at one end and Cisco router or access server at the other end. Use Distance Vector Multicast Routing Protocol (DVMRP) mode when a router or access server connects to a router to run DVMRP over a tunnel. It is required to configure Protocol-Independent Multicast (PIM) and an IP address on a DVMRP tunnel.

Do not configure a Cayman tunnel with an AppleTalk network address.

If you use GRE, you must have only Cisco routers or access servers at both ends of the tunnel connection. When you use GRE to tunnel AppleTalk, you must configure an AppleTalk network address and a zone. Perform the following tasks to tunnel AppleTalk using GRE:

Task	Command
Step 1 Enable tunneling on the interface.	**interface tunnel** *number*
Step 2 Assign a cable range to an interface.	**appletalk cable-range** *start-end* [*network.node*]
Step 3 Set a zone name for the connected AppleTalk network.	**appletalk zone** *zone-name*
Step 4 Specify the interface out which the encapsulated packets will be sent, or specify the router's IP address.	**tunnel source** {*ip-address* | *type number*}
Step 5 Specify the IP address of the router at the far end of the tunnel.	**tunnel destination** {*hostname* | *ip-address*}
Step 6 Enable GRE tunneling.	**tunnel mode gre ip**

Configuring End-to-End Checksumming

Some passenger protocols rely on media checksums to provide data integrity. By default, the tunnel does not guarantee packet integrity. By enabling end-to-end checksums, the Cisco IOS software drops corrupted packets. To enable such checksums on a tunnel interface, perform the following task in interface configuration mode:

Task	Command
Configure end-to-end checksumming.	**tunnel checksum**

Configuring a Tunnel Identification Key

You can enable an ID key optionally for a tunnel interface. This key must be set to the same value on the tunnel endpoints. Tunnel ID keys can be used as a form of *weak* security to prevent misconfiguration or injection of packets from a foreign source.

The tunnel ID key is available with GRE only.

NOTES

When using GRE, the ID key is carried in each packet. Cisco does *not* recommend relying on this key for security purposes.

To configure a tunnel ID key, perform the following task in interface configuration mode:

Task	Command
Configure a tunnel identification key.	**tunnel key** *key-number*

Configuring a Tunnel Interface to Drop Out-of-Order Datagrams

You can configure a tunnel interface optionally to drop datagrams that arrive out of order. This is useful when carrying passenger protocols that behave poorly when they receive packets out of order (for example, LLC2-based protocols). This option is available with GRE only.

To use this option, perform the following task in interface configuration mode:

Task	Command
Configure a tunnel interface to drop out-of-order datagrams.	**tunnel sequence-datagrams**

Configuring Asynchronous Host Mobility

Increasingly, remote users are accessing networks through dial-up telephone connections. In contrast to local users who can connect directly into the network, remote users must first dial into an access server.

The access server supports a packet tunneling strategy that extends the internetwork—in effect creating a virtual private link for the mobile user. When a user activates asynchronous host mobility, the access server on which the remote user dials into becomes a remote point-of-presence (POP) for the user's home network. Once logged in, users experience a server environment identical to the one that they experience when they connect directly to the "home" access server.

Once the network layer connection is made, data packets are tunneled at the physical and/or data-link layer instead of at the protocol layer. In this way, raw data bytes from dial-in users are transported directly to the "home" access server, which processes the protocols.

Figure 22–4 illustrates the implementation of asynchronous host mobility on an extended internetwork. A mobile user connects to an access server on the internetwork, and by activating asynchronous host mobility, is connected to a "home" access server configured with the appropriate user name. The user sees an authentication dialog or prompt from the "home" system and can proceed as if he or she were connected directly to that device.

Figure 22–4
Asynchronous Host Mobility

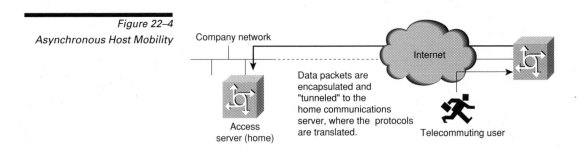

The remote user implements asynchronous host mobility by executing the **tunnel** command in the User EXEC mode. The **tunnel** command sets up a network layer connection to the specified destination. The access server accepts the connection, attaches it to a virtual terminal (VTY), and runs a command parser capable of running the normal dial-in services. After the connection is established, data is transferred between the modem and network connection with a minimum of interpretations. When communications are complete, the network connection can be closed and terminated from either end.

Refer to the *Cisco Access Connection Guide* for information about setting up the network layer connection with the **tunnel** command.

LOGICAL INTERFACE CONFIGURATION EXAMPLES

This section provides examples that illustrate configuration of IP tunnels.

IP Tunneling Examples

The following example shows an IP tunneling configuration with commented (!) explanations:

```
!Creates the interface
interface tunnel 0
 !enables IPX on the interface
 novell network 1e
 !enables appletalk
 appletalk cable-range 4001-4001 128
 !enables IP
 ip address 10.1.2.3. 255.255.255.0
 !enables DECnet
 DECnet cost 4
 !sets the source address, or interface, for packets
  tunnel source ethernet 0
!determines where the encapsulated packets are to go
 tunnel destination 131.108.14.12
 !sets the protocol
 tunnel mode gre
 !computes a checksum on passenger packets if protocol doesn't already have reliable
 !checksum
 tunnel checksum needed
 !sets the id key
```

```
tunnel key 42
!set to drop out of order packets
tunnel sequence-datagrams
```

Routing Two AppleTalk Networks Across an IP-Only Backbone Example

Figure 22–5 is an example of connecting multiprotocol subnetworks across a single-protocol backbone. The configurations of Router A and Router B follow.

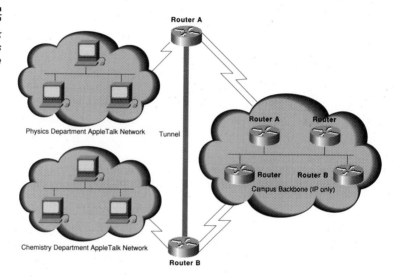

Figure 22–5

Connecting AppleTalk Networks across an IP-Only Backbone

Physics Department AppleTalk Network

Tunnel

Router A

Router

Router

Router B

Campus Backbone (IP only)

Chemistry Department AppleTalk Network

Router A

Router B

Router A

```
interface ethernet 0
 description physics department AppleTalk lan
 appletalk cable-range 4001-4001 32
 !
interface fddi 0
 description connection to campus backbone
 ip address 36.0.8.108 255.255.255.0
interface tunnel 0
 tunnel source fddi 0
 tunnel destination 36.0.21.20
 appletalk cable-range 5313-5313 1
```

Router B

```
interface ethernet 0
 description chemistry department appletalk lan
 appletalk cable-range 9458-9458 3
 !
interface fddi 0
```

```
description connection to campus backbone
ip address 36.0.21.20 255.255.255.0
interface tunnel 0
tunnel source fddi 0
tunnel destination 36.0.8.108
appletalk cable-range 5313-5313 2
```

Routing a Private IP Network and a Novell Net across a Public Service Provider Example

Figure 22–6 is an example of routing a private IP network and a Novell network across a public service provider.

Figure 22–6

Creating Virtual Private Networks across WANs

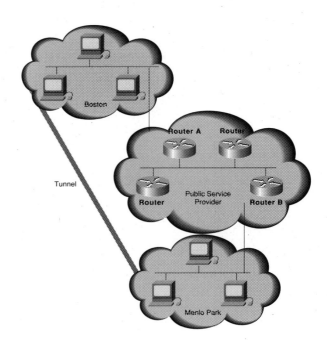

Router A

```
interface ethernet 0
 description boston office
 ip address 10.1.1.1 255.255.255.0
 novell network 1e
!
interface serial 0
 description connection to NEARnet
 ip address 192.13.2.1 255.255.255.0
!
interface tunnel 0
```

```
 tunnel source serial 0
 tunnel destination 131.108.5.2
 ip address 10.1.2.1 255.255.255.0
 novell network 1f
```

Router B

```
interface ethernet 0
 description menlo park office
 ip address 10.1.3.1 255.255.255.0
 novell network 31
 !
interface serial 4
 description connection to BARRnet
 ip address 131.108.5.2 255.255.255.0
 !
interface tunnel 0
 tunnel source serial 4
 tunnel destination 192.13.2.1
 ip address 10.1.2.2 255.255.255.0
 novell network 1f
```

## CHAPTER 23

Interface Commands

This chapter describes the commands that can be used on different types of interfaces.

For hardware technical descriptions, and for information about installing the router or access server interfaces, refer to the hardware installation and maintenance publication for your particular product.

NOTES

In Cisco IOS Release 11.3, all commands supported on the Cisco 7500 series are also supported on the Cisco 7000 series.

ACCESS-LIST (STANDARD)

Use the **access-list** global configuration command to establish MAC address access lists. Use the **no** form of this command to remove a single access list entry.

> **access-list** *access-list-number* {**permit** | **deny**} *address mask*
> **no access-list** *access-list-number*

Syntax	Description
access-list-number	Integer from 700 to 799 that you select for the list.
permit	Permits the frame.
deny	Denies the frame.
address mask	48-bit MAC addresses written in dotted triplet form. The ones bits in the *mask* argument are the bits to be ignored in the *address* value.

Default

No MAC address access lists are established.

Command Mode

Global configuration

Usage Guidelines

This command first appeared in Cisco IOS Release 10.0.

Related Commands

access-list (type-code)

ACCESS-LIST (TYPE-CODE)

Use the **access-list** global configuration command to build type-code access lists. Use the **no** form of this command to remove a single access list entry.

> **access-list** *access-list-number* {**permit** | **deny**} *type-code wild-mask*
> **no access-list** *access-list-number*

Syntax	Description
access-list-number	User-selectable number between 200 and 299 that identifies the list.
permit	Permits the frame.
deny	Denies the frame.
type-code	16-bit hexadecimal number written with a leading "0x"; for example, 0x6000. You can specify either an Ethernet type code for Ethernet-encapsulated packets, or a DSAP/SSAP pair for 802.3, or 802.5-encapsulated packets.
wild-mask	16-bit hexadecimal number whose ones bits correspond to bits in the *type-code* argument that should be ignored when making a comparison. (A mask for a DSAP/SSAP pair should always be at least 0x0101. This is because these two bits are used for purposes other than identifying the SAP codes.)

Default

No type-code access lists are built.

Command Mode

Global configuration

Usage Guidelines

This command first appeared in Cisco IOS Release 10.0.

Type-code access lists can have an impact on system performance. Therefore, keep the lists as short as possible and use wildcard bit masks whenever possible.

Access lists are evaluated according to the following algorithm:

- If the packet is Ethernet Type II or SNAP, the type-code field is used.
- For other packet types, the LSAP is used.

If the length/type field is greater than 1,500, the packet is treated as an LSAP packet unless the DSAP and SSAP fields are AAAA. If the latter is true, the packet is treated using type-code filtering.

If you have both Ethernet Type II and LSAP packets on your network, you should set up access lists for both.

Use the last item of an access list to specify a default action; for example, permit everything else or deny everything else. If nothing else in the access list matches, the default action is normally to deny access; that is, filter out all other type codes.

Related Commands

access-list (extended)
access-list (standard)

AUTO-POLARITY

To enable automatic receiver polarity reversal on a hub port connected to an Ethernet interface of a Cisco 2505 or Cisco 2507, use the **auto-polarity** hub configuration command. To disable this feature, use the **no** form of this command.

> **auto-polarity**
> **no auto-polarity**

Syntax   Description

This command has no arguments or keywords.

Default

Enabled

Command Mode

Hub configuration

Usage Guidelines

This command first appeared in Cisco IOS Release 10.3.

Part III

Command Reference

This command applies to a port on an Ethernet hub only.

Example

The following example enables automatic receiver polarity reversal on hub 0, ports 1 through 3:

```
hub ethernet 0 1 3
  auto-polarity
```

Related Commands

hub

BANDWIDTH

To set a bandwidth value for an interface, use the **bandwidth** interface configuration command. Use the **no** form of this command to restore the default values.

> **bandwidth** *kilobits*
> **no bandwidth**

Syntax	Description
kilobits	Intended bandwidth in kilobits per second. For a full bandwidth DS3, enter the value **44736**.

Default

Default bandwidth values are set during startup and can be displayed with the EXEC command **show interfaces**.

Command Mode

Interface configuration

Usage Guidelines

This command first appeared in Cisco IOS Release 10.0.

The **bandwidth** command sets an informational parameter only; you cannot adjust the actual bandwidth of an interface with this command. For some media, such as Ethernet, the bandwidth is fixed; for other media, such as serial lines, you can change the actual bandwidth by adjusting hardware. For both classes of media, you can use the **bandwidth** configuration command to communicate the current bandwidth to the higher-level protocols.

IGRP uses the minimum path bandwidth to determine a routing metric. The TCP protocol adjusts initial retransmission parameters based on the apparent bandwidth of the outgoing interface.

At higher bandwidths, the value you configure with the **bandwidth** command is not what is displayed by the **show interface** command. The value shown is that used in IGRP updates and also used in computing load.

NOTES

This is a routing parameter only; it does not affect the physical interface.

Example

The following example sets the full bandwidth for DS3 transmissions:

```
interface serial 0
  bandwidth 44736
```

Related Commands

vines metric

CABLELENGTH

To increase the pulse of a signal at the receiver and decrease the pulse from the transmitter using pulse equalization and line build-out for a T1 cable on an AS5200, use the **cablelength** interface configuration command. To return the pulse equalization and line build-out values to their default settings, use the **no** form of this command.

cablelength long {*dbgain-value dbloss-value*}
no cablelength long

Syntax	Description
long	Specifies a long cable length for channel service unit (CSU) connections.
dbgain-value	Number of decibels by which the receiver signal is increased. Use the keyword **gain26** or **gain36** to specify this value.
dbloss-value	Number of decibels by which the transmit signal is decreased. Use one of the following keywords to specify this value: • **0db** • **–7.5db** • **–15db** • **–22.5db**

Default

Long cable length, receiver gain of 36 dB, and transmitter loss of 0 dB.

Command Mode

Interface configuration

Usage Guidelines

Use this command for configuring the controller T1 interface on the AS5200 access server.

A pulse equalizer regenerates a signal that has been attenuated and filtered by a cable loss. Pulse equalization does not produce a simple gain, but it filters the signal to compensate for complex cable loss. A **gain26** receiver gain compensates for a long cable length equivalent to 26 dB of loss, while a **gain36** compensates for 36 dB of loss.

The lengthening or *building out* of a line is used to control far-end crosstalk. Line build-out attenuates the stronger signal from the customer installation transmitter so that the transmitting and receiving signals have similar amplitudes. A signal difference of less than 7.5 dB is ideal. Line build-out does not produce simple flat loss (also known as *resistive* flat loss). Instead, it simulates a cable loss of 7.5 dB, 15 dB, or 22.5 dB so that the resulting signal is handled properly by the receiving equalizer at the other end.

Example

The following example increases the receiver gain by 26 decibels and decreases the transmitting pulse by 7.5 decibels for a long cable:

```
AS5200(config)# controller t1 0
AS5200(config-controller)# cablelength long gain26 -7.5db
```

CAS-GROUP

To configure channelized T1 timeslots with channel-associated signaling (also known as *robbed bit signaling*), which enables an AS5200 modem to answer and send an analog call, use the **cas-group** controller configuration command. Use the **no** form of this command to disable channel-associated signaling for one or more timeslots.

> **cas-group** *channel-number* [**timeslots** *range*]
> **no cas-group** *channel-number* [**timeslots** *range*]

Syntax	Description
channel-number	Specifies a single channel-group number. The channel number can be between 0 and 23.
timeslots *range*	(Optional) Specifies a timeslot range of values from 1 to 24. The default value configures 24 timeslots with the channel-associated signal called E&M (Ear and Mouth), which is the default signal type.

Default

Disabled

Command Mode

Controller configuration

Usage Guidelines

Use this command to enable an AS5200 modem to receive and send incoming and outgoing analog calls through each T1 controller that is configured for a channelized T1 line, which has 24 possible channels.

Switched 56 digital calls are not supported under this new feature.

Example

The following example shows you how to configure all 24 channels to support robbed bit signaling on a Cisco AS5200:

```
AS5200(config)# controller T1 0
AS5200(config-controller)# cas-group 1 timeslots 1-24
AS5200(config-controller)#
%DSX0-5-RBSLINEUP: RBS of controller 1 timeslot 1 is up
%DSX0-5-RBSLINEUP: RBS of controller 1 timeslot 2 is up
%DSX0-5-RBSLINEUP: RBS of controller 1 timeslot 3 is up
%DSX0-5-RBSLINEUP: RBS of controller 1 timeslot 4 is up
%DSX0-5-RBSLINEUP: RBS of controller 1 timeslot 5 is up
%DSX0-5-RBSLINEUP: RBS of controller 1 timeslot 6 is up
%DSX0-5-RBSLINEUP: RBS of controller 1 timeslot 7 is up
%DSX0-5-RBSLINEUP: RBS of controller 1 timeslot 8 is up
%DSX0-5-RBSLINEUP: RBS of controller 1 timeslot 9 is up
%DSX0-5-RBSLINEUP: RBS of controller 1 timeslot 10 is up
%DSX0-5-RBSLINEUP: RBS of controller 1 timeslot 11 is up
%DSX0-5-RBSLINEUP: RBS of controller 1 timeslot 12 is up
%DSX0-5-RBSLINEUP: RBS of controller 1 timeslot 13 is up
%DSX0-5-RBSLINEUP: RBS of controller 1 timeslot 14 is up
%DSX0-5-RBSLINEUP: RBS of controller 1 timeslot 15 is up
%DSX0-5-RBSLINEUP: RBS of controller 1 timeslot 16 is up
%DSX0-5-RBSLINEUP: RBS of controller 1 timeslot 17 is up
%DSX0-5-RBSLINEUP: RBS of controller 1 timeslot 18 is up
%DSX0-5-RBSLINEUP: RBS of controller 1 timeslot 19 is up
%DSX0-5-RBSLINEUP: RBS of controller 1 timeslot 20 is up
%DSX0-5-RBSLINEUP: RBS of controller 1 timeslot 21 is up
%DSX0-5-RBSLINEUP: RBS of controller 1 timeslot 22 is up
%DSX0-5-RBSLINEUP: RBS of controller 1 timeslot 23 is up
%DSX0-5-RBSLINEUP: RBS of controller 1 timeslot 24 is up
```

CHANNEL-GROUP

Use the **channel-group** controller configuration command to define the timeslots that belong to each T1 or E1 circuit.

channel-group *number* **timeslots** *range* [**speed** {48 | 56 | 64}]

Syntax	Description
number	Channel-group number. When configuring a T1 data line, channel-group numbers can be values from 0 to 23. When configuring an E1 data line, channel-group numbers can be values from 0 to 30.
timeslots *range*	Timeslot or range of timeslots belonging to the channel group. The first timeslot is numbered 1. For a T1 controller, the timeslot range is from 1 to 24. For an E1 controller, the timeslot range is from 1 to 31.
speed {48 | 56 | 64}	(Optional) Specifies the line speed (in kilobits per second) of the T1 or E1 link.

Default

The default line speed when configuring a T1 controller is 56 kbps.

The default line speed when configuring an E1 controller is 64 kbps.

Command Mode

Controller configuration

Usage Guidelines

This command first appeared in Cisco IOS Release 10.0.

Use this command in configurations where the router or access server must communicate with a T1 or E1 fractional data line. The channel-group number may be arbitrarily assigned and must be unique for the controller. The timeslot range must match the timeslots assigned to the channel group. The service provider defines the timeslots that comprise a channel group.

Example

In the following example, three channel groups are defined. Channel group 0 consists of a single timeslot; channel group 8 consists of seven timeslots and runs at a speed of 64 kbps per timeslot, and channel group 12 consists of a single timeslot.

```
channel-group 0 timeslots 1
channel-group 8 timeslots 5,7,12-15,20 speed 64
channel-group 12 timeslots 2
```

Related Commands

framing
linecode

CLEAR CONTROLLER LEX

To reboot the LAN Extender chassis and restart its operating software, use the **clear controller lex** privileged EXEC command.

clear controller lex *number* [**prom**]
clear controller lex *slot/port* [**prom**] (for Cisco 7500 series routers)
clear controller lex [*type slot/port*] (Cisco 7200 series and for the Cisco 7500 series with a Packet over SONET Interface Processor)
clear controller lex [*type slot/port-adapter/port*] (for Cisco 7500 series with ports on VIP cards)

Syntax	Description
number	Number of the LAN Extender interface corresponding to the LAN Extender to be rebooted.
prom	(Optional) Forces a reload of the PROM image, regardless of any Flash image.
slot	Refer to the appropriate hardware manual for slot and port information.
port	Refer to the appropriate hardware manual for slot and port information.

Command Mode

Privileged EXEC

Usage Guidelines

This command first appeared in Cisco IOS Release 10.3.

The **clear controller lex** command halts operation of the LAN Extender and performs a cold restart.

Without the **prom** keyword, if an image exists in Flash memory, and that image has a newer software version than the PROM image, and that image has a valid checksum, then this command runs the Flash image. If any one of these three conditions is not met, this command reloads the PROM image.

With the **prom** keyword, this command reloads the PROM image, regardless of any Flash image.

Examples

The following example halts operation of the LAN Extender bound to LAN Extender interface 2 and causes the LAN Extender to perform a cold restart from Flash memory:

```
Router# clear controller lex 2
reload remote lex controller? [confirm] yes
```

Part
III

Command Reference

The following example halts operation of the LAN Extender bound to LAN Extender interface 2 and causes the LAN Extender to perform a cold restart from PROM:

```
Router# clear controller lex 2 prom
reload remote lex controller? [confirm] yes
```

CLEAR COUNTERS

To clear the interface counters, use the **clear counters** EXEC command.

> **clear counters** [*type number*]
> **clear counters** [*type slot/port*] [**ethernet** | **serial**] (for the Cisco 4000 series or Cisco 7500 series routers and a LAN Extender interface)
> **clear counters** [*type slot/port*] (for Cisco 7200 series, and for the Cisco 7500 with a Packet over SONET Interface Processor)
> **clear counters** [*type slot/port-adapter/port*]　(for Cisco 7500 series with ports on VIP cards)

Syntax	Description
type	(Optional) Specifies the interface type; one of the keywords listed in Table 23–1.
number	(Optional) Specifies the interface counter displayed with the **show interfaces** command.
ethernet	(Optional) If the *type* is **lex,** you can clear the interface counters on the Ethernet interface.
serial	(Optional) If the *type* is **lex,** you can clear the interface counters on the serial interface.
slot	Refer to the appropriate hardware manual for slot and port information.
port	Refer to the appropriate hardware manual for slot and port information.
port-adapter	Refer to the appropriate hardware manual for information about port adapter compatibility.

Command Mode
EXEC

Usage Guidelines
This command first appeared in Cisco IOS Release 10.0.

This command was modified in Cisco IOS Release 11.3 to include the **vg-anylan** interface type keyword and to change the **posi** keyword to **pos.**

This command clears all the current interface counters from the interface unless the optional arguments *type* and *number* are specified to clear only a specific interface type (serial, Ethernet, Token Ring, and so on). Table 23–1 lists the command keywords and their descriptions.

NOTES

This command will not clear counters retrieved using SNMP, but only those seen with the **show interface** EXEC command.

Table 23–1 *Clear Counters Interface Type Keywords*

Keyword	Interface Type
async	Asynchronous interface
bri	Integrated Services Digital Network (ISDN) Basic Rate Interface (BRI)
dialer	Dialer interface
ethernet	Ethernet interface
fast-ethernet	Fast Ethernet interface
fddi	Fiber Distributed Data Interface (FDDI)
hssi	High-Speed Serial Interface (HSSI)
lex	LAN Extender interface
loopback	Loopback interface
null	Null interface
pos	Packet OC-3 interface
serial	Synchronous serial interface
tokenring	Token Ring interface
tunnel	Tunnel interface
vg-anylan	100VG-AnyLAN port adapter

Part III

Command Reference

Examples

The following example clears all interface counters:

```
clear counters
```

The following example clears the Packet OC-3 interface counters on a POSIP card in slot 1 on a Cisco 7500 series router:

```
clear counters pos 1/0
```

The following example clears interface counters on the serial interface residing on a Cisco 1000 series LAN Extender:

```
clear counters lex 0 serial
```

Related Commands

show interfaces

CLEAR HUB

Use the **clear hub** EXEC command to reset and reinitialize the hub hardware connected to an interface of Cisco 2505 or 2507 routers.

clear hub ethernet *number*

Syntax	*Description*
ethernet	Indicates the hub in front of an Ethernet interface.
number	Hub number to clear, starting with 0. Because there is currently only one hub, this number is 0.

Command Mode

EXEC

Usage Guidelines

This command first appeared in Cisco IOS Release 10.3.

Example

The following example clears hub 0:

```
clear hub ethernet 0
```

Related Commands

hub

CLEAR HUB COUNTERS

Use the **clear hub counters** EXEC command to set to zero the hub counters on an interface of Cisco 2505 or 2507 routers.

clear hub counters [ether *number* [*port* [*end-port*]]]

Syntax	Description
ether	(Optional) Indicates the hub in front of an Ethernet interface.
number	(Optional) Hub number for which to clear counters. Because there is currently only one hub, this number is 0. If you specify the keyword **ether**, you must specify the *number*.
port	(Optional) Port number on the hub. On the Cisco 2505 router, port numbers range from 1 to 8. On the Cisco 2507 router, port numbers range from 1 to 16. If a second port number follows, then this port number indicates the beginning of a port range. If you do not specify a port number, counters for all ports are cleared.
end-port	(Optional) Ending port number of a range.

Command Mode
EXEC

Usage Guidelines
This command first appeared in Cisco IOS Release 10.3.

Example
The following example clears the counters displayed in a **show hub** command for all ports on hub 0:

```
clear hub counters ether 0
```

Related Commands
show hub

CLEAR INTERFACE

Use the **clear interface** EXEC command to reset the hardware logic on an interface.

clear interface *type number*
clear interface *type slot/port* (Cisco 7200, and 7500 series routers with a
  Packet OC-3 Interface Processor)
clear interface [*type slot/port-adapter/port*] (ports on VIP cards in 7500 series routers)
clear interface *type slot/port* [*:channel-group*] (Cisco 7500 series routers
clear interface *type slot/port-adapter/port* [*:t1-channel*]   (CT3IP in Cisco 7500 series routers)

Syntax	Description
type	Specifies the interface type; it is one of the keywords listed Table 23–2 in the "Usage Guidelines" section.
number	Specifies the port, connector, or interface card number.

Syntax	*Description*
slot	Refer to the appropriate hardware manual for slot and port information.
port	Refer to the appropriate hardware manual for slot and port information.
port-adapter	Refer to the appropriate hardware manual for information about port adapter compatibility.
:channel-group	(Optional) On Cisco 7500 series routers supporting channelized T1, specifies the channel from 0 to 23. This number is preceded by a colon.
:t1-channel	(Optional) For the CT3IP, the T1 channel is a number between 1 and 28.
	T1 channels on the CT3IP are numbered 1 to 28 rather than the more traditional zero-based scheme (0 to 27) used with other Cisco products. This numbering scheme ensures consistency with telco numbering schemes for T1 channels within channelized T3 equipment.

Command Mode

EXEC

Usage Guidelines

This command first appeared in Cisco IOS Release 10.0.

This command was modified in Cisco IOS Release 11.3 to include the **vg-anylan** interface type keyword and to change the **posi** keyword to **pos**.

Under normal circumstances, you do not need to clear the hardware logic on interfaces.

This command clears all the current interface hardware logic unless the optional arguments *type* and *number* are specified to clear only a specific interface type (serial, Ethernet, Token Ring, and so on). Table 23–2 lists the command keywords and their descriptions.

Table 23–2   *Clear Interface Type Keywords*

Keyword	Interface Type
async	Async interface
atm	Asynchronous Transfer Mode (ATM) interface
bri	Integrated Services Digital Network (ISDN) Basic Rate Interface (BRI)
ethernet	Ethernet interface
fddi	Fiber Distributed Data Interface (FDDI)

Table 23–2 *Clear Interface Type Keywords, Continued*

Keyword	Interface Type
hssi	High-Speed Serial Interface (HSSI)
loopback	Loopback interface
null	Null interface
pos	Packet OC-3 Interface Processor
serial	Synchronous serial interface
tokenring	Token Ring interface
tunnel	Tunnel interface
vg-anylan	100VG-AnyLAN port adapter

Examples

The following example resets the interface logic on HSSI interface 1:

```
clear interface hssi 1
```

The following example resets the interface logic on Packet OC-3 interface 0 on the POSIP in slot 1:

```
clear interface pos 1/0
```

The following example resets the interface logic on T1 0 on the CT3IP in slot 9:

```
clear interface serial 9/0/0:0
```

CLEAR INTERFACE FASTETHERNET

Use the **clear interface fastethernet** privileged EXEC command to reset the controller for a specified Fast Ethernet interface.

> **clear interface fastethernet** *number* (Cisco 4500 and 4700 series routers)
> **clear interface fastethernet** *slot/port* (Cisco 7200 and Cisco 7500 series routers)
> **clear interface fastethernet** *slot/port-adapter/port* (Cisco 7500 series routers)

Syntax	Description
number	Port, connector, or interface card number. On a Cisco 4500 or Cisco 4700 router, specifies the NPM number. The numbers are assigned at the factory at the time of installation or when added to a system.
slot	Refer to the appropriate hardware manual for slot and port information.

Syntax	*Description*
port	Refer to the appropriate hardware manual for slot and port information.
port-adapter	Refer to the appropriate hardware manual for information about port adapter compatibility.

Command Mode

Privileged EXEC

Usage Guidelines

This command first appeared in Cisco IOS Release 11.2.

Examples

The following example resets the controller for the Ethernet 0 interface on a Cisco 4500:

```
clear interface fastethernet 0
```

The following example resets the controller for the Ethernet interface located in slot 1 port 0 on a Cisco 7200 or Cisco 7500:

```
clear interface fastethernet 1/0
```

The following example resets the controller for the Ethernet interface located in slot 1 port adapter 0 port 0 on a Cisco 7500:

```
clear interface fastethernet 1/0/0
```

CLEAR RIF-CACHE

Use the **clear rif-cache** EXEC command to clear entries from the Routing Information Field (RIF) cache.

clear rif-cache

Syntax   *Description*

This command has no arguments or keywords.

Command Mode

EXEC

Usage Guidelines

This command first appeared in Cisco IOS Release 10.0.

Example

The following example clears the RIF cache:

```
clear rif-cache
```

Related Commands

multiring

CLEAR SERVICE-MODULE SERIAL

Use the **clear service-module serial** privileged EXEC configuration command to reset an integrated CSU/DSU.

clear service-module serial *number*

Syntax	*Description*
number	Number of the serial interface.

Command Mode

Privileged EXEC

Usage Guidelines

This command first appeared in Cisco IOS Release 11.2.

Use this command only in severe circumstances (for example, when the router is not responding to a CSU/DSU configuration command).

This command terminates all DTE and line loopbacks that are locally or remotely configured. It also interrupts data transmission through the router for up to 15 seconds. The software performs an automatic software reset in case of two consecutive configuration failures.

The CSU/DSU module is not reset with the **clear interface** command.

— **CAUTION** —

If you experience technical difficulties with your router and intend to contact customer support, refrain from using this command. This command erases the router's past CSU/DSU performance statistics. To clear only the CSU/DSU performance statistics, issue the **clear counters** command.

Example

The following example resets the CSU/DSU on a router:

```
router# clear service-module serial 0
router#
```

Related Commands

clear counters
test service-module

CLOCK RATE

Use the **clock rate** interface configuration command to configure the clock rate for the hardware connections on serial interfaces such as network interface modules (NIMs) and interface processors to an acceptable bit rate. Use the **no** form of this command to remove the clock rate if you change the interface from a DCE to a DTE device. Using the **no** form of this command on a DCE interface sets the clock rate to the hardware-dependent default value.

clock rate *bps*
no clock rate

Syntax	*Description*
bps	Desired clock rate in bits per second: 1,200 2,400 4,800 9,600 19,200 38,400 56,000 64,000 72,000 125,000 148,000 250,000 500,000 800,000 1,000,000 1,300,000 2,000,000 4,000,000 or 8,000,000.
	For the synchronous serial port adapters (PA-8T-V35, PA-8T-X21, PA-8T-232, and PA-4T+), a nonstandard clock rate can be used. You can enter any value from 300 to 8,000,000 bps. The clock rate you enter is rounded (adjusted), if necessary, to the nearest value your hardware can support except for the following standard rates: 1,200 2,400 4,800 9,600 14,400 19,200 28,800 38,400 56,000 64,000 128,000 or 2,015,232.

Default

No clock rate is configured.

Command Mode

Interface configuration

Usage Guidelines

This command first appeared in Cisco IOS Release 10.0.

This command was modified in Cisco IOS Release 11.3 to include nonstandard clock rates for the PA-8T-V35, PA-8T-X21, PA-8T-232, and PA-4T+ synchronous serial port adapters.

Cable Length

Be aware that the fastest speeds might not work if your cable is too long, and that speeds faster than 148,000 bits per second are too fast for EIA/TIA-232 signaling. It is recommended that you only use the synchronous serial EIA/TIA-232 signal at speeds up to 64,000 bits per second. To permit a faster speed, use EIA/TIA-449 or V.35.

Synchronous Serial Port Adapters

For the synchronous serial port adapters (PA-8T-V35, PA-8T-X21, PA-8T-232, and PA-4T+) on Cisco 7200 series routers, and on second-generation Versatile Interface Processors (VIP2s) in Cisco 7500 series routers, the clock rate you enter is rounded (if needed) to the nearest value that your hardware can support. To display the clock rate value for the port adapter, use the **show running-configuration** command.

If you plan to netboot your router over a synchronous serial port adapter interface and have a boot image prior to Cisco IOS Release 11.1(9)CA that does not support nonstandard (rounded) clock rates for the port adapters, you must use one of the following standard clock rates:

1200, 2400, 4800, 9600, 19200, 38400, 56000, 64000

Examples

The following example sets the clock rate on the first serial interface to 64,000 bits per second:

```
interface serial 0
 clock rate 64000
```

The following example sets the clock rate on a synchronous serial port adapter in slot 5, port 0 to 1234567. In this example, the clock rate is adjusted to 1,151,526 bps.

```
interface serial 5/0
 clock rate 1234567
%Clockrate rounded to nearest value that your hardware can support.
%Use Exec Command 'show running-config' to see the value rounded to.
```

The following example configures serial interface 5/0 with a clock rate that is rounded to the nearest value that is supported by the hardware:

```
Router# configure terminal
Enter configuration commands, one per line.  End with CNTL/Z.
Router(config)# interface serial 5/0
Router(config-if)# clock rate 1234567
%Clockrate rounded to nearest value that your hardware can support.
%Use Exec Command 'show running-config' to see the value rounded to.
Router(config-if)# exit
Router(config)#
```

The following example shows how to determine the exact clock rate that the serial interface was rounded to using the **show running-config** command. This example shows only the relevant information displayed by the **show running-config** command; other information was omitted.

```
Router# show running-config
Building configuration...
...
!
interface Serial5/0
 no ip address
 clockrate 1151526
!
...
```

CLOCK SOURCE

Use the **clock source** controller configuration command to specify where the clock source is obtained for use by the Channelized T3 Interface Processor (CT3IP) in Cisco 7500 series routers. Use the **no** form of this command to restore the default clock source.

> **clock source {internal | line}**
> **no clock source**

Syntax	Description
internal	Specifies that the internal clock source is used. This is the default.
line	Specifies that the network clock source is used.

Default

internal

Command Mode

Controller configuration

Usage Guidelines

This command first appeared in Cisco IOS Release 11.3.

If you do not specify the **clock source** command, the default clock source of internal is used by the CT3IP.

You also can set the clock source for each T1 channel by using the **t1 clock source** controller configuration command.

Example

In the following example, the clock source for the CT3IP is set to line:

```
controller t3 9/0/0
  clock source line
```

Related Commands

interface ethernet 2 squelch reduced

CLOCK SOURCE (CISCO AS5200)

Use the **clock source** interface configuration command to select the clock source for the time-division multiplexing (TDM) bus in a Cisco AS5200 access server. The **no** form of this command configures the clock source to its default setting.

> **clock source {line {primary | secondary} | internal}**
> **no clock source line {primary | secondary}**

Syntax	Description
line	Clock source on the active line.
primary	Primary TDM clock source.
secondary	Secondary TDM clock source.
internal	Selects the free-running clock (also known as internal clock) as the clock source.

Defaults

Primary TDM clock source from the T1 0 controller

Secondary TDM clock source from the T1 1 controller

Command Mode

Interface configuration

Usage Guidelines

This command first appeared in Cisco IOS Release 11.2.

To use the clocking coming in from a T1 line, configure the **clock source line primary** command on the T1 interface that has the most reliable clocking. Configure the **clock source line secondary** command on the T1 interface that has the next best known clocking. With this configuration, the primary line clocking is backed up to the secondary line if the primary clocking shuts down.

Example

The following example configures the Cisco AS5200 access server to use T1 controller 0 as the primary clock source and T1 controller 1 as the secondary clock source:

```
controller t1 0
clock source line primary
controller t1 1
clock source line secondary
```

CLOCK SOURCE (CONTROLLER)

Use the **clock source** controller configuration command to set the T1-line clock source for the MIP in the Cisco 7200 series and Cisco 7500 series or for the NPM in the Cisco 4000 series.

clock source {line | internal}

Syntax	Description
line	Specifies the T1 line as the clock source.
internal	Specifies the MIP (Cisco 7200 series and Cisco 7500 series) or the NPM (Cisco 4000) as the clock source.

Part III

Command Reference

Defaults

Primary TDM clock source from the T0 controller

Secondary TDM clock source from the T1 controller

Command Mode

Controller configuration

Usage Guidelines

This command first appeared in Cisco IOS Release 10.0.

To use the clocking coming in from a T1 line, configure the **clock source line primary** command on the controller that has the most reliable clocking. Configure the **clock source line secondary** command on the controller that has the next best known clocking. With this configuration, the primary line clocking is backed up to the secondary line if the primary clocking shuts down.

Example

The following example configures the Cisco AS5200 to use the T0 controller as the primary clocking source and the T1 controller as the secondary clocking source:

```
AS5200(config)# controller t1 0
AS5200(config-if)# clock source line primary
AS5200(config-if)# exit
AS5200(config)# controller t1 1
AS5200(config-if)# clock source line secondary
```

Related Commands

framing
linecode

CLOCK SOURCE (INTERFACE)

Use the **clock source** interface configuration command to control which clock a G.703 E1 interface will use to clock its transmitted data. The **no** form of this command restores the default value.

> **clock source** {**line** | **internal**}
> **no clock source**

Syntax	Description
line	Specifies that the interface will clock its transmitted data from a clock recovered from the line's receive data stream (default).
internal	Specifies that the interface will clock its transmitted data from its internal clock.

Default

By default, the applique uses the line's receive data stream.

Command Mode

Interface configuration

Usage Guidelines

This command first appeared in Cisco IOS Release 10.3.

This command applies to a Cisco 4000 router or Cisco 7500 series router. A G.703-E1 interface can clock its transmitted data from either its internal clock or from a clock recovered from the line's receive data stream.

Example

The following example specifies the G.703-E1 interface to clock its transmitted data from its internal clock:

```
clock source internal
```

CLOCK SOURCE (INTERFACE)

To control which clock a G.703-E1 interface will use to clock its transmitted data, use the **clock source** interface configuration command. The **no** form of this command restores the default value.

Part III

clock source {line | internal}
no clock source

clock source {line {primary | secondary} | internal} (Cisco AS5200 only)
no clock source line {primary | secondary}

Syntax	Description
line	Specifies that the interface will clock its transmitted data from a clock recovered from the line's receive data stream (default).
internal	Specifies that the interface will clock its transmitted data from its internal clock.
primary	Primary TDM clock source.
secondary	Secondary TDM clock source.

Default

By default, the applique uses the line's receive data stream.

Primary TDM clock source from the T0 controller on the Cisco AS5200.

Secondary TDM clock source from the T1 controller on the Cisco AS5200.

Command Reference

Command Mode

Interface configuration

Usage Guidelines

This command first appeared in Cisco IOS Release 10.3.

On the Cisco 4000 router and Cisco 7500 series router, a G.703-E1 interface can clock its transmitted data from either its internal clock or from a clock recovered from the line's receive data stream.

To use the clocking coming in from a T1 line for the Cisco AS5200, configure the **clock source line primary** command on the controller that has the most reliable clocking. Configure the **clock source line secondary** command on the controller that has the next best known clocking. With this configuration, the primary line clocking is backed up to the secondary line if the primary clocking shuts down.

Examples

The following example specifies the G.703-E1 interface to clock its transmitted data from its internal clock:

```
clock source internal
```

The following example configures the Cisco AS5200 to use the T0 controller as the primary clocking source and the T1 controller as the secondary clocking source:

```
AS5200(config)# controller t1 0
AS5200(config-if)# clock source line primary
AS5200(config-if)# exit
AS5200(config)# controller t1 1
AS5200(config-if)# clock source line secondary
```

CMT CONNECT

Use the **cmt connect** EXEC command to start the processes that perform the connection management (CMT) function and allow the ring on one fiber to be started.

cmt connect [*interface-name* [**phy-a** | **phy-b**]]

Syntax	Description
interface-name	(Optional) Specifies the FDDI interface.
phy-a	(Optional) Selects Physical Sublayer A.
phy-b	(Optional) Selects Physical Sublayer B.

Command Mode

EXEC

Usage Guidelines

This command first appeared in Cisco IOS Release 10.0.

In normal operation, the FDDI interface is operational once the interface is connected and configured. The **cmt connect** command allows the operator to start the processes that perform the CMT function.

The **cmt connect** command is not needed in the normal operation of FDDI; this command is used mainly in interoperability tests.

Examples

The following examples demonstrate use of the **cmt connect** command for starting the CMT processes on the FDDI ring.

The following command starts all FDDI interfaces:

```
cmt connect
```

The following command starts both fibers on the FDDI interface unit 0:

```
cmt connect fddi 0
```

The following command on the Cisco 7200 series or Cisco 7500 series starts both fibers on the FDDI interface unit 0:

```
cmt connect fddi 1/0
```

The following command starts only Physical Sublayer A on the FDDI interface unit 0:

```
cmt connect fddi 0 phy-a
```

The following command on Cisco 7500 series routers starts only Physical Sublayer A on the FDDI interface unit 0:

```
cmt connect fddi 1/0 phy-a
```

CMT DISCONNECT

Use the **cmt disconnect** EXEC command to stop the processes that perform the connection management (CMT) function and allow the ring on one fiber to be stopped.

cmt disconnect [*interface-name* [**phy-a** | **phy-b**]]

Syntax	Description
interface-name	(Optional) Specifies the FDDI interface.
phy-a	(Optional) Selects Physical Sublayer A.
phy-b	(Optional) Selects Physical Sublayer B.

Command Mode

EXEC

Usage Guidelines

This command first appeared in Cisco IOS Release 10.0.

In normal operation, the FDDI interface is operational once the interface is connected and configured, and is turned off using the **shutdown** interface configuration command. The **cmt disconnect** command allows the operator to stop the processes that perform the CMT function and allow the ring on one fiber to be stopped.

The **cmt disconnect** command is not needed in the normal operation of FDDI; this command is used mainly in interoperability tests.

Examples

The following examples demonstrate use of the **cmt disconnect** command for stopping the CMT processes on the FDDI ring.

The following command stops all FDDI interfaces:

```
cmt disconnect
```

The following command stops both fibers on the FDDI interface unit 0:

```
cmt disconnect fddi 0
```

The following command on the Cisco 7200 series or Cisco 7500 series stops both fibers on the FDDI interface unit 0:

```
cmt disconnect fddi 1/0
```

The following command stops only Physical Sublayer A on the FDDI interface unit 0. This command causes the FDDI media to go into a wrapped state so that the ring will be broken.

```
cmt disconnect fddi 0 phy-a
```

The following command on the Cisco 7500 series stops only Physical Sublayer A on the FDDI interface unit 0 in slot 1. This command causes the FDDI media to go into a wrapped state so that the ring will be broken.

```
cmt disconnect fddi 1/0 phy-a
```

COMPRESS

To configure compression for Link Access Procedure, Balanced (LAPB), Point-to-Point Protocol (PPP), and High-Level Data Link Control (HDLC) encapsulations, use the **compress** interface configuration command. On Cisco 7200 series routers and Cisco 7500 series routers, hardware compression on the compression service adapter (CSA) is supported for PPP links. To disable compression, use the **no** form of this command.

compress {predictor | stac}
no compress {predictor | stac}

compress {predictor | stac [distributed | software]}
compress {predictor | stac [csa *slot* | software]} (Cisco 7200 series)

Syntax	Description
predictor	Specifies that a predictor (RAND) compression algorithm will be used on LAPB and PPP encapsulation. Compression is implemented in the software installed in the router's main processor.
stac	Specifies that a Stacker (LZS) compression algorithm will be used on LAPB, HDLC, and PPP encapsulation. For all platforms except Cisco 7200 series and platforms that support the VIP2, compression is implemented in the software installed in the router's main processor.
	On Cisco 7200 series and on VIP2s in Cisco 7500 series specifying the **compress stac** command with no options, this causes the router to use the fastest available compression method for PPP encapsulation only:
	• If the router contains a compression service adapter (CSA), compression is performed in the CSA hardware (hardware compression).
	• If the CSA is not available, compression is performed in the software installed on the VIP2 (distributed compression).
	• If the VIP2 is not available, compression is performed in the router's main processor (software compression).
distributed	(Optional) Specifies that compression is implemented in the software that is installed in a VIP2. If the VIP2 is not available, compression is performed in the router's main processor (software compression).
software	(Optional) Specifies that compression is implemented in the Cisco IOS software installed in the router's main processor.
csa *slot*	(Optional) Specifies the CSA to use for a particular interface. This option applies only to Cisco 7200 series routers.

Default

Compression is disabled.

Command Mode

Interface configuration

Usage Guidelines

This command first appeared in Cisco IOS Release 10.0 (as **compress predictor**). The command **compress {predictor | stac}** first appeared in Cisco IOS Release 10.3.

This command was modified in Cisco IOS Release 11.3 P to include the **distributed**, **software**, and **csa** keywords.

Using CSA hardware compression on Cisco 7200 series routers and Cisco 7500 series routers removes the compression and decompression responsibilities from the VIP2 or the main processor installed in the router. By using the **compress stac** command, the router determines the fastest compression method available on the router.

When using hardware compression on Cisco 7200 series routers with multiple CSAs, you can specify optionally which CSA is used by the interface to perform compression. If no CSA is specified, the router determines which CSA is used. On Cisco 7500 series routers, the router uses the CSA on the same VIP2 as the interface.

You can configure point-to-point software compression for all LAPB, PPP, and HDLC encapsulations. Compression reduces the size of frames via lossless data compression. HDLC encapsulations support the Stacker compression algorithm. PPP and LAPB encapsulations support both predictor and Stacker compression algorithms.

When compression is performed in software installed in the router's main processor, it might affect system performance significantly. Cisco recommends that you disable compression if the CPU load exceeds 40 percent. To display the CPU load, use the **show process cpu** EXEC command.

Compression requires that both ends of the serial link be configured to use compression.

If the majority of your traffic is already compressed files, Cisco recommends that you not use compression. If the files are already compressed, the additional processing time spent in attempting unsuccessfully to compress them again will slow system performance.

Table 23–3 provides general guidelines for deciding which compression type to select.

Table 23–3 *Compression Guidelines*

Situation	Compression Type to Use
The bottleneck is caused by the load on the router.	Predictor
The bottleneck is the result of line bandwidth or hardware compression on theCSA is available.	Stacker
Most files are already compressed.	None

Software compression makes heavy demands on the router's processor. The maximum compressed serial line rate depends on the type of Cisco router you are using and which compression algorithm you specify. Table 23–3 shows a summary of the compressed serial line rates for software compression. The maximums shown in Table 23–4 apply to the "combined" serial compressed load on the router. For example, a Cisco 4000 series router could handle four 64-kbps lines using Stacker or one 256-kbps line. These maximums also assume there is very little processor load on the router, aside from compression. Lower these numbers when the router is required to do other processor-intensive tasks.

Table 23–4 *Combined Compressed Serial Line Rates (Software Compression)*

Compression Method	Cisco 1000 Series	Cisco 3000 Series	Cisco 4000 Series	Cisco 4500 Series	Cisco 4700 Series	Cisco 7000 Family
Stacker (kbps)	128	128	256	500	T1	256
Predictor (kbps)	256	256	500	T1	2xT1	500

Hardware compression can support a combined line rate of 16Mbps.

Cisco recommends that you do not adjust the maximum transmission unit (MTU) for the serial interface and the LAPB maximum bits per frame (N1) parameter.

Examples

The following example enables hardware compression and PPP encapsulation on serial interface 3/1/0.

```
interface serial 3/1/0
  encapsulate ppp
  compress stac
```

The following example enables predictor compression on serial interface 0 for a LAPB link:

```
interface serial 0
  encapsulation lapb
  compress predictor
```

Related Commands

encapsulation lapb
encapsulation ppp
encapsulation x25
ppp compress
show compress
show processes

CONTROLLER T3

To configure the Channelized T3 Interface Processor (CT3IP) in Cisco 7500 series routers, use the **controller t3** global configuration command.

controller t3 *slot/port-adapter/port*

Syntax	Description
slot	Refer to the appropriate hardware manual for slot and port information.
port	Refer to the appropriate hardware manual for slot and port information.
port-adapter	Refer to the appropriate hardware manual for information about port adapter compatibilty.

Default

No T3 controller is configured.

Command Mode

Global configuration

Usage Guidelines

This command first appeared in Cisco IOS Release 11.3.

This command is used to configure the CT3IP and the 28 T1 channels. After the T1 channels are configured, continue to configure each T1 channel as a serial interface by using the **interface serial** global configuration command.

Example

In the following example, the CT3IP in slot 3 is configured:

```
controller t3 3/0/0
```

Related Commands

interface serial

COPY FLASH LEX

To download an executable image from Flash memory on the core router to the LAN Extender chassis, use the **copy flash lex** privileged EXEC command.

> **copy flash lex** *number*

Syntax	Description
number	Number of the LAN Extender interface to which to download an image from Flash memory.

Command Mode

Privileged EXEC

Usage Guidelines

This command first appeared in Cisco IOS Release 10.3.

If you attempt to download a version of the software older than what is currently running on the LAN Extender, a warning message is displayed.

Example

The following example copies the executable image *namexx* to the LAN Extender interface 0:

```
Router# copy flash lex 0
Name of file to copy? namexx
Address of remote host [255.255.255.255] <cr>
writing namexx !!!!!!!!!!!!!!!!!!!!!!!!!!!!!copy complete
```

Related Commands

copy tftp lex

COPY TFTP LEX

To download an executable image from a TFTP server to the LAN Extender, use the **copy tftp lex** privileged EXEC command.

    copy tftp lex *number*

Syntax	Description
number	Number of the LAN Extender interface to which to download an image.

Command Mode

Privileged EXEC

Usage Guidelines

This command first appeared in Cisco IOS Release 10.3.

If you attempt to download a version of the software older than what is currently running on the LAN Extender, a warning message is displayed.

Example

The following example copies the file *namexx* from the TFTP server:

```
Router# copy tftp lex 0
Address or name of remote host (255.255.255.255]? 131.108.1.111
Name of file to copy? namexx
OK to overwrite software version 1.0 with 1.1 ?[confirm]
Loading namexx from 131.108.13.111!!!!!!!!!!!!!!!!!!!!!!!!!!!!!!
[OK - 127825/131072 bytes]

Successful download to LAN Extender
```

CRC

To set the length of the cyclic redundancy check (CRC) on a Fast Serial Interface Processor (FSIP), or HSSI Interface Processor (HIP) of the Cisco 7500 series routers, or on a 4-port serial adapter of the Cisco 7200 series routers, use the **crc** interface configuration command. To set the CRC length to 16 bits, use the **no** form of this command.

> **crc** *size*
> **no crc**

Syntax

Syntax	Description
size	CRC size (16 or 32 bits).

Default

16 bits

Command Mode

Interface configuration

Usage Guidelines

This command first appeared in Cisco IOS Release 10.0.

All interfaces use a 16-bit cyclic redundancy check (CRC) by default, but also support a 32-bit CRC. CRC is an error-checking technique that uses a calculated numeric value to detect errors in transmitted data. The designators 16 and 32 indicate the length (in bits) of the frame check sequence (FCS). A CRC of 32 bits provides more powerful error detection, but adds it overhead. Both the sender and receiver must use the same setting.

CRC-16, the most widely used throughout the United States and Europe, is used extensively with wide-area networks (WANs). CRC-32 is specified by IEEE 802 and as an option by some point-to-point transmission standards. It is often used on SMDS networks and LANs.

Example

In the following example, the 32-bit CRC is enabled on serial interface 3/0:

```
interface serial 3/0
  crc 32
```

DELAY

To set a delay value for an interface, use the **delay** interface configuration command. Use the **no** form of this command to restore the default delay value.

> **delay** *tens-of-microseconds*
> **no delay**

Syntax	*Description*
tens-of-microseconds	Integer that specifies the delay in tens of microseconds for an interface or network segment.

Default

Default delay values may be displayed with the EXEC command **show interfaces**.

Command Mode

Interface configuration

Usage Guidelines

This command first appeared in Cisco IOS Release 10.0.

Example

The following example sets a 30,000-microsecond delay on serial interface 3:

```
interface serial 3
  delay 30000
```

Related Commands

show interfaces

DCE-TERMINAL-TIMING ENABLE

When running the line at high speeds and long distances, use the **dce-terminal-timing enable** interface configuration command to prevent phase shifting of the data with respect to the clock. If SCTE is not available from the DTE, use **no** form of this command, which causes the DCE to use its own clock instead of SCTE from the DTE.

> **dce-terminal-timing enable**
> **no dce-terminal-timing enable**

Part
III

Command Reference

Syntax   *Description*

This command has no arguments or keywords.

Default

DCE uses its own clock.

Command Mode

Interface configuration

Usage Guidelines

This command first appeared in Cisco IOS Release 10.0.

On the Cisco 4000 platform, you can specify the serial Network Interface Module timing signal configuration. When the board is operating as a DCE and the DTE provides terminal timing (SCTE or TT), the **dce-terminal-timing enable** command causes the DCE to use SCTE from the DTE.

Example

The following example prevents phase shifting of the data with respect to the clock:

```
interface serial 0
  dce-terminal-timing enable
```

DESCRIPTION (CONTROLLER)

Use the **description** controller configuration command to add a description to an E1 or T1 controller or the Channelized T3 Interface Processor (CT3IP) in Cisco 7500 series routers. Use the **no** form of this command to remove the description.

> **description** *string*
> **no description**

Syntax   *Description*

string   Comment or a description to help you remember what is attached to the interface. Up to 80 characters.

Default

No description is added.

Command Mode

Controller configuration

Usage Guidelines

This command first appeared in Cisco IOS Release 10.3.

This command was modified in Cisco IOS Release 11.3 to include the CT3IP controller.

The **description** command is meant solely as a comment to be put in the configuration to help you remember what certain controllers are used for. The description affects the CT3IP and MIP interfaces only and appears in the output of the **show controller t3, show controller e1, show controller t1**, and **show running-config** EXEC commands.

Example

The following example describes a 3174 controller:

```
controller t1
  description 3174 Controller for test lab
```

Related Commands

show controller e1
show controller t1
show controller t3
show running-config

DOWN-WHEN-LOOPED

Use the **down-when-looped** interface configuration command to configure an interface to inform the system it is down when loopback is detected.

down-when-looped

Syntax   Description

This command has no arguments or keywords.

Default

Disabled

Command Mode

Interface configuration

Usage Guidelines

This command first appeared in Cisco IOS Release 10.0.

This command is valid for HDLC or PPP encapsulation on serial and HSSI interfaces.

Backup Interfaces

When an interface has a backup interface configured, it is often desirable that the backup interface be enabled when the primary interface is either down or in loopback. By default, the backup is only enabled if the primary interface is down. By using the **down-when-looped** command, the backup interface also will be enabled if the primary interface is in loopback.

Testing an Interface with the Loopback Command

If testing an interface with the loopback command, or by placing the DCE into loopback, **down-when-looped** should not be configured; otherwise, packets will not be transmitted out the interface that is being tested.

Example

In the following example, interface serial 0 is configured for HDLC encapsulation. It is then configured to let the system know that it is down when in loopback mode.

```
interface serial0
  encapsulation hdlc
  down-when-looped
```

Related Commands

backup interface serial
loopback (interface)

DTE-INVERT-TXC

Use the **dte-invert-txc** interface configuration command to invert the TXC clock signal received from the DCE. Use the **no** form of this command if the DCE accepts SCTE from the DTE.

> **dte-invert-txc**
> **no dte-invert-txc**

Syntax   Description

This command has no arguments or keywords.

Default

Disabled

Command Mode

Interface configuration

Usage Guidelines

This command first appeared in Cisco IOS Release 10.0.

Use this command if the DCE cannot receive SCTE from the DTE, the data is running at high speeds, and the transmission line is long. This prevents phase shifting of the data with respect to the clock.

On the Cisco 4000 series, you can specify the serial Network Processor Module timing signal configuration. When the board is operating as a DTE, the **dte-invert-txc** command inverts the TXC clock signal it gets from the DCE that the DTE uses to transmit data. If the DCE accepts SCTE from the DTE, use **no dte-invert-txc**.

Example

The following example inverts the TXC on serial interface 0:

```
interface serial 0
dte-invert-txc
```

EARLY-TOKEN-RELEASE

To enable early token release on Token Ring interfaces, use the **early-token-release** interface configuration command. Once enabled, use the **no** form of this command to disable this feature.

    early-token-release
    no early-token-release

Syntax   Description

This command has no arguments or keywords.

Default

Disabled

Command Mode

Interface configuration

Usage Guidelines

This command first appeared in Cisco IOS Release 10.0.

Early token release is a method whereby the Token Ring interfaces can release the token back onto the ring immediately after transmitting, rather than waiting for the frame to return. This feature helps increase the total bandwidth of the Token Ring.

The Token Ring Interface Processor (TRIP) on the Cisco 7500 series routers and the Token Ring adapters on the Cisco 7200 series routers all support early token release.

Examples

The following example enables the use of early token release on Token Ring interface 1:

```
interface tokenring 1
  early-token-release
```

On the Cisco 7500 series, to enable the use of early token release on your Token Ring interface processor in slot 4 on port 1, issue the following configuration commands:

```
interface tokenring 4/1
  early-token-release
```

ENCAPSULATION

To set the encapsulation method used by the interface, use the **encapsulation** interface configuration command.

  encapsulation *encapsulation-type*

Syntax	*Description*
encapsulation-type	Encapsulation type; one of the following keywords:

- **atm-dxi**—Asynchronous Transfer Mode-Data Exchange Interface.
- **bstun**—Block Serial Tunnel.
- **frame-relay**—Frame Relay (for serial interface).
- **hdlc**—High-Level Data Link Control (HDLC) protocol for serial interface. This encapsulation method provides the synchronous framing and error detection functions of HDLC without windowing or retransmission.
- **isl** — Inter-Switch Link (ISL) (for virtual LANs).
- **lapb**—X.25 LAPB DTE operation (for serial interface).
- **ppp**—Point-to-Point Protocol (PPP) (for serial interface).
- **sde**—IEEE 802.10 Security Data Exchange.
- **sdlc**—IBM serial SNA.
- **sdlc-primary**—IBM serial SNA (for primary serial interface).
- **sdlc-secondary**—IBM serial SNA (for secondary serial interface).
- **smds**—Switched Multimegabit Data Services (SMDS) (for serial interface).

Default

The default depends on the type of interface. For example, a synchronous serial interface defaults to HDLC.

Command Mode

Interface configuration

Usage Guidelines

This command first appeared in Cisco IOS Release 10.0.

To use SLIP or PPP, the router or access server must be configured with an IP routing protocol or with the **ip host-routing** command. This configuration is done automatically if you are using old-style **slip address** commands. However, you must configure it manually if you configure SLIP or PPP via the **interface async** command.

Examples

The following example resets HDLC serial encapsulation on serial interface 1:

```
interface serial 1
  encapsulation hdlc
```

The following example enables PPP encapsulation on serial interface 0:

```
interface serial 0
  encapsulation ppp
```

Related Commands

keepalive
ppp
ppp authentication
slip

FDDI BURST-COUNT

Use the **fddi burst-count** interface configuration command to allow the FCI card to preallocate buffers to handle bursty FDDI traffic (for example, NFS bursty traffic). Use the **no** form of this command to revert to the default value.

> **fddi burst-count** *number*
> **no fddi burst-count**

Syntax	Description
number	Number of preallocated buffers in the range from one to 10. The default is three buffers.

Default

3 buffers

Command Mode

Interface configuration

Usage Guidelines

This command first appeared in Cisco IOS Release 10.0.

This command applies to the FCI card only. The microcode software version should *not* be 128.45 or 128.43.

Example

The following example sets the number of buffers to 5:

```
interface fddi 0
  fddi burst-count 5
```

FDDI C-MIN

To set the C-Min timer on the PCM, use the **fddi c-min** interface configuration command. Use the **no** form of this command to revert to the default value.

> **fddi c-min** *microseconds*
> **no fddi c-min**

Syntax	Description
microseconds	Sets the timer value in microseconds. The default is 1,600 microseconds.

Default

1,600 microseconds

Command Mode

Interface configuration

Usage Guidelines

This command first appeared in Cisco IOS Release 10.0.

This command applies to the processor CMT only. You need extensive knowledge of the PCM state machine to tune this timer. Use this command when you run into PCM interoperability problems.

Example

The following example sets the C-Min timer to 2,000 microseconds:

```
interface fddi 0
  fddi c-min 2000
```

Related Commands

fddi tb-min
fddi tl-min-time
fddi t-out

FDDI CMT-SIGNAL-BITS

To control the information transmitted during the connection management (CMT) signaling phase, use the **fddi cmt-signal-bits** interface configuration command.

fddi cmt-signal-bits *signal-bits* [**phy-a** | **phy-b**]

Syntax	Description
signal-bits	A hexadecimal number preceded by 0x; for example, 0x208. The FDDI standard defines ten bits of signaling information that must be transmitted, as follows:

- bit 0—Escape bit. Reserved for future assignment by the FDDI standards committee.

- bits 1 and 2—Physical type, as defined in Table 23–5.

- bit 3—Physical compatibility. Set if topology rules include the connection of a physical-to-physical type at the end of the connection.

- bits 4 and 5—Link confidence test duration; set as defined in Table 23–6.

- bit 6—Media Access Control (MAC) available for link confidence test.

- bit 7—Link confidence test failed. The setting of bit 7 indicates that the link confidence was failed by the Cisco end of the connection.

- bit 8—MAC for local loop.

- bit 9—MAC on physical output.

phy-a	(Optional) Selects Physical Sublayer A.
phy-b	(Optional) Selects Physical Sublayer B.

Defaults

The default signal bits for the **phy-a** and **phy-b** keywords are as follows:

- **phy-a** is set to 0x008 (hexadecimal) or 00 0000 1000 (binary). Bits 1 and 2 are set to 00 to select Physical A. Bit 3 is set to 1 to indicate "accept any connection."

- **phy-b** is set to 0x20c (hexadecimal) or 10 0000 1100 (binary). Bits 1 and 2 are set to 10 to select Physical B. Bit 3 is set to 1 to indicate "accept any connection." Bit 9 is set to 1 to select MAC on output. The normal data flow on FDDI is input on Physical A and output on Physical B.

Command Mode

Interface configuration

Usage Guidelines

This command first appeared in Cisco IOS Release 10.0.

If neither the **phy-a** nor **phy-b** keyword is specified, the signal bits apply to both physical connections.

NOTES

Use of the **fddi cmt-signal-bits** configuration command is *not* recommended under normal operations. This command is used when debugging specific CMT implementation issues.

Table 23–5 lists the physical types.

Table 23–5 *FDDI Physical Type Bit Specifications*

Bit 2	Bit 1	Physical Type
0	0	Physical A
1	0	Physical B
0	1	Physical S
1	1	Physical M

Table 23–6 lists the duration bits.

Table 23–6 *FDDI Link Confidence Test Duration Bit Specification*

Bit 5	Bit 4	Test Duration
0	0	Short test (default 50 ms)
1	0	Medium test (default 500 ms)
0	1	Long test (default 5 seconds)
1	1	Extended test (default 50 seconds)

Example

The following example sets the CMT signaling phase to signal bits 0x208 on both physical connections:

```
interface fddi 0
  fddi cmt-signal-bits 208
```

FDDI DUPLICATE-ADDRESS-CHECK

Use the **fddi duplicate-address-check** interface configuration command to turn on the duplicate address detection capability on the FDDI. Use the **no** form of this command to disable this feature.

> **fddi duplicate-address-check**
> **no fddi duplicate-address-check**

Syntax   Description

This command has no arguments or keywords.

Default

Disabled

Command Mode

Interface configuration

Usage Guidelines

This command first appeared in Cisco IOS Release 10.0.

If you use this command, the Cisco IOS software will detect a duplicate address if multiple stations are sharing the same MAC address. If the software finds a duplicate address, it will shut down the interface.

Example

The following example enables duplicate address checking on the FDDI:

```
interface fddi 0
  fddi duplicate-address-check
```

FDDI ENCAPSULATE

Use the **fddi encapsulate** interface configuration command to specify encapsulating bridge mode on the CSC-C2/FCIT interface card. Use the **no** form of this command to turn off encapsulation bridging and return the FCIT interface to its translational, nonencapsulating mode.

> **fddi encapsulate**
> **no fddi encapsulate**

Syntax   Description

This command has no arguments or keywords.

Default

The FDDI interface by default uses the SNAP encapsulation format defined in RFC 1042. It is not necessary to define an encapsulation method for this interface when using the CSC-FCI interface card.

Command Mode

Interface configuration

Usage Guidelines

This command first appeared in Cisco IOS Release 10.0.

The **no fddi encapsulate** command applies only to CSC-C2/FCIT interfaces, because the CSC-FCI interfaces are always in encapsulating bridge mode. The CSC-C2/FCIT interface card fully supports transparent and translational bridging for the following configurations:

- FDDI to FDDI
- FDDI to Ethernet
- FDDI to Token Ring

The command **fddi encapsulate** puts the CSC-C2/FCIT interface into encapsulation mode when doing bridging. In transparent mode, the FCIT interface interoperates with earlier versions of the CSC-FCI encapsulating interfaces when performing bridging functions on the same ring.

CAUTION

Bridging between dissimilar media presents several problems that can prevent communications from occurring. These problems include bit-order translation (or usage of MAC addresses as data), maximum transfer unit (MTU) differences, frame status differences, and multicast address usage. Some or all of these problems might be present in a multimedia bridged LAN and might prevent communication from taking place. These problems are most prevalent when bridging between Token Rings and Ethernets or between Token Rings and FDDI nets. This is because of the different way Token Ring is implemented by the end nodes.

The following protocols have problems when bridged between Token Ring and other media: Novell IPX, DECnet Phase IV, AppleTalk, VINES, XNS, and IP. Further, the following protocols might have problems when bridged between FDDI and other media: Novell IPX and XNS. Cisco recommends that these protocols be routed whenever possible.

Example

The following example sets FDDI interface 1 on the CSC-C2/FCIT interface card to encapsulating bridge mode:

```
interface fddi 1
  fddi encapsulate
```

FDDI SMT-FRAMES

Use the **fddi smt-frames** interface configuration command to enable the SMT frame processing capability on the FDDI. Use the **no** form of this command to disable this feature and prevent the Cisco IOS software from generating or responding to SMT frames.

fddi smt-frames
no fddi smt-frames

Syntax   Description

This command has no arguments or keywords.

Default

Enabled

Command Mode

Interface configuration

Usage Guidelines

This command first appeared in Cisco IOS Release 10.0.

Use the **no** form of this command to turn off SMT frame processing for diagnosing purposes. Use the **fddi smt-frames** command to re-enable the feature.

Example

The following example disables SMT frame processing:

```
interface fddi 0
  no fddi smt-frames
```

FDDI TB-MIN

Use the **fddi tb-min** interface configuration command to set the TB-Min timer in the physical connection management (PCM). Use the **no** form of this command to revert to the default value.

fddi tb-min *milliseconds*
no fddi tb-min

Syntax	*Description*
milliseconds	Number that sets the TB-Min timer value. The default is 100 milliseconds.

Default

100 ms

Command Mode

Interface configuration

Usage Guidelines

This command first appeared in Cisco IOS Release 10.3.

This command applies to the processor CMT only. You need extensive knowledge of the PCM state machine to tune this timer. Use this command when you run into PCM interoperability problems.

Example

The following example sets the TB-Min timer to 200 ms:

```
interface fddi 0
 fddi tb-min 200
```

Related Commands

fddi c-min
fddi tl-min-time
fddi t-out

FDDI TL-MIN-TIME

Use the **fddi tl-min-time** interface configuration command to control the TL-Min time (the minimum time to transmit a Physical Sublayer, or PHY line state, before advancing to the next physical connection management [PCM] state, as defined by the X3T9.5 specification).

      fddi tl-min-time *microseconds*

Syntax	Description
microseconds	Number that specifies the time used during the connection management (CMT) phase to ensure that signals are maintained for at least the value of TL-Min, so the remote station can acquire the signal. The default is 30 microseconds.

Default

30 microseconds

Command Mode

Interface configuration

Usage Guidelines

This command first appeared in Cisco IOS Release 10.0.

Interoperability tests have shown that some implementations of the FDDI standard need more than 30 microseconds to sense a signal.

Examples

The following example changes the TL-Min time from 30 microseconds to 100 microseconds:

```
interface fddi 0
  fddi tl-min-time 100
```

The following example changes the TL-Min time from 30 microseconds to 100 microseconds on a Cisco 7500 series router:

```
interface fddi 3/0
  fddi tl-min-time 100
```

Related Commands

fddi c-min
fddi tl-min-time
fddi t-out

FDDI T-OUT

Use the **fddi t-out** interface configuration command to set the t-out timer in the physical connection management (PCM). Use the **no** form of this command to revert to the default value.

fddi t-out *milliseconds*
no fddi t-out

Syntax	Description
milliseconds	Number that sets the timeout timer. The default is 100 ms.

Default

100 ms

Command Mode

Interface configuration

Usage Guidelines

This command first appeared in Cisco IOS Release 10.0.

This command applies to the processor CMT only. You need extensive knowledge of the PCM state machine to tune this timer. Use this command when you run into PCM interoperability problems.

Example

The following example sets the timeout timer to 200 ms:

```
interface fddi 0
  fddi t-out 200
```

Related Commands

fddi c-min
fddi tb-min
fddi tl-min-time

FDDI TOKEN-ROTATION-TIME

Use the **fddi token-rotation-time** interface configuration command to control ring scheduling during normal operation and to detect and recover from serious ring error situations.

fddi token-rotation-time *microseconds*

Syntax	Description
microseconds	Number that specifies the token rotation time (TRT). The default is 5,000 microseconds.

Default

5,000 microseconds

Command Mode

Interface configuration

Usage Guidelines

This command first appeared in Cisco IOS Release 10.0.

The FDDI standard restricts the allowed time to be greater than 4,000 microseconds and less than 165,000 microseconds. As defined in the X3T9.5 specification, the value remaining in the TRT is loaded into the token holding timer (THT). Combining the values of these two timers provides the means to determine the amount of bandwidth available for subsequent transmissions.

Examples

The following example sets the rotation time to 24,000 microseconds:

```
interface fddi 0
  fddi token-rotation-time 24000
```

The following example sets the rotation time to 24,000 microseconds on a Cisco 7500 series router:

```
interface fddi 3/0
  fddi token-rotation-time 24000
```

FDDI VALID-TRANSMISSION-TIME

To recover from a transient ring error, use the **fddi valid-transmission-time** interface configuration command.

> **fddi valid-transmission-time** *microseconds*

Syntax	Description
microseconds	Number that specifies the transmission valid timer (TVX) interval. The default is 2,500 microseconds.

Default

2,500 microseconds

Command Mode

Interface configuration

Usage Guidelines

This command first appeared in Cisco IOS Release 10.0.

Examples

The following example changes the transmission timer interval to 3,000 microseconds:

```
interface fddi 0
  fddi valid-transmission-time 3000
```

The following example changes the transmission timer interval to 3,000 microseconds on a Cisco 7000 or Cisco 7200:

```
interface fddi 3/0
  fddi valid-transmission-time 3000
```

FDL

To set the facilities data link exchange standard for the CSU on the AS5200's T1 controllers, enter the **fdl** controller configuration command. The **no** form of this command disables this facilities data link support.

> **fdl** {att | ansi}
> **no fdl** {att | ansi}

Syntax	Description
att	Selects AT&T technical reference 54016 for extended superframe facilities data link exchange support.
ansi	Selects ANSI T1.403 for extended superframe facilities data link exchange support.

Default

Disabled

Command Mode

Controller configuration

Usage Guidelines

You must configure this command on both T1 controllers if you want to support the CSU function on each T1 line. However, you must use the same facilities data link exchange standard as your service provider. You can have a different standard configured on each T1 controller.

Example

The following example configures the ANSI T1.403 standard for both T1 controllers:

```
AS5200(config)# controller t1 0
AS5200(config-controller)# fdl ansi
AS5200(config-controller)# exit
AS5200(config)# controller t1 1
AS5200(config-controller)# fdl ansi
```

FRAMING

Use the **framing** controller configuration command to select the frame type for the T1 or E1 data line.

> **framing {sf | esf}**   (for T1 lines)
> **framing {crc4 | no-crc4} [australia]**   (for E1 lines)

Syntax	Description
sf	Specifies super frame as the T1 frame type.
esf	Specifies extended super frame as the T1 frame type.
crc4	Specifies CRC4 frame as the E1 frame type.
no-crc4	Specifies no CRC4 frame as the E1 frame type.
australia	(Optional) Specifies the E1 frame type used in Australia.

Defaults

Super frame is the default on a T1 line.

CRC4 frame is the default on an E1 line.

Command Mode

Controller configuration

Usage Guidelines

Use this command in configurations where the router or access server is intended to communicate with T1 or E1 fractional data line. The service provider determines which framing type, either **sf**, **esf**, or **crc4**, is required for your T1/E1 circuit.

Example

The following example selects extended super frame as the T1 frame type:

```
framing esf
```

Related Commands

cablelength
linecode

FRAMING (T3)

Use the **framing** controller configuration command to specify the type of framing used by the Channelized T3 Interface Processor (CT3IP) in Cisco 7500 series routers. Use the **no** form of this command to restore the default framing type.

> **framing {c-bit | m23 | auto-detect}**
> **no framing**

Syntax	Description
c-bit	Specifies that the C-bit framing is used as the T3 framing type.
m23	Specifies that the M23 framing is used as the T3 framing type.
auto-detect	Specifies that the CT3IP detects the framing type it receives from the far-end equipment. This is the default.

Default

auto-detect

Command Mode

Controller configuration

Usage Guidelines

This command first appeared in Cisco IOS Release 11.3.

If you do not specify the **framing** command, the default **auto-detect** is used by the CT3IP to determine automatically the framing type received from the far-end equipment.

Because the CT3IP supports the Application Identification Channel (AIC) signal, the setting for the framing might be overridden by the CT3IP firmware.

You also can set the framing for each T1 channel by using the **t1 framing** controller configuration command.

Example

In the following example, the framing for the CT3IP is set to C-bit:

```
controller t3 9/0/0
  framing c-bit
```

Related Commands

t1 framing

FULL-DUPLEX

Use the **full-duplex** interface configuration command to specify full-duplex mode on full-duplex single-mode and multimode port adapters available on the following:

- Cisco 7200 series routers
- Second-generation Versatile Interface Processors (VIP2s) in Cisco 7500 series routers
- Fast Ethernet Interface Processor (FEIP) port
- Serial interface port that uses bisynchronous tunneling.

Refer to the *Cisco Product Catalog* for hardware compatibility information and for specific model numbers of port adapters.

Use the **no** form of this command to restore the default half-duplex mode.

full-duplex
no full-duplex

Syntax   Description

This command has no arguments or keywords.

Default

Half-duplex mode is the default mode on a Cisco 7500 series router and a FEIP.

Half-duplex mode is the default mode for serial interfaces that are configured for bisynchronous tunneling.

Command Mode

Interface configuration

Usage Guidelines

This command first appeared in Cisco IOS Release 11.1.

This command was modified in Cisco IOS Release 11.3 to include information on FDDI full-duplex, single-mode, and multimode port adapters.

Use this command if the equipment on the other end is capable of full-duplex mode.

To enable half-duplex mode, use the **no full-duplex** or **half-duplex** commands.

Support for this Command

Use the question mark command (?) to find out which port adapters support this command. If the interface does not support full-duplex, an informational message similar to the one shown below is displayed, and no changes are made to the interface. To determine whether the interface supports full-duplex, use the **show interfaces** command. For example, the following message is displayed if the interface does not support full-duplex:

```
% interface does not support full-duplex.
```

Use on FDDI

Full-duplex on the FDDI full-duplex port adapters allows an FDDI ring with exactly two stations to transform the ring into a full-duplex, point-to-point topology. To operate in full-duplex mode, there must be only two stations on the ring, the two stations must be capable of operating in full-duplex mode, and both stations must complete a full-duplex autoconfiguration protocol. There is no FDDI token in full-duplex mode. Refer to the *Cisco Product Catalog* for specific model numbers of port adapters.

Full-duplex autoconfiguration protocol allows an FDDI station to operate dynamically and automatically in either half-duplex (or ring) or full-duplex mode and ensures that the stations fall back to ring mode when a configuration change occurs, such as a third station joining the ring.

After booting up, the FDDI stations begin operation in half-duplex mode. While the station performs the full-duplex autoconfiguration protocol, the station continues to provide data-link services to its users. Under normal conditions, the transition between half-duplex mode and full-duplex mode is transparent to the data-link users. The data-link services provided by full-duplex mode are functionally the same as the services provided by half-duplex mode.

If you change the full-duplex configuration (for example, from disabled to enabled) on supported interfaces, the interface resets.

Examples

The following example configures full-duplex mode on the Cisco 7000:

```
interface fastethernet 0/1
  full-duplex
```

The following example specifies full-duplex binary synchronous communications (BSC) mode:

```
interface serial 0
  encapsulation bstun
  full-duplex
```

The following example enables full-duplex mode on FDDI interface 0:

```
interface fddi 0/1/0
  full-duplex
```

Part III

Command Reference

Related Commands

half-duplex
interface fastethernet
interface fddi
interface serial

HALF-DUPLEX

Use the **half-duplex** interface configuration command to specify half-duplex mode on an SDLC interface or on the FDDI full-duplex, single-mode port adapter and FDDI full-duplex, multimode port adapter on the Cisco 7200 series, and Cisco 7500 series routers. Refer to the *Cisco Product Catalog* for specific model numbers of port adapters.

Use the **no** form of this command to reset the interface for full-duplex mode.

> **half-duplex**
> **no half-duplex**

Syntax   Description

This command has no arguments or keywords.

Default

Disabled

Command Mode

Interface configuration

Usage Guidelines

This command first appeared in Cisco IOS Release 11.1.

This command was modified in Cisco IOS Release 11.3 to include information on FDDI full-duplex, single-mode, and multimode port adapters.

Obsolete Commands Replaced by this Command

The **half-duplex** command replaces both the **sdlc hdx** and **media-type half-duplex** commands.

SDLC Interfaces

The **half-duplex** command is used to configure an SDLC interface for half-duplex mode and is used on a variety of port adapters. Use the question mark command (**?**) to find out which port adapters support this command.

Enable Full-Duplex Mode

To enable full-duplex mode, use the **no half-duplex** or **full-duplex** commands.

NOTES

The **media-type half-duplex** command exists in Cisco IOS Release 11.0 (5). As of Release 11.0 (6), the keyword **half-duplex** was removed from the **media-type** command. In Release 11.0 (6), the functionality for specifying half-duplex mode is provided by the **half-duplex** command.

Example

In the following example, an SDLC interface has been configured for half-duplex mode:

```
encapsulation sdlc-primary
half-duplex
```

Related Commands

full-duplex

HALF-DUPLEX CONTROLLED-CARRIER

Use the **half-duplex controlled-carrier** interface configuration command to place a low-speed serial interface in controlled-carrier mode, instead of constant-carrier mode. Use the **no** form of this command to return the interface to constant-carrier mode.

half-duplex controlled-carrier
no half-duplex controlled-carrier

Syntax   Description

This command has no arguments or keywords.

Default

Constant-carrier mode, where DCD is held constant and asserted by the DCE half-duplex interface.

Command Mode

Interface configuration

Usage Guidelines

This command first appeared in Cisco IOS Release 11.2.

This command applies only to low-speed serial DCE interfaces in half-duplex mode. Configure a serial interface for half-duplex mode by using the **media-type half-duplex** command. These interfaces are available on Cisco 2520 through 2523 routers.

Controlled-carrier operation means that the DCE interface will have DCD de-asserted in the quiescent state. When the interface has something to transmit, it will assert DCD, wait a user-configured amount of time, then start the transmission. When the interface has finished transmitting, it will again wait a user-configured amount of time, then de-assert DCD.

An interface placed in controlled-carrier mode can be returned to constant-carrier mode by using the **no** form of the command.

Examples

The following examples place the interface in controlled-carrier mode and back into constant-carrier operation.

Changing to controlled-carrier mode from the default of constant-carrier operation:

```
interface serial 2
  half-duplex controlled-carrier
```

Changing to constant-carrier operation from controlled-carrier mode:

```
interface serial 2
  no half-duplex controlled-carrier
```

Related Commands

half-duplex timer
physical-layer

HALF-DUPLEX TIMER

To tune half-duplex timers, use the **half-duplex timer** interface configuration command. Use the **no** form of this command, along with the appropriate keyword, to return to the default value for that parameter.

> **half-duplex timer** {**cts-delay** *value* | **cts-drop-timeout** *value* | **dcd-drop-delay** *value* | **dcd-txstart-delay** *value* | **rts-drop-delay** *value* | **rts-timeout** *value* | **transmit-delay** *value*}
>
> **no half-duplex timer** {**cts-delay** *value* | **cts-drop-timeout** *value* | **dcd-drop-delay** *value* | **dcd-txstart-delay** *value* | **rts-drop-delay** *value* | **rts-timeout** *value* | **transmit-delay** *value*}

You can configure more than one of these options, but each option must be specified as a separate command.

Syntax	Description
cts-delay *value*	Specifies the delay introduced by the DCE interface between the time it detects RTS to the time it asserts CTS in response. The range is dependent on the serial interface hardware. The default value is 0 ms.
cts-drop-timeout *value*	Determines the amount of time a DTE interface waits for CTS to be de-asserted after it has de-asserted RTS. If CTS is not de-asserted during this time, an error counter is incremented to note this event. The range is 0 to 1,140,000 ms (1,140 seconds). The default value is 250 ms.

Syntax	Description
dcd-drop-delay *value*	Applies to DCE half-duplex interfaces operating in controlled-carrier mode (see the **half-duplex controlled-carrier** command). This timer determines the delay between the end of transmission by the DCE and the deassertion of DCD. The range is 0 to 4,400 ms (4.4 seconds). The default value is 100 ms.
dcd-txstart-delay *value*	Applies to DCE half-duplex interfaces operating in controlled-carrier mode. This timer determines the time delay between the assertion of DCD and the start of data transmission by the DCE interface. The range is 0 to 1,140,000 ms (1,140 seconds). The default value is 100 ms.
rts-drop-delay *value*	Specifies the time delay between the end of transmission by the DTE interface and de-assertion of RTS. The range is 0 to 1,140,000 ms (1,140 seconds). The default value is 3 ms.
rts-timeout *value*	Determines the number of milliseconds the DTE waits for CTS to be asserted after the assertion of RTS before giving up on its transmission attempt. If CTS is not asserted in the specified amount of time, an error counter is incremented. The range is dependent on the serial interface hardware. The default value is 3 ms.
transmit-delay *value*	Specifies the number of milliseconds a half-duplex interface will delay the start of transmission. In the case of a DTE interface, this delay specifies how long the interface waits after something shows up in the transmit queue before asserting RTS. For a DCE interface, this dictates how long the interface waits after data is placed in the transmit queue before starting transmission. If the DCE interface is in controlled-carrier mode, this delay shows up as a delayed assertion of DCD.

This timer enables the transmitter to be adjusted if the receiver is a little slow and is not able to keep up with the transmitter. The range is 0 to 4,400 ms (4.4 seconds). The default value is 0 ms. |

Part III

Command Reference

Default

The default **cts-delay** value is 0 ms.

The default **cts-drop-timeout** value is 250 ms.

The default **dcd-drop-delay** value is 100 ms.

The default **dcd-txstart-delay** value is 100 ms.

The default **rts-drop-delay** value is 3 ms.

The default **rts-timeout** value is 3 ms.

The default **transmit-delay** value is 0 ms.

Command Mode

Interface configuration

Usage Guidelines

The **half-duplex timer** command is used to tune half-duplex timers. With these timer tuning commands you can adjust the timing of the half-duplex state machines to suit the particular needs of their half-duplex installation.

Commands Replaced by this Command

The **half-duplex timer cts-delay** command replaces the **sdlc cts-delay** command. The **half-duplex timer rts-timeout** command replaces the **sdlc rts-timeout** command.

Value Ranges

The range of values for the **cts-delay** and **rts-timeout** keywords are dependent on the serial interface hardware.

Example

The following example sets the cts-delay timer to 10 ms and the transmit-delay timer to 50 milliseconds:

```
interface serial 2
 half-duplex timer cts-delay 10
 half-duplex timer transmit-delay 50
```

Related Commands

half-duplex controlled-carrier
physical-layer

HOLD-QUEUE

To specify the hold-queue limit of an interface, use the **hold-queue** interface configuration command. Use the **no** form of this command with the appropriate keyword to restore the default values for an interface.

> **hold-queue** *length* {**in** | **out**}
> **no hold-queue** {**in** | **out**}

Syntax	Description
length	Integer that specifies the maximum number of packets in the queue.
in	Specifies the input queue.
out	Specifies the output queue.

Default

The default input hold-queue limit is 75 packets. The default output hold-queue limit is 40 packets. These limits prevent a malfunctioning interface from consuming an excessive amount of memory. There is no fixed upper limit to a queue size.

Command Mode

Interface configuration

Usage Guidelines

This command first appeared in Cisco IOS Release 10.0.

The input hold queue prevents a single interface from flooding the network server with too many input packets. Further input packets are discarded if the interface has too many input packets outstanding in the system.

If priority output queueing is being used, the length of the four output queues is set using the **priority-list** global configuration command. The **hold-queue** command cannot be used to set an output hold-queue length in this situation.

For slow links, use a small output hold-queue limit. This approach prevents storing packets at a rate that exceeds the transmission capability of the link. For fast links, use a large output hold-queue limit. A fast link may be busy for a short time (and thus require the hold queue), but can empty the output hold queue quickly when capacity returns.

To display the current hold-queue setting and the number of packets discarded because of hold-queue overflows, use the EXEC command **show interfaces**.

NOTES

Increasing the hold queue can have detrimental effects on network routing and response times. For protocols that use seq/ack packets to determine round trip times, do not increase the output queue. Dropping packets instead informs hosts to slow down transmissions to match available bandwidth. This is generally better than having duplicate copies of the same packet within the network (which can happen with large hold queues).

Example

The following example sets a small input queue on a slow serial line:

```
interface serial 0
  hold-queue 30 in
```

Related Commands

show interfaces

HSSI EXTERNAL-LOOP-REQUEST

Use the **hssi external-loop-request** interface configuration command to allow the router to support a CSU/DSU that uses the LC signal to request a loopback from the router. Use the **no** form of this command to disable the feature.

> **hssi external-loop-request**
> **no hssi external-loop-request**

Syntax   Description

This command has no arguments or keywords.

Default

Disabled

Command Mode

Interface configuration

Usage Guidelines

This command first appeared in Cisco IOS Release 10.0.

The HSA applique (on the HSSI) contains an LED that indicates the LA, LB, and LC signals transiting through the devices. The CSU/DSU uses the LC signal to request a loopback from the router. The CSU/DSU might want to do this so that its own network management diagnostics can check independently the integrity of the connection between the CSU/DSU and the router.

Use this command to enable a two-way, internal, and external loopback request on HSSI from the CSU/DSU.

NOTES

If your CSU/DSU does not support this feature, it should not be enabled in the router. Not enabling this feature prevents spurious line noise from accidentally tripping the external loopback request line, which would interrupt the normal data flow.

Example

The following example enables a CSU/DSU to use the LC signal to request a loopback from the router:

```
hssi external-loop-request
```

HSSI INTERNAL-CLOCK

To convert the HSSI interface into a 45 MHz clock master, use the **hssi internal-clock** interface configuration command. Use the **no** form of this command to disable the clock-master mode.

> **hssi internal-clock**
> **no hssi internal-clock**

Syntax   Description

This command has no arguments or keywords.

Default

Disabled

Command Mode

Interface configuration

Usage Guidelines

This command first appeared in Cisco IOS Release 10.0.

Use this command in conjunction with the HSSI null-modem cable to connect two Cisco routers together with HSSI. You must configure this command at both ends of the link, not just one.

Example

The following example converts the HSSI interface into a 45 MHz clock master:

```
hssi internal-clock
```

HUB

To enable and configure a port on an Ethernet hub of a Cisco 2505 or Cisco 2507, use the **hub** global configuration command.

> **hub ethernet** *number port* [*end-port*]

Syntax	Description
ethernet	Indicates that the hub is in front of an Ethernet interface.
number	Hub number, starting with 0. Because there is currently only one hub, this number is 0.

Syntax	Description
port	Port number on the hub. On the Cisco 2505, port numbers range from 1 to 8. On the Cisco 2507, port numbers range from 1 to 16. If a second port number follows, then the first port number indicates the beginning of a port range.
end-port	(Optional) Last port number of a range.

Default

No hub ports are configured.

Command Mode

Global configuration

Usage Guidelines

This command first appeared in Cisco IOS Release 10.3.

Examples

The following example enables port 1 on hub 0:

```
hub ethernet 0 1
no shutdown
```

The following example enables ports 1 through 8 on hub 0:

```
hub ethernet 0 1 8
no shutdown
```

Related Commands

shutdown

IGNORE-DCD

Use the **ignore-dcd** interface configuration command to configure the serial interface to monitor the DSR signal (instead of the DCD signal) as the line up/down indicator. Use the **no** form of this command to restore the default behavior.

> **ignore-dcd**
> **no ignore-dcd**

Syntax   Description

This command has no arguments or keywords.

Default

The serial interface, operating in DTE mode, monitors the DCD signal as the line up/down indicator.

Command Mode

Interface configuration

Usage Guidelines

This command first appeared in Cisco IOS Release 11.0.

This command applies to Quad Serial NIM interfaces on the Cisco 4000 series routers and Hitachi-based serial interfaces on the Cisco 2500 and 3000 series routers.

Serial Interfaces in DTE Mode

When the serial interface is operating in DTE mode, it monitors the Data Carrier Detect (DCD) signal as the line up/down indicator. By default, the attached DCE device sends the DCD signal. When the DTE interface detects the DCD signal, it changes the state of the interface to up.

SDLC Multidrop Environments

In some configurations, such as an SDLC multidrop environment, the DCE device sends the Data Set Ready (DSR) signal instead of the DCD signal, which prevents the interface from coming up. Use this command to tell the interface to monitor the DSR signal instead of the DCD signal as the line up/down indicator.

Example

The following example configures serial interface 0 to monitor the DSR signal as the line up/down indicator:

```
interface serial 0
  ignore-dcd
```

INTERFACE

Use the **interface** global configuration command to configure an interface type and enter interface configuration mode.

> interface *type number*
> interface *type slot/port* (for the Cisco 7200 series routers, and for the Cisco 7500 series routers with a Packet over SONET Interface Processor)
> interface [*type slot/port-adapter/port*] [**ethernet** | **serial**] (for ports on VIP cards in the Cisco 7500 series routers)
> interface serial *slot/port:channel-group* (for channelized T1 or E1 on Cisco 7500 series routers)
> interface serial *number:channel-group* (for channelized T1 or E1 on the Cisco 4000 series)

Part III

Command Reference

To configure a subinterface, use the **interface** global configuration command.

> **interface** *type slot/port-adapter/port.subinterface-number* {**multipoint** | **point-to-point**}
> (for ports on VIP cards in the Cisco 7500 series routers)
> **interface** *type slot/port.subinterface-number* {**multipoint** | **point-to-point**} (for the Cisco
> 7200 series routers)
> **interface** *type slot/port-adapter.subinterface-number* {**multipoint** | **point-to-point**} (for the
> Cisco 7500 series)

Syntax	Description
type	Type of interface to be configured. See Table 23–7.
number	Port, connector, or interface card number. On a Cisco 4000 series router, specifies the NPM number. The numbers are assigned at the factory at the time of installation or when added to a system, and can be displayed with the **show interfaces** command.
slot	Refer to the appropriate hardware manual for slot and port information.
port	Refer to the appropriate hardware manual for slot and port information.
port-adapter	Refer to the appropriate hardware manual for information about port adapter compatibility.
:channel-group	The Cisco 4000 series routers specifies the T1 channel-group number in the range of 0 to 23 defined with the **channel-group** controller configuration command. On a dual port card, it is possible to run channelized on one port and primary rate on the other port.
.subinterface-number	Subinterface number in the range 1 to 4294967293. The number that precedes the period (.) must match the number to which this subinterface belongs.
multipoint | **point-to-point**	(Optional) Specifies a multipoint or point-to-point subinterface. There is no default.

Default

No interface types are configured.

Command Mode

Global configuration

Usage Guidelines

This command first appeared in Cisco IOS Release 10.0 for the Cisco 7000 series routers. This command first appeared in Cisco IOS Release 11.0 for the Cisco 4000 series routers.

This command was changed in Cisco IOS Release 11.2 to add the **posi** keyword. This command was changed in Cisco IOS Release 11.3 to change the **posi** keyword to **pos**.

Subinterfaces can be configured to support partially meshed Frame Relay networks. See Chapter 21, "Configuring Serial Interfaces."

There is no correlation between the number of the physical serial interface and the number of the logical LAN Extender interface. These interfaces can have the same or different numbers.

Table 23–7 *Interface Type Keywords*

Keyword	Interface Type
async	Port line used as an asynchronous interface.
atm	ATM interface.
bri	Integrated Services Digital Network (ISDN) Basic Rate Interface (BRI). This interface configuration is propagated to each of the B channels. B channels cannot be configured individually. The interface must be configured with dial-on-demand commands in order for calls to be placed on that interface.
dialer	Dialer interface.
ethernet	Ethernet IEEE 802.3 interface.
fastethernet	100-Mbps Ethernet interface on the Cisco 4500, Cisco 4700, Cisco 7000 series, and Cisco 7500 series.
fddi	Fiber Distributed Data Interface (FDDI).
group-async	Master asynchronous interface.
hssi	High-Speed Serial Interface (HSSI).
lex	LAN Extender (LEX) interface.
loopback	Software-only loopback interface that emulates an interface that is always up. It is a virtual interface supported on all platforms. The *interface-number* is the number of the loopback interface that you want to create or configure. There is no limit on the number of loopback interfaces you can create.
null	Null interface.
pos	Packet OC-3 interface on the Packet-over-SONET Interface Processor.
serial	Serial interface.

Part III

Command Reference

Table 23–7   *Interface Type Keywords, Continued*

Keyword	Interface Type
tokenring	Token Ring interface.
tunnel	Tunnel interface; a virtual interface. The *number* is the number of the tunnel interface that you want to create or configure. There is no limit on the number of tunnel interfaces you can create.

Examples

In the following example, serial interface 0 is configured with PPP encapsulation:

```
interface serial 0
 encapsulation ppp
```

The following example enables loopback mode and assigns an IP network address and network mask to the interface. The loopback interface established here always will appear to be up:

```
interface loopback 0
 ip address 131.108.1.1 255.255.255.0
```

The following example for the Cisco 7500 router shows the interface configuration command for Ethernet port 4 on the EIP that is installed in (or recently removed from) slot 2:

```
interface ethernet 2/4
```

The following example begins configuration on the Token Ring interface processor in slot 1 on port 0 of a Cisco 7500:

```
interface tokenring 1/0
```

The following example shows how a partially meshed Frame Relay network can be configured. In this example, subinterface serial 0.1 is configured as a multipoint subinterface with three Frame Relay PVCs associated, and subinterface serial 0.2 is configured as a point-to-point subinterface.

```
interface serial 0
 encapsulation frame-relay
interface serial 0.1 multipoint
 ip address 131.108.10.1 255.255.255.0
 frame-relay interface-dlci 42 broadcast
 frame-relay interface-dlci 53 broadcast
interface serial 0.2 point-to-point
 ip address 131.108.11.1 255.255.0
 frame-relay interface-dlci 59 broadcast
```

The following example configures circuit 0 of a T1 link for Point-to-Point Protocol (PPP) encapsulation:

```
controller t1 4/1
circuit 0 1
interface serial 4/1:0
 ip address 131.108.13.1 255.255.255.0
 encapsulation ppp
```

The following example configures LAN Extender interface 0:

```
interface lex 0
```

Related Commands

circuit
controller
mac-address
ppp
show interfaces
slip

INTERFACE DIALER

To designate a dialer rotary group leader, use the **interface dialer** global configuration command.

interface dialer *interface-number*

Syntax	Description
interface-number	Integer that you select to indicate a dialer rotary group in the range 0 to 9.

Default

None

Command Mode

Global configuration

Usage Guidelines

Dialer rotary groups allow you to apply a single interface configuration to a set of interfaces. Once the interface configuration is propagated to a set of interfaces, those interfaces can be used to place calls using the standard dial-on-demand criteria. When many destinations are configured, any of these interfaces can be used for outgoing calls.

Dialer rotary groups are useful in environments that require many calling destinations. Only the rotary group needs to be configured with all of the **dialer map** commands. The only configuration required for the interfaces is the **dialer rotary-group** command that indicates which interface is part of a dialer rotary group.

Although a dialer rotary group is configured as an interface, it is not a physical interface. Instead, it represents a group of interfaces. Any number of dialer groups can be defined.

Interface configuration commands entered after the **interface dialer** command will be applied to all physical interfaces assigned to specified rotary group.

Example

The following example identifies dialer interface 1 as the dialer rotary group leader. Dialer interface 1 is not a physical interface, but represents a group of interfaces. The interface configuration commands that follow apply to all interfaces included in this group.

```
interface dialer 1
 encapsulation ppp
 dialer in-band
 dialer map ip 172.30.2.5 username YYY 14155553434
 dialer map ip 172.30.4.5 username ZZZ
```

Related Commands

dialer rotary-group

INTERFACE FASTETHERNET

To select a particular Fast Ethernet interface for configuration, use the **interface fastethernet** global configuration command.

interface fastethernet *number* (Cisco 4500 and 4700 routers)
interface fastethernet *slot/port* (Cisco 7200 series routers)
interface fastethernet *slot/port-adapter/port* (Cisco 7500 series routers)

Syntax	Description
number	Port, connector, or interface card number. On a Cisco 4500 or 4700 router, specifies the NIM or NPM number. The numbers are assigned at the factory at the time of installation or when added to a system.
slot	Refer to the appropriate hardware manual for slot and port information.
port	Refer to the appropriate hardware manual for slot and port information.
port-adapter	Refer to the appropriate hardware manual for information about port adapter compatibility.

Default

Standard Advanced Research Projects Agency (ARPA) encapsulation is configured.

Command Mode

Global configuration

Usage Guidelines

This command first appeared in Cisco IOS Release 11.2.

Default encapsulation type changed to ARPA in Cisco IOS Release 11.3.

Examples

The following example configures Fast Ethernet interface 0 for standard Advanced Research Projects Agency (ARPA) encapsulation (the default setting) on a Cisco 4500 or 4700 router: ·

```
interface fastethernet 0
```

Related Commands

show interfaces fastethernet

INTERFACE GROUP-ASYNC

To create a group interface that will serve as master, to which asynchronous interfaces can be associated as members, use the **interface group-async** command. Use the **no** form of the command to restore the default.

> **interface group-async** *unit-number*
> **no interface group-async** *unit-number*

Syntax	Description
unit-number	The number of the asynchronous group interface being created.

Default

No interfaces are designated as group masters.

Command Mode

Global configuration

Usage Guidelines

Using the **interface group-async** command, you create a single asynchronous interface to which other interfaces are associated as members using the **group-range** command. This one-to-many configuration allows you to configure all associated member interfaces by entering one command on the group master interface, rather than entering this command on each individual interface. You can create multiple group masters on a device; however, each member interface can be associated with only one group.

Examples

The following example defines asynchronous group master interface 0:

```
interface group-async 0
```

Related Commands

group-range
member

INTERFACE VG-ANYLAN

Use the **interface vg-anylan** global configuration command to specify the interface on a 100VG-AnyLAN port adapter and enter interface configuration mode on Cisco 7200 series routers and Cisco 7500 series routers.

> interface vg-anylan *slot/port-adapter/port* (VIP cards in Cisco 7500 series routers)
> interface vg-anylan *slot/port* (Cisco 7200 series routers)

Syntax	Description
slot	Refer to the appropriate hardware manual for slot and port information.
port	Refer to the appropriate hardware manual for slot and port information.
port-adapter	Refer to the appropriate hardware manual for information about port adapter compatibility.

Default

No interfaces are specified.

Command Mode

Global configuration

Usage Guidelines

This command first appeared in Cisco IOS Release 11.3.

The 100VG-AnyLAN port adapter provides a single interface port that is compatible with and specified by IEEE 802.12. The 100VG-AnyLAN port adapter provides 100 Mbps over Category 3 or Category 5 unshielded twisted-pair (UTP) cable with RJ-45 terminators, and supports IEEE 802.3 Ethernet packets.

You configure the 100VG-AnyLAN port adapter as you would any Ethernet or Fast Ethernet interface. The 100VG-AnyLAN port adapter can be monitored with the IEEE 802.12 Interface MIB.

Example

The following example specifies the 100VG-AnyLAN port adapter in the first port adapter in slot 1:

```
interface vg-anylan 1/0/0
```

Related Commands

frame-type
show interfaces vg-anylan

INVERT DATA

To invert the data stream, use the **invert data** interface configuration command. This command applies only to the Cisco 7200 series routers and Cisco 7500 series routers. Use the **no** form of this command to disable this feature.

> invert data
> no invert data

Syntax   Description

This command has no arguments or keywords.

Default

Data is not inverted.

Command Mode

Interface configuration

Part
III

Usage Guidelines

This command first appeared in Cisco IOS Release 11.3.

T1 Line without B8ZS Encoding

If the interface on the PA-8T and PA-4T+ synchronous serial port adapters is used to drive a dedicated T1 line that does not have B8ZS encoding (a method to avoid 15 zeros), the data stream must be inverted (both TXD and RXD) either in the connecting CSU/DSU or the interface.

By inverting the HDLC data stream, the HDLC zero insertion algorithm becomes a ones insertion algorithm that satisfies the T1 requirements. Be careful not to invert data both on the interface and on the CSU/DSU, as two data inversions will cancel each other out.

AMI Line Coding

If the interface on the CT3IP uses AMI line coding, you must also invert the data on the T1 channel. For more information, see the **t1 linecode** controller configuration command.

Command Reference

Example

The following example inverts data on serial interface 3/1/0:

```
interface serial 3/1/0
  invert data
```

Related Commands

t1 linecode

INVERT-TRANSMIT-CLOCK

The **invert txclock** command replaces this command. Refer to the description of **invert txclock** for information on the transmit clock signal.

INVERT TXCLOCK

Use the **invert txclock** interface configuration command to invert the transmit clock signal. Delays between the SCTE clock and data transmission indicate that the transmit clock signal might not be appropriate for the interface rate and length of cable being used. Different ends of the wire can have variances that differ slightly. The **invert txclock** command compensates for these variances. This command replaces the **invert data** command.

This command applies only to Cisco 7200 series and Cisco 7500 series routers. To return the transmit clock signal to its initial state, use the **no** form of this command.

> **invert txclock**
> **no invert txclock**

Syntax   Description

This command has no arguments or keywords.

Default

Transmit clock signal is not inverted.

Command Mode

Interface configuration

Usage Guidelines

This command first appeared in Cisco IOS Release 10.0.

This command was modified in Cisco IOS Release 11.3 to change the command from **invert-transmit-clock** to **invert txclock**.

Systems that use long cables or cables that are not transmitting the TxC signal (transmit echoed clock line, also known as TXCE or SCTE clock) can experience high error rates when operating at the higher transmission speeds. For example, if a PA-8T synchronous serial port adapter is reporting a high number of error packets, a phase shift might be the problem. Inverting the clock might correct this shift.

When a PA-8T or PA-4T+ port adapter interface is DTE, the **invert txclock** command inverts the TxC signal it received from the remote DCE. When the PA-8T or PA-4T+ port adapter interface is DCE, this command changes the signal back to its original phase.

Example

In the following example, the clock signal on serial interface 3/0 is inverted:

```
interface serial 3/0
 invert txclock
```

ISDN INCOMING-VOICE MODEM

To enable incoming ISDN voice calls to access the Cisco AS5200 call switch module and integrated modems, use the **isdn incoming-voice modem** interface configuration command. The **no** form of this command stops all incoming ISDN analog calls from routing to the modems.

isdn incoming-voice modem
no isdn incoming-voice modem

Syntax   Description

This command has no arguments or keywords.

Default

Disabled

Command Mode

Interface configuration

Usage Guidelines

Incoming ISDN digital calls are unaffected by this command. ISDN digital calls directly connect to network resources even when the **no isdn incoming-voice modem** command is configured.

Example

The following example enables incoming and outgoing ISDN calls to route to the modems using the D channel serial interface:

```
AS5200(config)# interface serial 0:23
AS5200(config-if)# isdn incoming-voice modem
AS5200(config-if)#
```

KEEPALIVE

To set the keepalive timer for a specific interface, use the **keepalive** interface configuration command. To turn off keepalives entirely, use the **no** form of this command.

> **keepalive** [*seconds*]
> **no keepalive** [*seconds*]

Syntax   *Description*

seconds   (Optional) Unsigned integer value greater than 0. The default is 10 seconds.

Default

10 seconds

Command Mode

Interface configuration

Usage Guidelines

This command first appeared in Cisco IOS Release 10.0.

You can configure the keepalive interval, which is the frequency at which the Cisco IOS software sends messages to itself (Ethernet and Token Ring) or to the other end (serial), to ensure a network interface is alive. The interval in previous software versions was 10 seconds; it is now adjustable in one-second increments down to one second. An interface is declared down after three update intervals have passed without receiving a keepalive packet.

Setting the keepalive timer to a low value is very useful for rapidly detecting Ethernet interface failures (transceiver cable disconnecting, cable unterminated, and so on).

A typical serial line failure involves losing the Carrier Detect (CD) signal. Because this sort of failure is typically noticed within a few milliseconds, adjusting the keepalive timer for quicker routing recovery is generally not useful.

NOTES

When adjusting the keepalive timer for a very low bandwidth serial interface, large datagrams can delay the smaller keepalive packets long enough to cause the line protocol to go down. You might need to experiment to determine the best value.

Example

The following example sets the keepalive interval to three seconds:

```
interface ethernet 0
 keepalive 3
```

LEX BURNED-IN-ADDRESS

To set the burned-in MAC address for a LAN Extender interface, use the **lex burned-in-address** interface configuration command. To clear the burned-in MAC address, use the **no** form of this command.

lex burned-in-address *ieee-address*
no lex burned-in-address

Syntax	Description
ieee-address	48-bit IEEE MAC address written as a dotted triplet of four-digit hexadecimal numbers.

Default

No burned-in MAC address is set.

Command Mode

Interface configuration

Usage Guidelines

This command first appeared in Cisco IOS Release 10.3.

Use this command only on a LAN Extender interface that is not currently active (not bound to a serial interface).

Example

The following example sets the burned-in MAC address on LAN Extender interface 0:

```
interface serial 4
 encapsulation ppp
interface lex 0
 lex burned-in-address 0000.0c00.0001
 ip address 131.108.172.21 255.255.255.0
```

LEX INPUT-ADDRESS-LIST

To assign an access list that filters on MAC addresses, use the **lex input-address-list** interface configuration command. To remove an access list from the interface, use the **no** form of this command.

lex input-address-list *access-list-number*
no lex input-address-list

Syntax	Description
access-list-number	Number of the access list you assigned with the **access-list** global configuration command. It can be a number from 700 to 799.

Part III
Command Reference

Default

No access lists are preassigned to a LAN Extender interface.

Command Mode

Interface configuration

Usage Guidelines

This command first appeared in Cisco IOS Release 10.3. (The **no lex input-address-list** command first appeared in Cisco IOS Release 10.0.)

Use the **lex input-address-list** command to filter the packets that are allowed to pass from the LAN Extender to the core router. The access list filters packets based on the source MAC address.

The LAN Extender interface does not process MAC-address masks. Therefore, you should omit the mask from the **access-list** commands.

For LAN Extender interfaces, an implicit permit-everything entry is automatically defined at the end of an access list. Note that this default differs from other access lists, which have an implicit deny everything entry at the end of each access list.

Example

The following example applies access list 710 to LAN Extender interface 0. This access list denies all packets from MAC address 0800.0214.2776 and permits all other packets.

```
access-list 710 deny 0800.0214.2776
interface lex 0
 lex input-address-list 710
```

Related Commands

access-list

LEX INPUT-TYPE-LIST

Use the **lex input-type-list** interface configuration command to assign an access list that filters Ethernet packets by type code. To remove an access list from the interface, use the **no** form of this command.

> **lex input-type-list** *access-list-number*
> **no lex input-type-list**

Syntax	Description
access-list-number	Number of the access list you assigned with the **access-list** global configuration command. It can be a number in the range 200 to 299.

Default

No access lists are preassigned to a LAN Extender interface.

Command Mode

Interface configuration

Usage Guidelines

This command first appeared in Cisco IOS Release 10.3.

Filtering is done on the LAN Extender chassis.

The LAN Extender interface does not process masks. Therefore, you should omit the mask from the **access-list** commands.

For LAN Extender interfaces, an implicit permit-everything entry is automatically defined at the end of an access list. Note that this default differs from other access lists, which have an implicit deny-everything entry at the end of each access list.

Example

The following example applies access list 220 to LAN Extender interface 0. This access list denies all AppleTalk packets (packets with a type field of 0x809B) and permits all other packets.

```
access-list 220 deny 0x809B 0x0000
interface lex 0
  lex input-type-list 220
```

Related Commands

access-list

LEX PRIORITY-GROUP

Use the **lex priority-group** interface configuration command to activate priority output queuing on the LAN Extender. To disable priority output queuing, use the **no** form of this command.

lex priority-group *group*
no lex priority-group

Syntax	Description
group	Number of the priority group. It can be a number in the range 1 to 10.

Default

Disabled

Command Mode

Interface configuration

Usage Guidelines

This command first appeared in Cisco IOS Release 10.3.

To define queuing priorities, use the **priority-list protocol** global configuration command. Note that you can use only the following forms of this command:

> **priority-list** *list* **protocol** *protocol* {**high** | **medium** | **normal** | **low**}

> **priority-list** *list* **protocol bridge** {**high** | **medium** | **normal** | **low**} **list** *list-number*

If you specify a protocol that does not have an assigned Ethernet type code, such as **x25**, **stun**, or **pad**, it is ignored and will not participate in priority output queuing.

Example

The following example activates priority output queuing on LAN Extender interface 0:

```
priority-list 5 protocol bridge medium list 701
lex interface 0
lex priority-group 5
```

Related Commands

priority-list protocol

LEX RETRY-COUNT

Use the **lex retry-count** interface configuration command to define the number of times to resend commands to the LAN Extender chassis. To return to the default value, use the **no** form of this command.

> **lex retry-count** *number*
> **no lex retry-count** [*number*]

Syntax	*Description*
number	Number of times to retry sending commands to the LAN Extender. It can be a number in the range 0 to 100. The default is 10 times.

Default

10

Command Mode

Interface configuration

Usage Guidelines

This command first appeared in Cisco IOS Release 10.3.

After the core router has sent a command the specified number of times without receiving an acknowledgment from the LAN Extender, it stops sending the command altogether.

Example

The following example resends commands 20 times to the LAN Extender:

```
lex interface 0
lex retry-count 20
```

Related Commands

lex timeout

LEX TIMEOUT

Use the **lex timeout** interface configuration command to define the amount of time to wait for a response from the LAN Extender. To return to the default time, use the **no** form of this command.

> **lex timeout** *milliseconds*
> **no lex timeout** [*milliseconds*]

Part
III

Command Reference

Syntax	Description
milliseconds	Time, in milliseconds, to wait for a response from the LAN Extender before resending the command. It can be a number in the range 500 to 60,000. The default is 2,000 ms (2 milliseconds).

Default

2,000 ms (2 milliseconds)

Command Mode

Interface configuration

Usage Guidelines

This command first appeared in Cisco IOS Release 10.3.

The **lex timeout** command defines the amount of time that the core router will wait to receive an acknowledgment after having sent a command to the LAN Extender.

Example

The following example causes unacknowledged packets to be re-sent at four-second intervals:

```
lex interface 0
lex timeout 4000
```

Related Commands

lex retry-count

LINECODE

Use the **linecode** controller configuration command to select the line-code type for the T1 or E1 line.

> **linecode {ami | b8zs | hdb3}**

Syntax	Description
ami	Specifies alternate mark inversion (AMI) as the line-code type. Valid for T1 or E1 controllers.
b8zs	Specifies B8ZS as the line-code type. Valid for T1 controller only.
hdb3	Specifies high-density bipolar 3 (hdb3) as the line-code type. Valid for E1 controller only.

Defaults

AMI is the default for T1 lines.

High-density bipolar 3 is the default for E1 lines.

Command Mode

Controller configuration

Usage Guidelines

Use this command in configurations where the router or access server must communicate with T1 fractional data lines. The T1 service provider determines which line-code type, either **ami** or **b8zs**, is required for your T1 circuit. Likewise, the E1 service provider determines which line-code type, either **ami** or **hdb3**, is required for your E1 circuit.

Example

The following example specifies B8ZS as the line-code type:

```
linecode b8zs
```

LINK-TEST

To re-enable the link-test function on a port on an Ethernet hub of a Cisco 2505 or Cisco 2507, use the **link-test** hub configuration command. Use the **no** form of this command to disable this feature if a pre-10BaseT twisted-pair device not implementing link test is connected to the hub port.

> **link-test**
> **no link-test**

Syntax   Description

This command has no arguments or keywords.

Default

Enabled

Command Mode

Hub configuration

Usage Guidelines

This command first appeared in Cisco IOS Release 10.3.

This command applies to a port on an Ethernet hub only. Disable this feature if a 10BaseT twisted-pair device at the other end of the hub does not implement the link-test function.

Example

The following example disables the link-test function on hub 0, ports 1 through 3:

```
hub ethernet 0 1 3
no link-test
```

Related Commands

hub

LOCAL-LNM

To enable Lanoptics Hub Networking Management of a PCbus Token Ring interface, use the **local-lnm** interface configuration command. Use the **no** form of this command to disable Lanoptics Hub Networking Management.

> **local-lnm**
> **no local-lnm**

Syntax   Description

This command has no arguments or keywords.

Default

Management is not enabled.

Command Mode

Interface configuration

Usage Guidelines

This command first appeared in Cisco IOS Release 10.3.

The Token Ring interface on the AccessPro PC card can be managed by a remote LAN manager over the PCbus interface. At present, the Lanoptics Hub Networking Management software running on an IBM-compatible PC is supported.

Example

The following example enables Lanoptics Hub Networking Management:

```
local-lnm
```

LOOPBACK (INTERFACE)

To diagnose equipment malfunctions between interface and device, use the **loopback** interface configuration command. The **no** form of this command disables the test.

> **loopback**
> **no loopback**

Syntax   Description

This command has no arguments or keywords.

Default

Disabled

Command Mode

Interface configuration

Usage Guidelines

This command first appeared in Cisco IOS Release 10.0.

On HSSI serial interface cards, the loopback function configures a two-way internal and external loop on the HSA applique of the specific interface.

On MCI and SCI serial interface cards, the loopback functions when a CSU/DSU or equivalent device is attached to the router or access server. The **loopback** command loops the packets through the CSU/DSU to configure a CSU loop, when the device supports this feature.

On the MCI and MEC Ethernet cards, the interface receives back every packet it sends when the **loopback** command is enabled. Loopback operation has the additional effect of disconnecting network server functionality from the network.

On the CSC-FCI FDDI card, the interface receives back every packet it sends when the **loopback** command is enabled. Loopback operation has the additional effect of disconnecting network server functionality from the network.

On all Token Ring interface cards (except the 4-megabit CSC-R card), the interface receives back every packet it sends when the **loopback** command is enabled. Loopback operation has the additional effect of disconnecting network server functionality from the network.

NOTES

Loopback does not work on an X.21 DTE, because the X.21 interface definition does not include a loopback definition.

To show interfaces currently in loopback operation, use the **show interfaces loopback** EXEC command.

Example

The following example configures the loopback test on Ethernet interface 4:

```
interface ethernet 4
  loopback
```

Related Commands

down-when-looped
show interfaces loopback

LOOPBACK (T1)

To loop individual T1 channels on the Channelized T3 Interface Processor (CT3IP) in Cisco 7500 series routers, use the **loopback** interface configuration command. Use the **no** form of this command to remove the loopback.

loopback [local | network {line | payload} | remote {line [fdl] [ansi] | inband} | payload [fdl] [ansi]}]
no loopback

Syntax	Description
local	(Optional) Loops the router output data back toward the router at the T1 framer and sends an AIS signal out toward the network.
network {line | payload}	(Optional) Loops the data back toward the network before the T1 framer and automatically sets a local loopback at the HDLC controllers (line) or loops the payload data back toward the network at the T1 framer and automatically sets a local loopback at the HDLC controllers (payload).
remote line [fdl] [ansi]	(Optional) Sends a repeating, 16-bit ESF data-link code word (00001110 11111111) to the remote end requesting that it enter into a network line loopback. Enables the remote line Facility Data Link (FDL) ANSI bit loopback on the T1 channel.
	You can specify **fdl** and **ansi** optionally, but it is not necessary.
remote line inband	(Optional) Sends a repeating, five-bit inband pattern (00001) to the remote end requesting that it enter into a network line loopback.
remote payload [fdl] [ansi]	(Optional) Sends a repeating, 16-bit ESF data-link code word (00010100 11111111) to the remote end requesting that it enter into a network payload loopback. Enables the remote payload Facility Data Link (FDL) ANSI bit loopback on the T1 channel.
	You can specify **fdl** and **ansi** optionally, but it is not necessary.

Default

Disabled

Command Mode

Interface configuration

Usage Guidelines

This command first appeared in Cisco IOS Release 11.3.

Use this command for troubleshooting purposes.

You also can loopback all the T1 channels by using the **loopback (CT3IP)** interface configuration command.

NOTES

You can specify **fdl** and **ansi** optionally, but it is not necessary. FDL ANSI is the default. There might be other options in a future release.

Example

The following example configures T1 channel 5 for a local loopback:

```
interface serial 3/0/0:5
  loopback local
```

Related Commands

loopback (T3)

LOOPBACK (T3)

To loop the entire T3 (all 28 T1 channels) on the Channelized T3 Interface Processor (CT3IP) in Cisco 7500 series routers, use the **loopback** controller configuration command. Use the **no** form of this command to remove the loopback.

> **loopback [local | network | remote]**
> **no loopback**

Syntax	Description
local	(Optional) Loops the data back toward the router and sends an AIS signal out toward the network.
network	(Optional) Loops the data toward the network at the T1 framer.
remote	(Optional) Sends a far-end alarm control (FEAC) request to the remote end requesting that it enter into a network line loopback. FEAC requests (and therefore remote loopbacks) are only possible when the T3 is configured for C-bit framing. The type of framing used is determined by the equipment you are connecting to (for more information, see the **framing** controller command).

Default

Disabled

Command Mode

Controller configuration

Usage Guidelines

This command first appeared in Cisco IOS Release 11.3.

Use this command for troubleshooting purposes.

You also can loopback each T1 channel by using the **loopback** interface configuration command.

For more information, see "Troubleshooting the T3 and T1 Channels" section in Chapter 21, "Configuring Serial Interfaces."

Example

The following example configures the CT3IP for a local loopback:

```
controller t3 3/0/0
  loopback local
```

Related Commands

loopback remote (interface)

LOOPBACK APPLIQUE

To configure an internal loop on the HSSI applique, use the **loopback applique** interface configuration command. To remove the loop, use the **no** form of this command.

> **loopback applique**
> **no loopback applique**

Syntax   Description

This command has no arguments or keywords.

Default

Disabled

Command Mode

Interface configuration

Usage Guidelines

This command first appeared in Cisco IOS Release 10.0.

This command loops the packets within the applique, to provide a way to test communication within the router or access server. It is useful for sending pings to yourself to check functionality of the applique.

To show interfaces currently in loopback operation, use the **show interfaces loopback** EXEC command.

Example

The following example configures the loopback test on the HSSI applique:

```
interface serial 1
loopback applique
```

Related Commands

show interfaces loopback

LOOPBACK DTE

To loop packets back to the DTE from the CSU/DSU, when the device supports this feature, use the **loopback dte** interface configuration command. To remove the loop, use the **no** form of this command.

> **loopback dte**
> **no loopback dte**

Syntax Description

This command has no arguments or keywords.

Default

Disabled

Command Mode

Interface configuration

Usage Guidelines

This command first appeared in Cisco IOS Release 10.0.

This command is useful for testing the DTE-to-DCE cable.

This command is used to test the performance of the integrated CSU/DSU. Packets are looped from within the CSU/DSU back to the serial interface of the router. Send a test ping to see whether the packets successfully looped back. To cancel the loopback test, use the **no loopback dte** command.

When using the 4-wire 56/64-kbps CSU/DSU module, an out-of-service signal is transmitted to the remote CSU/DSU.

To show interfaces currently in loopback operation, use the **show interfaces loopback** EXEC command.

Example

The following example configures the loopback test on the DTE interface:

```
router(config)# interface serial 0
router(config-if)# loopback dte
router(config-if)#
```

Related Commands

show interfaces loopback

LOOPBACK LINE

When the device supports this feature, use the **loopback line** interface configuration command to loop packets completely through the CSU/DSU to configure the CSU loop. To remove the loop, use the **no** form of this command.

> **loopback line** [payload]
> **no loopback line** [payload]

Syntax	Description
payload	(Optional) Configures a loopback point at the DSU and loops back data to the network on an integrated CSU/DSU.

Default

Disabled

Command Mode

Interface configuration

Usage Guidelines

This command first appeared in Cisco IOS Release 10.0.

This command is useful for testing the DCE device (CSU/DSU) itself. When the **loopback line** command is configured on the two-wire 56-kbps CSU/DSU module or the four-wire 56/64-kbps CSU/DSU modules, the network data loops back at the CSU and the router data loops back at the DSU. If the CSU/DSU is configured for switched mode, you must have an established connection to perform a payload-line loopback. To loop the received data through the minimum amount of CSU/DSU circuitry, issue the **loopback line** command.

When you issue the **loopback line payload** command on an integrated CSU/DSU module, the router cannot transmit data through the serial interface for the duration of the loopback. Choosing the DSU as a loopback point loops the received-network data through the maximum amount of CSU/DSU circuitry. Data is not looped back to the serial interface. An active connection is required when operating in switched mode for payload loopbacks.

If you enable the **loopback line** command on the fractional T1/T1 module, the CSU/DSU performs a full-bandwidth loopback through the CSU portion of the module and data transmission through the serial interface is interrupted for the duration of the loopback. No reframing or corrections of bipolar violation errors or cyclic redundancy check (CRC) errors are performed. When you configure the **loopback line payload** command on the FT1/T1 module, the CSU/DSU performs a loopback through the DSU portion of the module. The **loopback line payload** command reframes the data link, regenerates the signal, and corrects bipolar violations and Extended Super Frame CRC errors.

When performing a T1-line loopback with Extended Super Frame, communication over the facilities data link is interrupted, but performance statistics are still updated. To show interfaces currently in loopback operation, use the **show service-module** EXEC command.

To show interfaces currently in loopback operation on other routers, use the **show interfaces loopback** EXEC command.

Examples

The following example configures the loopback test on the DCE device:

```
interface serial 1
  loopback line
```

The following example shows how to configure a payload loopback on a Cisco 2524 or 2525 router:

```
Router1(config-if)#loopback line payload
Loopback in progress
Router1(config-if)#no loopback line
```

The following example shows the output on a Cisco 2524 or 2525 router when you loop a packet in switched mode without an active connection:

```
Router1(config-if)#service-module 56k network-type switched
Router1(config-if)#loopback line payload
Need active connection for this type of loopback
% Service module configuration command failed: WRONG FORMAT.
```

Related Commands

show interfaces loopback

Part
III

Command Reference

LOOPBACK REMOTE (INTERFACE)

To loop packets through a CSU/DSU, over a DS-3 link or a channelized T1 link, to the remote CSU/DSU and back, use the **loopback remote** interface configuration command. To remove the loopback, use the **no** form of this command.

loopback remote {full | payload | smart-jack} [0in1 | 1in1 | 1in2 | 1in5 | 1in8 | 3in24 | qrw | user-pattern *24bit-binary value*]
no loopback remote {full | payload | smart-jack}

loopback remote [2047 | 511 | stress-pattern *pattern number*]
no loopback remote

— **NOTES** ——————————————————————————————

The keywords **full, payload, smart-jack, 0in1** through **3in24, qrw,** and **user-pattern** *24bit-binary value* apply to the fractional T1/T1 CSU/DSU module. The keywords **2047, 511,** and **stress-pattern** apply to the 2- and 4-wire 56/64-kbps CSU/DSU module. The features for each module are grouped and described in the following two syntax descriptions.

Syntax	Description for FT1/T1 CSU/DSUModules
full	Transmits a full-bandwidth line loopback request to a remote device, which is used for testing the line and remote CSU.
payload	Transmits a payload-line loopback request to a remote device, which is used for testing the line and remote DSU.
smart-jack	Transmits a loopback request to the remote smart-jack, which some service providers attach on the line before the customer premises equipment (CPE). You cannot put the local smart-jack into loopback.
0in1	(Optional) Transmits an all-zeros test pattern used for verifying B8ZS line encoding. The remote end might report a loss of signal when using alternate mark inversion (AMI) line coding.
1in1	(Optional) Transmits an all-ones test pattern used for signal power measurements.
1in2	(Optional) Transmits an alternating ones and zeroes test pattern used for testing bridge taps.
1in5	(Optional) Transmits the industry standard test-pattern loopback request.
1in8	(Optional) Transmits a test pattern used for stressing timing recovery of repeaters.
3in24	(Optional) Transmits a test pattern used for testing the ones density tolerance on AMI lines.
qrw	(Optional) Transmits a quasi-random word test pattern, which is a random signal that simulates user data.
user-pattern *24bit-binary value*	(Optional) Transmits a test pattern that you define. Enter a binary string up to 24 bits long. For the fixed patterns such 0in1 and 1in1, the T1 framing bits are jammed on top of the test pattern; for the user pattern, the pattern is simply repeated in the timeslots.

Syntax	Description for 2- and 4-Wire 56/64-kbps CSU/DSU Modules
2047	Transmits a pseudo-random test pattern that repeats after 2,047 bits.
511	Transmits a pseudo-random test pattern that repeats after 511 bits.
stress-pattern *pattern number*	Transmits a DDS stress pattern available only on the four-wire 56/64-kbps CSU/DSU module. You may enter a stress pattern from 1 to 4. A 1 pattern sends 100 bytes of all 1s and then 100 bytes of all 0s to test the stress clocking of the network. A 2 pattern sends 100 bytes of a 0x7e pattern then 100 bytes of all 0s. A 3 pattern sends continuous bytes of a 0x46 pattern. A 4 pattern sends continuous bytes of 0x02 pattern.

Default

Disabled

Command Mode

Interface configuration

Usage Guidelines

This command applies only when the remote CSU/DSU device is configured for this function. It is used for testing the data communication channels along with or without remote CSU/DSU circuitry. The loopback is usually performed at the line port, rather than the DTE port, of the remote CSU/DSU.

For a multiport interface processor connected to a network via a channelized T1 link, the **loopback remote** interface configuration command applies if the remote interface is served by a DDS line (56 kbps or 64 kbps) and the device at the remote end is a CSU/DSU. In addition, the CSU/DSU at the remote end *must* react to latched DDS CSU loopback codes. Destinations that are served by other types of lines or that have CSU/DSUs that do not react to latched DDS CSU codes cannot participate in an interface remote loopback. Latched DDS CSU loopback code requirements are described in AT&T specification TR-TSY-000476, "OTGR Network Maintenance Access and Testing."

For the integrated FT1/T1 CSU/DSU module, the **loopback remote full** command sends the loopup code to the remote CSU/DSU. The remote CSU/DSU performs a full-bandwidth loopback through the CSU portion of the module. The **loopback remote payload** command sends the loopup code on the configured timeslots, while maintaining the D4-extended super framing. The remote CSU/DSU performs the equivalent of a loopback line payload request. The remote CSU/DSU loops back only those timeslots that are configured on the remote end. This loopback reframes the data link, regenerates the signal, and corrects bi polar violations and extended super frame CRC errors. The **loopback remote smart-jack** command sends a loopup code to the remote smart jack. You cannot put the local smart jack into loopback.

Failure to loopup or initiate a remote loopback request could be caused by enabling the **no service-module t1 remote-loopback** command or having an alternate remote loopback code configured on the remote end. When the loopback is terminated, the result of the pattern test is displayed.

For the 2- and 4-wire 56/64-kbps CSU/DSU module, an active connection is required before a loopup can be initiated while in switched mode. When transmitting V.54 loopbacks, the remote device is commanded into loopback using V.54 messages. Failure to loopup or initiate a remote loopback request could be caused by enabling the **no service-module 56k remote-loopback** command.

To show interfaces currently in loopback operation, use the **show interfaces loopback** EXEC command.

Examples

The following example configures a remote loopback test:

```
Router(config)#interface serial 0
Router(config-if)#loopback remote
```

The following example configures the remote device into full-bandwidth line loopback while spec-ifying the **qrw** test pattern over the T1 CSU/DSU module on a Cisco 2524 or Cisco 2525 router:

```
Router(config)#interface serial 0
Router(config-if)#loopback remote full qrw
Router(config-if)#
%LINEPROTO-5-UPDOWN: Line protocol on Interface Serial0, changed state to down
%LINK-3-UPDOWN: Interface Serial0, changed state to down
%SERVICE_MODULE-5-LOOPUPREMOTE: Unit 0 - Remote unit placed in loopback
```

The following example transmits a remote loopback stress pattern over the 4-wire 56/64-kbps CSU/DSU module, which tests the stress clocking of the network:

```
Router(config-if)#loopback remote stress-pattern 1
Router(config-if)#
%LINEPROTO-5-UPDOWN: Line protocol on Interface Serial1, changed state to down
%LINK-3-UPDOWN: Interface Serial1, changed state to down
%SERVICE_MODULE-5-LOOPUPREMOTE: Unit 1 - Remote unit placed in loopback
```

Related Commands

clear service-module
loopback dte
loopback line
service-module 56k remote-loopback
service-module t1 remote-loopback
show service-module

MDL

Use the **mdl** interface configuration command to configure the Maintenance Data Link (MDL) mes-sage defined in the ANSI T1.107a-1990 specification for the Channelized T3 Interface Processor (CT3IP) in Cisco 7500 series routers. Use the **no** form of this command to remove the message.

> **mdl** {transmit {path | idle-signal | test-signal} | string {eic | lic | fic | unit | pfi | port | generator} *string*}
> **no mdl** {transmit {path | idle-signal | test-signal} | string {eic | lic | fic | unit | pfi | port | generator} *string*}

Syntax	*Description*
transmit path	Enables transmission of the MDL Path message.
transmit idle-signal	Enables transmission of the MDL Idle Signal message.
transmit test-signal	Enables transmission of the MDL Test Signal message.

Syntax	Description
string eic *string*	Specifies the Equipment Identification Code; can be up to 10 characters.
string lic *string*	Specifies the Location Identification Code; can be up to 11 characters.
string fic *string*	Specifies the Frame Identification Code; can be up to 10 characters.
string unit *string*	Specifies the Unit Identification Code; can be up to 6 characters.
string pfi *string*	Specifies the Facility Identification Code sent in the MDL Path message; can be up to 38 characters.
string port *string*	Specifies the Port number string sent in the MDL Idle Signal message; can be up to 38 characters.
string generator *string*	Specifies the Generator number string sent in the MDL Test Signal message; can be up to 38 characters.

Default

No MDL message is configured

Command Mode

Interface configuration

Usage Guidelines

This command first appeared in Cisco IOS Release 11.3.

Use the **show controllers t3** command to display MDL information (received strings). MDL information is displayed only when framing is set to C-bit.

NOTES

MDL is supported only when the DS3 framing is C-bit parity.

Examples

The following examples show several of the **mdl** commands for the CT3IP in slot 9:

```
controller t3 9/0/0
  mdl string eic Router A
  mdl string lic Test Network
  mdl string fic Building B
  mdl string unit ABC
```

Related Commands

show controllers t3

MEDIA-TYPE

To specify the physical connection for one of the following configurations, use the **media-type** interface configuration command.

- Ethernet network interface module configuration on the Cisco 4000 series
- Fast Ethernet Interface Processor (FEIP) on the Cisco 7000 series, 7200 series, and 7500 series
- Full-duplex or half-duplex mode on a serial interface

Use the **no** form of this command to restore the default value.

> **media-type** {aui | 10baset | 100baset | mii}
> **no media-type** {aui | 10baset | 100baset | mii}

Syntax	Description
aui	Selects a 15-pin physical connection.
10baset	Selects an RJ45 10BaseT physical connection.
100baset	Specifies an RJ45 100BaseT physical connection.
mii	Specifies a media-independent interface.

Default

AUI 15-pin physical connection is the default setting on the Cisco 4000 series.

100BaseT physical connection is the default setting on the Cisco 7000 series and 7200 series.

Command Mode

Interface configuration

Usage Guidelines

This command first appeared in Cisco IOS Release 10.0.

Examples

The following example selects an RJ45 10BaseT physical connection on Ethernet interface 1:

```
interface ethernet 1
 media-type 10baset
```

The following example specifies a media-independent interface physical connection to Fast Ethernet slot 0, port 1 on the Cisco 7000 or 7200 series:

```
interface fastethernet 0/1
 media-type mii
```

The following example specifies a media-independent interface physical connection to Fast Ethernet slot 0, port-adapter 1, port 1 on the Cisco 7500 series:

```
interface fastethernet 0/1/1
 media-type mii
```

MOP ENABLED

Use the **mop enabled** interface configuration command to enable an interface to support the Maintenance Operation Protocol (MOP). To disable MOP on an interface, use the **no** form of this command.

> **mop enabled**
> **no mop enabled**

Syntax   Description

This command has no arguments or keywords.

Default

Enabled on Ethernet interfaces and disabled on all other interfaces.

Command Mode

Interface configuration

Usage Guidelines

This command first appeared in Cisco IOS Release 10.0.

Example

In the following example, MOP is enabled for serial interface 0:

```
interface serial 0
 mop enabled
```

Related Commands

mop retransmit-timer
mop retries
mop sysid

MOP SYSID

To enable an interface to send out periodic Maintenance Operation Protocol (MOP) system identification messages, use the **mop sysid** interface configuration command. To disable MOP message support on an interface, use the **no** form of this command.

mop sysid
no mop sysid

Syntax   Description

This command has no arguments or keywords.

Default

Enabled

Command Mode

Interface configuration

Usage Guidelines

This command first appeared in Cisco IOS Release 10.0.

You still can run MOP without having the background system ID messages sent. This lets you use the MOP remote console, but does not generate messages used by the configurator.

Example

In the following example, serial interface 0 is enabled to send MOP system identification messages:

```
interface serial 0
  mop sysid
```

Related Commands

mop device-code
mop enabled

MTU

To adjust the maximum packet size or maximum transmission unit (MTU) size, use the **mtu** interface configuration command. Use the **no** form of this command to restore the MTU value to its original default value.

mtu *bytes*
no mtu

Syntax   Description

bytes   Desired size in bytes.

Defaults

Table 23–8 lists default MTU values according to media type.

Table 23–8 *Default Media MTU Values*

Media Type	Default MTU
Ethernet	1,500
Serial	1,500
Token Ring	4,464
ATM	4,470
FDDI	4,470
HSSI (HSA)	4,470

Command Mode

Interface configuration

Usage Guidelines

This command first appeared in Cisco IOS Release 10.0.

Each interface has a default maximum packet size or maximum transmission unit (MTU) size. This number generally defaults to the largest size possible for that type interface. On serial interfaces, the MTU size varies, but cannot be set smaller than 64 bytes.

NOTES

Changing the MTU value with the **mtu** interface configuration command can affect values for the protocol-specific versions of the command (**ip mtu,** for example). If the value specified with the **ip mtu** interface configuration command is the same as the value specified with the **mtu** interface configuration command, and you change the value for the **mtu** interface configuration command, the **ip mtu** value automatically matches the new **mtu** interface configuration command value. However, changing the values for the **ip mtu** configuration command has no effect on the value for the **mtu** interface configuration command.

Example

The following example specifies an MTU of 1,000 bytes:

```
interface serial 1
  mtu 1000
```

Related Commands

encapsulation smds
ip mtu

NRZI-ENCODING

Use the **nrzi-encoding** interface configuration command to enable nonreturn-to-zero inverted (NRZI) line-coding format. Use the **no** form of this command to disable this capability.

>   **nrzi-encoding**
>   **no nrzi-encoding**

>   **nrzi-encoding [mark]** (Cisco 7200 series routers and Cisco 7500 series routers)

Syntax	*Description*
mark	(Optional) Specifies that NRZI mark encoding is required on the PA-8T and PA-4T+ synchronous serial port adapters on Cisco 7200 and 7500 series routers. If mark is not specified, NRZI space encoding is used.

Default

Disabled

Command Mode

Interface configuration

Usage Guidelines

This command first appeared in Cisco IOS Release 10.0.

This command was modified in Cisco IOS Release 11.3 to include the **mark** keyword.

All FSIP, PA-8T, and PA-4T+ interface types support nonreturn-to-zero (NRZ) and nonreturn-to-zero inverted (NRZI) format. This is a line-coding format that is required for serial connections in some environments. NRZ encoding is most common. NRZI encoding is used primarily with EIA/TIA-232 connections in IBM environments.

Examples

In the following example, serial interface 1 is configured for NRZI encoding:

```
interface serial 1
 nrzi-encoding
```

In the following example, serial interface 3/1/0 is configured for NRZI mark encoding:

```
interface serial 3/1/0
 nrzi-encoding mark
```

PHYSICAL-LAYER

To specify the mode of a slow-speed serial interface on a router as either synchronous or asynchronous, use the **physical-layer** interface configuration command. To return the interface to the default mode of synchronous, use the **no** form of this command.

physical-layer {sync | async}
no physical-layer

Syntax	Description
sync	Place the interface in synchronous mode.
async	Place the interface in asynchronous mode.

Default

Synchronous mode

Command Mode

Interface configuration

Usage Guidelines

This command first appeared in Cisco IOS Release 11.2.

This command applies only to low-speed serial interfaces available on Cisco 2520 through 2523 routers.

If you specify the **no physical-layer** command, you return the interface to its default mode (synchronous).

In synchronous mode, low-speed serial interfaces support all interface configuration commands available for high-speed serial interfaces, except the following two commands:

- **sdlc cts-delay**
- **sdlc rts-timeout**

When placed in asynchronous mode, low-speed serial interfaces support all commands available for standard asynchronous interfaces.

When you enter this command, it does not appear in the output of **show running config** and **show startup config** commands, because the command is a physical-layer command.

Example

This example changes a low-speed serial interface from synchronous to asynchronous mode:

```
interface serial 2
  physical-layer async
```

POS FRAMING-SDH

To select SDH STM-1 framing on a Packet OC-3 interface in Cisco 7500 series routers, use the **pos framing-sdh** interface configuration command. To revert to the default SONET STS-3c framing, use the **no** form of this command.

pos framing-sdh
no pos framing-sdh

Syntax   Description

This command has no arguments or keywords.

Default

SONET STS-3c framing

Command Mode

Interface configuration

Usage Guidelines

This command first appeared in Cisco IOS Release 11.2.

This command was modified in Cisco IOS Release 11.3 to change the **posi framing-sdh** command to **pos framing-sdh**.

Example

In the following example, the interface is configured for SDH STM-1 framing:

```
interface pos 3/0
 pos framing-sdh
 no shutdown
```

Related Commands

interface pos
pos internal-clock

POS INTERNAL-CLOCK

To set the internal clock as the transmission clock source on a Packet OC-3 interface in Cisco 7500 series routers, use the **pos internal-clock** interface configuration command. To revert to the default recovered-receive clock as the transmission clock source, use the **no** form of this command.

pos internal-clock
no pos internal-clock

Syntax   Description

This command has no arguments or keywords.

Default

The recovered receive clock

Command Mode

Interface configuration

Usage Guidelines

This command first appeared in Cisco IOS Release 11.2.

This command was modified in Cisco IOS Release 11.3 to change the **posi internal-clock** command to **pos internal-clock**.

Example

The following command reverts to the default recovered-receive clock:

```
interface pos 3/0
  no pos internal-clock
```

Related Commands

interface pos
pos framing-sdh

PRI-GROUP

To specify ISDN Primary Rate Interface (PRI) on a channelized E1 or T1 card on the Cisco 7500, use the **pri-group** controller configuration command. Use the **no** form of this command to remove the ISDN PRI.

pri-group [**timeslots** *range*]
no pri-group

Syntax	Description
timeslots *range*	(Optional) Specifies a single range of values from 1 to 23.

Default

Disabled

Command Mode

Controller configuration

Usage Guidelines

When you configure ISDN PRI, you must first specify an ISDN switch type for PRI and an E1 or T1 controller.

Example

The following example specifies ISDN PRI on T1 slot 1, port 0:

```
isdn switch-type primary-4ess
controllers t1 1/0
framing esf
linecode b8zs
pri-group timeslots 2-6
```

Related Commands

controller e1
controller t1
interface serial
isdn switch-type

PULSE-TIME

To enable pulsing DTR signal intervals on the serial interfaces, use the **pulse-time** interface configuration command. Use the **no** form of this command to restore the default interval.

> **pulse-time** *seconds*
> **no pulse-time**

Syntax	Description
seconds	Integer that specifies the DTR signal interval in seconds.

Default

0 seconds

Command Mode

Interface configuration

Usage Guidelines

This command first appeared in Cisco IOS Release 10.0.

When the serial line protocol goes down (for example, because of loss of synchronization) the interface hardware is reset and the DTR signal is held inactive for at least the specified interval. This function is useful for handling encrypting or other similar devices that use the toggling of the DTR signal to resynchronize.

Example

The following example enables DTR pulse signals for three seconds on serial interface 2:

```
interface serial 2
  pulse-time 3
```

RING-SPEED

To set the ring speed for the CSC-1R and CSC-2R Token Ring interfaces, use the **ring-speed** interface configuration command.

ring-speed *speed*

Syntax	Description
speed	Integer that specifies the ring speed, either 4 for 4-Mbps or 16 for 16-Mbps operation.

Default

16-Mbps operation

───── **CAUTION** ─────────────────────────────────────

Configuring a ring speed that is wrong or incompatible with the connected Token Ring will cause the ring to beacon, which effectively takes the ring down and makes it nonoperational.

───

Command Mode

Interface configuration

Usage Guidelines

This command first appeared in Cisco IOS Release 10.0.

Example

The following example sets a Token Ring interface ring speed to 4 Mbps:

```
interface tokenring 0
  ring-speed 4
```

SERVICE-MODULE 56K CLOCK RATE

To configure the network line speed for a serial interface on a four-wire 56/64-kbps CSU/DSU module, use the **service-module 56k clock rate** interface configuration command. Use the **no** form of this command to enable a network line speed of 56 kbps, which is the default.

service-module 56k clock rate *speed*
no service-module 56k clock rate *speed*

Syntax	*Description*
speed	Network line speed in kbps. The default speed is 56 kbps. Choose from one of the following optional speeds:

- **2.4**—2,400 kbps
- **4.8**—4,800 kbps
- **9.6**—9,600 kbps
- **19.2**—19,200 kbps
- **38.4**—38,400 kbps
- **56**—56,000 kbps
- **64**—64,000 kbps
- **auto**—Automatic line speed mode. Configure this option if your line speed is constantly changing.

Default

56 kbps

Command Mode

Interface configuration

Usage Guidelines

This command first appeared in Cisco IOS Release 11.2.

The 56-kbps line speed is available in switched mode, which is enabled using the **service-module 56k network-type** interface configuration command on the four-wire CSU/DSU. If you have a two-wire CSU/DSU module, the default is automatically set to switched mode.

The 64-kbps line speed cannot be used with back-to-back digital data service (DDS) lines. The sub-rate line speeds are determined by the service provider.

The keyword **auto** enables the CSU/DSU to decipher current line speed from the sealing current running on the network. Use **auto** only when transmitting over telco DDS lines and the clocking source is taken from the line.

Examples

The following example displays two routers connected in back-to-back DDS mode. However, notice that at first, the configuration fails because the **auto** option is used. Later in the example, the correct matching configuration is issued, which is **38.4** kbps.

```
Router1(config)# interface serial 0
Router1(config-if)#service-module 56k clock source internal
Router1(config-if)#service-module 56k clock rate 38.4
```

```
Router2(config-if)#service-module 56k clock rate auto

a1#ping 10.1.1.2
Type escape sequence to abort.
Sending 5, 100-byte ICMP Echos to 10.1.1.2, timeout is 2 seconds:
.....
Success rate is 0 percent (0/5)

Router2(config-if)#service-module 56k clock rate 38.4

Router1#ping 10.1.1.2
Type escape sequence to abort.
Sending 5, 100-byte ICMP Echos to 10.1.1.2, timeout is 2 seconds:
!!!!!
Success rate is 100 percent (5/5), round-trip min/avg/max = 52/54/56 ms
```

When transferring from DDS mode to switched mode, you must set the correct clock rate, as shown in the following example:

```
Router2(config-if)#service-module 56k network-type dds
Router2(config-if)#service-module 56k clock rate 38.4
Router2(config-if)#service-module 56k network-type switched
% Have to use 56k or auto clock rate for switched mode
% Service module configuration command failed: WRONG FORMAT.

Router2(config-if)#service-module 56k clock rate auto
% WARNING - auto rate will not work in back-to-back DDS.
Router2(config-if)#service-module 56k network-type switched
```

Related Commands

service-module 56k clock source
service-module 56k network-type

SERVICE-MODULE 56K CLOCK SOURCE

To set up the clock source on a serial interface for a four-wire 56/64-kbps CSU/DSU module, use the **service-module 56k clock source** interface configuration command. Use the **no** form of this command to specify the clocking come-from line.

service-module 56k clock source {line | internal}
no service-module 56k clock source {line | internal}

Syntax	Description
line	Use the clocking provided by the active line coming in to the router.
internal	Use the internal clocking provided by the hardware module.

Default

Line clock

Command Mode

Interface configuration

Usage Guidelines

This command first appeared in Cisco IOS Release 11.2.

In most applications, the CSU/DSU should be configured with the **clock source line** command. For back-to-back configurations, configure one CSU/DSU with the **clock source internal** command and the other with **clock source line** command.

Example

The following example configures internal clocking and transmission speed at 38.4 kbps.

```
router(config)# interface serial 0
router(config-if)# service-module 56k clock source internal
router(config-if)# service-module 56k clock rate 38.4
```

Related Commands

service-module 56k clock rate

SERVICE-MODULE 56K DATA-CODING

To prevent application data from replicating loopback codes when operating at 64 kbps on a 4-wire CSU/DSU, use the **service-module 56k data-coding** interface configuration command. Use the **no** form of this command to enable normal transmission.

service-module 56k data-coding {normal | scrambled}
no service-module 56k data-coding {normal | scrambled}

Syntax	Description
normal	Specifies normal transmission of data.
scrambled	Scrambles bit codes or user data before transmission. All control codes such as out-of-service and out-of-frame are avoided.

Default

Normal data transmission

Command Mode

Interface configuration

Usage Guidelines

This command first appeared in Cisco IOS Release 11.2.

Enable the scrambled configuration only in 64-kbps digital data service (DDS) mode. If the network type is set to switched, the configuration is refused.

If you transmit scrambled bit codes, both CSU/DSUs must have this command configured for successful communication.

Example

The following example scrambles bit codes or user data before transmission:

```
router(config)# interface serial 0
router(config-if)# service-module 56k clock rate 64
router(config-if)# service-module 56k data-coding scrambled
```

Related Commands

service-module 56k clock rate

SERVICE-MODULE 56K NETWORK-TYPE

To transmit packets in switched dial-up mode or digital data service (DDS) mode using a serial interface on a four-wire 56/64-kbps CSU/DSU module, use the **service-module 56k network-type** interface configuration command. Use the **no** form of this command to transmit from a dedicated leased line in DDS mode.

service-module 56k network-type {dds | switched}
no service-module 56k network-type {dds | switched}

Syntax	Description
dds	Transmits packets in DDS mode or through a dedicated leased line.
switched	Transmits packets in switched dial-up mode. On a two-wire switched 56-kbps CSU/DSU module, this is the default and only setting.

Default

DDS is enabled for the four-wire CSU/DSU.

Switched is enabled for the two-wire CSU/DSU.

Command Mode

Interface configuration

Usage Guidelines

This command first appeared in Cisco IOS Release 11.2.

Part III

Command Reference

In switched mode, you need additional dialer configuration commands to configure dial-out numbers. Before you enable the **service-module 56k network-type switched** command, both CSU/DSUs must use a clock source coming from the line and the clock rate configured to **auto** or **56** kbps. If the clock rate is not set correctly, this command will not be accepted.

The two-wire and four-wire 56/64-kbps CSU/DSU modules use V.25 *bis* dial commands to interface with the router. Therefore, the interface must be configured using the **dialer in-band** command. DTR dial is not supported.

NOTES

Any loopbacks in progress are terminated when switching between modes.

Example

The following example configures transmission in switched dial-up mode:

```
router(config)# interface serial 0
router(config-if)#service-module 56k clock rate auto
router(config-if)#service-module 56k network-type switched
router(config-if)#dialer in-band
router(config-if)#dialer string 2576666
router(config-if)#dialer-group 1
```

Related Commands

dialer in-band
service-module 56k clock rate
service-module 56k clock source
service-module 56k switched-carrier

SERVICE-MODULE 56K REMOTE-LOOPBACK

To enable the acceptance of a remote loopback request on a serial interface on a two- or four-wire 56/64-kbps CSU/DSU module, use the **service-module 56k remote-loopback** interface configuration command. Use the **no** form of this command to disable the module from entering loopback.

> **service-module 56k remote-loopback**
> **no service-module 56k remote-loopback**

Syntax   Description

This command has no arguments or keywords.

Default

Enabled

Command Mode

Interface configuration

Usage Guidelines

This command first appeared in Cisco IOS Release 11.2.

The **no service-module 56k remote-loopback** command prevents the local CSU/DSU from being placed into loopback by remote devices on the line. The line provider is still able to put the module into loopback by reversing sealing current. Unlike the T1 module, the two- or four-wire 56/64-kbps CSU/DSU module still can initiate remote loopbacks with the **no** form of this command configured.

Example

The following example enables transmitting and receiving remote loopbacks:

```
router(config)# interface serial 0
router(config-if)# service-module 56k remote-loopback
```

Related Commands

loopback remote (interface)

SERVICE-MODULE 56K SWITCHED-CARRIER

To select a service provider to use with a two- or four-wire 56/64 kbps dial-up serial line, use the **service-module 56k switched-carrier** interface configuration command. Use the **no** form of this command to enable the default service provider.

service-module 56k switched-carrier {att | sprint | other}
no service-module 56k switched-carrier {att | sprint | other}

Syntax	Description
att	AT&T or other digital network service provider.
sprint	Sprint or other service provider whose network requires echo cancelers.
other	Service provider besides AT&T or Sprint.

Default

ATT is enabled on the four-wire 56/64-kbps CSU/DSU module.

Sprint is enabled on the two-wire switched 56-kbps CSU/DSU module.

Command Mode

Interface configuration

Usage Guidelines

This command first appeared in Cisco IOS Release 11.2.

On a Sprint network, echo-canceler tones are sent during call setup to prevent the echo cancelers from damaging digital data. The transmission of echo-canceler tones may increase call setup times by eight seconds on the four-wire module. Having echo cancellation enabled does not affect data traffic.

This configuration command is ignored if the network type is DDS.

Example

The following example configures AT&T as a service provider:

```
router(config)# interface serial 0
router(config-if)# service-module 56k network-type switched
router(config-if)# service-module 56k switched-carrier att
```

Related Commands

service-module 56k network-type

SERVICE-MODULE T1 CLOCK SOURCE

To specify the clock source for the fractional T1/T1 CSU/DSU module, use the **service-module t1 clock source** interface configuration command. Use the **no** form of this command to enable the line clock.

> service-module t1 clock source {internal | line}
> no service-module t1 clock source {internal | line}

Syntax	Description
internal	Specifies the CSU/DSU internal clock.
line	Specifies the line clock.

Default

Line clock

Command Mode

Interface configuration

Usage Guidelines

This command first appeared in Cisco IOS Release 11.2.

Example

The following example sets an internal clock source on serial line 0:

```
interface serial 0
service-module t1 clock source line
```

Related Commands

service-module 56k clock source

SERVICE-MODULE T1 DATA-CODING

To guarantee the ones density requirement on an AMI line using the fractional T1/T1 module, use the **service-module t1 data-coding inverted** interface configuration command. Use the **no** form of this command to enable normal data transmission.

    service-module t1 data-coding {inverted | normal}
    no service-module t1 data-coding {inverted | normal}

Syntax	*Description*
inverted	Inverts bit codes by changing all 1 bits into 0 bits and all 0 bits into 1 bits.
normal	Requests that no bit codes be inverted before transmission.

Default

Normal transmission

Command Mode

Interface configuration

Usage Guidelines

This command first appeared in Cisco IOS Release 11.2.

Data inversion is used to guarantee the ones density requirement on an AMI line when using bit-oriented protocols such as High-Level Data Link Control (HDLC), Point-to-Point Protocol (PPP), X.25, and Frame Relay. If the timeslot speed is set to 56 kbps, this command is rejected because line density is guaranteed when transmitting at 56 kbps. Use this command with the 64-kbps line speed.

If you transmit inverted bit codes, both CSU/DSUs must have this command configured for successful communication.

Part III

Command Reference

Example

The following example inverts bit codes using a timeslot speed of 64 kbps:

```
service-module t1 timeslots all speed 64
service-module t1 data-coding inverted
```

Related Commands

service-module t1 linecode
service-module t1 timeslots

SERVICE-MODULE T1 FRAMING

To select the frame type for a line using the fractional T1/T1 (FT1/T1) module, use the **service-module t1 framing** interface configuration command. Use the **no** form of this command to select the default, which is Extended Super Frame as the T1 frame type.

service-module t1 framing {esf | sf}
no service-module t1 framing {esf | sf}

Syntax	*Description*
esf	Specifies Extended Super Frame as the T1 frame type.
sf	Specifies D4 Super Frame as the T1 frame type.

Default

esf

Command Mode

Interface configuration

Usage Guidelines

This command first appeared in Cisco IOS Release 11.2.

Use this command in configurations where the router communicates with FT1/T1 data lines. The service provider determines which framing type, either **esf** or **sf**, is required for your circuit.

Example

The following example enables Super Frame as the FT1/T1 frame type:

```
service-module t1 framing sf
```

SERVICE-MODULE T1 LBO

To configure the CSU line build out (LBO) on a fractional T1/T1 CSU/DSU module, use the **service-module t1 lbo** interface configuration command. Use the **no** form of this command to disable line build out.

> **service-module t1 lbo {-15 db | -7.5 db | none}**
> **no service-module t1 lbo {-15 db | -7.5 db | none}**

Syntax	Description
–15 db	Decreases outgoing signal strength by 15 dB.
–7.5 db	Decreases outgoing signal strength by 7.5 dB.
none	Transmits packets without decreasing outgoing signal strength.

Default

No line build out

Command Mode

Interface configuration

Usage Guidelines

This command first appeared in Cisco IOS Release 11.2.

Use this command to decrease the outgoing signal strength to an optimum value for a fractional T1 line receiver. The ideal signal strength should be –15 dB to –22 dB, which is calculated by adding the phone company loss + cable length loss + line build out.

You may use this command in back-to-back configurations, but it is not needed on most actual T1 lines.

Example

The following example shows an LBO setting of –7.5 dB:

```
service-module t1 lbo -7.5db
```

SERVICE-MODULE T1 LINECODE

To select the line code for the fractional T1/T1 module, use the **service-module t1 linecode** interface configuration command. Use the **no** form of this command to select the default, which is the B8ZS line code.

> **service-module t1 linecode {ami | b8zs}**
> **no service-module t1 linecode {ami | b8zs}**

Syntax	Description
ami	Specifies alternate mark inversion (AMI) as the line code.
b8zs	Specifies binary 8 zero substitution (B8ZS) as the line code.

Default
b8zs

Command Mode
Interface configuration

Usage Guidelines
This command first appeared in Cisco IOS Release 11.2.

Configuring B8ZS is a method of ensuring the ones density requirement on a T1 line by substituting intentional bipolar violations in bit positions four and seven for a sequence of eight zero bits. When the CSU/DSU is configured for AMI, you must guarantee the ones density requirement in your router configuration using the **service-module t1 data-coding inverted** command or the **service-module t1 timeslots speed 56** command.

Your T1 service provider determines which line code, either **ami** or **b8zs**, is required for your T1 circuit.

Example
The following example specifies AMI as the line code:

```
service-module t1 linecode ami
```

Related Commands
service-module t1 data-coding
service-module t1 timeslots

SERVICE-MODULE T1 REMOTE-ALARM-ENABLE

To generate remote alarms (yellow alarms) at the local CSU/DSU or detect remote alarms sent from the remote CSU/DSU, use the **service-module t1 remote-alarm-enable** interface configuration command. Use the **no** form of this command to disable remote alarms.

service-module t1 remote-alarm-enable
no service-module t1 remote-alarm-enable

Syntax   Description

This command has no arguments or keywords.

Default

Remote alarms disabled

Command Mode

Interface configuration

Usage Guidelines

This command first appeared in Cisco IOS Release 11.2.

Remote alarms are transmitted by the CSU/DSU when it detects an alarm condition, such as a red alarm (loss of frame) or blue alarm (unframed ones). The receiving CSU/DSU then knows there is an error condition on the line.

With D4 Super Frame configured, a remote alarm condition is transmitted by setting the bit 2 of each time slot to zero. For received user data that has the bit 2 of each time slot set to zero, the CSU/DSU interprets the data as a remote alarm and interrupts data transmission, which explains why remote alarms are disabled by default. With Extended Super Frame configured, the remote alarm condition is signalled out of band in the facilities data link.

You can see if the FT1/T1 CSU/DSU is receiving a remote alarm (yellow alarm) by issuing the **show service-module** command.

Example

The following example enables remote alarm generation and detection:

```
service-module t1 remote-alarm-enable
```

Related Commands

service-module t1 framing

SERVICE-MODULE T1 REMOTE-LOOPBACK

To specify if the fractional T1/T1 CSU/DSU module enters loopback mode when it receives a loopback code on the line, use the **service-module t1 remote-loopback** interface configuration command. Use the **no** form of this command to disable remote loopbacks.

service-module t1 remote-loopback {full | payload} [alternate | v54]
no service-module t1 remote-loopback {full | payload}

Syntax	Description
full	Configures the remote loopback code used to transmit or accept CSU loopback requests.
payload	Configures the loopback code used by the local CSU/DSU to generate or detect payload-loopback commands.

Syntax	Description
alternate	(Optional) Transmits a remote CSU/DSU loopback request using a 4-in-5 pattern for loopup and 2-in-3 pattern for loopdown. This is an inverted version of the standard loopcode request.
v54	(Optional) Industry standard loopback code. Use this configuration for CSU/DSUs that may not support the Accunet loopup standards. This keyword is used only with a **payload** request, not a **full** request.

NOTES

By entering the **service-module t1 remote-loopback** command without specifying any keywords, you enable the standard-loopup codes, which use a 1-in-5 pattern for loopup and a 1-in-3 pattern for loopdown.

Default

Full and payload loopbacks with standard-loopup codes

Command Mode

Interface configuration

Usage Guidelines

This command first appeared in Cisco IOS Release 11.2.

You can configure the **full** and **payload** loopback points simultaneously. However, only one loopback code can be configured at a time. For example, if you configure the **service-module t1 remote-loopback payload alternate** command, a **payload v54** request cannot be transmitted or accepted.

The **no** form of this command disables loopback requests. For example, the **no service-module t1 remote-loopback full** command ignores all full-bandwidth loopback transmissions and requests. Configuring the **no** form of the command may not prevent telco line providers from looping your router in esf mode, because fractional T1/T1 lines use facilities data link messages to initiate loopbacks.

If you enable the **service-module t1 remote-loopback** command, the **loopback remote** commands on the FT1/T1 CSU/DSU module will not be successful.

Example

The following example displays two routers connected back-to-back through a fractional T1/T1 line:

```
Router# no service-module t1 remote-loopback full
Router# service-module t1 remote-loopback payload alternate
```

```
Router# loopback remote full
%SERVICE_MODULE-5-LOOPUPFAILED: Unit 0 - Loopup of remote unit failed

Router# service-module t1 remote-loopback payload v54
Router# loopback remote payload
%SERVICE_MODULE-5-LOOPUPFAILED: Unit 0 - Loopup of remote unit failed

Router# service-module t1 remote-loopback payload alternate
Router# loopback remote payload
%SERVICE_MODULE-5-LOOPUPREMOTE: Unit 0 - Remote unit placed in loopback
```

Related Commands

loopback remote (interface)

SERVICE-MODULE T1 TIMESLOTS

To define timeslots that constitute a fractional T1/T1 (FT1/T1) channel, use the **service-module t1 timeslots** interface configuration command. Use the **no** form of this command to resume the default setting (all FT1/T1 timeslots transmit at 64 kbps).

service-module t1 timeslots {*range* | all} [speed {56 | 64}]
no service-module t1 timeslots {*range* | all}

Syntax	Description
range	The DS0 timeslots that constitute the FT1/T1 channel. The range is from 1 to 24, where the first timeslot is numbered 1 and the last timeslot is numbered 24. Specify this field by using a series of subranges separated by commas.
all	Selects all FT1/T1 timeslots.
speed	(Optional) Specifies the timeslot speed.
56	56 kbps.
64	64 kbps. This is the default for all timeslots.

Default

64 kbps

Command Mode

Interface configuration

Usage Guidelines

This command first appeared in Cisco IOS Release 11.2.

This command specifies which timeslots are used in fractional T1 operation and determines the amount of bandwidth available to the router in each FT1/T1 channel.

The timeslot range must match the timeslots assigned to the channel group. Your service provider defines the timeslots that comprise a channel group.

To use the entire T1 line, enable the **service-module t1 timeslots all** command.

Example

The following example displays a series of timeslot ranges and a speed of 64 kbps:

```
service-module t1 timeslots 1-10,15-20,22 speed 64
```

Related Commands

service-module t1 data-coding
service-module t1 linecode

SHOW COMPRESS

To display compression statistics, use the **show compress** EXEC command.

> **show compress**

Syntax   Description

This command has no arguments or keywords.

Command Mode

EXEC

Usage Guidelines

This command first appeared in Cisco IOS Release 10.0.

This information was modified in Cisco IOS Release 11.3 to include sample output for hardware compression (implemented in the CSA hardware).

Sample Displays

The following is sample output from the **show compress** command when software compression is used on the router:

```
Router# show compress
Serial0
 uncompressed bytes xmt/rcv 10710562/11376835
 1  min avg ratio xmt/rcv 2.773/2.474
 5  min avg ratio xmt/rcv 4.084/3.793
 10 min avg ratio xmt/rcv 4.125/3.873
 no bufs xmt 0 no bufs rcv 0
 resets 0
```

Table 23–9 describes the fields shown in the display.

Table 23–9 *Show Compress Field Descriptions—Software Compression*

Field	Description
Serial0	Name and number of the interface.
uncompressed bytes xmt/rcv	Total number of uncompressed bytes sent and received.
1 min avg ratio xmt/rcv 5 min avg ratio xmt/rcv 10 min avg ratio xmt/rcv	Static compression ratio for bytes sent and received, averaged over 1, 5, and 10 minutes.
no bufs xmt	Number of times buffers were not available to compress data being sent.
no bufs rcv	Number of times buffers were not available to uncompress data being received.
resets	Number of resets (for example, line errors could cause resets).

The following is sample output from the **show compress** command when hardware compression is enabled (that is, compression is implemented in the CSA hardware):

```
Router# show compress
Serial6/1
     Hardware compression enabled
     CSA in slot3 in use
     Compressed bytes sent:     402 bytes     0 Kbits/sec     ratio: 4.092
     Compressed bytes recv:     390 bytes     0 Kbits/sec     ratio: 3.476
     restarts:1
     last clearing of counters: 1278 seconds
```

Table 23–10 describes the fields shown in the display. The information displayed by the **show compress** command is the same for hardware and distributed compression. For Cisco 7200 series routers with multiple CSAs, an additional line is displayed indicating the CSA in use.

Table 23–10 *Show Compress Field Descriptions—Hardware or Distributed Compression*

Field	Description
Serial6/1	Name and number of the interface.
Hardware compression enabled	Type of compression.
CSA in slot3 in use	Identifies CSA that is performing compression service.
Compressed bytes sent	Total number of compressed bytes sent, including the kilobits per second.

Table 23–10 *Show Compress Field Descriptions—Hardware or Distributed Compression, Continued*

Field	Description
Compressed bytes recv	Total number of compressed bytes received, including the kilobits per second.
ratio	Compression ratio for bytes sent and received since the link last came up or since the counters were last cleared.
restarts	Number of times the compression process restarted or reset.
last clearing of counters	Duration since the last time the counters were cleared with the **clear counters** command.

Related Commands

compress

SHOW CONTROLLERS CBUS

To display all information under the cBus controller card, use the **show controllers cbus** privileged EXEC command on the Cisco 7500 or Cisco 7513 routers. This command also shows the capabilities of the card and reports controller-related failures.

> **show controllers cbus**

Syntax   Description

This command has no arguments or keywords.

Command Mode

Privileged EXEC

Usage Guidelines

This command first appeared in Cisco IOS Release 10.0.

Sample Displays

The following is partial sample output from the **show controllers cbus** command on a 7500 series router with one VIP2 interface processor. This example does not show output from additional interface processors that are usually installed in a Cisco 7500 series router.

```
Router# show controller cbus

MEMD at 40000000, 2097152 bytes (unused 2752, recarves 1, lost 0)
  RawQ 48000100, ReturnQ 48000108, EventQ 48000110
  BufhdrQ 48000138 (2849 items), LovltrQ 48000150 (42 items, 1632 bytes)
  IpcbufQ 48000158 (32 items, 4096 bytes)
```

```
        3570 buffer headers (48002000 - 4800FF10)
        pool0: 15 buffers, 256 bytes, queue 48000140
        pool1: 368 buffers, 1536 bytes, queue 48000148
        pool2: 260 buffers, 4544 bytes, queue 48000160
        pool3: 4 buffers, 4576 bytes, queue 48000168

    slot1: VIP2, hw 2.2, sw 200.50, ccb 5800FF30, cmdq 48000088, vps 8192
        software loaded from system
        FLASH ROM version 255.255
        FastEthernet1/0/0, addr 0000.0c41.6c20 (bia 0000.0c41.6c20)
          gfreeq 48000148, lfreeq 480001D0 (1536 bytes), throttled 0
          rxlo 4, rxhi 30, rxcurr 0, maxrxcurr 0
          txq 48001A00, txacc 48001A02 (value 0), txlimit 20
        Ethernet1/1/0, addr 0000.0c41.6c28 (bia 0000.0c41.6c28)
          gfreeq 48000148, lfreeq 480001D8 (1536 bytes), throttled 0
          rxlo 4, rxhi 30, rxcurr 0, maxrxcurr 0
          txq 48001A08, txacc 48001A0A (value 0), txlimit 20
        Ethernet1/1/1, addr 0000.0c41.6c29 (bia 0000.0c41.6c29)
          gfreeq 48000148, lfreeq 480001E0 (1536 bytes), throttled 0
          rxlo 4, rxhi 30, rxcurr 0, maxrxcurr 0
          txq 48001A10, txacc 48001A12 (value 0), txlimit 20
        Ethernet1/1/2, addr 0000.0c41.6c2a (bia 0000.0c41.6c2a)
          gfreeq 48000148, lfreeq 480001E8 (1536 bytes), throttled 0
          rxlo 4, rxhi 30, rxcurr 0, maxrxcurr 0
          txq 48001A18, txacc 48001A1A (value 0), txlimit 20
        Ethernet1/1/3, addr 0000.0c41.6c2b (bia 0000.0c41.6c2b)
          gfreeq 48000148, lfreeq 480001F0 (1536 bytes), throttled 0
          rxlo 4, rxhi 30, rxcurr 0, maxrxcurr 0
          txq 48001A20, txacc 48001A22 (value 0), txlimit 20
        Ethernet1/1/4, addr 0000.0c41.6c2c (bia 0000.0c41.6c2c)
          gfreeq 48000148, lfreeq 480001F8 (1536 bytes), throttled 0
          rxlo 4, rxhi 30, rxcurr 0, maxrxcurr 0
          txq 48001A28, txacc 48001A2A (value 0), txlimit 20
        Ethernet1/1/5, addr 0000.0c41.6c2d (bia 0000.0c41.6c2d)
          gfreeq 48000148, lfreeq 48000200 (1536 bytes), throttled 0
          rxlo 4, rxhi 30, rxcurr 0, maxrxcurr 0
          txq 48001A30, txacc 48001A32 (value 0), txlimit 20
        Ethernet1/1/6, addr 0000.0c41.6c2e (bia 0000.0c41.6c2e)
          gfreeq 48000148, lfreeq 48000208 (1536 bytes), throttled 0
          rxlo 4, rxhi 30, rxcurr 0, maxrxcurr 0
          txq 48001A38, txacc 48001A3A (value 0), txlimit 20
        Ethernet1/1/7, addr 0000.0c41.6c2f (bia 0000.0c41.6c2f)
          gfreeq 48000148, lfreeq 48000210 (1536 bytes), throttled 0
          rxlo 4, rxhi 30, rxcurr 0, maxrxcurr 0
          txq 48001A40, txacc 48001A42 (value 0), txlimit 20
```

Part III

Command Reference

The following is partial sample output of the **show controllers cbus** command for a Packet over SONET Interface Processor (POSIP) in slot 0; its single Packet OC-3 interface is Posi0/0:

```
    slot0: POSIP, hw 2.1, sw 200.01, ccb 5800FF30, cmdq 48000080, vps 8192
        software loaded from flash slot0:rsp_posip.new
        FLASH ROM version 160.4, VPLD version 2.2
```

```
Posi0/0, applique is SONET
  gfreeq 48000148, lfreeq 48000158 (4480 bytes), throttled 0
  rxlo 4, rxhi 226, rxcurr 0, maxrxcurr 186
  txq 48000160, txacc 48000082 (value 150), txlimit 150
```

The following is partial output of the **show controllers cbus** command for a Multichannel Interface Processor (MIP). Not all of the 23 channels defined on serial interface 1/0 are shown.

```
slot1: MIP, hw 1.1, sw 205.03, ccb 5800FF40, cmdq 48000088, vps 8192
  software loaded from system
  T1 1/0, applique is Channelized T1
    gfreeq 48000130, lfreeq 480001B0 (1536 bytes), throttled 0
    rxlo 4, rxhi 360, rxcurr 0, maxrxcurr 3
    Serial1/0:0, txq 480001B8, txacc 48000082 (value 3), txlimit 3
    Serial1/0:1, txq 480001B8, txacc 4800008A (value 3), txlimit 3
    Serial1/0:2, txq 480001B8, txacc 48000092 (value 3), txlimit 3
    Serial1/0:3, txq 480001B8, txacc 4800009A (value 3), txlimit 3
    Serial1/0:4, txq 480001B8, txacc 480000A2 (value 3), txlimit 3
    Serial1/0:5, txq 480001B8, txacc 480000AA (value 3), txlimit 3
    Serial1/0:6, txq 480001B8, txacc 480000B2 (value 3), txlimit 3
    Serial1/0:7, txq 480001B8, txacc 480000BA (value 3), txlimit 3
```

Table 23–11 describes significant fields in the per-slot part of these displays.

Table 23–11 *Show Controllers cBus Command Per-Slot Field Descriptions*

Field	Description
slot1:	Slot location of the specific interface processor (in this case, Packet over SONET Interface Processor).
hw	Version number of the card.
sw	Version number of the card's internal software (in read-only memory).
software loaded from	Source device and file name from which the router software was loaded.
FLASH ROM version VPLD version	Version of Flash ROM.
Pos1/0, applique is SONET	Location of the specific interface and the hardware applique type (in this case, a Packet OC-3 interface).
gfreeq	Location of the global free queue that is shared among similar interfaces.
lfreeq	Location of the local free queue, which is a private queue of MEMD buffers.
throttled	Number of times input packet processing has been throttled on this interface.

Table 23–11 *Show Controllers cBus Command Per-Slot Field Descriptions, Continued*

Field	Description
rxlo	Minimum number of MEMD buffers held on local free queue. When idle, the interface returns buffers from its local queue to the global free queue until only this number of buffers remains in the local queue.
rxhi	Maximum number of MEMD buffers that the interface can remove from the global free queue in order to populate its local queue.
rxcurr	Number of MEMD buffers currently on the local free queue.
maxrxcurr	Maximum number of MEMD buffers that were enqueued on the local free queue.
txq	Address of the transmit queue.
txacc	Address of the transmit queue accumulator.
txlimit	Maximum number of buffers allowed in the transmit queue.

The following is sample output from the **show controllers cbus** command on a Cisco 7500 series router:

```
Router# show controllers cbus

cBus 1, controller type 3.0, microcode version 2.0
   128 Kbytes of main memory, 32 Kbytes cache memory
   40 1520 byte buffers, 14 4484 byte buffers
   Restarts: 0 line down, 0 hung output, 0 controller error
HSCI 1, controller type 10.0, microcode version 129.3
   Interface 6 - Hssi0, electrical interface is Hssi DTE
      5 buffer RX queue threshold, 7 buffer TX queue limit, buffer size 1520
      ift 0004, rql 2, tq 0000 0000, tql 7
      Transmitter delay is 0 microseconds
 MEC 3, controller type 5.1, microcode version 130.6
   Interface 18 - Ethernet2, station address 0000.0c02.a03c (bia 0000.0c02.a03c)
      10 buffer RX queue threshold, 7 buffer TX queue limit, buffer size 1520
      ift 0000, rql 10, tq 0000 0000, tql 7
      Transmitter delay is 0 microseconds
   Interface 19 - Ethernet3, station address 0000.0c02.a03d (bia 0000.0c02.a03d)
      10 buffer RX queue threshold, 7 buffer TX queue limit, buffer size 1520
      ift 0000, rql 10, tq 0000 0000, tql 7
      Transmitter delay is 0 microseconds
```

Part
III

Command Reference

Table 23–12 describes the fields shown in the following lines of output from the display.

```
cBus 1, controller type 3.0, microcode version 2.0
   128 Kbytes of main memory, 32 Kbytes cache memory
   40 1520 byte buffers, 14 4484 byte buffers
   Restarts: 0 line down, 0 hung output, 0 controller error
```

Table 23–12 *Show Controllers cBus Field Descriptions—Part 1*

Field	Description
cBus 1	Card type and number (varies depending on card).
controller type 3.0	Version number of the card.
microcode version 2.0	Version number of the card's internal software (in read-only memory).
128 Kbytes of main memory	Amount of main memory on the card.
32 Kbytes cache memory	Amount of cache memory on the card.
40 1520 byte buffers	Number of buffers of this size on the card.
14 4484 byte buffers	Number of buffers of this size on the card.

Restarts
  0 line down
  0 hung output
  0 controller error
	Count of restarts due to the following conditions:
	  Communication line down
	  Output unable to transmit
	  Internal error

Table 23–13 describes the fields shown in the following lines of output from the display:

```
HSCI 1, controller type 10.0, microcode version 129.3
   Interface 6 - Hssi0, electrical interface is Hssi DTE
      5 buffer RX queue threshold, 7 buffer TX queue limit, buffer size 1520
      ift 0004, rql 2, tq 0000 0000, tql 7
      Transmitter delay is 0 microseconds
```

Table 23–13 *Show Controllers cBus Field Descriptions—Part 2*

Field	Description
HSCI 1	Card type and number (varies depending on card).
controller type 10.0	Version number of the card.
microcode version 129.3	Version number of the card's internal software (in read-only memory).
Interface 6	Physical interface number.
Hssi 0	Logical name for this interface.

Table 23–13 *Show Controllers cBus Field Descriptions—Part 2, Continued*

Field	Description
electrical interface is Hssi DTE	Self-explanatory.
5 buffer RX queue threshold	Maximum number of buffers allowed in the receive queue.
7 buffer TX queue limit	Maximum number of buffers allowed in the transmit queue.
buffer size 1520	Size of the buffers on this card (in bytes).
ift 0004	Interface type code. 0 = EIP 1 = FSIP 4 = HIP 5 = TRIP 6 = FIP 7 = AIP
rql 2	Receive-queue limit. Current number of buffers allowed for the receive queue. It is used to limit the number of buffers used by a particular inbound interface. When equal to 0, all of that interface's receive buffers are in use.
tq 0000 0000	Transmit-queue head and tail pointers.
tql 7	Transmit-queue limit. Current number of buffers allowed for transmit queue. It limits the maximum cBus buffers allowed to sit on a particular interface's transmit queue.
Transmitter delay is 0 microseconds	Transmitter delay between the packets.

The following is sample output of the **show controllers cbus** display for an AIP installed in IP slot 4. The running AIP microcode is Version 170.30, the PLIM type is 4B/5B, and the available bandwidth is 100 Mbps:

```
Router# show controllers cbus

Switch Processor 5, hardware version 11.1, microcode version 170.46
  Microcode loaded from system
  512 Kbytes of main memory, 128 Kbytes cache memory
  60 1520 byte buffers, 91 4496 byte buffers
  Restarts: 0 line down, 0 hung output, 0 controller error
 AIP 4, hardware version 1.0, microcode version 170.30
  Microcode loaded from system
  Interface 32 - ATM4/0, PLIM is 4B5B(100Mbps)
    15 buffer RX queue threshold, 36 buffer TX queue limit, buffer size 4496
    ift 0007, rql 12, tq 0000 0620, tql 36
    Transmitter delay is 0 microseconds
```

The following is sample output of the **show controllers cbus** display for SMIP:

```
Router# show controllers cbus

SMIP 2, hardware version 1.0, microcode version 10.0
 Microcode loaded from system
 Interface 16 - T1 2/0, electrical interface is Channelized T1
   10 buffer RX queue threshold, 14 buffer TX queue limit, buffer size 1580 ift 0001, rql
   7, tq 0000 05B0, tql 14
   Transmitter delay is 0 microseconds
```

SHOW CONTROLLERS ETHERNET

Use the **show controllers ethernet** EXEC command to display information on the Cisco 2500 series, Cisco 3000, or Cisco 4000 series.

> **show controllers ethernet** *number*

Syntax

number

Description

Interface number of the Ethernet interface.

Command Mode

EXEC

Usage Guidelines

This command first appeared in Cisco IOS Release 10.0.

Sample Display

The following is sample output from the **show controllers ethernet** command on the Cisco 4000:

```
Router# show controllers ethernet 0

LANCE unit 0, NIM slot 1, NIM type code 4, NIM version 1
Media Type is 10BaseT, Link State is Up, Squelch is Normal
idb 0x4060, ds 0x5C80, regaddr = 0x8100000
IB at 0x600D7AC: mode=0x0000, mcfilter 0000/0001/0000/0040
station address 0000.0c03.a14f  default station address 0000.0c03.a14f
buffer size 1524
RX ring with 32 entries at 0xD7E8
Rxhead = 0x600D8A0 (12582935), Rxp = 0x5CF0(23)
00 pak=0x60336D0 ds=0x6033822 status=0x80 max_size=1524 pak_size=98
01 pak=0x60327C0 ds=0x6032912 status=0x80 max_size=1524 pak_size=98
02 pak=0x6036B88 ds=0x6036CDA status=0x80 max_size=1524 pak_size=98
03 pak=0x6041138 ds=0x604128A status=0x80 max_size=1524 pak_size=98
04 pak=0x603FAA0 ds=0x603FBF2 status=0x80 max_size=1524 pak_size=98
05 pak=0x600DC50 ds=0x600DDA2 status=0x80 max_size=1524 pak_size=98
06 pak=0x6023E48 ds=0x6023F9A status=0x80 max_size=1524 pak_size=1506
07 pak=0x600E3D8 ds=0x600E52A status=0x80 max_size=1524 pak_size=1506
```

```
08 pak=0x6020990 ds=0x6020AE2 status=0x80 max_size=1524 pak_size=386
09 pak=0x602D4E8 ds=0x602D63A status=0x80 max_size=1524 pak_size=98
10 pak=0x603A7C8 ds=0x603A91A status=0x80 max_size=1524 pak_size=98
11 pak=0x601D4D8 ds=0x601D62A status=0x80 max_size=1524 pak_size=98
12 pak=0x603BE60 ds=0x603BFB2 status=0x80 max_size=1524 pak_size=98
13 pak=0x60318B0 ds=0x6031A02 status=0x80 max_size=1524 pak_size=98
14 pak=0x601CD50 ds=0x601CEA2 status=0x80 max_size=1524 pak_size=98
15 pak=0x602C5D8 ds=0x602C72A status=0x80 max_size=1524 pak_size=98
16 pak=0x60245D0 ds=0x6024722 status=0x80 max_size=1524 pak_size=98
17 pak=0x6008328 ds=0x600847A status=0x80 max_size=1524 pak_size=98
18 pak=0x601EB70 ds=0x601ECC2 status=0x80 max_size=1524 pak_size=98
19 pak=0x602DC70 ds=0x602DDC2 status=0x80 max_size=1524 pak_size=98
20 pak=0x60163E0 ds=0x6016532 status=0x80 max_size=1524 pak_size=98
21 pak=0x602CD60 ds=0x602CEB2 status=0x80 max_size=1524 pak_size=98
22 pak=0x6037A98 ds=0x6037BEA status=0x80 max_size=1524 pak_size=98
23 pak=0x602BE50 ds=0x602BFA2 status=0x80 max_size=1524 pak_size=98
24 pak=0x6018988 ds=0x6018ADA status=0x80 max_size=1524 pak_size=98
25 pak=0x6033E58 ds=0x6033FAA status=0x80 max_size=1524 pak_size=98
26 pak=0x601BE40 ds=0x601BF92 status=0x80 max_size=1524 pak_size=98
27 pak=0x6026B78 ds=0x6026CCA status=0x80 max_size=1524 pak_size=98
28 pak=0x6024D58 ds=0x6024EAA status=0x80 max_size=1524 pak_size=74
29 pak=0x602AF40 ds=0x602B092 status=0x80 max_size=1524 pak_size=98
30 pak=0x601FA80 ds=0x601FBD2 status=0x80 max_size=1524 pak_size=98
31 pak=0x6038220 ds=0x6038372 status=0x80 max_size=1524 pak_size=98
TX ring with 8 entries at 0xDA20, tx_count = 0
tx_head = 0x600DA58 (12582919), head_txp = 0x5DC4 (7)
tx_tail = 0x600DA58 (12582919), tail_txp = 0x5DC4 (7)
00 pak=0x000000 ds=0x600CF12 status=0x03 status2=0x0000 pak_size=118
01 pak=0x000000 ds=0x602126A status=0x03 status2=0x0000 pak_size=60
02 pak=0x000000 ds=0x600CF12 status=0x03 status2=0x0000 pak_size=118
03 pak=0x000000 ds=0x600CF12 status=0x03 status2=0x0000 pak_size=118
04 pak=0x000000 ds=0x600CF12 status=0x03 status2=0x0000 pak_size=118
05 pak=0x000000 ds=0x600CF12 status=0x03 status2=0x0000 pak_size=118
06 pak=0x000000 ds=0x600CF12 status=0x03 status2=0x0000 pak_size=118
07 pak=0x000000 ds=0x6003ED2 status=0x03 status2=0x0000 pak_size=126
0 missed datagrams, 0 overruns, 2 late collisions, 2 lost carrier events
0 transmitter underruns, 0 excessive collisions,  0 tdr, 0 babbles
0 memory errors, 0 spurious initialization done interrupts
0 no enp status, 0 buffer errors, 0 overflow errors
10 one_col, 10 more_col, 22 deferred, 0 tx_buff
0 throttled, 0 enabled
Lance csr0 = 0x73
```

SHOW CONTROLLERS FASTETHERNET

To display information about initialization block information, transmit ring, receive ring and errors for the Fast Ethernet controller chip on the Cisco 4500, Cisco 7200 series, or Cisco 7500 series, use the **show controllers fastethernet** EXEC command.

> **show controllers fastethernet** *number* (Cisco 4500)
> **show controllers fastethernet** *slot/port* (Cisco 7200 series)
> **show controllers fastethernet** *slot/port-adapter/port* (Cisco 7500 series)

Syntax	Description
number	Port, connector, or interface card number. On a Cisco 4500 or Cisco 4700 router, specifies the NPM number. The numbers are assigned at the factory at the time of installation or when added to a system.
slot	Refer to the appropriate hardware manual for slot and port information.
port	Refer to the appropriate hardware manual for slot and port information.
port -adapter	Refer to the appropriate hardware manual for information about port adapter compatibility.

Command Mode

EXEC

Usage Guidelines

This command first appeared in Cisco IOS Release 11.2.

The output of this command is generally useful for diagnostic tasks performed by technical support only.

Sample Displays

The following is sample output from the **show controllers fastethernet** command on a Cisco 4500 router:

```
c4500-1# show controllers fastethernet 0

DEC21140 Slot 0, Subunit 0
dec21140_ds=0x60001234, registers=0x3c001000, ib=0x42301563, ring entries=256
rxring=0x40235878, rxr shadow=0x64528745, rx_head=0, rx_tail=10
txring=0x43562188, txr shadow=0x65438721, tx_head=17, tx_tail=34, tx_count=17
DEC21140 Registers
CSR0=0x23457667, CSR3=0x12349878, CSR4=0x34528745, CSR5=0x76674565
CSR6=0x76453676, CSR7=0x76456574, CSR8=0x25367648, CSR9=0x87253674
CSR11=0x23456454, CSR12=0x76564787, CSR15=0x98273465
DEC21140 PCI registers
bus_no=0, device_no=0
CFID=0x12341234, CFCS=0x76547654, CFRV=0x87658765, CFLT=0x98769876
CBIO=0x12344321, CBMA=0x23454321, CFIT=0x34567654, CFDA=0x76544567
MII registers
Register 0x00: 0x1234 0x1234 0x2345 0x3456 0x4567 0x5678 0x6789 0x7890
Register 0x08: 0x9876 0x8765 0x7654 0x6543 0x5432 0x4321 0x3210 0x2109
Register 0x10: 0x1234 0x2345 0x3456          0x4567 0x5678 0x6789 0x7890
Register 0x18: 0x9876 0x8765 0x7654 0x6543 0x5432 0x4321
DEC21140 statistics
filtered_in_sw=1000, throttled=10, enabled=10
```

```
rx_fifo_overflow=10, rx_no_enp=12, rx_late_collision=18
rx_watchdog=15, rx_process_stopped=15, rx_buffer_unavailable=1500
tx_jabber_timeout=10, tx_carrier_loss=2, tx_deffered=15
tx_no_carrier=1, tx_late_collision=10, tx_excess_coll=10
tx_process_stopped=1, fata_tx_err=0
```

The following is sample output from the **show controllers fastethernet** command on a Cisco 7500
series router:

```
router# show controllers fastethernet 0/0

Interface FastEthernet0/0
Hardware is DEC21140
 dec21140_ds=0x60895888, registers=0x3C018000, ib=0x4B019500
 rx ring entries=128, tx ring entries=128
 rxring=0x4B019640, rxr shadow=0x60895970, rx_head=0, rx_tail=0
 txring=0x4B019EC0, txr shadow=0x60895B98, tx_head=77, tx_tail=77, tx_count=0
 CSR0=0xFFFA4882, CSR3=0x4B019640, CSR4=0x4B019EC0, CSR5=0xFC660000
 CSR6=0xE20CA202, CSR7=0xFFFFA241, CSR8=0xFFFE0000, CSR9=0xFFFDD7FF
 CSR11=0xFFFE0000, CSR12=0xFFFFFF98, CSR15=0xFFFFFEC8
 DEC21140 PCI registers:
  bus_no=0, device_no=6
  CFID=0x00091011, CFCS=0x02800006, CFRV=0x02000012, CFLT=0x0000FF00
  CBIO=0x7C5AFF81, CBMA=0x48018000, CFIT=0x0000018F, CFDA=0x0000AF00
 MII registers:
  Register 0x00:   2000   780B   2000   5C00   01E1   0000   0000   0000
  Register 0x08:   0000   0000   0000   0000   0000   0000   0000   0000
  Register 0x10:   0000   0000   0000   0000          0000   0000   8040
  Register 0x18:   8000   0000   0000   3800   A3B9
 throttled=0, enabled=0, disabled=0
 rx_fifo_overflow=0, rx_no_enp=0, rx_discard=0
 tx_underrun_err=0, tx_jabber_timeout=0, tx_carrier_loss=1
 tx_no_carrier=1, tx_late_collision=0, tx_excess_coll=0
 tx_collision_cnt=0, tx_deferred=0, fatal_tx_err=0, mult_ovfl=0
HW addr filter: 0x60895FC0, ISL Enabled
 Entry= 0: Addr=0100.0CCC.CCCC
 Entry= 1: Addr=0300.0000.0001
 Entry= 2: Addr=0100.0C00.0000
 Entry= 3: Addr=FFFF.FFFF.FFFF
 Entry= 4: Addr=FFFF.FFFF.FFFF
 Entry= 5: Addr=FFFF.FFFF.FFFF
 Entry= 6: Addr=FFFF.FFFF.FFFF
 Entry= 7: Addr=FFFF.FFFF.FFFF
 Entry= 8: Addr=FFFF.FFFF.FFFF
 Entry= 9: Addr=FFFF.FFFF.FFFF
 Entry=10: Addr=FFFF.FFFF.FFFF
 Entry=11: Addr=FFFF.FFFF.FFFF
 Entry=12: Addr=FFFF.FFFF.FFFF
 Entry=13: Addr=FFFF.FFFF.FFFF
 Entry=14: Addr=FFFF.FFFF.FFFF
 Entry=15: Addr=0060.3E28.6E00
```

Related Commands

show interface fastethernet

SHOW CONTROLLERS FDDI

To display all information under the FDDI Interface Processor (FIP) on the Cisco 7200 series and Cisco 7500 series, use the **show controllers fddi** user EXEC command.

   show controllers fddi

Syntax   Description

This command has no arguments or keywords.

Command Mode

User EXEC

Usage Guidelines

This command first appeared in Cisco IOS Release 10.0.

This command reflects the internal state of the chips and information the system uses for bridging and routing that is specific to the interface hardware. The information displayed is generally useful for diagnostic tasks performed by technical support personnel only.

Sample Display

The following is sample output from the **show controllers fddi** command:

```
Router# show controllers fddi

Fddi2/0 - hardware version 2.2, microcode version 1.2
  Phy-A registers:
    cr0 4, cr1 0, cr2 0, status 3, cr3 0
  Phy-B registers:
    cr0 4, cr1 4, cr2 0, status 3, cr3 0
  FORMAC registers:
    irdtlb  71C2, irdtneg F85E, irdthtt F5D5, irdmir  FFFF0BDC
    irdtrth F85F, irdtmax FBC5, irdtvxt 5959, irdstmc 0810
    irdmode 6A20, irdimsk 0000, irdstat 8060, irdtpri 0000
  FIP registers
    ccb:   002C  cmd:    0006  fr:   000F  mdptr: 0000  mema: 0000
    icb:   00C0  arg:    0003  app:  0004  mdpg:  0000  af:   0603
    clm:   E002  bcn:    E016  clbn: 0198  rxoff: 002A  en:   0001
    clmbc: 8011  bcnbc:  8011  robn: 0004  park:  0000  fop:  8004

    txchn: 0000  pend:   0000  act:  0000  tail:  0000  cnt:  0000
    state: 0003  check:  0000  eof:  0000  tail:  0000  cnt:  0000
    rxchn: 0000  buf0:   0534  nxt0: 0570  eof:   0000  tail: 0000
    eofch: 0000  buf1:   051C  nxt1: 0528  pool:  0050  err:  005C
```

```
head:   0984  cur:    0000  t0:    0030  t1:    0027  t2:    000F
tail:   0984  cnt:    0001  t3:    0000  rxlft: 000B  used: 0000
txq_s:  0018  txq_f:  0018  Aarm:  0000  Barm:  1388  fint: 8004
```

```
Total LEM: phy-a 6, phy-b 13
```

The last line of output indicates how many times the specific PHY encountered an "UNKNOWN LINE STATE" event on the fiber.

SHOW CONTROLLERS LEX

To show hardware and software information about the LAN Extender chassis, use the **show controllers lex** EXEC command.

> **show controllers lex** [*number*]
> **show controllers lex** [*slot/port*] (for the Cisco 7500 series)

Syntax	Description
number	(Optional) Number of the LAN Extender interface about which to display information.
slot	Refer to the appropriate hardware manual for slot and port information.
port	Refer to the appropriate hardware manual for slot and port information.

Command Mode

EXEC

Usage Guidelines

This command first appeared in Cisco IOS Release 11.0.

Use the **show controllers lex** command to display information about the hardware revision level, software version number, Flash memory size, serial number, and other information related to the configuration of the LAN Extender.

Sample Displays

The following is sample output from the **show controllers lex** command:

```
Router# show controllers lex 0

Lex0:
FLEX Hardware revision 1
FLEX Software version 255.0
128K bytes of flash memory
Serial number is 123456789
Station address is 0000.4060.1100
```

The following is sample output from the **show controllers lex** command when the LAN Extender interface is not bound to a serial interface:

```
Router# show controllers lex 1

Lex1 is not bound to a serial interface
```

Table 23–14 describes the fields shown in the output.

Table 23–14 *Show Controllers Lex Field Description*

Field	Description
Lex0:	Number of the LAN Extender interface.
FLEX Hardware revision	Revision number of the Cisco 1000 series LAN Extender chassis.
FLEX Software version	Revision number of the software running on the LAN Extender chassis.
128K bytes of Flash memory	Amount of Flash memory in the LAN Extender.
Serial number	Serial number of the LAN Extender chassis.
Station address	MAC address of the LAN Extender chassis.

SHOW CONTROLLERS MCI

Use the **show controllers mci** privileged EXEC command to display all information under the Multiport Communications Interface card or the SCI.

show controllers mci

Syntax   Description

This command has no arguments or keywords.

Command Mode

Privileged EXEC

Usage Guidelines

This command first appeared in Cisco IOS Release 10.0.

This command displays information the system uses for bridging and routing that is specific to the interface hardware. The information displayed is generally useful for diagnostic tasks performed by technical support personnel only.

Sample Display

The following is sample output from the **show controllers mci** command:

```
Router# show controllers mci

MCI 0, controller type 1.1, microcode version 1.8
    128 Kbytes of main memory, 4 Kbytes cache memory
22 system TX buffers, largest buffer size 1520
    Restarts: 0 line down, 0 hung output, 0 controller error
Interface 0 is Ethernet0, station address 0000.0c00.d4a6
    15 total RX buffers, 11 buffer TX queue limit, buffer size 1520
    Transmitter delay is 0 microseconds
Interface 1 is Serial0, electrical interface is V.35 DTE
    15 total RX buffers, 11 buffer TX queue limit, buffer size 1520
    Transmitter delay is 0 microseconds
    High speed synchronous serial interface
Interface 2 is Ethernet1, station address aa00.0400.3be4
    15 total RX buffers, 11 buffer TX queue limit, buffer size 1520
    Transmitter delay is 0 microseconds
Interface 3 is Serial1, electrical interface is V.35 DCE
    15 total RX buffers, 11 buffer TX queue limit, buffer size 1520
    Transmitter delay is 0 microseconds
    High speed synchronous serial interface
```

Table 23–15 describes significant fields shown in the display.

Table 23–15 *Show Controllers MCI Field Descriptions*

Field	Description
MCI 0	Card type and unit number (varies depending on card).
controller type 1.1	Version number of the card.
microcode version 1.8	Version number of the card's internal software (in read-only memory).
128 Kbytes of main memory	Amount of main memory on the card.
4 Kbytes cache memory	Amount of cache memory on the card.
22 system TX buffers	Number of buffers that hold packets to be transmitted.
largest buffer size 1520	Largest size of these buffers (in bytes).

Restarts
  0 line down
  0 hung output
  0 controller error
	Count of restarts due to the following conditions:
	  Communication line down
	  Output unable to transmit
	  Internal error

Interface 0 is Ethernet0	Names of interfaces, by number.
electrical interface is V.35 DTE	Line interface type for serial connections.

Table 23-15 *Show Controllers MCI Field Descriptions, Continued*

Field	Description
15 total RX buffers	Number of buffers for received packets.
11 buffer TX queue limit	Maximum number of buffers in transmit queue.
Transmitter delay is 0 microseconds	Delay between outgoing frames.
Station address 0000.0c00.d4a6	Hardware address of the interface.

NOTES

The interface type is only queried at startup. If the hardware changes *subsequent* to initial startup, then the wrong type is reported. This has *no* adverse effect on the operation of the software. For instance, if a DCE cable is connected to a dual-mode V.35 applique after the unit has been booted, then the display presented for **show interfaces** incorrectly reports attachment to a DTE device, although the software recognizes the DCE interface and behaves accordingly.

Related Commands

tx-queue-limit

SHOW CONTROLLERS PCBUS

To display all information about the ISA bus interface, use the **show controllers pcbus** privileged EXEC command.

> **show controllers pcbus**

Syntax   Description

This command has no arguments or keywords.

Command Mode

Privileged EXEC

Usage Guidelines

This command first appeared in Cisco IOS Release 11.0.

This command is valid on LanOptics' Branchcard or Stacknet 2000 products only.

Sample Display

The following is sample output from the **show controllers pcbus** command:

```
Router# show controllers pcbus

PCbus unit 0,  Name = PCbus0  Hardware is ISA PCbus shared RAM
IDB at 0x3719B0,  Interface driver data structure at 0x3735F8
Control/status register at 0x2110008,  Shared memory at 0xC000000
Shared memory is initialized

Shared memory interface control block :
Magic no = 0x41435A56 (valid)  Version = 1.0
Shared memory size = 64K bytes,  Interface is NOT shutdown
Interface state is up, line protocol is up

Tx buffer : (control block at 0xC000010)
Start offset = 0x30,  Size = 0x7FE8,  Overflows = 1
GET_ptr = 0x4F6C,  PUT_ptr = 0x4F6C,  WRAP_ptr = 0x3BB0

Rx buffer : (control block at 0xC000020)
Start offset = 0x8018,  Size 0x7FE8,  Overflows = 22250698
GET_ptr = 0x60,  PUT_ptr = 0x60,  WRAP_ptr = 0x7FD0

Interrupts received = 567
```

SHOW CONTROLLERS SERIAL

Use the **show controllers serial** privileged EXEC command to display information that is specific to the interface hardware.

show controllers serial

Syntax   Description

This command has no arguments or keywords.

Command Mode

Privileged EXEC

Usage Guidelines

This command first appeared in Cisco IOS Release 10.0.

The information displayed is generally useful for diagnostic tasks performed by technical support personnel only.

Part
III

Command Reference

Sample Display

Sample output of the **show controllers serial** command on the Cisco 4000 follows:

```
Router# show controllers serial

MK5 unit 0, NIM slot 1, NIM type code 7, NIM version 1
idb = 0x6150, driver structure at 0x34A878, regaddr = 0x8100300
IB at 0x6045500: mode=0x0108, local_addr=0, remote_addr=0
N1=1524, N2=1, scaler=100, T1=1000, T3=2000, TP=1
buffer size 1524
DTE V.35 serial cable attached
RX ring with 32 entries at 0x45560 : RLEN=5, Rxhead 0
00 pak=0x6044D78  ds=0x6044ED4 status=80 max_size=1524 pak_size=0
01 pak=0x60445F0  ds=0x604474C status=80 max_size=1524 pak_size=0
02 pak=0x6043E68  ds=0x6043FC4 status=80 max_size=1524 pak_size=0
03 pak=0x60436E0  ds=0x604383C status=80 max_size=1524 pak_size=0
04 pak=0x6042F58  ds=0x60430B4 status=80 max_size=1524 pak_size=0
05 pak=0x60427D0  ds=0x604292C status=80 max_size=1524 pak_size=0
06 pak=0x6042048  ds=0x60421A4 status=80 max_size=1524 pak_size=0
07 pak=0x60418C0  ds=0x6041A1C status=80 max_size=1524 pak_size=0
08 pak=0x6041138  ds=0x6041294 status=80 max_size=1524 pak_size=0
09 pak=0x60409B0  ds=0x6040B0C status=80 max_size=1524 pak_size=0
10 pak=0x6040228  ds=0x6040384 status=80 max_size=1524 pak_size=0
11 pak=0x603FAA0  ds=0x603FBFC status=80 max_size=1524 pak_size=0
12 pak=0x603F318  ds=0x603F474 status=80 max_size=1524 pak_size=0
13 pak=0x603EB90  ds=0x603ECEC status=80 max_size=1524 pak_size=0
14 pak=0x603E408  ds=0x603E564 status=80 max_size=1524 pak_size=0
15 pak=0x603DC80  ds=0x603DDDC status=80 max_size=1524 pak_size=0
16 pak=0x603D4F8  ds=0x603D654 status=80 max_size=1524 pak_size=0
17 pak=0x603CD70  ds=0x603CECC status=80 max_size=1524 pak_size=0
18 pak=0x603C5E8  ds=0x603C744 status=80 max_size=1524 pak_size=0
19 pak=0x603BE60  ds=0x603BFBC status=80 max_size=1524 pak_size=0
20 pak=0x603B6D8  ds=0x603B834 status=80 max_size=1524 pak_size=0
21 pak=0x603AF50  ds=0x603B0AC status=80 max_size=1524 pak_size=0
22 pak=0x603A7C8  ds=0x603A924 status=80 max_size=1524 pak_size=0
23 pak=0x603A040  ds=0x603A19C status=80 max_size=1524 pak_size=0
24 pak=0x60398B8  ds=0x6039A14 status=80 max_size=1524 pak_size=0
25 pak=0x6039130  ds=0x603928C status=80 max_size=1524 pak_size=0
26 pak=0x60389A8  ds=0x6038B04 status=80 max_size=1524 pak_size=0
27 pak=0x6038220  ds=0x603837C status=80 max_size=1524 pak_size=0
28 pak=0x6037A98  ds=0x6037BF4 status=80 max_size=1524 pak_size=0
29 pak=0x6037310  ds=0x603746C status=80 max_size=1524 pak_size=0
30 pak=0x6036B88  ds=0x6036CE4 status=80 max_size=1524 pak_size=0
31 pak=0x6036400  ds=0x603655C status=80 max_size=1524 pak_size=0
TX ring with 8 entries at 0x45790 : TLEN=3, TWD=7
tx_count = 0, tx_head = 7, tx_tail = 7
00 pak=0x000000 ds=0x600D70C status=0x38 max_size=1524 pak_size=22
01 pak=0x000000 ds=0x600D70E status=0x38 max_size=1524 pak_size=2
02 pak=0x000000 ds=0x600D70E status=0x38 max_size=1524 pak_size=2
03 pak=0x000000 ds=0x600D70E status=0x38 max_size=1524 pak_size=2
04 pak=0x000000 ds=0x600D70E status=0x38 max_size=1524 pak_size=2
```

```
05 pak=0x000000 ds=0x600D70E status=0x38 max_size=1524 pak_size=2
06 pak=0x000000 ds=0x600D70E status=0x38 max_size=1524 pak_size=2
07 pak=0x000000 ds=0x6000000 status=0x38 max_size=1524 pak_size=0
XID/Test TX desc at 0xFFFFFF, status=0x30, max_buffer_size=0, packet_size=0
XID/Test RX desc at 0xFFFFFF, status=0x0, max_buffer_size=0, packet_size=0
Status Buffer at 0x60459C8: rcv=0, tcv=0, local_state=0, remote_state=0
phase=0, tac=0, currd=0x00000, curxd=0x00000
bad_frames=0, frmrs=0, T1_timeouts=0, rej_rxs=0, runts=0
0 missed datagrams, 0 overruns, 0 bad frame addresses
0 bad datagram encapsulations, 0 user primitive errors
0 provider primitives lost, 0 unexpected provider primitives
0 spurious primitive interrupts, 0 memory errors, 0 tr
%LINEPROTO-5-UPDOWN: Linansmitter underruns
mk5025 registers: csr0 = 0x0E00, csr1 = 0x0302, csr2 = 0x0704
                  csr3 = 0x5500, csr4 = 0x0214, csr5 = 0x0008
```

SHOW CONTROLLERS T1

To display information about the T1 links, use the **show controllers t1** privileged EXEC command.

> **show controllers t1** [*slot/port*] (Cisco 7500 series)
> **show controllers t1** *number* (Cisco 4000 series)

Syntax	Description
slot/port	Backplane slot number and port number on the interface. See your hardware installation manual for the specific slot and port numbers.
number	Network processor module (NPM) number, in the range 0 through 2.

Command Mode

EXEC

Usage Guidelines

This command displays controller status that is specific to the controller hardware. The information displayed is generally useful for diagnostic tasks performed by technical support personnel only.

The NPM or MIP can query the port adapters to determine their current status. Issue a **show controllers t1** command to display statistics about the T1 link.

If you specify a slot and port number, each 15-minute period will be displayed.

Sample Display

The following is sample output from the **show controllers t1** command on the Cisco 7500 series:

```
Router# show controllers t1
T1 4/1 is up.
  No alarms detected.
```

```
Framing is ESF, Line Code is AMI, Clock Source is line
Data in current interval (0 seconds elapsed):
   0 Line Code Violations, 0 Path Code Violations 0 Slip Secs, 0 Fr Loss Secs,
   0 Line Err Secs, 0 Degraded Mins 0 Errored Secs, 0 Bursty Err Secs,
   0 Severely Err Secs, 0 Unavail Secs
Total Data (last 79 15 minute intervals):
   0 Line Code Violations, 0 Path Code Violations, 0 Slip Secs, 0 Fr Loss Secs,
   0 Line Err Secs, 0 Degraded Mins, 0 Errored Secs, 0 Bursty Err Secs,
   0 Severely Err Secs, 0 Unavail Secs
```

Table 23–16 describes the **show controllers t1** display fields.

Table 23–16 *Show Controller T1 Field Descriptions*

Field	Description
T1 0/0 is up.	The T1 controller 0 in slot 0 is operating. The controller's state can be up, down or administratively down. Loopback conditions are shown by (Locally looped) or (Remotely looped).
No alarms detected.	Any alarms detected by the controller are displayed here. Possible alarms are as follows: Transmitter is sending remote alarm. Transmitter is sending AIS. Receiver has loss of signal. Receiver is getting AIS. Receiver has loss of frame. Receiver has remote alarm. Receiver has no alarms.
Data in current interval (725 seconds elapsed)	Shows the current accumulation period, which rolls into the 24-hour accumulation every 15 minutes. Accumulation period is from 1 to 900 seconds. The oldest 15-minute period falls off the back of the 24-hour accumulation buffer.
Line Code Violations	Indicates the occurrence of either a Bipolar Violation (BPV) or Excessive Zeros (EXZ) error event.
Path Code Violations	Indicates a frame synchronization bit error in the D4 and E1-noCRC formats, or a CRC error in the ESF and E1-CRC formats.
Slip Secs	Indicates the replication or deletion of the payload bits of a DS1 frame. A slip may be performed when there is a difference between the timing of a synchronous receiving terminal and the received signal.

Table 23–16 *Show Controller T1 Field Descriptions, Continued*

Field	Description
Fr Loss Secs	Indicates the number of seconds an Out-of-Frame (OOF) error is detected.
Line Err Secs	Line Errored Second (LES) is a second in which one or more Line Code Violation errors are detected.
Degraded Mins	A Degraded Minute is one in which the estimated error rate exceeds 1E-6 but does not exceed 1E-3.
Errored Secs	In ESF and E1-CRC links, an Errored Second is a second in which one of the following are detected: one or more Path Code Violations; one or more Out-of-Frame defects; one or more Controlled Slip events, or a detected AIS defect. For D4 and E1-noCRC links, the presence of Bipolar Violations also triggers an Errored Second.
Bursty Err Secs	A second with fewer than 320 and more than 1 Path Coding Violation error, no Severely Errored Frame defects and no detected incoming AIS defects. Controlled slips are not included in this parameter.
Severely Err Secs	For ESF signals, a second with one of the following errors: 320 or more Path Code Violation errors; one or more Out-of-Frame defects, or a detected AIS defect. For E1-CRC signals, a second with one of the following errors: 832 or more Path Code Violation errors or one or more Out-of-Frame defects. For E1-noCRC signals, a second with 2048 Line Code Violations or more. For D4 signals, a count of 1-second intervals with Framing Errors, or an Out-of-Frame defect, or 1544 Line Code Violations.
Unavail Secs	A count of the total number of seconds on the interface.

SHOW CONTROLLERS T3

To display information about the Channelized T3 Interface Processor (CT3IP) on Cisco 7500 series routers, use the **show controllers t3** privileged EXEC command.

> **show controllers t3** [*slot/port-adapter/port* [*:t1-channel*]] [**brief** | **tabular** | **remote performance** [**brief** | **tabular**]]

Syntax	Description
slot	Refer to the appropriate hardware manual for slot and port information.
port-adapter	Refer to the appropriate hardware manual for information about port adapter compatibility.
port	Refer to the appropriate hardware manual for slot and port information.
:t1-channel	(Optional) For the CT3IP, the T1 channel is a number between 1 and 28.
remote performance	(Optional) Displays the far-end ANSI performance monitor information when enabled on the T1 channel with the **t1 fdl ansi** controller command.
brief	(Optional) Displays a subset of information.
tabular	(Optional) Displays information in a tabular format.

Command Mode

Privileged EXEC

Usage Guidelines

This command first appeared in Cisco IOS Release 11.3.

This command was modified in Cisco IOS Release 11.3 to include the **remote performance** keyword.

This command displays controller status that is specific to the controller hardware. The information displayed is generally useful for diagnostic tasks performed by technical support personnel only.

NOTES

T1 channels on the CT3IP are numbered 1 to 28 rather than the more traditional zero-based scheme (0 to 27) used with other Cisco products. This is to ensure consistency with telco numbering schemes for T1 channels within channelized T3 equipment.

The **show controllers t3** command also displays Maintenance Data Link (MDL) information (received strings) if MDL is configured and framing is set to C-bit.

Sample Displays

The following is partial sample output from the **show controller t3** command:

```
Router# show controller t3 3/0/0
T3 3/0/0 is up.
  CT3 H/W Version: 4, CT3 ROM Version: 0.116, CT3 F/W Version: 0.10.0
  Mx H/W version: 2, Mx ucode ver: 1.24
  Applique type is Channelized T3
  No alarms detected.
  FEAC code received: No code is being received
  Framing is M23, Line Code is B3ZS, Clock Source is Internal.
  Ext1: LOS, Ext2: LOS, Ext3: LOS, Test: OK
  Data in current interval (39 seconds elapsed):
     0 Line Code Violations, 0 P-bit Coding Violation
     0 C-bit Coding Violation
     0 P-bit Err Secs, 0 P-bit Severely Err Secs
     0 Severely Err Framing Secs, 0 Unavailable Secs
     0 Line Errored Secs, 0 C-bit Errored Secs, 0 C-bit Severely Errored Secs
  Total Data (last 1 15 minute intervals):
     0 Line Code Violations, 0 P-bit Coding Violation,
     0 C-bit Coding Violation,
     0 P-bit Err Secs, 0 P-bit Severely Err Secs,
     0 Severely Err Framing Secs, 0 Unavailable Secs,
     0 Line Errored Secs, 0 C-bit Errored Secs, 0 C-bit Severely Errored Secs

  T1 1 is down, speed: 1536 kbs, non-inverted data
  timeslots: 1-24
  FDL per ANSI T1.403 and AT&T 54016 spec.
  Configured for FDL Remotely Line Looped
  No alarms detected.
  Framing is ESF, LineCode is B8ZS, Clock Source is Internal.
  BERT test result (running)
       Test Pattern: All 0's, Status: Sync, Sync Detected: 1
       Interval: 4 minute(s), Tim Remain: 4 minute(s)
       Bit Errors (Sync BERT Started): 0 bits
       Bit Errors (Sync last Sync): 0 bits, Bits Received: 7 Mbits

  ...

  T1 15 is up, speed: 1536 kbs, non-inverted data
  timeslots: 1-24
  No alarms detected.
  Framing is ESF, LineCode is B8ZS, Clock Source is Internal.
  Data in current interval (69 seconds elapsed):
     0 Line Code Violations, 0 Path Code Violations
     0 Slip Secs, 0 Fr Loss Secs, 0 Line Err Secs, 0 Degraded Mins
     0 Errored Secs, 0 Bursty Err Secs, 0 Severely Err Secs
     0 Unavail Secs, 0 Stuffed Secs
  Total Data (last 1 15 minute intervals):
     0 Line Code Violations, 0 Path Code Violations,
     0 Slip Secs, 0 Fr Loss Secs, 0 Line Err Secs, 0 Degraded Mins,
     0 Errored Secs, 0 Bursty Err Secs, 0 Severely Err Secs
     0 Unavail Secs, 0 Stuffed Secs
```

The following is partial sample output from the **show controller t3 brief** command:

```
router# show controllers t3 3/0/0 brief
T3 3/0/0 is up.
  CT3 H/W Version: 4, CT3 ROM Version: 0.116, CT3 F/W Version: 0.10.0
  Mxt H/W version: 2, Mxt ucode ver: 1.24
  Applique type is Channelized T3
  No alarms detected.
  FEAC code received: No code is being received
  Framing is M23, Line Code is B3ZS, Clock Source is Internal.
  Ext1: LOS, Ext2: LOS, Ext3: LOS, Test: OK

  T1 1 is up, speed: 1536 kbs, non-inverted data
  timeslots: 1-24
  FDL per ANSI T1.403 and AT&T 54016 spec.
  Configured for FDL Remotely Line Looped
  No alarms detected.
  Framing is ESF, LineCode is B8ZS, Clock Source is Internal.
  BERT test result (done)
      Test Pattern: All 0's, Status: Not Sync, Sync Detected: 1
      Interval: 4 minute(s), Tim Remain: 0 minute(s)
      Bit Errors(Sync BERT Started): 0 bits
      Bit Errors(Sync last Sync): 0 bits, Bits Received: 368 Mbits
  ...
```

The following is partial sample output from the **show controllers t3 tabular** command:

```
router# show controllers t3 3/0/0 tabular
T3 3/0/0 is up.
  CT3 H/W Version: 4, CT3 ROM Version: 1.2, CT3 F/W Version: 2.1.0
  Mx H/W version: 2, Mx ucode ver: 1.25
  Applique type is Channelized T3
  No alarms detected.
  MDL transmission is disabled

  FEAC code received: No code is being received
  Framing is C-BIT Parity, Line Code is B3ZS, Clock Source is Internal.
  Ext1: AIS, Ext2: LOS, Ext3: LOS, Test: LOS
  INTERVAL     LCV   PCV   CCV   PES   PSES  SEFS  UAS   LES   CES   CSES
  08:56-09:11   0     0     0     0     0     0     0     0     0     0
  08:41-08:56   0     0     0     0     0     0     0     0     0     0
  08:26-08:41   0     0     0     0     0     0     0     0     0     0
  Total         0     0     0     0     0     0     0     0     0     0

  T1 2 is up, speed: 1536 kbs, non-inverted data
  timeslots: 1-24
  FDL per AT&T 54016 spec.
  No alarms detected.
  Framing is ESF, Line Code is B8ZS, Clock Source is Internal.
  INTERVAL     LCV   PCV   CSS   SELS  LES   DM    ES    BES   SES   UAS   SS
  08:56-09:11   0     0     0     0     0     0     0     0     0     0     0
  08:41-08:56   0     0     0     0     0     0     0     0     0     0     0
  08:26-08:41   0     0     0     0     0     0     0     0     0     0     0
  Total         0     0     0     0     0     0     0     0     0     0     0
```

The following is partial sample output from the **show controller t3 remote performance** command. This information is available if the **t1 fdl ansi** controller command is enabled for a T1 channel on a CT3IP.

```
Router# show controller t3 3/0/0 remote performance
T3 3/0/0 is up.
  CT3 H/W Version: 4, CT3 ROM Version: 0.116, CT3 F/W Version: 20.2.0
  Mx H/W version: 2, Mx ucode ver: 1.25

  T1 1 - Remote Performance Data
  Data in current interval (356 seconds elapsed):
     0 Line Code Violations, 0 Path Code Violations
     0 Slip Secs, 0 Fr Loss Secs, 0 Line Err Secs, 0 Degraded Mins
     0 Errored Secs, 0 Bursty Err Secs, 0 Severely Err Secs
     0 Unavail Secs
  Data in Interval 1:
     1 Slip Secs, 0 Fr Loss Secs, 0 Line Err Secs, 0 Degraded Mins
     2 Errored Secs, 0 Bursty Err Secs, 0 Severely Err Secs
     0 Unavail Secs
  Data in Interval 2:
     0 Line Code Violations, 0 Path Code Violations
     0 Slip Secs, 0 Fr Loss Secs, 0 Line Err Secs, 0 Degraded Mins
     0 Errored Secs, 0 Bursty Err Secs, 0 Severely Err Secs
     0 Unavail Secs
  Total Data (last 2 15 minute intervals):
     1 Path Code Violations
     1 Slip Secs, 0 Fr Loss Secs, 0 Line Err Secs, 0 Degraded Mins,
     2 Errored Secs, 0 Bursty Err Secs, 0 Severely Err Secs
     0 Unavail Secs
...
```

Table 23–17 describes the **show controller t3** display fields.

Table 23–17 *Show Controller T3 Field Descriptions*

Field	Description
T3 3/0/0 is up	T3 controller in slot 3 is operating. The controller's state can be up, down, or administratively down. Loopback conditions are shown by (Locally looped) or (Remotely looped).
CT3 H/W Version	Version number of the hardware.
CT3 ROM Version	Version number of the ROM.
CT3 F/W Version	Version number of the firmware.
Mx H/W version	Hardware version number of the HDLC controller chip.
Mx ucode ver	Microcode version of the HDLC controller chip.

Table 23–17   *Show Controller T3 Field Descriptions, Continued*

Field	Description
Applique type	Controller type.
No alarms detected	Any alarms detected by the controller are displayed here. Possible alarms are as follows: • Transmitter is sending remote alarm. • Transmitter is sending AIS. • Receiver has loss of signal. • Receiver is getting AIS. • Receiver has loss of frame. • Receiver has remote alarm. • Receiver has no alarms.
MDL transmission is disabled	Status of the maintenance data link (either enabled or disabled).
FEAC code received	Whether a far-end alarm code request is being received. Possible values are as follows: • DS3 Eqpt. Failure (SA) • DS3 LOS/HBER • DS3 Out-of-Frame • DS3 AIS Received • DS3 IDLE Received • DS3 Eqpt. Failure (NSA) • Common Eqpt. Failure (NSA) • Multiple DS1 LOS/HBER • DS1 Eqpt. Failure • Single DS1 LOS/HBER • DS1 Eqpts Failure (NSA) • No code is being received
Framing is M23	Framing type on the CT3IP. Values are: M23, C-Bit, and Auto-detect.
Line Code is B3ZS	Line coding format on the CT3IP.
Clock Source is Internal	Clock source on the CT3IP. Values are: internal or line.

Table 23–17 *Show Controller T3 Field Descriptions, Continued*

Field	Description
BERT test result	BERT test information is available if the **t1 bert** controller command is enabled for the T1 channel on the CT3IP. The BERT results include the following information:
	• Test Pattern—Type of test pattern selected.
	• Status—Status of the test.
	• Sync Detected—Number of times the pattern sync is detected (that is, the number of times the pattern goes from No Sync to Sync).
	• Interval—Duration selected.
	• Time Remain—Time remaining on the BERT test.
	• Bit Errors(Sync BERT Started)—Number of bit errors during the BERT test.
	• Bit Errors(Sync last Sync)—Number of bit errors since the last pattern sync was detected.
	• Bits Received—Total bits received.
	When the T1 channel has a BERT test running, the line state is DOWN. Also, when the BERT test is running and the Status field is Not Sync, the information in the total bit errors field is not valid. When the BERT test is done, the Status field is not relevant.
Data in current interval (39 seconds elapsed)	Shows the current accumulation period, which rolls into the 24-hour accumulation every 15 minutes. Accumulation period is from 1 to 900 seconds. The oldest 15-minute period falls off the back of the 24-hour accumulation buffer.
Line Code Violations	Line Code Violations (LCV) is a count of both Bipolar Violations (BPVs) and Excessive Zeros (EXZs) occurring over the accumulation period. An EXZ increments the LCV by one regardless of the length of the zero string.

Table 23–17   *Show Controller T3 Field Descriptions, Continued*

Field	Description
P-bit Coding Violation	For all DS3 applications, a P-bit coding violation (PVC) error event is a P-bit parity error event. A P-bit parity error event is the occurrence of a received P-bit code on the DS3 M-frame that is not identical to the corresponding locally calculated code.
C-bit Coding Violation	For C-bit parity and SYNTRAN DS3 applications, the C-bit coding violation (CCV) is the count of coding violations reported via the C-bits. For C-bit parity, it is the count of CP-bit parity errors occurring in the accumulation interval. For SYNTRAN, it is a count of CRC-9 errors occurring in the accumulation interval.
P-bit Err Secs	P-bit errored seconds (PES) is a second with one or more PCVs, one or more Out-of-Frame defects, or a detected incoming AIS. This gauge is not incremented when unavailable seconds are counted.
P-bit Severely Err Secs	P-bit severely errored seconds (PSES) is a second with 44 or more PCVs, one or more Out-of-Frame defects, or a detected incoming AIS. This gauge is not incremented when unavailable seconds are counted.
Severely Err Framing Secs	Severely errored framing second (SEFS) is a second with one or more Out-of-Frame defects or a detected incoming AIS.
Unavailable Secs	Unavailable seconds (UAS) are calculated by counting the number of seconds that the interface is unavailable. For more information, refer to RFC 1407.
Line Err Secs	Line errored second (LES) is a second in which one or more code violations occurred or one or more LOS defects.
C-bit Errored Secs	C-bit errored second (CES) is a second with one or more C-bit code violations (CCV), one or more Out-of-Frame defects, or a detected incoming AIS. This gauge is not incremented when UASs are counted.
C-bit Severely Errored Secs	C-bit severely errored second (CSES) is a second with 44 or more CCVs, one or more Out-of-Frame defects, or a detected incoming AIS. This gauge is not incremented when UASs are counted.

Table 23–17 *Show Controller T3 Field Descriptions, Continued*

Field	Description
Total Data (last 1 15 minute intervals)	Shows the last 15-minute accumulation period.
T1 1 is up	T1 channel is operating. The channel's state can be up, down, or administratively down. Loopback conditions are shown by (Locally looped) or (Remotely looped).
speed	Speed of the T1 channel in kbps.
non-inverted data	Indicates whether the T1 channel is configured for inverted data.
timeslots	Timeslots assigned to the T1 channel.
FDL per AT&T 54016 spec.	Performance monitoring is via Facility Data Link per ANSI T1.403.
No alarms detected	Any alarms detected by the T1 controller are displayed here. Possible alarms are as follows: • Transmitter is sending remote alarm. • Transmitter is sending AIS. • Receiver has loss of signal. • Receiver is getting AIS. • Receiver has loss of frame. • Receiver has remote alarm. • Receiver has no alarms.
Framing is ESF	Type of framing used on the T1 channel. Values are ESF or SF.
LineCode is B8ZS	Type of line coding used on the T1 channel. Values are B8ZS or AMI.
Clock Source is Internal	Clock source on the T1 channel. Values are internal or line.
Path Code Violations	Path coding violation (PCV) error event is a frame synchronization bit error in the D4 and E1-noCRC formats or a CRC error in the ESF and E1-CRC formats.
Slip Secs	Controlled slip second (CSS) is a one-second interval containing one or more controlled slips.

Table 23–17   *Show Controller T3 Field Descriptions, Continued*

Field	Description
Fr Loss Secs	Frame loss seconds (SELS) is the number of seconds an Out-of-Frame (OOF) error is detected.
Line Err Secs	Line errored second (LES) is a second in which one or more line code violation errors are detected.
Degraded Mins	Degraded minute (DM) is one in which the estimated error rate exceeds 1E-6 but does not exceed 1E-3. For more information, refer to RFC 1406.
Errored Secs	Errored second (ES) is a second with one or more path coding violations, one or more Out-of-Frame defects, or one or more controlled slip events or a detected AIS defect.
Bursty Err Secs	Bursty errored seconds (BES) is a second with fewer than 320 and more than one path coding violation error events, no Severely Errored Frame defects, and no detected incoming AIS defects. Controlled slips are not included in this parameter.
Severely Err Secs	Severely errored seconds (SES) is a second with 320 or more path code violation errors events, one or more Out-of-Frame defects, or a detected AIS defect.
Stuffed Secs	Stuffed second (SS) is a second in which one more bit stuffings take place. This happens when the Pulse Density Enforcer detects a potential violation in the output stream and inserts a 1 to prevent it. Such bit stuffings corrupt user data and indicate the network is misconfigured. This counter can be used to help diagnose this situation.

SHOW CONTROLLERS TOKEN

To display information about memory management and error counters on the Token Ring Interface Processor (TRIP) for the Cisco 7500 series, use the **show controllers token** privileged EXEC command.

> **show controllers token**

Syntax   Description

This command has no arguments or keywords.

Command Mode

Privileged EXEC

Usage Guidelines

This command first appeared in Cisco IOS Release 10.0.

Depending on the card being used, the output can vary. This command also displays information that is proprietary to Cisco Systems. Thus, the information that **show controllers token** displays is of primary use to Cisco technical personnel. Information that is useful to users can be obtained with the **show interfaces tokenring** command, which is described later in this chapter.

Sample Display

Sample output for the **show controllers token** command on the Cisco 7500 follows:

```
Router> show controllers token
Tokenring4/0: state administratively down
  current address: 0000.3040.8b4a, burned in address: 0000.3040.8b4a
  Last Ring Status: none
    Stats: soft: 0/0, hard: 0/0, sig loss: 0/0
           tx beacon: 0/0, wire fault 0/0, recovery: 0/0
           only station: 0/0, remote removal: 0/0
  Monitor state: (active), chip f/w: '000000........', [bridge capable]
    ring mode: 0"
    internal functional: 00000000 (00000000), group: 00000000 (00000000)
    internal addrs: SRB: 0000, ARB: 0000, EXB 0000, MFB: 0000
                    Rev: 0000, Adapter: 0000, Parms 0000
  Microcode counters:
    MAC giants 0/0, MAC ignored 0/0
    Input runts 0/0, giants 0/0, overrun 0/0
    Input ignored 0/0, parity 0/0, RFED 0/0
    Input REDI 0/0, null rcp 0/0, recovered rcp 0/0
    Input implicit abort 0/0, explicit abort 0/0
    Output underrun 0/0, tx parity 0/0, null tcp 0/0
    Output SFED 0/0, SEDI 0/0, abort 0/0
    Output False Token 0/0, PTT Expired 0/0
  Internal controller counts:
    line errors: 0/0,  internal errors: 0/0
    burst errors: 0/0, ari/fci errors: 0/0
    abort errors: 0/0, lost frame: 0/0
    copy errors: 0/0, rcvr congestion: 0/0
    token errors: 0/0, frequency errors: 0/0
  Internal controller smt state:
    Adapter MAC:    0000.0000.0000, Physical drop:    00000000
    NAUN Address:   0000.0000.0000, NAUN drop:        00000000
    Last source:    0000.0000.0000, Last poll:        0000.0000.0000
    Last MVID:      0000,           Last attn code:   0000
    Txmit priority: 0000,           Auth Class:       0000
    Monitor Error:  0000,           Interface Errors: 0000
    Correlator:     0000,           Soft Error Timer: 0000
```

```
        Local Ring:       0000,        Ring Status:        0000
        Beacon rcv type:  0000,        Beacon txmit type:  0000
        Beacon type:      0000,        Beacon NAUN:        0000.0000.0000
        Beacon drop:      00000000,    Reserved:           0000
        Reserved2:        0000
```

Table 23–18 describes key **show controllers token** display fields.

Table 23–18 *Show Controllers Token Field Descriptions for the Cisco 7500*

Field	Description
Tokenring4/0	Interface processor type, slot, and port.
Last Ring Status	Last abnormal ring condition. Can be any of the following: • Signal Loss • HW Removal • Remote Removal • Counter Overflow • Only station • Ring Recovery

Related Commands

show interfaces tokenring
show source bridge

SHOW CONTROLLERS VG-ANYLAN

Use the **show controllers vg-anylan** user EXEC command to display the controller information for the 100VG-AnyLAN port adapter on Cisco 7200 series routers and Cisco 7500 series routers.

> **show controllers vg-anylan** *slot/port-adapter/port* (on VIP cards in Cisco 7500 series)
> **show controllers vg-anylan** *slot/port* (Cisco 7200 series)

Syntax	Description
slot	Refer to the appropriate hardware manual for slot and port information.
port-adapter	Refer to the appropriate hardware manual for information about port adapter compatibility.
port	Refer to the appropriate hardware manual for slot and port information.

Command Mode

User EXEC

Usage Guidelines

This command first appeared in Cisco IOS Release 11.3.

The information displayed is generally useful for diagnostic tasks performed by technical support personnel only.

Sample Display

The following is sample output from the **show controllers vg-anylan** command:

```
Router# show controllers vg-anylan 3/0

Interface VG-AnyLAN3/0
Hardware is MC68852
 mc68852_ds=0x60A4C930, registers=0x3C300000, ib=0x4B056240
 rx ring entries=31, tx ring entries=31
 rxring=0x4B056340, rxr shadow=0x60A4CA08, rx_head=0, rx_tail=0
 txring=0x4B057180, txr shadow=0x60A4D07C, tx_head=0, tx_tail=2,
tx_count=2,

 MC68852 Registers:
 hw_id: 5048, hw_id & page: 7053, opr1=0x26, opr2=0x2C, opr3=0x00
  Page 0 - Performance:
  isr=0x3400, imr=0x0A0A, flreg=0x0000
  xfrct=0xC07E0080, rxcnt=0, txcnt=1F
  Page 1 - MAC Address/Hash Table:
  addrlow= 6009B9, addrhigh=9B1809B9,hash bytes=06 00 20 00 00 00 00 00
  Page 2 - Hardware Mapping:
  mmmsw=0x3785, mmlsw=0x0000, bmreg =0x04
  Page 4 - LAN Configuration:
  tccnf1=0x00, tccnf2=0x01
  vccnf=0x99, vtrrg=0x0020, valow1=0x0000, valow2=0x0000
  maccr1=0xBE, maccr2=0x00, maccr3=0x04, maccr4=0x03
  Page 5 - MMU Registers:
  rx mem stop addr=0xFF03, tx mem stop addr=0xFF07
 MC68852 PCI registers:
  bus_no=6, device_no=0
  CFID=0x0005101A, CFCS=0x02800005, CFRV=0x02000000, CFLT=0x0000F800
  CBIO=0x00006001, CBMA=0x00000000, CFIT=0x20080100, CFDA=0x0000000C

 Actel Hardware CAM Control Registers:
  CAM DEVICE BASE: 0x3C300800  Register Address: 0x3C300C00
  CSR: 0x8000  CAMCR: 0xFFFF
  USAR: 0000  MSAR: 0000  LSAR: 0000
  FIFOCR: 0x8000  WRMASK: 0x0080
  COMPARAND REG: 0000.0000.0000
  PERSISTENT SOURCE: 0x0   PERSISTENT DEST: 0xFD010000
```

Part III

Command Reference

```
ACTEL CAM PCI registers:
 bus_no=6, device_no=1
 CFID=0x555511AA, CFCS=0x04800003, CFRV=0xF0F0F001, CFLT=0x00000000
 CBIO=0x00006800, CBMA=0x00000000, CFIT=0x00000000, CFDA=0x00000000
 pak_to_host=0x0, filtered_pak=0
 throttled=0, enabled=0, disabled=0
 tx_carrier_loss=0
 fatal_tx_err=0, mult_ovfl=0
```

SHOW DIAGBUS

Use the **show diagbus** privileged EXEC command to display diagnostic information about the controller, interface processor, and port adapters associated with a specified slot of a Cisco 7200 series or Cisco 7500 series router.

show diagbus [*slot*]

Syntax	Description
slot	Refer to the appropriate hardware manual for slot and port information.

Command Mode
Privileged EXEC

Usage Guidelines
This command first appeared in Cisco IOS Release 11.2.

Sample Displays
The following is sample output for the Cisco 7513 with a VIP2 interface processor board in slot 8. This card has two four-port Token Ring port adapters located in port adapter bays 0 and 1.

```
Router# show diagbus 8
Slot 8:
        Physical slot 8, ~physical slot 0x7, logical slot 8, CBus 0
        Microcode Status 0x4
        Master Enable, LED, WCS Loaded
        Board is analyzed
        Pending I/O Status: None
        EEPROM format version 1
        VIP2 controller, HW rev 2.2, board revision UNKNOWN
        Serial number: 03341418  Part number: 73-1684-02
        Test history: 0x00        RMA number: 00-00-00
        Flags: cisco 7000 board; 7500 compatible

        EEPROM contents (hex):
          0x20: 01 15 02 02 00 32 FC 6A 49 06 94 02 00 00 00 00
          0x30: 07 2B 00 2A 1A 00 00 00 00 00 00 00 00 00 00 00
```

```
Slot database information:
Flags: 0x4      Insertion time: 0x3188 (01:20:53 ago)

Controller Memory Size: 8 MBytes

PA Bay 0 Information:
        Token Ring PA, 4 ports
        EEPROM format version 1
        HW rev 1.1, Board revision 0
        Serial number: 02827613  Part number: 73-1390-04

PA Bay 1 Information:
        Token Ring PA, 4 ports
        EEPROM format version 1
        HW rev 1.1, Board revision 88
        Serial number: 02023786  Part number: 73-1390-04
```

The following is sample output from the **show diagbus** command for the Ethernet interface in slot 2 on a Cisco 7200 series router:

```
Router# show diagbus 2

Slot 2:
        Ethernet port adapter, 8 ports
        Port adapter is analyzed
        Port adapter insertion time 1d18h ago
        Hardware revision 1.0        Board revision K0
        Serial number    2023387     Part number    73-1391-03
        Test history     0x0         RMA number     00-00-00
        EEPROM format version 1
        EEPROM contents (hex):
          0x20: 01 01 01 00 00 1E DF DB 49 05 6F 03 00 00 00 00
          0x30: A0 00 00 00 00 00 00 00 00 00 00 00 00 00 00 00
```

SHOW HUB

To display information about the hub (repeater) on an Ethernet interface of a Cisco 2505 or Cisco 2507, use the **show hub** EXEC command.

show hub [**ethernet** *number* [*port* [*end-port*]]]

Syntax	Description
ethernet	(Optional) Indicates that this is an Ethernet hub.
number	(Optional) Hub number, starting with 0. Because there is currently only one hub, this number is 0.

Syntax	Description
port	(Optional) Port number on the hub. On the Cisco 2505, port numbers range from 1 through 8. On the Cisco 2507, port numbers range from 1 through 16. If a second port number follows, then this port number indicates the beginning of a port range.
end-port	(Optional) Ending port number of a range.

Command Mode

EXEC

Usage Guidelines

This command first appeared in Cisco IOS Release 10.3.

If you do not specify a port or port range for the **show hub** command, the command displays all ports (for example, ports 1 through 16 on a Cisco 2507) by default. Therefore, the commands **show hub**, **show hub ethernet 0**, and **show hub ethernet 0 1 16** all produce the same result.

If no ports are specified, the command displays some additional data about the internal port. The internal port is the hub's connection to Ethernet interface 0 inside the box. Ethernet interface 0 still exists; physical access to the interface is via the hub.

Sample Displays

The following is sample output from the **show hub** command for hub 0, port 2 only:

```
Router# show hub ethernet 0 2

Port 2 of 16 is administratively down, link state is down
  0 packets input, 0 bytes
  0 errors with 0 collisions
      (0 FCS, 0 alignment, 0 too long,
       0 short, 0 runts, 0 late,
       0 very long, 0 rate mismatches)
  0 auto partitions, last source address (none)
  Last clearing of "show hub" counters never

Repeater information (Connected to Ethernet0)
  2792429 bytes seen with 18 collisions, 1 hub resets
  Version/device ID 0/1 (0/1)
  Last clearing of "show hub" counters never
```

The following is sample output from the **show hub** command for hub 0, all ports:

```
Router# show hub ethernet 0

Port 1 of 16 is administratively down, link state is up
  2458 packets input, 181443 bytes
```

```
    3 errors with 18 collisions
       (0 FCS, 0 alignment, 0 too long,
        0 short, 3 runts, 0 late,
        0 very long, 0 rate mismatches)
    0 auto partitions, last source address was 0000.0cff.e257
    Last clearing of "show hub" counters never
    .
    .
    .
  Port 16 of 16 is down, link state is down
    0 packets input, 0 bytes
    0 errors with 0 collisions
       (0 FCS, 0 alignment, 0 too long,
        0 short, 0 runts, 0 late,
        0 very long, 0 rate mismatches)
    0 auto partitions, last source address (none)
    Last clearing of "show hub" counters never

  Repeater information (Connected to Ethernet0)
    2792429 bytes seen with 18 collisions, 1 hub resets
    Version/device ID 0/1 (0/1)
    Last clearing of "show hub" counters never

  Internal Port (Connected to Ethernet0)
    36792 packets input, 4349525 bytes
    0 errors with 14 collisions
       (0 FCS, 0 alignment, 0 too long,
        0 short, 0 runts, 0 late,
        0 very long, 0 rate mismatches)
    0 auto partitions, last source address (none)
    Last clearing of "show hub" counters never
```

Table 23–19 describes significant fields shown in the display.

Table 23–19 *Show Hub Field Descriptions*

Field	Description
Port ... of ... is administratively down	Port number out of total ports; indicates whether the interface hardware is currently active, or down due to the following: • The link-state test failed. • The MAC address mismatched when source address configured. • It has been taken down by an administrator.
link state is up	Indicates whether port has been disabled by the link-test function. If the link-test function is disabled by the user, nothing will be shown here.
packets input	Total number of error-free packets received by the system.

Table 23–19 *Show Hub Field Descriptions, Continued*

Field	Description
bytes	Total number of bytes, including data and MAC encapsulation, in the error-free packets received by the system.
errors	Sum of FCS, alignment, too long, short, runts, very long, and rate mismatches.
collisions	Number of messages retransmitted due to Ethernet collisions.
FCS	Counter for the number of frames detected on the port with an invalid frame-check sequence.
alignment	Counter for the number of frames of valid length (64 bytes to 1,518 bytes) that have been detected on the port with an FCS error and a framing error.
too long	Counter for the number of frames that exceed the maximum valid packet length of 1,518 bytes.
short	Counter for the number of instances when activity is detected with a duration less than 74-82 bit times.
runts	Number of packets that are discarded because they are smaller than the medium's minimum packet size. For example, any Ethernet packet that is less than 64 bytes is considered a runt.
late	Counter for the number of instances when a collision is detected after 480-565 bit times in the frame.
very long	Counter for the number of times the transmitter is active in excess of 4 ms to 7.5 ms.
rate mismatches	Counter for the number of occurrences when the frequency, or data rate of incoming signal, is noticably different from the local transmit frequency.
auto partitions	Counter for the number of instances where the repeater has partitioned the port from the network.
last source address	Source address of last packet received by this port. Indicates "none" if no packets have been received since power on or a hub reset.
Last clearing of "show hub" counters	Elapsed time since **clear hub counters** command. Indicates "never" if counters have never been cleared.
Repeater information (Connected to Ethernet0)	Indicates that the following information is about the hub connected to the Ethernet interface shown.

Table 23-19 *Show Hub Field Descriptions, Continued*

Field	Description
... bytes seen with ... collisions, ... hub resets	Hub resets is the number of times the hub has been reset by network management software or by the **clear hub** command.
Version/device ID 0/1 (0/1)	Hub hardware version. IMR+ version device of daughter board.
Internal Port (Connected to Ethernet0)	Set of counters for the internal AUI port connected to the Ethernet interface.

Related Commands

hub

SHOW INTERFACES

Use the **show interfaces** EXEC command to display statistics for all interfaces configured on the router or access server. The resulting output varies, depending on the network for which an interface has been configured.

> **show interfaces** [*type number*] [*first*] [*last*] [**accounting**]
>
> **show interfaces** [*type slot/port*] [**accounting**] (for Cisco 7200 series, and for the Cisco 7500 series with a Packet over SONET Interface Processor)
>
> **show interface** [*type slot/port-adapter/port*] [**ethernet** | **serial**] (for ports on VIP cards in the Cisco 7500 series routers)

Syntax	Description
type	(Optional) Interface type. Allowed values for type include **async, bri0, ethernet, fastethernet, fddi, hssi, loopback, null, serial, tokenring,** and **tunnel**.

For the Cisco 4000 series, *type* can be **e1, ethernet, fastethernet, fddi, serial, t1,** and **token**. For the Cisco 4500 series, *type* can also include **atm**.

For the Cisco 7000 family, *type* can be **atm, e1, ethernet, fastethernet, fddi, serial, t1,** and **tokenring**.

For the Cisco 7500 series, *type* can also include **posi**. |
| *number* | (Optional) Port number on the selected interface. |

Syntax	Description
first last	(Optional) For the Cisco 2500 and 3000 ISDN Basic Rate Interface (BRI) only. The argument *first* can be either 1 or 2. The argument *last* can be only 2, indicating B-channels 1 and 2.
	D-channel information is obtained by using the command without the optional arguments.
accounting	(Optional) Displays the number of packets of each protocol type that have been sent through the interface.
slot	Refer to the appropriate hardware manual for slot and port information.
port	Refer to the appropriate hardware manual for slot and port information.
port -adapter	Refer to the appropriate hardware manual for information about port adapter compatibility.

Command Mode

EXEC

Usage Guidelines

This command first appeared in Cisco IOS Release 10.0.

The **show interfaces** command displays statistics for the network interfaces. The resulting display on the Cisco 7200 series shows the interface processors in slot order. If you add interface processors after booting the system, they will appear at the end of the list, in the order in which they were inserted.

If you use the **show interfaces** command on the Cisco 7200 series without the *slot/port* arguments, information for all interface types will be shown. For example, if you type **show interfaces ethernet,** you will receive information for all ethernet, serial, Token Ring, and FDDI interfaces. Only by adding the *type slot/port* argument can you specify a particular interface.

If you enter a **show interfaces** command for an interface type that has been removed from the router or access server, interface statistics will be displayed accompanied by the following text: "Hardware has been removed."

If you use the **show interfaces** command on a router or access server for which interfaces are configured to use weighted fair queueing through the **fair-queue** interface command, additional information is displayed. This information consists of the current and high-water mark number of flows.

You will use the **show interfaces** command frequently while configuring and monitoring devices. The various forms of the **show interfaces** commands are described in detail in the sections immediately following this command.

Sample Display

The following is sample output from the **show interfaces** command. Because your display will depend on the type and number of interface cards in your router or access server, only a portion of the display is shown.

```
Router# show interfaces

Ethernet 0 is up, line protocol is up
    Hardware is MCI Ethernet, address is 0000.0c00.750c (bia 0000.0c00.750c)
    Internet address is 131.108.28.8, subnet mask is 255.255.255.0
    MTU 1500 bytes, BW 10000 Kbit, DLY 100000 usec, rely 255/255, load 1/255
    Encapsulation ARPA, loopback not set, keepalive set (10 sec)
    ARP type: ARPA, ARP Timeout 4:00:00
    Last input 0:00:00, output 0:00:00, output hang never
    Last clearing of "show interface" counters 0:00:00
    Output queue 0/40, 0 drops; input queue 0/75, 0 drops
    Five minute input rate 0 bits/sec, 0 packets/sec
    Five minute output rate 2000 bits/sec, 4 packets/sec
        1127576 packets input, 447251251 bytes, 0 no buffer
        Received 354125 broadcasts, 0 runts, 0 giants
        0 input errors, 0 CRC, 0 frame, 0 overrun, 0 ignored, 0 abort
        5332142 packets output, 496316039 bytes, 0 underruns
        0 output errors, 432 collisions, 0 interface resets, 0 restarts
---More---
```

Sample Display with Custom Output Queuing

The following shows partial sample output when custom output queuing is enabled:

```
Last clearing of "show interface" counters 0:00:06
Input queue: 0/75/0 (size/max/drops); Total output drops: 21
Output queues: (queue #: size/max/drops)
    0: 14/20/14 1: 0/20/6 2: 0/20/0 3: 0/20/0 4: 0/20/0 5: 0/20/0
    6: 0/20/0 7: 0/20/0 8: 0/20/0 9: 0/20/0 10: 0/20/0
```

When custom queuing is enabled, the drops accounted for in the output queues result from bandwidth limitation for the associated traffic and leads to queue length overflow. Total output drops include drops on all custom queues as well as the system queue. Fields are described with the Weighted Fair Queuing output in Table 23–20.

Sample Display Including Weighted-Fair-Queuing Output

For each interface on the router or access server that's configured to use weighted fair queuing, the **show interfaces** command displays the information beginning with *Input queue:* in the following display:

```
Router# show interfaces

Ethernet 0 is up, line protocol is up
    Hardware is MCI Ethernet, address is 0000.0c00.750c (bia 0000.0c00.750c)
    Internet address is 131.108.28.8, subnet mask is 255.255.255.0
    MTU 1500 bytes, BW 10000 Kbit, DLY 100000 usec, rely 255/255, load 1/255
    Encapsulation ARPA, loopback not set, keepalive set (10 sec)
```

```
        ARP type: ARPA, ARP Timeout 4:00:00
        Last input 0:00:00, output 0:00:00, output hang never
        Last clearing of "show interface" counters 0:00:00
        Output queue 0/40, 0 drops; input queue 0/75, 0 drops
        Five minute input rate 0 bits/sec, 0 packets/sec
        Five minute output rate 2000 bits/sec, 4 packets/sec
            1127576 packets input, 447251251 bytes, 0 no buffer
            Received 354125 broadcasts, 0 runts, 0 giants
            0 input errors, 0 CRC, 0 frame, 0 overrun, 0 ignored, 0 abort
            5332142 packets output, 496316039 bytes, 0 underruns
            0 output errors, 432 collisions, 0 interface resets, 0 restarts
      Input queue: 0/75/0 (size/max/drops); Total output drops: 0
      Output queue: 7/64/0 (size/threshold/drops)
            Conversations 2/9 (active/max active)
```

Table 23–20 describes the input queue and output queue fields shown in this display.

Table 23–20   *Weighted-Fair-Queuing Output Fields*

Field	Description
Input queue:	
• size	Current size of the input queue.
• max	Maximum size of the queue.
• drops	Number of messages discarded in this interval.
• Total output drops	Total number of messages discarded in this session.
Output queue:	
• size	Current size of the output queue.
• threshold	Congestive-discard threshold. Number of messages in the queue after which new messages for high-bandwidth conversations are dropped.
• drops	Number of dropped messages.
• Conversations: active	Number of currently active conversations.
• Conversations: max active	Maximum number of concurrent conversations allowed.

Sample Display with Accounting Option

To display the number of packets of each protocol type that have been sent through all configured interfaces, use the **show interfaces accounting** EXEC command. When you use the **accounting** option, only the accounting statistics are displayed.

NOTES

Except for protocols that are encapsulated inside other protocols, such as IP over X.25, the accounting option also shows the total of all bytes sent and received, including the MAC header. For example, it totals the size of the Ethernet packet or the size of a packet that includes HDLC encapsulation.

Table 23–21 lists the protocols for which per-packet accounting information is kept.

Table 23–21 *Per-Packet Counted Protocols*

Protocol	Notes
Apollo	No note.
AppleTalk	No note.
ARP	For IP, Apollo, Frame Relay, SMDS.
CLNS	No note.
DEC MOP	The routers use MOP packets to advertise their existence to Digital Equipment Corporation machines that use the MOP protocol. A router periodically broadcasts MOP packets to identify itself as a MOP host. This results in MOP packets being counted, even when DECnet is not being actively used.
DECnet	No note.
HP Probe	No note.
IP	No note.
LAN Manager	LAN Network Manager and IBM Network Manager.
Novell	No note.
Serial Tunnel	SDLC.
Spanning Tree	No note.
SR Bridge	No note.
Transparent Bridge	No note.
VINES	No note.
XNS	No note.

Part
III

Command Reference

Sample Show Interfaces Accounting Display

The following is sample output from the **show interfaces accounting** command:

```
Router# show interfaces accounting

Interface TokenRing0 is disabled

Ethernet0
                Protocol    Pkts In    Chars In    Pkts Out   Chars Out
                      IP     873171   735923409       34624     9644258
                  Novell     163849    12361626       57143     4272468
                 DEC MOP          0           0           1          77
                     ARP      69618     4177080        1529       91740
Interface Serial0 is disabled

Ethernet1
                Protocol    Pkts In    Chars In    Pkts Out   Chars Out
                      IP          0           0          37       11845
                  Novell          0           0        4591      275460
                 DEC MOP          0           0           1          77
                     ARP          0           0           7         420

Interface Serial1 is disabled
Interface Ethernet2 is disabled
Interface Serial2 is disabled
Interface Ethernet3 is disabled
Interface Serial3 is disabled
Interface Ethernet4 is disabled
Interface Ethernet5 is disabled
Interface Ethernet6 is disabled
Interface Ethernet7 is disabled
Interface Ethernet8 is disabled
Interface Ethernet9 is disabled

Fddi0
                Protocol    Pkts In    Chars In    Pkts Out   Chars Out
                  Novell          0           0         183       11163
                     ARP          1          49           0           0
```

When the output indicates an interface is "disabled," the router has received excessive errors (over 5,000 in a keepalive period).

SHOW INTERFACES ETHERNET

Use the **show interfaces ethernet** privileged EXEC command to display information about an Ethernet interface on the router.

> **show interfaces ethernet** *unit* [**accounting**]
> **show interfaces ethernet** [*slot/port*] [**accounting**] (for the Cisco 7200 series and Cisco 7500)
> **show interfaces ethernet** [*type slot/port-adapter/port*] (for ports on VIP cards in the Cisco 7500 series routers)

Syntax	Description
unit	Must match a port number on the selected interface.
accounting	(Optional) Displays the number of packets of each protocol type that have been sent through the interface.
slot	Refer to the appropriate hardware manual for slot and port information.
port	Refer to the appropriate hardware manual for slot and port information.
port-adapter	Refer to the appropriate hardware manual for information about port adapter compatibility.

Command Mode

Privileged EXEC

Usage Guidelines

This command first appeared in Cisco IOS Release 10.0.

If you do not provide values for the argument *unit* (or *slot* and *port* on the Cisco 7200 series or slot and port adapter on the Cisco 7500 series), the command will display statistics for all network interfaces. The optional keyword **accounting** displays the number of packets of each protocol type that have been sent through the interface.

Sample Display

The following is sample output from the **show interfaces** command for the Ethernet 0 interface:

```
Router# show interfaces ethernet 0

Ethernet 0 is up, line protocol is up
    Hardware is MCI Ethernet, address is aa00.0400.0134 (bia 0000.0c00.4369)
    Internet address is 131.108.1.1, subnet mask is 255.255.255.0
    MTU 1500 bytes, BW 10000 Kbit, DLY 1000 usec, rely 255/255, load 1/255
    Encapsulation ARPA, loopback not set, keepalive set (10 sec)
    ARP type: ARPA, PROBE, ARP Timeout 4:00:00
    Last input 0:00:00, output 0:00:00, output hang never
    Output queue 0/40, 0 drops; input queue 0/75, 2 drops
    Five minute input rate 61000 bits/sec, 4 packets/sec
    Five minute output rate 1000 bits/sec, 2 packets/sec
        2295197 packets input, 305539992 bytes, 0 no buffer
        Received 1925500 broadcasts, 0 runts, 0 giants
        3 input errors, 3 CRC, 0 frame, 0 overrun, 0 ignored, 0 abort
        0 input packets with dribble condition detected
        3594664 packets output, 436549843 bytes, 0 underruns
        8 output errors, 1790 collisions, 10 interface resets, 0 restarts
```

Table 23–22 describes significant fields shown in the display.

Table 23–22 *Show Interfaces Ethernet Field Descriptions*

Field	Description
Ethernet ... is up ...is administratively down	Indicates whether the interface hardware is currently active and if it has been taken down by an administrator. "Disabled" indicates the router has received over 5,000 errors in a keepalive interval, which is 10 seconds by default.
line protocol is {up | down | administratively down}	Indicates whether the software processes that handle the line protocol believe the interface is usable (that is, whether keepalives are successful) or whether it has been taken down by an administrator.
Hardware	Hardware type (for example, MCI Ethernet, SCI, cBus Ethernet) and address.
Internet address	Internet address followed by subnet mask.
MTU	Maximum Transmission Unit of the interface.
BW	Bandwidth of the interface in kilobits per second.
DLY	Delay of the interface in microseconds.
rely	Reliability of the interface as a fraction of 255 (255/255 is 100 percent reliability), calculated as an exponential average over five minutes.
load	Load on the interface as a fraction of 255 (255/255 is completely saturated), calculated as an exponential average over five minutes.
Encapsulation	Encapsulation method assigned to interface.
ARP type:	Type of Address Resolution Protocol assigned.
loopback	Indicates whether loopback is set.
keepalive	Indicates whether keepalives are set.
Last input	Number of hours, minutes, and seconds since the last packet was successfully received by an interface. Useful for knowing when a dead interface failed.
Last output	Number of hours, minutes, and seconds since the last packet was successfully transmitted by an interface.

Table 23–22 *Show Interfaces Ethernet Field Descriptions, Continued*

Field	Description
output	Number of hours, minutes, and seconds since the last packet was successfully transmitted by the interface. Useful for knowing when a dead interface failed.
output hang	Number of hours, minutes, and seconds (or never) since the interface was last reset because of a transmission that took too long. When the number of hours in any of the "last" fields exceeds 24 hours, the number of days and hours is printed. If that field overflows, asterisks are printed.
Last clearing	Time at which the counters that measure cumulative statistics (such as number of bytes transmitted and received) shown in this report were last reset to zero. Note that variables that might affect routing (for example, load and reliability) are not cleared when the counters are cleared. *** indicates the elapsed time is too large to be displayed. 0:00:00 indicates the counters were cleared more than 2^{31}ms (and less than 2^{32}ms) ago.
Output queue, input queue, drops	Number of packets in output and input queues. Each number is followed by a slash, the maximum size of the queue, and the number of packets dropped due to a full queue.
Five minute input rate, Five minute output rate	Average number of bits and packets transmitted per second in the last five minutes. If the interface is not in promiscuous mode, it senses network traffic it sends and receives (rather than all network traffic). The five-minute input and output rates should be used only as an approximation of traffic per second during a given five-minute period. These rates are exponentially weighted averages with a time constant of five minutes. A period of four time constants must pass before the average will be within two percent of the instantaneous rate of a uniform stream of traffic over that period.
packets input	Total number of error-free packets received by the system.
bytes input	Total number of bytes, including data and MAC encapsulation, in the error-free packets received by the system.

Table 23-22   *Show Interfaces Ethernet Field Descriptions, Continued*

Field	Description
no buffers	Number of received packets discarded because there was no buffer space in the main system. Compare with ignored count. Broadcast storms on Ethernet networks and bursts of noise on serial lines are often responsible for no input buffer events.
Received ... broadcasts	Total number of broadcast or multicast packets received by the interface.
runts	Number of packets that are discarded because they are smaller than the medium's minimum packet size. For instance, any Ethernet packet that is less than 64 bytes is considered a runt.
giants	Number of packets that are discarded because they exceed the medium's maximum packet size. For example, any Ethernet packet that is greater than 1,518 bytes is considered a giant.
input error	Includes runts, giants, no-buffer, CRC, frame, overrun, and ignored counts. Other input-related errors also can cause the input-errors count to be increased, and some datagrams might have more than one error; therefore, this sum might not balance with the sum of enumerated input-error counts.
CRC	Cyclic redundancy checksum generated by the originating LAN station or far-end device does not match the checksum calculated from the data received. On a LAN, this usually indicates noise or transmission problems on the LAN interface or the LAN bus itself. A high number of CRCs is usually the result of collisions or a station transmitting bad data.
frame	Number of packets received incorrectly having a CRC error and a noninteger number of octets. On a LAN, this is usually the result of collisions or a malfunctioning Ethernet device.
overrun	Number of times the receiver hardware was unable to hand received data to a hardware buffer because the input rate exceeded the receiver's ability to handle the data.

Table 23–22 *Show Interfaces Ethernet Field Descriptions, Continued*

Field	Description
ignored	Number of received packets ignored by the interface because the interface hardware ran low on internal buffers. These buffers are different than the system buffers mentioned previously in the buffer description. Broadcast storms and bursts of noise can cause the ignored count to be increased.
input packets with dribble condition detected	Dribble bit error indicates that a frame is slightly too long. This frame-error counter is incremented just for informational purposes; the router accepts the frame.
packets output	Total number of messages transmitted by the system.
bytes	Total number of bytes, including data and MAC encapsulation, transmitted by the system.
underruns	Number of times that the transmitter has been running faster than the router can handle. This might never be reported on some interfaces.
output errors	Sum of all errors that prevented the final transmission of datagrams out of the interface being examined. Note that this might not balance with the sum of the enumerated output errors, as some datagrams might have more than one error, and others might have errors that do not fall into any of the specifically tabulated categories.
collisions	Number of messages retransmitted due to an Ethernet collision. This is usually the result of an overextended LAN (Ethernet or transceiver cable too long, more than two repeaters between stations, or too many cascaded multiport transceivers). A packet that collides is counted only once in output packets.

Table 23–22　*Show Interfaces Ethernet Field Descriptions, Continued*

Field	Description
interface resets	Number of times an interface has been completely reset. This can happen if packets queued for transmission were not sent within several seconds. On a serial line, this can be caused by a malfunctioning modem that is not supplying the transmit clock signal or by a cable problem. If the system notices that the carrier detect line of a serial interface is up, but the line protocol is down, it periodically resets the interface in an effort to restart it. Interface resets also can occur when an interface is looped back or shut down.
restarts	Number of times a Type 2 Ethernet controller was restarted because of errors.

Sample Display on Cisco 7500

The following sample output illustrates the **show interfaces ethernet** command on the Cisco 7500:

```
Router> show interfaces ethernet 4/2

Ethernet4/2 is up, line protocol is up
  Hardware is cxBus Ethernet, address is 0000.0c02.d0ce (bia 0000.0c02.d0ce)
  Internet address is 131.108.7.1, subnet mask is 255.255.255.0
  MTU 1500 bytes, BW 10000 Kbit, DLY 1000 usec, rely 255/255, load 1/255
  Encapsulation ARPA, loopback not set, keepalive set (10 sec)
  ARP type: ARPA, ARP Timeout 4:00:00
  Last input 0:00:00, output 0:00:09, output hang never
  Last clearing of "show interface" counters 0:56:40
  Output queue 0/40, 0 drops; input queue 0/75, 0 drops
  Five minute input rate 3000 bits/sec, 4 packets/sec
  Five minute output rate 0 bits/sec, 0 packets/sec
     4961 packets input, 715381 bytes, 0 no buffer
     Received 2014 broadcasts, 0 runts, 0 giants
     0 input errors, 0 CRC, 0 frame, 0 overrun, 0 ignored, 0 abort
     567 packets output, 224914 bytes, 0 underruns
     0 output errors, 168 collisions, 0 interface resets, 0 restarts
```

Sample Display with Accounting Option

The following is sample output from the **show interfaces ethernet** command with the **accounting** option on the Cisco 7500:

```
Router# show interfaces ethernet 4/2 accounting

Ethernet4/2
        Protocol    Pkts In   Chars In   Pkts Out   Chars Out
              IP       7344    4787842       1803     1535774
       Appletalk      33345    4797459      12781     1089695
         DEC MOP          0          0        127        9779
             ARP          7        420         39        2340
```

SHOW INTERFACES FASTETHERNET

Use the **show interface fastethernet** EXEC command to display information about the FastEthernet interfaces.

> **show interfaces fastethernet** [*number*] (Cisco 4500 and Cisco 4700)
> **show interfaces fastethernet** [*slot/port*] (Cisco 7200 series and Cisco 7500)
> **show interfaces fastethernet** [*slot/port-adapter/port*] (Cisco 7500 series with a VIP card)

Syntax	Description
number	(Optional) Port, connector, or interface card number. On a Cisco 4500 or Cisco 4700 router, specifies the NIM or NPM number. The numbers are assigned at the factory at the time of installation or when added to a system.
slot	Refer to the appropriate hardware manual for slot and port information.
port	Refer to the appropriate hardware manual for slot and port information.
port-adapter	Refer to the appropriate hardware manual for information about port-adapter compatibility.

Command Mode

EXEC

Usage Guidelines

This command first appeared in Cisco IOS Release 11.2.

Sample Displays

The following is a sample display for the **show interface fastethernet** on a Cisco 4500 router:

```
c4500-1# show interfaces fastethernet 0

FastEthernet0 is up, line protocol is up
  Hardware is DEC21140, address is 0000.0c0c.1111 (bia 0002.eaa3.5a60)
  Internet address is 11.0.0.1 255.0.0.0
  MTU 1500 bytes, BW 100000 Kbit, DLY 100 usec, rely 255/255, load 1/255
  Encapsulation ARPA, loopback not set, keepalive not set, hdx, 100BaseTX
  ARP type: ARPA, ARP Timeout 4:00:00
  Last input never, output 0:00:16, output hang 0:28:01
  Last clearing of "show interface" counters 0:20:05
  Output queue 0/40, 0 drops; input queue 0/75, 0 drops
  5 minute input rate 0 bits/sec, 0 packets/sec
```

```
      5 minute output rate 0 bits/sec, 0 packets/sec
        0 packets input, 0 bytes, 0 no buffer
        Received 0 broadcasts, 0 runts, 0 giants
        0 input errors, 0 CRC, 0 frame, 0 overrun, 1786161921 ignored, 0 abort
        0 watchdog, 0 multicast
        0 input packets with dribble condition detected
        67 packets output, 8151 bytes, 0 underruns
        0 output errors, 0 collisions, 1 interface resets, 0 restarts
        0 babbles, 0 late collision, 0 deferred
        0 lost carrier, 0 no carrier
        0 output buffer failures, 0 output buffers swapped out
```

The following shows information specific to the first FEIP port in slot 0 on a Cisco 7500:

```
Router# show interface fastethernet 0/1

FastEthernet0/1 is administratively down, line protocol is down
    Hardware is cxBus FastEthernet, address is 0000.0c35.dc16 (bia 0000.0c35.dc16)
    Internet address is 1.1.0.64 255.255.0.0
    MTU 1500 bytes, BW 100000 Kbit, DLY 100 usec, rely 255/255, load 1/255
    Encapsulation ARPA, loopback not set, keepalive not set, half-duplex, RJ45 (or MII)
    ARP type: ARPA, ARP Timeout 4:00:00
    Last input never, output 2:03:52, output hang never
    Last clearing of "show interface" counters never
    Output queue 0/40, 0 drops; input queue 0/75, 1 drops
    5 minute input rate 0 bits/sec, 0 packets/sec
    5 minute output rate 0 bits/sec, 0 packets/sec
        0 packets input, 0 bytes, 0 no buffer
        Received 0 broadcasts, 0 runts, 0 giants
        0 input errors, 0 CRC, 0 frame, 0 overrun, 0 ignored, 0 abort
        0 watchdog, 0 multicast
        0 input packets with dribble condition detected
        5 packets output, 805 bytes, 0 underruns
        0 output errors, 0 collisions, 4 interface resets, 0 restarts
        0 babbles, 0 late collision, 0 deferred
        0 lost carrier, 0 no carrier
        0 output buffer failures, 0 output buffers swapped out
```

Table 23–23 describes the fields in these displays.

Table 23–23   *Show Interfaces FastEthernet Field Descriptions*

Field	Description
FastEthernet0 is … is up …is administratively down	Indicates whether the interface hardware is currently active and whether it has been taken down by an administrator.
line protocol is	Indicates whether the software processes that handle the line protocol consider the line usable or whether it has been taken down by an administrator.
Hardware	Hardware type (for example, MCI Ethernet, SCI, cBus Ethernet) and address.

Table 23–23   *Show Interfaces FastEthernet Field Descriptions, Continued*

Field	Description
Internet address	Internet address followed by subnet mask.
MTU	Maximum Transmission Unit of the interface.
BW	Bandwidth of the interface in kilobits per second.
DLY	Delay of the interface in microseconds.
rely	Reliability of the interface as a fraction of 255 (255/255 is 100 percent reliability), calculated as an exponential average over five minutes.
load	Load on the interface as a fraction of 255 (255/255 is completely saturated), calculated as an exponential average over five minutes.
Encapsulation	Encapsulation method assigned to interface.
ARP type:	Type of Address Resolution Protocol assigned.
loopback	Indicates whether loopback is set.
keepalive	Indicates whether keepalives are set.
Last input	Number of hours, minutes, and seconds since the last packet was successfully received by an interface. Useful for knowing when a dead interface failed.
output	Number of hours, minutes, and seconds since the last packet was successfully transmitted by the interface. Useful for knowing when a dead interface failed.
output hang	Number of hours, minutes, and seconds (or never) since the interface was last reset because of a transmission that took too long. When the number of hours in any of the "last" fields exceeds 24 hours, the number of days and hours is printed. If that field overflows, asterisks are printed.
Last clearing	Time at which the counters that measure cumulative statistics (such as number of bytes transmitted and received) shown in this report were last reset to zero. Note that variables that might affect routing (for example, load and reliability) are not cleared when the counters are cleared. *** indicates the elapsed time is too large to be displayed. 0:00:00 indicates the counters were cleared more than 2^{31}ms (and less than 2^{32}ms) ago.

Table 23–23 *Show Interfaces FastEthernet Field Descriptions, Continued*

Field	Description
Output queue, input queue, drops	Number of packets in output and input queues. Each number is followed by a slash, the maximum size of the queue, and the number of packets dropped due to a full queue.
5 minute input rate, 5 minute output rate	Average number of bits and packets transmitted per second in the last five minutes. If the interface is not in promiscuous mode, it senses network traffic it sends and receives (rather than all network traffic). The five-minute input and output rates should be used only as an approximation of traffic per second during a given five-minute period. These rates are exponentially weighted averages with a time constant of five minutes. A period of four time constants must pass before the average will be within two percent of the instantaneous rate of a uniform stream of traffic over that period.
packets input	Total number of error-free packets received by the system.
bytes	Total number of bytes, including data and MAC encapsulation, in the error-free packets received by the system.
no buffer	Number of received packets discarded because there was no buffer space in the main system. Compare with ignored count. Broadcast storms on Ethernets and bursts of noise on serial lines are often responsible for no input buffer events.
Received ... broadcasts	Total number of broadcast or multicast packets received by the interface.
runts	Number of packets that are discarded because they are smaller than the medium's minimum packet size. For instance, any Ethernet packet that is less than 64 bytes is considered a runt.
giants	Number of packets that are discarded because they exceed the medium's maximum packet size. For example, any Ethernet packet that is greater than 1,518 bytes is considered a giant.
input errors	Includes runts, giants, no buffer, CRC, frame, overrun, and ignored counts. Other input-related errors also can cause the input-errors count to be increased, and some datagrams might have more than one error; therefore, this sum might not balance with the sum of enumerated input-error counts.

Table 23–23 *Show Interfaces FastEthernet Field Descriptions, Continued*

Field	Description
CRC	Cyclic redundancy checksum generated by the originating LAN station or far-end device does not match the checksum calculated from the data received. On a LAN, this usually indicates noise or transmission problems on the LAN interface or the LAN bus itself. A high number of CRCs is usually the result of collisions or a station transmitting bad data.
frame	Number of packets received incorrectly having a CRC error and a noninteger number of octets. On a LAN, this is usually the result of collisions or a malfunctioning Ethernet device.
overrun	Number of times the receiver hardware was unable to hand received data to a hardware buffer because the input rate exceeded the receiver's ability to handle the data.
ignored	Number of received packets ignored by the interface because the interface hardware ran low on internal buffers. These buffers are different than the system buffers mentioned previously in the buffer description. Broadcast storms and bursts of noise can cause the ignored count to be increased.
abort	Number of packets whose receipt was aborted.
watchdog	Number of times watchdog receive timer expired. It happens when receiving a packet with length greater than 2,048.
multicast	Number of multicast packets received.
input packets with dribble condition detected	Dribble bit error indicates that a frame is slightly too long. This frame-error counter is incremented just for informational purposes; the router accepts the frame.
packets output	Total number of messages transmitted by the system.
bytes	Total number of bytes, including data and MAC encapsulation, transmitted by the system.
underruns	Number of times that the transmitter has been running faster than the router can handle. This might never be reported on some interfaces.

Table 23–23　*Show Interfaces FastEthernet Field Descriptions, Continued*

Field	Description
output errors	Sum of all errors that prevented the final transmission of datagrams out of the interface being examined. Note that this might not balance with the sum of the enumerated output errors, as some datagrams might have more than one error, and others might have errors that do not fall into any of the specifically tabulated categories.
collisions	Number of messages retransmitted due to an Ethernet collision. This is usually the result of an overextended LAN (Ethernet or transceiver cable too long, more than two repeaters between stations, or too many cascaded multiport transceivers). A packet that collides is counted only once in output packets.
interface resets	Number of times an interface has been completely reset. This can happen if packets queued for transmission were not sent within several seconds. On a serial line, this can be caused by a malfunctioning modem that is not supplying the transmit clock signal, or by a cable problem. If the system notices that the carrier detect line of a serial interface is up, but the line protocol is down, it periodically resets the interface in an effort to restart it. Interface resets also can occur when an interface is looped back or shut down.
restarts	Number of times a Type 2 Ethernet controller was restarted because of errors.
babbles	The transmit jabber timer expired.
late collision	Number of late collisions. Late collision happens when a collision occurs after transmitting the preamble.
deferred	Deferred indicates that the chip had to defer while ready to transmit a frame because the carrier was asserted.
lost carrier	Number of times the carrier was lost during transmission.
no carrier	Number of times the carrier was not present during the transmission.
output buffer failures	Number of failed buffers and number of buffers swapped out.

SHOW INTERFACES FDDI

To display information about the FDDI interface, use the **show interfaces fddi** EXEC command.

> **show interfaces fddi** *number* [**accounting**]
> **show interfaces fddi** [*slot/port*] [**accounting**] (Cisco 7000 series and Cisco 7200 series)
> **show interfaces fddi** [*slot/port-adapter/port*] [**accounting**] (Cisco 7500 series routers)

Syntax	Description
number	Port number on the selected interface.
accounting	(Optional) Displays the number of packets of each protocol type that have been sent through the interface.
slot	Refer to the appropriate hardware manual for slot and port information.
port	Refer to the appropriate hardware manual for slot and port information.
port-adapter	Refer to the appropriate hardware manual for information about port-adapter compatibility.

Command Mode

EXEC

Usage Guidelines

This command first appeared in Cisco IOS Release 10.0.

This information was modified in Cisco IOS Release 11.3 to include sample output for FDDI full-duplex, single- and multimode port adapters (PA-F/FD-SM and PA-F/FD-MM).

Sample Displays

The following is a sample partial display of FDDI-specific data from the **show interfaces fddi** command on a Cisco 7500 series router:

```
Router> show interfaces fddi 3/0

Fddi3/0 is up, line protocol is up
  Hardware is cxBus Fddi, address is 0000.0c02.adf1 (bia 0000.0c02.adf1)
  Internet address is 131.108.33.14, subnet mask is 255.255.255.0
  MTU 4470 bytes, BW 100000 Kbit, DLY 100 usec, rely 255/255, load 1/255
  Encapsulation SNAP, loopback not set, keepalive not set
  ARP type: SNAP, ARP Timeout 4:00:00
  Phy-A state is  active, neighbor is  B, cmt signal bits 008/20C, status ILS
  Phy-B state is  active, neighbor is  A, cmt signal bits 20C/008, status ILS
  ECM is in, CFM is thru, RMT is ring_op
  Token rotation 5000 usec, ring operational 21:32:34
```

```
Upstream neighbor 0000.0c02.ba83, downstream neighbor 0000.0c02.ba83
Last input 0:00:05, output 0:00:00, output hang never
Last clearing of "show interface" counters 0:59:10
Output queue 0/40, 0 drops; input queue 0/75, 0 drops
Five minute input rate 69000 bits/sec, 44 packets/sec
Five minute output rate 0 bits/sec, 1 packets/sec
    113157 packets input, 21622582 bytes, 0 no buffer
    Received 276 broadcasts, 0 runts, 0 giants
    0 input errors, 0 CRC, 0 frame, 0 overrun, 0 ignored, 0 abort
    4740 packets output, 487346 bytes, 0 underruns
    0 output errors, 0 collisions, 0 interface resets, 0 restarts
    0 transitions, 2 traces, 3 claims, 2 beacons
```

The following is a sample display of the **show interfaces fddi** command for the full-duplex FDDI port adapter on a Cisco 7500 series router:

```
Router# show interfaces fddi 0/1/0

Fddi0/1/0 is up, line protocol is up
    Hardware is cxBus FDDI, address is 0060.3e33.3608 (bia 0060.3e33.3608)
    Internet address is 2.1.1.1/24
    MTU 4470 bytes, BW 100000 Kbit, DLY 100 usec, rely 255/255, load 1/255
    Encapsulation SNAP, loopback not set, keepalive not set
    ARP type: SNAP, ARP Timeout 04:00:00
    FDX supported, FDX enabled, FDX state is operation
    Phy-A state is maintenance, neighbor is Unknown, status HLS
    Phy-B state is active, neighbor is A, status SILS
    ECM is in, CFM is c_wrap_b, RMT is ring_op,
    Requested token rotation 5000 usec, negotiated 4997 usec
    Configured tvx is 2500 usec
    LER for PortA = 0A, LER for PortB = 0A ring operational 00:02:45
    Upstream neighbor 0060.3e73.4600, downstream neighbor 0060.3e73.4600
    Last input 00:00:12, output 00:00:13, output hang never
    Last clearing of "show interface" counters never
    Queueing strategy: fifo
    Output queue 0/40, 0 drops; input queue 0/75, 0 drops
    5 minute input rate 0 bits/sec, 0 packets/sec
    5 minute output rate 0 bits/sec, 0 packets/sec
        62 packets input, 6024 bytes, 0 no buffer
        Received 18 broadcasts, 0 runts, 0 giants
        0 input errors, 0 CRC, 0 frame, 0 overrun, 0 ignored, 0 abort
        71 packets output, 4961 bytes, 0 underruns
        0 output errors, 0 collisions, 0 interface resets
        0 output buffer failures, 0 output buffers swapped out
        3 transitions, 0 traces,  100 claims, 0 beacon
```

Table 23–24 describes the **show interfaces fddi** display fields.

Table 23–24 *Show Interfaces FDDI Field Descriptions*

Field	Description
Fddi is {up │ down │ administratively down	Gives the interface processor unit number and tells whether the interface hardware is currently active and can transmit and receive or whether it has been taken down by an administrator.
line protocol is {up │ down}	Indicates whether the software processes that handle the line protocol consider the interface usable.
Hardware	Provides the hardware type, followed by the hardware address.
Internet address	IP address, followed by subnet mask.
MTU	Maximum transmission unit of the interface.
BW	Bandwidth of the interface in kilobits per second.
DLY	Delay of the interface in microseconds.
rely	Reliability of the interface as a fraction of 255 (255/255 is 100 percent reliability), calculated as an exponential average over five minutes.
load	Load on the interface as a fraction of 255 (255/255 is completely saturated), calculated as an exponential average over five minutes.
Encapsulation	Encapsulation method assigned to interface.
loopback	Indicates whether loopback is set.
keepalive	Indicates whether keepalives are set.
ARP type	Type of Address Resolution Protocol assigned.
FDX	Displays full-duplex information. Values are: not supported or supported. When the value is supported, the display indicates whether full-duplex is enabled or disabled. When enabled, the state of the FDX negotiation process is displayed. The negotiation states only relate to the full-duplex negotiation process. You must also ensure that the interface is up and working by looking at other fields in the **show interfaces fddi** command, such as line protocol and RMT. Negotiation states are:

Table 23–24   *Show Interfaces FDDI Field Descriptions, Continued*

Field	Description
	• idle—Interface is working but not in full-duplex mode yet. If persistent, it could mean that the interface did not meet all negotiation conditions (for example, there are more than two stations in the ring).
	• request—Interface is working but not in full-duplex mode yet. If persistent, it could mean that the remote interface does not support full-duplex or full duplex is not enabled on the interface.
	• confirm—Transient state.
	• operation—Negotiations completed successfully, and both stations are operating in full-duplex mode.
Phy-{A | B}	Lists the state the Physical A or Physical B connection is in, which is one of the following: off, active, trace, connect, next, signal, join, verify, or break.
neighbor	State of the neighbor:
	• A—Indicates that the connection management (CMT) process has established a connection with its neighbor. The bits received during the CMT signaling process indicate that the neighbor is a Physical A type dual attachment station (DAS) or concentrator that attaches to the primary ring IN and the secondary ring OUT when attaching to the dual ring.
	• S—Indicates that the CMT process has established a connection with its neighbor and that the bits received during the CMT signaling process indicate that the neighbor is one Physical type in a single attachment station (SAS).
	• B—Indicates that the CMT process has established a connection with its neighbor and that the bits received during the CMT signaling process indicate that the neighbor is a Physical B dual attachment station or concentrator that attaches to the secondary ring IN and the primary ring OUT when attaching to the dual ring.
	• M—Indicates that the CMT process has established a connection with its neighbor and that the bits received during the CMT signaling process indicate that the router's neighbor is a Physical M-type concentrator serving as a Master to a connected station or concentrator.

Table 23–24 *Show Interfaces FDDI Field Descriptions, Continued*

Field	Description
	• unk—Indicates that the network server has not completed the CMT process and, as a result, does not know about its neighbor.
cmt signal bits	Shows the transmitted/received CMT bits. The transmitted bits are 0x008 for a Physical A type and 0x20C for Physical B type. The number after the slash (/) is the received signal bits. If the connection is not active, the received bits are zero (0); see the line beginning Phy-B in the display. This applies to FIP interfaces only.
status	Status value displayed is the actual status on the fiber. The FDDI standard defines the following values:
	• LSU—Line State Unknown, the criteria for entering or remaining in any other line state have not been met.
	• NLS—Noise Line State is entered upon the occurrence of 16 potential noise events without satisfying the criteria for entry into another line state.
	• MLS—Master Line State is entered upon the receipt of eight or nine consecutive HQ or QH symbol pairs.
	• ILS—Idle Line State is entered upon receipt of four or five idle symbols.
	• HLS—Halt Line State is entered upon the receipt of 16 or 17 consecutive H symbols.
	• QLS—Quiet Line State is entered upon the receipt of 16 or 17 consecutive Q symbols or when carrier detect goes low.
	• ALS—Active Line State is entered upon receipt of a JK symbol pair when carrier detect is high.
	• OVUF—Elasticity buffer Overflow/Underflow. The normal states for a connected Physical type are ILS or ALS. If the report displays the QLS status, this indicates that the fiber is disconnected from Physical B, or that it is not connected to another Physical type, or that the other station is not running.

Table 23–24   *Show Interfaces FDDI Field Descriptions, Continued*

Field	Description
ECM is...	ECM is the SMT entity coordination management, which overlooks the operation of CFM and PCM. The ECM state can be one of the following: • out—Router is isolated from the network. • in—Router is actively connected to the network. This is the normal state for a connected router. • trace—Router is trying to localize a stuck beacon condition. • leave—Router is allowing time for all the connections to break before leaving the network. • path_test—Router is testing its internal paths. • insert—Router is allowing time for the optical bypass to insert. • check—Router is making sure optical bypasses switched correctly. • deinsert—Router is allowing time for the optical bypass to deinsert.
CFM is...	Contains information about the current state of the MAC connection. The Configuration Management state can be one of the following: • isolated—MAC is not attached to any Physical type. • wrap_a—MAC is attached to Physical A. Data is received on Physical A and transmitted on Physical A. • wrap_b—MAC is attached to Physical B. Data is received on Physical B and transmitted on Physical B. • wrap_s—MAC is attached to Physical S. Data is received on Physical S and transmitted on Physical S. This is the normal mode for a single attachment station (SAS). • thru—MAC is attached to Physical A and B. Data is received on Physical A and transmitted on Physical B. This is the normal mode for a dual attachment station (DAS) with one MAC. The ring has been operational for 1 minute and 42 seconds.

Table 23–24 *Show Interfaces FDDI Field Descriptions, Continued*

Field	Description
RMT is...	RMT (Ring Management) is the SMT MAC-related state machine. The RMT state can be one of the following: • isolated—MAC is not trying to participate in the ring. This is the initial state. • non_op—MAC is participating in ring recovery, and ring is not operational. • ring_op—MAC is participating in an operational ring. This is the normal state while the MAC is connected to the ring. • detect—Ring has been nonoperational for longer than normal. Duplicate address conditions are being checked. • non_op_dup—Indications have been received that the address of the MAC is a duplicate of another MAC on the ring. Ring is not operational. • ring_op_dup—Indications have been received that the address of the MAC is a duplicate of another MAC on the ring. Ring is operational in this state. • directed—MAC is sending beacon frames notifying the ring of the stuck condition. • trace—Trace has been initiated by this MAC, and the RMT state machine is waiting for its completion before starting an internal path test.
token rotation	Token rotation value is the default or configured rotation value as determined by the **fddi token-rotation-time** command. This value is used by all stations on the ring. The default is 5,000 microseconds. For FDDI full-duplex, this indicates the value in use prior to entering full-duplex operation.
negotiated	Actual (negotiated) target token rotation time.
ring operational	When the ring is operational, the displayed value will be the negotiated token rotation time of all stations on the ring. Operational times are displayed by the number of hours:minutes:seconds the ring has been up. If the ring is not operational, the message "ring not operational" is displayed.
Configured tvx	Transmission timer.
LER	Link error rate.

Part
III

Command Reference

Table 23-24 *Show Interfaces FDDI Field Descriptions, Continued*

Field	Description
Upstream | downstream neighbor	Displays the canonical MAC address of outgoing upstream and downstream neighbors. If the address is unknown, the value will be the FDDI unknown address (0x00 00 f8 00 00 00).
Last input	Number of hours, minutes, and seconds since the last packet was successfully received by an interface. Useful for knowing when a dead interface failed.
output	Number of hours, minutes, and seconds since the last packet was successfully transmitted by an interface.
output hang	Number of hours, minutes, and seconds (or never) since the interface was last reset because of a transmission that took too long. When the number of hours in any of the "last" fields exceeds 24 hours, the number of days and hours is printed. If that field overflows, asterisks are printed.
Last clearing	Time at which the counters that measure cumulative statistics (such as number of bytes transmitted and received) shown in this report were last reset to zero. Note that variables that might affect routing (for example, load and reliability) are not cleared when the counters are cleared. *** indicates the elapsed time is too large to be displayed. 0:00:00 indicates the counters were cleared more than 2^{31}ms (and less than 2^{32}ms) ago.
Queueing strategy	First-in, first-out queuing strategy (other queueing strategies you might see are priority-list, custom-list, and weighted-fair).
Output queue, input queue, drops	Number of packets in output and input queues. Each number is followed by a slash, the maximum size of the queue, and the number of packets dropped due to a full queue.
5 minute input rate 5 minute output rate	Average number of bits and packets transmitted per second in the last five minutes. The five-minute input and output rates should be used only as an approximation of traffic per second during a given five-minute period. These rates are exponentially weighted averages with a time constant of five minutes. A period of four time constants must pass before the average will be within two percent of the instantaneous rate of a uniform stream of traffic over that period.

Table 23–24 *Show Interfaces FDDI Field Descriptions, Continued*

Field	Description
packets input	Total number of error-free packets received by the system.
bytes	Total number of bytes, including data and MAC encapsulation, in the error-free packets received by the system.
no buffer	Number of received packets discarded because there was no buffer space in the main system. Compare with ignored count. Broadcast storms on Ethernet networks and bursts of noise on serial lines are often responsible for no input buffer events.
broadcasts	Total number of broadcast or multicast packets received by the interface.
runts	Number of packets that are discarded because they are smaller than the medium's minimum packet size.
giants	Number of packets that are discarded because they exceed the medium's maximum packet size.
CRC	Cyclic redundancy checksum generated by the originating LAN station or far-end device does not match the checksum calculated from the data received. On a LAN, this usually indicates noise or transmission problems on the LAN interface or the LAN bus itself. A high number of CRCs is usually the result of collisions or a station transmitting bad data.
frame	Number of packets received incorrectly that have a CRC error and a noninteger number of octets. On a LAN, this is usually the result of collisions or a malfunctioning Ethernet device. On an FDDI LAN, this also can be the result of a failing fiber (cracks) or a hardware malfunction.
overrun	Number of times the serial receiver hardware was unable to hand received data to a hardware buffer because the input rate exceeded the receiver's capability to handle the data.
ignored	Number of received packets ignored by the interface because the interface hardware ran low on internal buffers. These buffers are different from the system buffers mentioned previously in the buffer description. Broadcast storms and bursts of noise can cause the ignored count to be increased.
packets output	Total number of messages transmitted by the system.
bytes	Total number of bytes, including data and MAC encapsulation, transmitted by the system.

Part III

Command Reference

Table 23–24 *Show Interfaces FDDI Field Descriptions, Continued*

Field	Description
underruns	Number of transmit aborts (when the router cannot feed the transmitter fast enough).
output errors	Sum of all errors that prevented the final transmission of datagrams out of the interface being examined. Note that this might not balance with the sum of the enumerated output errors, because some datagrams can have more than one error, and others can have errors that do not fall into any of the specifically tabulated categories.
collisions	Because an FDDI ring cannot have collisions, this statistic is always zero.
interface resets	Number of times an interface has been reset. The interface may be reset by the administrator or automatically when an internal error occurs.
restarts	Should always be zero for FDDI interfaces.
output buffer failures	Number of no-resource errors received on the output.
output buffers swapped out	Number of packets swapped to DRAM.
transitions	The number of times the ring made a transition from ring-operational to ring-nonoperational, or vice versa. A large number of transitions indicates a problem with the ring or the interface.
traces	Trace count applies to the FCI, FCIT, and FIP. Indicates the number of times this interface started a trace.
claims	Pertains to FCIT and FIP only. Indicates the number of times this interface has been in claim state.
beacons	Pertains to FCIT and FIP only. Indicates the number of times the interface has been in beacon state.

The following is an example that includes the **accounting** option. When you use the **accounting** option, only the accounting statistics are displayed.

```
Router> show interfaces fddi 3/0 accounting

Fddi3/0
        Protocol    Pkts In   Chars In   Pkts Out   Chars Out
              IP       7344    4787842       1803     1535774
        Appletalk     33345    4797459      12781     1089695
```

```
DEC  MOP        0          0         127      9779
     ARP        7        420          39      2340
```

Table 23–25 describes the **show interfaces fddi** display fields.

Table 23–25   *Show Interfaces FDDI Field Descriptions—Accounting*

Field	Description
Protocol	Protocol that is operating on the interface.
Pkts In	Number of packets received for that protocol.
Chars In	Number of characters received for that protocol.
Pkts Out	Number of packets transmitted for that protocol.
Chars Out	Number of characters transmitted for that protocol.

SHOW INTERFACES HSSI

Use the **show interfaces hssi** privileged EXEC command to display information about the HSSI interface.

>   **show interfaces hssi** *unit* [**accounting**]
>   **show interfaces hssi** [*slot/port*] [**accounting**] (for the Cisco 7500 series)

Syntax	Description
unit	Must match a port number on the selected interface.
accounting	(Optional) Displays the number of packets of each protocol type that have been sent through the interface.
slot	Refer to the appropriate hardware manual for slot and port information.
port	Refer to the appropriate hardware manual for slot and port information.

Command Mode

Privileged EXEC

Usage Guidelines

This command first appeared in Cisco IOS Release 10.0.

Sample Displays

The following is sample output from the **show interfaces hssi** command when HSSI is enabled:

```
Router# show interfaces hssi 0

HSSI 0 is up, line protocol is up
```

```
Hardware is cBus HSSI
Internet address is 150.136.67.190, subnet mask is 255.255.255.0
MTU 4470 bytes, BW 45045 Kbit, DLY 20000 usec, rely 255/255, load 1/255
Encapsulation HDLC, loopback not set, keepalive set (10 sec)
Last input 0:00:03, output 0:00:00, output hang never
Output queue 0/40, 0 drops; input queue 0/75, 0 drops
Five minute input rate 0 bits/sec, 0 packets/sec
Five minute output rate 0 bits/sec, 0 packets/sec
     0 packets input, 0 bytes, 0 no buffer
     Received 0 broadcasts, 0 runts, 0 giants
               0 parity, 0 rx disabled
  0 input errors, 0 CRC, 0 frame, 0 overrun, 0 ignored, 0 abort
  17 packets output, 994 bytes, 0 underruns
  0 output errors, 0 applique, 4 interface resets, 0 restarts
  2 carrier transitions
```

Table 23–26 describes significant fields shown in the display.

Table 23–26 *Show Interfaces HSSI Field Descriptions*

Field	Description
HSSI is {up | down | administratively down}	Indicates whether the interface hardware is currently active (whether carrier detect is present) and whether it has been taken down by an administrator. "Disabled" indicates the router has received over 5,000 errors in a keepalive interval, which is 10 seconds by default.
line protocol is {up | down | administratively down}	Indicates whether the software processes that handle the line protocol considers the line usable (that is, whether keepalives are successful).
Hardware	Specifies the hardware type.
Internet address	Lists the Internet address followed by subnet mask.
MTU	Maximum Transmission Unit of the interface.
BW	Bandwidth of the interface in kilobits per second.
DLY	Delay of the interface in microseconds.
rely	Reliability of the interface as a fraction of 255 (255/255 is 100 percent reliability), calculated as an exponential average over five minutes.
load	Load on the interface as a fraction of 255 (255/255 is completely saturated), calculated as an exponential average over five minutes.
Encapsulation	Encapsulation method assigned to interface.
loopback	Indicates whether loopback is set and type of loopback test.
keepalive	Indicates whether keepalives are set.
Last input	Number of hours, minutes, and seconds since the last packet was successfully received by an interface. Useful for knowing when a dead interface failed.

Table 23–26 *Show Interfaces HSSI Field Descriptions, Continued*

Field	Description
Last output	Number of hours, minutes, and seconds since the last packet was successfully transmitted by an interface.
output hang	Number of hours, minutes, and seconds (or never) since the interface was last reset because of a transmission that took too long. When the number of hours in any of the "last" fields exceeds 24 hours, the number of days and hours is printed. If that field overflows, asterisks are printed.
Last clearing	Time at which the counters that measure cumulative statistics (such as number of bytes transmitted and received) shown in this report were last reset to zero. Note that variables that might affect routing (for example, load and reliability) are not cleared when the counters are cleared. *** indicates the elapsed time is too large to be displayed. 0:00:00 indicates the counters were cleared more than 2^{31}ms (and less than 2^{32}ms) ago.
Output queue, drops Input queue, drops	Number of packets in output and input queues. Each number is followed by a slash, the maximum size of the queue, and the number of packets dropped due to a full queue.
5 minute input rate, 5 minute output rate	Average number of bits and packets transmitted per second in the last five minutes.
packets input	Total number of error-free packets received by the system.
bytes input	Total number of bytes, including data and MAC encapsulation, in the error-free packets received by the system.
no buffer	Number of received packets discarded because there was no buffer space in the main system. Compare with ignored count. Broadcast storms on Ethernet networks and bursts of noise on serial lines are often responsible for no input buffer events.
broadcasts	Total number of broadcast or multicast packets received by the interface.
runts	Number of packets that are discarded because they are smaller than the medium's minimum packet size.
giants	Number of packets that are discarded because they exceed the medium's maximum packet size.
parity	Report of the parity errors on the HSSI.

Table 23–26 *Show Interfaces HSSI Field Descriptions, Continued*

Field	Description
rx disabled	Indicates the HSSI could not find a free buffer on the ciscoBus controller to reserve for use for the HSSI receiver. When this happens, the HSSI shuts down its receiver and waits until a buffer is available. Data is not lost unless a packet comes in and overflows the HSSI FIFO. Usually, the receive disables are frequent but do not last for long, and the number of dropped packets is less than the count in the "rx disabled" field. A receive-disabled condition can happen in systems that are under heavy traffic load and that have shorter packets. In this situation, the number of buffers available on the ciscoBus controller is at a premium. One way to alleviate this problem is to reduce the mtu on the HSSI interface from 4,500 (FDDI size) to 1,500 (Ethernet size). Doing so allows the software to take the fixed memory of the ciscoBus controller and divide it into a larger number of smaller buffers, rather than a small number of large buffers. Receive disables are not errors, so they are not included in any error counts.
input errors	Sum of all errors that prevented the receipt of datagrams on the interface being examined. This might not balance with the sum of the enumerated output errors, because some datagrams might have more than one error and others might have errors that do not fall into any of the specifically tabulated categories.
CRC	Cyclic redundancy checksum generated by the originating LAN station or far-end device does not match the checksum calculated from the data received. On a LAN, this usually indicates noise or transmission problems on the LAN interface or the LAN bus itself. A high number of CRCs is usually the result of collisions or a station transmitting bad data. On a serial link, CRCs usually indicate noise, gain hits, or other transmission problems on the data link. CRC errors are also reported when a far-end abort occurs, and when the idle flag pattern is corrupted. This makes it possible to get CRC errors even when there is no data traffic.
frame	Number of packets received incorrectly having a CRC error and a noninteger number of octets. On a serial line, this is usually the result of noise or other transmission problems.
overrun	Number of times the serial receiver hardware was unable to hand received data to a hardware buffer because the input rate exceeded the receiver's capability to handle the data.

Table 23–26 *Show Interfaces HSSI Field Descriptions, Continued*

Field	Description
ignored	Number of received packets ignored by the interface because the interface hardware ran low on internal buffers. These buffers are different than the system buffers mentioned previously in the buffer description. Broadcast storms and bursts of noise can cause the ignored count to be increased.
abort	Number of packets whose receipt was aborted.
packets output	Total number of messages transmitted by the system.
bytes output	Total number of bytes, including data and MAC encapsulation, transmitted by the system.
underruns	Number of times that the far-end transmitter has been running faster than the near-end router's receiver can handle.
congestion drop	Number of messages discarded because the output queue on an interface grew too long. This can happen on a slow, congested serial link.
output errors	Sum of all errors that prevented the final transmission of datagrams out of the interface being examined. Note that this might not balance with the sum of the enumerated output errors, as some datagrams might have more than one error, and others might have errors that do not fall into any of the specifically tabulated categories.
applique	Indicates an unrecoverable error has occurred on the HSA applique. The system then invokes an interface reset.
interface resets	Number of times an interface has been completely reset. This can happen if packets queued for transmission were not sent within several seconds' time. On a serial line, this can be caused by a malfunctioning modem that is not supplying the transmit clock signal, or by a cable problem. If the system notices that the carrier detect line of a serial interface is up, but the line protocol is down, it periodically resets the interface in an effort to restart it. Interface resets also can occur when an interface is looped back or shut down.
restarts	Number of times the controller was restarted because of errors.
carrier transitions	Number of times the carrier detect signal of the interface has changed state. Indicates modem or line problems if the carrier detect line is changing state often.
Protocol	Protocol that is operating on the interface.

Table 23–26 *Show Interfaces HSSI Field Descriptions, Continued*

Field	Description
Pkts In	Number of packets received for that protocol.
Chars In	Number of characters received for that protocol.
Pkts Out	Number of packets transmitted for that protocol.
Chars Out	Number of characters transmitted for that protocol.

The following is an example of the **show interfaces hssi** command on a Cisco 7500:

```
Router# show interfaces hssi 1/0

Hssi1/0 is up, line protocol is up
   Hardware is cxBus HSSI
   Internet address is 131.108.38.14, subnet mask is 255.255.255.0
   MTU 1500 bytes, BW 45045 Kbit, DLY 1000000 usec, rely 255/255, load 1/255
   Encapsulation HDLC, loopback not set, keepalive set (10 sec)
   Last input 0:00:00, output 0:00:08, output hang never
   Last clearing of "show interface" counters never
   Output queue 0/40, 0 drops; input queue 0/75, 0 drops
   Five minute input rate 1000 bits/sec, 2 packets/sec
   Five minute output rate 0 bits/sec, 0 packets/sec
      630573548 packets input, 2077237628 bytes, 0 no buffer
      Received 2832063 broadcasts, 0 runts, 0 giants
            0 parity, 1970 rx disabled
      113 input errors, 20 CRC, 93 frame, 0 overrun, 0 ignored, 0 abort
      629721628 packets output, 1934313295 bytes, 0 underruns
      0 output errors, 0 applique, 62 interface resets, 0 restarts
      309 carrier transitions
```

The following is an example of the **show interfaces hssi** command with the **accounting** option on a Cisco 7500:

```
Router# show interfaces hssi 1/0 accounting

HIP1/0
        Protocol    Pkts In    Chars In    Pkts Out   Chars Out
              IP       7344     4787842        1803     1535774
       Appletalk      33345     4797459       12781     1089695
         DEC MOP          0           0         127        9779
             ARP          7         420          39        2340
```

SHOW INTERFACES IP-BRIEF

To display a brief summary of an IP interface's information and status, use the **show interfaces ip-brief** EXEC command.

show interfaces ip-brief

Syntax Description

This command has no arguments or keywords.

Command Mode

EXEC

Usage Guidelines

This command first appeared in Cisco IOS Release 10.0.

Sample Display

The following is sample output from the **show interfaces ip-brief** command:

```
Router# show interfaces ip-brief

Any interface listed with OK? value "NO" does not have a valid configuration
Interface   IP-Address     OK? Method  Status            Protocol
Ethernet0   172.30.160.22  YES NVRAM   up                up
```

SHOW INTERFACES LEX

To display statistics about a LAN Extender interface, use the **show interfaces lex** EXEC command.

show interfaces lex *number* [**ethernet** | **serial**]

Syntax	*Description*
number	Number of the LAN Extender interface that resides on the core router about which to display statistics.
ethernet	(Optional) Displays statistics about the Ethernet interface that resides on the LAN Extender chassis.
serial	(Optional) Displays statistics about the serial interface that resides on the LAN Extender chassis.

Command Mode

EXEC

Usage Guidelines

This command first appeared in Cisco IOS Release 10.3.

To display statistics about the LAN Extender interface on the core router, use the **show interfaces lex** command without any keywords.

Administratively, the physical serial interface that connects the core router to the LAN Extender is completely hidden. The **show interfaces serial** command will show only that the serial interface is present. However, it will not report any statistics about the traffic passing over the physical line. All statistics are reported by the **show interfaces lex** command.

Sample Displays

The following is sample output from the **show interfaces lex** command, showing the LAN Extender interface on the host router. Note the "Bound to ..." field, which is displayed only on a LAN Extender interface.

```
Router# show interfaces lex 0

Lex0 is up, line protocol is up
  Hardware is Lan Extender, address is 0204.0301.1526 (bia 0000.0000.0000)
  MTU 1500 bytes, BW 10000 Kbit, DLY 20000 usec, rely 255/255, load 1/255
  Encapsulation ARPA, loopback not set
  ARP type: ARPA, ARP Timeout 4:00:00
  Bound to Serial3
  Last input never, output never, output hang never
  Last clearing of "show interface" counters never
  Output queue 0/40, 0 drops; input queue 0/75, 0 drops
  Five minute input rate 1000 bits/sec, 0 packets/sec
  Five minute output rate 0 bits/sec, 0 packets/sec
     1022 packets input, 0 bytes, 0 no buffer
     Received 0 broadcasts, 0 runts, 0 giants
     0 input errors, 0 CRC, 0 frame, 0 overrun, 0 ignored, 0 abort
     2070 packets output, 23663 bytes, 0 underruns
     0 output errors, 0 collisions, 0 interface resets, 0 restarts
```

The following is sample output from the **show interfaces lex** command when you specify the **ethernet** keyword:

```
Router# show interfaces lex 0 ethernet

Lex0-Ethernet0 is up, line protocol is up
  Hardware is LAN-Extender, address is 0000.0c01.1526 (bia 0000.0c01.1526)
  Last input 6w3d, output 6w3d
  Last clearing of "show interface" counters 0:02:30
  Output queue 40/50, 60 drops; input queue 10/40, 2 drops
  Five minute input rate 0 bits/sec, 0 packets/sec
  Five minute output rate 0 bits/sec, 0 packets/sec
     3916 packets input, 960303 bytes, 3 no buffer
     Received 2 broadcasts, 3 runts, 3 giants
     2 input errors, 1 CRC, 1 frame, 1 overrun, 3 ignored, 2 abort
     2500 packets output, 128288 bytes, 1 underruns
     1 output errors, 1 collisions, 0 interface resets, 0 restarts
```

The following is sample output from the **show interfaces lex** command when you specify the **serial** keyword:

```
Router# show interfaces lex 0 serial

Lex0-Serial0 is up, line protocol is up
  Hardware is LAN-Extender
```

```
Last input 6w3d, output 6w3d
Last clearing of "show interface" counters 0:03:05
Input queue: 5/15/4 (size/max/drops); Total output drops: 450
Output queue: high 25/35/90, medium 70/80/180, normal 40/50/120, low 10/20/60
Five minute input rate 0 bits/sec, 0 packets/sec
Five minute output rate 0 bits/sec, 0 packets/sec
    1939 packets input, 30998 bytes, 6 no buffer
    Received 4 broadcasts, 6 runts, 6 giants
    4 input errors, 2 CRC, 2 frame, 2 overrun, 6 ignored, 4 abort
    1939 packets output, 219535 bytes, 2 underruns
    2 output errors, 2 collisions, 0 interface resets, 0 restarts
    2 carrier transitions
```

Table 23–27 describes the fields shown in these displays.

Table 23–27 *Show Interfaces Lex Field Descriptions*

Field	Description
Lex0 is up, line protocol is up	Indicates whether the logical LAN Extender interface on the core router is currently active (that is, whether carrier detect is present), inactive, or has been taken down by an administrator.
Lex0-Ethernet0 is up, line protocol is up Lex0-Serial0 is up, line protocol is up	Indicates whether the physical Ethernet and serial interfaces on the LAN Extender chassis are currently active (that is, whether carrier detect is present) and whether it has been taken down by an administrator.
Hardware is LAN-Extender	Hardware type of the interfaces on the LAN Extender.
address is...	Logical MAC address of the interface.
bia	Burned-in MAC address of the interface. The LAN Extender interface does not have a burned in address; hence it appears as all zeroes.
MTU	Maximum transmission unit size of the interface.
BW	Value of the bandwidth parameter that has been configured for the interface (in kilobits per second). The bandwidth parameter is used to compute IGRP metrics only. If the interface is attached to a serial line with a line speed that does not match the default (1,536 or 1,544 for T1 and 56 for a standard synchronous serial line), use the **bandwidth** command to specify the correct line speed for this serial line.
DLY	Delay of the interface in microseconds.

Part
III

Command Reference

Table 23-27 *Show Interfaces Lex Field Descriptions, Continued*

Field	Description
rely	Reliability of the interface as a fraction of 255 (255/255 is 100 percent reliability), calculated as an exponential average over five minutes.
load	Load on the interface as a fraction of 255 (255/255 is completely saturated), calculated as an exponential average over five minutes.
Encapsulation	Encapsulation method assigned to interface.
ARP type	Type of Address Resolution Protocol assigned.
ARP Timeout	Number of hours, minutes, and seconds an ARP cache entry will stay in the cache.
Bound to ...	Number of the serial interface to which the logical LAN Extender interface is bound.
Last input	Number of hours, minutes, and seconds (or never) since the last packet was successfully received by an interface. This is useful for knowing when a dead interface failed.
Last output	Number of hours, minutes, and seconds (or never) since the last packet was successfully transmitted by an interface.
output hang	Number of hours, minutes, and seconds (or never) since the interface was last reset because of a transmission that took too long. When the number of hours in any of the "last" fields exceeds 24 hours, the number of days and hours is printed. If that field overflows, asterisks are printed.
Last clearing of "show interface" counters	Time at which the counters that measure cumulative statistics (such as number of bytes transmitted and received) shown in this report were last reset to zero. Note that variables that might affect routing (for example, load and reliability) are not cleared when the counters are cleared. *** indicates the elapsed time is too large to be displayed. 0:00:00 indicates the counters were cleared more than 231ms (and less than 232ms) ago.
Output queue, drops input queue, drops	Number of packets in output and input queues. Each number is followed by a slash, the maximum size of the queue, and the number of packets dropped due to a full queue.

Table 23–27 *Show Interfaces Lex Field Descriptions, Continued*

Field	Description
5 minute input rate 5 minute output rate	Average number of bits and packets transmitted per second in the last five minutes. The five-minute input and output rates should be used only as an approximation of traffic per second during a given five-minute period. These rates are exponentially weighted averages with a time constant of five minutes. A period of four time constants must pass before the average will be within two percent of the instantaneous rate of a uniform stream of traffic over that period.
packets input	Total number of error-free packets received by the system.
bytes	Total number of bytes, including data and MAC encapsulation, in the error-free packets received by the system.
no buffer	Number of received packets discarded because there was no buffer space in the main system. Compare with ignored count. Broadcast storms on Ethernet networks and bursts of noise on serial lines are often responsible for no input buffer events.
Received ... broadcasts	Total number of broadcast or multicast packets received by the interface.
runts	Number of packets that are discarded because they are smaller than the medium's minimum packet size.
giants	Number of packets that are discarded because they exceed the medium's maximum packet size.
input errors	Total number of no buffer, runts, giants, CRCs, frame, overrun, ignored, and abort counts. Other input-related errors also can increment the count, so that this sum might not balance with the other counts.
CRC	Cyclic redundancy checksum generated by the originating station or far-end device does not match the checksum calculated from the data received. On a serial link, CRCs usually indicate noise, gain hits, or other transmission problems on the data link.

Part
III

Command Reference

Table 23–27 *Show Interfaces Lex Field Descriptions, Continued*

Field	Description
frame	Number of packets received incorrectly having a CRC error and a noninteger number of octets. On a serial line, this is usually the result of noise or other transmission problems.
overrun	Number of times the serial receiver hardware was unable to hand received data to a hardware buffer because the input rate exceeded the receiver's capability to handle the data.
ignored	Number of received packets ignored by the interface because the interface hardware ran low on internal buffers. Broadcast storms and bursts of noise can cause the ignored count to be increased.
abort	Illegal sequence of one bits on a serial interface. This usually indicates a clocking problem between the serial interface and the data link equipment.
input packets with dribble condition detected	Does not apply to a LAN Extender interface.
packets output	Total number of messages transmitted by the system.
bytes	Total number of bytes, including data and MAC encapsulation, transmitted by the system.
underruns	Number of times that the transmitter has been running faster than the router can handle. This might never be reported on some interfaces.
output errors	Sum of all errors that prevented the final transmission of datagrams out of the interface being examined. Note that this might not balance with the sum of the enumerated output errors, as some datagrams might have more than one error, and others might have errors that do not fall into any of the specifically tabulated categories.
collisions	Number of messages retransmitted due to an Ethernet collision. This usually is the result of an overextended LAN (Ethernet or transceiver cable too long, more than two repeaters between stations, or too many cascaded multiport transceivers). Some collisions are normal. However, if your collision rate climbs to around four or five percent, you

Table 23–27 *Show Interfaces Lex Field Descriptions, Continued*

Field	Description
	should consider verifying that there isn't any faulty equipment on the segment, and/or moving some existing stations to a new segment. A packet that collides is counted only once in output packets.
interface resets	Number of times an interface has been completely reset. This can happen if packets queued for transmission were not sent within several seconds' time. On a serial line, this can be caused by a malfunctioning modem that is not supplying the transmit clock signal, or by a cable problem. If the system notices that the carrier detect line of a serial interface is up, but the line protocol is down, it periodically resets the interface in an effort to restart it. Interface resets also can occur when an interface is looped back or shut down.
restarts	Number of times the controller was restarted because of errors.

SHOW INTERFACES LOOPBACK

Use the **show interfaces loopback** privileged EXEC command to display information about the loopback interface.

    show interfaces loopback [*number*] [**accounting**]

Syntax	Description
number	(Optional) Port number on the selected interface.
accounting	(Optional) Displays the number of packets of each protocol type that have been sent through the interface.

Command Mode

Privileged EXEC

Usage Guidelines

This command first appeared in Cisco IOS Release 10.0.

Sample Displays

The following is sample output from the **show interfaces loopback** command:

```
Router# show interfaces loopback 0

Loopback0 is up, line protocol is up
  Hardware is Loopback
  MTU 1500 bytes, BW 1 Kbit, DLY 50 usec, rely 255/255, load 1/255
  Encapsulation UNKNOWN, loopback not set, keepalive set (10 sec)
  Last input never, output never, output hang never
  Last clearing of "show interface" counters never
  Output queue 0/0, 0 drops; input queue 0/75, 0 drops
  Five minute input rate 0 bits/sec, 0 packets/sec
  Five minute output rate 0 bits/sec, 0 packets/sec
     0 packets input, 0 bytes, 0 no buffer
     Received 0 broadcasts, 0 runts, 0 giants
     0 input errors, 0 CRC, 0 frame, 0 overrun, 0 ignored, 0 abort
     0 packets output, 0 bytes, 0 underruns
     0 output errors, 0 collisions, 0 interface resets, 0 restarts
```

The following is sample output when the **accounting** keyword is included:

```
Router# show interfaces loopback 0 accounting

Loopback0
                   Protocol    Pkts In    Chars In    Pkts Out    Chars Out
   No traffic sent or received on this interface.
```

Table 23–28 describes significant fields shown in the displays.

Table 23–28 *Show Interfaces Loopback Field Descriptions*

Field	Description
Loopback is {up | down | administratively down}	Indicates whether the interface hardware is currently active (whether carrier detect is present), inactive, or has been taken down by an administrator.
line protocol is {up | down | administratively down}	Indicates whether the software processes that handle the line protocol considers the line usable (that is, whether keepalives are successful).
Hardware	Hardware is Loopback.
MTU	Maximum Transmission Unit of the interface.
BW	Bandwidth of the interface in kilobits per second.
DLY	Delay of the interface in microseconds.
rely	Reliability of the interface as a fraction of 255 (255/255 is 100 percent reliability), calculated as an exponential average over five minutes.

Table 23–28 *Show Interfaces Loopback Field Descriptions, Continued*

Field	Description
load	Load on the interface as a fraction of 255 (255/255 is completely saturated), calculated as an exponential average over five minutes.
Encapsulation	Encapsulation method assigned to interface.
loopback	Indicates whether loopback is set and type of loopback test.
keepalive	Indicates whether keepalives are set.
Last input	Number of hours, minutes, and seconds since the last packet was successfully received by an interface. Useful for knowing when a dead interface failed.
Last output	Number of hours, minutes, and seconds since the last packet was successfully transmitted by an interface.
output hang	Number of hours, minutes, and seconds (or never) since the interface was last reset because of a transmission that took too long. When the number of hours in any of the "last" fields exceeds 24 hours, the number of days and hours is printed. If that field overflows, asterisks are printed.
Last clearing	Time at which the counters that measure cumulative statistics (such as number of bytes transmitted and received) shown in this report were last reset to zero. Note that variables that might affect routing (for example, load and reliability) are not cleared when the counters are cleared. *** indicates the elapsed time is too large to be displayed. 0:00:00 indicates the counters were cleared more than 2^{31}ms (and less than 2^{32}ms) ago.
Output queue, drops Input queue, drops	Number of packets in output and input queues. Each number is followed by a slash, the maximum size of the queue, and the number of packets dropped due to a full queue.
5 minute input rate, 5 minute output rate	Average number of bits and packets transmitted per second in the last five minutes.
packets input	Total number of error-free packets received by the system.
bytes input	Total number of bytes, including data and MAC encapsulation, in the error-free packets received by the system.

Table 23–28 *Show Interfaces Loopback Field Descriptions, Continued*

Field	Description
no buffer	Number of received packets discarded because there was no buffer space in the main system. Compare with ignored count. Broadcast storms on Ethernet networks and bursts of noise on serial lines are often responsible for no input buffer events.
broadcasts	Total number of broadcast or multicast packets received by the interface.
runts	Number of packets that are discarded because they are smaller than the medium's minimum packet size.
giants	Number of packets that are discarded because they exceed the medium's maximum packet size.
input errors	Sum of all errors that prevented the receipt of datagrams on the interface being examined. This might not balance with the sum of the enumerated output errors, because some datagrams might have more than one error and others might have errors that do not fall into any of the specifically tabulated categories.
CRC	Cyclic redundancy checksum generated by the originating LAN station or far-end device does not match the checksum calculated from the data received. On a LAN, this usually indicates noise or transmission problems on the LAN interface or the LAN bus itself. A high number of CRCs is usually the result of collisions or a station transmitting bad data. On a serial link, CRCs usually indicate noise, gain hits, or other transmission problems on the data link. CRC errors are also reported when a far-end abort occurs, and when the idle flag pattern is corrupted. This makes it possible to get CRC errors even when there is no data traffic.
frame	Number of packets received incorrectly having a CRC error and a noninteger number of octets. On a serial line, this is usually the result of noise or other transmission problems.
overrun	Number of times the serial receiver hardware was unable to hand received data to a hardware buffer because the input rate exceeded the receiver's capability to handle the data.
ignored	Number of received packets ignored by the interface because the interface hardware ran low on internal buffers. These buffers are different than the system buffers mentioned previously in the buffer description. Broadcast storms and bursts of noise can cause the ignored count to be increased.

Table 23–28 *Show Interfaces Loopback Field Descriptions, Continued*

Field	Description
abort	Number of packets whose receipt was aborted.
packets output	Total number of messages transmitted by the system.
bytes output	Total number of bytes, including data and MAC encapsulation, transmitted by the system.
underruns	Number of times that the far-end transmitter has been running faster than the near-end router's receiver can handle. This might never happen (be reported) on some interfaces.
output errors	Sum of all errors that prevented the final transmission of datagrams out of the interface being examined. Note that this might not balance with the sum of the enumerated output errors, as some datagrams might have more than one error, and others might have errors that do not fall into any of the specifically tabulated categories.
collisions	A loopback interface does not have collisions.
interface resets	Number of times an interface has been completely reset. This can happen if packets queued for transmission were not sent within several seconds time. On a serial line, this can be caused by a malfunctioning modem that is not supplying the transmit clock signal, or by a cable problem. If the system notices that the carrier detect line of a serial interface is up, but the line protocol is down, it periodically resets the interface in an effort to restart it. Interface resets also can occur when an interface is looped back or shut down.
restarts	Number of times the controller was restarted because of errors.
Protocol	Protocol that is operating on the interface.
Pkts In	Number of packets received for that protocol.
Chars In	Number of characters received for that protocol.
Pkts Out	Number of packets transmitted for that protocol.
Chars Out	Number of characters transmitted for that protocol.

SHOW INTERFACES POS

To display information about the Packet OC-3 interface in Cisco 7500 series routers, use the **show interfaces pos** EXEC command.

> **show interfaces pos** [*slot/port-adapter/port*] (on VIP cards in Cisco 7000 series and Cisco 7500 series routers)

Syntax	Description
slot	Refer to the appropriate hardware manual for slot and port information.
port-adapter	Refer to the appropriate hardware manual for information about port adapter compatibility.
port	Refer to the appropriate hardware manual for slot and port information.

Command Mode

EXEC

Usage Guidelines

This command first appeared in Cisco IOS Release 11.2.

This command was modified in Cisco IOS Release 11.3 to change the **show interface posi** command to **show interface pos** and to update the sample output.

Sample Display

The following is sample output from the **show interfaces pos** command on a Cisco 7513 router with one Packet OC-3 Interface Processor (POSIP):

```
Router# show interfaces pos 2/0/0

POS2/0/0 is up, line protocol is up
  Hardware is cyBus Packet over Sonet
  Description: PRI-T1 net to zippy (4K) to Pac-Bell
  Internet address is 1.1.1.1/27
  MTU 4470 bytes, BW 1000 Kbit, DLY 40000 usec, rely 255/255, load 1/255
  Encapsulation HDLC, loopback not set, keepalive set (3 sec)
  Last input 00:00:00, output 00:00:00, output hang never
  Last clearing of "show interface" counters 00:23:09
  Queueing strategy: fifo
  Output queue 0/40, 0 drops; input queue 0/75, 0 drops
  5 minute input rate 0 bits/sec, 1 packets/sec
  5 minute output rate 1000 bits/sec, 1 packets/sec
     1046 packets input, 54437 bytes, 0 no buffer
     Received 485 broadcasts, 0 runts, 0 giants, 0 parity
     0 input errors, 0 CRC, 0 frame, 0 overrun, 0 ignored, 0 abort
```

```
4013 packets output, 1357412 bytes, 0 underruns
0 output errors, 0 applique, 0 interface resets
0 output buffer failures, 0 output buffers swapped out
0 carrier transitions
```

Table 23–29 describes significant fields in this output.

Table 23–29   *Show Interfaces POS Field Descriptions*

Field	Description
POS2/0/0 is up, line protocol is up	Indicates whether the interface hardware is currently active and can transmit and receive or whether it has been taken down by an administrator.
Hardware is cyBus Packet over Sonet	Hardware type.
Internet address is	Internet address and subnet mask.
MTU	Maximum transmission unit of the interface.
BW	Bandwidth of the interface in kilobits per second.
DLY	Delay of the interface in microseconds.
rely	Reliability of the interface as a fraction of 255 (255/255 is 100 percent reliability), calculated as an exponential average over five minutes.
load	Load on the interface as a fraction of 255 (255/255 is completely saturated), calculated as an exponential average over five minutes. The calculation uses the value from the **bandwidth** interface configuration command.
Encapsulation	Encapsulation method assigned to interface.
loopback	Indicates whether loopbacks are set.
keepalive	Indicates whether keepalives are set.
Last input	Number of hours, minutes, and seconds since the last packet was successfully received by an interface. Useful for knowing when a dead interface failed.
(Last) output	Number of hours, minutes, and seconds since the last packet was successfully transmitted by an interface.
(Last) output hang	Number of hours, minutes, and seconds (or never) since the interface was last reset because of a transmission that took too long. When the number of hours in any of the "last" fields exceeds 24 hours, the number of days and hours is printed. If that field overflows, asterisks are printed.

Table 23–29 *Show Interfaces POS Field Descriptions, Continued*

Field	Description
Last clearing	Time at which the counters that measure cumulative statistics (such as number of bytes transmitted and received) shown in this report were last reset to zero. Note that variables that might affect routing (for example, load and reliability) are not cleared when the counters are cleared. *** indicates the elapsed time is too large to be displayed. 0:00:00 indicates the counters were cleared more than 2^{31}ms (and less than 2^{32}ms) ago.
Queueing strategy	First-in, first-out queuing strategy (other queueing strategies you might see are priority-list, custom-list, and weighted-fair).
Output queue, drops input queue, drops	Number of packets in output and input queues. Each number is followed by a slash, the maximum size of the queue, and the number of packets dropped because a queue was full.
5 minute input rate 5 minute output rate	Average number of bits and packets received or transmitted per second in the last five minutes.
packets input	Total number of error-free packets received by the system.
bytes (input)	Total number of bytes, including data and MAC encapsulation, in the error-free packets received by the system.
no buffer	Number of received packets discarded because there was no buffer space in the main system. Compare with ignored count. Broadcast storms on Ethernets and bursts of noise on serial lines are often responsible for no input buffer events.
broadcasts	Total number of broadcast or multicast packets received by the interface.
runts	Number of packets that are discarded because they are smaller than the medium's minimum packet size.
giants	Number of packets that are discarded because they exceed the medium's maximum packet size.
parity	Report of the parity errors on the interface.
input errors	Total number of no buffer, runts, giants, CRCs, frame, overrun, ignored, and abort counts. Other input-related errors can also increment the count, so that this sum might not balance with the other counts.

Table 23–29 *Show Interfaces POS Field Descriptions, Continued*

Field	Description
CRC	Cyclic redundancy checksum generated by the originating LAN station or far-end device does not match the checksum calculated from the data received. On a LAN, this usually indicates noise or transmission problems on the LAN interface or the LAN bus itself. A high number of CRCs is usually the result of collisions or a station transmitting bad data. On a serial link, CRCs usually indicate noise, gain hits or other transmission problems on the data link.
frame	Number of packets received incorrectly having a CRC error and a noninteger number of octets. On a serial line, this is usually the result of noise or other transmission problems.
overrun	Number of times the serial receiver hardware was unable to hand received data to a hardware buffer because the input rate exceeded the receiver's capability to handle the data.
ignored	Number of received packets ignored by the interface because the interface hardware ran low on internal buffers. These buffers are different than the system buffers mentioned previously in the buffer description. Broadcast storms and bursts of noise can cause the ignored count to be incremented.
abort	Illegal sequence of one bits on the interface.
packets output	Total number of messages transmitted by the system.
bytes (output)	Total number of bytes, including data and MAC encapsulation, transmitted by the system.
underruns	Number of times that the far-end transmitter has been running faster than the near-end router's receiver can handle.
output errors	Sum of all errors that prevented the final transmission of datagrams out of the interface being examined. Note that this might not balance with the sum of the enumerated output errors, as some datagrams can have more than one error, and others can have errors that do not fall into any of the specifically tabulated categories.
applique	Indicates an unrecoverable error has occurred on the POSIP applique. The system then invokes an interface reset.

Table 23–29   *Show Interfaces POS Field Descriptions, Continued*

Field	Description
interface resets	Number of times an interface has been completely reset. This can happen if packets queued for transmission were not sent within a certain interval. If the system notices that the carrier detect line of an interface is up, but the line protocol is down, it periodically resets the interface in an effort to restart it. Interface resets also can occur when an unrecoverable interface processor error occurred, or when an interface is looped back or shut down.
carrier transitions	Number of times the carrier detect signal of the interface has changed state.

Related Commands

interface pos

SHOW INTERFACES SERIAL

To display information about a serial interface, use the **show interfaces serial** privileged EXEC command.

> **show interfaces serial** [*number*] [**accounting**]
> **show interfaces serial** [*number* [:*channel-group*] [**accounting**] (Cisco 4000 series)
> **show interfaces serial** [*slot/port* [:*channel-group*]] [**accounting**] (Cisco 7500 series)
> **show interfaces serial** [*type slot/port-adapter/port*] [**serial**] (ports on VIP cards in the Cisco 7500 series)
> **show interfaces serial** [*type slot/port-adapter/port*] [:*t1-channel*] [**accounting** | **crb**] (CT3IP in Cisco 7500 series)

Syntax	*Description*
number	(Optional) Port number.
accounting	(Optional) Displays the number of packets of each protocol type that have been sent through the interface.
:*channel-group*	(Optional) On the Cisco 4000 series with an NPM or Cisco 7500 series with a MIP, specifies the T1 channel-group number in the range of 0 to 23 defined with the **channel-group** controller configuration command.
slot	Refer to the appropriate hardware manual for slot and port information.
port-	Refer to the appropriate hardware manual for slot and port information.

Syntax	Description
port-adapter	Refer to the appropriate hardware manual for information about port adapter compatibility.
:t1-channel	(Optional) For the CT3IP, the T1 channel is a number between 1 and 28.
	T1 channels on the CT3IP are numbered 1 to 28 rather than the more traditional zero-based scheme (0 to 27) used with other Cisco products. This is to ensure consistency with telco numbering schemes for T1 channels within channelized T3 equipment.
crb	(Optional) Shows interface routing and bridging information.

Command Mode

Privileged EXEC

Usage Guidelines

This command first appeared in Cisco IOS Release 10.0 for the Cisco 4000 series. This command first appeared in Cisco IOS Release 11.0 for the Cisco 7000 series.

This command was modified in Cisco IOS Release 11.3 to include the CT3IP.

Sample Displays

The following is sample output from the **show interfaces** command for a synchronous serial interface:

```
Router# show interfaces serial
Serial 0 is up, line protocol is up
   Hardware is MCI Serial
   Internet address is 150.136.190.203, subnet mask is 255.255.255.0
   MTU 1500 bytes, BW 1544 Kbit, DLY 20000 usec, rely 255/255, load 1/255
   Encapsulation HDLC, loopback not set, keepalive set (10 sec)
   Last input 0:00:07, output 0:00:00, output hang never
   Output queue 0/40, 0 drops; input queue 0/75, 0 drops
   Five minute input rate 0 bits/sec, 0 packets/sec
   Five minute output rate 0 bits/sec, 0 packets/sec
       16263 packets input, 1347238 bytes, 0 no buffer
       Received 13983 broadcasts, 0 runts, 0 giants
       2 input errors, 0 CRC, 0 frame, 0 overrun, 0 ignored, 2 abort
 1 carrier transitions

       22146 packets output, 2383680 bytes, 0 underruns
       0 output errors, 0 collisions, 2 interface resets, 0 restarts
```

Table 23–30 describes significant fields shown in the display.

Table 23-30   *Show Interfaces Serial Field Descriptions*

Field	Description
Serial... is {up | down} ...is administratively down	Indicates whether the interface hardware is currently active (whether carrier detect is present) or whether it has been taken down by an administrator.
line protocol is {up | down}	Indicates whether the software processes that handle the line protocol consider the line usable (that is, whether keepalives are successful) or whether it has been taken down by an administrator.
Hardware is	Specifies the hardware type.
Internet address is	Specifies the Internet address and subnet mask.
MTU	Maximum transmission unit of the interface.
BW	Indicates the value of the bandwidth parameter that has been configured for the interface (in kilobits per second). The bandwidth parameter is used to compute IGRP metrics only. If the interface is attached to a serial line with a line speed that does not match the default (1,536 or 1,544 for T1 and 56 for a standard synchronous serial line), use the **bandwidth** command to specify the correct line speed for this serial line.
DLY	Delay of the interface in microseconds.
rely	Reliability of the interface as a fraction of 255 (255/255 is 100 percent reliability), calculated as an exponential average over five minutes.
load	Load on the interface as a fraction of 255 (255/255 is completely saturated), calculated as an exponential average over five minutes.
Encapsulation	Encapsulation method assigned to interface.
loopback	Indicates whether loopback is set.
keepalive	Indicates whether keepalives are set.
Last input	Number of hours, minutes, and seconds since the last packet was successfully received by an interface. Useful for knowing when a dead interface failed.
Last output	Number of hours, minutes, and seconds since the last packet was successfully transmitted by an interface.

Table 23–30 *Show Interfaces Serial Field Descriptions, Continued*

Field	Description
output hang	Number of hours, minutes, and seconds (or never) since the interface was last reset because of a transmission that took too long. When the number of hours in any of the "last" fields exceeds 24 hours, the number of days and hours is printed. If that field overflows, asterisks are printed.
Output queue, drops input queue, drops	Number of packets in output and input queues. Each number is followed by a slash, the maximum size of the queue, and the number of packets dropped due to a full queue.
5 minute input rate 5 minute output rate	Average number of bits and packets transmitted per second in the last five minutes. The five-minute input and output rates should be used only as an approximation of traffic per second during a given five-minute period. These rates are exponentially weighted averages with a time constant of five minutes. A period of four time constants must pass before the average will be within two percent of the instantaneous rate of a uniform stream of traffic over that period.
packets input	Total number of error-free packets received by the system.
bytes	Total number of bytes, including data and MAC encapsulation, in the error-free packets received by the system.
no buffer	Number of received packets discarded because there was no buffer space in the main system. Compare with ignored count. Broadcast storms on Ethernet networks and bursts of noise on serial lines are often responsible for no input buffer events.
Received... broadcasts	Total number of broadcast or multicast packets received by the interface.
runts	Number of packets that are discarded because they are smaller than the medium's minimum packet size.
giants	Number of packets that are discarded because they exceed the medium's maximum packet size.

Part III

Command Reference

Table 23–30 *Show Interfaces Serial Field Descriptions, Continued*

Field	Description
input errors	Total number of no buffer, runts, giants, CRCs, frame, overrun, ignored, and abort counts. Other input-related errors also can increment the count, so that this sum might not balance with the other counts.
CRC	Cyclic redundancy checksum generated by the originating station or far-end device does not match the checksum calculated from the data received. On a serial link, CRCs usually indicate noise, gain hits, or other transmission problems on the data link.
frame	Number of packets received incorrectly having a CRC error and a noninteger number of octets. On a serial line, this is usually the result of noise or other transmission problems.
overrun	Number of times the serial receiver hardware was unable to hand received data to a hardware buffer because the input rate exceeded the receiver's capability to handle the data.
ignored	Number of received packets ignored by the interface because the interface hardware ran low on internal buffers. Broadcast storms and bursts of noise can cause the ignored count to be increased.
abort	Illegal sequence of one bits on a serial interface. This usually indicates a clocking problem between the serial interface and the data link equipment.
carrier transitions	Number of times the carrier detect signal of a serial interface has changed state. For example, if data carrier detect (DCD) goes down and comes up, the carrier transition counter will increment two times. Indicates modem or line problems if the carrier detect line is changing state often.
packets output	Total number of messages transmitted by the system.
bytes output	Total number of bytes, including data and MAC encapsulation, transmitted by the system.
underruns	Number of times that the transmitter has been running faster than the router can handle. This might never be reported on some interfaces.

Table 23–30 *Show Interfaces Serial Field Descriptions, Continued*

Field	Description
output errors	Sum of all errors that prevented the final transmission of datagrams out of the interface being examined. Note that this might not balance with the sum of the enumerated output errors, as some datagrams can have more than one error, and others can have errors that do not fall into any of the specifically tabulated categories.
collisions	Number of messages retransmitted due to an Ethernet collision. This usually is the result of an overextended LAN (Ethernet or transceiver cable too long, more than two repeaters between stations, or too many cascaded multiport transceivers). Some collisions are normal. However, if your collision rate climbs to around four or five percent, you should consider verifying that there is no faulty equipment on the segment and/or moving some existing stations to a new segment. A packet that collides is counted only once in output packets.
interface resets	Number of times an interface has been completely reset. This can happen if packets queued for transmission were not sent within several seconds' time. On a serial line, this can be caused by a malfunctioning modem that is not supplying the transmit clock signal, or by a cable problem. If the system notices that the carrier detect line of a serial interface is up, but the line protocol is down, it periodically resets the interface in an effort to restart it. Interface resets also can occur when an interface is looped back or shut down.
restarts	Number of times the controller was restarted because of errors.
alarm indications, remote alarms, rx LOF, rx LOS	Number of CSU/DSU alarms, and number of occurrences of receive loss of frame and receive loss of signal.
BER inactive, NELR inactive, FELR inactive	Status of G.703-E1 counters for bit error rate (BER) alarm, near-end loop remote (NELR), and far-end loop remote (FELR). Note that you cannot set the NELR or FELR.

The following is sample output of the **show interfaces serial** command for the CT3IP serial interface:

```
Router# show interfaces serial 3/0/0:25
Serial3/0/0:25 is up, line protocol is up
  Hardware is cyBus T3
  Internet address is 25.25.25.2/24
  MTU 1500 bytes, BW 1536 Kbit, DLY 20000 usec, rely 255/255, load 12/255
  Encapsulation HDLC, loopback not set, keepalive not set
  Last input 00:19:01, output 00:11:49, output hang never
  Last clearing of "show interface" counters 00:19:39
  Input queue: 0/75/0 (size/max/drops); Total output drops: 0
  Queueing strategy: weighted fair
  Output queue: 0/64/0 (size/threshold/drops)
     Conversations  0/1 (active/max active)
     Reserved Conversations 0/0 (allocated/max allocated)
  5 minute input rate 69000 bits/sec, 90 packets/sec
  5 minute output rate 71000 bits/sec, 90 packets/sec
     762350 packets input, 79284400 bytes, 0 no buffer
     Received 0 broadcasts, 0 runts, 0 giants
     150 input errors, 0 CRC, 0 frame, 150 overrun, 0 ignored, 0 abort
     763213 packets output, 80900472 bytes, 0 underruns
     0 output errors, 0 collisions, 0 interface resets
     0 output buffer failures, 0 output buffers swapped out
     0 carrier transitions no alarm present
  Timeslot(s) Used:1-24, Transmitter delay is 0 flags, transmit queue length 5
  non-inverted data
```

Most fields are described in Table 23–30. Fields relevant to the CT3IP are described in Table 23–31.

Table 23–31 *Show Interfaces Serial Field Descriptions—CT3IP*

Field	Description
Timeslot(s) Used	Number of timeslots assigned to the T1 channel.
Transmitter delay	Number of idle flags inserted between each HDLC frame.
transmit queue length	Number of packets allowed in the transmit queue.
non-inverted data	Whether the interface is configured for inverted data.

The following is sample output of the **show interfaces serial** command for the HDLC synchronous serial interface on a Cisco 7500:

```
Router# show interfaces serial 1/0
Serial1/0 is up, line protocol is up
  Hardware is cxBus Serial
  Internet address is 150.136.190.203, subnet mask is 255.255.255.0
  MTU 1500 bytes, BW 1544 Kbit, DLY 20000 usec, rely 255/255, load 1/255
  Encapsulation HDLC, loopback not set, keepalive set (10 sec)
  Last input 0:00:07, output 0:00:00, output hang never
  Last clearing of "show interface" counters 2w4d
```

```
    Output queue 0/40, 0 drops; input queue 0/75, 0 drops
    Five minute input rate 0 bits/sec, 0 packets/sec
    Five minute output rate 0 bits/sec, 0 packets/sec
        16263 packets input, 1347238 bytes, 0 no buffer
        Received 13983 broadcasts, 0 runts, 0 giants
        2 input errors, 0 CRC, 0 frame, 0 overrun, 0 ignored, 2 abort
        22146 packets output, 2383680 bytes, 0 underruns
        0 output errors, 0 collisions, 2 interface resets, 0 restarts
        1 carrier transitions
```

The following is sample output of the **show interfaces serial** command for a G.703 interface on which framing is enabled:

```
Router# show interfaces serial 2/3
Serial2/3 is up, line protocol is up
  Hardware is cxBus Serial
  Internet address is 5.4.4.1, subnet mask is 255.255.255.0
  MTU 1500 bytes, BW 1544 Kbit, DLY 20000 usec, rely 255/255, load 1/255
  Encapsulation HDLC, loopback not set, keepalive not set
  Last input 0:00:21, output 0:00:21, output hang never
  Last clearing of "show interface" counters never
  Output queue 0/40, 0 drops; input queue 0/75, 0 drops
  Five minute input rate 0 bits/sec, 0 packets/sec
  Five minute output rate 0 bits/sec, 0 packets/sec
      53 packets input, 7810 bytes, 0 no buffer
      Received 53 broadcasts, 0 runts, 0 giants
      2 input errors, 2 CRC, 0 frame, 0 overrun, 0 ignored, 2 abort
      56 packets output, 8218 bytes, 0 underruns
      0 output errors, 0 collisions, 2 interface resets, 0 restarts
      1 carrier transitions
      2 alarm indications, 333 remote alarms, 332 rx LOF, 0 rx LOS
      RTS up, CTS up, DTR up, DCD up, DSR up
      BER inactive, NELR inactive, FELR inactive
```

Table 23–30 describes significant fields shown in the display.

Sample Display with Frame Relay Encapsulation

When using the Frame Relay encapsulation, use the **show interfaces** command to display information on the multicast DLCI, the DLCI of the interface, and the LMI DLCI used for the local management interface.

The multicast DLCI and the local DLCI can be set using the **frame-relay multicast-dlci** and the **frame-relay local-dlci** configuration commands or provided through the local management interface. The status information is taken from the LMI, when active.

The following is sample output from the **show interfaces serial** command when using Frame Relay encapsulation:

```
Router# show interfaces serial
Serial 2 is up, line protocol is up
   Hardware type is MCI Serial
   Internet address is 131.108.122.1, subnet mask is 255.255.255.0
```

```
       MTU 1500 bytes, BW 1544 Kbit, DLY 20000 usec, rely 255/255, load 1/255
       Encapsulation FRAME-RELAY, loopback not set, keepalive set (10 sec)
       multicast DLCI 1022,  status defined, active
       source DLCI   20, status defined, active
       LMI DLCI 1023, LMI sent 10, LMI stat recvd 10, LMI upd recvd 2
       Last input 7:21:29, output 0:00:37, output hang never
       Output queue 0/100, 0 drops; input queue 0/75, 0 drops
       Five minute input rate 0 bits/sec, 0 packets/sec
       Five minute output rate 0 bits/sec, 0 packets/sec
           47 packets input, 2656 bytes, 0 no buffer
           Received 5 broadcasts, 0 runts, 0 giants
           5 input errors, 0 CRC, 0 frame, 0 overrun, 0 ignored, 57 abort
           518 packets output, 391205 bytes
           0 output errors, 0 collisions, 0 interface resets, 0 restarts
           1 carrier transitions
```

In this display, the multicast DLCI has been changed to 1022 with the **frame-relay multicast-dlci** interface configuration command.

The display shows the statistics for the LMI are the number of status inquiry messages sent (LMI sent), the number of status messages received (LMI recvd), and the number of status updates received (upd recvd). See the *Frame Relay Interface* specification for additional explanations of this output.

Sample Display with ANSI LMI

For a serial interface with the ANSI LMI enabled, use the **show interfaces** command to determine the LMI type implemented.

The following is a sample display from the **show interfaces** output for a serial interface with the ANSI LMI enabled:

```
       Router# show interfaces serial
       Serial 1 is up, line protocol is up
         Hardware is MCI Serial
         Internet address is 131.108.121.1, subnet mask is 255.255.255.0
         MTU 1500 bytes, BW 1544 Kbit, DLY 20000 usec, rely 255/255, load 1/255
         Encapsulation FRAME-RELAY, loopback not set, keepalive set
         LMI DLCI   0, LMI sent 10, LMI stat recvd 10
         LMI type is ANSI Annex D
         Last input 0:00:00, output 0:00:00, output hang never
         Output queue 0/40, 0 drops; input queue 0/75, 0 drops
         Five minute input rate 0 bits/sec, 1 packets/sec
         Five minute output rate 1000 bits/sec, 1 packets/sec
             261 packets input, 13212 bytes, 0 no buffer
             Received 33 broadcasts, 0 runts, 0 giants
             0 input errors, 0 CRC, 0 frame, 0 overrun, 0 ignored, 0 abort
             238 packets output, 14751 bytes, 0 underruns
             0 output errors, 0 collisions, 0 interface resets, 0 restarts
```

Notice that the **show interfaces** output for a serial interface with ANSI LMI shown in this display is very similar to that for encapsulation set to Frame Relay, as shown in the previous display. Table 23–32 describes the few differences that exist.

Table 23–32 *Show Interfaces Serial Field Description—With ANSI LMI*

Field	Description
LMI DLCI 0	Identifies the DLCI used by the LMI for this interface. Default: 1023.
LMI sent 10	Number of LMI packets the router sent.
LMI type is ANSI Annex D	Indicates that the interface is configured for the ANSI-adopted Frame Relay specification T1.617 Annex D.

Sample Display with LAPB Encapsulation

Use the **show interfaces** command to display operation statistics for an interface using LAPB encapsulation.

The following is sample output from the **show interfaces** command for a serial interface using LAPB encapsulation:

```
Router# show interfaces
LAPB state is DISCONNECT, T1 3000, N1 12000, N2 20, K7, TH 3000
Window is closed
IFRAMEs 12/28 RNRs 0/1 REJs 13/1 SABMs 1/13 FRMRs 3/0 DISCs 0/11
```

Table 23–33 shows the fields relevant to all LAPB connections.

Table 23–33 *Show Interfaces Serial Field Descriptions—With LAPB Enabled*

Parameter	Description
LAPB state is DISCONNECT	State of the LAPB protocol.
T1 3000, N1 12000,...	Current parameter settings.
Window is closed	Indicates that no more frames can be transmitted until some outstanding frames have been acknowledged.
IFRAMEs 12/28 RNRs 0/1...	Count of the different types of frames in the form of sent/received.

Show Interfaces Serial with PPP

An interface configured for synchronous PPP encapsulation differs from the standard **show interface serial** output. An interface configured for PPP might include the following information:

```
lcp state = OPEN
ncp ipcp state = OPEN   ncp osicp state = NOT NEGOTIATED
```

```
ncp ipxcp state = NOT NEGOTIATED    ncp xnscp state = NOT NEGOTIATED
ncp vinescp state = NOT NEGOTIATED    ncp deccp state = NOT NEGOTIATED
ncp bridgecp state = NOT NEGOTIATED    ncp atalkcp state = NOT NEGOTIATED
```

Table 23–34 show the fields relevant to PPP connections.

Table 23–34 *Show Interfaces Serial Field Descriptions—With PPP Encapsulation*

Field	Description
lcp state	Link Control Protocol
ncp ipcp state	Network Control Protocol Internet Protocol Control Protocol
ncp osicp state	Network Control Protocol OSI (CLNS) Control Protocol
ncp ipxcp state	Network Control Protocol IPX (Novell) Control Protocol
ncp xnscp state	Network Control Protocol XNS Control Protocol
ncp vinescp state	Network Control Protocol VINES Control Protocol
ncp deccp state	Network Control Protocol DECnet Control Protocol
ncp bridgecp state	Network Control Protocol Bridging Control Protocol
ncp atalkcp state	Network Control Protocol AppleTalk Control Protocol

Sample Display with SDLC Connections

Use the **show interfaces** command to display the SDLC information for a given SDLC interface. The following is sample output from the **show interfaces** command for an SDLC primary interface supporting the SDLLC function:

```
Router# show interfaces

Serial 0 is up, line protocol is up
Hardware is MCI Serial
MTU 1500 bytes, BW 1544 Kbit, DLY 20000 usec, rely 255/255, load 1/255
Encapsulation SDLC-PRIMARY, loopback not set
    Timers (msec): poll pause 100 fair poll 500. Poll limit 1
    [T1 3000, N1 12016, N2 20, K 7] timer: 56608 Last polled device: none
    SDLLC [ma: 0000.0C01.14--, ring: 7 bridge: 1, target ring: 10
            largest token ring frame 2052]
SDLC addr C1 state is CONNECT
    VS 6, VR 3, RCNT 0, Remote VR 6, Current retransmit count 0
    Hold queue: 0/12 IFRAMEs 77/22 RNRs 0/0 SNRMs 1/0 DISCs 0/0
    Poll: clear, Poll count: 0, chain: p: C1 n: C1
    SDLLC [largest SDLC frame: 265, XID: disabled]
Last input 00:00:02, output 00:00:01, output hang never
Output queue 0/40, 0 drops; input queue 0/75, 0 drops
Five minute input rate 517 bits/sec, 30 packets/sec
Five minute output rate 672 bits/sec, 20 packets/sec
    357 packets input, 28382 bytes, 0 no buffer
```

```
Received 0 broadcasts, 0 runts, 0 giants
0 input errors, 0 CRC, 0 frame, 0 overrun, 0 ignored, 0 abort
926 packets output, 77274 bytes, 0 underruns
0 output errors, 0 collisions, 0 interface resets, 0 restarts
2 carrier transitions
```

Table 23–35 shows the fields relevant to all SDLC connections.

Table 23–35 *Show Interfaces Serial Field Descriptions—With SDLC Enabled*

Field	Description
Timers (msec): poll pause, fair poll, Poll limit	Current values of these timers, as described in the configuration section, for this interface.
T1, N1, N2, K	Values for these parameters, as described in the configuration section, for this interface.

Table 23–36 shows other data given for each SDLC secondary configured to be attached to this interface.

Table 23–36 *SDLC Secondary Descriptions*

SDLC Secondary	Description
addr	Address of this secondary.
state is	Current state of this connection, which is one of the following: • DISCONNECT—No communication is being attempted to this secondary. • CONNECT—A normal connect state exists between this router and this secondary. • DISCSENT—This router has sent a disconnect request to this secondary and is awaiting its response. • SNRMSENT—This router has sent a connect request (SNRM) to this secondary and is awaiting its response. • THEMBUSY—This secondary has told this router that it is temporarily unable to receive anymore information frames. • USBUSY—This router has told this secondary that it is temporarily unable to receive anymore information frames. • BOTHBUSY—Both sides have told each other that they are temporarily unable to receive anymore information frames. • ERROR—This router has detected an error and is waiting for a response from the secondary acknowledging this.

Table 23–36 *SDLC Secondary Descriptions, Continued*

SDLC Secondary	Description
VS	Sequence number of the next information frame this station sends.
VR	Sequence number of the next information frame from this secondary that this station expects to receive.
Remote VR	Last frame transmitted by this station that has been acknowledged by the other station.
Current retransm it count:	Number of times the current I-frame or sequence of I-frames has been retransmitted.
Hold Queue	Number of frames in hold queue/Maximum size of hold queue.
IFRAMEs, RNRs, SNRMs, DISCs	Sent/received count for these frames.
Poll	"Set" if this router has a poll outstanding to the secondary; "clear" if it does not.
Poll Count	Number of polls in a row that have been given to this secondary at this time.
Chain	Shows the previous (p) and next (n) secondary address on this interface in the *round robin loop* of polled devices.

Sample Display with SDLLC

Use the **show interfaces serial** command to display the SDLLC statistics for SDLLC configured interfaces.

The following is sample output from the **show interfaces serial** command for a serial interface configured for SDLLC:

```
Router# show interfaces serial

Serial 0 is up, line protocol is up
    Hardware is MCI Serial
    MTU 1500 bytes, BW 1544 Kbit, DLY 20000 usec, rely 255/255, load 1/255
    Encapsulation SDLC-PRIMARY, loopback not set
        Timers (msec): poll pause 100 fair poll 500. Poll limit 1
        [T1 3000, N1 12016, N2 20, K 7] timer: 56608 Last polled device: none
        SDLLC [ma: 0000.0C01.14--, ring: 7 bridge: 1, target ring: 10
            largest token ring frame 2052]
    SDLC addr C1 state is CONNECT
        VS 6, VR 3, RCNT 0, Remote VR 6, Current retransmit count 0
        Hold queue: 0/12 IFRAMEs 77/22 RNRs 0/0 SNRMs 1/0 DISCs 0/0
        Poll: clear, Poll count: 0, chain: p: C1 n: C1
        SDLLC [largest SDLC frame: 265, XID: disabled]
```

```
Last input 00:00:02, output 00:00:01, output hang never
Output queue 0/40, 0 drops; input queue 0/75, 0 drops
Five minute input rate 517 bits/sec, 30 packets/sec
Five minute output rate 672 bits/sec, 20 packets/sec
    357 packets input, 28382 bytes, 0 no buffer
    Received 0 broadcasts, 0 runts, 0 giants
    0 input errors, 0 CRC, 0 frame, 0 overrun, 0 ignored, 0 abort
    926 packets output, 77274 bytes, 0 underruns
    0 output errors, 0 collisions, 0 interface resets, 0 restarts
    6608 Last polled device: none
    SDLLC [ma: 0000.0C01.14--, ring: 7 brid2 carrier transitions
```

Most of the output shown in the display is generic to all SDLC encapsulated interfaces.

Table 23–37 shows the parameters specific to SDLLC.

Table 23–37 *SDLLC Parameter Descriptions*

Field	Description
SDLLC ma	Lists the MAC address configured for this interface. The last byte is shown as "--" to indicate that it is filled in with the SDLC address of the connection.
ring, bridge, target ring	Lists the parameters as configured by the **sdllc traddr** command.
largest token ring frame	Shows the largest Token Ring frame that is accepted on the LLC2 side of the connection.
largest SDLC frame	Shows the largest SDLC frame that is accepted and will be generated on the SDLC side of the connection.
XID	Enabled or disabled: Shows whether XID processing is enabled on the SDLC side of the connection. If enabled, it will show the XID value for this address.

Sample Display with Accounting Option

The following example illustrates the **show interfaces serial** command with the **accounting** option on a Cisco 7500:

```
Router# show interfaces serial 1/0 accounting

Serial1/0
        Protocol    Pkts In    Chars In    Pkts Out    Chars Out
              IP       7344     4787842        1803      1535774
       Appletalk      33345     4797459       12781      1089695
         DEC MOP          0           0         127         9779
             ARP          7         420          39         2340
```

SHOW INTERFACES TOKENRING

Use the **show interfaces tokenring** privileged EXEC command to display information about the Token Ring interface and the state of source route bridging.

> **show interfaces tokenring** *unit* [**accounting**]
>
> **show interfaces tokenring** *slot/port* [**accounting**] (for the Cisco 7500 series and Cisco 7200 series)
>
> **show interfaces tokenring** [*slot/port-adapter/port*] (for ports on VIP cards in the Cisco 7500 series routers)

Syntax	Description
unit	Must match the interface port line number.
accounting	(Optional) Displays the number of packets of each protocol type that have been sent through the interface.
slot	Refer to the appropriate hardware manual for slot and port information.
port	Refer to the appropriate hardware manual for slot and port information.
port-adapter	Refer to the appropriate hardware manual for information about port adapter compatibility.

Command Mode

Privileged EXEC

Usage Guidelines

This command first appeared in Cisco IOS Release 10.0.

The command description was modified in Cisco IOS Release 11.3 to account for support on new full-duplex token ring port adapters.

If you do not provide values for the parameters *slot* and *port*, the command will display statistics for all the network interfaces. The optional keyword **accounting** displays the number of packets of each protocol type that have been sent through the interface.

Sample Displays

The following is sample output from the **show interfaces tokenring** command:

```
Router# show interfaces tokenring

TokenRing 0 is up, line protocol is up
  Hardware is 16/4 Token Ring, address is 5500.2000.dc27 (bia 0000.3000.072b)
    Internet address is 150.136.230.203, subnet mask is 255.255.255.0
    MTU 8136 bytes, BW 16000 Kbit, DLY 630 usec, rely 255/255, load 1/255
```

```
         Encapsulation SNAP, loopback not set, keepalive set (10 sec)
         ARP type: SNAP, ARP Timeout 4:00:00
         Ring speed: 16 Mbps
         Single ring node, Source Route Bridge capable
         Group Address: 0x00000000, Functional Address: 0x60840000
         Last input 0:00:01, output 0:00:01, output hang never
         Output queue 0/40, 0 drops; input queue 0/75, 0 drops
         Five minute input rate 0 bits/sec, 0 packets/sec
         Five minute output rate 0 bits/sec, 0 packets/sec
         16339 packets input, 1496515 bytes, 0 no buffer
             Received 9895 broadcasts, 0 runts, 0 giants
               0 input errors, 0 CRC, 0 frame, 0 overrun, 0 ignored, 0 abort
           32648 packets output, 9738303 bytes, 0 underruns
     0 output errors, 0 collisions, 2 interface resets, 0 restarts
           5 transitions
```

Table 23–38 describes significant fields shown in the display.

Table 23–38   *Show Interfaces Tokenring Field Descriptions*

Field	Description
Token Ring is { up | down }	Interface is either currently active and inserted into ring (up) or inactive and not inserted (down). On the Cisco 7500 series, gives the interface processor type, slot number, and port number.
Token Ring is Reset	Hardware error has occurred.
Token Ring is Initializing	Hardware is up, in the process of inserting the ring.
Token Ring is Administratively Down	Hardware has been taken down by an administrator.
line protocol is {up | down | administratively down}	Indicates whether the software processes that handle the line protocol believe the interface is usable (that is, whether keepalives are successful).
Hardware	Hardware type. "Hardware is Token Ring" indicates that the board is a CSC-R board. "Hardware is 16/4 Token Ring" indicates that the board is a CSC-R16 board. Also shows the address of the interface.
Internet address	Lists the Internet address followed by subnet mask.
MTU	Maximum Transmission Unit of the interface.
BW	Bandwidth of the interface in kilobits per second.
DLY	Delay of the interface in microseconds.

Table 23-38   *Show Interfaces Tokenring Field Descriptions, Continued*

Field	Description
rely	Reliability of the interface as a fraction of 255 (255/255 is 100 percent reliability), calculated as an exponential average over five minutes.
load	Load on the interface as a fraction of 255 (255/255 is completely saturated), calculated as an exponential average over five minutes.
Encapsulation	Encapsulation method assigned to interface.
loopback	Indicates whether loopback is set.
keepalive	Indicates whether keepalives are set.
ARP type:	Type of Address Resolution Protocol assigned.
Ring speed:	Speed of Token Ring—4 or 16 Mbps.
{Single ring |multiring node}	Indicates whether a node is enabled to collect and use source routing information (RIF) for routable Token Ring protocols.
Group Address:	Interface's group address, if any. The group address is a multicast address; any number of interfaces on the ring may share the same group address. Each interface may have at most one group address.
Last input	Number of hours, minutes, and seconds since the last packet was successfully received by an interface. Useful for knowing when a dead interface failed.
Last output	Number of hours, minutes, and seconds since the last packet was successfully transmitted by an interface.
output hang	Number of hours, minutes, and seconds (or never) since the interface was last reset because of a transmission that took too long. When the number of hours in any of the "last" fields exceeds 24 hours, the number of days and hours is printed. If that field overflows, asterisks are printed.

Table 23–38 *Show Interfaces Tokenring Field Descriptions, Continued*

Field	Description
Last clearing	Time at which the counters that measure cumulative statistics (such as number of bytes transmitted and received) shown in this report were last reset to zero. Note that variables that might affect routing (for example, load and reliability) are not cleared when the counters are cleared.
	*** indicates the elapsed time is too large to be displayed. 0:00:00 indicates the counters were cleared more than 2^{31}ms (and less than 2^{32}ms) ago.
Output queue, drops Input queue, drops	Number of packets in output and input queues. Each number is followed by a slash, the maximum size of the queue, and the number of packets dropped due to a full queue.
5 minute input rate, 5 minute output rate	Average number of bits and packets transmitted per second in the last five minutes.
	The five-minute input and output rates should be used only as an approximation of traffic per second during a given five-minute period. These rates are exponentially weighted averages with a time constant of five minutes. A period of four time constants must pass before the average will be within two percent of the instantaneous rate of a uniform stream of traffic over that period.
packets input	Total number of error-free packets received by the system.
bytes input	Total number of bytes, including data and MAC encapsulation, in the error-free packets received by the system.
no buffer	Number of received packets discarded because there was no buffer space in the main system. Compare with ignored count. Broadcast storms on Ethernet networks and bursts of noise on serial lines are often responsible for no input buffer events.
broadcasts	Total number of broadcast or multicast packets received by the interface.
runts	Number of packets that are discarded because they are smaller than the medium's minimum packet size.
giants	Number of packets that are discarded because they exceed the medium's maximum packet size.

Table 23–38 *Show Interfaces Tokenring Field Descriptions, Continued*

Field	Description
CRC	Cyclic redundancy checksum generated by the originating LAN station or far-end device does not match the checksum calculated from the data received. On a LAN, this usually indicates noise or transmission problems on the LAN interface or the LAN bus itself. A high number of CRCs is usually the result of a station transmitting bad data.
frame	Number of packets received incorrectly having a CRC error and a noninteger number of octets.
overrun	Number of times the serial receiver hardware was unable to hand received data to a hardware buffer because the input rate exceeded the receiver's capability to handle the data.
ignored	Number of received packets ignored by the interface because the interface hardware ran low on internal buffers. These buffers are different than the system buffers mentioned previously in the buffer description. Broadcast storms and bursts of noise can cause the ignored count to be increased.
packets output	Total number of messages transmitted by the system.
bytes output	Total number of bytes, including data and MAC encapsulation, transmitted by the system.
underruns	Number of times that the far-end transmitter has been running faster than the near-end router's receiver can handle. This may never be reported on some interfaces.
output errors	Sum of all errors that prevented the final transmission of datagrams out of the interface being examined. Note that this might not balance with the sum of the enumerated output errors, as some datagrams might have more than one error, and others might have errors that do not fall into any of the specifically tabulated categories.
collisions	Because a Token Ring cannot have collisions, this statistic is nonzero only if an unusual event occurred when frames were being queued or dequeued by the system software.
interface resets	Number of times an interface has been reset. The interface may be reset by the administrator or automatically when an internal error occurs.

Table 23-38 *Show Interfaces Tokenring Field Descriptions, Continued*

Field	Description
restarts	Should always be zero for Token Ring interfaces.
transitions	Number of times the ring made a transition from up to down, or vice versa. A large number of transitions indicates a problem with the ring or the interface.

The following is sample output from the **show interfaces tokenring** command on a Cisco 7500:

```
Router# show interfaces tokenring 2/0

TokenRing2/0 is administratively down, line protocol is down
  Hardware is cxBus Token Ring, address is 0000.3040.8b4a (bia 0000.3040.8b4a)
  MTU 8136 bytes, BW 16000 Kbit, DLY 630 usec, rely 255/255, load 1/255
  Encapsulation SNAP, loopback not set, keepalive set (10 sec)
  ARP type: SNAP, ARP Timeout 4:00:00
  Ring speed: 0 Mbps
  Single ring node, Source Route Transparent Bridge capable
  Ethernet Transit OUI: 0x0000F8
  Last input never, output never, output hang never
  Last clearing of "show interface" counters never
  Output queue 0/40, 0 drops; input queue 0/75, 0 drops
  Five minute input rate 0 bits/sec, 0 packets/sec
  Five minute output rate 0 bits/sec, 0 packets/sec
     0 packets input, 0 bytes, 0 no buffer
     Received 0 broadcasts, 0 runts, 0 giants
     0 input errors, 0 CRC, 0 frame, 0 overrun, 0 ignored, 0 abort
     0 packets output, 0 bytes, 0 underruns
     0 output errors, 0 collisions, 1 interface resets, 0 restarts
     1 transitions
```

The following example on the Cisco 7500 includes the **accounting** option. When you use the **accounting** option, only the accounting statistics are displayed.

```
Router# show interfaces tokenring 2/0 accounting

TokenRing2/0
          Protocol    Pkts In   Chars In   Pkts Out  Chars Out
                IP       7344    4787842       1803    1535774
         Appletalk      33345    4797459      12781    1089695
           DEC MOP          0          0        127       9779
               ARP          7        420         39       2340
```

SHOW INTERFACES TUNNEL

To list tunnel interface information, use the **show interfaces tunnel** privileged EXEC command.

show interfaces tunnel *number* [**accounting**]

Syntax	Description
number	Port line number.
accounting	(Optional) Displays the number of packets of each protocol type that have been sent through the interface.

Command Mode

Privileged EXEC

Usage Guidelines

This command first appeared in Cisco IOS Release 10.0.

Sample Display

The following is sample output from the **show interfaces tunnel** command:

```
Router# show interfaces tunnel 4

Tunnel4 is up, line protocol is down
  Hardware is Routing Tunnel
  MTU 1500 bytes, BW 9 Kbit, DLY 500000 usec, rely 255/255, load 1/255
  Encapsulation TUNNEL, loopback not set, keepalive set (10 sec)
  Tunnel source 0.0.0.0, destination 0.0.0.0
  Tunnel protocol/transport GRE/IP, key disabled, sequencing disabled
  Last input never, output never, output hang never
  Last clearing of "show interface" counters never
  Output queue 0/0, 0 drops; input queue 0/75, 0 drops
  Five minute input rate 0 bits/sec, 0 packets/sec
  Five minute output rate 0 bits/sec, 0 packets/sec
    0 packets input, 0 bytes, 0 no buffer
    Received 0 broadcasts, 0 runts, 0 giants
    0 input errors, 0 CRC, 0 frame, 0 overrun, 0 ignored, 0 abort
    0 packets output, 0 bytes, 0 underruns
    0 output errors, 0 collisions, 0 interface resets, 0 restarts
```

Table 23–39 describes significant fields shown in the display.

Table 23–39   *Show Interfaces Tunnel Field Descriptions*

Field	Description
Tunnel is {up | down}	Interface is currently active and inserted into ring (up) or inactive and not inserted (down).
	On the Cisco 7500 series, gives the interface processor type, slot number, and port number.

Table 23-39 *Show Interfaces Tunnel Field Descriptions, Continued*

Field	Description
line protocol is {up | down | administratively down}	Shows line protocol up if a valid route is available to the tunnel destination. Shows line protocol down if no route is available, or if the route would be recursive.
Hardware	Specifies the hardware type.
MTU	Maximum Transmission Unit of the interface.
BW	Bandwidth of the interface in kilobits per second.
DLY	Delay of the interface in microseconds.
rely	Reliability of the interface as a fraction of 255 (255/255 is 100 percent reliability), calculated as an exponential average over five minutes.
load	Load on the interface as a fraction of 255 (255/255 is completely saturated), calculated as an exponential average over five minutes.
Encapsulation	Encapsulation method is always TUNNEL for tunnels.
loopback	Indicates whether loopback is set.
keepalive	Indicates whether keepalives are set.
Tunnel source	IP address used as the source address for packets in the tunnel.
destination	IP address of the host destination.
Tunnel protocol	Tunnel transport protocol (the protocol the tunnel is using). This is based on the **tunnel mode** command, which defaults to GRE.
key	ID key for the tunnel interface, unless disabled.
sequencing	Indicates whether the tunnel interface drops datagrams that arrive out of order. Can be disabled.
Last input	Number of hours, minutes, and seconds since the last packet was successfully received by an interface. Useful for knowing when a dead interface failed.
Last output	Number of hours, minutes, and seconds since the last packet was successfully transmitted by an interface.

Part III

Command Reference

Table 23–39   *Show Interfaces Tunnel Field Descriptions, Continued*

Field	Description
output hang	Number of hours, minutes, and seconds (or never) since the interface was last reset because of a transmission that took too long. When the number of hours in any of the "last" fields exceeds 24 hours, the number of days and hours is printed. If that field overflows, asterisks are printed.
Last clearing	Time at which the counters that measure cumulative statistics (such as number of bytes transmitted and received) shown in this report were last reset to zero. Note that variables that might affect routing (for example, load and reliability) are not cleared when the counters are cleared. *** indicates the elapsed time is too large to be displayed. 0:00:00 indicates the counters were cleared more than 2^{31}ms (and less than 2^{32}ms) ago.
Output queue, drops Input queue, drops	Number of packets in output and input queues. Each number is followed by a slash, the maximum size of the queue, and the number of packets dropped due to a full queue.
5 minute input rate, 5 minute output rate	Average number of bits and packets transmitted per second in the last five minutes. The five-minute input and output rates should be used only as an approximation of traffic per second during a given five-minute period. These rates are exponentially weighted averages with a time constant of five minutes. A period of four time constants must pass before the average will be within two percent of the instantaneous rate of a uniform stream of traffic over that period.
packets input	Total number of error-free packets received by the system.
bytes	Total number of bytes, including data and MAC encapsulation, in the error-free packets received by the system.
no buffer	Number of received packets discarded because there was no buffer space in the main system. Compare with ignored count. Broadcast storms on Ethernet networks and bursts of noise on serial lines are often responsible for no input buffer events.
broadcasts	Total number of broadcast or multicast packets received by the interface.
runts	Number of packets that are discarded because they are smaller than the medium's minimum packet size.

Table 23–39 *Show Interfaces Tunnel Field Descriptions, Continued*

Field	Description
giants	Number of packets that are discarded because they exceed the medium's maximum packet size.
CRC	Cyclic redundancy checksum generated by the originating LAN station or far-end device does not match the checksum calculated from the data received. On a LAN, this usually indicates noise or transmission problems on the LAN interface or the LAN bus itself. A high number of CRCs is usually the result of a station transmitting bad data.
frame	Number of packets received incorrectly having a CRC error and a noninteger number of octets.
overrun	Number of times the serial receiver hardware was unable to hand received data to a hardware buffer because the input rate exceeded the receiver's capability to handle the data.
ignored	Number of received packets ignored by the interface because the interface hardware ran low on internal buffers. These buffers are different than the system buffers mentioned previously in the buffer description. Broadcast storms and bursts of noise can cause the ignored count to be increased.
abort	Illegal sequence of one bits on a serial interface. This usually indicates a clocking problem between the serial interface and the data link equipment.
packets output	Total number of messages transmitted by the system.
bytes	Total number of bytes, including data and MAC encapsulation, transmitted by the system.
underruns	Number of times that the far-end transmitter has been running faster than the near-end router's receiver can handle. This may never be reported on some interfaces.
output errors	Sum of all errors that prevented the final transmission of datagrams out of the interface being examined. Note that this might not balance with the sum of the enumerated output errors, as some datagrams might have more than one error, and others might have errors that do not fall into any of the specifically tabulated categories.

Table 23–39   *Show Interfaces Tunnel Field Descriptions, Continued*

Field	Description
collisions	Number of messages retransmitted due to an Ethernet collision. This usually is the result of an overextended LAN (Ethernet or transceiver cable too long, more than two repeaters between stations, or too many cascaded multiport transceivers). Some collisions are normal. However, if your collision rate climbs to around four or five percent, you should consider verifying that there is no faulty equipment on the segment and/or moving some existing stations to a new segment. A packet that collides is counted only once in output packets.
interface resets	Number of times an interface has been reset. The interface may be reset by the administrator or automatically when an internal error occurs.
restarts	Number of times the controller was restarted because of errors.

Related Commands

show interfaces
show ip route
show route

SHOW INTERFACES VG-ANYLAN

Use the **show interfaces vg-anylan** EXEC command to display the information about the 100VG-AnyLAN port adapter on Cisco 7200 series routers, Cisco 7500 series routers.

> **show interfaces vg-anylan** [*slot/port-adapter/port*] (on VIP cards in Cisco 7500 series)
> **show interfaces vg-anylan** [*slot/port*] (Cisco 7200 series)

Syntax	Description
slot	Refer to the appropriate hardware manual for slot and port information.
port-adapter	Refer to the appropriate hardware manual for information about port adapter compatibility.
port	Refer to the appropriate hardware manual for slot and port information.

Command Mode

EXEC

Usage Guidelines

This command first appeared in Cisco IOS Release 11.3.

Sample Display

The following is sample output from the **show interfaces vg-anylan** command:

```
Router# show interfaces vg-anylan 3/0/0

VG-AnyLAN3/0/0 is up, line protocol is up
   Hardware is cyBus VG-AnyLAN Interface
   Frame type is 802.3, address is 0060.3e64.2460 (bia 0060.3e64.2460)
   Internet address is 10.1.1.5/16
   MTU 1500 bytes, BW 100000 Kbit, DLY 100 usec, rely 255/255, load 1/255
   Encapsulation ARPA, loopback not set, keepalive set (10 sec)
   ARP type: ARPA, ARP Timeout 04:00:00
   Last input 00:00:26, output 00:00:09, output hang never
   Last clearing of "show interface" counters never
   Queueing strategy: fifo
   Output queue 0/40, 0 drops; input queue 0/75, 0 drops
   5 minute input rate 0 bits/sec, 0 packets/sec
   5 minute output rate 0 bits/sec, 0 packets/sec
      5316 packets input, 857349 bytes, 0 no buffer
      Received 5310 broadcasts, 0 runts, 0 giants
      0 input errors, 0 CRC, 0 frame, 0 overrun, 0 ignored, 0 abort
      0 input packets with dribble condition detected
      7920 packets output, 754259 bytes, 0 underruns
      0 output errors, 0 collisions, 2 interface resets
      0 output buffer failures, 0 output buffers swapped out
      0 vg alignment error, 0 vg balance error
      0 vg invalid ipm  error, 0 vg symbol error
      0 vg skew error, 0 vg frame delimit error
      0 vg high priority packets, 0 vg high priority octets
```

Table 23–40 describes significant fields in this output.

Table 23–40 *Show Interfaces VG-AnyLAN Field Descriptions*

Field	Description
VG-AnyLAN3/0/0 is up, line protocol is up	Indicates whether the interface hardware is currently active and can transmit and receive or has been taken down by an administrator.
Hardware is cyBus VG-AnyLAN	Hardware type.
Frame type is 803.2	Currently the frame type supported is 803.2.
Internet address	Internet address and subnet mask.
MTU	Maximum transmission unit of the interface.

Table 23–40 *Show Interfaces VG-AnyLAN Field Descriptions, Continued*

Field	Description
BW	Bandwidth of the interface in kilobits per second.
DLY	Delay of the interface in microseconds.
rely	Reliability of the interface as a fraction of 255 (255/255 is 100 percent reliability), calculated as an exponential average over five minutes.
load	Load on the interface as a fraction of 255 (255/255 is completely saturated), calculated as an exponential average over five minutes. The calculation uses the value from the **bandwidth** interface configuration command.
Encapsulation	Encapsulation method assigned to the interface.
loopback	Indicates whether loopbacks are set.
keepalive	Indicates whether keepalives are set.
ARA type	ARP type on the interface.
Last input	Number of hours, minutes, and seconds since the last packet was successfully received by an interface. Useful for knowing when a dead interface failed.
output	Number of hours, minutes, and seconds since the last packet was successfully transmitted by an interface.
output hang	Number of hours, minutes, and seconds (or never) since the interface was last reset because of a transmission that took too long. When the number of hours in any of the "last" fields exceeds 24 hours, the number of days and hours is printed. If that field overflows, asterisks are printed.
last clearing	Time at which the counters that measure cumulative statistics (such as number of bytes transmitted and received) shown in this report were last reset to zero. Variables that might affect routing (for example, load and reliability) are not cleared when the counters are cleared. *** indicates the elapsed time is too large to be displayed. 0:00:00 indicates the counters were cleared more than 2^{31}ms (and less then 2^{32}ms) ago.

Table 23–40 *Show Interfaces VG-AnyLAN Field Descriptions, Continued*

Field	Description
Queueing strategy	First-in, first-out queuing strategy (other queueing strategies you might see are priority-list, custom-list, and weighted-fair).
Output queue, drops input queue, drops	Number of packets in output and input queues. Each number is followed by a slash, the maximum size of the queue, and the number of packets dropped because a queue was full.
5 minute input rate 5 minute output rate	Average number of bits and packets received or transmitted per second in the last five minutes.
packets input	Total number of error-free packets received by the system.
bytes (input)	Total number of bytes, including data and MAC encapsulation, in the error-free packets received by the system.
no buffer	Number of received packets discarded because there was no buffer space in the main system. Compare with ignored count. Broadcast storms on Ethernet networks and bursts of noise on serial lines are often responsible for no input buffer events.
broadcasts	Total number of broadcast or multicast packets received by the interface.
runts	Number of packets that are discarded because they are smaller than the medium's minimum packet size.
giants	Number of packets that are discarded because they exceed the medium's maximum packet size.
input errors	Total number of no buffer, runts, giants, CRCs, frame, overrun, ignored, and abort counts. Other input-related errors can also increment the count, so that this sum might not balance with the other counts.

Table 23-40 *Show Interfaces VG-AnyLAN Field Descriptions, Continued*

Field	Description
CRC	Cyclic redundancy checksum generated by the originating LAN station or far-end device does not match the checksum calculated from the data received. On a LAN, this usually indicates noise or transmission problems on the LAN interface or the LAN bus itself. A high number of CRCs is usually the result of collisions or a station transmitting bad data. On a serial link, CRCs usually indicate noise, gain hits, or other transmission problems on the data link.
frame	Number of packets received incorrectly having a CRC error and a noninteger number of octets. On a serial line, this is usually the result of noise or other transmission problems.
overrun	Number of times the serial receiver hardware was unable to hand received data to a hardware buffer because the input rate exceeded the receiver's capability to handle the data.
ignored	Number of received packets ignored by the interface because the interface hardware ran low on internal buffers. These buffers are different than the system buffers mentioned previously in the buffer description. Broadcast storms and bursts of noise can cause the ignored count to be incremented.
abort	Illegal sequence of one bits on the interface.
input packets with dribble condition detected	Dribble bit error indicates that a frame is slightly too long. This frame error counter is incremented just for informational purposes; the router accepts the frame.
packets output	Total number of messages transmitted by the system.
bytes (output)	Total number of bytes, including data and MAC encapsulation, transmitted by the system.
underruns	Number of times that the far-end transmitter has been running faster than the near-end router's receiver can handle.
output errors	Sum of all errors that prevented the final transmission of datagrams out of the interface being examined. Note that this might not balance with the sum of the enumerated output errors, as some datagrams can have more than one error, and others can have errors that do not fall into any of the specifically tabulated categories.

Table 23–40 *Show Interfaces VG-AnyLAN Field Descriptions, Continued*

Field	Description
collisions	Number of messages retransmitted due to an Ethernet collision. This is usually the result of an overextended LAN (Ethernet or transceiver cable too long, more than two repeaters between stations, or too many cascaded multiport transceivers). A packet that collides is counted only once in output packets.
interface resets	Number of times an interface has been completely reset. This can happen if packets queued for transmission were not sent within a certain interval. If the system notices that the carrier detect line of an interface is up, but the line protocol is down, it periodically resets the interface in an effort to restart it. Interface resets also can occur when an unrecoverable interface processor error occurred, or when an interface is looped back or shut down.
output buffer failures	Number of times that a packet was not output from the output hold queue because of a shortage of MEMD shared memory.
output buffers swapped out	Number of packets stored in main memory when the output queue is full; swapping buffers to main memory prevents packets from being dropped when output is congested. The number is high when traffic is bursty.
vg alignment error	Number of non-octets received.
vg balance error	Number of incorrect balanced symbols received.
vg invalid ipm error	Number of packets received with an invalid packet marker (IPM).
vg symbol error	Number of symbols received that were not correctly decoded.
vg skew error	Number of skews between four pairs of twisted-pair wire that exceeded the allowable skew.
vg frame delimit error	Number of start-of-frame errors or false-start errors received.
vg high priority packets	Number of high-priority packets received.
vg high priority octets	Number of high-priority octets received.

Related Commands

interface vg-anylan

SHOW IP INTERFACE

To list a summary of an interface's IP information and status, use the **show ip interface** privileged EXEC command.

> **show ip interface** [**brief**] [*type*] [*number*]

Syntax	*Description*
brief	(Optional) Displays a brief summary of IP status and configuration.
type	(Optional) Specifies that information be displayed about that interface type only. The possible value depends on the type of interfaces the system has. For example, it could be **ethernet, null, serial, tokenring,** and so forth.
number	(Optional) Interface number.

Command Mode

Privileged EXEC

Usage Guidelines

This command first appeared in Cisco IOS Release 10.3.

Sample Displays

The following is sample output from the **show ip interface** command:

```
Router# show ip interface

Ethernet0 is administratively down, line protocol is down
    Internet address is 1.0.46.10, subnet mask is 255.0.0.0
    Broadcast address is 255.255.255.255
    Address determined by setup command
    MTU is 1500 bytes
    Helper address is not set
    Directed broadcast forwarding is enabled
    Multicast groups joined: 224.0.0.1 224.0.0.2
    Outgoing access list is not set
    Inbound  access list is not set
    Proxy ARP is enabled
    Security level is default
    Split horizon is enabled
    ICMP redirects are always sent
    ICMP unreachables are always sent
    ICMP mask replies are never sent
```

```
    IP fast switching is enabled
    IP fast switching on the same interface is disabled
    IP SSE switching is disabled
    Router Discovery is disabled
    IP accounting is disabled
    TCP/IP header compression is disabled
    Probe proxy name replies are disabled
    Gateway Discovery is disabled
  PCbus0 is administratively down, line protocol is down
    Internet address is 198.135.1.43, subnet mask is 255.255.255.0
    Broadcast address is 255.255.255.255
    Address determined by setup command
    MTU is 1500 bytes
    Helper address is not set
    Directed broadcast forwarding is enabled
    Multicast groups joined: 224.0.0.1 224.0.0.2
    Outgoing access list is not set
    Inbound  access list is not set
    Proxy ARP is enabled
    Security level is default
    Split horizon is enabled
    ICMP redirects are always sent
    ICMP unreachables are always sent
    ICMP mask replies are never sent
    IP fast switching is enabled
    IP fast switching on the same interface is disabled
    IP SSE switching is disabled
    Router Discovery is disabled
    IP accounting is disabled
    TCP/IP header compression is disabled
    Probe proxy name replies are disabled
    Gateway Discovery is disabled
  Serial0 is administratively down, line protocol is down
    Internet address is 198.135.2.49, subnet mask is 255.255.255.0
    Broadcast address is 255.255.255.255
    Address determined by setup command
    MTU is 1500 bytes
    Helper address is not set
    Directed broadcast forwarding is enabled
    Multicast groups joined: 224.0.0.1 224.0.0.2
    Outgoing access list is not set
    Inbound  access list is not set
    Proxy ARP is enabled
    Security level is default
    Split horizon is enabled
    ICMP redirects are always sent
    ICMP unreachables are always sent
    ICMP mask replies are never sent
    IP fast switching is enabled
    IP fast switching on the same interface is disabled
    IP SSE switching is disabled
```

```
Router Discovery is disabled
IP accounting is disabled
TCP/IP header compression is disabled
Probe proxy name replies are disabled
Gateway Discovery is disabled
```

The following is sample output from the **show ip interface brief** command:

```
Router# show ip interface brief

Interface    IP-Address      OK?  Method  Status                    Protocol
Ethernet0    1.0.46.10       YES  manual  administratively down     down
PCbus0       198.135.1.43    YES  manual  administratively down     down
Serial0      198.135.2.49    YES  manual  administratively down     down
```

The following is sample output from the **show ip interface brief pcbus 0** command:

```
Router# show ip interface brief pcbus 0

Interface    IP-Address      OK?  Method  Status                    Protocol
PCbus0       198.135.1.43    YES  manual  administratively down     down
```

Related Commands

show interfaces

SHOW RIF

Use the **show rif** EXEC command to display the current contents of the RIF cache.

show rif

Syntax   Description

This command has no arguments or keywords.

Command Mode

EXEC

Usage Guidelines

This command first appeared in Cisco IOS Release 10.0.

Sample Display

The following is sample output from the **show rif** command:

```
Router# show rif

Codes: * interface, - static, + remote
Hardware Addr  How   Idle (min)  Routing Information Field
5C02.0001.4322 rg5        -      0630.0053.00B0
5A00.0000.2333 TR0        3      08B0.0101.2201.0FF0
```

```
5B01.0000.4444 -              -   -
0000.1403.4800 TR1        0   -
0000.2805.4C00 TR0        *   -
0000.2807.4C00 TR1        *   -
0000.28A8.4800 TR0        0   -
0077.2201.0001 rg5       10   0830.0052.2201.0FF0
```

In the display, entries marked with an asterisk (*) are the router/bridge's interface addresses. Entries marked with a dash (–) are static entries. Entries with a number are cached entries. If the RIF timeout is set to something other than the default of 15 minutes, the timeout is displayed at the top of the display.

Table 23–41 describes significant fields shown in the display.

Table 23–41 *Show RIF Cache Display Field Descriptions*

Field	Description
Hardware Addr	Lists the MAC-level addresses.
How	Describes how the RIF has been learned. Possible values include a ring group (rg), or interface (TR).
Idle (min)	Indicates how long, in minutes, since the last response was received directly from this node.
Routing Information Field	Lists the RIF.

SHOW SERVICE-MODULE SERIAL

To display the performance report for an integrated CSU/DSU, use the **show service-module serial** privileged EXEC command.

    show service-module serial *number* [**performance-statistics** [*interval-range*]]

Syntax	Description
number	Interface number 0 or 1.
performance-statistics	(Optional) Displays the CSU/DSU performance statistics for the past 24 hours. This keyword applies only to the fractional T1/T1 module.
interval-range	(Optional) Specifies the number of 15-minute intervals displayed. You can choose a range from 1 to 96, where each value represents the CSU/DSU activity performed in that 15-minute interval. For example, a range of 2-3 displays the performance statistics for the intervals two and three.

Command Mode

Privileged EXEC

Usage Guidelines

This command first appeared in Cisco IOS Release 11.2.

This command applies to the two- and four-wire 56/64-kbps CSU/DSU module and FT1/T1 CSU/DSU module. The **performance-statistics** keyword applies only to the FT1/T1 CSU/DSU module.

Sample Displays

The following example shows CSU/DSU performance statistics on a Cisco 2524 or Cisco 2525 router for intervals 30 to 32. Each interval is 15 minutes long. All the data is zero because no errors were discovered on the T1 line:

```
Router# show service-module serial 1 performance-statistics 30-32
Total Data (last 58 15 minute intervals):
    0 Line Code Violations, 0 Path Code Violations
    0 Slip Secs, 0 Fr Loss Secs, 0 Line Err Secs, 0 Degraded Mins
    0 Errored Secs, 0 Bursty Err Secs, 0 Severely Err Secs, 0 Unavail Secs
Data in current interval (131 seconds elapsed):
    0 Line Code Violations, 0 Path Code Violations
    0 Slip Secs, 0 Fr Loss Secs, 0 Line Err Secs, 0 Degraded Mins
    0 Errored Secs, 0 Bursty Err Secs, 0 Severely Err Secs, 0 Unavail Secs
Data in Interval 30:
    0 Line Code Violations, 0 Path Code Violations
    0 Slip Secs, 0 Fr Loss Secs, 0 Line Err Secs, 0 Degraded Mins
    0 Errored Secs, 0 Bursty Err Secs, 0 Severely Err Secs, 0 Unavail Secs
Data in Interval 31:
    0 Line Code Violations, 0 Path Code Violations
    0 Slip Secs, 0 Fr Loss Secs, 0 Line Err Secs, 0 Degraded Mins
    0 Errored Secs, 0 Bursty Err Secs, 0 Severely Err Secs, 0 Unavail Secs
Data in Interval 32:
    0 Line Code Violations, 0 Path Code Violations
    0 Slip Secs, 0 Fr Loss Secs, 0 Line Err Secs, 0 Degraded Mins
    0 Errored Secs, 0 Bursty Err Secs, 0 Severely Err Secs, 0 Unavail Secs
```

The following example is sample output from the **show service-module serial** command:

```
Router1# show service-module serial 0
Module type is T1/fractional
    Hardware revision is B, Software revision is 1.1 ,
    Image checksum is 0x2160B7C, Protocol revision is 1.1
Receiver has AIS alarm,
Unit is currently in test mode:
    line loopback is in progress
Framing is ESF, Line Code is B8ZS, Current clock source is line,
Fraction has 24 timeslots (64 Kbits/sec each), Net bandwidth is 1536 Kbits/sec.
Last user loopback performed:
    remote loopback
    Failed to loopup remote
Last module self-test (done at startup): Passed
Last clearing of alarm counters 0:05:50
    loss of signal      :    1, last occurred 0:01:50
    loss of frame       :    0,
```

```
        AIS alarm              :    1, current duration 0:00:49
        Remote alarm           :    0,
        Module access errors   :    0,
Total Data (last 0 15 minute intervals):
Line Code Violations, 0 Path Code Violations
        0 Slip Secs, 0 Fr Loss Secs, 0 Line Err Secs, 0 Degraded Mins
        0 Errored Secs, 0 Bursty Err Secs, 0 Severely Err Secs, 0 Unavail Secs
Data in current interval (351 seconds elapsed):
        1466 Line Code Violations, 0 Path Code Violations
        25 Slip Secs, 49 Fr Loss Secs, 40 Line Err Secs, 1 Degraded Mins
        0 Errored Secs, 0 Bursty Err Secs, 0 Severely Err Secs, 49 Unavail Secs

Router1# show service-module serial 1
Module type is 4-wire Switched 56
        Hardware revision is B, Software revision is 1.00,
        Image checksum is 0x44453634, Protocol revision is 1.0
Connection state: active,
Receiver has loss of signal, loss of sealing current,
Unit is currently in test mode:
        line loopback is in progress
Current line rate is 56 Kbits/sec
Last user loopback performed:
        dte loopback
        duration 00:00:58
Last module self-test (done at startup): Passed
Last clearing of alarm counters 0:13:54
        oos/oof                :    3, last occurred 0:00:24
        loss of signal         :    3, current duration 0:00:24
        loss of sealing curren:    2, current duration 0:04:39
        loss of frame          :    0,
        rate adaption attempts:    0,
```

The following example shows sample output from the **show service-module serial** command issued on a Cisco 3640 modular access router:

```
router# show service-module serial 0/1
Module type is 4-wire Switched 56
        Hardware revision is B, Software revision is 1.00,
        Image checksum is 0x42364436, Protocol revision is 1.0
Connection state: Idle
Receiver has no alarms.
CSU/DSU Alarm mask is 0
Current line rate is 56 Kbits/sec
Last module self-test (done at startup): Passed
Last clearing of alarm counters 4d02h
        oos/oof                :    0,
        loss of signal         :    0,
        loss of sealing curren:    0,
        loss of frame          :    0,
        rate adaptation attemp:    0,
```

The following example shows sample output from the **show service-module serial** command issued on a Cisco 1605 router:

```
router# show service-module serial 0
Module type is 4-wire Switched 56
    Hardware revision is B, Software revision is 1.00,
    Image checksum is 0x42364436, Protocol revision is 1.0
Receiver has oos/oof, loss of signal,
CSU/DSU Alarm mask is 4
Current line rate is 56 Kbits/sec
Last module self-test (done at startup): Passed
Last clearing of alarm counters 1d02h
    oos/oof              :   1, current duration 1d02h
    loss of signal       :   1, current duration 1d02h
    loss of frame        :   0,
    rate adaptation attemp:  0,
```

Table 23–42 describes the fields displayed by the **show service-module serial** command.

Table 23–42 *Show Service-Module Output Field Descriptions*

Field	Description
Module type	The CSU/DSU module installed in the router. The possible modules are T1/fractional, two-wire switched 56-kbps, and four-wire 56/64-kbps.
Receiver has AIS alarm	Alarms detected by the FT1/T1 CSU/DSU module or two- and four-wire 56/64-kbps CSU/DSU modules. Possible T1 alarms are as follows: • Transmitter is sending remote alarm. • Transmitter is sending AIS. • Receiver has loss of signal. • Receiver has loss of frame. • Receiver has remote alarm. • Receiver has no alarms. Possible switched 56k alarms are as follows: • Receiver has loss of signal • Receiver has loss of sealing current • Receiver has loss of frame • Receiver has rate adaptation attempts
Unit is currently in test mode	Loopback tests are in progress.

Table 23-42 *Show Service-Module Output Field Descriptions, Continued*

Field	Description
Framing is ESF	Indicates frame type used on the line. Can be extended super frame or super frame.
Line Code is B8ZS	Indicated line-code type configured. Can be alternate mark inversion (AMI) or binary 8-zero substitution (B8ZS).
Current clock source is line	Clock source configured on the line, which can be supplied by the service provider (line) or the integrated CSU/DSU module (internal).
Fraction has 24 timeslots	Number of timeslots defined for the FT1/T1 module, which can range from 1 to 24.
Net bandwidth	Total bandwidth of the line (for example, 24 timeslots multiplied by 64 kbps equals a bandwidth of 1,536 kbps).
Last user loopback performed	Type and outcome of the last performed loopback.
Last module self-test (done at startup): Passed	Status of the last self test performed on an integrated CSU/DSU module.
Last clearing of alarm counters	List of network alarms that were detected and cleared on the CSU/DSU module.
Total Data Data in current interval	Shows the current accumulation period, which rolls into the 24-hour accumulation every 15 minutes. The oldest 15-minute period falls off the back of the 24-hour accumulation buffer.
Line Code Violations	Indicates the occurrence of either a bipolar violation or excessive zeroes error event.
Path Code Violations	Indicates a frame synchronization bit error in the D4 and E1-no CRC formats or a CRC error in the ESF and E1-CRC formats.
Slip Secs	Indicates the replication or detection of the payload bits of a DS1 frame. A slip may be performed when there is a difference between the timing of a synchronous receiving terminal and the received signal.
Fr Loss Secs	Indicates the number of seconds an Out-of-Frame error is detected.
Line Err Secs	Line errored seconds is a second in which one or more line code violation errors are detected.

Part III

Command Reference

Table 23–42 *Show Service-Module Output Field Descriptions, Continued*

Field	Description
Errored Secs	In ESF and E1-CRC links, an errored second is a second in which one of the following is detected: one or more path code violations; one or more Out-of-Frame defects; one or more controlled slip events, or a detected AIS defect. For D4 and E1-no CRC links, the presence of bipolar violation also triggers an errored second.
Bursty Err Secs	A second with fewer than 320 and more than 1 path coding violation errors. No severely errored frame defects or incoming AIS defects are detected. Controlled slips are not included in this parameter.
Severely Err Secs	For ESF signals, a second with one of the following errors: 320 or more path code violation errors; one or more Out-of-Frame defects; a detected AIS defect. For D4 signals, a count of one-second intervals with framing errors, or an Out-of-Frame defect, or 1,544 line code violations.
Unavail Secs	Total time the line was out of service.

Related Commands

clear service-module

PART IV

System Management

## CHAPTER 24

Monitoring the Router and Network

This chapter describes the tasks that you can perform to monitor the router and network.

For a complete description of the router monitoring commands mentioned in this chapter, see Chapter 25, "Router and Network Monitoring Commands."

MONITORING THE ROUTER AND NETWORK TASK LIST

This chapter describes the tasks you can perform to manage the router and its performance on the network. Perform any of the tasks in the following sections:

- Configuring SNMP Support
- Configuring RMON Support
- Configuring the Cisco Discovery Protocol
- Configuring Response Time Reporter

CONFIGURING SNMP SUPPORT

The Simple Network Management Protocol (SNMP) system consists of the following three parts:

- An SNMP manager
- An SNMP agent
- A Management Information Base (MIB)

SNMP is an application-layer protocol that provides a message format for communication between SNMP managers and agents.

The SNMP manager can be part of a Network Management System (NMS) such as CiscoWorks. The agent and MIB reside on the router. To configure SNMP on the router, you define the relationship between the manager and the agent.

The SNMP agent contains MIB variables whose values the SNMP manager can request or change. A manager can get a value from an agent or store a value into that agent. The agent gathers data from the MIB, the repository for information about device parameters and network data. The agent also can respond to a manager's requests to get or set data.

An agent can send unsolicited traps to the manager. Traps are messages alerting the SNMP manager to a condition on the network. Traps can indicate improper user authentication, restarts, link status (up or down), closing of a TCP connection, loss of connection to a neighbor router, or other significant events.

Figure 24–1 illustrates the communications relationship between the SNMP manager and agent. A manager can send the agent requests to get and set MIB values. The agent can respond to these requests. Independent of this interaction, the agent can send unsolicited traps to the manager to notify the manager of network conditions.

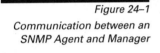

Figure 24–1

Communication between an SNMP Agent and Manager

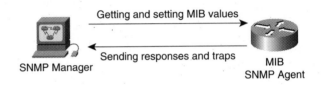

Getting and setting MIB values

Sending responses and traps

SNMP Manager

MIB
SNMP Agent

Versions of SNMP

Cisco IOS Release 11.3 software supports the following versions of SNMP:

- **SNMPv1**—The Simple Network Management Protocol, a Full Internet Standard, defined in RFC 1157.
- **SNMPv2C**, which consists of the following:
  - **SNMPv2**—Version 2 of the Simple Network Management Protocol, a Draft Internet Standard, defined in RFCs 1902 through 1907.
  - **SNMPv2C**—The Community-based Administrative Framework for SNMPv2, an Experimental Internet Protocol defined in RFC 1901.

Cisco IOS Release 11.3 ED removes support for the following version of SNMP:

- **SNMPv2Classic**—IETF Proposed Internet Standard of Version 2 of the Simple Network Management Protocol, defined in RFCs 1441 through 1451.

SNMPv2C replaces the Party-based Administrative and Security Framework of SNMPv2Classic with the Community-based Administrative Framework of SNMPv2C while retaining the bulk retrieval and improved error handling of SNMPv2Classic.

Both SNMPv1 and SNMPv2C use a community-based form of security. The community of managers able to access the agent's MIB is defined by an IP address access control list and password.

SNMPv2C support includes a bulk retrieval mechanism and more detailed error-message reporting to management stations. The bulk retrieval mechanism supports the retrieval of tables and large quantities of information, minimizing the number of round trips required. The SNMPv2C improved error-handling support includes expanded error codes that distinguish different kinds of error conditions; these conditions are reported through a single error code in SNMPv1. Error-return codes now report the error type. Three kinds of exceptions are also reported: no such object exceptions, no such instance exceptions, and end of MIB view exceptions.

You must configure the SNMP agent to use the version of SNMP supported by the management station. An agent can communicate with multiple managers; for this reason, you can configure the Cisco IOS software to support communications with one management station using the SNMPv1 protocol and another using the SNMPv2 protocol.

Supported MIBs

Cisco's implementation of SNMP supports all MIB II variables (as described in RFC 1213) and SNMP traps (as described in RFC 1215).

Cisco no longer supports RFC 1447, "SNMPv2 Party MIB" (April 1993) or RFC 1450, "SNMPv2 MIB" (April 1993).

Cisco provides its own private MIB extensions with every system. One of the set of MIB objects provided is the Cisco Chassis MIB that enables the SNMP manager to gather data on system card descriptions, serial numbers, hardware and software revision levels, and slot locations. Another set is the Entity MIB (RFC 2037), which describes the logical resources, physical resources, and logical-to-physical mappings of devices managed by a single SNMP agent. The Entity MIB also records the time of the last modification to any object in the Entity MIB and sends out a trap when any object is modified.

SNMP Configuration Task List

There is no specific command that you use to enable SNMP. The first **snmp-server** command that you enter enables both versions of SNMP.

To configure SNMP support, perform any of the tasks in the following sections. The second task is required; all other tasks are optional.

- Creating or Modifying an SNMP View Record
- Creating or Modifying Access Control for an SNMP Community
- Enabling the SNMP Agent Shutdown Mechanism
- Establishing the Contact, Location, and Serial Number of the SNMP Agent
- Defining the Maximum SNMP Agent Packet Size
- Limiting TFTP Servers Used Via SNMP
- Monitoring SNMP Status
- Disabling the SNMP Agent
- Defining SNMP Trap Operations

Creating or Modifying an SNMP View Record

You can assign views to community strings to limit which MIB objects an SNMP manager can access. You can use a predefined view, or create your own view. If you are using a predefined view or no view at all, skip this step.

To create or modify an SNMP view record, perform the following task in global configuration mode:

Task	Command
Create or modify a view record.	snmp-server view *view-name oid-tree* {included | excluded}

To remove a view record, use the **no snmp-server view** command.

You can enter this command multiple times for the same view record. Later lines take precedence when an object identifier is included in two or more lines.

Creating or Modifying Access Control for an SNMP Community

Use an SNMP community string to define the relationship between the SNMP manager and the agent. The community string acts like a password to permit access to the agent on the router. Optionally, you can specify one or more of the following characteristics associated with the string:

- An access list of IP addresses of the SNMP managers that are permitted to use the community string to gain access to the agent.
- A MIB view, which defines the subset of all MIB objects accessible to the given community.
- Read and write or read-only permission for the MIB objects accessible to the community.

To configure a community string, perform the following task in global configuration mode:

Task	Command
Define the community access string.	snmp-server community *string* [view *view-name*] [ro | rw] [*access-list number*]

You can configure one or more community strings. To remove a specific community string, use the **no snmp-server community** command.

For an example of configuring a community string, see the section "SNMP Examples" at the end of this chapter.

Enabling the SNMP Agent Shutdown Mechanism

Using SNMP packets, a network management tool can send messages to users on virtual terminals and the console. This facility operates in a similar fashion to the EXEC **send** command. However, the SNMP request that causes the message to be issued to the users also specifies the action to be taken after the message is delivered. One possible action is a shutdown request. After a system is shut down, typically it is reloaded. Because the ability to cause a reload from the network is a powerful feature, it is protected by the **snmp-server system-shutdown** global configuration command. If you do not issue this command, the shutdown mechanism is not enabled. To enable the SNMP agent shutdown mechanism, perform the following task:

Task	Command
Use the SNMP message reload feature and request a system shutdown message.	**snmp-server system-shutdown**

To understand how to use this feature with SNMP requests, read the document OLD-CISCO-SYSTEM-MIB.my, available on Cisco Connection Online.

Establishing the Contact, Location, and Serial Number of the SNMP Agent

You can set the system contact, location, and serial number of the SNMP agent so that these descriptions can be accessed through the configuration file. To do so, perform one or more of the following tasks in global configuration mode:

Task	Command
Set the system contact string.	**snmp-server contact** *text*
Set the system location string.	**snmp-server location** *text*
Set the system serial number.	**snmp-server chassis-id** *text*

Defining the Maximum SNMP Agent Packet Size

You can set the maximum packet size permitted when the SNMP agent is receiving a request or generating a reply. To do so, perform the following task in global configuration mode:

Task	Command
Establish the maximum packet size.	**snmp-server packetsize** *byte-count*

Limiting TFTP Servers Used Via SNMP

You can limit the TFTP servers used for saving and loading configuration files via SNMP to the servers specified in an access list. To do so, perform the following task in global configuration mode:

Task	Command
Limit TFTP servers used for configuration file copies via SNMP to the servers in an access list.	**snmp-server tftp-server-list** *number*

Monitoring SNMP Status

To monitor SNMP input and output statistics, including the number of illegal community string entries, errors, and requested variables, complete the following task in EXEC mode:

Task	Command
Monitor SNMP status.	**show snmp**

Disabling the SNMP Agent

To disable both versions of SNMP (SNMPv1 and SNMPv2C), perform the following task in global configuration mode:

Task	Command
Disable SNMP agent operation.	**no snmp-server**

Defining SNMP Trap Operations

The SNMP trap operations allow a system administrator to configure the agent router to send information to an SNMP manager when a particular event occurs.

To configure the router to send traps to a host, perform the following tasks in global configuration mode:

Task	Command
Step 1 Specify the recipient of the trap message.	**snmp-server host** *host* [**version** {1 | 2c}] *community-string* [**udp-port** *port*] [*trap-type*]
Step 2 Specify the types of traps sent.	**snmp-server enable traps** [*trap-type*] [*trap-option*]

The **snmp-server host** command specifies which hosts will receive traps. The **snmp-server enable traps** commands globally enables the trap production mechanism for the specified traps.

However, some traps are not controlled by the **snmp-server enable traps** command. These traps are either enabled by default or controlled through other commands. For example, by default, SNMP link traps are sent when an interface goes up or down. For interfaces expected to go up and down during normal usage, such as ISDN interfaces, the output generated by these traps might not be useful. Use the **no snmp trap link-status** interface configuration command to disable these traps.

In order for a host to receive a trap, a **snmp-server host** command must be configured for that host, and the trap must be enabled globally through the **snmp-server enable traps** command, through a different command, such as **snmp trap link-status,** or by default.

Optionally, you can specify a value other than the default for the source interface, message (packet) queue length for each trap host, or retransmission interval.

To change trap operation values, perform any of the following optional tasks in global configuration mode:

Task	Command
Specify the source interface (and hence IP address) of the trap message.	**snmp-server trap-source** *interface*
Establish the message queue length for each trap host.	**snmp-server queue-length** *length*
Define how often to resend trap messages on the retransmission queue.	**snmp-server trap-timeout** *seconds*

CONFIGURING RMON SUPPORT

The Remote Monitoring (RMON) option provides visibility of individual nodal activity and allows you to monitor all nodes and their interaction on a LAN segment. RMON, used in conjunction with the SNMP agent in the router, allows you to view both traffic that flows through the router and segment traffic not necessarily destined for the router. Combining RMON alarms and events with existing MIBs allows you to choose where proactive monitoring will occur.

Full RMON packet analysis as described in RFC 1757 is available only on an Ethernet interface of the Cisco 2500 series and Cisco AS5200 series routers. RMON requires that SNMP be configured. A generic RMON console application such as Frontier NETscout Manager or Traffic Director is recommended in order to take advantage of RMON's network management capabilities.

RMON can be very data and processor intensive. Users should measure usage effects to ensure that router performance is not degraded and to minimize excessive management traffic overhead. Native mode is less intensive than promiscuous mode.

All Cisco IOS software images ordered without the explicit RMON option include limited RMON support (RMON alarms and event groups only). Images ordered with the RMON option include support for all nine groups (statistics, history, alarms, hosts, hostTopN, matrix, filter, capture, and event). As a security precaution, support for the packet-capture group allows capture of packet header information only; data payloads are not captured.

To enable RMON on an Ethernet interface, perform the following task in interface configuration mode:

Task	Command
Enable RMON.	**rmon** {**native** | **promiscuous**}

In native mode, RMON monitors only the packets normally received by the interface. In promiscuous mode, RMON monitors all packets on the LAN segment.

The default size of the queue that holds packets for analysis by the RMON process is 64 packets. To change the size of the queue, perform the following task in global configuration mode:

Task	Command
Change the size of the RMON queue.	**rmon queuesize** *size*

To set an RMON alarm or event, perform one of the following tasks in global configuration mode:

Task	Command
Set an alarm on a MIB object.	**rmon alarm** *number variable interval* {**delta** | **absolute**} **rising-threshold** *value* [*event-number*] **falling-threshold** *value* [*event-number*] [**owner** *string*]
Add or remove an event in the RMON event table.	**rmon event** *number* [**log**] [**trap** *community*] [**description** *string*] [**owner** *string*]

You can set an alarm on any MIB object in the access server. To disable an alarm, you must enable the **no** form of this command on each alarm you configure. You cannot disable all the alarms you configure at once. Refer to RFC 1757 to learn more about alarms and events and how they interact with each other.

To display the current RMON status, perform one or more of the following tasks in EXEC mode:

Task	Command
Display general RMON statistics.	show rmon or show rmon task
Display the RMON alarm table.	show rmon alarms
Display the RMON buffer capture table. Available on Cisco 2500 series and Cisco AS5200 only.	show rmon capture
Display the RMON event table.	show rmon events
Display the RMON filter table. Available on Cisco 2500 series and Cisco AS5200 only.	show rmon filter
Display the RMON history table. Available on Cisco 2500 series and Cisco AS5200 only.	show rmon history
Display the RMON hosts table. Available on Cisco 2500 series and Cisco AS5200 only.	show rmon hosts
Display the RMON matrix table. Available on Cisco 2500 series and Cisco AS5200 only.	show rmon matrix
Display the RMON statistics table. Available on Cisco 2500 series and Cisco AS5200 only.	show rmon statistics
Display the RMON top-n hosts table. Available on Cisco 2500 series and Cisco AS5200 only.	show rmon topn

For an example of configuring RMON alarms and events, see the section "RMON Alarm and Event Examples" at the end of this chapter.

CONFIGURING THE CISCO DISCOVERY PROTOCOL

The Cisco Discovery Protocol (CDP) is a media- and protocol-independent protocol that runs on all Cisco-manufactured equipment including routers, bridges, access servers, and switches. With CDP, network management applications can learn the device type and the SNMP agent address of neighboring devices. This enables applications to send SNMP queries to neighboring devices.

CDP runs on all media that support Subnetwork Access Protocol (SNAP), including local-area network (LAN), Frame Relay, and Asynchronous Transfer Mode (ATM) media. CDP runs over the data-link layer only. Therefore, two systems that support different network-layer protocols can learn about each other.

Each device configured for CDP sends periodic messages to a multicast address. Each device advertises at least one address at which it can receive SNMP messages. The advertisements also contain time-to-live, or holdtime, information, which indicates the length of time a receiving device should hold CDP information before discarding it.

There is a CDP MIB for the management of CDP on Cisco devices.

CDP Configuration Task List

To configure CDP, perform the tasks in the following sections:

- Setting the CDP Transmission Timer and Hold Time
- Enabling CDP
- Enabling CDP on an Interface
- Monitoring and Maintaining CDP

NOTES

The **cdp enable**, **cdp timer**, and **cdp run** commands affect the operation of the IP-on-demand routing feature (that is, the **router odr** global configuration command).

Setting the CDP Transmission Timer and Hold Time

To set the frequency of CDP transmissions and the hold time for CDP packets, perform the following tasks in global configuration mode:

Task	Command
Step 1 Specify frequency of transmission of CDP updates.	**cdp timer** *seconds*
Step 2 Specify the amount of time a receiving device should hold the information sent by your device before discarding it.	**cdp holdtime** *seconds*

Enabling CDP

CDP is enabled by default. You can disable it with the **no cdp run** command.

To re-enable CDP after disabling it, perform the following task in global configuration mode:

Task	Command
Enable CDP.	**cdp run**

Enabling CDP on an Interface

CDP is enabled by default on all supported interfaces to send and receive CDP information. However, some interfaces, such as ATM interfaces, do not support CDP. You can disable CDP on an interface that supports CDP with the **no cdp enable** command.

To re-enable CDP on an interface after disabling it, perform the following task in interface configuration mode:

Task	Command
Enable CDP on an interface.	**cdp enable**

Monitoring and Maintaining CDP

To monitor and maintain CDP on your device, perform one or more of the following tasks in privileged EXEC mode:

Task	Command
Reset the traffic counters to zero.	**clear cdp counters**
Delete the CDP table of information about neighbors.	**clear cdp table**
Display global information such as frequency of transmissions and the holdtime for packets being transmitted.	**show cdp**
Display information about a specific neighbor. Display can be limited to protocol or version information.	**show cdp entry** *entry-name* **[protocol	version]**
Display information about interfaces on which CDP is enabled.	**show cdp interface** **[***type number***]**
Display information about neighbors. The display can be limited to neighbors on a specific interface, and expanded to provide more detailed information.	**show cdp neighbors [***type number***] [detail]**
Display CDP counters, including the number of packets sent and received and checksum errors.	**show cdp traffic**
Display information about the types of debugging that are enabled for your router.	**show debugging**

CONFIGURING RESPONSE TIME REPORTER

The response time reporter feature allows you to monitor network performance, network resources, and applications by measuring response times and availability. With this feature, you can perform troubleshooting, problem notifications, and pre-problem analysis based on response time reporter statistics.

The response time reporter feature is currently available only with the IBM feature set of the Cisco IOS software. A CiscoWorksBlue network management application will be available to support the response time reporter feature. Both the CiscoWorks Blue network management application and the router use the Cisco Round Trip Time Monitor (RTTMON) MIB.

You can use the response time reporter feature to troubleshoot problems by checking the time delays between devices (such as a router and an MVS host) and the time delays on the path from the source device to the destination device at the protocol level.

You also can use this feature to send any combination of SNMP traps and SNA Alerts/Resolutions when one of the following has occurred: a user-configured threshold is exceeded, a connection is lost and re-established, or a timeout occurs. Thresholds also can be used to trigger additional collection of time delay statistics.

You can use this feature to perform pre-problem analysis by scheduling the response time reporter and collecting the results as history and accumulated statistics. You can then use the statistics to model and predict future network topologies.

Response Time Reporter Configuration Task List

To configure the response time reporter feature, complete the tasks in the following sections. Configuring the probe and scheduling the probe are required tasks; the remaining tasks are optional.

- Configuring the Probe
- Capturing Statistics and Collecting Error Information
- Collecting History
- Setting Reaction Conditions
- Scheduling the Probe
- Resetting the Probe
- Monitoring the Response Time Reporter Feature

See the end of this chapter for "Response Time Reporter Examples."

Configuring the Probe

Response time and availability information is collected by probes that you configure on the router. To configure a new response time reporter probe, complete the following tasks starting in global configuration mode:

Task	Command
Step 1 Enter response time reporter configuration mode.	**rtr** *probe*
Step 2 Specify the type of probe.	**type** {echo | pathecho} **protocol** *type type-target*

You must configure the probe's type before you can configure any of the other characteristics.

— **NOTES** —————————————————————————————

When the probe type is **pathEcho**, statistics are recorded for each hop along the path that the probe takes to reach its destination.

To configure optional characteristics, perform the following tasks in response time reporter configuration mode:

Task	Command
Step 1 Set the rate at which the probe starts a response time reporter operation.	**frequency** *seconds*
Step 2 Configure the SNMP owner of the probe.	**owner** *text*
Step 3 Set the rising threshold (hysteresis) that generates a reaction event and stores history information for the probe.	**threshold** *milliseconds*
Step 4 Set the amount of time the probe waits for a response from its request packet.	**timeout** *milliseconds*
Step 5 Set the protocol data size in the payload of the probe's request packet.	**request-data-size** *bytes*
Step 6 Set the protocol data size in the payload of the probe's response packet.	**response-data-size** *bytes*

Task	Command
Step 7 Logically link probes together in a group.	**tag** *text*
Step 8 Check each probe response for corruption.	**verify-data**

Capturing Statistics and Collecting Error Information

The main purpose of the probe is to capture statistics and collect error information. By default, the following information is captured and collected:

- Minimum and maximum response times
- Number of completions
- Sum of completion times
- Sum of the squares of completion times
- Accumulation of errors for noncompletions
- Total attempts (errors plus number of completions)
- Statistical distributions of response times

In most situations, you do not need to change the statistical distribution interval or size. Only change the size when distributions are needed (for example, when performing statistical modeling of your network).

To control how much and what type of statistics are stored on the router, complete the following optional tasks in response time reporter configuration mode:

Task	Command
Step 1 Set the time interval for each statistical distribution kept.	**statistics-distribution-interval** *milliseconds*
Step 2 Set number of statistical distributions kept per hop during the probe's lifetime.	**distributions-of-statistics-kept** *size*
Step 3 Set the number of hops for which statistics are maintained per path for the probe.	**hops-of-statistics-kept** *size*
Step 4 Set the number of paths for which statistics are maintained per hour for the probe.	**paths-of-statistics-kept** *size*
Step 5 Set the number of hours for which statistics are maintained for the probe.	**hours-of-statistics-kept** *hours*

NOTES

When using a distribution size of 1 (the default), you do not need to set the **statistics-distribution-interval** response time reporter configuration command, because it has no effect on the statistics kept. For more information, refer to the command in Chapter 25, "Router and Network Monitoring Commands."

Collecting History

A probe can collect history and capture statistics. By default, history is not collected. When a problem arises where history is useful (for example, a large number of timeouts are occurring), you can configure the probe to collect history.

NOTES

Collecting history increases the RAM usage. Only collect history when you think there is a problem. For general network response time information, use statistics.

To control how much and what type of history is stored on the router, complete the following tasks in response time reporter configuration mode. The first task is required; the remainder are optional.

Task	Command
Step 1 Set the number of entries kept in the history table per bucket.	**samples-of-history-kept** *samples*
Step 2 Set the number of history buckets that are kept per lives-of-history-kept.	**buckets-of-history-kept** *size*
Step 3 Enable history collection and set the number of lives maintained in the history table for the probe.	**lives-of-history-kept** *lives*
Step 4 Define the type of information kept in the history table for the probe.	**filter-for-history** {none | all | overthreshold | failures}

To disable history collection, use the default value (0 lives) for the **lives-of-history-kept** command rather than the **filter-for-history none** response time reporter configuration command. The **lives-of-history-kept** command disables history collection before the probe's operation is attempted, and the **filter-for-history** command with the **none** keyword checks for history inclusion after the probe's operation attempt is made.

Setting Reaction Conditions

You can configure the probe to send threshold notifications and use those notifications to trigger additional collection of time delay statistics. You also can configure the probe to send notifications when the probe loses connection, re-establishes connections, times out, and first succeeds after a timeout.

To configure the probe's reaction conditions, perform the following optional tasks in global configuration mode:

Task	Command
Step 1 Configure certain actions to occur based on events under the control of the response time reporter.	**rtr reaction-configuration** *probe* [**connection-loss-enable**] [**timeout-enable**] [**threshold-falling** *milliseconds*] [**threshold-type** *option*] [**action-type** *option*]
Step 2 Define the target probe to make the transition from a "pending" state to an "active" state when one of the trigger action-type options is defined for the probe.	**rtr reaction-trigger** *probe target-probe*

Scheduling the Probe

After you have configured the probe, you must schedule the probe to begin capturing statistics and collecting error information. To do so, perform the following task in global configuration mode:

Task	Command
Schedule the probe by configuring the time parameters.	**rtr schedule** *probe* [**life** *seconds*] [**start-time** {**pending** | **now** | *hh:mm* [*month day* | *day month*]}] [**ageout** *seconds*]

───── **NOTES** ───

After you schedule the probe with the **rtr schedule** command, you cannot change the probe's configuration with the **rtr** global configuration command. To change the configuration of a probe that has been scheduled, use the **no** form of the **rtr** command. The **no** form removes all the probe's configuration information including the probe's schedule, reaction configuration, and reaction triggers. You now can create a new configuration for the probe.

If the probe is in a pending state (the default), you can define the conditions under which the probe makes the transition from pending to active with the **rtr reaction-trigger** global configuration command. When the probe is in an active state, it immediately begins collecting information.

Resetting the Probe

To perform a shutdown and restart of the response time reporter, perform the following task in global configuration mode:

Task	Command
Stop all probes and clear the response time reporter configuration information.	**rtr reset**

CAUTION

Use the **rtr reset** command only in extreme situations, such as the incorrect configuration of a number of probes.

In addition to stopping all probes and clearing the response time reporter configuration information, the **rtr reset** command returns the response time reporter feature to the startup condition. This command does not reread the configuration stored in NVRAM. You must retype the response time reporter's configuration or perform a **config memory** command (this has the side effect of reconfiguring the router to its startup configuration).

Monitoring the Response Time Reporter Feature

To display information about the status and configuration of the response time reporter feature, perform the following tasks in EXEC mode. You can display information in a tabular or full format. Tabular format displays information in a column, reducing the number of screens required to display the information. Full format displays all information using identifiers next to each displayed value.

Task	Command
Step 1 Display global information about the response time reporter feature.	**show rtr application** [tabular | full]
Step 2 Display error totals collected for all probes or the specified probe.	**show rtr collection-statistics** [*probe*] [tabular | full]
Step 3 Display configuration values including all defaults for all probes or the specified probe.	**show rtr configuration** [*probe*] [tabular | full]

Task	Command
Step 4 Display statistical distribution information (captured response times) for all probes or the specified probe.	**show rtr distribution-statistics** [*probe*] [**tabular** | **full**]
Step 5 Display history collected for all probes or the specified probe.	**show rtr history** [*probe*] [**tabular** | **full**]
Step 6 Display the operational state of all probes or the specified probe.	**show rtr operational-state** [*probe*] [**tabular** | **full**]
Step 7 Display the reaction trigger information for all probes or the specified probe.	**show rtr reaction-trigger** [*probe*] [**tabular** | **full**]
Step 8 Display the total statistic values (accumulation of error counts and completions) for all probes or the specified probe.	**show rtr totals-statistics** [*probe*] [**tabular** | **full**]

MONITORING THE ROUTER AND NETWORK CONFIGURATION EXAMPLES

The following sections provide system management examples:

- SNMP Examples
- RMON Alarm and Event Examples
- Response Time Reporter Examples

SNMP Examples

The following example enables SNMPv1 and SNMPv2C. The configuration permits any SNMP manager to access all objects with read-only permission using the community string *public*. This configuration does not cause the router to send any traps.

```
snmp-server community public
```

The following example permits any SNMP to access all objects with read-only permission using the community string *public*. The router also will send ISDN traps to the hosts 192.180.1.111 and 192.180.1.33 using SNMPv1 and to the host 192.180.1.27 using SNMPv2C. The community string *public* is sent with the traps.

```
snmp-server community public
snmp-server enable traps isdn
snmp-server host 192.180.1.27 version 2c public
snmp-server host 192.180.1.111 version 1 public
snmp-server host 192.180.1.33 public
```

The following example allows read-only access for all objects to members of access list 4 that specify the *comaccess* community string. No other SNMP managers have access to any objects. SNMP

Authentication Failure traps are sent by SNMPv2C to the host cisco.com using the community string *public*.

```
snmp-server community comaccess ro 4
snmp-server enable traps snmp authentication
snmp-server host cisco.com version 2c public
```

The following example sends Entity MIB traps to the host cisco.com. The community string is *restricted*. The first line enables the router to send Entity MIB traps in addition to any traps previously enabled. The second line specifies the destination of these traps and overwrites any previous **snmp-server host** commands for the host cisco.com.

```
snmp-server enable traps entity
snmp-server host cisco.com restricted entity
```

RMON Alarm and Event Examples

The following example enables the **rmon event** command:

```
rmon event 1 log trap eventtrap description "High ifOutErrors" owner sdurham
```

This example creates RMON event number 1, which is defined as *High ifOutErrors*, and generates a log entry when the event is triggered by an alarm. The user *sdurham* owns the row that is created in the event table by this command. This example also generates a Simple Network Management Protocol (SNMP) trap when the event is triggered.

The following example configures an RMON alarm using the **rmon alarm** command:

```
rmon alarm 10 ifEntry.20.1 20 delta rising-threshold 15 1 falling-threshold 0 owner
jjohnson
```

This example configures RMON alarm number 10. The alarm monitors the MIB variable *ifEntry.20.1* once every 20 seconds until the alarm is disabled, and checks the change in the variable's rise or fall. If the *ifEntry.20.1* value shows a MIB counter increase of 15 or more, such as from 100000 to 100015, the alarm is triggered. The alarm, in turn, triggers event number 1, which is configured with the **rmon event** command. Possible events include a log entry or an SNMP trap. If the *ifEntry.20.1* value changes by 0, the alarm is reset and can be triggered again.

Response Time Reporter Examples

The following sections contain examples of setting up probes on the router to monitor network performance and send notifications:

- Performing Normative Analysis for SNA LU2
- Performing Troubleshooting for IP/ICMP
- Configuring a Trigger for Connection Loss

Performing Normative Analysis for SNA LU2

In the example shown in Figure 24–2, probe 1 is configured from router A to host 2, and probe 2 is configured from router B to host 2 to perform a normative analysis of the network to determine a baseline from which triggers (and reactions in general) are then configured. Also, two SNA Physical Units (PUs) are assumed to be configured: CWBC0A and CWBC0B.

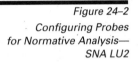

Figure 24–2

Configuring Probes
for Normative Analysis—
SNA LU2

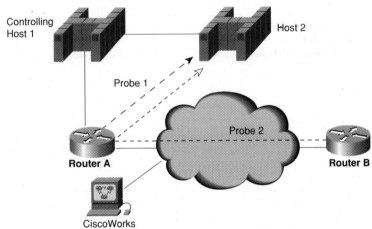

Router A's Configuration:

```
RouterA(config)# rtr 1
RouterA(config-rtr)# type echo protocol snaLU2EchoAppl CWBC0A
RouterA(config-rtr)# exit
RouterA(config)# rtr schedule 1 start-time now
RouterA(config)# exit
```

Router B's Configuration:

```
RouterB(config)# rtr 2
RouterB(config-rtr)# type echo protocol snaLU2EchoAppl CWBC0B
RouterB(config-rtr)# exit
RouterB(config)# rtr schedule 1 start-time now
RouterB(config)# exit
```

Configuration Files for Router A and Router B

After you save the configurations (using the **copy running-config startup-config** command), the following information is stored in the configuration files. Note the addition of the **"kept"** commands in the configuration file. They are automatically included, because they differ depending on the **type** you specify for the probe.

```
!Router A Configuration File
! Router A's PU Configuration
sna host CWBC0A xid-snd 05dcc00a rmac 4001.3745.1088 rsap 4 lsap 12 focalpoint
rtr 1
 type echo protocol snaLU2EchoAppl CWBC0A
 paths-of-statistics-kept 1
 hops-of-statistics-kept 1
```

```
   samples-of-history-kept 1
rtr schedule 1 start-time now

!Router B Configuration File
!Router B's PU Configuration from the Configuration File:
sna host CWBC0B xid-snd 05dcc00b rmac 4001.3745.1088 rsap 4 lsap 12 focalpoint
rtr 2
   type echo protocol snaLU2EchoAppl CWBC0B
   paths-of-statistics-kept 1
   hops-of-statistics-kept 1
   samples-of-history-kept 1
rtr schedule 2 start-time now
```

Performing Troubleshooting for IP/ICMP

In the example shown in Figure 24–3, probe 3 is configured from router B to router A to perform troubleshooting of the network to determine a network problem from which triggers (and reactions in general) are then configured.

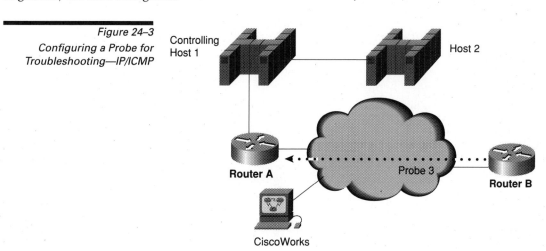

Figure 24–3

Configuring a Probe for Troubleshooting—IP/ICMP

This example sets up a **pathEcho** (with history) pending entry from router B to router A via IP/ICMP. It will attempt to execute three times in 25 seconds (first attempt starts at 0 seconds) and will keep those three times with three buckets. It can be started five times before wrapping over stored history (lives 5). Because this configuration keeps history, it uses more RAM on the router.

Router B's Configuration:

```
RouterB(config)# rtr 3
RouterB(config-rtr)# type pathEcho protocol ipIcmpEcho RouterA
RouterB(config-rtr)# frequency 10
RouterB(config-rtr)# lives-of-history-kept 5
RouterB(config-rtr)# buckets-of-history-kept 3
```

```
RouterB(config-rtr)# filter-for-history all
RouterB(config-rtr)# exit
RouterB(config)# rtr schedule 3 life 25
RouterB(config)# exit
```

Configuration File for Router B

After you save the configuration (using the **copy running-config startup-config** command), the following information is stored in the configuration file. Note the addition of commands in the configuration file. They are automatically included, because they differ depending on the **type** you specify for the probe.

```
rtr 3
 type pathEcho protocol ipIcmpEcho 172.28.161.21
 frequency 10
 response-data-size 1
 lives-of-history-kept 5
 buckets-of-history-kept 3
 filter-for-history all
rtr schedule 3 life 25 start-time pending
```

Configuring a Trigger for Connection Loss

Figure 24–4 shows probes 1, 2, and 3 in the network. This example shows how to configure a trigger if probe 2 encounters a connection loss from router B to host 2. If a connection loss occurs between router B and host 2, a trap is issued, an SNA NMVT Alert is issued, and probe 3's state is changed to "active."

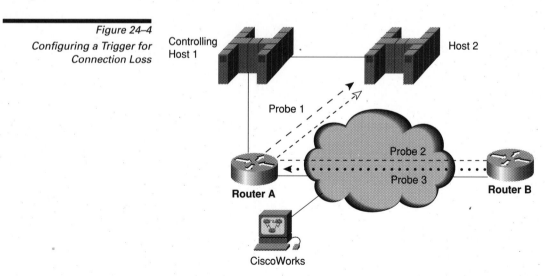

Figure 24–4

Configuring a Trigger for Connection Loss

Router B's Configuration:

```
RouterB(config)# rtr reaction-configuration 2 connection-loss-enable
                 action-type trapNmvtAndTrigger
RouterB(config)# rtr reaction-trigger 2 3
```

NOTES

The probe numbers need only be unique within one router. The examples shown use three different probe numbers for clarity.

## CHAPTER 25

Router and Network Monitoring Commands

This chapter describes the commands used to monitor the router and network.

For system management configuration tasks and examples, see Chapter 24, "Monitoring the Router and Network."

BUCKETS-OF-HISTORY-KEPT

To set the number of history buckets that are kept during the response time reporter probe's lifetime, use the **buckets-of-history-kept** response time reporter configuration command. Use the **no** form of this command to return to the default value.

> **buckets-of-history-kept** *size*
> **no buckets-of-history-kept**

Syntax	Description
size	Number of history buckets kept during the response time reporter probe's lifetime. The default is 50 buckets.

Default

50 buckets

Command Mode

Response time reporter configuration

Usage Guidelines

This command first appeared in Cisco IOS Release 11.2.

A response time reporter probe can collect history and capture statistics. By default, history is not collected. When a problem arises where history is useful (for example, a large number of timeouts are occurring), you can configure the **lives-of-history-kept** response time reporter configuration command to collect history. You can adjust the **buckets-of-history-kept, filter-for-history,** and **samples-of-history-kept** response time reporter configuration commands optionally.

When the number of buckets reaches the size specified, no further history for this life is stored.

NOTES

Collecting history increases the RAM usage. Only collect history when you think there is a problem. For general network response time information, use statistics.

If history is collected, each bucket contains one or more history entries from the probe. When the probe type is **pathEcho,** an entry is created for each hop along the path that the probe takes to reach its destination. The type of entry stored in the history table is controlled by the **filter-for-history** response time reporter configuration command. The total number of entries stored in the history table is controlled by the combination of **samples-of-history-kept, buckets-of-history-kept,** and **lives-of-history-kept** response time reporter configuration commands.

Each time the probe starts a response time reporter operation, a new bucket is created until the number of history buckets matches the specified size or the probe's lifetime expires. History buckets do not wrap. The probe's lifetime is defined by the **rtr schedule** global configuration command. The probe starts a response time reporter operation based on the seconds specified by the **frequency** response time reporter configuration command.

Example

In the following example, probe 1 is configured to keep 25 history buckets during the probe's lifetime:

```
rtr 1
 type echo protocol ipIcmpEcho 172.16.161.21
 buckets-of-history-kept 25
 lives-of-history-kept 1
```

Related Commands

filter-for-history
lives-of-history-kept
rtr
rtr schedule
samples-of-history-kept

CDP ENABLE

To enable Cisco Discovery Protocol (CDP) on an interface, use the **cdp enable** interface configuration command. Use the **no** form of this command to disable CDP on an interface.

> **cdp enable**
> **no cdp enable**

Syntax   Description

This command has no arguments or keywords.

Default

Enabled at the global level and on all supported interfaces.

Command Mode

Interface configuration

Usage Guidelines

This command first appeared in Cisco IOS Release 10.3.

CDP is enabled by default at the global level and on each supported interface in order to send or receive CDP information. However, some interfaces, such as ATM interfaces, do not support CDP.

NOTES

The **cdp enable**, **cdp timer**, and **cdp run** commands affect the operation of the IP on demand routing feature (that is, the **router odr** global configuration command).

Example

In the following example, CDP is enabled on Ethernet interface 0:

```
interface ethernet 0
  cdp enable
```

Related Commands

cdp run

CDP HOLDTIME

To specify the amount of time the receiving device should hold a CDP packet from your router before discarding it, use the **cdp holdtime** global configuration command. Use the **no** form of this command to revert to the default setting.

cdp holdtime *seconds*
no cdp holdtime

Syntax   *Description*

seconds   Specifies the hold time to be sent in the CDP update packets.

Default

180 seconds

Command Mode

Global configuration

Usage Guidelines

This command first appeared in Cisco IOS Release 10.3.

CDP packets are sent with time-to-live, or hold time, that is nonzero after an interface is enabled and a hold time of 0 immediately before an interface is idled down.

The CDP hold time must be set to a higher number of seconds than the time between CDP transmissions, which is set using the **cdp timer** command.

Example

In the following example, the CDP packets being sent from your router should be held by the receiving device for 60 seconds before being discarded. You might want to set the hold time lower than the default setting of 180 seconds if information about your router changes often, and you want the receiving devices to purge this information more quickly.

```
. cdp holdtime 60
```

Related Commands

cdp timer
show cdp

CDP RUN

To enable CDP, use the **cdp run** global configuration command. Use the **no** form of this command to disable CDP.

cdp run
no cdp run

Syntax   Description

This command has no arguments or keywords.

Default

Enabled

Command Mode

Global configuration

Usage Guidelines

This command first appeared in Cisco IOS Release 10.3.

CDP is enabled on your router by default, which means the Cisco IOS software will receive CDP information. CDP also is enabled on supported interfaces by default. To disable CDP on an interface, use the **no cdp enable** interface configuration command.

NOTES

The **cdp enable**, **cdp timer**, and **cdp run** commands affect the operation of the IP-on-demand routing feature (that is, the **router odr** global configuration command).

Example

In the following example, CDP is disabled:

```
no cdp run
```

Related Commands

cdp enable

CDP TIMER

To specify how often the Cisco IOS software sends CDP updates, use the **cdp timer** global configuration command. Use the **no** form of this command to revert to the default setting.

    cdp timer *seconds*
    no cdp timer

Syntax	*Description*
seconds	Specifies how often the Cisco IOS software sends CDP updates.

Default

60 seconds

Command Mode

Global configuration

Usage Guidelines

This command first appeared in Cisco IOS Release 10.3.

The trade-off with sending more frequent transmissions is providing up-to-date information versus using bandwidth more often.

NOTES

The **cdp enable**, **cdp timer**, and **cdp run** commands affect the operation of the IP-on-demand routing feature (that is, the **router odr** global configuration command).

Example

In the following example, CDP updates are sent every 80 seconds, less frequently than the default setting of 60 seconds. You might want to make this change if you are concerned about preserving bandwidth.

```
cdp timer 80
```

Related Commands

cdp holdtime
show cdp

CLEAR CDP COUNTERS

To reset CDP traffic counters to zero (0), use the **clear cdp counters** privileged EXEC command.

clear cdp counters

Syntax   Description

This command has no arguments or keywords.

Command Mode

Privileged EXEC

Usage Guidelines

This command first appeared in Cisco IOS Release 10.3.

Example

In the following example, the CDP counters have been cleared. The **show cdp traffic** output shows that all of the traffic counters have been reset to zero (0).

```
Router# clear cdp counters
Router# show cdp traffic
```

```
CDP counters:
        Packets output: 0, Input: 0
        Hdr syntax: 0, Chksum error: 0, Encaps failed: 0
        No memory: 0, Invalid packet: 0, Fragmented: 0
```

Related Commands

clear cdp table
show cdp traffic

CLEAR CDP TABLE

To clear the table that contains CDP information about neighbors, use the **clear cdp table** privileged EXEC command.

clear cdp table

Syntax   Description

This command has no arguments or keywords.

Command Mode

Privileged EXEC

Usage Guidelines

This command first appeared in Cisco IOS Release 10.3.

Example

In the following example, the CDP table is cleared. The output of the **show cdp neighbors** command shows that all information has been deleted from the table.

```
Router# clear cdp table

CDP-AD: Deleted table entry for neon.cisco.com, interface Ethernet0
CDP-AD: Deleted table entry for neon.cisco.com, interface Serial0
Router# show cdp neighbors

Capability Codes: R - Router, T - Trans Bridge, B - Source Route Bridge
                  S - Switch, H - Host, I - IGMP

Device ID       Local Intrfce     Holdtme    Capability  Platform  Port ID
```

Related Commands

clear cdp counters
show cdp neighbors

DISTRIBUTIONS-OF-STATISTICS-KEPT

To set the number of statistic distributions kept per hop during the response time reporter probe's lifetime, use the **distributions-of-statistics-kept** response time reporter configuration command. Use the **no** form of this command to return to the default value.

> **distributions-of-statistics-kept** *size*
> **no distributions-of-statistics-kept**

Syntax	*Description*
size	Number of statistic distributions kept per hop. The default is 1 distribution.

Default

1 distribution

Command Mode

Response time reporter configuration

Usage Guidelines

This command first appeared in Cisco IOS Release 11.2.

In most situations, you do not need to change the statistic distribution size for the response time reporter. Only change the size when distributions are needed (for example, when performing statistical modeling of your network).

NOTES

Increasing the distributions also increases the RAM usage. The total number of statistics distributions captured will be: the value of **distributions-of-statistics-kept** multiplied by the value of **hops-of-statistics-kept** multiplied by the value of **paths-of-statistics-kept** multiplied by the value of **hours-of-statistics-kept**.

When the number of distributions reaches the size specified, no further distribution information is stored.

Example

In the following example, the distribution is set to 5 and the distribution interval is set to 10 milliseconds. This means that the first distribution will contain statistics from 0 to 9 ms, the second distribution will contain statistics from 10 to 19 ms, the third distribution will contain statistics from 20 to 29 ms, the fourth distribution will contain statistics from 30 to 39 ms, and the fifth distribution will contain statistics from 40 ms to infinity.

```
rtr 1
 type echo protocol ipIcmpEcho 172.16.161.21
```

```
distributions-of-statistics-kept 5
statistics-distribution-interval 10
```

Related Commands

hops-of-statistics-kept
hours-of-statistics-kept
paths-of-statistics-kept
rtr
statistics-distribution-interval

FILTER-FOR-HISTORY

To define the type of information kept in the history table for the response time reporter probe, use the **filter-for-history** response time reporter configuration command. Use the **no** form of this command to return to the default value.

> **filter-for-history** {none | all | overThreshold | failures}
> **no filter-for-history** {none | all | overThreshold | failures}

Syntax	Description
none	No history kept. This is the default.
all	All probe operations attempted are kept in the history table.
overThreshold	Only packets that are over the threshold are kept in the history table.
failures	Only packets that fail for any reason are kept in the history table.

Default

none

Command Mode

Response time reporter configuration

Usage Guidelines

This command first appeared in Cisco IOS Release 11.2.

Use the **filter-for-history** command to control what gets stored in the history table for the response time reporter. To control how much history gets saved in the history table, use the **lives-of-history-kept, buckets-of-history-kept,** and the **samples-of-history-kept** response time reporter configuration commands.

A probe can collect history and capture statistics. By default, history is not collected. When a problem arises where history is useful (for example, a large number of timeouts are occurring), you can configure the **lives-of-history-kept** command to collect history.

NOTES

Collecting history increases the RAM usage. Only collect history when you think there is a problem. For general network response time information, use statistics.

Example

In the following example, only probe packets that fail are kept in the history table:

```
rtr 1
  type echo protocol ipIcmpEcho 172.16.161.21
  lives-of-history-kept 1
  filter-for-history failures
```

Related Commands

buckets-of-history-kept
lives-of-history-kept
rtr
samples-of-history-kept

FREQUENCY

To set the rate at which the response time reporter probe starts a response time operation, use the **frequency** response time reporter configuration command. Use the **no** form of this command to return to the default value.

    frequency *second*
    no frequency

Syntax	Description
second	Number of seconds between the probe's response time reporter operations. The default value is 60 seconds.

Default

60 seconds

Command Mode

Response time reporter configuration

Usage Guidelines

This command first appeared in Cisco IOS Release 11.2.

> **CAUTION**
>
> For normal operation, do not set the frequency value to fewer than 60 seconds for the following reasons: It is not needed when keeping statistics (the default), and it can slow down the WAN because of the potential overhead that numerous probes can cause.

If the probe takes longer to execute the current response time reporter operation than the specified frequency value, a statistics counter called *busy* is incremented in lieu of starting a second operation.

The value specified for the **frequency** command cannot be less than the value specified for the **time-out** response time reporter configuration command.

Example

In the following example, the probe is configured to execute a response time reporter operation every 90 seconds:

```
rtr 1
  type echo protocol ipIcmpEcho 172.16.1.176
  frequency 90
```

Related Commands

rtr
timeout

HOPS-OF-STATISTICS-KEPT

To set the number of hops for which statistics are maintained per path for the response time reporter probe, use the **hops-of-statistics-kept** response time reporter configuration command. Use the **no** form of this command to return to the default value.

> **hops-of-statistics-kept** *size*
> **no hops-of-statistics-kept**

Syntax	Description
size	Number of hops for which statistics are maintained per path. The default is 16 hops for type **pathEcho** and 1 hop for type **echo**.

Default

16 hops for type **pathEcho**

1 hop for type **echo**

Command Mode

Response time reporter configuration

Usage Guidelines

This command first appeared in Cisco IOS Release 11.2.

One hop is the passage of a timed packet from this router to another network device. The other network device is assumed to be a device along the path to the destination (including the destination) when the probe type is **pathEcho,** or just the destination when the type is **echo.**

When the number of hops reaches the size specified, no further hop information is stored.

Example

In the following example, probe 2's statistics are maintained for only 10 hops:

```
rtr 2
  type pathecho protocol ipIcmpEcho 172.16.1.177
  hops-of-statistics-kept 10
```

Related Commands

distributions-of-statistics-kept
hours-of-statistics-kept
paths-of-statistics-kept
rtr
statistics-distribution-interval

HOURS-OF-STATISTICS-KEPT

To set the number of hours for which statistics are maintained for the response time reporter probe, use the **hours-of-statistics-kept** response time reporter configuration command. Use the **no** form of this command to return to the default value.

>   **hours-of-statistics-kept** *hours*
>   **no hours-of-statistics-kept**

Syntax	Description
hours	Number of hours that the router maintains statistics. The default is two hours.

Default

2 hours

Command Mode

Response time reporter configuration

Usage Guidelines

This command first appeared in Cisco IOS Release 11.2.

When the number of hours exceeds the specified value, the statistics table wraps (that is, the oldest information is replaced by newer information).

Example

In the following example, probe 2's statistics are maintained for three hours:

```
rtr 2
 type pathecho protocol ipIcmpEcho 172.16.1.177
 hours-of-statistics-kept 3
```

Related Commands

distributions-of-statistics-kept
hops-of-statistics-kept
paths-of-statistics-kept
rtr
statistics-distribution-interval

LIVES-OF-HISTORY-KEPT

To set the number of lives maintained in the history table for the response time reporter probe, use the **lives-of-history-kept** response time reporter configuration command. Use the **no** form of this command to return to the default value.

> **lives-of-history-kept** *lives*
> **no lives-of-history-kept**

Syntax	Description
lives	Number of lives maintained in the history table for the probe. The default is 0 lives.

Default

0 lives

Command Mode

Response time reporter configuration

Usage Guidelines

This command first appeared in Cisco IOS Release 11.2.

The default value (0 lives) means that history is not collected for the probe. To disable history collection, use the default value for the **lives-of-history-kept** command rather than the **filter-for-history**

none response time reporter configuration command. The **lives-of-history-kept** command disables history collection before the probe's operation is attempted, and the **filter-for-history** command checks for history inclusion after the probe's operation attempt is made.

When the number of lives exceeds the specified value, the history table wraps (that is, the oldest information is replaced by newer information).

When a probe makes a transition from pending to active, a life starts. When a probe's life ends, the probe makes a transition from active to pending.

Example

In the following example, probe 1's history is maintained for five lives:

```
rtr 1
 type echo protocol ipIcmpEcho 172.16.1.176
 lives-of-history-kept 5
```

Related Commands

buckets-of-history-kept
filter-for-history
rtr
samples-of-history-kept

OWNER

To configure the SNMP owner of the response time reporter probe, use the **owner** response time reporter configuration command. Use the **no** form of this command to return to the default value.

> **owner** *text*
> **no owner**

Syntax	Description
text	Name of the SNMP owner from 0 to 255 ASCII characters. The default is none.

Default

No owner is specified.

Command Mode

Response time reporter configuration

Usage Guidelines

This command first appeared in Cisco IOS Release 11.2.

The owner name contains one or more of the following: ASCII form of the network management station's transport address, network management station name (that is, the domain name), and network management personnel's name, location, or phone number. In some cases, the agent itself will be the owner of the probe. In these cases, the name can begin with "agent."

Example

In the following example, probe 1's owner is set:

```
rtr 1
  type echo protocol ipIcmpEcho 172.16.1.176
  owner 172.16.1.189 cwb.cisco.com John Doe RTP 555-1212
```

Related Commands

rtr

PATHS-OF-STATISTICS-KEPT

To set the number of paths for which statistics are maintained per hour for the response time reporter probe, use the **paths-of-statistics-kept** response time reporter configuration command. Use the **no** form of this command to return to the default value.

> **paths-of-statistics-kept** *size*
> **no paths-of-statistics-kept**

Syntax	Description
size	Number of paths for which statistics are maintained per hour. The default is 5 paths for type **pathEcho** and 1 path for type **echo**.

Default

5 paths for type **pathEcho**

1 path for type **echo**

Command Mode

Response time reporter configuration

Usage Guidelines

This command first appeared in Cisco IOS Release 11.2.

A path is the route the probe's request packet takes through the network to get to its destination. The probe may take a different path to reach its destination for each response time reporter operation.

When the number of paths reaches the size specified, no further path information is stored.

Example

In the following example, probe 2's statistics are maintained for only 3 paths:

```
rtr 2
 type pathEcho protocol ipIcmpEcho 172.16.1.177
 paths-of-statistics-kept 3
```

Related Commands

distributions-of-statistics-kept
hops-of-statistics-kept
hours-of-statistics-kept
rtr
statistics-distribution-interval

REQUEST-DATA-SIZE

To set the protocol data size in the payload of the response time reporter probe's request packet, use the **request-data-size** response time reporter configuration command. Use the **no** form of this command to return to the default value.

> **request-data-size** *byte*
> **no request-data-size**

Syntax	Description
byte	size of the protocol data in the payload of the probe's request packet. Range is 0 to the protocol's maximum. The default is 1 byte.

Default

1 byte

Command Mode

Response time reporter configuration

Usage Guidelines

This command first appeared in Cisco IOS Release 11.2.

When the protocol name has the suffix "appl," the packet uses both a request and respond data size (see the **response-data-size** response time reporter configuration command), and the data size is 12 bytes smaller than the normal payload size (this 12 bytes is the ARR Header used to control send and data response sizes).

Example

In the following example, probe 3's request packet size is set to 40 bytes:

```
rtr 3
 type echo protocol snalu0echoappl cwbc0a
 request-data-size 40
```

Related Commands

response-data-size
rtr

RESPONSE-DATA-SIZE

To set the protocol data size in the payload of the response time reporter probe's response packet, use the **response-data-size** response time reporter configuration command. Use the **no** form of this command to return to the default value.

> **response-data-size** *byte*
> **no response-data-size**

Syntax	Description
byte	Size of the protocol data in the payload in the probe's response packet. For "appl" protocols, the default is 0 bytes. For all others, the default is the same value as the **request-data-size**.

Default

For "appl" protocols, 0 bytes

For all others, the same value as the **request-data-size**

Command Mode

Response time reporter configuration

Usage Guidelines

This command first appeared in Cisco IOS Release 11.2.

The **response-data-size** command is only applicable for protocols defined with the **type** command that end in "appl" (for example, **snalu0echoappl**). When the protocol ends in "appl," the response data size is 12 bytes smaller than normal payload size.

Example

In the following example, probe 3's response packet size is set to 1,440 bytes:

```
rtr 3
 type echo protocol snalu0echoappl cwbc0a
 response-data-size 1440
```

Related Commands

request-data-size
rtr

RMON

To enable Remote Network Monitoring (RMON) on an Ethernet interface, use the **rmon** interface configuration command. Use the **no** form of this command to disable RMON on the interface.

> **rmon** {**native** | **promiscuous**}
> **no rmon**

Syntax	Description
native	Enables RMON on the Ethernet interface. In native mode, the router processes only packets destined for this interface.
promiscuous	Enables RMON on the Ethernet interface. In promiscuous mode, the router examines every packet.

Default

RMON is disabled on the interface.

Command Mode

Interface configuration

Usage Guidelines

This command first appeared in Cisco IOS Release 11.1.

This command enables RMON on Ethernet interfaces of Cisco 2500 series and Cisco AS5200 series routers only. A generic RMON console application such as Frontier NETscout Manager™ or Traffic Director™ is recommended in order to use the RMON network management capabilities. SNMP must also be configured. RMON provides visibility of individual nodal activity and allows you to monitor all nodes and their interaction on a LAN segment. When the **rmon** command is issued, the router automatically installs an Ethernet statistics study for the associated interface.

NOTES

RMON can be very data and processor intensive. Users should measure usage effects to ensure that router performance is not degraded and to minimize excessive management traffic overhead. Native mode is less intensive than promiscuous mode.

All Cisco IOS software Release 11.3 feature sets support RMON alarm and event groups. Additional RMON groups are supported in certain feature sets. Refer to the Release Notes for feature set descriptions. As a security precaution, support for the packet-capture group allows capture of packet header information only; data payloads are not captured.

The RMON MIB is described in RFC 1757.

Example

The following example enables RMON on Ethernet interface 0 and allows the router to examine only packets destined for the interface:

```
interface ethernet 0
  rmon native
```

Related Commands

rmon alarm
rmon event
rmon queuesize
show rmon

RMON ALARM

To set an alarm on any MIB object, use the **rmon alarm global** configuration command. Use the **no** form of this command to disable the alarm.

rmon alarm *number variable interval* {**delta** | **absolute**} **rising-threshold** *value* [*event-number*]
falling-threshold *value* [*event-number*] [**owner** *string*]
no rmon alarm *number*

Syntax	Description
number	Alarm number, which is identical to the *alarmIndex* in the alarmTable in the Remote Monitoring (RMON) MIB.
variable	MIB object to monitor, which translates into the *alarmVariable* used in the alarmTable of the RMON MIB.
interval	Time in seconds the alarm monitors the MIB variable, which is identical to the *alarmInterval* used in the alarmTable of the RMON MIB.
delta	Tests the change between MIB variables, which affects the *alarmSampleType* in the alarmTable of the RMON MIB.
absolute	Tests each MIB variable directly, which affects the *alarmSampleType* in the alarmTable of the RMON MIB.
rising-threshold *value*	Value at which the alarm is triggered.

Default

No alarms configured

Command Mode

Global configuration

Usage Guidelines

This command first appeared in Cisco IOS Release 11.2.

To disable the RMON alarms, you must use the **no** form of the command on each configured alarm. For example, enter **no rmon alarm 1,** where the 1 identifies which alarm is to be removed.

See RFC 1757 for more information about the RMON alarm group.

Example

The following example configures an RMON alarm using the **rmon alarm** command:

```
rmon alarm 10 ifEntry.20.1 20 delta rising-threshold 15 1 falling-threshold 0
    owner jjohnson
```

This example configures RMON alarm number 10. The alarm monitors the MIB variable *ifEntry.20.1* once every 20 seconds until the alarm is disabled, and checks the change in the variable's rise or fall. If the *ifEntry.20.1* value shows a MIB counter increase of 15 or more, such as from 100,000 to 100,015, the alarm is triggered. The alarm, in turn, triggers event number 1, which is configured with the **rmon event** command. Possible events include a log entry or a SNMP trap. If the *ifEntry.20.1* value changes by 0 (falling-threshold 0), the alarm is reset and can be triggered again.

Related Commands

rmon
rmon event
show rmon

RMON EVENT

To add or remove an event in the RMON event table that is associated with an RMON event number, use the **rmon event** global configuration command. Use the **no** form of this command to disable RMON on the interface.

rmon event *number* [**log**] [**trap** *community*] [**description** *string*] [**owner** *string*]
no rmon event *number*

Syntax	Description
number	Assigned event number, which is identical to the *eventIndex* in the eventTable in the RMON MIB.
log	(Optional) Generates an RMON log entry when the event is triggered and sets the *eventType* in the RMON MIB to *log* or *log-and-trap*.

Syntax	Description
trap *community*	(Optional) SNMP community string used for this trap. Configures the setting of the *eventType* in the RMON MIB for this row as either *snmp-trap* or *log-and-trap*. This value is identical to the *eventCommunityValue* in the eventTable in the RMON MIB.
description *string*	(Optional) Specifies a description of the event, which is identical to the event description in the eventTable of the RMON MIB.
owner *string*	(Optional) Owner of this event, which is identical to the *eventOwner* in the eventTable of the RMON MIB.

Default

No events configured

Command Mode

Global configuration

Usage Guidelines

This command first appeared in Cisco IOS Release 11.2.

This command applies only to the Cisco 2500 series and Cisco AS5200 series.

See RFC 1757 for more information about the RMON MIB.

Example

The following example enables the **rmon event** command:

```
rmon event 1 log trap eventtrap description "High ifOutErrors" owner sdurham
```

This example configuration creates RMON event number 1, which is defined as High *ifOutErrors*, and generates a log entry when the event is triggered by an alarm. The user *sdurham* owns the row that is created in the event table by this command. This configuration also generates a Simple Network Management Protocol (SNMP) trap when the event is triggered.

Related Commands

rmon
show rmon

RMON QUEUESIZE

To change the size of the queue that holds packets for analysis by the Remote Network Monitoring (RMON) process, use the **rmon queuesize** global configuration command. Use the **no** form of this command to restore the default value.

rmon queuesize *size*
no rmon queuesize

Syntax	*Description*
size	Number of packets allowed in the queue awaiting RMON analysis. Default queue size is 64 packets.

Default

64 packets

Command Mode

Global configuration

Usage Guidelines

This command first appeared in Cisco IOS Release 11.1.

This command applies to the RMON function, which is available on Ethernet interfaces of Cisco 2500 series and Cisco AS5200 series routers only.

You might want to increase the queue size if the RMON function indicates it is dropping packets. You can determine this from the output of the **show rmon** command or from the etherStats-DropEvents object in the etherStats table. A feasible maximum queue size depends on the amount of memory available in the router and the configuration of the buffer pool.

Example

The following example configures the RMON queue size to be 128 packets:

```
rmon queuesize 128
```

Related Commands

rmon
show rmon

RTR

To configure a response time reporter probe, use the **rtr** global configuration command. Use the **no** form of this command to remove all configuration information for a probe including the probe's schedule, reaction configuration, and reaction triggers.

rtr *probe*
no rtr *probe*

Syntax	Description
probe	Number of the response time reporter probe (instance) to configure.

Default

None

Command Mode

Global configuration

Usage Guidelines

This command first appeared in Cisco IOS Release 11.2.

A probe is used for the purpose of collecting response time information.

Each platform has a limit on the number of probes that can be configured. In general, this limit is less than 20.

Debugging is supported only on the first 32 probe numbers.

The response time reporter feature allows customers to monitor the performance of their network, network resources, and applications by measuring response times and availability. With this feature, a customer can perform troubleshooting, problem notification, and pre-problem analysis. The response time reporter feature is currently available only with the IBM feature set of the Cisco IOS software. For more information, see Chapter 24, "Monitoring the Router and Network" and the Cisco Round-Trip Time Monitor (RTTMON) MIB.

This command places you in response time reporter configuration mode.

NOTES

After you schedule a probe with the **rtr schedule** global configuration command, you cannot modify the probe's configuration. To modify the probe's configuration after it is scheduled, use the **no rtr** command. You then can re-enter the probe's configuration with the **rtr** command.

Use the following response time reporter configuration commands (**config-rtr**) to configure the probe's characteristics:

- **buckets-of-history-kept**
- **distributions-of-statistics-kept**
- **filter-for-history**
- **frequency**

- hops-of-statistics-kept
- hours-of-statistics-kept
- lives-of-history-kept
- owner
- paths-of-statistics-kept
- request-data-size
- response-data-size
- samples-of-history-kept
- statistics-distribution-interval
- tag
- threshold
- type
- timeout
- verify-data

After you configure a probe, you must schedule the probe. For information on scheduling a probe, refer to the **rtr schedule** global configuration command. You also can set reaction triggers optionally for the probe. For information on reaction triggers, refer to the **rtr reaction-configuration** and **rtr reaction-trigger** global configuration commands.

To display the probe's current configuration settings, use the **show rtr configuration** EXEC command.

Example

In the following example, probe 1 is configured to perform end-to-end response time operations using an SNA LU Type 0 connection with the host name *cwbc0a*. Only the **type** response time reporter configuration command is required; all others are optional.

```
rtr 1
 type echo protocol snalu0echoappl cwbc0a
 request-data-size 40
 response-data-size 1440
```

NOTES

If probe 1 already existed and it has not been scheduled, you are placed into response time reporter configuration command mode. If the probe already exists and has been scheduled, this command will fail.

Related Commands

rtr reaction-configuration
rtr reaction-trigger
rtr reset
rtr schedule

RTR REACTION-CONFIGURATION

To configure certain actions to occur based on events under the control of the response time reporter, use the **rtr reaction-configuration** global configuration command. Use the **no** form of this command to return to the probe's default values.

> **rtr reaction-configuration** *probe* [**connection-loss-enable**] [**timeout-enable**]
> [**threshold-falling** *milliseconds*] [**threshold-type** *option*] [**action-type** *option*]
> **no rtr reaction-configuration** *probe*

Syntax	Description
probe	Number of the response time reporter probe to configure.
connection-loss-enable	(Optional) Enable checking for connection loss in connection-oriented protocols. The default is disabled.
timeout-enable	(Optional) Enable checking for response time reporting operation timeouts based on the timeout value configured for the probe with the **timeout** response time reporter configuration command. The default is disabled.
threshold-falling *milliseconds*	(Optional) Set the falling threshold (standard RMON-type hysteresis mechanism) in milliseconds. When the falling threshold is met, generate a resolution reaction event. The probe's rising over-threshold is set with the **threshold** response time reporter configuration command. The default value is 3,000 ms.
threshold-type *option*	(Optional) Specify the algorithm used by the response time reporter to calculate over- and falling-threshold violations. Option can be one of the following keywords: • **never**—Do not calculate threshold violations (the default). • **immediate**—When the response time exceeds the rising over-threshold or drops below the falling threshold, immediately perform the action defined by **action-type**.

Syntax	Description

- **consecutive** [*occurrences*]—When the response time exceeds the rising threshold five times consecutively or drops below the falling threshold five times consecutively, perform the action defined by **action-type**. Optionally specify the number of consecutive occurrences. The default is five.

- **xofy** [*x-value y-value*]—When the response time exceeds the rising threshold five out of the last five times or drops below the falling threshold five out of the last five times, perform the action defined by **action-type**. Optionally specify the number of violations that must occur and the number that must occur within a specified number. The default is five for both x-value and y-value.

- **average** [*attempts*]—When the average of the last five response times exceeds the rising threshold or when the average of the last five response times drops below the falling threshold, perform the action defined by **action-type**. Optionally specify the number of operations to average. The default is the average of the last five response time operations. For example: if the probe's threshold is 5,000 ms and the probe's last three attempts results are 6,000, 6,000, and 5,000 ms, the average would be 6,000+6,000+5,000=17,000/3>5,000, thus violating the 5,000-ms threshold.

Default

No reactions are generated.

Command Mode

Global configuration

Usage Guidelines

This command first appeared in Cisco IOS Release 11.2.

Triggers are used for diagnostic purposes and are not used in normal operation.

You can use triggers to assist you in determining where delays are happening in the network when excessive delays are being seen on an end-to-end basis.

The reaction applies only to attempts to the target (that is, attempts to any hops along the path in **pathEcho** do not generate reactions).

NOTES

Keywords are not case sensitive and are shown in mixed case for readability only.

Example

In the following example, probe 19 sends an SNMP trap when there is an over- or falling-threshold violation:

```
rtr reaction-configuration 19 threshold-type immediate action-type trapOnly
```

Figure 25–1 shows that an alert (rising trap) would be issued immediately when the response time exceeds the rising threshold and a resolution (falling trap) would be issued immediately when the response time drops below the falling threshold.

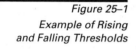

Figure 25–1

Example of Rising and Falling Thresholds

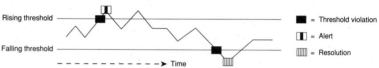

Related Commands

rtr
rtr reaction-trigger
threshold
timeout

RTR REACTION-TRIGGER

To define a second response time reporter probe to make the transition from a "pending" state to an "active" state when one of the trigger action-type options are defined with the **rtr reaction-configuration** global configuration command, use the **rtr reaction-trigger** global configuration command. Use the **no** form of this command to remove the trigger combination.

rtr reaction-trigger *probe target-probe*
no rtr reaction-trigger *probe*

Syntax	Description
probe	Number of the probe in the "active" state that has the **action-type** set with the **rtr reaction-configuration** global configuration command.
target-probe	Number of the probe in the "pending" state that is waiting to be triggered with the **rtr** global configuration command.

Default
None

Command Mode
Global configuration

Usage Guidelines
This command first appeared in Cisco IOS Release 11.2.

Triggers are usually used for diagnostic purposes and are not used in normal operation.

Example
In the following example, probe 1's state is changed from pending state to active state when probe 2's **action-type** occurs:

```
rtr reaction-trigger 2 1
```

Related Commands
rtr
rtr reaction-configuration
rtr schedule

RTR RESET

To perform a shutdown and restart of the response time reporter, use the **rtr reset** global configuration command.

rtr reset

Syntax   Description
This command has no arguments or keywords.

Default

None

Command Mode

Global configuration

Usage Guidelines

This command first appeared in Cisco IOS Release 11.2.

CAUTION

Use the **rtr reset** command only in extreme situations, such as the incorrect configuration of a number of probes.

The **rtr reset** command stops all probes, clears response time reporter configuration information, and returns the response time reporter feature to the startup condition. This command does not reread the response time reporter configuration stored in startup-config in NVRAM. You must retype the configuration or perform a **config memory** command.

Example

The following example resets the response time reporter feature:

```
rtr reset
```

Related Commands

rtr

RTR SCHEDULE

To configure the time parameters for a response time reporter probe, use the **rtr schedule** global configuration command. Use the **no** form of this command to stop the probe and restart it with the default parameters (that is, pending).

> **rtr schedule** *probe* [**life** *seconds*] [**start-time** {**pending** | **now** | *hh:mm* [*month day* | *day month*]}] [**ageout** *seconds*]
> **no rtr schedule** *probe*

Syntax	Description
probe	Number of the response time reporter probe to schedule.
life *seconds*	(Optional) Number of seconds the probe actively collects information. The default is 3,600 seconds (one hour).

Part IV

Command Reference

Syntax	Description
start-time	(Optional) Time when the probe starts collecting information. If the **start-time** is not specified, no information is collected until the **start-time** is configured or a trigger occurs that performs a **start-time now**.
pending	No information is collected. This is the default value.
now	Information is immediately collected.
hh:mm	Information is collected at the specified time (use a 24-hour clock). The time is the current day if you do not specify the month and day.
month	(Optional) Name of the month. If month is not specified, the current month is used. This requires a day.
day	Number of the day in the range 1 to 31. If day is not specified, the current day is used. This requires a month.
ageout *seconds*	(Optional) Number of seconds to keep the probe when it is not actively collecting information. The default is 0 seconds (never ages out).

Default

Place the probe in a pending state (that is, the probe is started but not actively collecting information).

Command Mode

Global configuration

Usage Guidelines

This command first appeared in Cisco IOS Release 11.2.

After you schedule the probe with the **rtr schedule** command, you cannot change the probe's configuration (with the **rtr** global configuration command). To change the probe's configuration, use the **no** form of the **rtr** global command and re-enter the configuration information.

If the probe is in a pending state, you can define the conditions under which the probe makes the transition from pending to active with the **rtr reaction-trigger** and **rtr reaction-configuration** global configuration commands. When the probe is in an active state, it immediately begins collecting information.

The following time line shows the probe's age-out process:

```
W- - - - - - - - - - - - - - - - - -X- - - - - - - - - - - - - - - - - - - -Y- - - - - - - - - - - - - - - - - -Z
```

where:

- W is the time the probe was configured with the **rtr** global configuration command.
- X is the probe's start time or start of life (that is, when the probe became "active").

- Y is the end of life as configured with the **rtr schedule** global configuration command (life seconds have counted down to zero).
- Z is the probe's age out.

Age out starts counting down at W and Y, is suspended between X and Y, and is reset to its configured size at Y.

It is possible for the probe to age out before it executes (that is, Z can occur before X). To ensure that this does not happen, the difference between the probe's configuration time and start time (X and W) must be less than the age-out seconds.

> **NOTES**
>
> The total RAM required to hold the history and statistics tables is allocated at this time. This is to prevent router memory problems when the router gets heavily loaded and to lower the amount of overhead the feature causes on a router when it is active.

Example

In the following example, probe 25 begins actively collecting data at 3:00 p.m. on April 5. This probe will age out after 12 hours of inactivity, which can be before it starts or after it has finished with its life. When this probe ages out, all configuration information for the probe is removed (that is, the configuration information is no longer in the running-config in RAM).

```
rtr schedule 25 life 43200 start-time 15:00 apr 5 ageout 43200
```

Related Commands

rtr
rtr reaction-configuration
rtr reaction-trigger

SAMPLES-OF-HISTORY-KEPT

To set the number of entries kept in the history table per bucket for the response time reporter probe, use the **samples-of-history-kept** response time reporter configuration command. Use the **no** form of this command to return to the default value.

> **samples-of-history-kept** *samples*
> **no samples-of-history-kept**

Syntax	Description
samples	Number of entries kept in the history table per bucket. The default is 16 entries for type **pathEcho** and 1 entry for type **echo**.

Default

16 entries for type **pathEcho**

1 entry for type **echo**

Command Mode

Response time reporter configuration

Usage Guidelines

This command first appeared in Cisco IOS Release 11.2.

Use the **samples-of-history-kept** command to control how many entries are saved in the history table. To control the type of information that gets saved in the history table, use the **filter-for-history** command. To set how many buckets get created in the history table, use the **buckets-of-history-kept** command.

A probe can collect history and capture statistics. By default, history is not collected. When a problem arises where history is useful (for example, a large number of timeouts are occurring), you can configure the **lives-of-history-kept** response time reporter configuration command to collect history.

NOTES

Collecting history increases the usage of RAM. Only collect history when you think there is a problem. For general network response time information, use statistics.

Example

In the following example, ten entries are kept in the history table for each of the of probe's three lives:

```
rtr 1
  type pathecho protocol ipIcmpEcho 172.16.1.176
  lives-of-history-kept 3
  samples-of-history-kept 10
```

Related Commands

buckets-of-history-kept
filter-for-history
lives-of-history-kept
rtr

SHOW CDP

To display global CDP information, including timer and hold-time information, use the **show cdp** privileged EXEC command.

    show cdp

Syntax   Description

This command has no arguments or keywords.

Command Mode

Privileged EXEC

Usage Guidelines

This command first appeared in Cisco IOS Release 10.3.

Sample Display

The following is sample output from the **show cdp** command. Global CDP timer and hold-time parameters are set to the defaults of 60 and 180 seconds, respectively.

```
Router# show cdp

Global CDP information:
        Sending CDP packets every 60 seconds
        Sending a holdtime value of 180 seconds
```

Related Commands

cdp holdtime
cdp timer
show cdp entry
show cdp interface
show cdp neighbors
show cdp traffic

SHOW CDP ENTRY

To display information about a neighbor device listed in the CDP table, use the **show cdp entry** privileged EXEC command.

> **show cdp entry** {* | *entry-name* [**protocol** | **version**]}

Syntax	*Description*
*	Shows all of the CDP neighbors.
entry-name	Name of neighbor about which you want information.
	You can enter an asterisk (*) at the end of an *entry-name*, such as show cdp entry dev*, which would show information about the neighbor, device.cisco.com.

Syntax	*Description*
protocol	(Optional) Limits the display to information about the protocols enabled on a router.
version	(Optional) Limits the display to information about the version of software running on the router.

Command Mode

Privileged EXEC

Usage Guidelines

This command first appeared in Cisco IOS Release 10.3.

Sample Displays

The following is sample output from the **show cdp** entry command with no limits. Information about the neighbor *device.cisco.com* is displayed, including device ID, address and protocol, platform, interface, hold time, and version.

```
Router# show cdp entry device.cisco.com


. . . . . . . . . . . . . . . . . . . . . .
Device ID: device.cisco.com
Entry address(es):
  IP address: 192.168.68.18
  CLNS address: 490001.1111.1111.1111.00
  DECnet address: 10.1
Platform: cisco 4500,  Capabilities: Router
Interface: Ethernet0/1,  Port ID (outgoing port): Ethernet0
Holdtime : 125 sec

Version :
Cisco Internetwork Operating System Software
IOS (tm) 4500 Software (C4500-J-M), Version 11.1(10.4), MAINTENANCE INTERIM SOFTWARE
Copyright (c) 1986-1997 by cisco Systems, Inc.
Compiled Mon 07-Apr-97 19:51 by dschwart
```

The following is sample output from the **show cdp entry protocol** command. Only information about the protocols enabled on *device.cisco.com* is displayed.

```
Router# show cdp entry device.cisco.com protocol

Protocol information for device.cisco.com:
  IP address: 192.168.68.18
  CLNS address: 490001.1111.1111.1111.00
  DECnet address: 10.1
```

The following is sample output from the **show cdp entry version** command. Only information about the version of software running on *device.cisco.com* is displayed.

```
Router# show cdp entry device.cisco.com version

Version information for device.cisco.com:
  Cisco Internetwork Operating System Software
IOS (tm) 4500 Software (C4500-J-M), Version 11.1(10.4), MAINTENANCE INTERIM SOFTWARE
Copyright (c) 1986-1997 by cisco Systems, Inc.
Compiled Mon 07-Apr-97 19:51 by dschwart
```

Related Commands

show cdp
show cdp interface
show cdp neighbors
show cdp traffic

SHOW CDP INTERFACE

To display information about the interfaces on which CDP is enabled, use the **show cdp interface** privileged EXEC command.

> **show cdp interface** [*type number*]

Syntax	Description
type	(Optional) Type of interface about which you want information.
number	(Optional) Number of the interface about which you want information.

Command Mode

Privileged EXEC

Usage Guidelines

This command first appeared in Cisco IOS Release 10.3.

Sample Displays

The following is sample output from the **show cdp interface** command. Status information and information about CDP timer and hold-time settings is displayed for all interfaces on which CDP is enabled.

```
Router# show cdp interface

Serial0 is up, line protocol is up, encapsulation is SMDS
  Sending CDP packets every 60 seconds
  Holdtime is 180 seconds
Ethernet0 is up, line protocol is up, encapsulation is ARPA
  Sending CDP packets every 60 seconds
  Holdtime is 180 seconds
```

Part IV

Command Reference

The following is sample output from the **show cdp interface** command with an interface specified. Status information and information about CDP timer and hold-time settings is displayed for Ethernet interface 0 only.

```
Router# show cdp interface ethernet 0

Ethernet0 is up, line protocol is up, encapsulation is ARPA
  Sending CDP packets every 60 seconds
  Holdtime is 180 seconds
```

Related Commands

show cdp
show cdp entry
show cdp neighbors
show cdp traffic

SHOW CDP NEIGHBORS

To display information about neighbors, use the **show cdp neighbors** privileged EXEC command.

>   **show cdp neighbors** [*type number*] [detail]

Syntax	Description
type	(Optional) Type of the interface connected to the neighbors about which you want information.
number	(Optional) Number of the interface connected to the neighbors about which you want information.
detail	(Optional) Displays detailed information about a neighbor (or neighbors) including network address, enabled protocols, hold time, and software version.

Command Mode

Privileged EXEC

Usage Guidelines

This command first appeared in Cisco IOS Release 10.3.

Sample Displays

The following is sample output from the **show cdp neighbors** command. Device ID, interface type and number, hold-time settings, capabilities, platform, and port ID information about neighbors is displayed.

```
Router# show cdp neighbors
```

```
Capability Codes: R - Router, T - Trans Bridge, B - Source Route Bridge
                  S - Switch, H - Host, I - IGMP, r - Repeater

Device ID         Local Intrfce    Holdtme    Capability  Platform   Port ID
device1.cisco.com    Eth 0/1       122          T S        WS-C2900   2/11
device2.cisco.com    Eth 0/1       179          R          4500       Eth 0
device3.cisco.com    Eth 0/1       155          R          2500       Eth 0
device4.cisco.com    Eth 0/1       155          R          2509       Eth 0
```

The following is sample output for one neighbor from the **show cdp neighbors detail** command. Additional detail is shown about neighbors, including network address, enabled protocols, and software version:

```
Router# show cdp neighbors detail


- - - - - - - - - - - - - - - - - - - - - - -
Device ID: device2.cisco.com
Entry address(es):
  IP address: 171.68.162.134
Platform: cisco 4500,  Capabilities: Router
Interface: Ethernet0/1,  Port ID (outgoing port): Ethernet0
Holdtime : 156 sec

Version :
Cisco Internetwork Operating System Software
IOS (tm) 4500 Software (C4500-J-M), Version 11.1(10.4), MAINTENANCE INTERIM SOFTWARE
Copyright (c) 1986-1997 by cisco Systems, Inc.
Compiled Mon 07-Apr-97 19:51 by dschwart
```

Related Commands

show cdp
show cdp entry
show cdp interface
show cdp traffic

SHOW CDP TRAFFIC

To display traffic information from the CDP table, use the **show cdp traffic** privileged EXEC command.

> **show cdp traffic**

Syntax   Description

This command has no arguments or keywords.

Command Mode

Privileged EXEC

Usage Guidelines

This command first appeared in Cisco IOS Release 10.3.

Sample Display

The following is sample output from the **show cdp traffic** command.

```
Router# show cdp traffic

CDP counters:
        Packets output: 94, Input: 75
        Hdr syntax: 0, Chksum error: 0, Encaps failed: 0
        No memory: 0, Invalid packet: 0, Fragmented: 0
```

In this example, traffic information is displayed, including the numbers of packets sent, the number of packets received, header syntax, checksum errors, failed encapsulations, memory problems, and invalid and fragmented packets. Header syntax indicates the number of packets CDP receives with an invalid header format.

Related Commands

show cdp
show cdp entry
show cdp interface
show cdp neighbors

SHOW RMON

Use the **show rmon** EXEC command to display the current RMON agent status on the router.

show rmon [alarms | capture | events | filter | history | hosts | matrix | statistics | task | topn]

Syntax	Description
alarms	(Optional) Displays the RMON alarm table.
capture	(Optional) Displays the RMON buffer capture table. Available on Cisco 2500 series and Cisco AS5200 series only.
events	(Optional) Displays the RMON event table.
filter	(Optional) Displays the RMON filter table. Available on Cisco 2500 series and Cisco AS5200 series only.
history	(Optional) Displays the RMON history table. Available on Cisco 2500 series and Cisco AS5200 series only.
hosts	(Optional) Displays the RMON hosts table. Available on Cisco 2500 series and Cisco AS5200 series only.
matrix	(Optional) Displays the RMON matrix table. Available on Cisco 2500 series and Cisco AS5200 series only.

Syntax	Description
statistics	(Optional) Displays the RMON statistics table. Available on Cisco 2500 series and Cisco AS5200 series only.
task	(Optional) Displays general RMON statistics. This is the default.
topn	(Optional) Displays the RMON top-n hosts table. Available on Cisco 2500 series and Cisco AS5200 series only.

Default

If no option is specified, the **task** option is displayed.

Command Mode

EXEC

Usage Guidelines

This command first appeared in Cisco IOS Release 11.1.

Refer to the specific **show rmon** command for an example and description of the fields.

For more information, see the RMON MIB described in RFC 1757.

Sample Display

The following is sample output from the **show rmon** command. All counters are from the time the router was initialized.

```
Router# show rmon

145678 packets input (34562 promiscuous), 0 drops
145678 packets processed, 0 on queue, queue utilization 15/64
```

Table 25–1 describes the fields shown in the display.

Table 25–1   *Show RMON Field Descriptions*

Field	Description
x packets input	Number of packets received on RMON-enabled interfaces.
x promiscuous	Number of input packets that were seen by the router only because RMON placed the interface in promiscuous mode.
x drops	Number of input packets that could not be processed because the RMON queue overflowed.
x packets processed	Number of input packets actually processed by the RMON task.

Table 25–1 *Show RMON Field Descriptions, Continued*

Field	Description
x on queue	Number of input packets that are sitting on the RMON queue, waiting to be processed.
queue utilization *x/y*	*y* is the maximum size of the RMON queue; *x* is the largest number of packets that were ever on the queue at a particular time.

Related Commands

rmon
rmon alarm
rmon event
rmon queuesize
show rmon alarms
show rmon capture
show rmon events
show rmon filter
show rmon history
show rmon hosts
show rmon matrix
show rmon statistics
show rmon topn

SHOW RMON ALARMS

Use the **show rmon alarms** EXEC command to display the contents of the router's RMON alarm table.

　　　show rmon alarms

Syntax Description

This command has no keywords or arguments.

Command Mode

EXEC

Usage Guidelines

This command first appeared in Cisco IOS Release 11.2.

For additional information, refer to the RMON MIB described in RFC 1757.

You must have enabled RMON on the interface first, and configured RMON alarms to display alarm information with the **show rmon alarms** command.

Sample Display

The following is sample output from the **show rmon alarms** command:

```
Router# show rmon alarms

Alarm 2 is active, owned by manager1
  Monitors ifEntry.1.1 every 30 seconds
  Taking delta samples, last value was 0
  Rising threshold is 15, assigned to event 12
  Falling threshold is 0, assigned to event 0
  On startup enable rising or falling alarm
```

Table 25–2 describes the fields shown in the display.

Table 25–2 *Show RMON Alarms Field Descriptions*

Field	Description
Alarm 2 is active, owned by manager1	Unique index into the alarmTable, showing the alarm status is active, and the owner of this row, as defined in the alarmTable of RMON.
Monitors ifEntry.1.1	Object identifier of the particular variable to be sampled. Equivalent to alarmVariable in RMON.
every 30 seconds	Interval in seconds over which the data is sampled and compared with the rising and falling thresholds. Equivalent to alarmInterval in RMON.
Taking delta samples	Method of sampling the selected variable and calculating the value to be compared against the thresholds. Equivalent to alarmSampleType in RMON.
last value was	Value of the statistic during the last sampling period. Equivalent to alarmValue in RMON.
Rising threshold is	Threshold for the sampled statistic. Equivalent to alarmRisingThreshold in RMON.
assigned to event	Index of the eventEntry that is used when a rising threshold is crossed. Equivalent to alarmRisingEventIndex in RMON.
Falling threshold is	Threshold for the sampled statistic. Equivalent to alarmFallingThreshold in RMON.
assigned to event	Index of the eventEntry that is used when a falling threshold is crossed. Equivalent to alarmFallingEventIndex in RMON.
On startup enable rising or falling alarm	Alarm that may be sent when this entry is first set to valid. Equivalent to alarmStartupAlarm in RMON.

Related Commands

rmon
rmon alarm
show rmon

SHOW RMON CAPTURE

Use the **show rmon capture** EXEC command to display the contents of the router's RMON capture table.

> **show rmon capture**

Syntax   Description

This command has no arguments or keywords.

Command Mode

EXEC

Usage Guidelines

This command first appeared in Cisco IOS Release 11.2.

For additional information, refer to the RMON MIB described in RFC 1757.

You must have enabled RMON on the interface first, and configured RMON alarms and events to display alarm information with the **show rmon capture** command.

This command is available on the Cisco 2500 series and Cisco AS5200 series only.

Sample Display

The following is sample output from the **show rmon capture** command:

```
Router# show rmon capture

Buffer 4096 is active, owned by manager1
 Captured data is from channel 4096
 Slice size is 128, download size is 128
 Download offset is 0
 Full Status is spaceAvailable, full action is lockWhenFull
 Granted 65536 octets out of 65536 requested
 Buffer has been on since 00:01:16, and has captured 1 packets
  Current capture buffer entries:
    Packet 1 was captured 416 ms since buffer was turned on
    Its length is 326 octets and has a status type of 0
    Packet ID is 634, and contains the following data:
00 00 0c 03 12 ce 00 00 0c 08 9d 4e 08 00 45 00
01 34 01 42 00 00 1d 11 e3 01 ab 45 30 15 ac 15
31 06 05 98 00 a1 01 20 9f a8 00 00 00 00 00 00
```

```
00 00 00 00 00 00 00 00 00 00 00 00 00 00 00 00
00 00 00 00 00 00 00 00 00 00 00 00 00 00 00 00
00 00 00 00 00 00 00 00 00 00 00 00 00 00 00 00
00 00 00 00
```

Table 25–3 describes the fields shown in the display.

Table 25–3 *Show RMON Capture Field Descriptions*

Field	Description
Buffer 4096 is active	Equates to bufferControlIndex in the bufferControlTable of RMON. Uniquely identifies a valid (active) row in this table.
owned by manager1	Denotes the owner of this row. Equates to bufferControlOwner in the bufferControlTable of RMON.
Captured data is from channel	Equates to the bufferControlChannelIndex and identifies which RMON channel is the source of these packets.
Slice size is	Identifies the maximum number of octets of each packet that will be saved in this capture buffer. Equates to bufferControlCaptureSliceSize of RMON.
download size is	Identifies the maximum number of octets of each packet in this capture buffer that will be returned in an SNMP retrieval of that packet. Equates to bufferControlDownloadSliceSize in RMON.
Download offset is	Offset of the first octet of each packet in this capture buffer that will be returned in an SNMP retrieval of that packet. Equates to bufferControlDownloadOffset in RMON.
Full Status is spaceAvailable	Shows whether the buffer is full or has room to accept new packets. Equates to bufferControlFullStatus in RMON.
full action is lockWhenFull	Controls the action of the buffer when it reaches full status. Equates to bufferControlFullAction in RMON.
Granted 65536 octets	Actual maximum number of octets that can be saved in this capture buffer. Equates to bufferControlMaxOctetsGranted in RMON.
out of 65536 requested	Requested maximum number of octets to be saved in this capture buffer. Equates to bufferControlMaxOctetsRequested in RMON.
Buffer has been on since	Indicates how long the buffer has been available.
and has captured 1 packets	Number of packets captured since buffer was turned on. Equates to bufferControlCapturedPackets in RMON.

Table 25–3   *Show RMON Capture Field Descriptions, Continued*

Field	Description
Current capture buffer entries:	Lists each packet captured.
Packet 1 was captured 416 ms since buffer was turned on Its length is 326 octets and has a status type of 0	Zero indicates the error status of this packet. Equates to captureBufferPacketStatus in RMON, where its value options are documented.
Packet ID is	Index that describes the order of packets received on a particular interface. Equates to captureBufferPacketID in RMON.
and contains the following data:	Data inside the packet, starting at the beginning of the packet.

Related Commands

rmon
rmon alarm
rmon event
show rmon

SHOW RMON EVENTS

Use the **show rmon events** EXEC command to display the contents of the router's RMON event table.

> **show rmon events**

Syntax   Description

This command has no arguments or keywords.

Command Mode

EXEC

Usage Guidelines

This command first appeared in Cisco IOS Release 11.2.

For additional information, refer to the RMON MIB described in RFC 1757.

You must have enabled RMON on the interface first, and configured RMON events to display alarm information with the **show rmon events** command.

Sample Display

The following is sample output from the **show rmon events** command:

```
Router# show rmon events

Event 12 is active, owned by manager1
 Description is interface-errors
 Event firing causes log and trap to community rmonTrap, last fired 00:00:00
```

Table 25–4 describes the fields shown in the display.

Table 25–4 *Show RMON Events Field Descriptions*

Field	Description
Event 12 is active, owned by manager1	Unique index into the eventTable, showing the event status is active, and the owner of this row, as defined in the eventTable of RMON.
Description is interface-errors	Type of event, in this case, an interface error.
Event firing causes log and trap	Type of notification that the router will make about this event. Equivalent to eventType in RMON.
community rmonTrap	If an SNMP trap is to be sent, it will be sent to the SNMP community specified by this octet string. Equivalent to eventCommunity in RMON.
last fired	Last time the event was generated.

Related Commands

rmon
rmon event
show rmon

SHOW RMON FILTER

Use the **show rmon filter** EXEC command to display the contents of the router's RMON filter table.

> **show rmon filter**

Syntax   Description

This command has no arguments or keywords.

Command Mode

EXEC

Usage Guidelines

This command first appeared in Cisco IOS Release 11.2.

For additional information, refer to the RMON MIB described in RFC 1757.

You must have enabled RMON on the interface first, and configured RMON alarms and events to display alarm information with the **show rmon filter** command.

This command is available on the Cisco 2500 series and Cisco AS5200 series only.

Sample Display

The following is sample output from the **show rmon filter** command:

```
Router# show rmon filter

Filter 4096 is active, and owned by manager1
 Data offset is 12, with
 Data of  08 00 00 00 00 00 00 00 00 00 00 00 00 00 ab 45 30 15 ac 15 31 06
 Data Mask is ff ff 00 00 00 00 00 00 00 00 00 00 00 00 ff ff ff ff ff ff ff ff
 Data Not Mask is 0
 Pkt status is 0, status mask is 0, not mask is 0
 Associated channel 4096 is active, and owned by manager1
 Type of channel is acceptFailed, data control is off
 Generate event index 0
 Event status is eventFired, # of matches is 1482
 Turn on event index is 0, turn off event index is 0
 Description:
```

Table 25–5 describes the fields shown in the display.

Table 25–5 *Show RMON Filter Field Descriptions*

Field	Description
Filter 4096 is active, and owned by manager1	Unique index of the filter, its current state, and the owner, as defined in the filterTable of RMON.
Data offset is	Offset from the beginning of each packet where a match of packet data will be attempted. Equivalent to filterPktDataOffset in RMON.
Data of	Data that is to be matched with the input packet. Equivalent to filterPktData in RMON.
Data Mask is	Mask that is applied to the match process. Equivalent to filterPktDataMask in RMON.
Data Not Mask is	Inversion mask that is applied to the match process. Equivalent to filterPktDataNotMask in RMON.
Pkt status is	Status that is to be matched with the input packet. Equivalent to filterPktStatus in RMON.

Table 25–5 *Show RMON Filter Field Descriptions, Continued*

Field	Description
status mask is	Mask that is applied to the status match process. Equivalent to filterPktStatusMask in RMON.
not mask is	Inversion mask that is applied to the status match process. Equivalent to filterPktStatusNotMask in RMON.
Associated channel 4096 is active, and owned by manager1	Unique index of the channel, its current state, and the owner, as defined in the channelTable of RMON.
Type of channel is acceptFailed	This object controls the action of the filters associated with this channel. Equivalent to channelAcceptType of RMON.
data control is off	This object controls the flow of data through this channel. Equivalent to channelDataControl in RMON.
Generate event index 0	Value of this object identifies the event that is configured to be generated when the associated channelDataControl is on and a packet is matched. Equivalent to channelEventIndex in RMON.
Event status is eventFired	When the channel is configured to generate events when packets are matched, this message indicates the means of controlling the flow of those events. Equivalent to channelEventStatus in RMON.
# of matches is	Number of times this channel has matched a packet. Equivalent to channelMatches in RMON.
Turn on event index is	Value of this object identifies the event that is configured to turn the associated channelDataControl from off to on when the event is generated. Equivalent to channelTurnOnEventIndex in RMON.
Turn off event index is	Value of this object identifies the event that is configured to turn the associated channelDataControl from on to off when the event is generated. Equivalent to channelTurnOffEventIndex in RMON.
Description:	Comment describing this channel.

Related Commands

rmon
rmon alarm

rmon event
show rmon

SHOW RMON HISTORY

Use the **show rmon history** EXEC command to display the contents of the router's RMON history table.

> **show rmon history**

Syntax   *Description*

This command has no arguments or keywords.

Command Mode

EXEC

Usage Guidelines

This command first appeared in Cisco IOS Release 11.2.

For additional information, refer to the RMON MIB described in RFC 1757.

You must have enabled RMON on the interface first, and configured RMON alarms and events to display alarm information with the **show rmon history** command.

This command is available on the Cisco 2500 series and Cisco AS5200 series only.

Sample Display

The following is sample output from the **show rmon history** command:

```
Router# show rmon history

Entry 1 is active, and owned by manager1
 Monitors ifEntry.1.1 every 30 seconds
 Requested # of time intervals, ie buckets, is 5
 Granted # of time intervals, ie buckets, is 5
  Sample # 14 began measuring at 00:11:00
   Received 38346 octets, 216 packets,
   0 broadcast and 80 multicast packets,
   0 undersized and 0 oversized packets,
   0 fragments and 0 jabbers,
   0 CRC alignment errors and 0 collisions.
   # of dropped packet events is 0
   Network utilization is estimated at 10
```

Table 25–6 describes the fields shown in the display.

Table 25–6 *Show RMON History Field Descriptions*

Field	Description
Entry 1 is active, and owned by manager1	Unique index of the history entry, its current state, and the owner as defined in the historyControlTable of RMON.
Monitors ifEntry.1.1	This object identifies the source of the data for which historical data was collected and placed in a media-specific table. Equivalent to historyControlDataSource in RMON.
every 30 seconds	Interval in seconds over which the data is sampled for each bucket in the part of the media-specific table associated with this historyControlEntry. Equivalent to historyControlInterval in RMON.
Requested # of time intervals, ie buckets, is	Requested number of discrete time intervals over which data is to be saved in the part of the media-specific table associated with this historyControlEntry. Equivalent to historyControlBucketsRequested in RMON.
Granted # of time intervals, ie buckets, is	Actual number of discrete time intervals over which data is to be saved in the part of the media-specific table associated with this historyControlEntry. Equivalent to historyControlBucketsGranted in RMON.
Sample # 14 began measuring at	Time at the start of the interval over which this sample was measured.
Received 38,346 octets	Total number of octets of data (including those in bad packets) received on the network (excluding framing bits but including FCS octets). Equivalent to etherHistoryOctets in RMON.
x packets	Number of packets (including bad packets) received during this sampling interval. Equivalent to etherHistoryPkts in RMON.
x broadcast	Number of good packets received during this sampling interval that were directed to the broadcast address. Equivalent to etherHistoryBroadcastPkts in RMON.
x multicast packets	Number of good packets received during this sampling interval that were directed to a multicast address. Equivalent to etherHistoryMulticastPkts in RMON.

Part
IV

Command Reference

Table 25–6 *Show RMON History Field Descriptions, Continued*

Field	Description
x undersized	Number of packets received during this sampling interval that were fewer than 64 octets long (excluding framing bits but including FCS octets) and were otherwise well formed. Equivalent to etherHistoryUndersizedPkts in RMON.
x oversized packets	Number of packets received during this sampling interval that were longer than 1,518 octets (excluding framing bits but including FCS octets) but were otherwise well formed. Equivalent to etherHistoryOversizePkts in RMON.
x fragments	Total number of packets received during this sampling interval that were fewer than 64 octets in length (excluding framing bits but including FCS octets), and had either a bad Frame Check Sequence (FCS) with an integral number of octets (FCS Error) or a bad FCS with a nonintegral number of octets (Alignment Error). Equivalent to etherHistoryFragments in RMON.
x jabbers	Number of packets received during this sampling interval that were longer than 1,518 octets (excluding framing bits but including FCS octets), and had either a bad Frame Check Sequence (FCS) with an integral number of octets (FCS Error) or a bad FCS with a nonintegral number of octets (Alignment Error). Note that this definition of jabber is different than the definition in IEEE-802.3 section 8.2.1.5 (10BASE5) and section 10.3.1.4 (10BASE2). Equivalent to etherHistoryJabbers in RMON.
x CRC alignment errors	Number of packets received during this sampling interval that had a length (excluding framing bits but including FCS octets) from 64 to 1,518 octets, inclusive, but had either a bad Frame Check Sequence (FCS) with an integral number of octets (FCS Error) or a bad FCS with a nonintegral number of octets (Alignment Error). Equivalent to etherHistoryCRCAlignErrors in RMON.
x collisions	Best estimate of the total number of collisions on this Ethernet segment during this sampling interval. Equivalent to etherHistoryCollisions in RMON.

Table 25–6 *Show RMON History Field Descriptions, Continued*

Field	Description
# of dropped packet events is	Total number of events in which packets were dropped by the probe because of resources during this sampling interval. Note that this number is not necessarily the number of packets dropped; it is just the number of times this condition has been detected. Equivalent to etherHistoryDropEvents in RMON.
Network utilization is estimated at	Best estimate of the mean physical-layer network usage on this interface during this sampling interval, in hundredths of a percent. Equivalent to etherHistoryUtilization in RMON.

Related Commands

rmon
rmon alarm
rmon event
show rmon

SHOW RMON HOSTS

Use the **show rmon hosts** EXEC command to display the contents of the router's RMON hosts table.

    show rmon hosts

Syntax   Description

This command has no arguments or keywords.

Command Mode

EXEC

Usage Guidelines

This command first appeared in Cisco IOS Release 11.2.

For additional information, refer to the RMON MIB described in RFC 1757.

You must have enabled RMON on the interface first, and configured RMON alarms and events to display alarm information with the **show rmon hosts** command.

This command is available on the Cisco 2500 series and Cisco AS5200 series only.

Sample Display

The following is sample output from the **show rmon hosts** command:

```
Router# show rmon hosts

Host Control Entry 1 is active, and owned by manager1
 Monitors host ifEntry.1.1
 Table size is 51, last time an entry was deleted was 00:00:00
  Creation Order number is 1
   Physical address is 0000.0c02.5808
   Packets: rcvd 6963, transmitted 7041
   Octets: rcvd 784062, transmitted 858530
   # of packets transmitted: broadcast 28, multicast 48
   # of bad packets transmitted is 0
```

Table 25–7 describes the fields shown in the display.

Table 25–7   *Show RMON Hosts Field Descriptions*

Field	Description
Host Control Entry 1 is active, and owned by manager1	Unique index of the host entry, its current state, and the owner as defined in the hostControlTable of RMON.
Monitors host ifEntry.1.1	This object identifies the source of the data for this instance of the host function. Equivalent to hostControlDataSource in RMON.
Table size is	Number of hostEntries in the hostTable and the hostTimeTable associated with this hostControlEntry. Equivalent to hostControlTableSize in RMON.
last time an entry was deleted was	Time when the last entry was deleted from the hostTable.
Creation Order number is	Index that defines the relative ordering of the creation time of hosts captured for a particular hostControlEntry. Equivalent to hostCreationOrder in RMON.
Physical address is	Physical address of this host. Equivalent to hostAddress in RMON.
Packets: rcvd	Number of good packets transmitted to this address. Equivalent to hostInPkts in RMON.
transmitted	Number of packets, including bad packets transmitted by this address. Equivalent to hostOutPkts in RMON.
Octets: rcvd	Number of octets transmitted to this address since it was added to the hostTable (excluding framing bits but including FCS octets), except for those octets in bad packets. Equivalent to hostInOctets in RMON.

Table 25–7 *Show RMON Hosts Field Descriptions, Continued*

Field	Description
transmitted	Number of octets transmitted by this address since it was added to the hostTable (excluding framing bits but including FCS octets), including those octets in bad packets. Equivalent to hostOutOctets in RMON.
# of packets transmitted:	Number of good packets transmitted by this address that were broadcast or multicast.
# of bad packets transmitted is	Number of bad packets transmitted by this address.

Related Commands

rmon
rmon alarm
rmon event
show rmon

SHOW RMON MATRIX

Use the **show rmon matrix** EXEC command to display the contents of the router's RMON matrix table.

> **show rmon matrix**

Syntax   Description

This command has no arguments or keywords.

Command Mode

EXEC

Usage Guidelines

This command first appeared in Cisco IOS Release 11.2.

For additional information, refer to the RMON MIB described in RFC 1757.

You must have enabled RMON on the interface first, and configured RMON alarms and events to display alarm information with the **show rmon matrix** command.

This command is available on the Cisco 2500 series and Cisco AS5200 series only.

Sample Display

The following is sample output from the **show rmon matrix** command:

```
Router# show rmon matrix

Matrix 1 is active, and owned by manager1
 Monitors ifEntry.1.1
 Table size is 451, last time an entry was deleted was at 00:00:00
```

Table 25–8 describes the fields shown in the display.

Table 25–8   *Show RMON Matrix Field Descriptions*

Field	Description
Matrix 1 is active, and owned by manager1	Unique index of the matrix entry, its current state, and the owner as defined in the matrixControlTable of RMON.
Monitors ifEntry.1.1	This object identifies the source of the data for this instance of the matrix function. Equivalent to matrixControlDataSource in RMON.
Table size is 451, last time an entry was deleted was at	Size of the matrix table and the time that the last entry was deleted.

Related Commands

rmon
rmon alarm
rmon event
show rmon

SHOW RMON STATISTICS

Use the **show rmon statistics** EXEC command to display the contents of the router's RMON statistics table.

show rmon statistics

Syntax   Description

This command has no arguments or keywords.

Command Mode

EXEC

Usage Guidelines

This command first appeared in Cisco IOS Release 11.2.

For additional information, refer to the RMON MIB described in RFC 1757.

You must have enabled RMON on the interface first, and configured RMON alarms and events to display alarm information with the **show rmon statistics** command.

This command is available on the Cisco 2500 series and Cisco AS5200 series only.

Sample Display

The following is sample output from the **show rmon statistics** command:

```
Router# show rmon statistics

Interface 1 is active, and owned by config
 Monitors ifEntry.1.1 which has
 Received 60739740 octets, 201157 packets,
 1721 broadcast and 9185 multicast packets,
 0 undersized and 0 oversized packets,
 0 fragments and 0 jabbers,
 0 CRC alignment errors and 32 collisions.
 # of dropped packet events (due to lack of resources): 511
 # of packets received of length (in octets):
  64: 92955, 65-127: 14204, 128-255: 1116,
  256-511: 4479, 512-1023: 85856, 1024-1518:2547
```

Table 25–9 describes the fields shown in the display.

Table 25–9 *Show RMON Statistics Field Descriptions*

Field	Description
Interface 1 is active, and owned by config	Unique index of the statistics entry, its current state, and the owner as defined in the etherStatsTable of RMON.
Monitors ifEntry.1.1	This object identifies the source of the data that this etherStats entry is configured to analyze. Equivalent to etherStatsDataSource in RMON.
Received 60739740 octets	Total number of octets of data (including those in bad packets) received on the network (excluding framing bits but including FCS octets). Equivalent to etherStatsOctets in RMON.
x packets	Number of packets (including bad packets) received. Equivalent to etherStatsPkts in RMON.
x broadcast	Number of good packets received that were directed to the broadcast address. Equivalent to etherStatsBroadcastPkts in RMON.
x multicast packets	Number of good packets received that were directed to a multicast address. Equivalent to etherStatsMulticastPkts in RMON.

Table 25–9 *Show RMON Statistics Field Descriptions, Continued*

Field	Description
x undersized	Number of packets received that were fewer than 64 octets long (excluding framing bits but including FCS octets) and were otherwise well formed. Equivalent to etherStatsUndersizedPkts in RMON.
x oversized packets	Number of packets received that were longer than 1,518 octets (excluding framing bits but including FCS octets) but were otherwise well formed. Equivalent to etherStatsOversizePkts in RMON.
x fragments	Total number of packets received that were fewer than 64 octets in length (excluding framing bits but including FCS octets), and had either a bad Frame Check Sequence (FCS) with an integral number of octets (FCS Error) or a bad FCS with a nonintegral number of octets (Alignment Error). Equivalent to etherStatsFragments in RMON.
x jabbers	Number of packets received that were longer than 1,518 octets (excluding framing bits but including FCS octets), and had either a bad Frame Check Sequence (FCS) with an integral number of octets (FCS Error) or a bad FCS with a nonintegral number of octets (Alignment Error). Note that this definition of jabber is different than the definition in IEEE-802.3 section 8.2.1.5 (10BASE5) and section 10.3.1.4 (10BASE2). Equivalent to etherStatsJabbers in RMON.
x CRC alignment errors	Number of packets received that had a length (excluding framing bits but including FCS octets) from 64 to 1,518 octets, inclusive, but had either a bad Frame Check Sequence (FCS) with an integral number of octets (FCS Error) or a bad FCS with a nonintegral number of octets (Alignment Error). Equivalent to etherStatsCRCAlignErrors in RMON.
x collisions	Best estimate of the total number of collisions on this Ethernet segment. Equivalent to etherHistoryCollisions in RMON.

Table 25-9 *Show RMON Statistics Field Descriptions, Continued*

Field	Description
# of dropped packet events (due to lack of resources):	Total number of events in which packets were dropped by the probe because of a lack of resources. Note that this number is not necessarily the number of packets dropped; it is just the number of times this condition has been detected. Equivalent to etherStatsDropEvents in RMON.
# of packets received of length (in octets):	Separates the received packets (good and bad) by packet size in the given ranges (64, 65 to 127,128 to 255, 256 to 511, 512 to 1,023, 1,024 to 1,516).

Related Commands

rmon
rmon alarm
rmon event
show rmon

SHOW RMON TOPN

Use the **show rmon topn** EXEC command to display the contents of the router's RMON Top-N host table.

show rmon topn

Syntax   Description

This command has no arguments or keywords.

Command Mode

EXEC

Usage Guidelines

This command first appeared in Cisco IOS Release 11.2.

For additional information, refer to the RMON MIB described in RFC 1757.

You must have enabled RMON on the interface first, and configured RMON events to display alarm information with the **show rmon events** command.

This command is available on the Cisco 2500 series and Cisco AS5200 series only.

Sample Display

The following is sample output from the **show rmon topn** command:

```
Router# show rmon topn

Host Entry 1 of report 1 is active, owned by manager1
 The rate of change is based on hostTopNInPkts
 This report was last started at 00:00:00
 Time remaining in this report is 0 out of 0
 Hosts physical address is 00ad.beef.002b
 Requested # of hosts: 10, # of hosts granted: 10
Report # 1 of Top N hosts entry 1 is recording
Host 0000.0c02.5808 at a rate of 12
```

Table 25–10 describes the fields shown in the display.

Table 25–10   *Show RMON Top-N Field Descriptions*

Field	Description
Host Entry 1 of report 1 is active, owned by manager1	Unique index of the hostTopN entry, its current state, and the owner as defined in the hostTopNControlTable of RMON.
The rate of change is based on hostTopNInPkts	Variable for each host on which the hostTopNRate variable is based.
This report was last started at	Time the report was started.
Time remaining in this report is	Number of seconds left in the report currently being collected. Equivalent to hostTopNTimeRemaining in RMON.
out of	Number of seconds that this report has collected during the last sampling interval, or if this report is currently being collected, the number of seconds that this report is being collected during this sampling interval. Equivalent to hostTopNDuration in RMON.
Hosts physical address is	Host address.
Requested # of hosts:	Maximum number of hosts requested for the Top-N table. Equivalent to hostTopNRequestedSize in RMON.
# of hosts granted:	Maximum number of hosts granted for the Top-N table. Equivalent to hostTopNGrantedSiz in RMON.
Report # 1 of Top N hosts entry 1 is recording	Report number and entry.
Host 0000.0c02.5808 at a rate of	Physical address of the host, and the amount of change in the selected variable during this sampling interval. Equivalent to hostTopNAddress and hostTopNRate in RMON.

Related Commands

rmon
rmon alarm
rmon event
show rmon

SHOW RTR APPLICATION

Use the **show rtr application** EXEC command to display global information about the response time reporter feature.

> **show rtr application [tabular | full]**

Syntax	Description
tabular	(Optional) Display information in a column format, reducing the number of screens required to display the information.
full	(Optional) Display all information using identifiers next to each displayed value. This is the default.

Default

Full format

Command Mode

EXEC

Usage Guidelines

This command first appeared in Cisco IOS Release 11.2.

Use the **show rtr application** command to display information such as supported operation types and supported protocols.

Sample Display

The following is sample output from the **show rtr application** command in full format.

```
Router# show rtr application

        Response Time Reporter
Version: 1.0.0 Initial Round Trip Time MIB
Max Packet Data Size (ARR and Data): 16384
Time of Last Change in Whole RTR: *16:49:53.000 UTC Thu May 16 1996
System Max Number of Entries: 20

        Supported Operation Types
Type of Operation to Perform: echo
```

Part
IV

Command Reference

```
Type of Operation to Perform: pathEcho

        Supported Protocols
Protocol Type: ipIcmpEcho
Protocol Type: snaRUEcho
Protocol Type: snaLU0EchoAppl
Protocol Type: snaLU2EchoAppl
```

Related Commands

show rtr configuration

SHOW RTR COLLECTION-STATISTICS

Use the **show rtr collection-statistics** EXEC command to display statistical errors for all response time reporter probes or the specified probe.

      show rtr collection-statistics [*probe*] [**tabular** | **full**]

Syntax	*Description*
probe	(Optional) Number of the response time reporter probe to display.
tabular	(Optional) Display information in a column format, reducing the number of screens required to display the information.
full	(Optional) Display all information using identifiers next to each displayed value. This is the default.

Default

Full format for all probes

Command Mode

EXEC

Usage Guidelines

This command first appeared in Cisco IOS Release 11.2.

Use the **show rtr collection-statistics** command to display information such as the number of failed operations and the failure reason. You also can use the **show rtr distribution-statistics** and **show rtr totals-statistics** commands to display additional statistical information.

Sample Display

The following is sample output from the **show rtr collection-statistics** command in full format.

```
Router# show rtr collection-statistics 1

    Collected Statistics
```

```
Entry Number: 1
Start Time Index: *17:15:41.000 UTC Thu May 16 1996
Path Index: 1
Hop in Path Index: 1
Number of Failed Operations due to a Disconnect: 0
Number of Failed Operations due to a Timeout: 0
Number of Failed Operations due to a Busy: 0
Number of Failed Operations due to a No Connection: 0
Number of Failed Operations due to an Internal Error: 0
Number of Failed Operations due to a Sequence Error: 0
Number of Failed Operations due to a Verify Error: 0
Target Address: 172.16.1.176
```

Related Commands

show rtr configuration
show rtr distributions-statistics
show rtr totals-statistics

SHOW RTR CONFIGURATION

Use the **show rtr configuration** EXEC command to display configuration values including all defaults for all response time reporter probes or the specified probe.

show rtr configuration [*probe*] [**tabular** | **full**]

Syntax	Description
probe	(Optional) Number of the response time reporter probe to display.
tabular	(Optional) Display information in a column format, reducing the number of screens required to display the information.
full	(Optional) Display all information using identifiers next to each displayed value. This is the default.

Default

Full format for all probes

Command Mode

EXEC

Usage Guidelines

This command first appeared in Cisco IOS Release 11.2.

Sample Display

The following is sample output from the **show rtr configuration** command in full format:

```
Router# show rtr configuration 1

        Complete Configuration Table (includes defaults)
Entry Number: 1
Owner: "Sample Owner"
Tag: "Sample Tag Group"
Type of Operation to Perform: echo
Reaction and History Threshold (milliseconds): 5000
Operation Frequency (seconds): 60
Operation Timeout (milliseconds): 5000
Verify Data: FALSE
Status of Entry (SNMP RowStatus): active
Protocol Type: ipIcmpEcho
Target Address: 172.16.1.176
Request Size (ARR data portion): 1
Response Size (ARR data portion): 1
Life (seconds): 3600
Next Start Time: Start Time already passed
Entry Ageout (seconds): 3600
Connection Loss Reaction Enabled: FALSE
Timeout Reaction Enabled: FALSE
Threshold Reaction Type: never
Threshold Falling (milliseconds): 3000
Threshold Count: 5
Threshold Count2: 5
Reaction Type: none
Number of Statistic Hours kept: 2
Number of Statistic Paths kept: 1
Number of Statistic Hops kept: 1
Number of Statistic Distribution Buckets kept: 1
Number of Statistic Distribution Intervals (milliseconds): 20
Number of History Lives kept: 0
Number of History Buckets kept: 50
Number of History Samples kept: 1
History Filter Type: none
```

Related Commands

show rtr application
show rtr collection-statistics
show rtr distributions-statistics
show rtr history
show rtr operational-state
show rtr reaction-trigger
show rtr totals-statistics

SHOW RTR DISTRIBUTIONS-STATISTICS

Use the **show rtr distributions-statistics** EXEC command to display statistic distribution information (captured response times) for all response time reporter probes or the specified probe.

show rtr distributions-statistics [*probe*] [**tabular** | **full**]

Syntax	Description
probe	(Optional) Number of the response time reporter probe to display.
tabular	(Optional) Display information in a column format, reducing the number of screens required to display the information. This is the default.
full	(Optional) Display all information using identifiers next to each displayed value.

Default

Tabular format for all probes

Command Mode

EXEC

Usage Guidelines

This command first appeared in Cisco IOS Release 11.2.

The distributions statistics consist of:

- The sum of completion times (used to calculate the mean)
- The sum of the completions times squared (used to calculate standard deviation)
- The maximum and minimum completion time
- The number of completed attempts

You also can use the **show rtr collection-statistics** and **show rtr totals-statistics** commands to display additional statistical information.

Sample Display

The following is sample output from the **show rtr distributions-statistics** command in tabular format.

```
Router# show rtr distributions-statistics

        Captured Statistics
        Multiple Lines per Entry
Line 1
Entry    = Entry Number
```

```
StartT   = Start Time of Entry (hundredths of seconds)
Pth      = Path Index
Hop      = Hop in Path Index
Dst      = Time Distribution Index
Comps    = Operations Completed
OvrTh    = Operations Completed Over Thresholds
SumCmp   = Sum of Completion Times (milliseconds)
Line 2
SumCmp2L = Sum of Completion Times Squared Low 32 Bits (milliseconds)
SumCmp2H = Sum of Completion Times Squared High 32 Bits (milliseconds)
TMax     = Completion Time Maximum (milliseconds)
TMin     = Completion Time Minimum (milliseconds)
Entry StartT      Pth Hop Dst Comps       OvrTh       SumCmp
   SumCmp2L  SumCmp2H   TMax       TMin
1     17417068    1   1   1   2           0           128
      8192      0          64         64
```

Related Commands

show rtr collection-statistics
show rtr configuration
show rtr totals-statistics

SHOW RTR HISTORY

Use the **show rtr history** EXEC command to display history collected for all response time reporter probes or the specified probe.

show rtr history [*probe*] [**tabular** | **full**]

Syntax	Description
probe	(Optional) Number of the response time reporter probe to display.
tabular	(Optional) Display information in a column format, reducing the number of screens required to display the information. This is the default.
full	(Optional) Display all information using identifiers next to each displayed value.

Default

Tabular format for all probes

Command Mode

EXEC

Usage Guidelines

This command first appeared in Cisco IOS Release 11.2.

The response return codes are listed in Table 25–11.

Table 25–11 *Response Return Codes*

Code	Meaning
1	Okay.
2	Disconnected.
3	Over threshold.
4	Timeout.
5	Busy.
6	Not connected.
7	Dropped.
8	Sequence error.
9	Verify error.
10	Application specific.

Sample Display

The following is sample output from the **show rtr history** command in tabular format:

```
Router# show rtr history

        Point by point History
          Multiple Lines per Entry
Line 1
Entry   = Entry Number
LifeI   = Life Index
BucketI = Bucket Index
SampleI = Sample Index
SampleT = Sample Start Time
CompT   = Completion Time (milliseconds)
Sense   = Response Return Code
Line 2 has the Target Address
Entry LifeI     BucketI   SampleI    SampleT    CompT    Sense
2     1         1         1          17436548   16       1
   AB 45 A0 16
2     1         2         1          17436551   4        1
   AC 12 7   29
2     1         2         2          17436551   1        1
   AC 12 5   22
```

```
2     1        2        3          17436552    4          1
   AB  45  A7  22
2     1        2        4          17436552    4          1
   AB  45  A0  16
```

Related Commands

show rtr configuration

SHOW RTR OPERATIONAL-STATE

Use the **show rtr operational-state** EXEC command to display the operational state of all response time reporter probes or the specified probe.

show rtr operational-state [*probe*] [**tabular** | **full**]

Syntax	Description
probe	(Optional) Number of the response time reporter probe to display.
tabular	(Optional) Display information in a column format, reducing the number of screens required to display the information.
full	(Optional) Display all information using identifiers next to each displayed value. This is the default.

Default

Full format for all probes

Command Mode

EXEC

Usage Guidelines

This command first appeared in Cisco IOS Release 11.2.

Use the **show rtr operational-state** command to determine whether a connection loss, timeout, and over-threshold occurred; how much life the probe has left; whether the probe is active, and the completion time. It also displays the results of the latest operation attempt.

Sample Display

The following is sample output from the **show rtr operational-state** command in full format:

```
Router# show rtr operational-state 1

        Current Operational State
Entry Number: 1
Modification Time: *17:15:41.000 UTC Thu May 16 1996
Diagnostics Text:
```

```
     Last Time this Entry was Reset: Never
     Number of Octets in use by this Entry: 2438
     Connection Loss Occurred: FALSE
     Timeout Occurred: FALSE
     Over Thresholds Occurred: FALSE
     Number of Operations Attempted: 6
     Current Seconds Left in Life: 3336
     Operational State of Entry: active
     Latest Completion Time (milliseconds): 60
     Latest Operation Return Code: ok
     Latest Operation Start Time: *17:19:41.000 UTC Thu May 16 1996
     Latest Target Address: 172.16.1.176
```

Related Commands

show rtr configuration

SHOW RTR REACTION-TRIGGER

Use the **show rtr reaction-trigger** EXEC command to display the reaction trigger information for all response time reporter probes or the specified probe.

>   **show rtr reaction-trigger** [*probe*] [**tabular** | **full**]

Syntax	*Description*
probe	(Optional) Number of the response time reporter probe to display.
tabular	(Optional) Display information in a column format, reducing the number of screens required to display the information.
full	(Optional) Display all information using identifiers next to each displayed value. This is the default.

Default

Full format for all probes

Command Mode

EXEC

Usage Guidelines

This command first appeared in Cisco IOS Release 11.2.

Use the **show rtr reaction-trigger** command to display the configuration status and operational state of target probes that will be triggered as defined with the **rtr reaction-configuration** global command.

Sample Display

The following is sample output from the **show rtr reaction-trigger** command in full format:

```
Router# show rtr reaction-trigger 1

        Reaction Table
Entry Number: 1
Target Entry Number: 2
Status of Entry (SNMP RowStatus): active
Operational State: pending
```

Related Commands

show rtr configuration

SHOW RTR TOTALS-STATISTICS

Use the **show rtr totals-statistics** EXEC command to display the total statistical values (accumulation of error counts and completions) for all response time reporter probes or the specified probe.

   show rtr totals-statistics [*probe*] [**tabular** | **full**]

Syntax	Description
probe	(Optional) Number of the response time reporter probe to display.
tabular	(Optional) Display information in a column format, reducing the number of screens required to display the information.
full	(Optional) Display all information using identifiers next to each displayed value. This is the default.

Default

Full format for all probes

Command Mode

EXEC

Usage Guidelines

This command first appeared in Cisco IOS Release 11.2.

The total statistics consist of the following items:

- The probe number
- The start time of the current hour of statistics
- The age of the current hour of statistics
- The number of attempted operations

You also can use the **show rtr distributions-statistics** and **show rtr collection-statistics** commands to display additional statistical information.

Sample Display

The following is sample output from the **show rtr totals-statistics** command in full format:

```
Router# show rtr totals-statistics

        Statistic Totals
Entry Number: 1
Start Time Index: *17:15:41.000 UTC Thu May 16 1996
Age of Statistics Entry (hundredths of seconds): 48252
Number of Initiations: 10
```

Related Commands

show rtr collection-statistics
show rtr configuration
show rtr distributions-statistics

SHOW SNMP

To check the status of SNMP communications, use the **show snmp** EXEC command.

   show snmp

Syntax   Description

This command has no arguments or keywords.

Command Mode

EXEC

Usage Guidelines

This command first appeared in Cisco IOS Release 10.0.

This command provides counter information for SNMP operations. It also displays the chassis ID string defined with the **snmp-server chassis-id** command.

Sample Display

The following is sample output from the **show snmp** command:

```
Router# show snmp

Chassis: 01506199
37 SNMP packets input
    0 Bad SNMP version errors
    4 Unknown community name
```

Part IV

Command Reference

```
          0 Illegal operation for community name supplied
          0 Encoding errors
          24 Number of requested variables
          0 Number of altered variables
          0 Get-request PDUs
          28 Get-next PDUs
          0 Set-request PDUs
      78 SNMP packets output
          0 Too big errors (Maximum packet size 1500)
          0 No such name errors
          0 Bad values errors
          0 General errors
          24 Response PDUs
          13 Trap PDUs

   SNMP logging: enabled
       Logging to 171.69.58.33.162, 0/10, 13 sent, 0 dropped.
```

Table 25–12 describes the fields shown in the display.

Table 25–12 *Show SNMP Field Descriptions*

Field	Description
Chassis	Chassis ID string.
SNMP packets input	Total number of SNMP packets input.
Bad SNMP version errors	Number of packets with an invalid SNMP version.
Unknown community name	Number of SNMP packets with an unknown community name.
Illegal operation for community name supplied	Number of packets requesting an operation not allowed for that community.
Encoding errors	Number of SNMP packets that were improperly encoded.
Number of requested variables	Number of variables requested by SNMP managers.
Number of altered variables	Number of variables altered by SNMP managers.
Get-request PDUs	Number of get requests received.
Get-next PDUs	Number of get-next requests received.
Set-request PDUs	Number of set requests received.
SNMP packets output	Total number of SNMP packets sent by the router.
Too big errors	Number of SNMP packets that were larger than the maximum packet size.
Maximum packet size	Maximum size of SNMP packets.

Table 25–12   *Show SNMP Field Descriptions, Continued*

Field	Description
No such name errors	Number of SNMP requests that specified an MIB object that does not exist.
Bad values errors	Number of SNMP set requests that specified an invalid value for a MIB object.
General errors	Number of SNMP set requests that failed due to some other error. (It was not a noSuchName error, badValue error, or any of the other specific errors.)
Response PDUs	Number of responses sent in reply to requests.
Trap PDUs	Number of SNMP traps sent.
SNMP logging	Indicates whether logging is enabled or disabled.
sent	Number of traps sent.
dropped	Number of traps dropped. Traps are dropped when the trap queue for a destination exceeds the maximum length of the queue, as set by the **snmp-server queue-length** command.

Related Commands

snmp-server chassis-id

SNMP-SERVER ACCESS-POLICY

This command is no longer valid. The functionality provided by this command has been removed from the Cisco IOS software.

SNMP-SERVER CHASSIS-ID

To provide a message line identifying the SNMP server serial number, use the **snmp-server chassis-id** global configuration command. Use the **no** form of this command to restore the default value, if any.

> **snmp-server chassis-id** *text*
> **no snmp-server chassis-id**

Syntax   *Description*

text   Message you want to enter to identify the chassis serial number.

Default

On hardware platforms where the serial number can be machine read, the default is the serial number. For example, a Cisco 7000 has a default value of its serial number.

Command Mode

Global configuration

Usage Guidelines

This command first appeared in Cisco IOS Release 10.0.

The Cisco MIB provides a chassis MIB variable that enables the SNMP manager to gather data on system card descriptions, chassis type, chassis hardware version, chassis ID string, software version of ROM monitor, software version of system image in ROM, bytes of processor RAM installed, bytes of NVRAM installed, bytes of NVRAM in use, current configuration register setting, and the value of the configuration register at the next reload. The following installed card information is provided: type of card, serial number, hardware version, software version, and chassis slot number.

The chassis ID message can be seen with **show snmp** command.

Example

In the following example, the chassis serial number specified is 1234456:

```
snmp-server chassis-id 1234456
```

Related Commands

show snmp

SNMP-SERVER COMMUNITY

To set up the community access string to permit access to the SNMP protocol, use the **snmp-server community** global configuration command. The **no** form of this command removes the specified community string.

snmp-server community *string* [**view** *view-name*] [**ro** | **rw**] [*number*]
no snmp-server community *string*

Syntax	Description
string	Community string that acts like a password and permits access to the SNMP protocol.
view view-name	(Optional) Name of a previously defined view. The view defines the objects available to the community.
ro	(Optional) Specifies read-only access. Authorized management stations are only able to retrieve MIB objects.

Syntax	Description
rw	(Optional) Specifies read-write access. Authorized management stations are able to both retrieve and modify MIB objects.
number	(Optional) Integer from 1 to 99 that specifies an access list of IP addresses that are allowed to use the community string to gain access to the SNMP agent.

Default

By default, an SNMP community string permits read-only access to all objects.

Command Mode

Global configuration

Usage Guidelines

This command first appeared in Cisco IOS Release 10.0.

The **no snmp-server** command disables both versions of SNMP (SNMPv1 and SNMPv2C).

The first **snmp-server** command that you enter enables both versions of SNMP.

Examples

The following example assigns the string *comaccess* to SNMP, allowing read-only access and specifies that IP access list 4 can use the community string:

```
snmp-server community comaccess ro 4
```

The following example assigns the string "mgr" to SNMP, allowing read-write access to the objects in the "restricted" view:

```
snmp-server community mgr view restricted rw
```

The following example removes the community "comaccess."

```
no snmp-server community comaccess
```

The following example disables both versions of SNMP:

```
no snmp-server
```

Related Commands

access-list
snmp-server view

SNMP-SERVER CONTACT

To set the system contact (sysContact) string, use the **snmp-server contact** global configuration command. Use the **no** form to remove the system contact information.

> **snmp-server contact** *text*
> **no snmp-server contact**

Syntax	Description
text	String that describes the system contact information.

Default

No system contact string is set.

Command Mode

Global configuration

Usage Guidelines

This command first appeared in Cisco IOS Release 10.0.

Example

The following is an example of a system contact string:

```
snmp-server contact Dial System Operator at beeper # 27345
```

Related Commands

snmp-server location

SNMP-SERVER CONTEXT

This command is no longer valid. The functionality provided by this command has been removed from the Cisco IOS software.

SNMP-SERVER ENABLE TRAPS

To enable the router to send SNMP traps, use the **snmp-server enable traps** global configuration command. Use the **no** form of this command to disable SNMP traps.

> **snmp-server enable traps** [*trap-type*] [*trap-option*]
> **no snmp-server enable traps** [*trap-type*] [*trap-option*]

Default

This command is disabled by default. No traps are enabled.

Syntax	Description
trap-type	(Optional) Type of trap to enable. If no type is specified, all traps are sent (including the **envmon** and **repeater** traps). The trap type can be one of the following keywords:

- **bgp**—Sends Border Gateway Protocol (BGP) state change traps.

- **config**—Sends configuration traps.

- **entity**—Sends Entity MIB modification traps.

- **envmon**—Sends Cisco enterprise-specific environmental monitor traps when an environmental threshold is exceeded. When the **envmon** keyword is used, you can specify a *trap-option* value.

- **frame-relay**—Sends Frame Relay traps.

- **isdn**—Sends Integrated Services Digital Network (ISDN) traps. When the **isdn** keyword is used on Cisco 1600 series routers, you can specify a *trap-option* value.

- **repeater**—Sends Ethernet hub repeater traps. When the **repeater** keyword is selected, you can specify a *trap-option* value.

- **rtr**—Sends response time reporter (RTR) traps.

- **snmp**—Sends Simple Network Management Protocol (SNMP) traps. When the **snmp** keyword is used, you can specify a *trap-option* value.

- **syslog**—Sends error message traps (Cisco Syslog MIB). Specify the level of messages to be sent with the **logging history level** command.

Syntax	Description
trap-option	(Optional) When the **envmon** keyword is used, you can enable a specific environmental trap type, or accept all trap types from the environmental monitor system. If no option is specified, all environmental types are enabled. The option can be one or more of the following keywords: **voltage, shutdown, supply, fan,** and **temperature.**

When the **isdn** keyword is used on Cisco 1600 series routers, you can specify the **call-information** keyword to enable an SNMP ISDN call information trap for the ISDN MIB subsystem, or you can specify the **isdnu-interface** keyword to enable an SNMP ISDN U interface trap for the ISDN U interface MIB subsystem.

Syntax	*Description*
	When the **repeater** keyword is used, you can specify the repeater option. If no option is specified, all repeater types are enabled. The option can be one or more of the following keywords:
	• **health**—Enables IETF Repeater Hub MIB (RFC 1516) health trap.
	• **reset**—Enables IETF Repeater Hub MIB (RFC 1516) reset trap.
	When the **snmp** keyword is used, you can specify the **authentication** option to enable SNMP Authentication Failure traps. (The **snmp-server enable traps snmp authentication** command replaces the **snmp-server trap-authentication** command.) If no option is specified, all SNMP traps are enabled.

Some trap types cannot be controlled with this command. These traps are either always enabled or enabled by some other means. For example, the linkUpDown messages are disabled by the **no snmp trap link-status** command.

If you enter this command with no keywords, the default is to enable all trap types.

Command Mode

Global configuration

Usage Guidelines

This command first appeared in Cisco IOS Release 11.1.

This command is useful for disabling traps that are generating a large amount of uninteresting or useless noise.

If you do not enter an **snmp-server enable traps** command, no traps controlled by this command are sent. In order to configure the router to send these SNMP traps, you must enter at least one **snmp-server enable traps** command. If you enter the command with no keywords, all trap types are enabled. If you enter the command with a keyword, only the trap type related to that keyword is enabled. In order to enable multiple types of traps, you must issue a separate **snmp-server enable traps** command for each trap type and option.

The **snmp-server enable traps** command is used in conjuction with the **snmp-server host** command. Use the **snmp-server host** command to specify which host or hosts receive SNMP traps. In order to send traps, you must configure at least one **snmp-server host** command.

For a host to receive a trap controlled by this command, both the **snmp-server enable traps** command and the **snmp-server host** command for that host must be enabled. If the trap type is not controlled by this command, just the appropriate **snmp-server host** command must be enabled.

The trap types used in this command all have an associated MIB object that allows them to be globally enabled or disabled. Not all of the trap types available in the **snmp-server host** command have notificationEnable MIB objects, so some of these cannot be controlled using the **snmp-server enable traps** command.

Examples

The following example enables the router to send all traps to the host myhost.cisco.com using the community string *public*:

```
snmp-server enable traps
snmp-server host myhost.cisco.com public
```

The following example enables the router to send Frame Relay and environmental monitor traps to the host myhost.cisco.com using the community string *public*:

```
snmp-server enable traps frame-relay
snmp-server enable traps envmon temperature
snmp-server host myhost.cisco.com public
```

The following example will not send traps to any host. The BGP traps are enabled for all hosts, but the only traps enabled to be sent to a host are ISDN traps.

```
snmp-server enable traps bgp
snmp-server host bob public·isdn
```

Related Commands

snmp-server host
snmp-server trap-source
snmp trap illegal-address

SNMP-SERVER HOST

To specify the recipient of an SNMP trap operation, use the **snmp-server host** global configuration command. Use the **no** form of this command to remove the specified host.

> **snmp-server host** *host* [**version** {**1** | **2c**}] *community-string* [**udp-port** *port*] [*trap-type*]
> **no snmp-server host** *host*

Syntax	Description
host	Name or Internet address of the host.
version	(Optional) Version of the Simple Network Management Protocol (SNMP) used to send the traps.
	• 1—SNMPv1
	• 2c —SNMPv2C
community-string	Password-like community string sent with the trap operation.

Syntax	Description
udp-port *port*	UDP port of the host to use. The default is 162.
trap-type	(Optional) Type of trap to be sent to the host. If no type is specified, all traps are sent. The trap type can be one or more of the following keywords:

- **bgp**—Sends Border Gateway Protocol (BGP) state change traps.
- **config**—Sends configuration traps.
- **dspu**—Sends downstream physical unit (DSPU) traps.
- **entity**—Sends Entity MIB modification traps.
- **envmon**—Sends Cisco enterprise-specific environmental monitor traps when an environmental threshold is exceeded.
- **frame-relay**—Sends Frame Relay traps.
- **isdn**—Sends Integrated Services Digital Network (ISDN) traps.
- **llc2**—Sends Logical Link Control, type 2 (LLC2) traps.
- **rptr**—Sends standard repeater (hub) traps.
- **rsrb**—Sends remote source-route bridging (RSRB) traps.
- **rtr**—Sends response time reporter (RTR) traps.
- **sdlc**—Sends Synchronous Data Link Control (SDLC) traps.
- **sdllc**—Sends SDLLC traps.
- **snmp**—Sends Simple Network Management Protocol (SNMP) traps defined in RFC 1157.
- **stun**—Sends serial tunnel (STUN) traps.
- **syslog**—Sends error message traps (Cisco Syslog MIB). Specify the level of messages to be sent with the **logging history level** command.
- **tty**—Sends Cisco enterprise-specific traps when a Transmission Control Protocol (TCP) connection closes.
- **x25**—Sends X.25 event traps.

Default

This command is disabled by default. No traps are sent.

If you enter this command with no keywords, the default is to send all trap types.

If no **version** keyword is present, the default is version 1.

Command Mode
Global configuration

Usage Guidelines
This command first appeared in Cisco IOS Release 10.0.

If you do not enter an **snmp-server host** command, no traps are sent. In order to configure the router to send SNMP traps, you must enter at least one **snmp-server host** command. If you enter the command with no keywords, all trap types are enabled for that host. In order to enable multiple hosts, you must issue a separate **snmp-server host** command for each host. You can specify multiple trap types in the command for each host.

When multiple **snmp-server host** commands are given for the same host, the community string in the last command is used, and the trap types set in the last command will be used to filter the SNMP trap messages sent to that host.

The **snmp-server host** command is used in conjuction with the **snmp-server enable traps** command. Use the **snmp-server enable traps** command to specify which SNMP traps are sent globally. In order to send most traps, you must configure at least one **snmp-server enable traps** command. However, some trap types are always enabled or enabled by other means.

For a host to receive most types of traps, both the **snmp-server enable traps** command and the **snmp-server host** command for that host must be enabled.

A trap-type option's availability depends on the router type and Cisco IOS software features supported on the router. For example, the **envmon** trap type is available only if the environmental monitor is part of the system.

Examples
The following example sends the SNMP traps defined in RFC 1157 to the host specified by the name myhost.cisco.com. The community string is defined as *comaccess*.
```
snmp-server enable traps
snmp-server host myhost.cisco.com comaccess snmp
```
The following example sends the SNMP and Cisco environmental monitor enterprise-specific traps to address 172.30.2.160:
```
snmp-server enable traps
snmp-server host 172.30.2.160 public snmp envmon
```
The following example enables the router to send all traps to the host *myhost.cisco.com* using the community string *public*:
```
snmp-server enable traps
snmp-server host myhost.cisco.com public
```

The following example will not send traps to any host. The BGP traps are enabled for all hosts, but only the ISDN traps are enabled to be sent to a host.

```
snmp-server enable traps bgp
snmp-server host bob public isdn
```

The following example will not send traps to any host. The BGP traps are enabled for all hosts, but only the ISDN traps are enabled to be sent to a host.

```
snmp-server enable traps bgp
snmp-server host bob public isdn
```

Related Commands

snmp-server enable traps
snmp-server trap-source
snmp-server trap-timeout

SNMP-SERVER LOCATION

To set the system location string, use the **snmp-server location** global configuration command. Use the **no** form of this command to remove the location string.

> **snmp-server location** *text*
> **no snmp-server location**

Syntax	*Description*
text	String that describes the system location information.

Default

No system location string is set.

Command Mode

Global configuration

Usage Guidelines

This command first appeared in Cisco IOS Release 10.0.

Example

The following example illustrates a system location string:

```
snmp-server location Building 3/Room 214
```

Related Commands

snmp-server contact

SNMP-SERVER PACKETSIZE

To establish control over the largest SNMP packet size permitted when the SNMP server is receiving a request or generating a reply, use the **snmp-server packetsize** global configuration command. Use the **no** form of this command to restore the default value.

> **snmp-server packetsize** *byte-count*
> **no snmp-server packetsize**

Syntax	Description
byte-count	Integer byte count from 484 to 8,192. The default is 1,500 bytes.

Default

1,500 bytes

Command Mode

Global configuration

Usage Guidelines

This command first appeared in Cisco IOS Release 10.0.

Example

The following example establishes a packet filtering of a maximum size of 1,024 bytes:

```
snmp-server packetsize 1024
```

Related Commands

snmp-server queue-length

SNMP-SERVER PARTY

This command is no longer valid. The functionality provided by this command has been removed from the Cisco IOS software.

SNMP-SERVER QUEUE-LENGTH

To establish the message queue length for each trap host, use the **snmp-server queue-length** global configuration command.

> **snmp-server queue-length** *length*

Syntax	Description
length	Integer that specifies the number of trap events that can be held before the queue must be emptied.

Default

10 events

Command Mode

Global configuration

Usage Guidelines

This command first appeared in Cisco IOS Release 10.0.

This command defines the length of the message queue for each trap host. Once a trap message is successfully transmitted, software will continue to empty the queue, but never faster than at a rate of four trap messages per second.

Example

The following example establishes a message queue that traps four events before it must be emptied:

```
snmp-server queue-length 4
```

Related Commands

snmp-server packetsize

SNMP-SERVER SYSTEM-SHUTDOWN

To use the SNMP message reload feature, the router configuration must include the **snmp-server system-shutdown** global configuration command. The **no** form of this command prevents an SNMP system-shutdown request (from an SNMP manager) from resetting the Cisco agent.

> **snmp-server system-shutdown**
> **no snmp-server system-shutdown**

Syntax   Description

This command has no arguments or keywords.

Default

This command is not included in the configuration file.

Command Mode

Global configuration

Usage Guidelines

This command first appeared in Cisco IOS Release 10.0.

Example

The following example enables the SNMP message reload feature:

```
snmp-server system-shutdown
```

SNMP-SERVER TFTP-SERVER-LIST

To limit the TFTP servers used via SNMP-controlled TFTP operations (saving and loading configuration files) to the servers specified in an access list, use the **snmp-server tftp-server-list** global configuration command. To disable this feature, use the **no** form of this command.

snmp-server tftp-server-list *number*
no snmp-server tftp-server-list

Syntax	*Description*
number	Standard IP access-list number from 1 to 99.

Default

Disabled

Command Mode

Global configuration

Usage Guidelines

This command first appeared in Cisco IOS Release 10.2.

Example

The following example limits the TFTP servers that can be used for configuration file copies via SNMP to the servers in access list 44.

```
snmp-server tftp-server-list 44
```

SNMP-SERVER TRAP-AUTHENTICATION

The **snmp-server enable traps snmp authentication** command replaces this command. Refer to the description of **snmp-server enable traps** for more information.

SNMP-SERVER TRAP-SOURCE

To specify the interface (and hence the corresponding IP address) from which an SNMP trap should originate, use the **snmp-server trap-source** global configuration command. Use the **no** form of the command to remove the source designation.

> **snmp-server trap-source** *interface*
> **no snmp-server trap-source**

Syntax	Description
interface	Interface from which the SNMP trap originates. The argument includes the interface type and number in platform-specific syntax.

Default

No interface is specified.

Command Mode

Global configuration

Usage Guidelines

This command first appeared in Cisco IOS Release 10.0.

When an SNMP trap is sent from a Cisco SNMP server, it has a trap address of whatever interface it happened to go out of at that time. Use this command if you want to use the trap address to trace particular needs.

Examples

The following example specifies that the IP address for interface Ethernet 0 is the source for all traps:

```
snmp-server trap-source ethernet 0
```

The following example specifies that the IP address for interface Ethernet 2/1 on a Cisco 7000 is the source for all traps:

```
snmp-server trap-source ethernet 2/1
```

Related Commands

snmp-server enable traps
snmp-server host

SNMP-SERVER TRAP-TIMEOUT

To define how often to try resending trap messages on the retransmission queue, use the **snmp-server trap-timeout** global configuration command.

> **snmp-server trap-timeout** *seconds*

Syntax	Description
seconds	Integer that sets the interval, in seconds, for resending the messages.

Default

30 seconds

Command Mode

Global configuration

Usage Guidelines

This command first appeared in Cisco IOS Release 10.0.

Before the Cisco IOS software tries to send a trap, it looks for a route to the destination address. If there is no known route, the trap is saved in a retransmission queue. The **server trap-timeout** command determines the number of seconds between retransmission attempts.

Example

The following example sets an interval of 20 seconds to try resending trap messages on the retransmission queue:

```
snmp-server trap-timeout 20
```

Related Commands

snmp-server host
snmp-server queue-length

SNMP-SERVER VIEW

To create or update a view entry, use the **snmp-server view** global configuration command. To remove the specified SNMP server view entry, use the **no** form of this command.

> **snmp-server view** *view-name oid-tree* {**included** | **excluded**}
> **no snmp-server view** *view-name*

Syntax	Description
view-name	Label for the view record that you are updating or creating. The name is used to reference the record.
oid-tree	Object identifier of the ASN.1 subtree to be included or excluded from the view. To identify the subtree, specify a text string consisting of numbers, such as *1.3.6.2.4*, or a word, such as *system*. Replace a single subidentifier with the asterisk (*) wildcard to specify a subtree family; for example 1.3.*.4.
**included	excluded**	Type of view. You must specify either **included** or **excluded**.

Default

None

Command Mode

Global configuration

Usage Guidelines

This command first appeared in Cisco IOS Release 10.0.

Other SNMP commands require a view as an argument. You use this command to create a view to be used as arguments for other commands that create records including a view.

Two standard predefined views can be used when a view is required, instead of defining a view. One is *everything*, which indicates that the user can see all objects. The other is *restricted,* which indicates that the user can see three groups: system, snmpStats, and snmpParties. The predefined views are described in RFC 1447.

The first **snmp-server** command that you enter enables both versions of SNMP.

Examples

The following example creates a view that includes all objects in the MIB-II subtree:

```
snmp-server view mib2 mib-2 included
```

The following example creates a view that includes all objects in the MIB-II system group and all objects in the Cisco enterprise MIB:

```
snmp-server view phred system included
snmp-server view phred cisco included
```

The following example creates a view that includes all objects in the MIB-II system group except for sysServices (System 7) and all objects for interface 1 in the MIB-II interfaces group:

```
snmp-server view agon system included
snmp-server view agon system.7 excluded
snmp-server view agon ifEntry.*.1 included
```

Related Commands

snmp-server community
snmp-server context

SNMP TRAP LINK-STATUS

To enable SNMP link trap generation, use the **snmp trap link-status** interface configuration command. To disable SNMP link traps, use the **no** form of this command.

> **snmp trap link-status**
> **no snmp trap link-status**

Syntax   Description

This command has no arguments or keywords.

Default

SNMP link traps are sent when an interface goes up or down.

Command Mode

Interface configuration

Usage Guidelines

This command appeared before Cisco IOS Release 10.0.

By default, SNMP link traps are sent when an interface goes up or down. For interfaces expected to go up and down during normal usage, such as ISDN interfaces, the output generated by these traps might not be useful. The **no** form of this command disables these traps.

Example

This example disables the sending of SNMP link traps related to the ISDN BRI 0 interface.

```
interface bri 0
  no snmp trap link-status
```

STATISTICS-DISTRIBUTION-INTERVAL

To set the time interval for each statistics distribution kept for the response time reporter, use the **statistics-distribution-interval** response time reporter configuration command. Use the **no** form of this command to return to the default value.

> **statistics-distribution-interval** *milliseconds*
> **no statistics-distribution-interval**

Syntax	Description
milliseconds	Number of milliseconds used for each statistics distribution kept. The default is 20 ms.

Default

20 ms

Command Mode

Response time reporter configuration

Usage Guidelines

This command first appeared in Cisco IOS Release 11.2.

In most situations, you do not need to change the statistical distribution interval or size. Only change the interval or size when distributions are needed, for example, when performing statistical modeling of your network. To set the statistical distributions size, use the **distributions-of-statistics-kept** response time reporter configuration command.

Example

In the following example, the distribution is set to five and the distribution interval is set to 10 ms. This means that the first distribution will contain statistics from 0 to 9 ms; the second distribution will contain statistics from 10 to 19 ms; the third distribution will contain statistics from 20 to 29 ms; the fourth distribution will contain statistics from 30 to 39 ms, and the fifth distribution will contain statistics from 40 ms to infinity.

```
rtr 1
  type echo protocol ipIcmpEcho 172.28.161.21
  distribution-of-statistics-kept 5
  statistics-distribution-interval 10
```

Related Commands

distributions-of-statistics-kept
hops-of-statistics-kept
hours-of-statistics-kept
paths-of-statistics-kept
rtr

TAG

To create a user-specified identifier for a response time reporter probe, use the **tag** response time reporter configuration command. It is normally used to logically link probes in a group. Use the **no** form of this command to remove a tag from a probe.

> **tag** *text*
> **no tag**

Syntax	Description
text	Name of a group to which this probe belongs. From 0 to 16 ASCII characters.

Default

None

Command Mode

Response time reporter configuration

Usage Guidelines

This command first appeared in Cisco IOS Release 11.2.

Tags can be used to support automation (for example, by using the same tag for two different probes on two different routers echoing the same target).

Example

In the following example, probe 1 is tagged with the label *bluebell*:

```
rtr 1
  type echo protocol ipIcmpEcho 172.16.1.176
  tag bluebell
```

Related Commands

rtr

THRESHOLD

To set the rising threshold (hysteresis) that generates a reaction event and stores history information for the response time reporter probe, use the **threshold** response time reporter configuration command. Use the **no** form of this command to return to the default value.

> **threshold** *millisecond*
> **no threshold**

Syntax	Description
millisecond	Number of milliseconds required for a rising threshold to be declared. The default value is 5,000 ms.

Default

5,000 ms

Command Mode

Response time reporter configuration

Usage Guidelines

This command first appeared in Cisco IOS Release 11.2.

The value specified for the **threshold** command must not exceed the value specified for the **timeout** response time reporter configuration command.

The threshold value is used by the **rtr reaction-configuration** and **filter-for-history** commands.

Example

In the following example, probe 1's threshold is set to 2,500 ms:

```
rtr 1
  type echo protocol ipIcmpEcho 172.16.1.176
  threshold 2500
```

Related Commands

filter-for-history
rtr
rtr reaction-configuration

TIMEOUT

To set the amount of time the response time reporter probe waits for a response from its request packet, use the **timeout** response time reporter configuration command. Use the **no** form of this command to return to the default value.

> **timeout** *millisecond*
> **no timeout**

Syntax	Description
millisecond	Number of milliseconds the probe waits to receive a response from its request packet. The default is 5,000 ms.

Default

5,000 ms

Command Mode

Response time reporter configuration

Usage Guidelines

This command first appeared in Cisco IOS Release 11.2.

Use the **timeout** command to set how long the probe waits to receive a response, and use the **frequency** command to set the rate at which the probe starts a response time report operation.

The value specified for the **timeout** command cannot be greater than the value specified for the **frequency** response time reporter configuration command.

Example

In the following example, the timeout is set for 2,500 ms:

```
rtr 1
 type echo protocol ipIcmpEcho 172.16.1.176
 timeout 2500
```

Related Commands

frequency
rtr

TYPE

To configure the type of response time reporter probe, use the **type** response time reporter configuration command. You must configure the probe's type before you can configure any of the other characteristics of the probe. Use the **no** form of this command to remove the type of configuration for the probe.

> **type** {echo | pathEcho} **protocol** *type type-target*
> **no type** {echo | pathEcho} **protocol** *type type-target*

Syntax	Description
echo	Perform end-to-end response time reporter operations only.
pathEcho	Perform response time reporter operations by using a route discovery algorithm to find a path to the destination and echo each device on the path.
protocol *type type-target*	Protocol used by the probe. Type can be one of the following keywords (whether the keyword is available depends on the Cisco

IOS software features installed on your router) followed by the required type parameter:

- **ipIcmpEcho** {*ip-address* | *ip-host-name*}—IP/ICMP Echo that requires a destination IP address or IP host name.

- **snaRUEcho** *sna-host-name*—SNA's SSCP Native Echo that requires the host name defined for the SNA's Physical Unit connection to VTAM.

- **snaLU0EchoAppl** *sna-host-name* [*sna-application*] [*sna-mode*]—An SNA LU Type 0 connection to Cisco's NSPECHO host application that requires the host name defined for the SNA's Physical Unit connection to VTAM. Optionally specify the host application name (the default is NSPECHO) and SNA mode to access the application.

- **snaLU2EchoAppl** *sna-host-name* [*sna-application*] [*sna-mode*]—An SNA LU Type 2 connection to Cisco's NSPECHO host application that requires the host name defined for the SNA's Physical Unit connection to VTAM. Optionally specify the host application name (the default is NSPECHO), and SNA mode to access the application.

Default

None

Command Mode

Response time reporter configuration

Usage Guidelines

This command first appeared in Cisco IOS Release 11.2.

Support of echo to a protocol and pathEcho to a protocol is dependent on the protocol type and implementation. In general, most protocols support echo and few protocols support pathEcho.

NOTES ───

Keywords are not case sensitive and are shown in mixed case for readability only.

Example

In the following example, probe 10 is created and configured as echo using the IP/ICMP Echo protocol and the destination IP address 172.16.1.175:

```
rtr 10
  type echo protocol ipIcmpEcho 172.16.1.175
```

Related Commands

rtr

VERIFY-DATA

To cause the response time reporter probe to check each response for corruption, use the **verify-data** response time reporter configuration command. Use the **no** form of this command to return to the default value.

> **verify-data**
> **no verify-data**

Syntax   Description

This command has no arguments or keywords.

Default

Disabled

Command Mode

Response time reporter configuration

Usage Guidelines

This command first appeared in Cisco IOS Release 11.2.

Only use the **verify-data** command when corruption might be an issue.

CAUTION

Do not enable this feature during normal operation, because it causes unnecessary overhead.

Example

In the following example, probe 5 is configured to verify the data for each response:

```
rtr 5
 type echo protocol ipIcmpEcho 172.16.1.174
 response-data-size 2
 verify-data
```

Related Commands

rtr

## CHAPTER 26

Managing System Performance

This chapter describes the basic tasks that you can perform to manage the general system performance.

For a complete description of the performance management commands in this chapter, see Chapter 27, "Performance Management Commands."

SYSTEM PERFORMANCE MANAGEMENT TASK LIST

Perform any of the tasks in the following sections to manage system performance:

- Setting the Interval for Load Data
- Limiting TCP Transactions
- Configuring Switching and Scheduling Priorities
- Establishing Queueing and Congestion Strategies
- Configuring Generic Traffic Shaping
- Modifying the System Buffer Size

See the "Performance Management Examples" section at the end of this chapter for examples.

SETTING THE INTERVAL FOR LOAD DATA

You can change the period of time over which a set of data is used for computing load statistics. Decisions, such as dial-backup decisions, are dependent on these statistics. If you decrease the load interval, the average statistics are computed over a shorter period of time and are more responsive to bursts of traffic.

To change the length of time for which a set of data is used to compute load statistics, perform the following task in interface configuration mode:

Task	Command
Set the length of time for which data is used for load calculations.	**load-interval** *seconds*

LIMITING TCP TRANSACTIONS

When using a standard TCP implementation to send keystrokes between machines, TCP tends to send one packet for each keystroke typed, which can use up bandwidth and contribute to congestion on larger networks.

John Nagle's algorithm (RFC 896) helps alleviate the small-packet problem in TCP. The first character typed after connection establishment is sent in a single packet, but TCP holds any additional characters typed until the receiver acknowledges the previous packet. Then the second, larger packet is sent, and additional typed characters are saved until the acknowledgment comes back. The effect is to accumulate characters into larger chunks, and pace them out to the network at a rate matching the round-trip time of the given connection. This method is usually good for all TCP-based traffic. However, do not enable the Nagle slow packet-avoidance algorithm if you have XRemote users on X Window sessions.

By default, the Nagle algorithm is not enabled. To enable the Nagle algorithm, and thereby reduce TCP transactions, perform the following task in global configuration mode:

Task	Command
Enable the Nagle slow packet avoidance algorithm.	**service nagle**

CONFIGURING SWITCHING AND SCHEDULING PRIORITIES

The normal operation of the network server allows the switching operations to use as much of the central processor as is required. If the network is running unusually heavy loads that do not allow the processor time to handle the routing protocols, you might need to give priority to the system process scheduler. To do so, perform the following task in global configuration mode:

Task	Command
Define the maximum amount of time that can elapse without running the lowest-priority system processes.	**scheduler interval** *milliseconds*

To change the amount of time that the CPU spends on fast switching and process-level operations on the Cisco 7200 series and Cisco 7500 series, perform the following task in global configuration mode:

Task	Command
For the Cisco 7200 series and Cisco 7500 series, change the default time the CPU spends on process tasks and fast switching.	**scheduler allocate** *network-microseconds process-microseconds*

> **CAUTION**
>
> Cisco recommends that you do not change the default values of the **scheduler allocate** command.

ESTABLISHING QUEUEING AND CONGESTION STRATEGIES

There are four possible queueing algorithms used: first-come-first-serve (FCFS), weighted fair queueing, priority queueing, and custom queueing. For serial interfaces at E1 (2.048 Mbps) and below, weighted fair queueing is used by default. When no other queueing strategies are configured, all other interfaces use FCFS by default. There is also one congestion-avoidance algorithm available: random early detection.

You can configure the Cisco IOS software to support the following types of queueing and congestion strategies for prioritizing network traffic:

- Weighted Fair Queueing
- Priority Queueing
- Custom Queueing
- Random Early Detection

You can configure weighted fair queueing, priority queueing, custom queueing, or random early detection, but you can assign only one type to an interface.

Weighted Fair Queueing

When enabled for an interface, weighted fair queueing provides traffic priority management that automatically sorts among individual traffic streams without requiring that you first define access lists.

Weighted fair queueing can manage duplex data streams, such as those between pairs of applications, and simplex data streams, such as voice or video. From the perspective of weighted fair queueing, there are two categories of data streams: high-bandwidth sessions and low-bandwidth sessions. Low-bandwidth traffic has effective priority over high-bandwidth traffic, and high-bandwidth traffic shares the transmission service proportionally according to assigned weights.

When you enable weighted fair queueing for an interface, new messages for high-bandwidth conversations are discarded after the congestive-messages threshold you set or the default one has been met. However, low-bandwidth conversations, which include control-message conversations, continue to enqueue data. As a result, the fair queue might occasionally contain more messages than are specified by the threshold number.

Priority Queueing

Priority output queueing is a mechanism that allows the administrator to set priorities on the type of traffic passing through the network. Packets are classified according to various criteria, including protocol and subprotocol type, and then queued on one of four output queues (high, medium, normal, and low).

When the server is ready to transmit a packet, it scans the priority queues in order, from highest to lowest, to find the highest-priority packet. After that packet is completely transmitted, the server scans the priority queues again. If a priority output queue fills up, packets are dropped and, for IP, quench indications are sent to the original transmitter.

Although you can enable priority output queueing for any interface, the intended application was for low-bandwidth, congested serial interfaces. Cisco's priority output queueing mechanism allows traffic control based on protocol or interface type. You also can set the size of the queue and defaults for what happens to packets that are not defined by priority output queue rules.

The priority output queueing mechanism can be used to manage traffic from all networking protocols. Additional fine-tuning is available for IP and for setting boundaries on the packet size.

NOTES

Priority queueing introduces extra overhead that is acceptable for slow interfaces, but might not be acceptable for higher-speed interfaces such as Ethernet.

The four priority queues—high, medium, normal, and low—are listed in order from highest to lowest priority. Keepalives sourced by the network server are always assigned to the high-priority queue; all other management traffic (such as IGRP updates) must be configured. Packets that are not classified by the priority list mechanism are assigned to the normal queue.

A priority list is a set of rules that describes how packets should be assigned to priority queues. A priority list might also describe a default priority or the queue size limits of the various priority queues.

Custom Queueing

Priority queueing introduces a fairness problem in that packets classified to lower-priority queues might not get serviced in a timely manner or at all, depending upon the bandwidth used by packets sent from the higher-priority output queues.

With custom output queueing, a "weighted-fair" queueing strategy is implemented for the processing of interface output queues. You can control the percentage of an interface's available bandwidth that is used by a particular kind of traffic. When custom queueing is enabled on an interface, the system maintains 17 output queues for that interface that can be used to modify queueing behavior. You can specify queues 1 through 16.

For queue numbers 1 through 16, the system cycles through the queues sequentially, delivering packets in the current queue before moving on to the next. Associated with each output queue is a configurable byte count, which specifies how many bytes of data the system should deliver from the current queue before it moves on to the next queue. When a particular queue is being processed, packets are sent until the number of bytes sent exceed the queue byte count or the queue is empty. Bandwidth used by a particular queue can only be indirectly specified in terms of byte count and queue length.

Queue number 0 is a system queue; it is emptied before any of the queues numbered 1 through 16 are processed. The system queues high-priority packets, such as keepalive packets, to this queue. Other traffic cannot be configured to use this queue.

On most platforms, all protocols are classified in the fast switching path.

NOTES

With custom or priority queueing enabled, the system takes longer to switch packets because the packets are classified by the processor card.

Random Early Detection

Random early detection is useful in high-speed networks to provide a congestion-avoidance mechanism (as opposed to a congestion-management mechanism such as queueing). When enabled on an interface, random early detection begins dropping packets at a rate you select during configuration when congestion occurs.

Random early detection is recommended only for TCP/IP networks. You can use random early detection as a way to cause TCP to back off traffic. TCP not only pauses, but also restarts quickly and adapts its transmission rate to the rate that the network can support.

Random early detection is not recommended for protocols, such as AppleTalk or Novell NetWare, that respond to dropped packets by retransmitting the packets at the same rate. Random early detection should only be configured on an interface where most of the traffic is TCP/IP traffic.

For interfaces configured to use RSVP, random early detection chooses packets from other flows rather than the RSVP flows to drop. Also, IP precedence governs which packets are dropped—traffic that is at a lower precedence has a higher drop rate and therefore is more likely to be throttled back.

Queueing Task List

You can set up weighted fair queueing, priority queueing, custom queueing, or random early detection on your network, but you can assign only one of the four to an interface.

The following sections describe the tasks that you can choose from, depending on the needs of your network:

- Setting Weighted Fair Queueing for an Interface
- Enabling Priority Queueing
- Enabling Custom Queueing
- Enabling Random Early Detection on an Interface

Setting Weighted Fair Queueing for an Interface

To enable weighted fair queueing for an interface, set the congestion threshold after which messages for high-bandwidth conversations are dropped, and specify the number of dynamic and reservable queues, perform the following task in interface configuration mode after specifying the interface:

Task	Command
Configure an interface to use weighted fair queueing.	**fair-queue** [*congestive-discard-threshold* [*dynamic-queues* [*reservable-queues*]]]

To disable weighted fair queueing for an interface, use the **no fair-queue** command.

Fair queueing is enabled by default for physical interfaces whose bandwidth is less than or equal to 2.048 megabits per second (Mbps) and that do not use Link Access Procedure, Balanced (LAPB), X.25, or Synchronous Data Link Control (SDLC) encapsulations. (Fair queueing is not an option for these protocols.) However, if custom queueing or priority queueing is enabled for a qualifying link, it overrides fair queueing, effectively disabling it. Additionally, fair queueing is automatically disabled if you enable autonomous or SSE switching. Fair queueing is now enabled by default on interfaces configured for Multilink PPP.

Enabling Priority Queueing

To enable priority queueing, perform the tasks in the following sections. The first and third tasks are required.

- Assigning Packets to Priority Queues
- Specifying the Maximum Packets in the Priority Queues
- Assigning a Priority Group to an Interface
- Monitoring the Priority Queueing Lists

Assigning Packets to Priority Queues

You can assign packets to priority lists based on the protocol type or the interface where the packets enter the router. In addition, you can set the default queue for packets that do not match other assignment rules. To define the priority lists, perform the following tasks in global configuration mode:

Task	Command
Step 1 Establish queueing priorities based upon the protocol type.	**priority-list** *list-number* **protocol** *protocol-name* {**high**	**medium**	**normal**	**low**} *queue-keyword keyword-value*
Step 2 Establish queueing priorities for packets entering from a given interface.	**priority-list** *list-number* **interface** *interface-type interface-number* {**high**	**medium**	**normal**	**low**}
Step 3 Assign a priority queue for those packets that do not match any other rule in the priority list.	**priority-list** *list-number* **default** {**high**	**medium**	**normal**	**low**}

All protocols supported by Cisco are allowed. The *queue-keyword* variable provides additional options including byte-count, TCP service and port number assignments, and AppleTalk, IP, IPX, VINES, or XNS access-list assignments. See the **priority-list** command syntax description in Chapter 27, "Performance Management Commands."

When using multiple rules, remember that the system reads the **priority-list** commands in order of appearance. When classifying a packet, the system searches the list of rules specified by **priority-list** commands for a matching protocol or interface type. When a match is found, the packet is assigned to the appropriate queue. The list is searched in the order it is specified, and the first matching rule terminates the search.

Specifying the Maximum Packets in the Priority Queues

You can specify the maximum number of packets allowed in each of the priority queues. To do so, perform the following task in global configuration mode:

Task	Command
Specify the maximum number of packets allowed in each of the priority queues.	**priority-list** *list-number* **queue-limit** *high-limit medium-limit normal-limit low-limit*

Assigning a Priority Group to an Interface

You can assign a priority list number to an interface. Only one list can be assigned per interface. To assign a priority group to an interface, perform the following task in interface configuration mode:

Task	Command
Assign a priority list number to the interface.	**priority-group** *list-number*

Monitoring the Priority Queueing Lists

You can display information about the input and output queues when priority queueing is enabled on an interface. To do so, perform the following task in EXEC mode:

Task	Command
Show the status of the priority queueing lists.	**show queueing priority**

Enabling Custom Queueing

To enable custom queueing, perform the tasks in the following sections. The first and third tasks are required.

- Assigning Packets to Custom Queues
- Specifying the Maximum Packets and Bytes in the Custom Queues
- Assigning a Custom Queue to an Interface
- Monitoring the Custom Queueing Lists

Assigning Packets to Custom Queues

You can assign packets to custom queues based on the protocol type or the interface where the packets enter the router. In addition, you can set the default queue for packets that do not match other assignment rules. To define the custom queueing lists, perform the following tasks in global configuration mode:

Task	Command
Step 1 Establish queueing priorities based upon the protocol type.	**queue-list** *list-number* **protocol** *protocol-name queue-number queue-keyword keyword-value*
Step 2 Establish custom queueing based on packets entering from a given interface.	**queue-list** *list-number* **interface** *interface-type interface-number queue-number*

Task	Command
Step 3 Assign a queue number for those packets that do not match any other rule in the custom queue list.	**queue-list** *list-number* **default** *queue-number*

All protocols supported by Cisco are allowed. The *queue-keyword* variable provides additional options, including byte-count, TCP service and port number assignments, and AppleTalk, IP, IPX, VINES, or XNS access-list assignments. See the **queue-list** command syntax description in Chapter 27, "Performance Management Commands."

When using multiple rules, remember that the system reads the **queue-list** commands in order of appearance. When classifying a packet, the system searches the list of rules specified by **queue-list** commands for a matching protocol or interface type. When a match is found, the packet is assigned to the appropriate queue. The list is searched in the order it is specified, and the first matching rule terminates the search.

Specifying the Maximum Packets and Bytes in the Custom Queues

You can specify the maximum number of packets allowed in each of the custom queues or the maximum queue size in bytes. To do so, perform one of the following tasks in global configuration mode:

Task	Command
Specify the maximum number of packets allowed in each of the custom queues.	**queue-list** *list-number* **queue** *queue-number* **limit** *limit-number*
Designate the byte size allowed per queue.	**queue-list** *list-number* **queue** *queue-number* **byte-count** *byte-count-number*

Assigning a Custom Queue to an Interface

You can assign a custom queue list number to an interface. Only one list can be assigned per interface. To assign a custom queue to an interface, perform the following task in interface configuration mode:

Task	Command
Assign a custom queue list number to the interface.	**custom-queue-list** *list-number*

Monitoring the Custom Queueing Lists

You can display information about the input and output queues when custom queueing is enabled on an interface. To do so, perform one of the following tasks in EXEC mode:

Task	Command
Show the status of the custom queueing lists.	show queueing custom
Show the current status of the custom output queues when custom queueing is enabled.	show interface type number

Enabling Random Early Detection on an Interface

To enable random early detection on the interface, perform the following task in interface configuration mode:

Task	Command
Enable random early detection on an interface.	random-detect [weighting]

To monitor the various drop statistics for early random detection, perform the following tasks in EXEC mode:

Task	Command
Show the drop statistics for the interface.	show interface [type number]

CONFIGURING GENERIC TRAFFIC SHAPING

Traffic shaping allows you to control how fast packets are sent out on the interface to avoid congestion and meet the needs of remote interfaces. You might want to configure traffic shaping on the interface if you have a network with differing access rates or if you are offering a subrate service. For example, if one end of the link in a Frame Relay network is 256 kbps and the other end of the link is only 128 kbps, sending packets at 256 kbps could cause failure of the applications using the link.

Traffic shaping is supported on all media and encapsulation types on the router. Traffic shaping also can be applied to a specific access list on an interface. To perform traffic shaping on Frame Relay virtual circuits, you also can use the **frame-relay traffic-shaping** command.

To enable traffic shaping for outbound traffic on an interface, perform one of the following tasks in interface configuration mode:

Task	Command
Enable traffic shaping for outbound traffic on an interface.	**traffic-shape rate** *bit-rate* [*burst-size* [*excess-burst-size*]]
Enable traffic shaping for outbound traffic on an interface for a specified access list.	**traffic-shape group** *access-list bit-rate* [*burst-size* [*excess-burst-size*]]

If traffic shaping is performed on a Frame Relay network with the **traffic-shape rate** command, you also can use the **traffic-shape adaptive** command to specify the minimum bit rate to which the traffic is shaped.

To configure a Frame Relay subinterface to estimate the available bandwidth when backward explicit congestion notifications (BECNs) are received, perform the following task in interface configuration mode:

Task	Command
Configure minimum bit rate to which traffic is shaped when BECNs are received on an interface.	**traffic-shape adaptive** [*bit-rate*]

The **traffic-shape adaptive** command uses the configured bit rate as a lower bound of the range and the bit rate specified by the **traffic-shape rate** command as the upper bound. The rate to which the traffic is actually shaped will be between those two rates. Configure the **traffic-shape adaptive** command at both ends of the link, because it also configures the device at the flow end to reflect forward explicit congestion notification (FECN) signals as BECNs, enabling the router at the high-speed end to detect and adapt to congestion even when traffic is flowing primarily in one direction.

To display the current traffic-shaping configuration and statistics, perform the following tasks in EXEC mode:

Task	Command
Step 1 Display the current traffic-shaping configuration.	**show traffic-shape** [*interface*]
Step 2 Display the current traffic-shaping statistics.	**show traffic-shape statistics** [*interface*]

For an example of configuring traffic shaping, see the section "Generic Traffic Shaping Example" at the end of this chapter.

MODIFYING THE SYSTEM BUFFER SIZE

You can adjust initial buffer pool settings and the limits at which temporary buffers are created and destroyed. To do so, perform the following tasks in global configuration mode:

Task	Command
Step 1 Adjust the system buffer sizes.	**buffers {small	middle	big	verybig	large	huge |** *type number*} **{permanent	max-free	min-free	initial}** *number*
Step 2 Dynamically resize all huge buffers to the value that you supply.	**buffers huge size** *number*

> **CAUTION**
>
> Normally, you need not adjust these parameters; do so only after consulting with technical support personnel. Improper settings can affect system performance adversely.

During normal system operation, there are two sets of buffer pools: public and interface.

- The buffers in the public pools grow and shrink based upon demand. Some public pools are temporary and are created and destroyed as needed. Other public pools are permanently allocated and cannot be destroyed. The public buffer pools are small, middle, big, large, very big, and huge.

- Interface pools are static—that is, they are all permanent. One interface pool exists for each interface. For example, a Cisco 4000 1E 4T configuration has one Ethernet buffer pool and four serial buffer pools. In the **buffers** command, the *type* and *number* arguments allow the user to tune the interface pools.

See the section "Buffer Modification Examples" at the end of this chapter.

The server has one pool of queueing elements and six public pools of packet buffers of different sizes. For each pool, the server keeps count of the number of buffers outstanding, the number of buffers in the free list, and the maximum number of buffers allowed in the free list. To display statistics about the buffer pool on the system, perform the following tasks in EXEC mode:

Task	Command
Step 1 Display all public pool information.	**show buffers**
Step 2 Display all public and interface pool information.	**show buffers all**
Step 3 Display a brief listing of all allocated buffers.	**show buffers alloc**

Task	Command
Step 4 Display interface pool information.	**show buffers** [*type number*]
Step 5 Dump all allocated buffers.	**show buffers alloc dump**
Step 6 Display all interface pool information.	**show buffers interface**
Step 7 If the specified interface has its own buffer pool, display information for that pool.	**show buffers interface** *type number*
Step 8 Display a brief listing of buffers allocated for this interface.	**show buffers interface** *type number* **alloc**
Step 9 Dump the buffers allocated to this interface.	**show buffers interface** *type number* **alloc dump**

PERFORMANCE MANAGEMENT EXAMPLES

The following sections provide performance management examples:

- Generic Traffic Shaping Example
- Buffer Modification Examples

Generic Traffic Shaping Example

This example shows the configuration of two traffic-shaped interfaces on a router. Ethernet 0 is configured to limit User Datagram Protocol (UDP) traffic to 1 Mbps. Ethernet 1 is configured to limit all output to 5 Mbps.

```
access-list 101 permit udp any any
interface Ethernet0
 traffic-shape group 101 1000000 125000 125000
!
interface Ethernet1
 traffic-shape rate 5000000 625000 625000
```

The following is a sample display for the **show traffic-shape** command for the example shown:

```
Router# show traffic-shape

        access Target   Byte   Sustain   Excess    Interval  Increment Adapt
  I/F   list   Rate     Limit  bits/int  bits/int  (ms)      (bytes)   Active
  Et0   101    1000000  23437  125000    125000    63        7813      -
  Et1          5000000  87889  625000    625000    16        9766      -
```

The following is a sample display for the **show traffic-shape statistics** command for the example shown:

```
Router# show traffic-shape statistics

          Access Queue    Packets   Bytes    Packets   Bytes    Shaping
  I/F     List   Depth                        Delayed   Delayed  Active
  Et0     101    0         2         180      0         0        no
  Et1            0         0         0        0         0        no
```

Buffer Modification Examples

The following example instructs the system to keep at least 50 small buffers free:

```
buffers small min-free 50
```

The following example instructs the system to keep no more than 200 medium buffers free:

```
buffers middle max-free 200
```

The following example instructs the system to create one large temporary extra buffer, just after a reload:

```
buffers large initial 1
```

The following example instructs the system to create one permanent huge buffer:

```
buffers huge permanent 1
```

## CHAPTER 27

Performance Management Commands

This chapter describes the commands used to manage router performance on the network. To manage system performance, you can perform load-balancing and modify system parameters. For example, priority queueing allows you to prioritize traffic order.

For performance management configuration tasks and examples, see Chapter 26, "Managing System Performance."

BUFFERS

Use the **buffers** global configuration command to make adjustments to initial buffer pool settings and to the limits at which temporary buffers are created and destroyed. Use the **no** form of this command to return the buffers to their default size.

> **buffers** {**small** | **middle** | **big** | **verybig** | **large** | **huge** | *type number*} {**permanent** | **max-free** | **min-free** | **initial**} *number*
> **no buffers** {**small** | **middle** | **big** | **verybig** | **large** | **huge** | *type number*} {**permanent** | **max-free** | **min-free** | **initial**} *number*

Syntax	Description
small	Buffer size of this public buffer pool is 104 bytes.
middle	Buffer size of this public buffer pool is 600 bytes.
big	Buffer size of this public buffer pool is 1,524 bytes.
verybig	Buffer size of this public buffer pool is 4,520 bytes.
large	Buffer size of this public buffer pool is 5,024 bytes.
huge	Default buffer size of this public buffer pool is 18,024 bytes. This value can be configured with the **buffers huge size** command.

Syntax	Description
type number	Interface type and interface number of the interface buffer pool. The type value cannot be **fddi**.
permanent	Number of permanent buffers that the system tries to create and keep. Permanent buffers are normally not trimmed by the system.
max-free	Maximum number of free or unallocated buffers in a buffer pool. A maximum of 20,480 small buffers can be constructed in the pool.
min-free	Minimum number of free or unallocated buffers in a buffer pool.
initial	Number of additional temporary buffers that are to be allocated when the system is reloaded. This keyword can be used to ensure that the system has necessary buffers immediately after reloading in a high-traffic environment.
number	Number of buffers to be allocated.

Default

The default number of buffers in a pool is determined by the hardware configuration and can be displayed with the EXEC **show buffers** command.

Command Mode

Global configuration

Usage Guidelines

This command first appeared in Cisco IOS Release 10.0.

Normally you need not adjust these parameters; do so only after consulting with technical support personnel. Improper settings can affect system performance adversely.

You cannot configure FDDI buffers.

Examples of Public Buffer Pool Tuning

In the following example, the system will try to keep at least 50 small buffers free:

```
buffers small min-free 50
```

In the following example, the permanent buffer pool allocation for big buffers is increased to 200:

```
buffers big permanent 200
```

Example of Interface Buffer Pool Tuning

A general guideline is to display buffers with the **show buffers** command, observe which buffer pool is depleted, and increase that one.

In the following example, the permanent Ethernet 0 interface buffer pool on a Cisco 4000 is increased to 96 because the Ethernet 0 buffer pool is depleted:

```
buffers ethernet 0 permanent 96
```

Related Commands

buffers huge size
show buffers

BUFFERS HUGE SIZE

Use the **buffers huge size** global configuration command to resize all huge buffers dynamically to the value you specify. Use the **no** form of this command to restore the default buffer values.

> **buffers huge size** *number*
> **no buffers huge size** *number*

Syntax	*Description*
number	Huge buffer size, in bytes.

Default

18,024 bytes

Command Mode

Global configuration

Usage Guidelines

This command first appeared in Cisco IOS Release 10.0.

Use only after consulting with technical support personnel. The buffer size cannot be lowered below the default.

Example

In the following example, the system will resize huge buffers to 20,000 bytes:

```
buffers huge size 20000
```

Related Commands

buffers
show buffers

CUSTOM-QUEUE-LIST

To assign a custom queue list to an interface, use the **custom-queue-list** interface configuration command. To remove a specific list or all list assignments, use the **no** form of the command.

> **custom-queue-list** *list*
> **no custom-queue-list** [*list*]

Syntax	Description
list	Number of the custom queue list you want to assign to the interface. An integer from 1 to 16.

Default

No custom queue list is assigned.

Command Mode

Interface configuration

Usage Guidelines

This command first appeared in Cisco IOS Release 10.0.

Only one queue list can be assigned per interface. Use this command in place of the **priority-list** command (not in addition to it). Custom queueing allows a fairness not provided with priority queueing. With custom queueing, you can control the interfaces' available bandwidth when it is unable to accommodate the aggregate traffic enqueued. Associated with each output queue is a configurable byte count, which specifies how many bytes of data should be delivered from the current queue by the system before the system moves on to the next queue. When a particular queue is being processed, packets are sent until the number of bytes sent exceeds the queue byte count or until the queue is empty.

Use the **show queueing custom** and **show interface** commands to display the current status of the custom output queues.

Example

In the following example, custom queue-list number 3 is assigned to serial interface 0:

```
interface serial 0
custom-queue-list 3
```

Related Commands

queue-list default
queue-list interface
queue-list protocol
queue-list queue byte-count
queue-list queue limit

FAIR-QUEUE

To enable weighted fair queueing for an interface, use the **fair-queue** interface configuration command. To disable weighted fair queuing for an interface, use the **no** form of this command.

> **fair-queue** [*congestive-discard-threshold* [*dynamic-queues* [*reservable-queues*]]]
> **no fair-queue**

Syntax	Description
congestive-discard-threshold	(Optional) Number of messages allowed in each queue in the range 1 to 4,096. The default is 64 messages. When the number of messages in the queue for a high-bandwidth conversation reaches the specified threshold, new high-bandwidth messages are discarded.
dynamic-queues	(Optional) Number of dynamic queues used for best-effort conversations (that is, a normal conversation not requiring any special network services). Values are 16, 32, 64, 128, 256, 512, 1,024, 2,048, and 4,096. The default is 256.
reservable-queues	(Optional) Number of reservable queues used for reserved conversations in the range 0 to 1,000. The default is 0. Reservable queues are used for interfaces configured for the Resource Reservation Protocol (RSVP) feature.

Default

Fair queuing is enabled by default for physical interfaces whose bandwidth is less than or equal to 2.048 megabits per second (Mbps) and for those that do not use Link Access Procedure, Balanced (LAPB), X.25, or Synchronous Data Link Control (SDLC) encapsulations. (Fair queuing is not an option for these protocols). However, if custom queuing or priority queuing is enabled for a qualifying link, it overrides fair queueing, effectively disabling it. Additionally, fair queuing is automatically disabled if you enable autonomous or SSE switching.

Fair queueing is now enabled automatically on interfaces configured for Multilink PPP.

Congestive-discard-threshold: 64 messages; dynamic-queues: 256; reservable-queues: 0.

Command Mode

Interface configuration

Usage Guidelines

This command first appeared in Cisco IOS Release 11.0.

When enabled for an interface, weighted fair queueing provides traffic priority management that automatically sorts among individual traffic streams without requiring that you first define access lists. Enabling weighted fair queueing requires use of this command only.

Part IV

Command Reference

Weighted fair queuing can manage duplex data streams, such as those between pairs of applications, and simplex data streams, such as voice or video. From the perspective of weighted fair queueing, there are two categories of sessions: high-bandwidth sessions and low-bandwidth sessions. Low-bandwidth traffic has effective priority over high-bandwidth traffic, and high-bandwidth traffic shares the transmission service proportionally according to assigned weights.

When weighted fair queuing is enabled for an interface, new messages for high-bandwidth traffic streams are discarded after the configured or default congestive-messages threshold has been met. However, low-bandwidth conversations, which include control-message conversations, continue to enqueue data. As a result, the fair queue might occasionally contain more messages than its configured threshold number specifies.

Weighted fair queuing uses a traffic data stream discrimination registry service to determine to which traffic stream a message belongs. For each forwarding protocol, Table 27–1 shows the attributes of a message that are used to classify traffic into data streams.

Table 27–1   *Weighted Fair Queuing Traffic Stream Discrimination Fields*

Forwarder	Fields Used
AppleTalk	• Source net, node, socket • Destination net, node, socket • Type
CLNS	• Source NSAP • Destination NSAP
DECnet	• Source address • Destination address
Frame Relay switching	• DLCI value
DDN IP	• TOS • IP Protocol • Source IP address (if message is not fragmented) • Destination IP address (if message is not fragmented) • Source TCP/UDP port • Destination TCP/UDP port
Transparent bridging	• Unicast: Source MAC, Destination MAC • Ethertype SAP/SNAP multicast: Destination MAC address
Source-route bridging	• Unicast: Source MAC, Destination MAC • SAP/SNAP multicast: Destination MAC address

Table 27–1 *Weighted Fair Queuing Traffic Stream Discrimination Fields, Continued*

Forwarder	Fields Used
VINES	• Source Network/Host • Destination Network/Host • Level 2 Protocol
Apollo	• Source Network/Host/Socket • Destination Network/Host/Socket • Level 2 protocol
XNS	• Source/Destination Network/Host/Socket • Level 2 Protocol
Novell NetWare	• Source/Destination Network/Host/Socket • Level 2 Protocol
All others (default)	Control protocols (one queue per protocol)

It is important to note that IP precedence, congestion in Frame Relay switching, and discard eligibility flags affect the weights used for queuing.

IP precedence, which is set by the host or by policy maps, is a number in the range of 0 to 7. Data streams of precedence *number* are weighted so that they are given an effective bit rate of *number*+1 times as fast as a data stream of precedence 0, which is normal.

In Frame Relay switching, message flags for congestion (FECN and BECN) and discard eligible (DE) message flags cause the algorithm to select weights that effectively impose reduced queue priority, providing the application with "slow down" feedback and sorting traffic, giving the best service to applications within their Committed Information Rate.

Fair queuing is supported for all LAN and line (WAN) protocols except X.25. These protocols are listed in "Default." Because tunnels are software interfaces that are themselves routed over physical interfaces, fair queuing is not supported for tunnels. Fair queuing is on by default for interfaces with bandwidths less than or equal to 2 Mbps.

Part
IV

Command Reference

> **NOTES**
>
> For Release 10.3 and earlier for the Cisco 7000 and 7500 with an RSP card, if you used the **tx-queuelimit** command to set the transmit (tx-queue) limit available to an interface on an MCI or SCI card and you configured custom queuing or priority queuing for that interface, the configured transmit (tx-queue) limit was automatically overridden and set to 1. With this release, for weighted fair queuing, custom queuing, and priority queuing, the transmit (tx-queue) limit is derived from the bandwidth value set for the interface using the **bandwidth** command. Bandwidth value divided by 512 rounded up yields the effective transmit (tx-queue) limit. However, the derived value only applies in the absence of a **tx-queue-limit** command; that is, a configured transmit (tx-queue) limit overrides this derivation.

When Resource Reservation Protocol (RSVP) is configured on an interface that supports fair queuing or on an interface that is configured for fair queuing with the reservable queues set to 0 (the default), the reservable queue size is automatically configured using the following method: interface bandwidth divided by 32 kbps. You can override this by specifying a reservable queue other than 0.

Examples

The following example enables use of weighted fair queuing on Serial 0, with a congestive threshold of 300. This means that messages will be discarded from the queuing system only when 300 or more messages have been queued and the message is in a data stream that has more than one message in the queue. The transmit queue limit is set to 2, based on the 384-kilobit (kb) line set by the **bandwidth** command:

```
interface serial 0
  bandwidth 384
  fair-queue 300
```

The following example requests a fair queue with 512 dynamic queues, 18 RSVP queues, and a congestive discard threshold of 64 messages:

```
interface Serial 3/0
  ip unnumbered Ethernet 0/0
  fair-queue 64 512 18
```

Related Commands

custom-queue-list
ip rsvp bandwidth
priority-group
priority-list default
queue-list default
random-detect
show interface

LOAD-INTERVAL

To change the length of time for which data is used to compute load statistics, use the **load-interval** interface configuration command. Use the **no** form of this command to revert to the default setting.

> **load-interval** *seconds*
> **no load-interval** *seconds*

Syntax	Description
seconds	Length of time for which data is used to compute load statistics. A value that is a multiple of 30, from 30 to 600 (30, 60, 90, 120, and so forth).

Default

300 seconds (or 5 minutes)

Command Mode

Interface configuration

Usage Guidelines

This command first appeared in Cisco IOS Release 10.3.

If you want load computations to be more reactive to short bursts of traffic, rather than averaged over five-minute periods, you can shorten the length of time over which load averages are computed.

If the load interval is set to 30 seconds, new data is used for load calculations over a 30-second period. This data is used to compute load statistics, including input rate in bits and packets per second, output rate in bits and packets per second, load, and reliability.

Load data is gathered every five seconds. This data is used for a weighted average calculation in which more recent load data has more weight in the computation than older load data. If the load interval is set to 30 seconds, the average is computed for the last 30 seconds of load data.

The **load-interval** command allows you to change the default interval of five minutes to a shorter or longer period of time. If you change it to a shorter period of time, the input and output statistics that are displayed when you use the **show interface** command will be more current, and based on more instantaneous data, rather than reflecting a more average load over a longer period of time.

This command is often used for dial-backup purposes to increase or decrease the likelihood of a backup interface being implemented, but it can be used on any interface.

Example

In the following example, the default five-minute average is set it to a 30-second average. A burst in traffic that would not trigger a dial backup for an interface configured with the default five-minute interval might trigger a dial backup for this interface that is set for a shorter, 30-second interval.

```
interface serial 0
load-interval 30
```

Related Commands

show interfaces

PRIORITY-GROUP

To assign the specified priority list to an interface, use the **priority-group** interface configuration command. Use the **no** form of this command to remove the specified priority group assignment.

priority-group list
no priority-group

Syntax	Description
list	Priority list number assigned to the interface. An integer from 1 to 16.

Default

None

Command Mode

Interface configuration

Usage Guidelines

This command first appeared in Cisco IOS Release 10.0.

Only one list can be assigned per interface. Priority output queueing provides a mechanism to prioritize packets transmitted on an interface.

Use the **show queuing priority** and **show interface** commands to display the current status of the output queues.

Example

The following example causes packets on serial interface 0 to be classified by priority list 1:

```
interface serial 0
  priority-group 1
```

Related Commands

priority-list default
priority-list interface
priority-list queue-limit
queue-list default

PRIORITY-LIST DEFAULT

To assign a priority queue for those packets that do not match any other rule in the priority list, use the **priority-list default** global configuration command. Use the **no** form of this command to return to the default or assign **normal** as the default.

> **priority-list** *list-number* **default** {high | medium | normal | low}
> **no priority-list** *list-number* **default** {high | medium | normal | low}

Syntax	Description
list-number	Arbitrary integer between 1 and 16 that identifies the priority list selected by the user.
**high	medium	normal	low**	Priority queue level.

Default

The **normal** queue, if you use the **no** form of the command.

Command Mode

Global configuration

Usage Guidelines

This command first appeared in Cisco IOS Release 10.0.

When using multiple rules, remember that the system reads the priority settings in order of appearance. When classifying a packet, the system searches the list of rules specified by **priority-list** commands for a matching protocol or interface type. When a match is found, the packet is assigned to the appropriate queue. The list is searched in the order it is specified, and the first matching rule terminates the search.

Example

The following example sets the priority queue for those packets that do not match any other rule in the priority list to a low priority:

```
priority-list 1 default low
```

Related Commands

priority-group
show queueing

PRIORITY-LIST INTERFACE

To establish queuing priorities on packets entering from a given interface, use the **priority-list interface** global configuration command. Use the **no** form of this command with the appropriate arguments to remove an entry from the list.

> **priority-list** *list-number* **interface** *interface-type interface-number* {**high** | **medium** | **normal** | **low**}
> **no priority-list** *list-number* **interface** *interface-type interface-number* {**high** | **medium** | **normal** | **low**}

Syntax	Description
list-number	Arbitrary integer between 1 and 16 that identifies the priority list selected by the user.
interface-type	Specifies the name of the interface.
interface-number	Number of the specified interface.
high | **medium** | **normal** | **low**	Priority queue level.

Default

No queuing priorities are established.

Command Mode

Global configuration

Usage Guidelines

This command first appeared in Cisco IOS Release 10.0.

When using multiple rules, remember that the system reads the priority settings in order of appearance. When classifying a packet, the system searches the list of rules specified by **priority-list** commands for a matching protocol or interface type. When a match is found, the packet is assigned to the appropriate queue. The list is searched in the order it is specified, and the first matching rule terminates the search.

Example

The following example sets any packet type entering on Ethernet interface 0 to a medium priority:

```
priority-list 3 interface ethernet 0 medium
```

Related Commands

priority-group
show queueing

PRIORITY-LIST PROTOCOL

To establish queuing priorities based upon the protocol type, use the **priority-list protocol** global configuration command. Use the **no** form of this command with the appropriate list number to remove an entry from the list.

> **priority-list** *list-number* **protocol** *protocol-name* {**high** | **medium** | **normal** | **low**}
>   *queue-keyword keyword-value*
> **no priority-list** *list-number* **protocol** [*protocol-name* {**high** | **medium** | **normal** | **low**}
>   *queue-keyword keyword-value*]

Syntax	Description
list-number	Arbitrary integer between 1 and 16 that identifies the priority list selected by the user.
protocol-name	Specifies the protocol type: **aarp, arp, apollo, appletalk, bridge** (transparent), **clns, clns_es, clns_is, compressedtcp, cmns, decnet, decnet_node, decnet_router-l1, decnet_router-l2, ip, ipx, pad, rsrb, stun, vines, xns,** and **x25.**

Syntax	Description
high | **medium** | **normal** | **low**	Priority queue level.
queue-keyword keyword-value	Possible keywords are **fragments**, **gt**, **lt**, **list**, **tcp**, and **udp**. See Table 27–2.

Default

No queuing priorities are established.

Command Mode

Global configuration

Usage Guidelines

This command first appeared in Cisco IOS Release 10.0.

When using multiple rules for a single protocol, remember that the system reads the priority settings in order of appearance. When classifying a packet, the system searches the list of rules specified by **priority-list** commands for a matching protocol type. When a match is found, the packet is assigned to the appropriate queue. The list is searched in the order it is specified, and the first matching rule terminates the search.

The **decnet_router-l1** keyword refers to the multicast address for all level 1 routers, which are intra-area routers, and the **decnet_router-l2** keyword refers to all level 2 routers, which are inter-area routers.

Use Table 27–2, Table 27–3, and Table 27–4 to configure the queuing priorities for your system.

Table 27–2 *Protocol Priority Queue Keywords and Values*

Option	Description
fragments	Assigns the priority level defined to fragmented IP packets (for use with IP protocol only). More specifically, IP packets whose fragment offset field is nonzero are matched by this command. The initial fragment of a fragmented IP packet has a fragment offset of zero, so such packets are not matched by this command. Note: Packets with a nonzero fragment offset do not contain TCP or UDP headers, so other instances of this command that use the **tcp** or **udp** keyword will always fail to match such packets.
gt *byte-count*	Specifies a greater-than count. The priority level assigned goes into effect when a packet size exceeds the value entered for the argument *byte-count*. The size of the packet must also include additional bytes because of MAC encapsulation on the outgoing interface.

Table 27–2   *Protocol Priority Queue Keywords and Values, Continued*

Option	Description
lt *byte-count*	Specifies a less-than count. The priority level assigned goes into effect when a packet size is less than the value entered for the argument *byte-count*. The size of the packet must also include additional bytes because of MAC encapsulation on the outgoing interface.
list *list-number*	Assigns traffic priorities according to a specified list when used with AppleTalk, bridging, IP, IPX, VINES, or XNS. The *list-number* argument is the access list number as specified by the **access-list** global configuration command for the specified *protocol-name*. For example, if the protocol is AppleTalk, *list-number* should be a valid AppleTalk access-list number.
tcp *port*	Assigns the priority level defined to TCP segments originating from or destined to a specified port (for use with the IP protocol only). Table 27–3 lists common TCP services and their port numbers.
udp *port*	Assigns the priority level defined to UDP packets originating from or destined to a specified port (for use with the IP protocol only). Table 27–4 lists common UDP services and their port numbers.

Table 27–3   *Common TCP Services and Their Port Numbers*

Service	Port
Telnet	23
SMTP	25

Table 27–4   *Common UDP Services and Their Port Numbers*

Service	Port
TFTP	69
NFS	2049
SNMP	161
RPC	111
DNS	53

NOTES

The TCP and UDP ports listed in Table 27–3 and Table 27–4 include some of the more common port numbers. However, you can specify any port number to be prioritized; you are not limited to those listed. For some protocols, such as TFTP and FTP, only the initial request uses port 69. Subsequent packets use a randomly chosen port number. For these types of protocols, the use of port numbers fails to be an effective method to manage queued traffic.

Use the **no priority-list** global configuration command followed by the appropriate *list-number* argument and the **protocol** keyword to remove a priority-list entry assigned by protocol type.

Examples

The following example assigns 1 as the arbitrary priority-list number, specifies DECnet as the protocol type, and assigns a high-priority level to the DECnet packets transmitted on this interface:

```
priority-list 1 protocol decnet high
```

The following example assigns a medium-priority level to every DECnet packet with a size greater than 200 bytes:

```
priority-list 2 protocol decnet medium gt 200
```

The following example assigns a medium-priority level to every DECnet packet with a size less than 200 bytes:

```
priority-list 4 protocol decnet medium lt 200
```

The following example assigns a high-priority level to traffic that matches IP access list 10:

```
priority-list 1 protocol ip high list 10
```

The following example assigns a medium-priority level to Telnet packets:

```
priority-list 4 protocol ip medium tcp 23
```

The following example assigns a medium-priority level to UDP Domain Name service packets:

```
priority-list 4 protocol ip medium udp 53
```

The following example assigns a high-priority level to traffic that matches Ethernet type code access list 201:

```
priority-list 1 protocol bridge high list 201
```

Related Commands

priority-group
show queueing

PRIORITY-LIST QUEUE-LIMIT

To specify the maximum number of packets that can be waiting in each of the priority queues, use the **priority-list queue-limit** global configuration command. The **no** form of this command selects the normal queue.

priority-list *list-number* queue-limit *high-limit medium-limit normal-limit low-limit*
no priority-list *list-number* queue-limit

Syntax	Description
list-number	Arbitrary integer between 1 and 16 that identifies the priority list selected by the user.
high-limit medium-limit normal-limit low-limit	Priority queue maximum length. A value of 0 for any of the four arguments means that the queue can be of unlimited size for that particular queue.

Default

The default queue-limit arguments are listed in Table 27–5.

Table 27–5   *Priority Queue Packet Limits*

Priority Queue Argument	Packet Limits
high-limit	20
medium-limit	40
normal-limit	60
low-limit	80

Command Mode

Global configuration

Usage Guidelines

This command first appeared in Cisco IOS Release 10.0.

If a priority queue overflows, excess packets are discarded and quench messages can be sent, if appropriate, for the protocol.

Example

The following example sets the maximum packets in the priority queue to 10:

```
priority-list 2 queue-limit 10 40 60 80
```

Related Commands

priority-group
show queueing

QUEUE-LIST DEFAULT

To assign a priority queue for those packets that do not match any other rule in the queue list, use the **queue-list default** global configuration command. To restore the default value, use the **no** form of this command.

queue-list *list-number* **default** *queue-number*
no queue-list *list-number* **default** *queue-number*

Syntax Description

list-number   Number of the queue list. An integer from 1 to 16.

queue-number   Number of the queue. An integer from 1 to 16.

Default

Queue number 1

Command Mode

Global configuration

Usage Guidelines

This command first appeared in Cisco IOS Release 10.0.

When using multiple rules, remember that the system reads the **queue-list** commands in order of appearance. When classifying a packet, the system searches the list of rules specified by **queue-list** commands for a matching protocol or interface type. When a match is found, the packet is assigned to the appropriate queue. The list is searched in the order it is specified, and the first matching rule terminates the search.

Queue number 0 is a system queue. It is emptied before any of the other queues are processed. The system enqueues high-priority packets, such as keepalives, to this queue.

Use the **show interface** command to display the current status of the output queues.

Example

In the following example, the default queue for list 10 is set to queue number 2:

```
queue-list 10 default 2
```

Related Commands

custom-queue-list
show queueing

QUEUE-LIST INTERFACE

To establish queuing priorities on packets entering on an interface, use the **queue-list interface** global configuration command. To remove an entry from the list, use the **no** form of the command.

>   **queue-list** *list-number* **interface** *type number queue-number*
>   **no queue-list** *list-number* **interface** *queue-number*

Syntax	Description
list-number	Number of the queue list. An integer from 1 to 16.
type	Required argument that specifies the name of the interface.
number	Number of the specified interface.
queue-number	Number of the queue. An integer from 1 to 16.

Default

No queuing priorities are established.

Command Mode

Global configuration

Usage Guidelines

This command first appeared in Cisco IOS Release 10.0.

When using multiple rules, remember that the system reads the **queue-list** commands in order of appearance. When classifying a packet, the system searches the list of rules specified by **queue-list** commands for a matching protocol or interface type. When a match is found, the packet is assigned to the appropriate queue. The list is searched in the order it is specified, and the first matching rule terminates the search.

Example

In the following example, queue list 4 established queuing priorities for packets entering on interface tunnel 3. The queue number assigned is 10.

```
queue-list 4 interface tunnel 3 10
```

Related Commands

custom-queue-list
show queueing

QUEUE-LIST PROTOCOL

To establish queuing priority based upon the protocol type, use the **queue-list protocol** global configuration command. Use the **no** form of this command with the appropriate list number to remove an entry from the list.

> **queue-list** *list-number* **protocol** *protocol-name queue-number queue-keyword keyword-value*
> **no queue-list** *list-number* **protocol** *protocol-name*

Syntax	Description
list-number	Number of the queue list. An integer from 1 to 16.
protocol-name	Required argument that specifies the protocol type: **aarp, arp, apollo, appletalk, bridge** (transparent), **clns, clns_es, clns_is, compressedtcp, cmns, decnet, decnet_node, decnet_routerl1, decnet_routerl2, dlsw, ip, ipx, pad, rsrb, stun, vines, xns,** and **x25.**
queue-number	Number of the queue. An integer from 1 to 16.
queue-keyword keyword-value	Possible keywords are **gt, lt, list, tcp,** and **udp.** See Table 27–2.

Default

No queuing priorities are established.

Command Mode

Global configuration

Usage Guidelines

This command first appeared in Cisco IOS Release 10.0.

When using multiple rules, remember that the system reads the **queue-list** commands in order of appearance. When classifying a packet, the system searches the list of rules specified by **queue-list** commands for a matching protocol or interface type. When a match is found, the packet is assigned to the appropriate queue. The list is searched in the order it is specified, and the first matching rule terminates the search.

The **decnet_router-l1** keyword refers to the multicast address for all level 1 routers, which are intra-area routers, and the **decnet_router-l2** keyword refers to all level 2 routers, which are inter-area routers.

The **rsrb** keyword refers only to RSRB direct encapsulation.

Use Table 27–2, Table 27–3, and Table 27–4 from the **priority-list protocol** command to configure custom queueing for your system.

Examples

The following example assigns 1 as the custom queue list, specifies DECnet as the protocol type, and assigns 3 as a queue number to the packets transmitted on this interface:

```
queue-list 1 protocol decnet 3
```

The following example assigns DECnet packets with a size greater than 200 bytes to queue number 2:

```
queue-list 2 protocol decnet 2 gt 200
```

The following example assigns DECnet packets with a size less than 200 bytes to queue number 2:

```
queue-list 4 protocol decnet 2 lt 200
```

The following example assigns traffic that matches IP access list 10 to queue number 1:

```
queue-list 1 protocol ip 1 list 10
```

The following example assigns Telnet packets to queue number 2:

```
queue-list 4 protocol ip 2 tcp 23
```

The following example assigns UDP Domain Name service packets to queue number 2:

```
queue-list 4 protocol ip 2 udp 53
```

The following example assigns traffic that matches Ethernet type code access list 201 to queue number 1:

```
queue-list 1 protocol bridge 1 list 201
```

Related Commands

custom-queue-list
show queueing

QUEUE-LIST QUEUE BYTE-COUNT

To designate the byte size allowed per queue, use the **queue-list queue byte-count** global configuration command. To return the byte size to the default value, use the **no** form of the command.

> **queue-list** *list-number* **queue** *queue-number* **byte-count** *byte-count-number*
> **no queue-list** *list-number* **queue** *queue-number* **byte-count** *byte-count-number*

Syntax	Description
list-number	Number of the queue list. An integer from 1 to 16.
queue-number	Number of the queue. An integer from 1 to 16.
byte-count-number	Specifies the lower boundary on how many bytes the system allows to be delivered from a given queue during a particular cycle.

Default

1,500 bytes

Command Mode

Global configuration

Usage Guidelines

This command first appeared in Cisco IOS Release 10.0.

Example

In the following example, queue list 9 establishes the byte-count as 1,400 for queue number 10:

```
queue-list 9 queue 10 byte-count 1400
```

Related Commands

custom-queue-list
show queueing

QUEUE-LIST QUEUE LIMIT

To designate the queue-length limit for a queue, use the **queue-list queue limit** global configuration command. To return the queue length to the default value, use the **no** form of the command.

> **queue-list** *list-number* **queue** *queue-number* **limit** *limit-number*
> **no queue-list** *list-number* **queue** *queue-number* **limit** *limit-number*

Syntax	Description
list-number	Number of the queue list. An integer from 1 to 16.
queue-number	Number of the queue. An integer from 1 to 16.
limit-number	Maximum number of packets that can be enqueued at any time. Range is 0 to 32,767 queue entries. A value of 0 means that the queue can be of unlimited size.

Default

20 entries

Command Mode

Global configuration

Usage Guidelines

This command first appeared in Cisco IOS Release 10.0.

Example

In the following example, the queue length of queue 10 is increased to 40:

```
queue-list 5 queue 10 limit 40
```

Related Commands

custom-queue-list
show queueing

RANDOM-DETECT

To enable random early detection on an interface, use the **random-detect** interface configuration command. Use the **no** form of this command to disable random early detection on the interface.

> **random-detect** [*weighting*]
> **no random-detect**

Syntax	Description
weighting	(Optional) Exponential weighting constant in the range 1 to 16 used to determine the rate that packets are dropped when congestion occurs. The default is 10 (that is, drop 1 packet every 2^{10}).

Default

Random early detection is disabled.

Command Mode

Interface configuration

Usage Guidelines

This command first appeared in Cisco IOS Release 11.2.

Random early detection (RED) is useful in high-speed TCP/IP networks to avoid congestion by dropping packets at a controlled rate. RED is not recommended for protocols, such as AppleTalk or Novell Netware, that respond to dropped packets by retransmitting the packets at the same rate. RED should be configured only on an interface where most of the traffic is TCP/IP traffic.

Cisco recommends using the default value for the exponential weighting constant; however, you might need to change this value depending on your operational environment. For example, a value of 10 (the default), which might achieve a loss rate of 10^{-4}, is recommended for high-speed links such as DS3 and OC3, whereas a value of 7, which might achieve a loss rate of 10^{-3}, is recommended for T1 links.

Random early detection cannot be configured on an interface already configured with custom, priority, or fair queueing.

When RSVP is configured on the interface, packets from other traffic flows are dropped before RSVP flows (when possible). Also, the IP precedence of the packet determines whether the packet is dropped. Lower-precedence traffic is dropped before higher-precedence traffic. Therefore, lower-precedence traffic is more likely to be throttled back.

Example

The following example enables random early detection on a serial interface:

```
interface serial 0
random-detect
```

Related Commands

custom-queue-list
fair-queue
ip rsvp bandwidth
priority-group
priority-list default
queue-list default
random-detect
show interface

SCHEDULER ALLOCATE

To guarantee CPU time for processes, use the **scheduler allocate** global configuration command on the Cisco 7200 series and Cisco 7500 series. The **no** form of this command restores the default.

> **scheduler allocate** *interrupt-time process-time*
> **no scheduler allocate**

Syntax	Description
interrupt-time	Integer (in microseconds) that limits the maximum number of microseconds to spend on fast switching within any one network-interrupt context. The range is 400 to 60,000 microseconds. The default is 4,000 microseconds.
process-time	Integer (in microseconds) that guarantees the minimum number of microseconds to spend at the process level when network interrupts are disabled. The range is 100 to 4,000. The default is 200 microseconds.

Default

Approximately five percent of the CPU is available for process tasks.

Command Mode

Global configuration

Usage Guidelines

This command first appeared in Cisco IOS Release 11.2.

This command applies to the Cisco 7200 series and Cisco 7500 series.

CAUTION

Cisco recommends that you do not change the default values.

Example

The following example makes 20 percent of the CPU available for process tasks:

```
scheduler allocate 2000 500
```

Related Commands

scheduler interval

SCHEDULER INTERVAL

To control the maximum amount of time that can elapse without running system processes, use the **scheduler interval** global configuration command. The **no** form of this command restores the default.

> scheduler interval *milliseconds*
> no scheduler interval

Syntax	Description
milliseconds	Integer that specifies the interval, in milliseconds. The minimum interval that you can specify is 500 milliseconds; there is no maximum value.

Default

High-priority operations are allowed to use as much of the central processor as needed.

Command Mode

Global configuration

Usage Guidelines

This command first appeared in Cisco IOS Release 10.0.

The normal operation of the network server allows the switching operations to use as much of the central processor as is required. If the network is running unusually heavy loads that do not allow the processor the time to handle the routing protocols, give priority to the system process scheduler. High-priority operations are allowed to use as much of the central processor as needed.

On the Cisco 7200 series and Cisco 7500 series, use the **scheduler allocate** global configuration command.

Example

The following example changes the low-priority process schedule to an interval of 750 milliseconds:

```
scheduler interval 750
```

Related Commands

scheduler allocate

SERVICE NAGLE

To enable the Nagle congestion-control algorithm, use the **service nagle** global configuration command. Use the **no** form of this command to disable this feature.

> **service nagle**
> **no service nagle**

Syntax   Description

This command has no arguments or keywords.

Default

Disabled

Command Mode

Global configuration

Usage Guidelines

This command first appeared in Cisco IOS Release 10.0.

When using a standard TCP implementation to send keystrokes between machines, TCP tends to send one packet for each keystroke typed. On larger networks, many small packets use up bandwidth and contribute to congestion.

John Nagle's algorithm (RFC 896) helps alleviate the small-packet problem in TCP. In general, it works this way: The first character typed after connection establishment is sent in a single packet, but TCP holds any additional characters typed until the receiver acknowledges the previous packet.

Then the second, larger packet is sent, and additional typed characters are saved until the acknowledgment comes back. The effect is to accumulate characters into larger chunks, and pace them out to the network at a rate matching the round-trip time of the given connection. This method is usually good for all TCP-based traffic. However, do not use the **service nagle** command if you have XRemote users on X Window sessions.

Example
The following example enables the Nagle algorithm:
```
service nagle
```

SHOW BUFFERS

Use the **show buffers** EXEC command to display statistics for the buffer pools on the network server.

> **show buffers** [*type number* | **alloc** [**dump**]]

Syntax	Description
type number	(Optional) Displays interface pool information. If the specified interface *type* and *number* has its own buffer pool, displays information for that pool. Value of *type* can be **ethernet, serial, tokenring, fddi, bri, atm, e1, t1.**
alloc	(Optional) Displays a brief listing of all allocated buffers.
dump	(Optional) Dumps all allocated buffers. This keyword must be used with the **alloc** keyword, not by itself.

Command Mode
EXEC

Usage Guidelines
This command first appeared in Cisco IOS Release 10.0.

Sample Displays
The following is sample output from the **show buffers** command with no arguments, showing all buffer pool information:
```
Router# show buffers

Buffer elements:
    398 in free list (500 max allowed)
    1266 hits, 0 misses, 0 created
```

```
Public buffer pools:
Small buffers, 104 bytes (total 50, permanent 50):
     50 in free list (20 min, 150 max allowed)
     551 hits, 0 misses, 0 trims, 0 created
Middle buffers, 600 bytes (total 25, permanent 25):
     25 in free list (10 min, 150 max allowed)
     39 hits, 0 misses, 0 trims, 0 created
Big buffers, 1524 bytes (total 50, permanent 50):
     49 in free list (5 min, 150 max allowed)
     27 hits, 0 misses, 0 trims, 0 created
VeryBig buffers, 4520 bytes (total 10, permanent 10):
     10 in free list (0 min, 100 max allowed)
     0 hits, 0 misses, 0 trims, 0 created
Large buffers, 5024 bytes (total 0, permanent 0):
     0 in free list (0 min, 10 max allowed)
     0 hits, 0 misses, 0 trims, 0 created
Huge buffers, 18024 bytes (total 0, permanent 0):
     0 in free list (0 min, 4 max allowed)
     0 hits, 0 misses, 0 trims, 0 created

Interface buffer pools:
Ethernet0 buffers, 1524 bytes (total 64, permanent 64):
     16 in free list (0 min, 64 max allowed)
     48 hits, 0 fallbacks
     16 max cache size, 16 in cache
Ethernet1 buffers, 1524 bytes (total 64, permanent 64):
     16 in free list (0 min, 64 max allowed)
     48 hits, 0 fallbacks
     16 max cache size, 16 in cache
Serial0 buffers, 1524 bytes (total 64, permanent 64):
     16 in free list (0 min, 64 max allowed)
     48 hits, 0 fallbacks
     16 max cache size, 16 in cache
Serial1 buffers, 1524 bytes (total 64, permanent 64):
     16 in free list (0 min, 64 max allowed)
     48 hits, 0 fallbacks
     16 max cache size, 16 in cache
TokenRing0 buffers, 4516 bytes (total 48, permanent 48):
     0 in free list (0 min, 48 max allowed)
     48 hits, 0 fallbacks
     16 max cache size, 16 in cache
TokenRing1 buffers, 4516 bytes (total 32, permanent 32):
     32 in free list (0 min, 48 max allowed)
     16 hits, 0 fallbacks

0 failures (0 no memory)
```

Table 27–6 describes significant fields shown in the display.

Table 27–6 *Show Buffers Field Descriptions*

Field	Description
Buffer elements	*Buffer elements* are small structures used as placeholders for buffers in internal operating system queues. Buffer elements are used when a buffer might need to be on more than one queue.
free list	Total number of the currently unallocated buffer elements.
max allowed	Maximum number of buffers that are available for allocation.
hits	Count of successful attempts to allocate a buffer when needed.
misses	Count of buffer allocation attempts that resulted in growing the buffer pool to allocate a buffer.
created	Count of new buffers created to satisfy buffer allocation attempts when the available buffers in the pool have already been allocated.
Public buffer pools:	
Small buffers	Buffers that are 104 bytes long.
Middle buffers	Buffers that are 600 bytes long.
Big buffers	Buffers that are 1,524 bytes long.
VeryBig buffers	Buffers that are 4,520 bytes long.
Large buffers	Buffers that are 5,024 bytes long.
Huge buffers	Buffers that are 18,024 bytes long.
total	Total number of this type of buffer.
permanent	Number of these buffers that are permanent.
free list	Number of available or unallocated buffers in that pool.
min	Minimum number of free or unallocated buffers in the buffer pool
max allowed	Maximum number of free or unallocated buffers in the buffer pool
hits	Count of successful attempts to allocate a buffer when needed.
misses	Count of buffer allocation attempts that resulted in growing the buffer pool in order to allocate a buffer.
trims	Count of buffers released to the system because they were not being used. This field is displayed only for dynamic buffer pools, not interface buffer pools, which are static.

Table 27–6 *Show Buffers Field Descriptions, Continued*

Field	Description
created	Count of new buffers created in response to misses. This field is displayed only for dynamic buffer pools, not interface buffer pools, which are static.
Interface buffer pools:	
total	Total number of this type of buffer.
permanent	Number of these buffers that are permanent.
free list	Number of available or unallocated buffers in that pool.
min	Minimum number of free or unallocated buffers in the buffer pool.
max allowed	Maximum number of free or unallocated buffers in the buffer pool.
hits	Count of successful attempts to allocate a buffer when needed.
fallbacks	Count of buffer allocation attempts that resulted in falling back to the public buffer pool that is the smallest pool at least as big as the interface buffer pool.
max cache size	Maximum number of buffers from that interface's pool that can be in that interface buffer pool's cache. Each interface buffer pool has its own cache. These are not additional to the permanent buffers; they come from the interface's buffer pools. Some interfaces place all of their buffers from the interface pool into the cache. In this case, it is normal for the *free list* to display 0.
failures	Total number of allocation requests that have failed because no buffer was available for allocation; the datagram was lost. Such failures normally occur at interrupt level.
no memory	Number of failures that occurred because no memory was available to create a new buffer.

The following is sample output from the **show buffers** command with an interface *type* and *number*:

```
Router# show buffers Ethernet 0

Ethernet0 buffers, 1524 bytes (total 64, permanent 64):
     16 in free list (0 min, 64 max allowed)
     48 hits, 0 fallbacks
     16 max cache size, 16 in cache
```

The following is sample output from the **show buffers** command when **alloc** is specified:

```
Router# show buffers alloc

Buffer elements:
     398 in free list (500 max allowed)
     1266 hits, 0 misses, 0 created

Public buffer pools:
Small buffers, 104 bytes (total 50, permanent 50):
     50 in free list (20 min, 150 max allowed)
     551 hits, 0 misses, 0 trims, 0 created
Middle buffers, 600 bytes (total 25, permanent 25):
     25 in free list (10 min, 150 max allowed)
     39 hits, 0 misses, 0 trims, 0 created
Big buffers, 1524 bytes (total 50, permanent 50):
     49 in free list (5 min, 150 max allowed)
     27 hits, 0 misses, 0 trims, 0 created
VeryBig buffers, 4520 bytes (total 10, permanent 10):
     10 in free list (0 min, 100 max allowed)
     0 hits, 0 misses, 0 trims, 0 created
Large buffers, 5024 bytes (total 0, permanent 0):
     0 in free list (0 min, 10 max allowed)
     0 hits, 0 misses, 0 trims, 0 created
Huge buffers, 18024 bytes (total 0, permanent 0):
     0 in free list (0 min, 4 max allowed)
     0 hits, 0 misses, 0 trims, 0 created

Interface buffer pools:
Ethernet0 buffers, 1524 bytes (total 64, permanent 64):
     16 in free list (0 min, 64 max allowed)
     48 hits, 0 fallbacks
     16 max cache size, 16 in cache
Ethernet1 buffers, 1524 bytes (total 64, permanent 64):
     16 in free list (0 min, 64 max allowed)
     48 hits, 0 fallbacks
     16 max cache size, 16 in cache
Serial0 buffers, 1524 bytes (total 64, permanent 64):
     16 in free list (0 min, 64 max allowed)
     48 hits, 0 fallbacks
     16 max cache size, 16 in cache
Serial1 buffers, 1524 bytes (total 64, permanent 64):
     16 in free list (0 min, 64 max allowed)
     48 hits, 0 fallbacks
     16 max cache size, 16 in cache
TokenRing0 buffers, 4516 bytes (total 48, permanent 48):
     0 in free list (0 min, 48 max allowed)
     48 hits, 0 fallbacks
     16 max cache size, 16 in cache
TokenRing1 buffers, 4516 bytes (total 32, permanent 32):
     32 in free list (0 min, 48 max allowed)
     16 hits, 0 fallbacks
```

```
0 failures (0 no memory)
```

Address	PakAddr	Data Area	Off set	Data Size	Pool	Ref Cnt	Link Type	Enc Type	Flags (Hex)	Output Idb	Input Idb
604B37A0	604B37C0	40004A38	62	60	Big	1	65	3	0	Et0	
604C6DA0	604C6DC0	40007038	84	0	Ether	1	0	0	0		
604C6F60	604C6F80	400076E4	84	0	Ether	1	0	0	0		
604C7120	604C7140	40007D90	84	0	Ether	1	0	0	0		
604C72E0	604C7300	4000843C	84	0	Ether	1	0	0	0		
604C74A0	604C74C0	40008AE8	84	0	Ether	1	0	0	0		
604C7660	604C7680	40009194	84	0	Ether	1	0	0	0		
604C7820	604C7840	40009840	84	0	Ether	1	0	0	0		

.
.
.

SHOW QUEUEING

To list the current state of the queue lists, use the **show queueing** privileged EXEC command.

show queueing [custom | fair | priority | virtual-access *interface-number***]**

Syntax	Description
custom	(Optional) Shows status of custom queueing list configuration.
fair	(Optional) Shows status of the fair queueing configuration. This is the default.
priority	(Optional) Shows status of priority queueing list configuration.
virtual-access *interface-number*	(Optional) Shows information about interleaving on a virtual access interface.

Default

Fair queueing configuration

Command Mode

Privileged EXEC

Usage Guidelines

This command first appeared in Cisco IOS Release 10.3.

If no keyword is entered, this command shows the status of fair queueing configuration.

Sample Displays

The following is sample output from the **show queueing custom** EXEC command:

```
Router# show queueing custom

Current custom queue configuration:

List   Queue  Args
3      10     default
3      3      interface Tunnel3
3      3      protocol ip
3      3      byte-count 444 limit 3
```

The following is sample output from the **show queueing** command. On interface Serial0, there are two active conversations. Weighted fair queueing ensures that both of these IP data streams—both using TCP—receive equal bandwidth on the interface while they have messages in the pipeline, even though there is more FTP data in the queue than rcp data.

```
Router# show queueing

Current fair queue configuration:
Interface Serial0
   Input queue: 0/75/0 (size/max/drops); Total output drops: 0
   Output queue: 18/64/30 (size/threshold/drops)
      Conversations 2/8 (active/max active)
      Reserved Conversations 0/0 (allocated/max allocated)

   (depth/weight/discards) 3/4096/30
   Conversation 117, linktype: ip, length: 556, flags: 0x280
   source: 172.31.128.115, destination: 172.31.58.89, id: 0x1069, ttl: 59,
   TOS: 0 prot: 6, source port 514, destination port 1022

   (depth/weight/discards) 14/4096/0
   Conversation 155, linktype: ip, length: 1504, flags: 0x280
   source: 172.31.128.115, destination: 172.31.58.89, id: 0x104D, ttl: 59,
   TOS: 0 prot: 6, source port 20, destination port 1554
```

Related Commands

custom-queue-list
priority-group
priority-list interface
priority-list queue-limit
queue-list default
queue-list default
queue-list interface
queue-list protocol
queue-list queue byte-count
queue-list queue limit

SHOW TRAFFIC-SHAPE

Use the **show traffic-shape** EXEC command to display the current traffic-shaping configuration.

> **show traffic-shape** [*interface*]

Syntax	Description
interface	(Optional) Name of the interface.

Command Mode

EXEC

Usage Guidelines

This command first appeared in Cisco IOS Release 11.2.

You must have enabled traffic shaping first using the **traffic-shape rate, traffic-shape group,** or **frame-relay traffic-shaping** command to display traffic-shaping information with the **show traffic-shape** command.

Sample Display

The following is sample output from the command.

```
Router# show traffic-shape

         access Target  Byte   Sustain   Excess    Interval  Increment Adapt
I/F      list   Rate    Limit  bits/int  bits/int  (ms)        (bytes) Active
Et0      101    1000000 23437  125000    125000    63          7813    -
Et1             5000000 87889  625000    625000    16          9766    -
```

Table 27–7 describes the fields shown in the display.

Table 27–7 *Show Traffic-Shape Field Descriptions*

Field	Description
I/F	Interface.
access list	Number of the access list.
Target Rate	Rate that traffic is shaped to in bps.
Byte Limit	Maximum number of bytes transmitted per internal interval.
Sustain bits/int	Configured sustained bits per interval.
Excess bits/int	Configured excess bits in the first interval.

Table 27-7   *Show Traffic-Shape Field Descriptions, Continued*

Field	Description
Interval (ms)	Interval being used internally. This interval may be smaller than the Committed Burst divided by the committed information rate if the router determines that traffic flow will be more stable with a smaller configured interval.
Increment (bytes)	Number of bytes that will be sustained per internal interval.
Adapt Active	Contains "BECN" if Frame Relay has BECN Adaptation configured.

Related Commands

frame-relay traffic-shaping
show traffic-shape statistics
traffic-shape adaptive
traffic-shape group
traffic-shape rate

SHOW TRAFFIC-SHAPE STATISTICS

Use the **show traffic-shape statistics** EXEC command to display the current traffic-shaping statistics.

> **show traffic-shape statistics** [*interface*]

Syntax	Description
interface	(Optional) Name of the interface.

Command Mode

EXEC

Usage Guidelines

This command first appeared in Cisco IOS Release 11.2.

You must first have enabled traffic shaping using the **traffic-shape rate, traffic-shape group,** or **frame-relay traffic-shaping** command to display traffic-shaping information with the **show traffic-shape statistics** command.

Sample Display

The following is sample output from the **show traffic-shape statistics** command.

```
Router# show traffic-shape statistics

          Access Queue    Packets  Bytes     Packets  Bytes    Shaping
   I/F    List   Depth                        Delayed  Delayed  Active
   Et0    101    0         2        180        0        0        no
   Et1           0         0        0          0        0        no
```

Table 27–8 describes the fields shown in the display.

Table 27–8 *Show Traffic-Shape Statistics Field Descriptions*

Field	Description
I/F	Interface.
Access List	Number of the access list.
Queue Depth	Number of messages in the queue.
Packets	Number of packets sent through the interface.
Bytes	Number of bytes sent through the interface.
Packets Delayed	Number of packets sent through the interface that were delayed in the traffic-shaping queue.
Bytes Delayed	Number of bytes sent through the interface that were delayed in the traffic-shaping queue.
Shaping Active	Contains "yes" when timers indicate that traffic shaping is occurring and "no" if traffic shaping is not occurring.

Related Commands

frame-relay traffic-shaping
show traffic-shape
traffic-shape adaptive
traffic-shape group
traffic-shape rate

TRAFFIC-SHAPE ADAPTIVE

To configure a Frame Relay subinterface to estimate the available bandwidth when backward explicit congestion notifications (BECNs) are received, use the **traffic-shape adaptive** interface configuration command. Use the **no** form of this command to stop adapting to congestion signals.

traffic-shape adaptive [*bit-rate*]
no traffic-shape adaptive

Syntax	Description
bit-rate	(Optional) Lowest bit rate that traffic is shaped to in bits per second. The default is half the value specified for the **traffic-shape rate** or **traffic-shape group** *bit-rate* option.

Default

No available bandwidth is estimated when BECNs are received.

Command Mode

Interface configuration

Usage Guidelines

This command first appeared in Cisco IOS Release 11.2.

You must enable traffic shaping on the interface with the **traffic-shape rate** command before you can use the **traffic-shape adaptive** command.

The bit rate specified for the **traffic-shape rate** command is the upper limit, and the bit rate specified for the **traffic-shape adaptive** command is the lower limit to which traffic is shaped when BECNs are received on the interface. The rate actually shaped to will be between these two rates. The **traffic-shape adaptive** command should be configured at both ends of the link, as it also configures the device at the flow end to reflect forward explicit congestion notification (FECN) signals as BECNs, enabling the router at the high-speed end to detect and adapt to congestion even when traffic is flowing primarily in one direction.

Example

The following example configures traffic shaping on interface 0.1 with an upper limit of 128 kbps and a lower limit of 64 kbps. This allows the link to run from 64 to 128 kbps, depending on the congestion level.

```
interface serial 0
 encapsulation-frame-relay
interface serial 0.1
 traffic-shape rate 128000
 traffic-shape adaptive 64000
```

Related Commands

traffic-shape group
traffic-shape rate

TRAFFIC-SHAPE GROUP

To enable traffic shaping based on a specific access list for outbound traffic on an interface, use the **traffic-shape group** interface configuration command. Use the **no** form of this command to disable traffic shaping on the interface for the access list.

> **traffic-shape group** *access-list bit-rate* [*burst-size* [*excess-burst-size*]]
> **no traffic-shape group** *access-list*

Syntax	Description
access-list	Number of the access list that controls the packets that traffic shaping is applied to on the interface.
bit-rate	Bit rate that traffic is shaped to in bits per second. This is the access bit rate that you contract with your service provider or the service level you intend to maintain.
burst-size	(Optional) Sustained number of bits that can be transmitted per interval. On Frame Relay interfaces, this is the committed burst size contracted with your service provider. The default is the *bit-rate* divided by 8.
excess-burst-size	(Optional) Maximum number of bits that can exceed the burst size in the first interval in a congestion event. On Frame Relay interfaces, this is the excess burst size contracted with your service provider. The default is equal to the *burst-size*.

Default

Traffic shaping is disabled.

Command Mode

Interface configuration

Usage Guidelines

This command first appeared in Cisco IOS Release 11.2.

Traffic shaping uses queues to limit surges that can congest a network. Data is buffered and then sent into the network in regulated amounts to ensure that traffic will fit within the promised traffic envelope for the particular connection.

The **traffic-shape group** command allows you to specify one or more previously defined access lists to shape traffic on the interface. You must specify one **traffic-shape group** command for each access list on the interface.

You would use traffic shaping if you have a network with differing access rates or if you are offering a subrate service. You can configure the values according to your contract with your service provider or the service levels you intend to maintain.

An interval is calculated as follows:

- If the *burst-size* is not equal to zero, the interval is the *burst-size* divided by the *bit-rate*.
- If the *burst-size* is zero, the interval is the *excess-burst-size* divided by the *bit-rate*.

Traffic shaping is supported on all media and encapsulation types on the router. To perform traffic shaping on Frame Relay virtual circuits, you also can use the **frame-relay traffic-shaping** command.

If traffic shaping is performed on a Frame Relay network with the **traffic-shape rate** command, you also can use the **traffic-shape adaptive** command to specify the minimum bit rate to which the traffic is shaped.

Example

The following example enables traffic that matches access list 101 to be shaped to a certain rate and traffic matching access list 102 to be shaped to another rate on the interface:

```
interface serial 1
  traffic-shape rate 128000 16000 8000 group 101
  traffic-shape rate 130000 10000 1000 group 102
```

Related Commands

access-list
traffic-shape adaptive
traffic-shape rate

TRAFFIC-SHAPE RATE

To enable traffic shaping for outbound traffic on an interface, use the **traffic-shape rate** interface configuration command. Use the **no** form of this command to disable traffic shaping on the interface.

traffic-shape rate *bit-rate* [*burst-size* [*excess-burst-size*]]
no traffic-shape rate

Syntax	Description
bit-rate	Bit rate that traffic is shaped to in bits per second. This is the access bit rate that you contract with your service provider or the service level you intend to maintain.
burst-size	(Optional) Sustained number of bits that can be transmitted per interval. On Frame Relay interfaces, this is the committed burst size contracted with your service provider. The default is the *bit-rate* divided by 8.

Syntax	Description
excess-burst-size	(Optional) Maximum number of bits that can exceed the burst size in the first interval in a congestion event. On Frame Relay interfaces, this is the excess burst size contracted with your service provider. The default is equal to the *burst-size*.

Default

Traffic shaping is disabled.

Command Mode

Interface configuration

Usage Guidelines

This command first appeared in Cisco IOS Release 11.2.

Traffic shaping uses queues to limit surges that can congest a network. Data is buffered and then sent into the network in regulated amounts to ensure that traffic will fit within the promised traffic envelope for the particular connection.

You would use traffic shaping if you have a network with differing access rates or if you are offering a subrate service. You can configure the values according to your contract with your service provider or service levels you intend to maintain.

An interval is calculated as follows:

- If the *burst-size* is not equal to zero, the interval is the *burst-size* divided by the *bit-rate*.
- If the *burst-size* is zero, the interval is the *excess-burst-size* divided by the *bit-rate*.

Traffic shaping is supported on all media and encapsulation types on the router. To perform traffic shaping on Frame Relay virtual circuits, you also can use the **frame-relay traffic-shaping** command.

If traffic shaping is performed on a Frame Relay network with the **traffic-shape rate** command, you also can use the **traffic-shape adaptive** command to specify the minimum bit rate to which the traffic is shaped.

Example

The following example enables traffic shaping on a serial interface using the bandwidth required by the service provider:

```
interface serial 0
  traffic-shape rate 128000 16000 8000
```

Related Commands

traffic-shape adaptive
traffic-shape group

## CHAPTER 28

Troubleshooting the Router

This chapter describes basic tasks that you can perform to troubleshoot your router and network.

For a complete description of the troubleshooting commands in this chapter, see Chapter 29, "Troubleshooting Commands."

UNDERSTANDING FAULT MANAGEMENT

To manage network faults, you need to discover, isolate, and fix the problems. You can discover problems with the system's monitoring commands, isolate problems with the system's test commands, and resolve problems with other commands, including **debug** commands.

To perform general fault management, complete the tasks in the following sections:

- Displaying System Information Using Show Commands
- Receiving Automatic Warning Messages
- Receiving the Automatic Shutdown Message
- Testing Network Connectivity
- Testing Memory and Interfaces
- Logging System Error Messages
- Enabling Debug Operations

DISPLAYING SYSTEM INFORMATION USING SHOW COMMANDS

To provide information about system processes, the Cisco IOS software includes an extensive list of EXEC commands that begin with the word **show**, which, when executed, display detailed tables of system information. Following is a list of the more common system management **show** commands. Perform these tasks in EXEC mode to display the information described:

Task	Command
Step 1 Display information about the CPU and midplane for the Cisco 7200 series routers.	**show c7200**
Step 2 Display information stored in NVRAM when the router crashes. This command is only useful to your technical support representative. This command is supported on the Cisco 7000 family routers.	**show context**
Step 3 Display a message indicating whether an environmental warning condition currently exists, the temperature and voltage information, the last measured value from each of the six test points stored in nonvolatile memory, or the environmental specifications. This command is supported on the Cisco 7000 family routers.	**show environment [all | last | table]**
Step 4 Display all GT64010 internal registers and interrupt status on the Cisco 7200 series routers.	**show gt64010**
Step 5 Display memory pool statistics, including summary information about the activities of the system memory allocator and a block-by-block listing of memory use.	**show memory** [*type*] [**free**] [**summary**]
Step 6 Display information about the peripheral component interconnect (PCI) hardware registers or bridge registers for the Cisco 7200 series routers.	**show pci {hardware | bridge** [*register*]**}**
Step 7 Display information about all active processes.	**show processes** [**cpu**]
Step 8 Display information about memory usage.	**show processes memory**
Step 9 Display the configured protocols.	**show protocols**

Task	Command
Step 10 Display stack usage of processes and interrupt routines, including the reason for the last system reboot. This command is only useful to your technical support representative.	**show stacks**
Step 11 Display the status of TCP connections.	**show tcp** [*line-number*]
Step 12 Display a concise description of TCP connection endpoints.	**show tcp brief** [**all**]
Step 13 Display a snapshot of the time-division multiplexing (TDM) bus connection or data memory in a Cisco AS5200 access server.	**show tdm** {**connections** I **data**} [**motherboard** I **slot** *number*]
Step 14 Display general information about the router when reporting a problem.	**show tech-support** [**page**] [**password**]

Look for specific **show** commands and their descriptions in the tables of configuration tasks found throughout the chapters in this book.

RECEIVING AUTOMATIC WARNING MESSAGES

Some routers have an environmental monitor that monitors the physical condition of the router. If a measurement exceeds acceptable margins, a warning message is printed to the system console. The system software collects measurements once every 60 seconds, but warnings for a given test point are printed at most once every four hours. If the temperature measurements are out of specification more than the shutdown margin, the software shuts the router down, but the fan will stay on. The router has to be manually turned off and on after such a shutdown. You can query the environmental monitor using the **show environment** command at any time to determine whether a measurement is out of tolerance. Refer to the *System Error Messages* publication for a description of environmental monitor warning messages.

RECEIVING THE AUTOMATIC SHUTDOWN MESSAGE

On routers with an environmental monitor, if the software detects that any of its temperature test points have exceeded maximum margins, it performs the following steps in this order:

1. Saves the last measured values from each of the six test points to internal nonvolatile memory.

2. Interrupts the system software and causes a shutdown message to be printed on the system console.

3. Shuts off the power supplies after a few milliseconds of delay.

The following is the message the system displays if temperatures exceed maximum margins, along with a message indicating the reason for the shutdown:

```
Router#
%ENVM-1-SHUTDOWN: Environmental Monitor initiated shutdown
%ENVM-2-TEMP: Inlet temperature has reached SHUTDOWN level at 64(C)
```

Refer to the hardware installation and maintenance publication for your router for more information about environmental specifications.

TESTING NETWORK CONNECTIVITY

Complete the tasks in the following sections to test basic network connectivity:

- Setting Up the TCP Keepalive Packet Service
- Testing Connections with the Ping Command
- Tracing Packet Routes

Setting Up the TCP Keepalive Packet Service

The TCP keepalive capability allows a router to detect when the host with which it is communicating experiences a system failure, even if data stops being transmitted (in either direction). This is most useful on incoming connections. For example, if a host failure occurs while talking to a printer, the router might never notice, because the printer does not generate any traffic in the opposite direction. If keepalives are enabled, they are sent once every minute on otherwise idle connections. If five minutes pass and no keepalives are detected, the connection is closed. The connection is also closed if the host replies to a keepalive packet with a reset packet. This will happen if the host crashes and comes back up again.

To set up the TCP keepalive packet service, perform the following task in global configuration mode:

Task	Command
Generate TCP keepalive packets on idle network connections, either incoming connections initiated by a remote host, or outgoing connections initiated by a user.	service {tcp-keepalives-in | tcp-keepalives-out}

Testing Connections with the Ping Command

As an aid to diagnosing basic network connectivity, many network protocols support an echo protocol. The protocol involves sending a special datagram to the destination host, then waiting for a reply datagram from that host. Results from this echo protocol can help in evaluating the path-to-host reliability, delays over the path, and whether the host can be reached or is functioning.

To use the echo protocol, perform the following task in either user or privileged EXEC mode:

Task	Command
Invoke a diagnostic tool for testing connectivity.	**ping** [*protocol*] {*host*	*address*}

Look for specific **ping** commands and command descriptions in the tables of configuration tasks found throughout this book.

Tracing Packet Routes

To discover the routes that packets actually will take when traveling to their destinations, perform the following task in either user or privileged EXEC mode:

Task	Command
Trace packet routes through the network (privileged level).	**trace** [*protocol*] [*destination*]

TESTING MEMORY AND INTERFACES

You can test the status of the following items:

- Flash memory
- System memory
- Interfaces

CAUTION

We do not recommend using these test commands; they are intended to aid manufacturing person-nel in checking system functionality.

Testing Flash Memory

To test the status of Flash memory, perform the following task in privileged EXEC mode:

Task	Command
Test Flash memory on MCI and envm Flash EPROM interfaces.	**test flash**

Testing System Memory

To test the status of system memory, perform the following task in privileged EXEC mode:

Task	Command
Diagnose Multibus memory, including nonvolatile memory.	**test memory**

Testing Interfaces

CAUTION

Do not use this test to diagnose problems with an operational server.

To test the status of the interfaces, perform the following task on a nonoperational server in privileged EXEC mode:

Task	Command
Check network interfaces.	**test interfaces**

LOGGING SYSTEM ERROR MESSAGES

By default, routers send the output from the **debug** EXEC command and system error messages to a logging process. The logging process controls the distribution of logging messages to the various destinations, such as the logging buffer, terminal lines, or a UNIX syslog server, depending on your configuration. The process also sends messages to the console. When the logging process is on, the messages are displayed on the console after the process that generated them has finished.

NOTES

The syslog format is compatible with 4.3 BSD UNIX.

When the logging process is disabled, messages are sent only to the console. The messages are sent as they are generated, so error and debug output will be interspersed with prompts or output from the command.

You can set the severity level of the messages to control the type of messages displayed for the console and each of the destinations. You can timestamp log messages or set the syslog source address to enhance real-time debugging and management.

Refer to the *System Error Messages* publication for information on possible error messages.

Enabling Message Logging

Message logging is enabled by default. It must be enabled in order to send messages to any destination other than the console.

To disable message logging, use the **no logging on** command. Disabling the logging process can slow down the router, because a process must wait until the messages are written to the console before continuing.

To re-enable message logging after it has been disabled, perform the following task in global configuration mode:

Task	Command
Enable message logging.	**logging on**

Enabling Message Logging for a Slave Card

To enable slave Versatile Interface Processor (VIP) cards to log important messages to the console, perform the following task in global configuration mode:

Task	Command
Enable slave message logging.	**service slave-log**

Setting the Error Message Display Device

If message logging is enabled, you can send messages to specified locations, in addition to the console.

To specify the locations that receive messages, perform one or more of the following tasks in global configuration mode:

Task	Command
Log messages to an internal buffer.	**logging buffered** [*size*]
Log messages to a nonconsole terminal.	**terminal monitor**
Log messages to a UNIX syslog server host.	**logging** *host*

The **logging buffered** command copies logging messages to an internal buffer. The buffer is circular, so newer messages overwrite older messages after the buffer is full. To display the messages that are logged in the buffer, use the **show logging** EXEC command. The first message displayed is the oldest message in the buffer. To clear the current contents of the buffer, use the **clear logging** privileged EXEC command.

The EXEC command **terminal monitor** locally accomplishes the task of displaying the system error messages to a nonconsole terminal.

The **logging** command identifies a syslog server host to receive logging messages. The argument *host* is the name or Internet address of the host. By issuing this command more than once, you build a list of syslog servers that receive logging messages. The **no logging** command deletes the syslog server with the specified address from the list of syslogs.

Configuring Synchronization of Logging Messages

You can configure the system to synchronize unsolicited messages and **debug** command output with solicited device output and prompts for a specific line. You can identify the types of messages to be output asynchronously based on the level of severity. You also can determine the maximum number of buffers for storing asynchronous messages for the terminal after which messages are dropped.

When synchronous logging of unsolicited messages and **debug** command output is turned on, unsolicited device output is displayed on the console or printed after solicited device output is displayed or printed. Unsolicited messages and **debug** command output are displayed on the console after the prompt for user input is returned. Therefore, unsolicited messages and **debug** command output are not interspersed with solicited device output and prompts. After the unsolicited messages are displayed, the console displays the user prompt again.

To configure for synchronous logging of unsolicited messages and **debug** command output with solicited device output and prompts, perform the following tasks, beginning in global configuration mode:

Task		Command
Step 1	Specify the line to be configured for synchronous logging of messages.	**line [aux	console	vty]** *line-number* [*ending-line-number*]
Step 2	Enable synchronous logging of messages.	**logging synchronous** [**level** *severity-level*	**all**] [**limit** *number-of-buffers*]

Enabling Timestamps on Log Messages

By default, log messages are not timestamped. You can enable timestamping of log messages by performing the following task in global configuration mode:

Task	Command
Enable log timestamps.	**service timestamps log uptime**
	or
	service timestamps log datetime [**msec**] [**localtime**] [**show-timezone**]

Defining the Error Message Severity Level and Facilities

You can limit messages displayed to the selected device by specifying the severity level of the error message. To do so, perform one of the following tasks in global configuration mode:

Task	Command
Limit messages logged to the console.	**logging console** *level*
Limit messages logged to the terminal lines.	**logging monitor** *level*
Limit messages logged to the syslog servers.	**logging trap** *level*

If you have enabled syslog message traps to be sent to an SNMP network management station with the **snmp-server enable trap** command, you also can change the level of messages sent and stored in a history table on the router. You also can change the number of messages that get stored in the history table.

Messages are stored in the history table, because SNMP traps are not guaranteed to reach their destination. By default, one message of the level warning and above (see Table 28–1) is stored in the history table, even if syslog traps are not enabled.

To change the level and table size defaults, perform the following tasks in global configuration mode:

Task		Command
Step 1	Change the default level of syslog messages stored in the history file and sent to the SNMP server.	**logging history** *level*
Step 2	Change the number of syslog messages that can be stored in the history table.	**logging history size** *number*

> **NOTES**
>
> Table 28–1 lists the level keywords and severity level. For SNMP usage, the severity level values use +1. For example, **emergency** equals 1 not 0 and **critical** equals 3 not 2.

The **logging console** command limits the logging messages displayed on the console terminal to messages with a level number at or below the specified severity level, which is specified by the *level* argument. Table 28–2 lists the error message *level* keywords and corresponding UNIX syslog definitions in order from the most severe level to the least severe level.

Table 28–1 *Error Message Logging Keywords*

Level Keyword	Level	Description	Syslog Definition
emergencies	0	System unusable	LOG_EMERG
alerts	1	Immediate action needed	LOG_ALERT
critical	2	Critical conditions	LOG_CRIT
errors	3	Error conditions	LOG_ERR
warnings	4	Warning conditions	LOG_WARNING
notifications	5	Normal but significant condition	LOG_NOTICE
informational	6	Informational messages only	LOG_INFO
debugging	7	Debugging messages	LOG_DEBUG

The **no logging console** command disables logging to the console terminal.

The default is to log messages to the console at the **debugging** level and those level numbers that are lower, which means all levels. The **logging monitor** command defaults to **debugging** also. The **logging trap** command defaults to **informational**.

To display logging messages on a terminal, use the **terminal monitor** EXEC command.

Current software generates four categories of error messages:

- Error messages about software or hardware malfunctions, displayed at level **warnings** through **emergencies**
- Output from the **debug** commands, displayed at the **debugging** level
- Interface up/down transitions and system restart messages, displayed at the **notifications** level
- Reload requests and low-process stack messages, displayed at the **informational** level

Defining the Syslog Facility

You also can configure the syslog facility in which error messages are sent by performing the following task in global configuration mode:

Task	Command
Configure system log facilities.	**logging facility** *facility-type*

Table 28–2 lists the logging facility type keywords and their descriptions.

Table 28–2 *Logging Facility Type Keywords*

Facility Type Keyword	Description
auth	Indicates the authorization system.
cron	Indicates the cron facility.
daemon	Indicates the system daemon.
kern	Indicates the Kernel.
local0–7	Reserved for locally defined messages.
lpr	Indicates line printer system.
mail	Indicates mail system.
news	Indicates USENET news.
sys9	Indicates system use.
sys10	Indicates system use.
sys11	Indicates system use.
sys12	Indicates system use.
sys13	Indicates system use.
sys14	Indicates system use.
syslog	Indicates the system log.
user	Indicates user process.
uucp	Indicates UNIX-to-UNIX copy system.

Refer also to your syslog manual pages.

To display logging information, perform the following task in EXEC mode:

Task		Command
Step 1	Display the state of syslog error and event logging, including host addresses, whether console logging is enabled, and other logging statistics.	show logging
Step 2	Display information in the syslog history table such as the table size, the status of messages, and the text of the messages stored in the table.	show logging history

Logging Errors to a UNIX Syslog Daemon

To set up the syslog daemon on a 4.3 BSD UNIX system, include a line such as the following in the /etc/syslog.conf file:

```
local7.debugging /usr/adm/logs/cisco.log
```

The **debugging** keyword specifies the syslog level; see Table 28–1 for a general description of other keywords. The **local7** keyword specifies the logging facility to be used; see Table 28–2 for a general description of other keywords.

The syslog daemon sends messages at this level or at a more severe level to the file specified in the next field. The file must already exist, and the syslog daemon must have permission to write to it.

Setting the Syslog Source Address

By default, a syslog message contains the IP address of the interface it uses to leave the router. To require that all syslog messages contain the same IP address, regardless of which interface they use, perform the following task in global configuration mode:

Task	Command
Set the syslog source address.	**logging source-interface** *type number*

ENABLING DEBUG OPERATIONS

Your router includes hardware and software to aid in tracking down internal problems and problems with other hosts on the network. The privileged **debug** EXEC commands start the console display of several classes of network events. The following tasks describe in general the system debug message feature.

Task		Command
Step 1	Display the state of each debugging option.	**show debugging**
Step 2	Display a list and brief description of all the **debug** command options.	**debug ?**
Step 3	Begin message logging for the specified **debug** command.	**debug** *command*
Step 4	Turn message logging off for the specified **debug** command.	**no debug** *command*

> **CAUTION**
>
> The system gives high priority to debugging output. For this reason, debugging commands should be turned on only for troubleshooting specific problems or during troubleshooting sessions with technical support personnel. Excessive debugging output can render the system inoperable.

You can configure timestamping of system debug messages. Timestamping enhances real-time debugging by providing the relative timing of logged events. This information is especially useful when customers send debugging output to your technical support personnel for assistance. To enable timestamping of system debug messages, perform the following task in global configuration mode:

Task	Command
Enable timestamping of system debug messages.	**service timestamps debug uptime** or **service timestamps debug datetime [msec] [localtime] [show-timezone]**

Normally, the messages are displayed only on the console terminal. See the section "Setting the Error Message Display Device" earlier in this chapter to change the output device.

CHAPTER 29

Troubleshooting Commands

This chapter describes the commands used to troubleshoot your router. To troubleshoot, you need to discover, isolate, and fix the problems. You can discover problems with the system's monitoring commands, isolate problems with the system's test commands, and resolve problems with other commands, including **debug**.

This chapter describes general fault-management commands.

For troubleshooting tasks and examples, see Chapter 28, "Troubleshooting the Router."

CLEAR LOGGING

To clear messages from the logging buffer, use the **clear logging** privileged EXEC command.

> **clear logging**

Syntax   *Description*

This command has no arguments or keywords.

Command Mode

Privileged EXEC

Usage Guidelines

This command first appeared in Cisco IOS Release 11.2.

Example

In the following example, the logging buffer is cleared:

```
Router# clear logging            .

Clear logging buffer [confirm]
Router#
```

Related Commands

logging buffered
show logging

EXCEPTION CORE-FILE

To specify the name of the core dump file, use the **exception core-file** global configuration command. To return to the default core filename, use the **no** form of this command.

exception core-file *name*
no exception core-file

Syntax	Description
name	Name of the core dump file saved on the server.

Default

The core file is named *hostname*-core, where *hostname* is the name of the router.

Command Mode

Global configuration

Usage Guidelines

This command first appeared in Cisco IOS Release 10.3.

CAUTION

Use the **exception** commands only under the direction of a technical support representative. Creating a core dump while the router is functioning in a network can disrupt network operation. The resulting binary file, which is very large, must be transferred to a TFTP, FTP, or rcp server and subsequently interpreted by technical personnel who have access to source code and detailed memory maps.

If you use TFTP to dump the core file to a server, the router will dump only the first 16 MB of the core file. If the router's memory is larger than 16 MB, the whole core file will not be copied to the server. Therefore, use rcp or FTP to dump the core file.

Example

The following example configures a router to use FTP to dump a core file named *dumpfile* to the FTP server at 172.17.92.2 when it crashes:

```
ip ftp username red
ip ftp password blue
exception protocol ftp
exception dump 172.17.92.2
exception core-file dumpfile
```

Related Commands

exception dump
exception memory
exception protocol
ip ftp password
ip ftp username

EXCEPTION DUMP

To configure the router to dump a core file to a particular server when the router crashes, use the **exception dump** global configuration command. To disable core dumps, use the **no** form of this command.

> **exception dump** *ip-address*
> **no exception dump**

Syntax	*Description*
ip-address	IP address of the server that stores the core dump file.

Default

Disabled

Command Mode

Global configuration

Usage Guidelines

This command first appeared in Cisco IOS Release 10.3.

CAUTION

Use the **exception** commands only under the direction of a technical support representative. Creating a core dump while the router is functioning in a network can disrupt network operation. The resulting binary file, which is very large, must be transferred to a TFTP, FTP, or rcp server and subsequently interpreted by technical personnel who have access to source code and detailed memory maps.

If you use TFTP to dump the core file to a server, the router will dump only the first 16 MB of the core file. If the router's memory is larger than 16 MB, the whole core file will not be copied to the server. Therefore, use rcp or FTP to dump the core file.

The core dump is written to a file named *hostname*-core on your server, where *hostname* is the name of the router. You can change the name of the core file by configuring the **exception core-file** command.

This procedure can fail for certain types of system crashes. However, if successful, the core dump file will be the size of the memory available on the processor (for example, 16 MB for a CSC/4).

Example

The following example configures a router to use FTP to dump a core file to the FTP server at 172.17.92.2 when it crashes:

```
ip ftp username red
ip ftp password blue
exception protocol ftp
exception dump 172.17.92.2
```

Related Commands

exception core-file
exception memory
exception protocol
ip ftp password
ip ftp username
ip rcmd remote-username

EXCEPTION MEMORY

To cause the router to create a core dump and reboot when certain memory size parameters are violated, use the **exception memory** global configuration command. To disable the rebooting and core dump, use the **no** form of this command.

> **exception memory** {**fragment** *size* | **minimum** *size*}
> **no exception memory** {**fragment** | **minimum**}

Syntax	Description
fragment *size*	The minimum contiguous block of memory in the free pool, in bytes.
minimum *size*	The minimum size of the free memory pool, in bytes.

Default

Disabled

Command Mode

Global configuration

Usage Guidelines

This command first appeared in Cisco IOS Release 10.3.

CAUTION

Use the **exception** commands only under the direction of a technical support representative. Creating a core dump while the router is functioning in a network can disrupt network operation. The resulting binary file, which is very large, must be transferred to a TFTP, FTP, or rcp server and subsequently interpreted by technical personnel who have access to source code and detailed memory maps.

This command is useful to troubleshoot memory leaks.

The size is checked every 60 seconds. If you enter a size that is greater than the free memory, a core dump and router reload is generated after 60 seconds.

The **exception dump** command must be configured in order to generate a core file. If the **exception dump** command is not configured, the router reloads without generating a core dump.

Example

The following example configures the router to monitor the free memory. If the amount of free memory falls below 250,000 bytes, the router will dump the core file and reload.

```
exception dump 131.108.92.2
exception core-file memory.overrun
exception memory minimum 250000
```

Related Commands

exception core-file
exception dump
exception protocol
ip ftp password
ip ftp username

EXCEPTION PROTOCOL

To configure the protocol used for core dumps, use the **exception protocol** global configuration command. To configure the router to use the default protocol, use the **no** form of this command.

exception protocol {ftp | rcp | tftp}
no exception protocol

Syntax	Description
ftp	Use FTP for core dumps.
rcp	Use rcp for core dumps.
tftp	Use TFTP for core dumps. This is the default.

Default

TFTP

Command Mode

Global configuration

Usage Guidelines

This command first appeared in Cisco IOS Release 10.3.

CAUTION

Use the **exception** commands only under the direction of a technical support representative. Creating a core dump while the router is functioning in a network can disrupt network operation. The resulting binary file, which is very large, must be transferred to a TFTP, FTP, or rcp server and subsequently interpreted by technical personnel who have access to source code and detailed memory maps.

If you use TFTP to dump the core file to a server, the router will dump only the first 16 MB of the core file. If the router's memory is larger than 16 MB, the whole core file will not be copied to the server. Therefore, use rcp or FTP to dump the core file.

Example

The following example configures a router to use FTP to dump a core file to the FTP server at 172.17.92.2 when it crashes:

```
ip ftp username red
ip ftp password blue
exception protocol ftp
exception dump 172.17.92.2
```

Related Commands

exception core-file
exception dump
exception memory
ip ftp password
ip ftp username

IP FTP PASSIVE

To configure the router to use only passive FTP connections, use the **ip ftp passive** global configuration command. To allow all types of FTP connections, use the **no** form of this command.

> **ip ftp passive**
> **no ip ftp passive**

Syntax Description

This command has no arguments or keywords.

Default

All types of FTP connections are allowed.

Command Mode

Global configuration

Usage Guidelines

This command first appeared in Cisco IOS Release 10.3.

Example

The following example configures the router to use only passive FTP connections:

```
ip ftp passive
```

Related Commands

ip ftp password
ip ftp source-interface
ip ftp username

IP FTP PASSWORD

To specify the password to be used for FTP connections, use the **ip ftp password** global configuration command. Use the **no** form of this command to return the password to its default.

> **ip ftp password** [*type*] *password*
> **no ip ftp password**

Syntax Description

type	(Optional) Type of encryption to use on the password. A value of 0 disables encryption. A value of 7 indicates proprietary encryption.
password	Password to use for FTP connections.

Default

The router forms a password *username@routername.domain*. The variable *username* is the username associated with the current session, *routername* is the configured host name, and *domain* is the domain of the router.

Command Mode

Global configuration

Usage Guidelines

This command first appeared in Cisco IOS Release 10.3.

Example

The following example configures the router to use the username *red* and the password *blue* for FTP connections:

```
ip ftp username red
ip ftp password blue
```

Related Commands

ip ftp passive
ip ftp source-interface
ip ftp username

IP FTP SOURCE-INTERFACE

To specify the source IP address for FTP connections, use the **ip ftp source-interface** global configuration command. Use the **no** form of this command to use the address of the interface where the connection is made.

ip ftp source-interface *interface*
no ip ftp source-interface

Syntax	Description
interface	The interface type and number to use to obtain the source address for FTP connections.

Default

The FTP source address is the IP address of the interface the FTP packets use to leave the router.

Command Mode

Global configuration

Usage Guidelines

This command first appeared in Cisco IOS Release 10.3.

Use this command to set the same source address for all FTP connections.

Example

The following example configures the router to use the IP address associated with the Ethernet 0 interface as the source address on all FTP packets, regardless of which interface is actually used to transmit the packet:

```
ip ftp source-interface ethernet 0
```

Related Commands

ip ftp passive
ip ftp password
ip ftp username

IP FTP USERNAME

To configure the username for FTP connections, use the **ip ftp username** global configuration command. To configure the router to attempt anonymous FTP, use the **no** form of this command.

> **ip ftp username** *username*
> **no ip ftp username**

Syntax	Description
username	Username for FTP connections.

Default

The Cisco IOS software attempts an anonymous FTP.

Command Mode

Global configuration

Usage Guidelines

This command first appeared in Cisco IOS Release 10.3.

The remote username must be associated with an account on the destination server.

Example

The following example configures the router to use the username *red* and the password *blue* for FTP connections:

```
ip ftp username red
ip ftp password blue
```

Related Commands

ip ftp passive
ip ftp password
ip ftp source-interface

LOGGING

To log messages to a syslog server host, use the **logging** global configuration command. The **no** form of this command deletes the syslog server with the specified address from the list of syslogs.

>   **logging** *host*
>   **no logging** *host*

Syntax	*Description*
host	Name or IP address of the host to be used as a syslog server.

Default

No messages are logged to a syslog server host.

Command Mode

Global configuration

Usage Guidelines

This command first appeared in Cisco IOS Release 10.0.

This command identifies a syslog server host to receive logging messages. By issuing this command more than once, you build a list of syslog servers that receive logging messages.

Example

The following example logs messages to a host named *johnson*:

```
logging johnson
```

Related Commands

logging trap
service timestamps

LOGGING BUFFERED

To log messages to an internal buffer, use the **logging buffered** global configuration command. The **no** form of this command cancels the use of the buffer. The **default** form of this command returns the buffer size to the default size.

logging buffered [*size*]
no logging buffered
default logging buffered

Syntax	Description
size	(Optional) Size of the buffer from 4,096 to 4,294,967,295 bytes. The default size varies by platform.

Default

For most platforms, the Cisco IOS software logs messages to the internal buffer.

Command Mode

Global configuration

Usage Guidelines

This command first appeared in Cisco IOS Release 10.0.

This command copies logging messages to an internal buffer. The buffer is circular in nature, so newer messages overwrite older messages after the buffer is filled.

To display the messages that are logged in the buffer, use the EXEC command **show logging**. The first message displayed is the oldest message in the buffer.

Do not make the buffer size too large, because the router could run out of memory for other tasks. You can use the **show memory** EXEC command to view the free processor memory on the router; however, this is the maximum available and should not be approached. The command **default logging buffered** resets the buffer size to the default for the platform.

Example

The following example enables logging to an internal buffer:

```
logging buffered
```

Related Commands

clear logging
show logging

LOGGING CONSOLE

To limit messages logged to the console based on severity, use the **logging console** global configuration command. The **no** form of this command disables logging to the console terminal.

> **logging console** *level*
> **no logging console**

Part IV

Command Reference

Syntax

level

Description

Limits the logging of messages displayed on the console terminal to a specified level. See Table 29–1 for a list of the *level* keywords.

Default

debugging

Command Mode

Global configuration

Usage Guidelines

This command first appeared in Cisco IOS Release 10.0.

Specifying a *level* causes messages at that level and numerically lower levels to be displayed at the console terminal.

The EXEC command **show logging** displays the addresses and levels associated with the current logging setup, as well as any other logging statistics.

Table 29–1 *Error Message Logging Priorities*

Level Name	Level	Description	Syslog Definition
emergencies	0	System unusable	LOG_EMERG
alerts	1	Immediate action needed	LOG_ALERT
critical	2	Critical conditions	LOG_CRIT
errors	3	Error conditions	LOG_ERR
warnings	4	Warning conditions	LOG_WARNING
notifications	5	Normal but significant condition	LOG_NOTICE
informational	6	Informational messages only	LOG_INFO
debugging	7	Debugging messages	LOG_DEBUG

The effect of the **log** keyword with the IP **access list** (**extended**) command depends on the setting of the **logging console** command. The **log** keyword takes effect only if the logging console level is set to 6 or 7. If you change the default to a level lower than 6 and specify the **log** keyword with the IP **access list** (**extended**) command, no information is logged or displayed.

Example

The following example changes the level of messages displayed to the console terminal to **alerts,** which means alerts and emergencies are displayed:

```
logging console alerts
```

Related Commands

logging facility
access-list (extended)

LOGGING FACILITY

To configure the syslog facility in which error messages are sent, use the **logging facility** global configuration command. To revert to the default of **local7,** use the **no** form of this command.

> **logging facility** *facility-type*
> **no logging facility**

Syntax	Description
facility-type	Syslog facility. See Table 29–2 for the *facility-type* keywords.

Default

local7

Command Mode

Global configuration

Usage Guidelines

This command first appeared in Cisco IOS Release 10.0.

Table 29–2 describes the acceptable options for the *facility-type* keyword.

Table 29–2 *Logging Facility-Type Keywords*

Keyword	Description
auth	Authorization system
cron	Cron facility
daemon	System daemon
kern	Kernel
local0–7	Reserved for locally defined messages
lpr	Line printer system

Table 29–2   *Logging Facility-Type Keywords, Continued*

Keyword	Description
mail	Mail system
news	USENET news
sys9	System use
sys10	System use
sys11	System use
sys12	System use
sys13	System use
sys14	System use
syslog	System log
user	User process
uucp	UNIX-to-UNIX copy system

Example

The following example configures the syslog facility to the kernel facility type.

```
logging facility kern
```

Related Commands

logging console

LOGGING HISTORY

To limit syslog messages sent to the router's history table and the SNMP network management station based on severity, use the **logging history** global configuration command. The **no** form of this command returns the logging of syslog messages to the default level.

    logging history *level*
    no logging history

Syntax	Description
level	Limits the messages saved in the history table and sent to the SNMP network management station to the specified set of levels. See Table 29–3 for a list of the *level* keywords.

Default

warnings, errors, critical, alerts, and **emergencies** messages

Command Mode

Global configuration

Usage Guidelines

This command first appeared in Cisco IOS Release 11.2.

Sending syslog messages to the SNMP network management station occurs when you enable syslog traps with the **snmp-server enable trap** global configuration command. Because SNMP traps are inherently unreliable and much too important to lose, at least one syslog message (the most recent message) is stored in a history table on the router. The number of messages stored in the table is governed by the **logging history size** command.

Specifying a *level* causes messages at that severity level and numerically lower levels to be stored in the router's history table and sent to the SNMP network management station. Severity levels are numbered 1 to 8 with 1 being the most important message and 8 being the least important message (that is, the lower the number, the more critical the message). For example, specifying the level **critical** causes critical (3), alerts (2), and emergencies (1) messages to be stored to the history table and sent to the SNMP network management station. See Table 29–3 for a list of severity levels.

The EXEC command **show logging history** displays information about the history table such as the table size, the status of messages, and text of the messages stored in the table.

Table 29–3 *Error Message Logging Priorities for History Table and SNMP Server*

Level Keyword	Severity Level	Description	Syslog Definition
emergencies	1	System unusable	LOG_EMERG
alerts	2	Immediate action needed	LOG_ALERT
critical	3	Critical conditions	LOG_CRIT
errors	4	Error conditions	LOG_ERR
warnings	5	Warning conditions	LOG_WARNING
notifications	6	Normal but significant condition	LOG_NOTICE
informational	7	Informational messages only	LOG_INFO
debugging	8	Debugging messages	LOG_DEBUG

Part
IV

Command Reference

Example

The following example changes the level of messages sent to the history table and to the SNMP server to **alerts,** which means alerts (2) and emergencies (1) are sent:

```
logging history alerts
```

Related Commands

logging history size
show logging
snmp-server enable traps

LOGGING HISTORY SIZE

To change the number of syslog messages stored in the router's history table, use the **logging history size** global configuration command. The **no** form of this command returns the number of messages to the default value.

> **logging history size** *number*
> **no logging history size**

Syntax   *Description*

number   Number from 1 to 500 that indicates the maximum number of messages stored in the history table.

Default

1 message

Command Mode

Global configuration

Usage Guidelines

This command first appeared in Cisco IOS Release 11.2.

When the history table is full (that is, it contains the maximum number of message entries specified with the **logging history size** command), the oldest message entry is deleted from the table to allow the new message entry to be stored.

Example

The following example sets the number of messages stored in the history table to 20:

```
logging history size 20
```

Related Commands

logging history
show logging

LOGGING MONITOR

To limit messages logged to the terminal lines (monitors) based on severity, use the **logging monitor** global configuration command. This command limits the logging messages displayed on terminal lines other than the console line to messages with a level at or above *level*. The **no** form of this command disables logging to terminal lines other than the console line.

> **logging monitor** *level*
> **no logging monitor**

Syntax	*Description*
level	One of the *level* keywords listed in Table 29–1.

Default

debugging

Command Mode

Global configuration

Usage Guidelines

This command first appeared in Cisco IOS Release 10.0.

Specifying a *level* causes messages at that level and numerically lower levels to be displayed to the monitor.

Example

The following example specifies that only messages of the levels **errors, critical, alerts,** and **emergencies** be displayed on terminals:

```
logging monitor errors
```

Related Commands

terminal monitor

LOGGING ON

To control logging of error messages, use the **logging on** global configuration command. This command sends debug or error messages to a logging process, which logs messages to designated locations asynchronously to the processes that generated the messages. The **no** form of this command disables the logging process.

logging on
no logging on

Syntax   Description

This command has no arguments or keywords.

Default

The Cisco IOS software sends messages to the asynchronous logging process.

Command Mode

Global configuration

Usage Guidelines

This command first appeared in Cisco IOS Release 10.0.

The logging process controls the distribution of logging messages to the various destinations, such as the logging buffer, terminal lines, or syslog server. You can turn logging on and off for these destinations individually using the **logging buffered, logging monitor**, and **logging** commands. However, if the **logging on** command is disabled, no messages are sent to these destinations. Only the console receives messages.

Additionally, the logging process logs messages to the console and the various destinations after the processes that generated them have completed. When the logging process is disabled, messages are displayed on the console as soon as they are produced, often appearing in the middle of command output.

CAUTION

Disabling the **logging on** command significantly slows down the router. Any process generating debug or error messages will wait until the messages have been displayed on the console before continuing.

The **logging synchronous** command also affects the displaying of messages to the console. When the **logging synchronous** command is enabled, messages will appear only after the user types a carriage return.

Examples

The following example shows command output and message output when logging is enabled. The ping process finishes before any of the logging information is printed to the console (or any other destination).

```
Router(config)# logging on
Router(config)# end
Router#
```

```
%SYS-5-CONFIG_I: Configured from console by console
Router# ping dirt

Type escape sequence to abort.
Sending 5, 100-byte ICMP Echos to 172.16.1.129, timeout is 2 seconds:
!!!!!
Success rate is 100 percent (5/5), round-trip min/avg/max = 4/5/8 ms
Router#
IP: s=172.21.96.41 (local), d=172.16.1.129 (Ethernet1/0), len 100, sending
IP: s=171.69.1.129 (Ethernet1/0), d=172.21.96.41, len 114, rcvd 1
IP: s=172.21.96.41 (local), d=172.16.1.129 (Ethernet1/0), len 100, sending
IP: s=171.69.1.129 (Ethernet1/0), d=172.21.96.41, len 114, rcvd 1
IP: s=172.21.96.41 (local), d=172.16.1.129 (Ethernet1/0), len 100, sending
IP: s=171.69.1.129 (Ethernet1/0), d=172.21.96.41, len 114, rcvd 1
IP: s=172.21.96.41 (local), d=172.16.1.129 (Ethernet1/0), len 100, sending
IP: s=171.69.1.129 (Ethernet1/0), d=172.21.96.41, len 114, rcvd 1
IP: s=172.21.96.41 (local), d=172.16.1.129 (Ethernet1/0), len 100, sending
IP: s=171.69.1.129 (Ethernet1/0), d=172.21.96.41, len 114, rcvd 1
```

In the next example, logging is disabled. The message output is displayed as messages are generated, causing the debug messages to be interspersed with the message, "Type escape sequence to abort."

```
Router(config)# no logging on
Router(config)# end

%SYS-5-CONFIG_I: Configured from console by console
Router#
Router# ping dirt

IP: s=172.21.96.41 (local), d=172.16.1.129 (Ethernet1/0), len 100, sendingTyp
IP: s=171.69.1.129 (Ethernet1/0), d=172.21.96.41, len 114, rcvd 1e
IP: s=172.21.96.41 (local), d=172.16.1.129 (Ethernet1/0), len 100, sending esc
IP: s=171.69.1.129 (Ethernet1/0), d=172.21.96.41, len 114, rcvd 1
IP: s=172.21.96.41 (local), d=172.16.1.129 (Ethernet1/0), len 100, sendingape
IP: s=171.69.1.129 (Ethernet1/0), d=172.21.96.41, len 114, rcvd 1
IP: s=172.21.96.41 (local), d=172.16.1.129 (Ethernet1/0), len 100, sendingse
IP: s=171.69.1.129 (Ethernet1/0), d=172.21.96.41, len 114, rcvd 1
IP: s=172.21.96.41 (local), d=172.16.1.129 (Ethernet1/0), len 100, sendingquen
IP: s=171.69.1.129 (Ethernet1/0), d=172.21.96.41, len 114, rcvd 1ce to abort.
Sending 5, 100-byte ICMP Echos to 172.16.1.129, timeout is 2 seconds:
!!!!!
Success rate is 100 percent (5/5), round-trip min/avg/max = 152/152/156 ms
Router#
```

Related Commands

logging
logging buffered
logging monitor
logging synchronous

LOGGING SOURCE-INTERFACE

To specify the source IP address of syslog packets, use the **logging source-interface** global configuration command. Use the **no** form of this command to remove the source designation.

> **logging source-interface** *type number*
> **no logging source-interface**

Syntax	Description
type	Interface type.
number	Interface number.

Default

No interface is specified.

Command Mode

Global configuration

Usage Guidelines

This command first appeared in Cisco IOS Release 11.2.

Normally, a syslog message contains the IP address of the interface it uses to leave the router. The **logging source-interface** command specifies that syslog packets contain the IP address of a particular interface, regardless of which interface the packet uses to exit the router.

Examples

The following example specifies that the IP address for Ethernet interface 0 is the source IP address for all syslog messages:

```
logging source-interface ethernet 0
```

The following example specifies that the IP address for Ethernet interface 2/1 on a Cisco 7000 series router is the source IP address for all syslog messages:

```
logging source-interface ethernet 2/1
```

Related Commands

logging

LOGGING SYNCHRONOUS

To synchronize unsolicited messages and debug output with solicited Cisco IOS software output and prompts for a specific console port line, auxiliary port line, or virtual terminal line, use the **logging synchronous** line configuration command. Use the **no** form of this command to disable synchronization of unsolicited messages and debug output.

logging synchronous [**level** *severity-level* | **all**] [**limit** *number-of-buffers*]
no logging synchronous [**level** *severity-level* | **all**] [**limit** *number-of-buffers*]

Syntax	Description
level *severity-level*	(Optional) Specifies the message severity level. Messages with a severity level equal to or higher than this value are printed asynchronously. Low numbers indicate greater severity and high numbers indicate lesser severity. The default value is 2.
all	(Optional) Specifies that all messages are printed asynchronously, regardless of the severity level.
limit *number-of-buffers*	(Optional) Specifies the number of buffers to be queued for the terminal after which new messages are dropped. The default value is 20.

Defaults

This feature is turned off by default.

If you do not specify a severity level, the default value of 2 is assumed.

If you do not specify the maximum number of buffers to be queued, the default value of 20 is assumed.

Command Mode

Line configuration

Usage Guidelines

This command first appeared in Cisco IOS Release 10.0.

When synchronous logging of unsolicited messages and debug output is turned on, unsolicited Cisco IOS software output is displayed on the console or printed after solicited Cisco IOS software output is displayed or printed. Unsolicited messages and debug output are displayed on the console after the prompt for user input is returned. This is to keep unsolicited messages and debug output from being interspersed with solicited software output and prompts. After the unsolicited messages are displayed, the console displays the user prompt again.

When specifying a severity level number, consider that for the logging system, low numbers indicate greater severity and high numbers indicate lesser severity.

When a terminal line's message-queue limit is reached, new messages are dropped from the line, although these messages might be displayed on other lines. If messages are dropped, the notice "%SYS-3-MSGLOST *number-of-messages* due to overflow" follows any messages that are displayed. This notice is displayed only on the terminal that lost the messages. It is not sent to any other lines, any logging servers, or the logging buffer.

___CAUTION___

By configuring abnormally large message-queue limits and setting the terminal to "terminal moni-tor" on a terminal that is accessible to intruders, you expose yourself to "denial of service" attacks. An intruder could carry out the attack by putting the terminal in synchronous output mode, making a Telnet connection to a remote host, and leaving the connection idle. This could cause large num-bers of messages to be generated and queued, and these messages would consume all available RAM. Although unlikely to occur, you should guard against this type of attack through proper config-uration.

Example

The following example identifies line 4 and enables synchronous logging for line 4 with a severity level of 6. Then the example identifies another line, line 2, and enables synchronous logging for line 2 with a severity level of 7 and specifies a maximum number of buffers to be 70,000:

```
line 4
logging synchronous level 6
line 2
logging synchronous level 7 limit 70000
```

Related Commands

line
logging on

LOGGING TRAP

To limit messages logged to the syslog servers based on severity, use the **logging trap** global config-uration command. The command limits the logging of error messages sent to syslog servers to only those messages at the specified level. Use the **no** form of this command to disable logging to syslog servers.

> **logging trap** *level*
> **no logging trap**

Syntax	*Description*
level	One of the *level* keywords listed in Table 29–1.

Default

Informational

Command Mode

Global configuration

Usage Guidelines

This command first appeared in Cisco IOS Release 10.0.

The EXEC command **show logging** displays the addresses and levels associated with the current logging setup. The command output also includes ancillary statistics.

Table 29–1 lists the syslog definitions that correspond to the debugging message levels. Additionally, there are four categories of messages generated by the software, as follows:

- Error messages about software or hardware malfunctions at the LOG_ERR level.
- Output for the **debug** commands at the LOG_WARNING level.
- Interface up/down transitions and system restarts at the LOG_NOTICE level.
- Reload requests and low process stacks are at the LOG_INFO level.

Use the **logging** and **logging trap** commands to send messages to a UNIX syslog server.

Example

The following example logs messages to a host named *johnson*:

```
logging johnson
logging trap notifications
```

Related Commands

logging

PING (PRIVILEGED)

Use the **ping** (packet internet groper) privileged EXEC command to diagnose basic network connectivity on Apollo, AppleTalk, Connectionless Network Service (CLNS), DECnet, IP, Novell IPX, VINES, or XNS networks.

    ping [*protocol*] {*host* | *address*}

Syntax	Description
protocol	(Optional) Protocol keyword, one of **apollo**, **appletalk**, **clns**, **decnet**, **ip**, **ipx**, **vines**, or **xns**.
host	Host name of system to ping.
address	Address of system to ping.

Command Mode

Privileged EXEC

Usage Guidelines

This command first appeared in Cisco IOS Release 10.0.

The ping program sends an echo request packet to an address, then awaits a reply. Ping output can help you evaluate path-to-host reliability, delays over the path, and whether the host can be reached or is functioning.

To terminate a ping session abnormally, type the escape sequence—by default, **Ctrl-^ X**. You type the default by simultaneously pressing and releasing the **Ctrl, Shift,** and **6** keys, and then pressing the **X** key.

Table 29–4 describes the test characters that the ping facility sends.

Table 29-4 *Ping Test Characters*

Char	Meaning
!	Each exclamation point indicates receipt of a reply.
.	Each period indicates the network server timed out while waiting for a reply.
U	A destination unreachable error PDU was received.
C	A congestion experienced packet was received.
I	User interrupted test.
?	Unknown packet type.
&	Packet lifetime exceeded.

NOTES

Not all protocols require hosts to support pings. For some protocols, the pings are Cisco-defined and are answered only by another Cisco router.

Example

After you enter the **ping** command in privileged mode, the system prompts for one of the following keywords: **appletalk, clns, ip, novell, apollo, vines, decnet,** or **xns.** The default protocol is IP.

If you enter a host name or address on the same line as the **ping** command, the default action is taken as appropriate for the protocol type of that name or address.

While the precise dialog varies somewhat from protocol to protocol, all are similar to the ping session using default values shown in the following display.

```
Router# ping
Protocol [ip]:
Target IP address: 192.168.7.27
Repeat count [5]:
```

```
Datagram size [100]:
Timeout in seconds [2]:
Extended commands [n]:
Sweep range of sizes [n]:
Type escape sequence to abort.
Sending 5, 100-byte ICMP Echos to 192.168.7.27, timeout is 2 seconds:
!!!!!
Success rate is 100 percent, round-trip min/avg/max = 1/2/4 ms
```

Table 29–5 describes the default **ping** fields shown in the display.

Table 29–5 *Ping Field Descriptions*

Field	Description
Protocol [ip]:	Prompts for a supported protocol. Enter **appletalk, clns, ip, novell, apollo, vines, decnet,** or **xns**. Default: **ip**.
Target IP address:	Prompts for the IP address or host name of the destination node you plan to ping. If you have specified a supported protocol other than IP, enter an appropriate address for that protocol here. Default: none.
Repeat count [5]:	Number of ping packets that will be sent to the destination address. Default: 5.
Datagram size [100]:	Size of the ping packet (in bytes). Default: 100 bytes.
Timeout in seconds [2]:	Timeout interval. Default: 2 (seconds).
Extended commands [n]:	Specifies whether a series of additional commands appears. Many of the following displays and tables show and describe these commands.
Sweep range of sizes [n]:	Allows you to vary the sizes of the echo packets being sent. This capability is useful for determining the minimum sizes of the MTUs configured on the nodes along the path to the destination address. Packet fragmentation contributing to performance problems can then be reduced.
!!!!!	Each exclamation point (!) indicates receipt of a reply. A period (.) indicates the network server timed out while waiting for a reply. Other characters might appear in the ping output display, depending on the protocol type.
Success rate is 100 percent	Percentage of packets successfully echoed back to the router. Anything less than 80 percent is usually considered problematic.
round-trip min/avg/ max = 1/2/4 ms	Round-trip travel time intervals for the protocol echo packets, including minimum/average/maximum (in milliseconds).

Part
IV

Command Reference

Related Commands

ping (user)

PING (USER)

Use the **ping** (packet internet groper) user EXEC command to diagnose basic network connectivity on AppleTalk, CLNS, IP, Novell, Apollo, VINES, DECnet, or XNS networks.

> **ping** [*protocol*] {*host* | *address*}

Syntax	Description
protocol	(Optional) Protocol keyword, one of **apollo, appletalk, clns, decnet, ip, ipx, vines,** or **xns.**
host	Host name of system to ping.
address	Address of system to ping.

Command Mode

EXEC

Usage Guidelines

This command first appeared in Cisco IOS Release 10.0.

The user-level ping feature provides a basic ping facility for users who do not have system privileges. This feature allows the Cisco IOS software to perform the simple default ping functionality for a number of protocols. Only the terse form of the **ping** command is supported for user-level pings.

If the system cannot map an address for a host name, it returns an "%Unrecognized host or address" error message.

To terminate a ping session abnormally, type the escape sequence—by default, **Ctrl-^ X**. You type the default by simultaneously pressing and releasing the **Ctrl, Shift,** and **6** keys and then pressing the **X** key.

Table 29–6 describes the test characters that the ping facility sends.

Table 29–6 *Ping Test Characters*

Char	Meaning
!	Each exclamation point indicates receipt of a reply.
.	Each period indicates the network server timed out while waiting for a reply.
U	A destination unreachable error PDU was received.
C	A congestion experienced packet was received.

Table 29-6 *Ping Test Characters, Continued*

Char	Meaning
I	User interrupted test.
?	Unknown packet type.
&	Packet lifetime exceeded.

Example

The following display shows sample ping output when you ping the IP host named *donald*:

```
Router> ping donald
Type escape sequence to abort.
Sending 5, 100-byte ICMP Echos to 192.168.7.27, timeout is 2 seconds:
!!!!!
Success rate is 100 percent, round-trip min/avg/max = 1/3/4 ms
```

Related Commands

ping (privileged)

SERVICE SLAVE-LOG

To allow slave Versatile Interface Processor (VIP) cards to log important error messages to the console, use the **service slave-log** global configuration command. Use the **no** form of this command to disable slave logging.

> service slave-log
> no service slave-log

Syntax   Description

This command has no arguments or keywords.

Default

This command is enabled by default.

Command Mode

Global configuration

Usage Guidelines

This command first appeared in Cisco IOS Release 11.1.

This command allows slave slots to log error messages of level 2 or higher (critical, alerts, and emergencies).

Part
IV

Command Reference

Examples

The following example logs important messages from the slave cards to the console:

```
service slave-log
```

The following example illustrates sample output when this command is enabled:

```
%IPC-5-SLAVELOG: VIP-SLOT2:
  IPC-2-NOMEM: No memory available for IPC system initialization
```

The first line indicates which slot sent the message. The second line contains the error message.

SERVICE TCP-KEEPALIVES-IN

To generate keepalive packets on idle incoming network connections (initiated by the remote host), use the **service tcp-keepalives-in** global configuration command. The **no** form of this command with the appropriate keyword disables the keepalives.

> **service tcp-keepalives-in**
> **no service tcp-keepalives-in**

Syntax   Description

This command has no arguments or keywords.

Default

Disabled

Command Mode

Global configuration

Usage Guidelines

This command first appeared in Cisco IOS Release 10.0.

Example

The following example generates keepalives on incoming TCP connections:

```
service tcp-keepalives-in
```

Related Commands

service tcp-keepalives-out

SERVICE TCP-KEEPALIVES-OUT

To generate keepalive packets on idle outgoing network connections (initiated by a user), use the **service tcp-keepalives-out** global configuration command. The **no** form of this command with the appropriate keyword disables the keepalives.

service tcp-keepalives-out
no service tcp-keepalives-out

Syntax   Description

This command has no arguments or keywords.

Default

Disabled

Command Mode

Global configuration

Usage Guidelines

This command first appeared in Cisco IOS Release 10.0.

Example

The following example generates keepalives on outgoing TCP connections:

```
service tcp-keepalives-out
```

Related Commands

service tcp-keepalives-in

SERVICE TIMESTAMPS

To configure the system to timestamp debugging or logging messages, use one of the **service timestamps** global configuration commands. Use the **no** form of this command to disable this service.

service **timestamps** *type* [**uptime**]
service **timestamps** *type* **datetime** [**msec**] [**localtime**] [**show-timezone**]
no service **timestamps** *type*

Syntax	*Description*
type	Type of message to timestamp: **debug** or **log**.
uptime	(Optional) Timestamp with time since the system was rebooted.
datetime	Timestamp with the date and time.
msec	(Optional) Include milliseconds in the date and timestamp.
localtime	(Optional) Timestamp relative to the local time zone.
show-timezone	(Optional) Include the time zone name in the timestamp.

Default

No timestamping.

If **service timestamps** is specified with no arguments or keywords, default is **service timestamps debug uptime**.

The default for **service timestamps** *type* **datetime** is to format the time in UTC, with no milliseconds and no time zone name.

The command **no service timestamps** by itself disables timestamps for both debug and log messages.

Command Mode

Global configuration

Usage Guidelines

This command first appeared in Cisco IOS Release 10.0.

Timestamps can be added to either debugging or logging messages independently. The **uptime** form of the command adds timestamps in the format HHHH:MM:SS, indicating the time since the system was rebooted. The **datetime** form of the command adds timestamps in the format MMM DD HH:MM:SS, indicating the date and time according to the system clock. If the system clock has not been set, the date and time are preceded by an asterisk (*) to indicate that the date and time are probably not correct.

Examples

The following example enables timestamps on debugging messages, showing the time since reboot:

```
service timestamps debug uptime
```

The following example enables timestamps on logging messages, showing the current time and date relative to the local time zone, with the time zone name included:

```
service timestamps log datetime localtime show-timezone
```

Related Commands

clock set
debug
ntp

SHOW C7200

Use the **show c7200** EXEC command to display information about the CPU and midplane for Cisco 7200 series routers.

> **show c7200**

Syntax   Description

This command has no arguments or keywords.

Command Mode

EXEC

Usage Guidelines

This command first appeared in Cisco IOS Release 11.2.

You can use the output of this command to determine whether the hardware version level and upgrade are current. The information is generally useful for diagnostic tasks performed by technical support only.

Sample Display

The following is sample output from the **show c7200** command:

```
Router# show c7200

C7200 Network IO Interrupt Throttling:
 throttle count=0, timer count=0
 active=0, configured=0
 netint usec=3999, netint mask usec=200

C7200 Midplane EEPROM:
        Hardware revision 1.2        Board revision A0
        Serial number    2863311530  Part number    170-43690-170
        Test history     0xAA        RMA number     170-170-170
        MAC=0060.3e28.ee00, MAC Size=1024
        EEPROM format version 1, Model=0x6
        EEPROM contents (hex):
          0x20: 01 06 01 02 AA AA AA AA AA AA AA AA 00 60 3E 28
          0x30: EE 00 04 00 AA AA AA AA AA AA AA 50 AA AA AA AA

C7200 CPU EEPROM:
        Hardware revision 2.0        Board revision A0
        Serial number    3509953     Part number    73-1536-02
        Test history     0x0         RMA number     00-00-00
        EEPROM format version 1
        EEPROM contents (hex):
          0x20: 01 15 02 00 00 35 8E C1 49 06 00 02 00 00 00 00
          0x30: 50 00 00 00 FF FF FF FF FF FF FF FF FF FF FF FF
```

SHOW CONTEXT

Use the **show context** EXEC command to display information stored in NVRAM when the router crashes. This command works only on the Cisco 7000 family platforms.

> **show context**

Syntax   Description

This command has no arguments or keywords.

Command Mode

EXEC

Usage Guidelines

This command first appeared in Cisco IOS Release 10.3.

The display from the **show context** command includes the following information:

- Reason for the system reboot
- Stack trace
- Software version
- The signal number, code, and router uptime information
- All the register contents at the time of the crash

This information is of use only to your technical support representative in analyzing crashes in the field. It is included here in case you need to read the displayed statistics to an engineer over the phone.

Sample Display

The following is sample output from the **show context** command following a system failure:

```
Router> show context

System was restarted by error - a Software forced crash, PC 0x60189354
GS Software (RSP-PV-M), Experimental Version 11.1(2033) [ganesh 111]
Compiled Mon 31-Mar-97 13:21 by ganesh
Image text-base: 0x60010900, data-base: 0x6073E000
Stack trace from system failure:
FP: 0x60AEA798, RA: 0x60189354
FP: 0x60AEA798, RA: 0x601853CC
FP: 0x60AEA7C0, RA: 0x6015E98C
FP: 0x60AEA7F8, RA: 0x6011AB3C
FP: 0x60AEA828, RA: 0x601706CC
FP: 0x60AEA878, RA: 0x60116340
FP: 0x60AEA890, RA: 0x6011632C
Fault History Buffer:
GS Software (RSP-PV-M), Experimental Version 11.1(2033) [ganesh 111]
Compiled Mon 31-Mar-97 13:21 by ganesh
Signal = 23, Code = 0x24, Uptime 00:04:19
$0 : 00000000, AT : 60930120, v0 : 00000032, v1 : 00000120
a0 : 60170110, a1 : 6097F22C, a2 : 00000000, a3 : 00000000
t0 : 60AE02A0, t1 : 8000FD80, t2 : 34008F00, t3 : FFFF00FF
t4 : 00000083, t5 : 3E840024, t6 : 00000000, t7 : 11010132
s0 : 00000006, s1 : 607A25F8, s2 : 00000001, s3 : 00000000
s4 : 00000000, s5 : 00000000, s6 : 00000000, s7 : 6097F755
t8 : 600FABBC, t9 : 00000000, k0 : 30408401, k1 : 30410000
gp : 608B9860, sp : 60AEA798, s8 : 00000000, ra : 601853CC
EPC : 60189354, SREG : 3400EF03, Cause : 00000024
```

Related Commands

show processes
show stacks

SHOW DEBUGGING

To display information about the types of debugging that are enabled for your router, use the **show debugging** privileged EXEC command.

show debugging

Syntax   Description

This command has no arguments or keywords.

Command Mode

Privileged EXEC

Usage Guidelines

This command first appeared in Cisco IOS Release 11.1.

Sample Display

The following is sample output from the **show debugging** command. In this example, three types of CDP debugging are enabled.

```
Router# show debugging

CDP:
   CDP packet info debugging is on
   CDP events debugging is on
   CDP neighbor info debugging is on
```

Related Commands

debug

SHOW ENVIRONMENT

Use the **show environment** EXEC command to display temperature and voltage information on the Cisco 7000 series, Cisco 7200 series, and Cisco 7500 series routers.

show environment [all | last | table]

Syntax	Description
all	(Optional) Displays a detailed listing of the power supplies, temperature readings, and voltage readings.
last	(Optional) Displays the reason for the last system shutdown that was related to voltage or temperature and the environmental status at that time.
table	(Optional) Displays the temperature and voltage thresholds and a table that lists the ranges of environmental measurements that are within specification.

Default

If no options are specified, the router displays the date and time that the environmental measurements were last checked and whether the environmental measurements were within specifications. For the Cisco 7500 series, the router displays only measurements that are out of normal range.

Command Mode

EXEC

Usage Guidelines

This command first appeared in Cisco IOS Release 10.0.

Once a minute, a routine is run that gets environmental measurements from sensors and stores the output into a buffer. This buffer is displayed on the console when **show environment** is invoked.

If a measurement exceeds desired margins, but has not exceeded fatal margins, a warning message is printed to the system console. The system software queries the sensors for measurements once a minute, but warnings for a given test point are printed at most once every hour for sensor readings in the warning range and once every five minutes for sensor readings in the critical range. If a measurement is out of line within these time segments, an automatic warning message appears on the console. As noted, you can query the environmental status with the **show environment** command at any time to determine whether a measurement is at the warning or critical tolerance.

If a shutdown occurs because of detection of fatal environmental margins, the last measured value from each sensor is stored in internal nonvolatile memory.

For environmental specifications, refer to the hardware installation and maintenance publication for your individual chassis.

Sample Displays

The following example shows the typical **show environment** display when there are no warning conditions in the system for the Cisco 7000 series and Cisco 7200 series. This information might vary slightly depending on the platform you are using. The date and time of the query are displayed, along with the data refresh information and a message indicating that there are no warning conditions.

```
Router> show environment

Environmental Statistics
    Environmental status as of 13:17:39 UTC Thu Jun 6 1996
    Data is 7 second(s) old, refresh in 53 second(s)

    All Environmental Measurements are within specifications
```

Table 29–7 describes the fields shown in the display.

Table 29–7   *Show Environment Field Descriptions*

Field	Description
Environmental status as of...	Current date and time.
Data is..., refresh in...	Environmental measurements are output into a buffer every 60 seconds, unless other higher-priority processes are running.
Status message	If environmental measurements are not within specifications, warning messages are displayed.

Sample Displays for the Cisco 7000 Series

The following are examples of messages that display on the system console when a measurement has exceeded an acceptable margin:

```
ENVIRONMENTAL WARNING: Air flow appears marginal.
ENVIRONMENTAL WARNING: Internal temperature measured 41.3(C)
ENVIRONMENTAL WARNING: +5 volt testpoint measured 5.310(V)
```

The system displays the following message if voltage or temperature exceeds maximum margins:

```
SHUTDOWN: air flow problem
```

In the following example, there have been two intermittent power failures since a router was turned on, and the lower power supply is not functioning. The last intermittent power failure occurred on Monday, June 10, 1996, at 11:07 p.m.

```
7000# show environment all

Environmental Statistics
    Environmental status as of 23:19:47 UTC Wed Jun 12 1996
    Data is 6 second(s) old, refresh in 54 second(s)

    WARNING: Lower Power Supply is NON-OPERATIONAL

    Lower Power Supply:700W, OFF    Upper Power Supply: 700W, ON

    Intermittent Powerfail(s): 2    Last on 23:07:05 UTC Mon Jun 10 1996
```

```
+12 volts measured at  12.05(V)
 +5 volts measured at   4.96(V)
-12 volts measured at -12.05(V)
+24 volts measured at  23.80(V)
Airflow temperature measured at 38(C)
Inlet temperature measured at 25(C)
```

Table 29–8 describes the fields shown in the display.

Table 29–8   *Show Environment All Field Descriptions for the Cisco 7000*

Field	Description
Environmental status as of...	Date and time of last query.
Data is..., refresh in...	Environmental measurements are output into a buffer every 60 seconds, unless other higher-priority processes are running.
WARNING:	If environmental measurements are not within specifications, warning messages are displayed.
Lower Power Supply	Type of power supply installed and its status (On or Off).
Upper Power Supply	Type of power supply installed and its status (On or Off).
Intermittent Powerfail(s)	Number of power hits (not resulting in shutdown) since the system was last booted.
Voltage specifications	System voltage measurements.
Airflow and inlet temperature	Temperature of air coming in and going out.

The following example is for the Cisco 7000 series router. The router retrieves the environmental statistics at the time of the last shutdown. In this example, the last shutdown was Friday, May 19, 1995, at 12:40 p.m., so the environmental statistics at that time are displayed:

```
Router# show environment last

Environmental Statistics
    Environmental status as of 14:47:00 UTC Sun May 21 1995
    Data is 6 second(s) old, refresh in 54 second(s)

    WARNING: Upper Power Supply is NON-OPERATIONAL

LAST Environmental Statistics
    Environmental status as of 12:40:00 UTC Fri May 19 1995
    Lower Power Supply: 700W, ON     Upper Power Supply: 700W, OFF

    No Intermittent Powerfails
```

```
 +12 volts measured at  12.05(V)
  +5 volts measured at   4.98(V)
 -12 volts measured at -12.00(V)
 +24 volts measured at  23.80(V)

Airflow temperature measured at 30(C)
Inlet   temperature measured at 23(C)
```

Table 29–9 describes the fields shown in the display.

Table 29–9 *Show Environment Last Field Descriptions for the Cisco 7000*

Field	Description
Environmental status as of...	Current date and time.
Data is..., refresh in...	Environmental measurements are output into a buffer every 60 seconds, unless other higher-priority processes are running.
WARNING:	If environmental measurements are not within specifications, warning messages are displayed.
LAST Environmental Statistics	Displays test point values at time of the last environmental shutdown.
Lower Power Supply: Upper Power Supply:	For the Cisco 7000, indicates the status of the two 700W power supplies. For the Cisco 7010, indicates the status of the single 600W power supply.

The following sample output shows the current environmental status in tables that list voltage and temperature parameters. There are three warning messages: one each about the lower power supply, the airflow temperature, and the inlet temperature. In this example, voltage parameters are shown to be in the normal range, airflow temperature is at a critical level, and inlet temperature is at the warning level:

```
Router> show environment table

Environmental Statistics
   Environmental status as of Mon 11-2-1992 17:43:36
   Data is 52 second(s) old, refresh in 8 second(s)

   WARNING: Lower Power Supply is NON-OPERATIONAL
   WARNING: Airflow temperature has reached CRITICAL level at 73(C)
   WARNING: Inlet temperature has reached WARNING level at 41(C)

Voltage Parameters:
```

```
SENSE        CRITICAL              NORMAL              CRITICAL
-------|-------------------|--------------------------|-------------------

+12(V)                    10.20      12.05(V)      13.80
 +5(V)                     4.74       4.98(V)       5.26
-12(V)                   -10.20     -12.05(V)     -13.80
+24(V)                    20.00      24.00(V)      28.00

Temperature Parameters:

SENSE     WARNING    NORMAL     WARNING     CRITICAL     SHUTDOWN
-------|-------------|------------|-------------|-------------|----------

Airflow        10          60          70    73(C)        88
Inlet          10          39    41(C)       46           64
```

Table 29–10 describes the fields shown in the display.

Table 29–10   *Show Environment Table Field Descriptions for the Cisco 7000*

Field	Description
SENSE (Voltage Parameters)	Voltage specification for DC line.
SENSE (Temperature Parameters)	Air being measured. Inlet measures the air coming in, and Airflow measures the temperature of the air inside the chassis.
WARNING	System is approaching an out-of-tolerance condition.
NORMAL	All monitored conditions meet normal requirements.
CRITICAL	Out-of-tolerance condition exists.
SHUTDOWN	Processor has detected condition that could cause physical damage to the system.

Sample Displays for the Cisco 7200 Series

The system displays the following message if the voltage or temperature enters the "Warning" range:

```
%ENVM-4-ENVWARN: Chassis outlet 3 measured at 55C/131F
```

The system displays the following message if the voltage or temperature enters the "Critical" range:

```
%ENVM-2-ENVCRIT: +3.45 V measured at +3.65 V
```

The system displays the following message if the voltage or temperature exceeds the maximum margins:

```
%ENVM-0-SHUTDOWN: Environmental Monitor initiated shutdown
```

The following message is sent to the console if a power supply has been inserted or removed from the system. This message relates only to systems that have two power supplies:

```
%ENVM-6-PSCHANGE: Power Supply 1 changed from Zytek AC Power Supply to removed
```

The following message is sent to the console if a power supply has been powered on or off. In the case of the power supply being shut off, this message can be due to the user shutting off the power supply or to a failed power supply. This message relates only to systems that have two power supplies:

```
%ENVM-6-PSLEV: Power Supply 1 state changed from normal to shutdown
```

The following is sample output from the **show environment all** command on the Cisco 7200 series router when there is a voltage warning condition in the system:

```
7200# show environment all

Power Supplies:
        Power supply 1 is unknown. Unit is off.
        Power supply 2 is Zytek AC Power Supply. Unit is on.

Temperature readings:
        chassis inlet    measured at 25C/77F
        chassis outlet 1 measured at 29C/84F
        chassis outlet 2 measured at 36C/96F
        chassis outlet 3 measured at 44C/111F
Voltage readings:
        +3.45 V measured at +3.83 V:Voltage in Warning range!
        +5.15 V measured at +5.09 V
        +12.15  measured at +12.42 V
        -11.95  measured at -12.10 V
```

Table 29–11 describes the fields shown in the display.

Table 29–11 *Show Environment All Field Descriptions for the Cisco 7200*

Field	Description
Power Supplies:	Current condition of the power supplies, including the type and whether the power supply is on or off.
Temperature readings:	Current measurements of the chassis temperature at the inlet and outlet locations.
Voltage readings:	Current measurement of the power supply test points.

The following example is for the Cisco 7200 series router. This example shows the measurements immediately before the last shutdown and the reason for the last shutdown (if appropriate).

```
7200# show environment last

        chassis inlet      previously measured at 27C/80F
        chassis outlet 1   previously measured at 31C/87F
        chassis outlet 2   previously measured at 37C/98F
        chassis outlet 3   previously measured at 45C/113F
        +3.3 V             previously measured at 4.02
        +5.0 V             previously measured at 4.92
```

```
  +12.0 V              previously measured at 12.65
  -12.0 V.             previously measured at 11.71

last shutdown reason - power supply shutdown
```

Table 29–12 describes the fields shown in the display.

Table 29–12   *Show Environment Last Field Descriptions for the Cisco 7200*

Field	Description
chassis inlet	Temperature measurements at the inlet area of the chassis.
chassis outlet	Temperature measurements at the outlet areas of the chassis.
voltages	Power supply test point measurements.
last shutdown reason	Possible shutdown reasons are power supply shutdown, critical temperature, and critical voltage.

The following example is for the Cisco 7200 series router. This information lists the temperature and voltage shutdown thresholds for each sensor.

```
7200# show environment table

Sample Point       LowCritical     LowWarning      HighWarning      HighCritical
chassis inlet                                      40C/104F         50C/122F
chassis outlet 1                                   43C/109F         53C/127F
chassis outlet 2                                   75C/167F         75C/167F
chassis outlet 3                                   55C/131F         65C/149F
+3.45 V            +2.76           +3.10           +3.80            +4.14
+5.15 V            +4.10           +4.61           +5.67            +6.17
+12.15 V           +9.72           +10.91          +13.37           +14.60
-11.95 V           -8.37           -9.57           -14.34           -15.53
Shutdown system at 70C/158F
```

Table 29–13 describes the fields shown in the display.

Table 29–13   *Show Environment Table Field Descriptions for the Cisco 7200*

Field	Description
Sample Point	Area for which measurements are taken.
LowCritical	Level at which a critical message is issued for an out-of-tolerance voltage condition. The system continues to operate; however, the system is approaching shutdown.
LowWarning	Level at which a warning message is issued for an out-of-tolerance voltage condition. The system continues to operate, but operator action is recommended to bring the system back to a normal state.

Table 29–13 *Show Environment Table Field Descriptions for the Cisco 7200, Continued*

Field	Description
HighWarning	Level at which a warning message is issued. The system continues to operate, but operator action is recommended to bring the system back to a normal state.
HighCritical	Level at which a critical message is issued. For the chassis, the router is shut down. For the power supply, the power supply is shut down.
Shutdown system at	The system is shut down if the specified temperature is met.

Sample Displays for the Cisco 7500 Series

The sample output for the Cisco 7500 series routers might vary depending on the specific model (for example, the Cisco 7513). The following is sample output from the **show environment all** command on the Cisco 7500 series router:

```
7500# show environment all

Arbiter type 1, backplane type 7513 (id 2)
Power supply #1 is 1200W AC (id 1), power supply #2 is removed (id 7)
Active fault conditions: none
Fan transfer point: 100%
Active trip points: Restart_Inhibit
15 of 15 soft shutdowns remaining before hard shutdown


                      1
              0123456789012
Dbus slots:   X     XX   X

card          inlet       hotpoint      exhaust
RSP(6)        35C/95F     47C/116F      40C/104F
RSP(7)        35C/95F     43C/109F      39C/102F

Shutdown temperature source is 'hotpoint' on RSP(6), requested RSP(6)

+12V measured at 12.31
+5V measured at 5.21
-12V measured at -12.07
+24V measured at 22.08
+2.5 reference is 2.49

PS1 +5V Current       measured at 59.61 A (capacity 200 A)
PS1 +12V Current      measured at 5.08 A (capacity 35 A)
PS1 -12V Current      measured at 0.42 A (capacity 3 A)
PS1 output is 378 W
```

Table 29–14 describes the fields shown in the display.

Command Reference

Table 29-14 *Show Environment All Field Descriptions for the Cisco 7500*

Field	Description
Arbiter type 1	Numbers indicating the arbiter type and backplane type.
Power supply	Number and type of power supply installed in the chassis.
Active fault conditions:	If any fault conditions exist (such as power supply failure, fan failure, and temperature too high), they are listed here.
Fan transfer point:	Software controlled fan speed. If the router is operating below its automatic restart temperature, the transfer point is reduced by 10 percent of the full range each minute. If the router is at or above its automatic restart temperature, the transfer point is increased in the same way.
Active trip points:	Temperature sensor is compared against the values displayed at the bottom of the **show environment table** command output.
15 of 15 soft shutdowns remaining	When the temperature increases above the "board shutdown" level, a soft shutdown occurs (that is, the cards are shut down, and the power supplies, fans, and CI continue to operate). When the system cools to the restart level, the system restarts. The system counts the number of times this occurs and keeps the up/down cycle from continuing forever. When the counter reaches zero, the system performs a hard shutdown, which requires a power cycle to recover. The soft shutdown counter is reset to its maximum value after the system has been up for six hours.
Dbus slots:	Indicates which chassis slots are occupied.
card, inlet, hotpoint, exhaust	Temperature measurements at the inlet, hotpoint, and exhaust areas of the card. The (6) and (7) indicate the slot numbers. Dual-RSP chassis can show two RSPs.
Shutdown temperature source	Indicates which of the three temperature sources is selected for comparison against the "shutdown" levels listed with the **show environment table** command.
Voltages (+12V, +5V, -12V, +24V, +2.5)	Voltages measured on the backplane.
Power supply current (PS1)	Current measured on the power supply.

The following example is for the Cisco 7500 series router. This example shows the measurements immediately before the last shutdown.

```
7500# show environment last

RSP(4) Inlet        previously measured at 37C/98F
RSP(4) Hotpoint     previously measured at 46C/114F
RSP(4) Exhaust      previously measured at 52C/125F
+12 Voltage         previously measured at 12.26
+5 Voltage          previously measured at 5.17
-12 Voltage         previously measured at -12.03
+24 Voltage         previously measured at 23.78
```

Table 29–15 describes the fields shown in the display.

Table 29–15 *Show Environment Last Field Descriptions for the Cisco 7500*

Field	Description
RSP(4) Inlet, Hotpoint, Exhaust	Temperature measurements at the inlet, hotpoint, and exhaust areas of the card.
Voltages	Voltages measured on the backplane.

The following example is for the Cisco 7500 series router. This information lists the temperature and voltage thresholds for each sensor. These thresholds indicate when error messages occur. There are two level of messages: warning and critical.

```
7500# show environment table

Sample Point       LowCritical    LowWarning       HighWarning     HighCritical
RSP(4) Inlet                                       44C/111F        50C/122F
RSP(4) Hotpoint                                    54C/129F        60C/140F
RSP(4) Exhaust
+12 Voltage        10.90          11.61            12.82           13.38
+5 Voltage         4.61           4.94             5.46            5.70
-12 Voltage        -10.15         -10.76           -13.25          -13.86
+24 Voltage        20.38          21.51            26.42           27.65
2.5 Reference                     2.43             2.51
Shutdown boards at                70C/158F
Shutdown power supplies at        76C/168F
Restart after shutdown below 40C/104F
```

Table 29–16 describes the fields shown in the display.

Table 29–16 *Show Environment Table Field Descriptions for the Cisco 7500*

Field	Description
Sample Point	Area for which measurements are taken.
LowCritical	Level at which a critical message is issued for an out-of-tolerance voltage condition. The system continues to operate; however, the system is approaching shutdown.

Table 29–16 *Show Environment Table Field Descriptions for the Cisco 7500, Continued*

Field	Description
LowWarning	Level at which a warning message is issued for an out-of-tolerance voltage condition. The system continues to operate, but operator action is recommended to bring the system back to a normal state.
HighWarning	Level at which a warning message is issued. The system continues to operate, but operator action is recommended to bring the system back to a normal state.
HighCritical	Level at which a critical message is issued. For the chassis, the router is shut down. For the power supply, the power supply is shut down.
Shutdown boards at	The card is shut down if the specified temperature is met.
Shutdown power supplies at	The system is shut down if the specified temperature is met.
Restart after shutdown	The system will restart when the specified temperature is met.

SHOW GT64010

Use the **show gt64010** EXEC command to display all GT64010 internal registers and interrupt status on the Cisco 7200 series routers.

    show gt64010

Syntax   *Description*

This command has no arguments or keywords.

Command Mode

EXEC

Usage Guidelines

This command first appeared in Cisco IOS Release 11.2.

This command displays information about the CPU interface, DRAM/device address space, device parameters, DMA channels, timers and counters, and PCI internal registers. The information is generally useful for diagnostic tasks performed by technical support only.

Sample Display

The following is a partial sample output for the **show gt64010** command:

```
Router# show gt64010

GT64010 Channel 0 DMA:
 dma_list=0x6088C3EC, dma_ring=0x4B018480, dma_entries=256
 dma_free=0x6088CECC, dma_reqt=0x6088CECC, dma_done=0x6088CECC
 thread=0x6088CEAC, thread_end=0x6088CEAC
 backup_thread=0x0, backup_thread_end=0x0
 dma_working=0, dma_complete=6231, post_coalesce_frames=6231
 exhausted_dma_entries=0, post_coalesce_callback=6231

GT64010 Register Dump: Registers at 0xB4000000

CPU Interface:
 cpu_interface_conf  : 0x80030000 (b/s 0x00000380)
 addr_decode_err     : 0xFFFFFFFF (b/s 0xFFFFFFFF)
Processor Address Space :
 ras10_low           : 0x00000000 (b/s 0x00000000)
 ras10_high          : 0x07000000 (b/s 0x00000007)
 ras32_low           : 0x08000000 (b/s 0x00000008)
 ras32_high          : 0x0F000000 (b/s 0x0000000F)
 cs20_low            : 0xD0000000 (b/s 0x000000D0)
 cs20_high           : 0x74000000 (b/s 0x00000074)
 cs3_boot_low        : 0xF8000000 (b/s 0x000000F8)
 cs3_boot_high       : 0x7E000000 (b/s 0x0000007E)
 pci_io_low          : 0x00080000 (b/s 0x00000800)
 pci_io_high         : 0x00000000 (b/s 0x00000000)
 pci_mem_low         : 0x00020000 (b/s 0x00000200)
 pci_mem_high        : 0x7F000000 (b/s 0x0000007F)
 internal_spc_decode : 0xA0000000 (b/s 0x000000A0)
 bus_err_low         : 0x00000000 (b/s 0x00000000)
 bus_err_high        : 0x00000000 (b/s 0x00000000)
 ...
```

SHOW LOGGING

Use the **show logging** EXEC command to display the state of logging (syslog).

show logging [history]

Syntax	Description
history	(Optional) Display information in the syslog history table only.

Command Mode

EXEC

Usage Guidelines

This command first appeared in Cisco IOS Release 10.0.

This command displays the state of syslog error and event logging, including host addresses, and whether console logging is enabled. This command also displays Simple Network Management Protocol (SNMP) configuration parameters and protocol activity.

When you use the optional **history** keyword, information about the syslog history table is displayed such as the table size, the status of messages, and text of messages stored in the table. Messages stored in the table are governed by the **logging history** global configuration command.

Sample Display

The following is sample output from the **show logging** command:

```
Router# show logging

Syslog logging: enabled
     Console logging: disabled
     Monitor logging: level debugging, 266 messages logged.
     Trap logging: level informational, 266 messages logged.
     Logging to 192.180.2.238

SNMP logging: disabled, retransmission after 30 seconds
     0 messages logged
```

Table 29–17 describes significant fields shown in the display.

Table 29–17   *Show Logging Field Descriptions*

Field	Description
Syslog logging	When enabled, system logging messages are sent to a UNIX host that acts as a syslog server; that is, it captures and saves the messages.
Console logging	If enabled, states the level; otherwise, this field display is disabled.
Monitor logging	Minimum level of severity required for a log message to be sent to a monitor terminal (not the console).
Trap logging	Minimum level of severity required for a log message to be sent to a syslog server.
SNMP logging	Shows whether SNMP logging is enabled and the number of messages logged, and the retransmission interval.

The following is sample output from the **show logging history** command:

```
Router# show logging history

Syslog History Table: 1 maximum table entry, saving level notifications or higher
0 messages ignored, 0 dropped, 15 table entries flushed,
```

```
SNMP notifications not enabled
  entry number 16: SYS-5-CONFIG_I
  Configured from console by console
  timestamp: 1110
```

Table 29–18 describes the significant fields shown in the display.

Table 29–18 *Show Logging History Field Descriptions*

Field	Description
maximum table entry	Number of messages that can be stored in the history table. Set with the **logging history size** command.
saving level notifications or higher	Level of messages that are stored in the history table and sent to the SNMP server (if SNMP notification is enabled). Set with the **logging history** command.
messages ignored	Number of messages not stored in the history table because the severity level is greater than that specified with the **logging history** command.
dropped	Number of messages that could not be processed due to lack of system resources. Dropped messages do not appear in the history table and are not sent to the SNMP server.
table entries flushed	Number of messages that have been removed from the history table to make room for newer messages.
SNMP notifications	Whether syslog traps of the appropriate level are sent to the SNMP server. Syslog traps are either enabled or not enabled through the **snmp-server enable** command.
entry number	Number of the message entry in the history table.
SYS-5-CONFIG_I Configured from console by console	Cisco IOS syslog message consisting of the facility name (SYS) that indicates where the message came from, the severity level (5), the message name (CONFIG_I), and the message text.
timestamp	Time, based on the router's up time, that the message was generated.

Related Commands

logging history size

Part
IV

Command Reference

SHOW MEMORY

Use the **show memory** EXEC command to show statistics about memory, including memory-free pool statistics.

show memory [*memory-type*] [**free**] [**summary**]

Syntax	Description
memory-type	(Optional) Memory type to display (**processor, multibus, io, sram**). If *type* is not specified, statistics for all memory types present are displayed.
free	(Optional) Displays free memory statistics.
summary	(Optional) Displays a summary of memory usage, including the size and number of blocks allocated for each address of the system call that allocated the block.

Command Mode

EXEC

Usage Guidelines

This command first appeared in Cisco IOS Release 10.0.

The **show memory** command displays information about memory available after the system image decompresses and loads.

Sample Displays

The following is sample output from the **show memory** command:

```
Router# show memory

                Head    Total(b)   Used(b)    Free(b)    Lowest(b)  Largest(b)
Processor       B0EE38   5181896    2210036    2971860    2692456    2845368

                Processor memory
Address   Bytes Prev.    Next     Ref  PrevF  NextF  Alloc PC  What
B0EE38    1056 0         B0F280    1                  18F132    List Elements
B0F280    2656 B0EE38    B0FD08    1                  18F132    List Headers
B0FD08    2520 B0F280    B10708    1                  141384    TTY data
B10708    2000 B0FD08    B10F00    1                  14353C    TTY Input Buf
B10F00     512 B10708    B11128    1                  14356C    TTY Output Buf
B11128    2000 B10F00    B11920    1                  1A110E    Interrupt Stack
B11920      44 B11128    B11974    1                  970DE8    *Init*
B11974    1056 B11920    B11DBC    1                  18F132    messages
B11DBC      84 B11974    B11E38    1                  19ABCE    Watched Boolean
B11E38      84 B11DBC    B11EB4    1                  19ABCE    Watched Boolean
B11EB4      84 B11E38    B11F30    1                  19ABCE    Watched Boolean
B11F30      84 B11EB4    B11FAC    1                  19ABCE    Watched Boolean
Router#
```

The following is sample output from the **show memory free** command:

```
Router# show memory free

                  Head    Total(b)   Used(b)    Free(b)  Lowest(b) Largest(b)
Processor       B0EE38    5181896   2210076    2971820   2692456    2845368

                Processor memory
Address   Bytes Prev.     Next     Ref  PrevF    NextF    Alloc PC  What
            24     Free list 1
CEB844      32 CEB7A4    CEB88C      0  0          0       96B894    SSE Manager
            52     Free list 2
            72     Free list 3
            76     Free list 4
            80     Free list 5
D35ED4      80 D35E30    D35F4C      0  0          D27AE8  96B894    SSE Manager
D27AE8      80 D27A48    D27B60      0  D35ED4     0       22585E    SSE Manager
            88     Free list 6
            100    Free list 7
D0A8F4      100 D0A8B0   D0A980      0  0          0       2258DA    SSE Manager
            104    Free list 8
B59EF0      108 B59E8C   B59F84      0  0          0       2258DA    (fragment)
```

The display of **show memory free** contains the same types of information as the **show memory** display, except that only free memory is displayed, and the information is displayed in order for each free list.

The first section of the display includes summary statistics about the activities of the system memory allocator. Table 29–19 describes significant fields shown in the first section of the display.

Table 29–19 *Show Memory Field Descriptions—First Section*

Field	Description
Head	Hexadecimal address of the head of the memory allocation chain.
Total(b)	Sum of used bytes plus free bytes.
Used(b)	Amount of memory in use.
Free(b)	Amount of memory not in use.
Lowest(b)	Smallest amount of free memory since last boot.
Largest(b)	Size of largest available free block.

The second section of the display is a block-by-block listing of memory use. Table 29–20 describes significant fields shown in the second section of the display.

Part
IV

Command Reference

Table 29–20 *Characteristics of Each Block of Memory—Second Section*

Field	Description
Address	Hexadecimal address of block.
Bytes	Size of block in bytes.
Prev.	Address of previous block (should match Address on previous line).
Next	Address of next block (should match address on next line).
Ref	Reference count for that memory block, indicating how many different processes are using that block of memory.
PrevF	Address of previous free block (if free).
NextF	Address of next free block (if free).
Alloc PC	Address of the system call that allocated the block.
What	Name of process that owns the block, or "(fragment)" if the block is a fragment, or "(coalesced)" if the block was coalesced from adjacent free blocks.

The **show memory io** command displays the free I/O memory blocks. On the Cisco 4000, this command quickly shows how much unused I/O memory is available.

The following is sample output from the **show memory io** command:

```
Router# show memory io

Address  Bytes   Prev.     Next      Ref  PrevF     NextF     Alloc PC  What
6132DA0  59264   6132664   6141520   0    0         600DDEC   3FCF0     *Packet Buffer*
600DDEC  500     600DA4C   600DFE0   0    6132DA0   600FE68   0
600FE68  376     600FAC8   600FFE0   0    600DDEC   6011D54   0
6011D54  652     60119B4   6011FE0   0    600FE68   6013D54   0
614FCA0  832     614F564   614FFE0   0    601FD54   6177640   0
6177640  2657056 6172E90   0         0    614FCA0   0         0
Total: 2723244
```

The **show memory sram** command displays the free SRAM memory blocks. For the Cisco 4000, this command supports the high-speed static RAM memory pool to make it easier to debug or diagnose problems with allocation or freeing of such memory.

The following is sample output from the **show memory sram** command:

```
Router# show memory sram

Address  Bytes  Prev.  Next  Ref  PrevF  NextF  Alloc PC  What
7AE0     38178  72F0   0     0    0      0      0
Total    38178
```

The **show memory** command on the Cisco 4000 includes information about SRAM memory and I/O memory, and appears as follows:

```
Router# show memory

              Head    Total(b)  Used(b)   Free(b)   Lowest(b) Largest(b)
Processor    49C724   28719324  1510864   27208460  26511644  15513908
      I/O    6000000  4194304   1297088   2897216   2869248   2896812
     SRAM    1000     65536     63400     2136      2136      2136


Address  Bytes Prev.   Next    Ref  PrevF  NextF  Alloc PC  What
1000     2032 0        17F0    1                   3E73E     *Init*
17F0     2032 1000     1FE0    1                   3E73E     *Init*
1FE0     544  17F0     2200    1                   3276A     *Init*
2200     52   1FE0     2234    1                   31D68     *Init*
2234     52   2200     2268    1                   31DAA     *Init*
2268     52   2234     229C    1                   31DF2     *Init*
72F0     2032 6E5C     7AE0    1                   3E73E     Init
7AE0     38178 72F0    0       0    0      0       0
```

The **show memory summary** command displays a summary of all memory pools as well as memory usage per Alloc PC (address of the system call that allocated the block).

The following is a partial sample output from the **show memory summary** command. This command shows the size, blocks, and bytes allocated. Bytes equal the size multiplied by the blocks. For a description of the other fields, see Table 29–19 and Table 29–20.

```
Router# show memory summary

Head    Total(b)   Used(b)   Free(b)   Lowest(b) Largest(b)
Processor  B0EE38  5181896   2210216   2971680   2692456   2845368


            Processor memory
Alloc PC     Size    Blocks   Bytes    What
0x2AB2       192     1        192      IDB: Serial Info
0x70EC       92      2        184      Init
0xC916       128     50       6400     RIF Cache
0x76ADE      4500    1        4500     XDI data
0x76E84      4464    1        4464     XDI data
0x76EAC      692     1        692      XDI data
0x77764      408     1        408      Init
0x77776      116     1        116      Init
0x777A2      408     1        408      Init
0x777B2      116     1        116      Init
0xA4600      24      3        72       List
0xD9B5C      52      1        52       SSE Manager
. . . . . . . . . . . . . . . . . . . .
0x0          0       3413     2072576  Pool Summary
0x0          0       28       2971680  Pool Summary (Free Blocks)
0x0          40      3441     137640   Pool Summary(All Block Headers)
0x0          0       3413     2072576  Memory Summary
0x0          0       28       2971680  Memory Summary (Free Blocks)
```

Related Commands

show processes memory

SHOW PCI

Use the **show pci** EXEC command to display information about the peripheral component interconnect (PCI) hardware registers or bridge registers for the Cisco 7200 series routers.

show pci {hardware | bridge [*register*]}

Syntax	Description
hardware	Displays PCI hardware registers.
bridge	Displays PCI bridge registers.
register	(Optional) Number of a specific bridge register in the range 0 to 7. If not specified, this command displays information about all registers.

Command Mode

EXEC

Usage Guidelines

This command first appeared in Cisco IOS Release 11.2.

The output of this command is generally useful for diagnostic tasks performed by technical support only.

NOTES

The **show pci hardware** command displays a significant amount of information.

Sample Displays

The following is sample output for the PCI bridge register 1 on a Cisco 7200 series router:

```
Router# show pci bridge 1

Bridge 4, Port Adaptor 1, Handle=1
DEC21050 bridge chip, config=0x0
(0x00): cfid  = 0x00011011
(0x04): cfcs  = 0x02800147
(0x08): cfccid = 0x06040002
(0x0C): cfpmlt = 0x00010010

(0x18): cfsmlt = 0x18050504
(0x1C): cfsis  = 0x22805050
(0x20): cfmla  = 0x48F04880
(0x24): cfpmla = 0x00004880
```

```
(0x3C): cfbc  = 0x00000000
(0x40): cfseed = 0x00100000
(0x44): cfstwt = 0x00008020
```

The following is partial sample output for the PCI hardware register, which also includes information on all the PCI bridge registers on a Cisco 7200 series router:

```
Router# show pci hardware

GT64010 External PCI Configuration registers:
  Vendor / Device ID  : 0xAB114601 (b/s 0x014611AB)
  Status / Command    : 0x17018002 (b/s 0x02800117)
  Class / Revision    : 0x00000006 (b/s 0x06000000)
  Latency             : 0x0F000000 (b/s 0x0000000F)
  RAS[1:0] Base       : 0x00000000 (b/s 0x00000000)
  RAS[3:2] Base       : 0x00000001 (b/s 0x01000000)
  CS[2:0] Base        : 0x00000000 (b/s 0x00000000)
  CS[3] Base          : 0x00000000 (b/s 0x00000000)
  Mem Map Base        : 0x00000014 (b/s 0x14000000)
  IO Map Base         : 0x01000014 (b/s 0x14000001)
  Int Pin / Line      : 0x00010000 (b/s 0x00000100)

Bridge 0, Downstream MB0 to MB1, Handle=0
DEC21050 bridge chip, config=0x0
(0x00): cfid   = 0x00011011
(0x04): cfcs   = 0x02800143
(0x08): cfccid = 0x06040002
(0x0C): cfpmlt = 0x00011810

(0x18): cfsmlt = 0x18000100
(0x1C): cfsis  = 0x02809050
(0x20): cfmla  = 0x4AF04880
(0x24): cfpmla = 0x4BF04B00

(0x3C): cfbc   = 0x00000000
(0x40): cfseed = 0x00100000
(0x44): cfstwt = 0x00008020
...
```

SHOW PROCESSES

Use the **show processes** EXEC command to display information about the active processes.

    show processes [cpu]

Syntax	*Description*
cpu	(Optional) Displays detailed CPU utilization statistics.

Command Mode

EXEC

Usage Guidelines

This command first appeared in Cisco IOS Release 10.0.

Sample Displays

The following is sample output from the **show processes** command:

```
Router# show processes

CPU utilization for five seconds: 21%/0%; one minute: 2%; five minutes: 2%
PID QTy      PC Runtime (ms)    Invoked    uSecs    Stacks      TTY  Process
  1 Mwe   2FEA4E       1808         464     3896    1796/3000     0   IP-EIGRP Router
  2 Lst    11682      10236         109    93908    1828/2000     0   Check heaps
  3 Mst     3AE9C          0         280        0    1768/2000     0   Timers
  4 Lwe    74AD2          0          12        0    1492/2000     0   ARP Input
  5.ME     912E4          0           2        0    1892/2000     0   IPC Zone Manager
  6.ME     91264          0           1        0    1936/2000     0   IPC Realm Manager
  7.ME     91066          0          30        0    1784/2000     0   IPC Seat Manager
  8.ME    133368          0           1        0    1928/2000     0   CXBus hot stall
  9.ME    1462EE          0           1        0    1940/2000     0  Microcode load
 10 Msi   127538          4          76       52    1608/2000     0  Env Mon
 11.ME    160CF4          0           1        0    1932/2000     0  MIP Mailbox
 12 Mwe   125D7C          4         280       14    1588/2000     0  SMT input
 13 Lwe    AFD0E          0           1        0    1772/2000     0  Probe Input
 14 Mwe    AF662          0           1        0    1784/2000     0  RARP Input
 15 Hwe    A1F9A        228         549      415    3240/4000     0  IP Input
 16 Msa    C86A0          0         114        0    1864/2000     0  TCP Timer
 17 Lwe    CA700          0           1        0    1756/2000     0  TCP Protocols
 18.ME     CCE7C          0           1        0    1940/2000     0  TCP Listener
 19 Mwe    AC49E          0           1        0    1592/2000     0  BOOTP Server
 20 Mwe   10CD84         24          77      311    1652/2000     0  CDP Protocol
 21 Mwe   27BF82          0           2        0    1776/2000     0  ATMSIG Input
```

The following is sample output from the **show processes cpu** command:

```
Router# show processes cpu

CPU utilization for five seconds: 5%/2%; one minute: 3%; five minutes: 2%
 PID  Runtime (ms)    Invoked    uSecs   5Sec   1Min   5Min   TTY Process
   1          1736         58    29931    0%     0%     0%     0   Check heaps
   2            68        585      116   1.00%  1.00%   0%     0   IP Input
   3             0        744        0    0%     0%     0%     0   TCP Timer
   4             0          2        0    0%     0%     0%     0   TCP Protocols
   5             0          1        0    0%     0%     0%     0   BOOTP Server
   6            16        130      123    0%     0%     0%     0    ARP Input
   7             0          1        0    0%     0%     0%     0   Probe Input
   8             0          7        0    0%     0%     0%     0   MOP Protocols
   9             0          2        0    0%     0%     0%     0   Timers
  10           692         64    10812    0%     0%     0%     0   Net Background
  11             0          5        0    0%     0%     0%     0   Logger
  12             0         38        0    0%     0%     0%     0   BGP Open
  13             0          1        0    0%     0%     0%     0   Net Input
```

```
14       540      3466     155     0%     0%     0%   TTY Background
15         0         1       0     0%     0%     0%   BGP I/O
16      5100      1367    3730     0%     0%     0%   IGRP Router
17        88      4232      20  0.20%  1.00%     0%   BGP Router
18       152     14650      10     0%     0%     0%   BGP Scanner
19       224        99    2262     0%     0%  1.00%   Exec
```

Table 29–21 describes significant fields shown in the two displays.

Table 29–21   *Show Processes Field Descriptions*

Field	Description
CPU utilization for five seconds	CPU utilization for the last five seconds. The second number indicates the percent of CPU time spent at the interrupt level.
one minute	CPU utilization for the last minute.
five minutes	CPU utilization for the last five minutes.
PID	Process ID.
Q	Process queue priority. Possible values: H (high), M (medium), L (low).
Ty	Scheduler test. Possible values: * (currently running), E (waiting for an event), S (ready to run, voluntarily relinquished processor), rd (ready to run, wakeup conditions have occurred), we (waiting for an event), sa (sleeping until an absolute time), si (sleeping for a time interval), sp (sleeping for a time interval (alternate call)), st (sleeping until a timer expires), hg (hung; the process will never execute again), xx (Dead. The process has terminated, but not yet been deleted).
PC	Current program counter.
Runtime (ms)	CPU time the process has used, in milliseconds.
Invoked	Number of times the process has been invoked.
uSecs	Microseconds of CPU time for each process invocation.
Stacks	Low water mark/Total stack space available, shown in bytes.
TTY	Terminal that controls the process.
Process	Name of process.
5Sec	CPU utilization by task in the last five seconds.
1Min	CPU utilization by task in the last minute.
5Min	CPU utilization by task in the last five minutes.

Part
IV

Command Reference

NOTES

Because the network server has a four-millisecond clock resolution, runtimes are considered reliable only after a large number of invocations or a reasonable, measured runtime.

Related Commands

show processes memory

SHOW PROCESSES MEMORY

Use the **show processes memory** EXEC command to show memory used.

    show processes memory

Syntax   Description

This command has no arguments or keywords.

Command Mode

EXEC

Usage Guidelines

This command first appeared in Cisco IOS Release 10.0.

Sample Display

The following is sample output from the **show processes memory** command:

```
Router# show processes memory

Total: 5611448, Used: 2307548, Free: 3303900
 PID  TTY  Allocated    Freed   Holding   Getbufs   Retbufs  Process
   0    0     199592     1236   1907220         0         0  *Init*
   0    0        400    76928       400         0         0  *Sched*
   0    0    5431176  3340052    140760    349780         0  *Dead*
   1    0        256      256      1724         0         0  Load Meter
   2    0        264        0      5032         0         0  Exec
   3    0          0        0      2724         0         0  Check heaps
   4    0      97932        0      2852     32760         0  Pool Manager
   5    0        256      256      2724         0         0  Timers
   6    0         92        0      2816         0         0  CXBus hot stall
   7    0          0        0      2724         0         0  IPC Zone Manager
   8    0          0        0      2724         0         0  IPC Realm Manager
   9    0          0        0      2724         0         0  IPC Seat Manager
  10    0        892      476      3256         0         0  ARP Input
  11    0         92        0      2816         0         0  SERIAL A'detect
  12    0        216        0      2940         0         0  Microcode Loader
```

```
       13    0          0         0       2724        0        0 RFSS watchdog
       14    0   15659136  15658584       3276        0        0 Env Mon
     ...
       77    0        116         0       2844        0        0 IPX-EIGRP Hello
                                      2307224 Total
```

Table 29–22 describes significant fields shown in the display.

Table 29–22 *Show Processes Memory Field Descriptions*

Field	Description
Total	Total amount of memory held.
Used	Total amount of used memory.
Free	Total amount of free memory.
PID	Process ID.
TTY	Terminal that controls the process.
Allocated	Bytes of memory allocated by the process.
Freed	Bytes of memory freed by the process, regardless of who originally allocated it.
Holding	Amount of memory currently allocated to the process.
Getbufs	Number of times the process has requested a packet buffer.
Retbufs	Number of times the process has relinquished a packet buffer.
Process	Process name.
Init	System initialization.
Sched	The scheduler.
Dead	Processes as a group that are now dead.
Total	Total amount of memory held by all processes.

Related Commands

show memory
show processes

SHOW PROTOCOLS

Use the **show protocols** EXEC command to display the configured protocols.

This command shows the global and interface-specific status of any configured Level 3 protocol; for example, IP, DECnet, IPX, AppleTalk, and so forth.

  show protocols

Syntax   Description

This command has no arguments or keywords.

Command Mode

EXEC

Usage Guidelines

This command first appeared in Cisco IOS Release 10.0.

Sample Display

The following is sample output from the **show protocols** command:

```
Router# show protocols

Global values:
  Internet Protocol routing is enabled
  DECNET routing is enabled
  XNS routing is enabled
  Appletalk routing is enabled
  X.25 routing is enabled
Ethernet 0 is up, line protocol is up
  Internet address is 192.168.1.1, subnet mask is 255.255.255.0
  Decnet cost is 5
  XNS address is 2001.AA00.0400.06CC
  AppleTalk address is 4.129, zone Twilight
Serial 0 is up, line protocol is up
  Internet address is 192.168.7.49, subnet mask is 255.255.255.240
Ethernet 1 is up, line protocol is up
  Internet address is 192.168.2.1, subnet mask is 255.255.255.0
  Decnet cost is 5
  XNS address is 2002.AA00.0400.06CC
  AppleTalk address is 254.132, zone Twilight
Serial 1 is down, line protocol is down
  Internet address is 192.168.7.177, subnet mask is 255.255.255.240
  AppleTalk address is 999.1, zone Magnolia Estates
```

SHOW STACKS

Use the **show stacks** EXEC command to monitor the stack usage of processes and interrupt routines.

show stacks

Syntax   Description

This command has no arguments or keywords.

Command Mode

EXEC

Usage Guidelines

This command first appeared in Cisco IOS Release 10.0.

The display from this command includes the reason for the last system reboot. If the system was reloaded because of a system failure, a saved system stack trace is displayed. This information is of use only to your technical support representative in analyzing crashes in the field. It is included here in case you need to read the displayed statistics to an engineer over the phone.

Sample Display

The following is sample output from the **show stacks** command following a system failure:

```
Router# show stacks

Minimum process stacks:
Free/Size  Name
 652/1000  Router Init
 726/1000  Init
 744/1000  BGP Open
 686/1200  Virtual Exec

Interrupt level stacks:
Level    Called  Free/Size   Name
  1          0   1000/1000   env-flash
  3        738    900/1000   Multiport Communications Interfaces
  5        178    970/1000   Console UART
System was restarted by bus error at PC 0xAD1F4, address 0xD0D0D1A
GS Software (GS3), Version 9.1(0.16), BETA TEST SOFTWARE
Compiled Tue 11-Aug-92 13:27 by jthomas
Stack trace from system failure:
FP: 0x29C158, RA: 0xACFD4
FP: 0x29C184, RA: 0xAD20C
FP: 0x29C1B0, RA: 0xACFD4
FP: 0x29C1DC, RA: 0xAD304
FP: 0x29C1F8, RA: 0xAF774
FP: 0x29C214, RA: 0xAF83E
FP: 0x29C228, RA: 0x3E0CA
FP: 0x29C244, RA: 0x3BD3C
```

Related Commands

show processes

SHOW TCP

Use the **show tcp** EXEC command to display the status of TCP connections.

    show tcp [*line-number*]

Syntax

line-number

Description

(Optional) Absolute line number of the line for which you want to display Telnet connection status.

Command Mode

EXEC

Usage Guidelines

This command first appeared in Cisco IOS Release 10.0.

Sample Display

The following is sample output from the **show tcp** command:

```
Router# show tcp

tty0, connection 1 to host cider
Connection state is ESTAB, I/O status: 1, unread input bytes: 0
Local host: 172.31.232.17, Local port: 11184
Foreign host: 172.31.1.137, Foreign port: 23

Enqueued packets for retransmit: 0, input: 0, saved: 0

Event Timers (current time is 67341276):
Timer:         Retrans   TimeWait    AckHold    SendWnd   KeepAlive
Starts:             30          0         32          0           0
Wakeups:             1          0         14          0           0
Next:                0          0          0          0           0

iss:   67317172  snduna:   67317228  sndnxt:   67317228    sndwnd:    4096
irs: 1064896000  rcvnxt: 1064897597  rcvwnd:       2144  delrcvwnd:      0

SRTT: 317 ms, RTTO: 900 ms, RTV: 133 ms, KRTT: 0 ms
minRTT: 4 ms, maxRTT: 300 ms, ACK hold: 300 ms
Flags: higher precedence, idle user, retransmission timeout

Datagrams (max data segment is 536 bytes):
Rcvd: 41 (out of order: 0), with data: 34, total data bytes: 1596
Sent: 57 (retransmit: 1), with data: 35, total data bytes: 55
```

Table 29–23 describes the first five lines of output shown in the display:

Table 29–23 *Show TCP Field Descriptions—First Section of Output*

Field	Description
tty0	Identifying number of the line.
connection 1	Number identifying the TCP connection.
to host xxx	Name of the remote host to which the connection has been made.
Connection state is ESTAB	A connection progresses through a series of states during its lifetime. These states follow in the order in which a connection progresses through them. • LISTEN—Waiting for a connection request from any remote TCP and port. • SYNSENT—Waiting for a matching connection request after having sent a connection request. • SYNRCVD—Waiting for a confirming connection request acknowledgment after having both received and sent a connection request. • ESTAB—Indicates an open connection; data received can be delivered to the user. This is the normal state for the data transfer phase of the connection. • FINWAIT1—Waiting for a connection termination request from the remote TCP or an acknowledgment of the connection termination request previously sent. • FINWAIT2—Waiting for a connection termination request from the remote TCP host. • CLOSEWAIT—Waiting for a connection termination request from the local user. • CLOSING—Waiting for a connection termination request acknowledgment from the remote TCP host. • LASTACK—Waiting for an acknowledgment of the connection termination request previously sent to the remote TCP host. • TIMEWAIT—Waiting for enough time to pass to be sure the remote TCP host has received the acknowledgment of its connection termination request. • CLOSED—Indicates no connection state at all. For more information, see RFC 793, Transmission Control Protocol Functional Specification.

Table 29–23   *Show TCP Field Descriptions—First Section of Output, Continued*

Field	Description
I/O status:	Number describing the current internal status of the connection.
unread input bytes:	Number of bytes that the lower-level TCP processes have read, but the higher-level TCP processes have not yet processed.
Local host:	IP address of the network server.
Local port:	Local port number, as derived from the following equation: *line-number* + (512 * *random-number*). (The line number uses the lower nine bits; the other bits are random).
Foreign host:	IP address of the remote host to which the TCP connection has been made.
Foreign port:	Destination port for the remote host.
Enqueued packets for retransmit:	Number of packets waiting on the retransmit queue. These are packets on this TCP connection that have been sent but have not yet been acknowledged by the remote TCP host.
input:	Number of packets that are waiting on the input queue to be read by the user.
saved:	Number of received out-of-order packets that are waiting for all packets comprising the message to be received before they enter the input queue. For example, if packets 1, 2, 4, 5, and 6 have been received, packets 1 and 2 would enter the input queue, and packets 4, 5, and 6 would enter the saved queue.

The following line of output shows the current time according to the system clock of the local host:

```
Event Timers (current time is 67341276):
```

The time shown is the number of milliseconds since the system started.

The following lines of output display the number of times that various local TCP timeout values were reached during this connection. In this example, the local host retransmitted 30 times, because it received no response from the remote host, and it transmitted an acknowledgment many more times because there was no data on which to piggyback.

```
Timer:       Retrans   TimeWait   AckHold   SendWnd   KeepAlive
Starts:           30          0        32         0           0
Wakeups:           1          0        14         0           0
Next:              0          0         0         0           0
```

Table 29–24 describes the fields in the preceding lines of output.

Table 29–24 *Show TCP Field Descriptions—Second Section of Output*

Field	Description
Timer:	The names of the timers in the display.
Starts:	The number of times the timer has been started during this connection.
Wakeups:	Number of keepalives transmitted without receiving any response. (This field is reset to zero when a response is received).
Next:	The system clock setting that will trigger the next time this timer will go off.
Retrans	The Retransmission timer is used to time TCP packets that have not been acknowledged and are waiting for retransmission.
TimeWait	The TimeWait timer is used to ensure that the remote system receives a request to disconnect a session.
AckHold	The Acknowledgment timer is used to delay the sending of acknowledgments to the remote TCP in an attempt to reduce network use.
SendWnd	The Send Window is used to ensure that there is no closed window due to a lost TCP acknowledgment.
KeepAlive	The KeepAlive timer is used to control the transmission of test messages to the remote TCP to ensure that the link has not been broken without the local TCP's knowledge.

The following lines of output display the sequence numbers that TCP uses to ensure sequenced, reliable transport of data. The local host and remote host each use these sequence numbers for flow control and to acknowledge receipt of datagrams. Table 29–25 describes the specific fields in these lines of output:

```
iss:   67317172  snduna:   67317228  sndnxt:   67317228    sndwnd:    4096
irs: 1064896000  rcvnxt: 1064897597  rcvwnd:       2144  delrcvwnd:       0
```

Table 29–25 *Show TCP Field Descriptions—Sequence Number*

Field	Description
iss:	Initial send sequence number.
snduna:	Last send sequence number the local host sent but for which host has not received an acknowledgment.
sndnxt:	Sequence number the local host will send next.
sndwnd:	TCP window size of the remote host.
irs:	Initial receive sequence number.

Table 29–25 *Show TCP Field Descriptions—Sequence Number, Continued*

Field	Description
rcvnxt:	Last receive sequence number the local host has acknowledged.
rcvwnd:	Local host's TCP window size.
delrcvwnd:	Delayed receive window—data the local host has read from the connection, but has not yet subtracted from the receive window the host has advertised to the remote host. The value in this field gradually increases until it is larger than a full-sized packet, at which point it is applied to the rcvwnd field.

The following lines of output display values that the local host uses to keep track of transmission times so that TCP can adjust to the network it is using. Table 29–26 describes the fields in the following line of output:

```
SRTT: 317 ms, RTTO: 900 ms, RTV: 133 ms, KRTT: 0 ms
minRTT: 4 ms, maxRTT: 300 ms, ACK hold: 300 ms
Flags: higher precedence, idle user, retransmission timeout
```

Table 29–26 *Show TCP Field Descriptions—Line Beginning with SRTT*

Field	Description
SRTT:	A calculated smoothed round-trip timeout.
RTTO:	Round-trip timeout.
RTV:	Variance of the round-trip time.
KRTT:	New round-trip timeout (using the Karn algorithm). This field separately tracks the round-trip time of packets that have been retransmitted.
minRTT:	Smallest recorded round-trip timeout (hard wire value used for calculation).
maxRTT:	Largest recorded round-trip timeout.
ACK hold:	Time the local host will delay an acknowledgment in order to piggyback data on it.
Flags:	Properties of the connection.

For more information on these fields, refer to "Round Trip Time Estimation," P. Karn & C. Partridge, ACM SIGCOMM-87, August 1987.

Table 29–27 describes the fields in the following lines of output:

```
Datagrams (max data segment is 536 bytes):
Rcvd: 41 (out of order: 0), with data: 34, total data bytes: 1596
Sent: 57 (retransmit: 1), with data: 35, total data bytes: 55
```

Table 29-27 *Show TCP Field Descriptions—Last Section of Output*

Field	Description
Rcvd:	Number of datagrams the local host has received during this connection (and the number of these datagrams that were out of order).
with data:	Number of these datagrams that contained data.
total data bytes:	Total number of bytes of data in these datagrams.
Sent:	Number of datagrams the local host sent during this connection (and the number of these datagrams that had to be retransmitted).
with data:	Number of these datagrams that contained data.
total data bytes:	Total number of bytes of data in these datagrams.

Related Commands

show tcp brief

SHOW TCP BRIEF

To display a concise description of TCP connection endpoints, use the **show tcp brief** EXEC command.

> **show tcp brief** [all]

Syntax	*Description*
all	(Optional) Displays status for all endpoints. Without this keyword, endpoints in the LISTEN state are not shown.

Command Mode

EXEC

Usage Guidelines

This command first appeared in Cisco IOS Release 11.2.

Sample Display

The following is sample output from the **show tcp brief** command while a user has connected into the system via Telnet:

```
Router> show tcp brief

TCB         Local Address         Foreign Address        (state)
609789AC    Router.cisco.com.23   cider.cisco.com.3733   ESTAB
```

Table 29–28 describes the fields shown in the display.

Table 29–28   *Show TCP Brief Field Descriptions*

Field	Description
TCB	An internal identifier for the endpoint.
Local Address	The local IP address and port.
Foreign Address	The foreign IP address and port (at the opposite end of the connection).
(state)	The state of the connection. States are described in Syntax Description of the **show tcp** command.

Related Commands

show tcp

SHOW TDM CONNECTIONS

To display a snapshot of the time-division multiplexing (TDM) bus connection memory in a Cisco AS5200 access server, use the **show tdm connections** EXEC command.

> **show tdm connections [motherboard | slot** *number***]**

Syntax   *Description*

motherboard   (Optional) Motherboard in the Cisco AS5200 access server.

slot *number*   (Optional) Slot number.

Command Mode

EXEC

Usage Guidelines

This command first appeared in Cisco IOS Release 11.2.

The **show tdm connections** command shows the connection memory for all TDM bus connections in the access server if you do not limit the display to the motherboard or a slot.

Sample Display

The following example shows source stream 3 (ST3) channel 2 switched out of stream 6 (ST6) channel 2:

```
AS5200# show tdm connections motherboard

MT8980 motherboard unit 0, Control Register = 0x1F, ODE Register = 0x06
Connection Memory for ST6:
Ch0:  0x62, Ch1:  0x00, Ch2:  0x00, Ch3:  0x00
```

```
Ch4:  0x00, Ch5:  0x00, Ch6:  0x00, Ch7:  0x00
Ch8:  0x00, Ch9:  0x00, Ch10: 0x00, Ch11: 0x00
Ch12: 0x00, Ch13: 0x00, Ch14: 0x00, Ch15: 0x00
Ch16: 0x00, Ch17: 0x00, Ch18: 0x00, Ch19: 0x00
Ch20: 0x00, Ch21: 0x00, Ch22: 0x00, Ch23: 0x00
Ch24: 0x00, Ch25: 0x00, Ch26: 0x00, Ch27: 0x00
Ch28: 0x00, Ch29: 0x00, Ch30: 0x00, Ch31: 0x00
```

To interpret the hexadecimal number 0x62 into meaningful information, you must translate it into binary code. These two hexadecimal numbers represent a connection from any stream and a channel on any stream. The number 6 translates into the binary code 0110, which represents the third-source stream. The number 2 translates into the binary code 0010, which represents the second-source channel.

Stream 6 (ST6) channel 0 is the destination for source stream 3 (ST3) channel 2 in this example.

Related Commands

show tdm data

SHOW TDM DATA

To display a snapshot of the time-division multiplexing (TDM) bus data memory in a Cisco AS5200 access server, use the **show tdm data** EXEC command.

   show tdm data [**motherboard** | **slot** *number*]

Syntax	Description
motherboard	(Optional) Motherboard in the Cisco AS5200 access server.
slot *number*	(Optional) Slot number.

Command Mode

EXEC

Usage Guidelines

This command first appeared in Cisco IOS Release 11.2.

The data memory for all TDM bus connections in the access server is displayed if you do not specify a motherboard or slot.

Sample Display

The following example shows a snapshot of TDM memory where the normal ISDN idle pattern (0x7E) is present on all channels of the TDM device resident on the motherboard:

```
AS5200# show tdm data motherboard
MT8980 motherboard unit 0, Control Register = 0x1F, ODE Register = 0x06
```

```
Data Memory for ST0:
Ch0:  0x7E, Ch1:  0x7E, Ch2:  0x7E, Ch3:  0x7E
Ch4:  0x7E, Ch5:  0x7E, Ch6:  0x7E, Ch7:  0x7E
Ch8:  0x7E, Ch9:  0x7E, Ch10: 0x7E, Ch11: 0x7E
Ch12: 0x7E, Ch13: 0x7E, Ch14: 0x7E, Ch15: 0x7E
Ch16: 0x7E, Ch17: 0x7E, Ch18: 0x7E, Ch19: 0x7E
Ch20: 0x7E, Ch21: 0x7E, Ch22: 0x7E, Ch23: 0x7E
Ch24: 0x7E, Ch25: 0x7E, Ch26: 0x7E, Ch27: 0x7E
Ch28: 0x7E, Ch29: 0x7E, Ch30: 0x7E, Ch31: 0x7E
Data Memory for ST1:
Ch0:  0x7E, Ch1:  0x7E, Ch2:  0x7E, Ch3:  0x7E
Ch4:  0x7E, Ch5:  0x7E, Ch6:  0x7E, Ch7:  0x7E
Ch8:  0x7E, Ch9:  0x7E, Ch10: 0x7E, Ch11: 0x7E
Ch12: 0x7E, Ch13: 0x7E, Ch14: 0x7E, Ch15: 0x7E
Ch16: 0x7E, Ch17: 0x7E, Ch18: 0x7E, Ch19: 0x7E
Ch20: 0x7E, Ch21: 0x7E, Ch22: 0x7E, Ch23: 0x7E
Ch24: 0x7E, Ch25: 0x7E, Ch26: 0x7E, Ch27: 0x7E
Ch28: 0x7E, Ch29: 0x7E, Ch30: 0x7E, Ch31: 0x7E
```

Related Commands

show tdm connections

SHOW TECH-SUPPORT

To display general information about the router when reporting a problem, use the **show tech-support** privileged EXEC command.

> show tech-support [page] [password]

Syntax	*Description*
page	(Optional) Causes the output to display a page of information at a time. Use the return key to display the next line of output or use the space bar to display the next page of information. If not used, the output scrolls (that is, does not stop for page breaks).
password	(Optional) Leaves passwords and other security information in the output. If not used, passwords and other security-sensitive information in the output are replaced with the label "<removed>" (this is the default).

Default

Display output without page breaks and remove passwords and other security information.

Command Mode

Privileged EXEC

Usage Guidelines

This command first appeared in Cisco IOS Release 11.2.

Use this command to help collect general information about the router when you are reporting a problem. This command displays the equivalent of the following **show** commands:

- **show version**
- **show running-config**
- **show controllers**
- **show stacks**
- **show interfaces**
- **show buffers**
- **show processes memory**
- **show processes cpu**

For a sample display of the output of the **show tech-support** command, refer to these **show** commands.

Related Commands

show buffers
show controllers
show interfaces
show processes cpu
show processes memory
show running-config
show stacks
show version

TEST FLASH

To test Flash memory on MCI and envm Flash EPROM interfaces, use the **test flash** EXEC command.

> **test flash**

Syntax   Description

This command has no arguments or keywords.

Command Mode

EXEC

Usage Guidelines

This command first appeared in Cisco IOS Release 10.0.

Example

The following example tests the Flash memory:

```
test flash
```

Related Commands

test interfaces
test memory

TEST INTERFACES

To test the system interfaces on the modular router, use the **test interfaces** EXEC command.

    test interfaces

Syntax   *Description*

This command has no arguments or keywords.

Command Mode

EXEC

Usage Guidelines

This command first appeared in Cisco IOS Release 10.0.

The **test interfaces** EXEC command is intended for the factory checkout of network interfaces. It is not intended for diagnosing problems with an operational router. The **test interfaces** output does not report correct results if the router is attached to a "live" network. For each network interface that has an IP address that can be tested in loopback (MCI and ciscoBus Ethernet and all serial interfaces), the **test interfaces** command sends a series of ICMP echoes. Error counters are examined to determine the operational status of the interface.

Example

The following example tests the system interfaces:

```
test interfaces
```

Related Commands

test flash
test memory

TEST MEMORY

To perform a test of Multibus memory (including nonvolatile memory) on the modular router, use the **test memory** EXEC command. The memory test overwrites memory.

>   **test memory**

Syntax   Description

This command has no arguments or keywords.

Command Mode

EXEC·

Usage Guidelines

This command first appeared in Cisco IOS Release 10.0.

CAUTION

The memory test overwrites memory. If you use the **test memory** command, you will need to rewrite nonvolatile memory. For example, if you test Multibus memory, which is the memory used by the CSC-R 4-Mbps Token Ring interfaces, you will need to reload the system before the network interfaces will operate properly. The **test memory** command is intended primarily for use by Cisco personnel.

Example

The following example tests memory:

```
test memory
```

Related Commands

test flash
test interfaces

TRACE (PRIVILEGED)

Use the **trace** privileged EXEC command to discover the routes that packets actually will take when traveling to their destination.

>   **trace** [*protocol*] [*destination*]

Syntax	*Description*
protocol	(Optional) Protocols that can be used are **appletalk**, **clns**, **ip** and **vines**.
destination	(Optional) Destination address or host name on the command line. The default parameters for the appropriate protocol are assumed and the tracing action begins.

Default

The *protocol* argument is based on the Cisco IOS software's examination of the format of *destination*. For example, if the software finds a *destination* argument in IP format, the *protocol* value defaults to **ip**.

Command Mode

Privileged EXEC

Usage Guidelines

This command first appeared in Cisco IOS Release 10.0.

The **trace** command works by taking advantage of the error messages generated by routers when a datagram exceeds its time-to-live (TTL) value.

The **trace** command starts by sending probe datagrams with a TTL value of one. This causes the first router to discard the probe datagram and send back an error message. The **trace** command sends several probes at each TTL level and displays the round-trip time for each.

The **trace** command sends out one probe at a time. Each outgoing packet might result in one or two error messages. A "time exceeded" error message indicates that an intermediate router has seen and discarded the probe. A "destination unreachable" error message indicates that the destination node has received the probe and discarded it, because it could not deliver the packet. If the timer goes off before a response comes in, **trace** prints an asterisk (*).

The **trace** command terminates when the destination responds, when the maximum TTL is exceeded, or when the user interrupts the trace with the escape sequence. By default, to invoke the escape sequence, type **Ctrl-^ X**—by simultaneously pressing and releasing the **Ctrl**, **Shift**, and **6** keys, and then pressing the **X** key.

To use nondefault parameters and invoke an extended **trace** test, enter the command without a *destination* argument. You will be stepped through a dialog to select the desired parameters.

Common Trace Problems

Due to bugs in the IP implementation of various hosts and routers, the IP **trace** command might behave in odd ways.

Not all destinations will respond correctly to a `probe` message by sending back an "ICMP port unreachable" message. A long sequence of TTL levels with only asterisks, terminating only when the maximum TTL has been reached, might indicate this problem.

There is a known problem with the way some hosts handle an "ICMP TTL exceeded" message. Some hosts generate an "ICMP" message but they reuse the TTL of the incoming packet. Because this is zero, the ICMP packets do not make it back. When you trace the path to such a host, you might see a set of TTL values with asterisks (*). Eventually, the TTL gets high enough that the *ICMP* message can get back. For example, if the host is six hops away, **trace** will time out on responses 6 through 11.

Sample Display Showing Trace IP Routes

The following display shows sample IP **trace** output when a destination host name has been specified:

```
Router# trace ABA.NYC.mil

Type escape sequence to abort.
Tracing the route to ABA.NYC.mil (26.0.0.73)
  1 DEBRIS.CISCO.COM (192.180.1.6) 1000 msec 8 msec 4 msec
  2 BARRNET-GW.CISCO.COM (192.180.16.2) 8 msec 8 msec 8 msec
  3 EXTERNAL-A-GATEWAY.STANFORD.EDU (192.42.110.225) 8 msec 4 msec 4 msec
  4 BB2.SU.BARRNET.NET (192.200.254.6) 8 msec 8 msec 8 msec
  5 SU.ARC.BARRNET.NET (192.200.3.8) 12 msec 12 msec 8 msec
  6 MOFFETT-FLD-MB.in.MIL (192.52.195.1) 216 msec 120 msec 132 msec
  7 ABA.NYC.mil (26.0.0.73) 412 msec 628 msec 664 msec
```

Table 29–29 describes the fields shown in the display.

Table 29–29 *Trace Field Descriptions*

Field	Description
1	Indicates the sequence number of the router in the path to the host.
DEBRIS.CISCO.COM	Host name of this router.
192.180.1.6	Internet address of this router.
1000 msec 8 msec 4 msec	Round-trip time for each of the three probes that are sent.

Sample Display Showing Extended IP Trace Dialog

The following display shows a sample **trace** session involving the extended dialog of the **trace** command.

```
Router# trace

Protocol [ip]:
Target IP address: mit.edu
Source address:
```

```
Numeric display [n]:
Timeout in seconds [3]:
Probe count [3]:
Minimum Time to Live [1]:
Maximum Time to Live [30]:
Port Number [33434]:
Loose, Strict, Record, Timestamp, Verbose[none]:
Type escape sequence to abort.
Tracing the route to MIT.EDU (18.72.2.1)
  1 ICM-DC-2-V1.ICP.NET (192.108.209.17) 72 msec 72 msec 88 msec
  2 ICM-FIX-E-H0-T3.ICP.NET (192.157.65.122) 80 msec 128 msec 80 msec
  3 192.203.229.246 540 msec 88 msec 84 msec
  4 T3-2.WASHINGTON-DC-CNSS58.T3.ANS.NET (140.222.58.3) 84 msec 116 msec 88 msec
  5 T3-3.WASHINGTON-DC-CNSS56.T3.ANS.NET (140.222.56.4) 80 msec 132 msec 88 msec
  6 T3-0.NEW-YORK-CNSS32.T3.ANS.NET (140.222.32.1) 92 msec 132 msec 88 msec
  7 T3-0.HARTFORD-CNSS48.T3.ANS.NET (140.222.48.1) 88 msec 88 msec 88 msec
  8 T3-0.HARTFORD-CNSS49.T3.ANS.NET (140.222.49.1) 96 msec 104 msec 96 msec
  9 T3-0.ENSS134.T3.ANS.NET (140.222.134.1) 92 msec 128 msec 92 msec
 10 W91-CISCO-EXTERNAL-FDDI.MIT.EDU (192.233.33.1) 92 msec 92 msec 112 msec
 11 E40-RTR-FDDI.MIT.EDU (18.168.0.2) 92 msec 120 msec 96 msec
 12 MIT.EDU (18.72.2.1) 96 msec 92 msec 96 msec
```

Table 29–30 describes the fields that are unique to the extended trace sequence, as shown in the display.

Table 29–30   *Trace Field Descriptions*

Field	Description
Target IP address	You must enter a host name or an IP address. There is no default.
Source address	One of the interface addresses of the router to use as a source address for the probes. The router normally will pick what it feels is the best source address to use.
Numeric display	The default is to have both a symbolic and numeric display; however, you can suppress the symbolic display.
Timeout in seconds	The number of seconds to wait for a response to a probe packet. The default is three seconds.
Probe count	The number of probes to be sent at each TTL level. The default count is three.
Minimum Time to Live [1]	The TTL value for the first probes. The default is 1, but it can be set to a higher value to suppress the display of known hops.
Maximum Time to Live [30]	The largest TTL value that can be used. The default is 30. The **trace** command terminates when the destination is reached or when this value is reached.

Table 29-30 *Trace Field Descriptions, Continued*

Field	Description
Port Number	The destination port used by the UDP probe messages. The default is 33434.
Loose, Strict, Record, Timestamp, Verbose	IP header options. You can specify any combination. The **trace** command issues prompts for the required fields. Note that **trace** will place the requested options in each probe; however, there is no guarantee that all routers (or end nodes) will process the options.
Loose	Allows you to specify a list of nodes that must be traversed when going to the destination.
Strict	Allows you to specify a list of nodes that must be the only nodes traversed when going to the destination.
Record	Allows you to specify the number of hops for which to leave room.
Timestamp	Allows you to specify the number of time stamps needing room.
Verbose	If you select any option, the verbose mode is automatically selected and **trace** prints the contents of the option field in any incoming packets. You can prevent verbose mode by selecting it again, toggling its current setting.

Table 29-31 describes the characters that can appear in **trace** command output.

Table 29-31 *IP Trace Text Characters*

Char	Description
nn msec	For each node, the round-trip time in milliseconds for the specified number of probes.
*	The probe timed out.
?	Unknown packet type.
A	Administratively unreachable. Usually, this output indicates that an access list is blocking traffic.
H	Host unreachable.
N	Network unreachable.
P	Protocol unreachable.
Q	Source quench.
U	Port unreachable.

Related Commands

trace (user)

TRACE (USER)

Use the **trace** EXEC command to discover the IP routes that packets actually will take when traveling to their destination.

> **trace** [*protocol*] [*destination*]

Syntax	Description
protocol	(Optional) Protocols that can be used are **appletalk, clns, ip** and **vines**.
destination	(Optional) Destination address or host name on the command line. The default parameters for the appropriate protocol are assumed and the tracing action begins.

Default

The *protocol* argument is based on the Cisco IOS software examination of the format of the *destination* argument. For example, if the software finds a *destination* in IP format, the *protocol* defaults to **ip**.

Command Mode

EXEC

Usage Guidelines

This command first appeared in Cisco IOS Release 10.0.

The **trace** command works by taking advantage of the error messages generated by routers when a datagram exceeds its time-to-live (TTL) value.

The **trace** command starts by sending probe datagrams with a TTL value of one. This causes the first router to discard the probe datagram and send back an error message. The **trace** command sends several probes at each TTL level and displays the round-trip time for each.

The **trace** command sends out one probe at a time. Each outgoing packet might result in one or two error messages. A "time exceeded" error message indicates that an intermediate router has seen and discarded the probe. A "destination unreachable" error message indicates that the destination node has received the probe and discarded it, because it could not deliver the packet. If the timer goes off before a response comes in, **trace** prints an asterisk (*).

The **trace** command terminates when the destination responds, when the maximum TTL is exceeded, or when the user interrupts the trace with the escape sequence. By default, to invoke the escape sequence, type **Ctrl-^ X** by simultaneously pressing and releasing the **Ctrl, Shift,** and **6** keys, and then pressing the **X** key.

Common Trace Problems

Due to bugs in the IP implementation of various hosts and routers, the IP **trace** command might behave in odd ways.

Not all destinations will respond correctly to a probe message by sending back an "ICMP port unreachable" message. A long sequence of TTL levels with only asterisks, terminating only when the maximum TTL has been reached, might indicate this problem.

There is a known problem with the way some hosts handle an "ICMP TTL exceeded" message. Some hosts generate an *ICMP* message, but they reuse the TTL of the incoming packet. Because this is zero, the ICMP packets do not make it back. When you trace the path to such a host, you might see a set of TTL values with asterisks (*). Eventually, the TTL gets high enough that the "ICMP" message can get back. For example, if the host is six hops away, **trace** will time out on responses 6 through 11.

Sample Display Showing Trace IP Routes

The following display shows sample IP **trace** output when a destination host name has been specified:

```
Router# trace ip ABA.NYC.mil

Type escape sequence to abort.
Tracing the route to ABA.NYC.mil (26.0.0.73)
  1 DEBRIS.CISCO.COM (192.180.1.6) 1000 msec 8 msec 4 msec
  2 BARRNET-GW.CISCO.COM (192.180.16.2) 8 msec 8 msec 8 msec
  3 EXTERNAL-A-GATEWAY.STANFORD.EDU (192.42.110.225) 8 msec 4 msec 4 msec
  4 BB2.SU.BARRNET.NET (192.200.254.6) 8 msec 8 msec 8 msec
  5 SU.ARC.BARRNET.NET (192.200.3.8) 12 msec 12 msec 8 msec
  6 MOFFETT-FLD-MB.in.MIL (192.52.195.1) 216 msec 120 msec 132 msec
  7 ABA.NYC.mil (26.0.0.73) 412 msec 628 msec 664 msec
```

Table 29–32 describes the fields shown in the display.

Table 29–32 *Trace Field Descriptions*

Field	Description
1	Indicates the sequence number of the router in the path to the host.
DEBRIS.CISCO.COM	Host name of this router.
192.180.1.61	Internet address of this router.
1000 msec 8 msec 4 msec	Round-trip time for each of the three probes that are sent.

Table 29–33 describes the characters that can appear in **trace** output.

Table 29–33   *IP Trace Text Characters*

Char	Description
nn msec	For each node, the round-trip time in milliseconds for the specified number of probes.
*	The probe timed out.
?	Unknown packet type.
A	Administratively unreachable. Usually, this output indicates that an access list is blocking traffic.
H	Host unreachable.
N	Network unreachable.
P	Protocol unreachable.
Q	Source quench.
U	Port unreachable.

Related Commands

trace (privileged)

## CHAPTER 30

Performing Basic System Management

This chapter describes the basic tasks that you can perform to manage the general system features of the Cisco IOS software—those features that are generally not specific to a particular protocol.

For a complete description of the basic system management commands in this chapter, see Chapter 31, "Basic System Management Commands."

BASIC SYSTEM MANAGEMENT TASK LIST

This chapter describes the basic system management tasks you can perform. Perform any of the tasks in the following sections:

- Customizing the Router Prompt
- Setting the Router Name
- Creating and Monitoring Command Aliases
- Enabling Minor Services
- Enabling the Finger Protocol
- Hiding Telnet Addresses
- Generating a Donward-Compatible Configuration
- Setting Time and Calendar Services
- Delaying EXEC Startup
- Handling Idle Telnet Connection

See the "Basic System Management Examples" section at the end of this chapter for examples.

CUSTOMIZING THE ROUTER PROMPT

By default, the prompt consists of the router name followed by an angle bracket (>) for EXEC mode or a pound sign (#) for privileged EXEC mode. To customize your prompt, perform the following task in global configuration mode:

Task	Command
Step 1 Customize the prompt.	**prompt** *string*
Step 2 Remove the configuration prompt (config).	**no service prompt config**

SETTING THE ROUTER NAME

One of the first basic tasks is to name your router. The name is considered the host name and is the name that is displayed by the system prompt. If no name is configured, the system default name is Router. You can name the router in global configuration mode as follows:

Task	Command
Set the host name.	**hostname** *name*

For an example of configuring a router name, see the section "System Configuration File Example" at the end of this chapter.

CREATING AND MONITORING COMMAND ALIASES

You can create aliases for commonly used or complex commands. Use word substitutions or abbreviations to tailor command syntax for you and your user community.

To create and display command aliases, perform the tasks in the following sections:

- Creating a Command Alias
- Displaying Command Aliases

Creating a Command Alias

To create a command alias, perform the following task in global configuration mode:

Task	Command
Configure a command alias.	**alias** *mode alias-name alias-command-line*

Displaying Command Aliases

To display alias names and the original command syntax, perform the following task in EXEC mode:

Task	Command
Show all command aliases and original command syntax, or specify the aliases in a particular command mode.	show aliases [*mode*]

ENABLING MINOR SERVICES

You can access minor TCP, UDP, and BOOTP services available from hosts on the network. These services are enabled by default.

To enable these services, perform the following tasks in global configuration mode:

Task		Command
Step 1	Access minor TCP services such as echo, chargen, discard, and daytime.	service tcp-small-servers
Step 2	Access minor UDP services such as echo, chargen, and discard.	service udp-small-servers
Step 3	Access the BOOTP service.	ip bootp server

ENABLING THE FINGER PROTOCOL

You can enable the Finger protocol so that people throughout the network can get a list of the users currently using the router. The information displayed includes the processes running on the system, the line number, connection name, idle time, and terminal location. To enable the Finger protocol, perform the following task in global configuration mode:

Task	Command
Enable the Finger protocol requests.	service finger

HIDING TELNET ADDRESSES

You can hide addresses while attempting to establish a Telnet session. To configure the router to suppress Telnet addresses, perform the following task in global configuration mode:

Task	Command
Hide addresses while establishing a Telnet session.	service hide-telnet-address

The hide feature suppresses the display of the address and continues to display all other messages that normally would display during a connection attempt, such as detailed error messages if the connection was not successful.

Use the **busy-message** command with the **service hide-telnet-address** command to customize the information displayed during Telnet connection attempts. If the connection attempt is not successful, the router suppresses the address and displays the message specified with the **busy-message** command.

GENERATING A DOWNWARD-COMPATIBLE CONFIGURATION

In Cisco IOS Release 10.3, IP access lists changed format. If you decide to downgrade from Release 11.0 to Release 10.2, you can configure the software to regenerate a configuration in the format of Release 10.2, thereby saving time and making your IP access lists compatible with the software.

To have the software regenerate a configuration in the format prior to Release 10.3, perform the following task in global configuration mode:

Task	Command
Generate a backward-compatible configuration.	**downward-compatible-config** *version*

SETTING TIME AND CALENDAR SERVICES

All Cisco routers provide an array of time-of-day services. These services allow the products to keep track of the current time and date accurately, to synchronize multiple products to the same time, and to provide time services to other systems. The following sections describe the time and calendar tasks:

- Understanding Time Sources
- Configuring NTP
- Configuring SNTP
- Configuring VINES Time Service
- Configuring Time and Date Manually
- Monitoring Time and Calendar Services

Understanding Time Sources

The heart of the time service is the system clock. This clock runs from the moment the system starts up and keeps track of the current date and time. The system clock can be set from a number of sources and, in turn, can be used to distribute the current time through various mechanisms to other systems. When a router with a system calendar is initialized, the system clock is set based on the time in its internal battery-powered calendar; on other models, the system clock is set to midnight on March 1, 1993. The system clock can then be set from the following sources:

- Network Time Protocol (NTP)
- Simple Network Time Protocol (SNTP)
- VINES Time Service
- Manual configuration

The system clock can provide time to the following services:

- NTP
- VINES Time Service
- User **show** commands
- Logging and debugging messages

NOTES

The system clock cannot provide time to the NTP or VINES Time Service if it was set using SNTP.

The system clock keeps track of time internally based on Coordinated Universal Time (UTC), also known as Greenwich Mean Time (GMT). You can configure information about the local time zone and summer time (daylight savings time) so that the time is displayed correctly relative to the local time zone.

The system clock keeps track of whether the time is "authoritative" (that is, whether it has been set by a time source considered to be authoritative). If it is not authoritative, the time will be available only for display purposes and will not be redistributed.

Network Time Protocol

The Network Time Protocol (NTP) is a protocol designed to time-synchronize a network of machines. NTP runs over UDP, which, in turn, runs over IP. NTP is documented in RFC 1305.

An NTP network usually gets its time from an authoritative time source, such as a radio clock or an atomic clock attached to a time server. NTP then distributes this time across the network. NTP is extremely efficient; no more than one packet per minute is necessary to synchronize two machines to within a millisecond of one another.

NTP uses the concept of a "stratum" to describe how many NTP "hops" away a machine is from an authoritative time source. A "stratum 1" time server has a radio or atomic clock directly attached; a "stratum 2" time server receives its time via NTP from a "stratum 1" time server, and so on. A machine running NTP automatically will choose as its time source the machine with the lowest stratum number that it is configured to communicate with via NTP. This strategy effectively builds a self-organizing tree of NTP speakers.

NTP is careful to avoid synchronizing to a machine whose time might not be accurate. It avoids doing so in two ways. First of all, NTP never will synchronize to a machine that is not in turn synchronized itself. Secondly, NTP will compare the time reported by several machines, and will not synchronize to a machine whose time is significantly different than the others, even if its stratum is lower.

The communications between machines running NTP (known as "associations") are usually statically configured; each machine is given the IP address of all machines with which it should form associations. Accurate timekeeping is made possible by exchanging NTP messages between each pair of machines with an association. However, in a local-area network (LAN) environment, NTP can be configured to use IP broadcast messages instead. This alternative reduces configuration complexity, because each machine can be configured simply to send or receive broadcast messages. However, the accuracy of timekeeping is marginally reduced because the information flow is one-way only.

The time kept on a machine is a critical resource, so Cisco strongly recommends that you use the security features of NTP to avoid the accidental or malicious setting of incorrect time. Two mechanisms are available: an access list-based restriction scheme and an encrypted authentication mechanism.

Cisco's implementation of NTP does not support stratum 1 service; in other words, it is not possible to connect to a radio or atomic clock. It is recommended that time service for your network be derived from the public NTP servers available in the IP Internet. If the network is isolated from the Internet, Cisco's implementation of NTP allows a machine to be configured so that it acts as though it is synchronized via NTP, when in fact it has determined the time using other means. Other machines then synchronize to that machine via NTP.

When multiple sources of time (VINES, system calendar, manual configuration) are available, NTP is always considered to be more authoritative. NTP time overrides the time set by any other method.

A number of manufacturers include NTP software for their host systems, and a publicly available version for systems running UNIX and its various derivatives is also available. This software allows host systems to be time-synchronized as well.

Simple Network Time Protocol (SNTP)

Simple Network Time Protocol (SNTP) is a simplified, client-only version of NTP for use on Cisco 1003, Cisco 1004, and Cisco 1005 routers. SNMP can receive the time only from NTP servers; it cannot be used to provide time services to other systems.

SNTP typically provides time within 100 milliseconds of the accurate time, but it does not provide the complex filtering and statistical mechanisms of NTP. In addition, SNTP does not authenticate traffic, although you can configure extended access lists to provide some protection. An SNTP client is more vulnerable to misbehaving servers than an NTP client and should only be used in situations where strong authentication is not required.

You can configure SNTP to request and accept packets from configured servers or to accept NTP broadcast packets from any source. When multiple sources are sending NTP packets, the server with the best stratum is selected. (See the "Network Time Protocol" section earlier in this chapter for a description of strata). If multiple servers are at the same stratum, a configured server is preferred over a broadcast server. If multiple servers pass both tests, the first one to send a time packet is selected. SNTP will choose a new server only if it stops receiving packets from the currently selected server, or if a better server (according to the above criteria) is discovered.

VINES Time Service

Time service is also available when Banyan VINES is configured. This protocol is a standard part of VINES. Cisco's implementation allows the VINES time service to be used in two ways. First, if the system has learned the time from some other source, it can act as a VINES time server and provide time to other machines running VINES. It also can use the VINES time service to set the system clock if no other form of time service is available.

Calendar System

Some routers contain a battery-powered calendar system that tracks the date and time across system restarts and power outages. This calendar system is always used to initialize the system clock when the system is restarted. It also can be considered to be an authoritative source of time and be redistributed via NTP or VINES time service if no other source is available. Furthermore, if NTP is running, the calendar can be periodically updated from NTP, compensating for the inherent drift in the calendar time.

Configuring NTP

NTP services are enabled on all interfaces by default. The optional tasks you can perform are documented in the following sections:

- Configuring NTP Authentication
- Configuring NTP Associations
- Configuring NTP Broadcast Service
- Configuring NTP Access Restrictions
- Configuring the Source IP Address for NTP Packets
- Configuring the System as an Authoritative NTP Server
- Configuring NTP to Update the Calendar

Configuring NTP Authentication

If you want to authenticate the associations with other systems for security purposes, perform the tasks that follow. The first task enables the NTP authentication feature. The second task defines each of the authentication keys. Each key has a key number, a type, and a value. Currently, the only key type supported is **md5**. Third, a list of "trusted" authentication keys is defined. If a key is trusted, this system will be ready to synchronize to a system that uses this key in its NTP packets.

To configure NTP authentication, perform the following tasks in global configuration mode:

Task	Command
Step 1 Enable the NTP authentication feature.	**ntp authenticate**
Step 2 Define the authentication keys.	**ntp authentication-key** *number* **md5** *value*
Step 3 Define trusted authentication keys.	**ntp trusted-key** *key-number*

Configuring NTP Associations

An NTP association can be a peer association (meaning that this system is willing either to synchronize to the other system or to allow the other system to synchronize to it), or it can be a server association (meaning that this system will synchronize to the other system, and not the other way around). If you want to form an NTP association with another system, perform one of the following tasks in global configuration mode:

Task	Command
Form a peer association with another system.	**ntp peer** *ip-address* [**version** *number*] [**key** *keyid*] [**source** *interface*] [**prefer**]
Form a server association with another system.	**ntp server** *ip-address* [**version** *number*] [**key** *keyid*] [**source** *interface*] [**prefer**]

Note that only one end of an association needs to be configured; the other system automatically will establish the association.

See the example "Clock, Calendar, and NTP Configuration Examples" at the end of this chapter.

Configuring NTP Broadcast Service

The system can either send broadcast packets or listen to them on an interface-by-interface basis. The estimated round-trip delay for broadcast packets also can be configured. Perform one or more of the following tasks in global configuration mode if you want to use NTP's broadcast feature:

Task	Command
Send NTP broadcast packets.	**ntp broadcast** [**version** *number*]

Task	Command
Receive NTP broadcast packets.	**ntp broadcast client**
Adjust estimated delay.	**ntp broadcastdelay** *microseconds*

See the example "Clock, Calendar, and NTP Configuration Examples" at the end of this chapter.

Configuring NTP Access Restrictions

You can control NTP access on two levels by completing the tasks in the following sections:

- Creating an Access Group and Assigning a Basic IP Access List to It
- Disabling NTP Services on a Specific Interface

Creating an Access Group and Assigning a Basic IP Access List to It

To control access to NTP services, you can create an NTP access group and apply a basic IP access list to it. To do so, perform the following task in global configuration mode:

Task	Command
Create an access group and apply a basic IP access list to it.	**ntp access-group** {**query-only** | **serve-only** | **serve** | **peer**} *access-list-number*

The access-group options are scanned in the following order from least restrictive to most restrictive:

1. Peer—Allows time requests and NTP control queries and allows the system to synchronize itself to a system whose address passes the access-list criteria.

2. Serve—Allows time requests and NTP control queries, but does not allow the system to synchronize itself to a system whose address passes the access-list criteria.

3. Serve-only—Allows only time requests from a system whose address passes the access-list criteria.

4. Query-only—Allows only NTP control queries from a system whose address passes the access-list criteria.

If the source IP address matches the access lists for more than one access type, the first type is granted. If no access groups are specified, all access types are granted to all systems. If any access groups are specified, only the specified access types will be granted.

For details on NTP control queries, see RFC 1305 (NTP version 3).

Disabling NTP Services on a Specific Interface

NTP services are enabled on all interfaces by default. You can disable NTP packets from being received through an interface by performing the following task in interface configuration mode:

Task	Command
Disable NTP services on a specific interface.	ntp disable

Configuring the Source IP Address for NTP Packets

When the system sends an NTP packet, the source IP address is normally set to the address of the interface through which the NTP packet is sent. Perform the following task in global configuration mode if you want to configure a specific interface from which the IP source address will be taken:

Task	Command
Configure an interface from which the IP source address will be taken.	ntp source *interface*

This interface will be used for the source address for all packets sent to all destinations. If a source address is to be used for a specific association, use the **source** parameter on the **ntp peer** or **ntp server** command shown earlier in this chapter.

Configuring the System as an Authoritative NTP Server

Perform the following task in global configuration mode if you want the system to be an authoritative NTP server, even if the system is not synchronized to an outside time source:

Task	Command
Make the system an authoritative NTP server.	ntp master [*stratum*]

CAUTION

Use this command with extreme caution. It is very easy to override valid time sources using this command, especially if a low stratum number is configured. Configuring multiple machines in the same network with the **ntp master** command can cause instability in timekeeping if the machines do not agree on the time.

For an example of configuring an authoritative NTP server, see the section "Clock, Calendar, and NTP Configuration Examples" at the end of this chapter.

Configuring NTP to Update the Calendar

On systems that have calendars, you can configure NTP to update the calendar periodically.

Perform the following task in global configuration mode if the system is synchronized to an outside time source via NTP, and you want the calendar to be synchronized periodically to NTP time:

Task	Command
Configure NTP to update the calendar.	**ntp update-calendar**

For an example of configuring NTP to update the calendar, see the section "Clock, Calendar, and NTP Configuration Examples" at the end of this chapter.

Configuring SNTP

SNTP is disabled by default. In order to enable SNTP on a Cisco 1003, Cisco 1004, or Cisco 1005 router, perform one or both of the following tasks in global configuration mode:

Task	Command
Configure SNTP to request NTP packets from an NTP server.	**sntp server** {*address* | *hostname*} [**version** *number*]
Configure SNTP to accept NTP packets from any NTP broadcast server.	**sntp broadcast client**

Enter the **sntp server** command once for each NTP server. The NTP servers must be configured to respond to the SNTP messages from the router.

If you enter both the **sntp server** command and the **sntp broadcast client** command, the router will accept time from a broadcast server but prefers time from a configured server, assuming the strata are equal.

To display information about SNTP, use the **show sntp** EXEC command.

Configuring VINES Time Service

Perform the following task in global configuration mode if you want to distribute the system clock to other VINES systems:

Task	Command
Distribute the system clock to other VINES systems.	**vines time use-system**

To receive VINES time service to control the system clock, perform the following task in global configuration mode:

Task	Command
Receive VINES time service.	**vines time set-system**

Configuring Time and Date Manually

If no other source of time is available, you can configure the current time and date manually after the system is restarted. The time will remain accurate until the next system restart. Cisco recommends that you use manual configuration only as a last resort.

To set up time services, complete the tasks in the following sections as needed. If you have an outside source to which the router can synchronize, you do not need to set the system clock manually.

- Configuring the Time Zone
- Configuring Summer Time (Daylight Savings Time)
- Setting the System Clock
- Setting the System Calendar

Configuring the Time Zone

Complete the following task in global configuration mode to configure manually the time zone used by the Cisco IOS software:

Task	Command
Set the time zone.	**clock timezone** *zone hours* [*minutes*]

For an example of configuring the time zone, see the section "Clock, Calendar, and NTP Configuration Examples" at the end of this chapter.

Configuring Summer Time (Daylight Savings Time)

To configure summer time (daylight savings time) in areas where it starts and ends on a particular day of the week each year, perform the following task in global configuration mode:

Task	Command
Configure summer time.	**clock summer-time** *zone* **recurring** [*week day month hh:mm week day month hh:mm* [*offset*]]

If summer time in your area does not follow this pattern, you can configure the exact date and time of the next summer time events by performing one of the following tasks in global configuration mode:

Task	Command
Configure summer time.	**clock summer-time** *zone* **date** *month date year hh:mm month date year hh:mm* [*offset*]
	or
	clock summer-time *zone* **date** *date month year hh:mm date month year hh:mm* [*offset*]

For an example of configuring summer time, see the section "Clock, Calendar, and NTP Configuration Examples" at the end of this chapter.

Setting the System Clock

If you have an outside source on the network that provides time services (such as an NTP server or VINES time service), you do not need to set the system clock manually.

However, if you do not have any time service source, complete one of the following tasks in EXEC mode to set the system clock:

Task	Command
Set the system clock.	**clock set** *hh:mm:ss date month year*
	or
	clock set *hh:mm:ss month date year*

Setting the System Calendar

Some routers have a separate system calendar in addition to the system clock. The calendar can set the system time and control the system clock, as well as enable the router to act as a time service for the network.

You can complete the tasks in the following sections to enable the calendar capabilities:

- Setting the Router Calendar
- Setting the Router as a Network Time Source
- Setting the System Clock from the Calendar
- Setting the Calendar from the System Clock

Setting the Router Calendar

The calendar maintains time separately from the system clock. It continues to run when the system is restarted or power is turned off. Typically, it only needs to be set manually once, when the system is first installed. If time is available from an external source using NTP, the calendar can be updated from the system clock instead.

If you do not have an external time source, perform the following task in EXEC mode to set the system calendar:

Task	Command
Set the calendar.	**calendar set** *hh:mm:ss day month year*
	or
	calendar set *hh:mm:ss month day year*

Setting the Router as a Network Time Source

Although the system clock is always initialized from the calendar when the system is restarted, by default it is not considered to be authoritative and so will not be redistributed with NTP or VINES Time Service. To make the calendar be authoritative, complete the following task in global configuration mode:

Task	Command
Enable the router to act as a valid time source to which network peers can synchronize.	**clock calendar-valid**

For an example of making the calendar authoritative, see the section "Clock, Calendar, and NTP Configuration Examples" at the end of this chapter.

Setting the System Clock from the Calendar

To set the system clock to the new calendar setting, perform the following task in EXEC mode:

Task	Command
Set the system clock from the calendar.	**clock read-calendar**

Setting the Calendar from the System Clock

To update the calendar with the new clock setting, perform the following task in EXEC mode:

Task	Command
Set the calendar from the system clock.	clock update-calendar

Monitoring Time and Calendar Services

To monitor clock, calendar, and NTP EXEC services, complete the following tasks in EXEC mode:

Task		Command
Step 1	Display the current calendar time.	show calendar
Step 2	Display the current system clock time.	show clock [detail]
Step 3	Show the status of NTP associations.	show ntp associations [detail]
Step 4	Show the status of NTP.	show ntp status
Step 5	Display information about SNTP (Cisco 1003, Cisco 1004, and Cisco 1005 only).	show sntp

DELAYING EXEC STARTUP

You can delay the startup of the EXEC on noisy lines until the line has been idle for three seconds. To do so, perform the following task in global configuration mode:

Task	Command
Delay startup of the EXEC.	service exec-wait

This command is useful on noisy modem lines or when a modem attached to the line is configured to ignore MNP or V.42 negotiations, and MNP or V.42 modems may be dialing in. In these cases, noise or MNP/V.42 packets might be interpreted as usernames and passwords, causing authentication failure before the user can type a username/password. The command is not useful on nonmodem lines or lines without some kind of login configured.

HANDLING IDLE TELNET CONNECTION

You can configure the Cisco IOS software to set the TCP window to zero (0) when the Telnet connection is idle. To do so, perform the following task in global configuration mode:

Task	Command
Set the TCP window to zero when the Telnet connection is idle.	service telnet-zero-idle

Normally, data sent to noncurrent Telnet connections is accepted and discarded. When **service telnet-zero-idle** is enabled, if a session is suspended (that is, some other connection is made active or the EXEC is sitting in command mode), the TCP window is set to zero. This action prevents the remote host from sending any more data until the connection is resumed. Use this command when it is important that all messages sent by the host be seen by the users and the users are likely to use multiple sessions. Do not use this command if your host eventually will time out and log out a TCP user whose window is zero.

BASIC SYSTEM MANAGEMENT EXAMPLES

The following sections provide system management examples:

- System Configuration File Example
- Clock, Calendar, and NTP Configuration Examples

System Configuration File Example

The following is an example of a typical system configuration file:

```
! Define line password
line 0 4
 password secret
 login
!
! Define privileged-level password
enable-password Secret Word
!
! Define a system hostname
hostname TIP
! Specify a configuration file to load at system startup
boot host host1-confg 192.168.1.111
boot host host2-confg 192.168.1.111
! Specify the system image to boot at startup
boot system sys1-system 192.168.13.111
boot system sys2-system 192.168.1.111
boot system rom
!
```

```
! Enable SNMP
snmp-server community red
snmp-server enable traps snmp authentication
snmp-server host 192.168.1.27 public
snmp-server host 192.168.1.111 public
snmp-server host 192.168.2.63 public
!
! Define TACACS server hosts
tacacs-server host 192.168.1.27
tacacs-server host 192.168.13.33
tacacs-server host 192.168.1.33
!
! Define a message-of-the-day banner
banner motd ^C
The Information Place welcomes you

Please call 1-800-555-2222 for a login account, or enter
your password at the prompt.
^C
```

Clock, Calendar, and NTP Configuration Examples

In the following example, a router with a system calendar has server associations with two other systems; transmits broadcast NTP packets; periodically updates the calendar, and redistributes time into VINES:

```
clock timezone PST -8
clock summer-time PDT recurring
ntp update-calendar
ntp server 192.168.13.57
ntp server 192.168.11.58
interface Ethernet 0/0
 ntp broadcast
vines time use-system
```

In the following example, a router with a calendar has no outside time source, so it uses the calendar as an authoritative time source and distributes the time via NTP broadcast packets.

```
clock timezone MET 2
clock calendar-valid
ntp master
interface fddi 0/0
 ntp broadcast
```

## CHAPTER 31

Basic System Management Commands

This chapter describes the commands used to perform basic system management tasks, such as naming the router and setting time services.

For basic system management configuration tasks and examples, see Chapter 30, "Performing Basic System Management."

ALIAS

To create a command alias, use the **alias** global configuration command. Use the **no** form of this command to delete all aliases in a command mode or to delete a specific alias, and to revert to the original command syntax.

> **alias** *mode alias-name alias-command-line*
> **no alias** *mode* [*alias-name*]

Syntax	Description
mode	Command mode of the original and alias commands. See Table 31–1 for a list of options for this argument.
alias-name	Command alias.
alias-command-line	Original command syntax.

Defaults

Default aliases are in EXEC mode as follows:

Command Alias	Original Command
h	help
lo	logout
p	ping
r	resume
s	show
w	where

Command Mode

Global configuration

Usage Guidelines

This command first appeared in Cisco IOS Release 10.3.

You can use simple words or abbreviations as aliases. The aliases in the "Defaults" section are pre-defined. They can be turned off using the **no alias** command.

Table 31–1 shows the acceptable options for the *mode* argument in the **alias** global configuration command.

Table 31–1   *Mode Argument Options*

Argument Options	Mode
configuration	Global configuration
controller	Controller configuration
exec	EXEC
hub	Hub configuration
interface	Interface configuration
ipx-router	IPX router configuration
line	Line configuration
map-class	Map class configuration
map-list	Map list configuration

Table 31-1 *Mode Argument Options, Continued*

Argument Options	Mode
route-map	Route map configuration
router	Router configuration

See the summary of command modes in Chapter 2, "Basic Command Line Interface Commands" for more information about command modes.

When you use online help, command aliases are indicated by an asterisk (*), as follows:

```
Router#lo?
*lo=logout  lock  login  logout
```

When you use online help, aliases that contain spaces (for example, telnet device.cisco.com 25) are displayed as follows:

```
Router# configure terminal
Enter configuration commands, one per line. End with CNTL/Z.
Router(config)# alias exec device-mail telnet device.cisco.com 25
Router(config)# end
Router# device-mail?
*device-mail="telnet device.cisco.com 25"
```

When you use online help, the alias is expanded and replaced with the original command, as shown in the following example with the **td** alias:

```
Router(config)# alias exec td trace device
Router(config)# ^Z
Router# t?
*td="trace device" telnet terminal test tn3270
trace
```

To list only commands and omit aliases, begin your input line with a space. In the following example, the alias **td** is not shown, because there is a space before the **t?** command line.

```
Router# t?
telnet terminal test tn3270 trace
```

As with commands, you can use online help to display the arguments and keywords that can follow a command alias. In the following example, the alias **td** is created to represent the command **telnet device**. The **/debug** and **/line** switches can be added to **telnet device** to modify the command:

```
Router(config)# alias exec td telnet device
Router(config)# ^Z
Router# td ?
/debug    Enable telnet debugging mode
     /line     Enable telnet line mode
   ...
```

```
        whois      Whois port
      · <cr>
  Router# telnet device
```

You must enter the complete syntax for the **alias** command. Partial syntax for aliases are not accepted. In the following example, the parser does not recognize the command **t** as indicating the alias **td**.

```
  Router# t
  % Ambiguous command: "t"
```

Example

In the following example, the alias **fixmyrt** is created for the IP route198.92.116.16:

```
  alias exec fixmyrt clear ip route 198.92.116.16
```

Related Commands

show aliases

CALENDAR SET

To set the system calendar, use one of the formats of the **calendar set** EXEC command.

> **calendar set** *hh:mm:ss day month year*
> **calendar set** *hh:mm:ss month day year*

Syntax	Description
hh:mm:ss	Current time in hours (military format), minutes, and seconds.
day	Current day (by date) in the month.
month	Current month (by name).
year	Current year (no abbreviation).

Command Mode

EXEC

Usage Guidelines

This command first appeared in Cisco IOS Release 10.0.

Some platforms have a calendar that is separate from the system clock. This calendar runs continuously, even if the router is powered off or rebooted. After you set the calendar, the system clock automatically will be set from the calendar when the system is restarted or when the **clock read-calendar** EXEC command is issued. The time specified in this command is relative to the configured time zone.

Example

In the following example, the system calendar is set manually to 1:32 p.m. on July 23, 1997:

```
  calendar set 13:32:00 23 July 1997
```

Related Commands

clock read-calendar
clock set
clock summer-time
clock timezone
clock update-calendar

CLOCK CALENDAR-VALID

To configure a router as a time source for a network based on its calendar, use the **clock calendar-valid** global configuration command. Use the **no** form of this command to specify that the calendar is not an authoritative time source.

>   clock calendar-valid
>   no clock calendar-valid

Syntax   Description

This command has no arguments or keywords.

Default

The router is not configured as a time source.

Command Mode

Global configuration

Usage Guidelines

This command first appeared in Cisco IOS Release 10.0.

Some platforms have a calendar that is separate from the system clock. This calendar runs continuously, even if the router is powered off or rebooted. If you have no outside time source available on your network, use this command to make the calendar an authoritative time source.

Example

In the following example, a router is configured as the time source for a network based on its calendar:

```
clock calendar-valid
```

Related Commands

ntp master
vines time use-system

CLOCK READ-CALENDAR

To read the calendar into the system clock manually, use the **clock read-calendar** EXEC command.

clock read-calendar

Syntax   Description

This command has no arguments or keywords.

Command Mode

EXEC

Usage Guidelines

This command first appeared in Cisco IOS Release 10.0.

Some platforms have a calendar that is separate from the system clock. This calendar runs continuously, even if the router is powered off or rebooted. When the router is rebooted, the calendar is automatically read into the system clock. However, you may use this command to read the calendar setting into the system clock manually. This command is useful if the **calendar set** command has been used to change the setting of the calendar.

Example

In the following example, the system clock is configured to set its date and time by the calendar setting:

```
clock read-calendar
```

Related Commands

calendar set
clock set
clock update-calendar
ntp update-calendar

CLOCK SET

To set the system clock manually, use one of the formats of the **clock set** EXEC command.

clock set *hh:mm:ss day month year*
clock set *hh:mm:ss month day year*

Syntax   *Description*

hh:mm:ss   Current time in hours (military format), minutes, and seconds.

day   Current day (by date) in the month.

Syntax	Description
month	Current month (by name).
year	Current year (no abbreviation).

Command Mode

EXEC

Usage Guidelines

This command first appeared in Cisco IOS Release 10.0.

Generally, if the system is synchronized by a valid outside timing mechanism, such as an NTP or VINES clock source, or if you have a router with calendar capability, you do not need to set the system clock. Use this command if no other time sources are available. The time specified in this command is relative to the configured time zone.

Example

In the following example, the system clock is set manually to 1:32 p.m. on July 23, 1997:

```
clock set 13:32:00 23 July 1997
```

Related Commands

calendar set
clock read-calendar
clock summer-time
clock timezone

CLOCK SUMMER-TIME

To configure the system to switch to summer time (daylight savings time) automatically, use one of the formats of the **clock summer-time** global configuration command. Use the **no** form of this command to configure the Cisco IOS software not to switch to summer time automatically.

> **clock summer-time** *zone* **recurring** [*week day month hh:mm week day month hh:mm* [*offset*]]
> **clock summer-time** *zone* **date** *date month year hh:mm date month year hh:mm* [*offset*]
> **clock summer-time** *zone* **date** *month date year hh:mm month date year hh:mm* [*offset*]
> **no clock summer-time**

Syntax	Description
zone	Name of the time zone (PDT,...) to be displayed when summer time is in effect.
recurring	Indicates that summer time should start and end on the corresponding specified days every year.

Syntax	Description
date	Indicates that summer time should start on the first specific date listed in the command and end on the second specific date in the command.
week	Week of the month (1 to 5 or **last**).
day	Day of the week (Sunday, Monday,...).
date	Date of the month (1 to 31).
month	Month (January, February,...).
year	Year (1993 to 2035).
hh:mm	Time (military format) in hours and minutes.
offset	(Optional) Number of minutes to add during summer time (default is 60).
zone	Name of the time zone (PDT,...) to be displayed when summer time is in effect.

Default

Summer time is disabled. If **clock summer-time** *zone* **recurring** is specified without parameters, the summer time rules default to United States rules. Default of *offset* is 60.

Command Mode

Global configuration

Usage Guidelines

This command first appeared in Cisco IOS Release 10.0.

Use this command if you want to switch to summer time (for display purposes only) automatically. Use the **recurring** form of the command if the local summer time rules are of this form. Use the **date** form to specify a start and end date for summer time if you cannot use the first form.

In both forms of the command, the first part of the command specifies when summer time begins, and the second part specifies when it ends. All times are relative to the local time zone. The start time is relative to standard time. The end time is relative to summer time. If the starting month is after the ending month, the system assumes that you are in the Southern Hemisphere.

Examples

In the following example, summer time starts on the first Sunday in April at 2:00 and ends on the last Sunday in October at 2:00:

```
clock summer-time PDT recurring 1 Sunday April 2:00 last Sunday October 2:00
```

If you live in a place where summer time does not follow the pattern in the first example, you could set it to start on October 12, 1997 at 2:00, and end on April 26, 1998 at 2:00, with the following example:

```
clock summer-time date 12 October 1997 2:00 26 April 1998 2:00
```

Related Commands

calendar set
clock timezone

CLOCK TIMEZONE

To set the time zone for display purposes, use the **clock timezone** global configuration command. To set the time to Coordinated Universal Time (UTC), use the **no** form of this command.

> **clock timezone** *zone hours* [*minutes*]
> **no clock timezone**

Syntax	Description
zone	Name of the time zone to be displayed when standard time is in effect.
hours	Hours offset from UTC.
minutes	(Optional) Minutes offset from UTC.

Default

UTC

Command Mode

Global configuration

Usage Guidelines

This command first appeared in Cisco IOS Release 10.0.

The system internally keeps time in UTC, so this command is used only for display purposes and when the time is set manually.

Example

In the following example, the time zone is set to Pacific Standard Time and is offset eight hours behind UTC:

```
clock timezone PST -8
```

Related Commands

calendar set
clock set
clock summer-time
show clock

CLOCK UPDATE-CALENDAR

To set the calendar from the system clock, use the **clock update-calendar** EXEC command.

   clock update-calendar

Syntax   Description

This command has no arguments or keywords.

Command Mode

EXEC

Usage Guidelines

This command first appeared in Cisco IOS Release 10.0.

Some platforms have a calendar that is separate from the system clock. This calendar runs continuously, even if the router is powered off or rebooted.

If the system clock and calendar are not synchronized, and the system clock is more accurate, use this command to update the calendar to the correct date and time.

Example

In the following example, the current time is copied from the system clock to the calendar:

```
clock update-calendar
```

Related Commands

clock read-calendar
ntp update-calendar

DOWNWARD-COMPATIBLE-CONFIG

To generate a configuration that is compatible with an earlier Cisco IOS release, use the **downward-compatible-config** global configuration command. To remove this feature, use the **no** form of this command.

   downward-compatible-config *version*
   no downward-compatible-config

Syntax	Description
version	Cisco IOS Release number, not earlier than 10.2.

Default

Disabled

Command Mode

Global configuration

Usage Guidelines

This command first appeared in Cisco IOS Release 11.1.

In Cisco IOS Release 10.3, IP access lists changed format. Use this command to regenerate a configuration in a format prior to Release 10.3 if you are going to downgrade from a Release 10.3 or later to an earlier release. The earliest release this command accepts is 10.2.

When this command is configured, the router attempts to generate a configuration that is compatible with the specified version. Currently, this command affects only IP access lists.

Under some circumstances, the software might not be able to generate a fully backward-compatible configuration. In such a case, the software issues a warning message.

Example

In the following example, the router attempts to generate a configuration file compatible with Cisco IOS Release 10.2:

```
downward-compatible-config 10.2
```

Related Commands

access-list (extended)
access-list (standard)

HOSTNAME

To specify or modify the host name for the network server, use the **hostname** global configuration command. The host name is used in prompts and default configuration filenames. The **setup** command facility also prompts for a host name at startup.

    hostname *name*

Syntax	Description
name	New host name for the network server.

Default

The factory-assigned default host name is *router*.

Command Mode

Global configuration

Usage Guidelines

This command first appeared in Cisco IOS Release 10.0.

The order of display at startup is banner message-of-the-day (MOTD), then login and password prompts, then EXEC banner.

Do not expect case to be preserved. Uppercase and lowercase characters look the same to many internet software applications (often under the assumption that the application is doing you a favor). It might seem appropriate to capitalize a name the same way you might do in English, but conventions dictate that computer names appear all lowercase. For more information, refer to RFC 1178, *Choosing a Name for Your Computer.*

The name also must follow the rules for ARPANET host names. They must start with a letter, end with a letter or digit, and have as interior characters only letters, digits, and hyphens. Names must be 63 characters or fewer. For more information, refer to RFC 1035, *Domain Names—Implementation and Specification.*

Example

The following example changes the host name to *sandbox*:

```
hostname sandbox
```

Related Commands

setup

IP BOOTP SERVER

To access the BOOTP service available from hosts on the network, use the **ip bootp server** global configuration command. Use the **no** form of the command to disable these services.

> **ip bootp server**
> **no ip bootp server**

Syntax   Description

This command has no arguments or keywords.

Default

Enabled

Command Mode

Global configuration

Usage Guidelines

This command first appeared in Cisco IOS Release 11.2.

By default, the BOOTP server is enabled.

When you disable the BOOTP server, access to the BOOTP ports causes the Cisco IOS software to send an "ICMP port unreachable" message to the sender and discard the original incoming packet.

NOTES

Unlike defaults for other commands, this command displays when you perform **show running config** to display current settings, whether or not you have changed the default using the **no ip bootp server** command.

Example

The following example disables the BOOTP service on the router:

```
no ip bootp server
```

IP TELNET SOURCE-INTERFACE

Use the **ip telnet source-interface** global configuration command to allow a user to select an address of an interface as the source address for Telnet connections. Use the **no** form of this command to reset the source address to the default for each connection.

> **ip telnet source-interface** *interface*
> **no ip telnet source-interface**

Syntax	Description
interface	The interface whose address is to be used as the source for Telnet connections.

Default

The address of the closest interface to the destination as the source address. If the selected interface is *not* "up," the Cisco IOS software selects the address of the closest interface to the destination as the source address.

Command Mode

Global configuration

Usage Guidelines

This command first appeared in Cisco IOS Release 11.1.

Use this command to set an interface's IP address as the source for all Telnet connections.

Example

The following example makes the IP address for Ethernet interface 1 as the source address for Telnet connections:

```
ip telnet source-interface e 1
```

Related Commands

ip tacacs source-interface
ip tftp source-interface
ip radius source-interface

IP TFTP SOURCE-INTERFACE

Use the **ip tftp source-interface** global configuration command to allow a user to select the interface whose address will be used as the source address for TFTP connections.

   ip tftp source-interface *interface*
   no ip tftp source-interface

Syntax	*Description*
interface	The interface whose address is to be used as the source for TFTP connections.

Default

The address of the closest interface to the destination as the source address. If the selected interface is not "up," the Cisco IOS software selects the address of the closest interface to the destination as the source address.

Command Mode

Global configuration

Usage Guidelines

This command first appeared in Cisco IOS Release 11.1.

Use this command to set an interface's IP address as the source for all TFTP connections.

Example

The following example makes the IP address for Ethernet interface 1 as the source address for TFTP connections:

```
ip tftp source-interface e 1
```

Related Commands

ip radius source-interface
ip tacacs source-interface
ip telnet source-interface

NTP ACCESS-GROUP

To control access to the system's Network Time Protocol (NTP) services, use the **ntp access-group** global configuration command. To remove access control to the system's NTP services, use the **no** form of this command.

    ntp access-group {query-only | serve-only | serve | peer} *access-list-number*
    no ntp access-group {query-only | serve-only | serve | peer}

Syntax	Description
query-only	Allows only NTP control queries. See RFC 1305 (NTP version 3).
serve-only	Allows only time requests.
serve	Allows time requests and NTP control queries, but does not allow the system to synchronize to the remote system.
peer	Allows time requests and NTP control queries and allows the system to synchronize to the remote system.
access-list-number	Number (1 to 99) of a standard IP access list.

Default

No access control (full access granted to all systems)

Command Mode

Global configuration

Usage Guidelines

This command first appeared in Cisco IOS Release 10.0.

The access-group options are scanned in the following order from least restrictive to most restrictive:

1. peer
2. serve
3. serve-only
4. query-only

Access is granted for the first match that is found. If no access groups are specified, all access is granted to all sources. If any access groups are specified, only the specified access is granted. This facility provides minimal security for the time services of the system. However, it can be circumvented by a determined programmer. If tighter security is desired, use the NTP authentication facility.

Example

In the following example, the system is configured to allow itself to be synchronized by a peer from access list 99. However, the system restricts access to allow only time requests from access list 42.

```
ntp access-group peer 99
ntp access-group serve-only 42
```

Related Commands

access-list

NTP AUTHENTICATE

To enable Network Time Protocol (NTP) authentication, use the **ntp authenticate** global configuration command. Use the **no** form of this command to disable the feature.

> **ntp authenticate**
> **no ntp authenticate**

Syntax   Description

This command has no arguments or keywords.

Default

No authentication

Command Mode

Global configuration

Usage Guidelines

This command first appeared in Cisco IOS Release 10.0.

Use this command if you want authentication. If this command is specified, the system will not synchronize to a system unless it carries one of the authentication keys specified in the **ntp trusted-key** command.

Example

In the following example, the system is configured to synchronize only to systems providing authentication key 42 in their NTP packets:

```
ntp authenticate
ntp authentication-key 42 md5 aNiceKey
ntp trusted-key 42
```

Related Commands

ntp authentication-key
ntp trusted-key

NTP AUTHENTICATION-KEY

To define an authentication key for Network Time Protocol (NTP), use the **ntp authentication-key** global configuration command. Use the **no** form of this command to remove the authentication key for NTP.

> **ntp authentication-key** *number* **md5** *value*
> **no ntp authentication-key** *number*

Syntax	Description
number	Key number (1 to 4294967295).
md5	Authentication key. Message authentication support is provided using the Message Digest (MD5) algorithm. The key type **md5** is currently the only key type supported.
value	Key value (an arbitrary string of up to eight characters).

Default

No authentication key is defined for NTP.

Command Mode

Global configuration

Usage Guidelines

This command first appeared in Cisco IOS Release 10.0.

Use this command to define authentication keys for use with other NTP commands in order to provide a higher degree of security.

NOTES

When this command is written to NVRAM, the key is encrypted so that it is not displayed when the configuration is viewed.

Example

In the following example, the system is configured to synchronize only to systems providing authentication key 42 in their NTP packets:

```
ntp authenticate
ntp authentication-key 42 md5 aNiceKey
ntp trusted-key 42
```

Related Commands

ntp authenticate
ntp peer
ntp server
ntp trusted-key

NTP BROADCAST

To specify that a specific interface should send Network Time Protocol (NTP) broadcast packets, use the **ntp broadcast** interface configuration command. Use the **no** form of this command to disable this capability.

> **ntp broadcast** [**version** *number*]
> **no ntp broadcast**

Syntax	Description
version *number*	(Optional) Number from 1 to 3 indicating the NTP version.

Default

Disabled

Command Mode

Interface configuration

Usage Guidelines

This command first appeared in Cisco IOS Release 10.0.

Example

In the following example, Ethernet interface 0 is configured to send NTP version 2 packets:

```
interface ethernet 0
  ntp broadcast version 2
```

Related Commands

ntp broadcast client
ntp broadcastdelay

NTP BROADCAST CLIENT

To allow the system to receive NTP broadcast packets on an interface, use the **ntp broadcast client** interface configuration command. Use the **no** form of this command to disable this capability.

> **ntp broadcast client**
> **no ntp broadcast client**

Syntax   Description

This command has no arguments or keywords.

Default

Disabled

Command Mode

Interface configuration

Usage Guidelines

This command first appeared in Cisco IOS Release 10.0.

Use this command to allow the system to listen to broadcast packets on an interface-by-interface basis.

Example

In the following example, the Cisco IOS software synchronizes to NTP packets broadcast on Ethernet interface 1:

```
interface ethernet 1
  ntp broadcast client
```

Related Commands

ntp broadcast
ntp broadcastdelay ·

NTP BROADCASTDELAY

To set the estimated round-trip delay between the Cisco IOS software and a Network Time Protocol (NTP) broadcast server, use the **ntp broadcastdelay** global configuration command. Use the **no** form of this command to revert to the default value.

     ntp broadcastdelay *microseconds*
     no ntp broadcastdelay

Syntax	*Description*
microseconds	Estimated round-trip time (in microseconds) for NTP broadcasts. The range is from 1 to 999999.

Default

3,000 microseconds

Command Mode

Global configuration

Usage Guidelines

This command first appeared in Cisco IOS Release 10.0.

Use this command when the router is configured as a broadcast client, and the round-trip delay on the network is other than 3,000 microseconds.

Example

In the following example, the estimated round-trip delay between a router and the broadcast client is set to 5,000 microseconds:

```
ntp broadcastdelay 5000
```

Related Commands

ntp broadcast
ntp broadcast client

NTP CLOCK-PERIOD

—◖ **CAUTION** ◗——

Do not enter this command; it is documented for informational purposes only. The system automatically generates this command as Network Time Protocol (NTP), determines the clock error, and compensates.

——

As NTP compensates for the error in the system clock, it keeps track of the correction factor for this error. The system automatically saves this value into the system configuration using the **ntp clock-period** global configuration command. The system uses the **no** form of this command to revert to the default.

> **ntp clock-period** *value*
> **no ntp clock-period**

Syntax	Description
value	Amount to add to the system clock for each clock hardware tick (in units of 2^{-32} seconds).

Default

17179869 2^{-32} seconds (4 milliseconds)

Command Mode

Global configuration

Usage Guidelines

This command first appeared in Cisco IOS Release 10.0.

If a **copy running-config startup-config** command is entered to save the configuration to NVRAM, this command automatically will be added to the configuration. It is a good idea to perform this task after NTP has been running for a week or so; this will help NTP synchronize more quickly if the system is restarted.

NTP DISABLE

To prevent an interface from receiving Network Time Protocol (NTP) packets, use the **ntp disable** interface configuration command. To enable receipt of NTP packets on an interface, use the **no** form of this command.

> **ntp disable**
> **no ntp disable**

Syntax	Description
	This command has no arguments or keywords.

Default

Enabled

Command Mode

Interface configuration

Usage Guidelines

This command first appeared in Cisco IOS Release 10.0.

This command provides a simple method of access control.

Example

In the following example, Ethernet interface 0 is prevented from receiving NTP packets:

```
interface ethernet 0
 ntp disable
```

NTP MASTER

To configure the Cisco IOS software as a Network Time Protocol (NTP) master clock to which peers synchronize themselves when an external NTP source is not available, use the **ntp master** global configuration command. To disable the master clock function, use the **no** form of this command.

> **ntp master** [*stratum*]
> **no ntp master** [*stratum*]

CAUTION

Use this command with *extreme* caution. It is very easy to override valid time sources using this command, especially if a low stratum number is configured. Configuring multiple machines in the same network with the **ntp master** command can cause instability in keeping time if the machines do not agree on the time.

Syntax	Description
stratum	(Optional) Number from 1 to 15. Indicates the NTP stratum number that the system will claim.

Default

By default, the master clock function is disabled. When enabled, the default stratum is 8.

Command Mode

Global configuration

Usage Guidelines

This command first appeared in Cisco IOS Release 10.0.

Because Cisco's implementation of NTP does not support directly attached radio or atomic clocks, the router is normally synchronized, directly or indirectly, to an external system that has such a clock. In a network without Internet connectivity, such a time source might not be available. The **ntp master** command is used in such cases.

If the system has **ntp master** configured, and it cannot reach any clock with a lower stratum number, the system will claim to be synchronized at the configured stratum number, and other systems will be willing to synchronize to it via NTP.

NOTES

The system clock must have been set from some source, including manually, before **ntp master** will have any effect. This protects against distributing erroneous time after the system is restarted.

Example

In the following example, a router is configured as an NTP master clock to which peers may synchronize:

```
ntp master 10
```

Related Commands

clock calendar-valid

NTP PEER

To configure the system clock to synchronize a peer or to be synchronized by a peer, use the **ntp peer** global configuration command. To disable this capability, use the **no** form of this command.

ntp peer *ip-address* [**version** *number*] [**key** *keyid*] [**source** *interface*] [**prefer**]
no ntp peer *ip-address*

Syntax	Description
ip-address	IP address of the peer providing, or being provided, the clock synchronization.
version	(Optional) Defines the Network Time Protocol (NTP) version number.
number	(Optional) NTP version number (1 to 3).
key	(Optional) Defines the authentication key.
keyid	(Optional) Authentication key to use when sending packets to this peer.
source	(Optional) Names the interface.

Syntax	Description
interface	(Optional) Name of the interface from which to pick the IP source address.
prefer	(Optional) Makes this peer the preferred peer that provides synchronization.

Default

No peers are configured by default. If a peer is configured, the default NTP version number is 3, no authentication key is used, and the source IP address is taken from the outgoing interface.

Command Mode

Global configuration

Usage Guidelines

This command first appeared in Cisco IOS Release 10.0.

Use this command if you want to allow this machine to synchronize with the peer, or vice versa. Using the **prefer** keyword reduces switching back and forth between peers.

If you are using the default version of 3 and NTP synchronization does not occur, try using NTP version number 2. Many NTP servers on the Internet run version 2.

Example

In the following example, a router is configured to allow its system clock to be synchronized with the clock of the peer (or vice versa) at IP address 192.168.22.33 using NTP version 2. The source IP address is the address of Ethernet 0.

```
ntp peer 192.168.22.33 version 2 source ethernet 0
```

Related Commands

ntp authentication-key
ntp server
ntp source

NTP SERVER

To allow the system clock to be synchronized by a time server, use the **ntp server** global configuration command. To disable this capability, use the **no** form of this command.

> **ntp server** *ip-address* [**version** *number*] [**key** *keyid*] [**source** *interface*] [**prefer**]
> **no ntp server** *ip-address*

Syntax	Description
ip-address	IP address of the time server providing the clock synchronization.
version	(Optional) Defines the Network Time Protocol (NTP) version number.
number	(Optional) NTP version number (1 to 3).
key	(Optional) Defines the authentication key.
keyid	(Optional) Authentication key to use when sending packets to this peer.
source	(Optional) Identifies the interface from which to pick the IP source address.
interface	(Optional) Name of the interface from which to pick the IP source address.
prefer	(Optional) Makes this server the preferred server that provides synchronization.

Default

No peers are configured by default. If a peer is configured, the default NTP version number is 3, no authentication key is used, and the source IP address is taken from the outgoing interface.

Command Mode

Global configuration

Usage Guidelines

This command first appeared in Cisco IOS Release 10.0.

Use this command if you want to allow this machine to synchronize with the specified server. The server will not synchronize to this machine.

Using the **prefer** keyword reduces switching back and forth between servers.

If you are using the default version of 3 and NTP synchronization does not occur, try using NTP version number 2. Many NTP servers on the Internet run version 2.

Example

In the following example, a router is configured to allow its system clock to be synchronized with the clock of the peer at IP address 172.16.22.44 using NTP version 2:

```
ntp server 172.16.22.44 version 2
```

Related Commands

ntp authentication-key
ntp peer
ntp source

NTP SOURCE

To use a particular source address in Network Time Protocol (NTP) packets, use the **ntp source** global configuration command. Use the **no** form of this command to remove the specified source address.

>   **ntp source** *type number*
>   **no ntp source**

Syntax	Description
type	Type of interface.
number	Number of the interface.

Default

Source address is determined by the outgoing interface.

Command Mode

Global configuration

Usage Guidelines

This command first appeared in Cisco IOS Release 10.0.

Use this command when you want to use a particular source IP address for all NTP packets. The address is taken from the named interface. This command is useful if the address on an interface cannot be used as the destination for reply packets. If the **source** keyword is present on an **ntp server** or **ntp peer** command, that value overrides the global value.

Example

In the following example, a router is configured to use the IP address of Ethernet 0 as the source address of all outgoing NTP packets:

```
ntp source ethernet 0
```

Related Commands

ntp peer
ntp server

NTP TRUSTED-KEY

To authenticate the identity of a system to which Network Time Protocol (NTP) will synchronize, use the **ntp trusted-key** global configuration command. Use the **no** form of this command to disable authentication of the identity of the system.

>   **ntp trusted-key** *key-number*
>   **no ntp trusted-key** *key-number*

Syntax	Description
key-number	Key number of authentication key to be trusted.

Default
Disabled

Command Mode
Global configuration

Usage Guidelines
This command first appeared in Cisco IOS Release 10.0.

If authentication is enabled, use this command to define one or more key numbers (corresponding to the keys defined with the **ntp authentication-key** command) that a peer NTP system must provide in its NTP packets, in order for this system to synchronize to it. This provides protection against accidentally synchronizing the system to a system that is not trusted because the other system must know the correct authentication key.

Example
In the following example, the system is configured to synchronize only to systems providing authentication key 42 in their NTP packets:

```
ntp authenticate
ntp authentication-key 42 md5 aNiceKey
ntp trusted-key 42
```

Related Commands
ntp authenticate
ntp authentication-key

NTP UPDATE-CALENDAR
To update the calendar from Network Time Protocol (NTP) periodically, use the **ntp update-calendar** global configuration command. Use the **no** form of this command to disable this feature.

> **ntp update-calendar**
> **no ntp update-calendar**

Syntax   Description
This command has no arguments or keywords.

Default

The calendar is not updated.

Command Mode

Global configuration

Usage Guidelines

This command first appeared in Cisco IOS Release 10.0.

Some platforms have a calendar that is separate from the system clock. This calendar runs continuously, even if the router is powered off or rebooted.

If a router is synchronized to an outside time source via NTP, it is a good idea to update the calendar periodically with the time learned from NTP. Otherwise, the calendar will tend to lose or gain time gradually. The calendar will be updated only if NTP has synchronized to an authoritative time server.

Example

In the following example, the system is configured to update the calendar periodically from the system clock:

```
ntp update-calendar
```

Related Commands

clock read-calendar
clock update-calendar

PROMPT

To customize the prompt, use the **prompt** global configuration command. To revert to the default prompt, use the **no** form of this command.

prompt *string*
no prompt [*string*]

Syntax	Description
string	Prompt. It can consist of all printing characters and the escape sequences listed in Table 31–2.

Default

The default prompt is either Router or the name defined with the **hostname** global configuration command, followed by an angle bracket (>) for EXEC mode or a pound sign (#) for privileged EXEC mode.

Command Mode

Global configuration

Usage Guidelines

This command first appeared in Cisco IOS Release 10.3.

You can include escape sequences when specifying the prompt. All escape sequences are preceded by a percent sign (%). Table 31–2 lists the valid escape sequences.

Table 31–2 *Custom Prompt Escape Sequences*

Escape Sequence	Interpretation
%h	Host name. This is either *Router* or the name defined with the **hostname** global configuration command.
%n	Physical terminal line (TTY) number of the EXEC user.
%p	Prompt character itself. It is either an angle bracket (>) for EXEC mode or a pound sign (#) for privileged EXEC mode.
%s	Space.
%t	Tab.
%%	Percent sign (%).

Issuing the **prompt %h** command has the same effect as issuing the **no prompt** command.

Examples

The following example changes the EXEC prompt to include the TTY number, followed by the name and a space:

```
prompt TTY%n@%h%s%p
```

The following are examples of user and privileged EXEC prompts that result from the previous command:

```
TTY17@Router1 >
TTY17SRouter1 #
```

Related Commands

hostname

SERVICE DECIMAL-TTY

To specify that line numbers be displayed and interpreted as decimal numbers rather than octal numbers, use the **service decimal-tty** global configuration command. Use the **no** form of this command to restore the default.

> **service decimal-tty**
> **no service decimal-tty**

Syntax   Description

This command has no arguments or keywords.

Default

Decimal numbers on the 500-CS and Cisco 2500 Series.

Command Mode

Global configuration

Usage Guidelines

This command first appeared in Cisco IOS Release 10.0.

Example

The following example shows how to display decimal rather than octal line numbers:

```
service decimal-tty
```

SERVICE EXEC-WAIT

To delay the startup of the EXEC on noisy lines, use the **service exec-wait** global configuration command. Use the **no** form of this command to disable this feature.

> **service exec-wait**
> **no service exec-wait**

Syntax   Description

This command has no arguments or keywords.

Default

Disabled

Command Mode

Global configuration

Usage Guidelines

This command first appeared in Cisco IOS Release 10.0.

This command delays startup of the EXEC until the line has been idle (no traffic seen) for three seconds. The default is to enable the line immediately on modem activation.

This command is useful on noisy modem lines or when a modem attached to the line is configured to ignore MNP or V.42 negotiations, and MNP or V.42 modems may be dialing in. In these cases, noise or MNP/V.42 packets may be interpreted as usernames and passwords, causing authentication failure before the user gets a chance to type a username/password. The command is not useful on non-modem lines or lines without some kind of login configured.

Example

The following example delays the startup of the EXEC:

```
service exec-wait
```

SERVICE FINGER

To allow Finger protocol requests (defined in RFC 742) to be made of the network server, use the **service finger** global configuration command. This service is equivalent to issuing a remote **show users** command. Use the **no** form of this command to remove this service.

> **service finger**
> **no service finger**

Syntax   Description

This command has no arguments or keywords.

Default

Enabled

Command Mode

Global configuration

Usage Guidelines

This command first appeared in Cisco IOS Release 10.0.

Example

The following example disables the Finger protocol:

```
no service finger
```

Part
IV

Command Reference

SERVICE HIDE-TELNET-ADDRESS

To hide addresses while trying to establish a Telnet session, use the **service hide-telnet-address** global configuration command. Use the **no** form of this command to remove this service.

> **service hide-telnet-address**
> **no service hide-telnet-address**

Syntax   Description

This command has no arguments or keywords.

Default

Addresses are displayed.

Command Mode

Global configuration

Usage Guidelines

This command first appeared in Cisco IOS Release 11.2.

When you attempt to connect to a device, the router displays addresses and other messages (for example, Trying router1 (171.69.1.154, 2008)...). With the hide feature, the router suppresses the display of the address (for example, Trying router1 address #1...). The router continues to display all other messages that normally would display during a connection attempt, such as detailed error messages if the connection was not successful.

The hide feature improves the functionality of the busy-message feature. When you configure only the **busy-message** command, the normal messages generated during a connection attempt are not displayed; only the busy-message is displayed. When you use the hide and busy features together, you can customize the information displayed during Telnet connection attempts. When you configure the **service hide-telnet-address** command and the **busy-message** command, the router suppresses the address and displays the message specified with the **busy-message** command if the connection attempt is not successful.

Example

The following example shows how to hide Telnet addresses:

```
service hide-telnet-address
```

Related Commands

busy-message

SERVICE PROMPT CONFIG

To display the configuration prompt (config), use the **service prompt config** global configuration command. Use the **no** form of this command to remove the configuration prompt.

> **service prompt config**
> **no service prompt config**

Syntax   Description

This command has no arguments or keywords.

Default

The configuration mode prompts (*hostname*(config)#) appear in all configuration modes.

Command Mode

Global configuration

Usage Guidelines

This command first appeared in Cisco IOS Release 11.1.

Example

In the following example, the **no service prompt config** command prevents the configuration prompt from being displayed. The prompt is still displayed in EXEC mode. When the **service prompt config** command is entered, the configuration mode prompt reappears.

```
Router# configure terminal
Enter configuration commands, one per line.  End with CNTL/Z.
Router(config)# no service prompt config
hostname bob
end
bob# configure terminal
Enter configuration commands, one per line.  End with CNTL/Z.
service prompt config
bob(config)# hostname Router
Router(config)# end
Router#
```

Related Commands

hostname
prompt

SERVICE TCP-SMALL-SERVERS

To access minor TCP/IP services available from hosts on the network, use the **service tcp-small-servers** global configuration command. Use the **no** form of the command to disable these services.

> **service tcp-small-servers**
> **no service tcp-small-servers**

Syntax   Description

This command has no arguments or keywords.

Default

Enabled

Command Mode

Global configuration

Usage Guidelines

This command first appeared in Cisco IOS Release 11.1.

By default, the TCP servers for Echo, Discard, Chargen, and Daytime services are enabled.

When you disable the minor TCP/IP servers, access to the Echo, Discard, Chargen, and Daytime ports cause the Cisco IOS software to send a TCP RESET packet to the sender and discard the original incoming packet.

NOTES

Unlike defaults for other commands, this command will display when you perform **show running config** to display current settings whether or not you have changed the default using the **no service tcp-small-servers** command.

Example

The following example enables minor TCP/IP services available from the network:

```
service tcp-small-servers
```

SERVICE TELNET-ZERO-IDLE

To set the TCP window to zero (0) when the Telnet connection is idle, use the **service telnet-zero-idle** global configuration command. Use the **no** form of this command to disable this feature.

> **service telnet-zero-idle**
> **no service telnet-zero-idle**

Syntax *Description*

This command has no arguments or keywords.

Default

Disabled

Command Mode

Global configuration

Usage Guidelines

This command first appeared in Cisco IOS Release 10.0.

Normally, data sent to noncurrent Telnet connections is accepted and discarded. When **service telnet-zero-idle** is enabled, if a session is suspended (that is, some other connection is made active or the EXEC is sitting in command mode), the TCP window is set to zero. This action prevents the remote host from sending anymore data until the connection is resumed. Use this command when it is important that all messages sent by the host be seen by the users, and the users are likely to use multiple sessions.

Do not use this command if your host eventually will time out and log out a TCP user whose window is zero.

Example

The following example sets the TCP window to zero when the Telnet connection is idle:

```
service telnet-zero-idle
```

Related Commands

resume

SERVICE UDP-SMALL-SERVERS

To access minor User Datagram Protocol (UDP) services available from hosts on the network, use the **service udp-small-servers** global configuration command. Use the **no** form of the command to disable these services.

service udp-small-servers
no service udp-small-servers

Syntax *Description*

This command has no arguments or keywords.

Default

Enabled

Command Mode

Global configuration

Usage Guidelines

This command first appeared in Cisco IOS Release 11.2.

By default the UPD servers for Echo, Discard, and Chargen services are enabled.

When you disable the servers, access to Echo, Discard, and Chargen ports causes the Cisco IOS software to send an "ICMP port unreachable" message to the sender and discard the original incoming packet.

NOTES

Unlike defaults for other commands, this command will display when you perform **show running config** to display current settings, whether or not you have changed the default using the **no service udp-small-servers** command.

Example

The following example disables minor UDP services on the router:

```
no service udp-small-servers
```

SHOW ALIASES

To display all alias commands, or the alias commands in a specified mode, use the **show aliases** EXEC command.

    show aliases [*mode*]

Syntax	Description
mode	(Optional) Command mode. See Table 31–1 in the description of the **alias** command for acceptable options for the *mode* argument.

Command Mode

EXEC

Usage Guidelines

This command first appeared in Cisco IOS Release 10.3.

All of the modes listed in Table 31–1 have their own prompts, except for the null interface mode. For example, the prompt for interface configuration mode is *Router(config-if)*.

Sample Display

The following is sample output from the **show aliases exec** commands. The aliases configured for commands in EXEC mode are displayed.

```
Router# show aliases exec

Exec mode aliases:
  h               help
  lo              logout
  p               ping
  r               resume
  s               show
  w               where
```

Related Commands

alias

SHOW CALENDAR

To display the calendar hardware setting, use the **show calendar** EXEC command:

> show calendar

Syntax   Description

This command has no arguments or keywords.

Command Mode

EXEC

Usage Guidelines

This command first appeared in Cisco IOS Release 10.0.

Some platforms have a calendar that is separate from the system clock. This calendar runs continuously, even if the router is powered off or rebooted.

You can compare the time and date shown with this command with the time and date listed via the **show clock** command to verify that the calendar and system clock are in sync with each other. The time displayed is relative to the configured time zone.

Sample Display

In the following sample display, the hardware calendar indicates the timestamp of 12:13:44 p.m. on Friday, July 19, 1996:

```
Router# show calendar

12:13:44 PST Fri Jul 19 1996
```

Related Commands

show clock

SHOW CLOCK

To display the system clock, use the **show clock** EXEC command.

> **show clock** [detail]

Syntax	*Description*
detail	(Optional) Indicates the clock source (NTP, VINES, system calendar, and so forth) and the current summer-time setting (if any).

Command Mode

EXEC

Usage Guidelines

This command first appeared in Cisco IOS Release 10.0.

The system clock keeps an "authoritative" flag that indicates whether the time is authoritative (believed to be accurate). If the system clock has been set by a timing source (system calendar, NTP, VINES, and so forth), the flag is set. If the time is not authoritative, it will be used only for display purposes. Until the clock is authoritative and the "authoritative" flag is set, the flag prevents peers from synchronizing to the clock when the peers' time is invalid.

The symbol that precedes the **show clock** display indicates the following:

Symbol	Description
*	Time is not authoritative.
(blank)	Time is authoritative.
.	Time is authoritative, but NTP is not synchronized.

Sample Display

The following sample output shows that the current clock is authoritative and that the time source is NTP:

```
Router# show clock detail

15:29:03.158 PST Mon Mar 3 1997
Time source is NTP
```

Related Commands

clock set
show calendar

SHOW NTP ASSOCIATIONS

To show the status of Network Time Protocol (NTP) associations, use the **show ntp associations** EXEC command.

show ntp associations [detail]

Syntax	*Description*
detail	(Optional) Shows detailed information about each NTP association.

Command Mode

EXEC

Usage Guidelines

This command first appeared in Cisco IOS Release 10.0.

Sample Displays

Detailed descriptions of the information displayed by this command can be found in the NTP specification (RFC 1305).

The following is sample output from the **show ntp associations** command:

```
Router# show ntp associations

        address         ref clock      st  when  poll  reach  delay  offset   disp
 ~172.31.32.2    172.31.32.1       5    29  1024   377    4.2   -8.59    1.6
+~192.168.13.33  192.168.1.111     3    69   128   377    4.1    3.48    2.3
*~192.168.13.57  192.168.1.111     3    32   128   377    7.9   11.18    3.6
 * master (synced), # master (unsynced), + selected, - candidate, ~ configured
```

Table 31–3 describes significant fields shown in the display.

Table 31–3   *Show NTP Associations Field Descriptions*

Field	Description
(leading characters in display lines)	The first characters in a display line can be one or more of the following characters: * Synchronized to this peer # Almost synchronized to this peer + Peer selected for possible synchronization - Peer is a candidate for selection ~ Peer is statically configured
address	Address of peer.
ref clock	Address of peer's reference clock.
st	Peer's stratum.
when	Time since last NTP packet received from peer.
poll	Polling interval (seconds).
reach	Peer reachability (bit string, in octal).
delay	Round-trip delay to peer (milliseconds).
offset	Relative time of peer's clock to local clock (milliseconds).
disp	Dispersion.

The following is sample output of the **show ntp associations detail** command:

```
Router# show ntp associations detail

172.31.32.2 configured, insane, invalid, stratum 5
ref ID 172.31.32.1, time AFE252C1.6DBDDFF2 (00:12:01.428 PDT Mon Jul 5 1993)
our mode active, peer mode active, our poll intvl 1024, peer poll intvl 64
root delay 137.77 msec, root disp 142.75, reach 376, sync dist 215.363
delay 4.23 msec, offset -8.587 msec, dispersion 1.62
precision 2**19, version 3
org time AFE252E2.3AC0E887 (00:12:34.229 PDT Mon Jul 5 1993)
rcv time AFE252E2.3D7E464D (00:12:34.240 PDT Mon Jul 5 1993)
xmt time AFE25301.6F83E753 (00:13:05.435 PDT Mon Jul 5 1993)
filtdelay =     4.23    4.14    2.41    5.95    2.37    2.33    4.26    4.33
filtoffset =   -8.59   -8.82   -9.91   -8.42  -10.51  -10.77  -10.13  -10.11
filterror =     0.50    1.48    2.46    3.43    4.41    5.39    6.36    7.34
```

```
192.168.13.33 configured, selected, sane, valid, stratum 3
ref ID 192.168.1.111, time AFE24F0E.14283000 (23:56:14.078 PDT Sun Jul 4 1993)
our mode client, peer mode server, our poll intvl 128, peer poll intvl 128
root delay 83.72 msec, root disp 217.77, reach 377, sync dist 264.633
delay 4.07 msec, offset 3.483 msec, dispersion 2.33
precision 2**6, version 3
org time AFE252B9.713E9000 (00:11:53.442 PDT Mon Jul 5 1993)
rcv time AFE252B9.7124E14A (00:11:53.441 PDT Mon Jul 5 1993)
xmt time AFE252B9.6F625195 (00:11:53.435 PDT Mon Jul 5 1993)
filtdelay =     6.47    4.07    3.94    3.86    7.31    7.20    9.52    8.71
filtoffset =    3.63    3.48    3.06    2.82    4.51    4.57    4.28    4.59
filterror =     0.00    1.95    3.91    4.88    5.84    6.82    7.80    8.77

192.168.13.57 configured, our_master, sane, valid, stratum 3
ref ID 192.168.1.111, time AFE252DC.1F2B3000 (00:12:28.121 PDT Mon Jul 5 1993)
our mode client, peer mode server, our poll intvl 128, peer poll intvl 128
root delay 125.50 msec, root disp 115.80, reach 377, sync dist 186.157
delay 7.86 msec, offset 11.176 msec, dispersion 3.62
precision 2**6, version 2
org time AFE252DE.77C29000 (00:12:30.467 PDT Mon Jul 5 1993)
rcv time AFE252DE.7B2AE40B (00:12:30.481 PDT Mon Jul 5 1993)
xmt time AFE252DE.6E6D12E4 (00:12:30.431 PDT Mon Jul 5 1993)
filtdelay =    49.21    7.86    8.18    8.80    4.30    4.24    7.58    6.42
filtoffset =   11.30   11.18   11.13   11.28    8.91    9.09    9.27    9.57
filterror =     0.00    1.95    3.91    4.88    5.78    6.76    7.74    8.71
```

Table 31–4 describes significant fields shown in the display.

Table 31–4 *Show NTP Associations Detail Field Descriptions*

Field	Descriptions
configured	Peer was statically configured.
dynamic	Peer was dynamically discovered.
our_master	Local machine is synchronized to this peer.
selected	Peer is selected for possible synchronization.
candidate	Peer is a candidate for selection.
sane	Peer passes basic sanity checks.
insane	Peer fails basic sanity checks.
valid	Peer time is believed to be valid.
invalid	Peer time is believed to be invalid.
leap_add	Peer is signaling that a leap second will be added.
leap-sub	Peer is signaling that a leap second will be subtracted.

Table 31–4   *Show NTP Associations Detail Field Descriptions, Continued*

Field	Descriptions
unsynced	Peer is not synchronized to any other machine.
ref ID	Address of machine to which peer is synchronized.
time	Last timestamp peer received from its master.
our mode	Our mode relative to peer (active / passive / client / server / bdcast / bdcast client).
peer mode	Peer's mode relative to us.
our poll intvl	Our poll interval to peer.
peer poll intvl	Peer's poll interval to us.
root delay	Delay along path to root (ultimate stratum 1 time source).
root disp	Dispersion of path to root.
reach	Peer reachability (bit string in octal).
sync dist	Peer synchronization distance.
delay	Round-trip delay to peer.
offset	Offset of peer clock relative to our clock.
dispersion	Dispersion of peer clock.
precision	Precision of peer clock in Hz.
version	NTP version number that peer is using.
org time	Originate time stamp.
rcv time	Receive time stamp.
xmt time	Transmit time stamp.
filtdelay	Round-trip delay in milliseconds of each sample.
filtoffset	Clock offset in milliseconds of each sample.
filterror	Approximate error of each sample.

Related Commands

show ntp status

SHOW NTP STATUS

To show the status of Network Time Protocol (NTP), use the **show ntp status** EXEC command.

> **show ntp status**

Syntax   Description

This command has no arguments or keywords.

Command Mode

EXEC

Usage Guidelines

This command first appeared in Cisco IOS Release 10.0.

Sample Display

The following is sample output from the **show ntp status** command:

```
Router# show ntp status

Clock is synchronized, stratum 4, reference is 192.168.13.57
nominal freq is 250.0000 Hz, actual freq is 249.9990 Hz, precision is 2**19
reference time is AFE2525E.70597B34 (00:10:22.438 PDT Mon Jul 5 1993)
clock offset is 7.33 msec, root delay is 133.36 msec
root dispersion is 126.28 msec, peer dispersion is 5.98 msec
```

Table 31–5 shows the significant fields in the display.

Table 31–5 *Show NTP Status Field Descriptions*

Field	Description
synchronized	System is synchronized to an NTP peer.
unsynchronized	System is not synchronized to any NTP peer.
stratum	NTP stratum of this system.
reference	Address of peer to which we are synchronized.
nominal freq	Nominal frequency of system hardware clock.
actual freq	Measured frequency of system hardware clock.
precision	Precision of this system's clock (in Hz).
reference time	Reference timestamp.
clock offset	Offset of our clock to synchronized peer.
root delay	Total delay along path to root clock.

Table 31–5 *Show NTP Status Field Descriptions, Continued*

Field	Description
root dispersion	Dispersion of root path.
peer dispersion	Dispersion of synchronized peer.

Related Commands

show ntp associations

SHOW SNTP

Use the **show sntp** EXEC command on a Cisco 1003, Cisco 1004, or Cisco 1005 router to show information about the Simple Network Time Protocol (SNTP).

> **show sntp**

Syntax   Description

This command has no arguments or keywords.

Command Mode

EXEC

Usage Guidelines

This command first appeared in Cisco IOS Release 11.2.

Sample Display

The following is sample output from the **show sntp** command:

```
Router# show sntp

SNTP server      Stratum   Version   Last Receive
171.69.118.9        5         3       00:01:02
172.21.28.34        4         3       00:00:36    Synced  Bcast

Broadcast client mode is enabled.
```

Table 31–6 describes the fields show in this display.

Table 31–6 *Show SNTP Field Descriptions*

Field	Description
SNTP server	Address of the configured or broadcast NTP server.
Stratum	NTP stratum of the server. The stratum indicates how far away from an authoritative time source the server is.
Version	NTP version of the server.
Last Receive	Time since the last NTP packet was received from the server.
Synced	Indicates the server chosen for synchronization.
Bcast	Indicates a broadcast server.

Related Commands

sntp broadcast client
sntp server

SNTP BROADCAST CLIENT

Use the **sntp broadcast client** global configuration command to configure a Cisco 1003, Cisco 1004, or Cisco 1005 router to use the Simple Network Time Protocol (SNTP) to accept Network Time Protocol (NTP) traffic from any broadcast server. The **no** form of the command prevents the router from accepting broadcast traffic.

> sntp broadcast client
> no sntp broadcast client

Syntax   Description

This command has no arguments or keywords.

Default

The router does not accept SNTP traffic from broadcast servers.

Command Mode

Global configuration

Usage Guidelines

This command first appeared in Cisco IOS Release 11.2.

SNTP is a compact, client-only version of the Network Time Protocol (NTP). SNMP can only receive the time from NTP servers; it cannot be used to provide time services to other systems.

SNTP typically provides time within 100 milliseconds of the accurate time, but it does not provide the complex filtering and statistical mechanisms of NTP. In addition, SNTP does not authenticate traffic, although you can configure extended access lists to provide some protection.

You must configure the router with either this command or the **sntp server** command in order to enable SNTP.

Example

The following example enables the router to accept broadcast NTP packets and shows sample **show sntp** command output:

```
Router(config)# sntp broadcast client
Router(config)# end
Router#
%SYS-5-CONFIG: Configured from console by console
Router# show sntp

SNTP server     Stratum   Version   Last Receive
172.21.28.34       4         3       00:00:36   Synced  Bcast

Broadcast client mode is enabled.
```

Related Commands

show sntp
sntp server

SNTP SERVER

Use the **sntp server** global configuration command to configure a Cisco 1003, Cisco 1004, or Cisco 1005 router to use the Simple Network Time Protocol (SNTP) to request and accept Network Time Protocol (NTP) traffic from a time server. The **no** form of the command removes a server from the list of NTP servers.

> **sntp server** {*address* | *hostname*} [version *number*]
> **no sntp server** {*address* | *hostname*}

Syntax	Description
address	IP address of the time server.
hostname	Host name of the time server.
version *number*	(Optional) Version of NTP to use. The default is 1.

Default

The router does not accept SNTP traffic from a time server.

Command Mode

Global configuration

Usage Guidelines

This command first appeared in Cisco IOS Release 11.2.

SNTP is a compact, client-only version of the Network Time Protocol (NTP). SNMP can only receive the time from NTP servers; it cannot be used to provide time services to other systems.

SNTP typically provides time within 100 milliseconds of the accurate time, but it does not provide the complex filtering and statistical mechanisms of NTP. In addition, SNTP does not authenticate traffic, although you can configure extended access lists to provide some protection.

Enter this command once for each NTP server.

You must configure the router with either this command or the **sntp broadcast client** command in order to enable SNTP.

Example

The following example enables the router to request and accept NTP packets from the server at 172.21.118.9 and shows sample **show sntp** command output:

```
Router(config)# sntp server 172.21.118.9
Router(config)# end
Router#
%SYS-5-CONFIG: Configured from console by console
Router# show sntp

SNTP server     Stratum   Version   Last Receive
172.21.118.9       5         3        00:01:02    Synced
```

Related Commands

show sntp
sntp broadcast client

PART V

Appendixes

ASCII Character Set

Some commands described in this documentation set, such as the **escape-character** line configuration command, require that you enter the decimal representation of an ASCII character.

Table A–1 provides code translations from the decimal numbers to their hexadecimal and ASCII equivalents. It also provides the keyword entry for each ASCII character. For example, the ASCII carriage return (CR) is decimal 13. Entering Ctrl-M at your terminal generates decimal 13, which is interpreted as a CR.

Table A–1 *ASCII Translation Table*

Numeric Values Decimal	Hex	ASCII Character	Meaning	Keyboard Entry
0	00	NUL	Null	Ctrl-@
1	01	SOH	Start of heading	Ctrl-A
2	02	STX	Start of text	Ctrl-B
3	03	ETX	Break/end of text	Ctrl-C
4	04	EOT	End of transmission	Ctrl-D
5	05	ENQ	Enquiry	Ctrl-E
6	06	ACK	Positive acknowledgment	Ctrl-F
7	07	BEL	Bell	Ctrl-G
8	08	BS	Backspace	Ctrl-H
9	09	HT	Horizontal tab	Ctrl-I
10	0A	LF	Line feed	Ctrl-J

Table A–1   *ASCII Translation Table, Continued*

Numeric Values Decimal	Hex	ASCII Character	Meaning	Keyboard Entry
11	0B	VT	Vertical tab	Ctrl-K
12	0C	FF	Form feed	Ctrl-L
13	0D	CR	Carriage return	Ctrl-M
14	0E	SO	Shift out	Ctrl-N
15	0F	SI	Shift in/XON (resume output)	Ctrl-O
16	10	DLE	Data link escape	Ctrl-P
17	11	DC1	Device control character 1	Ctrl-Q
18	12	DC2	Device control character 2	Ctrl-R
19	13	DC3	Device control character 3	Ctrl-S
20	14	DC4	Device control character 4	Ctrl-T
21	15	NAK	Negative acknowledgment	Ctrl-U
22	16	SYN	Synchronous idle	Ctrl-V
23	17	ETB	End of transmission block	Ctrl-W
24	18	CAN	Cancel	Ctrl-X
25	19	EM	End of medium	Ctrl-Y
26	1A	SUB	Substitute/end of file	Ctrl-Z
27	1B	ESC	Escape	Ctrl-[
28	1C	FS	File separator	Ctrl-\
29	1D	GS	Group separator	Ctrl-]
30	1E	RS	Record separator	Ctrl-^
31	1F	US	Unit separator	Ctrl-_
32	20	SP	Space	Space
33	21	!	!	!
34	22	"	"	"
35	23	#	#	#
36	24	$	$	$

Table A–1 *ASCII Translation Table, Continued*

Numeric Values Decimal	Hex	ASCII Character	Meaning	Keyboard Entry
37	25	%	%	%
38	26	&	&	&
39	27	'	'	'
40	28	(	(	(
41	29	)	)	)
42	2A	*	*	*
43	2B	+	+	+
44	2C	,	,	,
45	2D	-	-	-
46	2E	.	.	.
47	2F	/	/	/
48	30	0	Zero	0
49	31	1	One	1
50	32	2	Two	2
51	33	3	Three	3
52	34	4	Four	4
53	35	5	Five	5
54	36	6	Six	6
55	37	7	Seven	7
56	38	8	Eight	8
57	39	9	Nine	9
58	3A	:	:	:
59	3B	;	;	;
60	3C	<	<	<
61	3D	=	=	=
62	3E	>	>	>

Table A–1 *ASCII Translation Table, Continued*

Numeric Values Decimal	Hex	ASCII Character	Meaning	Keyboard Entry
63	3F	?	?	?
64	40	@	@	@
65	41	A	A	A
66	42	B	B	B
67	43	C	C	C
68	44	D	D	D
69	45	E	E	E
70	46	F	F	F
71	47	G	G	G
72	48	H	H	H
73	49	I	I	I
74	4A	J	J	J
75	4B	K	K	K
76	4C	L	L	L
77	4D	M	M	M
78	4E	N	N	N
79	4F	O	O	O
80	50	P	P	P
81	51	Q	Q	Q
82	52	R	R	R
83	53	S	S	S
84	54	T	T	T
85	55	U	U	U
86	56	V	V	V
87	57	W	W	W
88	58	X	X	X

Table A–1 _ASCII Translation Table, Continued_

Numeric Values Decimal	Hex	ASCII Character	Meaning	Keyboard Entry
89	59	Y	Y	Y
90	5A	Z	Z	Z
91	5B	[	[	[
92	5C	\	\	\
93	5D	]	]	]
94	5E	^	^	^
95	5F	_	_	_
96	60	`	`	`
97	61	a	a	a
98	62	b	b	b
99	63	c	c	c
100	64	d	d	d
101	65	e	e	e
102	66	f	f	f
103	67	g	g	g
104	68	h	h	h
105	69	i	i	i
106	6A	j	j	j
107	6B	k	k	k
108	6C	l	l	l
109	6D	m	m	m
110	6E	n	n	n
111	6F	o	o	o
112	70	p	p	p
113	71	q	q	q
114	72	r	r	r

Table A–1 *ASCII Translation Table, Continued*

Numeric Values Decimal	Hex	ASCII Character	Meaning	Keyboard Entry
115	73	s	s	s
116	74	t	t	t
117	75	u	u	u
118	76	v	v	v
119	77	w	w	w
120	78	x	x	x
121	79	y	y	y
122	7A	z	z	z
123	7B	{	{	{
124	7C	|	|	|
125	7D	}	}	}
126	7E	~	Tilde	~
127	7F	DEL	Delete	Del

APPENDIX B

References and Recommended Reading

This appendix contains the following lists of publications related to networks and networking:

- Books and Periodicals
- Technical Publications and Standards
- Cisco-Supported RFCs

BOOKS AND PERIODICALS

Apple Computer, Inc. *AppleTalk Network System Overview*. Reading, Massachusetts: Addison-Wesley Publishing Company, Inc.; 1989.

Black, U. *Data Networks: Concepts, Theory and Practice*. Englewood Cliffs, New Jersey: Prentice Hall; 1989.

Black, U. *Physical Level Interfaces and Protocols*. Los Alamitos, California: IEEE Computer Society Press; 1988.

Case, J.D., J.R. Davins, M.S. Fedor, and M.L. Schoffstall. "Introduction to the Simple Gateway Monitoring Protocol." *IEEE Network:* March 1988.

Case, J.D., J.R. Davins, M.S. Fedor, and M.L. Schoffstall. "Network Management and the Design of SNMP." *ConneXions: The Interoperability Report,* Vol. 3: March 1989.

Clark, W. "SNA Internetworking." *ConneXions: The Interoperability Report*, Vol. 6, No. 3: March 1992.

Coltun, R. "OSPF: An Internet Routing Protocol." *ConneXions: The Interoperability Report*, Vol. 3, No. 8: August 1989.

Comer, D.E. *Internetworking with TCP/IP: Principles, Protocols, and Architecture*, Vol. I, 2nd ed. Englewood Cliffs, New Jersey: Prentice Hall; 1991.

Davidson, J. *An Introduction to TCP/IP*. New York, New York: Springer-Verlag; 1992.

Garcia-Luna-Aceves, J.J. "Loop-Free Routing Using Diffusing Computations." Publication pending in *IEEE/ACM Transactions on Networking*, Vol. 1, No. 1, 1993.

Green, J.K. *Telecommunications*, 2nd ed. Homewood, Illinois: Business One Irwin; 1992.

Hagans, R. "Components of OSI: ES-IS Routing." *ConneXions: The Interoperability Report*, Vol. 3, No. 8: August 1989.

Hares, S. "Components of OSI: Inter-Domain Routing Protocol (IDRP)." *ConneXions: The Interoperability Report*, Vol. 6, No. 5: May 1992.

Hughes Jr., Larry J. *Actually Useful Internet Security Techniques*, New Riders Publishing.

Kaufman, Charlie and Perlman, Radia and Specinen, Mike *Network Security: Private Communication in a Public World*, Prentice-Hall, Inc. ISBN 0-13-061466-1.

Kousky, K. "Bridging the Network Gap." *LAN Technology*, Vol. 6, No. 1: January 1990.

Leinwand, A. and K. Fang. *Network Management: A Practical Perspective*. Reading, Massachusetts: Addison-Wesley Publishing Company, Inc.; 1993.

Lippis, N. "The Internetwork Decade." *Data Communications*, Vol. 20, No. 14: October 1991.

Martin, J. *SNA: IBM's Networking Solution*. Englewood Cliffs, New Jersey: Prentice Hall; 1987.

Martin, J., with K.K. Chapman and the ARBEN Group, Inc. *Local Area Networks. Architectures and Implementations*. Englewood Cliffs, New Jersey: Prentice Hall; 1989.

McNamara, J.E. *Local Area Networks*. Digital Press, Educational Services, Digital Equipment Corporation, 12 Crosby Drive, Bedford, MA 01730.

Medin, M. "The Great IGP Debate—Part Two: The Open Shortest Path First (OSPF) Routing Protocol." *ConneXions: The Interoperability Report*, Vol. 5, No. 10: October 1991.

Meijer, A. *Systems Network Architecture: A tutorial*. New York, New York: John Wiley & Sons, Inc.; 1987.

Miller, M.A. *LAN Protocol Handbook*. San Mateo, California: M&T Books; 1990.

O'Reilly, T. and G. Todino. *Managing UUCP and Usenet*, 10th ed. Sebastopol, California: O'Reilly & Associates, Inc.; 1992.

Perkins, D. and E. McGinnis, *Understanding SNMP MIBs*, Englewood Cliffs, New Jersey: Prentice Hall PTR; 1997.

Perlman, R. *Interconnections: Bridges and Routers*. Reading, Massachusetts: Addison-Wesley Publishing Company, Inc.; 1992.

Perlman, R. and R. Callon. "The Great IGP Debate—Part One: IS-IS and Integrated Routing." *ConneXions: The Interoperability Report*, Vol. 5, No. 10: October 1991.

Rose, M.T. *The Open Book: A Practical Perspective on OSI*. Englewood Cliffs, New Jersey: Prentice Hall; 1990.

Rose, M.T. *The Simple Book: An Introduction to Management of TCP/IP-based Internets*. Englewood Cliffs, New Jersey: Prentice Hall; 1991.

Ross, F.E. "FDDI—A Tutorial." *IEEE Communications Magazine*, Vol. 24, No. 5: May 1986.

Schlar, S.K. *Inside X.25: A Manager's Guide*. New York, New York: McGraw-Hill, Inc.; 1990.

Schneier, Bruce *Applied Cryptography*, John Wiley & Sons, Inc. ISBN 0-471-11709-9.

Schwartz, M. *Telecommunications Networks: Protocols, Modeling, and Analysis*. Reading, Massachusetts: Addison-Wesley Publishing Company, Inc.; 1987.

Sherman, K. *Data Communications: A User's Guide*. Englewood Cliffs, New Jersey: Prentice Hall; 1990.

Sidhu, G.S., R.F. Andrews, and A.B. Oppenheimer. *Inside AppleTalk*, 2nd ed. Reading, Massachusetts: Addison-Wesley Publishing Company, Inc.; 1990.

Spragins, J.D. et al. *Telecommunications Protocols and Design*. Reading, Massachusetts: Addison-Wesley Publishing Company, Inc.; 1991.

Stallings, W. *Data and Computer Communications*. New York, New York: Macmillan Publishing Company; 1991.

Stallings, W. *Handbook of Computer-Communications Standards*, Vols. 1–3. Carmel, Indiana: Howard W. Sams, Inc.; 1990.

Stallings, W. *Local Networks*, 3rd ed. New York, New York: Macmillan Publishing Company; 1990.

Sunshine, C.A. (ed.). *Computer Network Architectures and Protocols*, 2nd ed. New York, New York: Plenum Press; 1989.

Tannenbaum, A.S. *Computer Networks*, 2nd ed. Englewood Cliffs, New Jersey: Prentice Hall; 1988.

Terplan, K. *Communication Networks Management*. Englewood Cliffs, New Jersey: Prentice Hall; 1992.

Tsuchiya, P. "Components of OSI: IS-IS Intra-Domain Routing." *ConneXions: The Interoperability Report*, Vol. 3, No. 8: August 1989.

Tsuchiya, P. "Components of OSI: Routing (An Overview)." *ConneXions: The Interoperability Report*, Vol. 3, No. 8: August 1989.

Zimmerman, H. "OSI Reference Model—The ISO Model of Architecture for Open Systems Interconnection." *IEEE Transactions on Communications* COM-28, No. 4: April 1980.

TECHNICAL PUBLICATIONS AND STANDARDS

Advanced Micro Devices. *The Supernet Family for FDDI*. Technical Manual Number 09779A. Sunnyvale, California; 1989.

————. *The Supernet Family for FDDI*. 1989 Data Book Number 09734C. Sunnyvale, California; 1989.

American National Standards Institute X3T9.5 Committee. *FDDI Station Management (SMT)*. Rev. 6.1; March 15, 1990.

———. Revised Text of ISO/DIS 8802/2 for the Second DIS Ballot, "Information Processing Systems—Local Area Networks." Part 2: Logical Link Control. 1987-01-14.

———T1.606. Integrated Services Digital Network (ISDN)—Architectural Framework and Service Description for Frame-Relaying Bearer Service. 1990.

——— T1.617. Integrated Services Digital Network (ISDN)—Signaling Specification for Frame Relay Bearer Service for Digital Subscriber Signaling System Number 1 (DSS1). 1991.

——— T1.618. Integrated Services Digital Network (ISDN)—Core Aspects of Frame Protocol for Use with Frame Relay Bearer Service. 1991.

ATM Data Exchange Interface (DXI) Specification, Version 1.0. Document ATM_FORUM/93-590R1; August 4, 1993.

Banyan Systems, Inc. *VINES Protocol Definition*. DA254-00, Rev. 1.0. Westboro, Massachusetts; February 1990.

Bellcore. *Generic System Requirements in Support of a Switched Multi-Megabit Data Service*. Technical Advisory, TA-TSY-000772; October 1989.

———. *Local Access System Generic Requirements, Objectives, and Interface Support of Switched Multi-Megabit Data Service*. Technical Advisory TA-TSY-000773, Issue 1; December 1985.

———. *Switched Multi-Megabit Data Service (SMDS) Operations Technology Network Element Generic Requirements*. Technical Advisory TA-TSY-000774.

Chapman, J.T. and M. Halabi. *HSSI: High-Speed Serial Interface Design Specification*. Menlo Park, California and Santa Clara, California: Cisco Systems and T3Plus Networking, Inc.; 1990.

Consultative Committee for International Telegraph and Telephone. *CCITT Data Communications Networks—Services and Facilities, Terminal Equipment and Interfaces, Recommendations X.1–X.29*. Yellow Book, Vol. VIII, Fascicle VIII.2; 1980.

———. *CCITT Data Communications Networks—Interfaces, Recommendations X.20–X.32*. Red Book, Vol. VIII, Fascicle VIII.3; 1984.

DDN Protocol Handbook. Four volumes; 1989.

Defense Communications Agency. *Defense Data Network X.25 Host Interface Specification*. Order number AD A137 427; December 1983.

Defense Trade Regulations (Parts 120 to 126).

Digital Equipment Corporation. *DECnet/OSI Phase V: Making the Transition From Phase IV*. EK-PVTRN-BR; 1989.

———. *DECserver 200 Local Area Transport (LAT) Network Concepts*. AA-LD84A-TK; June 1988.

———. *DIGITAL Network Architecture (Phase V)*. EK-DNAPV-GD-001; September 1987.

Digital Equipment Corporation, Intel Corporation, Xerox Corporation. *The Ethernet, A Local-Area Network, Data Link Layer and Physical Layer Specifications*. Ver. 2.0; November 1982.

Feinler, E.J., et al. *DDN Protocol Handbook*, Vols. 1–4, NIC 50004, 50005, 50006, 50007. Defense Communications Agency. Alexandria, Virginia; December 1985.

FIPS140, Federal Information Processing Standard.

Garcia-Luna-Aceves, J.J. "A Unified Approach to Loop-Free Routing Using Distance Vectors or Link States." ACM 089791-332-9/89/0009/0212, pp. 212–223; September 1989.

Hemrick, C. and L. Lang. "Introduction to Switched Multi-megabit Data Service (SMDS), an Early Broadband Service." *Proceedings of the XIII International Switching Symposium* (ISS 90), May 27– June 1, 1990.

Hewlett-Packard Company. X.25: The PSN Connection; An Explanation of Recommendation X.25. 5958-3402; October 1985.

IEEE Project 802—*Local & Metropolitan Area Networks. Proposed Standard: Distributed Queue Dual Bus (DQDB) Subnetwork of a Metropolitan Area Network (MAN)*; February 7, 1990.

IEEE 802.2—*Local Area Networks Standard, 802.2 Logical Link Control.* ANSI/IEEE Standard; October 1985.

IEEE 802.3—*Local Area Networks Standard, 802.3 Carrier Sense Multiple Access.* ANSI/IEEE Standard; October 1985.

Information Security and Privacy in Network Environments, Office of Technology Assessment (OTA)— Congress of the United States.

International Business Machines Corporation. ACF/NCP/VS Network Control Program, System Support Programs: General Information. GC30-3058.

————. *Advanced Communications Function for VTAM (ACF/VTAM), General Information: Introduction.* GS27-0462.

————. *Advanced Communications Function for VTAM, general information: concepts. GS27-0463.*

————. *Dictionary of Computing.* SC20-1699-7; 1987.

————. *Local Area Network Technical Reference.* SC30-3883.

————. *Network Problem Determination Application: general information.* GC34-2010.

————. *Synchronous Data Link Control: general information.* GA27-3093.

————. *Systems Network Architecture: concepts and products.* GC30-3072.

————. *Systems Network Architecture: technical overview.* GC30-3073-1; 1985.

————. *Token-Ring Network Architecture Reference.* SC30-3374.

International Organization for Standardization. *Information Processing System—Open System Interconnection; Specification of Abstract Syntax Notation One (ASN.1).* International Standard 8824; December 1987.

McGraw-Hill/Data Communications. *McGraw-Hill's Compilation of Data Communications Standards.* Edition III; 1986.

National Security Agency. *Blacker Interface Control Document*. March 21, 1989.

Novell, Inc. IPX Router Specification, Version 1.10. Part Number 107-000029-001. October 16, 1992.

————. NetWare Link Services Protocol (NLSP) Specification, Revision 0.9. Part Number 100-001708-001. March 1993.

StrataCom. *Frame Relay Specification with Extensions*. 001-208966, Rev.1.0; September 18, 1990.

Transmission Control Protocol/Internet Protocol TCP/IP Version 2 Release 2.1 for MVS: Planning and Customization, SC31-6085 (or later version).

Transmission Control Protocol/Internet Protocol TCP/IP Version 2 Release 2 for VM: Planning and Customization, SC31-6082 (or later version).

Xerox Corporation. *Internet Transport Protocols*. XNSS 029101; January 1991.

CISCO-SUPPORTED RFCS

Table B–1 lists the Requests for Comments (RFCs) supported by the Cisco Internetwork Operating System (Cisco IOS) software as of Cisco IOS Release 11.3, in descending numerical order. RFCs that have been superseded or replaced are identified, as are RFCs that are partially supported or supported only from Software Release 9.21 forward.

Table B–1   *Cisco-Supported Requests for Comments*

Standard Number		Standard Title
RFC 2125		PPP Bandwidth Allocation Protocol (BAP) PPP Bandwidth Allocation Control Protocol (BACP)
RFC 2037[1]		Entity MIB
RFC 2018		TCP Selective Acknowledgment Options
RFC 1997		BGP Communities Attribute
RFC 1994	Supersedes RFC 1334	PPP Challenge Handshake Authentication Protocol (CHAP)
RFC 1990	Supersedes RFC 1717	The PPP Multilink Protocol (MP)
RFC 1989	Supersedes RFC 1333	PPP Link Quality Monitoring
RFC 1918		Address Allocation for Private Internet Space
RFC 1907		Management Information Base for Simple Network Management Protocol (SNMPv2)
RFC 1906		Transport Mappings for Version 2 of the Simple Network Management Protocol (SNMPv2)

Table B–1 *Cisco-Supported Requests for Comments, Continued*

Standard Number		Standard Title
RFC 1905		Protocol Operations for Version 2 of the Simple Network Management Protocol (SNMPv2)
RFC 1904		Conformance Statements for Version 2 of the Simple Network Management Protocol (SNMPv2)
RFC 1903		Textual Conventions for Version 2 of the Simple Network Management Protocol (SNMPv2)
RFC 1902		Structural Management for Version 2 of the Simple Network Management Protocol (SNMPv2)
RFC 1901	Supersedes RFC 1441-1450	Introduction to Community-based SNMPv2
RFC 1889		RTP—A Transport Protocol for Real-Time Applications
RFC 1850		OSPF Version 2 MIB
RFC 1812		Requirements for IP Version 4 Routers
RFC 1795		DLSw: Switch-to-Switch Protocol
RFC 1793		Extending OSPF to Support Demand Circuits
RFC 1771		A Border Gateway Protocol 4
RFC 1745		BGP4/IDRP for IP—OSPF Interaction
RFC 1724		RIP Version 2 MIB Extension
RFC 1723		RIP Version 2 Carrying Additional Information
RFC 1722		RIP Version 2 Protocol Applicability Statement
RFC 1717	Replaced by RFC 1990	The PPP Multilink Protocol (MP)
RFC 1695		Definitions of Managed Objects for ATM Management Version 8.0 using SMIv2
RFC 1661	Supersedes RFC 1548	PPP (Point-to-Point Protocol)
RFC 1654		A Border Gateway Protocol (BGP-4)
RFC 1647		TN3270 Enhancements
RFC 1646		Cisco supports LU name selection method only
RFC 1638		PPP Bridging Control Protocol (BCP)

Table B–1   *Cisco-Supported Requests for Comments, Continued*

Standard Number		Standard Title
RFC 1634	Supersedes 1362 and 1551	Novell Routing over Various WAN Media (IPXWAN)
RFC 1633		Integrated Services in the Internet Architecture: An Overview
RFC 1631		The IP Network Address Translator
RFC 1618		PPP over ISDN
RFC 1604		Definitions of Managed Objects for Frame Relay Service
RFC 1587		The OSPF Not-So-Stubby Area (NSSA) Option
RFC 1583	Supersedes RFC 1247	OSPF Version 2
RFC 1577		Classical IP and ARP over ATM
RFC 1576		TN3270 Current Practices
RFC 1559		DECnet Phase IV MIB Extensions
RFC 1552		The PPP Internetwork Packet Exchange Control Protocol (IPXCP)
RFC 1549		PPP in HDLC Framing
RFC 1548	Replaced by RFC 1661	PPP (Point-to-Point Protocol)
RFC 1541	Supersedes RFC 1531	Dynamic Host Configuration Protocol
RFC 1531	Replaced by RFC 1541	Dynamic Host Configuration Protocol
RFC 1519		Classless Inter-Domain Routing (CIDR): An Address Assignment and Aggregation Strategy
RFC 1510		The Kerberos Network Authentication Service (V5)
RFC 1492		Access Control Protocol or TACACS
RFC 1490		Multiprotocol Interconnect over Frame Relay
RFC 1483[1]		Multiprotocol Encapsulation over ATM Adaptation Layer 5
RFC 1469		IP Multicast over Token-Ring Local Area Network

Table B-1   *Cisco-Supported Requests for Comments, Continued*

Standard Number		Standard Title
RFC 1450	Replaced by RFC 1907	MIB for SNMP Version 2
RFC 1403		BGP OSPF Interaction
RFC 1397		Default Route Advertisement in BGP2 and BGP3
RFC 1395		BootP Extensions
RFC 1393		Traceroute using an IP Option
RFC 1390		Transmission of IP and ARP over FDDI Networks
RFC 1382[1,2]		SNMP MIB Extension for X.25 Packet Layer
RFC 1381[1,2]		SNMP MIB Extension for X.25 LAPB
RFC 1378[1]		PPP AppleTalk Control Protocol (ATCP)
RFC 1377		PPP OSI Network Layer Control Protocol (OSINLCP)
RFC 1376		PPP DECnet Phase IV Control Protocol (DNCP)
RFC 1370		Applicability Statement for OSPF
RFC 1362		Novell IPX Over Various WAN Media (IPXWAN)
RFC 1356		Multiprotocol Interconnect on X.25 and ISDN in the Packet Mode
RFC 1350		TFTP Version 2
RFC 1349		Type of Service in the Internet Protocol Suite
RFC 1348		DNS NSAP RRs
RFC 1334	Replaced by RFC 1994	PPP Authentication Protocols
RFC 1333	Replaced by RFC 1989	PPP Link Quality Monitoring
RFC 1332		PPP Internet Protocol Control Protocol (IPCP)
RFC 1331	Replaced by RFC 1548	PPP for the Transmission of Multi-protocol Datagrams over Point-to-Point Links
RFC 1323		TCP Extensions for High Performance
RFC 1315 [1,2]		MIB for Frame Relay DTE's

Table B–1   *Cisco-Supported Requests for Comments, Continued*

Standard Number		Standard Title
RFC 1305		Network Time Protocol (NTP) Version 3
RFC 1294 [2]	Replaced by RFC1490	Multiprotocol Interconnect over Frame Relay
RFC 1293		Inverse ARP
RFC 1286		Definitions of Managed Objects for Bridges
RFC 1285 [1]		FDDI MIB
RFC 1269 [1]		Definitions of Managed Objects for the Border Gateway Protocol (Version 3)
RFC 1268		Application of BGP in the Internet
RFC 1267		BGP-3
RFC 1256		ICMP Router Discovery Messages
RFC 1253		MIB for OSPF Version 2
RFC 1247	Replaced by RFC 1583	OSPF Version 2
RFC 1236		IP-to-X.121 Address Mapping for DDN
RFC 1234		Tunneling IPX Traffic through IP Networks
RFC 1231 [1]		IEEE 802.5 Token Ring MIB
RFC 1220		Point-to-Point Protocol (PPP) Extensions for Bridging
RFC 1219		On the Assignment of Subnet Numbers
RFC 1215		Convention for Defining Traps for Use with SNMP
RFC 1213		Management Information Base for Network Management of TCP/IP-based Internets: MIB-II
RFC 1212		Concise MIB Definitions
RFC 1209		Transmission of IP Datagrams over SMDS Service
RFC 1196		Finger User Information Protocol
RFC 1195 [2]		Use of OSI IS-IS for Routing in TCP/IP in Dual Environments
RFC 1191		Path MTU Discovery

Table B–1 *Cisco-Supported Requests for Comments, Continued*

Standard Number		Standard Title
RFC 1188	Replaced by RFC 1390	Proposed Standard for the Transmission of IP Datagrams over FDDI Networks
RFC 1172		PPP Initial Configuration Options
RFC 1171	Replaced by RFC 1331	Point-to-Point Protocol for the Transmission of Multi-Protocol Datagrams over Point-to-Point links
RFC 1166		Internet Numbers
RFC 1164		Application of the BGP in the Internet
RFC 1163		Border Gateway Protocol (BGP)
RFC 1157		Simple Network Management Protocol (SNMP)
RFC 1156	Replaced by RFC 1213	MIB for TCP/IP
RFC 1155	Replaced by RFC 1212	Structure and Identification of Management Information for TCP/IP-Based Internets
RFC 1144		Compressing TCP/IP Headers for Low-Speed Serial Links
RFC 1141		Incremental Updating of the Internet Checksum
RFC 1139		Echo Function for ISO 8473 (PING)
RFC 1136		Administrative Domains and Routing Domains: A Model for Routing in the Internet
RFC 1122		Requirements for Internet Hosts—Communication Layers
RFC 1112		Host Extensions for IP Multicasting
RFC 1108	DCA Draft	IP Security Option (IPSO)
RFC 1101		DNS Encoding of Network Names and Other Types
RFC 1091		Telnet Terminal-Type Option
RFC 1084		BootP Extensions
RFC 1080		Telnet Remote Flow Control Option
RFC 1079		Telnet Terminal Speed Option

Table B–1 *Cisco-Supported Requests for Comments, Continued*

Standard Number		Standard Title
RFC 1069		Guidelines for the use of Internet-IP Addresses in the ISO Connectionless-Mode Network Protocol
RFC 1060		Assigned Numbers
RFC 1058		Routing Information Protocol (RIP)
RFC 1055		Standard for the Transmission of IP Datagrams Over Serial Lines: SLIP
RFC 1042		Standard for the Transmission of IP Datagrams Over IEEE 802 Networks
RFC 1035		Domain Names—Implementation and Specification
RFC 1034		Domain Names—Concepts and Facilities
RFC 1027		Using ARP to Implement Transparent Subnet Gateways (Proxy ARP)
RFC 1009		Requirements for Internet Gateways
RFC 995	Replaced by ISO 9542	ES-to-IS Routing Exchange Protocol for Use in Conjunction with ISO 8473
RFC 994	Replaced by ISO 8473	Protocol for Providing the Connectionless-Mode Network Service
RFC 982		Guidelines for the Specification of the Top of the Structure of the Domain Specific Part (DSP) of the ISO Standard NSAP Address
RFC 951		Bootstrap Protocol (BootP)
RFC 950		Internet Standard Subnetting Procedure
RFC 925		Multi-LAN Address Resolution (PROXY ARP)
RFC 922		Broadcasting Internet Datagrams in the Presence of Subnets (IP_BROAD)
RFC 919		Broadcasting Internet Datagrams
RFC 906		Bootstrap Loading Using TFTP
RFC 904		Exterior Gateway Protocol (EGP) Formal Specification
RFC 903		Reverse Address Resolution Protocol (RARP)
RFC 896		Congestion Control in TCP/IP Internetworks

Table B–1 *Cisco-Supported Requests for Comments, Continued*

Standard Number		Standard Title
RFC 895		Standard for the transmission of IP datagrams over experimental Ethernet networks
RFC 894		Standard for the Transmission of IP Datagrams over Ethernet
RFC 891		Hello Protocol
RFC 879		The TCP Maximum Segment Size and Related Topics
RFC 877		Standard for the Transmission of IP Datagrams Over Public Data Networks
RFC 874		Telnet Protocol Specification
RFC 863		Discard Service (TCP discard)
RFC 862		Echo Service (TCP echo)
RFC 860		Telnet Timing Mark Option
RFC 858		Telnet Suppress Go Ahead option
RFC 857		Telnet Echo Option
RFC 856		Telnet Binary Transmission
RFC 855		Telnet Option Specification
RFC 854	MIL STD 1782	Telnet Protocol Specification
RFC 827		Exterior Gateway Protocol (EGP)
RFC 826		Address Resolution Protocol (ARP)
RFC 815		IP Datagram Re-assembly Algorithms
RFC 813		Window and Acknowledgment Strategy in TCP/IP
RFC 793	MIL STD 1778	Transmission Control Protocol (TCP)
RFC 792		Internet Control Message Protocol (ICMP)
RFC 791	MIL STD 1777	Internetwork Protocol (IP)
RFC 783		Trivial File Transfer Protocol (TFTP) (version 2)
RFC 779		Telnet Send-Location Option
RFC 768		User Datagram Protocol (UDP)

[1] This RFC is only partially supported by the Cisco IOS.
[2] This RFC is supported from Software Release 9.21 forward.

Where to Obtain RFCs

RFCs are maintained by Government Systems, Inc. (GSI). Both electronic and printed copies can be obtained. GSI can be contacted in the following ways:

- By mail:

  Government Systems, Inc.
  Attn: Network Information Center
  14200 Park Meadow Drive, Suite 200
  Chantilly, Virginia 22021

- By telephone:

  1–800–365–3642
  1–703–802–8376
  1–703–802–8376 (FAX)

- By electronic mail:

  NIC@NIC.DDN.MIL
  Network address: 192.112.36.5

Index

Symbols

! (exclamation points), adding comments to
     configuration files, 240
(pound sign), initializing Flash memory, 298
? (question mark), listing commands, 14

Numerics

100VG-AnyLAN port adapter
     configuring, 553
     examples, 580
10BaseT capability, 552
2-wire 56/64-kbps CSU/DSU service module,
     performing loopback tests, 538
4-wire 56/64-kbps CSU/DSU module, 623
     line speed, setting, 621–622
     scrambled data coding, enabling, 622
     service providers, selecting, 623–624
7-bit character set, special characters, 148
8-bit character set
     changing for session, 148
     displaying, 96–97

special characters, 148
specifying for all lines, 147

A

abbreviating commands, 38
access-list command, 571–572
access lists
     assigning to HTTP servers, 79–80
     MAC, establishing, 657–658
     removing from interfaces, 732–733
     type code, establishing, 658–659
access servers
     Cisco AS5200
          CSU, setting FDL, 705–706, 708
          enabling voice calls, 729
          setting FDL, 705–706, 708
          TDM clock source selection,
               676–677
          voice calls, enabling, 729
     home page, accessing, 56–58
     initializing, 19

Q

CISCO CERTIFIED INTERNETWORK EXPERT

Cisco's CCIE certification programs set the professional benchmark for internetworking expertise. CCIEs are recognized throughout the internetworking industry as being the most highly qualified of technical professionals. And, because the CCIE programs certify individuals—not companies— employers are guaranteed any CCIE with whom they work has met the same stringent qualifications as every other CCIE in the industry.

To ensure network performance and reliability in today's dynamic information systems arena, companies need internetworking professionals who have knowledge of both established and newer technologies. Acknowledging this need for specific expertise, Cisco has introduced three CCIE certification programs:

WAN Switching

ISP/Dial

Routing & Switching

CCIE certification requires a solid background in internetworking. The first step in obtaining CCIE certification is to pass a two-hour Qualification exam administered by Sylvan-Prometric. The final step in CCIE certification is a two-day, hands-on lab exam that pits the candidate against difficult build, break, and restore scenarios.

Just as training and instructional programs exist to help individuals prepare for the written exam, Cisco is pleased to announce its first CCIE Preparation Lab. The CCIE Preparation Lab is located at Wichita State University in Wichita, Kansas, and is available to help prepare you for the final step toward CCIE status.

Cisco designed the CCIE Preparation Lab to assist CCIE candidates with the lab portion of the actual CCIE lab exam. The Preparation Lab at WSU emulates the conditions under which CCIE candidates are tested for their two-day CCIE Lab Examination. As almost any CCIE will corroborate, the lab exam is the most difficult element to pass for CCIE certification.

Registering for the lab is easy. Simply complete and fax the form located on the reverse side of this letter to WSU. For more information, please visit the WSU Web page at www.engr.twsu.edu/ cisco/ or Cisco's Web page at www.cisco.com.

CISCO CCIE PREPARATION LAB

REGISTRATION FORM

Please attach a business card or print the following information:

Name/Title: _____

Company: _____

Company Address: _____

City/State/Zip: _____

Country Code (_____) Area Code (_____) Daytime Phone Number _____

Country Code (_____) Area Code (_____) Evening Phone Number _____

Country Code (_____) Area Code (_____) Fax Number _____

E-mail Address: _____

Circle the number of days you want to reserve lab: 1   2   3   4   5

Week and/or date(s) preferred (3 choices):

_____

_____

_____

Have you taken and passed the written CCIE exam?   Yes   No

List any CISCO courses you have attended:

Registration fee: _____ $500 per day × _____ day(s) = Total _____

Check Enclosed (Payable to WSU Conference Office)

Charge to: _____   MasterCard or Visa exp. Date _____

CC# _____

Name on Card _____

Cardholder Signature _____

Refunds/Cancellations: The full registration fee will be refunded if your cancellation is received at least 15 days prior to the first scheduled lab day.

Wichita State University
University Conferences
1845 Fairmount
Wichita, KS 67260
Attn: Kimberly Moore
Tel: 800-550-1306
Fax: 316-686-6520